THE BEST OF

P L A N N I N G

PLANNERS PRESS   American Planning Association   Chicago, Illinois   Washington, D.C.

Two Decades of Articles
From the Magazine of the
American Planning Association

THE BEST OF

P L A N N I N G

Contents

3.   Land Use and the Environment   188

4.   Housing   245

8. Urban Design   478

9. Planning Issues: Parcels and Panoramas   532

Preface

For the editors of *Planning* magazine, looking back over 17 years of articles is like looking through a family photo album: The images are both familiar and fresh. That combination results in part from the way the pieces were chosen for publication in the first place. A word, then, seems in order about how stories are selected for *Planning* magazine.

When *Planning* first began publication in 1972, it defined the field of city planning quite broadly. Any article that concerned land-use management, whether city planners were directly involved in the issue or not, was fair game. Those were the days when *Planning* concentrated on the big picture (national trends, legal strategies, the philosophy underlying systems of land ownership).

In the last decade, in part because of changes in the planning field, the magazine has narrowed its focus (stressing local issues as well as national ones) while also changing its definition of planning to include topics other than land-use management. Topics that might have seemed out of place in the old days—for example, how cities scramble after new industry—are now common. In short, sights now are fixed on workaday problems and professional techniques.

The changes occurred partly because the readers demanded them, saying they wanted more information that would be helpful on the job. But the readers have also changed over the years. *Planning,* which originally had a circulation of about 12,000, was published by the American Society of Planning Officials, whose membership was open to all. In 1978, ASPO merged with the American Institute of Planners (AIP), whose membership was limited to professional planners. The result of that merger was the American Planning Association. APA membership is open to everyone, but many members are professional planners who have a deep interest in enhancing the planning profession. Taking the lead in that effort is one of the institutes under the APA umbrella, the American Institute of Certified Planners (AICP), whose membership is open only to planners with certain qualifications. Today, the magazine's circulation is about 25,000.

A few more clues to the use of the book: First, the editors have updated biographical information about all the authors whose articles appear in these pages. However, that is the only information that has been updated. All facts, figures, and prices are current as of their original date of publication—a date that is noted at the beginning of each story. Second, what you see in this book is not what the readers saw in *Planning* magazine. Most magazine articles, and especially the most recent ones, have been generously illustrated with photographs, maps, drawings, and cartoons. Lacking the space to do the illustrations full justice, this book includes fewer pieces of art.

Now to the reasons for choosing the articles that appear in this book. The reader shouldn't be misled by the book's title, *The Best of Planning.* The stories included here are good, to be sure—timely, well-written, some even classics of their type—but what's most important is that they are representative. They explain a person, place, situation, or concept that was important to a part of the planning field at a particular time. Yet something about them is still fresh, possibly because the issues they address are still with us.

Nearly everyone who has served as an editor of *Planning* magazine is represented in the book, and so are faithful contributors, those who have continued to write for the magazine through various changes in format and philosophy. To all contributors—and to the readers of *Planning* magazine through the years—the editors give their thanks.

Sylvia Lewis
Editor and Associate Publisher, Planning

Ruth Eckdish Knack
Senior Editor, Planning

Introduction

For nearly two decades, *Planning* has been the lively, prizewinning magazine published by the American Planning Association. *Planning* features short, readable articles reflecting the professional concerns of the day and offering the combined skills of contributors and the editorial staff.

It is obvious that the use and impact of a monthly periodical are constrained by the understandable tendency of readers to file and partially forget. The ability to compare programs and assess results is minimized when the subject matter is tucked away in discrete packages.

For that reason alone, a *Planning* reader that groups, assorts, classifies, and analyzes 17 years of the magazine's highlights seems justified. But there is a further reason: This volume offers an enticing sampler of the scope, the concerns, and the techniques of a small profession whose public image is still somewhat blurred. Professionals will find the text useful, and students, members of other professions, and the civic-minded public are likely to be intrigued and stimulated. Planning will never again be as mysterious, and planners will be less likely to be dismissed as bureaucratic dullards addicted to creating unnecessary problems. In these reports from the firing line, planners show up as thoughtful, sensitive, and often effective individuals. One can hope that their accounts will influence undergraduates casting about for an interesting career to give serious consideration to planning as a profession. In addition, this volume provides bite-sized glimpses into American planning practice for the benefit of foreign professionals.

In scanning the selections in this book, one is struck by the relatively minor amount of puffery in which planners indulge. As a matter of fact, the opposite is more often true: Much of the volume is a litany of problems and unfinished business, of promising programs that ease and alleviate, that offer hope but no definite solutions.

To a great degree, planners function as an urban social conscience, flagellating themselves and others for failing to meet the needs of the poor, for breaching standards of civil amenity and design, for failing to preserve the best of the old and to achieve the highest possible quality in new development. For this reason, readers should not be surprised by the pervasive tone of dissatisfaction. As a profession, we are not smug and complacent; even in the midst of celebrating a particular achievement there is a persistent undertone, an overt or tacit implication, that we can do better.

A survey of the readings also gives little aid or comfort to those fossils who cherish the notion that planning in practice is somehow alien and un-American. If mainstream American politics is a game played between the 40-yard lines, most planners are near the middle, slightly left of center. Right-wing allegations that planning is by its very nature radical and socialistic are seen to be delusions without substance. Unlike some right-wingers who maintain that government is the problem, not the solution, however, planners by profession are governmental activists. They are reformers, profoundly conservative in the sense of making the system work better for everyone's benefit, including the disadvantaged.

Gone, however, are the epic illusions of earlier decades, when planners were called on to remake a sick society, to prepare plans of utopian scope and sweeping scale and cost. Gone, too, is the constant preoccupation with federal leadership and federal programs and grantsmanship. The current focus, startling to the older generation, is on local and state initiatives, on using private investment to meet public needs in creative partnership arrangements.

A fascinating subtext in the readings is the salutary example or horror story, which serves as a warning against following its path to disaster. Planners have taken to granting awards for good practice, but for good reasons they have never followed the author's advice to single out the egregious bunglers, the venal, the uglifiers, and the vandals for special mention as most outstanding in class. Discerning readers may, however, catch references to the dangers of 'Manhattanization' as a warning to San Francisco to control building height limits, and to guard against the Chinese Walls of beachfront high rises for which Miami is famous. Further, they will note that up until recently, New Jersey was cited as a vivid example of the dangers of environmental laxity. Such are the uses of adversity.

PROFESSION AND PROFESSIONALS

One of the striking changes in the profession has been its heightened self-awareness, not simply as a repository of frequently ignored wisdom on improving the urban condition, but as a functioning career. The 1980s have seen much more in the way of surveys and analysis of employment topics: How many planners are there, where do they work, what do they earn, what are their careers like? Overall, the tone reflected in these selections becomes increasingly self-confident, a reflection of higher status and better salaries.

Another aspect of self-consciousness is the attention paid to our most prominent planners, some of whom are profiled in these pages. Doubtless the initiation of the professional association's landmark awards will stimulate further attention to this type of recognition. A profession with a 70-year history of official organization is old enough to have generated a substantial number of human monuments.

A useful byproduct of preparing this reader was the revelation of gaps in the literature pertaining to some of the serious day-to-day concerns of practicing planners. In the critical area of planning ethics, for example, there has been perfunctory notice of whistle-blowing and nothing at all on the revolving door—the tendency of planners to emulate retiring Pentagon generals by taking on jobs with firms they formerly supervised. On a more mundane level, there has been little on the nuts-and-bolts topics of public finance, legislative drafting, or public speaking. Such subjects may be considered boring, but *Planning* contributors have demonstrated a remarkable ability at treating ostensibly dull subjects in a sprightly, readable fashion.

Inevitably, a collection of readings is fragmentary rather than systematic and comprehensive. To fill the gaps and to provide necessary perspectives in time and space, each of the nine chapters is preceded by a brief introduction, whose objective is to step back and assess the topic, places the readings in context, and offer a timely overview of the field.

LOOKING AHEAD

Do the collected works of planners in the 1970s and 1980s offer any guidelines for the 1990s and beyond? Most planners probably agree that the profession badly needs replenishment of its intellectual capital, that there is no realistic prospect for rewarming and recycling the programs of the 1960s. Most would probably agree that the feds are unlikely to recapture the central role fostered by some of our more urban-minded presidents. They would also concur that there remains a crying need for federal dynamism, leverage funds, leadership, and vigor, all sadly lacking in the Washington of the 1980s.

The readings also demonstrate that, while the electorate may have been sedated with rosy "Morning in America" propaganda, as a profession planners travel in gloom. They have consistently confronted the unfinished, often expensive business that many conservatives, wary of taxes, regulation, and government intervention, prefer to ignore. Problems of the poor, the gaps in housing affordability, the woes of displaced workers, the lagging maintenance of public facilities all show up in these pages. To a degree, planners are bringing bad news to the unheeding; we resemble killjoy adults among frolicking children.

But more and more, we discern that the profession has discovered how to sell its product. Planning proposals designed to help the poor tend to be packaged as economically viable investments with a promise of indispensable contributions to development rather than visions of gleaming cities on a hill. We can also see a growing understanding of the intricacies of business and the uses of political power, factors that will have major consequences in the 1990s.

Increasingly, planners are becoming significant players rather than frustrated benchwarmers. This is not to suggest that there is a total consensus on approach, outlook, or method. One of the benefits of this book is to demonstrate the differences in programs and personalities associated with success, failure, celebration, or frustration. And there is awareness in looking to the future that our most serious challenges are not technical but social; engineering is easy, people are difficult. Finally, there is recognition that in the future, as in the past, planning is protracted warfare, an endless series of guerrilla actions rather than a single, sweeping victory. Indeed, we recognize that as in foreign affairs, each achievement is not a destination, but rather a ticket of admission to tackle the next set of problems. Planners also know that gains must be defended and that any slackening of vigorous effort is usually followed by inertia and disappointment.

But these are personal implications and conclu-sions; depending on experience and outlook, the reader may draw different lessons from the text. In any event, this book offers a generous sampling of material on an interesting 17 years. A follow-up 10 years hence is likely to prove equally productive as a trove for planning professionals, students, and the civic-minded.

Melvin R. Levin, AICP
Professor of Urban Studies and Planning
University of Maryland, College Park

1

The Profession

"Who's a planner," asks a contributor to *Planning's* June 1988 letters section. It is a question that has troubled academics and practitioners alike for decades, along with its corollary, "What do planners do?" Most of the debate has been carried out in the pages of the *Journal of the American Planning Association.* But *Planning* has also tackled the question from time to time, in such articles as Mel Levin's "Conscience of the Planner" (January 1976) and Lawrence Livingston's "Confessions of a Planner" (March 1980).

In fact, soul searching seems to be a characteristic of the profession. Some of the reason may well be the economic insecurity of the last decade. Hard times often cause people to cast around for new roles, new ways to make themselves useful. In the case of planners, the era of cutbacks has brought a rethinking of the old dependence on federal funds, a new look at the private provision of services, and a broadening of job possibilities in the private sector.

Not everyone, however, is agreed about what planners' new roles should be. At the spring 1988 national conference of the American Planning Association in San Antonio, speakers at a session on "New Visions" exhorted a large audience to become go-getters, entrepreneurs who move freely from the public to the private to the nonprofit sector. In this framework, a successful planner is a doer, someone who makes things happen.

What happens to social planners in such a period? That's the question tackled by a group of "advocate planners" in an October 1985 magazine roundtable. Their conclusions: that, for many planners, social issues are as important as ever and that, as renowned advocate Paul Davidoff once said, "all public planning must be considered social planning."

A danger is that the current hands-on view of planning will conflict with the traditional view of the planner as coordinator. In the spring 1988 issue

of the *APA Journal,* Virginia Commonwealth University professor Michael Brooks worried that planners were, in effect, losing their soul by ignoring the very features that made the profession distinctive.

There's also the danger of faddishness, of falling in love with the newest phenomenon and newest buzzword—until the inevitable disappointment occurs. In the 17 years that *Planning* has been published as a magazine, we have lived through advocacy planning and strategic planning, new age planning, and planning for success. The word isn't yet in on all the labels, but fickleness is always a cause for caution.

COMMON GROUND

As the keynote speaker at the APA conference, San Antonio mayor Henry Cisneros said planners were uniquely trained to deal with a rapidly changing society. And many of the articles reprinted in this anthology reflect the profession's constant effort to educate itself to keep pace with change. That's most obvious in the features specifically focused on education, the September 1983 roundtable, for instance, or the stories on Harvard and MIT (March 1981) and the University of North Carolina (June 1987). But the emphasis on learning is equally present in articles like "How to Survive as a Big City Planning Director" (December 1983), where practitioners demonstrate their ability to adjust to new political situations.

In a world of specialists, that's an important skill. Nowhere is its value made more important than in the careers and writings of such figures as Lewis Mumford, subject of an April 1983 profile. Other profiles show the range of the profession and suggest what issues are on planners' minds, from the grand urban vision of Edmund Bacon (December

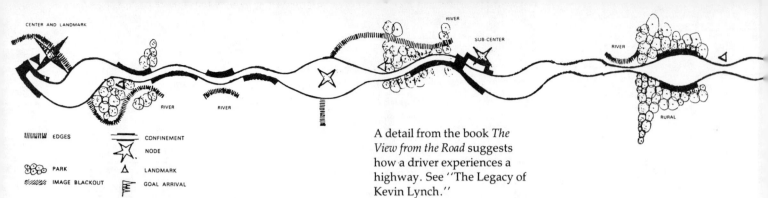

A detail from the book *The View from the Road* suggests how a driver experiences a highway. See "The Legacy of Kevin Lynch."

Lawrence Livingston, Jr. (left), helped plan the Bay Area Rapid Transit District. See "Confessions of a Planner." Photo: John Kelly.

It takes political savvy to hold a top job in local government. Baltimore's Larry Reich (below) and Allan Jacobs of San Francisco (bottom) explain the steps in "How to Survive as a Big City Planning Director." Photos: Bruce Smallwood, Allan Jacobs.

"Lewis Mumford: Critic, Colleague, Philosopher."

Famed developer James Rouse (right) has used festival marketplaces to upgrade cities and give housing rehab a boost. See ''James Rouse: The Robin Hood of Real Estate.'' Photo: Jeanne Marklin.

''Every thoughtful practitioner in the country has read his works and been deeply influenced by them,'' says one planner of William Whyte (below). See ''William Whyte: The Observation Man.'' Photo: Janet Charles.

Twenty-five years ago, Jane Jacobs (below) upset the apple cart by writing a book with an unconventional view of American cities. Below left, a street in the New York City neighborhood she made famous. See ''Eyes on Jane Jacobs.'' Photos: Maggie Steber (below); Janet Charles (below left).

1983) to the legal reminiscences of Richard Babcock (August 1987).

A series of articles on consultants forms a sort of group profile of an important segment of the profession. Articles like "Start-ups and Spin-offs" (December 1986) show that consultants often cross the lines between disciplines, while first-person accounts by such practitioners as Tom Roberts (July 1979) and Robert Leary (December 1986) describe the particular problems of running a consulting business.

GROUPS

The articles in this chapter fall into six categories, arranged as follows:

Soul searching, including "Here's Looking at You" (March 1986); Mel Levin's "Conscience of the Planner"; and Lawrence Livingston's "Confessions of a Planner"; a December 1981 piece on whistle blowing; "Where Have All the Radicals Gone"; and "Woman's Work" (October 1986).

Politics, with the Jacobs piece on San Francisco and "How to Survive as a Big City Planning Director" (December 1983).

Education, including "Why Can't Johnny Plan?" by Mel Levin (September 1976); "Meeting of the Minds" (September 1983); and the pieces on Harvard and MIT (March 1981) and Chapel Hill (June 1987).

Consultants, with "Why I Left a Cushy Job to Be My Own Boss" by Tom Roberts (July 1979); the consultants' roundtable (November 1984); "Start-ups and Spin-offs: Consulting Today" (December 1986); and Robert Leary's "A Practice Built for One (or Two)" in December 1986.

Profiles: Lewis Mumford (April 1983); Kevin Lynch (October 1984); James Rouse (May 1985); Edward Logue (August 1985); William Whyte (March 1986); Denise Scott Brown (May 1986); Jane Jacobs (September 1986); John Reps (November 1986); Richard Babcock (August 1987).

Commissioners, "For the Record: Planning Commissioners Speak Out" (August 1984).

Ruth Eckdish Knack
Senior Editor, Planning

Here's Looking at You
Ruth Eckdish Knack
(March 1986)

Steve Tuckerman has been practicing planning for six years. He does most of his work in zoning and subdivision review, policy planning, and economic development, and he believes that a planner's ideal role is interagency coordination. Tuckerman considers himself a liberal Democrat, he's married, and he's a Protestant.

In many respects, Tuckerman, who is the planning director of Southington, Connecticut, is also that most elusive of creatures—a typical planner. At least that's what a special *Planning* survey tells us. A few months ago, the magazine mailed questionnaires to almost the entire APA membership, excluding students and foreign addresses. Out of some 20,000 questionnaires, there were 6,369 responses. We followed up by interviewing some of the respondents.

APA regularly surveys its members about such job-related issues as salary and employment trends. . . . *Plannings's* aim was to go beyond employment data into the vaguer realms of beliefs and life styles. Some of what we asked has been touched on in more scientific inquiries by such researchers as Jerome Kaufman and Elizabeth Howe, Michael Vasu, Francine Rabinovitz, and Howell Baum. But generally, planners as people remain unknown territory. We thought it was time to take a closer look.

Here's what we found.

The big three

Asked to choose the three areas in which they did most of their planning, our respondents did what we thought they might do. Almost 44 percent checked off the old workhorse, zoning and subdivision regulation; in fact, nearly 4 percent (231 people) checked *only* that area. The other two top choices were policy planning and coordination (40 percent) and—the field of the 1980s—economic development (35 percent).

We suspect that a decade ago, environmental planning, fourth on our list with 24 percent, would have come in higher, and so would housing—eighth on our list with 14 percent—and historic preservation, eleventh with 8 percent. And two decades ago, transportation, sixth today with 15 percent, would surely have ranked near the top.

And where are the newcomers—those with less than a year of experience? Besides the popular fields noted above, they're doing more demographics (5 percent vs. 2 percent for those with more than 25 years experience); information processing (7 percent vs. 3 percent); and mapping (3 percent vs. 1 percent). Fewer seem to be going into environmental planning: 5 percent vs. 8 percent of the group with over 25 years of experience.

Ideal role

People's views of what they *should* be doing often differ greatly from what they, in fact, do. And planners, apparently, are no exception. For only 4 percent picked zoning and subdivision approvals—the number one area of work—as their "ideal role."

What did reach the top of this list was interagency coordination (20 percent) and providing data (13 percent). We note with interest that political liaison (fourth on the list) picks up adherents from the old-timers (25-plus years of experience) and that many more of the newcomers chose social advocacy than their older counterparts.

Our results—with the heavy emphasis on technical aspects of the profession—back up a survey of a cross-section of American Institute of Planners members by researcher Michael Vasu. He reported in *Politics and Planning* (University of North Carolina Press, 1979) that almost half of his respondents thought planners should be "technicians," assuming a strictly advisory role.

Vasu also found that planners tended to identify themselves as political liberals and, when asked party affiliation, as Democrats or "independents" (each group accounted for about 44 percent of his sampling). . . .

Beyond statistics

We knew when we started our survey that the numbers would not tell the whole story. To define a planner, we would have to talk to planners. . . .

Margaret Garrington is a 35-year-old county planner in southern Oregon. Her questionnaire caught our eye because she wrote in above her ideal role choice—providing data—the words "in an en-

vironmentally sound manner." Clearly, here was someone for whom environmental planning was still important—despite the 1980s emphasis on the practicalities of economic development.

"I probably approach almost everything from the environmental planning direction," Garrington told us by phone from Medford, the Jackson County seat. But like her colleagues on the county's small advanced planning staff, she does a little bit of everything. Always, she says, she must balance the interests of the environment and the state land-use laws designed to protect it with the strong property rights ethic that characterizes the area. Much of the county's land is federally owned, further complicating regulatory issues. And sometimes there's conflict among the three major sources of employment: lumbering, agriculture, and tourism—the latter particularly strong in Ashland, site of an annual Shakespeare festival.

"When the economy is bad around here, as it has been recently, environmental issues tend to take the back seat," says Garrington. "I'm really torn then because I live here, too, and when I see people out of work, I feel for them. The most satisfying part of the job is when we can follow state law and also help people.

"I want economic development, too," she adds, "but not at the expense of what's nice about the county." . . .

Lure of the West

Roy Fronczyk was also drawn west from Illinois, but he wound up in a Denver-area consulting firm, where he does work in site planning, transportation, and environmental planning. In his case, the environmental planning is likely to involve water supply or oil and gas exploration, the big issues in his region.

Fronczyk, 42, started out to be an architect, first at a Chicago junior college (he's from Pullman, the model industrial town, which is now a city neighborhood). In the early 1960s, his interest in design drew him to Southern Illinois University, where Buckminster Fuller had established a design program that was a generalist's dream—with community planning as one of the elements. Next stop for Fronczyk, who by then had opted for planning rather than architecture, was the University of Washington's graduate program in urban planning. His interest: "how people interact with the physical environment."

Fronczyk's consulting career started at Barton-Aschman in Chicago, where he worked on a variety of renewal projects for midwestern cities. His liking for the West drew him to Denver and a job with THK Associates in 1971. The firm had 12 professionals then. Now it's up to 40, and Fronczyk is one of five with the title "planner," although he notes that office titles are not particularly meaningful. He is an AICP member but agrees with others we spoke with that state registration of planners is unnecessary.

For three years, between 1979 and 1982, Fronczyk worked for ARCO's land development arm, doing planning for oil shale new towns. When the shale boom fizzled, he returned to THK. He sees little difference between his approach to planning as a consultant—he too checked providing data as a planner's ideal role—and that of public planners. Once in a while, he says, he finds it refreshing to sit down at a drawing board to do some mapping, thereby exercising his long-ago-learned graphic skills. . . .

The feminist

"Basically," says Charlotte Birdsall, "I'm a midlife planner." Trained as a social worker, Birdsall, known generally by her nickname, Tommie, was an activist in her Cincinnati neighborhood when her three children were growing up. Ten years ago, at age 40, she joined the city planning department, after earning a master's degree in community planning from the University of Cincinnati.

"I never expected to go into a traditional land-use agency," she says. "But I've never regretted my decision. I feel there's a definite place in an agency like this for someone with a social policy orientation."

As senior planner in the advanced planning division, Birdsall heads a small housing section, which, in addition to planning and monitoring programs, works on such special projects as shared housing for the elderly. She defines her job as "using traditional land-use skills and background as the basis for recommending social policy." . . .

California conservative

At the other end of the political spectrum is Roger Baker, a 40-year-old planner for the Burbank, California, planning department. Until December,

Baker worked for neighboring Glendale, where he had been since 1978. . . .

On the survey, Baker said he was a conservative Republican, but he notes that he doesn't always follow party labels. "I believe people should take care of themselves," he explains, "and I believe in the free enterprise system." At the same time, he says he recognizes that developers today are not always as responsible as their predecessors, making it necessary at times for government to step in. . . .

The rural life

Instead of answering our survey question about "how you spend your leisure hours," Lawrence Carter scribbled in the margin, "You don't know anything about rural life, do you?"

Willing to concede the point, we called him to find out what we were missing. First, he said that our leisure choices—sports, gardening, cultural activities, and so on—were "so suburban." Carter, it turns out, is a part-time farmer (two acres of produce, several hogs, 1,000 chickens), besides being planning director of very rural Bedford County, near Altoona, Pennsylvania.

Most planners, he says, occupy an "alien world" with far different values from Carter's. It's the world he saw as a teacher in a Cleveland suburb in the early 1970s—"middle-class American, Organization Man, not for me." He left in midyear, and after a short stint running the county's children's home ("a quick burnout"), returned to the Altoona area, where he grew up. For several years, he worked for a newly formed health systems agency, acquiring on-the-job training in systems analysis and health planning, skills that he says separate him from typical planners, who, in Carter's view, are hung up on land use.

In 1981, Carter, who is now 40, became county planning director. He describes himself as "a bit of a maverick" because he isn't a "trained planner—whatever that is." But he insists that his undergraduate social sciences degree qualifies him to deal with a job that he sees as primarily educational. "Our job is to help local governments determine what policy direction *they* want to take."

In practice, that means that Carter spends a lot of time "soapbox stumping—teaching people about themselves." When they understand, he says, they may be ready to accept some land-use controls (the county now has almost none). . . .

Opposite number

We weren't necessarily looking for an exact opposite to Larry Carter when we called our next planner. But we found it anyway in Mark Strauss. Not only is Strauss traditionally trained in land-use planning and a city dweller—but he believes anyone involved with physical planning should be trained as an architect, as he himself is. . . . As head of planning for the New York architecture firm, Kohn Pederson Fox Associates, he views planning as a "support for architecture," and he spends much of his time going after projects. His forte is showing clients and local officials how a proposed development will fit into the character of a city. A smaller proportion of his time is spent on such master planning projects as the multimillion-dollar Garrison Channel Place in downtown Tampa. Registered as an architect, Strauss has not taken the AICP exam. "As an architect," he says, "I feel I have a license to do planning." . . .

Man in the middle

Finally, we come back to our "typical planner," Steve Tuckerman. He comes from East Providence, Rhode Island, where his father was an engineer. And Tuckerman himself intended to study civil engineering when he enrolled at Worcester Polytechnic Institute. A freshman course in city planning sidetracked him permanently. He went straight from WPI to the graduate regional planning program at the University of Massachusetts.

Tuckerman's first job in 1979, and where he stayed until last year, was with East Hampton, Connecticut, a growing community of 9,000 20 miles from Hartford. He was the first inhouse planner in the town's history, and his job included revamping the zoning and subdivision regulations. He's proud of having gotten a new mixed-use zoning district passed to encourage people to invest in unused factory sites (East Hampton used to be a big bell manufacturing center).

In East Hampton, Tuckerman was, as he puts it, "a one-man show." Because he wanted to get experience in management, he decided a year ago to take a job in nearby Coventry, a rural town near the University of Connecticut. Things didn't work out, though, and a few months ago, he moved again, this time to Southington (pop. 40,000), another of the contiguous semi-industrial towns in the Hartford metropolitan area.

As Tuckerman views his job, interagency coordination—"getting different agencies to talk to each other"—and zoning and subdivision approvals are equally important roles. The latter he refers to as "the meat and potatoes of planning."

Tuckerman is 31 years old and married to a pediatrician. They live in neighboring New Britain in the downstairs portion of a two-family house they own. Southington, he notes, does not have a residency requirement for city employees, but if it did, he would be opposed. In fact, he thinks planners can be more impartial if they don't live in the town they work in. He's a nonpracticing Episcopalian who checked liberal Democrat for our political question and added the word "ultra." With a laugh, he says that means he "subverts from within."

Not a big TV watcher, Tuckerman nevertheless "tries not to miss 'Hill Street Blues.' " He reads Stephen King thrillers, *Consumer Reports,* and *Backpacking.* An avid hiker, he's active in the Appalachian Mountain Club.

He's an AICP member but doesn't believe in registration or licensing beyond that. "Ours is too diverse a field," he says.

Tuckerman's comment is reminiscent of the definition once offered by the late Harvey Perloff, dean of UCLA's planning and architecture school. A planner, said Perloff, is a "generalist with a specialty." And after reviewing the results of our survey and the interviews that followed, we think Perloff was on to something.

Ruth Knack is the senior editor of Planning.

The Conscience of the Planner

Melvin R. Levin
(January 1976)

In recent years much of the blame for the decay of the cities and the sprawl of the suburbs has fallen on the planning profession. In a way, this attention is flattering. After all, there are only about 15,000 professional planners in the nation—less than 50 percent of the number of architects and only five percent of the doctors and lawyers. They earn only 60 percent as much as lawyers and half as much as doctors. Planners have been neglected in serious fiction and the mass media. Where are the novels or television series illustrating the drama of zoning referrals, the romance of subdivision control, or the comic relief of floor-area ratios?

Planners have by no means closed ranks against outside critics. In fact, planners are their own severest and most persistent critics. The self-flagellation which characterized the profession in the latter part of the 1960s was attributable in large measure to the planners' role in the wholesale clearance of slums for urban renewal and highways. This era was the planning profession's Vietnam. We have never quite recovered the certainty, the tendency toward ex-cathedra prescriptions (concealing vast areas of ignorance) that was ours in the fifties. The profession is racked by doubts concerning its legitimacy, its honesty, its mission, and its effectiveness. For the sake of convenience, these moral dilemmas can be grouped under five main headings.

The Little Tin Box. From time to time a planner surfaces in news stories as a party to land fraud or as an influence-peddling defendant in a zoning scandal. Planners have taken some comfort from the fact that such reported cases are rare. But there is more to the story than meets the press. Certain consulting firms are notorious for their success in operating in corrupt environments. Outright bribery, kickbacks, phony subcontracts, dummy partners, tips, and laundered fees are all part of the game.

This business of sticky fingers is not as simple as it may appear, however. It is not uncommon for many, if not most, employees of consulting firms to be unaware of the financial calisthenics taking place in the upper echelons. Indeed, it is common practice to seal off the fixers and bag men from the rest of the firm; partners and senior staff are careful to avoid any direct knowledge of the shady side of the street, so that they can plead ignorance in the event of legal action. Under these circumstances, morality is often divorced from efficiency; and staff planners, unaware of the sordid details of contract procurement, can perform their duties as competent professionals.

So far as the big money is concerned, however, most planners are no closer than rumor and suspicion; they lack the opportunity. Like the good folk of Mark Twain's Hadleyburg, most planners are honest because no one has offered them an alternative. Since critical decisions are made outside their jurisdiction, they are rarely considered worth corrupting. In money, as in sex, the appearance of virtue may be due to a lack of a good offer.

Most planners have to settle for lesser spoils—typing paper, colored pencils, paper clips, personal calls on the office phone, and minor expense padding. This is kid stuff. So is goofing off on the job, occupying space, drawing a salary but doing nothing productive. Some planners may comfort themselves with the notion that they are learning their trade. But much of this is self-delusion and comforting rationalization. Like the rest of the army of useless public and private bureaucrats, far too many planners are engaging in this most costly game.

Why does a professional engage in conduct that even by charitable standards is demeaning in its vacuous triviality and utter waste? To be sure, hard times may be partly responsible: Even a dull job is better than no job. And there are civil service benefits, security, on-the-job socializing, generous vacations and sick leaves and pensions. But there are still a horrifying number of presumably professional planners clinging year after deadly year to positions that, except for salary, are one step above work relief.

The Bully Boys. Some planners are shoved around by supervisors they heartily dislike and fear; others linger on in a work environment they detest. Many others are pushed into nasty practices—favors for chosen developers, political shenanigans (including forced contributions to favored candidates), concealment of data and reports embarrassing to big-money operators.

It is possible for planners to mature and ripen (or more accurately, sour) into satraps, responsive to corrupt pressures and given to vicious and tyrannical behavior with their subordinates. There is an excellent reason for rough treatment of junior professionals in agencies whose director has established cozy working arrangements with the boodlers. Rudeness is an effective way of chastening idealists who want to poke their young, inquisitive noses into important business matters.

There are far too many docile, browbeaten planners working at jobs that hurt both their pride and their conscience. Equally sad is the fact that we have produced our share of obsequious servants to networks of the powerful and corrupt who simultaneously are despicably mean-spirited bullies to their subordinates.

The benign cabal. The practice of conferring in private to make plans for the benefit of client-constituencies is a feature of most bureaucracies, including planning agencies. Most planners are aware of the dangers inherent in paternalistic, class-biased, traditional planning and are theoretically and emotionally in favor of broad public participation and informed feedback. In practice, however, their commitment is substantially weakened by political and administrative realities.

As a practical matter, the public has limited time and technical expertise at its disposal. Attempts to secure a wide spectrum of citizen participants usually fail. As a result, citizen participation generally takes on a representative character: trusted volunteers or paid experts represent the interests of the hitherto neglected segments of the population. In contrast, effective mass participation usually occurs only as a negative response to a specific proposal, such as the construction of a highway through a residential neighborhood.

There is always the risk that citizen representatives are virtually self-appointed rather than truly representative. Only five percent of the potential voters turn out for certain elections. As a result, citizen participation may turn out to be a dialogue between a handful of ambitious, young activists and the technical staff. Some of the Young Turks may even be co-opted into well-paying establishment jobs. The aged, housewives, children, and the institutionalized population have little voice in planning decisions.

By its very nature, give-and-take with different citizen groups is a time-consuming, frustrating process. A crafty administrator wedded to the status quo can easily restrain attempts at reform and innovation by requiring painstaking checking and rechecking with the various citizen groups and government agencies. In most cases broad citizen participation leads to paralysis and stagnation. Some planners feel that process is more important than product—that participation, even if it means only wheel-spinning, is its own reward. Others expect concrete results; and if it means using a significant amount of secret, private conferences, they are prepared to let part of their conscience trouble them. They know, too, that the agency that spends its time "participating," not writing reports, may be left at the funding post.

Finally, there is a serious, vexing, and unresolved issue involving potential conflicts between the democratic system and planning decisions. The battle lines are clear. In the mid-1970s many democratically elected political figures faithfully reflect the sentiments of their constituents in their strong resistance to desegregation of any kind. By and large planners support desegregation. Some have deliberately conspired with like-minded lawyers, newspaper reporters, and federal agencies to sabotage and overturn the exclusionary policies of democratically elected public officials. They have, in fact, sought to bypass a public sentiment that obviously reflects a participatory consensus, albeit one that they find unacceptable.

This dilemma seems to impose little strain on the planner's conscience. Apparently many planners view themselves as agents of a larger community. Hence, a lapse from their professed adherence to the principles of participatory democracy is not troublesome when, as in this case, the consequences are considered inappropriate.

Professor beware, or the doctor's dilemma. For many fortunate folk, academia offers one of the most pleasant working environments conceived by man. But even in paradise, there are worms in the apples.

Take the case of the tenured freeloader. Given a light teaching load for the purpose of scholarly research and publishing, he is incapable of either. Even so, the tenured professor has one cheering thought. He *is* in the education business; and, if he is unable or unwilling to serve at the front, he can train tomorrow's combatants. Depending on his talents, that may be a significant contribution.

Then there are the academic snipers. In the mid-1960s it became fashionable and profitable for academicians to perform autopsies, biopsies, and occasional lobotomies on government reform programs. A number of youngish professors directed their criticism to deficiencies in the public sector rather than the private sector. In the process, they helped to kill off a number of marginal, useless, or counterproductive programs; but they also helped to poison the climate for reform. From the comfort and safety of the academy they not only criticized, maligned, and ridiculed well-meaning, if often inept, government efforts but also soured the prospects for future programs. The upshot is a scholarly contribution to conservative standpattism, reinforcing a fairly widespread public sentiment that government is always wrong and always incompetent.

The snipers seem happy in their work. After a barrage of criticism from a group of unsympathetic academics, one of the nation's outstanding planning directors asked, "Am I the enemy?" From their viewpoint, perhaps he was.

Hired guns are another type. A lot of dyed-in-the-wool academics who have never worked for a planning agency are in great demand from developers and lawyers skilled in busting zoning laws. For sizable fees they lend their academic prestige to all sorts of proposals, often after only cursory study of local planning needs and objectives.

This illustrates a basic difference between the legal and planning professions. Most lawyers see themselves as clinicians selling their talents to any client who can pay their fee. Planning faculty or planning consultants who do this are regarded as conscienceless guns for hire. This is another example of the planner's tendency to be judge and jury as well as advocate. The legal profession applauds a brilliant performance in the service of a shoddy client. In contrast, the planning profession castigates such efforts as pandering to greedy developers.

Political gamesmanship. Some planners appreciate the intimate relationship between planning and politics. But many planners, aware only of the surface outcroppings of the political landscape, view political activity as an ecology of friendly games—preparation of reasoned policy statements, polite calls on legislators, adoption of high-minded resolutions, financing full-page newspaper advertisements. They dismiss the active subterranean movement as either worthless or demeaning.

If it can be assumed that political influence rests primarily on the ability to muster votes or money, planning ranks far, far behind such professions as medicine, law, or education. Since the kind of high-minded pageantry in which the profession is now engaged hasn't worked, other methods—coalition building, infiltration, or bureaucratic maneuvering—are worth trying. They all seem promising until one examines their implications.

Fashioning effective coalitions is a task calling for considerable energy, shrewdness, tolerance, patience, and a willingness to compromise. The most politicized members of the profession, however, are hot-blooded, dogmatic sectarians who are convinced that compromise is tantamount to selling

out. They do not find it easy to work with a variety of groups with differing viewpoints, and they are constantly on the lookout for signs of backsliding on the part of their colleagues. On balance, it is likely that the planning profession's role in political coalitions is likely to be that of endorser and validator, adding a professional imprimatur to a reform candidate who has already marshaled his resources elsewhere.

Planners don't seem to be much better at infiltrating the inner temples of power. In the first place, planners are perpetually astonished by the mendacious, venal, rough-and-tumble tactics of harder working, ruthless, public administration or business types slavishly devoted to serving their masters. The planner who breaks through to the inner circle is likely soon to become indistinguishable from his bright, tense colleagues. For a time, he may feel a few twinges of conscience as he jettisons some of his past values and beliefs in favor of the criteria of political realism that now govern his actions, but planners must exhibit the same degree of adaptability as other staff if they are to survive.

If he is indeed one of the lucky survivors, he may be awarded with an upper-echelon appointment in a planning agency. He then discovers that he has been promoted into a supergrade target for invective, misrepresentation, and vilification. His fate hangs on the fortunes of his political sponsor, and he may be sacrificed as a liability.

Even if he lacks outstanding ability, all is not lost for the upper level planner. Should there develop a consensus that the planning agency must be retained but must not pose a threat to the power structure, then there is a very good chance that an impressive-looking but not very aggressive planner may be used as a kind of front man. He serves as a screen to hide the real decision making. Bland, solemn, and pompous—it helps if he is bald or at least graying—he dignifies conferences with his persona, drawing a high salary for his services.

And so we come to the final twist of the ethical pretzel. Like the young and useless occupant of a desk and title, there are some in the profession whose conscience does (or should) trouble them, not because of peculation but because their talents have grown rusty from disuse in a planning job that calls for the presence of ectoplasm rather than substantive effort. If there is contempt for thieves, there might also be a modicum of sympathy for the pathetic molluscs who have thrown their professional lives away for tenure, salary, and pension.

This examination of the state of the planner's conscience suggests that in outlook planners are perhaps closer to ministers and social workers than lawyers or businessmen. That the profession is its own severest critic is a compliment to both its principles and the quality of the people it attracts. But how is the profession to grapple with the restless stirrings of ethical disquiet? Surely laceration in print is not the answer, even if the pummeling is performed by academic moralists, quick to consign their colleagues to the thumbscrew, rack, and stake. We need a better method.

One possibility is the equivalent of the religious retreat, a prolonged change of scene, a year or so of sabbatical to permit the kind of perspective and understanding that can only be achieved through a substantial period of service in someone else's shoes.

Meanwhile a great debate on the proper role and ethical function of planners can continue.

Foremost among the topics for debate is the role of the planner within the broad sweep of economic, social, and technological convulsions that have ripped the urban landscape to shreds. In some respects planners are akin to social workers, restricted to tinkering with symptoms rather than causes. They're not attracted to pure scholarship as a career. They want to help shape urban patterns and trends; are frustrated by their lack of influence; and, pinched by conscience, often consider dropping out in favor of a career (like law) that seems to promise a closer relationship between energy input and tangible output.

Yet, despite the unquenchable optimism of many planners and the purblindness or callousness of others, there is a nagging, persistent, and fundamental question: Is planning in the United States irrelevant? Are we no more than marginal professionals, spear carriers in the urban drama, fit—"to swell a progress, start a scene or two . . ., an easy tool, deferential, glad to be of use, politic, cautious, and meticulous. Full of high sentence but a bit obtuse; at times, indeed, almost ridiculous . . ."?

Did T.S. Eliot know any planners?

Melvin R. Levin, AICP, is a professor of urban studies and planning at the University of Maryland, College Park.

Confessions of a Planner

Lawrence Livingston, Jr.
(March 1980)

Thirty years ago, armed with a government-financed MIT graduate degree and brimming over with an intoxicating blend of professional ambition and reformer's zeal, I embarked on a career in city planning, then a relatively new field. Today, looking back over three decades of service to local and state government agencies, as a public employee in the early years and as a consultant for the past 27, I find myself disillusioned by the consequences of city planning in general and by my own contributions in particular. Too often, planners' proposals have proved to be unjustifiably costly, ineffective, or, in some cases, even harmful to the public interest. The best that can be said of the mixed results of public planning is that the benefits probably have outweighed the costs by a slight margin.

Most of my work was done in California, the state that leads the nation not only in population growth and urbanization, but also in experimenting with planning solutions to its problems. California heads the nation both in number of planners employed and in the size of public planning budgets. In general, the consequences of the programs in California have been the same as in other heavily urbanized states. But, because of its size, population, rapid growth, and penchant for accepting planners' advice, the golden state has suffered more than most.

In fairness, it must be recognized that some farsighted leaders of the profession and some critics and commentators have foreseen the consequences of ill-conceived planning policies and have warned against them. Most planners, however, have supported or at least have not opposed such costly and harmful programs as these: the sprawl-inducing freeway system; the California Aqueduct, which provides northern California water to the Los Angeles area and thus encourages growth; the establishment of new university and college campuses in outlying locations, where they have stimulated unwanted, costly growth, instead of in urban centers; and downtown redevelopment projects that have destroyed the homes of thousands of low-income residents and, more often than not, still failed to restore the health of the CBD.

The recent taxpayers' revolts are signs that voters in California and elsewhere have finally recognized such costly, socially harmful mistakes. But the message seems to have been heard only dimly in Washington, and vast sums continue to flow to the states and local governments for the same sorts of public programs. Unfortunately for the cause of reform, most of the federal assistance programs that make it possible to translate planners' proposals into action are administered by HUD, the agency with probably the worst record of effective problem solving in the entire federal establishment.

Now, I must confess that I share the blame for the failures of city planning in California. While in some cases I foresaw the adverse consequences of planning programs—such as those that fostered suburban sprawl—I was unable to block them, sometimes because I did not present my case convincingly, and sometimes because the odds against me were too great. On one occasion I advised a Bank of America executive to halt mortgage lending in badly located, poorly designed subdivisions. He refused on the grounds that a change in lending policy might undermine public confidence in the bank. In other cases, I myself was one of the villains, and I must accept my share of the blame for the results.

BART

My first commission as an independent consultant in 1953 was to assist what now is the Bay Area Rapid Transit District (BART) in planning the rapid transit system. From my student days, I had been an enthusiastic advocate of rail mass transit as the solution to urban traffic congestion. Now my great opportunity had arrived! With the other planners working on the job, I concluded that the system should connect the core areas of San Francisco, Oakland, and Berkeley with outlying residential districts and suburbs, thus facilitating commutation and strengthening the dominance of the central cities. We purposely did not plan to provide service to outlying commercial and industrial centers.

While this choice was theoretically sound, the results were not exactly what we foresaw. San

Francisco's dominant role as the regional headquarters indeed has been reinforced, but reinforced to the point of generating justifiable opposition to further proliferation of closely packed high-rise buildings. Many city planners agree with the environmentalists' battle cry, "Stop the Manhattanization of San Francisco." Further, downtown Oakland and Berkeley have gained relatively little strength from rapid transit service. And the suburban shopping centers and industrial parks, unserved by BART, have become focal points of traffic congestion with impacts far beyond their immediate vicinity.

To minimize costs and community disruption, BART lines followed existing rail rights-of-way wherever possible. In order to maintain high average train speeds, planners located stations at widely spaced intervals. Most BART patrons drive to the stations and park all day. Thus, the typical BART rider is an affluent suburbanite who travels to his downtown white collar job on a heavily subsidized transit system, while blue collar workers whose jobs are in outlying areas share the cost through their sales taxes and receive few benefits.

Market Street

I was retained in 1962 by the San Francisco Planning and Urban Research Association (SPUR) to head a team, including landscape architect Lawrence Halprin and architect George Rockrise, to develop a concept for the rejuvenation of Market Street, the city's run-down main business artery. The assignment was timely because the street was about to be torn up for construction of the underground BART line and a local subway. In our report, *What to Do About Market Street*, we proposed eliminating two traffic lanes; widening sidewalks; creating plazas at the new BART stations; and embellishing Market Street with ornamental paving, landscaping, lighting, signs, kiosks, benches, and other street furniture. We envisioned Market Street as San Francisco's Champs Elysees.

Voters approved a $25 million Market Street bond issue in 1965, although it took more than a decade to complete the improvements. Halprin was a member of the team that proposed the final designs, which, for the most part, were consistent with the concepts outlined in our report.

No expense was spared: brick sidewalks with granite curbs, double rows of sycamores, refurbished light standards (originally installed during the 1915 World's Fair), granite benches, bronze trash receptacles and bicycle racks, handsomely lettered street signs, and specially designed traffic signals. The city banished all overhanging signs, even theater marquees. But, despite these improvements, the landscaped plazas of the new office skyscrapers in the financial district, and new construction and remodeling in the retail sector, the basic character of the Market Street area remains unchanged. The amusement sector, with its X-rated movie theaters, pornographic bookstores, and penny arcades, is as tawdry as it ever was.

The obvious fact, overlooked by the planners, is that improving a street's appearance does not change the uses of adjacent properties in the absence of economic demand for new development. The people who use the street are still those who patronize its businesses and amusements. Market is still the people's street.

The growth of the city's low-income minority population is reflected in the character of Market Street. Public spaces like the plaza at the Powell Street BART station have become havens for down-and-outers, unemployed youths, and street entertainers. The new landscaping and street furniture have been vandalized, the walls defaced with spray paint, the brick sidewalks littered with trash. Unhappily, but inevitably, the cosmetic surgery on Market Street has cured no basic ills.

Yerba Buena Center

A year after the Market Street report, my firm was hired by Justin Herman, the dynamic director of the San Francisco Redevelopment Agency, to plan the South of Market Redevelopment Project, later renamed Yerba Buena Center. Herman had strong ideas about the future uses of the redevelopment area, the central feature of which was to be a convention complex and adjacent sports arena.

Our plan called for clearance of virtually all buildings in the project area except historic St. Patrick's Church and a few industrial buildings in the south portion. Studies prepared by other consultants gave assurance that adequate housing was available to relocate the 300 families and 3,000 elderly single men who lived in the project area. But because I had some reservations about moving the single men into residential hotels in the sleazy Tenderloin district north of Market Street, I proposed construction of 400 units of public housing for the elderly within the project area. This done, I pretty

much dismissed my concerns about relocation and enthusiastically addressed myself to designing plans for transforming the area to accommodate Herman's development proposals. I assumed that demolition and reconstruction would be under way within a few years.

Yerba Buena Center moved more slowly than I had anticipated. Support from City Hall was not strong, primarily because of justified doubts that the convention center could be self-supporting. The federal money needed to buy and clear the land was slow in coming. When it did become available in 1969, Herman launched an all-out effort to get the convention center built, retaining the world-famous Japanese architect, Kenzo Tange, to head a team to design a detailed development plan for the central blocks of the project area. I was a member of the team, along with architects Gerald McCue and John Bolles and landscape architect Lawrence Halprin. The Tange plan and the public relations campaign that accompanied it won city approval of the convention complex, and site clearance was accelerated.

We should not have been surprised—but we were—when residents of the area organized to oppose the project. While the Redevelopment Agency insisted that it met all legal requirements governing relocation, some of the elderly hotel tenants were displaced summarily. Represented by public interest lawyers, a group called Tenants and Owners in Opposition to Redevelopment (TOOR) went to court, demanding construction of 2,000 new low-rent housing units. That court case, a subsequent lawsuit based on failure to comply with environmental impact assessment requirements, plus financing problems and controversy over design of the convention center, delayed construction until 1979. One newspaper observed that it took longer to build than the Panama Canal.

In retrospect, it is clear to me that, while the Yerba Buena Center was a sound proposal, the project should not have been undertaken until relocation facilities had been provided for the low-income residents of the area. This means that relocation housing should have been built both inside and outside the project area, and the entire relocation process should have been handled with greater sensitivity and humanity.

Palo Alto foothills

One final example of a planning project that yielded mixed results is a study I led in 1969 and 1970 to determine the best use of some 7,500 acres of undeveloped land in the foothills of Palo Alto. After annexing the area 10 years earlier, the city had purchased 2,500 acres for a rural park and installed water mains and sewers on more than half of the remaining land.

The city had little interest in any type of commercial or industrial development in the foothills. Palo Alto already contains a highly successful regional shopping center, office park, and industrial park, all on land owned by Stanford University. But the city is plagued by severe traffic congestion and a chronic shortage of moderate-price housing. Our study examined 20 different residential patterns from all the standpoints now required in environmental impact assessments.

We also looked at what would happen if the foothills remained entirely undeveloped. Our calculations assumed that if the land were to remain in open space, the city would have to buy it at fair market value and repay with interest the taxes levied for the water and sewer lines that already had been installed. We found that the open-space alternative actually would cost the taxpayers less over a 20-year period than any of the development alternatives, despite the high cost of purchasing the land and repaying the taxes.

After months of debate, the city decided to turn down a pending planned unit development to be built in the foothills and to preserve the entire area as open space. When the necessary funds were found to be unavailable, the city rezoned the land as an open-space district, permitting only certain agricultural and open-space uses or residential development at a maximum density of one house per 10 acres. The applicant for the planned unit development sued the city, claiming inverse condemnation (taking of his land without payment) and won a $7.5 million judgment, although of course the land is worth far more today. Another inverse condemnation suit by an owner who had never proposed any type of development is pending, but a recent California supreme court decision indicates that the outcome is likely to be in the city's favor.

Palo Alto's action received widespread national publicity, both in professional planning publications and in the popular press. Conservationists were particularly delighted by our finding that in Palo Alto open-space preservation was financially as well as environmentally advantageous. Unfortunately, many zealots hastily concluded that what is true in Palo Alto must be true anywhere, overlooking the fact that residential development in Palo Alto is unusually costly to the taxpayers because of the city's lavish public service program and excellent school system.

As a result of the Palo Alto study, I received dozens of invitations to talk about urban planning and open-space conservation. On each occasion I stressed that Palo Alto is a special case and that open-space preservation results in a net cost to the taxpayers in cities with lower levels of public services. But people typically hear only what they want to hear, and, without real justification, I became a minor hero to many conservationists. On the strength of an undeserved reputation as an uncompromising advocate of open-space preservation, I received commissions to prepare comprehensive plans for such environmentally sensitive areas as Santa Barbara and Jackson Hole. Some residents of these areas were disappointed when the plans I prepared did not rule out all development possibilities. They were unable to accept a balanced view of the consequences of urban growth.

In retrospect

In most instances, the disillusionment I describe here did not set in until many years after the job was completed. In some cases, such as the BART plan, our mistakes did not become apparent for as long as 15 years. These time lapses help to explain why I enthusiastically embarked on project after project with a conviction that the public would benefit from my efforts. My optimism was neither unreasonable nor totally unwarranted. To some degree the public interest was well served by the assignments I have discussed, and there were many others where the benefits clearly outweighed the negative results.

In a sense, a public planning project is like a war. Either a good cause or an unworthy one may prevail, but there is certain to be a substantial number of innocent victims. It takes a considerable degree of foresight to decide whether the purpose of a major planning project is justifiable in terms of the public interest. If justification is seriously questionable, the planner should decline the assignment. I have done this a number of times.

It is much more difficult to judge how harmful a project's side effects will be. For instance, it is tough but not impossible to foretell whether a central district redevelopment project will revitalize an area. But deciding whether the results are warranted in the light of the human suffering and the financial cost involved is far more difficult.

My inability as a planner to make sound, far-sighted judgments on such side-effects issues is primarily what accounts for my frustration with the profession. I find it hard to believe that other planners do not have the same problem. As time passes and mistakes become evident, it seems logical that the mistakes will not be repeated. In many instances, however, logic does not prevail. I was dismayed to learn in 1979 that Houston is planning a rapid transit system and basing its decisions on many of the same erroneous judgments we made 25 years ago.

Like elected officials, public planners make decisions that cause some people to be winners and some to be losers. If there are too many losers, the public official eventually goes down to defeat. The public has no such protection from the mistakes of planners. Only an obvious, outrageous error or a long chain of errors with disastrous, cumulative effects discredits a planner.

In fairness, it must be granted that planners have tried to devise systems to evaluate the inevitable trade-offs implicit in their proposals. Statistical matrices, computer models, and a host of other devices have been utilized in attempting to measure just how much the winners will win and how much the losers will lose. None of these attempts has been fully successful.

Perhaps I am being unrealistic in seeking foolproof answers to such complex questions as are involved in most major public planning projects. But 30 years of seeing human values ignored, individuals unfairly treated, and public funds misspent have convinced me that planners must be held accountable for the consequences of their proposals. Planners must seek and find an accurate way to gauge the gains and losses that will stem from their proposals and identify unmistakably who will reap the gains and who will suffer the losses.

A voter or an elected official who is presented with such an accounting and who knows that it is valid then can accept or reject the planner's proposal with confidence. Until such an analytical system becomes available, plans made by planners should be treated with skepticism, ranging, as is appropriate in each case, from caution to distrust.

Lawrence Livingston, Jr., AICP, is the retired head of a San Francisco-based city and regional planning firm.

Warning From a Whistle Blower

Anonymous
(December 1981)

I was, until recently, the planning director of an areawide planning agency. While I was there, I witnessed widespread corruption. High-level employees of the agency conducted personal business on agency time, using office phones, and billed personal travel to the agency, misspending as much as $10,000 in public funds. They also may have violated federal law in their hiring practices.

Finally, I decided to blow the whistle—an experience that opened my eyes to the realities of investigative bodies. My agency's board of directors, which was supposed to handle such complaints, never questioned any of the activities of its employees, so I knew it would do no good to go to it. The state followed up on my complaint, but with little immediate effect. And the Federal Bureau of Investigation, where I went first, was remarkably slow to act. Moreover, I was unable to protect myself from retribution, as I had hoped to do.

Others, I hope, can benefit from what I learned.

It's important for any potential whistle blower to know what he's getting into. First, he must stop believing in myths. One such myth is that public agencies at any level are effective in exposing and stopping corruption. When I contacted the FBI, I half expected an Efrem Zimbalist type to be at my door in a matter of days. Instead, it was four months until I got an official inquiry and over a year until the bureau took its first, limited action, confiscating some of the agency's records.

The state's investigation was hampered by a shortage of funds. The attorney general's office, which was charged with the responsibility of ferreting out white collar crime, was consistently shortchanged by the state legislature. Also, the staff of the watchdog agency established by the state legislature includes a state senator who was implicated in the investigation of my agency and who leaked details of the investigation to my executive director, according to the latter's statements to me.

The second myth is that you can protect yourself. I was exposed by the good state senator and a fellow employee. Nor are whistle blowers immune from retaliation. The fact is that employers can either fire you at will or else make your job so miserable that you will quit voluntarily. Sure, the boss won't officially fire you because you have launched an investigation—unless he's unusually stupid; but he will manipulate the books so that he can let you go for lack of funds or some other trumped up reason. In my case, the reason given was the termination of the HUD and Intergovernmental Personnel Act programs I had been working on. Yet a week before my exposure as a whistle blower, I had been assured by my boss that I would be shifted to another program.

If you have any backbone at all, you won't take this lying down, and neither did I. I explored all my options, and all failed me. First, there was the grievance procedure established by the agency's board of directors. The problem here was that the board meetings generally were called only by the president, who was himself implicated in the various investigations; he refused to call a meeting to hear my grievance. Like many such boards, this one was handpicked and manipulated by the executive director and his cronies.

Since the board would not hear me out, I went to the state Equal Employment Opportunity Commission. Unfortunately, a male WASP does not have a lot of clout in using Title VII of the Civil Rights Act of 1964. I was informed that, although my situation was unfortunate, I could not be helped by EEOC unless I could document some sort of discrimination recognized by the agency. That I couldn't do.

Another option was to sue. The problems in doing so are substantial, however. First, there is the matter of legal costs. Estimates given to me by two different attorneys ranged from $2,000 to $7,000, and both felt that victory was chancy.

Second, the time involved in reaching the first rung of judicial review could be as much as three years. A third problem was what to charge the agency with. My first thought was to sue for breach of promise and breach of contract, but all our agreements were verbal and there were no witnesses.

My lawyer thought a slander charge was our best approach. This charge did not materialize, however. I could not prove that my reputation was being damaged. All I could prove was that I was fired for blowing the whistle. I had significant corroboration on that point. But it was all meaningless because of three significant factors:

First, I discovered that the deputy director, who was my main corroborator, was lying about his support of me and was secretly doing some empire building himself in anticipation of the executive director's departure. Second, the investigative heat put on by the local press caused various local officials to wilt in their support. Third, my attorney determined that in my state an employer could fire an employee at will in the absence of clear-cut discrimination. These factors essentially negated any case I might have had.

Last resort

A final option was to go to the press—which I did, solving some problems and creating others. The press can investigate such matters very thoroughly, and in my case the reporters did a better job than the government investigators.

Also, a bureaucrat may stonewall endlessly to another bureaucrat, but such an action can seem like guilt to a questioning reporter and subsequently to the reader or television viewer. Being in the dailies or on the six o'clock news as a whistle blower is not a good way to get another job, however. Some form of blackballing is a danger, even if the whistle blower acts anonymously.

I went to the various investigative authorities because of my indignation at such large-scale squandering of federal, state, and local tax monies and not because of some sort of grudge against my superiors. I encountered officials at all levels who honestly did not give a damn about the misuse of funds. And those that did care often moved too slowly to do any good. Moreover, the same officials continued to fund the agency, even after being shown evidence of abuse.

Some people, including members of my family, believe that nothing positive came out of the whole affair. I disagree. My former agency has been investigated to the hilt and the wrongs will be ferreted out. What will be done about them is another matter. Although I was disgusted with the apathy demonstrated by most agencies, particularly at the federal level where most of the funding came from, there were exceptions. These exceptions are still plugging along with their investigations.

All of this leads me to offer three pieces of advice to prospective whistle blowers. First, do it for the right reason: because an abuse has occurred, not because you dislike your boss or for some other reason that can be attacked as "sour grapes." Second, get into an offensive posture instead of a defensive one. That means making your allegations directly while you are still on the job and without leaking your intentions. Third, remember that there is usually a Judas in any organization. Act with discretion.

If I had it to do over again, knowing what I know now, would I do it again? Yes. Even though it cost me my job. I would do it again if the abuse I observe is so flagrant that I cannot ignore it without violating my ethical standards, as it was in this case. But in the future, I will blow the whistle only after consulting with my attorney, and I'll be better prepared to pay the price.

The author of this article is the former planning director of an areawide planning organization in a southern state. He now works for a city agency.

Where Have All the Radicals Gone?

Ruth Eckdish Knack and James Peters
(October 1985)

This Planning *roundtable is dedicated to the memory of Paul Davidoff, who died last December. Davidoff was a leading exponent of the view that planners should be advocates for those whose interests may not be represented, a view shared by a group of planners gathered in Montreal during the APA national planning conference in April, 1985.* Planning *asked them to consider the role of advocacy today and to reminisce about their involvement in the past. What follows is an edited version of the transcript of that two-hour discussion.*

PARTICIPANTS
(Titles correct as of 1985)

Pierre Clavel. Professor of city planning, Cornell University, Ithaca, New York.
Chester Hartman. Fellow, Institute for Policy Studies, Washington, D.C.
William Harris. Associate professor of city planning and director of the Center for Housing and the Social Environment, University of Virginia, Charlottesville.
Charles Hoch. Assistant professor of urban planning, University of Illinois at Chicago.
Jacqueline Leavitt. Acting associate professor of urban planning, University of California at Los Angeles.
Lewis Lubka. Associate professor of community and regional planning, North Dakota State University, Fargo.
Anshel Melamed. Associate professor and coordinator of urban studies, Concordia University, Montreal.
Ruth Price. Formerly a planner with the New Haven, Connecticut, Housing Authority.
Joel Werth. Director of planning, Department of Housing, City of Chicago.

Planning. In 1965, Paul Davidoff wrote a widely quoted article called "Advocacy and Pluralism in Planning." In it, he said that a planner should be an advocate for what he deems "proper" and that there should be "plural plans," including plans in opposition to official agency doctrine. How much of an effect did this article actually have on the planning of the 1960s and later?

Chester Hartman. Paul's article was important because it challenged a common misconception on the part of planners—that they are all serving the public interest. What he was saying was that all planners are, in fact, advocates for some definition of interest—but not necessarily the public interest.

No matter where they stood on the political spectrum, I think that his analysis changed people's views of what planning did and who planners were. It's very difficult nowadays for planners to disregard their class background, who they work for, the fact that there are competing interests, and that there are two sides to issues.

The other thing the article did was to spark a more progressive, more community-oriented view of what planners ought to be doing. People started to say, "Hey, if all those other planners out there are serving a certain set of interests, we should be defining our own set of interests." The idea came out of the urban renewal days when the government presented the notion that it was in the public interest to rebuild cities. But some of us were discovering that people were paying a high price for someone else's benefit. What Paul was saying was that those who traditionally paid that price needed their own planners, people who would help them express their own interests. . . .

Andy Melamed. Henry Fagin, the educator who influenced scores of students during the late 1950s and 60s, used to say that we've all been advocate planners—advocates for the power structure. Davidoff was calling on us, as technocrats, to be advocates for the powerless, for the people who haven't really got a voice.

Jackie Leavitt. The other thing that's important about the article is that it didn't define the outermost of what you could do as a planner but actually pushed you to think about other possibilities. For some people, the term "advocacy" was too confining.

Planning. Yet some people took offense when we invited them to a roundtable on "radical" planning. . . .

Lew Lubka. I agree that the concept of advocacy is quite narrow. "Radical" goes further, but it suggests far out things—people parading down the street nude. That's radical, but what does it get you? I consider myself a revolutionary rather than a radical. I want to see some fundamental change in society. On the whole, though, I prefer the term "progressive" because it suggests a broader range of things. There's another point, too, and that is that all of us here look at planning in a larger context. The first time I met Chester Hartman, for instance, was at a peace meeting in Maine. We were both planners, but we were both doing other things. And the first time I met Paul Davidoff, at a conference of Planners for Equal Opportunity, he wasn't talking about planning; he was talking about the Vietnam War.

Ruth Price. I had a similar experience. When Paul spoke in Connecticut before the last national election, he started out by saying that, if we don't have peace, the other issues don't matter. Then he talked about the election and how important it was to be involved, and a planner in the audience took issue with the fact that he was interjecting politics into the discussion. . . .

Charlie Hoch. Talking about all this in the past tense upsets me a lot. You make it sound as though it's over. But none of this stuff is dead for me or for a lot of my colleagues for that matter—it's our life. It's important to us to have this broader sense of what planning might be, to recognize that it's part of a broader social process. The excitement that the women's movement generated within the organization in the 1970s is a particularly powerful example to me because that's when I came into the profession. . . .

The last thing Davidoff would want is for us to be memorializing about advocacy. We may be going through politically hard times. But for me it's no less a time of important political significance.

Price. I don't think any of us want this to be a memorial. I think it's an impetus to continue.

Lubka. Besides, there are still some radical planners around—or progressive, or whatever you want to call them. True, I see a lot of "privatizing"—a lot of fine planning minds spending their time figuring out how to keep business profitable. But I'm still fighting. I'm still involved. My state, through the efforts of some of the planners, voted for nuclear freeze and against spending money for phony nuclear relocation plans. It's clear that there are still people who are looking for alternatives. . . .

William Harris. I have a problem with this whole issue because when we talk about advocacy planning we're talking about primarily a *white* response to a social problem. Years ago, white planners captured the advocacy movement and gave it a "safe" orientation. That was clearly demonstrated when the movement displaced its goals from challenging white racism to opposing the Vietnam War, to, now, protecting Central American refugees and similar issues. Yet the issue of white racism in the planning community is just not discussed.

The fact remains that advocacy planning has failed, and the biggest reason for the failure is the desire of planners to do something *for* someone. I don't know anyone in this country, even in the most depressed group of people, who needs to have planning done for them.

Hartman. I think most advocacy planners believe in empowerment and using whatever skills they have to help community groups fight their own battles. I don't know where your idea comes from.

Harris. It comes from the failure of that to happen—the failure of that empowerment to occur.

Leavitt. When we were organizing APA's women's technical division, the first title proposed was "Planning for Women." I objected that it seemed a bit patronizing, patriarchal if you will. It's been changed, but the point remains that a lot of people have difficulty confronting their own racism and their own sexism. I'm not excusing. I'm just trying to show that these problems exist for other groups as well.

Harris. You point up the great difficulty in speaking to whites about white racism. They simply say, "Yes, but there is also the issue of sexism and the issue of hungry people in other countries and the issue of peace."

People say to you, "I went to Mississippi on a freedom march." Well, I was in Mississippi two months ago, and, I'll tell you, things haven't changed a whole lot, and that's frightening.

Leavitt. I don't think we're the audience for what you're saying. The people in this room try to deal with some of these issues, and try to write and teach from the people's perspective, if you will.

Price. Can you suggest any strategies to change things?

Harris. I ran out of strategies in the sixties. What I say now when asked that question is, "Tell me your commitment and that will define your strategy." But that question—"What is your commitment?"—is one that advocate planners often find hard to answer honestly.

Lubka. Commitment might be the basis, but the key is how you organize it into a movement. I think many of us here tried to build a movement among planners that would focus their commitment into constructive channels.

Joel Werth. I find this discussion frustrating, again speaking from within a bureaucracy that day in and day out is trying to do something about affirmative action. The issues you're raising, though they might be important in the abstract, would not interest the blacks and whites I work with every day who are trying to do something to change the city of Chicago. They're busy trying to figure out how to get things past the city council.

Pierre Clavel. I think it's important to put the advocacy movement in the context of what has gone before. Did the planners of the day have an answer to Burnham in 1909, for instance, when he said "Make no little plans"? And then in the 1920s,

what was the position of the Regional Planning Association of America on the way zoning was developing? And in the 1940s, how did planners react to McCarthyism?

The point is that we've been through lots of different phases. And blacks and other minorities have been through different phases also, in the way they approach things. For me, the thing that seems most useful about the advocacy planning of the sixties and seventies is that a generation of white folks made contact with other kinds of people. The results might not have been exactly what the minorities had hoped for, but they did provide a bridge. I think that, in many respects, we're way ahead of where we were in the 1960s.

Lubka. I think we're getting a bit tangled up here. Let me get this thing back on course. We're in a profession called planning. We're also progressive-minded people. Now, how do we work toward social change, toward improving society? It's true, as Bill Harris said, that we're concerned with 35 million issues. From soup to nuts, we're concerned about it. And sometimes our efforts—and our results—may not be of the best quality. So what do we do? . . .

All of us are here because we're concerned. We're searching for the best way to operate. Should we be more radical and maybe isolate ourselves? Should we merge in with the profession? I don't know.

For myself, I believe in being upfront. I take part in demonstrations in town—about South Africa, El Salvador—whatever issue comes up in our area. I don't change my identity at five o'clock. I'm involved in the community, and I'm trying to use some of the skills I learned in planning to make myself a better, more progressive person.

Melamed. We're talking about being planners with a social conscience. I always found that when I was a practicing planner, I managed to get involved in local battles because those were the ones I was living with. I felt that I couldn't do a damn thing about the larger issues. After all, revolutions are basically won and lost by the people who are fighting for their own country. That's what will happen in Central America. We can send books down, we can send medical supplies. But it's always a drop in the bucket. So I simply chose to work at the local level.

Hoch. I've been accused of being idealistic about this, but the promise of planning to me is that it doesn't claim to be procedurally rational, that knowing the efficient techniques isn't all that counts. The important thing is that we understand what's worth doing. And that puts us in danger of being elitist, of saying what *should* be. But it's also in the old Enlightenment tradition of believing that reasoning and reflecting make a difference in the development of our culture. It's an idea that's being questioned in many quarters today. We encounter a lot of antiintellectualism.

But for me, there's no doubt. Being a planner means being reasonable, and that means making a fundamental claim about justice in our society. Yes, we're going to disagree about what that means. Yes, we have a lot to learn about what that means. But it should be a part of what we claim as a vision and a part of what our profession says to its membership and to the rest of the world. And that's what Paul Davidoff symbolized to me and why his work had such an impact.

It bothers me that we no longer seem to have this shared vision within the profession. But even so, many of the planners I meet, and many of my students too, though they often don't share my values, all have a tremendous ambivalence about justice. They want to do good, although they're not sure how to do it. And that ambivalence, it seems to me, we can shape, we can have an influence on. That's partly why I'm a teacher—because I want to say, "Yes, it does matter. It does make a difference. Justice *is* important."

Leavitt. I don't want to sound like a West Coast Pollyanna, but I think the planning program at UCLA keeps some of us on our toes. Many of the students we attract are active in Feminist Planners and Designers and the Minority Association of Planners and Architects, and they have cooperated on sponsoring programs. And many of the faculty, while they are interested in theoretical issues, are also active in local politics.

Allan Heskin and I are a doing a class on the homeless in this quarter, and we spend half of our time walking around Skid Row and talking with providers. We're dealing with issues not only of race and sex, but also of mental impairment and everything else. We're trying to raise issues and provide models for students so that when they go out there, they will get involved on an emotional level, because, unless they're involved personally, the work alone won't be enough to sustain them.

Ruth Knack is Planning's *senior editor; Jim Peters was formerly associate editor.*

Woman's Work
Ruth Eckdish Knack
(October 1986)

THE PARTICIPANTS
(Titles correct as of 1986)

Carol D. Barrett. Manager of the Community Development Bureau of the Greater Washington, D.C., Board of Trade and former planning director of Annapolis, Maryland.
Susan E. Brody. Planning director of Eugene, Oregon.
Patricia Casler. Community development director of Aurora, Illinois.
Corinne L. Gilb. Professor of urban studies at Wayne State University and former planning director of Detroit.
Florence Beck Kurdle. Planning director of Anne Arundel County, Annapolis, Maryland.
Ann Leviton. Former director of the Whitman County Regional Planning Council, Colfax, Washington.
Marjorie W. Macris. Planning director of Berkeley, California, and former planning director of Marin County, California.

Planning. Certainly women have come a long way in the last decade. But where do we really stand? How much discrimination persists today?

Marge Macris. Things have improved a lot since I started planning school at the University of Illinois in Urbana in the mid-1950s. In fact, I was the only woman in my class. I went into planning in large part because my other interest, journalism, simply did not have opportunities for women—except to do things like write wedding stories. But planning was expanding at that time, and women were being hired. So it seemed like a good field to go into.

It's different today. From the classes I've taught at the University of California at Berkeley, it looks to me as if about half the planning students are women, and so are the people in the entry-level and mid-range planning positions. That's not true on the planning director level, though. That's partly because not many women in my age group got in when I did. But it's also because some discrimination—even if it's not conscious—occurs when it comes to appointing women planning directors.

Becky Kurdle. I agree that time has made a difference. When I became planning director 10 years ago, I was the only woman department head in the county, and the county executive who appointed me frequently—and publicly—referred to me as the administration's "token woman."

Ann Leviton. But still discrimination does persist today. I experienced discrimination early in my career, in the mid-1970s, and also as recently as last year. In Tucson, where I started out, I was part of a class-action suit with two other women in a case where a male with less education and experience was promoted ahead of us. It was resolved when the city intervened and moved us all up.

Then I thought I might have a better opportunity to become a director in a small town or rural area. But I soon learned that a lot of people in rural areas simply don't believe that women can be good managers. In Albert Lea, Minnesota, I was kept as acting director for a year and then my position was removed from the budget in order to get rid of me. The moment I left, the position was reinstated and they hired a male.

Kurdle. A lot depends on the political climate. In less sophisticated jurisdictions, where there's a good old boy network, you don't get many points for hiring women. My county executive said recently that there are no longer any "political bennies"—benefits—for hiring women.

Susan Brody. In contrast, in Eugene, we have a situation where half of the council members are women. So appointing a woman department head is actually a politically popular thing to do.

Corinne Gilb. In my case, the mayor [Detroit mayor Coleman Young], who is very political, consciously chose to appoint a woman. But there's a big difference between getting the job and how you're treated after you have it. I soon learned that the administration wanted me to be much less capable than I turned out to be.

Pat Casler. It seems to me that whether women are appointed depends a lot on how politically active they've been in the community. Aurora has a strong League of Women Voters that has been involved in a lot of very high-profile political activities, including a change of government. So appointing a woman as head of a community de-

velopment department wasn't viewed so much as invading male turf. Other women had already laid the groundwork.

Planning. Once women are in the director's job, do they have special problems—or advantages—in dealing with other agency heads, politicians, and so on?

Brody. If there are problems, they're likely to be with public works because, traditionally, relations between planning and public works have been strained. But our public works director happens to be a woman, and we have a wonderful relationship.

Carol Barrett. I had so much trouble with public works in the community where I was planning director that at their Christmas party they toasted the fact that they didn't have to work for a woman. Interestingly enough, the director of that public works department is now in the private sector, and I deal with him from time to time. Only now I can provide something he needs, and he's a lot more cordial. . . .

Planning. What are the workplace issues that most concern you as women managers?

Brody. The issue that interests me is the question of promotions. When I have particularly talented women working for me, I'm inclined to want to give them the opportunities—rather than the men. And that makes me uncomfortable sometimes.

Kurdle. I don't think you should be uncomfortable. I recently, with regret, filled two top-level positions in my office with men because I couldn't find the right women. I have six divisions and six male division chiefs. I really feel an obligation as a female planning director to try to change that.

Barrett. APA should be providing resources to help in such situations. You should be able to call the national office or the Planning and Women Division and get names and resumes of qualified women.

I was faced with a dilemma as city planning director when a female staff member first asked for a two-month extension of her maternity leave and then asked to come back part-time.

The city turned me down when I asked for another part-time position so I would have the equivalent of a full-time staff person. Then I had to tell my employee that she either had to come back to work full-time or resign. I took a lot of grief from women for doing it, but I felt that my responsibility as a planning director required me to make that decision, although other sensibilities made me wish it could have been otherwise.

Gilb. My sensibilities go to the men because women in professions sometimes have an advantage over men. There has been a transformation in the situation for men, at least in Detroit, and I felt alert to their psychological needs.

Macris. That may be true, but women still face enormous problems, especially when they have kids. Our system is simply not set up to accommodate working mothers. I would really like to make it possible for people to have flexible hours and work part-time when their kids are little and then come back to work and share jobs and have child care readily available. But when you're working in local government, which is terribly strapped for resources, and when you've got to deliver a product, you often have to make awful choices like the one Carol had to make.

Brody. I would do what you did—try to make it possible for the employee to return to work and still accommodate the need to be home with the child for a while. But I would hope that I would exhibit the same kind of sensitivity to a male who might be in that kind of situation.

Kurdle. In a small shop like Carol's was, that half a person made a very large impact. I might have been able to swing the part-time position because I have a staff of 85, so I can shuffle people around a little bit more. We don't have a flextime policy in the county, but in my shop we have flextime, because I just quietly allow it.

Barrett. A lot of women I've talked to are frustrated by what the *Wall Street Journal* recently called "invisible ceilings" for women in management. They've gotten promotions and better staff jobs, but they don't get the line jobs that allow them to move all the way up. They get to be executive assistant to the planning director, but not chief of comprehensive planning, where they would have budgeting and hiring authority.

Obviously, the barriers would be even greater for minority women—Hispanics, blacks, Asians. We can't find out because there aren't any here—which is a problem in itself. But I'm curious about the women at this table. How did you crash through the invisible ceiling?

Kurdle. I had a mentor—a man who was very close to the county executive. The county executive wanted to put in a new planning director, and my mentor was influential in the decision to choose me. That's one way to get the job, although it's not how you keep it.

Gilb. In my case, a woman who had taken a course with me and who was close to the mayor pushed me as a candidate without my ever knowing it. The job offer came to me out of the blue. I was teaching full time and had no thought of a different career. I stepped right into a 75-person department ridden with intense racial problems in a city that was in terrible shape economically.

I think the mayor thought I was going to fall on my face in six weeks. To everybody's amazement, I did not. I stayed for six years under enormous pressure, but I got the job done, completing a master plan for the city. It was a trial by fire, but I live best under pressure and respond best to exotic and extreme challenge. That's when I feel my oats. So I was psychologically able to cope. But there is no formula that one can pass on to help somebody else do the same.

Kurdle. I think it helps, as you're going up the ladder, to try to find highly visible projects and to be competent at them. That's how you attract the attention of those who do the appointing.

Brody. Having someone who takes an interest in you makes all the difference in the world. In Alaska, where I had my first important administrative job, the person who hired me spent an enormous amount of time training me for the position. He was a very strong feminist, and I think he picked me in part *because* I was a woman.

Casler. I had a similar experience. The community development director, when I was a division head, made it clear that he wouldn't stand for anyone giving me any lip, any negative comments. By the time I got promoted to community development director, people were used to treating me in a certain way. By that time, too, I'd been head of two of the four divisions within community development, and people were used to seeing me in that context.

Macris. I like to hear that people had mentors, but I never did. My support came from my peers, from other women professionals, most of them a bit younger than I. They always encouraged me to try for the next step, and if I said I didn't know if I was ready, they would ask why not. Then we'd go through it again, and I'd say, "Well, OK, maybe I am." All along, the men I reported to were very skeptical about my ability to do the job. They were of the age and of the school that assumed that I wouldn't be able to, although of course I always proved that I could.

Kurdle. The mentor thing can be harmful as well. You have to be careful not to try to ride somebody's coattails, because you might ride them right out the door when your mentor is no longer in favor. . . .

Planning. With all that power, will women be corrupted?

Macris. A lot of people think women are not as power hungry as men, which may or may not be true and may or may not be good if it is true. But as a result, women are often perceived as more trustworthy than men. And that's very important to politicians. They won't necessarily agree with you, but they know they can trust you, that you're not going to stab them in the back.

Kurdle. Women often see power as something that you don't touch and certainly don't talk about. They're sometimes unwilling to try to understand the arithmetic of power, to really think it through and play the numbers and figure out how it works. Yet women have traditionally wielded great power, without necessarily understanding what they were doing.

Gilb. But sometimes to have power, you have to seem not to have it.

Kurdle. That's true, but you still have to understand how to manipulate it.

Brody. I recognize that from my own professional development. I used to think, naively perhaps, that I could simply present the facts and everyone would accept them. I've learned a lot about the importance of having a sharp political sense and how to lobby and all those other things I never expected to have to do.

Leviton. That's been my hardest lesson—that people don't always do the rational thing and that almost everything is political. In essence, you have to learn what people want and then develop their egos to get them to do what you want.

Kurdle. Some people never become comfortable with the politics involved, especially in local government.

Brody. What women bring to that aspect of planning is a skill at mediation. It's a particularly valuable skill in local government.

Casler. It can also be a weakness, though. There are times when I think I should stand up and scream about things instead of trying to work out

a resolution. I'm still not comfortable in the role of fist banger.

Macris. I always put getting power in terms of simply empowering the community to get what it wants. But it's true that there comes a time when you have to say what you're after.

Kurdle. Yet power is simply the ability to make things happen. Whether it's good or bad depends on the things you want to make happen.

Brody. On the one hand, we're conditioned to think of power as being ugly. Yet I think we all have to admit that we have a certain drive for power. It's certainly what's behind some of my ambition—and achievement too. Recognizing that helps me to deal with it.

Gilb. It's power for its own sake that is corrupt, not the kind that is really enablement, the kind that Michelangelo was talking about when he said he "merely freed the statue from the stone."

Ironically, perhaps, I got out of planning because I didn't think there was enough power in it. Theoretically, it's a tremendous field, but in the real world, it's highly limited. I felt that I actually had more scope as a university professor.

Planning. Women talk a lot today about "wanting it all"—careers and family. Is that particularly difficult for women in planning?

Kurdle. In some ways it is because of the irregular hours and night meetings.

Barrett. I encountered a lot of hostility when I had a baby and continued to work as a planning director. Bringing the baby in to a meeting generated a letter to the mayor. People seemed to be saying, you can be a woman, and you can be a planning director, but you can't be a mother and a woman *and* a planning director.

Brody. I feel guilty when I have two evening meetings in a row and can't be with my three-year-old. Yet being in management also gives you flexibility.

Kurdle. I think these things will sort themselves out as women no longer feel the need to be super everything. My generation certainly did. I almost ran myself into the ground trying to be all things to my family and to my job. Women today are beginning to put things back in perspective.

Macris. So much so that my daughter, who is also a planner, simply doesn't understand what I'm talking about when I describe the problems I faced when I started out. I'm glad, by the way, that she decided, on her own, to go into planning. It's a good field—and for women it's getting better.

Ruth Knack is the senior editor of Planning.

Making City Planning Work
Allan B. Jacobs
(September 1978)

My first recommendation on a major city planning issue to the San Francisco City Planning Commission was a loser.

At a joint meeting of the planning commission and the San Francisco Redevelopment Agency, held in the formal, wood paneled, heavily draped chambers of the Board of Supervisors in late March 1967, I recommended against changing the plan for the Embarcadero Center section of the Golden Gateway redevelopment project to permit buildings of over 25 stories. The commissioners, who had only recently hired me, voted against my recommendation. Instead, they voted for changes that would permit one building near the waterfront to rise 60 floors and another to jump to over 40 floors. They also voted for a third building that would be exactly 25 stories tall but would stretch two blocks in length; it would create a new Chinese wall in small-scaled San Francisco. The only holdout was a new commissioner who had not been involved in my hiring. He abstained.

A few days later I flew back to Philadelphia, where I was winding up teaching at the University of Pennsylvania, and began to wonder why I had accepted the San Francisco job in the first place. During an earlier visit I had tangled with Justin Herman, director of the Redevelopment Agency, and John Portman, architect-developer for the Embarcadero Center project. We met at the San Francisco Museum of Art, around a model of the proposed project. Portman said that my opinion of his design was subjective and that he didn't see why he should have to be concerned with what I thought. My screaming reply—that as long as the project had to come before the planning department for my recommendation, he had goddamned well better be concerned with my opinion—was not considered friendly.

Then, too, on my first day in the city, I was greeted by a headline announcing that my department, without first informing either the planning commission or its new director, had just made public a report stating its opposition to any future freeway construction in the city. While the conclusion may have been reasonable, the report was less than perfect; and as a new boy in town I was not looking to make instant enemies among bureaucrats like the director of public works or the chamber of commerce.

At first glance, the staff seemed a mixed blessing in terms of quality and the caution with which they received me. After meeting with the head of Civil Service, I was left with the impression that he was serious about my not having any say over hiring and firing. Indeed, I was to learn very shortly that I might not even be able to fire an employee who was on probation, a period during which I supposedly had absolute authority. . . .

Why then was I leaving the University of Pennsylvania to become director of the San Francisco Department of City Planning?

There were reasons, of course. Not the least of them was simple, old-fashioned ego satisfaction. In late 1966, when I was first contacted about the position, I was about to finish my thirty-eighth year. I felt that I had served my apprenticeship as a city planner. Twelve years earlier I had earned my graduate degree in city planning from the University of Pennsylvania. After studying new towns in England for a year, I had learned the nuts and bolts of my craft and art in Cleveland, Pittsburgh, and Calcutta. . . . I had been fortunate to work with some inspired and outstanding people, and now it was time to try my own hand. I told my friend, Dave Wallace, an incredibly gifted city planner, that I wanted a shot at being boss. He was sympathetic, but he couldn't resist throwing in a gratuitous "You never are."

San Francisco itself had something to do with my decision to go there. I had enjoyed myself immensely on three brief visits in the late fifties and early sixties. The hills, the views, the climate, the water, the street activity, the bridges, the small-scaled but intensely urban development—all these created an impression of an extremely livable city, unlike so many of its eastern counterparts. San Francisco was a city I wanted to live in.

More important to my decision was the nature of the times. The middle and late sixties were days of urban riots and long, hot summers. After years of unfulfilled promises, the minorities and the poor were tired of waiting. They wanted their share. They were intent, too, on making such phrases as "maximum feasible participation" mean what they said. In 1965, on the way home after two years in Calcutta, I read about the rioting in Watts. Watts was followed by dozens of other riots in major cities, and San Francisco was not immune. A black teenager in Hunter's Point was fatally shot by a policeman on September 27, 1966. In the aftermath of that shooting, the city went through what some call its worst outbreak of racial violence, complete with shooting, the National Guard, fires, and looting. Eighty arrests were made. The violence subsided within a day or two, but the tension remained.

In 1966, then, it seemed more important to be doing city planning than to be teaching it. City planning had to be made meaningful to the lives of all the people of a community. I believed then that I should and could help solve some urban problems and that I could do this best by being where the action was.

Another issue concerned me as well. That was the matter of making planning relevant within the decision-making process of local government. In the early fifties, when I was in school, city planning seemed to be an important part of government in cities like Cleveland, Detroit, Philadelphia, Cincinnati, Chicago, New York, and Pittsburgh. I was left with the impression that real attention was given to the city planners' plans; that roads got built where planners said they should be; that parks, playgrounds, schools, and other public facilities had a good chance of being built if they were part of a public plan; that programs conceived by planners to help eliminate social inequities would become reality; and that city planners not only talked to but were listened to by mayors and councilmen, who sought and welcomed their advice on all sorts of matters related to the development and well-being of their communities. My early experience in Cleveland, where Mayor Anthony Celebrezze regularly met with and listened to his planners (even young ones like me just out of school), supported my belief in the efficacy of planning. "Plans that gather dust on the shelves" was not yet a universally known phrase.

But by the mid-1960s things had changed. It seemed possible then to count on the fingers of one hand the communities where city planning was relevant to decision making. Urban renewal agencies, not planning departments, had the money and power and they "got things done." If a citywide plan existed, it was likely to be changed to conform to the dictates of a marketable redevelopment project. But the redevelopment project was rarely changed to carry out the policies of a master plan. Except in a few cities—Philadelphia was the shining example—planning departments were more often to be bypassed than consulted. That, at least, was the way it seemed to me in December 1966 when I was trying to make up my mind about this job. And so there was the challenge of making city planning work in San Francisco, a city where I had the impression, right or wrong, that it did not.

I had also heard from friends both in the East and in California that the staff of the San Francisco Department of City Planning was less than outstanding. Morale was low, the staff was occupied almost exclusively with zoning matters, and civil service regulations made it nearly impossible to hire competent people or to fire the incompetent ones. Although I wasn't sure that any of this was true—it simply could not be all that bad—I wanted the chance to build and to keep a high-quality staff.
· · ·

Cooperative effort

No one plans a city alone. It takes a good-sized staff to run a city planning department and to make the day-to-day decisions that are needed. In 1967, there were 62 permanent employees in the San Francisco Department of City Planning. My initial assessment, based on their resumes, comments they made at staff meetings, and personal contacts, was that they were indeed a mixed lot.

On the one hand, there were a few extremely bright, dedicated, experienced, and well-trained professionals. They were underpaid and overworked, and sometimes they were abused by the public and even by their colleagues. I wondered often what kept them at their jobs. Their presence, I concluded, reflected a value system, too seldom found, that says public service is the noblest calling and that it deserves the best. This group was augmented by four or five equally talented, although untrained and inexperienced, young people. . . .

[The strength that some of the staff members exhibited was matched by the mediocrity and incompetence of others.] One planner insisted that it was impossible to analyze neighborhood traffic properly without having lived in the neighborhood for at least a year. A demographer related local population projections to famine in India centuries ago. Some had problems in writing the English language and in adding columns of figures. Some senior people seemed to have been there forever and to have reached their protected civil service slots by reason of endurance rather than merit. Other than dreaming about their removal, there was nothing to be done about these people. By far the largest group was made up of those who were neither good nor bad. Some simply suffered from an inadequate education. Others were showing the strains and insecurities that develop when talents are unappreciated and unrecognized. Years earlier, one staff member had proposed an underground freeway where the monstrous, never-to-be-completed Embarcadero freeway now stands. For his daring he was publicly chastised by his director with words to the effect of "How can I do my job when I have staff that proposes stuff like this?" So they came to work every day and did their jobs, but without spark or enthusiasm. Maybe it would be possible to light a few fires among them. . . .

If one were to think hard about the problems of getting and keeping a high-quality city planning staff in San Francisco, one could reasonably conclude that to do so is legally impossible. It became clear that I would have to capitalize on low-level openings, filling them with top-notch young people who would forgo the better salaries paid elsewhere in favor of exciting and socially relevant work. I also would have to try to make the few new senior openings specialty positions that could be filled from the outside. I intended to elevate two of the most senior positions, which were then vacant, to the level of assistant director; the new positions would be equal with the one assistant director slot that already existed. In conjunction with this last move, and in order to have a semblance of power consistent with my responsibilities, it was decided to ask for an amendment that would make the three assistant director positions and the administrative assistant post appointive by the director, rather than filling them through civil service hiring mechanisms. That charter amendment was to be listed on the November ballot as "Proposition J." . . .

There was no dearth of issues that required immediate attention and resolution in the last half of 1967. From late May until the end of the year over 100 official actions were taken by the city planning commission that required some kind of staff recommendation. They ranged from approval of a proposal for major rezoning of the downtown area (it took two and one-half years of staff work to prepare for this decision) to disapproval of a plan for a downtown garage, to endorsement, with reservations, of the city-centered regional plan of the Association of Bay Area Governments. This says nothing, of course, of the myriad matters that required meetings with the mayor (about ways to modernize the municipal transit system), with the Board of Supervisors (O'Shaughnessy Boulevard should be rebuilt), with other city officials (about the accuracy of the information on housing vacancy that was being used to determine the pace of the redevelopment program), with developers and their representatives ("I cannot support the International Market Center as you propose it"), and with citizen groups (the Model Cities program seems reasonable in the South Bayshore).

The downtown zoning study, which had been prepared by the staff with the aid of consultants, was probably the most pressing matter to come before the planning commission during this early period. The zoning that it called for downtown was more restrictive and more finely drawn than the existing zoning. Among the more significant proposals were these: Allow less space for prime office and commercial development and direct such development toward planned transit improvements and away from residential and historic areas; offer development bonuses in exchange for such privately built conveniences as plazas and direct access to transit; reduce development intensities; and, for the first time, impose height restrictions in some critical areas. Although there was no explicit downtown plan to which the proposed zoning was tied, it soon became apparent that the zoning staff did have some kind of implicit plan in mind. It was clear, for example, that they were trying to create a more compact, transit-oriented downtown; that they wanted to maintain retail shopping continuity where it was strongest; that they wanted to keep parking away from the center of downtown; and that they wanted to lower drastically the number and size of office buildings that could be built under existing zoning. In any case, it would be untoward for a new director to suggest that after years of staff work, adoption of the new ordinance should be postponed until a plan was prepared.

I learned quite a bit about San Francisco and its people during the public hearings and negotiations. For one thing, I learned that the chamber of commerce was extremely well funded and had a large staff. It had extensive associations with elected officials, commissioners, architects, and the media, and it was understandably opposed to constraints on development. Bigger is better was the prevailing philosophy at the chamber. Government should keep its hands off. Although that position was predictable, the chamber's strength was a modest surprise. More surprising was the philosophy of the committee of the local chapter of the American Institute of Architects that was monitoring the proposed ordinance. Its chairman and some of its members seemed philosophically in tune with Ayn Rand's Howard Roark and were at heart opposed to any zoning. Later, I was to find that this committee was not wholly representative. . . .

Fast track

Boredom was not a problem during those early months in San Francisco. In addition to finding out what the staff was doing and beginning to direct its efforts, it was important to get to know San Francisco and its people. I learned about the city more in weekend walks and quick visits to particular sites that were at issue than by making use of the blocks of office time that I reserved for that purpose. Unscheduled—but always "urgent"— meetings with this official or that group often intruded on time scheduled for field trips.

Getting to know the people of San Francisco seemed no task at all. Their attendance and participation at planning commission meetings, especially at hearings on zoning issues, was remarkable, much greater than I had experienced elsewhere. They even attended general meetings and committee meetings of the Board of Supervisors in considerable numbers. Once there, they had few reservations about speaking their piece, not hesitating to castigate the processes of government that denied them adequate participation. Beyond these formal meetings, many people acting as individuals or as part of a group found no problem in telephoning their concerns to the planning director or in coming to the office for meetings. Accessibility was as important for me as it was for them.

Many of the neighborhood associations that abound in the city sought out the new planning director either to ask him to speak or to let him know

early in his tenure what their problems were and what they might want. I do not recall declining an invitation to a neighborhood association meeting during the period. I tried to be as informal as possible, to ask and to answer questions about the concerns of the residents, and to find out what they thought the department should be doing. The only problem with the neighborhood meetings was that there were few invitations from minority or poor neighborhoods. But even so, these meetings taught me more about the city than any other source. . . .

From all these sources [including the press], as well as from discussions with public officials, reflections on the results of recent elections, and observations of the actions of the Board of Supervisors, it was possible over a four- or five-month period to get a sense of the major issues in San Francisco. Most significant was the issue of citizen distrust. Simply put, it appeared that there were very few public officials that people trusted. The reason for the distrust was not entirely clear, but it had something to do with promises unfulfilled; with a growing awareness that the data and projections of the technicians were sometimes inaccurate and always subject to divergent interpretations; and with a sense that the process of physical, social, and economic change was almost out of control.

Housing was a major issue. There simply was not enough housing at prices that people could afford, especially for the poor and for minorities—in San Francisco mainly blacks, Chicanos, and Chinese. The problem was made worse by the dislocation of low-income, minority families, especially blacks, that was brought about by freeway construction and the redevelopment program. The excesses of the redevelopment program were in large measure responsible for the coalitions of moderate- and low-income people organized to stop it, for the alertness of the neighborhood associations to anything that smacked of renewal, and for the high degree of public awareness about all housing matters.

Transportation was another issue. San Franciscans had made it clear that they wanted no more freeways. In what has been called the country's first major freeway revolt, the Board of Supervisors rejected a federal expenditure of some $280 million to complete two of them, the Embarcadero and the Central. The antihighway forces looked at almost any proposed roadway change with jaundiced eyes—"It's a freeway in disguise!"—and were convinced that improved public transit was the only solution. At the same time, the city's gridiron street pattern, together with what seemed to me as excessively wide streets with little or no landscaping, invited auto traffic and made many streets unpleasant and unsafe places to be. Neighborhoods with streets like that seemed less than totally desirable places to live and therefore vulnerable to competition from the suburbs. I said as much at early neighborhood meetings.

In perhaps no other major American city was urban design a significant issue. For those few not already aware that this was an extremely attractive and joyful place to live, well-publicized surveys showed San Francisco to be just about every American tourist's favorite city. Residents, especially those living in the most favored locations, were alert to building proposals that offended them, and they were prepared to do public battle to stop them. . . .

Finally, zoning was a continuing issue, not in a citywide sense but in that many, many individual proposals for change, often initiated by someone wanting to develop property at a greater density than was permitted under the zoning code, were hotly contested. These contests involved considerable effort by all parties concerned, including representations by lawyers, architects, and other professionals, and they often filled the hearing chambers to overflowing. Five to 10 cases were heard at the first planning commission meeting of each month.

The backdrop for these issues was a governmental and political structure that was new and strange to me. It seemed a naive and cumbersome government, hardly suited to efficient, contemporary methods of management, and incapable of being responsive to the kinds of issues that demanded attention. Nor was it clear in this supposedly nonpartisan government whether top elected officials were void of strong leadership qualities or if they were indeed without significant power. Mayor John Shelley's staff was unusually small, with four or five assistants at best. In my few meetings with the mayor and other department executives, he gave few orders and was undemanding of actions or programs. Although department heads seemed knowing and confident when I met with them alone, many appeared uneasy in the mayor's presence, and I wondered what, if anything, was going to happen as a result of the decisions made in that

office. By far the strongest presence was that of Chief Administrative Officer Tom Mellon—red-faced, white-haired, the epitome of everyone's favorite, kindly, political father figure. A goodly number of the city's operating departments were under him and, as an ex officio member of the planning commission, he was reserved a seat of honor, which he usually filled, at meetings of the Board of Supervisors.

If public officials appeared strong and confident in the mayor's office or in meetings with their peers, they were clearly less confident when asked to testify before the Board of Supervisors. Despite their reputed job security they often stood mute before outlandish attacks by a few board members. Perhaps power did not reside with the civil servants. Or were they just being smart by holding their tongues?

The 11-member Board of Supervisors, with six or seven conservative downtown business and development-oriented members, might have been quite typical of the governing boards of many large cities, but it also seemed rather incongruous in a city that was then giving birth to the "hippies." Except for their antifreeway position, most of the supervisors did not see the issues I did during this period. Although members of the board were then without individual staff aides, most of them were remarkably accessible. One phone call was usually all that was required.

Most notable to me were the rules under which all these people operated. The *Charter of the City and County of San Francisco* is a long document. It goes on for over 300 pages, dealing with such matters as the cable car routes and the compensation to be given planning commissioners for their attendance at meetings ($15). It requires a line-item budget form that tells a citizen how much a department will spend for janitorial services but says almost nothing about the duties and responsibilities of that department. Departments did not have the flexibility to transfer allotted funds from one purpose to another. I was reminded that the charter says that elected officials may not meddle in the affairs of a department under penalty of being removed from office. Over and over again one heard, "The charter says . . . ," in response to "Why doesn't someone do this or that?" It took a vote of the people to change any part of the document. I read the parts related to the department of city planning, but I have to admit that I never got around to reading the rest.

I was coming to the conclusion that no one had much power in San Francisco. This was a situation that did not coincide with my preconceptions about government, especially the need for local government to be responsive. There was a naive, textbook nature to it all, hardly "big city." It was the kind of government about which a newcomer might shake his head in disbelief and smile, as yet unaware that he was comfortable within it.

I end my account of this period in November of 1967—but not because there was a local election in that month, or because the honeymoon was drawing to a close. There was no honeymoon. If anything, my first months in San Francisco might be termed a period of discovering new hurdles at every turn, each one apparently invented to keep a new planning director from doing his job. But I was much too busy, working much too hard, experiencing too much that was new, and too full of energy and thoughts of the future to be anything but optimistic. . . .

Allan B. Jacobs, AICP, San Francisco's city planning director from 1967 to 1974, teaches in the Department of City and Regional Planning at the University of California, Berkeley. This article was exerpted from Making City Planning Work, *published by APA in 1978.*

How to Survive as a Big City Planning Director

Sylvia Lewis
(December 1983)

What does it take to succeed as the planning director of a large city—to derive personal and professional satisfaction from the job, to see your policies upheld and programs put into effect—and to stay in office? The experts say it takes both technical expertise and political acumen, for starters. But those who have held the office—and hung on to it for a long time—say that planning directors also need a thick skin and, judging by the shouting matches some of them gleefully describe, a good set of lungs as well.

While no one has invented a blueprint for the

perfect planning director—an impossible task, given the varied nature of U.S. cities—the pros tend to have some traits in common and generally agree about the ingredients needed for success. These traits may not be the same for people who serve in small agencies, where the planning director also writes all the zoning and subdivision ordinances. But in the agencies with million-dollar budgets and dozens or even hundreds of employees, directors must, above all, be good at plotting strategy to make sure their policies fly. They leave the hands-on work—tasks such as budgeting, administration, and technical reports—to their staff. In many respects, the planning office is like the military, except that the battles aren't so bloody. The lieutenants do the field work while the generals mull over tactics in the war room.

Like other people in the public eye, planning directors are better off being tough-minded, not easily wounded by insult, calumny, or attacks on their job or, indeed, on their character. Calvin Hamilton, the long-time planning director of Los Angeles, says he's been called all sorts of names, including Communist. At one time, he was accused by the *Los Angeles Times* of a conflict of interest in buying some land—a charge that led to a six-week investigation by the Los Angeles Police Department before it was dismissed.

Hamilton's job has been in jeopardy at least twice—once when the city council was after his hide and once when a mayor was annoyed with him over a citywide downzoning scheme (eventually adopted). He survived both times—mostly, he recalls, because the parties involved couldn't muster enough planning commission votes to get rid of him. Does he get flustered by the *sturm und drang*? Apparently not. "I'm willing to take a lot of guff, a lot of heat in the press," he says. "Then I go back to the office the next day and forget about it. You can't take these things seriously."

Hamilton, of course, can afford to be thick-skinned. After 20 years in the job, the longest tenure of any Los Angeles city official, he's weathered many storms, and he's become something of an institution along the way. During his time, he has developed an international reputation for state-of-the-art planning (such as the city's massive downzoning, which would redirect growth and cut the projected population in half); lectured on three continents; and served as consultant to mayors and planning officials in several foreign countries.

Aside from having a thick skin, you have a better chance of success, according to Hamilton and others, if you are willing to take risks and to stand on principle, even if your job is at stake. In his book, *Making City Planning Work,* Allan Jacobs says that when he served as planning director of San Francisco between 1968 and 1974, he put his planning commission on notice that they were welcome to fire him at any time. That way, he wouldn't compromise his principles just to keep his job.

First, though, you have to get the job. Even if the position is vacant, the planning director's job may not be easy to secure from inside. It took some doing for Richard Counts, the Phoenix planning director, to muscle his way into the job. In 1978, when the city was hiring to fill the director's spot, Counts had been the city's zoning administrator and a planning department deputy for five years, but he was told that the city wanted to hire from the outside.

What he had going against him, he says, was that he was a lawyer by training (and thus was pigeonholed as a land-use expert with narrow interests) and a Young Turk by nature. "I think it's fair to say that I was the most difficult deputy my predecessor had to deal with," he recalls. What he had going for him, though, was chutzpah. "The planning commission said, 'We want a new brush—no one from the staff.' I told them, 'I'll be the new guy'—but I really had to do a hard sell."

Rules of the game

If life were fair, new planning directors would have a firm agenda and all the necessary laws, budget, and power to put the agenda into effect. . . . Not everyone is so lucky, though some get close. For example, Baltimore's city charter requires that the planning department do all the capital improvements programming for the city. Larry Reich, the planning director there for 17 years, sees two advantages in this arrangement. Capital improvements programming, he says, gives the mayor a tangible tool, and "it's a way of making the planning department directly useful to the city administration."

The Baltimore planning department reviews all programs with the mayor and the city council and—through a surveillance system—keeps track of all developments in the pipeline. The planning department can provide the mayor with a monthly status report on every project that has been funded.

That arrangement keeps the boss happy because he never gets a nasty surprise about a lagging project.

"You have to recognize that most chief operating officers in city government aren't terribly interested in long-term plans, but they *are* interested in implementing plans that were adopted in their administration," Reich says. He also notes that the individuals who preceded him as planning director had the same mandate to do capital improvements programming but hadn't exploited the opportunity. Mayor William Donald Schaefer (under whom Reich has worked for 12 years) saw the value of the system and insisted that it be carried out—with some help from his planning director. "I lobbied for capital improvements programming, although I did it gradually," Reich says.

Reich is low-key about his political activities inside city government. He speaks of liaisons with other city departments, not battles. Other planning directors are more combative, either by nature or because the planning department is in a weaker position in their local government. In many cases, the directors may have to fight and maneuver for power—although they argue that they are fighting for good planning rather than for power per se.

Allan Jacobs, in *Making City Planning Work,* describes how much his perspective differed from that of the city's Redevelopment Agency and how he tried to circumvent his rival: "Our involvement with urban redevelopment projects would be minimal. I was convinced that the Redevelopment Agency's approach to renewal was unsound, and clearly there was growing citizen disenchantment and fear of the program. Nevertheless, the agency had all the marbles. It had a large, high-quality staff; it had money; it had political and media support; and its staffers knew their way around city hall. Unfortunately, there was no way of becoming a colleague of the agency's director without also becoming his servant. We would, therefore, try to stand apart from the city's redevelopment efforts, instead assembling information about housing that anyone could use and developing separate programs, such as those related to slum prevention. Slowly, we would attempt to build a fence around the Redevelopment Agency's power and influence."

At the same time, Jacobs says, he hated to prevail on a particular issue only because he was a better politician, not because he was technically competent or because a planning principle had won out.

Winning in such a situation was "a little shameful," he says. For that reason, he worked to develop a competent staff—which became a hub of power because, above all, the planning department served as adviser to other departments and to the mayor and board of supervisors (the San Francisco equivalent of a city council).

Every planning director interviewed for this story agrees with Jacobs: Technical competence—good planning—comes first. Norman Krumholz, the former planning director of Cleveland, who obviously loves a good fight and is politically savvy, notes that his staff spent many years in the trenches.

An example, which Krumholz mentions in the spring 1982 issue of the *Journal of the American Planning Association,* involved a reorganization of the city's garbage collection department to update collection routes, reassign workers, and buy cost-saving equipment. "By the time we ended our work with them," he writes, "the division commissioner (a former garbageman) was a frequent speaker at national solid waste conferences, where he would talk of picking up garbage 'heuristically.'

"Our work was quiet, completely behind the scenes, and long term," Krumholz continues. "The division's willingness to accept our advice was based on the trust that our advice was worthy, that we would stay with them over the long pull, and that we would take some of the political heat as they sought to implement our recommendations."

Likewise, Larry Reich points out that his department has worked with the city's criminal justice system; specific proposals about the city jails eventually wound up in the capital improvements program.

Still, the technical work is performed by staff. The big-city planning director is principally a strategist—and therefore a political animal. Anthony Catanese, in a book he compiled with Paul Farmer (*Personality, Politics, and Planning*), writes, "The chief planner will often set guidelines for technical work, and sometimes even refine the results for presentation purposes to decision makers, but usually will not personally do the technical analysis and findings."

How, then, do planning directors spend their days? In meetings, mostly. A typical day in Allan Jacobs's busy schedule included a meeting with the mayor's deputy for development, a meeting with staff and would-be developers over use of the

shoreline in San Francisco's South Bayshore area, 40 minutes of paperwork and telephone calls, a meeting with the mayor regarding the Embarcadero Center renewal project, and a lunch meeting with local architects to discuss a comprehensive urban design plan. Lunch might be followed by a two-hour meeting with key staff on salaries, job classifications, and recruiting—and so on until bedtime.

Larry Reich meets daily with his two top deputies to review current issues and anticipate new ones. Calvin Hamilton says he spends 40 percent of his time on the technical aspects of planning, reviewing all reports and policy issues, and the rest meeting with committees, agency heads, and the mayor. He also meets with nine senior managers on Monday morning to review the previous week's meetings. He writes a weekly summary of everything going on in the department, which is then circulated to 80 individuals. He spends almost all day Wednesday reviewing the mayor's current programs.

"I delegate everything—all budgeting, all administration, all subdivision regulations," Hamilton says. "Staff come to me for advice on a sticky political situation or something that's very difficult technically. I offer to help; otherwise, they have full responsibility."

Planning directors also spend time nurturing their staff. Every director tries to bring people along, educate, and encourage them—with the result that they often leave for other jobs, including other positions in the city government. The advancement of subordinates can be a mark of the boss's success—and besides, it never hurts to have a trusted ally working for another agency.

Controlling staff

A downside of the planning director's job is that he or she can't always control the quality or size of the staff. Allan Jacobs complains about how little control he had over hiring, simply because the San Francisco Civil Service Commission had a stranglehold on hiring procedures. In recent years, planning directors have been in an even worse position. Faced with large budget cuts, they have had to lay off staff.

Larry Reich says that he had to lay off 10 percent of his staff this year. And Alan Canter, who resigned this fall after serving as Denver's planning director for 12 years, found that his last years in office were made particularly difficult by big budget cuts. His 1982 budget was trimmed so severely that he lost 15 of his 38 staff positions.

"The end result was that long-range planning became a casualty," says Canter. When interviewed earlier this year, Canter was still working under Mayor William McNichols, who subsequently lost his job to Frederico Pena. Although he didn't complain about his budget cuts, Canter must have found them tough to swallow, particularly because his big successes, in the early 1970s, had involved long-range planning and capital improvements programming.

Behind the strategy and tactics and all the staff effort lies an overall goal, the heart of the planning director's job. This doesn't mean a comprehensive plan. It means a personal belief or philosophy about what is best for a particular city. That conviction may be derived from past experience—or it may evolve from close contact with the community.

Calvin Hamilton's goal in Los Angeles, he says, has been to turn around a situation in which developers and speculators call the tune in land development; he has worked to have the city take control. Norman Krumholz says he started in Cleveland with a firm notion of what was important and stuck to it through 10 years in office.

Here's how he explains that goal in his APA *Journal* article:

"Regardless of who was mayor, the staff of the Cleveland City Planning Commission consistently operated in a way that was activist and interventionist in style and redistributive in objective. Our overriding goal was to provide a wider range of choices for those Cleveland residents who have few, if any choices. Why would this particular group of city planners act in a way that was highly visible and frequently politically risky? The urgent reality of conditions in Cleveland, the inherent unfairness and exploitative nature of our urban development process, the inability of local politics to address these problems, and our conception of the ethics of professional planning practice."

More recently, Krumholz described in a conversation why it's essential for a planning director to have an overriding goal. "Such a goal," he says, "gives you great clarity and great power. You can think clearly about each issue: 'Who gets? Who pays?' If it's the wrong group, you can chart a course."

Sometimes, sticking to a principle can be dangerous because it can jeopardize a career. Richard Counts and Calvin Hamilton say they were almost fired for sticking to the principle of controlled growth—Counts for opposing a large development in a low-density area (unsuccessfully, it turned out) and Hamilton for pushing the concept of downzoning (which eventually succeeded).

On the other hand, it helps to have an operating principle because that makes it easy to gauge success. Allan Jacobs, whose implicit goal was to maintain the quality of streetscape and skyline in San Francisco, knew he'd won big when the city adopted an ambitious urban design plan in 1971—after much planning department effort. Conversely, he knew he'd lost big when the Transamerica Corporation outmaneuvered him to build its big pyramid downtown—on the wrong site and with the wrong shape, at least from Jacobs's perspective.

Along the same lines, Norman Krumholz says his biggest success was getting the Cleveland public transit system transferred to a new regional transportation authority. As he recounts in the Catanese and Farmer book, the politicians in city hall wanted to settle for control of the regional transportation authority board, but Krumholz successfully pushed for guarantees on service and fares—thereby serving the low-income residents of the city, whom he took to be his primary clients.

Give and take

On a day-to-day basis, though, compromise is the modus operandi of local government. Sticking to a principle without compromise on details can be the equivalent of sticking with a sinking ship. That is why Allan Jacobs and Norman Krumholz both chuckle over old fights—a now-famous anecdote has Jacobs confronting Embarcadero Center developer John Portman in the San Francisco Museum of Art—but, in many other instances, both were willing to negotiate on fine points.

Calvin Hamilton clarifies this point. "I fight for principle," he says. "I compromise on little things. The next time around, I can strengthen the plan with amendments."

That's common sense. The planning director, after all, is a functionary, serving at the pleasure of the mayor or commission or council. Be willing to give on details, the pros say, but keep the overriding goal firmly in mind—and put your job on the line only for the principle. Have your bags packed mentally, Jacobs advises in his book, in case those you work for demand that you waffle on that principle.

Gauging the style of the community—and matching one's style to it—can be one of the hardest tasks for a new planning director, as Jack Schoop learned in Dallas. Schoop had left his job with the California Coastal Commission to take the top planning job in Dallas in 1979. His first big project in Texas involved putting together a study of Far North Dallas, a booming area plagued by traffic congestion and other problems that accompany fast growth.

The study involved six local governments. Everywhere else he had worked, Schoop says, the top guy represented the whole city. That was not true in Texas. The mayors and city managers of the communities surrounding Dallas couldn't deliver the vote of their city councils, Schoop says. As a result, the cities continued to grab whatever development came their way, and Schoop's plan sank without a trace.

"In each city, it's a game of assessing the political situation. I missed the ball that time," Schoop says. "After that, I didn't do anything on an inter-city basis unless the city councils were involved." Schoop stayed in Dallas two more years, overseeing two plans that he considers more successful—the Dallas 2000 study and a plan for the downtown arts district that was adopted while he was there.

It's interesting to note that of all the planning directors interviewed for this article, Schoop alone says that he had no particular goal in mind when he took his job. "I went to Dallas to work in a big-city context," he says. "I didn't go with an agenda. I went to do what was needed and do-able."

Clearly, many other planning directors have a different personal style. Hamilton says he had expected to leave his post in Los Angeles after 10 years but found that there was still too much planning to do. And Krumholz thinks longevity is a necessity if a planning director expects to have any impact on a community.

"The curse of the profession—and why planning is called ineffective—is that the model is to stay for a couple of years, look for your chance, and move up," says Krumholz. "But that almost guarantees that you're a political neophyte in any situation. If you stay, then you have a much higher chance of affecting decisions. You've paid your dues and are accepted by others as being legitimate. It's not

only longevity that's important. It's the willingness to keep pressing forward with your objectives. Then the other players in the game have to adjust their strategies. Pretty soon, you can negotiate."

Friends and foes

How, then, to survive long enough to pay those dues? One way is to build bridges. Richard Counts says the first thing he did upon becoming planning director in Phoenix was to get members of the chamber of commerce involved in task forces. Calvin Hamilton says that when he came to Los Angeles from Pittsburgh, he phoned the 50 most important people in town and asked them for the names of other important people. His VIP list soon included 250 people, and he talked with all of them.

Hamilton also keeps a file on people so that he can anticipate where they might stand on any given issue. He has computer files on community groups and a matrix worked out that shows how city council members have voted on various issues. These lists help him decide who his friends and enemies will be on any given issue. Friends are asked to help eliminate opposition, and opponents are brought around or outvoted.

Hamilton sums up the planning director's need for friends: "You have to have allies and support among business groups and in the city council. You have to have a circle of other department heads and contacts in the wider community—both for political viability and to get the job done."

Allan Jacobs—whose book can be read as an instruction manual for planning directors—is particularly informative about how he built bridges (and sometimes detours). Often, the coalitions shifted, although he always tried to stick close to the mayor and planning commission. Sometimes he worked with other city agencies to isolate a maverick; at other times, he went directly to neighborhood groups. He focused on the board of supervisors when his relationship with the mayor cooled. And, when nearly everyone was against him (for example, with the Transamerica Building), he tried all sorts of tactics but, in that instance, failed to rally support even from citizen groups.

Although the San Francisco city charter put the planning department in an inherently weak position, Jacobs nurtured his connections so well that, after a few years, his currency went up with citizen groups and other city agencies. "[Neighborhood] people were beginning to understand that we were fairly independent, that we were likely to advocate what we thought best from a city planning point of view, and that they could get a fair share from us," he writes.

The tactics worked with other city agencies, too: "Our familiarity with neighborhood issues may have suggested that we could help other agencies achieve their objectives. Our sense of what was politically possible and our ability to get programs funded also helped our relations. Most significant, I suspect, is that other departments thought of us as having a very good rapport with top decision makers, including the mayor. Whether or not they were correct is less important than the fact that that was their perception."

Jacobs's last point, about the need for the planning director to be close to the city's top politician, is something that every planning director stresses. "It's essential to be compatible with the mayor," says Calvin Hamilton, "because he can thwart everything you are trying to do, and I'm not sure it's worth it to fight that kind of obstacle."

However, being close doesn't necessarily mean sharing the same politics—merely the same style of operation or compatible personalities. Norman Krumholz, who served under three mayors in Cleveland between 1969 and 1979, says he was most productive under Mayor Ralph Perk, a Republican, although he was more in tune with the politics of the mayors who preceded and followed Perk: Carl Stokes, a Democrat, and Dennis Kucinich, a self-styled populist.

Looking back on his experiences, Krumholz recalls that Stokes's agenda had little to do with planning; he wanted to keep the city solvent, reform the police department, and build black political power. Kucinich, though more sympathetic to planning, was a confrontational type who alienated nearly everyone, Krumholz says. The lesson, says Krumholz, "is that it is less important to be politically in sync with the mayor than to provide a consistent point of view that the mayor can use."

As Allan Jacobs learned, however, a political rift between the planning director and the mayor can be unbridgeable, regardless of how compatible the two may have been in the past. In his book, Jacobs says that he and Mayor Joseph Alioto were close and explains how the two drifted apart—over a scruple. "For reasons that I will never fully understand, I seemed to have had it 'made' with the

mayor from the beginning," Jacobs writes. "I was considered to be 'one of the team' or 'one of the inner circle,' as a mayor's aide put it."

That was 1967. Four years later, Jacobs refused to campaign for Alioto, then running for re-election. After that, Jacobs writes, he was on Alioto's blacklist. His meetings with the mayor became infrequent and uncomfortable: "Even though I discussed the matter privately with him in an attempt to clear the air, that incident colored all our future relationships," Jacobs says.

Now, nine years after leaving his post, Jacobs says that his falling out with Alioto was only one reason for quitting. But after the 1971 mayoral election, his triumphs became less frequent and his interest in the job less profound. In addition, during his second term, Alioto outflanked Jacobs by setting up a mayor's Office of Community Development, funded with federal money, and by hiring Jacobs's deputy, Dean Macris, to head it. (Macris, by the way, eventually succeeded Jacobs in the job of San Francisco planning director—a post he now holds.)

Knowing when to exit gracefully is also part of the job of a planning director. Jacobs says the time is at hand when the personal stakes in staying (the lure of money, a nice home, job security) become more important than your principles. Another sign is when you get impatient with all those meetings or blow up without provocation. If peace becomes more important than negotiation, even a tough-minded planning director may begin to look elsewhere—or begin a book of memoirs.

Sylvia Lewis is the editor and associate publisher of Planning.

Why Can't Johnny Plan?
Melvin R. Levin
(September 1976)

The trouble with America's graduate schools of planning is that they are not teaching young people to be planners. This is not the same as saying that the curricula are "irrelevant," to use that much-overused phrase from the sixties. The schools seem to be going out of their way to be with it. No, I'm not talking about the focus of professional education. I'm saying that planning school graduates have not been given sufficient technical training of any type to make them employable in today's tight job market.

Much of the blame for that failure must fall on the planning school faculties. They can't teach planning because they have not spent enough time in the real world of planning agencies and consulting firms. They have given their energies to earning Ph.D.'s and writing scholarly tomes, not drafting and implementing zoning ordinances. If they can't teach their students how to do the practical work of a planner, it's because they've never been real planners themselves.

A quick look at the trends in planning education shows how this remarkable situation has come about.

Twenty years ago only the rare planning school graduate could have complained of having insufficient training in practical work. Graduate programs were run by land-use planners, most of them without Ph.D.'s, but possessing extensive agency and consulting experience. Like their fellows in architecture, the planning faculty operated an extensive consulting practice, including long-term, comprehensive planning contracts with nearby comunities. To help churn the work out, the faculty hired students to take care of the mundane parts of the job.

Even in this golden era, there were problems. In many cases the planning departments were simply grafted on to architecture schools. They became warped or stunted as a result. Many of the faculty were resistant, even hostile, to change. As the immutability of the Eisenhower years yielded to the rapid change of the early sixties, the sentiment grew that planning curricula—and the Old Guard who devised them—were too rigid and narrow-minded.

The verdict came down that many of the Old Guard had to be replaced. The new troops were a different breed. The first assault of doctorate-bearing academics into the planning schools was made by technocrats whose first love was mathematics. They thought of planning in terms of measurements, planimetrics, models, and regional science. They filled the technical literature with formulas and charts. . . .

Then came the Great Society, model cities, and the racial upheavals of the 1960s, all of which had a profound effect on planning education. Rallying round the banner of "relevance," students demanded a share in departmental governance and a focus on the planner's role as a "change agent" in the service of oppressed minorities. As curricula shifted toward the problems of race, poverty, and other social concerns, university planning departments began to draw heavily on a second wave of academics from other disciplines, particularly political science, sociology, economics, and the law.

This is not to suggest that this changeover in faculty was universal. Some smaller planning departments, particularly those linked to schools of architecture, virtually ignored the new wave. Others made token changes by adding a course or two in "hot" areas. But most departments were thoroughly altered in character. In a few instances the emphasis on the technocratic and social change role was so profound that these newly hatched planning departments never bothered to develop a serious land-use component.

The new breed of faculty was not only different, it was antagonistic. For the most part these young faculty possessed Ph.D.'s. Moreover, there was a deep sense that the old gang were abysmal failures, ignorant of math, lackeys of the establishment, blind to the nation's social problems, and not very bright. True, the Old Guard had published a great deal, but these were simple-minded technical reports for communities, just one step above a cookbook in profundity.

None of this is meant to suggest that the new regimes were barren of accomplishment. In contrast to the seat-of-the-pants operations of the Old Guard, the academics helped to provide a solid base of research and theory capable of being transmitted to students and working professionals. What was missing was a base of planning practice.

A mismatch

Hopes that government programs and private foundations would create a permanent market for the new breed of planning change agents proved overly sanguine. As a result, academically oriented faculty found themselves in the anomalous position of attempting to train planning students in skills they were not really prepared to teach for service in agencies they held in low esteem.

The capture of planning schools by the academics led to a growing mandarinism in planning education. This is a reference, of course, to the civil servant class of nineteenth-century China. These elite workers were masters at calligraphy and knew all the classics, but they were totally ignorant of industrial arts or weaponry. They were bright people who possessed none of the skills or knowledge needed to prevent China from being taken over by foreigners.

The academic mandarins also live in a closed world not unlike that of nineteenth-century China. They have developed a careful pecking order, an impenetrable jargon, and an all-around aloofness, not to say arrogance, toward real-world practitioners. They live, if not in an ivory tower, in a kind of hothouse, visible to the outside world, yet insulated from it. The mandarins have chosen a world where they can flourish without having any outside interference.

But in the larger academic universe planning departments occupy a lowly position. The reason is simple: The loyalties of the new breed lie with the academic departments from which they received their Ph.D.'s. They share the view that planning is an ersatz, synthetic discipline like unto home economics rather than economics, an Elba on which the sociologist, economist, political scientist, or lawyer is condemned to live in exile until a triumphant book or a stroke of luck will enable him to return to the *real* academic world.

Planning departments are in fact full of people who dream of returning to home base at some prestigious—that is, nonplanning—department. They yearn to play for the Yankees, but are stuck for now with the Wichita farm club.

The domination by mandarins has had a profound impact on professional training in planning departments. To begin with, unlike other professional schools, many planning department faculties are composed of people who have not missed an academic step from kindergarten through the doctorate. Certainly there is no hint of any substantial field experience or even much sympathy with those who possess it. Taking two to five years away from one's academic career line for the purpose of picking up substantive experience with a planning agency is viewed as a form of insanity. Career progress in the academic world depends on *academic* credentials, degrees, and publications, not one's success in drafting a planning proposal, having it adopted, and supervising its implementation.

What does the mandarin think of planners?

Some comments culled over the years from various planning faculty are instructive.

"We're training students for dull jobs so we (i.e., the faculty) can have interesting jobs."

"Cindy is too bright to be a land-use planner. I told her she should go on for her Ph.D."

"I've met only one planner with real conceptual ability."

"Tom is much too good to remain a planner. I've recommended law school."

"If you want to teach, stay around and finish your dissertation. A job would only sidetrack you and slow you down."

These are the merest tip of a very large iceberg. What they suggest is that a large proportion of planning faculty have little or no experience as practitioners, despise people who do (including their students who are ostensibly being trained as practitioners), and are incapable of providing usable professional training. It is clear that something has to be done to correct an educational system which is not doing its job.

Possible reforms

Now what can be done to reform the system? History has shown that bureaucracies rarely reform themselves, and the tendency for self-perpetuation among the academic mandarinates surely is as marked as in other bureaucracies. Department chairmen are locked into the system. The upper levels of university administration—the deans, provosts, and presidents—are content to leave well enough alone. As one high-ranking administrator put it, "We know our planning department is mediocre, but it seems to attract plenty of students. We'll let things rock along for a while."

How about the students? After all, they're the ones who are being exploited. But students rely on their professors for grades and recommendations, and they're gone in a couple of years anyway. Only a few kamikazes, Maoists, or hotheads are likely to call for a revolution in the composition of planning faculties.

That leaves the profession itself—the agency heads and consultants who do most of the hiring and who grumble about the people they're getting to fill the jobs. If there is to be reform, it will have to come from this quarter.

Reform is not likely to be easy or quick. Some of the professionals are awestruck by the academics, deferring to the pomp and circumstance of their caps and gowns. Other practitioners may themselves have their eye on a Ph.D. or a part-time teaching assignment. They are unlikely candidates to bring about the necessary changes.

The answer seems to be the establishment of a small, select commission composed of respected consultants and senior officials of planning agencies and beholden to no one. Such a panel could have a clear mandate to determine the extent to which planning departments are governed by academics with little or no practical experience, the manner in which graduates of these schools are suffering from the deficiencies in their education caused by a lack of practical experience, and the necessary corrective action.

Such a commission can gain legitimacy and authority by going over the heads of the departmental junta directly to the university presidents and boards of trustees. The panel could inform the universities that any lack of cooperation could result in their planning-school graduates not being given top-priority consideration for jobs.

If the panel works and the university administrations agree that planning faculties should have practical experience, what needs to be done then? The primary goal should be to fashion a reward-penalty system under which faculty are required to have stipulated amounts of field experience as part of the procedure for hiring, promoting, or granting tenure. Under such a system, the recommendations of agency officials and other practitioners would be given considerable weight in determining whether academics are hired, promoted, or given tenure. The Ph.D. and a list of academic publications would not be enough to assure a steady climb to the academic top.

The answer is to get the academics out into the real world. This won't be much of a problem for the younger, untenured faculty, who could be granted one- or two-year leaves of absence to work for agencies and consultants. They are bright, ambitious, hungry, and flexible and should work out fine for their employers.

The problem comes as you proceed up the hierarchy, through the tenured assistant and associate professors, right up to the hard-core academic mandarins. Exactly what can be done with the latter group is a puzzle. In academia as in haute cuisine, the oldest chickens are the toughest to make palatable. The qualities that make the mandarins troublesome as teachers make them equally unpro-

ductive as potential practitioners. By definition the mandarin is arrogant, receptive only to credentialized information—scholarly books, learned journals, and an occasional article on the *Times's* op-ed page. In such a celestial world, it's hard to imagine the mandarins getting worked up over a PUD ordinance for Tuscaloosa.

It may be that the only way to get rid of the mandarins is to transfer them to the "pure" disciplines they so love anyway—sociology, economics, political science. That may be the only feasible way of disintegrating the hard core of mandarins to the point where they no longer control the planning schools.

One thing seems clear—the profession cannot afford to drift along on the assumption that there are more pressing problems than the reform of planning education.

We must resolve to never again permit a fissure between the practice of planning and the teaching of planning. New faculty should be required not only to have substantial practical experience, but the criteria for hiring, promotion, and tenure should be revised to give substantial weight to agency and consulting background.

The working professionals have to take charge of planning education. The job is too important to be left to the educators themselves. It will be tough and time-consuming, but it's a job that must be done.

Melvin Levin, AICP, is a professor of urban studies and planning at the University of Maryland. He has had 11 years' experience working for planning agencies and consulting firms.

Harvard and MIT: Where It All Began

Bernard Cohen
(March 1981)

Zoning was no longer a novelty, there were some 400 planning boards across the country, and, for the first time in U.S. history, city dwellers constituted a majority of the population when Harvard University made its historic announcement 51 years ago. "A School of City Planning, the first in the country, will be founded at Harvard University this fall with the aid of the Rockefeller Foundation," proclaimed the four-page press release dated September 3, 1929. The statement quoted from the report of a 1928 conference at Columbia University that stressed the "need for trained guidance of city growth" in the face of predictions of unprecedented urban development in the coming 25 years.

Several events had set the stage for the momentous announcement, starting with the establishment in 1909 of the National Conference on City Planning (NCCP), headed by John Nolen, later of Harvard. Eight years later, 52 charter members, 13 of them associated with Harvard at one time or another, founded the American City Planning Institute (ACPI).

Equally influential was the unveiling in 1922 of the Regional Plan of New York and Its Environs, the first detailed regional plan for a large city undertaken in the United States. Charles Dyer Norton, in whose memory a chair was endowed when Harvard opened its new program in 1929, was the first chairman of the Committee on the Regional Plan for New York.

The decision to set up the degree-granting program at Harvard was a milestone not only because it launched planning education in the U.S. but also because it marked the end of the formative era of American planning practice. Exactly eight weeks after Harvard's announcement, the stock market crashed. Planning came to a standstill, to reemerge later with a different focus and sphere of interest.

It was during the low-point years of the Depression in 1931–32 that Harvard's neighbor, the Massachusetts Institute of Technology, inaugurated its five-year bachelor of architecture in city planning degree. In 1935, the Institute added a master of city planning program.

Two other planning divisions were established during the 1930s, at Cornell in 1935 and at Columbia in 1937. But as the largest and the first, Harvard and MIT remained preeminent. Of the 538 graduates of the 21 university planning programs that existed in 1952, 248—nearly half—were Harvard and MIT alumni, according to Frederick Adams's major study, *Urban Planning Education in the United States,* published in 1954.

Beginning of a dynasty

But the prodigious influence of the two schools from 1923 to 1949 goes beyond numbers. Graduates and faculty from those years have headed doz-

ens of city and regional planning departments, and they have played important roles in major federal agencies. Harvard–MIT alumni also have headed, and in some cases founded, at least a dozen university planning schools, including the University of Michigan, Cornell University, University of North Carolina, Ohio State University, Georgia Tech, and the University of Liverpool in England. They have been influential in the establishment and the advancement of the professional organizations, dominating the rosters of past presidents and important committee chairmanships. In fact, from 1935 to 1957, ACPI and later the American Institute of Planners (AIP) were based in Cambridge, first at Harvard and then, after a 1941–44 wartime lapse, at MIT.

"Dynasty" is perhaps too strong a word to describe the influence of Harvard and MIT men and women from 1923 to 1949. But not by much. Roland Greeley, who taught at MIT from 1944 to 1961 points out with excusable exaggeration, "There were few leaders in planning education during those years who were not from one of the two schools."

The new school at Harvard more or less weaned city planning from the Department of Landscape Architecture, where it began in 1909 as a few side credits in a course taught by James Sturgis Pray with an assist from Frederick Law Olmsted.

From 1923 to 1929, Harvard offered an optional curriculum leading to a master's of landscape architecture in city planning. It included two semesters of city planning design and two semesters of principles of city planning. The courses were taught by Pray, Hubbard, Nolen, Arthur Comey, Howard Menhinick and Arthur Shurtleff. They, along with Theodora Kimball and British town planner Thomas Adams, constituted the original faculty of the School of City Planning.

Students entering the four-year master's program in 1929 studied design, construction principles, planning principles, drawing and drafting, horticulture, topographic surveying, and fine arts during their first two years. In the first semester of the third-year studio, they drafted plans for parks, civic centers, zoning, transportation systems, and airports. In the second semester, the third-year students were asked to design an ideal town. The emphasis was always on the physical plan, although courses in real estate, economics, statistics, and public finance offered elsewhere in the university were recommended. The fourth year was devoted to the thesis.

Henry Hubbard, first chairman of the Harvard program, received a bachelor of science degree in landscape architecture from the university in 1901. His degree is believed to be the first such degree granted in the United States. Hubbard joined the faculty in 1906, helped to found *Landscape Architecture* magazine in 1910, and became a charter member of ACPI in 1917.

During World War I, Hubbard's involvement in designing emergency housing stimulated his interest in planning. In 1925, he helped found and became chief editor of the quarterly magazine *City Planning*. Hubbard was chairman of the school from 1929 until 1935 and of the new Department of Regional Planning of the Graduate School of Design from 1936 until 1941.

And now to MIT

A grant from the Carnegie Corporation enabled MIT to set up its bachelor of architecture in city planning program in 1933. Until then, city planning instruction had taken the form of a few lecture courses in the architecture department. Now Thomas Adams's son, Frederick Adams, was put in charge of the new program, whose faculty over the next few years consisted of both Adamses, Joseph Woodruff, and a series of lecturers, including Flavell Shurtleff, an authority on planning law.

MIT's master's program came along two years later. The curriculum included courses in engineering, sanitary and public health principles, theory and practice of city planning, color composition, European art and architecture, drawing, surveying, design, site planning, and urban sociology.

Frederick Adams, who headed the planning department at MIT until 1957, served as editor of the *AIP Journal* from 1937–40 and as president of AIP in 1948–49. Adams's long tenure at MIT gave the school stability and continuity, in contrast to Harvard, which followed a much more uneven course of productive and fallow periods.

In 1947, an AIP committee headed by MIT alumnus John Howard described an ideal planning curriculum as one that would endow a planner with foresight, social conscience, imagination, and an ability to analyze and synthesize. Also, in a passage for which the committee may prefer not to be remembered, the report said the planner "will not be financially ambitious but content with a moderate

income . . . willing to stake his accomplishments on the soundness and persuasiveness of his ideas rather than on any delegated powers to secure their accomplishment."

In 1935, Harvard reorganized again, and the School of City Planning became the Department of Regional Planning under the Graduate School of Design. Hubbard remained chairman. But times were difficult because the original Rockefeller Foundation grant had run out, and Harvard admitted no new students in 1936–37.

Although the money was low, planning jobs were plentiful in the latter years of the 1930s. Major federal recovery efforts provided jobs, but even more important, they stimulated planning at the state and local levels. In addition, housing and urban renewal emerged as important new issues for planners.

Hubbard resigned his chairmanship of the department at Harvard in 1941 and was succeeded by John M. Gaus. The following year, Harvard added the Ph.D. degree to its planning program.

One of Gaus's first jobs was to analyze the current state of planning and to define an appropriate educational role for the department. His 50-page report, "The Graduate School of Design and the Education of Planners," published in 1943, elaborated on the concept of the planner as the bridge between many related disciplines. "We can usefully convey to the students working primarily in design not only the essential techniques of design but also some sense of comradeship with the social analysts with whom they may be working in the future," Gaus wrote.

Gaus was succeeded as chairman by George Holmes Perkins in 1944. Also during the mid-1940s, a highly influential advocate of programs for low-income people became associated with both Harvard and MIT. Her name was Catherine Bauer, adviser to three presidents, lobbyist, educator, and critic of the urban scene. While much of planning was still rooted in land use, she was raising very different questions of social policy.

Her husband, William Wurster, joined MIT as dean of the School of Architecture and Planning in 1945 in a reorganization that set up architecture and planning as equal departments. Frederick Adams remained head of the Department of City and Regional Planning.

An important step in the drift of planning education away from land use and toward social, economic, and political issues took place at MIT about this time with the hiring of three new faculty members from untraditional backgrounds. Homer Hoyt was the leading specialist in the country in land economics when he joined the department in 1944. Roland Greeley, whose background was sociology and planning, joined in 1945.

Casting his line equally far in another direction, Adams hooked Lloyd Rodwin, whose background was in public administration with a special interest in land economics and housing. Rodwin joined the faculty in 1946. It was to the planners' credit that they recognized the need for diverse backgrounds in sociology, economics, and political science, says Rodwin today. He also observes that social scientists of the day were not interested in cities, so it was up to planners to take the initiative.

Differences

Most of the leaders in the profession from 1925 to 1949 wielded influence because they were good physical planners at a time when a growing country needed to know that some rational scheme lay between it and chaos. Planners were public servants, not visionaries. Their calling was to coordinate rather than create. They were process-oriented, so in a sense their job was never finished, their achievement obscured by the next set of problems. While architecture of the period produced the likes of Frank Lloyd Wright and Ludwig Mies van der Rohe, no cadre of household names exists in planning. "It was a good gray school," says Kevin Lynch, a 1947 grad and long-time faculty member, of the earlier years of planning education at MIT. But it was solid gray. Its administration was consistent. Its influence was steady. Its orientation was practical. Harvard, on the other hand, went through cycles of influence.

"I thought MIT's curriculum was more solidly organized," says Herbert Stevens, a 1942 MIT graduate. "At Harvard they were still trying to decide 'What is a city and what aspects of urban development should we look at?'" Says Louis Dolbeare (Harvard '42), "The running of the school [Harvard] was very much in the Beaux-Arts tradition. We had studios, and we all had projects. . . . Then we had a presentation in which we got up and defended them." There was a definite emphasis on drawing and design.

In a January 1980 *APA Journal* article on the history of the planning publications, Donald Kruecke-

berg of Rutgers University described the "distinct differences" between the Harvard and MIT programs: MIT was "the solid but perhaps conventional (if there was such a thing) professional program that produced a cadre of people who went off to establish new planning programs. . . . Harvard, as Perkins saw it, was more like a small school of visionaries, perhaps dreamers, who were challenging conventions."

Calling Harvard's program "somewhat effete" and MIT's "much more practical," J. Douglas Carroll, Jr., a 1947 Harvard grad, put the two venerable schools in this nutshell: An MIT graduate of the 1930s and 1940s was likely to proceed to a city and get a job as a planner; a Harvard graduate was more likely to think of his first job as building a new city.

Bernard Cohen has been a free-lance writer in Boston.

The Missionaries of Chapel Hill

Pat Verner
(June 1987)

When the city of Raleigh embarked on economic development planning a couple of years ago, planning director George Chapman wanted to be sure that his staff had a solid background in the subject. So he went to Emil Malizia at the department of city and regional planning at the University of North Carolina at Chapel Hill, who put together a short course on economic development for Chapman's staff. The short course was so well received in Raleigh that the North Carolina chapter of the American Planning Association took it to several other cities.

Helping North Carolina cities with their planning needs is nothing new for the university's planning department, which has been directly involved in statewide local planning since its establishment in 1946. On this task it works in concert with the university's Institute of Government, which presents short courses and workshops and provides consulting services in planning and other areas of government.

Planning in North Carolina was barely in its infancy when John Parker started the department just after World War II. "There were two planners in the state, I think," says Parker, who retired in 1974 after 28 years as the department's chairman. "Durham had Frank Dieter, and Winston–Salem had Harry Moore. It was absolutely virgin territory."

Nor was the virgin territory limited to North Carolina. There were only two other university planning departments in the U.S.—and none in the South.

From the beginning, the new department fit well in a university whose hallmark is service to its state. "Outreach is a major role of a great public university," says William Friday, who, until his retirement last year, was president of the 16-campus University of North Carolina system for 30 years. Friday himself was an active participant in a number of programs aimed at bettering the state.

Besides planning, the university has been a major player in promoting public health, quality government, culture, business entrepreneurship, economic growth, public schools, and even roads. The school has helped turn a once predominantly poor state into one of the nation's fastest growing. It is a tribute to the success of the university's planning department that there are so many planners—450 to 600, by most estimates—dispersed in so many towns, agencies, and firms. About half of them are University of North Carolina graduates. "There are UNC people everywhere," says longtime faculty member David Godschalk. "Every time you turn over a rock, a UNC graduate crawls out."

Despite its humble beginnings—Parker and six students comprised the department in the fall of 1946—the program is now considered among the best of the more than 100 university planning programs in the country. Its graduates and faculty have written some 80 books, held high-level positions with the federal government, and directed planning programs in small towns and large cities alike. The department is strengthened by its affiliation with a respected planning research organization, the university's Center for Urban and Regional Studies.

Nowhere has the department's influence been felt more than in its home state. About a quarter of its 1,200 graduates work in North Carolina, many in leadership roles in state government and local planning departments. Moreover, research and field work by both faculty and students often have far-reaching effects on local and statewide policies and decisions.

"The university has made planning a very legitimate enterprise in North Carolina," says Raleigh planning director George Chapman, a former state APA chapter president and a 1963 graduate of the program. "Because the department was accepted and had a good reputation, planning was started on a good footing with a good image."

A department is born

Good timing brought Jack Parker to North Carolina. A native of Canada, Parker earned two architecture degrees from the Massachusetts Institute of Technology. In 1944, he was director of the Lowethorpe School of Technology in Groton, Massachusetts, a non-degree-granting institution for women. Its trustees that year decided the school should affiliate with a larger college or university, and Parker was in charge of finding that institution.

He went knocking on the doors of 22 schools. Among them was the University of North Carolina, whose Institute for Research in Social Sciences had just decided to start a planning division in its graduate school. Parker's negotiations with Frank Porter Graham, president of the university, did not lead to the institution's taking the Lowethorpe School; they did lead, however, to Parker's returning to MIT for a master's degree in city and regional planning (there were no doctoral programs in planning at the time) with the idea of his heading UNC's new planning program afterward. Two years later, after moving the Lowethorpe School into the Rhode Island School of Design, Parker became the first department chair.

A second faculty member, James Webb, joined the department in January 1947, thanks to funding by the Tennessee Valley Authority. Webb's initial assignment was to split his time between teaching and helping local communities with planning. According to Parker, TVA, which operated numerous projects in North Carolina, saw the department as a way to stimulate planning in the state, and each summer it hired three or four students. Although it no longer plays as great a role as it did then, TVA still funds a summer internship as well as a student assistantship in the department.

TVA also played a role—although of a different sort—in bringing F. Stuart Chapin, Jr., to the department as the third faculty member in 1949. Two years earlier, Parker had gone to Greensboro, North Carolina, to help the city set up a municipal planning department. For director, he recommended Chapin, whom he had met when both worked at TVA in the summer of 1940. Like Parker and Webb, Chapin had a master's degree in planning from MIT and was interested in teaching and research, but he wanted to get some local planning experience first. Once he had that local experience, Parker used a Carnegie Foundation grant to bring him to Chapel Hill.

The triumvirate of Parker, Webb, and Chapin guided the department through its formative years. Although their roles overlapped, Parker was primarily the administrator, Webb the practitioner, and Chapin the researcher.

From the beginning, the department—one of the first in the country not affiliated with an architecture school—focused on social questions such as the role of planners and the consequences of planning, in addition to teaching the technical skills needed for traditional land-use planning. "Jack, Stu, and Jim instilled in all of us the importance of public service, that what we were doing essentially was trying to improve the life of a community," says Peter Larson, who graduated in 1951.

Almost as big a part of the duties of Parker, Webb, and Chapin as establishing a planning department in the university was establishing planning in North Carolina at a time when the value of the field had yet to be proved. Phillip Green, Jr., a faculty member at the Institute of Government who has taught planning law to hundreds of students and written much of the state's planning legislation, first heard about planning while he was a law student at Harvard in the late 1940s. He did not think much of the idea. "I thought it was the silliest thing I had ever heard," he says.

Parker, Webb, and Chapin did their best to win over the doubters with what Parker calls their "theme songs." First, they described how planning could help a community. Second, they stressed that planning was not a one-time effort, but something that should become a regular and continuing part of government.

Students helped spread the message. "Almost immediately, we neophytes were taken out of the classroom and pushed into planning in North Carolina," recalls Peter Larson. "We were immediately asked to practice what we were learning in class."

For many years, students were divided into groups of three or four, and each group was assigned to a town in North or South Carolina. The towns provided transportation and housing, although the latter could mean sleeping in the fire station; in exchange, the communities got free consulting.

Parker explains that the students first assessed the local situation, looking at such basics as population, local economy, and land use. Then they made recommendations about what the town should do. The data were compiled into a report, which the students presented to the town's governing board. The reports were not plans, says Parker, although they were the closest things to plans most of the towns had ever had.

The outcomes varied. "Some towns picked up the ball and really started moving," says Parker. "The chamber of commerce, civic groups—lots of people were involved. Others did absolutely nothing. In still others, nothing happened for 10 years, then someone would find the report and get some ideas."

Peter Larson remembers being assigned to three neighboring mill towns—Leaksville, Draper, and Spray. His team, in what Larson calls "the finest comprehensive plan ever developed," recommended that the three towns merge. A few years later, they did so, incorporating as the town of Eden.

Some years, Parker says, the planning students worked together on a major project for one city. One of these, a growth study for the city of Charlotte and surrounding Mecklenburg County, became the basis for a metropolitan planning program.

Faculty members also affected planning through their own consulting work. For example, Webb's firm, City Planning and Architectural Associates (which he formed with two alumni, Donald Stewart and Robert Anderson), developed the site plan for the internationally respected Research Triangle Park, located between Chapel Hill, Durham, and Raleigh.

Meanwhile, Phillip Green of the Institute of Government—by then a convert to the benefits of planning—wrote a book on zoning and planning aimed at local officials. He traveled around the state helping communities start planning boards and departments.

In many towns, interest in planning grew faster than budgets; often there was no money to hire professional planners. In 1949, Parker assembled a group of influential North Carolinians, who successfully persuaded the state government to begin assisting communities with planning. But large-scale local planning assistance did not come until the state received funds through the federal government's 701 program in the mid-1950s. When that happened, Green notes, there were suddenly more jobs than there were trained people available. Sometimes people were hired first and then trained with a short course developed by the Institute of Government in 1955.

As more and more North Carolina towns and counties hired professional planners, they were likely to be North Carolina graduates or were recommended by planning faculty members. By the early 1960s, planning was firmly established in the state.

During the same period, planning research was gaining a foothold under the leadership of Stuart Chapin, whose first large research grant came in the early 1950s from what is now HUD. The grant funded the Savannah River (South Carolina) Urbanization Study, which looked at the local impact of atomic energy plants. The department's next major contract was for a study of city and regional planning in the Soviet Union, financed by the U.S. Air Force, although because of the Cold War, no one actually went to Russia. Instead, international experts on the Soviet Union were brought to North Carolina.

Two landmark events occurred in 1957. First, Chapin published *Urban Land Use Planning,* which became the definitive textbook in the field. The book, now in its third edition with fellow North Carolina faculty member Edward Kaiser as coauthor, still is widely used. Second, the department received a five-year grant from the Ford Foundation to fund the urban studies program, which evolved into the Center for Urban and Regional Studies.

Like all the department's early grants, this one was made to the Institute for Research in Social Sciences and involved other departments—in this case, anthropology, economics, political science, social psychology, and sociology. Twenty faculty and staff members and 27 research assistants participated in the program, which was directed by Chapin.

Shirley Weiss, then a graduate student and now a professor in the department, was associate director. In 1969, the center, which had survived on

grant money since its inception, began getting ongoing state operating funds.

Before the five-year term of the Ford grant was over, the department had admitted its first doctoral student. Weiss notes that a series of fellowships and grants helped in recruiting outstanding students. Having these students on hand, in turn, made the department competitive for government and private grants. Those grants provided funding for new faculty members, who then attracted more outstanding students. The number of faculty members holding regular appointments grew from seven to 18 between 1963 and 1973, and the number of students more than doubled, from 53 to 109.

Six of today's leaders came to the faculty in that decade: Edward Bergman, David Godschalk, Edward Kaiser, Emil Malizia, David Moreau, and Michael Stegman. Parker retired in 1974, leaving the chairmanship with George C. Hemmens, a 1959 graduate of the department. Hemmens served as chairman until 1978, when he became director of the School of Urban Planning and Policy at the University of Illinois at Chicago.

In North Carolina today

The department and the urban studies center have continued to influence and aid planning in the state, although their role today probably is not as integral as it once was. "Certainly there is extensive involvement here," says David Godschalk, a 1964 master's and 1971 doctoral graduate who chaired the department from 1978 to 1983. "The faculty plays an important role in advising various state agencies, especially the Department of Natural Resources and Community Development. If a major planning issue in the state comes up, we're probably involved."

One area in which university planners have been particularly involved is coastal management. In 1974, the Coastal Area Management Act was enacted by the state legislature, making North Carolina one of the first states to set up a coastal program. "It probably wouldn't have happened without the center and the work of people like David Brower," says Jonathan Howes, director of the Center for Urban and Regional Studies and a 1961 department graduate.

The coastal management program, which is directed by department alumnus David Owens, has several components that can be tied directly to research done at the university. For example, Brower and Godschalk, along with another alum, William McElyea, did extensive research on the effects of hurricanes. Their book, *Before the Storm: Managing Development to Reduce Hurricane Damage,* was published by the coastal management office and formed the basis for the state's hurricane mitigation requirements.

A problem-solving course, which all students in the planning department are required to take, brings real-life planning issues into the classroom and takes students out into surrounding communities. Their efforts often influence planning decisions:

• Carrying capacity studies of Currituck Banks and Hatteras Island, on the Atlantic coast, tried to determine the potential of and limitations on future growth in each area. The studies looked at infrastructure, water supply, and evacuation schemes. The state coastal commission may soon require coastal communities to consider carrying capacity in their land-use plans. Both studies, led by Brower, Godschalk, and Kaiser, won state APA awards.

• A study commissioned by the Sierra Club in North Carolina's rapidly growing Research Triangle examined the impacts of population growth on natural resources in that area. David Moreau, Center for Urban and Regional Studies assistant director Raymond Burby, and David Godschalk were the leaders.

• A redevelopment plan for a Durham neighborhood looked at the pros and cons of developing the area as a business park. William Rohe was the leader.

• The Warren County Economic Development Commission commissioned a study on potential solutions to the problem of increasing jobs in the county, ranging from an equity retirement center to cultural arts development to main street revitalization. The following year, another group of students worked on the specifics of implementing proposals made in the original study. Shirley Weiss is the leader.

Faculty members also serve on all sorts of local boards and commissions. Not surprisingly, their presence is felt most in Chapel Hill, where Jonathan Howes and David Godschalk have been elected to the town council, and several faculty members are or have been on the planning board. A student, Meg Parker, currently serves on the planning board, and Edward Bergman is a member of the Orange County economic development commission.

Michael Stegman has chaired the Chapel Hill housing authority; David Moreau has headed the local water and sewer authority; and Raymond Burby has been on the recreation commission.

Stegman, who with former colleague Thomas Snyder devised an impact fee structure for Raleigh, also is the only nonresident on that city's affordable housing task force. Moreau directs the state Water Resources Research Institute. And Burby has been on the Governor's solar law task force.

In addition, local and state officials use the faculty members as experts. For example, Mary Joan Pugh, as assistant secretary of the Department of Natural Resources and Community Development, North Carolina's most highly placed planner, says she often calls Burby or Moreau for advice when dealing with watershed protection.

Local planners in North Carolina have even more day-to-day contact with the Institute of Government, notes William McNeill, High Point planning director and the current president of the state APA chapter. "The institute is set up to help the local practicing planner," says McNeill, "while the planning department is set up to train new planners and to do research."

McNeill says he wishes the department itself were more involved. Although some individual professors do a good job of disseminating their research in the state, he says, too often local planners have to wait until books are published to find out about research done in Chapel Hill. He would like to see a system through which local planners could learn about research earlier.

Department chair Stegman also says he would like to see more of the department's research put to immediate use by local planners and hopes the problem will be resolved through the department's upcoming merger with the Center for Urban and Regional Studies, which will be completed by June 1988. The merger "may help us redefine our service role," Stegman says.

National stature

As much as it has influenced planning in North Carolina, the department's impact extends beyond its home state. "In many ways, our national stature is easier to document," says Stegman, who was deputy assistant secretary for research in the U.S. Department of Housing and Urban Development from 1979 to 1981. Emil Malizia has been a special assistant in the U.S. Department of Labor's Office of National Programs and William Rohe a visiting scholar at HUD. Gorman Gilbert currently is on leave working as New York City's taxi commissioner.

Carl Goldschmidt of Michigan State University, who chaired the accreditation review committee that looked at the Carolina program in 1983, calls the department "one of the best." One of its consistent strengths, in Goldschmidt's opinion, is a "strong, productive faculty that has made significant contributions to the field as a whole—people who have been leaders in the field."

The department has some 1,200 alumni, many more than most other planning programs. Those graduates work in diverse and prominent positions all over the U.S. and in more than 25 foreign countries.

The department's stature is reflected in the kinds of research grants it is consistently awarded—grants that support studies that have major impact on policies, says Stegman. Recent examples of grants include a HUD contract for a national demonstration project on selling public housing to tenants; a Ford Foundation grant to study the economic effects of science and technology parks; and an Urban Mass Transit Administration contract to look at private contracting of transit services.

Stegman is especially excited about a U.S. Information Agency-funded exchange program that allows five faculty members—Bergman, Stegman, Malizia, Harvey Goldstein, and Linda Lacey—to collaborate with Viennese professors in research on comparative economic development policies and the restructuring of mature economies. The Center for Urban and Regional Studies currently has two National Science Foundation grants, one for studying floods as natural hazards and one to look at hurricane and growth management.

North Carolina planners hold a variety of nationally visible positions. Howes is president of the National League of Municipalities. Kaiser is vice-president of the Association of Collegiate Schools of Planning, and he, Stegman, and Weiss are on the organization's accreditation committee. Godschalk, Chapin, and Brower have served on the national APA board in recent years. . . .

Throughout the years, the university's planning program has had three consistent characteristics: an emphasis on public service, an emphasis on analytical thinking, and a willingness to change as the planning field and society change.

"The commitment to public interest stands out," says Kaiser, who in 1966 received one of the first doctorates awarded by the department. "Until very recently, work in the public sector was an unwritten expectation. That's moving away a bit, but there has always been a bias toward the public sector as being a higher calling."

The curriculum, which includes basic courses required of everyone and specific courses in five areas of concentration, has been criticized at times for focusing too much on methodology. The harshest critics say that North Carolina graduates sometimes do not have the technical skills to step into an entry-level planning job.

Mary Joan Pugh, whose duties at the state's natural resources department include responsibility for programs as diverse as community planning assistance, the state zoo, and jobs training, defends the university's approach. She says it bothers her that some planners and students expect easy answers—the three steps to writing a zoning ordinance, for instance.

"Planning is a thought process—it's not fill-in-the-blanks," Pugh says. "You have to tailor-make what you're doing, to bring people into the process, because if it's not implemented, it's absolutely no good. Technical skills are important, but when you go for a graduate degree, you want something more than technical expertise."

The department's willingness to change has meant that the curriculum has undergone many revisions. In the mid-1960s, interest and emphasis in the planning field moved away from traditional land-use planning to regional development. The decade from 1963 to 1973 also saw the creation of courses in environmental protection, planning for developing areas, and social planning and policy.

Concentrations in environmental and energy planning were added between 1978 and 1983 as concern and money for social planning lessened. With grant money less plentiful, economic development came to the forefront. In 1984, with a grant from the Urban Land Institute, the department began a curriculum in development and finance, in cooperation with the university's school of business.

Joining forces

The department currently offers five concentrations: land-use and environmental planning, real estate development and housing, economic and community development, urban services and infrastructure, and planning in developing areas. With the law school, it also offers a joint planning and law degree.

More curriculum changes and additions will come, says chairman Stegman. A joint planning and business program has been approved and will soon have its first students. Planning department and business faculty members had already been working together in the department's real estate development program. Stegman notes that a quarter to a third of the department's students are specializing in real estate development (sometimes in combination with another area, such as land-use planning).

Stegman believes much of the department's future expansion will be in two areas: public policy and international planning. The department has been in charge of the interdisciplinary undergraduate program in public policy since 1985. Next on the agenda is a doctoral program in public policy. A joint public administration/planning degree probably is in the future, Stegman says.

The addition next fall of a third faculty member with expertise in international planning—Gill-Chin Lem of the University of Illinois—will greatly strengthen this concentration, in Stegman's view. Linda Lacey and Dale Whittington already work in this area.

Ray Burby of the Center for Urban and Regional Studies will join the department as a professor this fall, bringing the number of full-time faculty members to 15—the largest it has been in about 15 years.

The department now has 90 to 100 students; Stegman would like to see that number go up by about 10 and thinks the program and faculty additions coming up should make that possible.

It has been more than 40 years since Jack Parker began his quest to show North Carolinians the benefits of planning. In some ways that job is not yet complete.

Stegman would like to see the department, through its teaching, service, research, and consulting, improve the image of the planner. Too often, he notes, the planner is seen either as a regulator who gets in the way of development or as a "visionary whose hopes for the future are never linked to workable means of getting there."

A better image, in Stegman's view, would be of the planner as a "regulator in the public interest and a visionary who can help define society's goals and provide the tools needed to meet them."

He hopes to see the department "use its growing strengths, especially in development and local public finance, to make planners central participants in efforts to improve the quality of the built environment and the lives of the people."

Pat Verner is a free-lance writer and editor in Concord, North Carolina, and a UNC graduate in journalism.

Why I Left a Cushy Job to Be My Own Boss

Thomas H. Roberts
(July 1979)

A year and a half ago, I left my job as a planning director and went into business for myself. I was 50 years old, with family responsibilities and no independent income. Since then, people—mostly other planners—have asked me why I did it, how I did it, and what differences this decision has made to me professionally and personally.

I'm not sure exactly when the idea for all this started, but I do remember that about three years ago I was musing, as everybody does now and then, about who I was and where I was going. At 48, I had for a number of years been a planning director for a respected public agency, dealing with "important" people and issues. I had been a planner for nearly all of my adult life. I had a fine staff, a well-appointed office in a fashionable downtown office building, enough salary and fringe benefits to get by and then some, and absolute job security. I had kept up with new developments in planning over the years, and I knew my craft—technically, politically, and administratively—and could do my job efficiently. Mine had been a good career, and by and large I had enjoyed my work.

Yet things were less than perfect. Without ever completely admitting it to myself, I had gradually become frustrated, bored, and impatient with my job. I was frustrated because almost every significant way that I could think of to improve the agency's effectiveness was impossible, given the political and organizational constraints that operated within and around it.

I was bored with an increasingly routine annual work program that was shaped more by the imperatives of grantsmanship than by the needs of the community. And, having spent a lifetime staffing boards and commissions of various kinds, I was bored with the repetitive monthly cycle of agendas, meetings, committee reports, and minutes.

I was impatient with what seemed to be an inexorable drift toward more and more bureaucracy, not just in my agency, but everywhere: personnel regulations, budgetary procedures, and countless progress reports in which people recorded what they wanted to do, had just done, or had decided not to do, and why.

And meetings! Departmental meetings, interdepartmental meetings, and interagency meetings took place like clockwork, whether you needed them or not, and forced you to sit around reporting on previous meetings, planning future meetings, and staffing other people's meetings.

I was also impatient because of a decreasing ratio between how hard or how effectively I worked and how much I was paid. Senior public officials often reach a plateau where their salaries either level off or inch up imperceptibly. In inflationary times, this trend usually amounts to an annual cut in pay. Legislators vote themselves raises, doctors and lawyers raise their fees, and union members strike; but I couldn't do any of these things.

I want to stress that these complaints were more a mark of what was wrong with me than with my place of employment. It was no worse than any other of its kind and, in fact, much better than most. No, this was clearly my problem, not someone else's, and it baffled me. I had been confronted with job-related dissatisfactions before, and I had always been able to deal with them. But, for whatever reasons, they were getting to me more now—bugging me—and it was not doing my employer, my staff, my family, or me any good.

The choices

The question was: What should I do about it? Being a planner, I considered the alternatives. An obvious choice was to stay where I was: continue adjusting to the realities of my job, lower my ex-

pectations, avoid making waves, and find creative outlets in hobbies and outside activities. According to the lights I had been brought up by (the Great Depression and all that), this was a compelling alternative. Where I came from, a 48-year-old executive in a secure position hung on to it; he didn't walk out on it.

But that was a depressing alternative, at least for me. I had seen how the spirit goes out of people who start counting the years until retirement, and I didn't want any part of it. Besides, I have never really liked the idea of retiring. I may slow down, but I would like to stay active in my career until I either die or become too senile to be of use to anyone.

I thought about getting another job. Like most planners, I had changed jobs a few times over the years, and I had no doubt that I could do it at least once more. One of the appealing things about this alternative was that I liked the city I lived in. Fortunately it had a lot of organizations that hire planners, so I would have a fairly good choice of opportunities without having to pull up roots and move. (I remembered how much fun moving had been in earlier years, but it's a lot less fun after you've done it several times, especially if you like your current location.)

I went down the list of federal, state, and local agencies, universities, and private firms that were likely to have suitable openings. In most cases, I just didn't see that they would offer anything different enough to justify a change. I wasn't interested in making a change for the sake of change, and I certainly didn't want to trade one set of institutional encumbrances and frustrations for another.

The plain truth was that, after a quarter century of being an employee, what I really wanted was to work for myself, not for some commission, department, or corporation. I had seen a growing willingness in young people, including my own children, to forgo traditional standards of status and security in favor of doing what they wanted to do. I had read articles about stockbrokers and corporate executives who dropped out of their respective rat races and turned to woodcarving or whatever. Now, just once in my life, I too wanted to know what it felt like to be my own boss, to be independent.

Such ideas had passed through my mind before, but I usually passed them off as pipe dreams. I had never really thought of planners as being on their own but always as a part of some organization, except for an occasional free-lancer or somebody at liberty between jobs. Besides, I was not financially independent, to say the least, and during the past 25 years I had become economically as well as emotionally dependent on the certainty of a biweekly paycheck. (And I had always faithfully observed the First Rule of Tree-Climbing: Don't let go of one limb until you have hold of another one.)

I even looked briefly at the possibility of leaving my chosen profession and finding another livelihood. But this option didn't seem right for me, either. First, although I do have some other interests and abilities, I didn't see how I could make a living at them. But, more importantly, planning is my line—I like to help communities solve their problems, and I believe I'm good at it. I had spent years learning my particular profession, and I had absolutely no desire to leave it. If anything, I wanted an opportunity to experience it in a wider, more challenging, and more fulfilling way.

So there I sat. Going through the paces, earning a salary. Surviving. Grumbling to myself and sometimes letting it spill over. Occasionally finding something creative or innovative to do. But not with the old zing I had when I was younger: working hard, worrying over my work, and enjoying the feeling that I was building something important and making a difference.

Then funny little changes began happening to me and to the way I thought. I came across a very helpful book for people who are not happy in their work, *Job Power,* by a man who had quit his job as the night city editor of the *Atlanta Constitution* to become a free-lance writer. He told about his own career frustrations and what he had done about them. He talked about the feeling many people have to want to "tend their own garden." In addition to helping me recognize my feelings, the book included a useful Career Workbook "for evaluating your current vocational situation, your aspirations, and your options." . . .

Making the switch

One afternoon in April 1977, a colleague and I were mulling over a particularly irksome matter—I don't even remember what it was now—when he half-seriously suggested that we both quit our jobs and go into consulting. We talked about it for a few minutes. Clearly, the national trend was in the other direction. Planning firms were shrinking or going under, not expanding. The drift toward new federal grant programs and expanded planning requirements had leveled off.

"But what if you stayed small and independent, kept expenses down, and offered high-quality, personal services within budget and on schedule—surely you could survive, because there must always be a demand for someone like that. . . ." We went on that way for a few more minutes. Then we agreed to go home and think about it overnight. I went home, thought about it, and something clicked inside me: I was going to work for myself. I decided I would rather try and fail than spend the rest of my life wondering if I could have done it and regretting that I hadn't tried. The only questions remaining were how and when. (My wife and I had discussed the idea from time to time, and I knew she supported it.) I felt enormously relieved. My colleague, as it turned out, was not prepared to make the same decision.

But for me there seemed to be no turning back. I made a list of people whom I could talk to in confidence—old friends in and out of planning, people who worked for themselves, people who were or had been in private practice of one kind or another. For weeks, over lunch with one after the other, I told them what I wanted to do and asked for their reactions. Their thoughts were very helpful in many ways, but there were two results of these discussions that were by far the most significant.

The first was the inescapable conclusion that self-employed people really liked what they were doing. Of the ones I talked to, drawn from a wide range of ages, lines of work, and financial conditions, all without exception said that, given a choice, they would have it no other way; the satisfaction of independence was worth all of the disadvantages it brought.

The other significant result came one day when I was having lunch with another planner who, although we had never really been close personal friends, was someone I had always liked and respected. He not only felt that my idea was feasible but had also been thinking along the same lines. Why not do it together?

Now there are advantages to going into business alone, and there are other advantages to doing it with one or more partners. If you go in with a partner, obviously you are not totally independent. You have to agree and compromise on all sorts of things. On the other hand, having a partner can give you a greater measure of flexibility in matters of illness, vacation, work load, and task sharing. It also lets you combine your strengths, compensate for each other's shortcomings, and take advantage of the germ of truth in the old adage that two heads are better than one.

My partner-to-be and I felt that a twosome made sense in our case but that one or more additional partners would geometrically increase the number of interpersonal issues to deal with (such as conflicting styles and goals) and make it a lot harder to get off the ground. Another very important part of our initial discussions was an agreement that there must always be absolute candor between us in all matters so that we could resolve our differences as we went along and not let them build up.

Looking back, though, by far the most important consequence of agreeing to a partnership was that it eliminated the option of my getting cold feet and backing out. Despite everything else, the security of a regular job with a certain paycheck can be very addictive after 25 years. If it had not been for our mutual commitment, there were times when I would probably have turned back.

Then followed months of sitting around the kitchen table at night, planning the details. What would we call ourselves? What should the stationery look like? What kind of office would we have, and where? Should we incorporate? How much does a business telephone cost? Should we get one incoming line or two?

Lining up enough money to survive on was, however, the overriding issue. Cash flow is a notorious problem in any small business venture, and we would be starting from scratch, with nothing in the pipeline and no contracts in our pockets. But, unlike many other small businesses, consulting requires no front-end money for inventory and relatively little initial investment in supplies and equipment. The biggest costs are money to live on the first year, money to meet whatever other continuing personal expenses you may have, and travel expenses.

With spouses who were willing to share the work, and by exercising constant care to buy, rent, or hire absolutely nothing we could do without until we had enough money, it is surprising how little cash it took to get started. Each of us projected our maximum negative cash-flow position under various assumptions of incoming work, and we made whatever arrangements we could to handle

it: saving, borrowing, selling things—whatever it took.

We found a very useful book called *Up Your OWN Organization!*, an informally written handbook on how to start and finance a new business. Although it is written more from the perspective of someone going into manufacturing or sales than for someone going into a professional service, it is really quite helpful for anyone wanting to strike off on his own. It contains good advice on the use of legal, accounting, banking, and insurance services; and it lists 40 possible sources of money, including some unexpected ones.

Although my partner had had some private business experience, I had had none, so I took a night school course sponsored by the U.S. Small Business Administration at a nearby university. The class was full of people (mostly a lot younger than I), working at all kinds of jobs, who wanted to spring loose and be on their own. Some planned to open small shops; one wanted to operate her own photography studio; another wanted to start a landscaping service; and so on. Although I was the only would-be planning consultant in the lot, I got a lot of moral support from meeting with them each week, sharing aspirations, and learning about the practicalities and pitfalls of self-employment. I was also reconciled to the fact that, if it didn't work out, I would swallow hard and look for another job.

Taking the plunge

The time finally came when my partner and I both resigned from our positions and opened for business, amid some raised eyebrows and a few gasps. The people who knew us best hired us first—less an act of charity, I hope, than an expression of confidence in our ability to perform. Much of our early work was subcontracted from other consultants, mostly overload work that they couldn't handle internally.

The first year, and especially the first six months, were sometimes exhilarating and sometimes discouraging. They required perseverence, patience, and a lot of simple faith. Things that seem little now were sources of great satisfaction at the time. It was a great thrill to get the first client of our very own, a small rural community. A former staff associate mentioned that he knew of a town that needed some help. He brought it up reluctantly, almost apologetically, saying that the community only had $7,500 available to do the work.

I grinned and said, *"Only* $7,500?" When I was an administrator of a large public planning program, we had routinely shuffled hundreds of thousands of dollars back and forth among budget categories, but now "only $7,500" was a lot of money. It not only offered a welcome opportunity to provide a service and prove our worth, but it would buy food and pay the telephone bill. Then, slowly at first and then faster, came a whole series of similar firsts.

It's been a year and half since we started, long enough to look back and identify some of the ways in which my life is different. For example, I find that I perform a lot more tasks myself, and I like that, at least for now. On a given day, you might find me not only reading, researching, or writing, but drafting, addressing envelopes, filing, or picking something up at the printer's. No more phalanxes of Division Chiefs and Planners I, II, and III at my beck and call. This change took some getting used to, but, for me at least, it's good hands-on therapy. I feel a closer identification with my work because I do it myself. As I tell my prospective clients, "What you see is what you get."

To a greater extent than before, I also choose my own hours, and they're fairly irregular. There are many times when the work bunches up because clients want what they want when they want it or because I'm on a creative streak and don't want to fall off. But there are other times when I may slow down to near-zero output in midweek just because I need to loaf a little. I go with my moods, and my time is less compartmentalized into weekdays, weekends, annual leave, and office holidays. (I have no idea whether I took off Veterans Day last year, and I don't care.)

I also get to choose *where* I want to work much of the time. We located our office in an older part of town, near a square that has the support services we need and where a subway station will open soon. The office is about a mile from my home, and I walk to work along pleasant neighborhood streets. Unless I have a meeting scheduled or want to impress somebody, I wear very informal clothes. (Our building is full of lawyers and accountants in three-piece suits, and sometimes I think I get a "There goes the neighborhood!" look from them on the elevator, but I'm still enjoying the small freedom of dressing the way I want to.) If I have a big report to get out or a complicated issue to

think through, I can go down to a little place at the seashore and stay there until I get it done.

I have always enjoyed traveling, which is fortunate because I have to travel a lot. It not only goes with the territory, but it provides a welcome change of scenery. I now participate in a larger variety of interesting planning issues—growth management, intergovernmental relations, coastal energy impact, inner-city revitalization, economic development, and environmental management, to name a few—and I get to do it in Florida, the District of Columbia, California, North Carolina, and points in between. (Maybe when I'm smarter I'll even learn how to do the Florida and California work in the winter and the northern work in the summer.)

My days are less alike than they used to be. I have some days when I work alone in absolute, uninterrupted silence and other days when I am juggling long-distance telephone calls or pursuing a hectic plane schedule.

I also enjoy the competitive nature of consulting work. For some reason, I have always liked competitive endeavors, even in my hobbies. Somehow I feel that competing for clients on the basis of higher quality and more efficient service is more savory than the institutional turf-and-budget type of competition that confronted me before.

I enjoy the variety of people I work with—not only different clients but different kinds of clients: planners, attorneys, managers, technicians, business people. I also enjoy putting together teams of specialists for different projects and selecting them on the basis of their competence, compatibility, and exact suitability for a particular planning problem.

I enjoy sharing my new career with my wife, because we work in the business together. (When you have your own business, nepotism is not only ethical, it is a wholesome opportunity for family togetherness.) For the first time in 29 years, we are mutually experiencing the problems, disappointments, and joys of our work in a way that was impossible when we worked apart all day long and didn't really understand what the other person was involved in.

That's the good part. Now for the other side. It was easier than I thought to accept the total lack of financial security that comes with self-employment, but insecurity is always there, hovering like a specter. No matter how busy we may be—and we have become constantly busier—I know of no dependable way to predict how much or what, if anything, we will be doing next year or even a few months from now.

There are ways to minimize the effects of this uncertainty, like putting aside savings when things are going well, looking for long-term assignments, and avoiding overdependence on one kind of work. But my self-employed friends, whether in advertising, hair styling, engineering, or planning, tell me that you eventually get used to it. What it seems to come down to is this: If you want to be free, you also have to be free to fall on your face.

Another fact of self-employment that takes some getting used to is that when you stop, everything stops. This problem is lessened somewhat, but not much, by having a partner. As a planning director who had learned to organize and delegate, I could always be absent for a period of time in the comfortable knowledge that work would proceed without my being there. The first month I was on my own, I enjoyed the thought that I could sleep as late as I wanted, until I quickly realized that nothing was going to happen unless I did it. As a self-employed friend put it when I first discussed my plans with him, when you are self-employed, you have more independence but not necessarily more freedom. The subtlety of that distinction escaped me until I experienced it personally.

There also is no getting around the fact that the kind of private consulting I do is very hard work. I'm not implying that public employment is easy because I know it isn't. But, although a self-employed person likes to say he has no boss, in a way he has many bosses: his customers or clients. I have a constant feeling that I should always be giving my best to all of them. There are many times when I am physically and mentally exhausted. Even though it is a satisfying kind of exhaustion, I find it absolutely essential to build deliberate relaxation periods into my daily and weekly life in a way that used to be unnecessary.

I have found, too, that being in business for myself has made me more conservative in some ways, and I must watch this tendency so it doesn't get out of hand. In the first year of keeping your own little corporate books, when you are just trying to survive from one month to the next, you sometimes wonder whether all of the withholding for Social Security (which doubles when you become your own employer), state and federal unemployment insurance, state and federal income taxes, and other miscellaneous exactions is really necessary. (But enough of this dangerous, reactionary nonsense! If there were no governmental programs, there'd be no need for planners, and then where would I be?)

Everyone would have a different mixture of advantages and disadvantages to evaluate in considering a step like mine. My major advantage was that I had been active in planning and professional societies and had been around awhile, so people knew me. Another advantage was that I had been a planning director for a long time and had hired a lot of consultants, so I had a pretty good feel for what clients need, want, and expect. I was also fortunate in finding the right partner.

But probably the biggest advantage is that I have a supportive spouse who not only was willing to give up security and a steady income, but even thinks it was a good idea, enjoys the business, and participates in it.

On the other hand, it gets a lot harder to make big life changes and take chances as you get older, even though I now realize that 51 is not as old as I thought it was when I was a mere lad of 41. You start to get little aches and pains. It's harder to read small print, and bifocals are awkward. You put on extra pounds more easily than you used to. You get tired faster and have to pace yourself. And you want little things your own way. Moreover, you have been around long enough to have acquired a full complement of family responsibilities—mortgage, kids who need to be educated—and a set of values that says you shouldn't jeopardize these things.

Another consideration was that I had had absolutely no experience in private consulting or, for that matter, in any kind of private business, and I had to learn a lot in a hurry. Finally, I was not poverty-stricken, but I had no real nest egg to use as a stake to avoid heavy debt.

The life of a self-employed planning consultant is clearly not for everybody. We are all different in the kinds of financial and emotional security we need, in the rewards we want, in the ways in which we want to be of service, and in the things that we are willing to put up with as a part of our job. And, as I have learned in my own case, these things can change within ourselves over the years. The things that satisfied me or bothered me 15 years ago are not the same as they are today. But for myself, for now at least, I have found a way to be independent and still do the kind of work I like best. And I am grateful.

Tom Roberts, AICP, heads his own planning firm in Decatur, Georgia.

Consulting With the Consultants

Ruth Eckdish Knack and James Peters
(November 1984)

THE PARTICIPANTS

(Titles correct as of 1984. Not all the participants are quoted in the following excerpt.)

Dean K. Boorman, 56, president of Dean Boorman and Associates of Montclair, New Jersey; his two-member firm specializes in community planning and development consulting.

Leon S. Eplan, 55, is president of Leon Eplan and Associates of Atlanta, a firm he founded in 1978.

Michael A. Garcia, Jr., 42, is a senior planner with the Breig Partnership, a seven-member San Antonio architecture and planning firm founded in 1972.

Bruce W. Heckman, 39, is executive vice-president of Robert B. Teska and Associates of Evanston, Illinois, an 11-member planning and landscape architecture firm founded in 1975.

Mary Lou Henry, 45, is vice-president of Vernon G. Henry and Associates, Inc., of Houston, a 13-member planning and landscape architecture firm founded in 1967.

Theodore R. Johnson, 33, is vice-president of Thompson Dyke and Associates, Ltd., of Northbrook, Illinois, a seven-member urban planning and landscape architecture firm founded in 1981.

Lane Kendig, 45, is president of Lane Kendig, Inc., a two-member firm in Mundelein, Illinois, founded in 1983.

Naphtali H. Knox, 51, is president of Naphtali H. Knox and Associates, a four-member Palo Alto, California, land-use and housing planning firm he started in 1981.

Robert M. Leary, 55, is president of Robert M. Leary Associates, Ltd., of Raleigh, North Carolina, a two-member firm he founded in 1969, specializ-

ing in land-use regulations, preservation planning, and management services.

Joseph A. Racine, 35, is the principal of Joseph A. Racine and Associates in Gillette, Wyoming, founded in 1980.

Kenneth H. Simmons, 51, is a principal of Community Design Collaborative of Oakland, California, a 14-member architecture and planning firm founded in 1979.

June Spencer is director of Opinion Research Associates, Inc., of Madison, Wisconsin, a professional arts, human and health services planning, and management consulting firm that was started in 1972.

Susan Stoddard, 42, is vice-president of Berkeley Planning Associates in Berkeley, California, a 20-member firm she joined in 1976; it specializes in policy analysis and program evaluation.

Joyce Whitley, 53, is vice-president for planning of Whitley/Whitley, Inc., a 12-member architecture and planning firm in Cleveland.

Planning. What sorts of ethical issues do small consulting firms face?

Naphtali Knox. I've had clients that I really didn't want to work for, because I didn't agree with their philosophy, although I didn't always know that going in. For instance, I found myself representing a developer who wouldn't take my advice, and I wasn't in harmony with what he wanted to do with his property. Nevertheless, I gave him what I thought was the best advice. At each decision point the matter got worse, and finally we just disassociated ourselves from each other. What do you do in that kind of situation—turn the potential client away?

Bob Leary. One approach we've learned comes from our handling of requests to appear as expert witnesses, and that's to make contracts a two-step process: first the letter offering services and then the letter of agreement. The first letter says we will examine the situation and render an opinion based on our evaluation of the facts. Then it's up to the client to decide whether that opinion agrees with his intended course of action or position in the litigation.

At that point, we move to the second stage of the agreement. But there are no commitments from either of us to go beyond that first stage. We make clear in our first letter that either side can withdraw at any time. You have to make the separation agreement while you're still friends, because trying to negotiate a withdrawal from an ironclad contract when the wheels have come off is a very sticky situation.

I'd say that 25 to 35 percent of our invitations to be expert witnesses result in opinions that don't coincide with the opinion our clients would like us to have. And word gets around rather quickly, I suspect, that you're not a hired gun. This raises your credibility in the field of expert witnessing.

Leon Eplan. I think it ought to be said to the clients, right up front, that your role is not as an advocate, but as an expert, and that you have to retain a level of objectivity about the findings. If they're not comfortable with that, then you're not the person they're seeking.

But I've drawn the line on expert witnessing at a different place, keeping in mind the special role of the planner. I simply never get involved in a project where I don't have a major part in the design. I've tended to take cases in which I'm called upon to defend a community's plan or its planning process, rather than those that fight the plan and the role of planning.

Lane Kendig. I think there are two kinds of situations: The legal kind that Bob was talking about, and the one where it's less clear what your role is going to be—where you take on a fairly complex planning program without knowing exactly where it's going. At that stage, Leon is right, you've got to make sure the client understands you're going to give your best professional advice, and that you're not necessarily going to be an advocate for any one position.

Bruce Heckman. There's another thing. Many attorneys now have an inventory of the expert witnesses who have been associated with various cases. The whole procedure of selecting witnesses is getting very sophisticated, and some of the people who have been very casual about testifying are going to be under the gun a little bit more. Another problem we've faced is with clients who misrepresent the materials we've produced for them. I don't have any solutions to that problem.

Leary. In some cases, particularly for a design, you can copyright it, which gives you a degree of control. You can also specify in the letter of agreement the use of any material you produce, whether it's going to be returned to you or whether you have to give up your working notes. We've developed a kind of checksheet for agreements, just like the ones that lawyers have for contracts. The only

sure way I know to handle this situation is to anticipate all the things that can go wrong.

Heckman. How about critiquing other consultants? Is there any good way to do it?

Eplan. I can think of an example. An independent planning board in Florida prepared a county plan that got an adverse reaction from some of the residents. The county administrator, who didn't have his own planning staff, asked me to come in and critique the plan, to see if the adverse reaction was fair. I tried to suggest ways to improve the plan and diminish the conflicts, rather than simply saying, "It's a lousy plan." I think this sort of thing can be done in a positive manner, so you're elevating the importance of the plan and showing that planning is important for the community.

Heckman. What if a consulting firm develops a rather consistent pattern of producing substandard products? Do any of you have experience in dealing with such a consultant directly?

Kendig. This gets to the larger issue that Leon was talking about—the special role of the planner. I've had an opportunity to look at a number of ordinances recently, and to do some testimony, and I see a lot of plans that have been devised solely to allow elected officials to browbeat developers into anything they want. Almost everything becomes a conditional use, and the planner is advised simply to keep everything the way it was. That, to me, is the antithesis of planning. The plan has become a political function. And I have no compunction whatsoever about walking into that kind of situation and telling a lawyer, under cross-examination, that it isn't a good plan because it doesn't recognize reality.

Leary. You also run into situations where plans were prepared by a strange conglomeration of engineers, architects, land surveyors, and God knows what else, who hold themselves out as planners. Not only aren't you dealing with a peer group in such a situation, you're dealing with people who may be completely unqualified.

Knox. I don't know if it's just a question of nonplanners. In the Bay Area now, a lot of communities are hiring supposedly legitimate planners to revise the housing elements of their comprehensive plans. And a lot of these "planners" are letting high-priced suburban communities get away with murder. They're saying that moderate-income housing isn't needed or is too expensive or something similar. I don't see anyone speaking out against such abuses. But neither do I want to put my business on the line by saying: "Hey, this particular planning firm, which I happen to compete with, is doing a pretty bad job in preparing housing elements." . . .

Joe Racine. How many of these issues are really that black and white? Three or four years after a document is written you can go back and see where some of the forecasts may have been way off base, but at the time it was probably the best effort. It may have been the community's first planning attempt, and the consultant's interaction with the planning commission may have taught the local people a lot about the planning process, even if the final document wasn't perfect. I wonder if anyone really is in a position to judge in very many cases.

Heckman. We're finding, in the Illinois APA chapter's investigation of ethics, that, one, it's very hard to get a consensus on many of these issues; two, it's very hard to get people to speak up; and three, we have almost no sanctions available to us. What are we going to do—kick the person out of APA? Expose him, or her, to public ridicule in the press?

Eplan. When it gets to the point of punishment, you've gone pretty far, and I agree there's not much you can do. But I do feel that the chapter has a vital role. It should note when someone is not following the laws of the state, or is not following the spirit of those laws. The chapter could sponsor a debate on it—in the chapter newsletter or at a meeting—just to heighten sensitivity.

Racine. Related to this business about ethics is the idea of taking on an assignment when the resources available are not sufficient to do a good job. A lot of the RFPs [requests for proposal] that come out of smaller communities are for preparing a comprehensive plan, complete with economic base studies and everything else—for $2,500. What do you say if you flat out know that you can't do a good plan for that amount of money? Do you just throw up your arms and walk away from the job?

Leary. We've got a project now in Florida where we believed that we couldn't do what we were being asked to do and said it, and the client turned us down. But when the first choice failed, the client reworked the budget and chose us. So sometimes it's not bad to lose the first time around.

Knox. Talking about RFPs raises another issue. I've responded to more RFPs than I've won, and they take a lot of time to prepare for. That's hard for a small firm. Do all of you respond to every RFP that comes along?

Heckman. Often there's a lack of sophistication on the part of the person who's in charge of putting together the RFP. Sometimes he gets carried away by bureaucratic zeal and adds more and more things to the form, many of them cribbed from other RFPs. We're also starting to see a very cavalier distribution of RFPs to an extraordinarily large number of people. The winnowing-down process then becomes very difficult—as many as 25 firms may be called in to interview on a project.

We've reached the point where we simply don't respond immediately. Instead, we contact the people who put out the RFP and try to diagnose the terms and understand the process. If the RFP is not clearly structured, and if the people issuing it are not clear about what they want, we're likely to avoid it. It's one of those things that, when you do it, you take a deep breath and say, "Well, if I start doing this, am I going to stop getting RFPs altogether, or am I going to gain a reputation for being uppity about critiquing RFPs?". . .

Racine. There's another touchy issue that hasn't been mentioned. That's when you respond to an RFP only to discover, after doing all the preparation, that the thing's been politically wired, and the job goes to a local consultant. I would bet that half of the RFPs are that way.

Kendig. It is a very political thing. You get listed by staff as being the number one choice, and then a local consultant goes complaining to the county commissioners. But I don't think there's any difference between that local consultant squealing about out-of-state competition and the squealing that you hear about competition from regional planning agencies that have gotten into the business of selling planning services.

Planning. In fact, the selling of services by regional agencies seems to be a growing point of controversy. Do you see it as a problem?

Leary. You get in trouble when you take off from an uneven starting line. I have a similar reaction to people who moonlight on nights and weekends from full-time jobs, or to academics who have access to resources and cheap labor that we have to pay for.

Mary Lou Henry. We reached agreement with the planning schools in Texas a long time ago that any outside consulting they do must be clearly recognized as student work. If they want to have some special educational program, it must be clearly stated that way to the community.

Kendig. I've been on both sides of the fence, as a public planner and as a consultant, and I happen to feel it's a very valid exercise for a county or regional agency to try to implement policy. After all, they have virtually no authority to implement any of their plans. Why shouldn't they be able to go out and sell their product? And if they've got a really good product, and the consultants can't match it, then that's the way the cookie's going to crumble.

Knox. Recently, when I was asked to respond to an RFP for a housing element, I found I was competing against a regional agency, which was offering to do the element for a reduced price because it had the data bank and the support staff. Several consultants in the area wrote a strongly worded letter to the agency saying this was not the type of business it should be in.

Eplan. I know of several regional planning agencies that have service centers that sell census information and other data. Do you feel that's unfair competition?

Knox. If it's equally available and usable by both the public and private sectors, then it seems as though it might be O.K. What I was referring to was a public agency getting into an area where private enterprise traditionally has competed with other private entrepreneurs.

Kendig. Most consultants recognize that when they're doing a project in an area they usually get free information from the regional agencies. So, if you believe that the point of planning is to get better plans, and a local agency is capable of competing quality-wise with consultants, then you just have to accept that competition. . . .

Planning. You all represent relatively small firms, and your ranks seem to be growing. Is this only because there are more unemployed planners who are calling themselves consultants?

Eplan. The whole thing is a recent phenomenon, partly because planning has become so varied and partly because there are more experienced planners around. It used to be that small firms simply tended to grow, whereas now we see an enormous proliferation of one- to five-people firms.

Henry. Another reason there are so many new firms starting up is that planners seem to be becoming less mobile. They're no longer so willing to move across the country for a new job. It's not so easy for a planning director to move on to the next town as it was 10 years ago when there were more jobs available.

Heckman. Our work is more varied, as Leon said, but, at the same time, I don't see a lot of specialists. I see many of us becoming supergeneralists. Most small planning consultants have a hard time explaining what they do. They usually wind up saying, "I'll do whatever you want me to do."

Susan Stoddard. It does vary, though. A number of planners in the San Francisco area have started companies that specialize in one type of service, such as walking applications through the development approval process.

Planning. Aren't there also more small firms today because the definition of "planner" has been expanded so greatly?

June Spencer. Yes, that's true for at least two of us here, who are not physical planners. We're social planners, and that means new directions for small consultants.

Dean Boorman. Yes, but I think there is a big difference between social planning and management consulting, say, and land-use planning. They are still largely separate fields.

Spencer. I disagree with that. I often see land-use planners getting into political situations where they don't have any clout. One of my roles is as an arts planner, and I use the arts as a mechanism for dealing with local opinion leaders, the people who control the political structure more than anyone. They're often on the local arts boards, and we get them to understand that community aesthetics is a part of art and that you have to have planning and zoning to get there.

It's a whole different type of planning than you're talking about and my role is quite different from most of yours, but we still call ourselves planners, and we still do many of the things that you do.

Kendig. One has to evolve to survive in this business. If anyone had told me in graduate school that I would end up writing computer programs, I would have considered him crazy. Obviously, there's plenty of room for growth, particularly in the area of new technology.

Planning. But not growth in firm size, evidently. How large a firm is ideal?

Leary. There is a growth knuckle at about five staff members. Any larger, and a whole different management system is needed. Also, your demand for space may exceed your ability to function as a cottage industry.

Knox. I think you're right about that knuckle of five. I'm at three now, and I've got just enough overhead that I can't really work it out economically unless I go to five.

Leary. From five to about 15 the profitability remains almost constant.

Heckman. It's a shock to find out that our firm is one of the larger ones represented here. We always think of ourselves as being very small. In fact, we work hard to *keep* ourselves small. My partners and I meet weekly to reevaluate our size and our management and overhead structure in an effort to keep ourselves small. But when you have a few successes, more people want you. That makes it hard to stay small. . . .

Ted Johnson. Three of the six people in our firm worked before for a large planning-engineering firm, with about 250 people, and they found they were getting away from that personal touch dealing with clients. That's why our firm was started, and we don't want it to grow any larger. We, too, have weekly brainstorming sessions, just to let everyone know what kind of projects we're working on, what happened during the week. That's our philosophy and that's how we want to continue. . . .

Ruth Eckdish Knack is Planning's *senior editor. Jim Peters was formerly associate editor.*

Start-ups and Spin-offs: Consulting Today

Ruth Eckdish Knack
(December 1986)

Sometimes, it really is hard to tell the players without a scorecard—especially when they're planning consultants. Part of the reason is the growth of the field. In 1927, pioneer planner John Nolen, himself a prolific consultant, counted up the comprehensive city plans commissioned since 1920 and found that all 87 of them had been done by 23 consultants. Yet this fall, 400 firms responded to an APA survey published in *Planning* in preparation for a new consultant directory.

Many of these firms are huge companies known for their work in other fields. Are they planning consultants in the same sense that Nolen's firms were? And what about the 1,500 AICP members who identified themselves as consultants in a survey conducted two years ago—many of them, no doubt, moonlighters with full-time agency or academic jobs? Should they be counted?

Even more than growth, there are other changes in the field that make the term *consultant* almost as elusive as *planner* itself. For one thing, consultants do different sorts of work nowadays than they did in the days when the comprehensive plan reigned supreme. Many firms have become more specialized, with some concentrating only on financial analysis, for instance. Some rely almost exclusively on private-sector clients, to a far greater extent than in the past. And more and more consultants are adopting bottom-line business tactics, emphasizing marketing and public relations, and opening regional offices to respond to new markets in the Sun Belt, particularly Florida, and to some extent overseas.

The biggest news in the numbers is the proliferation of small firms—those with fewer than five people—which account for 40 percent of the 400 APA survey respondents. Forty-seven of those 400 are single-member firms, a figure that coincides with the membership count of the American Society of Consulting Planners. Half of the 82 firms (no moonlighters allowed) listed in the group's 1986 directory are solo practices.

It's a safe bet that most of the new offices were opened by former public planners. Paul Sedway, a partner in the San Francisco-based Sedway Cooke Associates, dates the onslaught in his state to the 1979 passage of Proposition 13, the tax-cap measure that produced big cuts in public programs. "A lot of city planning directors either became disillusioned and quit, or were dismissed," says Sedway. "The next step was to become a consultant."

Many, of course, in California and across the nation, do not last. Lachlan Blair, a professor at the University of Illinois and a longtime consultant with an office in Urbana, notes that small planning firms have the same high failure rate as small businesses in general. "It's a gamble," says Blair, "and more lose than win."

Despite the risks, many small-timers say they

wouldn't change for anything. "It's tempting to expand, but this way, when there's a mistake, I know who did it," says Thomas Roberts, an Atlanta-area consultant who described his early days as a solo in a July 1979 *Planning* article. "When I need help," says Gainesville practitioner Ernest Bartley (who's also on the University of Florida faculty), "I put together an ad hoc team of experts."

The flip side, notes Harry Adley, proprietor of a midsized (12-person) firm in Sarasota, Florida, is that the lone practitioner denies himself some bigger jobs. "You have to spend all your time either getting work or doing it." But Adley adds that he felt like "Papa Robin" when he was a partner in a larger firm. "I had to keep scrambling to get work to keep so many people occupied."

Women and minorities make up a fairly high percentage of the small firm ranks. The APA survey elicited responses from 54 woman-owned firms, with almost half (21) no larger than three people and another 13 under five. (One respondent is co-owner of a 200-person firm, Jung/Brannen Associates of Boston). Of the nine black-owned firms, three have fewer than five members and four have between six and 10. The five Hispanic respondents own firms ranging from two to 154 people (Psomas Associates in California).

Loss leaders?

At the other end of the spectrum are the giants, the firms that consistently make *Engineering News-Record's* list of the top 500 design firms in terms of annual billings. These are the companies that made their reputation in engineering or architecture or management consulting, but add on specialties from time to time and then call themselves "multidisciplinary."

There are 25 firms with over 150 employees in the APA survey, and 19 with over 300. In most cases, the number of planners is tiny. The largest firm responding, Laventhol and Horwath management consultants, employs 20 planners out of a staff of 4,522. The Swerdrup Corporation, an engineering firm with a staff of 3,000, has seven planners, the same number as RTKL, a Baltimore-based architecture firm with 439 on its staff. Robinson and Cole, a law firm in Hartford, employs eight planners out of a total of 215.

Representatives of the big firms justify the small showing of planners by stressing that all the resources of the company are available to the plan-

ning arm. They also strongly dispute the charge that planning in the big shops is a "loss leader," offered at a cut rate to bring in the architectural or engineering or legal work, where the real money lies.

"Planning here is a separate profit center," says Bruce Yoder, a vice-president of Greenhorne & O'Mara, a big (850 employees, 11 planners), multidisciplinary firm in Greenbelt, Maryland, and an officer of the consulting planners society. "That's what I like about the firm, and that's what makes it different from some of the other big A&E firms, which may include planning on their letterhead, but that's all."

At the architectural giant Skidmore Owings & Merrill, a half-century old this year, the role of planning has grown from support of design projects to independent consulting, says Kim Goluska, head of the planning studio in the firm's Chicago office. "The difference between us and planners in a more traditional setting," he says, "is that we operate in a firm whose primary product is design-oriented. So we stress physical planning and take a three-dimensional approach to our work."

Similarly, David Wallace of Wallace, Roberts & Todd in Philadelphia insists that his firm, founded 30 years ago with Ian McHarg, views planning as a "professional discipline on its own," not as an adjunct to architectural work, "although, once in a while, there's a cross-fertilization and a master plan evolves into a commission for a building."

And at Sasaki Associates in Watertown, Massachusetts, planner Perry Chapman says the holistic approach of landscape architect Hideo Sasaki has colored all of the activities of the firm, even as it added new disciplines, including planning.

In fact, Allan Hodges of Parsons Brinckerhoff Quade & Douglas in Boston says there are certain advantages to being a planner in a big transportation-oriented engineering firm. "It's interesting work," he says, "because the public works jobs are so big. More important, they're likely to be implemented. So you get a chance to see something completed in your lifetime."

Meanwhile, the traditional midsized planning firms continue to hold their own, although in dwindling numbers and with all sorts of changes. "We've had fewer central city assignments in recent years, for instance, and fewer downtown plans," says Paul Sedway, whose 26-member firm is among the largest of the planning-only firms.

"Even so," he adds, "our practice remains wonderfully diverse. That's gratifying because it's why I went into planning in the first place. We do everything from expert witnessing to jail studies, with an increasing number of specific plans and transportation work." In contrast to the multidisciplinary firms, Sedway Cooke draws the line at crossing over into architecture, law, engineering, or other fields because doing so could lead to a conflict of interest.

"Going after that sort of work would also change the character of our practice," notes Sedway. "Above all, we want to be known as a planning firm."

Other firms have been less particular, picking up new work wherever they can find it, and adding new areas of expertise to their calling cards. In California, the phenomenon is most noticeable among the "EIR firms" that sprang up in the 1970s in response to the state's environmental quality act. Recently, environmental impact review work has been slow (because of an increasing number of exemptions to the law), so the firms have had to branch out into other areas, including traditional land-use planning.

Crossovers

Elsewhere, architecture and landscape architecture firms have also stepped into areas once reserved for planning firms, getting more involved at the front end of development, for instance. The Chicago-based architecture firm, Perkins & Will, with only one trained planner on its staff of about 150, now does strategic planning for developers and master plans for such projects as the new Chicago Technology Park. John LaMotte, the firm's planner, says the new work is a logical progression from the firm's early work on schools, college campuses, and, more recently, hospital complexes. He points out that he can tap into the whole firm for consultation on projects—better, he says, than having a single in-house planning group.

At Sasaki Associates, planner Perry Chapman reports a shift to "policy type planning," including zoning. "We're becoming increasingly eclectic," he says, although three-fourths of the practice continues to be project-oriented.

The shift to find new markets has been particularly taxing for firms that were dependent on such federally funded planning programs as Section 701 of the 1954 Housing Act, which provided money for local comprehensive plans, and the urban renewal program of the early 1960s. One of the largest, Candeub, Fleissig and Associates of Springfield, New Jersey, which had a staff of 150 in the mid-1960s, has shrunk to some 20 people, according to company president Burton Cohen. (Isadore Candeub, the planner who began the practice in 1953 with attorney Morris Fleissig, died earlier this year.)

Cohen says the firm has coped by shrinking geographically. It no longer markets itself nationally, for instance, except for a specific project like a recent zoning ordinance for Plano, Texas, winner of a Texas APA chapter award. Once known for its public work, it has taken on more development assignments, including site design and engineering, and has also landed federal contracts for military installations. This year, the firm won a competition to prepare a ward-level master plan for Washington, D.C.

Similar adjustments are reported by Malcolm Drummond, planning manager for Harland Bartholomew & Associates in St. Louis, the firm founded in 1929 by the man associated with the development of the comprehensive plan. "We have become specialists," says Drummond, who notes that comprehensive plans are only a small part of the firm's work today. Instead, it focuses on bridge and highway engineering and a potpourri of other projects, including environmental assessments, facility plans, and a smattering of comprehensive plans. The big interest now, adds Robert Duchek, manager of the firm's Chicago-area office, is not the document but the process—a major philosophical shift.

Duchek is one of the last planners in the firm to have been sent into the field as a "resident planner," a Bartholomew innovation in the early days. "Whenever there was a fairly sizable project," he explains, "a member of the firm would be sent to stay in the community until it was completed." In 1968–69, for example, Duchek lived in Decatur, Illinois, site of one of the last urban renewal-sponsored projects.

"We're more specialized, too," says Bruce Yoder of Greenhorn & O'Mara. "During the 701 days, we would work with a community on its entire planning program. Today, we're more likely to work on detailed studies for a specific area like a waterfront." No two firms are quite the same today, Yoder adds, "a big change from the old days when you'd hear the same things over and over again at ASCP meetings."

But, while recognizing the reasons for specialization, Florida planner Harry Adley says it is important to remember that the strong point of good planners is "precisely that they are not locked-up specialists. If they have a specialty, it is that they are generalists." Their other strong point, says Adley, is the ability "to think like a developer—or at least to speak developers' jargon."

Adley could have been talking about Michael Buckley, president of the 10-year-old real estate consulting and development firm called Halcyon Ltd. (after the seabird of Greek myth that settled on troubled waters). The firm's philosophy, says Buckley, is "to get as close to the developer's viewpoint as possible." That means not only giving advice but also occasionally stepping in and carrying out the development. Implementation is, in fact, a quarter of the firm's work.

"That makes us different from other consultants," says Buckley. "For one thing, it requires us to carry staff members with hands-on skills in leasing, marketing, and other areas." Halcyon claims expertise in six areas: mixed-use development, market research, project management, leasing, property management, and strategic planning. "We're known as development troubleshooters," says Buckley, and along those lines, the firm recently entered into a joint venture with Dade County, Florida, to program activities and manage the retail space in the 40-acre county government center in downtown Miami.

The 80-member Halcyon staff, distributed among the Hartford headquarters and four branch offices, includes "some planners," Buckley says, but more "financially oriented" types. Buckley himself earned a master's degree in MIT's joint program in management and urban studies. He is on the faculty of the MIT Center for Real Estate Development, where, he says, he tells students that strategic planning and "economic realities" are in and "future world planning" is out.

Unlike some firms, Halcyon is not committed to doing only private work. It served as national consultant to the UDAG program, for instance, a program whose loss Buckley laments. Yet New Orleans real estate consultant Jan Ramsey, vice-president of Robert L. Siegel & Associates, says she prefers not to work with public clients at all because of the bureaucratic procedures "you have to wade through just to get the job."

In contrast, Lawrence Livingston says that 95 percent of the dollars that have come into his office have been public dollars—and he likes it that way. "I prefer to work in the public sector because I want the public interest to be advanced," he says. "I also like the politics of public work. I'd never run for office myself, but I enjoy the give and take of public hearings."

Livingston has been practicing in the San Francisco Bay Area since 1953, when he started a firm (later joined by John Blayney) that grew to 12 people before the two split in the mid-1970s. Since 1981, Livingston has been a solo practitioner, "a consultant in the strict sense of the word," he says, "giving advice on planning instead of making plans." For years, his specialty has been open space preservation, including work in connection with litigation on the Lake Tahoe regional planning efforts. By now, he jokes, he has become "the gray eminence of open space preservation."

Selling

"Marketing," says Robert Gray, "is 80 percent of everything." Gray is the aggressive head of a Jacksonville, Florida, consulting firm, the Strategic Planning Group, that recently won two U.S. Navy planning contracts (both to study port facilities in the region). The firm garnered considerable local publicity by bringing in a team of outside experts led by Edmund Bacon for a design charette on downtown Jacksonville, subject of an SPG revitalization study. In Gray's view, marketing is what has enabled a new firm to compete successfully against nationally known consultants.

The emphasis on marketing is just one sign of change in the way consulting practice is conducted. Although traditional planning-only firms are still extremely discreet about advertising—relying on calling card ads and firm newsletters to get the word out—the large competitors from other fields are not. And when it comes to presentations, many planners have noted with chagrin, the big architecture firms are way ahead.

"Fifteen years ago, people would hear about us and call," says Malcolm Drummond of Harland Bartholomew, recalling the days before marketing became such an issue. "Now, clients look at several firms before they decide, and we find that our proposals are much more elaborate." Those elaborate proposals take time and money to prepare, but Drummond sees them as a sign that the public clients are much more sophisticated. "It's a healthy thing because it separates the truly competent planners from those who aren't."

Others are less sanguine about the request for proposal process that Drummond is referring to. "The selection process is debilitating," says Paul Sedway. "The RFP is a greatly misused device," adds Harry Adley. "We seldom respond to one." Similarly, Fred Bair, now retired from a longtime Florida practice, says that "when public agencies went to competitive bidding, consulting became a less professional thing."

While the RFP continues to be a sore point, some see hope in bypassing it by putting consulting on an hourly basis like legal work. "For some projects at least, it's a good thing," says Robert Teska of Teska and Associates in Evanston, Illinois.

Perhaps the greatest effect on practice has come from the merger phenomenon and its corollary, the trend toward spin-offs.

A growing number of planning firms are now part of large conglomerates. And that can mean changes in philosophy, staffing, and even location. For example, Burton Cohen says that his firm, Candeub Fleissig, has held its staff down since Hill International, the big New Jersey-based management consulting company, acquired a controlling interest in the firm in 1982. "The acquisition allowed us to draw on their specialists," says Cohen, "so we didn't need so many of our own."

For Harland Bartholomew, says Robert Duchek, a buy-out meant more joint ventures with a former competitor, Barton-Aschman Associates. Both were recently acquired by the Ralph M. Parsons Company, a California engineering and construction management firm. In the case of Perkins & Will, now owned by a London-based international holding company formed by a Lebanese engineering firm, the merger means more possibilities for international work, while retaining a considerable degree of autonomy, says planner John LaMotte.

Illinois consultant Lach Blair notes that one of the problems of running a big firm is that people tend to go off on their own, as for instance, SPG's Robert Gray did when he left the Plantec Corporation to open his own office across the street.

APA deputy executive director George Marcou (himself a former consultant whose firm, Marcou, O'Leary and Associates, was bought by Westing-

house in 1970), says that he has been struck by the "regionalization" of consulting and the decline of planning-only firms that operate nationwide. One reason, he suggests, is the smaller average size of contracts. Another is clearly the boom-bust cycle experienced periodically by different regions of the country. "Consultants are more sensitive to these regional ups and downs than public-sector planners," notes Pamela Wev, executive director of the American Society of Consulting Planners.

And where are today's hot spots? A few years ago, before oil prices tumbled, Texas was the draw. "We're glad now that we didn't open an office there," says Bruce Yoder of Greenhorne & O'Mara, which opened its first branch office in 1980 in Fairfax, Virginia. Now the firm is in 13 locations, including Atlanta, Raleigh, Denver, and—"of course"—Tampa, for Florida is the boom state of the 1980s. Sasaki's Chapman notes that there is also renewed interest in the Northeast, "which has turned out to be phenomenal." Halcyon's Buckley agrees and cites some other growth areas as well: the Midwest ("cities like Cleveland are getting their act together"); the Washington, D.C., area; Utah; and the "second cities" of California—Sacramento, for instance. . . .

Florida needs you

The ad in last July's *Planning* was an attention grabber. "Wanted: Planners for Florida," read the headline above the text, which included planning consultants among the types of professionals being sought. The ad was placed by the Florida APA chapter in the wake of new legislation that requires updated comprehensive plans for all of the state's 461 jurisdictions. The new law, coupled with the continuing strong real estate market and a slew of existing environmental requirements, make Florida a consultant's paradise, the Texas of the 1980s.

"Last year," explains James Murley, director of resources planning and management in the Department of Community Affairs, "each of the 67 counties got a start-up grant. Since then, the legislature has appropriated a total of $12 million, which has gone to the counties and to all the coastal cities. Next fiscal year, we'll go back to the legislature for further funding until we cover every jurisdiction." Each is required to produce a comprehensive plan, followed within a year by development regulations.

But already, although state funding has just

begun, the consulting firms are descending. "It's a very hot market," says Ronald Cossman of SPG in Jacksonville, one of the home-grown firms that are competing with the out-of-state consultants who have opened local branch offices. "We expect a lot more work there," says Robert Duchek of Harland Bartholomew, which has offices in Tampa and Jacksonville.

Among the most active out-of-staters are the large law firms like Chicago's Siemon Larsen Mattlin & Purdy. But some observers worry that their planning work could entail a conflict of interest if it eventually leads to litigation. And Ernest Bartley points out that litigation has, in fact, grown "by leaps and bounds" in Florida.

Nevertheless, Bartley believes that the lawyers serve a real need at a time when the "legalization of the planning process" seems to be the "wave of the future" in Florida. "Back in the 701 days," he notes, "no one ever worried about litigation." But then, he says, the 701 program produced a lot of lookalike plans. The new law is far more innovative, in Bartley's view.

Moreover, he says, the lawyers that come in often associate themselves with economists and other experts, giving them a broader base for planning work. Does that mean that the lead consultants of the future will be the lawyers? "I hope not," says Bartley, "although, since expert witnessing is 90 percent of my practice, I might be accused of having a vested interest. But it seems to me that the planner as generalist has to consider a lot of things that an attorney doesn't."

Harry Adley is just such a generalist. He's also been around long enough to put the current Florida boom in context. Owner of a Sarasota planning practice since 1971, he has served on numerous state boards and commissions, including the Florida Growth Management Advisory Committee, which worked on the standards for the new legislation. In addition, he's a former president and current board member of the consulting planners society.

He has high hopes for the new law, "although I know we've been accused of writing the planners and attorneys relief act. For the first time, though, we've assured continuity in the legislation, and for the first time we've tied planning to economics. Now, if a community says it will stick by its capital budget, it must do so. I think it will lead to more sophisticated planning."

But before out-of-state consultants start lining up to buy their plane tickets, Adley has a few warnings they might do well to heed. First, he notes that Floridians are wary of carpetbaggers and that outside firms should stock up with a couple of old Florida hands, who understand the local ecology, politics, and mores.

Second, he cautions against getting into the "701-type package plan frenzy." He sees a lot of firms racing around, drumming up business, and often promising more than they can deliver.

With these caveats in mind, Adley says, "Welcome aboard, we can use all the help we can get."

Adley also belongs to the World Future Society and thinks planners don't do enough prognosticating. So we asked him to consult his crystal ball, planning division. "I see more compartmentalization," he said, "with planners getting more sophisticated about public finance, and I see more highly specific problem-solving assignments."

Others agree. "We'll have more work in public-private partnerships, and public agencies will think more like developers, says David Wallace of Wallace Roberts & Todd. Malcolm Drummond of Harland Bartholomew foresees lots of "microplanning" for specific areas like riverfronts and historic districts. And Allan Hodges of Parsons Brinckerhoff predicts that consultants with technical expertise will find more work in small towns facing growth pressures and in states with strong environmental laws.

In short, if any consultant out there is looking for a firm motto, it might well be, "Privatization and Specialization—We Do It Better."

Ruth Knack is senior editor of Planning.

A Practice Built for One (or Two)

Robert M. Leary
(December 1986)

"Mr. Leary, I got your name from the Yellow Pages." (Ah, ha!, I said to myself, it pays to advertise. Visions of a megabuck contract flitted into my head.) "My son wants to be a planner—would you talk him out of that foolishness?"

This vignette occurred in 1970, soon after I decided to establish a one-man consulting firm in Raleigh, North Carolina. I had many of the same reasons that Tom Roberts described in "Why I Left a Cushy Job to Be My Own Boss." I had experienced the joys and frustrations of running large organizations engaged in significant undertakings, encrusted with bureaucratic procedures and creating few end products.

I had worked for the Port Authority of New York and New Jersey; spent five years as planning director of Ann Arbor, Michigan, and two as director of planning and zoning in Fairfax County, Virginia; and from 1966 to 1970 was in charge of planning and design for the National Capital Commission in Ottawa, Canada. After more than a decade of government service, I was curious to find out whether I could survive in the private sector.

My standard answer, when asked why I chose Raleigh, is that I started walking south from Ontario with a snow shovel on my shoulder and stopped when somebody said, "Hey, boy, what's that?" Actually, there were personal reasons for choosing Raleigh, as well as some practical ones. Among the latter were a salubrious climate; a socially, culturally, and educationally rich environment; relatively easy access to big cities such as Washington, Atlanta, Chicago, and New York; and North Carolina's large inventory of medium-sized communities, which, I hoped, might desire my services.

Anyone setting up a new organization should have an Organizational Philosophy. Mine was: Do some good, have some fun, make some money. It is a philosophy shared by my partner, Diane E. Lea, who joined the firm nine years ago. We still find it workable, although the emphasis changes according to the condition of our biorhythms and bank statement—and the personalities of our clients.

Another basic tenet of my philosophy was the decision to restrict the growth of the firm. Initially, it was to be a one-man operation so that clients could be assured of my direct responsibility and participation in every contract. Also, I was not interested in accumulating the myriad problems associated with a large staff, a complex organization, and a large payroll. I was very much aware that to keep a substantial portion of what I earned, subject to the vicissitudes of the federal tax code, I needed to remain small.

The decision to remain small also permitted me to establish the firm as a cottage industry operating out of a portion of my home. That eliminated the daily commute, but it also required a new type of discipline because of propinquity to family, toys, and other distractions.

It's tempting to say that all the decisions about starting a new firm followed each other logically, that once I had decided to start up, I began thinking about what the firm would do and how it would go about enticing clients for whom to do it. However, these decisions were not made seriatim but were intertwangled, one with the other. I had a long-standing interest and involvement in land-use regulations, particularly zoning ordinances and subdivision regulations, as well as training and experience in administration and management. Ergo, the firm would offer its services to clients, both public and private, in these areas.

These important and difficult decisions, when made, had the effect on the outside world of a whisper in the middle of a hurricane. With the exception of my family and a few close friends, the world was unaware of the nascent organization and its need for gainful employment.

To advertise in the conventional sense was inappropriate at that time. Calling cards in the publications of the American Society of Planning Officials and American Institute of Planners were not as commonplace as they are now. Also, I was not convinced that a media blitz would be effective. The Yellow Pages appeared to be a dry hole, a conclusion that was confirmed by that call from the distraught mother, the only one directly traceable to our listing, first under the title Zoning Consultants and, more recently, City and Town Planners. The latter listing is an amorphous one, containing a mix of architects, engineers, designers, planners, and landscape architects.

We did mail out a formal announcement of the birth of the firm to all AIP members in North Carolina, as well as friends, associates, and potential associates throughout the U.S. Many letters of encouragement and several leads resulted from this effort, and two jobs were directly traceable to it.

Contacts

Early contracts, such as appearances as an expert witness and a 10-month assignment to direct the Atlanta Central Area Study, came from friends and acquaintances who knew something of my qualifications and drew them to the attention of the appropriate people. That, however, was a shaky foundation on which to erect the future of the enterprise, so other methods had to be pursued.

Some assignments resulted from my participation in academic pursuits. I had always had connections with planning programs in various universities and colleges in North America. When I set up shop in Raleigh, I found a niche teaching part-time at the Institute of Government at the University of North Carolina at Chapel Hill. For the past 10 years, I have taught at the School of Design at North Carolina State University.

The work at the Institute of Government brought me in contact with local government officials across North Carolina, so that I was often called on to provide help in land-use matters by officials I had met in the classroom. In at least two instances, my teaching activities resulted in joint research assignments with colleagues.

These academic connections broadened my range of contacts, provided an opportunity to identify and employ part-time the pick of each new crop of students, and significantly sharpened my ability to articulate persuasive answers to my students' constant cries of "Why?" (This last skill also comes in handy when I face new clients.)

My planning students provide a constantly expanding pool of potential clients, as they move into positions of responsibility in local government, consulting firms, and development organizations. The same is true for students in other classes, like the law students whom I have encountered as a visiting lecturer.

In addition, I had to establish myself with local organizations, both professional associations and statewide special interest groups. I took on numerous committee assignments, agreed to edit the AIP chapter newsletter, and served as master of ceremonies and speaker at all types of gatherings of two or more people. All were methods of achieving name and face recognition and were a means to display the intellectual merchandise.

Not all the public appearances were positive occasions. Emerging spittle-covered from a confrontation with a deranged right-winger who was sure I represented the latest manifestation of the Trilateral Commission was not an edifying experience. Nor do I believe that my less than even-handed response to his harangue did much to enhance my reputation for equanimity.

Robert M. Leary and Associates survived as a solo practice for about seven years—defying the actuarial statistics for small businesses. The wolf was kept a reasonable distance from the door. After a couple of lean years, my earnings were well above what I would have made if I had stayed in public service. I could discern positive results from my efforts in the communities where I had worked. And all the time, I added to my store of chuckles and quiet satisfactions and occasional bursts of hilarity.

I had also recovered from the Centurion Syndrome, a malady commonly brought on by the loss of a staff. Moving from a large organization with many minions to one with no minions at all requires the centurion to become the cleaner of bottles, the filer of papers, the answerer of phones, and the doer of a number of things that, while not alien, are unfamiliar. I had learned to cope.

Also, the assignments from private and public clients had broadened somewhat from the initial concentration on land-use regulations and project management. Opportunities emerged (and were grasped) to conduct training sessions for planning commission and zoning board members, to prepare regulations implementing state legislation, and to put together general plans for municipalities facing a state mandate to prepare them.

It was a temptation, hard to surmount, to take on more and more assignments, beyond my capacity to accomplish. Nevertheless, I maintained my adherence to the "small is beautiful" philosophy. I tried to limit the number of jobs to no more than three to five at a time and to balance those that required extensive travel with those that were close at hand.

The length of each work week varied considerably. Fifteen-hour days were the rule when I was preparing for testimony in the Boca Raton population cap case. On the other hand, I saved time in not having to commute to the office and could take work breaks with a 10-foot stroll to my woodworking shop. The size of my contracts has varied as well. Some have been small—$3,000 to $7,000; others have exceeded $30,000. Some of the small ones have grown into larger ones or led to add-on assignments. For instance, one $5,000 subcontract led directly to additional work exceeding $200,000.

Time to grow

Even as I concentrated on land-use regulation and management work, I was always ready to take on challenges in related fields. For example, in 1977, a community foundation, set up to "improve the quality of life" in its area, sought my assistance in clarifying its grants strategy and policies. The foundation officers found out about me through my work at North Carolina State. My work for the foundation resulted in assignments that ranged from helping the surrounding county set up an economic development commission to finding a consultant to advise the local historical society on establishing a history museum.

My choice for the consultant job was a woman with experience in advising small museums and a good deal of grass-roots work in the state's expanding historic preservation movement, Diane Lea. She first worked for me as a subcontractor, consulting to the historical society. Eventually, she convinced the society and the town to apply for matching funds from the state to conduct an architectural and historic inventory. The firm was off in a new direction.

Serious discussions about doubling the size of the firm ensued. Each of us had strengths that could contribute to a combined effort. Diane's background in English, American studies, and museum management complemented my background of planning and public administration. Moreover, the professional and personal acquaintanceships Diane had built up over a number of years were definite assets and led to a number of contracts. During the past few years, we have undertaken five major architectural and historic inventories in North Carolina; prepared nominations to the National Register of Historic Places; prepared manuals for historic district commissions, historic properties commissions, and community appearance commissions; and assisted in the designation of local historic districts.

We have also found our mutual interest in the collection and use of antique tools to be an asset in our work in historic preservation. We know how the tools work and can recognize their marks on old buildings, which helps us identify the buildings' age and construction methods. In one case, our acceptance by a skeptical lawyer was hastened when he discovered that we were fellow tool nuts.

Our decision to associate permanently was not made easily or quickly. A one-man band does not easily give up responsibility for all solos, nor does he readily adjust to new keys and rhythms. But besides the skills and contacts, Diane's addition to the firm solved a problem that was becoming increasingly apparent—the lack of honest, intellectual feedback from a trusted associate, which is unavailable in a single-person organization. Access to a different viewpoint, value system, and approach overcame the difficulties of solitary decision making and production.

This doesn't mean everything went smoothly. It took a while for us to establish means for effective communication, the resolution of conflicts, and the sharing of authority and responsibility. We've even learned how to fight fairly.

Expansion

The increased flexibility of a two-person firm allowed me to accept a year-long assignment in Atlanta that required me to spend three days a week out of the office. This job grew out of associations established during the Central Area Study I conducted seven years before. Work on other contracts and the details of the office could now be shared, and we could take on jobs with greater complexity and scope. Thus, we accepted assignments to prepare development regulations for a major planned unit development in Jackson, Wyoming, and an administrative manual for Miami. Both would probably have been beyond my capacity, if I had had to handle them along with my other jobs, alone.

We have expanded our custom of associating with other firms in temporary joint arrangements. Landscape architects, architectural historians, graphic designers, soil scientists, geographers, economists, and lawyers are all available to us, and we to them. These arrangements allow us to complement them in large jobs and to take advantage of their marketing skills.

Our experience shows that the most effective marketing technique—leading to new, as well as repeat, business—is satisfied clients. Fully two-thirds of our work comes from referrals from such sources or from favorable recommendations in response to queries. We have never had an elaborate brochure, depending instead on a list of recent clients and projects, spartan resumes, and hard work.

We still market aggressively by participating in professional affairs and gatherings. For instance, this spring I will appear at my twentieth consecutive zoning clinic at the APA conference in New York—and I still devote one day a week to teaching. One of my courses, "The Ethics and Practice of Practice," is founded on our personal experience, trials, and errors as practitioners.

We welcome the lack of pressure of a large staff, whose mouths must be fed, just as we accept our sometimes roller coaster workload because the compensations offset the terrors. Among those compensations is the satisfaction of delivering a work product on time and within budget, a satisfaction not always available to the public servant.

We will continue to earn a buck, do some good, and have some fun. That's a good combination!

Bob Leary, AICP, is president of Robert M. Leary and Associates, Ltd., in Raleigh, and visiting lecturer in design at the School of Design, North Carolina State University.

Lewis Mumford: Critic, Colleague, Philosopher

David A. Johnson
(April 1983)

Lewis Mumford's extraordinary output includes no fewer than 30 books and countless articles and reviews. His latest book, and he says his last, Sketches from Life: The Autobiography of Lewis Mumford—The Early Years, *is a rich feast for the mind. It should be of special interest to urban planners, for it chronicles many of the ideas, people, and events that have shaped American planning.*

Lewis Mumford has had an extraordinary career or, more accurately, multiple careers—as literary critic, art critic, architectural critic, and social and urban historian. Less well known is his work as an urban planner. Had Mumford limited his attention to but one of these fields, his reputation would be secure—indeed, even more secure, since, as he has often reminded us, those who labor in many fields are too often discounted as inexpert by the specialists. But seeing the whole picture has been the essential quality of Mumford's thought and career.

In *Sketches from Life,* Mumford poignantly recalls his struggles as a young man to become a recognized and published author, to find romantic and sexual fulfillment, and simply to keep his young family fed and clothed. *Sketches* covers the period from his birth in 1895—illegitimate, we are surprised to learn—to 1938 and the advent of World War II. It nicely complements an earlier book, *The Letters of Lewis Mumford and Frederic J. Osborn,* which covers the period 1938 through 1970. Together,

these two books constitute a personal history of our time and of the evolution of the planning profession.

"I was a child of the city," he begins *Sketches.* The city is New York, Whitman's "Manahatta"—Mumford calls it his "university." His childhood on the Upper West Side was both difficult and enriching. The absence of his father was compensated for by the affection of his warm, supportive, extended family, especially of his grandfather. Mumford attended public schools and graduated in 1912 from Stuyvesant High School in Manhattan, one of New York's special schools for the scientifically and technically oriented. He took night classes at the City College of New York and also studied at Columbia University and the New School for Social Research, but he never completed a college degree.

In 1914, in the City College biology department library, Mumford came across the writings of Patrick Geddes, a Scottish professor of biology. From this point on, Mumford became a disciple, enthralled by Geddes's philosophy of integrating the natural and social worlds. There were other influences, such as William James; Peter Kropotkin; Frederick LePlay; and the Transcendentalists, Emerson, Thoreau, and Whitman. But none of these shaped Mumford's outlook on the world as did Patrick Geddes, particularly through his books, including *City Development* and the classic *Cities in Evolution.*

Early in life, Mumford knew he wanted to be a writer. In 1919, at age 24, he became an associate editor at the *Dial,* a lively fortnightly. The job lasted only seven months, but it brought him into contact with John Dewey, then an editor. More important, he met here his future wife, Sophia Wittenberg.

On a trip to England in 1920, Mumford was first exposed to the town planning movement led by Raymond Unwin, S. D. Adshead, and the aging Ebenezer Howard. Though he failed to see the great Geddes, who was off doing planning for Jerusalem and cities in India, Mumford was greatly stimulated by his British visit. It was the start of a lifetime association with the British town planning movement and the beginning of his role as a medium for the cross-Atlantic exchange of planning ideas. Mumford finally had an opportunity to meet his mentor when Geddes came to the U.S. in 1923 to lecture at the New School. In *Sketches,* Mumford describes how poorly the meeting went. (Geddes, it seems, demanded too much in the way of discipleship from those around him.)

Mumford's interest in planning and his ability as a writer brought him to the attention of Charles Harris Whitaker, the editor of the *Journal of the American Institute of Architects.* Soon after, in 1923, Whitaker, Benton MacKaye, Clarence Stein, Henry Wright, and a handful of others, including Mumford, formed the influential Regional Planning Association of America, an informal group dedicated to social betterment through planning.

Although the RPAA lasted only nine years, until 1932, it proved to be extraordinarily influential, thanks in large measure to Mumford's pen. The May 1925 issue of *Survey Graphic*—devoted to regional planning and edited by Mumford—is considered a classic expression of Geddes's theory of cyclical urban growth and decay (even though some modern critics have charged that Mumford misinterpreted and oversimplified Geddes's views).

The RPAA became a proponent of many of the ideas Mumford brought back from England: the value of garden cities and green belts, "recentralization," and the need to reduce urban congestion. [In Mumford's lexicon, recentralization refers to the creation of new regional centers.] Some of these ideas were absorbed into the ideology of the early New Deal, influencing the creation of the Tennessee Valley Authority, the Resettlement Administration's Greenbelt towns, and MacKaye's Appalachian Trail. One only wishes that Mumford, in *Sketches from Life* (and Stein and MacKaye in their own memoirs), had gone into more detail about the RPAA and its members.

Planning wars

At about the same time the RPAA was being formed, another effort was starting—this one to produce a regional plan for New York and environs. The work was directed by Thomas Adams, a Scotsman who had worked on Letchworth and Welwyn, garden cities outside London. Mumford was a severe critic of the monumental, multivolume survey and plan, which was underwritten by a $1 million grant from the Russell Sage Foundation and took a decade to complete.

It was, he wrote in his column in *The New Republic* in 1932, a mass of "well-meaning half-truths and contradictory plans and prescriptions" based on

unsound sociological assumptions. "The real task of transforming the inner area of the metropolis was shirked and the duty to prepare to receive larger increments of population in the immediate outlying areas was not even subjected to skeptical inquiry."

Adams was shocked at the severity of the criticism. He complained that Mumford was demanding nothing less than a total reconstruction of the economic and political organization of the New York area. Indeed, that was precisely what Mumford had in mind. His model of regional planning was Henry Wright's 1926 plan for New York State. Wright, planning adviser to New York State's housing and regional planning agency, called for rechanneling urban activities away from the New York metropolitan area and out toward the Hudson Valley and the old Erie Canal corridor. Implicit in Wright's plan was the dubious assumption that the state government had both the knowledge and the means to guide growth in this direction.

In his most influential book on planning, *The Culture of Cities,* published in 1938, Mumford said that he saw in the Adams and Wright plans a fundamental difference in planning philosophies: "Do not ignore the difference between these two orders of thinking: it underlies the approach to the whole problem of urban resettlement and rebuilding that now confronts the Western World."

In 1938—the year *Sketches from Life* concludes—Mumford's growing reputation as an urbanist resulted in an invitation to prepare a report for the Honolulu park board on the city's planning and development possibilities. His report, reprinted in *City Development,* stands as a practical symbol of his approach to local planning. Few planning reports have ever been better written, the images drawn so vividly that one hardly notices the absence of maps and graphic plans.

The report was filled with specific suggestions. For instance, noting that the city had failed to take advantage of its waterfront, Mumford called for improved access to the beaches and a new oceanfront parkway. He deplored the excesses of uncontrolled speculative development, observing that high land costs and exorbitant rents had resulted in some of the worst slums anywhere.

As in other proposals, Mumford assumed that land-use controls could achieve lower densities and more amenities without raising housing costs. He called for some of the same design elements he had observed in Sunnyside Gardens and Radburn, two New York-area planned developments of the 1920s—cul-de-sacs, narrow green strips to define neighborhoods, bypass roads around the business area, and even canals to the sea, a la Amsterdam. (Mumford lived in Sunnyside Gardens for 11 years.) Slum clearance and low-cost housing construction also were part of his plan.

Above all, the creation of parks, playgrounds, and green strips was, for Mumford, the key to Honolulu's development. He made numerous suggestions for new parks along the water and in the mountains. He shocked the commissioners by proposing the designation of several beaches for nude bathing, which he himself enjoyed.

Mumford understood that zoning ordinances alone would do little to realize his proposals. What was needed, he argued, was the appointment of a strong-minded planning commissioner. He also recommended that a "city plan council" of leading citizens be created to guide the staff and an advisory board of public works be established, comprising the heads of the various city departments. While this was hardly a radical reorganization proposal, it found little favor on the park board, and the board chairman, who had hired Mumford originally, was forced to resign.

Regrettably, little of Mumford's farsighted plan for Honolulu was followed. Its proposals were neither utopian nor impractical—but they were beyond the civic means and imagination of the community.

In 1939, a year after the Honolulu study, Mumford got his second big chance to do some actual planning. The Northwest Regional Council, a citizen's group concerned with the states of Washington, Oregon, Idaho, and Montana, invited him to "observe and critically appraise growth and development of the region." Mumford toured the area and prepared an incisive little report setting forth his ideas for "Regional Planning in the Pacific Northwest."

His proposals closely followed the Regional Planning Association of America's concepts and also those of the planning division of the Tennessee Valley Authority: Hold back the expansion of the largest metropolitan centers, Portland and Seattle, and—again the recentralization theme—build smaller centers, dispersed through the Columbia River gorge and tied to the growing

hydroelectric grid carrying power from the new Bonneville Dam.

The impact of Mumford's report is difficult to measure, but the message must have fallen on at least a few sympathetic ears in the Northwest. Oregon's well-known reluctance to accept unrestrained growth and its commitment to environmental quality were certainly reinforced by the report.

Mumford's planning-related work in 1939 was capped by the production of the now-classic film "The City," produced by the American Institute of Planners with a grant from the Carnegie Corporation. Mumford wrote the commentary and Aaron Copland created the musical score. It was and still is a powerful work of motion picture art. Its message was unequivocal: Build for people, recentralize, use the lessons learned in Radburn, the Greenbelt program, and the TVA.

Preparations for World War II diverted the country's—and Mumford's—attention from domestic concerns, however. Before many other intellectuals could muster the courage to do so, Mumford joined those who were calling for immediate mobilization against the threat of fascism.

His only son, Geddes, died in the fighting in Italy. It was a heavy blow, but, characteristically, Mumford turned his grief into a celebration of his son's short life in a touching recollection of Geddes's childhood and adolescent years, *Green Memories.* Hollywood offered to buy the book for a film but Mumford, not surprisingly, declined.

Mumford vigorously denounced the Allied firebombing of Tokyo and Dresden and the atomic attacks on Hiroshima and Nagasaki. We had, he declared, degraded our morality to the level of our foes.

Rebuilding London

The wartime destruction of London and other British cities offered an opportunity for rebuilding. In 1943, Mumford was invited by the British publication, *Architectural Review,* to comment on the new plan for the county of London prepared by Patrick Abercrombie and J. H. Forsham. (Like other American intellectuals, Mumford enjoyed a more appreciative audience in England than at home; his views were eagerly sought and respected there. He once complained to Frederic Osborn, "My own countrymen, who have an unholy respect for the 'expert,' never think of calling upon me for my opinion in the fashion that you or the *Architectural Review* did.")

Just as he had criticized Thomas Adams's plan for the New York region, Mumford rejected the underlying premises of Abercrombie's plan, which called for holding the population of London stable. Instead, Mumford wanted to reduce population, build more parks, and lower housing densities. A year later, his criticism probably influenced Abercrombie's regional plan for London, a follow-up to the county plan. Great Britain's Town and County Planning Act of 1946, with its greenbelt and new town features, also was a major victory for the recentralist views of Mumford and his British fellow believers.

Even though not all his criticisms took hold (witness the overbuilding of postwar London), Mumford was lionized by the British planning establishment. In 1946, he received the Ebenezer Howard Memorial Medal and was made an honorary member of the Royal Town Planning Institute.

Nor was he entirely ignored by American planners. In 1948, he addressed the conference of the American Society of Planning Officials in New York City, speaking on the "Goals of Planning." (The primary one: "the good life.") In 1951, he received an appointment as a professor of urban and regional planning at the University of Pennsylvania. He later was a visiting professor at MIT, and in 1955 he was named an honorary member of the American Institute of Planners.

Mumford's well-known *New Yorker* column, "Sky Line," which ran on an occasional basis for 32 years (from 1931 to 1963), provided a forum for his views on the changing urban and suburban scene. There was much grist for his mill in the 1950s and 1960s. The baby boom and rapid suburbanization resulted in an unprecedented decentralization, based on the automobile. It was not the kind of dispersal Mumford had hoped for. Moreover, the negative side effects of the automobile and its ubiquitous freeways were destroying the urban life and fabric he so ardently cherished.

Mumford attacked these issues head on in a series of *New Yorker* essays entitled "The Roaring Traffic's Boom" (reprinted in 1956 in *From the Ground Up*). In the series, Mumford, who in the 1920s and 1930s was an admirer of New York City parks commissioner Robert Moses, excoriated the "Master Builder" for wreaking havoc on his city in the name of progress. Moses returned the fire, denouncing Mumford as an "outspoken revolutionary" . . . "antiurban," and calling him unqualified, because he "has constructed little else" besides his writing.

What a pity these two contemporaries, both children of the same city, couldn't have merged their personas into one being, the doer and the thinker joined—Moses's action with Mumford's philosophy—the integrated figure that Frederick Law Olmsted, Sr., had embodied a century earlier. But the action and the thought were incompatible. Moses had succumbed to the idea of power, while Mumford clung to the power of the idea.

Despite his lifelong commitment to city rebuilding, Mumford was an early critic of the urban renewal program of the 1960s. In his view, urban renewal, though sound in its original intentions and legislation, had degenerated into a boondoggle for developers. But when Jane Jacobs, in *The Death and Life of Great American Cities,* rather unfairly attacked the planning profession for destroying rather than preserving cities, Mumford neatly placed the arguments for city renewal into perspective. In a *New Yorker* column entitled "Mother Jacobs's Home Remedies for Urban Cancer" (reprinted in *The Urban Prospect*), he rebutted Jacobs far better than any other writer or planner had done. By making development issues like these both important and understandable, Mumford greatly enhanced the standing and identity of the planning profession in the eyes of the public.

Other concerns were growing as well. In 1960, Mumford spoke on "Planning and Nuclear Warfare: The Non-Governmental Side" at the AIP annual conference. He also addressed the nuclear threat in his most successful book, *The City in History*. (Published in 1961, it was based partly on the earlier *The Culture of Cities,* which actually is a better book in its treatment of planning.) He repeated his warning about the nuclear peril later in "The Myth of the Machine" series. His early stand against American participation in the Vietnam War was equally controversial, although fully consistent with his philosophy.

Ecological planning

It was also in the mid-1960s that Mumford's commitment to regional planning brought him into contact with two ecological planners, Ian McHarg and Arthur Glikson. Mumford enthusiastically wrote the introduction to McHarg's influential 1969 book, *Design with Nature.*

Glikson, an Israeli architect–planner, shared Mumford's admiration for Patrick Geddes, and Mumford introduced Glikson to the remaining RPAA founders—Stein and MacKaye. It was a kind of passing of the torch to the next generation, with Glikson absorbing the old RPAA ideas and carrying them off to build new towns in Israel and Holland and prepare a regional plan for the island of Crete. The vigorous ideas of the Geddes disciples had found a new hearing thanks to the environmental movement, although Glikson's career was cut short by his death in 1966, at age 55. His writings subsequently were edited by Mumford and published as *The Ecological Basis of Planning.*

How do we assess this man, Lewis Mumford, and his influence on planning? For one thing, he has forced his ideas on us with a tenacity that we might envy and emulate. He has compelled us to think comprehensively, which is, after all, one of the claims of the planning profession. He has challenged us to see beyond the limits of our immediate constraints to a longer view (yet another of our professional claims). He has rooted the profession in the rich literary and aesthetic traditions of our country.

He has taught us to be wary of those quantifiers who obscure rather than enlighten us about the important issues and problems we face. He has shown us the way to a balanced view of city life and city planning—how to be simultaneously radical and conservative in the best meanings of those words. He has shown us how to love the good things in cities while hating the bad, without having to wear anti-city or pro-city labels.

He has shown us how a few committed people with powerful and humane ideas can make things happen. He has shown us the essential relationships between architecture, urban design, and planning. He has shown us how housing and planning are linked, how urban and regional planning must be fused, and how regional and national policy are necessarily connected. He has shown us how to be gentle, human, and civilized.

For all his criticism of planners as specialists, for all his asking us to do the impossible even as we struggle to do the difficult, for all that we sometimes disagree with his premises and proposals, we should be proud that he is a member of the American community of planners and that he and we may call each other colleague.

In a 1934 essay called "The Metropolitan Milieu," Mumford wrote: "An honest man looms high. He is a lighthouse on a low and treacherous coast." For six decades now, Lewis Mumford has been such a lighthouse, warning us of dangerous hidden shoals and guiding us to safe harbors.

May the lighthouse continue to shine for years to come.

David A. Johnson, AICP, a native New Yorker, is professor of planning at the University of Tennessee–Knoxville.

The Legacy of Kevin Lynch
Philip Langdon
(October 1984)

Two months ago, the *New York Times* told of a group of landscape architects who were trying to determine the scenic value of several stretches of land along the St. Lawrence River. They had collected a number of photographs—ranging from tree-framed riverfront panoramas to views of mobile homes and utility wires strung along the water's edge—and then asked college students and residents of the area to rate each scene on a scale of one to 10, from ugly to beautiful.

The researchers were happy to discover that beauty was not in the eye of each idiosyncratic beholder; on the contrary, the survey revealed that people generally agreed on what was pleasing and what was not. The head of a New York state regional commission said the findings would be useful in establishing a system of scenic easements to preserve the most highly prized vistas in the Thousand Islands.

Kevin Lynch, who had died four months earlier, was never involved in the study in Upstate New York. Yet Lynch unquestionably was one of the people who had helped make such people-oriented examinations of the environment increasingly commonplace.

Until Lynch's work began to be published about a quarter-century ago, neither landscape architects nor planners nor members of other professions concerned with the design of the environment generally consulted the public—at least not in any systematic way—before deciding what was esthetically important and consequently worthy of government action. Lynch demonstrated that there were fruitful methods of measuring people's feelings about such seemingly subjective issues as the quality of the environment and that those perceptions could be used to shape our surroundings, whether rural or urban, whether a small park or an entire metropolitan region.

Lynch died, at 66, on April 25, six years after retiring from the Massachusetts Institute of Technology's urban studies and planning program. His obituaries incorporated unusually specific bits of information—telling, for instance, that he died while sitting in a chair in the house he had built on Martha's Vineyard. The program for a memorial service at Trinity Church in Boston reproduced Lynch's diagram of his vegetable garden and his spring planting schedule.

What such details hinted at was that Lynch's interest in the environment extended beyond the theorizing that had established his reputation; it reached down to the small but emotionally significant ingredients of nature and of everyday life.

A simple life

Martha's Vineyard, summer address of a conspicuous portion of the Eastern elite, seems a long way from the North Side of Chicago where Lynch grew up, third-generation Irish. Yet this man with a crewcut and no formal degree beyond a bachelor's in city planning (received from MIT in 1947; he also studied at Yale and at Rensselaer Polytechnic Institute and spent two years at Taliesen with Frank Lloyd Wright) remained consistently modest all his life. His summer house on the Vineyard for years did without electricity and an indoor toilet. Chairs were hung on the wall, in the Shaker manner.

He rose early so that he could write without interruption from seven in the morning until one in the afternoon, six days a week. The seven books and dozens of articles authored, coauthored, or edited by Lynch constitute the most influential segment of his work.

At last count, MIT Press had printed 252,710 copies of his books—an extraordinary figure in university press publishing. Some 138,000 copies of *Image of the City* have been distributed in several languages. *Site Planning* sold 75,000 copies even be-

fore the recent release of a third edition, updated with Gary Hack of MIT as coauthor. A paperback edition of *A Theory of Good City Form,* the summation of Lynch's theoretical investigations, appeared in March. Of his other four books—*What Time Is This Place?, Managing the Sense of a Region, Growing Up in Cities,* and *The View from the Road*—only the road design book, written with John Myer and the late Donald Appleyard, is out of print. . . .

Before evaluating the importance of Lynch's writing and teaching, it's useful to look at his planning work. Though he spent only two years on the staff of a public planning agency—in Greensboro, North Carolina, in 1947–48—he was heavily involved in consulting, in some instances for projects that earned national prominence.

"You could feel he had no ax to grind and would give you the most rounded kind of judgment," says Morton Hoppenfeld, a student of Lynch, and former director of planning and design for the Rouse organization's Columbia, Maryland, new town, explaining why Lynch was called upon so often. In 1968 Lynch spent six months working on site planning and highway design and writing planning guidelines for Columbia.

Other projects illustrate the range of Lynch's consulting work: In 1957, for example, with the firm of Adams, Howard, and Greeley, Lynch helped bring together a major cluster of institutions in Cleveland's University Circle area, forging the cooperative arrangements that would produce 20 years of coordinated development.

More recently, with Carr, Lynch Associates, the Cambridge, Massachusetts, environmental design firm in which he was a partner for the last seven years, he helped establish a Dallas "arts district" close to the downtown commercial area. A new museum has been built and a symphony hall is under construction.

On a budget of about $15,000, Lynch and Donald Appleyard carried out a study of environmental alternatives for growth-threatened San Diego, a study that local officials say has been a source of the region's planning decisions in the past decade.

He was involved in designing a lively if less than elegant four-block pedestrian mall in Burlington, Vermont; in devising an innovative sign ordinance for Dallas; and in proposing Phoenix's ambitious Rio Salado master plan, which, if it is implemented, will result in the conversion of a mostly dry 40-mile-long riverbed area to a complex of parkland, lakes, sports facilities, high-density housing, and other development. In Boston, he helped fashion a plan for renovating the notorious Columbia Point housing project.

There were other studies as well, not all of them carried out to Lynch's satisfaction. He was principal consultant in 1959 on a plan for turning rundown Scollay Square in Boston into a new government center, but was not happy when later planning by others, particularly architect I.M. Pei, gave the area a more monumental scale.

In many respects, note numerous observers, his greatest triumph as a planning consultant was his 1962 plan for creation of a "Walk to the Sea" from the Statehouse at the top of Boston's Beacon Hill to what he envisioned as a revived waterfront.

At the time, the business community viewed the derelict harbor area as the site for expansion of the financial district. The importance of the old buildings near the waterfront, such as Quincy Market and Faneuil Hall, had failed to register on the city's Irish political establishment, which preferred to see them torn down. "Those were Yankee buildings, as far as they were concerned," says Stephen Carr, a Lynch student who later became his partner.

"Yet Kevin felt they were important and extremely beautiful buildings, and he felt it was important for a city to retain traces of its past," Carr says. Although much of the complex was vacant, Lynch felt it could be revived and occupied by at least some of its original enterprises, such as fish and meat markets. "It was," notes Carr, "one of the first struggles in which architects and others interested in saving historic buildings rallied successfully to do so."

The Rouse organization ultimately produced a more commercialized atmosphere than Lynch had wanted, but the core of his concept held firm—a preserved waterfront connected to the rest of the downtown.

It is almost impossible to overstate the significance of that accomplishment. The transformed Boston waterfront—though it is certainly not the only example of successful waterfront renewal in recent years—is one of the most widely noticed of such efforts. Lynch's planning work helped set a direction for many other communities, which began to think about turning their own neglected waterfronts into gathering places.

The theorist

But it is Lynch's books, articles, and teachings that have wielded the greatest impact. In *Image of the City* (1960), for example, he offered a profound analytical framework for looking at cities. In *Site Planning* (first published in 1962), he provided a textbook that is extraordinarily rich in the range of factors it considers and in how thoughtfully it deals with them. Those who traveled abroad with Lynch discovered that his writings had achieved an enthusiastic international reception; his books are used in China's planning schools, for example, and are familiar to planners in Europe.

However, he was, it should be noted, a writer who was primarily addressing scholars, students, and professionals. Other writers on urban planning and design—notably Lewis Mumford and Jane Jacobs—were far more effective in delivering their message directly to the public. Thus, for instance, *What Time Is This Place?* (1972) might have achieved a more prominent status within the burgeoning preservation movement if it had developed a stronger central theme instead of stringing together so many seemingly random thoughts.

Ronald Lee Fleming, president of the Townscape Institute in Cambridge, Massachusetts, believes Lynch sometimes failed to see the implications of the positions he took. For example, Lynch's rigid opposition in the mid-1970s to setting aside an arbitrary percentage of government construction budgets for public art had unforeseen consequences, according to Fleming. In the absence of a specific figure, the federal transportation department has devoted less money to public art than would have been the case if a one-percent figure then under consideration had been accepted.

Despite such minor cavils, Lynch was revered by many people in planning and related fields partly because, as *Landscape Architecture*'s long-time editor, Grady Clay, notes, "intellectually, he had a tremendously original way of looking at a subject." In more than 20 years, nothing has dislodged *Image of the City* from its position as a basic text in architecture and urban design programs. Lynch's "imageability" system of landmarks, nodes, paths, districts, and edges "is the vocabulary people still use," says Joan Gilbert of Yale University's architecture school.

Image of the City is based on the work led by Lynch and Gyorgy Kepes in Boston, Jersey City, and Los

Angeles, where researchers asked people to draw maps showing how they perceived their cities. Their hypothesis—which seems so commonsensical now—was that people had in their heads a bigger picture of the environment than what they could see at any one point. This concept of the "cognitive map" was seized and expanded upon by many other researchers in a variety of disciplines.

It continues to stimulate work by such individuals as the environmental psychologists Stephen and Rachel Kaplan, who made it the central theme of their recent book, *Cognition and Environment: Functioning in an Uncertain World.* "The concept was very little developed before Lynch," says Stephen Kaplan. "He made the world safe for environmental psychology."

Research by the Kaplans and others continues to explore the kinds of environments people prefer, and particularly the environmental cognition of such groups as children, the elderly, the handicapped, and transit travelers. Lynch's work also has spurred activity in a related field—behavioral geography. William H. Whyte says his own studies of how people use public spaces have benefited from Lynch's theories.

Lynch was instrumental in reviving the field of urban design which had languished for perhaps 30 years while planners focused on zoning, social and policy planning, and other activities that had little to do with the making of three-dimensional urban forms.

In Minneapolis at the start of the 1960s, Weiming Lu was working on a range of downtown, neighborhood, and regional planning problems. "When *Image of the City* was published," he recalls, "it got me to thinking about the city in a new way—about how people perceive the city." Subsequently, Minneapolis surveyed Hennepin County residents, asking them, for example, to sketch maps of downtown and to tell what they liked and disliked about the city. From this came state design review (enabling legislation not yet followed up by a city ordinance).

"Lynch was an incredible categorizer and lister," says Allan Jacobs of the University of California at Berkeley. The categorizing and listing—along with his insistence on finding out what people felt about the city—helped break through the vagueness that had afflicted earlier discussions of environmental quality. Things began to seem more researchable.

Donald Appleyard, one of Lynch's former research assistants at MIT, gauged the livability of various blocks in Berkeley by measuring the street traffic and correlating it with residents' comments about contacts with their neighbors—useful information for planners intent on making traffic patterns harmonize with a city's housing and neighborhood development objectives.

An earlier collaborative effort, *The View from the Road* (1964), influenced highway design in the U.S. and other countries, including Australia. And it's partly because of Lynch that development proposals in some cities are being subjected to analysis of each building's effect on sun exposure, wind, and temperature in the vicinity.

The teacher

MIT afforded Lynch a superb position from which to influence the way in which planning was taught and practiced. By the late 1950s, nearly a third of all the planners in the U.S. were graduates of MIT, according to Gary Hack, the planning department's current chair. With the initiation of a Ph.D. program in the 1960s, MIT further strengthened its ability to attract bright students who would go on to start planning and urban design programs elsewhere or to become practitioners. When the school's planning graduates were asked in 1974 to name the most influential teacher they'd encountered, Lynch was cited most often.

Lynch encouraged his students to see the environment as a setting that influenced human behavior. Robin Moore, a Lynch student now teaching at North Carolina State University, has focused on ways of making cities better for children. As an alternative to the usual asphalt playgrounds, Moore has proposed the "environmental yard," which would include a pond, meadow, stream, woods, and hillside.

The environmental yard proposal has been publicized internationally and is used as the basis for altering schoolyards in Sweden. "What I learned from Kevin," says Moore, "was a process of going about design from a human point of view—how to formulate a design objective and how to develop criteria for deciding whether the design is meeting its objective."

Another Lynch student, Michael Southworth, developed the idea of a national urban park in long-depressed Lowell, Massachusetts. The program Southworth worked out has led to new uses for some of the city's obsolete mills, to a turn-around in the city's economy, and to the creation of similar urban and cultural parks in other states.

But, while several dozen cities have carried out imageability studies, fewer have acted on them. Too frequently, planners and others have attempted to shortcut the process—relying on Lynch's and his students' writings rather than doing what Lynch had urged, getting out and asking people about their preferences.

In many planning departments today, urban design is neither a high priority nor is it carried out in the way that Lynch proposed. The urban design that is conducted often consists of negotiations over the details of particular buildings or blocks, not the systematic treatment of critical elements and attributes throughout the metropolis.

Such disappointments notwithstanding, Weiming Lu, now executive director of the Lowertown Redevelopment Corporation in St. Paul, judges Lynch to be "as important in his field as Le Corbusier was in architecture," referring to the way in which Le Corbusier's Modernism captured the architectural world's attention some 60 years ago. Yet Lynch's impact is not nearly so evident in the physical form of today's cities. Much of urban America remains ugly, disorganized, and uncomfortable—resistant to the clarifying and humanizing intentions of Lynch and his followers.

The reason might be that Le Corbusier's ideas went *with* the grain of both capitalist economics and American political attitudes, which allowed the individual property owner to reign supreme. Lynch's ideas went against the grain; they were predicated on a widespread willingness to cooperate at the metropolitan level and to put considerable influence at the disposal of planners. In the U.S., conditions favorable to Lynch's vision of planning have been the exception. And in any event, the hand of a planner, who must act in conjunction with so many other individuals, groups, and organizations, is harder to detect than that of an architect.

What is clear is that Lynch made the greatest personal impact of any planning teacher in the past 30 years, that he established the ways in which urban designers examine a city's physical form, and that he stimulated two decades of productive research in a variety of disciplines. As of 1984, his influence is pivotal, and it shows no signs of diminishing.

Philip Langdon, who lives in New Haven, Connecticut, is a writer specializing in design and urban affairs.

James Rouse: The Robin Hood of Real Estate

William Fulton
(May 1985)

Imagine a warm Friday afternoon in the summer, with thousands of people crowded along a riverfront in a celebratory mood. A band is playing. Beer is flowing by the gallon. Private boats are docked along the river, and their occupants join in the fun. Families stroll in and out of a large, colorful building filled with shops and restaurants of every description. Nearby stands a sculpture of a father, a mother, and their children—so lifelike that real children come along and try to play with them.

Now try to guess the city. Would you believe Toledo?

Toledo, a declining industrial center along the Maumee River in northwestern Ohio, is just one of the unlikely cities where James Rouse's Enterprise Development Company is trying to use the "festival marketplace" concept to help create a downtown turnaround. Others include Flint and Battle Creek, Michigan, and Richmond and Norfolk, Virginia. In each case, the effort is modeled after the large-scale retailing successes of the Rouse Company in Boston (Quincy Market), Baltimore (Harborplace), and, less so, New York (South Street Seaport).

At the Columbia, Maryland, headquarters of the Enterprise Development Company (which is not formally affiliated with the Rouse Company), the deluge of requests from cities seeking help on festival marketplaces is so great that an up-to-date list of projects is hard to come by. Clearly, the marketplace idea is considered by many planners and developers these days to be key to their downtown revitalization hopes.

For Rouse himself, though, the festival marketplaces are merely means to an end. He is trying, as he puts it, "to build a development company that will make a gigantic fortune—not for the rich, but for the poor."

At 70, Rouse has retired from the famous development company that bears his name, leaving behind a legacy that includes the development of numerous shopping centers, the creation of the country's most ambitious suburban new town (Columbia), and the invention of the festival marketplace idea that has given new life to some central cities.

Now, seeking to use his skill in creating wealth to help the poor, he has linked two areas of personal interest—commercial real estate and urban housing—and, typically, he is redefining both of them.

Enterprise Development, a for-profit development company founded by Rouse four years ago, has become a successful builder of festival marketplaces in secondary cities. But Enterprise's motives are unusual. When it begins turning a profit, all the money will flow to another Rouse creation, the Enterprise Foundation, a public nonprofit group dedicated to upgrading housing for the urban poor.

"Wealth is a resource to be used, just as health or mind is," James Rouse told the *Washington Post* last year. In setting up the two arms of the Enterprise organization, Rouse wanted to find out whether it was, in fact, possible to use the development business to benefit the poor.

"I was retiring from the Rouse Company, but I had no intention of retiring from life," he says, recalling the steps that led to the creation of Enterprise in 1981. "I had two objectives and they fit very well. One was to do something about housing for the poor, and the other was to use the real estate development process to create a flow of money for a social purpose." He credits his second wife, Patricia, once a member of the Norfolk Redevelopment and Housing Authority, with helping him work out the idea.

Rouse came by his concern for the poor not through armchair liberalism but from personal involvement. He had worked since the early 1970s with a remarkable self-help housing group in Washington, D.C., called Jubilee Housing. The Enterprise Foundation was created to seek out (or cause the creation of) similar groups in other cities, and Enterprise Development was created to provide the foundation with a long-term source of funds for those groups. At first Rouse wanted to call the organization the Robin Hood Trust, but dropped the idea because he thought the name might offend prospective donors.

The Enterprise Foundation is a public founda-

tion, which under IRS rules can own the for-profit Enterprise Development Company. Aside from the flow of profits to the foundation, however, the company and the foundation remain separate.

The Enterprise Foundation plans to help housing groups in all cities in which Enterprise Development builds a marketplace—but only after the marketplace is completed. "We don't go in and say, 'We'll come in and house the poor and also do this project,'" says Rouse. "Then it would look like we're using the poor to get a favorable deal."

The spark

Rouse, of course, first hit on the idea of the "festival marketplace" a decade ago when Boston officials asked his firm for assistance in revitalizing the Quincy Market area around historic Faneuil Hall. Though reluctant at first, Rouse proceeded because of his faith in "a very universal yearning . . . to have the center of the city be the center of the community." Even when building suburban shopping malls, Rouse claimed that he was fulfilling people's need for a sense of community.

Rouse had already built a successful downtown shopping mall in Philadelphia and was working on another in Santa Monica, California. But the "festival marketplace" idea came as much from desperation as from inspiration.

"After we finally got the financing and completed work on the first phase of the [Quincy Market] project . . . we couldn't lease it," he recalled in a speech last year. "We had never opened a project that wasn't 80, 85, 90 percent leased, and six weeks before the opening we were less than 50 percent leased. To face that disaster, we . . . reinvented the pushcart and the one-week lease."

On opening day in 1976, 43 pushcarts were "creating a spirit of festival and obscuring the vacant space," Rouse said. The idea was more successful than anyone could have imagined, and sales quickly rose to around $300 per square foot annually. (The typical shopping center averages around $130 per square foot in sales.)

Subsequently, the Rouse Company built Harborplace in Baltimore, which was even more successful, and, after Rouse himself had retired from the firm, it created a marketplace in the South Street Seaport section of lower Manhattan. The latter, though considered a success, was extremely expensive and has caused controversy.

Aside from their remarkable commercial success,

the festival marketplaces in Boston and, particularly, Baltimore, have served as catalysts for urban revitalization, attracting investors for other projects near them—hotels, office buildings, restaurants, even condominiums. Almost by accident, Rouse seemed to have found a way to bring downtown back to life, at least in a few large cities. In the process, he ignited the interest of what sometimes seems like every city in America.

"People go to see what happened in Baltimore," says Richard Starr, a downtown specialist with the Real Estate Research Corporation in Chicago, "and they come back wanting to do something in their own city." So when Rouse founded Enterprise and announced he would build more festival marketplaces, he had plenty of requests for help.

Rouse claims that Enterprise Development, with 50 employees, is not in competition with the gigantic Rouse Company, which employs 3,000 and which continues to work on festival marketplaces in large cities. Several Rouse Company veterans did follow their boss, though none of them directly from Rouse. They include Aubrey Gorman, Enterprise's president, and the late Morton Hoppenfeld, the Rouse Company's chief designer.

A Rouse aide says Enterprise decided to work on smaller projects simply because the company started small. Its first project was a 34,000-square-foot mixed-use restoration project in Baltimore called Brown's Arcade. The Waterside in Norfolk, an 80,000-square-foot festival marketplace, opened two years ago and quickly ascended into the retailing stratosphere. Its sales per square foot (about $340) rival Quincy Market's—in a city that Rouse himself had initially said was too small to support such a project.

Last year saw the opening of Portside in Toledo, a 60,000-square-foot marketplace, and this year Enterprise plans to open Water Street Pavilion in downtown Flint, Kellogg Square in Battle Creek, and the 6th Street Marketplace in Richmond. Enterprise is considering marketplaces in more cities, including some large ones.

Perhaps concerned about the rash of imitators beginning to pop up around the country, Rouse says the elements of success could easily be misconstrued.

While a location in the heart of downtown is vital, he points out, a marketplace by itself cannot turn a downtown around. "It takes other attractions at the marketplace to help in regenerating

that life at the center of the city." In Norfolk, for example, the contract with Enterprise required the city to build a park and marina and to establish an office to promote waterfront and downtown events.

Outside observers agree that it takes more than just the marketplace idea to turn a downtown around. In fact, it takes someone like Rouse.

"So much depends on the entrepreneurial skill of the individual," says Starr of RERC. "Rouse is a damned genius. He's got the ability to feel these things out. Someone else with just as much money and commitment might not be able to make it work."

The Rouse formula

Perhaps the most important element of the Rouse formula is partnership with the cities Enterprise works in. Enterprise typically provides development know-how but requires the city to put up the initial $10 million to $15 million in funding it then lends to Enterprise. Enterprise repays the loan, takes a developer's fee, and, when the project becomes profitable, splits the profits with the city.

"The cities have to see themselves as developers, willing to invest in the resources the city has in order to make possible projects that couldn't otherwise be done," Rouse told *Business Week* last year. Public financing is also needed because festival marketplaces are so expensive to build. Frequently, they need twice the sales of a conventional shopping center to turn a profit.

Norfolk is a good example of how the process works. The city had already begun to draw people back to the waterfront along the Elizabeth River. The arrival of the tall ships during the 1976 Bicentennial has turned into an annual event drawing a million people. First, the city lured an Omni Hotel to a riverfront site. Then, to get Waterside going, it lent Enterprise Development $10 million at 11.5 percent interest, using a combination of urban renewal cash, community development block grant funds, and revenue sharing money earmarked for economic development.

Because of the city involvement, Waterside, like most other Enterprise Development projects, has public purposes as well as private ones. Enterprise says it makes a concerted effort to encourage minority business ownership and employment; at Waterside there are eight minority-owned businesses and 42 percent of the employees are members of minority groups. Of these, Enterprise officials say, the "vast majority" were previously unemployed and, in many cases, considered unemployable.

Norfolk is considered a success. The city is realizing $1.1 million a year in mortgage payments from Enterprise and about $1 million a year in sales tax, and, when the project begins turning a profit, the city and Enterprise will split the funds. Projections show the city's share rising from $100,000 a year in 1988 to more than $800,000 in 1993 and $2.5 million in 1998. The money will be used for block grant–eligible and redevelopment purposes.

In addition, Waterside's success helped attract the Cousteau Center, a museum and headquarters building for the Cousteau Society, and has aided the city in marketing condominiums nearby.

Toledo made a similar commitment to its downtown riverfront, stirring Rouse's interest. Impressive headquarters buildings for Owens-Illinois and Toledo Trust anchor the riverfront site. Portside, which cost about $14.5 million to build, is part of a complex $81 million financing package put together by the Toledo Economic Planning Council for its SeaGate riverfront project, which includes the marketplace, an office tower, and a hotel.

The financing included $19 million in revenue bonds, $14 million in UDAG funds, a $9 million loan from Toledo Trust, $13.5 million from the local building trades council's pension fund, and $1 million from a church. Again, the city and Enterprise split the profits. Although local enthusiasm for the SeaGate/Portside project is high, Portside sales (about $280 a square foot) are below Enterprise's projections, partly, perhaps, because the hotel and an ice-skating rink are not yet open. Rouse concedes that "it's a bit of a struggle" in Toledo, and a local merchant notes that "everyone is waiting to see if Portside will work."

Although Enterprise works only in cities that have invited it in, the local reception isn't always positive. For example, St. Petersburg, Florida, voters turned down a festival marketplace last year in favor of retaining a more parklike waterfront.

Perhaps Enterprise's most controversial proposal is the one for Albuquerque, New Mexico, where the company was asked to study the feasibility of building on a 12-acre site that featured few of the now-familiar marketplace amenities, such as water. It returned with a plan that included a Japanese garden and artificial ponds. The plan also called for razing the Sunshine Building, a recently renovated, 60-year-old, Mediterranean–style office building and movie theater, and closing two blocks of Central Avenue, cherished locally as part of Route 66, America's "Main Street."

Local architecture critics dismissed the design as "Disneyland" and complained that it was out of keeping with the character of the downtown. And Nina Gruen, a San Francisco marketing analyst hired by the city, says the design could harm tourism by departing from the southwestern motif that characterizes Albuquerque. Rouse himself (who has praised Disneyland as good planning because it "brings joy to people") calls the Enterprise design "wonderfully Albuquerquian."

Enterprise's future in Albuquerque was to be determined in late April when voters decide whether to support a sales tax increase to finance the project.

The Albuquerque controversy raises perhaps the most frequent criticism of Rouse's festival marketplaces—their "cookie-cutter" design. And at first glance, the marketplaces the Rouse Company and Enterprise have built from scratch do look alike, although the ones that are part of historic renovations have more individuality. The basic design of both Portside and Waterside appears to be a simple knock-off of Baltimore's Harborplace: rounded at one end, with a pitched roof and large windows all the way around. Nevertheless, both Rouse and Morton Hoppenfeld, who was Enterprise's chief of planning and design until his death in March, said Enterprise seeks to include individual touches.

For example, Waterside, constructed on the site of a ferry ticketing building, features an attractive mural of early twentieth-century ferry scenes, and other nautical touches are included inside. The elevator is a Victorian tugboat cabin, and three wood bowsprit replicas hang in the center court.

On the other hand, in Toledo, Hoppenfeld said, "we scratched our heads until they were raw" without finding a cohesive theme. The result is what might be called a "generic" festival marketplace similar to Harborplace.

But both Hoppenfeld and Rouse said that the similarity of the buildings is beside the point. "The stamped-out Disneyland allegation is like saying the old city markets were 'stamped out,'" says Rouse. "Or you could even have said that of downtowns in America—the department stores, the shops in the streets. They were very much alike."

Hoppenfeld said that the marketplaces sometimes look alike because the elements of successful marketing are the same anywhere. "A flea market in a parking lot in Albuquerque on Saturday looks not unlike a market in a piazza in northern Italy," he said in an interview shortly before his death. "The fundamental idea is to create action."

It is, in fact, the flea-market type of intimacy that seems to explain the festival marketplace's draw. To create it, the Enterprise people, like their Rouse Company predecessors, break all the rules of marketing—mixing food and merchandise, introducing loud and colorful distractions, encouraging merchants to bust out of their stores with displays, and even seeking out inexperienced merchants because they want innovators.

How small is too small?

One question remaining is how small a city can be before it can't support a marketplace. From Boston to Battle Creek (pop. 39,000), Rouse has been going down in size, and he claims not to have found the bottom yet. He also says that even though the marketplaces must reach beyond their metropolitan area to draw people, he's not worried that the market is becoming saturated.

"To me, it's like asking, 40 years ago, was there a saturation point to downtowns," he says. As an example, he points to the Richmond project, located less than 100 miles from Norfolk's Waterside.

"If successful, we'll do $18 million to $21 million volume in Richmond," he says. "If you take that as a percentage of the purchases made in the Richmond metropolitan area, it's hardly significant. But that amount of purchasing at the center of Richmond . . . will bring two to three million people downtown that aren't now coming."

Richard Starr of RERC warns that the solution to central city decay is not the same for every city. "American cities have to be more interesting, more urbane," says Starr, "but it's one thing to try a marketplace in Savannah and New Orleans, where the transient tourist trade is great, and another to try it in Toledo. And what works in Toledo might be dead in the water in Madison, Wisconsin."

To Rouse, though, as noted above, festival marketplaces are still only a means to an end. The real issue is housing for the poor, and Rouse is typically optimistic about it. "We have the potential to eliminate all bad housing within a generation," he told

Engineering News-Record, which named him "Man of the Year" for 1984 for his efforts with Enterprise.

Rouse's involvement in low-income housing began more than a decade ago in Washington, D.C., when he met with two members of a local church that wanted to do something about providing housing for the poor.

"I said that there was really nothing they could do," he recalls, "that they were too small, didn't have the resources, and that they had to have a big program to work with the poor."

The church delegation ignored Rouse's advice and placed a nonrefundable deposit on two apartment buildings, in Washington's run-down Adams–Morgan neighborhood. Rouse was so impressed by their efforts that he agreed to finance their $625,000 purchase.

But the two buildings still needed some work—they had almost 1,000 housing code violations. "They were dreadful buildings," Rouse says. "But three years later, with $125,000 and 50,000 hours of volunteer time, they were very decent buildings."

For the next several years, Rouse and his wife, who is now secretary-treasurer of the Enterprise Foundation, served on the board of the group that came to be called Jubilee Housing, Inc., and which eventually grew into a full-service social services organization for residents of Adams–Morgan, providing a health care center, a "committee of compassion" to provide cash, and Jubilee Jobs, which produced 535 jobs last year.

Jubilee also serves as a good example of motivating the poor to improve their own housing. Living in a Jubilee apartment usually means taking on maintenance responsibilities as well as paying the rent. A seven-year plan adopted in 1983 set initial rent at about half the market rate, with raises every six months. The idea, according to the Jubilee people, is to give residents an incentive to find work.

"I believe what they were doing could be done in other neighborhoods for other cities," Rouse says. So, in 1981, he established the Enterprise Foundation and hired Edward Quinn, former head of the Sears Roebuck Foundation, to run it. Eventually, the foundation will be financed by the profits from Enterprise Development, which is expected to enter the black in 1987 and clear $10 million to $20 million a year in profits by the mid–1990s. To get the foundation started, however, Rouse set a goal of $25 million in contributions, and began by giving $1 million himself.

Four years later the total is over $16 million, and the contributors include the major foundations (Ford, Atlantic Richfield, Mott, Mellon, MacArthur, Hahn), the Rockefeller Brothers Fund, David and Laurence Rockefeller, Sohio, and AT&T. In addition, many businesses including the Rouse Company, lend staff members to Enterprise or the local groups it supports.

The money goes to housing groups that follow the Jubilee model by helping the poor help themselves. Right now, Enterprise is working in 15 cities with five more on the way, and the ambitious goal is to reach 50 cities within the next couple of years.

Groups that receive Enterprise grants remain part of the Enterprise "network," through which they share examples and techniques. Eight field officers work with the neighborhood groups, helping them find resources. For example, Good News Partners in Chicago, seeking to acquire a 21-unit apartment building, took a $79,000 loan from Enterprise and combined it with a syndication, a grant from Amoco, and loans from the University of Christian Ministry, the Community Investment Corporation, and other sources to create a $650,000 financing package.

To help its network groups lower construction costs, Enterprise set up the Rehabilitation Work Group, a 10-member organization that helps neighborhood groups draw up their own plans and specifications and act as general contractors.

Enterprise also established a for-profit subsidiary, the Enterprise Social Investment Corporation, to raise funds for the network and to help local groups come up with creative financing packages. In Cleveland, for example, ESIC guaranteed a loan so a neighborhood group's project could be underwritten by the Federal National Mortgage Association. And in Lynchburg, Virginia, Enterprise deposited $180,000 in a local bank and agreed to keep it there for 12 years so the bank could finance 20 new homes for low-income families. The six percent interest is being used to subsidize mortgage payments.

The fund-raising part of ESIC's work is modeled after a Jubilee Housing program. Through a direct-mail campaign, Jubilee has raised $1 million in two years from 300 socially minded investors, while paying an average interest rate of only 1.4 percent. Now ESIC will try to make the same idea work na-tionally, setting up a loan fund that will pay investors between 0 and 4 percent.

Director Quinn says he realizes that the Enterprise Foundation, by itself, isn't likely to make a big dent in the enormous problem of housing the urban poor. "But where I do think we can make a difference is in showing a way to do it," he adds.

"You've got to believe in success," Rouse said last year. "You've got to be bold in pushing for [what you want] and doing all those things that are going to bring it about."

He was referring to festival marketplaces, but he could have been referring to the entire Enterprise concept. In his boldness, Rouse is once again trying to set trends—to show how life can be brought to the center city and to show that it is possible to deal with housing for the poor on a block-by-block basis.

Of course, the problem trend setters sometimes run into is that they're followed by people who don't do a very good job of copying their ideas and, occasionally, even give the ideas a bad name. The suburban shopping mall is perhaps the most maligned type of development in modern planning circles, yet to this day Rouse, who built dozens of them, is a stout defender. Malls that see themselves as community centers, not just shopping areas, "have been a good force," he says.

As for festival marketplaces, he concedes: "Some will fail somewhere." And, in all likelihood, some Rouse follower will probably create a pale and unsuccessful imitation of the Enterprise housing program. But whatever the future of Enterprise and its inevitable progeny, at least Rouse has tried to tackle a few of the historically frustrating areas of planning.

William Fulton is a contributing editor of Planning *who is based in Los Angeles.*

Logue on Cities

William Lucy
(August 1985)

In conversation, Edward J. Logue describes himself, at different times, as "a planner first," a "Philadelphia lawyer," a "preservationist," someone who's in "the city business." Based on Logue's career, which has influenced urban development in at least three states, the last of those self-descriptions, in "the city business," seems most apt. Many would agree with the assessment of Jaquelin Robertson, dean of the School of Architecture at the University of Virginia, who calls Logue "the leading city developer of his time."

Not that cities are all that count to him. An integral dimension of Logue's beliefs is the effect of the intricacies of metropolitan and federal-state relationships on the quality of life in cities. The interview that follows demonstrates the importance of that dimension.

After graduation from Yale Law School in 1947, Logue began his career with a brief stint as a Philadelphia lawyer. During World War II, following his 1942 graduation from Yale College, he served three years in the Air Force. Today he says quite seriously that his planning education began during the eight hours he spent flying to and from Germany to perform his duties as a bombardier. By observation, from a height of thousands of feet, he says, he learned the pattern of the land and development on it.

But the "city business" is a political business. Logue prepared indirectly for his role in that realm by working as legal secretary to the governor of Connecticut, Chester Bowles, from 1949 to 1951. In 1951, he served as chief of staff to the state senate Democratic majority before becoming once again in 1952 a special assistant to Bowles, by this time U.S. ambassador to India.

In 1955, Logue became development administrator of New Haven, Connecticut, and, until 1960, he guided the city's urban renewal program—the largest, proportionate to population, in the U.S. The New Haven development program was diverse, with clearance downtown and in the neighborhoods, but with substantial attention at an early stage to rehabilitation. In fact, Logue's favorite New Haven project is Wooster Square, a project that featured substantial rehabilitation.

As an administrator, he was one of the first to see the importance of combining a development authority's acquisition and building powers with a comprehensive examination of the problems and opportunities presented by a project—in short, good planning. In New Haven, he combined these planning and development responsibilities in the office of the development administrator, a man-

agement pattern he continued at later stages of his career.

Ready for a new challenge and satisfied that the programs he had launched were reaching maturity, he left New Haven in 1960 for Boston.

There, until 1967, Logue directed a massive renewal effort by the Boston Redevelopment Authority. Again, he emphasized rehabilitation, particularly in the neighborhoods. Boston's central business district renewal was also a BRA project, and it meets Logue's test, more than New Haven, of a place he likes to return to because he likes how it turned out. He notes that the urban renewal project in the West End of Boston, made famous by the critiques of Herbert Gans (*The Urban Villagers*) and Jane Jacobs, was launched before his time. In fact, he was asked to come to Boston in part to revamp the city's renewal approach.

Logue's tenure in Boston ended in 1967, when the mayor who hired him and gave him unprecedented authority, John Collins, decided not to seek reelection for a third term. Logue himself decided to run for mayor. He lost in the Democratic primary and, understandably, decided it was time to move on.

From 1968 to 1975, Logue headed an organization that remains unique in U.S. history—the New York State Urban Development Corporation (UDC), created at the initiative of Gov. Nelson A. Rockefeller. The UDC is the only public, statewide corporation intended to carry out large-scale community development. During Logue's tenure, the agency's activities led to the development of three new towns and the construction of over 33,000 housing units in 27 communities and 115 separate development projects.

The beginning of the end came when Gov. Rockefeller left office in 1973. It was Rockefeller's persuasiveness that had garnered the support of New York financial institutions for all these projects, and without him, Logue says today, the bankers decided "not to be pushed around anymore." Instead, they withdrew their support and called for Logue's dismissal. He left, amid controversy and the threat of UDC bankruptcy, in 1975.

In each of these positions, Logue had the support of strong political leaders who were committed to urban redevelopment—Mayor Richard Lee in New Haven, Mayor Collins in Boston, and Rockefeller in New York. Logue says often that they deserve much of the credit for his success, that he "was just in the right place at the right time." And, in fact, each was unusual in some way. Lee was an organization Democrat, but one who was far more entrepreneurial, far less cautious, than the norm. Collins was an outsider who ran as an independent, owed few political debts, and found value, politically and in terms of development strategy, in bringing in another outsider.

Rockefeller was the quintessential Eastern Establishment Republican, but one who was committed to gathering immense resources and committing them to monumental projects and organizations. The Urban Development Corporation was but one example. Others were the remaking of the State University of New York and the commissioning of the complex of state government buildings in Albany known as the South Mall.

After leaving the UDC, Logue, who recently became a member of the American Institute of Certified Planners, spent several years consulting on various projects and teaching. In 1978, he became president of the South Bronx Development Organization, from which he resigned last January.

The South Bronx represented a challenge far different from Logue's previous jurisdictions. For one thing, much less federal funding was available. While $34 million had been committed to New Haven by 1960 and $200 million to Boston by 1967, the South Bronx was getting only $4 million in federal and state funds combined when SBDO launched its revitalization program in 1979. Thus, redevelopment necessarily had to be smaller in scale. The most publicized aspect of Logue's years with the South Bronx Development Organization is the construction of a group of three-bedroom, prefabricated ranch houses on Charlotte Street, the street made famous by a 1977 visit from President Jimmy Carter and, more recently, by a visit from President Reagan.

Since leaving the South Bronx, Logue, now 64, has lived in Lincoln, Massachusetts, outside Boston, where his wife Margaret is the director of a school for dyslexic children. Currently, he is organizing his papers in preparation for a book about his years with the BRA. He will be teaching planning at the Massachusetts Institute of Technology this fall. I interviewed him in April when he was Thomas Jefferson Professor of Architecture at the University of Virginia.

Lucy. When you look around the nation at our cities, what comes to mind? How do you feel about what is happening?

Logue. On the one hand, I feel good about our cities for a variety of reasons—not the least of which is that the excessive value has been extracted from them so that they now can develop again. After being overvalued downtown and generally, they have once again become good places to consider for rehabilitation, adaptive reuse, and new development. The federal income tax incentives—in particular those that encourage preservation and adaptive use—have had an extraordinary effect on stabilizing cities. Overcrowding, which was a real problem when I started out, has diminished greatly, and to a large extent disappeared.

On the other hand, I feel worse about the nation's diminished commitment to dealing with the ill-housed, ill-fed, and ill-clothed. With our riches, that is totally unnecessary.

Lucy. What do you see in the way of political support for revitalization?

Logue. Very little that is organized and directed. Revitalization is off the national agenda at this time, and so are the related issues of welfare reform and preservation of the family. Even preservation tax credits aren't regarded as a program for cities in the White House and in the Congress.

I don't think planning is held in any more esteem than when I started. Probably not as much. We continue to abuse our land with peripheral, incremental growth.

Lucy. What then can cities do for themselves?

Logue. They can do several things, but they all take strong political commitment and strong professionals. I would not spend any Community Development Block Grant money on routine projects. I would use those funds only to leverage capital investment. And even with their serious deficiencies, I would use all the Urban Development Action Grants I could get. I would be serious about code enforcement. Few cities are. I would stress preservation and far more serious and effective planning.

We can set higher performance standards for the public schools. In the South Bronx there are two school systems. One–the parochial school system—works, despite low salaries and poor facilities. The other—the public—doesn't work at all when measured by any serious objective standard.

We can deal seriously with government reorganization—which to me means decentralizing services in the largest cities, while making taxation a metropolitan function. I am a fan of London's system of decentralized boroughs.

To sum up, we need to involve the citizenry more than we do, and to spend the money we already spend far more effectively. That will be hard to do, very hard, but it is not impossible.

Lucy. When little public money is available to carry out large-scale redevelopment, are redevelopment plans still useful?

Logue. They are very useful. I am an activist, but I think of myself first as a planner. In the absence of public funds for major redevelopment projects, it becomes even more important to do competent, design-oriented, policy-based planning. If you have plans and a framework for forcing issues, then you can figure out what to do over time. You can help companies that invest in the public interest. If you have a plan and if people have a chance to participate, you can build public consensus and eventually control the development process in the public interest. I would never leave the development agenda to be set by the private development community.

Lucy. Are major clearance and redevelopment projects needed today?

Logue. We should do them in some places. I would love to do a major urban renewal project in the South Bronx. I am sure it would have overwhelming support within the community. But large-scale urban renewal rarely is politically feasible today.

There are three reasons for that. The first is that many black leaders believe that urban renewal was primarily "Negro removal," and sometimes it was. The second is that mayors perceive urban renewal as being too complicated, too long, with results that are too uncertain. Mayors want instant gratification even more than most people do. The third is that failed urban renewal projects are easily identified. Some, like one in Buffalo, have lain fallow for 30 years or more. Few people realize that many city successes, like Boston's successes, resulted from urban renewal.

Lucy. But is large-scale redevelopment for areas like the South Bronx feasible without federal or state assistance?

Logue. No. Large-scale redevelopment requires public assembly and control of land. To take down what should be taken down is very expensive. In the South Bronx alone, 2,500 abandoned five-story, walk-up apartment buildings should be demolished.

But there are things you can do without large federal or state support. In New York, I would gradually change every high-rise public housing project to an elderly housing project. I would let residents keep the extra bedrooms for their children or whatever, thus avoiding any structural modifications. The need of the elderly is there, and it will grow rapidly. High-rise housing is wrong for low-income families. It is unsafe. And in low-rise rental housing, you could cut maintenance costs overwhelmingly by requiring tenants to fix everything themselves except for major systems. You could also get rid of the public housing police, who spend a huge amount of time driving from project to project.

Lucy. What do you think of CDBG and UDAG as urban programs?

Logue. CDBG is just targeted revenue sharing. But it's difficult to keep it targeted. The money tends to be used in pedestrian ways, and once a spending pattern is established, it is difficult to break. Then, when the money is parceled out to nearly every city council district, it doesn't help anyone much.

UDAG provides the wrong subsidy at the wrong time. Projects that don't have local development and investment commitments are culled out. That means the feds commit to those that are most economically sound, but it also tends to eliminate most things that have social urgency. Also, it's very hard to highlight good design in UDAG projects—or sound planning for that matter.

Urban renewal gave us advance funding for surveys. So we used federal money to plan, and that helped us to be bold at the local level. It gave mayors the courage to try.

Lucy. What are your views on historic preservation?

Logue. We always should err on the side of more preservation because you can't put Humpty-Dumpty together again. Those who came before us generally had more taste and more concern.

But the preservationists themselves are often elitist and rigid. And while some adaptive reuse is inspired, some of it is outrageous. The old Boston City Hall was preserved as a shell. Nothing else was saved, not even the council chambers or the mayor's office. Now it houses a bank, lawyers' offices, and a restaurant. It's as though the University of Virginia were to convert Jefferson's academic village to a motel.

We've seen a remarkable decline in civic architecture, which used to provide the lead in design quality. In New Haven, we were the victims of International Style architecture, something we would prefer not to be remembered for.

Lucy: Other thoughts on urban design?

Logue. In general, the notion that urban design is a public responsibility is not an established idea in our society. For example, there still is no process in New York City for requiring developers to meet design standards. That is also the case in most other cities.

For signs of decline, compare today with the golden age of the early 1900s in both public and private architecture. In New York City, go to the tenth floor of a Fifth Avenue building and look across the park at Central Park West. You see a handsome row of rental apartment houses, built to last forever. Then look at the new buildings on the Upper East Side. They're all tax shelters or speculations.

The designs of the old post offices and courthouses were often chosen in competitions. The competition for new Boston City Hall in 1963 was the first such competition for a public building design in 50 years. Competitions are not a universal remedy, but they are an important statement of public concern about good design.

Lucy. What kind of form would you like to see our metropolitan areas take?

Logue. Ebenezer Howard had the right idea. We should have center cities, surrounded by greenbelts, with nodes outside—satellite cities—planned for a variety of people. All this is routine for most of Europe, and it is what should have happened in the United States. Cities in the U.S. are fundamentally affected by a lack of regional planning and regional government. In the U.S., with a handful of exceptions, cities and suburbs move in their own orbits. That's crazy. There's only one region that has been at all serious about metropolitan planning and development. That is the Minneapolis–St. Paul area, where tax sharing from commercial growth is one of the important signs of serious intent.

Lucy. You mention Europe as an example. Yet some argue that Europe has gone the way of the U.S. in becoming dependent on cars, building sprawling suburbs, and so on. Is that so?

Logue. That is not accurate, although there certainly is movement in that direction, particularly in West Germany. Generally, European cities still are the vital centers of their regions. Strip development is rare to nonexistent. Some limited-access highways have been built, of course, but they rarely dominate.

Train service is a vivid contrast. Nowhere in the U.S. is train service of any type as good today as it was in 1941, except for the Metroliner between New York City and Washington, D.C. In England, France, Germany, Holland, Sweden, Finland, and other places, commuter, intercity, and long distance train service is far superior to prewar days.

Lucy. Are you an optimist or a pessimist about the future of U.S. cities?

Logue. I expect to die an optimist—provided I die in good health. It's in my genes. In the city business, it's necessary.

William Lucy is professor of planning at the University of Virginia at Charlottesville.

William Whyte: The Observation Man

Eugenie L. Birch
(March 1986)

Perched in his office 55 stories above Rockefeller Center, William Hollingsworth Whyte surveys the city: Manhattan's brown and white skyscrapers give way to the blue-grey waters of the Hudson River and the green shores of New Jersey. But Holly (his longtime nickname) Whyte has never stayed long in this office. His mission has taken him into the streets and squares of cities, the fast-developing suburbs, and the sprawl-threatened countryside, into courtrooms, architects' studios, and planning board and city council meetings. He has gone to observe and later comment, often with practical suggestions for a design or a piece of legislation. As a critic and a teacher, he has recorded, analyzed, and explored the functioning of metropolitan environments for the past 30 years.

Whyte has shared his observations in several significant books, each more interesting to planners than the last. In 1956, he dissected the newly emerging postwar suburbs in his classic, *The Organization Man.* Two years later, he pointed out the evils of urban sprawl and thoughtless urban renewal in *The Exploding Metropolis.* In the 1960s, he outlined plans for conserving rural lands in *Open Space Action, Cluster Zoning,* and *The Last Landscape.*

Perhaps he is best known, however, for his most recent work on the design of urban open space. His highly acclaimed film and its companion book, *The Social Life of Small Urban Spaces,* reported the results of a decade-long research project observing human behavior patterns in streets, plazas, and malls.

Whyte is more than a writer. He is an activist, persuasively marketing his recommendations, translating words into laws and laws into livable environments. Few states in the nation have not been influenced by his conservation work; few downtowns of our largest cities have been left untouched by his findings on the use of public space.

Whyte began his writing career in 1946, when he joined *Fortune* magazine. Although a rookie, he brought with him a degree in English from Princeton and the experience of a Marine who had weathered the Guadalcanal campaign. At *Fortune,* he was a bit of a maverick, taking on unstructured assignments and often working several months before turning out a story. But those stories were always notable and often controversial, like the articles that became *The Organization Man.*

While his earliest work concentrated on the corporate world, he made the connection between planning and business in editing a series on metropolitan growth that later was published as *The Exploding Metropolis.* Here, he got Jane Jacobs to write her first attack on urban renewal, a precursor to her 1961 book-length critique, *The Death and Life of Great American Cities.* His contribution, an essay on urban sprawl, evolved from his dismay at seeing his own birthplace, Chester County, Pennsylvania, carelessly transformed from a rural to an urbanized area.

Struck by the conservation issues he touched on in this essay, Whyte left *Fortune* in 1959 to work on them full time. His basic concern, to preserve land in the most economical fashion, led to an Urban Land Institute report called *Conservation Easements.* In it he proposed legislation that became the model for open space statutes in California, New York, Connecticut, Massachusetts, and Maryland.

For the next 10 years, he drafted influential reports for the Outdoor Recreation Resources Review Commission and the American Conservation Foundation. He served as a consultant to Connecti-

cut and New Jersey, which both enacted his recommendations for open space programs financed by bond issues. He was a member of President Lyndon Johnson's Task Force on Natural Beauty and drafted its final report. It included his own proposal for urban beautification, which ultimately became a $50 million tree planting program. Later, he became codirector of the White House Conference on Natural Beauty and chairman of New York Governor Nelson Rockefeller's Conference on Natural Beauty. This period for Whyte culminated with the publication of *The Last Landscape* in 1968.

In the early 1970s, he turned his sights on central cities, attacking a recent flurry of regional plans premised on decentralization. During this time, he took on the year-long assignment of writing the text for the *Plan for New York City.* This 1969 official master plan was hailed by the *New York Times* for its concise and compelling writing and praised by the American Society of Planning Officials for its breadth of vision.

Work on the plan drew Whyte's attention to incentive zoning, particularly the provisions encouraging developers to create public plazas or arcades in exchange for additional floor space. While serving as distinguished professor of urban sociology at Hunter College of the City University of New York, he and some of his students organized the Street Life Project to study how people used streets and open spaces in the center of the city.

Using time-lapse photography, Whyte and his team recorded "schmoozing patterns, the rituals of street encounters" and sought to find out why "people flocked to some plazas and left others empty." Funded by grants from the National Geographic Society and others, Whyte had enough evidence by 1973 to stimulate a complete overhaul of the incentive zoning provisions in the New York City code.

Many other cities emulated this ordinance, with its specifications for seating, planting, food concessions, and other amenities. To disseminate his findings more widely, Whyte edited thousands of feet of time-lapse photographic film into a movie, "The Social Life of Small Urban Places," screened nationally on the Public Broadcasting System and currently being shown at the Pompidou Center in Paris.

Noting that he has always found a way to do what he enjoys doing, Whyte's face lights up as he describes his future plans. A book, an extension of

Social Life of Small Urban Places and another movie, one including footage on Japan and Europe, are immediate projects. And there is the ongoing work of the New York Landmarks Conservancy, which he helped found.

At age 69, Whyte keeps up a steady round of consulting. San Francisco, Dallas, Kansas City, Seattle, and San Diego have called for his advice. Yet New York is his base; he has lived there with his wife and daughter for about 40 years.

For these continuing efforts, last December Whyte was awarded an honorary membership in the American Institute of Certified Planners, joining such luminaries as Lewis Mumford and James Rouse.

One crisp morning last winter, Whyte took me on a walking tour to show me the workable spaces in midtown Manhattan. We paused in Rockefeller Center to watch natives and visitors enjoy the holiday display, then moved quickly to Paley Park, deserted on this subzero morning but still a perfect demonstration of the virtues of easy entry, movable furniture, trees, the soothing tones of a waterfall. On we went to the IBM Building's interior plaza, where Whyte expressed dismay at the removal of some of the seating, although it remains a haven for many.

Finally, we ended up at the Whitney Museum sculpture garden in the Philip Morris Building, a space Whyte worked on directly with architect Ulrich Franzen. It is not a big space, but a welcoming and interesting one, with a life-sized sculpture of dancing women, an ample supply of tables and chairs, and a little cappuccino stand. People of all ages came and went, and Whyte sighed contentedly.

After spending almost 10 years watching his fellow New Yorkers, Whyte knows what to expect of them. Walking on Madison Avenue, he spotted a pedestrian near the Urban Center. "Watch him," he ordered. Almost by command, the man stepped from the sidewalk, ignored the crosswalk, and paced diagonally across the street to the opposite corner. Whyte beamed. "They always do that," he observed. "I feel as if I'm controlling them, although I know I'm not. I have to be careful," he laughed with reference to his new AICP status, "or they really will have me certified."

In the following interview, conducted in his office later that day, Whyte shares both his philosophy about urban activism and his views on some contemporary planning techniques.

Birch. Planners from around the country are calling on you for advice. What are you saying?

Whyte. It's really my job and obligation to be frank. For instance, in the case of Dallas—not that it did any good—I was asked by the city council to do a study of the City Hall Plaza. It was an absolute bomb. I. M. Pei's wonderful monument—very striking, especially at night, but oh, that plaza, and all that concrete! In the plaza, there are a group of little stunted trees; Pei didn't want big trees interfering with the view. There were benches—horrible, concrete benches—and exactly four were within the shade of the trees. Now there are movable chairs, and people use the benches for footrests.

In addition, the city wanted me to look at the downtown. I've done enough counting to know that if you go to a downtown sidewalk at noon and you haven't got well over 1,000 people per hour per sidewalk, there's something very wrong. Dallas actually has a very high-density core. So where were all the people? Well, it's partly the southwest culture: clubs, in-house cafeterias, a short lunch hour.

But they also have an underground concourse, which they need like a hole in the head. These things are self-proving. The more underground links you have, the more pressure builds for them in every new development.

Birch. What's your opinion about using incentive zoning to obtain things that a city might need, like subway station improvements or a riverfront promenade?

Whyte. There's nothing wrong with the approach. But when you're thinking up innovative programs, you'd better be sure to check back to find out what's happened before.

For most of these things, you can tell in about a month whether or not they work. Look at arcaded sidewalks. It took us 15 years to acknowledge that these things don't work very well because they recess the stores away from the main traffic stream. That's why you see so many for sale signs. Well, we could have found that out very early, the second or third day out. So, on incentives, yes. But very few, and let's check to see if we're getting our money's worth.

Birch. How would you do such a check?

Whyte. Back in 1969, I proposed a little evaluative unit that would report directly to the chairman of the New York City Planning Commission—not to the Urban Design Group, not to the Office of Midtown Planning, but directly to the chairman, so he could say, "Check this thing out. Is Mr. Potemkin really doing the job?" But the idea never went anywhere. To my knowledge, in fact, there is no planning commission in the country that has built in an evaluative capability.

Birch. How would an evaluative unit work?

Whyte. It would be like the Inspector General's Office in the Army: Sometimes it works, sometimes it doesn't. When it does work, it can be very useful. It doesn't have the clout to go public—and you know what happens to someone within a department who does go public—but at least it can go to the boss.

I must say, though, for all my criticism of New York city planners, they've been pretty damn responsive.

Birch. What other cities are good models?

Whyte. San Francisco. They're leaning over backward to be responsive. I spent a day a while ago with George Williams and his whole urban design group. We talked about their new urban guidelines, and I thought they were pretty good. Philadelphia looks pretty good, too. Pittsburgh rates a salute. The planning commission did a fine survey of their downtown space and applied the findings in their guidelines.

Birch. So the large cities have been conscientious in trying to improve their downtowns, but are the medium and small cities less so?

Whyte. The medium-sized cities have a tougher job downtown. They are much more immediately hit than the big cities by the competition of the suburban shopping mall. They are much more apt to copy the shopping mall. That's a hideous mistake. For the form that works so well out on the interchange doesn't make much sense downtown. Developers can write their own ticket in most cities, and they get away with murder. But I've also found that when you bring in good legislation, they turn into pragmatists.

Birch. Then once something is legislated, the developers go along?

Whyte. They won't fight it. They've got other things to do. This is what I preach if I'm lecturing to a civic or planning group. I say, "You guys aren't asking for enough. The developers will give it to you, but you have to stretch for it. It's for their own

good. They might not know that, but in the long run, it is."

Birch. What's your opinion of the new festival marketplaces?

Whyte. I think Quincy Market [in Boston] and Harborplace [in Baltimore] are really exemplary in their way. Rouse is a very shrewd observer. He doesn't miss a trick. I was struck by the way he organized Quincy Market, with the street going through it and the very tight spaces. Of course, a lot of that was a given. I talked to him when he was working on Harborplace, and he said he realized how lucky he was in Boston to have so many key decisions already made for him by the site and the buildings. In Baltimore, he had much more of a clean slate.

Harborplace has worked very well. Some people complain that the activity is not vital, that it's not at the very core. No, it's not. It's a recreational place. You don't go there because you have to but because you want to. I'm persuaded that when you see the crowds there using it consistently and having a good time, something must be right. I think it has been very well done.

As for South Street Seaport, I always thought it would become the Wall Street office workers' place, and it did. Suddenly at 12 o'clock all these dark suits appear.

I'm not wild about some of the other festival marketplaces. The trouble is, you've seen them once too often, and some of the copies omit the key elements of the original. Rouse told me once he gets many requests from mayors who say, "We have a wonderful old warehouse with lots of brick. Come do it." He says, "They miss the point."

The Faneuil Hall Marketplace is a very workable place, for there are a lot of very tough merchandizing lessons demonstrated there: The street is central to it, as is a critical mass of people. It's a beneficently congested place. There is a wonderful second-story mix—which is important. There are lots of things to learn.

Birch. Talking about selling, you're pretty good at it, too. Your studies don't just lie around on shelves.

Whyte. Well, I knew, after finishing *Social Life of Small Urban Spaces*, that our findings were good. But we had to sell them, or they would have disappeared. Rather than wait for a full book, which was going to take forever to come out, I wanted to start the practical application of our ideas. I really wanted to get them known by the architects. Their assumptions are often so wrong that I thought it was really important to say something to them.

Birch. And what did you do to make sure your ideas got across?

Whyte. I did my homework. So I was able to anticipate the questions. The lawyers always ask the toughest questions. For instance, "If all this comes through, and we have more trees and this and that, aren't we going to attract too many people?"

It's nice, then, to be able to talk about the facts of the situation. To tell them that, in fact, there is no saturation point. And we have in no way begun to touch the demand for amenities. So the fact that Manhattan's Paley Park, for example, has been very, very well used doesn't mean that you shouldn't have a similar park maybe three blocks away.

Birch. Certainly you have encountered resistance to your proposals for zoning changes. Where did it come from?

Whyte. There was a lawyer who was appointed head of the parks and recreation committee of a community board, which oversaw development in midtown Manhattan. I'd run into him at conferences, and I could tell from his criticism that he didn't like what I was aiming for—more or less as-of-right legislation.

My as-of-right guidelines showed what developers could do. Then they wouldn't have to go through the conventional land-use review process. So, of course, stiff guidelines were needed. You couldn't be ambiguous. And we had them all: One linear foot of sitting space must be provided, a minimum for every 30 square feet of plaza. That is in the zoning of most big cities now. They all copy one another.

But this lawyer made unholy fun of that guideline. "Look," he said, "let's cut through all this red tape. Let's sit down with the developer and work it out case by case." Sounds good, but what it means is, tennis without the net and one man is in charge.

We went on about the issue for two full years. Finally, we had to cut out one of the best pieces of the legislation, the part that said, in effect, "Mr. Developer, there are a lot of places where it's best not to have a plaza. Instead of a plaza, find a lot within two blocks of your site and give us another Paley Park." My idea had been that we could make the developers work with us. We worked out quite

stiff guidelines. But in the end, John Zucotti, head of the planning commission, gave up this provision to get the rest through.

Birch. You have been involved in some very dramatic actions, haven't you?

Whyte. You can't go off in an ivory tower when you're dealing with issues like these. For example, we had a big fight on a sun question at Greenacre Park. I got involved through the New York Landmarks Conservancy. We were asked by the city's official landmarks commission to monitor a preservation easement on a landmark building whose air rights were being acquired by a developer. He was going to put up a high rise on Third Avenue. When I saw the plans for it, I thought that, at 34 stories, it might shadow Greenacre Park.

"No, no," said the developer and his people. "It's going to be a redundant shadow." In other words, the shadow would fall on the neighboring building, not on the park. When I started to do some sun angle analysis, I found that the new building would cause about 25 minutes' loss of sun at the critical midday period.

Well, the planning commission approved the project anyway. The last step was the Board of Estimate, which rarely goes against the planning commission. But we went there with our sun data. The developers were very confident. They had already started building the thing. They told the board that they had rented out the whole building, 34 stories and all. If they had to drop off some stories, many prospective tenants would have to leave New York. The lawyer didn't even address himself to the shadow issue, and we invoked it for all it was worth. The board reduced the building by three stories.

As the building was being built at the time, they had signed up every inch of space. It cost them $25 million. The *New York Times* took the developers' side. They said the environmentalists played dirty pool. But it put the fear of God into a lot of developers, let me tell you. They started doing their sun studies.

Birch. With all your lecturing, lobbying, and consulting, do you ever have the opportunity to talk to students, and if so, what do you tell them?

Whyte. I was just up at Winnipeg University in Manitoba, sitting on a jury for a design studio. The student projects are always the same—a redo of the downtown. They had all these overhead bridges encased in glass, all sorts of architectural acrobatics, sunken plazas, the works. You realize that this is a generation that never knew a city. They never knew a successful downtown. It's not their fault. Their image is of a suburban shopping mall. They recreate it. They don't know how important the street is.

That's where my mission is. I want to show them that the best contemporary developments, just like the best old ones, have a strong street presence. This is what unifies. It's what brings it together.

Eugenie Birch, AICP, is associate professor of planning at Hunter College in New York City.

Living With Las Vegas: A Profile of Denise Scott Brown

Ruth Eckdish Knack
(May 1986)

Some books are born to shock. An example, from 1972, is *Learning from Las Vegas,* which brought the wrath of architects, planners, and civic beautifiers down on the heads of its authors, Robert Venturi, Denise Scott Brown, and Steven Izenour. Scott Brown, whose early interest in the Las Vegas strip had started the whole thing, was denounced on the one hand as the high priestess of schlock—and acclaimed on the other as a prescient observer of the American landscape.

Now, almost 15 years later, the shock has worn off, roadside architecture is the subject of scholarly papers at meetings of the Society for Commercial Archeology, and Scott Brown applies what she learned in Las Vegas, and later Levittown, to a wide variety of planning projects.

"I call myself an architect-planner," she said in an interview last fall in the offices of Venturi, Rauch and Scott Brown, located appropriately enough on Main Street in the Philadelphia neighborhood of Manayunk. "But I seem to find my greatest delight in linkages." Linkages is a word she uses often, particularly in describing her efforts to explain social planning to architecture students—and vice versa—at Penn, Berkeley, UCLA, and Yale, where she taught in the 1960s.

But the idea works equally well to describe her catholic taste. Here's an intellectual "high-culture"

architect who watches "Miami Vice" (to catch a glimpse of Deco District architecture), shops in thrift stores, and furnished her house with two truckloads of furniture from the about-to-be demolished Traymore Hotel in Atlantic City. Comforting as it is to pigeonhole people into categories, it's hard to do so in the case of someone who's comfortable in *both* Levittown and Princeton.

So how did she get that way? She says some of it has to do with her exposure to both high art and folk art in South Africa, where she grew up, the oldest child of a well-to-do businessman.

She knew at five, she says, that she was going to become an architect because her mother had studied architecture, and "I thought that was woman's work." She spent four years at the University of the Witwatersrand, a "very nuts-and-bolts" program that gave her good basic training in construction and in old-fashioned rendering techniques. In 1951, at 20, she left for what was to be a year's study in London, at the Architectural Association, then dominated by the theories of the architects known as "the new Brutalists," whose heavily political agenda centered on providing housing for the working class.

Scott Brown says she found "irresistible" the Architectural Association's view that the "proper focus of architecture was urbanism." As a result, she and her husband, Robert Scott Brown, instead of returning to South Africa, headed for the United States to study urban planning at the University of Pennsylvania, which had a reputation in England as the best atmosphere for a socially committed architect, in part because of the presence of Louis Kahn—himself a major influence on the New Brutalists. She received a master's degree in city planning in 1960 and a master's in architecture in 1965. Robert Scott Brown was killed in an automobile accident in 1959.

A good learner

At Penn, which she later described as the "most interesting intellectual environment we had ever encountered," Scott Brown discovered that the most stimulating teachers were not the architects, but rather the social planners. And two lessons she learned there have stayed with her. One was from Paul Davidoff, who taught her that planning decisions are basically political decisions—but that those decisions can be made democratically if the planner presents alternatives and the implications of each alternative. The second lesson was from Herbert Gans, whose message was that cultural diversity was okay and that there is validity in a variety of life styles.

Gans's famous example is, of course, Levittown, and Scott Brown visited him in the New Jersey new town, some 20 miles from Philadelphia, when he was living there doing research for his book. That trip laid the foundation for an architecture studio called "Learning from Levittown" that Scott Brown and Robert Venturi taught at Yale in the late 1960s. Gans recalls that he was pleasantly surprised that any architect would have an interest in a development subject to so much scorn. But Scott Brown agreed with Gans that suburbs deserved analysis and, further, that studying Levittown impartially was not the same as endorsing it.

Scott Brown was also struck by Gans's taxonomy of "taste cultures," described in the 1974 book, *Popular Cultures and High Culture,* but disseminated earlier in several articles. We are "high culture architects who borrow from low culture and outrage the middle class," she joked in a 1980 interview.

She began to apply these lessons as a teacher at Penn, first in an introduction to urban design for nonarchitects. She has since talked about the frustration of getting those "nonarchitects" to accept the value of physical planning and design and of getting the designers to understand the importance of not being judgmental.

In the mid-1960s, the attraction of West Coast urbanism with its mixture of social and architectural theory drew Scott Brown to California, first to teach at the University of California, Berkeley, and then at UCLA, where she helped organize an interdisciplinary urban design program. She invited Philadelphia architect Robert Venturi to lecture to her classes, and that collaboration eventually led to Las Vegas, Levittown, and beyond. Venturi and Scott Brown were married in 1967.

During the time that Scott Brown was absorbing the thoughts of the Philadelphia social planners, Venturi had been promoting the idea of diversity in architectural design. "Soon, their ideas became so closely entwined that they became the same ideas," says former Penn colleague Tim Vreeland, who now teaches at UCLA. "In many ways, I think Denise has suffered from the fact that Bob has gotten major credit for ideas they developed jointly."

Among those ideas are the notions that complexity and contradiction in architecture (the title of Venturi's 1966 book) are good things in themselves and that the simplicity that was the goal of the early modern architects can be—well, boring. Venturi's comments stemmed in part from his study of the post-Renaissance Italian Mannerist architects, who exaggerated certain details to add variety to their facades.

In short, instead of Mies's less, let's have more—and particularly more decoration. Many of the most famous buildings in the world, in Venturi and Scott Brown's view, are nothing more than "decorated sheds." We remember the decoration because it symbolizes something that is important to us—in much the same way that a building sign is a modern cultural symbol. The sign may even be more important than the building, or it may be the whole building, like the famous roadside stand in the shape of a Long Island duckling. From that example came the term "duck" to define a building where symbolism has run amok. Ironically, the most flagrant examples are some of the stars of modern design.

From the decorated shed, Venturi and Scott Brown progressed to an analysis of the symbolism of billboards and commercial strips. Main Street, they concluded, could be studied in the same way any other space is studied.

Their ideas culminated in 1968 in a graduate architecture and planning studio at Yale University's School of Art and Architecture. It was called "Learning from Las Vegas, or Formal Analysis as Design Research," and it became the basis for the Las Vegas book. Their intention, they said in the written introduction to the studio, was "to define a new type of urban form . . . radically different from what we have known; one that we have been ill-equipped to deal with and that, from ignorance, we define today as urban sprawl." With understanding of this new form, they added, would come "new techniques for its handling."

A second Yale studio took Levittown as its departure, again with the idea of understanding the vernacular landscape and even getting a creative rush from it. In a 1969 article in the *Journal of the American Institute of Planners,* Scott Brown described the "aesthetic shiver that is engendered by trying to like what one does not like."

"Diatribes on the . . . immorality of sprawl won't make it go away," she added.

A few kindred spirits had already caught on to the importance of this new way of seeing the environment. Among those in Scott Brown's pantheon: landscape writer J. B. Jackson; architect Charles Moore, who considered Disneyland and the California freeway as contemporary monuments; and Berkeley planning professor Mel Webber, who argued against the hegemony of physical planning.

In 1967, Scott Brown joined Venturi's Philadelphia firm and also helped him run his family produce business (earning them the label "egghead fruit merchants"). Soon after, the firm was approached by a group of volunteers who were trying to stop a planned crosstown expressway, which would have destroyed three miles of the main street of a low-income black neighborhood along the southern edge of downtown.

"In the South Street plan," says Scott Brown, "are the ingredients of what I have done ever since." The order, she notes, comes from the planning process outlined by Paul Davidoff and Thomas Reiner in the early 1960s: Careful analysis of existing conditions, followed by the establishment of a democratic citizen participation process, and finally the plan.

Arguing that the expressway wasn't needed for through traffic, Scott Brown proposed that South Street be revived as a commercial strip. "We saw this part of the city not just as a service area for the hinterland—the suburbs," she says, "but as a service area to the inner city. And we wanted to use architecture to serve the purpose of revitalizing the neighborhood economy."

"What did we learn in Las Vegas that we could apply on South Street?" Scott Brown asked later. "Certainly not that the Crosstown Community should become a place for gambling, high life, and neon high readers. Rather that beauty could emerge from the existing fabric and that a none-too-apparent order should be sought from within instead of an easy one imposed from above. That piecemeal development need not spell disunity."

Moving on

Since that time, every Scott Brown planning project has begun with a "Learning from . . ." analysis, including a look at the project area's role in the region. "Only then," she says, "do we start talking about cosmetics." So, for example, a study of historic buildings in Jim Thorpe, Pennsylvania, turned into a broad strategy for the old mining town's economic revival. "The plan has had a dramatic effect on the community," says Carbon County community development planner Bruce Conrad, citing new downtown businesses and a new spurt of tourism.

"The remarkable thing about the study is that, even after seven years, it's still current. Denise anticipated the questions that would come up later."

In Miami Beach, the firm turned a commission for a simple public improvements plan into something approaching a comprehensive plan for Washington Avenue, the polyglot main street of the Art Deco District. The firm's strength, recalls Barbara Capitman, president of the nonprofit Miami Design Preservation League, was in dealing with the neighborhood's elderly residents, to the extent that it prepared special, brightly colored, oversized drawings for public presentations. Capitman adds, "They cautioned the city not to violate the district's low-rise scale and to allow signs to be painted on the buildings—a no-no at the time. They went to great lengths to avoid cuteness. Art Deco was an unknown style at the time, but they treated it with respect."

Perhaps because they were longtime fans of Miami Beach's Art Deco architecture, the Venturis did far more work than they were paid for. And that has proved to be a problem with almost every other plan the firm has done, says Scott Brown. "No town can afford everything it needs. So we have to make some very agonized choices. Something has to go, most often in the analysis of existing conditions."

One reason the plans are so costly is that the Scott Brown text is so elaborate. A plan now under way for downtown Memphis is an example. In this case, Scott Brown is heading a team of consultants hired by the city. Their initial proposal was a weighty, 100-plus page document that opened with what she calls a "sonnet"—a lyrical description of the city's history as a "good station." That was just to get the job. Now the team is working on detailed subarea plans, in each case—because this is a Scott Brown priority—stressing linkages among individual projects. Surprisingly, for plans produced in an architect's office, the resulting documents appear rather graphically cramped.

The only other planning project in the office at this time is on hold. It's an urban design strategy for a 25-block area of downtown Austin, commissioned by a private developer, the Watson–Casey Companies. The area includes the proposed site of a new municipal office complex and of a new art museum. Another architect has been chosen for the municipal complex, but the Venturi firm won the museum. Whether any of this will be built, however, depends on the city council's decision.

"Most of our planning," Scott Brown has written, "has to do with seeing what's happening and helping it happen better." That sort of insight worked spectacularly well in the case of the firm's plan for Philadelphia's Franklin Court, where Scott Brown suggested that a museum be put underground and that it be topped by a public park. The site of Ben Franklin's house is marked by a metal framed "ghost building."

Some projects have been significantly more problematic, producing a flurry of criticism and defense reminiscent of post-*Las Vegas* days. The firm's role as urban designer for a portion of Manhattan's Westway highway project is an example, with some critics claiming that the Venturis were on the "wrong side" of the controversial expressway plan.

In defense, Scott Brown, who was involved in this project only as an adviser, cites their efforts to stop the Philadelphia expressway. But, she notes, "that one wasn't needed for through traffic, and it would have removed 6,000 low-income people. Westway wouldn't have displaced anyone. The only good argument against it was that the money would have gone to transit. But what the New York transit system needs is operating money. The highway funds would have been a drop in the bucket. Our plan would have produced something very nice—a Central Park–type landscape—on the edge of Manhattan."

Earlier, an urban design plan for Hennepin Avenue in Minneapolis drew an angry response from local critics, who heaped scorn on the proposal for 40-foot-tall aluminum "reflector trees" along a six-block stretch. The firm defended the trees as a way of symbolically celebrating Hennepin's past glory as the city's "great white way."

A group of local architects satirized the effort with a counterproposal: La-Z-Boy recliners, pole lamps, and Lava lights. Others called for real trees—which Scott Brown insists are often *not* an appropriate solution.

Those are fighting words to people like Ron Fleming, a Boston-based consultant with a particular interest in public spaces and small towns. "The Venturis have demonstrated enormous wit and wisdom in some of the things they've done," he says, "but they've also had a negative influence on

a generation of younger architects and planners who have been anesthetized to the problem of the strip.

"Even worse, the big corporations—the oil companies, for instance—have used the Venturis' arguments as an apologia to continue their own visual assault on local community values."

It's the issue of design review that particularly riles Fleming. "The Venturis are afraid design guidelines will crimp creativity. I think guidelines force people who are producing junk to think about the community's opinions."

Scott Brown's long-held view is that architectural review as practiced by design review or historic review commissions in most cases does more harm than good. It's bad on two levels, she says. First, the review process is often unfairly administered, and second, it's harmful to the cause of good art. Such commissions, she wrote in the 1969 *JAIP* article, are too often composed of "aging modern architects with a neatness compulsion."

That is not to say that all review is bad. "To exert no control at all," Scott Brown wrote in the Hennepin Avenue plan, "is to court chaos." But she distinguishes between review and the use of suggestive guidelines, like those she did for "The Rambla," the tree-lined pedestrian mall proposed for downtown Austin. But the guidelines must conform to the character of the area they are serving, and those who administer them must know the difference between chaos and vitality. One street, she adds, may require several different kinds of guidelines for different types of buildings—including even the honky-tonks if their preservation is seen as desirable. "What looks terrible now may look okay later," she notes. "A city must take architectural risks. If it won't, it's not a city."

Scott Brown is known for such tart remarks. She's been particularly outspoken on the subject of sexism, whose sting she says she has felt for years. She was dismayed to discover when she left Penn in 1965 (she didn't get tenure) that her former students were being paid more than she was. At UCLA, she had to battle to get an associate professor ranking. "From such experiences," she wrote later, "I learned that if I didn't fight for my rights, no one else would. I became successively more bellicose."

What really turned her into an ardent feminist, she feels, is the star system she encountered in the architecture establishment and the architecture press, both of which she says have often ignored her contributions to the Venturi–Scott Brown collaborations.

Some critics have taken such reactions as a sign of supersensitivity. "Those are the people who talk about my 'woman's problem,' not about my work," she says.

Personal taste

People always ask if Denise Scott Brown practices what she preaches. And in many respects she doesn't—but then again, she points out, she wasn't *advocating* Las Vegas. She simply said we should study it.

She and Venturi and their 14-year-old son, Jimmie, live in a sprawling Art Nouveau house in the Mount Airy neighborhood. Fellow architects are often surprised, she says, to learn that they have neither altered the house structurally nor painted the walls white and installed designer furniture. Their eclectic furnishings include over 70 chairs of different periods, including some from the whimsical group they designed for Knoll a couple of years ago.

Scott Brown wrote about the house and her family for the spring 1983 issue of the *Journal of the American Planning Association,* which looked at changing family patterns. Her thesis was that domestic life is one of the social and economic forces that have influenced the physical form of the city but have not always been considered seriously by planners. She suggested numerous ways in which they could make amends, including allowing such imaginative zoning combinations as a "professional-residential" category. But her main point, consistent with her views on cultural pluralism, was that planners should accept diversity in family types and styles and should offer their constituents a choice of planning strategies.

"Main Street," according to the Venturis, "is almost all right." And Main Street, where the office is, still plays an important role in the family's life. "When Jimmie runs on Main Street, I can keep an eye on him from my office window, and the owner of the corner store will do the same for me from her window," wrote Scott Brown, who is eager to show off the dimestore and other treasures of her street—which shows some signs of impending gentrification. Recently, she has been dividing her time between the firm's newest design project, an addition to the National Gallery in London, and the

final phases of the plan for downtown Memphis. She has also been advising Venturi on the dimensions of a recently commissioned porcelain tea service. "That's what is interesting about us," she says, "the fact that we work in so many directions." She says it's also what makes them different from the postmodern architects with whom they are often lumped by critics. In Scott Brown's view, the postmodernists focus on surface attraction.

"What we do, in contrast, comes out of social planning, out of the social upheavals of the 1960s—as well as out of a knowledge of history. We don't *only* want to make things beautiful."

Ruth Knack is the senior editor of Planning.

Eyes on Jane Jacobs
Ed Zotti
(September 1986)

This year marks the twenty-fifth anniversary of Jane Jacobs's *The Death and Life of Great American Cities,* arguably one of the most influential and certainly one of the most controversial books ever written about large cities and how they work. Sharply criticized when it was first published, the book is now regarded by many as a classic and its author revered in some circles as a secular saint. More than 200,000 copies have been sold to date. The book is still in print, regularly turns up on college reading lists, and has been translated into six languages.

Did *Death and Life* have any real impact? Has Jacobs's analysis of cities been borne out by events? Is her message still relevant? Planners and other students of the modern city are as divided on these questions today as they were on the value of the book when it first appeared. But the fact that it still stirs them up testifies to the enduring power of Jane Jacobs's vision of city life.

Jacobs herself thinks the book made a difference in two ways. "One," she says, "was that a lot of people already knew the things I was writing about from their own experience of life. But they had been taught to mistrust their own experience in favor of what experts said. I think my book gave heart to a lot of people to trust what they knew. Before, if they fought city hall, they were told they were being selfish. The book helped people feel less guilty."

Second, she adds, the book made a difference with the younger generation. "I've seen a great difference in attitude on the part of young planners, and perhaps my books had some small part in that. I say a small part because the young planners also had the experience of seeing what the older generation of planners had done. When you see a Pruitt-Igoe blown up, that certainly tells you something."

Written chiefly as a screed against large-scale urban renewal projects and the mentality that produced them, *The Death and Life of Great American Cities* was a decidedly eccentric work. It was a critique of planning by someone who was neither a planner, an architect, nor a social scientist. Rather, Jacobs was a civic activist and journalist, who at the time her book was published was an associate editor for the now-defunct *Architectural Forum.* Her principal research tools were clippings from the New York newspapers and observations from her own life. She believed so passionately in cities that at times she was susceptible to a true believer's failings: a penchant for oversimplification and a tendency to make sweeping generalizations on the basis of limited evidence.

Now 70, Jacobs was born in Scranton, Pennsylvania, but as a young woman moved to New York City, where she married and raised three children. In 1968, the family moved to Toronto, where Jacobs lives today with her husband, an architect. She has continued to write: *The Economy of Cities* appeared in 1969, *The Question of Separatism* in 1980, and *Cities and the Wealth of Nations* in 1984.

She based many of her ideas in *Death and Life* on her experiences in Manhattan, particularly "the intricate sidewalk ballet" of Hudson Street in Greenwich Village, where she lived for many years. She believed that the creation of a vital city neighborhood could be reduced to four basic rules: short blocks, mixed uses, old buildings mingled with new, and residential densities of at least 100 units an acre. Not coincidentally, this was precisely the situation that prevailed in Greenwich Village.

The crime problem in New York's parks led her to attack with startling vehemence planners' calls for more open space. "More open space for what?" she asked. "For muggings? For bleak vacuums between buildings?" She believed that the center of urban life was the crowded, raucous city street, not an empty park or plaza, and she thought planners who criticized the former and admired the latter understood nothing about how cities really worked.

Planners, she wrote, are trained to simplify and clarify, whereas cities by their very nature are complex and diverse. To the extent that planners succeeded in their efforts to "clean up" urban areas, she said, the city's vitality was diminished.

She argued that planners were foolish to equate density with overcrowding. On the contrary, she wrote, density provided the vitality that was characteristic of all great cities. Moreover, busy streets were safe streets. In densely populated communities, she said, a cadre of neighborhood "proprietors" emerged to keep the street under informal surveillance. "Eyes on the street" became the watchword of a younger generation of planners.

She thought that wholesale slum clearance was foolhardy, and that inward-looking public housing projects were doomed to failure. She felt that urban highway building programs ate away at the city's heart. And she believed that efforts to sort cities into neat little zones for residence, commerce, and industry were counterproductive in the long run.

Becoming respectable

Many of these ideas are now the conventional wisdom. Slum clearance and high-rise public housing—indeed, public housing construction of any kind—have virtually ceased, and experts debate what to do with the high-rise slums already built. Highway projects have been halted in one city after another. Mixed-use real-estate developments have become commonplace, and many cities are now going to great lengths to attract shops and residents into their downtowns.

Most important, Jacobs forced planners to reassess their methods and assumptions. "She shook the profession out of its lethargy and challenged the self-satisfied orthodoxy," says Edmund Bacon, the former planning director of Philadelphia. "Planners had become accustomed to dealing with symbolic representations of the city rather than reality, and it affected the way they thought about things. Maps with different tones of gray represented different population densities, and so people thought in terms of averages. Other maps showed different colors for different land uses, and so people thought in terms of separation. Jane broke down the paradigm by going back to the hot, rich reality of the city itself. She told planners to use their eyes instead of seeing through symbols.

"One of the clear effects of her book was to smash the concept that separation of functions was a virtue. She was proven overwhelmingly right in that regard, and the concept of diversity remains an unchallenged ideal today.

"She did tend to carry things to ridiculous extremes. For instance, her idea that we shouldn't have playgrounds because somebody might get raped in them—that was ludicrous. Many of her particular recommendations sprang from an extremely narrow perspective on urban life that resulted from living in the middle of Manhattan. Her experiences in Greenwich Village were not necessarily translatable to the rest of the country. But overall, she did much to enlarge and vitalize the debate."

William H. Whyte, the journalist and urbanologist who first urged Jacobs to put her thoughts about cities into writing, echoes Bacon's comments. "The disturbing thing about the urban renewal era was that little of the planning was based on actual observation of how people used cities. In fact, I think a great vacuum in planning today is that there's seldom anybody on the staff whose job it is to check up on things and see if they're working. Her book was quite a blockbuster in that respect. She talked about what she saw with her own eyes. Her book was intemperate, as she often is, but planning is the better for it."

Jacobs is generally thought of as a liberal, but she expressed many views in *Death and Life* that today might be described as neoconservative. She believed firmly in economic growth—and in population growth, too. She was against government intervention in local affairs and against bigness in general. She celebrated the traditional and the domestic, emphasizing the importance of self-reliance and local initiative. Above all, she believed that people ought to have control over their own lives.

Against modernism

Her book struck one of the early blows against the modernist approach to planning and architecture, in many ways anticipating the more recent diatribe by Tom Wolfe, *From Bauhaus to Our House.* Like Wolfe, Jacobs was an opinionated amateur whose gift for invective won her a large popular following. Like Wolfe, her appeal and her methods were more emotional than intellectual. Indeed, her lyrical evocation of the joys of city life is one of the chief reasons *Death and Life* retains its appeal.

Its tone no doubt partly explains the widespread aversion to her work among planners and social scientists, even those who did not bear the direct brunt of her attacks. Planners accused her, with some justice, of attributing every evil in the world to misguided experts. For instance, she rejected the suggestion that postwar planners and legislators encouraged low-density suburban housing because that was what people preferred. People said they preferred it, she thought, because planners and legislators encouraged them to.

Her conception of the planner-as-Machiavelli was grating to many in the profession who thought the real problem was that nobody paid any attention to them. "I think she overestimated the power of the planners," says Herbert Gans, a Columbia University sociologist who wrote a good deal about cities and suburbs at the time *Death and Life* appeared. "I always meant to ask her where she got her inflated idea of planners' influence. On the other hand, it's true that planners were pretty sure of themselves in those days."

To this day, many social scientists and urban specialists regard Jacobs's work with scorn. "When I reviewed her book, I said it was a very bad book about a very important topic," says George Sternlieb, director of the Center for Urban Policy Research at Rutgers University. "I don't think much of her work, and I think it's a sad reflection on the field that they're taking her stuff seriously. It's by default of other insight. On a flat plain, pimples begin to look like the Rocky Mountains.

"In the context of the times, I suppose, her insistence that neighborhoods be considered one at a time was an important contribution. But the practical effect was that we built five-story walk-ups in the West Village. [Jacobs led a fight to build a low-rise middle-income housing project in the 1960s.] Her ideas are bourgeois romantic escapism that has a very negative impact as we try to confront economic reality. You can't reinvent the nineteenth century."

Gans is somewhat more sympathetic. "I think academics tend to be critical of freelancers who wander in and take potshots, particularly when they get the details wrong. The overall thrust of what she wrote had some impact. If one looks at the specifics, however, a lot of her ideas were tried without success. For instance, she talked about rehabilitating slum buildings. This had been tried before she wrote her book, and it was tried afterward, and it just doesn't work, except under special conditions. It's too expensive. If you want housing in large quantities, you have to tear things down and rebuild, and that means neo-Corbusian towers."

Gans also disputes some of Jacobs's basic assumptions about how cities worked. For instance, she wrote, "Great cities . . . differ from towns and suburbs in basic ways, and one of these is that cities are, by definition, full of strangers. . . . Even residents who live near each other are strangers, and must be, because of the sheer number of people in small geographical compass."

As a consequence, she thought, the social controls that operate in big cities, e.g., eyes on the street, are fundamentally different from those at work in small towns. Moreover, she believed, many social controls—eyes on the street again is a good example—are dependent on certain physical characteristics of cities.

Gans has his doubts about this sort of physical determinism. "I don't think city neighborhoods are necessarily all that different from suburban neighborhoods," he says. "The important thing is the degree of residential mobility. A neighborhood with constant turnover will be very different from one where people live all their lives, and that's true regardless of where the neighborhood is located."

Gans also feels that Jacobs was "basically wrong" in her assumption that people would flock to big cities if only they were more lively and exciting. "Surveys have repeatedly shown that the number of people who want to live in big cities is small."

But history has been kind to Jane Jacobs on this point. "There is definitely a population that likes the hustle and bustle—the yuppies, to use that dreadful word," Gans says.

On balance, he thinks Jacobs made a positive contribution. "She told planners 'This is how people live—pay some attention.' Others were trying to get the same message across, but she did it better, and she'll be read 50 years from now for that reason."

Her views today

And what does Mrs. Jacobs say about all this? I called her in Toronto recently to find out. Here are some of her comments:

On whether planning has improved. Not where traffic planners, and to some extent even transit planners, are concerned. Traffic planners have not really had any new ideas since the 1930s. They still live in the world of the General Motors pavilion at the 1939 New York World's Fair, no matter how much reality rubs in that if they keep on doing more of what they've been doing, it's just going to make things worse.

That's not true of other planners, or of architects or people concerned with the cityscape or with retrofitting older buildings. I've been enchanted with some of the imaginative, beautiful planning for cities that I see people are capable of—for instance, Harbourfront and the St. Lawrence neighborhood, both mixed-use developments in Toronto.

On separating uses. At the time I wrote my book, there was a lot of emphasis on the separation of uses, which was a very destructive notion. There's been a lot of progress in understanding that segregation of uses is not helpful. Now there's much more appreciation of mixed use, and I consider that progress.

I wasn't against planning per se when I wrote the book. I was against the kind of planning that was being done at the time. The important thing is whether or not you're really interested in cities. Many of the planners who objected to my book were not interested in cities; they were interested in planning. I'm against planning that hurts cities and works against the grain; I'm for planning that helps cities and goes with the grain. I'm not interested in the profession of planning for its own sake.

I was shocked when I first started looking at some of the plans that failed to turn out as intended. I remember one project that was accompanied by a beautiful artist's rendering. After it was built, I was walking through it with the planner, and there was not one soul in the street except for a bored kid who was kicking a tire. I asked the planner, "Why is nobody using this?" He said, "Stand here and look at this corner. Look how lovely the juxtaposition is." He wasn't in the least interested in the difference between the projection and the reality. We came upon another street that was crammed with people. He said, "In the next phase, we'll get rid of this." He wasn't interested in the city; he was interested in planning. The two are not synonymous.

On open space. I stand by my criticism of useless parks. The people who criticized me just don't look at how parks are used. Does it make sense, when city land is so valuable, when there are so many people around, to have parks that are the private preserve of a couple of gentlemen walking around with their hands behind their backs? It's absurd to think that parks can be like country estates. The reality is they're not safe for the solitary user. The less parks are used, the more dangerous they are.

On public housing. That's something I wish the book had had an influence on but hasn't yet. We must figure out how to replan these terrible projects. We can't afford to blow them all up. A lot could be done to knit them back into the fabric of the city. Maybe that can't happen until the present older generation of planners is gone. They have too much of a vested interest in saying they were right. But I think something will be done in time, and I think young people will do it. In Toronto, for instance, "assisted" housing, with a mixture of rent-assisted and market-rate tenants, has been put on small infill lots, so that the buildings are knit into the city, not set apart.

On gentrification. People who are against gentrification in principle have to ask themselves what the alternative is—should the neighborhood continue to go downhill? The trouble is excessive gentrification in certain spots. When there are only a few areas that have promise, of course they're landed on; the supply is too small for the demand. In part that's due to the sins of the older planners. They ruthlessly wiped out the older neighborhoods that people like to move into now. That terribly reduced the supply. I often think of New York—there are a lot of areas in Brooklyn that gentrifiers would have loved. But they're gone.

On density. Creating "eyes on the street" happens most easily when there are a lot of people using the streets. Anybody who's traveling by foot knows that; you don't want to be the only person on the street. But there are ways that eyes on the street can be stimulated in low-density areas, through "neighborhood watch" programs, for example. Having people along the street who take responsibility for it is vital.

People tend to confuse density with the idea of large structures, the way they used to confuse it with overcrowding. In fact, density can be deployed in all sorts of ways. The street I live in is mostly semi-detached houses that look like they're all single-family, but if you canvass for elections it's amazing how many units there are. It's not low density, but it has an attractive human scale.

On being called a romantic. That's a funny thing to say when cities are in so much trouble—to say, in effect, that this is progress, that it's romantic to want it any other way. It's like looking at an eroded hillside and saying, "Well, there aren't any forests here anymore, and it's romantic to want to have more." But the downtowns of cities in other countries aren't empty and deserted at 5:30 p.m. I don't think I'm a romantic about this at all—I think I'm hard-headed.

On cities today. Pretty nearly every city has one or two revitalized neighborhoods. But there are so pathetically few of them—probably fewer today than in 1961, even with gentrification. It varies quite a bit across the U.S. Boston by and large is a good deal better off now. Buffalo is not.

On what she would change if she were to rewrite Death and Life *today.* I can't answer that. It just bores me to think of rewriting anything. It was as true as I could make it at the time, and I hope those truths still come through today. But I've never looked back. In *The Economy of Cities* I wrote about the way one thing leads logically to another. Although I didn't think of myself as being an example of that, I realize now that I am one. I'm interested in going on to new things.

Ed Zotti is a Chicago writer who specializes in planning and design. Copyright 1986 by the author.

Mister Maps: A Profile of John Reps

Ruth Eckdish Knack
(November 1986)

Even at a 7 a.m. breakfast interview, John Reps is irrepressible when it comes to talking about the subject he loves—what bird's-eye views can tell us about American urban history. The setting is a cavernous poolroom cafe in Columbus, Ohio, the only place open so early on a Saturday morning.

The evening before, the distinguished Cornell University planning historian had been honored as "an inspiration to all" by the First National Conference on American Planning History, organized by Laurence Gerckens of Ohio State University. As he always does, Reps drew a crowd to hear his talk on nineteenth-century Savannah, a city that he said has "obsessed" him for over 35 years. He told about his latest discovery, a plan showing 74 squares, suggesting that the city's later expansion followed a pattern set in colonial times.

"I'm still bird-dogging that curious plat," he said recently, which probably means that we can expect a book on Savannah sometime soon. Such a publication would join a long list of acclaimed titles, beginning with *Making of Urban America* in 1965 up to the recent *Views and Viewmakers of Urban America,* and including *Cities of the American West,* cited in 1980 as the year's best book in American history.

Curiously, this scholarly output comes from a man who started his career as a practicing planner, and one oriented to policy rather than physical planning. "My intention was *not* to become an academic," says Reps, who, in fact, never did get a Ph.D., although the University of Nebraska conferred an honorary doctorate last year.

Born in St. Louis in 1921, Reps grew up in Springfield, Missouri, where his family had a dry goods store until the depression and where his father chaired the zoning commission. Springfield was then a town of 60,000, a county seat, centered on a square and typical of hundreds of towns that Reps has chronicled in his books.

In 1939, Reps left for Dartmouth College—a big deal, he says, for a young man from a provincial town. In his junior year, he took the only geography course offered, in North American regional geography, and was hooked on planning. That experience, he says today, makes it all the sadder that there is no geography program at Cornell.

That course led to a senior project, an in-depth study of a Vermont town, and to a job researching the same town for the National Resources Planning Board. In the same Boston office, he says, were renowned planners Roland Greeley and Arthur Comey. "Cats can look at kings," Reps says, "and I sat there looking at those guys."

His report on the town was his first publication, although by the time it came out in 1942 he was in the Army Air Corps, stationed just outside Denver. There, more good luck: an introduction to Carl Feiss, who had just arrived from Columbia University to become planning director of Denver and who, with his wife, "served as a personal USO" for Reps.

Reps's formal planning education began with a long bus and trolley ride to the night course Feiss taught at the University of Denver, and with a course on local planning administration offered through the Armed Services Institute. "By the end of the war, I had already decided to go to graduate school in planning," he recalls. The question was where, for only a few schools offered a program. He ruled out MIT because it required an architecture or engineering degree and a course in surveying. ("I thought life was too short," Reps jokes.) Instead, he went to Cornell, where architecture dean Thomas Mackesey, himself an MIT planning graduate, had started a planning program in 1935, and was virtually the sole teacher as well. Reps notes that the education of planners in that postwar period was spotty, to say the least.

He had another good mentor, though, in Mackesey, whose interests were wide-ranging. In 1947, Reps went to England to study planning law and administration in the Department of Civic Design at the University of Liverpool. He came back to what he describes as "the best postgraduate education in the world," a three-year stint as executive director of the Broome County, New York, planning board in Binghampton.

In the late 1940s, Broome County was a scene of wild suburban growth, sparked by the pent-up postwar housing demand. Reps saw his job both as helping the local towns and villages cope with the results of this growth and, even more important, trying to convince them of the need for planning.

A Fulbright grant lured him abroad again in 1950, this time for graduate studies in public administration at the London School of Economics, where he started—but never finished—a dissertation on the British new towns. When he returned, there was an offer of a full-time teaching job at Cornell. He said he would try teaching for three years, assuming at the time that he would return to practice. But he has been at Cornell ever since, a full professor since 1960 and chairman of the Department of City and Regional Planning from 1952 to 1964. For years, he was the only full-time faculty member—which, he says, "made department meetings a breeze." For the last four years, he has been on a "phased retirement" schedule, generally teaching only one course a semester.

But even while teaching, Reps kept his hand in as a practitioner by serving as a consultant to Upstate New York and Pennsylvania communities, including some of the towns affected by the building of the St. Lawrence Seaway. In the late 1950s and again in the 1960s, he served on the Ithaca planning board, and he was a member of the American Society of Planning Officials board of directors from 1966 to 1969.

The Requiem flap

Reps came to national attention with a speech called "Requiem for Zoning" at the 1964 ASPO conference. It was a polemical call for drastic changes in U.S. land policy to control development on the urban fringe. "Zoning," he began, "is seriously ill and its physicians—the planners—are mainly to blame. What is called for is legal euthanasia, a respectful requiem, and a search for a new legislative substitute sturdy enough to survive in the modern urban world."

Strong stuff. It was followed three years later from the same podium with "Requiem or Renascence?" which suggested a cure: Create a "metropolitan land corporation" with power to buy and condemn. Then lease or sell the land back to its present occupants—farmers, for example—or to developers, chosen in design competitions. Uses and development would be strictly controlled by the public agency. The result, said Reps, would be a way of providing effective public control over urban growth.

It was a powerful argument, vividly and at times humorously expressed. Reps talked about the "planability gap," the difference between what planners are capable of achieving and what they have achieved. Examples of the former: Washington, D.C., and Austin, Texas, both of which were built on land acquired by public bodies. "History would seem to indicate that what I am advocating is neither un-American or un-Texan," said Reps.

Even when writing on policy issues, as in the requiem pieces, Reps revealed his abiding interest in history. For example, he included his old favorite, Savannah, as prime evidence of the value of publicly acquiring and controlling land. His work in these essays and elsewhere seems all of a piece, with frequent references to the British new towns that he studied in the 1950s and, indirectly, to the problems of planning without sufficient authority in Broome County.

And even when his focus was on administration and law—teaching the planning law course at Cor-

nell, for instance—he was reading and writing history. In the late 1950s and early 1960s, he published articles in the *Journal of the Society of Architectural Historians* and the English *Town Planning Review* on early planning in the colonies; on the Detroit plan; and on "oddball cities"—Cairo, Illinois (the would-be metropolis that flopped); Circleville, Ohio (which had a circular plan); and Thomas Jefferson's "checkerboard towns." At the same time, he was churning out articles on subdivision control and zoning boards of appeal. ("Only a half-dozen lawyers paid any attention," he says.)

"Sometime in the 1950s, I began to think there might be a book in the historical stuff," he says. He used a Guggenheim grant in 1958 for seven months of travel and research on early town plans, although the following year he was back to policy studies with an Eisenhower Exchange Fellowship to look at urban development in European cities.

The book that resulted from "the historical stuff" in 1965 was the much-lauded *Making of Urban America*. In it, Reps confirmed what he had long suspected, that not all U.S. cities had been designed to conform to the gridiron pattern. The work showed his prodigious energy. He looked at more than 10,000 U.S.G.S. topographic maps; huge numbers of travel books and map catalogs; and almost all post–Civil War state and county atlases. He also visited most of the towns and cities described, noting that "there is no completely adequate substitute for such field inspection.

"If I had been traditionally trained as a historian, I wouldn't have dared to start with a grand synthesis," says Reps. "But it was useful as an overview. Then I could go back and sink some deeper shafts." In fact, the two books that followed had a narrower focus. *Monumental Washington* (1967) examined the Senate Park Commission of 1901–02, "an administrative case study," Reps calls it. *Tidewater Towns* (1972) is a study of city planning in colonial Virginia and Maryland.

The year 1973 was a milestone. "That's when I had to decide once and for all between history and land policy. I had another sabbatical coming up, and I was applying for two fellowships. One was to the National Endowment for the Humanities to study planning history in the Southeast. The other was to Resources for the Future to study large-scale public land acquisition. Both said yes. I chose NEH. Since then, I have been an extinct volcano as far as the land policy stuff goes."

He seems to have made the right choice. In 1980, the American Historical Association conferred its Albert J. Beveridge Award for the year's best book on American history on *Cities of the American West,* published the year before by the Princeton University Press and recipient as well of a design award from the Association of American University Presses. In the massive, 827-page volume, Reps successfully challenged Frederick Jackson Turner's thesis about the dominant influence of the American frontier.

From policy to planning history to the artifacts themselves—the lithographic "bird's-eye views" that flourished in the nineteenth century—there has been a progression in Reps's interest. "Somewhere along the line," he explains, "the Amon Carter Museum in Fort Worth proposed an exhibit of lithographs of the American West. It led to an essay and a series of lectures on the whole phenomenon of viewmaking." (The catalog was published as *Cities on Stone,* in 1976.)

That experience got Reps interested both in the documents and in the technical and business side of printing. Two years ago, the University of Missouri published the results of his labors in this area in *Views and Viewmakers of Urban America,* a 557-page, $90 book that includes a catalog of 4,500 city views. Hailed as the definitive reference in the field, the elegantly designed volume was included in the annual "book show" of the American Institute of Graphic Arts. In the same year, a series of lectures on lithographic views in the Pacific Northwest was published under the title *Panoramas of Promise.*

Judgment

To people who like their historians—and planners—neatly boxed and labeled, John Reps is something of an enigma. "Some geographers think what I do is geography, some historians think it's history, some planning. Others don't know what to make of it," he says. "The American studies people seem to understand best, because that's by nature an interdisciplinary field."

The Beveridge Award brought new respect but also raised the competitive hackles of some traditional historians. Reps acknowledges that "some people's noses were out of joint when I won," but it's not his wont to worry about others' reactions. Along those lines, he notes that he has a longstanding tradition of not responding to critics of his books.

Not that there has been much negative criticism to respond to. Reviewers have been effusive in their praise. "No one has traced the sequence of settlement in fuller detail across the width of the continent," wrote *San Francisco Chronicle* critic Allen Temko of *Cities of the American West.* And *Views and Viewmakers* drew forth a whole litany of encomiums: "A pioneering study" by "the dean of historians of the American urban lithograph" (*Winterthur Portfolio*); "visual delight, informed analysis, monument to dogged scholarship" (*Western Historical Quarterly*); "a scholarly tour de force" (*Landscape Journal*).

The dissenters are those who feel that Reps sacrifices theory for description, that he catalogs too much and analyzes too little. *Cities of the American West,* in the view of one such critic, is "too much of a good thing." Is it useful, he asks, to go on so long about a "seemingly endless number of gridiron towns"? *Tidewater Towns,* wrote another reviewer, is limited in value because of its author's "preoccupation" with physical plans. And recently, scholars such as Jon Peterson have suggested that Reps didn't understand the "hidden agenda" behind the events that led to the McMillan Plan for the nation's capital, subject of *Monumental Washington.*

One critic changed his mind. In reviewing *The Making of Urban America* for the *Journal of the American Institute of Planners* in 1965, John Hancock of the University of Washington said the book didn't deliver the analytic history promised by the preface. Today, he says, he wouldn't be so critical. "John Reps showed the way in uncovering plans as artifacts and putting them into a historical context. I faulted him for not dealing with the cultural context of planning, which happens to be my interest. But on reflection, I realize that what he wanted to do was to let us see what those plans were and then let us analyze them. That's an enormous contribution."

To all of that Reps has a simple reply. "Reviewers should look at what I do, not what they think I should do. I have written American history primarily from the standpoint of physical development patterns. I have indulged myself. I love it. But my work is mainly narrative history, not interpretive. I used to say that apologetically, but not any more.

"It seems to me important to establish what *did* occur in the development of American cities. So I approach history in a different way than a conventional historian would. I look for the graphic material first. The conventional historian, who relies only on the written word, can get a terribly skewed view. For example, according to his writings, Thomas Jefferson thought cities were terrible places. Yet at the same time he was saying that, he was helping design Richmond and Washington and collecting city plans and views. You have to look at what someone is doing as well as what he is saying.

"I'm not defensive about being 'preoccupied' with physical plans. My emphasis is on the city as artifact, and I think that's an important thing to study."

A young Turk

It was not always so. For Reps started out as an adherent of the views of Robert Walker, the University of Chicago professor who believed that planning's scope should be broadened to include almost all municipal government functions and that planners should be trained as social scientists rather than architects, engineers, or landscape architects, as most were in the 1930s. At Cornell, though, as Reps learned more about physical planning from his fellow students, he started to question those views. "I began to realize that if the Walker principle were carried to its ultimate conclusion, there would be nothing to separate the planner from the city manager," he says.

"I was a young Turk then. I saw the backlog of plans left on the shelf by the physical planners and thought the social scientists could do better. But then I realized that the new breed of planners was no more effective than the old. I also realized that many of the things the physical planners cared about are things we should care about. A city beautiful, for instance. That's a damned good thing to strive toward. A city in which all the social services are delivered efficiently isn't good if it isn't beautiful."

In 1962, Reps took part in an ASPO conference panel on "the qualifications of planners." Taking his cue from an essay by C.P. Snow on "the two cultures" of science and the humanities, he noted that planning was similarly divided between the design-trained planners, the "handicraft culture,"

and the social scientists, for whom computer modeling was becoming an all-consuming interest.

"I am deeply disturbed by what appears to me to be the widening gap of communications between two types of planners," Reps said. He adds today that even though he recently became a member of the computer culture—acquiring his first personal computer—he hopes planning will never lose its "handicraft sensitivity." Good design, he says, can't be reduced to numbers.

Cornell's planning program at one point seemed threatened by just such a communications gap. In 1971, the program split into two departments: policy planning and regional analysis, and urban planning and development. The former offered the increasingly popular social policy and capital budgeting courses. The latter was the traditional land-use program, and that's where Reps stayed until the programs merged again a few years later. Recently there has been talk of moving planning out of the College of Architecture, Art, and Planning into some other college. But Reps describes all of this as "healthy tension."

"If you have unanimity of opinion about how something should be taught," he says, "you can be pretty sure the field is rotten."

In another area, too, Reps's views have clearly changed. In the late 1940s and early 1950s, as a county planner and as a consultant, he was a strong believer in urban renewal. "I was a leveler," he says, "exalted" by the chance to replace the old environment with a new one. By the late 1950s, as a member of the Ithaca planning board, "guilt feelings" about renewal's mistakes started to pop up, and today he sounds very much like a confirmed preservationist.

In the mid-1950s, Laurence Gerckens, who this year retired from Ohio State, took a course from John Reps on the principles of city planning. "There was a lot more history than principles," recalls Gerckens. "And it was that course that inspired me to think about history and later to teach it myself."

Another testimonial: Norman Krumholz, director of Cleveland State University's neighborhood development center, was a dissatisfied businessman in Buffalo when he decided to apply to Cornell's planning program in 1963. "John Reps took a chance on me. He was enormously supportive, and for that, I have always regarded him as a special angel in my life."

And another: Pierre Clavel, now a colleague at Cornell, was a Reps teaching assistant in the early sixties and taught a course with him a decade later. "He was a silver-tongued lecturer," says Clavel. From watching him work, Clavel adds, he changed his own method of research to be less theoretical and more descriptive.

The qualities that make Reps a good scholar are the same ones that make him a good teacher, says Michael Fazio, a more recent teaching assistant, who now teaches in the architecture school at Mississippi State University. "A lecture was a discrete, carefully prepared piece of interesting scholarship, beautifully organized and clearly presented—to a packed class." In 1984, Reps was chosen outstanding planning educator by the Association of Collegiate Schools of Planning.

Fazio also remembers Reps's notably disciplined approach to his work. "I would walk back from class with him, and by the time I got to my mailbox at the end of the hall, I would hear him clacking away at his typewriter. He didn't waste a minute."

A dose of history

The profession needs a "dose of history," said University of Pennsylvania professor Seymour Mandelbaum at last spring's planning history conference. Others agree. Donald Krueckeberg of Rutgers notes that planning history has become a "legitimate" field in the last few years. A big question has been what kind of history is most valuable: social history? the history of the profession? general urban history? John Reps is important because he deals with all three, says Eugenie Birch of Hunter College.

Reps himself can think of a lot of reasons for reading and writing history. "It's part of our cultural baggage, for one thing, and it can give us confidence if we look back and see the successes that planning achieved in the past. I used history when I was writing about land banking, which sounds unAmerican until you point out that Washington and Jefferson stored up large tracts of urban land."

And you can learn from the cities themselves. From Williamsburg, for instance, and its approach to "total urban design." Reps has always been a traveler, and there are still lots of cities that he wants to visit and study: Paris; London ("my favorite city in the world"); and Moscow, where he wants to see what has changed since he was there in 1964. In the U.S., he says, his "spiritual batteries are recharged" every time he visits San Francisco. This spring, he will lecture in China.

Then it's back to Ithaca, where he says he will recover from the trauma of changing offices "after 27 years of never throwing anything away." And more writing: on views of St. Louis and of Washington, D.C., for its 200th anniversary in 1991, and an ambitious project to match up nineteenth-century views of Mississippi River towns with their modern aerial photography counterparts.

Reps and his wife Constance will stay in Ithaca, where "our roots are deep," and where they raised their two children, a son, who teaches computer science at the University of Wisconsin, and a daughter, who is a lawyer in Denver. Reps will continue to operate his unusual mail-order map business, Historic Urban Places, which he started 25 years ago when a Chicago museum wouldn't supply him with a facsimile of a view he needed for a book illustration. More books, more maps—and more inspiration—are likely to be forthcoming.

Ruth Knack is the senior editor of Planning.

Troubadour Babcock

Ruth Eckdish Knack
(August 1987)

If it's not too late for an alternative Supreme Court nomination, here's another one: Richard F. Babcock. Ten years ago, Washington, D.C., land-use lawyer Robert Linowes suggested that the nation would be better off if one of his confreres sat on the high court bench. And who better suited, he asked, than Babcock?

A generation of planners has grown up with Babcock's first book, *The Zoning Game,* published in 1966. In it, he makes the point that in zoning what you see is not always what you get, that the behind-the-scenes dealings and hidden motives of the players—the planners, lawyers, and judges, and the citizens who sit on the boards and commissions—are powerful influences on land-use decisions. "The book had a tremendous impact on the day-to-day practice of zoning," says Frank Schnidman, until recently a senior fellow of the Lincoln

Institute of Land Policy in Cambridge, Massachusetts.

In this volume and three that came after, Babcock chipped away at the legal mumbo jumbo to get at the real motives for zoning decisions. In the process, he helped put a fledgling legal specialty on the map and nurtured a flock of eager disciples. He made the land-use practice of Ross, Hardies, O'Keefe, Babcock & Parsons, the Chicago law firm he has been associated with since 1957, a model for others. And he showed the legal and planning worlds how a nonacademic could bridge the gap between practice and the printed page. Now 69 and officially retired for several years, Babcock continues to write, teach, and—occasionally—practice.

Making of a land-use lawyer

Although he says he knew "since I was a baby" that he would go to law school, Babcock's interest in land use wasn't sparked until, as a first-year student at the University of Chicago, he was asked to prepare a note on zoning in Illinois. "I started to read the cases," he recalls. "It was pretty dull stuff. Every opinion began with four pages of geographical description. There has to be more to it than this, I thought."

And there was. Establishing a working method that characterizes his writing to this day, he decided to look behind the scenes. He visited the city halls of several Illinois towns, searching for documentation relating to the amortization of nonconforming uses. "I found a horrible mess," he says. "No one ever kept any records. That gave me my first insight into the way the zoning system was administered."

His work was interrupted by World War II when, after being classified 4-F, he signed up as an ambulance driver with the American Field Service attached to the British Eighth Army and later the New Zealand Divisional Cavalry in the Middle East. Back in law school, he submitted the long-delayed note on zoning and was told that it wasn't "dignified" enough because the only footnotes referred to minutes of planning commission meetings. It was a foreshadowing of criticism to come.

In 1946, Babcock joined the big Chicago firm of Sidley, Austin, Burgess & Harper and seemed to be on his way to becoming a man in a gray flannel suit. "But I knew even then," he says, "that I didn't want to spend the rest of my life on railroad debentures."

His way out was zoning. He and a friend started their own firm, and Babcock began dropping in at the offices of the American Society of Planning Officials, then still headed by its first director, Walter Blucher, himself a lawyer. His first public job was rewriting a zoning ordinance for the university town of Urbana, Illinois. Dismayed even then, he recalls, by the "ubiquity of the single-family zone," he was surprised to learn that Urbana had none because the professors had always insisted on being able to create an income apartment.

Along the way, he also developed a strong interest in politics—particularly Democratic Party politics—and three times he abandoned the practice of law for a campaign. In 1952, Babcock directed the National Volunteers for Adlai Stevenson, who had been a partner at Sidley, Austin. Two years later, he quit another firm to become assistant campaign manager for Paul Douglas's successful U.S. Senate race.

"Then I really got the bug," he says. In 1956, he stumped the state—unsuccessfully—seeking the Democratic nomination for Illinois attorney general. He followed up with a try for the state senate. He didn't win, but he did fare better in his conservative exurban county than any Democrat before him. Democrats, he has observed, are scarcer in McHenry County than whooping cranes.

But by then Babcock and his wife Betty had five children—eventually, there were six—and it was time to get back to work. In 1957, he began his 30-year association with Ross, Hardies, which, to some extent, was willing to indulge his interest in land use. The firm gave him time off to do the research for *The Zoning Game* after the Ford Foundation agreed to put up some money. For the next several years, however, Babcock worked almost exclusively on public utility matters concerning People's Gas, one of the firm's biggest clients.

He kept up with land use during this time by writing for law reviews and planning journals; taking an active role in the American Law Institute's effort to produce a model land development code (he chaired the land-use subcommittee); and participating in planning association affairs (he was president of the ASPO board in 1970–71).

Always, Babcock's practice has been divided into three parts: litigation, drafting ordinances, and writing. He likes all three, recalling with equal relish courtroom battles on behalf of municipalities and developers all over the country, and taking great satisfaction in the legally defensible documents produced for New Jersey's Pinelands Commission.

But it's the writing for which he is best known—and, he acknowledges, which brought in the jobs by giving the firm's name national exposure. As he puts it, he was the "rainmaker," the firm's point man, a job well suited to his ebullient personality.

Moreover, he proved to be a natural writer, with a taut and witty style. "A poet of sorts," the late ASPO director Dennis O'Harrow called him in the forward to *The Zoning Game.*

In that book . . . Babcock expresses the frustrations of someone who has sat through too many suburban planning commission hearings. "It is my view," he writes, "that the plan commission, except, perhaps in the smallest communities, is a dodo." And the planner? A "schizoid" to whom zoning is "infra dig" and "who really is not sure what he is or what he wants to be."

In *Billboards, Glass Houses and The Law,* a collection of articles, some coauthored by colleagues, published in 1977, Babcock takes on "pretty committees," suburban design review boards that carry the definition of the public welfare to extreme lengths. In another piece, written while he himself was a member of the Northeastern Illinois Planning Commission, he expresses pessimism about the usefulness of metropolitan planning agencies. It's up to the states, he writes, to step in with regional policies—particularly for fair-share housing—and some mechanism for enforcing them, including, possibly, a board to review local zoning decisions.

Turning his attention from the suburbs, subject of most of his earlier work, to urban issues, Babcock collaborated with law firm colleague Clifford Weaver to produce *City Zoning,* published by APA in 1979. In it, the authors propose turning over some local zoning power to the neighborhoods and rethinking some of the more questionable consequences of such innovations in downtown zoning as development rights transfers and special districting.

Another collaboration, with Charles Siemon, resulted in *The Zoning Game Revisited* in 1985. It describes 11 zoning and planning conflicts, including several the authors were involved with. Once again, the focus is on what goes on outside the courtroom. "We believe it important," say the authors, "that lawyers, planners, and laymen understand the bargaining, haggling, and dealing that is part of the game."

In the works now is a book on special districts, with Wendy Larsen as coauthor. Babcock has already started following up a 50-city survey with interviews in New York and San Francisco, the two cities with most examples. Some disenchantment with the technique has set in in New York, he notes, because its provisions are so complex and hard to enforce.

Defense of zoning

Throughout the books runs a basic belief in the continuing usefulness of zoning. Babcock might gnash his teeth in print over an example of particularly inept administration or of the mindless enforcement of appearance codes. He might complain that zoning code-sanctioned "linkage" programs amount to "extortion by exaction," that too much negotiation threatens chaos, and that zoning has become a mulligatawny stew loaded with all sorts of responsibilities it was never meant to have.

"But what would you substitute for it?" he asked in an interview last fall. "Do you want no control over development at all? That would be turning back the clock.

"The problem is the way the process is operated. It's made worse by the fact that most planners are indifferent to process. It bores them. As a lawyer, I believe strongly in due process, in giving a guy a fair shake."

Great Britain, he notes with a wry smile, has found it necessary to reinvent the wheel. Measures recently passed by Parliament have superceded the Town and Country Planning Act of 1947, the law that eliminated zoning and made all development subject to special approval.

The last paragraph of *The Zoning Game* sums up Babcock's views, then and now: "I believe that public regulation of private use of land is worth reforming—saving if you please. There is little evidence in the history of land development in America that the private decision-maker, left to his own devices, can be trusted to act in the public interest."

That's not to say there aren't problems. "It's hard to justify some of the things that are done in zoning's name," says Babcock. He notes that, although this country's first zoning law was passed in New York, it's in the suburbs that it really caught on—often for the wrong reasons. Babcock has repeatedly criticized suburban attempts to block the development of multifamily housing, thus excluding the poor and minorities.

The courts, he has suggested, should become involved in the exclusionary zoning issue and in such related matters as the definition of family—an issue likely to grow in importance, he says, as our population shifts "and we have fewer six-child families."

A particular bugaboo is the use of zoning for purposes for which it wasn't intended, to preserve open space, for example. Be honest, writes Babcock in *The Zoning Game.* If a public agency wants to acquire some open space, it must condemn it and pay for it. What gets us into trouble, he says, "is our ever-broadening view of what is in the public welfare," and thus fair game for the zoning ordinance.

Unnecessary complication is another Babcock bete noir. "Instead of simplifying, we've made everything terribly complex, with as many as eight or nine residential districts, for example. On paper, it sounds good, but it's impossible to administer.

"And we've added condition after condition to planned unit developments. We make developers go through fiery hoops. I represented a developer just north of Los Angeles where the average temperature is 75. But the city insisted that every third house have a fireplace, 'so it would look attractive.' Negotiation is becoming the name of the game. We don't want to have anything as of right any more if we can avoid it." And that, Babcock thinks, is a mistake.

He's equally skeptical of the excesses of exactions. "I have often thought that requiring developers of a new subdivision to come up with additional fees—which they then pass on to the buyers anyway—is a sort of double tax. It's one thing if the developer is told up front what's due. It's another to slip something into the ordinance."

But no matter how critical he is of the way zoning is administered today, Babcock would not go so far as to require governments to pay for their sins with money damages. In this he differs fundamentally with those who criticize zoning from a more conservative perspective—and who applaud the Supreme Court's recent decision in the case of California's First English Evangelical Lutheran Church.

His views on damages are on the record in "The White River Junction Manifesto," a 1984 *Vermont Law Review* article attacking Supreme Court Justice

William Brennan's endorsement of the idea of compensation for "temporary takings" in *San Diego Gas & Electric.* Babcock and his four coauthors seemed to have great fun picking holes in Brennan's argument, which they said was based on a misreading of zoning law and practice. (The authors are listed in reverse alphabetical order: Norman Williams, Jr., R. Marlin Smith, Charles Siemon, Daniel R. Mandelker, and Babcock. In a footnote, Babcock says that's because Williams paid for the breakfast at which the ideas were hatched.)

He's not so sure, though, that the *First English* decision is as significant as some observers have made it out to be. "Two or three times," he notes, Justice William Rehnquist "emphasized that, to be a compensable taking, a regulation must totally destroy all value. Most regulations don't do that."

At one time, Babcock had hoped that the Court would become involved in such land-use issues as exclusionary zoning. Now, after this decision, he says he regrets that he ever said that. He notes that only one justice, former real estate lawyer John Paul Stevens, has a background in land use, and the general lack of knowledge shows.

"Stevens was right when he said in his dissent that this decision will lead to an enormous amount of litigation. And maybe the courts in California—which is so crazy—will find damages a reasonable thing. But there's still no excuse for the decision," Babcock says.

It's hard to pin down a man who holds such divergent views, who sides with developers at one moment and governments the next. But Babcock has always worked both sides of the fence, taking pride in the fact that he calls them as he sees them. While that stance has earned him criticism from both sides, it has also given him a considerable amount of credibility.

"I think many land-use lawyers make the mistake of representing only developers or only public agencies. I see it as an accomplishment that I could be called on by both. I never let my own opinion get in the way of a case."

Gus Bauman, the outspoken counsel to the National Home Builders Association, has known Babcock for a decade. The two are on opposite sides on issues like damages; Babcock calls him one of his "fallen children." Yet Bauman says they get along splendidly.

"We might disagree on this case, but when you

read all his horror stories about the irrationality of zoning decisions in this country, you wonder. *The Zoning Game Revisited* could have been written by Gideon Kanner and Mike Berger [lawyers for the plaintiffs in the *First English* case]. And the chapter on the California Coastal Commission and how it stopped development at Sea Ranch could have been written by any of the lawyers who have been battling the commission for the last 10 years."

Adds Bauman: "Labels like liberal and conservative get you nowhere in land use. It comes down to other ways of looking at things. Dick is not a rabid ideologist like a lot of people who admire him from the public sector. Dick and I are a lot alike. We're pragmatic. We know that neither developers nor land-use planners are perfect."

Harvard law school professor Charles Haar, reviewing *The Zoning Game Revisited,* placed Babcock and coauthor Siemon in the tradition of the "oral troubadour—handing down knowledge from one generation to the next." The description also fits the Babcock working method.

"His idea of doing a book is to set out with a tape recorder and find people to interview," explains Frank Schnidman, who helped Babcock get financial backing through the Lincoln Institute, a Cambridge think tank, for his last book and is doing the same for the forthcoming volume on special districts. Noting that some have criticized the books for lacking documentation, Schnidman adds, "Dick would be first to say he is not a legal scholar. He is a practitioner. But through his writing, he gives people an idea of what has to be done, not what has to be researched."

The case study, "war story" approach was Babcock's idea, says coauthor Siemon. The two divided up the chapters and told the stories in their own way, with Babcock contributing the first and last chapters.

Teachers find the books particularly useful. "The best kind of teaching is understanding that what you are doing is telling a story, and he tells stories," says Alan Weinstein of the Touro College of Law in New York.

He's even better in person, according to Lee Einsweiler, now a planner with a Chicago law firm. In the spring of 1984, Einsweiler was a student in a class taught by Babcock at the University of North Carolina. Since his retirement from active practice in 1982, he had taught for short periods at various universities across the country, and that semester

he was in residence at Duke but drove to Chapel Hill once a week for a late-afternoon planning course.

Einsweiler still remembers the two questions Babcock asked the class to get discussion started: How would you feel, he asked first, if someone bought the empty lot next door and put up an A-frame—on a street of colonial houses. "My first response was to say I would object. But then he asked if the newcomer had a right to build what he wanted. I had to say I wasn't sure."

The second question was whether front yards were needed. "That set us off, all right," Einsweiler recalls.

Begats

As a distinguished practitioner of planning law, Babcock is in a tradition that goes back to Edward Bassett, a prime mover of the nation's first comprehensive zoning ordinance, enacted by New York City in 1916, and of Alfred Bettman, the Cincinnati attorney best known for filing the winning Supreme Court brief in *Euclid v. Ambler Realty,* the 1926 case that held zoning constitutional.

From the start, notes APA executive director Israel Stollman, lawyers have figured prominently in the planning field. Babcock himself acknowledges the contributions of many of these people in his books. Besides Bassett and Bettman, his heroes include treatise writers Arden Rathkopf and Norman Williams, Jr., who was one of the "gang of five" (as Gideon Kanner called them) that produced the White River Junction Manifesto.

One judge is also on his list, New Jersey Supreme Court Justice Frederick Hall, who issued the landmark decision in the first *Mount Laurel* case. Others likely to be on anyone's list of "big names" include Charles Haar, Daniel Mandelker, Robert Linowes, Robert Freilich, Donald Connors, the late Donald Hagman, and a whole tribe of land-use lawyers that has come out of Babcock's firm, Ross, Hardies.

What's unusual about Babcock is that he has combined his quasi-academic pursuits with practice as part of a large firm. By all accounts, he is mainly responsible for giving Ross, Hardies a national reputation in land use. Typically, law firms that handle land-use matters are local, the better to deal with local politics and personalities. Ross, Hardies broke that mold, taking on cases all over the country.

"Between Dick and Fred Bosselman and John

Costonis and Marlin Smith [among the leading lights of the practice], I think it's fair to say that there has been no other firm like it before or since," says David Callies, an alumnus of the firm who now teaches at the University of Hawaii. It was Babcock, say Callies and others, who gave the firm its personality.

But writing ordinances for public clients is not especially lucrative, and at times the land-use section had rocky going. Then in 1983, shortly after Babcock retired, there came a major split, caused by disagreements over how the firm should be run (turning Ross, Hardies into the AT&T of land use, as one observer put it). In that year, Fred Bosselman and Clifford Weaver left the practice to start their own firm, followed soon after by Charles Siemon and Wendy Larsen. Marlin Smith, who died in 1985, was the only one of the big names to stay on, along with two of the younger group, Barbara Ross and Barbara Baran.

That's not the end of the story, though. For Babcock did such a good job of educating the next generation that they have gone out and done likewise. Siemon and Larsen, joined by another Ross, Hardies associate, Brian Blaesser, have begun a practice specifically modeled on the old firm.

"Dick had two rules," says Siemon. "Keep a balance between public and private work and keep writing. We're going to do both." Siemon, Larsen, Mattlin & Purdy now has 30 lawyers in three offices, one in Chicago and two in Florida. Twelve of the 30 specialize in land use.

There are, of course, many other land-use specialists, including Burke, Bosselman, & Weaver; Freilich & Leitner; and a host of solo practitioners around the country, some of them academics like Callies, Mandelker, and David Brower. Linowes & Blocher in the Washington, D.C., area, is somewhat different from firms in the Ross, Hardies mold in that it does only real estate and zoning law and almost exclusively represents developers.

In Hartford, Connecticut, someone who is not a Ross, Hardies alum is nevertheless following the Babcock model. "I measure many of my own decisions about the way our practice should go by what he did in Chicago," says Dwight Merriam, who heads the land-use section of Robinson & Cole.

Merriam jokes that he had always intended to become a planner with a law degree. He changed his mind when he discovered that he could do the work of a planner with the fees of a lawyer. More

important, he says, as a practicing lawyer, "I would be able to do advocacy in court." Robinson & Cole's land-use practice group transcends the firm's department structure, drawing in people from the real estate and litigation departments, among others. Some 70 percent of the group's work is for developers, and Merriam says the practice has become highly profitable. That allows the staff to do a considerable amount of pro bono work for neighborhood and environmental groups.

Merriam's advice to other land-use practitioners in large law firms: "Show that you can be profitable and work efficiently." There'll be no shortage of work, he adds, in the wake of the Supreme Court decisions on damages.

Recently, APA's Planning and Law Division (largest of the divisions) conducted a survey of its 600 members. Of the 40 percent that had responded by mid-June, 120 identified themselves as planners, 95 as lawyers, and 25 as both. To the surprise of division secretary-treasurer Alan Weinstein, "quite a few" of those in the planner-lawyer category were working as planners. Weinstein's theory: "Perhaps being an attorney doesn't allow you to do what planning trains you to do, including following through on long-range problems."

Times change

In the past, in fact, any sort of planner, even one with a dual degree, was likely to be odd man out in a law office. Nancy Stroud of Burke, Bosselman in Boca Raton notes that not too long ago she wasn't allowed to put "planner" on her law firm business card.

Yet today a number of planners are working quite happily *as planners* in law offices. An example is Gregory Dale, the new president of the Ohio APA chapter, who works for Manley, Jordan & Fischer in Cincinnati. Hired out of planning school in 1980, Dale works with municipalities "in effect as an in-house consultant"; does research to prepare for litigation; and coordinates project teams when seeking development approval.

The legal profession is still cautious, however. Dale's firm could not announce his hiring because a law firm cannot be perceived to be doing anything but law. "We are also very careful about not stepping over the line into planning," says Dale, who notes, however, that his law firm experience was accepted by the American Institute of Certified Planners.

Earlier this summer, Babcock addressed the Chicago Lawyers' Committee for Civil Rights Under Law, a group he helped found in 1968. The talk told a lot about him. First, it gave him a chance to show off his wit. "The only lawyer to address God on a first-name basis is Pat Robertson," said the cochair in his introduction. "But if God wants to know about zoning, he asks Dick Babcock."

Responded Babcock, "I deny that the Almighty is constantly consulting me about zoning—although I've had to put him straight once or twice about the difference between a floating zone and a variance. Unfortunately, it doesn't seem to have made much difference to his cohorts down here on the bench."

But the core of the talk was his dismay about the attitudes of today's young lawyers, who, he said, are more likely to ask about retirement benefits than about the possibilities for pro bono work. "We tend to assume that the problems are gone, but they're not. It's time once again to stand up for the rights of those less fortunate than we are," he said.

At home, in Bull Valley, in a part-rural, part-exurban area northwest of Chicago, Babcock has time these days to reflect on such issues. He also has more time for his one hobby—the wildflowers that peek through the woods and blanket the meadows of the idyllic landscape. The property was bought by his father, who died when Babcock was 14. Later his mother lived there. In 1949, Babcock and his family took up residence—abandoning a more conventional suburban life on the North Shore. A covenant on the land protects it from future subdivision.

Supposedly, frail health has slowed Babcock down since his retirement. Nevertheless, in the last four years he has been a visiting professor at several universities, including Dartmouth, his alma mater, and the University of Vermont, where he was this summer. He'll be at Duke next fall and at Florida State University in the winter. He has also been out with the tape recorder for the book on special districts. And he remains "of counsel" to his old firm, now known as Ross & Hardies.

"It's been great sport," he says, summing up a distinguished career, "a hell of a lot more fun than doing railroad debentures."

Ruth Knack is the senior editor of Planning.

For the Record: Planning Commissioners Speak Out

Ruth Eckdish Knack and James Peters
(August 1984)

THE PARTICIPANTS
(Titles correct as of 1984)

Estelle Berman. Chair of the Cincinnati planning commission.

Richard Brown. Former vice-chair of the Tacoma, Washington, planning commission and an architect.

William Forster. Chairman of the Golden Valley, Minnesota, planning commission, and a retired executive with General Mills.

Martin Gallent. Vice-chair of the New York City planning commission and a lawyer.

Kerry Kirschner. Vice-chair of the Sarasota, Florida, planning commission and owner of a fruit shipping company.

Derek Shearer. Vice-chair of the Santa Monica planning commission and director of urban studies at Occidental College.

Kirby Trumbo. Vice-chair of the Clark County, Nevada (Las Vegas area), planning commission and a mortgage banker.

Fred Witzig. Former member of the Duluth planning commission and a professor of geography and urban studies at the University of Minnesota, Duluth.

Planning. Planning commissions have a long history, dating back to the 1920s. But at a time of increasing professionalism, the role of a volunteer commission is not always clear. What *is* a planning commission supposed to be?

Derek Shearer. I worry that many of us are getting bogged down in technical details. Presumably, a planning commission represents some vision of what people want their communities to be like. But we spend a lot of time in Santa Monica making small, nickel-and-dime decisions.

Kerry Kirschner. I have been concerned about the nickel and diming, too. Last week, for example, our planning commission meeting started at 7 p.m. and lasted till 1:30 in the morning. And this is typical. Our meetings are so tied up with zoning and site plans that there's little time to look at the total picture.

We've asked the planning staff to look into establishing a "zoning season," which means that we'd look at all petitions for rezoning during a certain time every six months or even every 12 months.

Richard Brown. I get the idea from talking with other commissioners that almost everybody is in the trenches on rezonings. They take up such a bulk of your time. Tacoma has hearing examiners, who handle most of the documents you're talking about, and the planning commission develops guidelines for the examiners to follow, as well as reviewing the decisions.

Estelle Berman. Almost all planning commissions spend at least some time discussing policy issues. The trouble is that they don't make any final decisions.

Fred Witzig. To me, that's a central problem with planning commissions all over. All of us represent commissions that are advisory only. The Duluth planning commission can be overruled by a simple majority of the city council.

Berman. Two-thirds in Cincinnati's case.

Witzig. No matter what the numbers, the answer, it seems to me, is the same: The planning commission must develop an image and a standing in the community that makes it difficult for the city council to overrule it. I think that's the advantage a volunteer has over someone who's elected.

Shearer. Santa Monica has toyed around with the idea of an elected planning commission. My own view is that if it were at-large, it would be awful. If it were by neighborhood, it might make some sense, but even then you'd be forcing commissioners to go into the whole business of raising money to run for office. You'd be making them into city council people.

Berman. It seems to me, too, that our value is precisely that we're not elected. In our case, the planning commission membership includes both a member of the city council and the city manager. They're both voting members. I see that some of you are surprised, but actually it works very well. We have educated both of them, and we really do think we have more of an impact this way. . . .

William Forster. Several of our council members have been planning commissioners. But we have a peculiar situation. The council, which is nonpar-

tisan, decided to politicize our Housing and Redevelopment Authority, to appoint themselves as the HRA. And the HRA is where new projects originate. Then they come to the planning department as a fait accompli.

Witzig. I wonder whether any of you appear before the city council to explain or defend a planning commission recommendation. I did so sometimes even when I didn't agree with the majority decision. I think every time you do that you improve the image of the commission and make it more difficult for the council to overrule you in the future.

Kirschner. We have good interaction between the city council and the planning commission. Our city commission gets a report of the latest planning commission session at every meeting. And if the city commissioners have a question as to why the planning commission made a decision, they'll invite the chairman or the vice-chairman to a public meeting to explain why the planning board voted as it did.

Berman. We actually lobby council members on big issues.

Martin Gallent. We do, too. We are down at every Board of Estimate meeting. If it is a very heavy issue, the chairman himself is there. Otherwise designated staff people are there, who will tell the members of the Board of Estimate, in advance, what the issues are and why the commission voted the way it did.

Witzig. You make the presentation because you don't want the council to make a political decision?

Gallent. Just the opposite. The role of the city planning commission is a purely bureaucratic one. We put what we think is a rational consensus together. We've talked about all the issues, and we recommend what we believe is best for the city. Now, what is best for the city in our view may not be what is best for the city in a political view, and it's my personal opinion that if it *can't* pass political muster in the Board of Estimate, it shouldn't succeed. We are not elected, after all. We are doing what we think is correct, but if the elected representatives of seven million people say no, that should be it.

Berman. That's a pretty simplistic attitude. I'm not sure I agree.

Kirschner. Yet Martin has a point. In Sarasota, for example, zoning questions are handled by an appointed board of adjustment. The only appeal from there is to the courts. These appeals by law cannot be done by the elected city commission, which I think is grossly unfair because you can't do anything to get rid of the members of the board of adjustment.

Berman. A hearing examiner has the same kind of autonomy.

Brown. But he's subject to political pressure.

Gallent. We've partially resolved that problem. We have a Board of Standards and Appeals, which does the same thing as your board of adjustment. The only appeal from it is also right to the courts. But in the last charter revision, a provision was inserted to allow the Board of Estimate to look at the basis on which the decision of the Board of Standards and Appeals was made. If the Board of Estimate finds that the basis was inadequate, it has the authority to overturn the decision.

Berman. We have three zoning overlay districts—hillsides, neighborhood business districts, and areas of high public investment—that are handled by hearing examiners. The city council is the appeal in those cases.

Kirby Trumbo. I don't know if we're fortunate or unfortunate, but in Clark County, the end of the road is the county commission, which has jurisdiction over all the unincorporated areas—about 70 percent of the county. The only appeal is to the courts, and 99 percent of the courts will not touch the decisions of the commission.

Shearer. There's something I'm really curious about. We spend most of our time as planning commissioners modifying and channeling decisions that have already been made by somebody else—mostly someone from the private sector. What I'm wondering is where the *new* ideas come from.

Gallent. We have found that some of the most creative ideas come from our community groups.

Berman. Or from going some place that you've heard about that's doing something interesting.

Shearer. I'd like to do more of that. I'm always telling developers, when they ask "What do you *want?*" to go look at the market in Portland, or something. And of course they fly right up there, but I can't fly my colleagues up there. I wish there were more good visual materials. There are almost no good planning movies, for example.

Berman. We all feel the need to share creative ideas. We tend to get bogged down, and our staff does too.

Kirschner. A big problem, to back up a step, is

the basic education of planning commissioners. My first thought, when I was appointed to this job, was what the hell do I know about planning. My training consisted of getting a couple of books from the planning director, and then, within a week and a half, I was thrown into a rezoning hearing.

Gallent. You've got to keep after the staff to explain things to you. After all, the commissioners are supposed to be weighing the plans and recommendations that the department brings to you. If you can't understand them, then the guy down the block certainly isn't going to understand them.

Shearer. Finally, at my insistence, we got the staff to use visuals, slides, in every presentation to the commission. So now the audience can see what we're seeing. There's not a lot of material you can show your colleagues. What I've tended to do is copy an article in *Planning* or some other publication and pass it out.

Berman. The technique that we use that I think has helped commissioners most is to divide up into subcommittees. The zoning subcommittee in particular goes into great depth on issues and then tries to translate them for the rest of the commission.

Brown. Our commission takes a kind of parochial view; that what the staff does is its business. The commission sees its job as basically being the level head, the sounding board—giving the staff the broader input it can't get because of its own myopic view. . . .

Shearer. What I hear people saying is that there isn't any systematic way in which planning commissioners learn about all those different ways to do their job. APA certainly took a step in the right direction by making it easier for commissioners to become members, but I still have the sense that most planning commissioners don't feel all that much a part of the organization.

Kirschner. At APA meetings like this, people look at us and say, "Oh, you're a commissioner—what are you doing here?"

Berman. Planners turn up their noses at commissioners, as though they were dummies.

Trumbo. I think APA should provide some sort of training for commissioners, especially for smaller communities that don't have professional staff.

Shearer. At least it should have programs for new chairs, the way Harvard has programs for new mayors.

Forster. I think our staff does a super job of

training. They supply us with almost too much material. Every new commissioner gets a big book that has the minutes of the last six months of planning commission meetings. And we get the comprehensive plan, and the zoning code, and a couple of books on the function of the planning commission. If anybody reads those, I think they get a pretty good training. I have to admit, though, I got more out of some of these meetings here at the conference than out of those materials.

But we're different from some of the larger city commissions represented here. Our commissioners are just citizens who live on the block. There's a low level of interest in what the planning commission does. In fact, I don't think anybody knows who's on it. Most of the people, unless they've got an ax to grind, don't care. I think we have an indifference problem that is quite serious, particularly when we get into long-range projects. For instance, only five or six people show up when we're voting on the comprehensive plan.

Maybe part of the reason for the apathy is that we're so apolitical. We don't have any voting blocs on the commission. There are no developers, for instance.

Kirschner. We have the opposite situation. One member of our planning commission is one of the largest landholders in the city of Sarasota, and a lot of people feel that he has a conflict of interest.

Brown. In Tacoma, the big issue has been *apparent* conflict of interest, an issue that sooner or later is going to affect everybody at this table. The position I held on the planning commission—the architect's position—still isn't filled because nobody wants it. It means that you can't do any work for the city for two years after you leave the commission, and you can be sued if somebody can find a conflict of interest.

Berman. It's that way in Cincinnati, too.

Shearer. California law is real tough on obvious conflict of interest—if you have a monetary interest in the property in question for instance, you can't vote on it. Commissioners in California have to file the same conflict-of-interest statements that elected officials file. But the law is silent on the issue that seems to me where the real conflict of interest comes in. And that is that no city council member in any city is barred from voting on a project of a developer from whom they've received a campaign contribution. So you often have cases where the council overrules the planning commis-

sion and the deciding vote is cast by someone with that sort of conflict of interest. Studies show that something like 80 percent of all campaign contributions to city council races come from people who have an interest in the sale, disposal, or development of land.

Gallent. In New York, we've operated on the thesis that any planning commissioner who has even a suggestion of conflict, something that might not look proper, must disqualify himself before a vote. An extreme example was when we were voting on an issue that directly affected New York University. Another commissioner and I happen to be graduates of the NYU law school and the question came up of whether we should disqualify ourselves even though we weren't involved in this particular issue. It became a cause celebre. We decided that we would not disqualify ourselves because, if we did that, then we didn't know how far that sort of thing would reach.

If you *do* have a conflict, though, the way to handle it is to simply tell the commission's counsel that you will not vote on the issue. You should avoid even suggesting publicly that you might have a conflict. It is essential that commissioners be as free of conflict as possible because if your constituents—the local communities—think you're putting something over on them, you won't have any constituency.

Trumbo. What I've observed in the short time that I've been on my commission is that a good chairman makes all the difference. He's vitally instrumental in making sure that certain conditions are in the motions and in bringing up points that the staff is short on.

Gallent. In New York City, the planning commission chairman is a direct appointee and serves at the mayor's pleasure—and he is the director of the department—and that raises some rather interesting issues. We see the chairman as, in a sense, the mayor's representative on the commission, and that can, of course, present problems. But, on the whole, the system has worked extremely well in New York. In the 15 years I've been on the commission we've been fortunate in getting dynamic, and above all, honest, people as chairmen.

Planning. As a whole, are your commissions representative of your communities?

Witzig. Ours is now, although it didn't use to be. I did a study of our planning commissioners, from the first ones in 1922 on, and I found that only four or five women served until the early sixties. But in the early 1970s seven of our 13 members (our commission is unusually large) were women. An even more dramatic change in planning commission membership is the fact that the representation is broader. The early commissions were dominated by the business community—bankers, lawyers, people who had a real financial stake in the community. That's not true anymore. You also see a lot more retired people on planning commissions, and they bring another perspective entirely, particularly in matters relating to housing and similar issues.

Planning. Do any of your commissions have a quota for certain types of representation?

Brown. Ours isn't written, but there are slots for a "housewife," an educator, a labor representative (because Tacoma is an industrial town), a realtor, and an architect.

Forster. We don't have quotas, but we always seem to wind up with the ex-president of the League of Women Voters.

Kirschner. As I mentioned earlier, we have a large landowner on our commission. In his defense, I should say that he does represent one element of the community. In addition, we have an attorney, a black businessman, and a printer.

Trumbo. We also try to get a cross-section. The chairman of our commission is a woman, and she's also the president of the Las Vegas Chamber of Commerce. Generally, in fact, you get situations where people are wearing more than one hat. But I'm not sure what the point is. I'm not sure, for instance, that I represent the views of the particular area where I live. I probably don't, as a matter of fact. I look at my role as representing the whole area. If we all considered ourselves as representing a particular group or area, we'd all be antagonists instead of protagonists for the good of the whole. Can you imagine what it would be like if every five years the planning commission rolled over completely, and you had different people with totally different ideas?

Gallent. In 1976, when the New York city charter was changed, over the unanimous opposition of the city planning commission, it was decreed that commissioners must be appointed from each of our five boroughs. I felt that was unfortunate,

because when a commissioner comes in, he must understand that he doesn't represent the Borough of Manhattan or the Borough of Queens. He has to look at the entire city. My great fear was that there would be lots of ring kissing. Thank God it hasn't happened. If a developer wants to build something on Staten Island, for instance, he doesn't have to get the consent of the Staten Island commissioner beforehand. If that were to happen, the value of the planning commission would be nil.

Planning. In some of the communities represented here—New York, Tacoma, Cincinnati, Duluth—economic development is a prime concern. How involved is the planning commission in this area?

Witzig. Our community is looking at all sorts of ways to take up the slack caused by the decline in mining. What concerns some planning commissioners, though, is that we may be setting aside some fundamental planning principles and objectives in the hope of gaining a new business. We have to watch out for that, I think.

It's something that's true not just in Duluth, but in other cities as well. Economic development concerns become so dominant that we set aside for short-term gains some of the long-term objectives of planning. And that's where I think the planning commissioners come in. About two years ago, for example, the Duluth planning commission, working with the staff, decided to hold six conferences on the city of the future. They took place last spring and summer, and they were very successful. We brought in people from the outside who could talk about new ideas. Out of those sessions may come answers to some of our long-range concerns—how to develop our Lake Superior waterfront, to name just one.

In general, I think our planning commission is missing an opportunity to get an oar in for long-range planning through the community development process and capital improvements programming. We don't have much to say about either right now. Yet that, to me, is where the action is.

Ruth Knack is Planning'*s senior editor. Jim Peters was formerly associate editor. Joseph McElroy assisted with this article.*

CHAPTER

2

Nuts and Bolts

The phone rings. It's an old friend, the chairman of the planning department at a local university, who needs help with a seminar for students about to embark on a professional career. What are some of the subjects such a course would cover?

To start, I might recommend some sessions on modern drama and on tax shelters (to answer the developer who says there's no way a project can be scaled down). But above all, I'd suggest abnormal psychology—a topic that would help explain behavior at those public meetings where people who have in the past invited you to their homes for dinner accuse you of treason simply because you reported favorably on a minor two-lot subdivision.

In fact, though, none of these topics will show up in the planning curriculum, and for good reason. These are "experience" courses: You learn them only through suffering.

Still, there are skills that can be taught to those starting out on their first planning job. For example, Peter Dorram's article, "How to Be an Expert Witness," deals specifically with testifying in court, but it can be helpful in other settings as well. All planners testify—sometimes informally, as when a boss or client asks them to look at a piece of property to determine how it should be zoned and, after the review, asks them questions on the details. Sometimes the testifying is formal: when the planner actually appears in a courtroom as an expert witness and is subject to prescribed rules of evidence and testimony.

Dorram makes an important point about site visits. Developers are optimists. They see a piece of property and think about developing it. By the time they call to ask about your testifying as an expert witness on their behalf, it has become the best piece of property for whatever they're proposing. What they forget to tell you is that the property is mostly wetlands and surrounded by single-

family houses (if they're proposing warehouses) or by rendering factories (if they're proposing residences).

DEVELOPING A NETWORK

Another lesson for new professionals: Despite claims from all levels of government that they are trying to reduce paperwork, precisely the opposite is true. Applicants now need a myriad of permits from all sorts of agencies before development can occur. In New Jersey, for instance, a proposed development along the shoreline could conceivably require approval from the Army Corps of Engineers and the Environmental Protection Agency (federal agencies); the Port of New York and New Jersey (bistate); the New Jersey Department of Environmental Protection (state); and county and local planning boards.

Both the government planner who must review an application and the consulting planner working for the applicant must know the law that applies to the project in question. In particular, the applicant's planner must also be able to follow the application through each level of government. Here a flow chart is indispensable; it should include "ticklers" noting when phone calls should be made to agencies or individuals charged with each part of the review.

It's also critical for the applicant's planner to develop a network, getting to know the names, concerns, and work habits of the government planners being dealt with. The goal is not favored treatment but rather the information that is needed to clear each step of the application process.

To develop a network, the planner must seek out the key people involved—at their offices, at professional meetings, through mutual friends. That means that, if an application is going to the county planning board, for example, the applicant's plan-

Philadelphia's new downtown plan contains a series of sketch maps showing the city's history. See "Philadelphia Keeps the Faith." Maps: Robert Geddes.

William Penn's grid. The curved lines represent the city's two rivers.

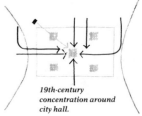

19th-century concentration around city hall.

A survey taken in 1984 showed that 300 communities had adopted some method of saving farmland. Shown here: contour farming used to reduce soil erosion. See "Ag Zoning Gets Serious." Photo: U.S. Department of Agriculture.

The new plan preserves the Chestnut-Walnut corridor as a buffer between the commercial and residential districts.

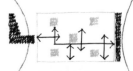

Proposed transit linkages: shuttle buses on Chestnut Street and along the Delaware, and a new subway station.

The 1963 plan led to the Chestnut Street transit mall and renewal of Society Hill.

The five development districts: Market West, Center City East, Broad Street, Parkway North, Delaware Riverfront.

In 1974, residents of Hardin County, Kentucky (right and below right), dumped the planning commission. Ten years later, the county approved an innovative development guidance system. Why? See ''Rebuilding a Rural Constituency.'' Photos: © 1984, Catherine C. Harned.

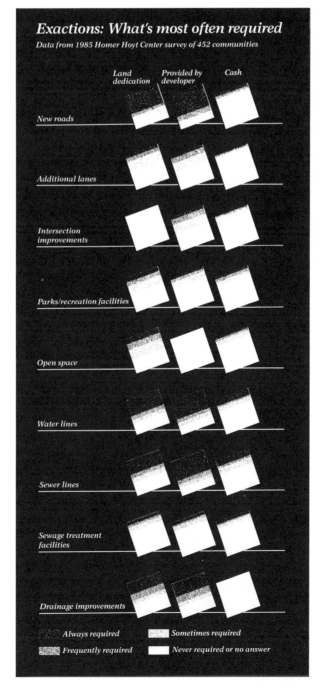

Exactions: *What's most often required*

Data from 1985 Homer Hoyt Center survey of 452 communities

	Land dedication	Provided by developer	Cash
New roads			
Additional lanes			
Intersection improvements			
Parks/recreation facilities			
Open space			
Water lines			
Sewer lines			
Sewage treatment facilities			
Drainage improvements			

Always required *Sometimes required*

Frequently required *Never required or no answer*

Faced with cutbacks in industrial revenue bonds and taxpayer revolts against property taxes, local governments across the country are counting on impact fees and other exactions to bail out their budgets. Recent court challenges are making them nervous. See ''Exactions Put to the Test.'' Chart: Dennis McClendon.

Hand-lettered labels look just right on this handsome map of Rancho Cucamonga, California. See "Tips for Better Maps." Map: The SWA Group.

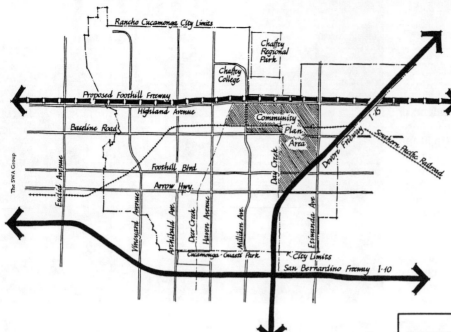

No one is too young to learn about the place where they live. Seattle's KidsPlace project asked local children what they would do if they were mayor. See "Getting an Early Start."

EVALUATION OF SELECTED DOWNTOWN PARKS & PLAZAS COMPARED WITH PROPOSED OPEN SPACE GUIDELINES

NAME OF PLAZA OR PARK	SEATING	SUN EXPOSURE	WIND PROTECTION	LANDSCAPING	WATER FEATURE	FOOD SERVICE	ACCESS
Crown Zellerbach Plaza	●	◐	○	○	○	●	●
Standard Oil Plaza	●	◐	○	○	○	●	●
One Metropolitan Plaza	◐	◐	○	○	●	●	○
333 Market Street Plaza	◐	●	○	○	●	●	○
Bechtel Plaza, Beale Street	○	●	○	○	●	●	○
Pacific Gas & Electric Plaza	◐	◐	○	●	●	●	○
Mutual Benefit Life Plaza	●	◐	○	●	●	●	○
Union Bank Plaza, 50 California St.	○	○	○	○	●	●	○
Steuart and Mission Plaza	◐	○	○	●	●	○	○
Bank of America Plaza	◐	●	●	●	●	●	○
101 California Plaza	●	●	●	○	○	●	○
St. Mary's Square	○	◐	○	○	●	●	◐

OPEN SPACE FEATURE RATING

○ SATISFACTORY

◐ FAIR

● UNSATISFACTORY

"There's no such thing as a flexible plan," says T.J. Kent, a guru of the planning profession. See "Notes on the Master Plan." Photo: Debra Jensen.

San Francisco's downtown plan, covering the area outlined in the photo, set tough standards by putting strict limits on the height and bulk of buildings in certain districts. Existing parks and plazas were rated according to open-space guidelines (chart opposite). See "Fine Points of the San Francisco Plan." Photo: Steve Proehl, San Francisco Convention and Visitors Bureau; chart: San Francisco Department of City Planning.

ner will find out who will be reviewing it and drop it off in person. Developing a network is good practice in government, as in business.

PERFORMANCE ZONING

A second major trend to watch is that of development taking place on land that was previously passed over because of environmental problems, limited access, or inappropriate surrounding land uses. The current paucity of prime quality vacant land has made such parcels targets for development. But the sites may, in fact, be environmentally sensitive and the planner, whether reviewing the application or assisting a client in preparing a site plan, must recognize the problems and devise solutions. The professional may also be called on to help prepare special ordinances and design appropriate standards.

A first step might be to read Lane Kendig's article, "Performance Zoning: An Update on Euclid," although there are problems with this approach. What Kendig recommends is to avoid the bad land and build on the rest. He suggests multiplying the permitted density by the total tract area to determine the total number of units for the site. As long as the minimum open space and maximum impervious surface standards are maintained, he argues, and the units are concentrated in the area free of environmental constraints, the maximum number of units may be built on the site. Presumably, the net density will suggest the type of housing to be built.

But there's a big gulf between reality and theory. Suppose three-quarters of the site is environmentally sensitive. Should the developer be permitted to concentrate all the units on one-quarter of the property? Would the community actually be bailing out a developer who made a poor business decision? Further, not all sites are suitable for all housing types. The buildable area may be so small that a mid-rise structure would be the only way to get all the units on the site. That solution may be acceptable in a city but wrong in a suburban setting. In short, while some flexibility is needed regarding uses, there should also be some sensitivity to the character of the surrounding area.

AUTOMATION AND MEDIATION

A third major change facing the new planner is that much development no longer takes place on a lot-by-lot basis. Many, if not most, proposals are for sizable projects, usually calling for a variety of densities, land uses, and open space. These are complex projects with complicated applications. Approval of the first section often triggers the need to review the entire plan because many of the support facilities (sewerage, circulation, recreation) needed for phase one are contingent on subsequent phases. This situation results in even more complicated applications—and the need to keep track of a vast amount of detail.

That's where the computer comes in handy. Large-scale projects with thousands of dwelling units on hundreds of acres push beyond the limits of conventional (uncomputerized) review and administration. This is particularly true when approval involves more than one level of government, when there are multiple conditions of approval, and when follow-up is needed both in the office and in the field to make sure that implementation is taking place as approved. Four articles on computers and related technology have been included here to help you get started.

Another major change in planning practice is that citizens no longer accept the premise that "government knows best." These days, the public notice of a perfectly legal development application can be counted on to generate opposition by legions of citizens and their attorneys and all sorts of "experts." ("Give me 10 objectors," one colleague recently told me, "and I can get any application turned down.") In such a case, the planner may be thrust into the role of negotiator, as well as (or instead of) the more traditional role of expert witness.

Resolving land-use disputes through negotiation is the newest trend in planning. Planning boards would prefer to consider applications involving little or no opposition. Consequently, it makes sense to eliminate the points of contention before the application is presented. Often, this can be done through a meeting of the municipal planner and the applicant's planner. William Claire's "Winning Through Negotiation" offers tips for dealing with such situations. To his list of suggestions, I would add two of my own:

First, don't promise the world. Tell the parties

involved that you can only make recommendations to the planning board (or governing body) and that you have no approval powers of your own. You can also point out, though, that the planning board often takes your advice.

Second, identify the issues, the major players (organizations, individuals) and the actions each wants to take. A matrix may help you sort out potential solutions: List the players horizontally; list vertically the issues and the actions each player wants to take. This way, you can see how many parties agree on each action and where each will have to compromise. With luck, most of the parties involved will get at least one thing they want.

THE BOTTOM LINE

Perhaps the stickiest problem facing planners today is that they find themselves with less and less money to meet more and more needs. One reason for this situation is that the federal government has for the past several years diminished its role in building housing and infrastructure. Because communities feel that the developer should pay more of these costs, the planner is forced to devise schemes to allocate costs and benefits equitably. The financing of off-tract improvements (often through exactions imposed on developers) has opened new opportunities—and new problems—for planners.

William Fulton's "Exactions Put to the Test," Joel Werth's "Tapping Developers," and Steven Rosen's "Linkage Programs Still Only for a Chosen Few" are worthwhile starting points in a financially complex and legally confusing area. It's important to realize that developer financing of off-tract improvements is not new. Where there is a "rational nexus" (a very close connection) between a development and its off-site impact, developers have always been required to contribute to the cost. Recently, though, the list of items that may be required has lengthened to include housing, schools, and child care centers—and the area included has expanded to cover the entire jurisdiction.

The question is who eventually pays. In new single-family developments where the exaction is used to subsidize housing for lower income families, the buyer paying full price is the one who pays, not the developer, because the cost of the subsidized units is passed along to the more expensive units. Still, planners who must write provisions for exactions into their ordinances should keep in mind that builders won't mind the fees so much if they are also offered bonuses. In fact, New Jersey communities must offer density bonuses whenever they require contributions from developers to fund housing programs.

For insights into some of the problems of exactions, read Robert Ponte's "New York's Zoning Solution." And for advice on the basics, read the articles on writing, ethics, zoning, master plans, and how to run a planning office. On the last point, read Stuart Meck's "Tips for Rookie Planning Directors," taking note of the second tip—the one where he explains how to plan your day.

Finally, I suggest two nonplanning books for your bookshelf. One is the classic *Elements of Style*, by William Strunk and E.B. White. It offers pointers on how to write concisely and is an excellent authority on grammar and punctuation. The other book is one you should carry in your briefcase: your state's municipal land-use law. When meetings get dull, you can pull it out and start to review it, suggesting to your client or employer that you are a wise practitioner well-grounded in legal fundamentals.

Harvey S. Moskowitz, AICP
President, Harvey S. Moskowitz, PP, PA
Florham Park, New Jersey

How to Be an Expert Witness

Peter B. Dorram
(April 1982)

There was a time when a witness needed only an Ivy League degree and a bow tie to be accepted as an expert. Times have changed. To be an expert today, you must do a lot of work, learn certain techniques, and communicate your knowledge in a concise, factual, and legal manner. And, you must do all this at a reasonable price. . . .

I operate on the theory that, in order to be a successful expert witness, one has to be the best informed person in the courtroom—better informed than the client, the opposition, the lawyers for both sides, and the judge. What brought me to this conclusion was a realization that knowledge is power and that the projection of power breeds confidence.

An experienced judge, or for that matter anyone else who is a heavyweight in a particular field, instantly recognizes another heavyweight, another person who is thoroughly knowledgeable in the field. Real knowledge cannot be faked. Thus, it behooves me, the expert, to be the single person in the room who is best informed—who can project that kind of expertise and, hence, see my testimony prevail over others'.

What this means is that, when I estimate my costs as an expert witness for a potential new client, I am never tempted to downplay the effort required. I know that I will not cut corners or content myself with flimsy preparation. On the contrary, the idea is to prepare so thoroughly that there will be ammunition to spare for the all-important conclusion of the case.

Make sure, in short, that your preparation will be superior to that of your adversaries, expert witnessing being primarily an adversary procedure.

To be sure, the expert will lose certain job opportunities because some potential clients are not prepared to foot the bill for such thorough preparation. On the other hand, well-grounded experts will build noteworthy track records by winning many more cases than they lose. Future clients will be willing to pay the going rate for their services to make success more likely in a particular case.

After all, the client who saves a few dollars on the costs of a witness and then loses the case obviously hasn't saved anything.

When to accept a case

As most experienced witnesses have learned, there is no point in hastily accepting or rejecting a potential job. The highest compliment that can be paid to an expert is being hired by a former antagonist. In response to such an inquiry, it is important to find out: What are the facts of the case? When is the hearing? Is the schedule agreeable? Is there a conflict of interest involving the locality or the issues?

The lawyer shopping for an expert witness knows these problems from experience and will tersely describe the time frame, the problem, and the situation so that, if for any reason a collaboration is not possible, little time will be wasted at this initial stage.

A planning expert often has to inspect the site in question before being sure a case can be accepted in good faith. Well-established experts may stipulate in such instances that the time spent for inspection will be billed at the customary rate should the case not be acceptable; otherwise, the cost will be absorbed in the overall fee.

In the field of community planning, as in other fields, professional ethics demand that the expert not be a human chameleon, changing views from case to case. Thus the expert occasionally has to back off a case if he feels he cannot represent the client's interest wholeheartedly.

Let's say, then, that an expert can represent a client in good faith. The next step is to estimate the time that will be needed to conduct field surveys, prepare photographs and other exhibits, conduct miscellaneous research, attend conferences with the attorney and other witnesses, draft an outline of the testimony, and actually deliver the testimony.

Hourly rates

The cost estimate will reflect the time allotted for the job. In most cases, the attorney will act as a go-between and will discuss the fee with the client. Only in very large law firms, and in very large cases, will the attorneys have a free hand to accept or reject the proposed fees of the miscellaneous expert witness.

The fees for a major witness in a typical zoning case could range from $2,000 to $20,000, with $3,000 a likely average. An hourly rate of $75 to $150 is common for heavyweight lawyers and miscellaneous experts-at-large.

There are variations on these costs. The real estate witness may not charge a fee at all for expert testimony—provided no extensive preparation is involved—with an understanding that, if the application is approved, that firm will get an exclusive listing of all the disposable real estate that the project will generate.

Similarly, some architects indulge in free preliminaries in anticipation of having a captive client for a multimillion-dollar project later on, but this practice is frowned upon by the American Institute of Architects and many practitioners. Finally, there are a few witnesses—and they are good ones and reputable ones at that—who have developed methods of testimony that require no substantial preparation. Such witnesses will charge considerably lower fees than the ones mentioned above.

One way to save money for the client is to cut down on the paper flow. Over the years, I have found that a lot of correspondence, drafting of contracts, and so on can be eliminated very simply by adding two sentences and some space for signatures at the bottom of the letter of proposal. For example: "If the above proposal meets with your approval, this letter can also serve as our agreement. Please sign in the space provided below and return one copy to us along with the retainer fee."

Those sentences are followed by the company name, the signatures of the principals, and the date. Then comes this phrase: "Authorization to proceed with work items as per scope of services I through X above," and the amount of the fee, followed by the client's name, spaces for signatures, and the date.

While this might not be the most sophisticated way to contract for professional services, I have found that not a single problem has arisen out of the informality of such agreements.

Preparation of the case

Following is a description of the preparations for a planning testimony in a typical zoning case.

• Step 1: Ordinarily, whatever information is readily available has been accumulated by the client's attorney, who started a file when the client first made the approach. It is logical, therefore, for the expert witness to begin with a visit to the attorney's office to obtain a copy of the application or brief that may already have been prepared and to obtain property maps, tax maps, topographical maps, site plans, deeds, and other pertinent documentation that could provide a basis for the development of the case to follow.

• Step 2: Next is a visit to the site (unless the site was visited before the case was accepted). This step is the most important of all because the expert can be sure that the head of the commission, the judge, or the cross-examining attorney will ask whether the site has been visited. If for any reason the answer is no, it is the end of the case so far as that particular witness is concerned. The entire testimony will be discounted.

• Step 3: The third step might be a visit to the municipal building or county or state offices to obtain any existing materials such as tax maps, zoning maps, and master plans. A most informative exhibit can be prepared by an ingenious expert from common, everyday sources. It is really the function of a good witness to provide illuminating information in an interesting and attractive form so that the expert's audience—a commission, judge, or board—will be better informed.

Surveys

One of the most interesting exhibits in planning litigation is the existing land-use survey, with its findings recorded on a composite of the official tax map sheets. Ordinarily, a single property and its immediate environs will fall on two or more official sheets.

The sheets can be spliced together in the drafting room to form a base map on which the land-use survey findings are entered. The various land uses (residential, commercial, industrial, public, vacant, utility, and so forth) are indicated in bright colors, and variations on each use are shown by different shadings. The objective is to make it easy for board members or a judge to view the exhibit from a distance.

Invariably, I have found hidden messages in these maps. The experienced eye can detect the past and present trends in land developments, which very often are independent of any zoning ordinance. Time and again I have found that the recording of the land use and its analysis is virtually indispensable in planning and zoning cases.

I have also discovered that interesting correlations appear when I juxtapose a series of photographs that I have taken at a site (depicting the land uses as the camera sees them—traffic conditions, road conditions, neighborhood) with an aerial photograph taken from a height of several thousand feet and enlarged to a scale of one inch to 400 feet.

These photos should also be compared with the land-use survey exhibit. To the expert, a stream of messages will flow from the analysis of land uses, the site photographs, and the aerial view.

Master plans

It's a safe bet that a lot can be learned by studying a community's formal master plan as well as those of the county, the region, and the state. Each will present in a rather orderly form—both in narrative and in maps and diagrams—the intentions, the aspirations, and the decisions arrived at in the jurisdiction. These studies, in turn, will yield exhibits related to the site in question—which might be in dispute in a particular case for alleged failure to adhere to the master plan in such areas as road improvements, community facilities, land uses, or zoning.

From all these comparisons evolves the testimony itself. This, of course, is where the good expert will be spellbinding.

Watching good testimony is like watching a spider weave a web. When it's all complete, one marvels at the symmetry and perfection and says, "But where did it come from?" This is the same kind of surprise and admiration an accomplished expert witness will elicit from his audience.

I used to hold my breath when watching the late Jack McCormick, one of the leading environmentalists of our age, testify before a public utilities commission or other bodies. I once witnessed a stunning performance Jack gave before the New Jersey Public Utilities Commission.

That time, testifying on behalf of an electric company, he proved (to everyone's astonishment) how the ecology of New Jersey's fragile Pinelands would be enhanced by permitting development of a high-tension power line at the perimeter of a series of state forests and conservation areas. His testimony was so excellent that no objections were entered and the line was approved.

The expert witness's role is to impart specialized information to a court or a board. A well-prepared, experienced witness will perform this task factually, impartially, and professionally, thereby making everyone's life a lot more efficient and agreeable. As a result, such an expert will be in great demand, will gain experience and insight, and will continue to grow professionally.

© *1982 by Peter Dorram. Dorram, AICP, a planning consultant in Totowa, New Jersey, has had 30 years' experience as an expert witness.*

Performance Zoning: An Update on *Euclid*

Lane Kendig
(November 1977)

Zoning has been knocked for many reasons, and the knee-jerk reaction of planners all too often is: "Zoning is alive and well in my town." It is easy to understand this reaction since zoning remains the major tool of planning at the local level and one of the most powerful.

The fact that zoning is alive does not necessarily mean, however, that it is well. If planning is to be meaningful, then planners must be able to take criticism, thoroughly evaluate zoning's weaknesses, and develop a better form of zoning.

That has happened in Bucks County, Pennsylvania, and now is occurring in Lake County, Illinois. The change began with an evaluation of the performance of existing ordinances and led to the formulation of a new type of zoning. Called performance zoning, the new system was designed to deal with many of the severe problems that have plagued Euclidean zoning over the years.

One way to evaluate zoning is to review the history of zoning in your community or in neighboring communities. The results are interesting. The first zoning ordinance in the community usually contains a simple map with a small number of zoning districts. Look at the zoning maps developed over five-year intervals. You'll see a proliferation of zoning districts. The zoning map has become increasingly spotty in character.

Large, uniform zoning districts are broken down into smaller districts that are all mixed together. Relationships between neighboring districts lack good planning. One has to ask: Is the plan that results at the end of 20 years anything like what the community set out to achieve? Or has the community simply reacted to various pressures and changed its zoning on the basis of personal beliefs and prejudices? It seems to me that zoning, as it is now practiced, is an ad hoc procedure with little relationship to planning goals.

Similar conclusions can be drawn by sampling a cross section of zoning maps from the center of an urban area out to its rural fringes. In the rural areas, you will find rather simple zoning maps that appear to have some logical basis. Toward the more built-up urban areas, zoning maps become a hodgepodge, influenced more by highways than good planning. Zoning consistently has failed as a planning tool.

Another way to evaluate a zoning ordinance is to look at the plats and land development proposals presented by developers. How often are these plans criticized by both the planners and the elected officials as not meeting the needs of the community? How often does the planning commission hassle developers to lower the density or to eliminate units? How often do we find the ordinances unable to cope with environmental problems of concern to planners and citizens? How often is traffic congestion a major issue in plat approval?

For each of these thoughts, a planner must ask himself: Does the zoning ordinance truly provide any assistance in dealing with the issues before us? The answer most probably will be that the zoning fails to deal with important issues.

My conclusion in evaluating zoning is that, while it should be the keystone of plan implementation, it has been a colossal failure in that role. The task is to create something to replace traditional zoning. Performance zoning is such an option.

Bucks County

Work on performance zoning was begun in the early 1970s in Bucks County, Pennsylvania. The county planning commission often had served as consultant to several of the 54 municipalities within the county, and staff planners had written a substantial number of zoning ordinances. I was a planner in Bucks County at the time and served as community planning director from 1972 to 1976. In the late 1960s, the county had drawn up several zoning ordinances using the land-use-intensity system as a basis for higher density zoning. The actual projects built according to those standards were terribly disappointing.

When planned unit development became popular, a new model was developed. Our initial experiences left substantial room for improvement: We found, for example, that the wording of environmental sections and site analysis and design criteria, whether written by the county or a consultant, led to confrontations between the developer's

planners and the local planners. This experience and others led to performance zoning.

One of the basic goals of performance zoning was to make zoning environmentally sensitive, something we achieved with only partial success in our planned development ordinances. Except for floodplain and sedimentation regulations, most ordinances failed to consider the environment.

A second important concern was the quality of design. Conventional zoning and even the planned development ordinances force cookiecutter design. The number of restrictions on lot size, building, spacing, density, and so on left the designer with little or no flexibility in working with the individual site and getting maximum density.

An important consideration in performance zoning, therefore, was to provide designers with enough flexibility to use their skills rather than to hamstring them with regulations that usually ensured mediocrity.

A third major goal was to address the exclusionary zoning cases that were becoming frequent in the state of Pennsylvania and in Bucks County in particular.

The term performance zoning was taken, of course, from the use of performance standards in industrial sections of zoning ordinances. The idea was to create performance criteria against which a plan could be judged and for which fairly simple tests could be made to see if the plan met the objectives of the ordinances. Differences of opinion in such areas as environmental protection were to be eliminated.

At the heart of performance zoning, as developed in Bucks County, were three criteria that specified the intensity of use in a district. Those criteria were density, open space ratio, and impervious surface ratio.

The density established and the imperious surface ratio were maximum measurements, while the open space ratio required was a minimum. Within each district, however, all types of dwellings, from single-family homes to apartment buildings, were permitted.

The standards in any zoning district thus provided the developer a wide variety of options for getting the most out of his density. There was flexibility in housing types and in the ways the units could be fitted on the property.

Use of three performance standards, however, meant that any one of them could be the controlling factor for a given proposal. For example, the selection of a given type of dwelling unit might mean that the minimum open space ratio would be reached without achieving the maximum density. Another dwelling type might reach the maximum density without approaching the limits on open space. Similarly, the choice of building large luxury dwellings might mean that the impervious surface ratio was exceeded before maximum density was reached.

For any proposal, the developer was free to alter his mix of dwellings to enhance profits or reach a specific market. These criteria are all easily measured and can be evaluated easily by a planner, landscape architect, or engineer—much more easily, in fact, than the difficulties encountered in trying to enforce noise vibration and other standards often found in zoning ordinances.

This new zoning concept was . . . first adopted in 1974 in New Britain Township, a Bucks County municipality. . . . In New Britain Township and Buckingham Township, performance zoning resulted in the elimination of most residential zoning districts. Only one or two residential classifications remained. However, a variety of densities was possible because in performance zoning the ordinance required a calculation of the environmental carrying capacity of each site.

The result was a dramatic shift from conventional Euclidean zoning. No longer did one turn to a specific page in the zoning ordinance to determine the density and value of property. The environmental calculation required the use of soil maps and other material to identify the carrying capacity of each site.

Specific open space ratios were developed for each of the natural resources that the community felt it important to protect. For example, floodplains were to remain 100 per cent open space, and forest was required to remain 80 per cent open space, with development permitted on only 20 per cent. The zoning district specified a maximum density to be applied to the buildable area of the site, and the calculation determined what portion of the site was buildable. Thus, within a single zoning district, individual properties could vary in gross density, depending on the resources present.

This concept is sympathetic with the design process taught in landscape architecture schools. Nonbuildable areas of the site are eliminated, and development is clustered on those portions of the site that can accept it. The process can be measured; calculations, which appear somewhat lengthy and confusing at first glance, can be done in less than 15 minutes once the characteristics of the site have been determined and measured. The calculations are easily checked by the municipal engineer or planner. Realtors and builders have quickly adjusted to the process. Now they obtain preliminary estimates of carrying capacity before determining an asking or purchase price.

In Bucks County, performance zoning was related largely to residential development. Overall, it seemed that design quality improved, and substantial progress was made in environmental protection. In addition, a wider variety of housing was being built in the county after these ordinances passed.

Initially, the Bucks County system did not deal with commercial, industrial, or other nonresidential land uses. It becomes evident, however, that the problems of other districts were similar to those of residential districts, and performance zoning seemed an appropriate solution.

It also became evident that many districts could be eliminated and the ordinance simplified by greatly expanding the permitted uses in each district and developing additional performance criteria. An analysis of many municipal zoning ordinances showed there was little logic in the placement of residential districts. Further, there was minimal protection, even though in theory the zoning classifications were supposed to segregate and protect one type of use from another.

One attempt was made to use performance zoning for regional shopping centers. As might be expected, the open space ratio was valueless for assessing nonresidential properties. On the other hand, the impervious surface ratio could serve the same purpose. Other problems, such as signs, transportation impact, lighting, and parking standards, were addressed on a preliminary basis in the Plumstead Township Planned Shopping Center Ordinance. It became evident even to elected officials that it was possible to do away with most conventional zoning districts.

Buffers

Performance zoning also addressed the question of protection of uses from one another. Frank Lloyd Wright, in commenting upon an architect whose work did not meet his standards, said that "greenery would hide a multitude of sins." This idea is the basis for the concept of a buffer yard.

In many zoning ordinances, a buffer yard is required along boundaries where commercial or industrial districts meet residential districts. Unfortunately, there has been little or no scientific study used in developing such standards. Often, in fact, it was decided arbitrarily that a certain number of feet of buffer yard should be provided or that a row of trees or hedges should be planted along the property line.

The buffer yard concept is one of the major areas of performance zoning still under study. Basic is the assumption that it is possible to develop a hierarchy of land uses from the highest and best to the lowest and worst. Such a hierarchy would rank uses much as we do presently with conventional districts. Next, a matrix would be created to indicate the level of buffer appropriate for one use against another.

Once an appropriate buffer for each of these uses is developed, an additional problem develops: how to provide some flexibility. For example, study might show that two rows of evergreens in a 50-foot buffer are appropriate between residential and a certain type of commercial use. That buffer yard may be workable on a property of 20 or more acres but becomes impractical on a one- or two-acre site in an older community.

Our research now has reached the stage where we can tentatively suggest a classification of uses. Further, for each class of buffer yard, a series of buffer alternatives ranging from a structure such as a wall or a berm to a largely unplanted open space would be available to the developer.

There are four variables in buffer designs: structure or land form, distance, type of plant material, and intensity of plant material—all of which can be used in different ways. Buffer yards, therefore, are a tool to reduce the number of zoning districts in a community.

Most suburban communities need relatively few zoning classifications. These might include nonurban uses such as an agricultural district, a conservation district, a scenic district, or a wilderness district—all of which would have little building and high open space ratios and low impervious surface ratios. The idea is to preserve the resources for a long time. Both agricultural districts and conservation districts have been established in Bucks County municipalities.

Such districts allow enough development to guarantee the landowner a reasonable use of his property—thus possibly avoiding the taking issue as a major concern. A district similar to these nonurban districts might replace the conventional large lot zoning districts used in many suburban areas. These districts, however, might change to allow more urban uses at regular intervals—for example, every five years.

In general, by setting up a single development district tied to a five-, 10-, or 20-year capital program, a community could identify land suitable for intensive uses over a period of time. In theory, the land could support any of various urban uses, depending on performance criteria.

Several key performance criteria are required. The first is a site capacity calculation based on the natural resources of the property. Performance zoning already covers this base. This calculation must be supplemented by a similar calculation that deals with the manmade environment or infrastructure—roads, mass transit, sewers, schools. The buffer yard system described previously would deal with those land-use questions other than infrastructure questions.

The basic design standards of the entire ordinance require critical review. Landscape requirements, road widths, and lighting requirements are a few of the standards that must be assessed. Traditional performance criteria on noise vibrations also may be needed. In reality, several districts may be needed, mostly because of people's reluctance to change. There is one exception: already developed areas. . . .

Road standards

There are many other areas in which zoning purports to regulate the quality of the living environment. Standards for roads and setbacks are an example. Most of these standards are rigid, and many of them regulate in such a manner as to ensure mediocrity.

Our research in developing performance zoning led us to the conclusion that existing standards in many suburban zoning ordinances often were borrowed from other cities without any thought as to their adequacy for the community adopting them. Some standards are so excessive that they are difficult to relate to the public health, safety, and welfare, and some are simply rule of thumb measures. What road width is required for the amount of traffic? Do we need, for example, a 30-foot cartway or a cul-de-sac? Does the road need curbs and storm drains? To develop more appropriate standards for streets, we are evaluating such variables as the number of dwellings or generating uses on a road, the frontage of each, the speed at which the road is designed to operate, the volume of traffic, safety factors, the need for on-street parking, and trip-generation characteristics.

Likewise, certain minimum design standards need to be written into ordinances. Several alternatives should be provided, since rigidity usually creates monotony and ultimately promotes mediocrity. Further, statements are needed regarding the purpose of the regulations, and ground rules should be specified for granting variances based on design.

We also must look at how uses are classified and attempt to evaluate what we are trying to achieve. Various industrial uses, all classified in a single district, may have very different impacts on their neighbors, depending on the design and layout of the buildings and such factors as lighting, advertising, parking, and landscaping.

Signs can be aesthetically pleasing, particularly when well designed and well placed. Can we not do this in our towns and along our major highways? It is possible to permit a variety of signs but to require buffering and setbacks to reduce their nuisance effects. Lighting also can be designated to use a wide variety of heights, types of locations and light sources, and buffering.

In any event, the classification of uses as to the degree of obnoxiousness can be done in the traditional way. Or the uses can be evaluated by their performance in a number of areas. Admittedly, this is a difficult job requiring rethinking of our normal mode of zoning, but it can be done. This system has the advantage of providing adequate protection while permitting the developer options.

Today the developer can get away with the adverse effects of sloppy design details. Neighbors pay the costs of screening them out with fences or vegetation. The performance approach would preserve choice for the developer but make him evaluate in economic terms the effects of his decisions.

Lane Kendig, AICP, was director of community planning for the Bucks County (Pennsylvania) Planning Commission and planning director of Lake County, Illinois. He is now a planning consultant in Waukegan, Illinois.

Winning Through Negotiation
William H. Claire III
(July/August 1983)

Most planners will be placed in a position to negotiate the details of a development project at some point in their career. Public sector planners already are familiar with the negotiating process. And now, private sector developers are beginning to hire planners to represent them in negotiations with public agencies.

For both sides, the following "Ten Commandments"—derived from my own 25 years of experience in negotiating development as both a public planner and a private sector consultant—can be helpful.

1. Negotiate in good faith and meet the other party's bottom line. Negotiating when you know there is no solid basis for agreement is the best way to poison a relationship. The party that does not come to the bargaining table in good faith will be unmasked quickly. Worse, the unmasked party can count on the story being told far and wide; future negotiations will surely be tainted.

If, conversely, each party tries to talk in terms of the other's interests, conflicts usually can be resolved to mutual satisfaction. The secret is for each party to recognize the opposite party's bottom line position—what is needed to ensure profit. For example, in negotiations on density, I have often asked developers to share their data on land cost so that I can understand their needs. Often, I can actually show a developer how to increase his profit and at the same time meet with many of my objectives.

2. Don't skin your opponent. In *Winning Through Intimidation*, Robert Ringer says, rather cynically, that if you treat your opponent gently—if you sandpaper him—you'll probably have a chance to sandpaper him again in the future. But if you seek to destroy him—to skin him—you could have a determined enemy who will take care never to place himself in a vulnerable position again. There is no percentage in utterly destroying the other party in a negotiation.

3. Do your homework. Organize and anticipate. Size up your opponent's track record beforehand

and anticipate the general direction issues will take. Before even the simplest negotiation on a development proposal, discuss the matter with other planners, review the possible political implications of the negotiations, and decide on your strategy.

4. Remember that you're dealing with creatures governed by emotions. You have to understand the motivation of the party sitting across the table. Move slowly in the discussion until you have a good sense of what that motivation is. And practice the four important arts of communication: responsive listening, being enthusiastic, stifling criticism, and giving praise where possible.

5. Don't have a hidden agenda. If you intend to ask for something, ask for it early in the negotiations. Anyone who has been involved with development bargaining has heard the classic afterthought that begins: "Oh, by the way, you won't object if we. . . I know we didn't discuss it, but . . . ." Most often it's the side that has lost the most that throws in these zingers. The result may be that the entire deal becomes unraveled.

6. Identify all the issues upfront. Don't tell a developer "Maybe" or "We'll see" if you know that what he's asking for is against the code requirements. Recognize that there are limits beyond which it is not possible to give. For instance, a developer might be shocked at a higher parking requirement than typical for a particular project. Obviously, the public planner can't change the requirement. What he can do is help the developer work out a solution, perhaps by modifying his site plan.

7. Don't get mad. "If you want to gather honey, don't kick over the beehive," says Dale Carnegie in *How to Win Friends and Influence People.* Occasionally—but only under carefully controlled circumstances—a deliberate temper tantrum can be a useful negotiating ploy. But the frequency of such events should be about the same as a total solar eclipse.

If anger flares up unintentionally in your role as a negotiator, you run the risk of losing not only all gains, but also credibility with the other side and any good will that has been built up during the negotiations.

A corollary to this commandment is never to bluff the opposite party if your bluff can be called. If it is and you lose, you lose face, credibility, and probably deal points. You may even render your-self permanently ineffective as a negotiator on that project or with that developer.

8. Know your limits. Every negotiator can only make a commitment up to a certain level on behalf of his organization. Nearly always, a deal is subject to review by someone higher up in the public sector—the planning director, planning commission, or city council. That's also true on the private side, where an architect or agent acting on behalf of a developer usually does not have latitude to commit his client to changes in a site plan or development proposal.

If time is a problem—and it usually is—it is incumbent on the public planner to recommend a full negotiating session with higher-ups present from both sides.

9. Observe the attorney-to-attorney respect rule. This is Robert Ringer's rule. His advice, in short, is to use an attorney to catch an attorney. That means that if the developer brings his attorney, you must have yours there, too. Otherwise, you're likely to lose on crucial points.

The opposite approach is to keep all attorneys out of the negotiations. In that case, you would seek legal counsel simply to confirm that what you want to do is legal.

10. Keep the negotiating package intact. This commandment is both a strategic and a tactical consideration. The main point is that you have to settle at some point. But you shouldn't negotiate piecemeal.

With the benefit of hindsight, one can examine every negotiating experience to pinpoint the ingredients that made for success. Ask yourself the following questions. The answer to each should be yes.

● Was something worthwhile received in terms of interpersonal relationships? In other words, would each party be comfortable if the negotiations were repeated?

● Did each side gain something from the encounter?

● Could each side have gotten more than it actually did?

● Did the parties on each side come away with their self respect largely intact?

● Could the negotiations have taken less time?

● Were both parties creative? In other words, did they develop alternatives and options that led to a successful settlement?

• Was the settlement implemented?

William H. Claire III, AICP, is president of Claire Associates, a planning consultant firm in Palos Verdes Estates, California.

Exactions Put to the Test

William Fulton
(December 1987)

Between February and October of this year, the Newport Mesa School District in Orange County, California, raised more than $1.3 million—about $81 for every student in the district—by imposing fees on local construction.

The fees ($1.50 a square foot on residential development, 25 cents a square foot on commercial and industrial projects) are supposed to help the school district come up with local matching funds for state school construction grants. But even though elementary enrollment is increasing, total enrollment remains stable at about 16,000 and the need for new schools remains questionable. The district has more than a dozen empty elementary schools, and the district's finance director says that most of the money will be used to upgrade high school science labs.

Legal under a package of bills passed by the California legislature last year, Newport-Mesa's development fees are being challenged in court by local builders, who say impact fees shouldn't be allowed when new growth doesn't have an impact. "Where's the link?" they ask.

The California example is not unusual. Throughout the country, pressures are growing on local governments to increase exactions on new development—to demand that developers provide land or public facilities or pay fees to handle the costs of growth in exchange for permission to build. With local jurisdictions unwilling or unable to raise taxes or float bond issues, exactions are one of the few tools both legally available and politically acceptable to handle the costs of growth.

Faced with such demands, local planners are hard pressed to answer the "Where's the link?" question. State courts have always required a "reasonable relationship" between the development in question and the exaction being demanded, partic-

ularly if the exaction is a fee. But following the U.S. Supreme Court's ruling in *Nollan v. California Coastal Commission* last June, the exaction linkage issue has become hotter than ever. Today, unless a direct link can be found, an exaction may be deemed to violate the U.S. Constitution.

Impact fees and other exactions nationwide are raising some $1 billion a year or more in cash and public improvements. The exact figure is hard to pinpoint, but regional estimates suggest the scope. In Florida, James Nicholas, an impact fee consultant associated with the University of Florida, estimates that impact fees are raising $345 million a year. Before the California legislature passed the school fee legislation last year, advocates estimated it would raise $200 million to $400 million, although they now believe the figure is lower.

A 1985 survey by Florida State University's Homer Hoyt Center (sponsor of an APA book, *Development Exactions*) indicates that for several decades the most common exactions have been requirements for new roads, water lines, sewer lines, and drainage facilities. But the fastest growing—and most talked-about—type of exaction today is the fee on new development, often called the impact fee. Once limited to payments in lieu of providing parkland or a sewer system, impact fees now include payments to cover the cost of additional roads, schools, libraries, affordable housing, and transit systems. . . .

Double bind

The underlying reason for all this activity is simple. State and federal infrastructure aid has dried up. In some states, property tax increases have been outlawed; in others they are difficult to pass. As for general obligation bonds, once the bread-and-butter of community growth, they are now viewed with suspicion by the electorate, which must approve them. APA president James Duncan, an impact fee consultant in Austin, Texas, notes that bond issues are often regarded as expensive and growth-inducing by local citizens unwilling to subsidize new development.

This situation leaves exactions as one of the few alternatives, a state of affairs not everybody is happy about. As many experts have noted, even the name *exactions* carries negative connotations, implying some feudal king's demand for a pound of flesh. To some planners, exactions are a solution, creating revenue where it's needed. To others, they are a problem, allegedly driving up the cost of doing business. Developers often have their own label for the device: exaction, extortion, ransom, tribute. Many gripe, but most pay in order to get their projects approved.

Exactions haven't always been asked to carry this big a load, but they have been around for decades. Their roots are in the Standard City Planning Enabling Act of 1927, the legislation that encouraged communities to draw up planning documents and regulations. The law recognized that local governments might require the dedication of streets or water and sewer lines "as a condition precedent to the approval of the plat." Close to 10 percent of the communities surveyed by the Homer Hoyt Center had adopted some sort of road exaction (land dedication, construction requirement, cash payment) before 1950.

During the suburban growth spurt of the 1950s and 1960s, developers were required to dedicate land for parks and schools, or to build roads or other public facilities and then turn them over to the municipality. Sometimes builders could buy their way out of the obligation with a payment in lieu of providing the actual land or building.

The 1970s brought two important developments: off-site exactions and negotiated exactions. Strapped for cash for needed improvements, some jurisdictions (particularly in California, where the courts were lenient) required in-lieu payments for roads, schools, or libraries that were nowhere near the development in question; they were acting on the theory that the development increased the overall demand for those facilities.

With the advent of environmental review laws, local governments also gained the power to demand that developers mitigate the adverse effects of their projects. Mitigation could take any form (land, buildings, cash) and was usually negotiated on a case-by-case basis. Again, California was the leader because its courts ruled as early as 1972 that the state's environmental laws applied to private development projects.

Recent surveys show that the vast majority of local jurisdictions in the United States still do not require exactions from developers. But the same polls also suggest that exactions play an important role in most jurisdictions where growth is an issue. For example, the National Association of Home Builders reports that most of its members have been required to provide some sort of exactions in

exchange for permission to build—most often an on-site exaction.

The NAHB survey also shows that California is the undisputed king of exactions—particularly the less traditional off-site exactions and impact fees; 82 percent of NAHB members in the state reported paying some kind of impact fee. In contrast, only 28 percent of homebuilders in the South (including Florida, where fees are a high-profile issue) were affected and absolutely none in the Northeast.

Legal challenges

At the same time that exactions have been growing, they have been subject to a series of rigid legal tests—particularly the impact fees, which have had rough going in the courts almost everywhere except California.

The *Nollan* case brought the legal issues to national prominence. But the same questions have been battled out in state courts for over 20 years— ever since 1961, when the Illinois Supreme Court ruled that exactions had to deal with demands that are "specifically and uniquely attributable" to the development for which they were intended.

In the 1960s, as cities began to seek off-site exactions, some legal scholars promoted the idea that such exactions were legally correct if there was a "rational nexus" or reasonable relationship between the exaction and the development. Thus, in-lieu payments for an interchange or park on the other side of town could be supported legally if the new development increased the demand for them.

But rational nexus meant different things in different states. In California, where the courts generally defer to local governments, the rule has been applied liberally. As early as 1971, California courts had concluded that the rational nexus test was met if an exaction had even an indirect connection to the project in question.

In other states, the battle for exactions—and, in particular, for impact fees—was tougher. In Florida, for example, where growth pressures and a conservative judiciary have not always coexisted peacefully, the courts have required a direct link and a strict accounting—when they've permitted exactions and fees at all.

Although impact fees became common practice in the state's fast-growing counties in the late 1970s, it wasn't until 1983 that a Florida appellate court ratified the concept. Today, Florida's tough rules include a requirement that an exaction represent a development's "fair share" of the community growth costs and that exaction funds be earmarked for projects directly benefiting the project.

Although many states adopted some version of the "rational nexus" test, other conservative state courts also sought to rein in their municipalities. In Utah, the courts went a step further than Florida had by ruling in 1982 that municipalities must calculate not just a new project's fair share of the community's infrastructure needs but also "past, present, and future fiscal contributions."

Nollan implications

The *Nollan* case provides, for the first time, a national standard for exactions—and it's far stricter than many planners wanted or expected. The Supreme Court ruled that, if the relationship between a proposed project and an exaction isn't strong enough, then the exaction is really a taking of private property by the government under the Fifth Amendment of the U.S. Constitution, meaning the government must pay for the property. Henceforth, the Court ruled, exactions must be directly linked to the project at hand, and the burden of proof must rest with the government agency doing the exacting.

Although the *Nollan* case at first appeared to deal a big blow to public agencies, in fact the rules the Supreme Court laid down are not very different from the rules many municipalities—particularly those outside California—are now following. For example, Florida's court requirements that impact fee systems calculate fair share and earmark funds in special accounts are just the sorts of steps *Nollan* encourages local governments to take. It's all part of proving the direct link.

In fact, even in California, many local governments had begun to establish post-*Nollan* systems even before *Nollan* came down. In San Francisco, downtown office developers must pay a transit impact fee, and in Santa Monica office builders must provide housing. In each case, however, the city did extensive statistical analysis beforehand to determine just what relationship exists between development and exaction.

As a result, when a California appellate court upheld San Francisco's transit fee, the judges remarked that the statistics would probably justify a fee even higher than the $5 per square foot currently being imposed. (The court's ruling, however,

turned on state constitutional tax issues rather than *Nollan*-type exaction questions.)

The one thing *Nollan* might do is push local governments toward fee systems instead of other kinds of exactions. It is hard to prove a direct link between construction of a new subdivision and the need for a freeway interchange several miles away. But it is relatively easy to calculate the overall need for new infrastructure and then assign each new project its fair share of the cost for that infrastructure. It's also possible to use this kind of statistically based fee structure for growth management purposes.

Robert Freilich, a Kansas City land-use lawyer and consultant, has helped local governments in San Diego, Sarasota, Florida, and elsewhere set up just such a system. Called "flexible benefit assessments" in San Diego, the method in effect places a fair share lien on each parcel of property, which is payable when the parcel is developed.

Also in San Diego, Freilich established three growth zones—essentially, urban, urbanizing, and rural—with three different fee systems. Developers in urban (already developed) areas pay no fee. Developers in urbanizing areas pay fees that are considerable but do not discourage growth. Developers in rural areas, because they must pay the full freight of long-distance infrastructure, must pay very high fees.

In growth management terms, the system has worked almost too well. Whereas Freilich expected older areas to attract only 10 percent of the new growth, they drew 60 percent. Rural areas remained virtually unchanged.

However, the San Diego example also points up a hazard of relying too much on fees rather than dedications or other kinds of exactions: Having the money on hand does not necessarily mean that it will be used. New construction in the city is running ahead of new infrastructure even though some $45 million in fees sits in the bank. Developers are asking for a more flexible system—one that would allow them to build the roads and sewers and then turn them over to the city, so they will be ready when the construction projects are complete.

State laws

With the *Nollan* case out of the way, it's possible that action on the exactions front may shift from the courts to the state legislatures. In the last few years, legislatures in several states have considered bills that would govern exactions, and in particular impact fees.

Up to this year, the California legislature had never explicitly authorized local governments to collect impact fees (the courts have taken care of that), although last year legislators gave the state's 1,000 school districts, such as Newport-Mesa Unified, the power to levy such fees. This year, the legislature passed a law, scheduled to take effect in 1989, that establishes rules for all impact fees. And earlier this year, the Texas legislature passed what may be the first comprehensive statewide impact fee legislation.

Originally proposed by developers, the Texas law took final shape with the involvement of James Duncan and others representing the Texas Municipal League.

The new law doesn't cover all possible impact fees. But it does authorize cities to assess fees for water, wastewater, road, and drainage facilities. It requires that a formal planning process precede the imposition of the fees. An advisory committee must be appointed, 10-year population and employment growth projections must be established, and a capital improvement plan must be prepared. Fair share costs must be determined; the land-use assumptions and capital plans must be updated every three years; and the funds realized must be spent within 10 years.

Although developers in Texas pushed for the law in part to limit the use of impact fees, Duncan notes that, because of the planning requirements, the legislation amounts to "the first land-use planning enabling legislation ever passed in Texas."

But state laws, too, must follow the *Nollan* guidelines, and that's why builders in Orange County, California, have challenged Newport-Mesa's fees in court. The builders claim that it's hard to determine a direct link between fees on new construction and the rehabilitation of high school science labs, especially when the high school population isn't growing.

The California law, drawn up in haste by the legislature and Gov. George Deukmejian's staff last year, isn't specific about making the rational nexus between need and exaction. In fact, the state's prime motivation in passing the law was not nexus but money—to allow school districts the ability to raise construction money that the state could no longer provide for them.

California legislators are currently arguing about how to work out the kinks in the law. They are eager to make this new revenue source work smoothly. But like lawmakers in other states—and on the city and county levels—they must first ask themselves, "Where's the link?" After *Nollan*, it's up to them—not the developers or the courts—to prove the connection.

William Fulton is a contributing editor of Planning.

Tapping Developers
Joel Werth
(January 1984)

For years, neighborhood housing activists have been exhorting local government officials to note the connection between gleaming skyscrapers downtown and disinvestment in the neighborhoods. Reinvestment in the resurgent central business districts, they said, comes at the expense of shelter-poor city residents. But as long as the federal government was providing deep housing subsidies, particularly through HUD's Section 8 rent supplement program, some low-income housing needs were being met, and the neighborhood voices were modulated.

It took the near death of most federal housing programs to spur local officials to look for ways of linking downtown revitalization to the generation of affordable housing. One such way is the housing trust fund, which has been tested in only a few cities so far, notably San Francisco and Santa Monica. Recently, however, other cities have considered potential applications of the trust fund idea to their own situations. In 1982, both Boston and New York established commissions to study ways of generating revenue to finance housing rehab and construction, and the mayors of both cities are now studying the commissions' final reports. . . .

The model

Officials in each of these cities have included San Francisco's three-year-old Office Housing Production Program (OHPP) in their investigation. . . . The 1981 law applies to all office developments of 50,000 square feet or more and is based on a formula that links housing demand to office space. Developers gain "housing credits" by contributing directly to a housing trust fund, building the housing themselves, or aiding other residential developers to build or rehabilitate housing units.

By late last year, the program had produced 2,600 dwelling units and exacted $19 million in contributions from 27 office developers. Of this amount, $4.88 million was contributed into the program's Home Mortgage Assistance Trust Fund, which has subsidized the mortgages of 76 low- and moderate-income families buying existing homes. Funds from the trust also will help finance the construction of new condominium and cooperative units and subsidize mortgage payments for their low- to moderate-income buyers.

San Francisco based its program on a creative interpretation of the California Environmental Quality Act of 1970. The city planning commission interpreted the term "environmental impact" to include social and economic impacts, reasoning that downtown office construction created increased demand on the city's tightly stretched housing supply. The program's designers devised a formula that crystallized this relationship: For every 1,000 square feet of office space built, a developer must build or cause to be built .9 housing units, or 640 square feet of housing.

However, last February, the California legislature amended the act to limit impact assessments to the effects on the physical environment. Consequently, city officials were forced to turn to the planning commission's discretionary review authority for legal authorization. An alternative, also being considered by the city, is to introduce an ordinance based on the local police power, which allows the city to pass a variety of laws, so long as they do not conflict with state law.

Useful as the exaction concept has been in San Francisco, it may have limited applicability in other cities. In places where housing vacancy rates are high and the office market is flat, housing exactions would be deemed an unreasonable and thus legally unjustifiable tax.

Another problem with tapping office development to capitalize a housing trust fund is its limited revenue potential. The final report of the advisory commission convened by former mayor Kevin White in Boston estimated that a $5 per-square-foot fee on developments over 100,000 square feet would raise less than $5 million in 10 years. At an average per-unit cost of $35,000 for substantial rehabilitation and $50,000 or more for new construction, this fee would finance the rehabilitation of fewer than 500 units a year and the construction of fewer than 100. In cities with softer office markets, the fee assessment approach is even more problematic as a source of revenue.

Many better than one

Thus, officials in other cities are looking into a variety of revenue sources. In New York, Mayor Edward Koch established the Mayor's Development Commitments Study Commission to review the city's widespread and much-criticized use of zoning bonuses to exact a variety of amenities. . . .

New York's investigation of the concept of a housing trust fund is set in the context of the city's particular approach to development, which allows development rights to be negotiated on a case-by-case basis. Negotiations are possible on any development over 100,000 square feet (as opposed to 500,000 square feet in Chicago, for instance). Over the past two decades, 33 special zoning districts—the results of these negotiations—have been added to the zoning map. In return for height and density bonuses, developers have provided on-site or near-site amenities, many of which have been criticized for doing little to improve the city.

Recently, the geographical relationship between building and amenity has been widened. In 1982, in return for a zoning change, the developer of the 4,300-unit Lincoln West project on the West Side agreed to fund a rail freight yard in the Bronx, and subway station and park improvements near the project.

Still, some critics oppose the principle of ad hoc development negotiations, regardless of the benefits. For example, in testimony before the Development Commitments Study Commission this fall, representatives of the Center for Metropolitan Action at Queens College and Pratt Institute's Center for Community and Environmental Development attacked the system of ad hoc negotiations as being unpredictable and geographically limited, and urged that the city adopt the trust fund approach instead. However, they also warned that developer contributions cannot substitute for public support for low- and moderate-income housing, and that any housing trust fund should not be dependent on one source of revenue alone.

Their proposal calls for office developers to contribute directly to the housing fund. Residential developers have the option of setting aside units for lower income tenants. Twenty-five percent of the cash contributions would be used within the same neighborhood, even more in poorer areas.

What's particularly interesting about this proposal is that the $200 million trust fund would come not from one, but over a dozen, sources: developer contributions ($30 to $60 million a year); the city's share of state mortgage recording fees ($22 million); repayments of UDAG and CDBG loans and sale of city-owned property ($17.5 million); higher building permit fees ($5 million); registration fees for real estate syndications and interest earned on escrow accounts set up to hold security deposits ($17.5 million); filing fees by newly formed cooperatives and condominiums ($7.5 million); revenues generated by tax increment financing districts ($7.5 million); taxes on major real estate transfers ($15 million); corporation filing fees ($7 million); the city's capital budget appropriations ($20 million); state budget appropriations ($20 million); inclusionary zoning payments made in lieu of providing on-site units ($20 million); annual repayment of loans made by the the housing trust fund ($11 million).

These numbers far surpass the projections made by low-income housing advocates in other cities. However, Phil Tegeler, one of those testifying at the commission's public hearings this fall, speaking on behalf of a group called New Yorkers for Equitable Development, warned that the housing trust fund concept would lead to large-scale displacement if developer contributions were based solely on density bonuses. Tegeler recommended the institution of inclusionary zoning districts as a protective measure.

Not surprisingly, the housing trust fund concept also has been attacked from the other end of the spectrum—the developers. The headline of an article in the March 21, 1983, *Fortune* read "'Robin Hood' Subsidies: A Dubious New Fad," and other private-sector critics have called the San Francisco approach "extortion" and "blackmail."

Lower income Bostonians face the same housing problems that plague other big cities. In 1980, for instance, two out of every five renters in Boston were paying over 30 percent of their income for rent.

Last March, in a partial response to this situation, the Boston city council unanimously passed a home rule petition sponsored by Councilor Bruce Bolling to establish an office/housing production program modeled on San Francisco's. Bolling's bill, which has not yet been signed into law, calls for commercial developers to build one housing unit for every 1,200 square feet of commercial space, or to contribute a fixed fee to a quasi-public housing development corporation. Its intent is to stimulate housing production generally, with extra credits granted for creating moderately priced units.

Subsequently, Mayor Kevin White created a 32-member advisory group to refine the Linkage Program, as it came to be called. The advisory group issued its report last October, just before the election in which White, who chose not to run, was replaced by Ray Flynn, who, during the campaign, also had gone on record as favoring the program. The advisory group recommended an assessment fee mechanism similar to San Francisco's, but it also emphasized that the program should not be viewed as the sole solution to the city's housing problems.

Central to the advisory group's recommendation is the designation of an overlay zoning district (Development Impact District), which would affect new and substantially rehabbed projects of over 100,000 square feet. Their developers would have to contribute a "neighborhood impact excise" of $5 a square foot, over a 12-year period, to a "neighborhood housing trust." Unlike San Francisco, Boston would not provide a large block of upfront capital for immediate use for housing production. The advisory group recommended that the housing trust fund be capitalized initially by the proceeds from the immediate sale of several city garages. The trust would make grants and loans to public entities like the Boston Housing Authority and private groups like the Boston Housing Partnership, which was formed by the city's financial institutions to help community organizations rehabilitate their low- and moderate-income housing. The advisory group also recommended the creation of a public service corporation as a conduit for additional developer contributions—in-lieu-of-tax money, for instance.

One linkage-type agreement has already been made in Boston. This is the Neighborhood Development Fund established under the terms of the Copley Place Urban Development Action Grant. Copley Place is the huge mixed-use downtown development now under construction by the Urban

Investment and Development Company. The neighborhood fund will benefit from the repayment of the low-interest loan made by the city to the developer, using the federal UDAG money. Interest on the loan is expected to total nearly $4 million by 1990. Sixty percent of that is to go to neighborhood housing.

Joel Werth, a former APA researcher, has worked in various capacities for the city of Chicago.

Linkage Programs Still Only for a Chosen Few

Steven Rosen
(September 1988)

When it comes to linkage fees, only Boston, Palo Alto, Menlo Park, San Francisco, and Santa Monica have rushed in where others fear to tread. In those cities, office developers paying a variety of linkage fees have helped build over 7,800 housing units—many of them for people of modest income. What those cities have, and many others lack, however, is a hot market for commercial space.

"There is a lot of interest," says Mary Brooks, director of the Housing Trust Fund Project, a nonprofit research group in San Pedro, California. "But only a handful of cities have the luxury of getting away with yet another development fee. Most cities are still trying to make their downtowns attractive enough to lure office development in the first place."

Palo Alto has had a linkage policy in place since 1979. In 1985, it passed an ordinance requiring developers with projects of 20,000 square feet or more to pay $2.69 per square foot of new space into a housing reserve fund. Some $2.4 million has been paid into the fund to date, and about 200 units have been built or renovated under the direction of the city planning department and the Palo Alto Housing Corporation, a local nonprofit redevelopment company.

Toby Kramer, who administers the linkage fee program for the planning department, says the program works well but has one drawback: It depends on commercial growth for revenue. "We're not growing, and we already have more jobs than housing," she notes.

Palo Alto, however, has a second method of providing affordable housing units. Because of a policy in the city's adopted housing plan, condominium and apartment builders are required to dedicate 10 percent of their projects to below-market-rate units. The planning director negotiates with each builder to set a fair reduced-rate price for those units, and the developer passes along the costs to more affluent buyers.

For purposes of determining affordability, the city assumes that any family of four with an annual income below $56,880 needs help to buy housing in Palo Alto, where market-rate condominiums typically sell for $200,000 or more. On the average, a reduced-rate two-bedroom condo sells for $105,000 and a three-bedroom unit for $120,000. Some 130 condos and 20 rental apartments had been underwritten in this manner by developers through the end of 1987, and the Palo Alto Housing Corporation, which finds occupants for these units, has a backlog of 200 families.

The city of Menlo Park, near Palo Alto, in May adopted a similar linkage policy for developers of commercial space. Office developers would pay $1.33 per square foot in excess of 10,000 square feet; developers of less intensive uses, such as warehouses, would pay 53 cents per square foot above 10,000 square feet. No money has been collected yet.

Slow payouts

Boston's linkage fee program, in effect since 1983, requires office developers to pay $5 per square foot toward housing on all space in excess of 100,000 square feet.

Unlike other cities, which require full payment of linkage fees before tenants can occupy a new office, Boston allows developers to pay off their exactions over several years. Those building offices in the neighborhoods have up to 12 years to pay; those building downtown have seven years. Developers may pay their fees all at once to a specific housing project, or they can pay in installments into the city-supervised Neighborhood Housing Trust.

Developers have made $46 million in linkage-fee commitments so far, and the trust has received $1.2 million. Because the trust can borrow against future payments to fund housing projects, it is now in the process of building 200 units. Of those, 138 are earmarked as affordable—locally defined as being for a family of four earning less than $29,000. Meanwhile, private housing developers who have received linkage-fee payments are working on 1,790 units, of which 1,530 are affordable.

Robert Gehret, a planner in the city's public facilities department, like his counterpart in Palo Alto, says the Boston program is working well but can't really put a dent in his city's need for affordable housing. To reach really poor people requires a heavy subsidy, he says, adding, "Do we try to help those families or go for numbers of units? That's always a question."

Eggs in one basket

San Francisco's linkage program, probably the most publicized in the nation, requires office developers to pay a one-time fee of $5.69 for each new foot of office space over 100,000 square feet. The money may go either to builders of affordable housing units or into a city fund; or developers may build their own housing.

Begun in 1981 and adopted by ordinance four years later, the San Francisco program has produced $28.3 million so far. Most of the money has gone directly from developers to specific housing projects, creating 5,532 units that have either been built or are in the pipeline. Of those units, nearly 4,000 are apartments and the rest are houses or cooperatives. Over half the total are affordable.

The city assumes that a family of four earning $52,000 or less needs help to buy housing in the city, and a family of four earning $35,000 needs a subsidy to rent an appropriate apartment.

Although the city planning department is in charge of the linkage program, the mayor's office of housing does day-to-day supervision by bringing together office developers and home builders looking for financing. The city approves the final arrangement between the two sides, and issues a certificate of occupancy to office tenants only when the linkage fees have been made in full.

One example of how the system works: In order to build a twin-tower mid-rise office building in downtown San Francisco, Marathon U.S. Realties in 1982 contributed $3.5 million toward construction of a housing cooperative for families in low-income Hunters Point. Then, to help the nonprofit developers, Catholic Charities of the Archdiocese of San Francisco, acquire additional financing,

Marathon hired a housing consultant and subsidized his $250,000 fee.

The cooperative opened in 1984, and Marathon's office buildings opened this year. "Absent Marathon's money, it would have been a lot more difficult, and perhaps could not have been done," says William Lightbourne, general director of Catholic Charities.

When the linkage fee was established in 1981, the city's downtown office vacancy rate was less than one percent and developers were clamoring to build. Changes in the local real estate market since then have cut into the revenues produced by the linkage program.

Over the past seven years, vacancy rates have risen to almost 15 percent, and average office rental rates have declined. In 1986, voters approved a slow-growth referendum limiting new office space to 475,000 square feet per year. As a result, the program can now generate no more than $2 million annually.

Richard Morten, associate planning director of the San Francisco Chamber of Commerce, says that the city's linkage program has a basic flaw: It is geared to poor people, whereas it should give first dibs on housing built with linkage fees to the people who actually work in the new office buildings.

Despite all the caveats, though, it appears that linkage programs may be getting a second look from a few more cities. Miami and Seattle, for example, provide some office developers with density bonuses if they contribute toward housing. And Jersey City, which negotiates on a case-by-case basis with office developers, so far has won commitments for 1,000 new units of housing.

Steven Rosen is a reporter for the Cincinnati Enquirer.

Rebuilding a Rural Constituency

Catherine C. Harned
(December 1984)

One of the most difficult, but essential, tasks of a public planner is gaining public acceptance and support for the idea of planning. Events of the past decade in Hardin County, Kentucky, illustrate how important such acceptance can be.

In the mid-1970s, a comprehensive plan prepared at the behest of the county planning commission was termed "a cancerous sore" and "a farce" at numerous public hearings. Organized opposition played on the fears of county residents, who saw planning as an infringement of individual property rights. Instead of accepting the proposed plan, the county's government dismantled the planning commission, leaving one of the state's largest, fastest growing counties (90,000 population) without any form of countywide planning.

Within three years, however, countywide planning had resumed, and public confidence was regained. Early this year, an innovative development guidance system, one of the few of its kind in the country, was adopted. What caused this major shift in public attitudes? . . .

'I can do what I want to'

In September 1973, Hardin County and five of its cities—Elizabethtown, Radcliff, Vine Grove, Upton, and West Point—funded the creation of a city-county planning commission. Its primary purpose was to develop a comprehensive plan, an effort embroiled in controversy almost from the start.

The commission hired a Louisville consultant to prepare the plan, a massive document that projected land-use, housing, and transportation needs from 1975 to 1995. Its land-use element was particularly controversial. Typical were the remarks of a local real estate broker, who identified himself as a "concerned citizen" when he addressed a packed commission hearing on the proposed plan in November 1975. "I believe every landowner in this country and in this county has the right to sell his property to a land developer," he said, "I can do what I want to."

Citizens voiced numerous fears at meetings of the fiscal court, the county's legislative body. One of the court magistrates said: "I think we all realize you have to plan. I plan my day. But the people I've talked to feel there's something hidden that's not coming out." . . . Some citizens complained about the plan itself, one calling it "too voluminous, ambiguous, and vague."

It soon became increasingly difficult to find citizens willing to serve on the commission. Some commissioners neglected to attend meetings, resulting in repeated failures to muster a quorum. Numerous postponements and reschedulings oc-

curred, and residents complained that it was difficult to ascertain where and when meetings would be held.

The influential Hardin County Board of Realtors complained that the plan was unrepresentative of local residents' wishes and that it discriminated against those owners of prime farmland who might want to develop their land. The realtors called for dissolution of the commission, and a group called Citizens for Property Rights threatened legal action.

Meanwhile, intercity rivalries flared, as each legislative body jockeyed for a plan that would be advantageous to its jurisdiction. An urban-rural dichotomy emerged between cities seeking industrial "growth at any cost" and rural areas with more traditional values. Many felt that urban interests dominated the planning commission.

The commission finally adopted the plan in early 1976, but none of the local legislative bodies voted to use it. Instead, "home rule" became the cry. Within a week, Elizabethtown, Radcliff, and Vine Grove all withdrew from the commission to establish their own planning agencies. In a letter to the fiscal court, the Elizabethtown mayor wrote that "objections to the proposed countywide master plan have been so intense that there is little chance of a truly cooperative effort for countywide planning."

In March 1976, the fiscal court voted to withdraw from the commission, even though some magistrates still supported the plan. Said one: "The days of Daniel Boone are over. When we see the smoke of our neighbors' chimneys, we cannot move on. We must live with it." Yet, when fiscal year funding ran out three months later, the commission was effectively dissolved.

Looking back on the battles, most local observers attribute the demise of the plan and the commission to several factors, among them: failure to establish good working relationships with the two local newspapers, one of which was dominated by real estate interests; use of an out-of-town consultant to devise the plan, particularly at a time when court-ordered school busing in nearby Louisville was causing "outside" plans to be viewed with suspicion; the perception that the county planner was also an "outsider" and inaccessible to boot; the suggestion by many opponents that the plan was inflexible and authoritarian; and organized opposition by real estate interests, who came to be viewed as representing the majority.

Try, try again

More than a year after the joint planning commission was abolished, planning became the major campaign issue in the 1977 general election. The close race for county judge, who serves as the county's chief executive, pitted the outspoken incumbent R. R. Thomas, who had strongly supported planning, against a candidate whose campaign was largely funded by local development interests.

Despite the continuing negative feelings toward planning and zoning, Thomas, running on a pro-planning platform, narrowly defeated his opponent. Area residents seemed to realize that local developers' interests were not necessarily their own. They were also impressed by the fact that the well-respected judge had risked defeat by running on such a controversial platform.

Soon after Thomas took office, the fiscal court voted to establish a new county planning commission. But this time, the three cities that had established their own planning departments decided not to join.

By early 1979, five planning commissioners had been appointed, and Dennis Gordon, formerly administrator of a seven-county regional planning agency in southeast Alabama, had been hired as commission director.

The first priority, the fiscal court told Gordon, was to draft new subdivision regulations. Aware of the commission's recent history, Gordon strongly encouraged participation by various local interests—builders, engineers, realtors, civic groups—in the preparation of the regulations.

After approving the subdivision regulations, the fiscal court asked for the planning commission's help in adopting an official roadways system. There was no county road department at all until 1970. Instead, magistrates were in charge of maintaining the roads in their districts. Even after formation of a road department, there was no systematic record keeping.

Development guide

With the fiscal court's adoption of both the subdivision regulations and the official roadways system inventory and map, the commission's public credi-

bility began to improve. In 1980, Gordon decided to propose a new comprehensive plan. Although many developers remained "leery of what was to come," Gordon says, "they were all willing to give us a chance."

The proposed plan was termed a "development guide," both "to stay away from what had gone on before," in Gordon's words, and more accurately to reflect the guide's policy planning approach. To avoid the negative connotations of hiring an outside consultant, Gordon decided to prepare the plan in-house.

The development guide was to consist of 11 planning elements, each about 35 to 40 pages long. This approach meant that more controversial segments could be reviewed in detail by citizen groups and public bodies, as other elements were being adopted. Thus, the plan stood a good chance of adoption and implementation.

Three plan elements—transportation, community facilities, and land use—were required by state law. The other proposed elements were to cover the commission's planning philosophy, basic community data, farmland analysis and protection techniques, energy alternatives, housing stock review, an inventory of historic structures, and environmental protection. A summary volume was to include methods for implementing the various plan elements.

Thus far, the court has adopted the four elements the commission has prepared: planning philosophy, transportation, community facilities, and land use. Key to their passage were a major public education effort and extensive publicity. Says Gordon: "One of the biggest problems I've found here is the misconception of what planning is all about and what it can achieve." The commission has distributed a pamphlet listing the 11 plan elements; the pamphlet emphasizes the importance of citizen participation and stresses the plan's flexibility. Gordon also has worked with the local media on stories about the plan and has spoken at dozens of civic organization meetings. . . .

Additional public contact and confidence have been created through the commission's handling of building and electrical inspections in both Hardin and neighboring LaRue counties. When a state-wide building code was phased in locally in 1981, the commission saw the new law as an opportunity, says Gordon, "to get a handle on where development was going."

A hybrid

Last January, after three years of study and numerous public surveys and hearings organized by the planning commission, the fiscal court adopted the "development guidance system" (DGS), which is essentially a hybrid of a land-use compatibility program developed in several Colorado cities and a soil classification system devised by the U.S. Soil Conservation Service. DGS provides the protection of standard zoning, Gordon says, but without zoning's inflexibility. It calls for a mixture of land uses, and helps guide growth to areas best prepared for it. In offering an alternative to a standard zoning ordinance, DGS has minimized the local fears of zoning that led to the downfall of the previous planning commission.

An aspect of the guidance system that has drawn praise is the requirement for a "compatibility" meeting between a developer and neighboring property owners regarding each development proposal. "This will give people a voice in land-use decisions where presently they have no voice," planning commission chair Bob Wade told the Elizabethtown *News-Enterprise*. These informal pre-site plan meetings, the newspaper later noted in an editorial, are "a key strength" of the new guidance system. "People living around any proposed development . . . will have a direct say."

In developing the DGS, Gordon and assistant planner Chris Hunsinger looked closely at the guidance systems used by Breckenridge and Fort Collins, Colorado. The basic premise of the Fort Collins system is that mixed land uses are not inherently bad, provided they are made compatible. An example is the use of buffers between industrial and residential uses.

The ideas gathered from the Colorado cities were combined with elements from the Land Evaluation Site Assessment (LESA) program developed by the Soil Conservation Service for the U.S. Department of Agriculture. Under the LESA system, soil types are identified and prime soils determined by local productivity data, i.e., corn yield per acre. In Hardin County, it is difficult to obtain approval for development on soils that are considered prime unless the site already has predominantly urban characteristics. Contiguous development also is sought. Because many of the county's development battles revolve around the loss of prime farmland to urban

annexation, the use of LESA was seen as of "extreme importance" by the commission.

An additional objective of the new regulations is to channel growth into an established corridor roughly paralleling U.S. 31-W and encompassing the triangle formed by Radcliff, Vine Grove, and Elizabethtown. "In pinpointing that growth corridor, we have made a trade-off," Gordon admits. "There is an awful lot of good, prime soil in that area, but we realize we can't preserve all of it." Instead, the preservation effort will be focused on the wide belt of agricultural land just outside the growth corridor.

How it's worked

During the first nine months the guidance system was in operation, 40 proposals were processed. Of these, 22 were for new development on undeveloped land. Sixteen were approved and six denied. Most of the approved requests were for development in the growth corridor. The remaining 18 proposals were for changes of use on previously developed sites.

The guidance system already has gained national attention. In July, the commission received an achievement award from the National Association of Counties for "improving the efficient delivery of county government services." In October, Kentucky's APA chapter cited the planning commission for an "outstanding planning project-program," and the American Farmland Trust has given the guidance system one of its five achievement awards for noteworthy "public policy development" aimed at farmland protection. The *Louisville Courier-Journal* has called DGS "an encouraging step forward in an area badly in need of imaginative approaches. . . . The result should be watched with keen interest wherever urban problems are impinging on the countryside."

Of course, there are a few questions about such a county-only planning effort. It is both a strength and weakness of the new planning commission that it is not a unified city-county agency. Because the three cities have not joined the commission, many of the intercity and city-county planning squabbles have been eliminated. And, since the LESA element of the guidance system is geared to protecting farmland, the regulations have a base of support among farmers. . . .

Presently, the commission is fine-tuning the guidance system, and gearing up to work on another element of the comprehensive plan, either farmland protection or historic preservation.

Catherine C. Harned is a preservation planner and free-lance journalist in Hodgenville, Kentucky. © *1984 by the author.*

U.S. Cities Face Combat in the Erogenous Zone

William Toner
(September 1977)

Porno shops, adult theaters, topless bars, massage parlors—the problem of what to do about these and other sex businesses drives people to extremes.

On the one hand are irate citizens, outraged by what they see as the excessive abuses caused by sex-related businesses. On the other are harried public officials who are forced to respond to these demands while assuring the legal and constitutional rights of all. Caught in between are—you guessed it—the planners, anxious to avoid the moral and emotional dimensions of the issue and hopeful of translating it into a simple land-use matter.

Take what happened in Chicago last May. One humid Friday afternoon, dozens of city policeman, accompanied by building and zoning inspectors, raided 34 adult bookstores, citing the owners for a multitude of building and licensing violations. The police padlocked the doors.

The following Monday, the store owners filed suit in federal court, charging harassment. The next afternoon, U.S. District Court Judge Frank McGarr commented on the city's action: "This [raid] raises the inescapable suggestion, if not conclusion, that the motivation [for the raid] lies more in the nature of the business than [in] the nature of the premises." On Wednesday, in ordering the bookstores reopened, he stated: "I must take notice of the improbability that [these] premises are imminent threats to public safety, all at the same time, and that it is only a coincidence they are all adult bookstores."

Chicago is a latecomer in the rush to control sex businesses. Yet its frantic, scatter-gun approach is the same as that taken by dozens of other cities.

Planners have adopted two basic approaches to control sex businesses. One is the "divide and regulate" scheme made famous by Detroit, which, in simple terms, forbids sex businesses from locating too close to one another or to a residential district. The other is the Boston-style "concentrate and regulate" approach, in which all the sex businesses are shoved into one area.

The difficulty is that most citizens don't see the control of sex businesses as a land-use question. To them, a massage parlor is not the same thing as a mobile home park or a fast-food restaurant. It's pornography or obscenity, not a "land-use." By ignoring the land-use issue, however, citizens often ignore the single most promising avenue of control over sex businesses. Instead, officials are pushed and prodded into adopting half-baked solutions. Planners are then left to figure it all out.

That's what happened to Michael Burnham, an associate planner for the city of Whittier, California, who had just returned from a week-long church conference. On his desk lay the newest addition to Whittier's zoning ordinance. California law permits cities to adopt so-called urgency ordinances—interim, emergency measures necessary to preserve the health, safety, or welfare of the community, which may be approved without long planning studies or extensive public hearings.

What Burnham had missed during his absence was the great race between the city council and the owner of a downtown theater that reportedly was going porn. Only hours before the council was to adopt the urgency ordinance, the theater owner showed his first X-rated film, *Deep Throat.* Thus the owner avoided the certain denial of a permit that would have followed under the urgency ordinance. Under the ordinance's "grandfather clause," he had the right to continue showing all the Linda Lovelace films he wanted to.

More important, for the first time Whittier had elevated adult bookstores and theaters to the crisis level of flood, famine, fire, and drought. That's how sex businesses drive people to extremes. . . .

The options

Some cities—Denver, Colorado; Norwalk, California; and Royal Oak, Michigan—have adopted regulations patterned after Detroit's anti-skid-row ordinance, which has been upheld by the U.S. Supreme Court. In Denver, the ordinance was adopted after several other anti-porn laws were ruled unconstitutional. Since adopting the regulation last

December, the city has had no new permit applications for adult entertainment uses.

Norwalk and Royal Oak were in a different position. Neither city had any adult entertainment uses, but both cities wanted to have some zoning insurance. "We adopted the regulation primarily as a preventive measure," said Richard Beltz, deputy director of community development in Royal Oak. "We felt we needed to get something in our ordinance rather than wait for someone to approach us." In both cities, the ordinance is mainly intended to discourage applications for sex businesses. Thus far it's working. Neither city has received any applications for a permit.

Other cities have discovered that even the most rational attempts to control sex businesses can fail. Three years ago the Boston Redevelopment Authority was hailed for its plan to control the sex businesses that had congregated in the so-called Combat Zone near the city's downtown retail district. BRA planners had the wisdom to recognize that, if sex businesses were driven out of the Combat Zone, they would simply locate in some other convenient, low-rent district. Instead of playing hide-and-seek, the BRA decided to establish an adult entertainment district that would rival those of London, Copenhagen, and San Francisco.

The BRA spelled out tough sign controls, upgraded streets and sidewalks, instituted a program to renovate storefronts, and even provided the zone with a new park, Liberty Tree Park. Former BRA director Robert Kennedy declared, "Within a year or so, the term 'Combat Zone' will be a thing of the past."

But on the way to becoming "Liberty Tree Park," the Combat Zone turned into a nightmare for the BRA planners. A Harvard football player was stabbed to death there, and an off-duty state trooper suffered a fatal heart attack after wrestling with a suspect in the Zone. . . .

What looked like a good idea has turned into a public embarrassment for the BRA planners, who must now reconsider the whole idea of concentrating sex businesses.

The effects of concentrating sex businesses are nowhere more evident than in New York City. "As the sex businesses proliferated, so did all kinds of crime," ABC News reported on its "Close-Up" series. "The New York police found that serious crime complaints ran almost 70 per cent higher on police posts that had sex business and prostitution problems. These posts with sex businesses showed sharply higher rates of rape, robbery, and assault."

Increased crime wasn't the only problem. "In two years the amount of money the Times Square area paid the city in sales taxes went down by 43 per cent," ABC News reported. "In roughly the same period, the amount of money owed the city by the area in back taxes went up sharply. In a two-year period Times Square lost 2.5 times as many retail jobs as the rest of the city lost. Put simply, the area produced much less income and much more debt for New York City."

These sad statistics, coupled with booming sex businesses and a growing sense of public outrage, earlier this year pushed the New York City Planning Commission to consider a new sex business ordinance as an amendment to the zoning ordinance. Patterned after the Detroit model, the ordinance prevented sex business concentrations—thereby encouraging dispersal—and also kept them out of residential areas and away from churches and schools. But this ordinance went one step further than any other in the nation, because, according to spokesman Jerry Miller, it "would have amortized current sex businesses. The effect of it was that any illegal [nonconforming] uses would have a year to get out of business."

On the day of the hearing before the Board of Estimate, though, the *New York Post* led off with a heading, "Porno Zone Set Up in Manhattan." The headline "scared a lot of people" into believing the city was "setting up a red light district or something," Miller said.

At the hearing itself, one woman, while waving a Bible at the board, declared, "You're all going to hell for breaking God's law." Others suggested that the board and city bureaucrats favored pornography. The ACLU threatened suit against the city, charging that the ordinance violated constitutional guarantees. And to round it off, a former massage parlor owner suggested what the city really needed was a committee made up of sex industry representatives and city representatives to work out the proper locations for the businesses.

Most upset of all were those people who felt that the ordinance would push sex businesses into their neighborhoods. This being an election year, the Board of Estimate was especially cautious about landing on the wrong side of neighborhood associations.

Still, most board members favored the ordinance

for its overall dampening effect on sex businesses, for it would have dispensed with as much as 80 per cent of the existing sex businesses in each of the city's five boroughs. But it also might allow some new sex businesses in each borough, and the idea of permitting even one new sex business would outweigh driving out 40 or 50 businesses. No politician could afford to run on a permissive pornography platform. Thus, no action will be taken until after the fall election. . . .

Is what happened in these cities unusual? No. Quite the reverse is true. In the regulation of sex businesses, oddity is the norm. While cities that have no sex businesses often find it easy to pass regulations, cities with sex businesses find it an especially torturous process.

The wording of regulations, for example, often generates blinding emotional reactions which make rational discussion nearly impossible. Public officials are careful to avoid any label that would put them on the side of obscenity or pornography.

Planners, on the other hand, are loath to get involved in anything that smacks of regulating morality. They want to define the problem as a land-use matter. But because of the crusading aura that surrounds the regulation of sex businesses, planners reluctantly, but necessarily, get caught up in the moral and emotional dimensions of the debate.

It seems to me that planners hurt themselves most in these debates when they fail to do what planners do best—detailed planning studies. If they were evaluating a proposed site plan ordinance, they would examine its tax consequences, its effect on commercial and residential areas, the consequences in terms of crime, and so on.

Perhaps because they're afraid to leap feet first into such a touchy area, planners avoid these nuts-and-bolts items when dealing with an ordinance to regulate sex businesses. As a result, they get caught up in an argument over morality that they have no chance to win.

If they stuck to what they do best—laying out the facts of the case in a clear, rational manner—they'd have a better chance of getting approval for the kinds of laws they think workable and valuable for the community.

William Toner teaches planning at Governors State University in University Park, Illinois.

Fine Points of the San Francisco Plan

George A. Williams
(February 1984)

The Downtown Plan: A Proposal for Citizen Review is the major written product to date of the San Francisco Department of City Planning's recent evaluation "of the potential and limits to development and preservation" in the city's central business district. Its focus "is to make possible appropriate growth but to manage vigorously its effects—preventing building where change would diminish the city's character or livability, but accommodating development that would further the city's economic and social objectives."

This article is a compilation of excerpts from the plan and from a summary of it prepared for WestPlan, *the magazine of APA's California chapter. The sections of the plan covered here are: preservation and transferable development rights, open space, building form, and solar access. Other key elements of the plan are transportation, housing, and the specific downtown zoning districts.*

Preservation and transferable development rights

One characteristic that makes San Francisco special is its legacy of architecture constructed just before or, in the downtown, just after the 1906 earthquake. Preservation of a substantial number of these buildings requires bold action. Mere encouragement and incentives by the public sector have proved inadequate. Building on the detailed inventory and evaluations prepared by the Foundation for San Francisco's Architectural Heritage, the downtown plan would require the retention of 266 "architecturally significant" downtown buildings.

Demolition of a significant building would be permitted only if: (1) The city planning commission finds that the building is unsafe for occupancy; that rehabilitation is not feasible because of fire, earthquake, or similar circumstances; or that the structure was irretrievably deteriorated prior to the adoption of the downtown plan; or (2) A court of last resort finds that no reasonable use can be made of the building.

The plan proposes the creation of five downtown "conservation districts" in areas that contain significant older buildings and that possess an overall scale and character worthy of protection. One such district embraces most of the retail district; the others are in the financial district.

In these districts, demolition and alteration of significant buildings would be subject to the same restrictions as described above. "Contributory" buildings—those that contribute to the character of the district but are not of the same quality as significant buildings—as well as unrated buildings, could be altered or replaced by new development. However, new buildings and alterations to existing ones would be subject to strict design controls to ensure the maintenance of the district's character.

The downtown plan continues to use floor area ratios (FAR) as a means of regulating building height. However, it no longer requires, for FAR purposes, that all parcels making up the development site be adjacent to one another.

To help preserve significant buildings, unused development rights—that is, the difference between the square footage of the existing building and the square footage that would be allowed in a proposed new building—may be transferred to another site in the same zoning district. Transferable development rights (TDR) also may be shifted to a special 33-acre "expansion" area south of the financial district. Contributory buildings in the five conservation districts also would be entitled to TDR as an incentive for retention.

Open space

Mandatory contributions of parkland are common in suburban subdivisions, and private open space is required in the city's residential districts. However, San Francisco could become the first major city to require that commercial development in a high-density downtown provide usable public open space.

The downtown plan envisions a central area where almost everyone would be within 900 feet (approximately two blocks) of a publicly accessible space in which to sit, eat a brown bag lunch, and people watch. Many of these spaces would be small and privately owned.

The plan's open space requirement is expressed not as a limit on lot coverage, but as a function of the amount of commercial space being built. The requirement is specific: one square foot of open space for every 50 square feet of commercial devel-

opment (1:100 in the retail district), but it can be met in a variety of ways: the traditional plaza, building terraces, lobby "sun areas," greenhouses, and "snippets" (small, sunny sitting areas). Guidelines have been worked out to ensure that these spaces become accessible "people places."

In the past, open spaces in the form of plazas were often provided as part of the development site. But, because the open space had to be adjacent to the building, it was not always located where it was most needed or where access to sunlight was greatest.

Consequently, the new plan also allows the open space requirement to be satisfied through a financial contribution by the developer to create a new park at another location in the downtown—not necessarily adjacent to the project itself. It is anticipated that several new downtown parks will be created by coupling this open space requirement with the TDR proposal discussed above.

It is also envisioned that a private group, such as the Trust for Public Land, will act as an intermediary in acquiring park sites. For example, such a private group could finance the acquisition of a park by selling its development rights to a builder; it would then finance development of the park with contributions from other builders looking for a way to meet their open space requirements. Finally, the group would deed the new park to the city.

Building form

The new plan proposes bulk rules that would, in essence, require a reduction in the upper portion of taller buildings to make them appear more slender and to create more distinctive building caps than the standard "flat-top box." Building heights would be set to preclude the skyline "benching" effect, which results from the development of a number of buildings at the same height. The rules also would create a softer skyline more in keeping with the city's hilly topography and the character of its older high-rise development.

The new bulk controls would apply to four components of a building: the base, lower tower, upper tower, and upper tower extension; the general principle is that, as a building increases in height, it should decrease in bulk. For example, at the base—the portion of the building that extends from a minimum height of 50 feet to a maximum of 1.25 times the width of the widest abutting street—no maximum lot coverage, horizontal dimensions, or floor area controls would apply. However, the plan would require the "streetwall" to be designed to harmonize with existing streetwalls and an appropriate setback and/or other means of delineating the base from the tower. The base's architectural treatment also would have to include a cornice line or equivalent projection(s) in order to harmonize with the traditional city streetscape.

Treatments of "distinctive building tops" could include: cornices, stepped parapets, hipped roofs, mansard roofs, stepped terraces, domes, and other forms of multifaceted sculptural tops. However, as the plan notes, "direct mimicry and replication of historical detailing would be discouraged."

Solar access

The plan also requires that new buildings be shaped to permit direct sunlight to reach public parks and certain sidewalks (such as those in the retail district) during "critical" hours of the day and months of the year. In the case of sidewalks, that critical time generally is considered to be around noon.

Using the resources of the Environmental Simulation Laboratory at the University of California-Berkeley, planners developed "solar fans" around public parks, and established solar access angles for sidewalk areas. (A solar fan is the curved plane, shaped something like a funnel, that describes the path of sunlight from the sun to the earth.)

For example, the solar fan around Union Square—the retail district's central open space—is approximated by height bands stepping up from the square. Taller buildings would cast shadows already on the park during the critical periods. However, if existing buildings already shadow the park—the St. Francis Hotel, for example—taller buildings may be constructed behind them.

The solar fans have been used, together with other criteria, to establish proposed new height limits around eight spaces. However, because the fan is a curving slope with varying angles of inclination, it is difficult to replicate it on a two-dimensional height map.

Height limits for specific development proposals in areas where solar access cannot be protected or where further shadow analysis is necessary would be established through the design review process. The shadow impacts of various building configurations would be studied and a configuration recom-

mended that eliminated shadows altogether or that minimized the amount.

George Williams is the San Francisco Department of City Planning's assistant director for plans and programs. He was in charge of preparing the downtown plan.

New York's Zoning Solution
Robert Ponte
(December 1982)

"As far as Manhattan skyscrapers are concerned," *New York Times* architecture critic Paul Goldberger wrote recently, the city's 1961 zoning ordinance "has so frequently been amended or altered—and even in special cases set aside altogether—that it has almost ceased to exist."

The inadequacies of that ordinance for dealing with development in Midtown Manhattan, the city's hottest growth area, were well documented in Roberta Gratz's December 1979 *Planning* article, entitled "New York's zoning predicament." She noted that incentive zoning in Midtown had become too complicated and too subject to negotiation, resulting in bulky, out-of-scale buildings.

Gratz was right. Many of the buildings erected under incentive zoning turned out to be bulky and unattractive. Thanks to the generous floor area bonuses allowed by the zoning, they were built at much higher densities than older buildings. In return, developers provided such amenities as plazas, indoor spaces, and covered arcades. In most cases, the amenity was not worth the bonus.

Even on midblock sites, where buildings traditionally had been smaller, developers were allowed to build to the maximum density by merging lots and piggybacking buildings. This was especially true on the narrow side streets in the east Midtown area around Park Avenue. (Fifth Avenue is the dividing line between the East and West sides. Madison and Park avenues lie just to the east; the Avenue of the Americas and Times Square to the west.)

The results were congestion and the loss of street character. Madison Avenue, which already had lost many of its retail shops, was becoming a canyon.

There were fears that the entire East Side would undergo a similar change.

Moreover, development activity had not spilled over to the West Side, which has underused land and excess utility and subway capacity. Blight around Times Square and the theater district had kept developers from investing west of the Avenue of the Americas. The city administration was eager to realize the West Side's development potential, and, of course, to bring in the maximum tax revenue.

New goals

How, though, to get change? The city planning department knew that changing the specifics of the zoning ordinance would not be enough. Midtown needed an overall plan to guide development—something it had never had.

The first step was the establishment of the Midtown Development Project, a working group whose charge was to formulate a planning strategy and then translate it into a revised zoning ordinance. The project was begun in 1980, by Robert Wagner, Jr., then planning chairman, and continued and intensified by his successor, Herbert Sturz. Heading the project was Richard Bernstein, formerly executive director of the planning department.

Six goals emerged from this group:
● To reduce pressures on the East Side by encouraging development elsewhere;
● To offer incentives to draw development westward to Times Square and south of 42nd Street;
● To protect areas of special character;
● To simplify the city's development review procedures and refocus them on basic needs like the openness of streets;
● To ensure that new buildings erected under Midtown's special zoning in the theater district and along Fifth Avenue would be compatible with their context;
● To emphasize the preservation of existing theaters.

To reach these goals, the working group proposed that the city encourage West Side development through zoning incentives, invest in capital improvements on the West Side, and offer tax concessions to potential developers. An elaborate "daylight evaluation chart" was proposed to calculate the allowable bulk of new buildings.

Almost everyone who is concerned about Midtown agreed that the entire proposal—both goals and strategy—was a step in the right direction. Few disagreed with the desirability of moving development westward and southward. However, several groups, including APA's New York Metro Chapter, expressed doubt that the zoning incentives, capital improvements, and tax concessions would suffice to lure developers to the West Side.

One group, the local chapter of the American Institute of Architects, called for much higher densities on the West Side as an inducement, but this was opposed by other civic and professional groups, including APA. Some also expressed concern about the fate of landmark buildings in areas where development was being encouraged. And others criticized the daylight evaluation chart as being unnecessarily complicated. ("Excessively cumbersome," said the New York Real Estate Board.)

These criticisms led to the revised development strategy and zoning text that the city's Board of Estimate adopted in May 1982. The revision offered stronger incentives for West Side development, including significant density differentials; assistance in site acquisition; subway station improvements; and four special publicly assisted projects designed to turn the area around. The strategy also promised to devise a program to preserve West Side theaters.

In answer to criticisms about midblock overdevelopment, the new zoning reduces densities in the midblocks of a 77-square-block portion of the East Side. The zoning also offers a simpler method of regulating height and bulk than the daylight evaluation chart. . . .

Real estate groups remain the most skeptical about the new zoning. The president of the New York City Real Estate Board argued, before adoption, that the new zoning would do little to encourage development on the West Side. Corporate tenants, he felt, would continue to insist on East Side locations, hampering rentals in new West Side developments.

Ratification by the Board of Estimate was delayed for two weeks by the real estate groups' efforts to add a liberal grandfather clause, which would have exempted development still in the planning stage. The board turned them down. A court challenge by the Real Estate Board and five developers also was dismissed. "Their position invites a degree of skepticism," said the judge who heard the case. "It is somewhat like a resolution from a convention of foxes deploring deficiencies in the incubation plans for the hen house."

The details

The new zoning divides Midtown into three zoning districts: a growth area, a stabilization area, and a preservation area. The growth area, generally west of the Avenue of the Americas, encompasses the theater district and the 34th Street shopping area. Larger buildings with a base floor area ratio of 18 are permitted on the avenues, while the midblock theaters are protected by a much lower floor area ratio. Special tax exemptions will be offered in the growth area. . . .

In the stabilization area, which covers most of the office core between the Avenue of the Americas and Third Avenue, a distinction is made between avenue and midblock sites. The base floor area ratio on avenue sites is 15, while midblocks are set at 12—a level that makes tower development too expensive.

Density controls in the preservation area are intended to curtail development on the side streets between Fifth Avenue and the Avenue of the Americas, from 52nd to 56th streets—the brownstone area surrounding the Museum of Modern Art (whose new apartment tower addition would not have been allowed under the new zoning). A similar preservation mechanism governs the theater district, where floor area ratios are kept at 10 and a special permit is required for demolition of any of the 45 theaters. . . .

The new Midtown zoning represents a shift away from the special districts and negotiated designs that had become common under the 1961 zoning. The point is to simplify the city's zoning law—one of the nation's most complex—as it applies to the city's most sought-after area. The text of the entire zoning law fills a weighty volume, including not only 115 provisions that apply citywide, but also 33 special districts that are tailored to particular areas. Hundreds of amendments have been made to cover unique situations. For major buildings, a complicated design review process usually supplements the written text.

The new zoning seeks to simplify existing procedures. While the new regulations are subject to complicated formulas and tables, they should, with practice, afford individual architects much more flexibility than they had before.

Moreover, the revisions emphasize the original concerns of zoning. For example, they avoid overpowering mass and minimize shadows, by requiring towers once again to be stepped back from the street. And exceptions are no longer made to achieve the particular design purposes of individual architects and urban designers. Little-used amenities like through-block arcades will no longer be rewarded throughout Midtown; simple improvements like wider subway stairs and broader sidewalks will be required.

Despite the fear that the Board of Estimate would make many amendments, the new zoning emerged basically intact. The most important amendment is a one-year moratorium on theater demolition and the establishment of the Theater Advisory Council—both steps taken in reaction to the demolition of three theaters. The council's role is to guide the planning commission on subsequent measures to protect and strengthen the city's legitimate theaters.

It is still too early to tell how effective the new zoning will be. Many towers are rising in Midtown, but all of them were approved before the zoning change. That change coincided with the end of a five-year office construction cycle, and no new buildings have been approved under the new rules.

Studies by the AIA and a number of architectural firms suggest, however, that the Midtown zoning will result in buildings that offer more daylight for their occupants and more light and air for pedestrians on the streets below. An example of an existing building that meets the new standards is Citicorp Center. This award-winning building by Hugh Stubbins is set back into the middle of its site. The base, which extends out to the sidewalk on three sides, encompasses stores and an enclosed public atrium.

The true test of the new zoning will be its ability to draw construction away from the East Side. Zoning that is as clear and predictable as the new Midtown regulations should encourage developers to invest in parts of the city that they previously shied away from. Yet, office building locations are chosen largely on the basis of market preference, and with such large investments at stake, developers do not like to take chances. By tightening up midblock zoning east of the Avenue of the Americas, the city may well have removed many of the remaining possible sites from consideration.

Nevertheless, the impact statement for the new

zoning estimates that, even if the regulations are very effective, only 12 million of the total 30 million square feet of new office space projected through the 1980s will be shifted to the growth area on the West Side. Thus, for the next decade, most office development will still be located on the popular East Side; most likely, it will spread throughout the stabilization area, as far east as Third Avenue.

Still, we can expect much more West Side development than under the old rules. Coupling zoning with tax measures and capital improvements is a good way for government to steer development to areas where infrastructure can, in fact, support greater density. And in central locations like Times Square, private development can produce the best of both worlds; much higher tax revenues and few additional public expenditures.

Robert Ponte, AICP, is a lecturer in urban planning at Princeton University.

Philadelphia Keeps the Faith

Roger Cohn
(September 1988)

With a tradition that dates back more than 300 years, from founder William Penn through legendary postwar planner Edmund Bacon, no American city has a more distinguished planning heritage than Philadelphia. And so it is hardly surprising that the new master plan for Center City Philadelphia, the first since Bacon's landmark document of 1963, has attracted national interest since it was unveiled by the city planning commission in May.

The plan, which took three years to complete, lacks the bold initiatives of the 1963 plan or the idealistic vision of Penn's original 1682 plan for a "green countrie town." Instead, Philadelphia's planners have given us a conservative, pro-growth concept of the city's future that seeks to accommodate major downtown development while preserving the human-scale streetscape and historic character of downtown neighborhoods.

The new plan accepts the basic concepts of the 1963 plan, many of which have been transformed into reality in the last 25 years, and proposes that

major new office development continue along the Market Street corridor, extending from the Delaware River waterfront westward to the 30th Street railroad station. In one of their most significant recommendations, the Philadelphia planners strongly support establishing buffer zones to protect Center City's historic neighborhoods from the encroachment of high-rise construction outside the Market Street corridor.

"I think the issues in 1963 were how to remake a 19th-century industrial city into a modern downtown, and we've now done that," says Barbara J. Kaplan, executive director of the Philadelphia City Planning Commission. "We now have a modern downtown, and we want it to continue to prosper and grow, but in a way that preserves the quality of life we've established."

Philadelphians pride themselves on that quality of life. One of the most commonly heard comments from those who live in the nation's fifth largest city is that Philadelphia is a "big small town," retaining 19th-century townhouse neighborhoods only a few blocks from the modern office and commercial corridor along Market Street.

Indeed, the decision to develop a new plan for Center City, only the third in the city's history, emerged from an emotional 1984 debate over developer Willard Rouse's proposal to break Philadelphia's long-standing tradition of constructing no building taller than the statue of the city's founder, William Penn, atop city hall. Rouse won the necessary approvals and last year completed construction of the 60-story One Liberty Place office tower (designed by architect Helmut Jahn), which far exceeds the old unofficial height limit of 491 feet. Four other buildings that will soar above Penn's tri-cornered hat, including Rouse's second Liberty Place tower, are currently under construction.

The controversy over the Rouse proposal raised the broader issue of how Center City, the three-square mile area that forms Philadelphia's commercial and residential core, could accommodate future growth while retaining the European ambience and open public spaces that Philadelphians so prize.

Unlike other American cities, including major northeastern cities like Boston, Philadelphia experienced relatively little downtown development in the 1970s. The development that did occur focused on the Market Street commercial corridor, leaving

Center City residential neighborhoods, particularly those south of Walnut Street, relatively intact.

The new plan for Center City concludes that the existing commercial core could support substantial new development without destroying those neighborhoods. The plan estimates that by the year 2000, Center City could accommodate 22 million square feet of new office space and a 25 percent increase in housing units (1,250 new units annually). In addition, taking into account the influx of visitors that would result from a planned new Center City convention center, the planners project a 30 percent increase in downtown retail sales.

While many in the Philadelphia business community consider these projections overly optimistic, they reflect the pro-growth vision of planners in a city that has not experienced the development boom that has caused cities like San Francisco and Boston to seek to limit future downtown development. As Kaplan and her staff see it, Philadelphia's task is to stimulate growth and channel it along the Market Street axis.

"Philadelphia is not like San Francisco," planning director Kaplan said in a recent interview. "This isn't a no-growth plan. It's a growth plan. We feel there's a dual goal here: stimulating growth and retaining the quality of life. And those goals are not mutually exclusive."

They are, however, potentially contradictory. To avoid conflict, the Philadelphia planners recommend expanding efforts to certify downtown historic buildings threatened by new development, as well as strengthening and extending height and use controls currently in effect along two of the city's primary retail streets, Walnut and Chestnut. That area will act as a significant buffer to prevent more intensive commercial development from encroaching on residential neighborhoods in the Rittenhouse Square, Washington Square West, and Society Hill areas.

The Philadelphia plan also proposes that the city revise its system of granting bonuses to developers in exchange for additional building density. Under the current system, developers are given bonus points that allow them to increase density above the zoning-code limit in exchange for providing certain public amenities; the choice of which amenities to include is left up to the developers. Kaplan and her planners believe that in Philadelphia, as in other cities, bonuses have been awarded for design features that provide few or no benefits for the general public: interior plazas not easily accessible from the street, sidewalk arcades that lead to dead-end walls, truck loading docks that are counted as open space.

Under the proposed new system, developers would be required to meet specific design standards before being allowed to increase building density. Among the amenities required would be contiguous public spaces, with standards for access and landscaping, covering at least 30 percent of the site; retail space equaling at least two percent of the gross floor space of a major building; and established standards to protect light and air at street level.

Developers could gain additional building density by including "extraordinary public amenities," such as public observation decks atop buildings or a theater or gallery. But even with these extra bonus points, Kaplan maintains, developers would not be able to build at any greater density than permitted under Philadelphia's existing zoning code. "The idea is not to increase densities over what we have now," Kaplan says. "The idea is to provide public amenities that truly serve the public."

In Philadelphia, the planning commission serves solely as an advisory body, and the zoning code changes proposed in the new plan must win the approval of the city council and Mayor W. Wilson Goode, who appointed the nine commission members, before they can be put into effect. If Philadelphia's ever-fractious city council does approve the changes, Goode, who has already publicly praised the new plan, is expected to sign them into law.

Loyal opposition

For a document that grew out of the heated debate over the Rouse project, the new Center City plan has met with surprisingly little criticism. Perhaps ironically, considering that the new plan pays homage to his 1963 plan and accepts most of his innovations, the lone outspoken opponent has been Edmund Bacon.

The 78-year-old Bacon, who retired from the commission in 1970 and still lives in Center City, showed up at the ceremonial public announcement of the plan with a written critique blasting the new document as "nothing more than a grab-bag of miscellaneous items, selected at random, with no connection with each other nor with any coherent body of planning principles to guide it."

"The plan for Center City is not a plan at all,"

Bacon added. "To produce a document that claims to be a plan does not automatically endow that document with the virtues of planning."

In a subsequent interview, Bacon, who has become something of a civic gadfly in his home city in recent years, had not tempered his view. He contended that the plan was little more than a hodgepodge of long-discussed ideas about Center City and lacked a coherent, creative vision of what Philadelphia could become. As Bacon sees it, such a lack of vision is endemic to the state of contemporary planning.

"I think this reflects 20 years of university teaching in which planners [have] become nothing more than automatons," Bacon said. "Everybody is taught the methodology of statistical extrapolation and computer printouts. They're not taught to trust themselves, their own thinking, their own creativity.

"What we're looking at now is a computer-prepared future as opposed to a future that is the product of imagination and human will," he said. "The Philadelphia planning commission is demeaning the whole planning profession by putting forth something that purports to be a vision and simply isn't."

Barbara Kaplan, who has been cautious in her public reactions to Bacon's criticism, was clearly annoyed at his blanket dismissal of her staff's three-year planning effort, which was conducted in conjunction with consulting architects Robert Geddes and Robert F. Brown, of the Philadelphia firm of Geddes, Breecher, Qualls and Cunningham.

"I could argue that Bacon's plan was simply a hodgepodge," Kaplan said in an interview. "It was a bunch of projects. He never looked at Center City in its entirety. He never looked at the neighborhoods. This plan is more comprehensive. We deal with preserving the residential neighborhoods. We deal with the economy of Center City. It's not just an urban design and land-use plan the way the 1963 plan was."

Four years ago, Bacon had led the opposition to Willard Rouse's proposal to exceed Philadelphia's unofficial height limit, which meant scrapping the "gentleman's agreement," conceived by Bacon and enforced during his 21 years at the planning commission, that kept all buildings below the top of the Penn statue on city hall tower, long the city's symbol and literally its focal point. The planning commission decided to approve Rouse's Liberty

Place project, in part because Kaplan and her staff determined that many of the existing views of city hall had already been obliterated by office buildings constructed within the 491-foot height limit. In its new plan, the commission proposes the establishment of "view corridors," located within the sightlines of remaining views of city hall, in which height restrictions (in some cases far less than 491 feet) should be imposed.

The plan recommends height restrictions of between 250 and 350 feet for the group of buildings that immediately surround city hall and additional restrictions that would project views of the tower from the Benjamin Franklin Parkway, the grand boulevard that is one of Philadelphia's true urban treasures, and from the highway approaches along Interstate 95 and the new Vine Street Expressway, currently under construction.

To Bacon, the proposed view corridors are "totally inadequate" to protect the prominence of the city hall tower on the city's skyline. He had proposed establishing a special zone along Broad Street, the city's primary north-south corridor, in which high-rise development would be prohibited. But the commission rejected that idea, concluding that its own plan would do more to preserve the remaining views of city hall most valued by the public.

Since the document was released in May, much of the public discussion in Philadelphia has focused on a topic given only brief mention in the plan, a proposal to establish a neighborhood employment fund, to be financed through voluntary contributions from developers and businesses. The fund would be a private, nonprofit organization that would contract with existing literacy and job-training programs to recruit and train neighborhood residents for Center City jobs.

The idea is being considered in the context of an ongoing debate over whether low-income and blue-collar Philadelphia neighborhoods are sharing the benefits of Center City development, a debate that focuses on a proposal by community groups to impose a mandatory linkage fee on downtown developers to raise money for a variety of neighborhood programs.

In the new plan, the planning commission acknowledges that with an adult illiteracy rate estimated at 40 percent, Philadelphia must take serious steps to provide training if neighborhood residents are to be equipped to fill the office jobs created by anticipated downtown development. But the planners contend that mandatory fees for such programs would only hinder Philadelphia's competitive position in attracting developers and companies that can opt for the suburbs. Mayor Goode is reviewing the linkage-fee proposal.

Fine points

While it may not fulfill Bacon's expectations for a creative vision of Center City's future, the new Philadelphia plan does contain some specific proposals and a strategy for implementing them. Among these are:

• Creating a nonprofit downtown management corporation, similar to existing organizations in Denver and Minneapolis, that would manage the central business and retail core in much the same way a private operator manages a shopping mall. The organization's responsibilities would include supplementing city maintenance and security services downtown and recruiting retailers to help create the proper mix of stores.

• Redesigning the Chestnut Street transitway, a 12-block stretch of the prime shopping street converted in 1976 into a partial pedestrian mall, open only to bus traffic. The plan supports efforts to remove the mall's clunky futuristic street furniture and to operate less polluting, "people-scale" shuttle buses along the full length of Chestnut Street, from the Delaware River to 30th Street.

• Encouraging the preservation of historic buildings through the establishment of programs that would allow the owner of an historic property to sell the development rights to another property owner, provided the proceeds are used to maintain and improve the historic structure. Similar transfer of development rights programs are in effect in New York, Seattle, San Francisco, Dallas, and Denver.

• A $50 million restoration of city hall, the ornate Victorian structure that was completed in 1901 and is now badly deteriorated. The plan revives a long-standing proposal to convert the building's ground floor, now used for city offices, for such public uses as an auditorium, a restaurant and a visitors' center. The plan also calls for redesigning Dilworth Plaza, the granite expanse just west of city hall that now is frequented by street people and used to unload buses bringing prisoners to the courts.

• Encouraging major development over the

railyards near the 30th Street Station on the west bank of the Schuylkill River. The station is owned by Amtrak, but a development partnership led by the Gerald D. Hines Interests of Houston has taken an option on the air rights to the 80-acre site, the largest remaining undeveloped parcel in downtown Philadelphia. With construction space still available closer to the central business core, local real estate observers believe the 30th Street development will not occur for at least a decade.

On the whole, the new plan for Center City respects the precedents of Penn's enduring city plan and Bacon's grand vision of 1963. Penn's plan, devised by the city's original surveyor, Thomas Holmes, laid out the concept of the original city, whose form is still visible in modern Center City. The Penn Plan produced an orderly grid proceeding westward from the Delaware River, with Market Street as the central east-west crossing, and five public squares (four of which still exist; the fifth now the site of city hall).

Bacon's plan, conceived in a boom period for federal funding for cities, proposed major public projects that would channel and spur development of a downtown that had only then begun its post-World War II transformation into a modern city. The 1963 plan called for the construction of a rail tunnel connecting the two Center City commuter stations, which was completed in 1984, and a major public investment along east Market Street, site of the publicly sponsored Gallery shopping mall that opened in 1977, and at Penn's Landing, where in the last two decades the city has built a public plaza and an esplanade along the Delaware.

Rather than proposing grandiose new public projects for a city experiencing recurring financial pressures, Philadelphia's new plan looks to encourage and steer private development in a central core that the planning commission believes still has room for growth.

"This city is really just coming to life in terms of realizing its development potential," Kaplan said. "We lagged behind a lot of cities in transforming from an industrial to a service-based economy, and in some ways that was an advantage. It gave us time to prepare. We've observed what's happened in other cities, and hopefully we learned from it."

Roger Cohn is a writer in New York; he was formerly the urban affairs reporter for the Philadelphia Inquirer.

Notes on the Master Plan

(September 1987)

COMING TO TERMS

Historically, the term *master plan* has been applied to developments ranging in scale from an individual lot to a region. Born in the City Beautiful era when plans were usually prepared by outside consultants, the term implies a certain superior authority. Over the years, it has gradually lost favor, to be replaced by *general plan,* a term championed by T. J. Kent, Jr., in an effort to emphasize a significant characteristic—one, sad to say, not usually found today. *General* has also been used to distinguish publicly sponsored plans from private-sector plans, which are often still called master plans.

Recently *comprehensive* has been used to indicate the expanded nature of the plan. Plans now contain, and indeed in some cases are required to do so by state law, social and economic elements of which earlier planners were not mindful. The resulting detailed documents become mid-range development plans, often losing the discipline, goals, objectives, and policies characteristic of a true general plan.

Policy plans list the community's goals and objectives. They don't qualify as master plans, however, because they do not contain a plan diagram portraying the spatial relationships between various land uses and the circulation network. They provide no answers to the inevitable question: "Where?"

Strategic plans derive from the business world and borrow heavily from its terminology. Critics have questioned whether the method can be successfully transferred from the private to the public sector. Much will depend on the willingness of government to devise new management, budgeting, and control systems.

Yet another variety of plan is the *sector plan,* popular in California, with examples in Texas in Fort Worth and Houston. The danger here is that planning becomes a cut-and-paste procedure, losing its overall vision and form.

Robert Cornish, AICP

Cornish is an associate professor in the Department of Urban and Regional Planning at Texas A&M University, College Station.

TRUE BELIEVER

"I believe that the preparation and maintenance of the general plan is the primary, continuing responsibility of the city-planning profession," wrote T. J. Kent, Jr., 23 years ago in the introduction to *The Urban General Plan,* a book that has since become a planning classic.

Long considered among the most articulate advocates of the traditional master plan (he prefers the term *general*), Kent, founder in 1948 of the planning program at the University of California in Berkeley, is still a believer. A community needs a long-range (20–30-year) framework for making decisions about its future, he says. "I don't understand short-term thinking in dealing with cities."

Kent's ideal plan is primarily a physical plan, although it makes clear the relationship between development policies and social and economic goals. It does *not* include implementation policies or zoning ordinances, which Kent says properly belong in separate documents. Most important, the plan is openly debated in public hearings, after which it is presented to the city council—not the city manager and not the mayor—for approval.

Over the years, Berkeley has served as a testing ground for Kent's ideas. A San Francisco native and 1939 graduate of the University of California's architecture program (with a master's in planning from the Massachusetts Institute of Technology), he served on the Berkeley planning commission for nine years, from 1948 to 1957, and later was elected to the city council. He also served two stints as San Francisco planning director, in 1948–49 and 1966–68.

"I realized soon after I started on the Berkeley planning commission," he says, "that we couldn't act on the issues that were confronting us—traffic, for instance—without some kind of general plan. We finally persuaded the city council to give us some planning staff, which it did, and within a couple of years we had a plan, which we then submitted to the council for adoption—a new idea at the time."

The commission and its first staff planner, Corwin Mocine, took on such controversial issues as the future of the waterfront and university expansion. Kent notes with satisfaction that the plan eventually led to a university decision to establish new campuses rather than continuing to expand in Berkeley and to a huge downzoning in the city's residential areas. "It took time—until 1961—but it worked because the plan clearly stated the reasons for its policy, and the city council understood them."

In his book, Kent singles out the city council as the most important element in local government and the principal "client" of the general plan. In a sense, the council is where the buck stops. "It is," he notes, "the final policy-making authority in municipal government" and thus the appropriate arbiter of physical development.

During his own tenure (1957–65) on the Berkeley city council, Kent was effective in shepherding through such liberal legislation as a fair housing ordinance. But it was also the time of the Free Speech Movement when, as he puts it, "all hell broke loose in Berkeley." The stress of that period contributed to his decision to take early retirement from the university in 1968.

Since then, Kent has devoted much of his time to regional activities. He has been particularly involved with People for Open Space, a group that he helped found in 1958, inspired by the British Garden City ideas of Ebenezer Howard. A long-range plan for a Bay Area greenbelt is now in the works.

From time to time, Kent trots out a proposal that he first made in the early 1970s when the Berkeley city charter was being revised. His idea, admittedly a minority view, he says, is to transform city government into a European-type parliamentary system with a 60- to 80-member council. Most members would be elected from very small districts, and a majority coalition would choose the leader. The result, he says, would be "the maximization of democracy and citizen participation."

Such a system would also allow local governments to realize the potential of their home rule powers. And Kent believes that there is much that city governments can do for themselves, freed from the strings attached to state and federal government grants.

"In time," he says, "people will come around to the idea of local control"—and to the idea of smaller size metropolitan areas. Kent quotes Lewis Mumford, a respected mentor, to back up his idea that smaller is better: "Just as with any other living creature or human organization, there is a limit be-

yond which things no longer work well," Mumford wrote.

In Kent's plain English, that translates to: "If it gets too big, it goes clunk."
Ruth Eckdish Knack

Knack is Planning's *senior editor.*

CALIFORNIA MEANS IT

In 1985, citizen activists in Walnut Creek, California, hailed the passage of a ballot initiative—Measure H—that tied the approval of new development permits to traffic congestion at certain city intersections. Just 14 months later, however, a Contra Costa County judge ruled Measure H invalid because it was inconsistent with Walnut Creek's general plan, which called for policies to enrich the city's position as a county office center.

Early this year, a Los Angeles judge dismissed a long-standing suit against L.A. County because the county had finally adopted an adequate general plan. The city of Los Angeles is also in the midst of a multi-year, multimillion-dollar effort to rezone hundreds of thousands of parcels in response to an order by yet another judge, who ruled that the city's zoning did not conform to its general plan.

In short, in California, the general plan—the local term of choice for the comprehensive or master plan—has teeth. Its legal basis is a 1972 law requiring local zoning ordinances to be consistent with general plans. As one judge put it, this law "transformed the general plan from just an 'interesting study' to the basic land-use charter governing the direction of future land use in the local jurisdiction."

The result is that California's 500 cities and counties have no choice but to put a lot of time and effort into preparing their general plans and making sure they're carried out.

"The general plan has become the single most important land-use document for local governments," says J. Laurence Mintier, a Sacramento planning consultant who specializes in general plans.

It has also given rise to a thriving consulting business. Most cities do not have the staff to handle all the complicated requirements of a general plan or a plan revision, and consultants fill the gap. Although most contracts are small, even in small cities the cost of a general plan can run into six figures.

State requirements for the general plan have become more and more complicated over the past 60 years. Now, all general plans must include seven mandatory elements: land use, circulation, housing, conservation, open space, noise, and safety. In certain jurisdictions, other elements are also required: coastal plans, airport plans, even timber plans.

"Every time there has been a problem the legislature has said, "Let's have local government deal with it on a local level and put it in the plan,' " says Los Angeles attorney Carlyle Hall, codirector of the Center for Law in the Public Interest.

In general, the consistency requirement gets high grades for encouraging cities and counties to deal head-on with hard issues. Part of the reason lies with the "Christmas tree" of requirements added periodically by the legislature. The general plan process often includes not only the overall document, but a variety of what might be called "subplans" that encourage local governments to think about implementation while they are formulating plans. The most important of these—and, at the moment, the trendiest—is known as the "specific plan."

The specific plan is defined in state law as an implementation tool for a specific "subarea" of the city or county, a bridge between the general plan and the zoning ordinance. In practice, it has become an umbrella under which local officials can place almost anything they want to for that area, so long as it conforms with the general plan.

"The neat thing about them is that you can, in fact, generate truly unique ideas without feeling you are obliged to do the same thing elsewhere in the city," says Al Bell of The Planning Center in Newport Beach, a consulting firm that has heavily promoted their use.

Because the specific plan is so handy, it is subject to overuse. Wherever a trouble spot arises in Los Angeles—at International Airport, for instance, or Westwood or Ventura Boulevard—a team of planning consultants is likely to swoop in to do a specific plan, often at considerable expense.

On the whole, though, the specific plan is simply further proof that California's cities and counties take their general plans seriously.
William Fulton

Fulton is a contributing editor of Planning.

A RURAL FABLE

"I'll tell you who planners are," said the dairy farmer before the conference audience. "They're the ones who don't know the difference between a nanny goat and a cow."

"As a planner," I responded, "I can assure you that I do know the difference. The goat is the one with the short tail."

But the farmer had a point. Rural planning is different. And the making of a good, rural, master plan is different, too. This tale of two adjacent rural counties shows exactly how different.

Our two counties—real ones but unidentified here for obvious reasons—are alike in many ways. Both share a similar geography, economy, and environment. Agriculture dominates the landscape, and small towns appear at crossroads and along river banks. In recent times, rates of population and economic growth have been high, but absolute levels remain distinctly rural.

I've worked in both places and was principally responsible for their latest plans. Both plans are policy-oriented, ready-made to be translated into regulations. In one county, which I'll name Everright, I was rehired to do just that, and the work is nearly complete. In the other, Everwrong, my work stopped when the plan was adopted.

In Everwrong, the plan was directed and controlled by a broad-based, hard-working citizens group that represented dominant interests. It included every member of the county board, most members of the planning commission, representatives of towns, and various other interests. The direction of the plan was further set by the results of a survey, a random sample of registered voters in Everwrong, that showed clearly what the citizens wanted in the way of planning and zoning.

The results showed extremely strong support for plans and regulations that would protect the county's agricultural base and its environmental resources. Similarly, citizens supported moderate growth rates and a series of desirable social policies, including low-cost housing. After an 18-month effort by the citizens group, the plan was adopted, unanimously, by the county board.

Since then, things have soured. While retaining the letter of the plan, the county board violated its spirit. The commitment to the protection of agricultural land and operations, still on the zoning books and in the plan, is giving way to zoning map amendments that retain the language, but alter geography and land use.

In Everright County, by contrast, the board, as well as the planning commission and zoning board of appeals, has kept its commitment to the new plan and has even gone on to revise the zoning ordinance to be consistent with it. It seems likely that the board will adopt the revised ordinance and retain its commitment to the spirit and letter of the new plan and revised ordinance.

So what might account for the difference? Both counties had experienced and competent zoning administrators. Both plans were policy-oriented and designed to be fed directly into the zoning ordinance, and in both cases the planning process was smooth—no great glitches, no lingering battles, a planner's delight.

The difference is that the politics of planning in Everwrong is a world apart from the politics of planning in Everright. In Everwrong, the county board chairman is antiplanning and antiregulation, but he's also a well-respected and well-liked politician. He appoints like-minded people to the board's planning and zoning committee, the key group in planning and zoning matters. Thus the board, while for political reasons keeping the language of the ordinance and the plan intact, can also pass map amendment after map amendment, subverting both.

In Everright, the board chairman supports planning and regulation, and the board's planning and zoning committee is similarly inclined. Both are interested in sustaining the spirit and language of the plan and the revised zoning ordinance.

Despite all this, as a long-term believer in the democratic theory of American government, I'm optimistic about Everwrong. Over the long term, it seems likely that the difference between appearance and reality will become clear to the citizens, and pressure and votes will be brought to bear to change things. Already one town in the county has begun revising its plan and is likely to go on to its ordinance.

There ends the tale of the two counties and their plans, one successful, one not. For the life of me, I can't figure out how I would have changed a thing.
William Toner

Toner teaches planning at Governors State University in University Park, Illinois.

FLORIDA: THE RUSH IS ON

Over the next five years, 66 counties and over 400 municipalities in Florida must complete comprehensive laws if they are to comply with the state's landmark 1985 Growth Management Act.

The most important feature of the new legislation, many planners believe, is the "adequate facilities" requirement, which makes the provision of public facilities—roads, schools and parks, police and fire protection, and solid waste disposal—a prerequisite for plan approval. The requirement is particularly important in Florida because much of the state was platted and sold off in the years following World War II yet remains basically unimproved to this day. This "committed" development will require an immense public investment in facilities to handle the expected population growth.

To aid its review of local plans—a gargantuan task—the Department of Community Affairs, the state's planning agency, has issued a set of model plan elements. But even with the models, many practitioners fear that local governments will try to get by with the minimum. The trick, says Charles Siemon, a land-use attorney frequently involved in Florida planning, is "to meet the 9J-5 [comprehensive planning] criteria without losing creativity."

The first plan deemed to be in compliance with the state law is one done by our firm for Monroe County (the Florida Keys). It includes such innovative features as the use of transferable development rights to protect wetlands and hammocks, provisions for affordable housing, and performance standards for various types of habitat. Because the plan and the development regulations are linked and the board of county commissioners is limited to amending the plan annually, comprehensive review of what are typically considered rezonings is built into the plan.

Also innovative is the state's use of "focal point" planning to deal with issues in areas where interests are in conflict. The process was used in North Key Largo, where the habitats of several endangered species are threatened by potential development. A steering committee was appointed by the governor to develop a habitat conservation plan (required under the federal Endangered Species Act). The committee held open meetings, landowners contributed toward a market survey, and the local planning department provided information about the area's vegetation.

The result of the two-year process is a recommendation to the county and the state concerning the appropriate level of development. The county will soon release a request for proposals to develop a plan for the area.
Lee D. Einsweiler

Einsweiler is a planner with Siemon, Larsen, Mattlin & Purdy in Chicago.

PROTECTING INDUSTRY FROM YUPPIES AND OTHER INVADERS

John King
(June 1988)

Like the young urban professionals who use them, renovated factory buildings have become symbols of cities on the upswing. Once-empty mills have filled up with lawyers and advertising firms, apartment dwellers are shopping for converted lofts, and old warehouses have been reborn as festival marketplaces. In some cities, entire industrial districts have been reclaimed without use of the wrecking ball.

At the same time, say the experts, it's possible to have too much of a good thing, to the point where the new city becomes a threat to the old. As the demand for renovated office space and residential lofts continues to grow, local officials and manufacturers see potential problems for inner-city industry. Faced with a market that puts a higher value on commercial and residential uses than it does on industry, some planners argue that adaptive reuse of older structures will displace manufacturers that otherwise would stay in the area.

"In most cases, the conversion of industrial space has been the best example of resurgence within the city, but resurgence can't be allowed to drive out industry," says Gregory Longhini, director of industrial land-use policy for the Chicago planning department. "The image may be positive 80 percent of the time, but we have to identify the 20 percent where change shouldn't be allowed to happen."

Increasingly, the tool being used to prevent industrial displacement is zoning. Chicago is one of several cities that has recently rewritten its zoning code to inhibit the spread of other uses within industrial districts. In April, the city council passed an ordinance allowing the creation of "planned manufacturing districts," in which most nonindustrial uses would be prohibited.

Even if land in such a district is empty or a building vacant, redevelopment must be industrial in nature; variances will be granted only in exceptional cases. While the ordinance did not spell out the specific boundaries of such districts, city planners say that legislation will be filed this summer for two north-side areas, Goose Island and the Clybourn corridor. . . .

Districts of this nature are not new. Portland, Oregon, has had an industrial sanctuary policy in place since 1981. But the Chicago experience has raised the national profile of the approach, and planners anticipate that other cities will follow suit.

"The needs of cities have changed. Zoning has to reflect that," says Marilyn Swartz Lloyd, director of Boston's Economic Development and Industrial Corporation, sponsor of a similar initiative. "This approach is an important tool to preserve urban industry into the next century."

The new districts are a departure from traditional industrial zoning, which allowed most commercial development to coexist alongside manufacturing. As a result, attempts to create the new zones have met strong opposition: The passage of the Chicago ordinance took three years, Boston's initiative faces widespread opposition, and a New York City effort in the garment district is now being challenged in court.

"We had to prove that there was still a substantial industrial economy in the city and that it deserved assistance," says Elizabeth Hollander, Chicago's planning commissioner. "Manufacturing has always been the zone where you could put *anything*. It was hard to convince people that it shouldn't be a grab bag anymore."

Chicago offers the most vivid example of how the concept of industrial zoning is being redefined. With approximately 6,000 factories employing 250,000 people, Chicago still has the image of a blue-collar town, though in fact thousands of industrial jobs have been lost in recent decades and many factories stand empty. But on the north side, in the upper income Lincoln Park neighborhood, developers have spotted a market for residential lofts in empty factories along the Clybourn corridor, an industrial area between the lakefront and the Chicago River to the west.

Chicago's existing industrial zoning, like that of most cities, allows almost everything *except* housing. But when a developer bought an old paint factory on Clybourn Avenue in 1983 and sought a variance to convert the building to residential lofts, permission was granted despite the proximity of a scrap yard and a plumbing supplies distributor.

"The developer said he would make sure the people who bought units would understand the nature of the area," recalls Donna Ducharme, executive director of the Chicago-area YMCA's Local Economic and Employment Development Council and a force behind the new district. "Once that project went in, the dam was broken. Within the next year there were six or eight similar proposals."

To large manufacturers in the Clybourn corridor and on nearby Goose Island, another old industrial area, the residential invasion posed two problems. First, it encouraged potential sellers to hold out for residential developers; the square foot value of a residential property is roughly twice that of industrial. And after the homeowners moved into manufacturing areas, they began to complain about the night shift noises and early morning loading.

"The city was spending all sorts of money on infrastructure improvements and low-interest loans to fortify its manufacturing base, yet it routinely allowed zoning changes. There was no coordination, and the policies were in blatant contradiction," Ducharme says. "Manufacturers saw that if the conversion trend continued, this would force them out."

It took three years to create the protected districts, Ducharme explains: one year for the idea to gain credibility, one year to build support in the proposed districts, and one year to forge the coalition needed to get the zoning category approved.

By the time of passage, that group included union workers, the Illinois Manufacturing Association, and even nearby residential groups. Although some developers fought the new classification, the local board of real estate brokers declined to take a position on the proposal.

Boston begins

By contrast, the effort in Boston is barely a year old. Compared to Portland or Chicago, Boston is a dense city with relatively small industrial districts. The entire city is only 47 square miles, less than half the size of Portland. Except for the Fort Point Channel area of South Boston, a 900-acre district where printers and fish processors coexist with newly restored offices and empty land, industrial areas tend to be sandwiched between residential areas and the waterfront.

Two city agencies, the Boston Redevelopment Authority and the EDIC, want to amend the zoning code to allow light manufacturing districts. If approved, district boundaries would probably be drawn around at least two existing industrial areas. But the city also hopes to win residential support to create small districts on vacant land in certain neighborhoods. For instance, it has proposed a seven-acre district for the Jamaica Plain neighborhood on publicly owned land left over from a mass transit project. The city's approach is similar to an industrial park, although land within the districts would be developed privately.

To make industrial development acceptable to nearby residents, the list of allowed uses would be restricted to nine types of light manufacturing, including the production of electrical machinery, pharmaceuticals, office equipment, and pottery. Scientific research and development would be encouraged, as would printing and publishing. By contrast, grittier industries—smelting, waste disposal, manufacture of asphalt or fertilizers—would be forbidden.

Lloyd admits that Boston's approach is unorthodox. "It's like a compact," she says. "We tell the neighborhoods, 'You want jobs? Manufacturing brings jobs. This is a way to meet your needs.' And we say to industry, 'We have a zone for you, but you have to meet certain standards.'"

The districts' zoning, in fact, would include explicit standards for performance and design. Vibrations, dust, and odors would be strictly regulated, and five-foot wide strips of trees or shrubs would be required as buffers between residential and nonresidential uses. Parking facilities, loading areas, and dumpsters would be screened from public view, and outside storage of supplies would not be allowed. "We wanted to make the rules clear, so that manufacturers didn't have to come to us for every detail," says Linda Bourque, head of the zoning staff at the redevelopment authority.

Bourque admits that the proposed districts are designed to squelch real estate speculation and might frustrate landowners who planned to replace industry or empty space with offices. "Manufacturers who want the option of selling out to office developers feel they're losing value, but it's speculative value," Bourque says. "They're saying, 'We can't sell out," and we're saying, "That's the point.' "

New York conflicts

In New York City, where pressure on industry is often intense, city planners have explored the use of zoning as a protective mechanism in such diverse areas as Manhattan's West Chelsea district and outlying Queens. Since 1981, converters of loft space in the SoHo section of Lower Manhattan have been charged a $9-per-square-foot fee that helps relocate displaced manufacturers in the outer boroughs.

In March 1987, responding to a rash of office conversions in Manhattan's West Side garment district, the planning commission imposed a new set of zoning restrictions. The district encompasses some 4,800 clothing firms—manufacturers, wholesalers, shippers, small retailers—and employs about 60,000 people in a 30-block area.

According to the new regulations, developers who convert manufacturing space to office use must guarantee that an equal amount of space in the district will remain industrial. They can do this by keeping manufacturing on lower floors, or—if they want to convert the entire structure—by buying another manufacturing building with a promise that its use will not be changed.

Supporters of the change admit that it is a stopgap measure. "It does not generate space. It only comes into action when some is taken away," says William Ryan, district manager for community planning board 4, the area's officially sanctioned citizens' group. "We're trying to protect as much of the manufacturing base as possible. We aren't really changing zoning, just adding to it." . . .

What the critics say

Such protective measures face an uphill battle, even when the initial idea for the district comes from the manufacturers themselves, as was the case in Chicago. Much opposition to the zoning changes is rooted in the notion that the market should not be reined in. . . .

To make the Chicago ordinance more palatable, the name was changed from *protected* manufacturing districts to *planned* manufacturing districts and the guidelines for creating a district were revised. Before a district is approved, studies must be made to assess its potential, the opinion of landowners, and the evidence of encroachment by nonindustrial uses.

In Boston, the battle is still being fought. At a public hearing in April, light manufacturing districts were attacked not only by real estate groups—the Building Owners and Managers criticized "the infringement of property rights"—but also by manufacturers who feared that the district's stringent criteria would hamper expansion.

Because of the objections, city officials are now reviewing the proposal, which will probably be resubmitted this summer. It has the support of several neighborhood residential advisory committees and a group of manufacturers and landowners in the Newmarket district. Privately, however, city planners acknowledge that work must be done to satisfy the concerns raised by critics.

Those concerns include skepticism about interest on the part of manufacturers. The economic development corporation has done studies showing that more than half of Boston's printers will need to expand or move within five years, which suggests that a market exists for new industrial space in the city. However, critics point to a citywide industrial vacancy rate near 25 percent as proof that space is available for companies that need it. Boston's industrial job base has eroded by roughly two percent per year since 1977 and statewide slippage is even worse. Between June 1984 and last February, the number of industrial jobs available in Massachusetts dropped by 14.2 percent. . . .

In Chicago, however, there are signs that developers are willing to build industrial space if their options are restricted. Even before approval of the planned manufacturing districts, city officials last year said that they would refuse to allow any more residential conversions on Goose Island, a traditional large manufacturing area in the Chicago River. A few months later, developers unveiled plans for a 42-acre industrial park on the island.

The key, say planners, is to reinforce zoning changes with other planning initiatives. "We're attempting to depress land values, no doubt about it, but we also have to set the stage for growth," says Greg Longhini. "If nothing happens five years down the line, and even more companies leave, we'll be hard pressed to defend the changes."

Portland's results

This view is endorsed by Ken Swan, Portland's project manager for urban renewal. "Just because you don't allow housing or retail doesn't mean you'll get manufacturing," Swan says. "Policy can't be adopted in a vacuum. Planners have to think about what tools are necessary to implement the policy." Among those tools: infrastructure improvements, low-interest loans for manufacturers seeking to expand, even government assistance in assembling parcels large enough for modern industrial buildings of one or two stories. Portland has used all these tools, particularly tax-increment financing.

Since 1981, Portland has established 16 industrial sanctuaries, which are spread throughout the city. In some cases, the districts are designed to impede gentrification or conversion; that was so with a 500-acre sanctuary across the Willamette River from the central business district. In other areas, the sanctuaries are designed to set the stage for future industrial development. The largest is a 2,000-acre tract of land annexed by Portland in the mid-1980s; it is currently agricultural land but has been rezoned for industrial use so as to forestall other types of development.

As it turned out, the creation of industrial sanctuaries in Portland hasn't triggered the hostility that's been seen elsewhere, in part, Swan says, because the districts came about through a citywide, comprehensive zoning overhaul.

Portland's policy is straightforward: In all areas zoned for industrial use, office and retail space that is not ancillary to manufacturing is either forbidden or a conditional use. Only two residential uses are permitted: caretakers and artists' living and working space. (The Boston proposal also embraces artists, though one official wondered aloud at a hearing if Michelangelo ever thought of himself as a light manufacturer.)

So far, Portland's sanctuary policy seems to have lived up to its promise. Although industrial jobs in the city have declined by 10 percent in the past decade, blue-collar employment within the sanctuaries has increased 30 percent. The most active

sanctuary area, the one near the central business district, contains 1,400 businesses with 17,000 workers, 60 percent of them employed by industrial firms.

While, as some critics note, commercial development may actually employ more people, manufacturing jobs tend to pay higher wages and require less education than service jobs. In Boston, for example, the average blue-collar wage in 1986 was $25,400, compared to $20,203 in the service sector. And that, in the end, seems to be the reason that cities will continue to push for protected manufacturing zones.

"Without a manufacturing base, a city won't survive," says Boston's Marilyn Swartz Lloyd, who is also president of the National Council for Urban Economic Development. "We can't talk about blue-collar jobs and then stand back and let all the buildings be turned into retail spaces or offices."

John King covers business and planning issues for the Boston Globe.

STRATEGIC PLANNING: REINVENTING THE WHEEL?

Frank S. So
(February 1984)

You have probably noticed how the national media, when reporting on military actions in the world's all too many trouble spots, constantly refer to "strategic roads," "strategic hamlets," and "strategic valleys." It isn't very long before you realize that not every place or thing being described can be strategic. If everything is strategic, then one of two things is probably true: Nothing is strategic, or the language is being debased.

I am experiencing a very similar feeling as I look at the increasing interest in borrowing the business concept of strategic planning as an approach to planning cities.

Something else also is bothersome. New ideas are continually being infused into all professional fields, and planning is no exception. This, of course, is good. Without new ideas, the field would become stale, incompetent, and irrelevant. Sometimes, however, a new idea has striking similarities to things we have been through before—the notion of strategic planning for local government is an example. But so are such "new ideas" of the past as management by objective, zero base budgeting, and planning-programming-budgeting systems (PPBS). If we look at each of these in terms of its "life cycle," we begin to spot a predictable pattern.

First, a new or better system for some aspect of public management or planning is announced— maybe in a conference speech, maybe in a magazine article. Usually the idea is borrowed from another field or another institutional framework.

Next, the idea is promoted as a way to solve the problems of the present system by substituting a new system. For example, replace line item budgets with program budgets. Rarely are these new ideas promoted as a way of changing or adapting the present system by improving it; rather, it is the revolutionary aspect of the idea that counts. Little or no thought is given to the adaptability of a system taken from somewhere else, or, for that matter, to evaluation. Measurement might, after all, interfere with the promotion of the system.

At this point, a few scattered early experiments are tried. They are publicized in conferences and by academics (who must publish *something*), by consultants (who have a new service to sell), and by local officials and private citizens (who want to improve the local situation, but who also want to look innovative and progressive).

If the early experiences work out well, the idea spreads. It is likely then to be integrated into a local system and adapted to local conditions. If, however, early experiences are not positive, the idea withers away. In that case, a lot of money, time, and effort have been wasted.

The idea of applying business strategic planning to government is a new idea, with a life cycle like that of other new ideas. It is too early at this point to predict whether it will be a solid contribution to planning practice or simply a short-lived fad. There is no question, however, that if we, as planners, approach the idea as informed consumers, we will be better off down the road.

What is strategic planning?

Planning in the public sector came long before planning in the private sector. Some day a business historian might be able to identify the Daniel Burnham of business strategic planning, but for our purpose we can say that interest in long-range corporate planning began in the late 1950s and early 1960s in such companies as General Electric.

Over the next two decades, corporate planning evolved to the point where management consultants were being called in and corporate planning divisions were being established. As the concept evolved, it came to be known as strategic planning.

Perhaps the best way to compare strategic planning with traditional urban planning is operationally—that is, by singling out the major steps in both types of processes.

We note first that the traditional urban planning process is usually described as having five steps: setting goals, developing and analyzing alternatives, adopting plans, implementing plans, and establishing some sort of feedback or monitoring system.

The business strategic plan goes through a process that is partly similar and partly different. The differences offer the more creative and potentially useful concepts for public planning. Thus, the first step of strategic planning is to ask the question "How are we doing?" To answer it, corporate planning departments develop data on sales, markets, costs, and so on. But perhaps of greater importance to us is that the question forces those involved to be absolutely honest and self-critical. In contrast, traditional planning analyses are rarely critical of government performance.

The second step is to analyze the external factors—political, social, economic, and technological—that affect the corporation. The "environmental scan," as this process is sometimes called, includes those trends and factors over which the corporation has little control. (If you are in the oil business, you know who Yasser Arafat is.) Traditional planning might on occasion identify such factors, but rarely are the implications examined.

The third step is to examine critically the workings of the various elements of the corporation. How good is the marketing department? The research department? What is the condition of the production facilities? And so on. Again, traditional planning doesn't ask these questions.

The fourth step is to analyze the implications of the first three.

The first four steps are frequently referred to as the situation analysis or the situation audit. They involve the identification of four areas—in corporate argot, the "WOTS" of the situation: weaknesses, opportunities, threats, and strengths. These four areas are, of course, applicable to organizations that exist in a competitive world. Can we also speak of local governments as being in competition? Yes, we can. Think, for instance, of the competition between cities and suburbs or between Snow Belt and Sun Belt.

The fifth step of strategic planning is to develop strategic objectives and subobjectives, or as they are sometimes called, mission statements—the terminology varies in the literature. These objectives seek to correct weaknesses, take advantage of opportunities, deal with threats, and build on strengths. To be strategic, these objectives must be few in number, and they must relate to the bottom line of any business: return on investment, return on equity, and expanding markets. Here the difference between public and private planning is profound, even though at first glance the casual observer sees great similarities. Both processes develop goals. But, whereas public goals statements usually read like wish lists, the situation analysis raises fundamental questions and issues and should therefore help lead to more realistic objectives.

The sixth strategic planning step involves implementation—the preparation of programs, budgets, and marketing plans. Implementation strategies deal with basic management questions: why, what, when, who, and where? Traditional planning rarely goes into such details before the plan is published—and sometimes not at all.

Finally, we come to the last step, monitoring and feedback. Typically, at this stage corporations institute computer-based budgeting and amass production and sales data to measure progress toward strategic objectives. While monitoring is often discussed in public planning theory, it is rarely practiced.

Why the interest?

Cities and their planners are becoming interested in strategic planning for a variety of reasons—some good, some bad. Whether a reason is good or bad may vary from place to place, depending on the situation. . . .

One reason for the interest stems from the dissatisfaction of many practitioners with traditional planning models. In the late 1960s, the field abandoned the rigid map-oriented approach to planning that more properly belonged to engineering and architecture. Policy planning became the in thing.

Yet some disillusionment with the policy planning approach has resulted in a situation where many major urban areas have not updated their plans for at least a decade. For some, corporate strategic planning seems to offer a new and relevant approach to arriving at policy decisions.

It's also appealing to those who are impatient with the long time it takes to prepare the studies that precede the traditional comprehensive plan. Strategic planning seems to be something that can be done a lot faster. Strategic planners don't find it necessary, for example, to reinvent the analytical wheel. Instead, they tend to exploit existing data and past studies. The process also relies heavily on the knowledge of participants, knowledge that is often widely known and widely shared; there is no need to study the obvious. This is not to say that preparing a strategic plan is cheap. The plan prepared for one major city by a consultant cost about $500,000.

It's obvious that it is still much too early to assess strategic planning's long-range impact on government. I am bothered, however, by the promotional nature of the early literature. For example, only a few writers spend any significant amount of time discussing the problems involved in transferring a technique from the private sector to the public sector. Thus, a lot of the literature does not point out that the typical business corporation is a very top-down organization in which the chief executive officer and key staff have life and death decision-making powers. No local or state elected official has that kind of power. . . .

Private plans

A particularly troublesome point is that the early literature rarely differentiates between public and private strategic planning endeavors, instead fuzzily referring to strategic plans that have been prepared by private groups as a city or state plan.

Surely we know that a private plan is not a public plan. In one city, for instance, the list of people who were involved in the private strategic planning effort included an impressive number of corporate representatives. Representation from the public sector, however, was exceedingly small. Moreover, the handful of public-sector representatives often sent subordinates to key committee meetings—a practice that is always an indicator of a meeting's importance to the official invited. In the corporate sector, strategic planning is a management tool, which means that the people who run the business are heavily involved. A recent *Fortune* article, for example, points out that line managers are taking an increasingly active role in corporate strategic planning, supplementing or replacing the work of outside consultants and the corporate planning staff. In public agencies, officials, in effect, run the business, and they must be involved if the project is to succeed.

Where the sponsorship and direction of the strategic planning process are private, local merchants, conservationists, and political leaders may not be included. The planning director of the city mentioned above referred to the local strategic planning effort as "fundamentally a lobbying device for the local chamber of commerce." It was the chamber's way of getting its agenda into the public consciousness. But, he added, "as a means of decision making for government it has no value and is not particularly effective. A small group of knowledgeable people could have produced as much in a weekend." He concluded that "only government can convene the broad-based group that is required for government planning, and only the government can plan." . . .

Different mind sets

Strategic planners often use a variety of techniques of group dynamics to arrive at consensus. Thus, the government strategic planner may have to shift his role slightly from being a proposer of policies and plans (which he then tries to sell) to being a facilitator of a strategic planning process.

The strategic planner must also be incisive, never using a lack of data as an excuse for inaction. In other words, the planner must get to the point of the problem, the solution, or the policy.

A corollary point is that strategic planners stress the use of intuition. Business planners started out trying to get business leaders, who often relied on intuitive solutions, to act on more rational grounds. Recent experience indicates that intuition is extremely important. Public planners, too, need to get away from the fear of acting intuitively.

Another key element of strategic planning is a shift of emphasis away from long-range end states to the decisions that need to be made today. The literature calls this "emphasizing the futurity of present decisions." While forecasting plays a role, choosing a specific course of action is seen as even more important.

Strategic planning, especially through the situation analysis, sorts out those things about which you can do something and those things about which you can't do much of anything at all. Strategic planning, for example, may require that local government weed out unnecessary programs, activities, or units. This sorting out requires a degree of realism that may be very difficult to achieve in a political environment.

Private strategic planners pay a great deal of attention to money, and, if public planners are to follow their lead, they will have to do the same. Effectively administered, strategic planning can in fact provide a better framework for public service programming and budgeting.

Strategic planning also can play an important role in involving elected officials. The process demands interaction between technicians and administrators and policymakers. Further, a good strategic plan states its missions and objectives in clearly understandable language.

Strategic planning in government can provide a vehicle for improving managerial effectiveness. Forcing top administrators to concentrate on key strategic issues means that a better sense of mission and purpose can be achieved. Strategic planning can be a mindstretching exercise for top managers, a way of promoting creativity and innovative thinking and of forcing department heads to ask and answer questions of the highest importance to government.

Corporate strategic planners stress the preparation of action plans and budgets. As yet, it may be too early to know whether public strategic plans will move beyond broad, and sometimes inevitably vague, statements of mission. If the strategic planning process really works, new budgeting, management, and control systems will be put into place. If they are not, it's not strategic planning.

Finally, we come to the most important characteristic of strategic planning. That is the demand it places on us to ask such fundamental questions as these: Should some services be spun off to the private sector? Should user fees be charged for services that were formerly "free"? Is promoting industrial development in a declining community worthwhile? Should transit be subsidized if most of the riders are middle class? These questions and others have been raised, and answered, recently by a number of newly elected chief executives in both declining cities and cutback environments. These officials have been acting like strategic planners.

A couple of years ago I was talking with a key aide to a top municipal official. In our conversation I learned that he had a Ph.D. in philosophy. I asked if such a background was helpful in his job. His answer was that "philosophers ask fundamental questions." So do strategic planners.

Frank S. So, AICP, is a deputy executive director of APA. Materials for this article were gathered by Lisa Linowes, formerly of the APA research staff.

AG ZONING GETS SERIOUS

William Toner
(December 1984)

When I was a child in the mid-1950s, my father would drive my brothers and me to school each day. We would make the trip from Garden Grove, California, to Long Beach in about 30 minutes. And often, coming or going, we would pass through the towns of Dairy City, Dairyland, and Dairy Valley. I didn't know it then, but all three towns had been incorporated to keep us and those like us out.

As former South Dakotans, we were part of a huge migration into Orange County, a migration that increased the county's population by 500,000 during the 1950s and a decade later would add another 700,000. In the 1950s, dairy farmers began to experience the hazards of rural subdivisions and of elected officials who viewed every farm as a subdivision-in-waiting.

It was a classic land-use confrontation of the sort described by Gordon J. Fielding in a 1962 *Professional Geographer* (vol. 14, no. 1) article entitled "Dairying in Cities Designed to Keep People Out." It pitted new suburbanites against old-time dairymen, who found their property taxes rising, their neighbors hostile, their operations damaged, and their county supervisors decidedly unsympathetic. The way out, they thought, was to incorporate themselves into cities, where the dairies, not the suburbanites, would control the vote, the taxes, the land, and the zoning.

And, so in the mid-1950s, Dairy City, Dairyland, and Dairy Valley were incorporated. Together,

they covered 18 square miles, held a population of 5,000 people and 75,000 cows, and were protected by rigorous agricultural zoning.

The experiment failed. You won't find Dairy City, Dairy Valley, or Dairyland in any recent atlas. Instead you will find Cypress, La Palma, and Cerritos, name changes that tell you who won and who lost. For the most part, the only animals around are the quarterhorses that spring around the racetrack in nearby Los Alamitos. The dairies have long since moved to San Bernardino and Tulare counties, places where dairy owners were convinced they could escape the suburban invasion.

Thus ended one of the first, if not the first, attempts to use agricultural zoning and other controls to protect farms and farm operations.

Seeds of change

Roughly 10 years after the dairies left Orange County, I did too. And, ironically, after being part of the force that moved them out, I became interested in the ways in which communities could protect their farms. In 1978, I wrote *Saving Farms and Farmland,* a technical report published by APA. It recorded the experience of a handful of counties and townships that had ventured into the fight the dairymen had lost.

The report was difficult to write because examples were so scarce. Only a few jurisdictions at that time were using agricultural zoning in a serious way to protect agriculture. Yet, even then, the nation seemed to be on the verge of a major shift in its attitude toward the preservation of farmland.

By 1981, the federally sponsored National Agricultural Lands Study (NALS) had reported an enormous increase in the number of communities (a whopping 270 jurisdictions, 104 counties and 166 municipalities) that had adopted some form of agricultural zoning.

Serious business

Agricultural zoning was, in fact, the most commonly used farmland preservation technique cited by NALS. Other methods reported were: differential tax assessment to help discourage farmland speculation, right-to-farm laws designed to protect farmers from nuisance suits, and land trusts. Only a few jurisdictions reported buying or transferring development rights.

But not all agricultural zoning is equal. Serious

agricultural zoning has two distinguishing features. The first is that the basic purpose of the ordinance is to protect and maintain farms and farm operations. The second is that nonfarm uses, especially housing, are curtailed or excluded altogether.

The word agriculture attached to a zoning district does not in itself indicate a serious effort toward preservation. Quite the reverse is often true. Typically, the uses and standards applied to such districts are based on a conception of agriculture as vacant land rather than as a resource to be conserved. A wide variety of nonfarm uses, especially housing, may be permitted, and the standards applied may actually encourage rather than discourage the conversion of land to nonfarm use.

One of the main reasons that so few communities have used agricultural zoning to protect agriculture lies in zoning's urban origins. In 1936 Edward M. Bassett noted in his classic text, *Zoning,* that 1,200 municipalities had zoning but only 42 counties did, and 34 of those counties were concentrated in two states, Wisconsin and California. In most early zoning texts, agriculture is discussed, if at all, in terms of its compatibility with residential and business uses and rarely the reverse—in terms of the compatibility of urban uses with agriculture.

A stunning example of zoning's typical mismatch with rural needs is Stanley Township (pop. 1,730) in Cass County, North Dakota. It adopted a zoning ordinance drawn up by a local attorney and complete with single-family districts, multi-family districts, public districts, mobile home districts, commercial districts, industrial districts, and agricultural districts. Yet, according to Tracey Anderson of the Lake Agassiz Regional Council in Fargo, the township has never had a zoning map and the district boundaries are not described in the ordinance.

But, as I suggested above, things are changing. And the National Agricultural Lands Study documented that change. It found heavy concentrations of agricultural zoning activity in the northern tier of states (including Pennsylvania, Minnesota, Wisconsin, Illinois, Iowa, and Oregon); in California; and, to a lesser extent, in Maryland, the Dakotas, and Washington, with isolated examples in several other states.

New survey

Still, roughly five years after NALS first examined local zoning activity, numerous questions remain about the 270 cases cited. Critics continue to complain that agricultural zoning is "exclusionary," that it is "environmental zoning in disguise," and that it ignores agricultural interests. Given zoning's historic urban bias, the criticism is not surprising. Moreover, agriculture is the single largest private land user in the nation, and attempts to restrict it to agricultural use are bound to affect other land uses, especially in the populous regions.

Recently, APA undertook a survey of the jurisdictions represented in NALS to find out how local officials assess their experience. We wanted to know, first, if elected officials felt that agricultural zoning was working to accomplish their goals. Second, we asked about the nature of those goals: What did the communities want zoning to do? Third, we asked what special interest groups were involved in the design or administration of agricultural zoning. Fourth, did the communities put agricultural zoning in a comprehensive planning context before adopting it, and finally, what were the technical weaknesses and strengths of the zoning?

We sent surveys to 97 communities, mostly counties, that covered the 270 jurisdictions identified by NALS, and we asked those most familiar with agricultural zoning, typically zoning administrators and planners, to fill out the questionnaire. We have received 86 responses to date, an 89 percent rate of return.

As the returns began to come in, it became clear that agricultural zoning activity had increased substantially since NALS. We had asked respondents to identify other communities that had adopted agricultural zoning in the last five years and found the numbers growing. So we decided to expand our coverage to include the additional communities. Thus, the survey continues. But preliminary figures from three states show agricultural zoning in at least 80 counties and 242 townships—more than the 270 communities found in NALS. Wisconsin, for example, reports that 32 counties and 242 townships are using agricultural zoning as compared with 13 counties and 116 townships shown by NALS. Iowa reports 17 counties today (seven at the time of NALS); Minnesota, 31 counties today (12 then). . . .

Are you satisfied?

Three questions we asked were aimed at determining whether local officials felt that agricultural zoning was effective. Given that agricultural zoning remains experimental, we wanted to get an idea of the level of satisfaction and the degree of support given to it. The responses would also suggest the likelihood of other communities using this type of land-use control.

In general, how satisfied is your chief elected body with agricultural zoning? 45 percent responded "very satisfied"; 49 percent "somewhat satisfied"; 5 percent "somewhat dissatisfied"; 1 percent "very dissatisfied."

The support given agricultural zoning by your elected and appointed decision makers has been. . .? 78 percent said "good"; 19 percent "fair"; and 3 percent "poor." As a check on these responses, we asked about any changes made since the agricultural zoning ordinance was adopted. No changes or changes that resulted in a strengthening of agricultural zoning would seem to indicate that officials are basically satisfied.

Since you first adopted agricultural zoning, the changes that have occurred have made it. . .? 72 percent said "stronger" (more protective of farms and/or farming); 5 percent "weaker"; and 23 percent "about the same."

The responses to these questions were consistent. In the main, officials seem to be satisfied with agricultural zoning and their satisfaction was reinforced by their actions. Most of the changes that had been made in the zoning strengthened it, indicating a basic satisfaction with the approach. To one observer, John Keller, a professor in the regional and community planning program at Kansas State University, the responses suggest that "the level of awareness of county officials has changed drastically." Adds Keller, "They know a lot of things now, and they demand far more sophisticated zoning."

In a few cases, however, support has declined. Melanie Tyler, associate planner in Whitman County, Washington, described the local situation in these words: "There seems to be a willingness to sacrifice agricultural land for other economic uses—almost anything except residential development. Whenever an opportunity arises for development, the landowner lambastes the ag zoning restrictions." Jack Schoop, planning director of Santa Clara County, California, wrote: "The problem here is that the county is booming—Silicon Valley is spreading out. Despite our 1980 general plan and our recently adopted ag zoning, speculation has driven the price of the remaining farmland out of reach of farmers. They've retreated to intensive flower culture and mushroom growing."

There's trouble on the East Coast, too. Auburn, Maine, a city of 21,000, has had restrictive agricultural zoning since 1960, making it one of the oldest programs in the country. It is also one of the most restrictive. The agricultural district now covers 17,500 acres—40 percent of the city's land area. The restrictive zoning has been supported by citizens, officials, and farmers alike, and it has substantially changed patterns of development. Recently, however, it was challenged by three council members. No decisions have yet been made, but any serious weakening of such a successful program would not bode well for agricultural zoning elsewhere.

The next series of questions addressed the issue of what the zoning was intended to accomplish. We wanted to know about the status of farms in the agricultural district and, specifically, whether agriculture was given priority use and whether farmland was being set aside for long-term agricultural use rather than established as a transitional use (from farming to urban uses). Historically, designation as a transitional use has been a characteristic of urban bias in agricultural zoning.

Do you consider the farmlands in your most restrictive agricultural district as being set aside for long-term agricultural use? 93 percent said yes; 7 percent no.

In the most restrictive agricultural district, is agriculture considered the highest and best use of land? 94 percent said yes; 6 percent no.

Clearly, agriculture is viewed as both a long-term land use and as the highest and best use. But we also know from NALS that communities adopt agricultural zoning for a variety of purposes. And that variety might explain why so many communities have adopted agricultural zoning. If the controls appeal to a variety of interest groups for various reasons, public support for them is likely to be widespread. To understand what these purposes are and how widely they are shared, we asked these five questions about the community's principal purpose in adopting agricultural zoning:

Was it to keep a lid on public service costs associated with sprawl? 61 percent said yes; 39 percent no.

Was it to protect natural resources (water quality, woodlands, groundwater recharge areas, wetlands, etc.) 65 percent said yes; 35 percent no.

Was it to protect the agricultural economic base? 96 percent said yes; 4 percent no.

Was it to curtail farmland loss? 90 percent said yes; 10 percent no.

Was it to curtail conflicts between farms and nearby subdivisions? 79 percent said yes; 21 percent no.

Thus, we learned that communities adopted agricultural zoning for reasons ranging from stopping sprawl to protecting environmental resources. But the reasons cited most often had to do with protecting the agricultural economy, stopping farmland conversion, and curtailing conflict between farm and nonfarm residents. Regarding the last point, Bob Peterson, planning director of Merced County, California, wrote: "Our opinion is that if you live in an area that is planned and zoned for agriculture, you will experience agricultural noise, dust, and odors. If that disturbs a resident, he should relocate."

Bottom line

Of all the stated purposes, more respondents (96 percent) identified protecting the agricultural economic base than any other. "In our agricultural district," wrote Bryon Whiting, zoning administrator of Calhoun County, Iowa, "we're not interested in industrial growth, we're interested in agricultural development." Robert Gray, director of policy development for the American Farmland Trust in Washington, D.C., and former director of NALS, also sees the economic argument as central to agricultural zoning: "Local communities are now aware of the contribution of the agricultural economy," he says. "They recognize that scattered development is costly."

In at least one place, Chester County, Pennsylvania, local officials have come up with a novel idea, an agricultural development council—an agricultural version of an industrial development program. But instead of concentrating on manufacturing, the agricultural development council is designed to support farming as economic development. Stephen Kehs, formerly a Chester County planner and now assistant planning director for Cumberland County, New Jersey, explained why the council is needed: "City people don't look at farming as a business," he said, "they look at the land as a place to build. The ag council is trying to

turn that idea around, and I think they're successful."

Sometimes nice-sounding statements of public purpose can mask real motives. It is essential, therefore, to understand the role of special interest groups in the design and administration of agricultural zoning. If, as critics charge, environmental interests are dominant in getting the zoning adopted, they are more likely to be interested in environmental protection than in agriculture. Similarly, if antidevelopment interests are strong, it can be assumed that the real purpose of agricultural zoning is to keep newcomers out rather than to keep agriculture in. Finally, if agricultural interests are central, one can expect the public purpose to reflect agricultural sentiments. Thus, several questions centered on the role of special interests in supporting agricultural zoning:

The support given agricultural zoning by the agricultural community has been . . .? 74 percent said "good"; 22 percent "fair"; and 4 percent "poor."

In developing your agricultural zoning, how influential was the role played by the agricultural community? 51 percent said "very influential"; 45 percent "moderately influential"; 4 percent "minor." None chose "no influence."

Identify the interest groups involved in the development of your agricultural zoning. 36 percent said "agricultural interest groups"; 16 percent "environmental groups"; 13 percent "business groups"; 13 percent "urban development groups"; 10 percent "good government groups"; 6 percent "antidevelopment groups"; and 6 percent "other."

Evaluate the extent of influence of each of these interest groups on the design or administration of your agricultural zoning.

Interest Groups	Very	Moderate	Not Very	None
Ag	51%	23%	3%	1%
Environmental	12	26	24	11
Business	5	12	19	24
Urban Dev.	12	10	26	21
Good Gov.	10	18	10	30
Anti-dev.	5	5	16	9
Other	6	6	1	3

The responses to all of these questions indicate that the agricultural community plays a far more important role in supporting agricultural zoning than either environmental interests or antidevelopment interests. Indeed, business and urban development interests are as significant as environmental or antidevelopment interests. Thus the evidence does not support those who attack agricultural zoning as environmental zoning in disguise or as the tool of antidevelopment interests. The evidence indicates that the agricultural community played a strong role in developing agricultural zoning and remains committed to it.

Effects on development

A related series of questions addressed the issue of the effect of agricultural zoning on new urban development and housing construction. We wanted to get at the place of agricultural zoning in the broader planning process and, in particular, to see if it seriously impinged on lands available for additional housing.

In adopting your agricultural zoning, did you evaluate its effect on new urban development? 44 percent said yes; 56 percent no.

If you answered yes, did you determine its effect on new housing construction? 49 percent said yes; 51 percent no. (Because of a flaw in the design of the questionnaire, more people responded to this question than should have been possible.)

Do you have enough land set aside to meet projected housing demands? 97 percent said yes; 3 percent said no.

The response indicates that most of the communities did not evaluate the effect of agricultural zoning on new urban development generally, or on new housing construction specifically. But, by a large margin, respondents did indicate that they had enough land set aside to meet projected housing demands.

The final set of questions revolved around the nature and consistency of zoning administration. We were interested in knowing whether written criteria were used in evaluating rezoning petitions in the agricultural district and whether the recommendations of the planning staff were generally supported by local appointed officials. The answers indicate that written criteria are more important to the staff, the planning commission, and the zoning board of appeals than to the chief elected body. Still, 40 percent of our respondents indicated that the chief elected body used written criteria in evaluating rezonings. A clear majority said that the staff prepared recommendations for elected and/or appointed officials and that, in most cases, their recommendations were followed, indicating that the public purpose in adopting agricultural zoning is likely to be served. . . .

What can be said at this point is that the historic, urban-biased practice of agricultural zoning is changing so that now an agricultural district is more likely to be one seriously devoted to agriculture and not simply a residential district in disguise. It can also be said that the experience of our respondents has been largely satisfactory and that they have made their agricultural zoning more restrictive over time, not less. The agricultural community has played the dominate role in shaping these local programs, and it appears that its support continues. Finally, because agricultural zoning serves several public purposes, its political appeal is broad. One is not surprised, then, to find that the list of communities adopting it continues to grow.

William Toner teaches planning at Governors State University in University Park, Illinois. He was a consultant to NALS.

TIPS FOR BETTER MAPS

Dennis McClendon
(August 1988)

In several years of observing maps prepared for planning reports and other publications, I have been struck by how often the same mistakes are made. The tips that follow are intended to help planning mapmakers come up with maps that are easy to use and pleasant to look at.

Prepare the map for printing instead of display. Too many of the maps I see in planning reports obviously started life as oversized graphics prepared for display at a public hearing or commission meeting. The mapmaker started with a huge base map and colored directly on it in dozens of subtle shades. Lettering machine labels were pasted directly on the map.

When the time comes to put out a printed report, the original map must be photographed and reproduced in full color. Not only is that a costly process, but the finished product is hard to read. Labels and legends that could be crisply reproduced from an original are muddied by being screened for color printing.

A better approach would be to prepare the maps for printing. Prepare the map only slightly larger than the size it will be printed. Place ruby masking film overlays on areas to be printed in color and put labels and legends on a separate overlay, which the printer can then overprint neatly on the map. If you need a large version to place on an easel, ask the printer to produce an oversized proof.

Don't work too large. The biggest single defect in planners' maps may be the fact that they have been reduced to a fraction of their original size. While that makes them look precise—too much so, usually—it also makes them unreadable. Lines become too thin to reproduce and type too small to read; it's impossible to make out details.

I don't like to work at more than 150 percent of reproduction size. Type sizes must be calculated so that nothing will be smaller than six-point type *when reproduced.* The same is true for line weights: Nothing finer than one-half point (about the same as a 000 technical pen) will reproduce, so use thicker rules on any map that will be reduced.

Start with a good base map. In high-growth areas, finding an up-to-date base map to work from is always a problem. U.S. Geological Survey topographic maps set the standard for accuracy, but are usually hopelessly out of date for suburban areas. In some cases, because of the Census Bureau's TIGER file project, the USGS's 1:100,000 series may be more up-to-date than the better known 1:24,000 quads.

A little-known resource is the color separates (individual overlays of map features) available from USGS for its maps. Overlaying the blue and black portions, for instance, provides a map of water features and culture (streets and landmarks), without the distractions of contours, woodland cover, urban tint, or survey lines.

Another resource is the sets of county maps maintained by state highway departments. Often these sets include large-scale up-to-date sheets for urban areas. Be aware, though, that the lines for U.S. and state highways may be drawn so thick that they dominate the maps, making them unattractive for general use. Small-scale state highway maps often present another problem: They have been distorted in order to make them easier for mo-

torists to read. Unwary cartographers may find that intersections have been moved, downtown streets spread apart, and winding routes straightened.

Most cities maintain some sort of official map, but generally it makes a poor base map. The official maps are usually double-line street maps, drawn at such a large scale that they look wispy when reduced and the street names become unreadable. The maps may include irrelevant alleys or, inexplicably, show freeways as blank strips of right-of-way.

Most of the base maps now being maintained on computers and drawn by plotters are even worse, with no attention paid to proportion in line weight. Agencies with geographic information systems are not going back to ink on linen, however, and computerized maps are improving. ESRI, a GIS vendor whose ARC/Info system was recently chosen for use by the National Geographic Society, annually publishes a book of maps produced by its customers, and the examples get better each year. As part of the TIGER mapping project, the Census Bureau has also been working to develop symbols, particularly coincident boundary markings, that are better suited to their computers' electrostatic plotters than the traditional hand-scribed lines.

Don't be afraid to redraw. A lot of people accept an unsatisfactory base map because they think it's too much trouble to do anything about it. The right tools can make it easy to redraw in just a few minutes. Start by putting a sheet of acetate over the original base map and then put in the highway route markers and interchange symbols that you will need to work around. Flexible (crepe) border tape, such as Formaline or Letraline, goes over the roads and streets. (I curve it as needed and tear it off at intersections with my thumbnail.) Within minutes, you can cover all the streets visible on the original base map.

Generalize. Just as it's silly to carry a numerical estimate to several decimal places, it's silly to let complex boundaries or winding watercourses dominate a map made to illustrate another point. Every jot and title of a city's legal boundaries need not be shown, for instance, on a simple map locating a neighborhood within the city. In fact, it's distracting.

Generalization when redrawing at a smaller scale is an old and distinguished cartographic tradition, one sometimes forgotten as it became easier to photoreduce maps. Now the biggest threat is from computers, which can reproduce every detail of a shoreline, for instance, no matter what scale the map is.

Use standard symbols. The value of symbols is that they are easily recognized. Yet a surprising number of newspaper maps confuse the highway route markers that Americans have spent 60 years learning to recognize, putting U.S. highway numbers inside Interstate shields and vice versa.

Sometimes planners on a desperate search for Zip-A-Tone patterns to represent various land uses end up with patterns that have different common meanings. As a result, "agricultural" areas are shown in the stippled pattern that usually means sand, and little tufts of grass are used to represent industrial areas instead of wetlands.

Don't crowd. Many planning maps suffer from overcrowding. Just about every plan, for instance, includes a map of current land uses, often done in dozens of shades; such a map is costly to reproduce and of questionable value. Even worse are maps that use different patterns in a single color to represent use classifications (industrial, commercial, multifamily). Since the real point of such a map is to show where uses are concentrated—where the commercial strips are, for instance—a series of smaller maps showing only one classification each would be more useful.

I suggest replacing the big land-use map with several smaller maps, each showing only a single category. The smaller maps are simpler and less expensive, for they don't have to be printed in color. Distinctions—between single-family and multifamily on the residential map, for instance—can be made with tints.

Use maps to make a point. The often-cited justification for a big single map of land uses is that it is a reference document. And sometimes that's a valid reason to make a map. But more often, maps are included in a report to make a point, and they should be drawn to communicate that point. The smaller maps say directly: "Commercial is strung along the strips," or "All the multifamily is south of the freeway."

Making any map involves hundreds of choices—what streets or towns to leave out, what features to simplify, how to symbolize features, how to divide data into classes for thematic maps. The best way to make those choices is to keep in mind why the map is being made.

Take advantage of the printing process. On a printed document, you can do things you can't do easily by hand. For example, virtually all my maps use a 30 percent screen for the ground, with streets, water features, and boundaries reversed out. That allows me to show important features in black, right on the base map. If I have redrawn the base map using border tape on acetate, as described earlier, the acetate can be used to contact print a reverse print. Flaws can be corrected and grade separations drawn in on the print, which shows white streets on a black background. Put labels and names on a separate overlay. The printer can combine them with the base map so names can overprint tints or thin lines.

For a small number of copies to be run off on a copying machine, or using plastic offset printing plates, prepare the artwork as if it were going to be printed using traditional negatives, flats, and plates. But ask the printer to use the composite negatives to produce a Velox proof instead of a metal plate. The Velox proof can then be used as camera-ready artwork for reproduction.

You should also ask the printer to strip in screen tints. The results will usually be much smoother than you get with Zip-A-Tone film.

Beware of bad reproduction. Think about the limits of the reproduction process before you begin. Screen tints, for instance, present serious problems for unsophisticated print shops. Usually in such a case you must limit yourself to coarse screens—no finer than 85 lines per inch—and expect them to reproduce as much as 20 percent darker or lighter than the original. Because many of these shops use photostat-type platemakers, originals must be camera-ready just as if they were going to be photocopied.

Planners often apply adhesive screen tints such as Zip-A-Tone film directly to maps. But be careful. Any cut marks or lines (even in non-repro blue) under the shaded areas will show up as a dark area. Any type or lines must go on top of the screen, both because the Zip-A-Tone is not perfectly transparent and because it will be ruined if moved. Border tape with a clear carrier film can also mask whatever is underneath just enough to keep it from reproducing well.

If you use a second color, do everything you can to ensure proper registration. Use stable material for overlays (Mylar is best; 5-mil acetate is better than the more common 3-mil thickness) and include registration marks. You can deliberately design a map so misregistration will be less noticeable by, for example, not outlining color areas in black. If there is no place where the two colors touch, you can usually get better results by putting everything on a single original and marking the color breaks on a tissue overlay. The printer will make two identical negatives, opaquing out the black on one and the color on the other.

I often make several overlays from the same piece of ruby litho film, guaranteeing that they will fit together properly when printed. There's no danger of an island overlapping the water, for instance, if the island overlay consists of the missing portion of the water overlay.

Observe lettering conventions. Many people don't realize—until it's pointed out—that mapmakers have traditional ways of distinguishing labels. Water features, for example, are nearly always italicized. Salt water features are usually all capital letters, and letterspaced to span the feature. Names of streams usually curve along the watercourse. Mountain ranges are set in all caps, but peaks are caps and lowercase. City names follow a variety of rules, but most mapmakers use all caps for other political subdivisions, parks, and areas such as airports.

Amateur mapmakers often use all caps for everything, perhaps in the misguided belief that they are more readable (the opposite is true). To make matters worse, they invariably use sans-serif typefaces, which are at their ugliest when set in all caps. Eight-point type is large enough for most maps.

Labels are generally set straight with the map borders, except when they are aligned with linear features such as streets. Vertical labels read best from top to bottom. On a crowded downtown map, however, it is sometimes best to turn building labels at a consistent 45 degree angle, so they don't interfere with street names.

Watch those patterns. On thematic maps, use patterns that have a recognizable progression. The viewer should not have to refer to a legend to see which pattern denotes, for example, the high-income census tracts. There should be a clear progression from a light pattern for low-income areas to the darkest pattern for high-income tracts. The easiest way to do this for five classes or less is with screen tints, changing in increments of 20 percent. Screen tints closer in value than that are hard to distinguish from each other.

When color is available, avoid the temptation to range through the spectrum. The progression from red to yellow to green to blue may be a phenomenon of physics but the eye does not perceive it as a clear progression. In a book published in 1982, *Mapping Information,* the late Howard T. Fisher suggested using related colors from the same side of the color wheel. A three-color progression might consist of yellow, orange, and red; a four-color sequence could use yellow, green, blue, violet. The most common problem, five classes, can be solved by using yellow, green, blue, violet, red, taking care that the violet doesn't overwhelm the red. The intensity of intermediate colors must be carefully adjusted so that the highest value is also the most dominant color.

Color makes it possible to show two variables on the same thematic map, and the Census Bureau's 1980 *Urban Atlas* series shows some fine examples, progressing from yellow to blue along one axis and from yellow to red along the other. Areas in which both variables are equal are shown in purple. In most instances, though, it's clearer to use two maps.

The best solution to the dilemma of creating patterns that have a clear progression but can easily be linked to the legend is the Fisher cartographic patterns, designed (and patented) by the author of *Mapping Information* and now sold by Letraset. From a distance, these patterns give the impression of screen tints, progressing from a very light pattern to a dense near-solid. But the pattern is composed of polygons whose shape tells where they fall in the progression. Thus, the third in the series is composed of tiny triangles, the fourth of squares, and so on. Using these patterns, it is possible to represent 10 different shades, all in a clear progression, yet distinguishable.

Unfortunately, about the time Fisher's patterns became available, computer software for thematic mapping became popular. Making thematic maps is much easier with these programs, but the results usually require the viewer to remember that the progression of values goes from green crosshatch to blue slanting lines to a red brick pattern.

In response to complaints about this problem, software vendors respond that users can design their own patterns. If that's true, more planners should do so. Electrostatic printers are certainly capable of emulating Fisher's patterns or producing screen tints. Even pen plotters can produce a progressive series of patterns based on increasing crosshatch density, or on color—but, please, not both, and not one based on what direction the crosshatching runs.

Question the value of a thematic map. Think for a moment about the big map NBC will have behind Tom Brokaw on election night. As the big Western states turn blue, the map will make it seem that Bush is winning in a landslide even though the red (Democratic) states like New York and Massachusetts represent more electoral votes. The meaning of the data is perverted when its display is dominated by something unrelated—the size of the states. Planners see the same skewing when large suburban high-income census tracts dominate a map that actually shows serious urban poverty.

One way around the problem is to combine the base map with a bar chart. The base map can be redrawn into an oblique, or bird's-eye, projection to show the bars rising out of the districts.

Another technique is to use a dasymetric (dot-frequency) map. Instead of coloring the high-population tract red, the mapmaker places one dot for every 100 people inside the tract. You can place the dots using your knowledge of an area to show, for example, high density along the edge of a park but no one living in the park. Even a rudimentary knowledge of an area lets you spread out the dots around the edges to avoid the "cliffs" endemic to thematic maps: the appearance that a value changes dramatically at the tract boundary.

Think about your data classes. The range of data displayed on a thematic map can be broken into classes several ways, none of them always "correct." Let's say, for example, that a thematic map of Illinois counties by population is to include five classes, each represented by a different color. If we divide the range of values into five equal segments, the map will be dominated by the great number of counties in class two (low-moderate population), Cook County (Chicago) will be the only county in the top class, and the next-to-highest class may have no qualifying counties.

If we set the values so that there are an equal number of counties in each class, we will see more differentiation among the mass of moderate-population Downstate counties, but the whole northern tier of the state will be in the same class as Cook County, making it look as if the population is spread evenly from Lake Michigan to the Mississippi River.

A third way to break the classes would be to space them along the bell-shaped curve beloved of statisticians. This would differentiate the very-high- and very-low-population counties well, and would also distinguish fairly well among the many moderately populated counties.

Which way should I do it? It depends on what I'm trying to show. Luckily, the new microcomputer software is ideal for trying several different breakdowns in just a few minutes, making it possible to decide by trial and error.

Dennis McClendon is the managing editor of Planning.

THE MOUSE THAT ROARED

Dennis McClendon
(January 1988)

What is desktop publishing good for? For laying out inexpensively produced, frequently revised publications that incorporate graphics. Since that pretty well describes most planning documents, it's easy to understand the growing popularity of such software in planning offices.

Consider the general plan produced for Petaluma, California, last year by Palo Alto planning consultants Naphtali Knox and Associates. Instead of the typical typewritten document, it is a handsome two-column book. Large chapter headings are accompanied by small drawings, policy objectives are set apart by an overprinted screen, and charts are integrated with the text.

All that could have been done without desktop publishing, says Knox, but not by the staff of his small office. And a small city like Petaluma could not afford to typeset and keyline the plan using traditional methods. So Knox put the plan together on an Apple Macintosh microcomputer, using Aldus PageMaker software and a laser printer.

By using desktop publishing, says Knox, the Petaluma plan was compressed into fewer pages and made more readable. The plan won the California chapter's 1987 award for best comprehensive plan, partly for its graphics.

Desktop publishing is also useful for flyers, meeting notices, and newsletters. Alwin Kloeb, a senior planner with the Hillsborough County

(Florida) City-County Planning Commission, says her agency uses PageMaker for flyers and will soon use it to produce newsletters. Last year Kloeb used the program to create new page designs for the Florida APA chapter's Sun Coast section newsletter and then turned the disks over to an outside design firm with desktop publishing equipment. Now the copy for each issue is "flowed" into the existing page layouts and masters are created for the printer's use.

Presentation graphics can also be improved markedly with desktop publishing programs. Agencies that previously relied on transfer lettering or Kroy machines can quickly set type in a variety of sizes and styles, and charts and graphs can be imported from graphics or spreadsheet programs. Overhead transparencies can be printed directly by most laser printers, and best of all, a change of wording or an updated figure means simply correcting the file and reprinting.

Defining terms

"Desktop publishing" is something of a misnomer. The programs described here are really page layout programs, which organize areas of text, electronically stored illustrations, and rules and boxes. The resulting files, which describe all these elements for the computer using a single page-description language, are usually printed on a high-resolution laser printer.

The layout designer starts by opening a new page on the computer screen and giving it a basic format. Working either with predefined layouts or starting from scratch, the designer determines the size of the page, how many columns and what margins the page will have, and the presence of any recurring elements such as column rules, page numbers, or running heads.

Desktop publishing programs have only limited word processing and illustration capabilities, so a document usually begins with text files that have been composed separately on a word processor. The page designer imports these files and places them into the page layout, using a mouse to point to the area on the screen where text should go. Some word processors allow the text files to be formatted—with types and sizes of subheads, for example. Otherwise, the designer uses the desktop publishing software to specify type size and style.

Different desktop publishing programs use different methods to place text in a document. Page-Maker, the most popular program, uses something of a "drafting table" system. The first column of type is placed in the proper position, and the excess hangs off the bottom. It can be cut at the bottom of the page and placed at the top of the next column, or temporarily laid somewhere else on the "drafting table."

Ventura, the most popular software for MS-DOS computers, uses a slightly different system. A series of columns is first selected and linked, and then the text is permitted to flow into the selected areas. Controls can be set to avoid subheads at the bottom of columns and "widows" (short lines) at the tops. In either system, the various parts of an article are now linked, so that deleting a paragraph in the first column causes the remaining text to automatically ripple forward.

That's a big advantage for documents that are frequently revised. The freedom of the word processor—and the subtle ways that it changes people's working habits—is now brought to page layout as well. Galleys of type laid down with desktop publishing software are always straight, never fall off the page, and can be "snapped to" invisible guide lines for precise placement.

The software includes tools for creating such miscellany as rules, boxes, screen tints, and circles. Other graphics are imported from specialized graphics programs, such as pie or bar charts from spreadsheet or business graphics programs. More complex graphics can come from paint, draw, and computer-aided drafting programs. Capabilities vary, but most bit-mapped (raster) or object-oriented (vector) graphics can be cropped, resized, and even stretched or compressed once placed into the page design. . . .

Once the page layout is completed, it is usually printed on a laser printer, which looks and works like a small photocopier. Laser printers form images from dots, as do dot-matrix printers, but the resolution is so much higher (usually 300 dots per inch) that most people don't notice.

Documents are sent to the laser printer using a page description language—and PostScript, the most popular one, is something of a breakthrough. Instead of describing characters as bit-mapped images, it uses formulas to describe a curve or a character mathematically. This means that type can be any size or be printed at the highest possible resolution of 1,200 dots per inch.

The resulting copy is a vast improvement over

typewritten copy. Proportional typefaces (laser versions of the most popular phototypesetting fonts) dramatically improve readability and usually take up less room. Changes in type style and size add emphasis and organize the document, and a multicolumn layout improves legibility and makes the use of photos or drawings easier.

But it is important to realize that laser printer output is not typesetting. Letter edges are not smooth, typeface selection is limited, letterspacing and kerning (closely fitting adjacent letters) are unsophisticated, and hypenation and justification routines are usually so bad that it's better to do without.

The leaders

Some 60,000 desktop publishing systems have been sold to date, the vast majority of them using Aldus's PageMaker software on some variety of Apple Computer's Macintosh. These two companies invented the field, but a market with this much promise quickly attracted competitors. In addition to programs for the Macintosh there are now several packages available for the rival IBM-compatible PCs, also called MS-DOS machines.

Only one package (PageMaker) is available for both kinds of machine, so the choice of hardware and software is closely linked. The Macintosh's great advantages include its high-resolution screen and a mouse, both necessary for moving around detailed items. Another natural advantage is the "user interface": the way in which all Macintosh software uses pull-down menus, point and click selection, and dialogue boxes. Even a first-time user, if familiar with the general way all Macintosh software works, can stumble around in PageMaker or its competitors without being totally mystified. The unshakable standards used by all Macintosh software to store data make it easier to exchange files, and these standards and the more advanced operating system make setting up a system much easier.

But there are at least eight million MS-DOS machines already installed, many in large corporations and governments where it can be tough to get approval to buy a Macintosh. While there are MS-DOS desktop publishing packages, they are not always the best solution.

To begin with, only AT-class machines (using the 80286 or an equivalent chip) are fast enough to run desktop publishing programs without frus-

tration. Desktop publishing will also require a high-resolution EGA standard) monitor (plus card) and a mouse. The cost of these additions or upgrades can come close to the cost of a separate Macintosh system.

MS-DOS machines so far have not proven well-suited for desktop publishing or other graphic applications. Even the fastest ("386") machines are noticeably slower than the Mac. The MS-DOS "desktop environments," such as Digital Research's GEM and Microsoft's Windows, are slow and hard to use. A relative of Windows, called the Presentation Manager, is being developed for IBM's new PS/2 computers, but software that can use its capabilities is still in the future.

Another disadvantage for MS-DOS machines is the unfriendly commands of DOS itself, from paths and file names to serial port parameters. Downloadable PostScript files have finally become available for MS-DOS machines, but screen fonts are so crude that typefaces can't be distinguished from each other.

MS-DOS machines are better for word processing, though, and many offices have mountains of data in that format or have invested in an MS-DOS local area network. That's one reason for the popularity of such MS-DOS desktop publishing software as Ventura. Another possibility is to export the text from an MS-DOS machine to a Macintosh running desktop publishing software. Software-hardware combinations like MacLink Plus or the new 5.25 inch MS-DOS disk drive for the Macintosh SE and II allow communication using the universal data language of ASCII. . . .

Costs are similar for both Macintosh and MS-DOS systems. MS-DOS turnkey packages (AT-compatible computer, EGA monitor, software, and laser printer) sell for just under $10,000. A Macintosh SE with a 20-megabyte hard disk can be bought for around $3,500, the Apple LaserWriter Plus for $5,700, and PageMaker software for $500. A large-screen display for the Macintosh will cost about $1,800; the MS-DOS equivalent about $1,000.

Picking software

Choosing software is no less complicated. The best known is Aldus's PageMaker (street price about $500), first developed for the Macintosh but released last spring for MS-DOS machines. Its interactive "drafting table" metaphor is easy to work with for newsletters and other short, graphics-filled documents. The main competition in the MS-DOS world is Xerox's Ventura Publisher (about $550), whose ability to tag parts of documents with type specifications and batch-style text placement better suits it to long documents with lots of text.

Competing with PageMaker for the Mac is Letraset's Ready Set Go! ($165). Its advantages include larger page sizes, automatic runarounds, and more word processing features. Another competitor, Quark's Xpress, offers automatic text placement for long documents and more typographic refinements, but it is expensive ($550), copy-protected, and reportedly more difficult to learn.

None of this software is effortless, planners warn. "It takes a lot of patience to learn the software and use it right," says Colette Gerstenberg, office supervisor for the Bucks County Planning Commission, which uses Ready Set Go! Kirby Metcalfe, manager of the Dallas planning department's graphics division, has found Ready Set Go! easier to teach to planners than PageMaker.

Moreover, not everyone thinks desktop publishing is worth the time. Kathy Oniskey, in Bucks County, says using the software is frustrating because everything has to be moved indirectly, using the mouse. "Most things I work on are not repetitive enough to save any time," she says. "I did two newsletters on it, but then I could no longer justify as training the time it was taking—three times as long as by hand."

Other projects are better candidates for desktop publishing. Metcalfe points to Dallas's zoning use charts, which took his department about 450 manhours using traditional pasteup techniques. With the department's new Macintosh, the project took about 100 manhours, he says, and was a "big seller" in convincing people of the system's worth.

And desktop publishing software needn't be at odds with traditional pasteup. Some jobs are best done as combinations of both: Galleys of type from the laser printer can be easily hand-pasted into a short newsletter, or a frame, with title and legend, can be created for a hand-drawn map.

It's also a mistake to think of the software as an end in itself. Some users have let the software's limits control the look of their publications, accepting bad typography, shoehorned layouts, and other compromises. Others, suddenly confronted with a large choice of typefaces and special effects, have used them all, producing newsletters that look like ransom notes. Aldus has begun to offer discounts on graphic design books to help educate users and now offers a package of well-designed newsletter templates for users to build on.

Many of the features of desktop publishing are available with other software. Some word processing programs, particularly for the Macintosh, can access laser printers' proportional typefaces or produce multicolumn documents. Most Macintosh draw, paint, drafting, charting, and even spreadsheet software can integrate slick typefaces and screen tints. Metcalfe says his department has "parked the Kroy machine" and instead produces map legends and street names on applique film run through the LaserWriter's single sheet feed.

One related application of particular interest is Adobe's new Illustrator software, a sophisticated drawing program that takes full advantage of PostScript to produce smooth curves, fill patterns, and embedded lettering. Metcalfe redrew a base map of Dallas using Illustrator, adding screens in certain areas for the maps in the city's growth policy plan. He notes that the base can be updated as needed and used "forevermore," and that it can be embedded directly into desktop publishing documents. . . .

Kloeb, in Hillsborough County, has found advantages in creating documents that look more finished earlier in production. Last year she used PageMaker to produce comps for the agency's annual report, a project she says elected officials feel a "personal stake" in. The project went through several revisions, but at each stage officials were seeing an essentially finished document. "If you had to do those permutations using traditional tools," she says, "it would have cost thousands and taken months. Showing officials a polished document at an early stage seems to facilitate the process."

Dennis McClendon is the managing editor of Planning.

THE NEXT PICTURE SHOW

Sylvia Lewis
(July 1988)

To David Ciaccio, paper is a thing of the past. Ciaccio, owner of an Omaha planning and landscape architecture firm, is using a combination of videotape and still photos for planning presentations. What he's come up with is a low-cost version of the simulations that others are doing with expensive scale models or sophisticated CADD systems.

Ciaccio first used his system in Council Bluffs, Iowa, where the Iowa West Racing Association (the nonprofit group that runs the local greyhound racetracks) contracted with him for a preliminary plan to upgrade West Broadway, the city's 20-block commercial strip. Later, as a result of local television stories and a *Wall Street Journal* article, he began to branch out, using video for a variety of site planning projects. Interest in his technique has been so widespread that he is thinking of spinning off a separate company to use video for nonplanning uses, including surveying, interior design, and real estate appraisals.

Ciaccio calls his product visual simulation; others call it image editing, image processing, or electronic cut-and-paste. To show how a site could be changed, he makes a videotape of it and then adds other images (photos, drawings, models, maps). The result is a more lifelike television substitute for traditional renderings.

One drawback is that the images are stationary, not animated; animation, Ciaccio says, would require more computer memory than his small firm can afford. "At the moment the microcomputer doesn't have the horsepower for animation," says Brian Orland, a pioneer in simulation techniques who teaches landscape architecture at the University of Illinois in Urbana. "Increasing realism is accompanied by increasing costs."

Without animation, Ciaccio cannot replicate a windshield survey of a street, for example, or a walk around a city block. Nor can he change images on demand during a presentation—to show what a building would look like if it were oriented differently on its site or if it were shorter or bulkier. That type of animation is next on his agenda.

What's involved

What Ciaccio has come up with is a relatively cheap way to produce lively presentations. The equipment and software needed to produce his video simulations cost about $20,000. The equipment includes an IBM PC AT with one hard disk drive and one tape drive, a Minolta camcorder, and a JVC editing deck. For software, he uses a Truevision product.

To produce his simulations, Ciaccio starts with a videotaped scene. This is transferred in digital form to the computer, where it can be retouched or combined with other images using Truevision software. An editing deck is used to combine the altered images with other videotaped scenes, resulting in the simulations.

Ciaccio says that, while it's no cheaper or faster to produce video simulations than traditional renderings, the audience is invariably more enthusiastic about what they see. Even a heavily retouched image looks more realistic than an artist's rendering. "People believe what they see on television," he says.

In Council Bluffs, Ciaccio offered recommendations for upgrading an unsightly commercial strip that is also the main route to Omaha, across the Missouri River. He videotaped all 20 blocks and then added photos to show what the strip would look like if trees were added—and overhead power lines and freestanding signs were taken away. Both the city and the racing association liked what they saw and hired Ciaccio's firm to help put the changes into effect. Seven projects are now in the works, and he is involved in all of them.

Ciaccio's is not the only method of video simulation. Instead of superimposing still photos on videotape, other planners transfer 35mm color slides to videotape. In addition, AutoCAD images can be superimposed on videotape or sandwiched onto aerial photos. Finally, the end product of video simulation can be something besides videotape—photos or slides, for instance.

Charles Cornwall, an environmental planner with the San Francisco office of consultants Dames and Moore, says his firm is using a variety of video simulation techniques for both big and small projects on the West Coast. Among the major projects: design concepts for a 15-mile stretch of U.S. 101 in Oregon; siting new roads and bridges on national forest land in Arizona; design guidelines for highway corridors in Thousand Oaks, California; and proposals for scenic overlooks along the Columbia River Gorge.

To produce his simulations, Cornwall uses photos, CAD drawings, and digital terrain data from a geographic information system as well as videotape. He notes that videotape is never wasted; besides simulations, it can be stored as documentation and to provide backup for field notes and aerial photos.

What's ahead

As for the future of video simulation, Ciaccio says animation is definitely the way to go. Meanwhile, though, he continues to get inquiries not only from public agencies but from a slew of private firms ranging from sign companies and utilities to real estate developers and appraisers, telecommunications companies, and the fast food industry.

Other experts also see an expanded horizon for video simulations. Joseph Gerdom, a planner with the Lincoln-Lancaster County Planning Department in Nebraska, says that site plan review would be much improved if public agencies used video simulations to assess development proposals. His agency is taking the first step by budgeting for software that can be used for simulations.

"Video simulations are to the built environment what Lotus 1-2-3 is to financial calculations," he says. In other words, both systems extend the possibilities for playing with new ideas.

One caveat: Having used video simulations for the last 18 months, Chuck Cornwall says that, while the planning benefits are obvious, there are potential problems, too. Above all, he says he worries about bad simulations—those that look good but are based on weak field work or sloppy analysis. The result might be completed projects that look only vaguely like the simulations presented during public hearings. To avoid such an outcome, he suggests that public agencies should take a hard look not only at simulations but at the background data used to create them.

Sylvia Lewis is the editor and associate publisher of Planning.

MAKING SUPERMAPS

Gilbert H. Castle III
(May 1986)

One of the most intriguing and potentially significant computer applications for planners is the geographic information system (GIS). GIS unites computerized mapping and data base management; the result is a "supermap" that stores far more information in a computer's memory than could ever be packed onto a printed map: census tract statis-

tics, traffic capacity, zoning designations, fiscal impacts, even telephone survey responses. Traditional computer systems can store this data, too, but in a GIS all the data in the system can be integrated on the basis of location.

But the value of GIS to planners is less in what can be stored than in what can be produced. Because a GIS can retrieve data in any combination, it can produce maps of nearly anything the planner might be interested in—at any scale or level of detail.

What it can do

As a result, the GIS can do far more than draw maps. A few examples:

• By combining a current land-use inventory with a zoning map, a GIS can show where the two are in conflict.

• By looking for vacant parcels of a certain size, properly zoned, in a low-crime area, and within 100 yards of a bus route, a GIS can identify potential sites for a housing project for the elderly.

• It can calculate the cost of providing water to a new subdivision by determining the distance to the nearest water line, how many feet of pipe would be needed, and where lines with slack capacity can be found.

• By comparing a proposed subdivision's boundaries with other maps in the data base that show development constraints, a GIS could flag such problems as flood hazards, poor soils, inadequate sewers, or critical wildlife habitats. . . .

Planners who would like to do computer graphics or mapping often begin by assuming that the system will be self-contained in one department. Yet they often find themselves involved in an interdepartmental venture. The reason is cost. Even for systems based on personal computers, the cost of adequate digitizers, plotters, and software pushes the entry price to $35,000 or beyond. Suddenly, the idea of distributing costs over several departmental budgets—planning, public works, assessor, public safety, city administrative officer—has great appeal. . . .

Another intriguing possibility is a joint venture with a local utility. Utilities also need accurate, comprehensive, large-scale base maps and may already have done some of the homework. Some cities have found ways to piggyback on private systems by allowing the utility to resell some public data—on property valuations or development restrictions, for example.

Consultants

Faced with an unfamiliar and complex product, many agencies bring in a GIS consultant to oversee the acquisition process. As in any consulting arrangement, there are potential pitfalls. Be sure to find out:

• How frequently and how recently the consultant has been involved in a "soup to nuts" GIS acquisition and installation.

• Who the consultant's past clients have been: planning departments, assessors' offices, public works departments? A consultant who has specialized in nonplanning applications (where most of the money has been so far) is likely to be more at ease with a computer-aided design and drafting (CADD) or other non-GIS approach.

• How familiar the consultant is with the vendors. Since most GIS innovations come from the vendors, a consultant who is not well connected professionally may not be up to date.

The agency must also decide how much of the acquisition and installation process it wants the consultant to oversee. And it must decide whether to hire a consultant who can provide a complete system—or one with no connections to a particular system.

Some agencies resolve not to buy a complete GIS. They count on being able to assemble a sophisticated, customized system from a few cheap, generic computer graphic tools. In fact, some highly sophisticated installations have been largely home-grown: Minnesota's Land Resources Information System is an example. But these are rare—and they are certainly not inexpensive. Many organizations (including leading federal agencies), following such an approach, have invested huge sums over many years without producing a reliable GIS.

But if an agency's emphasis is on relatively unsophisticated, "magic marker" planning applications where cartographic accuracy is not critical, there are a number of inexpensive options. As a rule, though, you get what you pay for in GIS.

Software

As in most current computer applications, it's the software—not the hardware—that determines what a system should include. And the software

requirements depend on the user's interests, priorities, finances, and data. In general, however, a sophisticated GIS should have these capabilities:

• Digitizing. There must be a way to encode existing maps. The best is an "arc-based" program design, which reduces problems with shared boundaries.

• Plotting. It includes the capacity to map at multiple scales, add insets and legends, use multiple colors and typefaces, and draw on various materials.

• Polygon processing. The ability to overlay coterminous areas, recognize adjacent areas, and merge and extract from polygon files.

• Topographic data processing. Processing of contours, slopes, and three-dimensional perspectives.

In addition, a system should include a relational data base manager to integrate attribute data and provide for accommodation of such third-party data as census data, marketing information, and geographic data from outside sources.

I would place special emphasis on the data base management system. Some vendors have tied into existing systems, while others have developed their own. Each agency must decide which approach suits its needs and which will make it easier to transfer data from existing computer files.

Hardware

The hardware needed also depends on the user's needs, but a GIS nearly always includes:

• A minicomputer, almost always a 32-bit CPU manufactured by DEC, Data General, or Prime. Some vendors use IBM 43xx or 30xx computers and the VM/CMS operating systems. Less sophisticated software is available on IBM PCs (usually XT or AT versions) and a few other PCs.

• A digitizer, which is an input device (in computerspeak, a "peripheral") that resembles a drafting table. Usually a hand-held "mouse" is used to point to and enter physical coordinates on the surface. This allows existing base maps to be "traced" into the computer. The most common size, 36 by 48 inches, costs about $7,500. Common manufacturers are Calcomp, Calma, and Summa-Graphics.

• A plotter—the device that draws the maps. The two basic types are pen plotters for vector data (data stored as mathematical or geometric formulas) and electrostatic plotters for raster data (data stored as a televisionscreen representation). Pen plotters are more versatile and more common. Although small letter-size plotters start around $1,000, plotters used for planning applications usually accommodate 32-inch rolls of paper, vellum, or acetate and cost between $13,000 and $23,000. Manufacturers include Calcomp, Nicolet Zeta, Hewlett-Packard, and Houston Instruments.

• A graphics CRT to depict a map on a terminal. The cost of high-resolution color graphics CRTs has fallen dramatically in recent years, and they are now frequently preferred over traditional and monochromatic CRTs. An industry standard is the Tektronix 4100 series, which, for about $4,000, provides sufficient resolution for planning applications. A very-high-resolution color CRT for detailed engineering work may cost up to $60,000.

Other typical components of a GIS are alphanumeric CRTs for nongraphic analysis and data entry, high-speed and letter-quality printers, disk and tape drives, and film recorders for making 35mm slides and 8-by-10-inch Polaroid photos of CRT screen images.

All this adds up to an expensive system—typically $250,000 to $300,000, including installation and training, for a "medium-range" system for a city of 500,000. Many agencies will want to space the cash flow over several years. The hardware, for instance, may be leased for a set time period. Software, however, is usually obtained under a perpetual licensing agreement, rather than a lease or outright purchase. Software can sometimes be leased, but the total lease payments will likely equal the licensing fee plus interest. The only advantage is that leasing spaces out the cash flow.

Perhaps the least carefully examined—but potentially the most important—part of the GIS system is getting the data into it. Some types of data, such as census tract boundaries, jurisdictional boundaries, and topographic contours, can be purchased pre-encoded. Other types of information are already in-house and need only be linked to a map; a good example is assessor data on parcels, which need only to be linked to a digitized map. A considerable amount of information will still have to be encoded, though, such as flood zones, soils, roads, special district boundaries, and—most notably—assessor parcels.

Assessor parcels are a popular GIS focus, because of the promise they hold for creating a multipurpose cadastre. The basic idea is that all the departments will be able to link their information to one basic analysis unit, or common denominator: the assessor parcel.

The concept is fine, but not inexpensive. The experiences of cities such as Edmonton, Milwaukee, and Houston suggest that the cost of building a comprehensive data base, complete with digitized boundaries and connected tabular data, can run $3 to $15 per parcel. Once in place, however, the multiple uses of such a comprehensive data base can yield an impressive return on investment.

An agency may want to subcontract the bulk of the initial digitizing work to an experienced service bureau, taking advantage of the outside firm's knowledge, economies of scale, and quality control. Encoding thousands of assessor parcels, street networks, and elevation contours is not an easy job. Once the initial data base has been built, the agency must set up procedures for encoding new maps, updating existing files, and processing custom requests.

Installation

The actual installation of the GIS is usually the vendor's responsibility (unless the software is for a personal computer). If the installation is a turnkey system, the vendor will coordinate buying, installing, and testing the hardware as well as the software. Installation is typically followed by an acceptance period, during which any system bugs are tracked down and training initiated.

Training classes are usually held on site, though some vendors have training facilities elsewhere. Expect different training programs, depending on the employee's job and responsibilities. Digitizing skills, for example, are substantially different from relational data base management skills. Training usually lasts two to four weeks, and acceptable productivity requires no longer than four to eight weeks. It may be a year, though, before users feel truly proficient in all facets of GIS use.

Most vendors offer ongoing software support and maintenance, at an annual cost of five to 15 percent of the purchase price. Subscribing to such a service is a prudent idea. For hardware, it means insurance against expensive repair bills. For software, the advantages include software updates and someone to talk to when questions arise. Indeed, the absence of a well-defined, fully staffed customer support group is a sign of a weak vendor.

Most good vendors also have an established, active users group. Users keep each other informed of successful applications of the software, swap internally developed utilities (small programs and subroutines), share publications and contacts, and occasionally join in trying to influence a vendor's research and development plans.

New uses

Once a city or county begins to see productivity gains from the GIS in traditional areas, it is likely to begin thinking of new uses. For example, the fire chief might want to overlay an arson incidence map on maps of socioeconomic data to develop an arson prediction model. Or the assessor might want to test computer-aided mass appraisal methods by overlaying land-use, zoning, and economic data, thus being able to identify homogeneous assessment zones, and fitting a predictive model to actual recent sales mapped by parcel. Some new applications will require new hardware—for example, a terminal with user-friendly menus at the public information counter so patrons can do their own research on the zoning or assessment for specific parcels. . . .

A word about seemingly everyone's favorite wish: sophisticated GIS capability on a personal computer. Although virtually all GIS vendors have looked into this, don't expect such products to flood the market or be an economic panacea. Sophisticated GIS software is expensive to develop, but even if software were free, the costs of hardware peripherals for this specialized application quickly add up. For the foreseeable future, at least, expect to get graphics on a PC but not an inexpensive full-blown GIS.

Gilbert Castle III, a former planner, is senior manager with Deloitte Haskins and Sells, in San Francisco.

CADD TAKES HOLD

Ed Zotti
(January 1987)

In just a few years, the use of computer-aided drafting and design (CADD) has become widespread among planners in both the public and private sectors. The equipment ranges from

inexpensive personal computers running $80 software to state-of-the-art systems that produce three-dimensional drawings and cost thousands of dollars. The applications include maps, presentation graphics, site planning, and streetscape studies. Whatever the task, many planners find that CADD increases their productivity—and their creativity—by enabling them to investigate alternative solutions to planning and design problems.

"I can sit down and get something just the way I like it," says John Fregonese, director of community development for Ashland, Oregon, who's using a common personal computer-based software package called AutoCAD to prepare a downtown plan. "I can play with rerouting traffic, see what if we did this, what if we did that. It's seat-of-the-pants stuff that allows me to be much more creative than if I were tied to paper and pencil."

"I find myself trying different things," says Tim Gilbert, a landscape architect for the Ann Arbor, Michigan, parks and recreation department who's using a souped-up AutoCAD system to design some park renovations. "The system enables me to make mistakes. If something doesn't work, I just try something else instead of laboriously erasing and starting all over again."

"Anything you would do on a drafting table in a planning office you can do on a program like AutoCAD," says Dale Himes, a client manager for David Evans and Associates, a consulting firm in Portland, Oregon. Himes finds AutoCAD particularly useful for updating maps. "You only have to digitize [draw the basic map] once," he notes. "Then you can make alterations, do reductions or enlargements, or change colors. That's where you really save time."

That's not to say that CADD doesn't have limitations. For one thing, CADD programs for personal computers are limited in the amount of map information they can store. . . .

It is also hard to do the sort of thematic mapping offered by a geographic information system (GIS)—the kind of computer system many planners would prefer if they could afford one. Unlike a CADD system, a GIS isn't primarily a drafting tool; rather, it's an electronic data base with mapmaking capability. With a GIS it's possible, for example, to generate maps showing all the vacant parcels zoned for commercial use within 100 yards of an expressway exit. While that's not impossible using CADD, it's a lot tougher. . . .

Planners who want to produce thematic maps with CADD software must use it in conjunction with a data base management program like dBase III or Lotus 1-2-3. That means manually switching back and forth between the two programs, a tedious process. A "what-if" inquiry that might take a few minutes on a full-fledged GIS like Intergraph or Synercom might take half an hour using Auto-CAD and 1-2-3 or dBase.

Nonetheless, some agencies say they've succeeded in using AutoCAD to create a poor man's GIS. The Pikes Peak Area Council of Governments in Colorado Springs uses a marriage of AutoCAD and another software package called PC Map to do transportation planning. To do maps showing transportation projections, planners feed numbers into a computer modeling program called Tran-Plan, generating a data file that is then fed into PC Map. PC Map correlates the simulation data with map data from AutoCAD to produce a finished thematic map.

"The time saving is remarkable," says Maureen Araujo, transportation program manager. A map showing the lanes for all the area's principal roadways would take two weeks to draw by hand, she notes. With AutoCAD and PC Map, it can be done in half an hour.

"We can find errors rapidly, and it's also useful as a presentation tool," Araujo says. A road segment that was incorrectly described during data entry will show up in a different color from the rest of the road when the map is plotted, making it easier to spot the mistake.

The cost of the system? About $36,000 for the basic hardware and software, plus $3,500 for the consultant who wrote the custom software package that makes the whole thing work. Another $7,500 went to another consultant, who put the area's road network into electronic form.

Some public agencies view CADD mapping as an interim measure, a way to get some computer experience until they can afford a GIS.

"We see AutoCAD as an entry-level tool," says Donald Stence, the director of comprehensive planning for the Capital Area Planning Council, a regional agency in Austin, Texas. The council is now putting together an RFP for a full-blown GIS.

"We felt we had to get our feet wet," echoes Fred Bohl, manager of the computer graphics and urban information systems for Ann Arbor, Michigan. "What we've got now [the ubiquitous AutoCAD]

we call our throwaway system. We're learning a lot while we wait for our needs to become clearer."

Both agencies put much of their initial investment into top-of-the-line peripheral devices, such as a king-size plotter (used to draw maps) and digitizer (used to copy existing maps), which can be used even when the systems are upgraded.

In anticipation of the eventual arrival of a GIS, the Austin council is investigating ways to convert electronic files from the Texas highway department and the state's natural resources information system. It's also about to undertake a pilot program in cooperation with the city of Austin to map crime data, clearly a GIS-type project, although CADD equipment will be used for mapping and file translation.

Meanwhile, the council uses AutoCAD for mapping and presentation graphics, such as the charts and maps for its annual growth trends assessment report. The council also has used the system to make flip charts with maps and graphics for a group of touring Japanese businessmen, and it has used AutoCAD's SCRIPT and SLIDE commands to put together computer-generated "slide shows" for visitors. Charts and maps appear on the computer screen in a pre-timed sequence while the presenter narrates.

The Ann Arbor, Michigan, parks and recreation department planners are using their CADD system for several park renovation projects. With an Auto-CAD add-on called LandCADD, they can get ready-made graphic depictions of common landscaping features ranging from tennis courts to trees. The program allows them to specify tree height, crown width, even tree type—and when they're done, LandCADD's "easy estimate" module will calculate a list of the needed materials, complete with the cost. Another module can calculate the volume of cut and fill required for a project. The end product will be finished construction drawings for use by the contractor.

Bare bones

Ann Arbor spent $35,000 for its system, which seems fairly typical for smaller cities. But it's possible to get by with less. John Fregonese's AutoCAD package cost just $10,000. Dale Himes estimates that a bare bones CADD could be set up for about $3,700, which will buy a personal computer, a "mouse" instead of a digitizer, a small plotter, and a greatly simplified version of AutoCAD called AutoSketch that costs about $80.

In fact, Himes says, some planners might be better off with such a system, especially those who are put off by the complicated AutoCAD manual. With AutoSketch, Himes notes, planners can also generate zoning amendment hearing notices, complete with map and text, and a variety of charts, graphs, and forms.

High end

The use of CADD by public agencies is a tribute to how much can be accomplished on a limited budget. But the most exciting work these days is being done by private consultants who can afford expensive systems.

Design Workshop, an Aspen-based landscape architecture and planning firm, is a good example. The company doesn't use a conventional CADD system but rather a custom-designed animation program that generates a sophisticated three-dimensional representation of a site plan that can be viewed from any perspective on the screen, providing instant feedback on a particular design.

The system got a workout during the creation of a master plan for a 14,000-unit residential development called the Meadows, being built by Lincoln Savings and Loan near Interstate 25 on the outskirts of Castle Rock, Colorado.

The primary concern of both planners and local officials during the design process for the Meadows was to preserve the natural beauty of the site, some 3,500 acres of rolling pasture land at the foot of the Rocky Mountains.

Design Workshop decided to adopt the reverse of the usual strategy for developing hilly or mountainous sites, leaving the high ground open and clustering the buildings in the lowlying areas. From a distance, particularly from the interstate, this would create the impression that much of the site was open space.

The planners used their CADD system to convince the engineers to change the routing of a road to make it less obtrusive visually and to convince local officials of the wisdom of their unusual approach. Computer-generated drawings were used as the basis for handdrawn renderings of the completed project, and a slide presentation about the process demonstrated that no artistic liberties had been taken.

Eventually, says landscape architect Howard Hahn, Design Workshop hopes to develop a "drive-through" video that will take viewers on a simulated automobile tour of the Meadows. The video will be shown to prospective developers and architects to bring them up to speed on the intended "look" of the project when complete.

The firm already produced such a video in connection with the new downtown Denver plan. In this case, the simulation shows what portions of the city would look like if the plan were built as proposed.

Making life easier

Another important application of CADD with implications for planners is its use by architects. In this case, planners are likely to be in the position of inspecting computer-generated architectural drawings during the design review process rather than doing the actual work. . . .

A case in point is the approval process for the new headquarters of the National Conference of Catholic Bishops in Washington, D.C., designed by the Washington office of the Leo A. Daly Company, an Omaha-based architecture, engineering, planning, and interior design firm.

Working with staff members of the bishops' conference and the city zoning commission, the architects used their GDS computer system to draw up a traditional-style building that would be "contextual" with its neighbors. But when the bishops saw it, they wanted a more "progressive" design. The architects went back to the terminal to put in more glass, take out some of the limestone, and flatten the roof.

Both designs, the modern and the traditional, were presented to community groups and to the zoning commission. Both were illustrated with computer-generated 3-D perspective drawings that showed the building from different vantage points, including bird's-eye and street views.

The zoning commissioners, not surprisingly, decided they preferred the traditional look. It was only after a good deal more discussion and a flurry of additional computer drawings, including some quite detailed facade renderings, that a compromise was finally reached. Despite everything, says Al O'Konski, director of computer services for Daly, the project was on time and on budget, chiefly because of CADD.

Ed Zotti is a Chicago writer who covers planning and architecture.

GETTING AN EARLY START

Ruth Eckdish Knack
(August 1986)

Sometimes it takes a while for a good idea to germinate. Almost 10 years ago, the late Kevin Lynch, influenced by the environmental psychologists, admonished fellow planners to pay attention to the observations of the "child client." Lynch was the editor in 1977 of *Growing Up in Cities,* a UNESCO-sponsored study of the environmental perceptions of children and adolescents in Poland, Australia, and Mexico. He found the children to be remarkably accurate observers, in contrast to local public officials, who seemed to know little about what children really do.

"If children's rights and needs are to be represented in public decisions," Lynch concluded, "there must be formal bodies concerned with children's welfare at the local and national levels."

Today, we see signs of such formalization all over the country, with several West Coast cities in the forefront. . . . One major focus of activity is planning with children, and here the model is Seattle, whose "KidsPlace" project has led to similar efforts elsewhere.

The Seattle model

The kids' planning effort in Seattle coincided with an attempt to stem the exodus of middle-class families from the city. It's too early to say if it has done that, but it has led to an "action agenda" and the implementation of several items. The KidsPlace effort started in July 1984, spurred by the enthusiasm of a local pediatrician, a devotee of the planning-with-children ideas of the Greek architect Constantine Doxiadis. The action agenda is based on the work of several officially sanctioned task forces, which used surveys and other citizen participation techniques to set priorities.

A high priority for Donna James, the KidsPlace coordinator, is making downtown "kid friendly," one of the 30 agenda items. At a KidsPlace conference this spring, organized by the Project for Public

Spaces, children said they would like: a downtown skating rink, a park, a gathering place, and "a place to touch the water." Their ideas are being passed along to the developers of several downtown projects now under way.

To make the city less dangerous for "kids at risk," another agenda item, the KidsPlace staff applied to HUD for a grant to help single parents find housing and other aid. It also organized a day camp for Southeast Asian refugee children at one apartment complex. And it is working with the metropolitan bus system to try to lower children's fares.

"What we hope to do," says James, "is to institutionalize these concerns." A step in that direction is the local "KidsBoard," whose 40 members, middle and high school students, advise city agencies on a variety of issues. A promising spinoff is the appointment of two KidsBoard members to a city commission studying ways of revamping Seattle Center, the cultural center left over from the 1962 world's fair. . . .

Going farther

Berkeley, California, incorporated a plan produced by young people into the city's downtown plan. The youth plan was produced by a group of some 30 youngsters, ages 10 to 17, organized by consultant Susan Goltsman of the Berkeley planning firm, Moore Iacofano Goltsman. The firm was paid out of a $5,000 grant authorized by the Berkeley city council.

Goltsman recruited the youth planning team members and helped them design and administer a survey of some 275 local teens and preteens. Several of the teens' recommendations were accepted by the city planning department as part of the downtown specific plan, which is expected to be adopted this summer. An outgrowth of the project is the establishment of a "youth corporation," which will run a downtown teen center.

Berkeley planning director Marjorie Macris points out that the teen plan included some recommendations that are at odds with city policy—adding downtown parking spaces, for instance. But on the whole, Macris says she found the exercise useful and the participants' enthusiasm "inspirational." . . .

The success in Berkeley led to a bid from the city of Portland, which has hired Goltsman's firm to lead young people in a downtown planning exercise. In this case, the youth plan will become part of Portland's ongoing central city planning effort, and it hooks into a series of related activities. One example is the "Kidmapped" project, organized by a local architect to involve elementary school children in mapping various parts of the city.

Goltsman says the initial planning focus in Portland will be downtown recreation, and the young planners will pay particular attention to Pioneer Courthouse Square, a popular central gathering place.

Portland is a step ahead of other cities in that local young people sit on the Metropolitan Youth Commission, an advisory group to the city council. The youth commission also has an advisory relationship with the school district and, in the future, hopes to establish something similar with the park district.

As in Berkeley, a new central city planning effort seemed a good time to strengthen the youth commission by involving a greater variety of participants. To kick off the effort, in July 1985, a former youth commission chair, Gerald Blake, an urban studies professor at Portland State University, organized a workshop at which the theory and practice of youth participation were discussed. Later, the MYC singled out one problem area, recreation, for follow-up. . . .

A central city planning day gave the elementary and middle-school children who participated in "Kidmapped" a chance to show off their designs, which had been drawn on plastic triangles and fashioned into a geodesic dome by a local architect-teacher, Elijuh Mirochnik. Metropolitan Youth Commission director Alice Simpson says the group is now seeking funding for a Berkeley-style youth planning project. A primary goal is to create a cadre of trained youth volunteers, who would be available to advise city agencies. . . .

Jacquie Swaback, whose Sacramento consulting firm is called Urban Dependencies, has done several surveys of local school children. The most recent, compiled under the auspices of the nonprofit Urban Planning for Children Project, was released in March in a report called *Planning Sacramento: Views of Students and Parents.* In includes the views of both children and parents, and it suggests to Swaback that young people are more serious than we give them credit for. Jobs, for example, are ranked high as a "desired activity," as are music, art, and drama.

The kids also thought there should be more frequent bus service, more bike lanes, and wide shad-

ed sidewalks to shopping areas and transportation centers. They wanted computers in libraries and practical classes in after-school centers. Asked about residential planning, they said they preferred small multifamily complexes to single-family houses (because they're better for children at home alone). And they said they liked front porches. . . .

Essentially a one-person effort, a Louisville, Kentucky, survey attracted community attention to the issue of what children like and dislike about their neighborhoods. Louisville planner Theresa Stanley devised the questionnaire and presented the survey to 746 sixth-, seventh-, and eighth-grade students in 10 Catholic elementary schools in Louisville and its eastern suburbs. Asked first to define a neighborhood, the children surprised Stanley by singling out its people as the identifying factor. Adults surveyed earlier had tended to define their neighborhoods in terms of property or safety.

Here's a sampling of Stanley's survey:

A neighborhood is: A lot of friends, where people know each other; togetherness; a street of families.

*The thing I like **best** about my neighborhood is:* The people; having stores, schools, and parks nearby; grass and trees and nice houses; not too much traffic; block parties.

*The thing I like **least** is:* Not enough kids my own age; run-down appearance; too much traffic; no place for kids to go.

What can children do to make their neighborhood a better place to live? Pick up trash; help elderly neighbors; watch out for strangers and prowlers.

My favorite place to hang out in my neighborhood is: My house; a fast-food restaurant; skating rink; bowling alley; park; a vacant lot; "down the street." . . .

In the schools

Planning was one of the fields that benefited from the consciousness-raising efforts stimulated by the 1976 Bicentennial. With the recent cuts in federal funds, however, programs like the National Endowment for the Arts' "Architects in the Schools" have suffered. We're glad to note that in many places locally funded projects—often staffed by volunteers—have helped to fill the gap.

In Portsmouth, New Hampshire, planner Susan Thoresen developed a program on community planning for fourth to sixth graders, which she has presented some 25 times over the last several years. The program includes a 45-minute slide show on changes in the city, designed to elicit student responses. As a follow-up, teachers are asked to lead walking tours of the school neighborhood, using a map supplied by Thoresen.

Thoresen, who is part of a consulting firm called the Thoresen Group, went into the schools as a volunteer. She recommends that other planners do the same—in part out of self-interest. "Children are an untouched audience for planners. They are honest and tough, and their observations can tell practitioners a lot about their community." . . .

Back in the Midwest, the Affiliate Council of the nonprofit Historic Landmarks Foundation of Indiana is focusing on training teachers and volunteers to incorporate built environment education into the regular school cirriculum. The council is composed of representatives of 21 preservation groups throughout the state. Its goal is to produce model teaching units that can be adapted to several grade levels in any Indiana community.

The idea, says Lisbeth Henning, the foundation's community services director, is to expand the network of volunteers who are trained to educate young people about historic architecture and local history. A useful tool is the foundation's "Architecture Education Resource Guide," which includes a bibliography of source materials in several fields. . . .

A similar effort at Cornell University won an honorable mention in the 1985 student project awards competition sponsored by the American Institute of Certified Planners. Since 1976, Cornell planning and design students have spent time teaching in local schools as part of the university's community service program. The students get academic credit for their work. For the last two years, the classroom teachers themselves have been invited to a three-day workshop designed to help them develop their own materials.

Ruth Knack is senior editor of Planning.

TIPS FOR ROOKIE PLANNING DIRECTORS
Stuart Meck
(April 1983)

For a planner in a management position, the first six months are key, the period in which both style and credibility are established. I had always thought that I would hit the ground running when I became a planning director. Last July, I had an opportunity to turn theory into practice.

That month, after nine years with a regional planning commission in Dayton, Ohio, I became assistant city manager and planning director of Oxford, Ohio. Located near the Indiana border and about an hour's drive from both Dayton and Cincinnati, Oxford has some 18,000 people, about two-thirds of them students at Miami University, a state-supported graduate and undergraduate institution.

The city planning staff consists of a secretary, a couple of student interns, and me. Although my secretary deftly limits public access to me at certain times when I am working on deadline, people, particularly students, still slip through. I don't mind the interruptions (in fact, I relish them). Still, limited staff resources and constant public contact have made it necessary to develop a relatively driven approach to planning matters. It's one that anticipates those routine problems that consume inordinate amounts of time, preventing us from addressing long-range issues. I think planners, after all, should plan, and that's what I set out to do.

Here's my 10-point program for professionals starting out in similar situations:

1. Develop a work program and stick to it. On the basis of exchanges with city council members and planning commissioners, a review of planning commission and board of zoning appeals minutes (valuable, but often overlooked, sources of data for the planner), and conversations with other department heads, I devised a year-long work program. My number-one-priority: Finish the city's comprehensive plan, which dates from 1963 and, despite various attempts to do so, has never been revised.

2. Plan your day. I keep a master list of objectives for the month. At the end of each day, I sit down for 15 to 20 minutes and identify tasks from that list that I hope to undertake the next day. I jot them down on a desk calendar and, as I go through the day, check them off. I try to do the unpleasant things first—dictating minutes, proofing—and the activities I enjoy later. This approach is fairly simple stuff, but having a daily schedule of activities facing me when I come to work is the way I make myself my own boss, instead of a slave to brush fires.

3. Update all maps. By the third day on the job, I had taken steps to update the city's zoning and base maps, which hadn't been amended since 1979. Such maps are public policy documents and decisions based on them are made every day. Clearly, they should be accurate. Since I'm a lousy draftsman, I hired a graduate cartography student to help out. The new zoning district map uses removable tape to delineate zoning district boundaries, so I can change them without redrafting. There's also a box showing dates and ordinance numbers for map amendments. The updated zoning map was officially adopted by the planning commission and the city council, and now I do a fairly brisk trade in selling both maps to the public.

4. Buy good equipment. When our cranky electric typewriter broke down for the second time in a month the day of a planning commission mailout, I knew it was time for decisive action. After shopping around, my secretary and I settled on an IBM electronic memory typewriter, one that almost does its own typing, and the city manager found money in the budget to pay for it. Agendas, memos, and reports get out faster and look better. . . .

Speaking of computers, I bought one as a gift for myself, a portable Osborne about the size of a small suitcase. It comes with a bunch of software, most notably an electronic spreadsheet program that takes the tedium out of numbers crunching. I use it every day for forecasting, budgeting, and dealing with cost-revenue problems. Like the electronic typewriter, the computer enables us to work smarter. . . .

5. Review all plans and studies. Specific plans that provide policy guidance for a city often have the same force and effect as the comprehensive plan. These documents include wastewater treatment plans, traffic studies, water supply plans, and park plans. Knowing what's in them may save

work later; Oxford's federally mandated sewage treatment facilities plan, for example, is supplying much of the physical inventory for the comprehensive plan update with minimal editing. Moreover, changes proposed in a comprehensive plan may affect and compel modifications in other plans. In sum, the planner should serve as the advocate for these plans, the one who, by mastering the details, can convey an integrated view of the city's future physical development. If the plans are bad, change them, but don't let them go unused.

6. Devise clear application forms. Like most planners, I spend a lot of time telling people how to apply for development permissions—rezonings, variances, conditional uses, sign permits, and subdivisions. Application forms should furnish much of the data necessary for good staff reports. I revised them all during the first month, checking the development codes to make certain that they reflected city policy and asked the questions I wanted answered. I also prepared a citizen's guide to development permits, a simple, three-page handout that explains the procedures. Many of the questions citizens have (few of Oxford's applicants are attorneys) fall into several categories: "How long will it take?" "How much will it cost?" and (asked with considerable apprehension) "Will I have to appear at the public hearing?" Having the guide available saves time, eliminates possible misunderstandings, and creates good public relations.

7. Educate your city council, planning commission, and board of zoning appeals. Planners often forget that sitting on such bodies can be a bewildering experience. New, and even seasoned, members need guidance. I supplied council members and planning commissioners with a handbook I wrote on how to evaluate zoning and other development requests. Planning commissioners also are provided with copies of Herbert H. Smith's *Citizen's Guide to Planning,* along with the commission's rules. Board of zoning appeals members receive material on what does and does not constitute a variance. When the planning commission was debating how to modify the sign ordinance, I showed the film, "Street Graphics," which helped the commissioners understand the issue of sign regulation. (The film is based on a book of the same title by William R. Ewald, Jr., and Daniel R. Mandelker.)

Remember, though, that "education" should never be patronizing. Assume some native intelligence on the part of local officials, or you'll be headed for rocky shoals in a hurry.

8. Develop in-house research capacity. It's satisfying to have information at arm's reach. This means having a solid professional library, copies of the most recent censuses of population, housing, and business for your jurisdiction; and—I can't emphasize this enough—a subscription to APA's Planning Advisory Service (PAS) to answer questions that are beyond a general planning library. PAS has helped me with a sign ordinance, guidelines for noise regulations, and standards for sidewalk cafes.

9. Prepare for public presentations. Planners are judged by the quality of their public presentations. I am of the transparency/overhead projector/flipchart school and rehearse meticulously for hearings. A good presentation should reduce a staff report to three or four main points and, through the use of appropriate graphics, clarify the spatial relationships inherent in land-use decisions. Graphics needn't be elaborate, but they must be accurate.

10. Be a straight shooter. Nobody loves a smart-ass, least of all a smart-ass planner. In my relations with the public and city employees I try to maintain a cordial, helpful, and consultative posture. Similarly, with the city council and appointed boards, I present my staff reports with a "this-is-my-best-recommendation, what-do-you-think?" attitude. I probe for alternate points of view, resist being dogmatic.

A planner's stock-in-trade is advice, a carefully researched and reasoned counsel that asks municipal officials to consider the alternatives and their consequences, and then select the best course of action. But gaining confidence takes time, preparation, organization and tact. That's where these tips might come in handy.

Stuart Meck, AICP, is assistant city manager and planning director of Oxford, Ohio.

ETHICS IN PLANNING: YOU BE THE JUDGE

Carol D. Barrett
(November 1984)

The specific ethical concepts that underlie the Code of Professional Conduct adopted by the American Institute of Certified Planners in 1981—public interest, conscientiousness, pursuit of excellence, fair treatment of colleagues, consideration, equity, integrity—are the stuff of apple pie and the flag. While their statement in the AICP code evokes little controversy, their day-to-day application may be quite problematical.

How one makes certain ethical decisions is usually more dependent on family and religious training than on the view of professional colleagues. Planning schools devote little time to the subject, and the sessions on ethics at recent national planning conferences have not drawn nearly as well as those featuring computers. The upshot is that planners often feel they have no guide to evaluating their own behavior.

Most planners would agree, of course, that no one should accept bribes left in shoeboxes. However, the subtleties that characterize life with public and private decision makers make it difficult to achieve such clear-cut agreement as to whether a particular course of action is ethical.

Published research by University of Wisconsin-Madison planning professors Elizabeth Howe and Jerome Kaufman on the subject of ethics finds agreement among planners that certain kinds of behavior *are* acceptable:

• Dramatizing a problem or issue to overcome apathy.

• Making tradeoffs in negotiating situations.

• Assisting citizen groups, on a planner's own time, to prepare a counterproposal to an official agency decision.

Likewise, there is consensus that the following tactics are *not* acceptable:

• Making threats.

• Distorting information.

• "Leaking" information.

Last year, the AICP Ethics Committee published

Ethical Awareness in Planning, a report designed to encourage more systematic attention to planning ethics. The 66-page report was distributed to planning schools and APA chapters for use in their classes, newsletters, meetings, and AICP exam preparation sessions. Seventeen "scenarios," all developed by planners, are included in the report. Six of those scenarios are reprinted here in slightly edited form.

Potential conflict of interest

The county council is considering an ordinance that would drastically increase the water and sewage fees for rental units. The county's housing planner has analyzed the proposal and feels that the proposed fees are excessive because the amount of water consumed by apartment units is far less than that of single-family houses. The planner also feels the rate hikes will exacerbate the county's existing rental housing shortage by encouraging the conversion of rental units to condominiums.

The planner prepares a staff report that recommends that the revised fee structure not be approved. However, the planner does not declare a potential conflict of interest, even though her husband owns a small rental property.

The behavior of the planner who prepared the staff report was: ethical, probably ethical, probably unethical, unethical? Not sure?

Release of development information

The staff of a state planning agency is reviewing a development proposal. Most of the data it has assembled show the project in an unfavorable light. The state's policy is that all working files should be open to the public, but the staff planners are concerned about releasing information in a piecemeal fashion because it could be misconstrued.

The president of a citizens group opposed to the project has requested an appointment to see the file. The president has also stated her intention to seek the state's help in organizing opposition to the project. The state's director of planning decides to remove the single most critical document and keep it in his desk for "further study" during the time when the leader of the citizens group is reviewing the file.

The behavior of the planner who edited the file was: ethical, probably ethical, probably unethical, unethical? Not sure?

Letter to the editor

A city planner writes a letter to the editor of a local newspaper. The letter compliments the county's planning commission on its refusal to approve a rezoning request that would have allowed further industrial development. The planner signs the letter with his name and home address only. The city's planning director agrees with the planner's conclusions and even notes that the comments expressed are of a professional, not a political, nature.

The letter to the editor provokes behind-the-scenes activity in which pressure is put on the planning director to fire the planner. The director refuses. Instead, he inserts a memo in the office file listing several "legitimate vehicles"—going to meetings and giving speeches—through which staff planners can express themselves publicly. The planner also is told to use more discretion in the future and never to sign his own name to such a letter. (This scenario is excerpted from a 1971 Planning Advisory Service Report, No. 269, *Dissent and Independent Initiative in Planning Offices,* by Earl Finkler.)

The behavior of the planner who wrote the letter was: ethical, probably ethical, probably unethical, unethical? Not sure?

Gag order

Several city planners oppose a freeway system plan that was adopted by a regional planning agency. They contend that the original staff plan has been emasculated and that the final product discredits the profession.

The city's planning director, who supports the freeway system plan, refuses to allow her staff to express public opposition to the plan, either as professionals or as citizens. She threatens to fire any planners who disobey her orders in this matter.

The planners draft a statement for presentation at the local APA chapter meeting, but then receive word from a reliable source that pressure will be put on the planning director to fire them if such a statement is presented. Fearing for their jobs, the planners do not make any statements in opposition to the freeway system. But they do tell the local APA chapter, at a meeting attended by the director, that they have been forbidden from taking a public position on the freeway system plan. (This scenario is also excerpted from Planning Advisory Service Report No. 269.)

The behavior of the planning director in threatening to fire her employees was: ethical, probably ethical, probably unethical, unethical? Not sure?

Employment opportunity

A small city of 25,000 on a lovely lake is being wooed by several hotel entrepreneurs. In evaluating the various proposals, the city's planning staff has asked for information about the number and types of jobs to be made available and, also, how many of these jobs would be targeted to city residents.

In reviewing the data submitted, the staff notices that the jobs are segregated by sex. For example, women are to be employed in the coffee shop as waitresses and men are to work in the main restaurant as waiters.

A member of the planning staff meets with a planning commissioner to discuss this matter, and the commissioner volunteers to contact the developer and challenge the hotel's policies. A debate develops among the planners, with some arguing that the management of the hotel is outside the purview of their responsibilities.

How do you regard the behavior of the planner who contacted the commissioner: ethical, probably ethical, probably unethical, unethical? Not sure?

Save the wetlands

A regional planner who worked on a wetlands preservation study gives certain findings to an environmental group, without receiving authorization from the director of the agency. The planner took this action because he felt the director had purposely left out of the study report those findings that did not support the agency's official policies. The findings that were deleted had been well documented. (This scenario is used with permission of Jerome Kaufman.)

The behavior of the planner who released the information was: ethical, probably ethical, probably unethical, unethical? Not sure?

Carol D. Barrett, AICP, is a senior associate with the Austin, Texas, consulting firm of James Duncan and Associates. She is a member of the AICP Ethics Committee and the author of Ethical Awareness in Planning, *from which this article is adapted.*

SAY IT IN ENGLISH

Richard B. Dymsza
(August 1981)

"Let us beware of the plight of our colleagues, the behavioral scientists, who by use of a proliferating jargon have painted themselves into a corner—or isolation ward—of unintelligibility. They *know* what they mean, but no one else does. . . . *Their condition might be pitied if one did not suspect it was deliberate."* BARBARA TUCHMAN

Tuchman, a Pulitzer Prize-winning historian, could have been talking about those of us who are practicing planners. Indeed, our plight might be more serious than that of behavioral scientists. Our writing is aimed at the public more than our profession, yet we are apt to write in a way that can be understood only by other planners.

We have to view this situation with alarm. The planning message gets out mainly by writing. Our failure to write clearly to legislators and to the general public can only mean that our ideas will not take hold and will not be put into effect.

Tuchman suggests that the behavioral scientist's unintelligibility might be deliberate. Some planners, too, might choose to make their writing obscure to give it an aura of expertise and to conceal the simplicity of their concepts. But most practicing planners, I believe, make an honest effort to write for broad public understanding. They simply are not sure how to go about it and can find few good examples to follow within the profession.

To make planning reports more readable, three guidelines must be followed:
- Guideline 1: Get rid of clutter.
- Guideline 2: Be concrete.
- Guideline 3: Do not try to say too much.

Journalists interpret these guidelines very restrictively when they write for the general public. But planners write for a more narrowly defined and better educated public, and their reports must often convey technical information. Planners, therefore, need not apply these guidelines as restrictively as a journalist would, but they should adopt some of the qualities of a journalistic style to make their reports more readable.

Get rid of clutter

A planning report that I recently read begins like this: "This most significant and important innovations. . . ." This is clutter. The writer has used two words where one would have done as well. Perhaps the subtle distinctions between "significant" and "important" are important (or is it significant?) to the writer, but they are not to most readers.

Two words instead of one may appear to be a small matter. But in so many planning reports the small matters, like bricks, get piled up until an impenetrable wall is built between the planner and the reader.

Clutter is not only the use of two words where one would do as well. It is also the long, loosely constructed sentence that bewilders the reader, and it is the use of a long word where a short one will serve. Clutter is contagious; it spreads into all of our writing—even when we try our best to keep it out.

Here are a few of the problems to watch out for in the fight against clutter.

Long paragraphs. You were probably taught that paragraphs must be constructed around a given topic or idea. But if, in meeting this rule, a paragraph gets too long, break it down anyway. A paragraph is probably too long for the lay reader if it goes beyond 10 typewritten lines.

Long sentences. Write short sentences rather than long sentences, but do not overreact by using only short sentences. Good style requires sentences of varying lengths to create rhythm and flow.

If you must use a long sentence, make sure that it is under very tight grammatical control. Here's an example of one that's not: "Considering the high volume of traffic on north-south arterials such as Lamont Highway, which have been obstructed by unrestricted access to abutting land uses and have resulted not only in congestion but also major traffic hazards, improvements to these must be given a high priority in the county capital program along with similar highways within the city limits."

Strung-together nouns. These are series of nouns used as adjectives. Some planners think that the longer the series, the better the writing. The planner who wrote this designation for a transportation planning project thought so: "Northwest corridor transportation improvements alternatives feasibility study project."

Indirect expressions. "It is felt that," "it should be noted that," "it must be emphasized that," "it is safe to say that"—indirect expressions like these are epidemic in planning reports. Most of them should be wiped out. Usually the indirect expressions are not needed for meaning, or if they are, the same idea often can be conveyed through the use of appropriate adverbs (e.g., "probably," "certainly") in the main clause of the sentence.

Jargon. Some jargon cannot be reduced. It conveys in a few words meanings that might take several paragraphs to put into lay language. Most planning jargon, however, is just the opposite: It conveys in many complex words no more than what can be said in a few simple words. There is no reason to use such jargon.

Below are a few examples of swollen language and their simpler, more graceful, and more forthright equivalents:

Decision-making process. "Our purpose is to facilitate the legislative decision-making process." Translation: "Our purpose is to help legislators in making decisions."

Ecosystem. "Environment," or a more specific term like "plant and animal life" or "water quality."

Educational facilities, transportation facilities, sewerage facilities. "Schools," "highways," "sewers."

In close proximity to. "Near."

Infrastructure. "Streets," "sewers," "water mains." If you must use a general term, "public facilities" would be an improvement.

Input. Borrowed from the argot of computer programming. Instead of calling for the public to provide input into your plan, you can call for the public to comment on it or to take part in its preparation.

Interface with. "Meet with," "work with."

Optimize. "Make the most of."

Pedestrian-oriented facilities. "Sidewalks," usually.

Residential land uses, commercial land uses, institutional land uses. . . . These tedious constructions are needed on occasion, but more often they are not. They can be replaced by simple words like "housing," "shopping areas," and "schools" when their more general meanings are not needed.

Significantly severe topography. "Steep slopes," "hills."

Subject. Do not use as an adjective, as in "the subject parcel." Say "this parcel."

Sufficient. "Enough" is enough.

Urban scatteration. "Urban sprawl" has been worn threadbare, but it still is the better way to say it.

Utilize. "Use."

Viability. If you work at it, you will find a more lively way to express this idea.

Be concrete

A published housing report for a metropolitan county starts this way: "There are three basic dimensions to the housing problem: (1) inadequate conditions, (2) affordability, and (3) locational concentration due to price discrimination. These dimensions combine to make housing one of the most significant problems in our metropolitan area."

Loading a paragraph with abstractions is not the way to capture the interest of the reader.

Here's an example of a more readable opening paragraph: "In (name of county) many people live in dilapidated, overcrowded housing. They live there not by choice, but by necessity; they cannot afford housing that meets acceptable standards. Furthermore, they are denied the opportunity to live in most areas of the county because these areas offer no low-cost housing."

If you compare this paragraph with the original, you will see that it conveys the same three basic dimensions of the housing problem: the inadequate conditions, the affordability, and the locational concentration. But it conveys them in specific terms that are more easily understood.

Another example, this one from an agricultural preservation report by a regional planning board: "The process of urban expansion results in disinvestment in agricultural capital and the premature withdrawal of land from the production of agricultural goods. Urbanization creates within the agricultural community excessive speculation arising from unrealistic expectations on the potential for capital gains in a transitional land market. Such expectations lead to less than optimal agricultural investment decisions."

The more concrete rewrite: "As an urban area expands, farm investments decline and land is retired from farming long before it is needed for urban use. The development of new housing nearby awakens farmers' interest in speculating on their land.

Often, they expect to get a much higher price for their land than it is worth, and they would be better off investing in their farms than looking for a windfall in the land market."

Don't say too much

Most planning reports are much too long for their readers. Part of the problem is that the reports try to serve both technical and public information purposes. Unfortunately, both purposes cannot be well served within the same report.

Planning offices would do well to publish their plans in two reports, one for the technician, the other for the general public. Few planning offices, though, find the time to do this.

Where planning material must be confined to a single report, a compromise must be reached between the technical and the public information requirements. Unfortunately, the impulse is to err in the direction of meeting technical requirements, resulting in a report that is too long and complicated for most readers.

Challenge everything you intend to write. Is it important? If it is not, omit the material or relegate it to an appendix. Appendices help to meet technical requirements and to keep the body of the report readable. They should be used more often.

Beware, also, of the packed paragraph, in which too many ideas are crammed into too small a space. The paragraph below, taken from a published planning report, is an example:

"Urban sprawl has resulted in excessive energy use. With the spatial arrangement of existing activities to a large extent fixed, the potential of achieving greater efficiency in energy use through land-use planning is limited, but still significant. The energy efficiency of existing development and activities can be improved in some ways through land-use planning. The principal opportunities, however, lie in the development of policies related to the type, location, and number of future facilities and structures and the ways in which they are used; and in the implementation of those policies through land-use controls and infrastructural investments. . . ."

A more readable style would require a number of paragraphs to impress these concerns on the reader. For this reason, the more readable style sometimes requires more space than highly condensed technical writing. If the report gets too long, though, there is a simple alternative: Eliminate the extraneous material.

Finally, be on your guard against unneeded qualifiers. These two examples were found in published planning reports: "Although there are many exceptions, communities are coming to recognize the need for somewhat more flexible ways to control land use than through traditional zoning." And: "It can be logically argued that many of the problems facing our metropolitan community today have their roots in the largely unbridled growth of the past three decades."

The first sentence has two qualifiers that are not needed: the clause "although there are many exceptions" and the word "somewhat." The writer who cannot resist the urge to qualify the statement should begin by simply saying "Many communities. . . ."

In the second sentence, the word "largely" and the initial construction "It can be logically argued that" should be deleted. Guideline 1 calls for deleting the initial construction because it is an indirect expression, a form of clutter. Guideline 3 calls for deleting it because it qualifies a statement that is almost self-evident and would not be contested.

It will not be easy for planners to change their writing to a more readable style. The change will require planners to work outside their acquired idiom.

But the more readable style will come over time, if planners work at it. And the payoff of having planning reports read and understood by more people will make the effort worthwhile.

Richard Dymsza is an Atlanta free-lance writer who has worked as a planning consultant.

3

Land Use and the Environment

American land-use planning has probably changed more since 1972, when *Planning* first appeared as a magazine, than in any comparable period of the nation's history. Two decades ago, land-use planning and regulation in the United States consisted almost entirely of municipal and county zoning. No longer. Now planning and regulation are far more centralized, increasingly originating with regional, state, or federal agencies rather than local ones, and they are more environmental, aimed increasingly at controlling the harmful effects of land development and other economic activity. Further, planning and regulation have become more complicated and pervasive—their political opponents would say intrusive. These changes have transformed American planning: its intentions, its practice, its role in American government, even its attractiveness as a career.

THE RISE OF CENTRALIZED PLANNING

There may never have been a time when it was as challenging to be an American land-use planner as the late 1960s and early 1970s. The post-World War II building boom, culminating in the record-high development rates of the late 1960s, had produced a professionally exhilarating set of environmental problems. Development projects of all kinds—commercial, residential, industrial, and governmental—were getting bigger and polluting more. The interstate highway system, undertaken in 1956 and reaching completion after the middle 1960s, had created vast new stretches of urban or potentially urban land—much of it succumbing to formless sprawl and strip development, shoddy leisure-home projects, ruinous strip mines, and polluting power plants.

Under these pressures, long-standing deficiencies in local land-use planning became obvious. Zoning, the action arm of local planning and the nation's most prevalent device for land-use regulation, seemed especially fallible. Most zoning agencies and ordinances had originated in the 1920s and 1930s and were often inadequate to cope with the 1960s development. They could not handle huge suburban residential projects that might affect dozens of rapidly growing localities beyond the boundaries of the regulating one. They could not deal with big energy facilities that might have regional, statewide, or even national consequences, or with large, complicated public works projects. In all such cases, lone communities were dealing with land-use issues that had regional or state impact but were making their decisions without consideration of the consequences for surrounding communities.

Another reason why local planning and zoning did not work well was that in most of the country, particularly in the small rural communities in the path of urban expansion, they had never really existed in the first place. Such communities espoused the American ideal of rugged individualism; many of their residents thought zoning verged on socialism. To counter this ragged local performance, a liberal coalition of environmentalists, land-use planners, lawyers, state and federal officials, progressive business people and developers, and citizen activists of all kinds emerged, bearing an alternative—more precisely, a supplement—to local land-use planning: centralized land-use planning. The coalition's goal was new planning that would operate at higher levels of government and apply mainly to projects that were large and thus had regional impact or were proposed for environmentally sensitive areas.

This coalition was remarkably effective. In 1969, only Hawaii—a state whose development patterns, land market, and local government structure differed substantially from those of the rest of the country—had a law providing for state land-use planning, and it had been passed in 1961, another era entirely. By 1975 the coalition had achieved at least 20 new environmentally oriented state land-use laws, mostly in the Northeast, the upper Midwest, and the West. These laws variously regulated the siting and operation of all large development projects, particular kinds of large projects such as power plants or strip mines, and projects in environmentally sensitive areas. Thirty-seven states had new programs of statewide planning or statewide review of local regulatory decisions.

The coalition also succeeded in obtaining funding for land-use planning programs at the federal level. Through the 1972 Coastal Zone Management Act, the Commerce Department gave the 30 Atlantic, Pacific, Gulf, and Great Lakes states grants totalling about $16 million a year to plan for and regulate coastal development. The 1977 Surface Mine Control and Reclamation Act gave the states $110 million annually in Interior Department grants to regulate strip mining. The 1970 Clean Air Act, the 1972 Clean Water Act, and the 1974 Safe Drinking Water Act gave the states a total of nearly $3 billion yearly in Environmental Protection Agency grants to carry out regulatory and construction programs with complex but definite land-use implications, including controls on the location of new projects. The 1973 Flood Disaster Protection Act required that states and localities regulate development in floodplains before they (and their residents) could buy federal flood insurance or receive flood disaster aid.

This trend toward centralization is examined in articles on state land-use planning by John DeGrove and Robert Cassidy, on the California Coastal Commission by Gladwin Hill, and on the effort to clean up Chesapeake Bay by Sandra Martin. The saga of land-use planning in Florida has received special attention in the pages of *Planning,* and articles on that topic by Ed McCahill, Nancy Stroud, and Daniel O'Connell appear in this chapter.

THE FALL OF CENTRALIZED PLANNING

After the middle 1970s, centralized land-use planning seemed to lose its political momentum. The liberals who support it and the conservatives who oppose it offer widely different explanations for the decline, with liberals arguing that there never was enough centralized planning, probably never would be. They note that few new state land-use laws have been passed in recent years and that most states still lack genuinely strong land-use planning. Moreover, in the states that have statewide regulations, they have often been weakened in scope, budget, staffing, and enforcement. Throughout the 1970s, for instance, the Florida and California programs had no enforcement staff whatever.

By the early 1980s, conservative state and local politicians were finding support for positions opposed to centralized land-use planning. In 1972, for example, California Gov. Ronald Reagan opposed a voters' initiative to create state commissions to regulate development along the coast. But when the initiative passed, Reagan made environmentalist appointments to those commissions that were in regions where regulatory sentiment was powerful—around San Francisco and Santa Cruz, for instance. In contrast, in his 1982 gubernatorial race, George Deukmejian made the coastal commissions a special target, and once in office, he substantially reduced their personnel and funding.

There was comparable deterioration of federal support for state planning programs. At the urging of many developers and localities, the Reagan administration in effect abandoned, for example, the Coastal Zone Management Act, never asking for funding for it in any of its annual budget proposals. The Reagan-era directors of the program were always publicly committed to terminating it. The Clean Air, Clean Water, Safe Drinking Water, Flood Disaster Protection, and Surface Mine Control and Reclamation acts experienced similar neglect.

Land-use conservatives—most developers, many local officials, nearly all libertarians, and political figures like former Interior Secretary James Watt—view the recent history of centralized land-use planning quite differently. They emphasize the vast amount of centralized land-use legislation that has passed since 1970, as well as the bureaucratic toils in which the laws have enmeshed homeown-

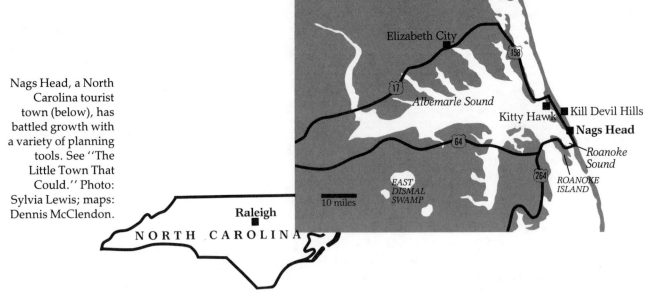

Nags Head, a North Carolina tourist town (below), has battled growth with a variety of planning tools. See ''The Little Town That Could.'' Photo: Sylvia Lewis; maps: Dennis McClendon.

State environmental laws have affected development patterns in Florida (above) and the mid-Atlantic states (right). See ''The Quiet Revolution 10 Years Later'' and ''Last Chance for Chesapeake Bay.'' Photo: Sylvia Lewis; map: Dennis McClendon.

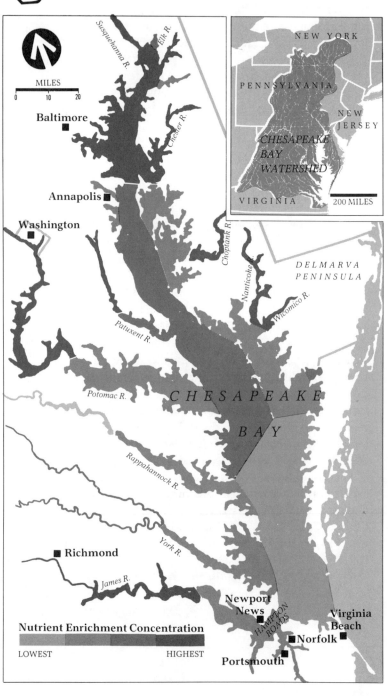

Nutrient Enrichment Concentration

LOWEST   HIGHEST

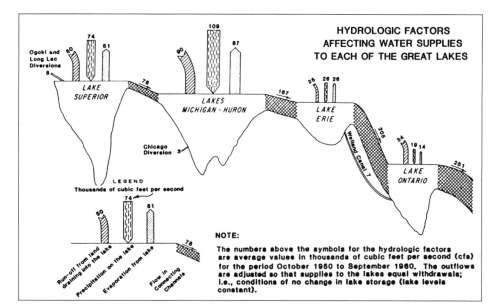

With a surface area of 95,000 square miles, the five Great Lakes form the largest freshwater lake system in the world. See ''Shore Wars.'' Drawing: U.S. Army Corps of Engineers.

HYDROLOGIC FACTORS AFFECTING WATER SUPPLIES TO EACH OF THE GREAT LAKES

NOTE:

The numbers above the symbols for the hydrologic factors are average values in thousands of cubic feet per second (cfs) for the period October 1950 to September 1960. The outflows are adjusted so that supplies to the lakes equal withdrawals; i.e., conditions of no change in lake storage (lake levels constant).

Older landfills feel the pressure when new sites can't be found—as with this 25-year-old facility in New Jersey (above). See ''Garbage In, Garbage Out.'' Photos: Jack Whitman, Edgeboro Disposal (above); Ron Gordon (left).

ers, developers, and localities. The conservatives like to count up numbers of laws, the contradictions between them, and the resulting long application processing times, leading to predictable horror stories. Conservatives use the stories to embarrass and cow the agencies administering the laws.

At the state level, for example, the growth of laws and regulations for centralized land-use planning was highly objectionable to conservatives. By the early 1980s California had 41 state agencies besides the coastal commissions with overlapping responsibilities for planning land use in the coastal zone—the Energy Commission, the Forestry Board, the State Lands Commission, and the Public Utilities Commission, to name a few. Six Minnesota agencies exercised several hundred land-use planning powers. These clear-it-with-yet-another-planning-agency programs inevitably antagonized many of those for whom the planning was intended, as well as conservatives opposed to the very concept of centralized land-use planning.

PUBLIC LAND

Just as centrally planned are America's public lands—the third of the nation, primarily in the deep-rural intermountain West and Alaska, that is owned by the federal government. These are the lands of the Interior Department's Bureau of Land Management (the largest federal land agency, holding a fifth of the entire United States), Interior's National Park Service and Fish and Wildlife Service, and the Agriculture Department's Forest Service: the country's national parks, forests, wildlife refuges, public grazing areas, and the federally designated wilderness areas within all these lands. California, the nation's most populous and in many ways most urban state, is nonetheless 45 percent public land, primarily away from the coast and especially east of the Central Valley. Arizona is 44 percent public land, Wyoming 48 percent. Alaska, Idaho, Nevada, Oregon, and Utah are over half public land; Nevada is an astonishing 86 percent public land.

The federal holdings are governed by a body of land-use planning laws that is entirely separate from those applying to private land. After 1970, this body of public-land law expanded rapidly, just like other forms of centralized land-use planning. The prime federal statute for planning the public lands is the Federal Land Policy and Management Act, passed in 1976. Also enacted that year was the

National Forest Management Act, allowing the Forest Service to conduct what may be the largest, most detailed land-use planning exercise in American history on the 298,000 square miles of Forest Service-owned land. In 1980, the Alaska National Interest Lands Conservation Act created 10 new national parks, most bigger than any in the lower 48 states. At least 10 other major pieces of legislation to preserve the federal lands passed between 1970 and 1980.

All these public land planning laws greatly resemble the post-1970 private land planning laws passed by the federal government. Both sets of laws deal with impacts that cross local and state boundaries, have a strong environmental focus, and are aimed at managing growth (on public land by, for example, establishing moratoriums on new coal leasing). In addition, both sets of laws try to blend conservation and development (on public lands, through the doctrine of multiple use) and seek to preserve environmentally sensitive areas.

As with the private lands, the public land planning efforts provoked a conservative counterreaction symbolized by Ronald Reagan; James Watt, Reagan's first Interior Secretary; and the Sagebrush Rebellion, the grass-roots Western attempt to shrink the public-land holdings and loosen the laws planning them. (See "Let's Reopen the West.") Reagan, Watt, and the rebellion were highly successful, at least at the latter task: Oil, gas, mineral, and timber leasing accelerated, and more land was opened to such uses.

The conservatives found other reasons to dislike the new centralized programs. The programs' attempts either to compel or to stimulate stronger local land-use planning have often been ineffectual in the face of local resistance. Many rural localities still have weak zoning or lack it entirely. Almost 30 percent of New York State's municipalities, for instance, lack zoning in the late 1980s—an improvement over the 60 percent figure of the early 1970s, but not huge progress. Most localities are years behind in their attempts to comply with the local planning requirements of the Florida comprehensive and California coastal laws.

More revealingly, after nearly two decades of centralized programs, many land-use planners are beginning to lose patience with their deficiencies. Much of the criticism is reminiscent of the late-1960s liberal criticism of local planning or, most strikingly, adopts the conservative position that almost any planning or regulation at any level of government is objectionable excess, doomed to frustration that is also publicly harmful.

THE QUIET SUCCESS OF CENTRALIZED PLANNING

Nevertheless, centralized land-use planning continues to expand, but more slowly than liberals hope and conservatives fear. Its fortunes ebb and flow, depending mainly on the politics of the individual states or federal agencies that apply it. Yet on the whole it is thriving. It is more tempered, more narrowly focused than it was in the early 1970s, less a subject of extravagant ideological claims (or even attention) from either liberals or conservatives.

The basic problem of centralized planning was that no one had much practical experience with it. But now that its unfamiliarity has diminished, the agencies and laws embodying it are melting into an almost boring respectability. The price of achieving familiarity is that centralized land-use planning is evolving in directions neither its friends nor its enemies could expect. Thus there is more centralized planning today than there has ever been, but it is less likely to be comprehensive, more likely to be specialized, oriented to particular purposes: programs for hazardous waste facilities, farmland protection, wetlands and floodplain regulation, groundwater protection, industrial- and energy-facility siting, sensitive-area preservation, state parks and forests. Every state now has some form of farmland protection legislation, and state parks are a newly exciting land-use field.

The new acceptability of centralized planning also means that the combination of even a few single-purpose laws can be as effective as a comprehensive land-use law of the Florida-Vermont-Oregon variety. New Jersey has become a leader in combining single-purpose laws. It has state-required and state-reviewed local planning; regional planning for the rural quarter of the state in the Pinelands near Philadelphia and Atlantic City and for the urban 30-square-mile, high-growth Hackensack Meadowlands near New York City and Newark; state hazardous waste, coastal zone, wetlands, and farmland protection laws that are among the strongest in the country; and the nationally unique Mount Laurel legislation governing the local placement and amount of new low-income housing. And now, as Robert Guskind's article in-

dicates, the state is seriously considering a demanding state land-use plan as well.

In some states, the 1970s centralized programs have found especially high public acceptance and made hefty political gains in the 1980s. Florida passed a package of legislation in 1984, 1985, and 1986 that amounted to an entire second-generation effort at centralized planning (see Stroud and O'Connell), a revamping and expansion of the state's 1972 comprehensive land-use laws. Many programs tried to consolidate their political support, often by at least partially winning over such former enemies as developers and local governments—for instance, by persuading developers that the programs could improve their product and so help them charge higher prices for it.

At the federal level, the Reagan administration always professed opposition to centralized land-use planning. But when forced or embarrassed by Congress, it still undertook such measures, albeit specialized, hedged, and relatively unpublicized ones. In 1981, it agreed to the Farmland Protection Policy Act, intended to prevent federal agencies' actions from contributing to agricultural land loss, but then used the law mainly as a way to defer to state farmland protection programs. In 1982 it actively promoted the Coastal Barrier Resources Act, intended to restrain growth in selected barrier areas, such as islands and exposed mainland beaches, that are vulnerable to damage from hurricanes, erosion, and other natural hazards (and thus often necessitate large federal flood insurance payments). In 1987 the administration proposed to triple the size of the protected area—although it would still have totaled barely 2,000 square miles.

In 1987 the administration agreed to an expansion of the 1977 Surface Mine Control and Reclamation Act to cover strip mines of less than two acres, closing a serious loophole. On the public lands, it has added nearly 11,000 square miles of federally designated wilderness since 1981, and put over 7,000 square miles of river banks into the federally protected wild and scenic river system.

On close examination, the Reagan administration did not prove as uniformly hostile to land-use planning as its liberal critics assumed. But because it was perceived as hostile (and not just by liberals), an interesting spillover effect appeared: a 1980s revival of local land-use planning. Especially in big cities, planning is now more pervasive, sophisticated, and effective than it has ever been. Zoning and local regulation generally have, in fact, shown a practical adaptiveness and political feasibility that could not have been anticipated in 1970.

THE IMPLICATIONS OF SUCCESS

This interpretation has intriguing political and professional consequences that are largely hopeful for planners. There is now more land-use planning—centralized and local, for big projects and small, on private and public land—than ever before. The future will probably see even more planning. The membership of environmental organizations keeps climbing steadily. The public's support for land-use and environmental planning has remained high and constant throughout the 1970s and 1980s, and shows no signs of wavering. The Reagan administration was not able to alter this consensus, and sometimes had to accommodate to it. The liberal impulses that produced centralized land-use planning did not decline or disappear. They won out, and nobody noticed.

Yet in one respect the Reagan-conservative approach to land-use planning achieved an odd triumph: No one expects major federal initiatives anymore. No one, including state and local governments and planners and environmentalists, relies on such initiatives (or the prospect of them) as they did in the late 1960s and early 1970s. Under Reagan federalism, each level of government and each individual government goes its own way, develops and manages and finances its own programs. Free administrative enterprise prevails.

Thus land-use planning can bubble up from the local level (see the Lewis articles) and simultaneously trickle down from the state (or even federal) one. Alternatively, it need not appear at all, at any level. Or it may appear at one level and then be resisted at another, as when the federal government tries to cut back funding for state surface-mine planning or opposes state coastal-zone planning intended to restrain oil and gas drilling on the federal Outer Continental Shelf. Or the federal, state, and local levels may plan together with varying degrees of cooperation, as they often do for government-owned lands.

The result can be remarkable variation across governments, a flexible responsiveness to the relevant constituencies, with the population getting the particular land-use planning it wants. Thus state planning flourishes in Florida, New Jersey, and Oregon, languishes in Colorado. Local plan-

ning booms in California, busts in Kansas. State planning thrives in Vermont while local planning falters; just across the Connecticut River in New Hampshire, the situation is reversed. State and local planners work together poorly in Maine, well in Florida and North Carolina. Federally funded state coastal zone planning performs nicely in Washington State, does not exist at all in Georgia or Illinois.

American land-use planners have plenty to do in the late 1980s. The development boom that began in 1982 now dwarfs the late-1960s one that led to centralized planning. But the new boom is more geographically uneven, leaving a big hole in the center of the country. Metropolitan areas in the Northeast and the far West experience near-boomtown capitalism while much of the South, the Midwest, the Great Plains, and the intermountain West undergoes near-depression.

Moreover, planners across the nation face a daunting menu of emerging land-use issues: acid rain, the cutoff of federal subsidies for low-income housing construction, hazardous waste, foreign land ownership, suburban traffic gridlock, deindustrialization, high-tech growth corridors, affordable housing for the middle class, the greenhouse effect, local unwanted land uses, aging strip developments, the disappearance of small- and mid-scale farming and ranching, gentrification that displaces the poor, homelessness, and—most extensively—the plain ugliness, inconvenience, indistinctiveness, and sterility of much of the new 1980s development. Large areas of, for example, New Jersey, Los Angeles's San Fernando Valley, and urban and suburban Florida are highly affluent, boast an impressive array of land-use planning devices, and still look vile. Improving the devices will provide work for planners at all levels of government, including the federal one. So will formulating new concepts of land and how to plan for it. (See the Healy and Krohe articles.) In truth, the professional opportunities for planners—and the chances for true political and intellectual power—have never been greater.

Frank J. Popper
Chair, Urban Studies Department
Rutgers University
New Brunswick, New Jersey

Portions of the preceding article appeared in the summer 1988 issue of the *Journal of the American Planning Association.*

Preaching the Good Life

Robert Cassidy
(October 1974)

Jehovah did not think "Lawson" was in the best tradition of Shadrach, Meshach, Abednago, Obadiah, Nahum, Michah, Jeremiah, Ezekiel, Malachi, Habakkuk, Zechariah, and the other Chosen Few with whom he was populating Creation. So God renamed him and called him Great Tom, for he was exceeding tall.

And Great Tom, the Lord God's prophet, went to the Great Council in Salaam. And he cast a spell on the two tribes of Oregon—for, in those days, there were only two tribes, the Republicans and the Democrats; the other 10 were yet but a twinkle in God's all-seeing eye—and they agreed to cast away their false gods and restore the land to Paradise.

That's one version of the Oregon story: How a tough former television newsman named Thomas Lawson McCall won first the secretary of state job and then the governorship and then pushed the legislature to pass the most far-reaching land-use and environmental legislation in the country. The story has taken on the aura of scripture.

The distinctive record of accomplishment began shortly after McCall took the governor's chair in 1966. One of the administration's first achievements was to clean up the Willamette River, referred to by some as perhaps America's filthiest river. To do this, McCall appointed himself state pollution control director, then instituted one of the toughest pollution-control systems in the country. Today, the chinook salmon have returned to the river. The entire river valley will be preserved through acquisition of land under the Willamette River Park Systems Act of 1967 and the Willamette Greenways Act of 1973.

Protection of other valuable resources also has been emphasized. The Scenic Waterways Act of 1970 has resulted in parts or all of seven rivers being preserved in their wild, rambling state. Concern for the beautiful Oregon coast led in 1971 to the creation of the Oregon Coastal Conservation and Development Commission.

Then there were what Charles E. Little calls the "B" bills. (Little is the author of an excellent account of the passage of state land-use legislation in Oregon, called *The New Oregon Trail.*) The bottle bill outlawed pop-top cans and nonreturnable bottles and cans. As a result, Oregon is one of the least-littered states in the Union. The bikeways bill set aside one per cent of highway funds for bikeways. The billboard law got rid of billboards. The beach bill declared that Oregon's beaches belonged to the people: now, access has to be provided at least every three miles.

These and other more important laws were not created out of a vacuum. Oregonians have a liberal and dynamic approach to government, dating back to the early part of this century, when they approved such reform measures as the direct primary and initiative, referendum, and reform. The state had a liberal abortion law long before the Supreme Court ruled on that touchy issue. Possession of less than an ounce of marijuana is a crime punishable by a traffic ticket. Hitchhiking is permitted everywhere. . . .

But the major effort in the last few years has been in land use. In 1969 the legislature passed Senate Bill 10, a draconian measure which required the counties to plan—or have the state do it. "We didn't do a damn thing to help them," said Governor McCall, during a recent interview. "We just put in the law, required planning, and if they didn't do it, we'd go in and change things." There was no money for local planning, nor any guidelines to direct the predominantly rural counties. "I had so much power I wouldn't even use it," said McCall.

This was remedied at least in part in 1973, with the passage of Senate Bill 100. S.B. 100 was approved for three basic reasons. First, there was the general recognition that S.B. 10 was not working. Second, there was the almost unheard-of personal effort of Hector Macpherson, a farmer from Eugene who decided to make a political issue of the decline of the environment in the Willamette Valley—even though he was not a politician at the time, and had never been. He got himself elected to the state legislature and, when the legislative leaders refused to give him funds to investigate land-use problems, set up a voluntary committee to do the job.

The final contribution came from the McCall administration, which, in cooperation with the Willamette Valley Environmental Protection and Development Council, created Project Foresight. Foresight was nothing more than a slide show which presented two different scenarios: the first showing continued development in the customary automobile-oriented, land-consuming, urban sprawl pattern; the second, a planned system which encouraged the use of mass transit, preservation of agricultural lands, and advanced methods of subdivision controls. Of course the presentations were somewhat simplistic. But some 25,000 people from Portland to Eugene saw them, and this created an awareness of the problems of growth that laid a foundation for popular acceptance of S.B. 100.

"One of the important things we've done is to point out the importance of land use," said Robert K. Logan of the governor's Local Government Relations Office. "Land use is a conflict. We don't know what is 'good' in land use. What is needed is a conflict-resolution system. The proper place for conflict resolution is the legislature. That forces the issue into the public arena."

The public domain

S.B. 100 has indeed pushed land use into the public forum. The law established a Land Conservation and Development Commission to obtain citizen input on various controversial matters. Arnold Cogan, the commission's staff director, said, "One of the big mandates of the bill was to get the public involved." To that end, the commission has been holding hearings all over the state. More than 90,000 invitations were sent out—70,000 at random, because, as Cogan said, "It's critically important to get in contact with the public at large," not just the lobbying groups.

At each meeting, the attendees were asked to break up into groups and make recommendations on specific problems. This material, plus information gathered from a questionnaire, will help the commission complete its major tasks by next January. These include recommendations on land-use regulations for farm lands, forests, energy generators, and coastal and shore areas, and other controls on economic development, urbanization, employment patterns, housing, pollution, and transportation. The commission will have to define standards of comprehensive land-use planning, so that the

cities and counties will not be left rudderless as they were under S.B. 10. It will most likely develop a permit system for regulating the five "activities of statewide significance" mentioned in this bill: public transportation, public sewerage, water supply, solid waste sites, and public schools sites. (Power sites and activities may be added to the list.)

And the commission will have to decide on eight or so environmentally critical geographical areas for special stewardship by the state. In addition, the commission is charged with assuring that, throughout the planning process, from the governor's office to the local planning commission, the voices of citizens are heard.

S.B. 100 also has clout. If local planning commissions fail to conform to state guidelines once the commission adopts them, the commission can appropriate the delinquent county's liquor and cigarette tax share and hire a consultant to develop a plan. When asked if he thought the commission would ever actually follow through with this threat, Cogan shook his head no.

But this is not the end of the state's effort in land-use protection. A tough bill puts restrictions on what McCall has termed "sagebrush saboteurs"—rural land subdividers who are selling lots in the Cascades without providing necessary public services, particularly water. There is a new law requiring stricter subdivision regulation by the counties. Planning commissions have been reorganized to reduce the influence of the real estate lobby. A program called Feedback has been continuing the work of Project Foresight, giving citizens a way to get information about planning. An Oregon Futures Foundation is being set up to coordinate long-range state planning. And Bob Logan's office is looking into the possibility of compensable zoning, under which landowners who find their property values reduced due to public action will be paid for their loss.

Perhaps more important than any specific legislative accomplishment of the eight-year administration of Tom McCall has been a change in attitude. There may be some public relations hype and political-flag waving involved, but there also is something to be said for the way in which McCall has conducted his governorship. Perhaps after seeing him for years on television, Oregonians feel they know him. But he has made an effort to be open with them, and the mutual respect has pushed Oregon ahead of the other states in the environmental field.

As he enters the last days of his administration—by law, he cannot succeed himself to a third term; furthermore, he is still recovering from a cancer operation—McCall is contemplative. "We're running quite a bit ahead of the people of the state," he said, referring to his administration. "One of the arguments of one of the gubernatorial candidates is that we need some quiet years." McCall shakes his head in disagreement. "What we've done is create a relationship between the legislature and the governor," he said. Now that 61-year-old McCall is sure to be out of public life, the good working relationship between governor and legislature may not carry over into the next administration.

The McCall years have given Oregon a respected place among the states and have made government interesting and fun. During one of his recent staff meetings, which are open to the press, 20 members of his administration were tackling some weighty issues: an important antitrust case, new electric utility rates, energy problems. In the midst of all this McCall brought up his recent television appearance in which he demonstrated his golf swing. He told the staff that he was later introduced at a benefit as the worst golfer, but the best governor, the state had ever had. "I just wish it had been the other way around," McCall said.

As we left the staff meeting, McCall pointed to a newspaper clipping that took the smile from his face. "Atiyeh criticizes Councils of Government," the headline read, referring to Victor Atiyeh, the Republican candidate for governor. "I spent eight years fighting for COGs, and here the candidate of my own party comes out against them," said McCall.

McCall need not be so downcast. There is yet hope in sight, as the Bible—at least that apocryphal version—points out:

> *And the seventh angel poured out his vial into the air; and there came a great voice out of the temple of heaven, from the throne, saying, It is done.*
>
> *And there were voices, and thunders, and lightnings; and there was a great earthquake, such as was not since men were upon the earth, so mightly an earthquake, and so great.*
>
> *And every island fled away, and the mountains were not found.*

Respected scientists already predict that an earthquake will wash California into the sea in the near future. That simple act of God could solve at least half of Oregon's problems.

Robert Cassidy is a former editor of Planning.

The Quiet Revolution 10 Years Later

John M. DeGrove
(November 1983)

Over the past decade, a number of states have taken actions in the area of land and growth management that have changed the nature of both state and local land regulation. In my view, these actions represent a public policy initiative of major and lasting importance, both to the substantive issue of growth management and to the intergovernmental issue of state and local relationships.

The degree of control ranges from very slight (Colorado) to extensive (Oregon). What has been done in the way of adopting new laws and regulations and of implementing them also varies widely among the states. However, they all share certain characteristics, including a broadening of state authority for growth management; a mandate to strengthen local authority; a new relationship—and new tensions—between state and local governments; and implementing laws that tend to join planning and regulation more directly—and in many cases more effectively—than in the past.

The significance of these new state initiatives lies in the fact that, for the first time, state legislatures are acting on the recognition that land decisions made by local government often have a regional or statewide impact. Once this recognition is made, it becomes imperative that statutory and supporting regulatory and administrative mechanisms be put in place to account for this impact.

One way to do this is to remove the decision-making authority from local government. But, while this approach has been supported at one time or another in almost all the states I have looked at, it has not survived as the major thrust in any one of them. What we see emerging instead is a new partnership between state and local governments in the area of land and growth management.

After looking closely at land and growth management in seven states—an effort that has engaged my attention over the past eight years—I've concluded that there is no quick-fix model that can be adopted by other states. One can, however, pick out certain ingredients that are essential to success.

First, no program is likely to get off the ground unless there is a reasonably widespread perception that serious problems require a new look at how state and local governments manage growth. Characteristically, this perception has existed only in states with heavy growth pressures and a public conviction that growth was degrading the environment.

Typically, it has been environmental groups that have mobilized public support for state laws, but these groups have had to appeal to a broad cross-section of the population—including the governor and key legislators, who in turn respond to citizen concern about growth pressures.

A second ingredient for success is the ability to keep the land and growth management issue free of partisan politics. Politics dominated the process in only one state in my sample—Colorado. It is not a coincidence that this is also the only state of the seven where the effort failed to accomplish most of the original goals.

While former Colorado governor John Love, a Republican, did support a state land-use law in 1973 and 1974, as did some Republicans in the legislature, the effort to pass a law in 1974 produced a schism along party lines that has remained to this day. That division involves Gov. Richard Lamm, a Democrat elected in 1974, who has supported a relatively strong state role in growth management, and a legislature dominated by conservative Republicans strongly opposed even to a minor state role in such a system. The result has been a steady erosion of support in the legislature to the point where the Colorado Land Use Commission has been stripped of almost all of its funding and survives only because it has the support of the governor.

Despite such setbacks, Colorado continues to seem a natural for an effective growth management system. Growth pressures affect both the mountain resort areas and the urban areas of the front range. These growth pressures have degraded the environment and the quality of life in both places, and the people of the state seem concerned about these impacts. Yet the stalemate between the governor and the legislature threatens to impede all progress.

Finally, success requires support from the top. My data suggest that it may be easier for growth management systems to survive neglect by the governor than by the legislature. Strong gubernatorial support in Colorado was not enough to make the program effective there. In contrast, the lack of support by then governor Ronald Reagan was not enough to make the program ineffective in California. In every other state I examined, both legislative and gubernatorial support was sustained in the decade following the adoption of the growth management legislation. Obviously, this is the ideal situation. It does not come about by itself, however. Environmental groups played a large part in broadening the base of support for growth management systems in several of the states I studied. Their impact has been clearest in Oregon and Florida, and visible to some extent in California.

Money talks

Any assertion of state responsibility in an area as sensitive politically as land and growth management is bound to encounter local resistance. This has been the case in every state in my sample. Yet, in most of these states, a new partnership is emerging in which state and local governments are working together in new ways to manage growth—albeit with varying degrees of stress stemming from the state's assertion of new authority and added financial burdens on local governments.

Several actions seem effective in easing this strain. First, the state can contribute to the costs of the growth management systems, thus making the sometimes bitter pill of state oversight more palatable. The states in my sample vary widely in their willingness to provide the necessary funds. Florida has done very little in this area, and local governments, especially cities, have expressed strong resentment at the state government's failure to back up its demands with dollars. Oregon, California, and North Carolina have done better in this regard, and their actions have helped make some new initiatives acceptable to local government.

There is no way to avoid the issue of home rule in these new state partnerships. Clear definitions of state, regional, and local responsibilities are needed. Often this need for clarity has not been met; the result has been needless conflict between the state and local governments.

In some areas, localities may even welcome a state role in certain kinds of land-use decisions. In Florida, this is certainly true concerning LULUS— "locally unwanted land uses" (a phrase coined by Frank Popper in an article in the April 1981 issue of *Planning*). Examples of LULUs are airports, solid waste facilities, hazardous waste transfer stations, electric generating facilities, prisons, and forensic hospitals. City and county officials view them as political nightmares because of pressures by the state on the one hand to find suitable sites and objections by citizens groups on the other. In such a politically charged atmosphere, local governments may welcome a state override in site selection. . . .

It's hard to pinpoint how much difference the new state initiatives in growth management have made. Evaluation of impact has not been a strong point of any of the programs. Indeed, if there is a single weak link that can be identified in all of the growth management efforts that I have studied over the last decade, it is a striking lack of monitoring, evaluation, and enforcement.

All the programs follow a similar pattern. Citizen group concerns generate enough political pressure to bring about the passage of new laws. This concern is sustained to provide at least a minimum amount of funding for the implementation of the program, but it is never enough for meaningful monitoring and enforcement—which would ensure that actions taken under the new system, including permits that have important conditions attached to them, achieved the desired goals and objectives.

Even without the follow-up, however, there is an imposing body of evidence that suggests that growth management initiatives have substantially improved the quality of local planning and implementation. In addition, the systems have brought pressure on state governments to get their own houses in order—to coordinate their growth management efforts with regional and local efforts. Participants and observers in all the states analyzed agreed that this impact is a positive one, whether or not they supported the growth management program.

John DeGrove, AICP, is director of the Joint Center for Environmental and Urban Problems at Florida Atlantic University/Florida International University. He is the author of Politics, Growth, and Land, *published by APA.*

California's Coastal Commission: Ten Years of Triumphs
Gladwin Hill
(January 1982)

One day last fall the word went out that a Little League baseball team was about to be evicted from its longtime playing field on the edge of California's Malibu Lagoon, to permit construction of a parking lot. At first it sounded like a typical clash between white hats and black hats—some rapacious developer encroaching yet further on recreational space. But that wasn't the case. The heavy turned out to be none other than the state's Department of Parks and Recreation, which wanted to make the lagoon more accessible to the public as a nature preserve.

That dispute is a microsample of the thousands of dilemmas about appropriate land use that have arisen to tax the ingenuity of the California Coastal Commission, now in the tenth year of the nation's most comprehensive experiment in state-level land regulation.

Basic mandate

"We've sweated over everything from multi-million-dollar hotel projects to the paint on a single house," sighs Michael L. Fischer, the commission's unflappable 40-year-old executive director.

California's coast stretches for 1,100 miles. About half of it is privately owned. A decade ago, like most of the nation's shores, this coastline was rapidly disappearing behind an opaque wall of private homes, subdivisions, apartments, hotels, industrial facilities, marinas, fast-food emporiums, bait shops, and anything else an entrepreneur could dream up.

In 1972, at the instigation of conservationists, the state yanked away from cities and counties land-use jurisdiction over a coastal strip running up to five miles inland, encompassing one-tenth of the state's area. It consigned the authority to a new state agency, which was given one simple mandate: "Preserve."

The result is remarkable. In less than 10 years runaway coastal development has been arrested, and a long-range conservation program has been put into operation. Both the program and the coastal commission have survived a barrage of legal and legislative attacks; and the public seems reasonably satisfied with the results.

Last July brought a milestone that could be described as the start of the program's home stretch. The state commission began turning back to local jurisdictions the authority that had been taken from them in 1972. From here on out, qualified cities and counties will make the decisions about development—with the 12-member state commission remaining in existence indefinitely as a sort of supreme court of appeal to ensure that decisions conform to policies prescribed in the inch-thick California Coastal Plan, enacted in 1976.

Its basic principles are that coastal open space, farmland, wetlands, beaches, and the marine ecology in the 15 coastal counties are to be preserved wherever possible; development concentrated in areas where it exists already; and public access to the shore maximized. The coastal zone contains 75 percent of the state's population.

The chief devices for accomplishing the plan's objectives have been, first, a permit system under which it was hardly possible to drive a nail on shoreline property without minute public scrutiny of a project's likely impacts; and, second, long-range local land-use plans subject to approval by the state commission.

The critical ingredient in the employment of these tools has been the democratic process. The coastal plan itself was the product of countless public hearings. All permit applications were reviewed initially by one of six regional commissions, essentially citizen bodies. Their decisions could be appealed by anybody to the state commission, whose staff conclusions likewise were aired at public hearings before final rulings. Since 1973 the regional commissions have processed some 55,000 development applications. Ninety-five percent ultimately were approved—although often with radical changes and imposed conditions.

Adding up the score

What has the program in fact accomplished? For starters, it spurred state and local government efforts to acquire coastal land as recreational preserves. In 1973, 273 miles of the coast were in state,

county, and municipal ownership; today the commission estimates the total at 447 miles.

The coastal plan earmarked 600 square miles of private property for eventual government purchase; to date, 30 square miles have been acquired. The state's 120 square miles of wetlands—the remnant of an area once four times as large—have been protected from further dredging, filling, and diking.

Formerly, the first thought was that new power plants should be located on the shore because of the easy availability of water; since 1973, none has been built there. Industrial development generally has been confined to port areas. About one-third of the coastal zone is classified as agricultural land. Most of it has been kept in this condition, with protracted arguments over the disposition of even 50-acre vegetable plots.

A basic principle of the program has been that nothing could be built on the coast that would obstruct the view from the nearest highway. That put an end to the high-rise apartments and hotels that had been mushrooming all along the coast and drastically altered the type of construction permitted.

But development has by no means been paralyzed. For instance, a 17-lot subdivision at Big Sur, one of the choicest locations in the state, had only two homes on it in 1973; now only a couple of lots remain unbuilt. But, to conform with the clear-view regulation, the new homes are low-lying.

A before-and-after example of the regulatory process is the case of a 582-acre Avco Community Developers project near Laguna, one of the largest the commission has dealt with. The company spent three years, going all the way to the U.S. Supreme Court, in a vain effort to carry out its pre-1972 plan to build 8,000 dwelling units, including some six-story structures.

Legal avenues exhausted, the company engaged Ronnie Rogers, an Orange County planning consultant, who spent the next 18 months attending coastal commission hearings and gradually ironing out an approvable plan. It was trimmed to 3,000 units, with no high rises, and with the dedication of some 33 acres to public parks. The overall economics of the project have not been detailed, but one 7.5-acre park tract alone was said to represent a $16 million outlay. Even so, said the company's president, Barry McComic: "We would still expect it to be a highly profitable project." . . .

Inequities

There being no such thing as a free lunch, the coastal program inevitably has had negative aspects. The limitation of coastal development has put a premium on existing properties and tended to make the rich richer, despite the program's basic objective of democratizing the use of the coast, and despite efforts to incorporate "affordable" housing and other facilities. Projects have taken anywhere from several months to several years to gain approval, during which costs have soared.

There have been acknowledged inequities—cases in which property owners in sensitive locations found there was no way they could build even modest homes and still conform with regulations. Some owners of beachfront property have complained that, to obtain permits for improvements, they were blackmailed into granting special beach access easements.

Apart from the federal-state squabbling over oil leases, oil companies with valid offshore drilling permits have been embroiled in years of negotiation about shoreside facilities. In several pending situations, sponsors of major development projects have, along with commission officials, been perplexed over workable definitions of where wetlands begin and end.

A big disappointment of the program stems from the law's provision that the coastal zone should be regulated with special regard for low- and moderate-income people (defined as those whose incomes range from 80 percent to 120 percent of the area's median). The commission set a target stating that 25 percent of new housing should be within reach of these groups.

The system proved difficult both economically and politically. Many would-be buyers found their incomes did not qualify them for the open-market financing needed. The commission issued permits covering some 7,000 lower income units, and 700 are occupied. But what some critics call unworkable social experimentation became a focus of attacks in the state legislature. The mandate had become an increasing headache for the commission—so much so that the commissioners did not oppose its elimination from the law last September.

Naysayers

Any reformist venture as sweeping as the coastal program was bound to arouse great opposition. At one point or another it has riled almost every interest group in the state—property owners, developers, the construction industry, labor unions, local governments, and even environmentalists.

Initially some business interests predicted that the program would precipitate economic disaster—which has not materialized. At the other extreme, some environmentalists have contended that the program has worked out as just a piecemeal coastal giveaway.

Property owners formed an organization called the California Coastal Council to buck the commission's mandates. Another group, the Alliance of the Coast, says it seeks only constructive modifications in the law. The state chamber of commerce, the League of California Cities, organizations of county officials, and the business-oriented Council on Environmental and Economic Balance all take intermittent potshots at the commission's activities.

At one time, lawsuits were hitting the agency almost daily, but the commission has not lost a significant court action. Two individuals have been jailed, briefly, for contempt of court in defying commission orders.

To date, the opposition has failed to derail the program. It is difficult to challenge a clear electoral mandate whose implementation is spelled out in 200 pages of text arrived at only after exhaustive public hearings. Accordingly, outright hostility has largely mellowed into various degrees of acceptance, sometimes grudging, sometimes hearty. . . .

In a statewide opinion poll in mid-1980, only half of the respondents had heard of the coastal commission, but 80 percent of those questioned endorsed its objectives, and 35 percent of those familiar with it rated its work from "good" to "excellent."

Some communities have found fulfillment of their end of the coastal program difficult. Los Angeles does not expect to finish its coastal plan until 1983, two years behind the statutory schedule. Long Beach, by contrast, by dint of more than 150 citizen committee meetings and thousands of hours of professional and volunteer work, won timely commission approval of an elaborate development plan.

Under the law, on last July 1 the six regional commissions, whose functions had been to screen permit applications, hold public hearings, and grant or deny approvals, ceased to exist. By then, it was expected that local governments would have received approval for long-term regulatory programs for their segments of the coast and would take over permit issuance. However, only 22 of 67 cities and counties have so qualified, and only a few more are expected to be in the fold this year. Then the state commission's main work will be overseeing compliance. Meanwhile, it has to do most of the permit screening.

Half of the commission's 12 members are state appointees, half of them elected representatives of local government. All serve with only token compensation. The current panel includes several lawyers, an engineer, a biologist, an insurance agent, and a travel agent. The commission meets seven days a month, alternating between northern and southern California. There is a staff of 200 at its San Francisco headquarters.

The agency's tentative 1982–83 budget is $13.8 million. The Reagan economy program cut the federal contribution from $5.5 million last year to $1.6 million for 1982–83. Altogether, the agency has spent about $58 million—less than $3 per citizen, or about $1 for every foot of coastline.

Threats remain

In 1981 some 50 bills were introduced in the legislature to either abolish the commission or trim its powers. Except for the ending of the "affordable housing" effort, none of the bills got anywhere. Michael Fischer, the commission's executive director, thinks that perhaps, after nine years of such unavailing efforts, the program "may have passed a watershed."

But another threat has arisen. There has been a flurry of special-interest bills to remove particular tracts of land from the commission's jurisdiction on one pretext or another—a device malleable legislators have tried unabashedly with noncoastal land as well.

"If this sort of thing got out of hand, there's a possibility we could be Swiss-cheesed to death," Fischer says. "But I don't think it's going to happen."

More gnawing a question, looking far down the road, is how coastal values can be preserved for all time in the face of relentless pressure for develop-ment—to provide recreation facilities, to convert farmland to settlement, to extend densely developed areas until they abut in a solid ribbon of development.

In Fischer's view, preservation hinges on public acquisition of terrain that citizens believe it's important to preserve.

"What we're involved in now," he says, "is the regulatory approach, and that's essentially a weak reed. We can't depend indefinitely on the rulings of local bodies; they're subject to local pressures that ignore statewide interests.

"What we can depend on is acquired land. There's no way we can buy up the whole coast. But we can, through devices like easements, create a new structure of property rights that can be enduring and serve our real constituents: people who won't be born for several generations."

For all its complexities and travail, the coastal program seems to be working. And many observers—including Fischer—believe it also offers a model for government management of noncoastal areas that are particularly worthy of preservation.

Gladwin Hill is former national environmental correspondent for the New York Times. *He lives in Los Angeles.*

Last Chance for Chesapeake Bay

Sandra Olivetti Martin
(June 1986)

Each dawn illuminates a new mood of the Chesapeake Bay. Sun, haze, or tempest, every weather compliments the world's largest estuary. The wind ripples and froths the slate waters. Screaming, soaring gulls welcome the day. Ducks dive and dabble. A heron freezes into fishing point. Beneath the sun- and wind-pied surface of the waters, hungry plankton fill each drop like stars in a bay night sky, and fin and shell fish dwarf populations of human cities. Throughout the changing day and into the night, the bay's resources seem boundless.

They are not, of course. Over the years, the people who have been drawn irresistibly to the bay have bred problems that have mounted like heaps of discarded oyster shells, until they threaten the vitality of the great Chesapeake. Today, even as we assault them with our best tools—planning, money, and regulation—the problems seem limitless and the cures elusive.

In shape and in the complexity of its ecosystem, the bay resembles a massive oak tree. It's a long, narrow estuary, stretching 200 miles south from Baltimore to the Norfolk-Portsmouth-Newport News-Hampton, Virginia megalopolis. From a broad base, it branches into 150 tributaries, 15 of them major rivers. The larger—the James, Elizabeth, York, Rappahannock, Patuxent, Potomac, and, to the north, the Susquehanna, from which the bay was born—drain the western shore, the mainland. These giants dwarf the Elk and Chester, Choptank, Nantico, and Wicomico of the eastern shore or Delmarva Peninsula.

Like the oak, the bay is a living body, sustained by lively interaction with the elements around it. Twisting and tangling, it forms a great estuarine watershed of deep waters, shallows, and marshlands. The tributaries carry fresh water—and whatever by act of man or nature enters those waters—into the salty, ocean-fed trunk of the bay.

In the bay's two-way circulatory system, the lighter freshwater flows downstream and the heavier saltwater flows up. Mingling, the two waters nourish an ecosystem that supports some 2,700 species: 280 kinds of fish; oysters; soft-shelled clams; and Atlantic blue crabs, both hard-shelled and soft.

Some 12.7 million people live, work, farm, and fish on the 64,000 square miles of land surrounding Chesapeake Bay—eroding the soil, flushing sewage, generating power, refining petroleum, concocting chemicals, emitting sulfur and carbon dioxide, building ships, and even splitting atoms.

"As more and more people move into the Chesapeake basin, their development and the byproducts of their towns and industries cause the quality and productivity of the bay to decline inexorably," notes James M. Seif, chairman of the Chesapeake Bay Executive Council. "The bay has changed dramatically over the last century, and since 1950, the change has accelerated even faster."

With few exceptions, change has not yet spoiled the beauty of the Chesapeake. But increasingly, it has clouded her waters, blighted her vegetation, and assaulted her creatures.

A crusade

To reverse the tide of degradation, a massive effort was mounted in 1983. In an unmatched planning crusade, forces with starkly conflicting goals joined in a rescue operation—only to find the money drying up.

The crusaders include the states of Maryland, Virginia, Pennsylvania, and the District of Columbia, plus a score of federal agencies—among them the Soil Conservation Service, National Oceanic and Atmospheric Administration, Fish and Wildlife Service, Army Corps of Engineers, U.S. Geological Survey, and the Department of Defense.

Much of the effort is coordinated by the U.S. Environmental Protection Agency, advised by independent groups with sometimes conflicting goals; one such is the Chesapeake Bay Foundation, the private-sector authority of record on bay issues. Then there are all the special interest groups representing, among others, farmers, landowners, developers, and scientists.

The crusade demands not only unprecedented cooperation but also unprecedented staying power, requiring its planners to spread scarce resources far into the future.

Until 1983, when the federal EPA completed its multiyear, $27 million Chesapeake Bay study, the bay was assumed to be infinitely able to cleanse itself of the effects of use and abuse. The study proved that assumption wrong. It discovered a massive burden of human-generated pollution that threatened to overwhelm the bay. Toxics and nutrients, the EPA concluded, have polluted the waters of the bay and, directly and indirectly, poisoned its resources.

The toxic threat

Toxics—the heavy metals and the hundreds of organic wastes such as pesticides—may be the least-understood danger in the pollution equation. Conclusions about their effects remain tentative but alarming. "Research has shown a relationship between elevated levels of toxic compounds in the sediments and the survival and diversity of individual organisms necessary to have a balanced bay ecology," said the Chesapeake Executive Council's cautiously worded Chesapeake Bay Restoration and Protection Plan of 1985. "Toxic materials are present in concentrations sufficient to kill aquatic organisms, especially in Baltimore Harbor and

Hampton Roads," stated the less equivocal Chesapeake Bay Foundation.

The toxics enter the bay from industrial facilities; sewage treatment plants; runoff from cities, suburbs, and farms; and acid rain. Today, the entire trunk of the bay and many of its major tributaries endure at least low-level contamination. Areas near its major urban centers—Baltimore, Washington, and the quad cities of the Virginia capes—suffer heavy contamination.

What is certain is that toxics already in the bay remain there. "Like a giant sink, the bay is filling up. The circulation pattern washes only a small percentage of the pollutants into the ocean," says Rod Coggin of the Chesapeake Bay Foundation. A decade ago, the insecticide Kepone was dumped into Virginia's James River. Today, blind and lesion-scarred fish are still taken from the James. One prominent marine biologist, Michael Bender of the Virginia Institute of Marine Science, says that cleaning the river could take 100 years.

Better understood is the damage caused by nutrients—the benign name given to the nitrogen and phosphorus that wreck the balance of bay life. They are actually the supernutrients that fertilize a hazardous crop of blue-green algae—floating fields that block sunlight from the acres of water beneath them. When they decay, they starve other plant and animal life of oxygen.

Ever-increasing areas of the bay's trunk and two of its tributaries, the Potomac and Patuxent rivers, are oxygen-deprived. Since 1950, the area of deprivation has increased 15-fold. A starvation band follows the bay's central channel at depths below 30 feet from the Patapsco River in the north to the Rappahannock in the south. This area, according to Chesapeake Executive Council chair Seif, "supports no life."

By the year 2000, scientists expect even higher levels of these oxygen killers. Phosphorus loads could rise from 14 to as much as 21 million pounds, and nitrogen from over 140 to an astronomical 160 million pounds. The major sources: farm chemicals, sewage, automobiles, and the industries around the bay. With the population of the basin expected to swell to 14.6 million by 2000, the poisonous effluents can only be expected to increase.

"I think it's interesting to note that the pollutants that most impact the Chesapeake are precisely those which we have done the least in controlling up until now," Seif told legislators and others assembled for the first review of the bay program last September.

The EPA study got action. Months after it was released in December 1983, the bay states, the District of Columbia, and the federal government joined in partnership with the goal of "restoring the Chesapeake Bay to the conditions that existed in mid-century."

Their compact, the Chesapeake Bay Agreement, spells out responsibilities. "EPA and the states share the responsibility for management decisions and resources regarding the high priority issues of the Chesapeake Bay." The partners agreed to support both "site-specific, discrete state efforts and baywide undertakings." They formed a "government"; identified the enemy (toxics and nutrients); pledged funding; and promised a plan of action.

Last September, the governors of Maryland, Virginia, and Pennsylvania, as well as Lee M. Thomas, administrator of the Environmental Protection Agency, and Mayor Marion S. Barry, Jr., of Washington, D.C., presented their Chesapeake Bay Restoration and Protection Plan. That appropriately thick document is the bible of bay believers. The first comprehensive blueprint for saving the bay, it is a triumph of systems thinking, organizing an array of facts about bay ills and remedies into a strategy for action based on priorities, goals, and objectives. In its implementation, each of the signatories has a role to play.

The federal government

A decade earlier, the federal government had set the stage for bay recovery through the Clean Water Act of 1972. Under the act, state-set water quality standards are achieved by controlling wastes discharged by municipalities and industry (through the National Pollutant Discharge Elimination System Permits) and by improving sewage systems with the help of the Construction Grants Program. The federal government has spent a whopping $150 million for each of the past several years to help build municipal sewage treatment systems within the bay basin. But now that ambitious construction program is winding down. Both total funding and the federal grant percentage have been cut back, and in 1990 federal grants will cease. The bay area's share of funding this year for sewer construction—a crucial part of restoration—is down to $84 million from $170 million in 1985.

The Chesapeake Bay Program is never again

likely to see such bountiful spending. In 1984, the year President Ronald Reagan proclaimed the bay a national treasure in his State of the Union message, $4 million in federal funds bankrolled the beginning of EPA's bay program. The federal government pledged $10 million a year to the program through fiscal year 1988. (The six other federal agencies that also contribute to the bay program receive independent funding.)

Then this year, the Gramm-Rudman-Hollings Deficit Reduction Act sliced 4.3 percent off that federal budget item. And the cuts could be substantially worse if Congress doesn't meet its deficit goals this year. The first $2.75 million of each year's federal contribution (figured at the $10 million pre-Gramm-Rudman level) supports baywide activities—administration, monitoring and modeling, and public education. The remaining $7.25 million per year is reserved for the states as matching grants. Maryland, Virginia, and Pennsylvania are each eligible for 30 percent and the District of Columbia for 10 percent.

The states

The states' programs and funding vary as widely as their situation on the bay basin. Within each jurisdiction, the goals are translated into strategies to recover the bay's integrity watershed by watershed. Maryland has gone even further. The state's landmark critical areas criteria, approved this year by the General Assembly, push the battlefront onto the land.

Maryland and Virginia are the biggest bay holders. Both span the bay. Though Virginia controls more bay waters than Maryland—985 square miles as opposed to 703—Maryland's bay lands are more extensive and more populous. Historically the more aggressive bay protector, Maryland has spent $81 million on the bay over the last two years and has allocated $50 million in its FY87 budget. Virginia spent approximately $15 million for its bay cleanup initiatives in 1985–86 and has allocated close to $40 million for the next two years.

Neither Pennsylvania nor the District of Columbia borders the bay. But Pennsylvania's major river, the Susquehanna, brings the bay almost half of its unwanted load of sediment and nutrients. And the District's 625,000 residents—plus tens of thousands more workers and tourists—wash their sewage and stormwater into the bay by way of the Potomac River. Pennsylvania has contributed just

$2 million to the bay since 1984 and the District over $10 million in that time.

What are those millions buying? A quarter of the EPA's grant money—over $1.75 million a year—is spent to stop pollutants at their sources.

Despite a decade and a half of heavy funding, the most obvious sources of nutrient and toxic pollution—sewage and industrial discharges—continue to be major problems. Little wonder: More than 1,000 sewage plants return treated waters to the bay and its tributaries. In Maryland alone, 700 industrial sources also pump their waste into bay waters.

Millions of pounds of heavy metals, chemicals, nitrogen, phosphorus, and sediments continue to pour in. Even the chlorine that is used to purify wastewater eventually poisons the bay water and its creatures. "Wastewater frequently does not meet the requirements established by the government, even when those requirements are lax, as they often are," says Ann Powers, lawyer for the Chesapeake Bay Foundation.

Improving technology and enforcement are the means to staunching these flows. Bay states are increasing their control over point sources of pollution. Limitations on what can be discharged have become more stringent throughout the bay basin. Enforcement and prosecution are following suit. New tracking systems monitor the stages of compliance. Maryland now employs 2,000 inspectors and has empowered an attorney general's hazardous waste strike force. The state collected $421,000 in fines through civil and criminal actions against polluters last year, by far the most ever. This year, Virginia reached half that level in one swoop, assessing a $200,000 fine against Perdue Farms, Inc., for the devastation its chickens caused in Parker Creek, a bay tributary. . . .

Hidden sources

Fifteen years of multi-million-dollar spending have reduced point-source pollution of the Chesapeake. But the pollution has not stopped. For in that time we've learned that pollution not only pours into the bay from telltale pipes. It also seeps from the land and falls from the sky. The second target of bay cleanup efforts is all those "nonpoint sources" of pollution.

Three-fourths of each year's EPA Bay Program spending—$5.6 million a year—is devoted to curbing this devastating seepage. The states add several times that amount on "best management practices" to keep the land and its burden of chemicals, fertilizer, and petroleum residue out of the bay.

Maryland's efforts range from its ban on phosphates in detergent to its Agriculture Cost-Share Program. Three thousand applications are in for soil conservation projects that can bring as much as $25,000 to each approved farm. Virginia and Pennsylvania also are subsidizing soil conservation efforts. The District of Columbia is concentrating on preventing heavy storms from pushing raw sewage into bay-feeding rivers, allocating over three-quarters of its $10 million contribution to the cleanup for this purpose. Stormwater and runoff controls are in effect in Virginia and Maryland as well.

The newest frontier is state-regulated land management. In legislation approved this year, Maryland has designated a strip extending 1,000 feet from the bay waters and its tributaries as critical areas and has enacted strict criteria for its use—despite opposition from real estate and development lobbies and some legislators. Planners hope to move the regulation line farther inland. "Because of the pressure population puts on the bay, this is an incredibly important beginning," says Ann Powers of the Bay Foundation. . . .

The biggest worry is where the money will come from. Federal priorities continue to shift away from jurisdictions shared with state and local governments—areas like the bay. Gramm-Rudman-Hollings hangs like a sword, with the threat of huge across-the-board cuts that may be as deep as 25 percent. So the planners and the scientists weigh priorities. "What do you want? Can it get done? How can you get it paid for?" Those, according to Seif, are the questions of the day.

"Maintaining state funding in changing political climates is very much the issue," says Pat Bonner of the EPA Bay Program. In Virginia, Charles S. Robb, who signed the Bay Agreement, has ended his term as governor. And Maryland Gov. Harry Hughes, a supporter, is seeking to replace retiring U.S. Sen. Charles Mathias, Jr., another longtime friend of the bay. Will the bay remain a high priority for the leaders who replace them? Will state legislatures continue to be generous as money gets tighter and competition sharper?

The answers, everybody agrees, depend on citizen support for a restored Chesapeake Bay. "As long as the public is concerned, the legislatures and regulatory agencies will be concerned, too," says EPA's Bonner. For that reason, substantial sums of each jurisdiction's funding are earmarked for public education and citizen participation.

At the same time, alternative funding is being explored. Virginia's $20 million commitment to financing improved wastewater treatment through loans rather than outright grants and to establishing a bonding authority sets the pattern for the future. Across the board, it is likely that all bay "users" will be paying more of their own way.

To make change easier, the profit motive is being tapped through investment strategies encouraging users to "invest" in the bay. Instead of paying farmers to adopt good soil management practices, for example, Pennsylvania has adopted a low-cost program to educate farmers about conservation. The state sends a "mobile nutrient laboratory" throughout the Susquehanna basin testing farm soils and animal wastes and teaching farmers that they can save money by reducing their use of fertilizers and insecticides.

In the future, local governments will also have more responsibility. Already, progressive local authorities have taken steps to regulate pressures on the bay. Maryland's Calvert County, winner of a 1984 APA honorable mention award, has enacted a land-use plan that not only balances growth with preservation but also protects the bay.

Because local jurisdictions are on the line of change, they have the most to win or lose. By overcoming hands-off habits of the past, they stand to improve their economies through revenues, taxes, and user fees, while protecting their resources—public health, the environment, land values, and soil, as well as less tangible values like the pleasantness that makes bay land so attractive.

In the decade since we first recognized the bay's fragility, we've made a promise to the future. In beginning to keep that promise, we've learned enough to mock our every assumption, challenge our every goal—even the meaning of recovery. "We now question whether the standards set 10 years ago will support life," EPA's Morris says. We've learned enough to know bay protection has only just begun.

"The lantern has been hung in the old North Church. Now Paul Revere has to get riding," warns Mo Lynch, head of the Bay Scientific and Technical Advisory Committee.

Sandra Martin is a writer who lives in Dunkirk, Maryland.

New Jersey Says, 'Enough'

Robert Guskind

(June 1988)

Nabisco's corporate headquarters rise on what used to be a rolling golf course in East Hanover, New Jersey, part of a development boom that has brought 14 million square feet of office space to rural Morris County in a decade. The good times have made Morris one of New Jersey's wealthiest counties, but planners are now warning that by the turn of the century only land deemed unsuitable for development or protected by law will remain untouched.

The same kind of breakneck development has overtaken U.S. Route 1, the two-lane highway that forms the spine of the corridor between Princeton and New Brunswick, where 12 million square feet of office space has sprouted since 1980. Postmodern corporate campuses and their residential satellites—an endless progression of treeless cul-de-sacs and modern colonials abutting the cornfields—freckle the landscape. The agglomeration of 14 towns along Route 1 will be Jersey's largest "city" by 2000.

As suburban and exurban growth has proliferated, so have its well-known side effects: traffic congestion and acute housing shortages in the newer suburbs; local governments pushed to the fiscal edge; and older cities left to decay. For a long time, New Jersey cast a benevolent eye on what was happening, not surprising in a state where helter-skelter suburban development has become an art form and municipal home rule has been defended as akin to holy writ.

Now it seems that a political turnabout has taken place, for New Jersey is about to become the nation's first industrial state to enact a wide-reaching set of statewide land-use controls. If the new plan succeeds, and the odds are long at best, new development will be directed to designated suburban areas and depressed inner cities and the brakes will be applied to growth in relatively undeveloped rural areas.

"In New Jersey you're seeing the first wave of what is going to wash over the rest of the United States," predicts James Gilbert, the Merrill Lynch vice-president who chairs the 17-member New Jersey State Planning Commission, which was set up by the legislature in early 1986 to draft the plan. A final draft is to be released this month, with a finished document due sometime next year.

"There is no alternative to growth," said New Jersey's Republican Gov. Thomas H. Kean in an interview. "But it has to be planned growth. General growth really doesn't make sense anymore."

Road to nowhere?

The sense of urgency isn't misplaced. Nearly every corner of New Jersey, from the swamps of the Meadowlands in the shadow of Manhattan to the bedroom communities near the Jersey shore, has been touched by an explosion of office construction and the dispersal of business and people into far-flung suburbs.

Northern New Jersey's 99.1 million square feet of office space today exceeds the combined volume of downtown Chicago and Los Angeles. One-third of the office space has been built since 1984, and another 35 million square feet is expected to be built by 1990. In the Princeton corridor alone, one recent survey found 51 million square feet of office space planned, proposed, approved, or under construction.

In the tiny village of Plainsboro, some 7.1 million square feet of office space is coming up, including a two-million-square-foot complex adjoining the Princeton Forrestal Center, the 3.2-million-square-foot office park that touched off the boom in the 1970s. The corridor is zoned for 34 million square feet of office space, enough for 1.2 million new employees, and about the total volume of office space in Manhattan.

Such rapid development has increased personal income and reduced the state's unemployment rate. It has also spawned what Bruce Coe, the executive director of the New Jersey Business and Industry Association, calls "the problems of prosperity."

"There's a limited amount of pavement you can put in any square mile before the quality of life deteriorates and the economy comes to a halt," says Rep. Robert Torricelli (D-N.J.), a backer of state planning, who adds that an unfettered market place is no substitute for such planning.

The ever-lengthening traffic pile-ups, the most

visible manifestation of sprawl, are as much symbols of modern-day New Jersey as the belching oil refineries along the turnpike were in years past. "New Jersey doesn't have rush hours anymore," jokes James Hughes, a professor of planning at Rutgers University in New Brunswick. "We have rush mornings and rush evenings punctuated by noontime backups." State planners estimate it will cost $13.8 billion over the next 20 years—close to double what will be available—simply to accommodate projected growth, let alone pay for the huge backlog of infrastructure needs.

Along the traffic-clogged stretch of Route 1 from the state capitol of Trenton to New Brunswick in the north, for example, transportation planners say some $750 million in improvements will be needed simply to keep traffic moving at today's sluggish pace. Without improvements, a trip that takes half an hour today could take over five hours by the turn of the century. And in Morris County, the average commuter will be spending the equivalent of six weeks a year sitting in a car stuck in traffic.

Yet another prominent concern is that the booming economy of the 1980s has, by and large, bypassed New Jersey's industrial-era cities. Between 1970 and 1985, while the number of jobs available statewide increased by 25 percent, the six largest cities *lost* 25 percent of theirs. In addition, minority residents of the older cities have been closed off from suburban housing by price and from suburban jobs because development has spread dozens of miles into the countryside.

Prime mover

Even though statewide sentiment for growth management has been mounting on its own in the last few years, planning was, in fact, forced by the New Jersey Supreme Court's 1970s *Mount Laurel* rulings requiring municipalities to provide for low- and moderate-income housing. To estimate the extent of those needs, the court ordered the state to come up with a plan reflecting New Jersey's recent growth patterns.

Once the door was kicked open by the courts, a broader effort to redirect growth found allies among environmentalists disturbed about vanishing open space; local officials whose municipalities have been overwhelmed by megaprojects in neighboring towns; suburbanites upset with traffic tie-ups and escalating housing prices; and corporate leaders facing labor shortages, skyrocketing costs,

and their employees' increasing reluctance to move to New Jersey.

The plan's goals are ambitious, especially for a state that is at once the nation's most densely populated, most suburban, and most dominated by home-rule municipalities. It attempts to curb suburban development in parts of the state where growth has only recently begun, to concentrate rural development around selected towns, to steer new development to mixed-use centers along transportation corridors in areas like Princeton, and to spur new growth in the older cities and suburbs that have the infrastructure to accommodate it.

Designed to accommodate the 1.2 million new residents expected in the next 20 years, the plan carves New Jersey into seven categories, or "tiers." The first four, including transportation corridors and older cities, are designated for growth, and the remaining three, including rural areas, farmland, and conservation areas, are defined as limited-growth areas. The goals for the cities are modest: to halt their slide of people and jobs so that by 2010 they return to 1985 population and employment levels.

The plan leaves zoning and land-use decisions to individual towns. It could, however, be used to control state funding for infrastructure projects in limited growth areas, while—in theory at least—channeling funds to older cities and suburbs and to mass transit. The plan leaves it up to developers to pay for roads and other infrastructure in areas targeted for limited growth; development would be phased in as infrastructure is built to accommodate it. State environmental permits would be withheld for projects in areas where the plan says they aren't appropriate.

In general, the New Jersey plan is based more on incentives than regulatory provisions, according to state transportation commissioner Hazel Gluck. "It's a very fine line," says Gluck. "If it appears too regulatory, there will be a lot more opposition to it. But you can't leave it open-ended because if you do people will keep coming in and paving things over." . . .

Now in its second draft, the plan must go through a "cross-acceptance" process that gives individual towns and counties a chance to comment on preliminary drafts and to amend their own plans accordingly.

When it's finished, the plan will take its place along with other New Jersey land-use regulations and entities: the Pinelands Commission, a regional body that controls development in a vast portion of southern New Jersey; the regional planning commission for the 32-square-mile Hackensack Meadowlands near New York City; a stringent wetlands protection law passed after Gov. Kean threatened a development moratorium last year; and a soon-to-be-rejuvenated coastal commission, now working its way through the legislature.

Mixed reviews

Environmentalists and some suburban officials worry that the plan has already been watered down to pacify developers and municipalities. Developers and municipalities, meanwhile, are concerned that the document will be too heavy-handed. "Depending on where you sit, you are enthused, ecstatic, annoyed, hostile, or outright ready to kill," says state senator Gerald Stockman, a Democrat who sponsored the planning bill in 1985.

"The plan is couched in terms that lack definition in order to allow everyone the freedom to do their own thing," says David Moore, executive director of the New Jersey Conservation Foundation, which advocated a much tougher, mandatory state planning system. "But the freedom to do their own thing is what caused the problems in the first place." Moore believes that many of the original targets and specifications contained in an early draft of the plan have been removed in favor of broadly stated, and nonbinding, goals. The document "lacks specificity," he claims.

But the planning effort has come under the heaviest fire from New Jersey builders, who say the opposite: that it has too many growth restrictions. Designating a large swath of the state for limited growth "is going to cause some severe dislocations within the economy," says Joanne Harkins, director of land use and planning for the New Jersey Builders Association.

A key concern of the builders is that the state may find it easier to slow growth than to stimulate it in the designated growth areas—particularly those unwilling to accept certain kinds of development. The builders' group, whose Foundation for the Preservation of the American Dream has a bankroll of $900,000 to fight the plan, also alleges that housing prices will skyrocket if developable land is limited.

Perhaps the most serious concern, however, is that the plan will follow in the footsteps of Jersey land-use plans of previous decades and simply collect dust. . . . The last time New Jersey tried state planning—in the mid-1970s—the state was, in fact, in the throes of a severe recession. Jersey's rejuvenated economy, plus the dedication of the state's leaders, provide the plan's supporters with more hope this time. But even they concede that new laws will be needed, probably after the 1989 gubernatorial election, in which Kean is barred from running for reelection.

Supplementary bills are already pending in the legislature. One package submitted by the Kean administration, called "Transplan," would give counties approval of large developments, limiting the eligibility of individual towns to rule on projects that affect dozens of their neighbors. It would also severely restrict highway access for some projects and set up "transportation assessment districts" to enable counties to impose fees on developers for infrastructure improvements necessitated by their projects. Another bill would create a transfer of development rights program to protect open space.

Avoiding the issue

Still, a troubling question remains: Have New Jersey's planners avoided the key issues? Some officials say the answer is yes. They note that development is driven by two forces: local dependence on property tax revenue and home rule, which allows one town to make development decisions that have wide repercussions throughout an entire region. The planning effort has addressed neither issue.

"Home rule allows one town to do another one in," says the Conservation Foundation's David Moore. Case-in-point: an ongoing dispute between Lawrence and Hopewell, two adjoining communities along the Princeton corridor. Hopewell has zoned land along the Lawrence border for high-density housing; it is now taking applications from developers interested in building some 1,000 units on the land.

While Hopewell would receive all of the property tax revenue, the traffic impacts and much of the costs of services would be borne by Lawrence. Sewage treatment, for instance, will be provided by a regional authority that Lawrence subsidizes. Hopewell doesn't even belong to it.

"Communities are now realizing that their concern is not necessarily with the state or the county but with decisions their fellow municipalities are making," says the Municipal League's Jack Trafford.

The solution, advocates argue, is countywide or regional planning. "Local planning boards process applications. They don't do planning," says Sam Hammill, executive director of the Mercer-Somerset-Morris Regional Council, a privately funded study group. "Shifting decision making to the county level will allow us to bring more talent and more sophisticated technical resources to bear."

Whether areawide planning should be the responsibility of counties or of new regional planning bodies is a matter of considerable discussion. But an even testier subject—taxes—may decide the final outcome for Jersey's plan. Effective growth management, Rep. Torricelli argues, requires New Jersey to "solve the problem that local government is financed largely by real estate taxes. We have a tax system with the incentive for the very kind of sprawl we want to stop."

A variety of tax changes have been suggested. Among them: that the state assume a bigger share of the cost of welfare and the courts to lower the tax burden in the cities; that property tax rates be lowered in areas targeted for development; that regional property tax base sharing be instituted, following the model of the state's Hackensack Meadowlands, where a regional commission controlling development apportions property tax revenue among 14 municipalities, some of which have severe restrictions on growth. Gov. Kean has consistently rejected the need for tax reform, however.

Second generation

New Jersey's push to rein in growth follows by two years Florida's enactment of a statewide growth management system, and there are indications that Georgia, Maine, and other states may be getting ready to act on similar controls. Hawaii, Oregon, and Vermont led the way in the 1960s and 1970s with plans that emphasized protecting scenic beauty and preserving open space.

The modern era of state planning dawned with Florida's Growth Management Act of 1985, which is designed to protect environmentally sensitive areas, particularly the state's coastline, ensure more compact development patterns, and guarantee that development doesn't outstrip infrastructure. Over the next three years, Florida's cities and counties

are supposed to draft or update their plans and set standards for a host of services, from traffic flow to health care and education.

Once the plan is approved by the state, local governments are prohibited from approving developments that adversely affect their service levels unless they provide enough money to upgrade public facilities. Governments that break with the plan face the loss of state aid. Florida now estimates that implementing the plan's goals will cost $52.9 billion over the next decade. The state's share of that tab will be $35 billion.

The first local plans began trickling in to the state in April, but one gaping loophole has already become apparent: Local governments may still gorge on development. It's possible under the growth management law to settle for congested roads and inadequate sewers and public facilities as the local service level, although whether the state will approve such plans remains to be seen.

Growth management in Florida received its worst blow last year when Republican Gov. Robert Martinez, after flip-flopping on the issue for months, finally repealed the new state tax on services, which was supposed to raise $1.5 billion a year to implement the plan. Only a few local governments have accepted the option of imposing a one-cent sales tax.

The land-use debate is building in other states this year, too. The Maine legislature is considering the recommendations of a nine-member legislative commission on a statewide growth management system. And in Georgia, where suburban growth has been fast-moving, particularly in the Atlanta area, Democratic Gov. Joe Frank Harris has appointed a panel to look into state land-use controls. It is expected to suggest a state planning effort that would redirect growth to targeted areas and ration state infrastructure and economic development funds accordingly.

But New Jersey's foray into state planning remains the most unusual—and the most problematic—of the undertakings now gathering steam among the 50 states. . . . [It is happening because] Jerseyites have begun to spot signs that the state's good fortune may soon boomerang, its office boom threatened by a combination of traffic, rising housing costs, labor shortages, and a looming political backlash. And that may be the spur needed for the state plan.

"No corporation is going to build a large office

facility where they're concerned about the availability of water or adequate sewerage or an adequate road system," says Stanley W. Smith, a former AT&T real estate executive who is now assistant postmaster general for facilities at the U.S. Postal Service. AT&T chose to expand several current facilities in neighboring Pennsylvania rather than around its New Jersey base in Morristown.

Instead of corporate headquarters, New Jersey is getting back-office operations, says state treasurer Feature O'Connor, whose office oversees the planning commission. "The cost advantages that helped fuel the growth over the last five years are disappearing," she says, adding that "the state will lose even its back-office operations if something isn't done about growth."

Some see the state plan as warding off a stronger no-growth movement, as two officials on opposite sides of the political fence agree. "We're at the point where growth has created a political backlash," says Torricelli, who is expected to run for the 1989 Democratic gubernatorial nomination. "We're right on the edge of tipping into an antigrowth movement that would put us into an economy that won't help anybody," says Gluck, an expected candidate for the Republican gubernatorial nomination, who also favors the planning effort.

Meanwhile, an early March poll by Rutgers University's Eagleton Institute found ample evidence of mounting public frustration with growth. More than half of those polled said New Jersey has grown too fast; exactly half said they want no more growth. Most interesting is the fact that 55 percent indicated that they were willing to surrender some local autonomy for more planned growth.

"Any planning effort of this magnitude faces a very difficult time of being accepted, enacted, and viable," says Smith, the ex-AT&T executive. "It's not a matter of whether or not it's going to happen, it's a matter of what the penalty will be before it does happen."

As more and more states begin to realize that they have paid a high price for their suburban prosperity, state planning could well turn out to be the wave of the future—and not only in New Jersey.

Robert Guskind is a contributing editor of Planning *and of the* National Journal, *from which this story is adapted.*

Florida's Not-So-Quiet Revolution
Ed McCahill
(March 1974)

Lately, anytime more than two people get together in Florida, the subject of stopping, slowing, redirecting, or managing growth seems to come up. About 6,000 people a week are moving into Florida, and about 57,000 acres of land each year are becoming urbanized. Florida's population, which has doubled since 1920, will double again by 2000. "Some day soon, about 100,000 people in a new town here are going to wake up in a swamp with no fresh water to drink, and they're going to wonder how a town got there," a worried state official said recently.

In response to this influx of people, Florida has elected to close the door on some of the growth. "No one can put up a gate," says Dade County Commissioner Harvey Ruvin, "but we'll eventually reach our carrying capacity. The problem is not just numbers. It's distribution." Ruvin was elected because he led the fight to stop all construction in his district. He, like most of his neighbors, wanted some time to think about and plan where in the hell they were going to put all those people. . . .

No one gave a tinker's damn about growth in Florida until 1971, when the Everglades caught fire after a two-year drought. Water rationing in urban areas was then, and still is, commonplace. When Governor Reubin Askew called for a conference on the crisis, he got an overwhelming response from state, business, and civic officials and a whole lot of private citizens. Witnesses to Askew's keynote speech at the conference three years ago say that he so fired the 160 members of the audience with zeal for preserving the balance between man and his environment that it led eventually to the biggest revolution in land-use thinking the state has ever had. At that conference the governor called for and got a task force of land-use experts from all over the state to come up with legislation for handling the problem.

Fortunately for the task force, Fred Bosselman, a Chicago zoning lawyer, meanwhile had coauthored a book called *The Quiet Revolution in Land-Use Control.* The book gave some of the task force members the idea that maybe the state, in its efforts to protect the rights of its citizens, had itself the right to take back some of the powers for controlling the use of land it had given up to Florida's 400 municipalities over the years. They called Bosselman, and he suggested that their approach should approximate the one spelled out in the American Law Institute's Model Land Development Code. Ultimately, they did in fact use Article 7 of the ALI code, which spells out the regulation of land use. The task force also discovered a legislative committee working on a water resources bill, so they adopted its chairman as a member. Because of this, the task force was able to go to the legislature just six months later and propose a package of bills that would make the state leap from being the most backward to one of the leading states in environmental planning.

The laws

The package of bills presented to the legislature in 1972 included: (1) The Florida Environmental Land and Water Management Act of 1972; (2) The Water Resources Act of 1972; (3) The Land Conservation Act of 1972; and (4) The Comprehensive Planning Act of 1972. The approach was to establish a statewide planning system by assigning localities certain responsibilities for controlling the use of land. The bills did not extensively standardize the administrative procedures statewide nor did it assign any particular local jurisdiction, such as the county, with the responsibility. This was to be worked out later.

"Environment and water were easy to sell to voters at that time," says Dr. John DeGrove, a professor of political science at the Joint Center for Environmental and Urban Problems at Florida Atlantic University in Boca Raton. "We were getting support from two kinds of people: the environmentalists who are worried about ecosystems, and the people just bothered by too many people. It's a powerful coalition." The League of Women Voters served as one of the grass roots organizations, and the governor put some of his key legislators behind the package of bills. Florida has just redistricted its legislature to comply with the U.S. Supreme Court's one-man, one-vote ruling; and this changed it from a rural-oriented body to urban-

oriented. The bills were quickly passed and signed into law.

The most important bill was the Environmental Land and Water Management Act, which gave the state control over two categories of land use: It had control of areas of critical ecological concern to the state, such as an environmentally sensitive marsh important to a large area; and although the act left to localities the right to zone or not to zone, it asserted that in instances where a development, such as a shopping center, was large enough to have an impact beyond the borders of the affected town, some agency would have to review the project to make sure the rights of the neighboring localities were not diminished.

Next in importance was the Water Resources Act, which called for the state to manage its water and related land resources properly. It asked that the state conserve wetlands, protect surface and ground water, and assist in maintaining the navigability of rivers and harbors. In general, it promoted the health, safety, and welfare of the thirsty people of the state.

The Land Conservation Act was simply the instrument to let the state float a bond issue so that it could be provided with enough money to buy up land that was environmentally important to the state. Seventy per cent of the voters approved the bond issue when it later appeared on the ballot.

The Comprehensive Planning Act ordered the new state division of planning to evaluate the projects that qualified as "developments of regional impact," commonly called DRIs. DRI guidelines would cover housing, transportation, health, land, and water. Regional planning councils, regional water management districts, and, in some areas, a combination of these two types of agency would actually be doing the reviewing. The state division of planning would set the rules and regulations used by the regional agencies for determining which areas were of critical ecological concern and which projects were developments of regional impact.

As is usual with new laws, the principal problem was money. The legislators wanted the state planning division to supervise the DRI review process and the critical areas process, but it allowed only $300,000 for the job. The chief of the bureau of land planning, Robert Rhodes, had asked for $900,000. The state division currently has only half as many planners in its planning department as

Dade County. "Maybe there are 100 DRIs that we missed in the first six months," a state planner said. Nevertheless, the four state planners working on DRIs did manage to process requests from 145 builders who wanted to throw up 294,000 houses. "The bill was grossly underfunded," Professor De-Grove says. "It was peanuts, but it was not disastrous because in the first year we were busy creating regulations. It would be disastrous if we didn't get the money this year. We're all geared up to start enforcing the DRI concept."

Controlling large developments

The DRI concept was the key to slowing down growth. Housing was the principal target. The number of units qualifying a project as a DRI was tied to a sliding scale proportionate to the population. In Dade County, the most populous, a developer could put in as many as 3,000 units and escape having to subject himself to state scrutiny and state-imposed guidelines. In smaller counties, 250 units would qualify for state examination. This would force a builder in Dade County to build smaller projects so he would not have to file an impact statement with the city or county. If the project qualified as a DRI, the city or county would send the impact statement to the regional agency for review and recommendation. The city or county would not necessarily have to follow the recommendations made by the regional agency; but, if it did not, the state planning division was charged with asking the governor and his cabinet not to allow the project to go ahead. Since 40,000 to 60,000 housing units are being proposed each month, it can readily be seen that four planners are too few to do the job.

So far, developers have been cooperative; but, if they begin experiencing delays in the maze of permit granting, their tolerance of the new law will disappear. Developers, unlike real estate interests, have not strongly opposed the law thus far. They prefer Florida's laws to the brush-fire nongrowth laws that are cropping up around the country, which include, in some instances, complete moratoriums on building. If the implementation is bad, however, developer support could disappear overnight; and the state division of planning might find itself suddenly without funds. . . .

Besides the state planning division, the regions, the counties, and the localities need funding. When the impact statements are filed, a staff is needed to review the various elements. In Dade County, for example, there's a good planning agency with a big staff. When a developer submits a proposal, the Metropolitan Dade County Planning Department can parcel out the various elements to the departments involved. If what the developer has provided meets the necessary requirements, then the county can go ahead and issue the permit.

The system seems to be working. Reginald Walters, director of the Dade County planning department, says his department is going to parallel the state's criteria by having developers submit impact statements regarding transportation, school, fire, and police. "But we will require finer information than the state gets. We may say, for example, that 200 units will qualify as a DRI while the state sets the level at 2,000. As a countywide planning agency, we're responsible for providing a countywide land-use plan." The impact statement would be the only way the planning department could get enough information together to keep the plan updated. Right now the county agencies do not have to provide recommendations on a DRI, mainly because there's no money. But DeGrove and others want to amend the present laws so that it will be the county's job to make recommendations to the politically weak regional agencies on the acceptability of proposals. . . .

The Water Resources Act

Floridians are not just being mean in wanting to keep others away. (There are even TV commercials sponsored by the Miami Chamber of Commerce and others telling Floridians to be kind to tourists.) They are up against it in the drain on their natural resources. In the Tampa area, where the problem first cropped up at least 40 years ago, the fight over water has escalated into a major range war, with hired hydrologists being brought into the county water departments to gun down adjacent county's hydrologists.

One such hired hit man, John Logan, water resources director for Hillsborough County (serving Tampa), smiles as he says that his main job is cutting off the water flowing from his county to his neighbors in St. Petersburg. "St. Pete's two well fields in Hillsborough County were pumping 31.4 million gallons a day average for 30 months, up to June 1973. Everybody near those fields had to deepen their wells. The new maximum average allowance for St. Pete is 24 million gallons. That's the first step toward our ultimate goal of zero for St. Pete." The Water Resources Act gives authority in the area to the Southwest Florida Water Management District ("Swiftmud," as it's affectionately known) to determine who should get how much water.

Although this device has not been tested yet in the courts, the act already has brought about the first agreement in the 40-year St. Petersburg–Tampa water battle, with St. Petersburg agreeing to limit the amount of water it pumps from the aquifer, the large underground bubble of fresh water from which most of Florida draws its supply. Swiftmud elected a figure of 640,000 gallons a square mile as the water crop figure—the amount of water that can be taken from the aquifer and that will be returned to it through natural processes.

Developers have not yet felt the full force of the Water Resources Act. Swiftmud usually discourages builders through "Maximum Administrative Delay," but, when the full force of the law is felt, both the present residents and new developers will feel the pinch. Logan estimates that Pinellas County, which includes St. Petersburg, is drawing off 40 to 50 times what it should. To St. Petersburg residents that means that eventually the town will have to go possibly a hundred miles north to draw water. If it has to be carried to them in a 72-inch pipe, the costs will soar.

Developers in the area have to receive permission to build from the board of Swiftmud; builder applications no longer can be approved by the staff as in the old days. Swiftmud's board has been denying permits to half the builders coming before it. Whenever a builder wants to draw out more water than is replaced, the permit is denied. Swiftmud has also forbidden daytime irrigation of crops. Legislation has been introduced in Tallahassee to create a marketing authority to sell water based on water crop figures. A debate is taking place now on whether agencies such as Swiftmud should sell water, thus eliminating need for a new staff in a new regional agency, or whether new agencies should be created. There is some feeling that the agency selling water should not be the agency deciding how much to sell.

"What we're trying to understand is the limits of growth," says Harry Merritt, chairman of the graduate design department of architecture of the University of Florida in Gainesville. "I think we ought to handle our natural systems with trembling hands. Natural systems do things for you for free. The whole goddamn state is using too much water. They're having to move the well fields inland, and they're beginning to eliminate their potential for growth. They are selling their birthright." . . .

The aquifer under Florida has dropped 20 feet in nine years, so Merritt has reason to be upset when he sees precious potable water being used to flush toilets or water golf courses. The bubble of water thins along the coast (St. Petersburg's own water supply dried out 30 years ago). Once more water is being used than is replaced, the wells have to be moved inland or they'll be pumping saltwater.

Merritt is presently writing a work proposal for the state on the time and cost of inventorying the natural systems of the state, calculating the carrying capacity of Florida's natural systems, and devising a practical method for implementation. "We're not saying the growth of the population should be constrained, but we will have to pay for the energy it will take to support additional population," he says. Most states are going to have to look at two things: one, what their natural systems can support, and two, how much external energy will be needed to support any additional population. Under the Water Act even the present users are going to have to reapply for a permit and prove that the water is being used for a reasonable and beneficial use and not damaging the source.

Negative effects on housing

Through concepts such as DRIs and the state purchase of endangered areas, Florida is trying to keep Malthus from the door. These measures are adding greatly to the price of housing—$1,800 can be added to the cost of a home, for example. The 1972 environmental package has received the support, or at least the tolerance, of builders in Florida because they can just pass the cost along to the consumer. Also, having one set of statewide standards is easier than having one in each locality. But developers do have problems with the act.

Jay Janis, a Miami developer formerly with HUD, dislikes the land-use law because it does not provide for low- and moderate-income housing needs. He notes that it could be repaired by providing for a statewide override of local zoning that is exclusionary. On DRIs he believes that it's necessary to have a sliding scale that will give a bottom limit for qualifying. He also believes that if development is curtailed it is a taking, and the law should provide for fast and fair compensation. He also feels that, if five per cent of the state lands can be taken out of the market as environmentally endangered, then the government has an obligation to see to it that other lands are provided for housing.

Areas designated as of critical concern should conform to a statewide comprehensive plan, Janis said, adding "But they also should be reviewable so that if technology improves, say for building in a flood plain, then the designation could be altered." He also wants public hearings whenever the state designates an area of critical concern, in order to give the builder an opportunity to show the deleterious economic effects.

"It all came on Florida so suddenly. They call it things like 'ecology' and 'environment,' but sometimes it's a cloak that hides the issues of the poor," a black college professor said recently. These measures are of concern to lower income people because they involve zoning, and zoning is by definition exclusionary. Dade County Commissioner Harvey Ruvin notes that it is in the best interest of any group advocating slowed growth to advocate a housing program to go along with it. There is a severe shortage of housing in Dade, where the vacancy rate is about one per cent. Ruvin wants a housing corporation formed to float loans to developers at reduced rates and to issue bonds to provide low- and moderate-income housing. However, a rehabilitation program involving only $10 million recently failed to win voter confidence.

. . .

Indifference toward the poor

There is a lot to learn from the Florida experience. As the zoning web broadens, it is going to restrict the movement of people across boundaries. There will be more zoning at the local, county, and regional levels than at the state level. There will be a plan for each of the 67 counties.

In Florida, one can drive down the new Interstate 10 between Jacksonville and Tallahassee on a weekday and not see another car. This would obviously be the place to put people if jobs were available, just as Orlando was a good place to put Disney World.

Disney World was supposedly the "best-planned" private development in the state, but in January it announced the layoff of 1,700 people because of the energy crisis. The biggest question seems to be not whether Malthus was right or wrong but whether Keynes was right or wrong. Keynes said you could play the economy just like a piano, and a lot of presidents have tried to do just that. It was the opinion of many that the ALI Model Land Development Code approach, the basis for Florida's law, was a good approach to land-use planning; but many thought that it needed a housing element in it.

In Florida, it's tough to get an unemployment compensation check because it's a conservative state when it comes to providing for social needs. In contrast to Illinois, for example, which spends $8 billion on 11 million people, Florida spends only $2 billion on its 7 million people. In the case of housing, a soon-to-be-introduced growth policy resolution proposes that, since the state can't provide any low- and moderate-income housing, the federal government should do so. It seems as though the piano is out of tune, because the federal government isn't going to be providing enough housing for Florida's needs.

Florida is basing its land-use laws on the concept that developments of regional impact should be reviewed by the state. The list of DRIs is not large. But times are a-changing. "Right now we are setting threshold standards tied to the population of the county," says Eastern Tin of the state division of planning. "We did this to provide for the easy identification of DRIs. But there are other approaches. We could identify them on the basis of the extent to which the proposed project places a demand on the natural systems."

His proposal is that, if the natural system is in a balanced state, it will have to be kept in that condition by requiring the builder to provide all of the facilities necessary to maintain the land's carrying capacity. When the carrying capacity is exceeded, an impact fee will have to be levied so that new water and sewer pipes can be paid for by the locality. This would call for a sophisticated system wherein one would have to weigh current demand on the system against future demand. It would require a good capital facilities program. . . .

"I would hate to have to determine what the carrying capacity is," said John Woodlief, chief of the metropolitan planning division of the Metropolitan Dade County Planning Department. "It would be a very subjective definition based on the quality of life you want to achieve." Woodlief recently headed the staff which assisted a citizens advisory task force in producing a comprehensive development master plan for Dade. This group came up with a plan sensitive to the growth issue but also sensitive to the social needs, calling for a minimum amount of low- and moderate-income housing. Other plans and planners are not that sensitive.

A bill before the state legislature would require all cities and counties to adopt comprehensive plans within three years. It would prohibit development inconsistent with the plan and calls for a four-fifths majority vote to change the zoning at the local level. To pay for this fine-tuning of the zoning system the bill would increase the real estate transaction tax. Under the bill, municipalities that failed to plan would have their planning done by the next highest agency, the county, under the force of law.

This measure was proposed by the Environmental Land Management Study committee created by the land management act and funded to operate for one year. It has set the wheels in motion to put the brakes on growth. Its task is finished and its recommendations printed, and it is just about to be dissolved. Its December report asked for a number of new laws and some procedural changes to strengthen the original laws.

Planners will have to improve their tools to handle legislation such as the Florida package. They will have to grapple with the carrying capacity concept at a time when nobody knows how to define it, much less analyze it. But the job for elected officials is even tougher. The energy crisis has proven beyond any shadow of a doubt that the steady-state economy is a pipe dream.

Ed McCahill is a former editor of Planning.

Florida Toughens Up Its Land-Use Laws

Nancy E. Stroud and
Daniel W. O'Connell
(January 1986)

Florida continues to bust out all over. By the year 2000, it could add population equal to that of the state of Georgia. This is, of course, a familiar story—so much so that Florida has had a much-heralded package of state land-use laws in place since the early 1970s.

The new growth—most of which is expected to be on the coast—will tax the resources of local governments, which like most throughout the nation have fallen behind their current infrastructure needs. In the past, the state has chosen to rely heavily on local government planning—but with a strong state oversight.

This year, though, Florida took a quantum leap in land-use control by adopting a network of planning laws that takes an integrated approach to tackling the state's high growth rate and attendant problems.

In brief, the state has adopted both a state plan and a requirement that local comprehensive plans be approved by the state planning agency. This means that the 461 cities and counties must revise their plans to include capital improvements programs and more stringent coastal zone protection. It also means that 28 state agency plans and 11 regional policy plans will have to be written—and that all three levels of plans must dovetail.

The legislation

Unlike the first wave of state land-use laws, which the state legislature passed without providing significant local planning funds, the lawmakers this time appropriated more than $2 million to help local governments during the first year alone. They also appropriated almost $7 million for the additional planning efforts the new laws require.

The new planning system is contained in two major laws, both passed last spring: the State Comprehensive Plan Act and the Growth Management

Act. Together, they represent an omnibus package of major and minor changes to Florida's growth management laws. The new laws are the result of extraordinary attention given to growth management in the previous two years by a series of state blue ribbon committees, a persistent governor, legislative conferences, and interested legislators.

The state comprehensive plan is composed of 25 goals and accompanying policies, addressing concerns of every state agency: education, health, housing, public safety, transportation, energy, natural systems, and so on. The goals also address concerns that cross agency lines, such as property rights, the elderly, and plan implementation. The legislation requires all state agencies to prepare "functional plans" for the governor's approval by July 1986, and every other year beginning in 1987.

Like the functional plans of state agencies in Hawaii (the only other state with a similar setup), Florida's plans are intended to provide policy guidance; unlike the Hawaii plans, Florida's plans must identify for the legislature the financial resources necessary to implement them. Although legislative approval is not necessary, legislative leaders are to be consulted about the organization of the functional plans. After public hearings and review by the governor, the plan will be transmitted to the legislature.

Two special functional plans for water resources and state land development must be prepared in time for the spring legislative session. Of these, the state land development plan may be the most controversial because it is the least well defined. The plan has been authorized since 1972 as part of the Environmental Land and Water Management Act, which deals with developments of regional impact and areas of critical state concern. However, the state has never attempted to prepare such a plan.

The second new law, the growth management act, provides deadlines for revising local comprehensive plans beginning in December 1987. The local plans must meet expanded legislative criteria as well as criteria to be developed by the state land planning agency. Local governments whose plans do not meet state approval may be ineligible for certain funding, including revenue sharing and specified grants.

Once the local plan is adopted, the local government must adopt land development regulations, including subdivision regulations and sign regulations. It must also restrict new development until public facilities and services can be provided at the level of service established by the plan's capital improvement element.

The regulations, along with the plan and the development orders issued by the local government, are subject to citizen challenges and formal administrative hearings. The new laws continue the Florida tradition of ultimately submitting most of those challenges to the governor and cabinet for resolution.

Key issues

Most local governments in Florida already have local government comprehensive plans and basic land development regulations. But the new growth management act provides a strong measure of accountability for planning by endorsing closer scrutiny by the state and by opening up a citizens forum at the state level. The law also focuses attention on issues of particular importance to the state.

One such issue is the preparation of capital improvement programs, which will now be required as part of local comprehensive plans. Background studies for the state comprehensive plan predicted that public facility needs for the year 2000, including catch-up costs, will require $60 billion. The requirement for a capital facilities plan will hasten the hard choices that must be made as a result of the state's backlog of needed improvements and rapid growth coupled with historically low tax rates.

The new law requires the capital improvements element to adopt standards to ensure adequate public facilities at acceptable levels of service. The level-of-service standard may be changed only during the biennial plan amendment process, and all decisions about public facilities and development permits must be consistent with the standard. Timing, location, costs, and revenues for the facilities must be included in the element, although they may be changed by ordinance.

During the next year, a new state comprehensive plan committee will review the local government tax structure and alternative means of financing the infrastructure and operations called for in the state and local comprehensive plans.

A second emphasis of the growth management act is coastal management. Eighty percent of the new growth in Florida occurs in coastal counties, and, with thousands of miles of coastal shoreline, the importance of the coast cannot be overstated.

Among the coastal concerns are limitations on public expenditures in high hazard areas, redevelopment to eliminate unsafe development, planning for natural disasters, port development, and public access.

Although coastal elements have been required in local plans since 1975, the new law significantly expands and strengthens the criteria for the element and requires state approval. The law strengthens direct state responsibility for the coast by creating new building code requirements within several thousand feet of the shore, prohibiting construction within a 30-year erosion zone, requiring disclosure statements regarding coastal control regulations as part of all real property purchases, and prohibiting the construction of new bridges to coastal barrier islands. The result is to strengthen local government plans for more restricted development on the coast.

Funding and implementation

Florida planners now face a formidable task. Over the next several years, they must produce an integrated planning system composed of hundreds of plans at the state, regional, and local levels. Fortunately, the state legislature budgeted almost $7 million to help with the task.

The state's primary growth management agency, the Department of Community Affairs (DCA), has received $6.7 million to administer and implement growth management programs. This appropriation includes 40 new full-time positions. By way of contrast, the DCA has operated its local plan review process since 1975 with only one full-time employee. (This year, however, DCA received $835,000 and 21 new positions to carry out its responsibilities under the new "Local Government Comprehensive Planning and Land Development Regulation Act.")

DCA will also administer a $2.3 million grant program to help local governments comply with the new requirements. The Governor's Office of Planning and Budgeting (OPB) and DCA are expected to recommend that this grant program be expanded and continued through at least 1989, at funding levels of $5 million to $7 million a year.

The legislature also committed substantial funds for state and regional planning. Florida's 11 regional planning agencies received $2 million this year to continue work on their mandated comprehensive regional policy plans, and OPB and DCA are

expected to recommend an additional $2 million next year.

Other growth management programs in DCA were also expanded. Fifteen new positions were added to the Development of Regional Impact program, and four new positions were created to administer the new Apalachicola Bay Protection Act. Other agencies, such as the Department of Environmental Regulation and the Department of Natural Resources, also received additional funding to administer and enforce related growth management programs.

New people needed

This new demand for plans and land development regulations presents a great opportunity for planners. But the state now faces the challenge of quickly locating a supply of experienced planners. According to a rough estimate, more than 100 new staff planners will be needed, along with specialized staff such as engineers, lawyers, and economists. Most of the 461 local governments in Florida will need to enhance their planning capabilities, as will the 11 regional planning councils. Part of the planning assistance will no doubt be provided by private consultants, or by technical assistance from state and regional agencies.

Anticipating a similar problem resulting from the Local Government Comprehensive Planning Act of 1975, a 1973 state agency report recommended crash training courses for professional planners and those in related fields. Joint planning efforts, including technical advisory committees, were also suggested.

Florida now has three graduate schools of planning. The University of Florida graduates about 15 masters of urban planning each year, Florida State University about 25, and the University of Miami about five. Other disciplines and state schools produce graduate planning personnel in programs of architecture, business, engineering, geography, law, and public administration. But these programs don't produce the number of experienced planners that will be needed.

The University of Miami, which says it could triple the number of students in its program, has recommended that the DCA directly fund the training of additional planners as part of its local aid grant program. Others have suggested that the state support planning internships and fellowships. And it's always possible that out-of-state planners would have to be recruited.

Whatever approach the state finally takes, it's clear that Florida must organize all its available resources immediately.

Nancy Stroud is a partner in the law firm of Burke, Bosselman and Weaver, with offices in Florida and Chicago. Daniel O'Connell, AICP, is a West Palm Beach planning consultant.

Let's Reopen the West

Frank J. Popper
(May 1983)

It is still possible to surprise an eastern or West Coast listener with the fact that the federal government owns a third of the nation's land. The vast bulk is in Alaska and the intermountain West (from the Sierra-Cascades to the Rockies), and it is all but uninhabited.

The public lands contain a prodigious share of the resources of the United States. Forest Service land, mainly in Oregon, Washington, and northern California, produces 40 percent of its salable timber and 60 percent of its softwood sawtimber. Public lands in Wyoming and Montana contain a third of the nation's known coal reserve. A third of its uranium reserve is in the Wyoming Basin and Colorado Plateau. Eighty percent of its oil shale lies under the Green River formation in Colorado, Utah, and Wyoming.

These national storehouses are often state and local headaches. The governments of Alaska, Idaho, Nevada, Oregon, and Utah have no formal jurisdiction over more than half their territory. Arizona, California, Colorado, New Mexico, and Wyoming lack jurisdiction over more than a third of theirs. The average citizen of a western state cannot live, work, or even vacation on much of the federal land, let alone buy, sell, or develop it.

Almost every town in the intermountain West and Alaska amounts to an urban island in a sea of public land. Federal landholdings around such cities as Albuquerque, Anchorage, Las Vegas, and Phoenix have the direct or indirect effect of constraining urban growth, raising land prices, and forcing construction into environmentally risky areas. Energy boomtowns like Rock Springs, Wyoming, and Colstrip, Montana, are overcrowded, slumlike, and expensive partly because they cannot expand to surrounding public land.

Federal land policies have enormous effects on western economies. Small changes in federal logging contracts, mineral leases, grazing permits, and irrigation allowances can have boom-or-bust consequences for western localities, particularly small ones. Some towns exist essentially at the sufferance of federal agencies.

There are compensations. The federal government has rarely charged western industries high prices for the use of public lands, and the charges have often amounted to subsidies. Federal agencies pay the states and localities large sums as replacements for lost property taxes and as royalties for the resources extracted from the public lands. The federal agencies also pay for what would otherwise be state and local public services, and national parks anchor many local economies. Yet the federal government—viewed as a distant, intrusive, locally uncontrollable force—is resented anyway.

The Rebellion rampant

Thus, the "Sagebrush Rebellion" of recent years was predictable. The Rebellion was kicked off in 1979 when Nevada filed a lawsuit claiming the land controlled by the Interior Department's Bureau of Land Management. The basic outlines of the public lands and their management had not changed for nearly half a century. Prices for the commodities they produced—especially energy and timber—had risen dramatically in the 1970s. The West was growing fast in population and in wealth—no longer a poor-relative region that needed special federal tutelage. Conservatism was resurgent, environmentalism losing its bloom, federal regulation increasingly seen as onerous, particularly in the poorer parts of the rural, rugged-individualist West. The federal holdings began to rankle as an anomaly.

The Sagebrush Rebellion could count on some tacit support outside the West. Those parts of the rural East with heavy federal holdings have traditionally had complaints much like those of the Rebels. In the late 1970s Northeast Minnesota, for example, fought a long battle against Forest Service wilderness designations in the million-acre Boundary Waters Canoe Area. A 1981 Appalachian Regional Commission report quoted a resident of

North Carolina's Swain County (80 percent federally owned) as saying that the Great Smoky Mountains National Park "is the most visited national park in the U.S., but that doesn't help our economy any." County residents have set fire to land in the Great Smokies as a way of harassing the National Park Service.

The federal government has been a self-admittedly mediocre manager of its western holdings. In 1975 the BLM estimated that 83 percent of its rangeland was in environmentally "unsatisfactory" or worse condition because of overgrazing. The Forest Service's figures showed that its timberland yielded 60 percent less than what the land could produce were it managed by private corporations.

Many national parks are decrepit and overextended, some national wildernesses overused by seekers of solitude. Large parts of the public lands produce neither the commodities nor the amenities they should. In a practical, economic sense they are ownerless. The Sagebrush Rebellion appealed to its supporters because it suggested the lands—or some of them—could have large numbers of active owner-operators. It outraged its opponents for the same reason.

To the Westerners, the Sagebrush Rebellion seemed historically justifiable, economically sensible, and regionally equitable. It appeared to be (even if it was not) a new wrinkle in the settlement of the West—a right-wing land reform. Yet in September 1981, U.S. Interior Secretary James Watt told the Western Governors Conference, meeting in Jackson, Wyoming, that the Rebellion was over: "I'm a rebel without a cause. You hardly hear about the Rebellion in Washington anymore." The governors cheered. Suddenly the Rebellion was history.

What went wrong? Very little; the Rebellion got a great deal of what it sought. But on examination, some of its objectives proved impractical, alienated possible supporters, and were abandoned by the Rebels. The western governors, for instance, observed that if they acquired responsibility for the public lands, they would also acquire new costs and duties and eventually lose the federal replacement payments, royalties, and public services—which were generous subsidies. The governors also realized that state agencies might be no better managers than federal ones.

Moreover, the Rebels—macho masters of rural

West blowhard speechifying, capable of invoking the Boston Tea Party as a precedent for resisting a small increase in BLM grazing fees—had antagonized western liberals and citydwellers, groups that might have supported a large-scale land transfer as a way to promote locally sensitive regulation and environmentally balanced economic growth.

Conservative Republican Westerners—the natural supporters of the Rebellion—also had second thoughts. Disposal would still leave most of the land arid, isolated, rocky, and difficult to cultivate. It was also unclear how disposal would occur, what prices (if any) would be charged for the newly available land, and whether neighbors harmed by disposal would be compensated. Rural land and housing markets were already down; putting more land on the private market would depress them further. Moreover, the Westerners reasoned, much of the land was likely to remain in the hated public sector, simply shifting from federal hands to state and local ones. Then too, the corporations that were the likely buyers of the land were generally based in the East, on the West Coast, or abroad—and thus were anathema to the rural West. The corporations were even more likely than the federal government to lock the public out of their land holdings. The federal dominance no longer seemed so bad.

Another factor was the election of Ronald Reagan. Now the rural West could get what it wanted without land transfers. Regulation became less stringent, and oil, gas, coal, and timber leasing accelerated; parkland and wildlife refuge acquisitions were frozen and wilderness designations slowed down. Short-term economic considerations began to override long-term environmental ones.

The Reagan administration also found clever, politically appealing ways to start to transfer some public lands without having to ask Congress for new legislation. Watt's Interior Department established a "Good Neighbor Policy," which allowed state and local governments to request the department's "surplus" public lands for their own use. The initiative was soon broadened to a program under which all federal agencies could sell their excess land, in the West and elsewhere; the eventual sale of 35 million acres—an area the size of Iowa—was anticipated.

Separately, the Forest Service began moves to sell up to 15 to 18 million acres of small tracts, most of which would probably be in the West. The federal land management agencies speeded up the Alaska land transfers authorized by the 1958 Statehood Act, the 1971 Native Claims Settlement Act, and the 1980 National Interest Lands Conservation Act. A range of federal-western state land exchanges were in exploratory stages and seemed most advanced in Utah.

Defused, the Sagebrush Rebellion wound down. Nevada's lawsuit, which began it all, was rejected by a federal district court in Reno in 1981. The state has appealed the decision to the circuit court level, but with little hope. To state and local officials in the West, the politics of the Rebellion had always been uncertain, for in truth it was hard to tell what the western public thought.

Washington's voters rejected the state's Sagebrush Rebellion legislation in a 1980 referendum. Voters in Arizona and Alaska supported their legislation in 1982 referendums, but the votes came too late to make a difference. The only state consistently to support the Rebellion was Nevada, but in 1982 Reno's Republicans refused to endorse a Sagebrush Rebellion plank in a party statement.

Privatization

The West will probably see more land transfers in coming decades, and the Sagebrush Rebellion will have made them possible by making them thinkable. A number of plausible alternatives to outright transfer have surfaced recently. Dean Rhoads, the Nevada state legislator and rancher often considered the father of the Rebellion, now supports allowing cattle and sheep raisers to buy surface rights to public land, keeping the mineral rights in federal hands, and letting the states take over day-to-day management and regulation.

The 1982 report of the President's Commission on Housing advocates "townsteading" on public land. Others have suggested the creation of public-private development corporations; direct transfers to private interests ("privatization" in the language of the economists); long-term leases to private interests for terms as long as 100 years; procedures to allow private interests, environmentalists, and state and local governments to challenge particular bids for public land; or—most sensibly—a series of experimental programs on relatively small parcels to test different approaches to land management. . . .

Over the long term, we are almost certainly entering a new phase of America's growth into its gi-

gantic physical setting. From the Articles of Confederation to the Taylor Grazing Act, federal policy essentially was to acquire and dispose of public land. From the Taylor Act to the advent of James Watt, it was to retain it. The Sagebrush Rebellion marks the transition back to what will probably be a lengthy period of disposal, prompted by new land demands and new technologies that make more of the land usable.

Nor will disposal necessarily lead to environmental, economic, or intergovernmental debacle. The environmental movement and its laws are here to stay. Many public lands—nearly all national parks, monuments, and wildernesses, some national forests, other high-grade recreation areas—are politically sacred places that disposal cannot touch. If disposal—mainly of the more numerous, less distinctive BLM lands, especially those near big cities—takes place gradually, it need not invite fraud, disrupt local land markets, or overburden states and localities. A key problem will be weaning western governments and resource-based industries from their dependence on federal subsidies.

Frank Popper chairs the urban studies department at Rutgers University.

Siting LULUs

Frank J. Popper
(April 1981)

Last November the U.S. Environmental Protection Agency issued regulations requiring large numbers of new disposal sites for hazardous wastes. Yet, as a 1979 EPA report makes clear, the agency is nervous: "Public opposition to the siting of hazardous waste management facilities, particularly landfills, is . . . the most critical problem in developing new facilities. . . . If public opposition continues to frustrate siting attempts, there may be no place to put all this hazardous waste, and the national effort to regulate hazardous waste may collapse."

I would argue that federal, state, and local governments, along with private companies, have faced this apparently awesome problem many times before and have for the most part found effective ways of coping with it. Hazardous waste facilities are just one instance of development projects that are needed regionally or nationally but are objectionable to the people who must live near them. Such projects share a common characteristic: They are what I call Locally Unwanted Land Uses, or LULUs.

LULUs abound. Some of the most obvious are low-income housing projects, power plants, airports, prisons, halfway houses, and sewage treatment plants. Then there are strip mines, power lines, highways, dams, oil refineries, rail lines, military installations, junkyards, cemeteries, amusement parks, taverns, and sex businesses.

Strip development generally is a LULU, as are many of its components—gas stations, car dealerships, repair shops, parking lots and garages, rental outlets, carwashes, motels, and drive-in restaurants.

In many cases public parks, factories, stadiums, hotels, hospitals, marinas, office buildings, and residential developments (especially high-rises, suburban apartment buildings, and trailer parks) may qualify. The most prominent LULUs are large, built by the public sector rather than private enterprise, and sited primarily by local governments.

Why they're unpopular

Few people want to live near a LULU, much less in one. A LULU is noisy (highways), dangerous (airports), ugly (power plants), polluting (all of the above), or otherwise unwelcome to those who must live close by (halfway houses). A LULU, or the threat of a LULU, frequently lowers property values, especially residential ones.

A large LULU is generally unpleasant during construction and inconvenient if it causes a large influx of new people—construction workers, residents, customers, or employees. Areas whose land uses are primarily LULUs—slums, industrial neighborhoods, energy boomtowns, red-light districts, skid rows—are considered undesirable places to live.

Personal preferences about living near LULUs vary considerably, of course. Parents and children usually want to live close to a school, if not necessarily next to it; the childless, on the other hand, may want to live far from it. Similarly, people who don't drive may have a special aversion to living near commercial strips.

But there seems to be general consensus on which LULUs are most unwanted. A 1980 Council on Environmental Quality poll found that only about 10 percent of the population would voluntarily live within a mile of a nuclear power plant or hazardous waste disposal site. Twenty-five percent would live that near a coal-fired power plant or large factory, and 60 percent that near a 10-story office building.

Since a LULU always threatens its surroundings, its neighbors usually resist its siting. They may do so far in advance of a siting decision or in an attempt to forestall an imminent one—for instance, a middle- or upper-income community may enact an exclusionary zoning ordinance to keep out low-income housing, apartments, high-rises, trailers, factories, or strip development.

Yet by definition a LULU meets a strong, usually regional public need or private demand and offers (or appears to offer) large regional or national benefits. The problem is that its economic and environmental costs fall mainly on its locality or neighborhood.

This imbalance often cannot be rectified. The local few must suffer for the sake of the regional many. The local opponents frequently will concede that the LULU at issue is needed, but they confine their arguments to citing reasons for not putting it near them.

Land-use strategies

Governments and the private sector use four land-use strategies in siting LULUs.

Concentration. A community's LULUs may be crowded into a few areas. For instance, a community may deliberately decide to concentrate new LULUs in an undeveloped or industrial area.

Zoning for some kinds of factories, industries, and residences, as well as for strip development, often operates this way; so, too, may zoning specifically for fast-food and drive-in restaurants. On a larger scale, this approach recurs in proposals for declaring parts of the West "national sacrifice areas" where intensive energy development can proceed with a minimum of environmental restrictions.

In other cases concentrations of LULUs arise naturally and then are confirmed by the community's land-use controls. A good deal of zoning consists of reacting to the presence of existing LULUs. For example, Boston's decision to confine its sex businesses to a seven-acre "combat zone" seems to have been motivated partly by the fact that nearly all the city's sex shops and porno movies were already there.

In still other cases the actions of one community may indirectly push LULUs elsewhere. Exclusionary zoning in the suburbs typically has the effect of restricting low-income housing, apartments, and high-rises to the inner city and of relegating strip development and trailers to less affluent suburbs or rural areas. Similarly, local or neighborhood sentiment against halfway houses may force such facilities to concentrate in areas that are relatively willing to accept them.

The concentration strategy will work best when the areas of concentration have natural or man-made features that make them especially suitable for the LULUs in question—for instance, environmental resiliency or pre-existing factories, strip development, or combat zones. Yet the strategy may unfairly force LULUs into the places least able to resist them—poor or minority communities, politically underrepresented neighborhoods, unincorporated or thinly populated areas.

Dispersal. Another strategy is to spread out a community's LULUs. . . .

The dispersal strategy is being used when "scattered-site" housing is spread throughout a metropolitan region as an antidote to confining low-income people to the inner city. The Miami Valley region around Dayton, Ohio, requires each city to take on a "fair share" of the region's low-income housing. Orange County, California, part of the Los Angeles metropolitan area, requires most new projects with five or more dwelling units to price one of every 10 units low enough so that households making 80 percent or less of the county's median income can afford them.

The dispersal strategy will work best when its LULUs are likely to lower the intensity of the land use at issue because they are small and widely separated from each other: "vest-pocket" low-income housing projects, small strip mines, lightly traveled rural and suburban highways, spread-out strip development, and the like.

Yet, the strategy sometimes fails to provide serious guarantees that disadvantaged communities will not be saddled with an unfairly large share of LULUs. The strategy may also create urban sprawl. And it tends to ignore the valid environmental, economic, and social reasons for not locating particular LULUs in certain areas.

Randomization. A third strategy is to deliberately site LULUs in a seemingly haphazard way. This strategy in effect renounces any ordered governmental land-use or spatial rationale for siting LULUs. It frequently amounts to a decision to leave siting to the private market. A government may choose to locate its LULUs at random because strong home-rule or neighborhood sentiment precludes a communitywide approach, or because it wishes to avoid specific responsibility for siting unpopular land uses.

The LULUs most likely to be sited at random are ones that can be divided into small pieces and then scattered by the happenstance of local economics and politics. The prime examples are the components of strip development, but parks, factories, halfway houses, and many kinds of residential development also can be sited at random.

The randomization strategy eliminates the costs of government intervention in siting and is often responsive to local needs and desires. It can be highly efficient in purely economic terms. On the other hand, it produces an erratic siting process with unpredictable environmental or social results. Moreover, it may ignore the overall requirements and wishes of the larger region.

On-site mitigation. The final strategy tries to minimize a LULU's adverse effects on its immediate vicinity, while accepting its placement as a given. The strategy either leaves the LULU where it is or makes only minor adjustments in its location.

But the mitigation measures undertaken can be substantial. Stringent antipollution regulations, zoning and subdivision ordinances, and public health and building codes can diminish a LULU's environmental impacts. A community also may mitigate a LULU's economic impacts; for example, by insisting that developers make concessions or improve public services—by donating land for a school site, generating their own electric power, or making a beach more accessible to the public.

On-site mitigation may lower a LULU's social costs and ensure that they are borne mainly by those who receive benefits from it (usually because they built or operate it). The primary drawback of mitigation measures is that they may not deliver on their promise. Public acceptance is not certain, the LULU's developer may not pursue the measures in good faith, and they may not work in practice.

Political tactics

A range of political tactics for siting LULUs is also available. The tactics appear below roughly in order of assertiveness, with ownership at the most aggressive end of the scale.

Planning. LULUs usually figure prominently in a community's long-term planning. Most proposals for LULUs also require specific planning devices—zoning classifications, capital budgets, maps, environmental impact statements, long-range forecasts. But planning is not by itself legally binding, and later development decisions may not be consistent with it. For that reason, governments or industries seeking strong control over the siting of LULUs rarely confine their efforts to planning.

Persuasion. There may be an effort to convince the residents of the area where the LULU is to be located that every reasonable step is being taken to minimize its harm. Persuasion takes a variety of forms: public hearings, presentations by the LULU's sponsor, debates, establishing local advisory boards, bringing in outside experts, enlisting the support of allied local industries, establishing grievance committees.

As a general rule, this tactic will work only if it shows good faith. It must provide for genuine citizen participation, clear presentation of arguments for and against the LULU, and a willingness to alter the location or design of the LULU if the opposition finds large flaws.

Conflict resolution. A slightly more assertive tactic uses a variety of techniques drawn from labor relations and the social sciences. A go-between sets up negotiations between the parties to the siting decision. The go-between may be a mediator who simply structures the negotiations so that the parties can resolve the conflict themselves or an arbitrator who actually decides the conflict.

The techniques used may range from opinion surveys and simulation exercises to public workshops and marathon private meetings. To work well, the techniques must deal with such issues as the legitimacy of the go-between, the representativeness of the negotiators, and the varying constraints and values of the parties to the negotiations.

Economic incentives. There may be an attempt to pay a LULU's neighbors for the difficulties it causes them. In some cases, a LULU indirectly provides its own payment, as when a large energy de-velopment gives a poor rural area its only hope for a solid economic base.

But in most cases, the payment must be provided directly in the form of state or federal subsidies. The "impact assistance" grants that federal agencies offer to communities with a large number of federal installations, many of them LULUs, are one example. So are the grants, loans, and bond guarantees the Commerce Department's Coastal Energy Impact Fund gives the states to help coastal communities affected by rapid energy development.

Legal approaches. Another tactic brings to bear the power of the courts. For example, under the eminent domain power, governments or such quasi-public corporations as utilities may condemn private property, pay its owner a fair price, and take it for public use, thus solving the siting problem directly. For some LULUs, especially low-income housing, indirect legal approaches have worked. Minority organizations, developers, and aggrieved individuals have successfully sued suburban communities to force them to undo their exclusionary zoning and allow low-income projects. Recently, the Justice Department has filed similar suits against suburbs of Detroit, Cleveland, and Buffalo.

Regulation. Through its police power, a government has the power to approve, reject, or put conditions on a proposed LULU before it is built. Regulatory devices range from local zoning and subdivision ordinances to a growing number of state and regional land-use and pollution controls.

The Massachusetts Housing Appeals Law, for instance, established a state regulatory board to review cases in which publicly subsidized low- or middle-income housing is denied a rezoning or other locally required approval; the board may reverse a local ruling if it harms the larger region. State boards that regulate land use in Maine, Vermont, Florida, and Hawaii and statewide coastal management, strip-mining, and public utilities agencies have comparable powers to site large LULUs.

Ownership. With this tactic, government assumes total responsibility for siting, building, operating, and maintaining the LULU. Many large LULUs—highways, airports, schools, public parks, prisons, sewage treatment plants, and mass transit stations—are sited this way.

Sometimes governments deliberately avoid ownership. For philosophical, operational, or pork barrel reasons, they allow private contractors to build or maintain publicly owned LULUs (highways or airports) or to operate them (low-income housing projects and mass transit systems).

Implications for siting

This review of strategies and tactics for siting LULUs suggests that the EPA's despairing conclusion regarding hazardous waste facilities is not justified. The political, administrative, and technical difficulties of particular siting cases may be formidable. But at least in principle, the facilities can be sited.

They are being sited in practice as well. Chicago has concentrated its three facilities in or near the heavily industrial neighborhood of Pullman. Maryland and Michigan have turned to regulation in establishing state hazardous waste boards that can override local vetoes on proposed facilities. Planning and persuasion tactics are used nearly everywhere.

Among the political tactics, economic incentives seem most promising. They can take an unusual number of forms—grants, loans, bond guarantees, taxation devices, cash payments, in-kind contributions, improvements in public services, perhaps even auction bidding or property tax reductions—that with imagination can be adapted to suit almost any site, government, developer, political climate, or local opposition.

In general, a necessary LULU probably will get sited eventually, but the siting procedures are becoming longer and more expensive, bureaucratic, acrimonious, and prone to stalemate.

In recent years some LULUs have been nearly stymied. Since 1970, at least 12 attempts to site an oil refinery on the East Coast have resulted in only one successful proposal (in Hampton Roads, Virginia), and that one is still being litigated. No new nuclear power plant has been undertaken in nearly three years, no metropolitan airport in 10. In many states, even projects as relatively innocuous as marinas are now almost impossible to site.

Put another way, the number of locally *wanted* land uses is dropping fast. Perhaps the only land uses left that are universally acceptable to their immediate neighborhoods are open space and research parks, which are not live options in most cases. The public has, understandably, become extremely sensitive to the environmental and economic effects of LULUs and other projects.

Yet a large number of seemingly necessary new LULUs—hazardous waste facilities, nuclear disposal sites, synthetic fuels plants, the MX missile system—loom in the near future. At a minimum, we ought to be trying to find ways to speed siting that allow for the public's new environmental and economic awareness.

Frank J. Popper chairs the urban studies department at Rutgers University.

Garbage In, Garbage Out

Jim Schwab
(October 1986)

Nine years ago, Betty and Robert Boesen knew nothing about toxic waste. Now they're experts. Their story illustrates what is happening to landfills all around the country and to the people who rely on them.

In 1977, the Boesens bought a 10-acre lot near Waterloo, Iowa. The property was part of a 160-acre landfill, but they were assured that the operators would close it within seven years and convert it into a park. Several years later, though, the landfill owner, Landfill Services, learned that hazardous waste disposal could be profitable and started using part of the site for hazardous waste. Last year, the Boesens and their neighbors learned that an Idaho firm sought to purchase the site solely for hazardous waste disposal. That would have left the county without enough landfill space for its municipal waste.

Galvanized into action by the prospect of hazardous waste arriving from other states, Boesen and her neighbors launched a petition drive to convince the Black Hawk County Solid Waste Commission to buy the site. In December, the commission did so, spending $2.2 million and keeping Landfill Services as the operator.

The site is now closed to further disposal of hazardous waste, and Boesen says she and her neighbors "have learned to live" with the remainder of the landfill. But Boesen has become committed to a citizen watchdog role and now serves on the county's Resource Recovery Commission, which is seeking alternative methods for handling solid waste disposal.

While Waterloo wrestles with its problem, Iowans along the Minnesota border have become alarmed over increasing amounts of out-of-state waste arriving in their landfills. Minnesota companies have found dumping in Iowa a convenient way of avoiding increased costs stemming from stringent Minnesota regulations that require counties to prove they have explored all workable alternatives to landfills before a permit is issued. The state regulations also toughen environmental performance and financial assurance rules for landfills.

Concern over these issues has led to a flurry of legislation in Iowa. In the last two years, the Sierra Club, the Iowa Citizen Action Network, and the Black Hawk County group have campaigned hard for passage of laws to halt the disposal of hazardous material in landfills and to require local and regional governments to prepare long-term solid waste disposal plans.

The state has also imposed a fee of 25 cents per ton on solid waste dumped in landfills to finance groundwater monitoring. According to state representative Paul Johnson, leader of the solid waste legislative effort, one in five of Iowa's 150 landfills is leaking. Johnson lives in Decorah, in far northeast Iowa, where the limestone karst geology is permeated with fissures that guarantee leakage into groundwater. "We'd rather march in step with Minnesota" in regulating landfills than be vulnerable to landfill shopping by disposal firms, he says.

State oversight

Minnesota and Iowa are only two states joining a nationwide trend toward more vigilant state-level supervision of landfills. In Florida, for instance, where a burgeoning population has resulted in a growing mound of garbage, landfills entail serious environmental problems. Water tables as high as three feet below the surface in south Florida often prevent excavation, forcing landfills to become "Mount Trashmores." State performance standards, adopted last December, require landfill operators to install synthetic liners or their equivalent along with stormwater, methane, and leachate (polluted water that seeps out of decomposed waste) control systems in order to minimize groundwater contamination. Many Florida counties were unable to meet deadlines for the stringent

landfill requirements set out in Florida's 1982 Water Quality Assurance Act. With assistance from the legislature, 14 counties in the north central part of the state are now studying the feasibility of disposing of their solid waste in two or three centrally located landfills. Some of the counties generate only 200 to 300 tons of waste per month, not enough for efficient hauling to separate locations. The study will also consider baling and shredding waste to save landfill space.

Without state intervention, regional cooperation in solid waste planning is hard to achieve. Most small communities lack the funds and the expertise to plan new facilities, and county government is often equally inadequate.

The need for a strong state planning role became apparent in a recent waste management study by Iowa's Energy Policy Council. The study concluded that many tipping fees—the amount haulers pay to dump their waste at a landfill—were too low. They range from $2 to $25 per ton. Bureau chief Philip Svanoe notes that most local governments lack data on which to base fees that would cover the real costs of landfill operation, including liability, monitoring, and eventual closing and cleanup.

The study was also Iowa's first statewide canvass of industrial markets for recycled materials and waste energy. Local plans are intensifying the search. In northeast Iowa, the five-county Upper Explorerland Regional Planning Commission hired an engineering firm to identify potential markets for steam, electricity, and refuse-derived fuel. While the firm found that landfills were the cheapest alternative at $10 a ton, compared to $31 for energy recovery and even higher costs for recycling, it nevertheless recommended a trial recycling program to reduce future reliance on landfills. That conclusion will probably be common in rural Iowa, says Department of Natural Resources program planner Darrell McAllister, because Iowans are conservation-oriented and do not consider cost the only issue.

A measure that may aid energy recovery efforts—if it survives current litigation—is an Iowa State Commerce Commission requirement that private utilities buy electricity from small producers at 6.5 cents per kilowatt hour. That would assure waste-to-energy projects of both a stable price and a long-term market. The ruling is based on a federal law requiring utilities to pay for such electricity at a price that reflects the cost they avoided by not producing it themselves. A Cedar Rapids utility has already negotiated the state's first contract for production of methane gas from a city-owned landfill.

Local headaches

A landfill in Lycoming County, near Williamsport in north central Pennsylvania, offers a textbook example of the trials that faced waste management innovators before passage of the federal Resource Conservation and Recovery Act in 1974, the precursor of more recent state laws. When planning director Jerry Walls arrived in 1970, the sprawling county had already spent a year developing a solid waste systems plan. It started out as merely a standard landfill plan, says Walls, but residents wanted something different. So they got a modern solid waste disposal system that incorporates leachate collection and recirculation for recovery of methane gas.

Before 1974, Walls says, hundreds of local dumps in Lycoming and nearby counties were poorly managed and charged no fees. "Periodically," he says, "the municipality would go out and throw dirt on top, or torch them to burn off some of the volume."

Even after federal law prohibited open dumping, Walls notes, old habits were hard to break. But citizens agreed to accept an upgraded system if the added cost was held to $1.50 per ton. The county developed a lined landfill at a federal prison site. The facility now accepts 1,000 tons per day, taking municipal waste from eight counties and nonhazardous industrial waste from 18 counties.

But the cost limitation on the 1973 plan caused several system failures, Walls notes, so his department explored alternatives. Then a local citizens' group challenged the landfill permit in court. That led to almost three years in delays and $600,000 in increased costs before the dispute was resolved. Because the state had no standards at the time, the county had to provide extensive engineering justification for its system, but it won consistently in state and federal courts.

But the additional costs imposed on the system forced the county to try to increase its waste intake to at least 750 tons a day to avoid losing money. With only 200 to 300 tons arriving a day, the system lost nearly $1 million in its first four years.

Despite further turmoil—including a haulers' boycott over a fee increase and the loss of custom-

ers for the energy that went ungenerated—Walls managed to pull the operation together, while county officials aided the state in identifying and closing 235 roadside dumps. The county has added paper and metal recycling components to the program, and now sells its energy to Pennsylvania Power and Light Company. Its contract maintains a floor price commitment of six cents per kilowatt-hour, with adjustments to reflect the utility's avoided costs.

At capacity

In 1981, the Illinois legislature effectively granted cities and counties veto power, after public hearings on specified health and safety criteria, over landfill siting within their jurisdictions. No new area sites have been approved since the law's passage, and only four sites have gained permission to expand.

The Northwest Municipal Conference, a voluntary association of 27 Chicago-area suburbs, recently faced the implications of this stalemate. When planning for a new landfill began in 1981, the conference area still had four operating landfills. Only one remains, with capacity only until early 1988. With new landfill capacity needed, the conference proposed a site west of Bartlett, in an unincorporated corner of Cook County, and asked Bartlett to annex it.

The conference proposed that part of the 289-acre site—the one-third that lies in neighboring Kane County—be converted into a recreation area. Another third, in Cook County, would become an industrial park with outdoor amenities, where the conference would take a loss on land values to attract industrial occupants. Only the middle would become a "state-of-the-art" landfill, with a tree buffer along the road and an equestrian park proposed as an end use.

Baling at three transfer stations—where loose waste is compacted and then loaded on trailers to go to the landfill—would be used to reduce volume and eliminate loose debris. The site would use leachate collection and treatment and a system to recover methane gas. Tipping fees would be set high enough to compensate Bartlett as the host community and to finance future solid waste alternatives. To alleviate community fears, the conference also proposed a mediation program for disputes on environmental concerns.

After six months of hearings on the proposal,

Bartlett's combined zoning board of appeals and plan commission in July rejected the plan. The conference's remaining option is to seek rezoning of the unincorporated parcel through the Cook County Board of Commissioners. Cook County is the only county exempted from the public hearing requirement of the 1981 law.

The Illinois legislature has thus far been reluctant to force the kind of cooperation some states have required, but a 1985 law may at least encourage it by establishing the authority of counties to plan all aspects of solid waste management on a cooperative basis with municipalities. Another law primarily aids plans for waste-energy incinerators by relieving cities and counties of antitrust liability for agreements controlling waste disposal.

But landfills remain the cheapest alternative in Illinois. Incineration is largely being saved for the future, when landfill space runs out. The crisis, says Lake County solid waste consultant Jeanne Becker, is not "around the corner as it is on the East Coast."

Many cities elsewhere have been forced to look at alternatives to landfills. The leading alternative recently has been waste-to-energy projects, in many ways a modernization of older solid waste incinerators that sent their energy up the stack. Cities generate either steam or electricity to help pay for the facility and the increasing costs of environmental regulations. Some burn raw garbage in "mass-burn" incinerators, while others compact or shred garbage into "refuse-derived" fuel, either burning that or selling it to utilities or industries with coal-fired boilers.

A burning issue

The first communities to turn to such systems often did so because they had little choice. In the late 1960s, Saugus, Massachusetts, had only one landfill—and it was being picketed by citizens for its persistent public health hazards. Its mass-burn facility, begun in 1975, was developed by the former landfill operator. About the same time, Akron, Ohio, was running out of landfill space and, for geological reasons, was unlikely to find much more. Since Akron's garbage-shredding, steam-generating Recycle Energy System was planned, the flammable combination of underground natural gas seams and the movement of biologically created landfill gas has proven the area's geology even more hazardous.

Population and space pressures have also made Florida a leader in shifting to waste-to-energy facilities. Dade County now has the nation's largest incinerator, processing up to 3,000 tons per day, though it is rivaled by several other Florida plants.

Large municipalities are usually able to find energy customers to pay for the enterprise. Ensuring the reliability of the energy had been a problem, however, for those that did not collect the waste themselves. Akron spent several years in court in the early 1980s defending an ordinance that mandates disposal of trash at its plant. In 1985, the U.S. Supreme Court resolved the issue in a similar case, *City of Eau Claire v. Hallie,* by holding that local governments are not liable for antitrust damages if their actions further a stated and legitimate state interest, even in the absence of state supervision. The ruling removed a major roadblock to cities' ability to finance resource recovery processes.

Smaller cities face other obstacles, though. Modular units allow them to burn as few as 50 tons per day, but finding appropriate industrial customers in rural areas for long-term steam contracts is often a challenge. Still, Iowa planners are placing increased emphasis on resource recovery simply because landfilling ultimately will prove wasteful and environmentally unsound.

Incineration has special problems. Older facilities usually failed to meet new emissions standards, and their numbers fell from 299 in 1965 to 67 by 1979. But the new waste-to-energy facilities have become increasingly attractive in the last 10 years. *Waste Age,* a magazine devoted to the waste disposal industry, last October listed 117 such operations in the U.S. and five in Canada. (The same issue also listed 95 landfill gas recovery operations.) The U.S. plants had a combined design capacity in excess of 87,000 tons per day. . . .

The soft path

The battle lines were drawn very clearly early last year in Philadelphia when Mayor W. Wilson Goode proposed to deal with that city's mounting solid waste problems by building a new, 2,250-ton-per-day incinerator at the Philadelphia Navy Yard. The city council's rules committee commissioned the Institute for Local Self-Reliance, an advocate of soft-path energy and recycling, to study alternatives for managing the city's solid waste. The institute outlined a number of alternatives using intermediate-scale neighborhood recycling facilities, combined with greater source separation prior to collection, as a way to both salvage a significant percentage of waste and create low-skilled jobs. With that report as weaponry, and with South Philadelphians angry over the proposed incinerator's location, the city council overwhelmingly rejected the facility.

In the face of that stormy history, Pennsylvania Governor Richard Thornburg earlier this year embraced a series of Pennsylvania Department of Environmental Resources initiatives designed to increase landfill tipping fees by $3 to $5 a ton to finance a resource recovery trust fund for mass-burn incinerators. . . .

Such state-level reliance on a single technology would have been new. Most new state legislation mandating and consolidating solid waste planning has emphasized either source reduction or landfill volume reduction. In most states, enough landfill space still exists—and costs are low enough—that other alternatives would raise collection and disposal costs. But the new planning mandates examine future choices. Most local governments can still choose among recycling, energy conversion, landfilling, and source reduction—or some balance of them all. The enabling legislation merely creates new tools for analyzing those choices and creating policy.

Recycling

But alternative plans require markets—for energy, for recycled materials, for compost. Of course, markets for some materials like aluminum and glass are well developed, but others are limited, nonexistent, or strictly in developmental stages. In addition, distance from potential markets was an added economic deterrent in many rural areas the Iowa planners examined.

To Walls, such questions are at the heart of governmental philosophy. He contends that the markets for many recycled materials are weak precisely because of a lack of concerted government effort. Once a government commitment exists, he contends, creative planning can result in entrepreneurial activity to capitalize on that commitment. This sort of activist government role, using the solid waste dilemma for economic development and job creation, was precisely the object of the Philadelphia study.

Walls cites as a result of such commitment Lycoming County's current work with a West German company seeking an American location for plastics manufacturing. A key problem in recycling plastics has been manufacturers' insistence on having sellers presort types of plastic—a cumbersome, very expensive operation, except for programs like mandatory container deposit laws. The West German firm, Walls says, does not require presorting but will extrude cast products from the combined plastic ingredients.

Recycling is no longer a purely voluntary, ragtag effort where such planning takes hold. From California to New Jersey, cities and states are aiming to recycle upwards of 30 percent of their solid waste, first by separating it at the curbside, then by finding or developing local markets, often through incentives.

By next year, Austin, Texas, will have a citywide voluntary source-separation curbside collection program, with local markets for newspaper, glass, and metal cans. It recycles 18 percent of its waste. Landfill use is still economical in the Austin area, at $7 per ton, and the program, with an operating budget of $537,000, brought in only $100,000 in fiscal year 1985. But program manager Richard Abramowitz notes that it is not the city's goal to make the program pay for itself because its long-term benefits, though difficult to calculate, are considered a higher priority.

Cost will always play a major role in such decisions, but so will philosophy and public attitudes. Public support for any option, says consultant Jeanne Becker, will depend on planners' efforts to build consensus behind the most logical alternatives. She observes ruefully that Lake County 10 years ago had a technically sound waste management plan that died for lack of public support within a week of its release simply because the public had no input until the planners had already completed their work.

Virtually any solid waste facility—be it an incinerator, transfer station, recycling facility, or landfill—is a potential target of protest. The role of planning is to find a way—with public input—to make a sow's ear into a project that makes sense to the people of Bartlett, Waterloo, and South Philadelphia. That is seldom easy, and Becker is not sure planners will always succeed, even with their best efforts. But the concerns people have are very real, Becker says. And, as in Iowa, those concerns are often the foundation of the new laws that will govern solid waste planning.

Jim Schwab is the assistant editor of Planning.

The Little Town That Could

Sylvia Lewis
(June 1987)

Nags Head may be the planningest little town in North Carolina. This community of 1,100 has either tried or considered nearly every planning scheme dreamed up by the aficionados: PUDs, large-lot zoning, impact fees, and height and bulk restrictions (in place); a hurricane mitigation strategy (in the works); transfer of development rights (at the talking stage).

According to many observers, Nags Head has also set a standard for local planning along the North Carolina coast. It's no coincidence, they say, that surrounding Dare County last year spent $100,000 on a carrying capacity study after seeing what Nags Head had produced on its own. Further, hurricane mitigation strategies, which figure prominently in the Nags Head land-use plan, are now being included in the plans of every other coastal community—by order of the state's coastal management agency. While the state didn't necessarily follow Nags Head's lead, it's noteworthy that the town had addressed an issue of regional importance.

Part of the reason for all this activity is that Nags Head, like other communities on North Carolina's Outer Banks, is literally built on shifting sands. The Outer Banks are barrier islands wedged between two massive—and powerful—bodies of water, sounds and bays to the west and the Atlantic Ocean to the east. Wave and wind sculpt the islands at will, with occasional disastrous results to manmade objects like houses, roads, and bridges.

Nags Head's interest in planning has been growing for the last decade. "After I was here a relatively short time, I saw that this place would experience great changes, and I wanted a hand in guiding them," says Donald Bryan, a retired Air Force colonel who moved to Nags Head in 1972 and has served as the town's mayor since 1978.

Bryan and other Nags Head residents (half of them 45 years or older, many of them retired military people) saw the benefits of planning early on.

By 1980, when the town's first land-use plan was completed, many full-time residents had already decided that they wanted to retain the small-town atmosphere that had drawn them to Nags Head in the first place. In 1981, the town hired the first full-time planner to work in Dare County; he apparently set to work with a vengeance—with the help of the state and of friends at the University of North Carolina.

Shifting sands

The area around Nags Head has a distinguished history. It's the site of the continent's first, though ill-fated, English settlement and of many Civil War battles (the Union warship *Monitor* sank offshore). And it was here that the Wright brothers soared above the dunes in the world's first successful airplanes.

Still, the dunes and everything on them are fragile. Beach erosion is a constant headache, especially for those who have built at the very lip of the Atlantic. In some parts of Nags Head, threatened houses are dragged back from the foredunes; when that's impossible, the houses are sacrificed to the ocean. Groins, jetties, and other breakwaters have been banned—as indeed they have been banned along the entire North Carolina coast.

Despite these drawbacks—or perhaps because of them—oceanfront property remains the most valuable, and Nags Head remains a target of development. Adding to the pressure is the fact that the town occupies a strategic location, only 80 miles south of Norfolk and Virginia Beach and within easy driving distance of Washington, D.C. It's also the first seaside community one reaches by bridge from the mainland. Except for the small towns scattered on the northernmost islands, much of the Outer Banks—including nearly everything to the south of Nags Head—is national seashore. Small towns are scattered on the northernmost islands.

These factors account in part for the growth spurt in Nags Head, whose year-round population grew by 146 percent (from 414 to 1,020) between 1970 and 1980. At the peak of the summer season, the population of this little resort reaches 30,000. There to service them are run-of-the mill motels, restaurants, and shops—plus a nine-mile beachfront that now has 33 public access points.

Not counting a state park and a forest reserve within its boundaries, the town occupies 7.2 square miles and has about 4,000 dwelling units and 2,600 undeveloped platted lots. Planners say that the town's permanent population could swell to as much as 6,000 by the end of the century. It was the recognition by town officials of the potentially harmful effects of growth that led to the decision to hire a full-time planner.

Some planning had already taken place. The North Carolina Coastal Area Management program requires coastal communities to update their land-use plans every five years, and Nags Head and its neighbors had complied with the help of circuit riders they had hired.

Bill Collins was one of the first full-time planners in Nags Head. He spent nearly five years there before moving to Dover, New Hampshire, last year. In some ways, he followed standard procedure: Ask residents what they want to do with their town, write a land-use plan based on the answers, and devise ordinances based on the plan. Then came creative license.

Instead of holding a few hearings to take the public pulse, the town mailed out 4,000 seven-page questionnaires. Survey forms were sent to everyone living or owning land or a business in the town; they generated a 60 percent response. Instead of stopping with a standard land-use inventory, Collins put together a carrying capacity study to figure out how much development the town could support. The study included computerized spreadsheets showing how development would affect sewer and water resources, police and fire services, recreation facilities, and so on.

From the data—and from the town's constant refrain, "We don't want to be another Virginia Beach" (that is, choked with beachfront hotels), Collins concluded that some growth management policies might be in order—and town officials agreed. Here are some of the policies they adopted in their 1985 land-use plan—the town's second plan:

● *Move back from the Atlantic.* "Our policy is to retreat rather than to fight the ocean," says Mayor Don Bryan, the ex-military officer. This means no hard structures for beach protection; it means that bigger buildings like hotels should be located west of the beach road (which is only about 100 yards from the high tide line); and it means that new houses should be built well behind the foredunes.

● *Build only to the limit of the town's capacity.* Because fresh water is scarce, people who want to build in Nags Head must compete for tap permits, paying a $2,000 permit fee for each single-family unit or its equivalent. (Half the fee is put aside to fund expansion of the town's water system.) Further, the town annually issues new permits for only 132 single-family units and duplexes, 57 multi-family and motel/hotel units, and 25 commercial units.

The competition for water taps takes the form of a point system. Conceptual site plans are graded according to conformance with the land-use plan. Developers with the highest grades are given tentative water allocations and then may submit their final plans to the planning board. Town officials say that the quality of site plans has definitely improved in the 18 months since the water allocation system began.

The water tap fee is Nags Head's only impact fee to date, but the town has permission from the state legislature to impose other impact fees as needed (for roads or emergency services, for example). For now, Dare County communities and the city of Raleigh are the only North Carolina municipalities that are allowed to impose local impact fees.

● *Stay residential.* "Nags Head does not wish to become a regional commercial center," says the land-use plan. As a result, the town is reducing the amount of land zoned for commercial uses and will prohibit most industries.

● *Don't do anything to encourage major growth.* The most telling policy in the land-use plan—a policy that town officials wrestled with—is the one outlawing a public sewer system. Nine-tenths of the town's dwelling units have septic systems; the rest use packaged treatment facilities.

"A lot of people on the North Carolina coast advocate a public sewer," says Bill Collins, "but then density would explode because that more than anything else is the limiting factor on growth in this area. I remember vividly the workshop in which the planning board said, 'We don't want a public sewer because it would increase density.' I was proud of them for putting it in writing and adopting a policy."

A little help from friends

Collins credits other people for providing a supportive atmosphere for planning and for sharing their ideas. Town officials took an open-minded attitude: "If no one in a 200-mile radius had tried it, who cared?" And they came through with money (usually from state grants in the low four figures) so that Collins could hire consultants for individual tasks.

That's where the University of North Carolina came in. The journalism school at Chapel Hill helped with the citizens' survey. Lawyers at the Institute of Government spent hours on the phone with Collins when he was writing the Nags Head water allocation ordinance. And David Brower, associate director of the university's Center for Urban and Regional Studies, was hired as a very part-time consultant to work on the carrying capacities and hurricane mitigation policies.

Brower is becoming something of a growth management guru (he has written two APA Planners Press books on the topic with David Godschalk of the university's planning department). He also spends a lot of his free time on the North Carolina coast and has served as a consultant to other Dare County communities besides Nags Head.

He and Collins became a two-man planning team. "This was not the case of a consultant plopping down a document and saying, 'Here's what I've done for you.' I was an extension of Bill's staff," Brower says. What that meant was lots of brainstorming—to the point that the two men can't sort out where one person's ideas ended and the other's began.

At any rate, what they concocted—and the town eventually adopted as policies or ordinances—has made life a little easier for other planners. Stephen Davenport, who has worked throughout North Carolina and who replaced Collins as the Nags Head planning director, says that he sees a tighter relationship between planning and zoning in Nags Head than in any other community he's worked in.

"The system of site plan approval, the point system in water allocations, the way the zoning ordinance is conceived, the density allocations are all directly related to the land-use plan," says Davenport.

Building a tight ship

Still, lots of work remains. Hurricane mitigation and fiscal impact analysis are on the front burner. The town's biggest planned unit development—with a total of 700 units—is under way with the construction of a golf course. About 30 site plans for multifamily and commercial developments are in various stages of completion, and Steve Davenport (with a staff of two code enforcement officers and two building inspectors) must police them all.

And then there is the future—particularly, what happens when a $10 million desalination plant is completed in the county in 1989. According to project engineer David Todd, with the engineering firm of Black and Veatch in Asheboro, the plant will draw brackish water from an aquifer in the northeast part of the state and purify it through reverse osmosis (which removes the dissolved solids). Five million gallons of potable water per day will be added to the capacity of Dare County and its partners in the project, the towns of Kill Devil Hills and Nags Head. The Nags Head allotment will be two million gallons a day—a 56 percent increase in the town's fresh water supply.

Todd says that the Dare County desalination plant will be one of the largest in the nation (it is also one of a very few such plants). To Nags Head, the plant will mean abundant water—and the end of the competitions for water allocations.

Despite the development that is bound to occur as the result of the added water supply, the chances are good that Nags Head will continue on its present course. Like all converts, this town approaches its new religion with particular zeal.

A recent clue to the future is afforded by the example of Nags Head Woods. This 1,400-acre, largely undeveloped patch of woods lies on the western side of the island, on Roanoke Sound. It is the most diverse maritime forest on the East Coast—home to several species of flora and fauna that have chosen this windy spot to make their last stand. Some species refuse to live any farther south, others any farther north.

In the late 1970s, the Nature Conservancy, a national environmental group, targeted Nags Head Woods as one of the top 10 critical natural areas in the U.S. The Conservancy bought 400 acres there (the Nags Head Woods Ecological Preserve); it manages another 300 acres belonging to the town of Nags Head.

It happens that another 650 acres lie within the town boundaries. On this privately owned land stand a small farm, three houses, and another four or five houses under construction. For years the private owners have resisted zoning changes that would increase the minimum acreage for building sites.

In March the town created a special environmental district for its portion of Nags Head Woods.

Anyone who wants to build there must now have twice as much land as in the past: approximately two acres per dwelling unit instead of one. Six years earlier, Bill Collins had suggested a similar downzoning scheme—without results. "I went to the planning board and got beaten to the ground," he says, cheerfully fessing up to a rare failure.

The next item on the Nags Head agenda is hurricanes, specifically how to get people off the island during a storm and how to deal with the aftermath. The task is daunting: to prevent major damage to the lives and property of those who like to live on the edge. The people of Nags Head may not be miracle workers, but they're bound to figure out some interesting ways to cope.

Sylvia Lewis is the editor and associate publisher of Planning.

Shore Wars

Sylvia Lewis
(August 1988)

The residents of Whitefish Bay, Wisconsin, had something extra to celebrate this July 4. For the first time in over a year, their popular lakefront park was open for business, the serious business of swimming, fishing, and picnicking. After the local parade, thousands of people flocked to the park to climb down the regraded slope, dig their toes into the brand-new beach, and swim out to the "floats"—actually mounds of 5-to-10-ton rocks serving as breakwaters against the greedy waves of Lake Michigan. Klode Park had been reclaimed.

This modest—and temporary—triumph of man over nature is being repeated all around the Great Lakes, often with an array of hold-back-the-water structures whose life expectancy is one generation. In places where lakefront properties are very valuable and the lake uncomfortably close, buildings are being moved back. In Chicago, where moving back is not an option, a recent lakefront plan takes an aggressive approach—not unexpected in a city whose 30-mile shoreline is completely manmade and mostly public. If the lake wants to fight, says the plan, let's get in the next punch by building

even farther out than in the past. Estimated cost for the Chicago endeavor: $841 million.

In these straitened times, of course, a debt that size may be too large even for the city of big shoulders. And what is true for Chicago is also true on a smaller scale elsewhere. For every Whitefish Bay, Wisconsin, or Lake Forest, Illinois (where another beach has been reclaimed with breakwaters), there are dozens of communities wondering how to repair the damage to their lakefront beaches and bluffs. And so the alternative strategy: Three of the eight Great Lakes states have passed laws saying, "Let's not build too close to the edge," and a fourth state is about to do the same.

None of this effort would be needed if the lakes would just stay still, or at least maintain their "normal" levels. But, as numerous lakefront property owners have learned to their distress, there is no such thing as a normal level on the Great Lakes; there are merely the averages recorded since the mid-nineteenth century.

Looking at the Great Lakes as a whole, Army Corps of Engineers figures show that for long periods water levels were relatively low on most of the lakes until the mid-1960s, when they began to climb. In 1986, four of the five lakes reached their highest recorded levels, with storms that year sometimes pushing the lakes five feet above average.

If anyone wanted dramatic proof of what a lake can do, it came that winter. In February 1987, with Lake Michigan already a foot above its historic level, a fierce northeastern storm whipped up 20-foot waves that came crashing onto the Chicago shoreline, swamped Lake Shore Drive, flooded lakeside apartment buildings, and tore up great chunks of public parkland.

Whitefish Bay

That winter was rough in Whitefish Bay, too. In early December, crashing waves destroyed 240 feet of seawall in Klode Park, at a spot precariously close to the water pumping station that serves the village and two of its neighbors. To shore up the pumping station, the village spent $70,000 for a stone revetment, but it left the adjacent slope temporarily unprotected. The next April, on the same stormy night that village manager Michael Harrigan was meeting with the area's erosion management task force, the unfortified bluff in Klode Park abruptly and soundlessly slid into Lake Michigan.

Gone was a scoop of lake frontage engineers estimated to be 240 feet long, 100 feet wide, and 60 feet high.

"The next day," Harrigan recalls, "my public works staff said, 'You'd better come look at the park. A big chunk of it's missing.' I thought they were kidding."

The intervening year has been no joke for the people of Whitefish Bay (pop. 14,200), an affluent suburb north of Milwaukee whose lakefront bluffs hold not only Klode Park and two other public parks, but $300,000 houses as well. It's one thing to read studies, like the one begun in 1986 by the Southeastern Wisconsin Regional Planning Commission, which warns that three-quarters of the shore protection structures in northern Milwaukee County are in danger of failing. It's quite another to see nearly half a public beach disappear overnight.

But if nature wasn't cooperating with the residents of Whitefish Bay, at least the relevant government agencies were. For starters, there was the regional planning commission, whose plan for controlling erosion along 7.3 miles of county shoreline was well under way. At the time of the Klode Park slide, the commission had already inventoried much of the shoreline and examined shore protection devices. In fact, according to planner David Kendziorski, the commission's slope stability analysis had predicted the park slide.

More important to Whitefish Bay, the regional commission had reached definite conclusions about the relative effectiveness of various erosion control structures. Seawalls, like the one that collapsed in Klode Park, weren't a good solution, the agency said. Instead, it recommended a series of groins and nourished gravel beaches. With the regional planning commission's information on tap, Whitefish Bay could "jump into this project with both feet," says Mike Harrigan.

Only two months after the slide, the village board approved a scheme for regrading the fallen bluff, rebuilding the beach, and protecting the shoreline with groins and breakwaters. A year after that, the project was complete.

Backup was provided by at least eight other government agencies besides the regional planning commission, including the U.S. Army Corps of Engineers and U.S. Coast Guard, which issued needed permits, and the Metropolitan Milwaukee Sewer-

age District, which supplied some 30,000 cubic yards of rock.

It happened that the sewer district had lots of rock. About 2,000 cubic yards of limestone a day were being hauled out of underground tunnels as part of the county's "deep tunnel" (stormwater retention) project. However, the county had already arranged to dump the rock spoil at quarries in the area. To persuade it to give part of the spoil to Whitefish Bay—for free—the village agreed to two conditions: The rock would be accepted as soon as it was available (without intermediate storage), and Klode Park would be open to all county residents, not just to village residents.

Despite some grumbling from local people about the potential for overcrowding in the park, the second condition was easy to comply with, Harrigan says, because the park had always been open to everyone. Meeting the first condition was a bit harder, though. It meant that over $1 million had to be lined up for park restoration while the rock was still being hauled out of the tunnels.

Last June, two months after the slide, the village issued $5 million in general obligation notes. Of that amount, about $840,000 was spent on the two new acres of land in Klode Park, Harrigan says. The rest of the money for the project (about $400,000 worth) came from other government agencies: $257,000 from the North Shore Water Commission (to protect the water pumping station) and $150,000 from the county sewer district, which had saved that amount in rock-hauling fees. Without the free tunnel debris, the project would have cost an additional $700,000.

Construction began last November and ended with the official reopening of Klode Park last month, although property owners will get annual reminders in their tax bills. Harrigan estimates that for every $100,000 of assessed valuation, property owners will pay $14.55 annually to retire the debt for restoring Klode Park.

What they're paying for is completely new lake frontage. The bluff has been shaved back and replanted to form a stable slope, and a drainage system installed to reduce groundwater leakage. Instead of a seawall running parallel to the shore, there are three groins made of steel sheet piling running perpendicular to the shoreline and out to the three breakwaters.

Beachcombers who take a close look at the two new pocket beaches between the groins will see that only one beach is made of sand. The other is crushed limestone trucked in from the Milwaukee County deep tunnel project. The big rocks that make up the three breakwaters are also limestone, but not tunnel debris. These monsters were barged in from Michigan.

And so the people of Whitefish Bay can claim a modest victory—or at least a truce—in their fight with Lake Michigan. But their northern Milwaukee County neighbors are staring at another $17 million in construction costs for shore protection measures that may be just as critical as those recently completed at Klode Park.

The estimate—and the rationale for it—are the result of the two-year study of erosion control now nearing completion by the Southeastern Wisconsin Regional Planning Commission. The $108,000 study, paid for equally by the state coastal zone program and the communities of northern Milwaukee County, is up for adoption before the countywide erosion control committee that serves as a liaison between the planning commission and the communities. After adoption by the committee, it goes to the local governments for adoption and implementation.

As usual, implementation may be the sticking point, not only because of the $17 million price tag (and an additional $1 million annual maintenance cost), but because four-fifths of the 7.3-mile shoreline is privately owned. Besides, much of the shoreline—nearly 30 percent, according to Dave Kendziorski of the regional planning commission—has been subject to the experiments of private property owners eager to save their bluffs. At great cost in dollars and appearance, they have dumped truckloads of rubble and soil over the cliff edge to the toe of the bluffs, 60 to 130 feet below. As the soil washed away, the concrete rubble formed revetments, but eventually those, too, have begun to wash away. "There's substantial erosion from fill done 10 to 15 years ago," Kendziorski says. "The piecemeal approach has not worked well in the North Shore area."

Partly to avoid piecemeal solutions in the future, the plan suggests that the shoreline be divided into no more than 18 project areas. Among the recommendations are schemes for protecting the upper portions of the bluffs and for fortifying the toe. For toe protection, the plan suggests stone revetments, groins and pocket beaches, offshore breakwaters—and better maintenance.

Two factors may sweeten the deal for the 274 property owners in the study area. The first is that, until the lake level dropped dramatically this year, many owners were facing a crisis; recent high levels had caused the bluffs to recede up to 1.6 feet a year. The other factor is that the planning commission suggests that the improvements be paid for according to benefits received, not according to the amount of lake frontage owned. The recommended projects will proceed only if a majority of the affected owners agree to them. Still, half the cost of improvements will have to be picked up by private property owners, either through taxes or by other means, the plan says. . . .

Hard solutions

The breakwater systems in use in Lake Forest, Illinois, and Whitefish Bay, Wisconsin, are "hard solutions" to the erosion control problem, as are the now-discredited seawalls and rubble-and-soil revetments popular in the past. What gives credibility to the breakwaters is that they have been tested scientifically by experts using computers and scale models. Lake Forest spent $120,000 and Whitefish Bay $45,000 for the wave-action tests performed by the Ottawa, Ontario, engineering firm of W.F. Baird and Associates. Videotapes of the tests helped convince local officials in each community that the new devices would, in fact, fend off the lake.

Hard (i.e. structural) solutions are being tried elsewhere, too. In Milwaukee, for instance, breakwaters and pocket beaches are being installed in McKinley Park, at a cost of $3.3 million. According to Cyrus Ingraham of Warzyn Engineering—the Madison, Wisconsin, firm that also designed the Whitefish Bay and Lake Forest systems—McKinley Park is being built in part with Milwaukee County tunnel debris. And the city is using tunnel debris to build a $4.4 million, 17-acre peninsula to protect the downtown Summerfest grounds.

In Chicago, since the 1987 storm that chewed up the lakefront, the park district has spent $2.5 million to build dikes behind the most damaged portions of the city's 50-year-old step-stone revetments, which run for several miles along the shoreline. Park district officials say the dikes are stopgap measures and that repairs to the existing system will be extremely expensive.

To the north, five major erosion control projects

are in the works along the Scarborough Bluffs, on Lake Ontario just outside Toronto. To protect the bluffs, the Metropolitan Toronto and Region Conservation Authority is building some 2.5 miles of offshore revetments and using landfill obtained for free from local construction projects to extend the shoreline. Total cost: $5.5 million (Canadian) over five years.

Because three of the five projects are on private land, the conservation authority (a provincial agency) is asking the landowners to make a trade. The province will provide erosion control at no cost in exchange for ownership of the beach. All but five of the many landowners involved have accepted the deal to date, says Nigel Cowey, a project engineer with the conservation authority.

Softer is better

Some experts say that the hard solutions may not be the best way to go. "What shoreline management means around the Great Lakes is big fills, not erosion control," says William Brah, president of the Center for the Great Lakes. "We're coming around, though," he adds. "Each crisis makes us see there are things to be done landside."

This was also the conclusion of several speakers at the conference on Great Lakes erosion control that Brah's group held last fall in Grand Rapids, Michigan. Although many strategies were suggested—public acquisition of endangered areas, state setback requirements, local zoning overlay districts—the common element in the various landside (or "soft") solutions is a provision that allows municipalities to keep development away from the water's edge.

Ohio, for instance, has proposed a setback regulation that would prohibit development in 30-year hazard areas (i.e., where shoreline would be eroded within 30 years) anywhere along Ohio's 262-mile Lake Erie shoreline. The law was first drafted in 1978 but only now, after several years of high lake levels, does it have a serious chance of passing, says Richard Bartz, special assistant for Lake Erie in the water division of the Ohio Department of Natural Resources.

In addition, Bartz says, the state is organizing a coastal zone management program, to be run by his department and funded in part by $800,000 a year in federal funds. The state will issue a policy plan for the coastal zone program this summer and a document outlining management strategies by next January.

In taking these steps, Ohio is belatedly following the lead of several other Great Lakes states. New York, Pennsylvania, Michigan, and Wisconsin all have federally approved coastal zone programs, and all of these but Wisconsin have setback requirements in place. Illinois, a notable holdout, has no coastal zone plan. Although it is impossible to say how much damage has been avoided because of setbacks, state officials claim that property owners are much better off with the regulations than without.

Pennsylvania, for example, imposed setback requirements on new development along the 63-mile Lake Erie shoreline in 1980. Since then, the shoreline has been badly battered by high lake levels and seiches, wave oscillations that are most common in Lake Erie because it is the shallowest of the Great Lakes. According to Shamus Malone, a natural resources specialist with the state Department of Environmental Resources, two-thirds of the Pennsylvania shoreline is highly erodible, with an average recession rate of one foot a year. Ninety percent is privately owned.

Several houses were lost to erosion before the setback requirements were in place, Malone says, and even now several more houses sit within 20 feet of the edge of a bluff. Yet, Malone notes, the law has prevented development where it ought not to be. Setbacks are determined by shoreline recession rates and the presumed lifespan of various types of development: 50 years for houses, 75 years for commercial development, 100 years for industry.

To monitor enforcement, staff members from Malone's agency fly over the coastline once a year, and this year they have begun to visit each shoreline property. Strict monitoring is needed, he says, because improvements are often made on the lake side, out of sight of local officials traveling by road. Sometimes, too, local code enforcement officers "get a little lazy and don't want to make note of an improvement," says Malone.

One place he says is doing a good job with enforcement is Fairview Township (pop. 8,000), one of eight townships along the Lake Erie shoreline. Like the other townships, Fairview includes setback regulations in its zoning ordinance. Since 1981, its 5.3 miles of lake frontage have been designated a special district where new structures require a variance and building additions are strictly limited. This year, the cost of enforcement in Fairview Township, according to code enforcement officer Ralph Heidler, has come to $4,400. The state has picked up half the tab.

Among all the Great Lakes states, Michigan has the longest coastline (3,288 miles along four lakes) and is the only one to put its money where the mess *might* be. The state provides three percent interest subsidies on loans of up to $25,000 to help move houses threatened by erosion. About 70 relocation loans have been made since the program began in 1985, says Martin Jannereth, head of the shoreline management unit in the Michigan Department of Natural Resources.

Michigan's setbacks are fixed at the 30-year hazard line, based on local shoreline recession rates. However, those setbacks apply only in "high-risk" lakefront areas where recession is at least one foot a year. At the moment, only one-tenth of the Michigan shoreline is defined as high risk, and therefore only that one-tenth is subject to setbacks.

That situation could change as a result of two provisions now before the state legislature. One of them, a proposed bill, would apply setbacks to all erodible shoreland, about 70 percent of the state total. The second provision, which could be accomplished through a rule amendment, would double setbacks for nonmovable structures (buildings bigger than houses) to 60-year hazard lines. Explaining the need for expanding the setbacks, Jannereth says the emergency house moving program has shown that erosion is a problem throughout the state. Nearly a third of the houses the state has helped relocate were outside high-risk areas.

Even with the more modest setbacks, people building in high-risk areas seem to be taking the danger to heart. Jannereth says that nearly three-quarters of the 102 building applications received in 1986 and 1987 in high-risk areas were for structures sited farther back than the mandatory setbacks, many of them twice as far.

The danger now is that people may be lulled into dropping their guard. After the high levels of 1986, the Great Lakes have receded, in part because of dry winters and the current summer drought conditions throughout the Midwest. The Army Corps of Engineers predicts that all five lakes will have near-average levels through 1988.

As erosion loses its place in the headlines, the Great Lakes governors are debating whether to di-

vert water from Lake Michigan to the Mississippi River, not to lower lake levels but to deepen the river's shipping lanes. Regardless of whether diversion makes sense under any circumstances (many experts and interest groups oppose it), legislators' attention is fixed on too little water, not too much.

Under the circumstances, erosion protection laws may become casualties. In Michigan, whose coastal program has been called the best of the bunch by Bill Brah of the Center for the Great Lakes, the shift in focus may mean an end to the emergency house moving program. The program was due to expire at the end of July, and because of the lower water levels, says Martin Jannereth, "there's no interest in reauthorization."

Sylvia Lewis is the editor and associate publisher of Planning.

Hallmarks of a New Decade in Land Use
Robert G. Healy
(August 1983)

For the first time in two decades, the study of land use and the formulation of land policy are without a unifying theme or focus. During the 1960s, the interest of researchers and policy makers was focused to a large extent on what was then called "the urban problem," emphasizing housing policy, urban economics, new towns, population redistribution, urban-suburban fiscal relationships, and zoning as an element of racial and class exclusion.

Then, starting about 1971, a new environmental focus came to dominate thinking about land use. Dominant themes during the "environmental decade" were management of large-scale development, suburban growth, impact analysis, legal limits of regulation, and protection of environmentally sensitive lands. Toward the end of the 1970s, in somewhat belated response to the 1973–74 upsurge in oil and food prices, attention turned toward the productive attributes of land, including farmland preservation and conservation of publicly owned timber and minerals.

In the last two years, however, thinking about land use has been without a focus. The change is due partly to the lack of new policy initiatives in the Reagan administration. Indeed, several moderately important ideas being developed under President Carter, including HUD's proposals for discouraging outlying shopping centers, some innovative Interior Department programs for protecting natural areas, and the Agriculture Department's study of the implications of changing farm size, were either abruptly terminated or given low priority. Substitutes such as enterprise zones and federal land divestiture have failed to generate much intellectual excitement.

In part, the current lack of direction is due to the severe slump in the construction industry. In part, however, thinking about land use has reached the kind of inevitable dead end associated with the maturing of any broad concept.

That the 1970s land-use paradigm has run out of steam is evident in several ways. For one thing, there is less vigor in the idea that the natural environment is the primary constraint to development. This change actually is testimony to the success of this idea during the 1970s—projects doing severe damage to the natural environment are simply not proposed to the extent that they were in the early years of that decade. Moreover, the methodology of environmental analysis is now so well established that major breakthroughs in research are less likely now than they were in the early years.

Growth control also has lost its popularity, not only because the rate of growth has slowed, but because so few communities were ever successful in controlling it. Finally, the idea that natural resources are getting scarcer has, at least temporarily, been shaken in the popular mind by falling prices for a broad range of commodities. Water appears to be a notable exception; the perception of its increasing scarcity has been matched by a corresponding increase in research interest.

If these observations are correct, where might we search for a paradigm for land-use researchers in the 1980s? First, though, I should ask why we need one at all. Certainly, using a single concept to characterize several years of activity around the country is an oversimplification of reality, whether the label is "environmental decade" or "era of the city beautiful." And it's true that much useful work on the environment was accomplished in the 1960s and much good urban research was done in the 1970s. But despite the imperfection, a paradigm or theme gives us a tool for finding patterns, a sort of template against which we can compare isolated facts, attitudes, and events.

Let me suggest a broad approach to land use that might be a beginning. Briefly put, it rests on the observation that it has become much more difficult and expensive to convert land to new uses than to raise the efficiency of existing uses. This observation applies to all classes of land—agricultural, residential, commercial, and industrial.

Our new era of land use can best be described by contrasting it with the old. A notable characteristic of land use in the U.S. has been the ease with which successive users have been able to exploit the land, damage its productivity, and then move on to a new area to begin the process again. This pattern of use and abandonment was obvious in the timber and mining industries, which moved southward and westward across the nation during the nineteenth and early twentieth centuries.

In less obvious ways, the same pattern has held in housing and industrial development. In housing, it has meant the abandonment of center-city land in favor of suburban or exurban sites (often former farms or forests). In industry, the process has involved the construction of new plants on "greenfield" sites, rather than modernization or replacement at already industrialized, "brownfield" locations. This process has even occurred at a regional level, as industry and population have migrated from old central locations, such as the midwestern-middle Atlantic industrial belt, to new, peripheral locations.

The result of this long-standing process has been continuing damage to productive and environmentally significant land and a troublesome legacy of abandoned or underutilized properties within already developed areas. These developed sites represent not only raw land but also huge capital investments in infrastructure. Americans have become accustomed to thinking that the natural course of economic development, whether in forest exploitation or residential building, is a cycle of boom and bust, of frantic investment followed by economic hemorrhage.

So little left

Recently, though, it has become more difficult simply to abandon existing development and move on. First, the stock of suitable land that is available for a given use and unclaimed by any other use has been declining. Despite some of the extravagant claims of various doomsayers during the 1970s, there is little prospect of a land shortage in the form of a sudden and insurmountable limit to the expansion of any particular use. But there is increasing evidence of land scarcity. Much more often these days, several uses compete for the same land.

Perhaps the most obvious example of this change is offered by the timber industry. Lumber companies are now harvesting the nation's remaining old-growth timber in the Pacific Northwest. As these firms draw down their own stocks of trees, they face three alternatives. Each of them involves competition, and often conflict, with other uses. They can try to obtain increased harvests of old-growth timber from federal lands, thereby incurring the wrath of recreationists and wilderness advocates. They can intensify the management of their own land in the Northwest, where new rural settlers are likely to object to their spraying and clearcutting. Or they can turn to the Southeast, where the raising of southern pines must compete for land with soybeans and cattle and still more rural settlement.

A second factor in the general shift toward redevelopment is an improvement in the economics of renovation and reuse of structures as compared to the cost of new construction. Over the past 300 years, the U.S. has built up a prodigious capital stock of structures, roads, bridges, drainage canals, and irrigation projects. Although some of this infrastructure is physically obsolete, much of it is quite functional. Given that its initial capital cost has long since been amortized, it is available to society for the cost of maintenance alone, plus whatever upgrading is necessary.

Third, interest groups—including environmentalists, local governments, and neighborhood groups—have been notably successful over the past decade in raising the cost of land conversion. They have made it more expensive and more time-consuming to drain wetlands, to cut highways through old neighborhoods or scenic areas, to build new housing tracts, and to locate new industrial plants. In most cases, those involved argue, they are simply shifting to the developers some of the environmental, fiscal, and social costs generated by their projects.

The evidence is strong that the change in attitudes pervades U.S. society. In 1982, residential property owners spent almost as much ($45.3 billion) on various improvements as on new housing

units ($52 billion). And according to *Commercial Remodeling,* a trade journal, $51.6 billion was spent on remodeling commercial structures in 1982, a figure that equals or exceeds the volume of new commercial construction. (The magazine's forecast for 1983 is $58.7 billion.) When the American Institute of Architects met in New Orleans in May for its annual meeting, the convention theme for the first time was related to historic preservation and adaptive reuse. The president of the AIA explained in a recent interview that the theme was selected because so many current development projects include existing buildings.

Recent reports by the Census Bureau indicate that the geographic mobility of the U.S. population also is declining. This trend could reflect the high costs of relocation or the natural tendency of an aging population. There also are indications, though few available statistics, that industrial firms are choosing to renovate old plants rather than build new ones.

The next step

Within this context, what are the implications for land-use planning and land-use research? First, one might expect a greater emphasis on the built environment. To be sure, the natural environment remains important. Some aspects, such as water and natural hazards, appear to be of growing, not declining, interest to researchers and policymakers. But overall, I expect a relative shift of interest away from nature and toward the built environment.

Second, I suspect that more attention will be paid to mixing land uses, both in space and in time. Where climate permits, farmers are coping with the high price of land by growing more than one crop a year—soybeans in the summer and wheat in the winter. There is interest in intercropping—starting one crop between the maturing rows of another. And there is growing interest in such "agroforestry" techniques as raising cattle and trees on the same land, or even planting crops among the trees.

In developed areas, the limitations of the Euclidean separation of uses are widely recognized. New developments tend to mix office, commercial, and residential functions, with each producing positive spillovers for the others. And the role of planning has shifted from one of trying to keep the uses apart to one of maximizing their relationships.

Third, I expect that planners—and some environmentalists—will become more entrepreneurial. At the moment, the American business community seems particularly unwilling to take risks—the result, no doubt, of a decade of high uncertainty, inflated interest rates (which make long-term projects unprofitable), and, some argue, a management approach that emphasizes quarterly profits at the expense of long-term strategy.

If the planning problem of the early 1970s was how to restrain an overexpansive, almost reckless, development industry, the problem of the 1980s may be to point out large-scale opportunities to a private sector too timid to take the lead. Thus, planning, especially at the local level, will emphasize negotiation and partnership, rather than regulation and unilateral government action.

Fourth, I suspect that history and context will become more important as a guide to development. For the first time since the Bauhaus, architects are turning back to historical references. It's true that the wry historical allusions of such post-modernists as Michael Graves and Charles Moore may have little to do with what the average architect or builder does in practice. But these opinion leaders have made history and context respectable for the first time in half a century. I suspect that this shift in taste, unrelated to the physical and economic forces I have been describing, may prove to be one of the most important changes of all.

Robert Healy teaches both in the School of Forestry and Environmental Studies and the Institute of Policy Sciences and Public Affairs at Duke University.

Buy Now, Save Later: A Farmland Proposal

James Krohe Jr.
(November 1986)

Planners are not often asked to help save the world, but they were in the 1970s, a time when harvests were so bad that responsible observers were predicting mass starvation by the end of the century. Farmland in the United States suddenly became what oil was to the Saudis: a precious national resource. At the same time, government reports were suggesting that the nation was losing its farmland (mainly to urbanization) at a rate of one to three million acres a year. The U.S. had a farmland "crisis," and planners were put on notice to solve it.

As it turned out, though, the dire predictions were proved wrong as the scarcity of the 1970s became the bankrupting surpluses of the 1980s. Nor did the stepped-up attempts to save farmland live up to their promise: Witness the miles of linear suburbs and "ranchettes" scattered across the landscape.

Looking back after a decade, it is easier to see that, if preservation programs permanently saved little farmland, it was because they were never really designed to. While saving farmland is usually justified in terms of protecting the nation's food supply, or at least its food production capacity, preservationists have always had other, usually unspoken objectives. Some are noble: to protect open space and rationalize urban growth and generally to assert a public interest in private land use. Others are open to criticism: to provide tax breaks for owners of rural land, for example, or to keep out "undesirables." In some cases, the specter of land scarcity has been used as a smokescreen, a proxy issue of other, more controversial objectives. Dishonesty, in short, has often proved the best preservation policy.

Then why preserve?

Despite widespread recognition of the smokescreen, the connection between food supply and farmland preservation continues to be made by preservationists. This, despite the fact that land is no longer the decisive factor in output. Equipment, technology (in the form of hybrid plant varieties), and energy (in the form of fertilizers) matter far more.

Should we then abandon attempts to preserve farmland, or at least slow its conversion to other uses? I would answer no, even though food production (except for the limited case of specialty crops and produce grown for local fresh markets) should no longer be considered the only or even the best reason to save it. Food is only one of the useful products of farms along the urban periphery, just as farmland is only one useful way to develop land. More on this topic below.

First though, we should look at some of the cultural forces underlying land economics. The urbanite tends to see rural land as a natural resource, to be harvested for a range of public goods of which food is only one; he feels a vested interest in the land which owes itself to nostalgia rather than bank notes.

Farmers, on the other hand, look at land as an exploitable private resource. Not speculators in the usual sense, farmers seldom expect a quick return on their investment. But while their commitment to working the land may be permanent, their commitment to working a particular piece of it seldom is. Farmers tend to be sentimental about land only when selling prices are low.

Such differences, of course, have deep roots in history. In his early essays in *Landscape* magazine more than 20 years ago, J.B. Jackson noted that the contest over land use is not a simple one between the city and the countryside. Americans were not then, nor have they become, an urban people except by demographic convention. Cities simply supply the jobs.

Interestingly, by the 1970s, large numbers of people had found it possible to enjoy both, as the era of the 90-minute commute began. The resulting phenomenon of the "city-in-the-country" or "plug-in city," typified by the linear suburb, the highway, and the strip shopping center, is by now older than many of its critics. The newcomers continued to work in the city or in new industrial parks transplanted from the city, and thus remained part of the nonfarm urban economy, confirming predictions that future settlement patterns will be less driven by economics than by the congregation of people according to life style.

Whatever impulse it is owed to, the new city remains by every conventional planning standard a wasteful way to array people on the land. But it is a popular one. The strung-out roadside residential development seems to satisfy a basic craving for Americans.

Americans may be country people at heart, but they have two distinct, indeed antithetical, visions of the countryside. One was described most eloquently by Jefferson, who saw the countryside as Utopia, not a refuge from civilization but a place to rebuild it as a community of independent farmers. It is to this tradition of Jeffersonian agrarianism that U.S. farmers still hark. Against that ideal is a Romantic tradition whose spokesman was Thoreau. He saw the countryside (or rather its unspoiled corners) as a refuge from the inevitable corruption of civilization. J.B. Jackson sees Thoreau's influence in the early generations of U.S. land planners—Olmsted, for example—whose

banner has been kept aloft by modern rural preservationists.

The outmigration of the 1970s did not see exiles from the city trading urban for rural values. Instead, it saw people use their new affluence to express an impulse toward a Thoreau-type separateness that lies dormant in a great many Americans. That impulse contradicts most planners' notions of rationality, which derive, however indirectly, from the Jeffersonian idea of imposing order on the rural landscape.

New definitions

The familiar distinctions between city and countryside are thus rendered increasingly moot. As popularly understood, such distinctions were always over-simple anyway. Agriculture itself, especially in its current form, is a form of development, and by no means a completely benign one. And while it remains true as ever that cities destroy farmland—not only by direct conversion to urban use but by "parcelization" or the breakup of farm tracts into uneconomically small units—it is also true that a countryside filled with open land and willing sellers is destructive of cities.

To date, it has been assumed that preserving farmland required stopping urbanization. Yet the 1970s, when the U.S. tried to do both, proved that the cities' impulse to spread is unstoppable. Preferential tax treatment for farmland is less a land-use control than a concession to locally powerful special interests. Minimum lot size requirements in areas where development pressures are strong only makes sprawl sprawlier. Exclusively agricultural zoning is only a stopgap, while the purchase of development rights is permanent but burdensomely expensive. Rural land-use controls in general have been of temporary and limited usefulness, mere fingers in a dike. As a suburban Chicago planner put it, recalling the 1970s, "More agricultural lands have been saved by high interest rates, OPEC, and the pill than by anything we've done."

Clearly, preservation needs new tools. It also needs a new rationale. There is no shortage of food or farmland in the U.S. There is a shortage of close-in farmland capable of producing specialty crops for big-city markets. There is an even more pressing shortage of open space near cities for wildlife habitat, woodlots, and outdoor recreation.

People enjoy the "city in the country." So why not make the country part of the new city? This is hardly a new idea, but the moment offers new possibilities for its realization, and perhaps for a common cure for the two crises facing our rural areas: haphazard urbanization and the economic decline of the family farm.

To begin with, we need to appreciate that, for all its changes, the countryside is still not simply a city with too few people in it. It is not just location that sets rural land apart from urban land, for example, but versatility. A hayfield is at once a food factory, a solar energy converter, a wildlife habitat, a flood control structure, and a scenic vista. A scrub forest will reclaim a depleted hillside cornfield in only a few years, and mined land can, with careful reconstruction, recover a useful future as pasture, even cropland.

Planners have traditionally not paid much attention to this versatility. Traditional urban planning has been biased, not just toward single uses of land but against "non-productive" uses. J.B. Jackson has noted that planning in the U.S. evolved along the lines of the Romantic design tradition and did not (as was the case in Europe) have close contract with what he has called "the workaday countryside." We can see the result in generations of land-use planners who have tended to see the countryside in either-or terms of conservation or recreation.

The preservation of farmland thus can be seen as both means and end of rational rural planning. Farming remains central to any land-use scheme in developing rural areas, and not just for political reasons. William H. Whyte's 1968 observation in *The Last Landscape* remains true: "The best landscape program would be one that revivified the family farm"—the family farm, we might add, as it was known 20 years ago, meaning a diversified grain-and-livestock operation using traditional crop rotation and other land-saving cultivation techniques.

Farmers and planners, so long antagonistic, thus might find themselves on common ground, perhaps for the first time. Both would benefit from a new approach that would enable farmers to make a living from farms on the urban periphery, subject to restrictions protecting both public benefits and the farmers' right to realize the profit in the long-term appreciation of their land. Such mechanisms would allow the continued movement of land into and out of compatible nonurban uses as circumstances and the market suggest, and would do so without overburdening taxpayers or putting local land-use decisions into the hands of state or national governments.

The case for public control

Few would disagree that zoning, tax incentives, and agricultural districting have had little effect. It is in light of that recognition that the argument for wider public control (including outright ownership) of land in the developing countryside becomes compelling. We already have successful examples in the public purchase and resale or lease-back of wilderness areas, parkland, and historic properties. Extending the concept to farmland is a novel variation—but one that offers the same opportunities to planners to direct development away from environmentally or visually sensitive areas.

Typically, the power to purchase land is vested in some local authority such as a quasi-independent commission or a private conservancy. That group then leases or sells the land back to private parties, its use subject to restriction in the form of covenants, easements, and so on. Details vary, but analysts tend to agree that in order to be effective, such authorities must have the power to take land for designated preservation purposes and/or to preempt private purchasers who might convert the land for inappropriate uses. The technique has most appeal in areas such as the California coast, where local environmental interests are politically persuasive and the resource at risk is unique. Farmland presents other problems, but also other opportunities.

The advantages to the public are obvious. For one thing, land kept in working farms, unlike land acquired for parks, remains on the tax rolls and is maintained at private rather than public expense. Meanwhile, the farmer gets the benefit of lower capital costs and greater profit potential through reasonable lease and purchase terms that take into account the reduction in value of land subject to use restrictions.

The principal problem is cost. Although agricultural land values have dropped from the inflated levels of the late 1970s, farmland still costs more per acre than rangeland or wilderness, and there is a lot of it, even if planners limit their ambitions to key tracts. Farmland in developing areas costs even more. (Fiscal prudence would almost certainly dictate that acquisitions in such areas be preventative rather than restorative, limited to purchases in remote areas where development is anticipated.)

A revolving fund similar to that set up under the French system of local nonprofit land corporations would ease revenue requirements over the long run. While in theory land stripped of development rights brings significantly less at resale, in practice the general inflation of land values in growing areas compensates for such losses. In some cases such land has actually sold for more than was paid for it. But such an acquisition program still needs sizeable upfront capital, and while potential for more local funds exists—from the sale of zoning rights at auction and from taxes on real estate transfers, for example—they are unlikely to be sufficient.

And Washington? The federal government is expected to spend as much as $35 billion this year on price supports and other farm subsidies whose aim, indirectly, is farmland preservation. But for all the infusions of cash into the countryside, the number of small farms continues to dwindle. The continuing crisis has touched off a debate about the need for a fundamental reorganization of U.S. agriculture. Among the proposals being heard in Congress is a system of national production quotas intended to cut production and thus buoy prices. More radical are suggestions for a dramatic downsizing of the farm system, perhaps by a one-time buyout of existing farm debt by Washington. In effect, the feds would buy the farm instead of continuing the deficit-accumulating subsidies.

A look at Europe, which faces similar problems, also suggests some solutions. In Great Britain, for instance, where subsidies bolster acres of economically marginal small farms near the cities, the chairman of a national countryside commission has called for a new system of financing rural enterprises—a system that would stress public amenity and access.

France has gone farther, actually targeting subsidies to specific valleys in order to sustain small farms and local handicrafts. The aid is contingent upon the residents' continued use of traditional farm methods and machines. The results are living farm museums that both provide local income and preserve natural beauty under relatively low-intensity cultivation. The farms have also proven popular with urban tourists, thus stimulating the local service economy.

While such European ventures in rural land policy seem unlikely to be adopted wholesale in the U.S., there are possibilities in areas like rural New England, which is already dependent for its livelihood on seasonal tourist traffic.

Even in Europe, the search for new economic uses to replace farming and other traditional rural industries has encountered opposition; an unemployed Cornish tin miner, when he was apprised of a similar, tourist-oriented plan, bitterly complained to the press about a government that wanted him and his neighbors to "dress up as country yokels in smocks and pose for the tourists."

U.S. variation

The partnership between city and country would undoubtedly be less theatrical in most U.S. farming regions. Ideally, most of the land best fit for farming would stay in farming, although the mix of crops would be likely to shift with the markets. But the farms would be subject to scenic easements (especially along roadsides), public access covenants for hunting, for example, and similar restrictions.

Buyouts are not new to U.S. agriculture. The Shawnee National Forest, which covers much of the southernmost one-fifth of Illinois, consists of failed farms bought by federal agents (usually at tax foreclosures) during the depression and that either have been replanted or allowed to revert to second-growth timber. And in the 1960s, Washington responded to the grain glut by offering modest grants to convert surplus cropland to parks and conservation areas. Once acquired, such parcels can be deeded to local authorities for resale or lease or conversion to preserves or parks, all subject to local planning approvals. Properly planned, such a program would revitalize agriculture and secure a public interest in land use.

Farm policy is planning policy, in short. The failure of each to inform the other is drearily apparent; billions of dollars pumped into farm programs since World War II has purchased little except a littered countryside. An aggressive program linking debt retirement with land acquisition in rural areas would not stop the push into the countryside, but it could help redirect it; farming and residential uses aren't incompatible, although farms and houses often are if they are placed in too close proximity. Jefferson understood better than Thoreau that private utopias have their public costs.

James Krohe Jr. is the associate editor of the Illinois Times, *published in Springfield, and regularly writes on land-use issues.*

4

Housing

In *A New Housing Policy for America,* David Schwartz documents the federal government's recent retreat "from the great goal of decent, affordable housing to all Americans." Across the spectrum of national housing concerns, Schwartz says, "on issues of homeownership, homelessness, the affordability and quality of the rental stock, and planning for future housing needs, recent federal policies would appear to be largely irrelevant, inadequate, or counterproductive." While the period 1981–88 has indeed been very unkind to low-income housing, there are four things we should be grateful for as the Reagan era draws to a close.

First, the U.S. Department of Housing and Urban Development has survived the Reagan onslaught, albeit in a terribly weakened and demoralized state. For this reason, we are far better off entering the post-Reagan era with a cabinet-level housing agency than we would be without one. However, the severe attrition in skilled program and production personnel that HUD has suffered during the past eight years means that a major restructuring job awaits a new administration. Therefore, for the foreseeable future, it would be unwise to lodge within HUD any project-level underwriting and processing responsibilities for new low-income production programs. Fortunately, as discussed below, the growing experience of states, localities, the community sector, and private developers in building and rehabilitating affordable housing through partnerships and joint ventures means that the resumption of federal leadership in housing no longer requires programs to be micromanaged from Washington.

Second, with 44 percent of the nation's inventory of substandard housing in rural areas, the survival of the Farmers Home Administration's rural housing programs is another important victory. Moreover, Congress's reluctance to consolidate rural housing programs into HUD, and its unwill-ingness to abandon FmHA's decentralized, county-based housing delivery system, will be politically important in winning the rural and southern votes needed to secure support for the next generation of low-income housing programs.

Third, with the half-life of federal low-income housing programs no more than a half-dozen years and the landscape littered with long-lived housing produced under short-lived programs, we should take note that public housing celebrated its 50th anniversary during the decade. This is good news because, on balance, public housing has proven to be relatively cost-effective; and, because the buildings remain in public ownership even after they are paid off, it enjoys an even greater cost advantage over other forms of subsidized development. If it has not exactly thrived under an administration committed to privatization, the public housing program has certainly held its own. While most other production programs have been abolished or severely curtailed, funds for public housing modernization have held steady since 1981, while appropriations for operating subsidies have grown by nearly 40 percent.

Meanwhile, demand continues to grow. Nationally, there are an estimated one million families on waiting lists for public housing even though some lists have been closed to applicants to prevent false hopes of obtaining affordable housing anytime soon. Rather than resuming volume production at this time, however, housing agencies should focus their efforts on the redevelopment of the most seriously distressed family projects, mostly high-rise developments in major cities, which have become breeding grounds for crime, despair, and social disorganization. It is these relatively few disasters, symbols of the program's failures, that continue to overshadow the considerable success that public housing has enjoyed in cities and towns across the country.

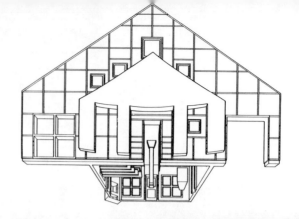

Smaller and smarter houses may be the wave of the future. Right: the winner of a small house competition sponsored by the National Council of the Housing Industry; below: high ceiling and mirrors enhance a small space. See ''Downsizing Gracefully.'' Drawing: Booth/Hansen & Associates; photo: David Mosena.

For nearly two decades, a small New Jersey city has been at the eye of a nationwide storm over the lack of affordable housing. ''The Road to Mount Laurel'' describes how this particular community was chosen for a legal test case. Photo: Neil Benson.

Recycling urban scrap has long been a means of livelihood for the down and out. See ''Sheltering the Homeless.'' Photo: Los Angeles Community Redevelopment Agency.

Public housing was the subject of a charette. See ''Public Housing: A Status Report.'' Drawing: New Haven Housing Authority.

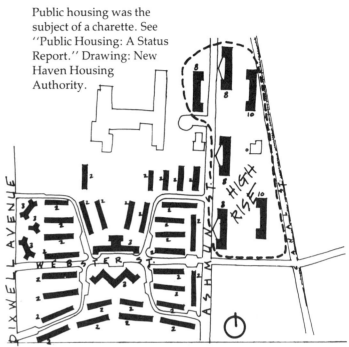

Accessory apartments are becoming more popular, but that doesn't mean communities are happy about legalizing them. See ''Carving Up the American Dream.'' Drawing: Richard Sessions.

Even without a general resumption of new construction, additional public housing units could be freed up by creating a new homeownership program that would be targeted to higher income, upwardly mobile families in public housing. Most of the parameters for such a program have already been defined by the Congress in the Nehemiah Housing Opportunities Grant program, a pilot project contained in the 1987 Housing and Community Development Act.

Named for the biblical prophet who rebuilt Jerusalem, the Nehemiah program is based on the highly successful program of a consortium of New York City churches that built 5,000 single-family houses in a devastated area of East Brooklyn. Built on city-owned land by a nonprofit developer with the aid of zero-interest construction loans from the consortium, tax-exempt financing from the state, and $15,000 deferred payment second mortgages from the Urban Development Action Grant Program, Nehemiah houses are affordable to the higher income end of the public housing community.

Finally, as suggested earlier, in light of the federal retreat, the most exciting recent developments in low-income housing have, of necessity, taken place in states and localities. To a greater extent than ever before, housing needs are being recognized as a legitimate area of state and local concern. Thus, the legitimacy of housing's claim to a growing share of locally generated revenues is now more widely accepted than it ever has been, and the most active units of state and local government are becoming exporters of new program ideas.

Many localities (and a few states) that have not previously financed low-income housing are not yet prepared to proceed. However, reports issued by numerous legislative study commissions, affordable-housing task forces, and other groups across the country whose job is to educate decision makers and citizens about local housing problems suggest that both the aggregate volume and the geographic representation of nonfederal housing activities will substantially increase in the years ahead. The diversity of local program approaches is also likely to increase as jurisdictions begin to implement housing strategies that are tailored to their own political, social, and fiscal situations.

LOCAL INITIATIVES

This decentralization of activities will also broaden the political support for an expanded federal role in low-income housing in the post-Reagan era. A recent national survey of nonfederal housing initiatives documented the following developments, all of which should be viewed as positive impacts, albeit indirect ones, of the Reagan revolution:

● In addition to appropriating more general revenues for housing, states and localities are using new revenue sources, including real estate-related taxes, fees on new development, bond reserves, and community loan funds.

● As a direct result of the 1986 tax reform law, a smaller amount of tax-exempt capital is available for financing low-income housing; the low-income housing tax credit will be less effective than the host of exemptions it replaces, so that large state and local subsidies will prove necessary to make its use worthwhile.

● Despite great reluctance to do so, some states and localities are finding the problem of excessive housing costs for low-income renters so serious that they must now fund their own housing voucher (rent certificate) programs. Local reluctance to take over this function is based on the continuing high subsidy costs and on the fact that vouchers do little to increase the permanent supply of affordable housing.

● An important new kind of housing delivery system has emerged consisting of formally and informally structured partnerships among the corporate, financial, public, and community sectors. Each partner has a specific role to play in planning, financing, building, and operating low-income housing projects. If any one partner is not up to speed, the concept will not work. Housing partnerships should, therefore, be thought of as part of a sophisticated housing delivery system that cannot be readily replicated in all states and localities.

● Despite these trends, and although the search for new revenues and revenue sources for housing seems to be succeeding in many places, the total of all state and local housing activities equals only a small fraction of the federal programs that this activity is trying to replace.

● In general, the subsidy term of locally assisted units is shorter than it is under many of the vanishing federal programs. Local programs also emphasize ownership more than their federal counterparts have done. These two factors are stimulating experimentation in such things as limited-equity cooperatives and community land trusts.

• Most state- and locally funded housing programs are too limited to reverse the fortunes of older, deteriorating neighborhoods. For this reason, these programs can complement but can never replace comprehensive neighborhood revitalization programs.

FEDERAL ROLE

While virtually all advocates of an expanded federal low-income housing presence are calling for renewed production, none has proposed the creation of a new, major production initiative that would be centrally managed by HUD. Instead, there is a decided preference for a decentralized housing program that would make federal dollars available to states or localities "with a minimum of regulation and a maximum of flexibility to meet distinctive local housing needs."

Advocates of federal housing block grants argue that local production capabilities have gained strength over the past eight years because of having to go it alone. But, while the flexibility that comes with block grants is a positive feature, the growing problem of housing affordability, the imminent expiration of subsidy contracts and low-income use restrictions on more than 600,000 federally assisted housing units, and the national tragedy of homelessness are far too serious to leave exclusively to states and localities to deal with. Strategies to deal with these problems should be designed locally, but federal funds must be specifically earmarked to ensure that these urgent problems receive priority attention.

Moreover, there is a downside to the Reagan legacy that overshadows the victories that housing interests have earned. First, we note that housing deprivation is rising. The Harvard-MIT Joint Center for Urban Studies has documented this phenomenon in substantial detail. Despite major gains in the elimination of slums and blight, there were still 7.6 million occupied substandard units in the United States in 1983, 5.5 million of them occupied by lower income renters and owners. With respect to housing costs, despite the economic recovery that began in 1982, the joint center reports that the housing expenses of lower income families have increased to dangerously high levels as the supply of affordable housing has fallen. With respect to

the loss of supply, almost half of the 4.5 million housing units that were permanently removed from the housing inventory between 1973 and 1983 had been occupied by low-income families.

As a result, according to the 1988 report of the National Housing Task Force, more renters than ever before—some 16 million—are now paying more than 30 percent of their income on housing and there has been a steady decline in the rate of homeownership as well.

A second byproduct of the Reagan revolution that will haunt us for years to come has to do with the huge budget cuts the housing sector has already suffered. The depressing numbers have by now become all too familiar. From 1976 to 1982, more than a million new, federally subsidized units of lower income housing were added to the supply. In recent years, fewer than 25,000 units have been produced annually. In real terms, the Reagan administration has cut low-income housing programs more than 80 percent.

Another way of assessing how badly assisted housing has fared since 1981 is to understand that just to replicate fiscal year 1981 programs, which consisted of 300,000 units—60 percent newly built or substantially rehabilitated and 40 percent existing units—would require new budget authority of more than $33 billion (in 1988 dollars).

Despite recent surveys that show public opinion drifting back toward increased government social spending, a convincing case can be made that the huge federal budget deficit has institutionalized the Reagan revolution by defunding the welfare state. The revenue problem has, of course, been compounded by tax reform. By relinquishing an important means of implementing social policy, Congress has severely limited its ability to use tax preferences to implement a broad new low-income and affordable housing agenda.

LAND USE AND HOUSING

The continued scarcity of federal subsidies and the clear need to strengthen the production capacities of nonprofit developers suggests the growing importance of state and local financing and technical assistance programs. In developing the next generation of housing programs, however, it would be shortsighted to ignore the critical role that local land-use controls play both in facilitating and discouraging the production of affordable housing. Planners can help develop new financing schemes, represent the city in negotiations with private developers, and help empower the community sector; but their most central and direct role is to rationalize local development regulations with affordable housing goals.

It is fitting, therefore, that the housing chapter of this book starts with a set of articles on the complex relationship between land-use controls and affordable housing. The articles in this section are as diverse as the views on the subject. The chapter begins with Ernest Erber's essay, "The Road to Mount Laurel," which discusses the planning and legal precedents behind the momentous *Mount Laurel* exclusionary zoning decisions of the New Jersey Supreme Court in the 1970s. Next is a strident attack on inclusionary land-use controls by attorney-economist Robert Ellickson, who refers to this planning innovation as "yet another misguided urban policy." Then follow three articles on zoning and subdivision regulatory issues. The first, by Daniel Lauber, "Mainstreaming Group Homes," shows how zoning can be used in a positive way to help meet the unique housing needs of developmentally disabled adults. "Downsizing Gracefully," by David Mosena, discusses how a reduction in minimum lot size and frontage requirements reduces development costs; and the third article, by Welford Sanders, explores the cost-reducing effects of zero lot-line zoning.

The second part of the chapter deals with changing market conditions and local initiatives to meet the affordable housing challenge. In "Carving Up the American Dream," Patrick Hare discusses accessory apartments as a rational response to the greying of suburbia. Moving down the income ladder and inward to the central city, William Fulton and Jim Schwab describe, respectively, local initiatives to preserve rapidly vanishing supplies of single-room-occupancy units, which house the hidden homeless, and local initiatives to produce emergency and transitional shelter for those who are without any housing at all.

In "Housing '87," Sandra Olivetti Martin continues the analysis of local initiatives to produce affordable housing. She also explains why, despite the widespread emergence of public/private housing partnerships, the new low-income housing tax credit created by the Tax Reform Act of 1986 is an inadequate substitute for a direct federal role in the production of low-income housing. Picking up on the theme that public housing is an under-

appreciated resource, in "Public Housing: A Status Report," Ruth Price describes the efforts of several local housing authorities to create innovative opportunities for low-income families; Jerry DeMuth discusses the origins of the concept of scattered site housing as a policy alternative; and J.S. Fuerest explains why the concept has not always worked in practice. Concluding the chapter, Stanley Ziemba updates the status of public housing and describes what lies ahead.

Michael A. Stegman, AICP
Chair, Department of City and Regional Planning
University of North Carolina, Chapel Hill

The Road to Mount Laurel

Ernest Erber
(November 1983)

In its recent *Mount Laurel II* opinion, New Jersey's supreme court said that it was acting to end a situation that forever zoned poor people out of much of the state, "not because housing could not be built for them but because they are not wanted." It is a situation, said the court, "at variance with all concepts of fundamental fairness and decency that underpin many constitutional obligations."

In saying this, the court reaffirmed the doctrine it laid down in its first *Mount Laurel* opinion in 1975. But *Mount Laurel II* goes beyond its predecessor in a number of important ways. It requires that zoning and other land-use regulations be inclusionary not only in "developing communities" but in all others as well; that local planning and zoning conform to the State Development Guide Plan; and that local planning and zoning be subject to review by the courts under the supervision of three special judges, each empowered to appoint experts as masters where needed to expedite the rewriting of flawed ordinances.

Taken together, the two cases constitute the most far-reaching judicial pronouncements on the regulation of land use and urban development since the U.S. Supreme Court's *Euclid v. Ambler* decision gave the green light to planning and zoning in 1926. Although the Mount Laurel doctrine is currently in force only in New Jersey, its impact will be felt by the courts of every other state and, in time, by the federal bench. It is a judgment whose time has come—not only in New Jersey, but everywhere else.

To some extent, the new *Mount Laurel* decision points an accusing finger at local planning officials and professional planners everywhere who have been engaged in erecting barriers of the type the New Jersey court seeks to dismantle. As with much else in American life, the purposes of planning and zoning at times have been warped to accommodate established mores. Members of local planning boards often reflect their communities on these issues. Professional planners—overwhelmingly from white, middle-class backgrounds—tend to be oblivious of the effect of discriminatory land-use arrangements upon poor people, or, if aware, feel powerless to resist the tide of community opinion and peer pressure.

At the same time, however, planners have led the way in opposing the exclusionary practices identified by the court in *Mount Laurel.* They created the rationale—the intellectual underpinning—for the inclusionary planning and zoning that was ultimately spelled out in the 247 pages of the *Mount Laurel II* opinion, and they were active in litigation at every stage along the way. The work of these planners, however unrepresentative it might have been of the profession as a whole, deserves to be better known. . . .

Watershed years

In retrospect, it is now clear that the years 1969–71 were a watershed in the fight against exclusionary zoning. . . . Norman Williams was working with Thomas Norman on his article, "Exclusionary Land Use Controls: The Case of North-Eastern New Jersey" (published in the *Syracuse Law Review* in 1971). The article served as a comprehensive guide to the evolving case law on this subject and created the intellectual framework for a litigative strategy.

And 1969 was the year that Paul Davidoff launched the Suburban Action Institute, greeting the new decade in the January 1970 issue of the *Journal of the American Institute of Planners* with his article, "Suburban Action: Advocate Planning for an Open Society." This was a time when the planning profession was being exposed to the findings of the Commission on Building the American City, chaired by Paul Douglas, with penetrating analyses of exclusionary practices by Davidoff, George

Raymond, and other planners. In Dayton, Ohio, Dale Bertsch was putting together the first metropolitan fair-share housing plan. In Minnesota, Trudy McFall was using her unique advantage as director of housing and redevelopment for the Metropolitan Council of the Twin Cities to pioneer balanced allocation of subsidized housing throughout the area, giving low-income families the choice of living in city or suburb.

In Chicago, Mary E. Brooks was putting together a publication entitled *Exclusionary Zoning,* containing her findings as a researcher for the American Society of Planning Officials—its first recognition of this subject area. In 1969, too, the National Committee Against Discrimination in Housing filed its first lawsuits against exclusionary zoning, going to federal courts to challenge zoning that excluded subsidized housing in Lawton, Oklahoma, and in Union City, California, and to a state court to oppose zoning in Montclair, New Jersey, that required a minimum construction cost. (All three cases proved substantially successful.)

In Philadelphia, Yale Rabin was using the planning research skills he had sharpened in school segregation cases to investigate residential exclusion, resulting in 1970 in a think piece, called "Challenging Discriminatory Development Controls: Some Thoughts on Future Directions," for an informal network of planners and civil rights lawyers. The future came quickly; before the year was out, he was asked to help two legal services lawyers in Camden, New Jersey, prepare statistical and mapped evidence of exclusionary zoning in a nearby, sprawling, highway-oriented suburban municipality called Mount Laurel.

In the decades before this watershed period, a few rare planners were aware that there might be something unfair in the manner in which planning and zoning were shaping the burgeoning development of America's suburbs, and these few were struggling to articulate the problem. But, for the planning profession as a whole, the task of the time was to protect zoning from the attacks of developers, builders, and landowners. Their instinct was to protect the local zoning ordinance at all costs. So, for example, Hugh R. Pomeroy, perhaps the best-known zoning authority among practicing planners in the decades after World War II and a widely used expert witness, made it a principle never to testify against a local government in zoning cases. Planners in this period were riding high on the zoning wave set in motion by the *Euclid* deci-sion, and they ignored its reference to "the possi-bility of cases where the general public interest would so far outweigh the interest of the munici-pality that the municipality would not be allowed to stand in the way."

Norman Williams was one of the first planners to articulate the idea that the police power inherent in zoning could easily be used to protect parochial interests in ways that would be destructive of the broader public interest. He addressed the question of the discriminatory use of public powers as early as 1949 while serving as senior analyst for the re-zoning of New York City—a position he took after five years of private law practice. In 1950, he be-came director of the planning division in New York City's department of city planning and chief of the office of master planning, and he used his enlarged perspective to write a seminal article on planning law and democratic living (which appeared in *Law and Contemporary Problems* in 1955). In that article, he documented the alarming trend toward using plan-ning and zoning to discriminate and exclude. But Williams was not discouraged. "What is needed," he wrote, "is a conscious overall strategy for inte-gration into a more democratic society." He saw the development of such a strategy to be "the cre-ative task of the planning lawyer in a democracy" and made it the lodestar for his career.

His published works, above all his monumental, five-volume, *American Land Planning Law: Land Use and the Police Power* (1975), are evidence of his role in this creative task, without which *Mount Laurel II* would not have come so soon or been so encom-passing. It is evident that New Jersey justice Fred-erick Hall, author of the first *Mount Laurel* opinion, was a devoted student of Williams's work.

Williams has conveyed his concern for demo-cratic values in urban planning to generations of planning and law students at the University of Vermont Law School and the University of Arizo-na. Earlier, while he was lecturing at Yale's school of city planning in 1952, a law student in his audi-ence, Paul Davidoff, caught a vision of a new cause—the fight for democratic values in urban planning—and was inspired to do something about it.

The troops

Paul Davidoff had gone to law school to follow the example of his boyhood hero, Clarence Darrow, re-nowned for defending society's victims and un-popular causes. Even before hearing Williams lecture, Davidoff questioned some of the things taught about zoning in a course on property law. He decided then to switch from law to planning, enrolling at the University of Pennsylvania's plan-ning school at a time when it was bubbling with debates on urban renewal and related issues of public power and residents' rights, many triggered by Charles Abrams, then on the faculty. A paper by a student, Harry Schwartz, on the effect of large-lot zoning upon housing opportunities in Philadelphia's suburbs, helped Davidoff, by then on the school's planning faculty, decide that the zoning of vacant land in suburban areas was the central issue on which the battle for fairness in planning would be joined.

To be more effective in this battle, Davidoff de-cided that it would be advantageous to have a law degree after all. He earned one from the University of Pennsylvania in 1961, sandwiching in some ex-perience with the New York City and New Ca-naan, Connecticut, planning offices. As a portent of things to come, he resigned from his New Ca-naan job to protest the city's exclusionary policies.

The social and political climate of the 1960s seemed specially made for Davidoff's tempera-ment, outlook, and professional skills. As a faculty member, he spent the decade on campuses that were rife with activities on behalf of civil rights and against the war in Vietnam. In 1964, together with Walter Thabit, he organized Planners for Equal Opportunity, bringing together younger planners in a loose network for the purpose of sen-sitizing the profession and planning schools to the fairness issue in planning.

In 1969, in association with Linda Davidoff and others, Davidoff spearheaded the launching of the Suburban Action Institute as a center for studies, litigation, and the mobilization of public opinion on behalf of equality in access to suburban hous-ing. Initial funding came from several smaller foundations that were interested in social change programs. Davidoff continues to direct the SAI program, now known as the Metropolitan Action Institute, at Queens College in New York City.

Davidoff showed a genius for the exploitation

of issues to force media attention upon his chosen targets. But he knew that, in the last analysis, litigation was the most potent weapon for securing the rights of the disadvantaged in American society and that all other actions could only be auxiliary to it.

Litigation against exclusionary land-use controls was, however, an unexplored territory, sure to be filled with hazards. Those who set out to explore were mainly lawyers with experience in litigation against racial segregation in schools, housing, public accommodations, and employment. Coming upon zoning, with its anchor in *Euclid,* they envisioned a definitive and conclusive U.S. Supreme Court victory that would replace the old doctrine with a new one in the way that *Brown v. Board of Education* replaced the "separate but equal" doctrine of the 1890s. There also were a few "planning lawyers" who were familiar with case law in state courts, although most of those cases were confined to site-specific litigation seeking a "builder's remedy," i.e., a court-ordered building permit for a given piece of land. And *sui generis,* there was Norman Williams.

Seeking to cross-fertilize the skills of these two groups of lawyers, the National Committee Against Discrimination in Housing (which I served as director of research and policy planning) convened a conference in May 1969. Besides Williams, I recall that Ann Louise Strong, Daniel Mandelker, Allen Fonoroff, and Clarence Funnye were among the planners who attended. It was my impression that the civil rights lawyers barely understood what Williams was talking about when he analyzed state courts' attitudes on land-use controls. These lawyers saw race-related suits in federal courts as the only hope.

But the participants parted feeling challenged to design a workable strategy for a problem that had been identified a bit more clearly. Several key concepts had emerged: Exclusionary zoning, though having racial implications, was not primarily a matter of race discrimination. An anti-exclusionary legal strategy would have to relate to the case law of zoning as fashioned in the various state court systems. The choice of states in which to litigate was, therefore, all-important. Finally, representatives of the excluded classes would have to replace the traditional builder, developer, or landowner as plaintiff. . . .

Davidoff was attracted in 1970 to what seemed

a promising case in Madison, New Jersey, filed by a builder seeking to construct multifamily housing on an environmentally questionable site. This was *Oakwood at Madison, Inc. v. Madison.* The Suburban Action Institute joined the suit to broaden it into a challenge of the town's whole zoning ordinance as being in conflict with the general welfare provisions of the state constitution. The trial court invalidated Madison's zoning ordinance as exclusionary on the unprecedented ground that it did not meet its fair share of regional housing needs and thus did not serve the general welfare. (Later, though, Davidoff's group was out-lawyered before the state supreme court, which reduced Madison's obligation to zoning for "least cost" housing, thereby diluting the full force of the original Mount Laurel opinion.)

Oakwood at Madison was a great breakthrough; the framework of a litigative strategy was now clear. The plaintiff status of nonresidents and nonowners was established, at least in New Jersey. Even more important, the case validated the concept of regional housing needs as a general welfare obligation in zoning, with the subject municipality required to provide for its fair share.

The courts were now talking planners' language—gone was the mumbo jumbo about "highest and best use"—and beginning to look to planners, rather than real estate people and appraisers, for expertise. But the new doctrine was still subject to higher court review. From the perspective of 1971, the road to *Mount Laurel II* still stretched beyond the horizon.

Other developments

Meanwhile, outside the courtrooms, planners like Dale Bertsch in Dayton and Trudy McFall in the Twin Cities were using their professional skills to put together fair share housing programs—a new development that the courts would note.

Bertsch's "Dayton Plan," conceived when he was director of the Miami Valley Regional Planning Commission, included an allocation formula by which each locality in the region would take its allotted share of low- and moderate-cost housing. The idea was to offset the concentration of such housing in Dayton, the central city of the region.

Within a short time, the plan was known from coast to coast, and HUD officials in both the Ford and Carter administrations responded to Bertsch's entreaties to make it a national showcase. The approach was crystallized in the requirement for Areawide Housing Opportunity Plans (AHOPs) by HUD Assistant Secretary Robert Embry and, later, in the Regional Housing Mobility Plan by Trudy McFall, who directed HUD's planning office from 1977 to 1981. Earlier, McFall had directed housing programs in the Twin Cities. At HUD, she infused the housing and planning programs she directed with the inclusionary doctrine enunciated in *Mount Laurel,* making it possible for lawyers to cite the intent of federal programs in litigation against exclusionary land-use controls.

Despite the success of public advocacy against exclusionary practices, the courts still had to be educated on the nature of the exclusionary phenomenon. Those devising legal strategies during this time often referred to the need for a "scenario" that would give the judges a panoramic view of the effects of the urbanization that was rolling over the countryside. Such a scenario would be most important in cases that did not focus on a given piece of property.

The first planner challenged to do such documentation was Yale Rabin (now at the University of Virginia). As an expert witness during the first *Mount Laurel* case, he prepared the factual underpinning of the specific charges set forth in the NAACP's complaint against the Township of Mount Laurel. His brilliant performance in the original *Mount Laurel* trial in 1972 set a pattern for all such presentations in the cases that followed.

Immediately before getting into the *Mount Laurel* case, Rabin had had valuable experience in school segregation studies as related to land-use and housing policy. He also became a regular attendee at Herbert Franklin's sessions on legal strategy, where he believes he first met Carl Bisgaier and Peter O'Connor, the Camden Regional Legal Services attorneys who were sketching in the outlines of a challenge to the zoning in Mount Laurel township.

Bisgaier was, in fact, the heart and soul of the 12-year effort challenging the township of Mount Laurel. Unlike the plaintiffs in the other cases that eventually became part of *Mount Laurel II,* the plaintiffs in the case involving Mount Laurel had no backing from a Suburban Action Institute or a National Committee Against Discrimination in Housing. Bisgaier and O'Connor were pretty much on their own.

As for Yale Rabin . . . His documented and illus-

trated testimony spelled out for the *Mount Laurel* trial court the injustice of exclusionary land-use controls articulated earlier by Williams. When the case came before the state supreme court, Williams's amicus curiae arguments, based on Rabin's factual data, presented a planner's indictment of exclusionary zoning.

Overall, to understand the planner's role in creating the *Mount Laurel* doctrine, one must understand what is unique about *Mount Laurel II.* And that, simply put, is that the New Jersey courts will now administer local planning to conform with an otherwise legally toothless state development plan. Such a system is new in the history of planning in this country. Although it is not ideal, it is the New Jersey supreme court's way of giving the state comprehensive planning, as dreamed of by planners, despite the cowardly, essentially anti-planning, stance of the state's governors and legislators. At last, the long road of litigation that led to *Mount Laurel II* has brought us to a destination marked "planning."

Ernest Erber, AICP, is a planning consultant in Columbia, Maryland. He was director of the Regional Plan Association's New Jersey program from 1959 to 1969 and director of research and policy planning for the National Committee Against Discrimination in Housing from 1969 to 1980.

Inclusionary Zoning: Who Pays?
Robert C. Ellickson
(August 1985)

The landscape of urban policy in the United States is littered with the wreckage of bad ideas. Well-intended programs often go wrong.

The script is familiar. Urban reformers propose a new government policy to help remedy a perceived (and usually real) social problem. Elected officials then adopt and implement the policy. After a few years, commentators—often members of the next generation of reformers—conclude that the previous generation's policies have, in fact, aggravated urban woes. Thus, zoning of residential areas, a darling of urban reformers of the 1920s, had become by the 1980s the arch enemy of the Center for Metropolitan Action. Massive public housing projects, the 1940s solution to perceived housing problems, by the 1960s were being regarded as nothing short of an urban calamity. Bulldozer-style urban renewal, the 1950s route to upgrading the cities, had few friends remaining two decades later.

This dismal record cautions policymakers to look carefully before embracing the latest fashion in urban policy. Interventions into housing markets often have unanticipated and harmful side effects. In my view, history is likely to prove inclusionary zoning—a policy now in ascendance in many parts of the United States, and one recently blessed by the New Jersey Supreme Court in *Mount Laurel II*—to be yet another misguided urban policy.

Doubtful at best

Pared to its essentials, an inclusionary zoning program consists of three components: (1) the taxation of new development to raise revenue for municipal purposes; (2) the spending of municipal funds to provide large in-kind housing subsidies to selected middle-income (and, less commonly, low-income) households; (3) the ironclad linkage of the taxation and spending policies just identified (say by means of a housing trust fund) so that municipal legislators cannot divert the revenues raised from the taxes on new development to any nonhousing purpose.

I believe that the first of these policies is doubtful and that the latter two policies are plainly wrong.

Henry George, the noted nineteenth-century reformer, persuasively argued that taxes on land are among the best kinds of taxes. But George made a sharp distinction between taxes on land and taxes on land improvements. He opposed taxes on improvements because he predicted that such taxes would inhibit useful enterprise.

Under Georgist criteria, inclusionary zoning, which imposes a tax on new construction, is suspect. A tax on construction is not only likely to reduce the amount of development that occurs but may also increase the rents landlords can command for both new and existing buildings. (Rents on existing buildings may rise because the tax inhibits the production of new buildings that would compete with them.)

Aggravation, not alleviation

The magnitude of these effects depends on the elasticity of supply and demand for land improvements in the relevant market and thus is extremely difficult to estimate. One can, nevertheless, predict with some confidence that, if New York City, for example, were to tax all forms of new construction, rent levels would rise throughout the city. As its residents are proud to point out, there are no perfect substitutes for New York City. This means that the elasticity of demand for its buildings is not infinite. In a market of this sort, a construction tax will be partly passed on to consumers in the form of higher rents. It is thus possible that, if New York City were to adopt an inclusionary program that included a tax on new residential construction, the program would, on balance, *aggravate* the housing problems of the groups it was assigned to assist.

In some places, in contrast, the tax component of an inclusionary program would not raise rents. If a small suburb were to place an unusual tax on new development, most, if not all, of the tax burden would be passed backward and borne by local landowners. In such a jurisdiction, a construction tax would largely satisfy Georgist criteria.

George might have pointed out, however, that he favored the taxation of *all* site values so that no landowner would receive an unearned increment. An inclusionary tax—whether imposed by city or suburb—falls unequally on landowners. Owners of land ripe for development or redevelopment bear the brunt of the tax, while owners of recently built buildings are free of the inclusionary taxes until they choose to redevelop. In fact, in a real estate market such as New York City's, owners of existing structures may actually profit from an inclusionary program because they benefit immediately from the higher rents caused by the stifling of new construction.

Despite its shortcomings, I do not regard a tax on new construction as a ludicrously bad tax. Virtually all tax systems are problematic when judged according to the usual standards of efficiency and equity. Moreover, it is possible that taxes on new construction are useful counterweights to the unjustified subsidies that exist elsewhere in the tax system. Proponents of inclusionary zoning should recognize, however, that the taxation component of an inclusionary program is almost certain to reduce the amount of development in the taxing jurisdiction and, in some markets, may raise housing prices to the detriment of consumers.

Bizarre redistribution

Less defensible is the expenditure policy that an inclusionary program carries in its train. The provision of massive in-kind housing subsidies to a few (mostly middle-income) families is a truly bizarre redistributive policy.

A half-century of experience indicates that in-kind housing subsidies are an extremely inefficient way to improve the welfare of recipient families. Since the adoption of the first federal public housing program in 1937, the federal government has delivered housing subsidies by virtually every method imaginable—leased public housing, Section 221(d)(3), Section 236, Section 8, and on and on. In countless studies of the effectiveness of these programs, most analysts have given extremely low marks to the programs that provide *nontransportable* subsidies.

Subsidies of this sort are inherently inferior to cash transfers or other transportable subsidies. Yet, although the spending prongs of inclusionary zoning programs vary, most require developers to offer particular housing units to program beneficiaries rather than allowing them to transport their subsidies to other locations. Inclusionary programs thus tend to use the most wasteful form of housing subsidy.

The expenditure side of a typical inclusionary program is not only inefficient, it is unfair. In California, where inclusionary zoning first flowered, local officials have directed a large majority of their inclusionary units to middle-income families. A beneficiary household may receive a discount of as much as $50,000 when purchasing an inclusionary unit. Inclusionary units are few, yet most city programs identify a substantial majority of the city's households as eligible beneficiaries. As a result, the program can at best serve only a few percent of the targeted families. Why should a government transfer large amounts of wealth to a few fortuitously selected middle-income households?

Inclusionary programs typically use "trust funds" to prevent elected officials from spending program revenues for nonhousing purposes. Yet someone who believes in political visibility and accountability should be wary of government trust funds of any stripe.

Advocates of inclusionary housing programs have at least two reasons for wanting to embrace the trust fund device. The first is legal. Courts tend to be hostile to general taxes on new construction. City attorneys might, therefore, conclude that a program of exactions on developers is more likely to pass legal muster if the revenues raised are automatically spent to cure problems that new development (allegedly, if not actually) creates.

The second reason is political. The trust fund device helps the interest groups that favor in-kind housing subsidies to obtain funding that would otherwise not be forthcoming. It is inconceivable that a city council would ever appropriate general municipal funds to enable a few low- and middle-income families to buy or rent housing units at large discounts. The interest groups that favor the local funding of in-kind housing subsidies, therefore, prefer a nondiscretionary funding system, such as a trust fund, that promises to reduce the political visibility of their potentially vulnerable spending program.

"Professional housers" have been the most ardent proponents of inclusionary zoning. I use this phrase to describe anyone who specializes in the production of the governmental approvals necessary for the construction and occupancy of subsidized housing units. The label can fittingly be attached to many individuals connected to local planning departments, nonprofit housing organizations, and private development firms. I suspect that inclusionary zoning programs are currently popular with these individuals because federal sources of in-kind housing subsidies have recently been drying up. Professional housers are struggling to maintain their place in the sun despite dwindling federal funds. When appealing for local funds, they recognize that elected city officials will be hesitant to appropriate general municipal revenue for inclusionary programs. Professional housers, therefore, prefer trust fund systems. To put it bluntly, professional housers seem to have structured inclusionary zoning with a close eye to their own interests.

Robert C. Ellickson is a law professor at Stanford University.

Mainstreaming Group Homes

Daniel Lauber
(December 1985)

Zoning made it to the U.S. Supreme Court this year in the form of a case regarding group homes for developmentally disabled adults. The result was a landmark decision that should change the way most zoning ordinances treat group homes. Further, the decision will force local officials to confront the popular misconceptions about group homes and their residents that so frequently lead to stiff neighborhood opposition.

Group homes pose a zoning challenge that nearly every community in the country eventually will face. Over the past decade, the number of group homes increased from 700 to over 6,000. There's no end in sight because the need for them remains so great. The disabled are living longer, thanks to better health care and increasing deinstitutionalization.

Local officials often are at a loss when it comes to zoning for group homes. Most zoning ordinances fail to provide for them, as cities typically (and improperly) treat group homes as hospitals for the insane or feeble-minded. In other places, ordinances contain exclusionary provisions that keep group homes out of the very residential districts in which they function best.

Here are answers to some of the most frequent questions local officials and planners ask about zoning for group homes, particularly in light of the Supreme Court's latest edict on this type of zoning provision.

What are they?

Q. Before we go any further, what are group homes and who lives in them?

A. A group home usually houses individuals who are mentally ill or developmentally disabled. Congress defines "developmental disability" as a severe, chronic, and permanent disability due to a mental and/or physical impairment, manifested before age 22, that results in substantial functional limitations in at least three of the following major life activities: self-care, language, learning, mobili-

ty, capacity for independent living, economic self-sufficiency, and self-direction.

Traditionally, these special, "service-dependent" individuals were warehoused in large institutions. But as the professionals who work with these special populations came to understand them, they realized that large institutions hindered the recovery of the mentally ill and the progress of the developmentally disabled. If they are ever to overcome or cope with their conditions, these people need to live in a relatively normal household environment in the community.

The group home provides that setting. Depending on the size of the house, anywhere from two to about 15 service-dependent people live in the group home with professional staff, who function as surrogate parents. Residents and staff seek to emulate a traditional family. The group home constitutes a single housekeeping unit in which residents share responsibilities, meals, and recreation.

The group home's primary purpose is to provide supervision and support, in a family-like setting, for persons unable to live independently in the community. It is not a clinic or hospital, where treatment is the principal or essential service. While a treatment regime may be incorporated into the daily routine of handicapped persons wherever they live—whether with their own families, in an institution, or in a group home—treatment is merely incidental to the group home's primary purpose of helping residents adjust to community living, and in many cases, to live on their own in the community.

Q. Then why are group homes a zoning problem?

A. Many zoning ordinances simply don't provide for group homes. When a group home sponsor seeks to open a group home under such an ordinance, city officials often stretch their imaginations to fit the proposed group home under the zoning definition of some other use. Most often, they'll call the group home a nursing home or hospital for the insane or feeble-minded."

Q. We have to do that all the time with uses that didn't exist when our zoning ordinances were written. What's so bad about that?

A. Group homes are not nursing homes or hospitals. A group home is a residential use—a place where inhabitants live as a family, albeit a generic family, as one court put it. In contrast, nursing homes and hospitals are primarily medical institutions that provide no education or simulated family setting for patients. Group homes are most appropriate in residential areas, while nursing homes and hospitals belong in commercial areas.

Q. Didn't the U.S. Supreme Court case deal with a Texas city that treated group homes for the developmentally disabled as a hospital for the feeble-minded?

A. Yes, the zoning ordinance for Cleburne, Texas, didn't provide for group homes. So city officials decided that the Cleburne Living Center's proposed group home for 13 developmentally disabled adults would be treated as a "hospital for the insane or feeble-minded."

Q. How did that decision lead all the way to the Supreme Court?

A. Cleburne's zoning ordinance allows all hospitals, except those for the "insane or feeble-minded or alcoholics or drug addicts," as permitted uses in the R-3 residential zone where the Cleburne Living Center (CLC) sought to locate its group home. It also allows apartments, boarding and lodging houses, and fraternities, sororities, and dormitories as of right in that zone.

Although the proposed group home complied with all federal and state licensing regulations that ensured the house itself would be adequate to house the 13 mentally retarded residents plus staff, Cleburne denied the special use permit application. CLC sued. While the federal district court found that the city's denial "was motivated primarily by the fact that the residents of the homes would be persons who are mentally retarded," it held that no fundamental rights had been violated and that the ordinance, as written and applied, was rationally related to the city's legitimate interests in "the legal responsibility of CLC and its residents, . . . the safety and fears of residents in the adjoining neighborhood," and the number of people to be housed in the home.

After the Fifth Circuit U.S. Court of Appeals reversed in favor of CLC, the city appealed to the U.S. Supreme Court. The Court unanimously invalidated the zoning ordinance as applied to CLC (although three justices would have invalidated the ordinance on its face) in *City of Cleburne v. Cleburne Living Center,* 105 S.Ct. 3249 (1985).

The Court speaks

Q. Why is this decision so important?
A. The Court put cities on notice that they need

a clear, rational reason if they want to treat group homes for the developmentally disabled (and probably for other service-dependent populations as well) differently from other residential uses. The Court started its analysis by noting that the equal protection clause of the Fourteenth Amendment essentially requires that "all persons similarly situated should be treated alike."

Cleburne, though, had created a classification in which a group home for the mentally retarded must obtain a special use permit in an R-3 zone even though apartment houses, boarding and lodging houses, fraternity and sorority houses, nursing homes for the aged, and other specific uses were allowed as of right. Although a city's zoning ordinance is presumed valid, the classifications it creates must be "rationally related to a legitimate state interest" to be upheld.

The Court noted that while the "mentally retarded as a group are indeed different from others" who don't share "their misfortune" and are allowed to locate in an R-3 zone without a special use permit, "this difference is largely irrelevant unless the [group] home and those who would occupy it would threaten legitimate interests of the city in a way that other permitted uses such as boarding houses and hospitals would not." The Court searched the trial record and could find no rational basis to believe that the group home "would pose any threat to the city's legitimate interests."

Q. You mean that none of the city's reasons for denying the special use permit were legitimate?

A. Right. Opposition from neighbors, based on unsubstantiated fears, continues to be the major reason that cities deny special use permits for group homes. But the Court confirmed a long line of rulings that "mere negative attitudes, or fear, unsubstantiated by factors which are properly cognizable in a zoning proceeding, are not permissible bases for treating a home for the mentally retarded differently from apartment houses, multiple dwellings, and the like." While neighbors may have biases against group home residents, "the law cannot, directly or indirectly, give them effect."

The Court rejected all of the city's reasons for denying the permit. The city council had doubts about who had legal responsibility for the actions of the mentally retarded group home residents. But the Court found that the council had no concern about the legal responsibility for other uses permitted in the zoning district, such as boarding houses and fraternities. The Court could not see how the group home would present a hazard different from these other uses. Nor could the Court understand how the city could object to the location of the group home because it was on a 500-year floodplain, yet not be concerned about other uses located on the floodplain.

Q. Given the Court's decision, for what reasons can a city deny a special use permit for a group home?

A. Remember that the Court said the denial was based on prejudices and unsubstantiated fears. The most common fears are that group home residents will engage in criminal behavior, that the home will be poorly maintained, and that the mere presence of the home will depress property values in the neighborhood. If true, these are legitimate reasons to deny a special-use permit.

Q. Can any of these fears be substantiated?

A. So far, fairly extensive research says, "Not at all!" A large body of research shows that the mentally ill are no more criminally prone than the rest of us. And 66 years of studies have found the developmentally disabled to be harmless. The most pertinent study covered the state of Virginia. The *Report on the Incidence of Client Crime Within Community-Based Programming* (1979) found a crime rate of 0.8 percent among the developmentally disabled who lived in group homes, as compared to a four to six percent crime rate among the general population.

Q. But what about property maintenance and property values?

A. Every one of the 20 or so studies on this topic has found that group homes simply do not affect the selling prices of neighboring properties or the turnover rate of properties. The studies uniformly report that group homes are invariably well-maintained—often better maintained than neighboring private homes. The few studies that have inquired have found that group homes are so inconspicuous that barely half the people on the same block know they exist, fewer than half on the next block know of them, and fewer than 30 percent of the residents three blocks away are aware of them. Small wonder that group homes have virtually no effect on property values.

Q. If group homes are so innocuous, why regulate them at all?

A. One study did find that five group homes on the same block might, in fact, have an adverse effect on the neighborhood. Further, if large numbers of group homes cluster on the same block or in the same neighborhood, they could undermine a basic premise of group homes—namely that, to be effective, they must locate in "normal" residential neighborhoods where able-bodied neighbors can serve as role models for the disabled or mentally ill.

At some indeterminate point, the capacity of the neighborhood to absorb service-dependent people could be exceeded, and the proportion of service-dependent persons in the neighborhood could become so great as to recreate the institutional atmosphere from which the group home is supposed to provide an escape. So there is a need to ensure that group homes do not cluster on the same block and that they are spread throughout the safe neighborhoods of a city. . . .

The bottom line

Q. Given the *Cleburne* ruling, what's the bottom line? How should my city or county zone for group homes?

A. In a word, rationally. The *Cleburne* decision is a bit deceptive. While the Court says it is applying the standard "rational relationship" test, its inquiry into Cleburne's reasons for denying the special use permit is really an example of the sort of heightened judicial scrutiny usually reserved for cases of discrimination based on sex, race, or religion. The lesson of *Cleburne* is that the zoning provisions for group homes must be based on the sound planning principles that call for zoning provisions grounded in an understanding of what group homes are, what their impacts are, and the types of neighborhoods in which they function best.

Q. What are these sound principles on which we should base our zoning provisions for group homes?

A. There are four. By following them, you'll be able to write zoning provisions that should withstand even the Supreme Court's new version of the rational relationship test.

• Group homes, being residential in nature, are appropriate uses in all residential zoning districts.

• Group home residents are service-dependent persons who require special protection to ensure their safety in the home. Those protections—that the group home meet adequate safety, sanitation, and program standards—form the subject matter of licensing requirements.

However, the zoning ordinance is not the place to specify licensing criteria—that's the business of the licensing agency. One of the simplest ways to require licensing is to include the licensing requirement in your ordinance's definition of a group home.

• Controls are needed to prevent concentrations of group homes. Two types of controls will prevent clustering and ensure dispersal throughout a community. The first is a spacing requirement by which the zoning ordinance imposes a minimum distance between group homes and between group homes and institutions.

It is vital, however, that there be some rational basis for this distance. According to one widely accepted theory, the most elementary form of social impact is the degree to which neighborhood residents become aware of a change. Because the research shows that few residents living three blocks from a group home even know it exists, it seems appropriate to establish a spacing requirement equal to at least three city blocks so that each group home will be beyond the "impact area" of any other group home or institution.

However, the ability of a neighborhood to absorb service-dependent residents is thought to vary with density. Presumably, higher-density neighborhoods have a higher absorption level that would warrant a shorter spacing requirement than lower-density neighborhoods.

The Westchester County Planning Department has suggested spacing requirements of 1,700 to 1,300 feet for suburban areas where the population density is less than 1,000 persons per square mile; 1,400 to 1,000 feet for densities of 1,000 to 4,999; 1,000 to 700 feet for densities of 5,000 to 9,999; and 800 to 400 feet for densities over 10,000 persons per square mile. In contrast, Evanston, Illinois, has arbitrarily established an unusually high 2,500-foot spacing requirement between group homes. With no rational reason for that great a distance in an inner-ring suburb like Evanston, *Cleburne*-style judicial review could invalidate Evanston's requirement.

The second control is a dispersal or density requirement that establishes a cap on the total population permitted to live in group homes and institutions in a designated geographic area. Ideally, this figure should approximate the proportion of service-dependent individuals a neighborhood can absorb. For example, if three percent of a state's population is service-dependent, the proportion of service-dependent population per census tract could be limited to three percent.

• Zoning should recognize that group homes come in different sizes. The smaller home, for six or fewer residents, is roughly the size of a large family. There is no sound planning reason not to allow such "family homes" in all residential zoning districts as of right as long as they obtain or prove they are eligible for a license, meet the specified spacing and density requirements, and obtain an administrative occupancy permit.

This permit is needed to ensure that the home complies with these requirements and to provide a record for the planning agency so it can enforce spacing and density requirements. The ordinance should provide a special use permit process to allow for circumstances that might justify exceptions to the spacing and dispersal requirements for family homes. These should be similar to those suggested below for larger group homes.

Because group homes for seven to 15 persons exceed the size of all but the very largest families, municipalities should subject proposals for these "family group homes" to somewhat greater scrutiny than the smaller family homes. Family group homes, however, should be allowed in all residential districts as special uses. There's no sound planning principle for excluding family group homes from even the largest-lot single-family district. In fact, when the sponsoring agency can afford the cost, the larger houses in lowest-density districts offer excellent sites.

However, to minimize subjectivity and lessen the influence of fear, prejudice, and political pressure on decisions about group homes, the zoning ordinance should state reasonably objective relevant standards by which the special use permit application is to be evaluated. Appropriate standards should require the applicant to: obtain a license or evidence of eligibility for a license from the appropriate agency; meet specified spacing and density requirements; register with the municipality's planning department; submit a statement of the exact nature of the home planned, the qualifications of the home operator, the type and number of personnel, and the number of residents; conform to the general zoning requirements for the residential district, with the exception of the number of unrelated individuals permitted and the off-street parking requirements; and conform, to the extent possible, to the type and outward appearance of the residences in the area.

The ordinance should allow for a waiver of the spacing and dispersal requirements under certain conditions. Primarily, the decision-making body must find that the cumulative effect of allowing the group home (in addition to existing group homes and institutions for service-dependent populations) will not alter the residential character of the neighborhood, create an institutional setting, nor exceed the capacities of existing community recreational and social service facilities.

Daniel Lauber, AICP, is a River Forest, Illinois, planning consultant and attorney who has been involved in zoning for group homes since 1974.

Downsizing Gracefully

David R. Mosena
(January 1984)

The American Dream is in trouble. The possibility of owning a single-family house on an individual lot has collided hard with the unpleasant economic realities of the 1980s, putting it out of reach of the large majority of newly formed households. The results of this phenomenon have major implications not only for home buyers and the building industry, but also for planners and public officials, who must come up with new strategies to meet a more diverse array of housing needs than in the past, provide services and infrastructure on a limited budget, and devise new regulations that encourage the construction of a variety of housing types.

The housing cost and median income curves, once on parallel paths, have crossed and started off in opposite directions. Housing costs, including land, labor, materials, and especially the cost of money, increased at more than twice the rate of median family income during the last decade. In fact, as George Sternlieb and James Hughes [of Rutgers University have noted], when measured in constant 1982 dollars, median income has actually fallen. The value of existing houses also appreciated at an unprecedented level during the 1970s. As a result, the National Association of Home Builders estimates that only 29 percent of all households in

the United States earn enough to qualify for a conventional mortgage at today's interest rates. The assumption of the home builders association is that mortgage payments should total no more than a third of a family's gross income, and most lending institutions have, in fact, raised their qualifying rule-of-thumb from one-quarter to one-third of gross family income.

The consumer profile of the housing market is also changing. Factors such as delayed marriage and childbearing, smaller families, an increased divorce rate, and growing numbers of young single people and older "empty nesters" have altered the shape of the home-buying market in profound ways. In 1950, the average household size was 3.37 people. Today, the average is down to 2.75 and predicted to continue falling. In 1960, 80 percent of all households were composed of related family members; by 1975, this number had fallen to 60 percent, and it is still falling. Today, one out of four households consists of a single person. Analysts see the strongest areas of growth in the market segments of singles, mingles (two unrelated adults), and married couples without children. Households composed of a single parent and one or more children are also a growing segment of the market.

These fundamental demographic and life-style shifts suggest a more complex and diverse market with new types of shelter needs. For example, Fox and Jacobs, a major Dallas home builder, offers eight different single-family house styles targeted to different segments of the market. While similar in exterior appearance, all the houses have different floor plans, different amenities, different architectural details, and other special features.

The most dramatic change in new housing is the trend toward smaller houses on smaller lots at higher densities—what the building industry calls "smaller and smarter" housing. After five decades of steady increase in average house size, the trend has reversed and virtually all forms of housing are shrinking in size. In 1950, the average single-family detached house was 983 square feet. In 1979, average house size peaked at 1,760 square feet. Since then, the average has dropped to around 1,500 square feet. Some analysts predict it will level off here; others predict a continued decline to as low as 1,200 square feet by 1990.

Considerable pressure is being put on local governments, primarily by the building industry, to revise their development standards to accommodate the downsized, more affordable single-family house. Minimum lot sizes and frontage requirements, which control densities, are being relaxed in a growing number of communities throughout the country. The building industry also has pressed for revision of other development standards considered to add unnecessarily to the cost of housing, including standards governing street width, sidewalk and street lighting, curbs and gutters, parking, and open space. . . .

Riverside County's incentive zone

Riverside County, one of the fastest growing counties in California, offers a classic example of the housing affordability problem and an interesting public response. In 1970, 82 percent of the households in Riverside County could afford the median-priced resale house of the day. By 1977, only 21 percent could. During the 1970s, the median price of an existing house rose 225 percent while median income rose only 131 percent. By 1980, the median price of an existing house was $73,582, requiring a gross family income of $32,976 to qualify for a mortgage; the median family income in Riverside County was $19,000.

In August 1981, Riverside County adopted an "R-6 Residential Incentive" zone for the express purpose of "facilitating . . . the construction of affordable housing." This new ordinance was developed as a part of the county's state-mandated housing element. It was the first local housing element approved by the state that offered an incentive approach as an alternative to the mandatory inclusionary housing approach made famous by neighboring Orange County.

The residential incentive zone, which is not mapped and requires a rezoning, grants significant density increases in return for a developer's compliance with a pricing formula aimed at making lower priced housing available to consumers. The new zone reduces the minimum lot size from 7,200 to 3,600 square feet and drops frontage requirements from 60 feet to 30 feet. (Previously, developers in Riverside County could build to a 3,500 square foot minimum lot size by going through the planned unit development process, but the accompanying 40 percent open space requirement left that option generally ignored.) The new incentive zone requires projects to go through a site plan review process, at which time a variety of design features are negotiated with developers and actual

densities are set, depending on the characteristics of each specific site.

In return for the higher density offered by the county, developers must comply with one of three price control formulas:

● The average selling price [of all units in the project] shall not exceed 80 percent of the average home sales price in the market area;

● The selling price of 25 percent of the dwelling units shall be affordable to families earning no more than 120 percent of the median county income; or

● The selling price of 15 percent of the dwelling units shall be affordable to families earning no greater than 80 percent of the median county income.

Most developers, with some encouragement from the county board, have chosen the first option. The county established the median income in 1982 at $19,707, and the average sales price ceiling for the R-6 zone was set at $62,998 (80 percent of the median price of new homes). No attempt was made to control who bought the units—only to control their sales price—and no restrictions were put on resales.

Riverside County's residential incentive zone unleashed a flurry of development proposals. As of last June, 26 projects totaling some 5,000 housing units had been approved under the incentive provision with seven projects either completed or under construction. The market response was brisk—in some cases overwhelming. For example, Woodhaven Cottages, the first project completed under the R-6 zone, sold 160 of 262 units in 10 hours. The entire project sold out in 10 days. People stood in line for hours to tour the models and sign sales contracts. Houses in Woodhaven Cottages range from 800 to 1,457 square feet in size and were priced from $49,950 to $70,950. A similar project built by another firm sold 300 of 393 homes in two weeks from the blueprints in the field office, even before the model homes were finished.

Riverside County has since raised the minimum lot size from 3,600 square feet to 5,000 square feet, in part because of concern over the lack of usable yard space and in part because of political pressure from neighboring residents, who are concerned about the possible negative effects of higher density.

Riverside County's residential incentive zone has permitted and encouraged the construction of smaller, but perfectly sound and adequate, housing at substantially below prevailing average prices. It also has helped a depressed building industry get back to work. But whether it will help relieve the county's housing needs remains to be seen. Buyer profiles from the first few projects completed show that as many as 90 percent of all sales were made to first-time home buyers from neighboring Orange, Los Angeles, and San Bernardino counties, rather than to residents of Riverside County. And the out-of-county buyers' median income is $28,000, as opposed to $19,000 in Riverside County. . . .

Slums of tomorrow?

"Slums of tomorrow!" "Throw-away neighborhoods!" You hear these charges in every community where development standards are being relaxed in the interests of adding lower priced housing. The charge comes most often from neighboring residents, afraid of the effects that smaller homes at higher densities will have on their property values and afraid of the types of people such housing will attract. These claims are emotionally charged and unsupported by facts. The few studies that have been done show no negative effects on property values caused by the mixing of different sizes of single-family houses in different price ranges. So far the market for "affordable" housing has been dominated by first-time house buyers in their late twenties and early thirties with incomes in the $25,000 to $30,000 range.

The issue of density is central to the affordable housing debate. Clearly, the density question is more political than technical in nature. Sound, attractive houses can be built at 800 square feet on 3,600-square-foot lots. While builders and site planners will have to pay closer attention to virtually all of the design details, it's perfectly feasible to produce technically good housing at this scale. And given the prospects of continually rising energy costs and other constraints on consumers, in some parts of the U.S., smaller, more efficient houses may have a higher relative value than their larger counterparts.

Compatibility with existing housing is also a solvable problem. Providing a diverse, integrated mix of different housing types and sizes as opposed to high concentrations of small-lot housing is one part of the solution. Good buffering is another.

Amending development standards to give build-

ers more flexibility to meet the needs of the new housing market can be good for both communities and the industry. In competitive markets, the cost savings achieved will be passed on to consumers in the form of lower priced housing. This is not to say that some standards, such as those for street width and sewer mains, don't have physical limits beyond which they can't be relaxed and still function properly. Better, more careful planning will be needed at the project, neighborhood, and community level to ensure good design, maintain compatibility with existing neighborhoods, and schedule and finance needed public improvements. But these technical issues can be hammered out by reasonable parties.

The biggest problem in accommodating downsized housing is how to deal with entrenched neighborhood resistance—the proverbial, pull-up-the-gangplank syndrome. Developers and builders need to demonstrate they can and will provide well-designed projects. And communities need to examine their development policies and decide if they are going to help foster a mix of housing opportunities that better fit the needs of today's and tomorrow's consumers. Given the rampant land speculation in most hot housing markets, smaller homes at higher densities may be the only way to serve the entry-level homeownership market.

David R. Mosena, AICP, formerly APA's director of research, is now the planning commissioner for the city of Chicago.

Zero Lot Lines Can Trim Housing Costs

Welford Sanders
(April 1982)

As housing costs continue to rise, the demand for smaller, less expensive housing grows. Equally responsible for the demand are the growing ranks of smaller families and single people, who don't need as much space as the larger families of 20 years ago but still seek the advantages of single-family, detached housing.

An increasingly popular way for local governments to encourage small-lot development is to make use of the zero lot line concept. ZLL building is a way of obtaining many of the characteristics of conventional, single-family-detached housing but at a lower cost. While not an entirely new residential development concept, it is one that seems to be coming of age, primarily out of economic necessity.

ZLL houses abut one side lot line and sometimes also the rear or front lot line. In developments where lots are under 6,000 square feet, the use of this concept is the only way to ensure that the side yards will be usable and easily maintained. ZLL is also a way of preserving privacy in small-lot developments, since most communities that permit ZLL don't allow windows or doors in walls abutting side lot lines.

In the past, the ZLL concept has not had a significant impact on housing costs. In Huntington Beach, California, for example, where a well-publicized zero lot line development was built in 1966, prices for ZLL houses range from $150,000 to over $300,000. Clearly, Huntington Beach used the concept to provide more ocean frontage, not to bring down prices.

One reason ZLL has not had a greater impact on costs is the way it is regulated. Most communities allow relaxation of setback requirements only in planned unit developments. But the purpose of a PUD is usually to gain certain amenities in return for higher density, and amenities often add to the cost of housing.

The Sugar Tree development in Nashville is an example of a zero lot line PUD. Houses range in value from about $200,000 to over $400,000, with lots selling for about $65,000. By using the ZLL concepts, developers are able to get six or seven houses (averaging some 2,000 square feet of floor area) per acre in a residential district otherwise zoned for one-acre lots.

Nashville's PUD ordinance also illustrates the problems that can occur if specific siting requirements aren't included—especially when the ZLL concept is used at this level of density and involves large houses. Some of the Sugar Tree houses are only three or four feet apart, resulting in side yards that are difficult to maintain.

Dade County

The current trend seems to be to enact specific ZLL regulations rather than to regulate this form of development under existing PUD provisions. Leading the way is Dade County, Florida, where high land costs and a growing population of empty-nesters have created substantial demand for small-lot development.

Zero lot line housing is not new to Dade County. The county's first ZLL development on small lots was completed three years ago. But it required over 1,200 variances. Subsequent demands for similar variances by other developers convinced local officials that a new ordinance was in order. Now the county has an ordinance that may well represent the nation's most flexible non-PUD approach to zero lot line housing.

Despite its flexibility, however, the Dade County law contains design safeguards that protect privacy and allow for proper maintenance. The new ordinance was drawn up with the aid of the county's zoning review committee, a citizens committee with representation by community leaders, developers, architects, and lawyers.

Dade's ordinance allows ZLL housing in five of the county's residential districts, including its most restrictive single-family district (RU-1), which has a 7,500-square-foot minimum lot size. ZLL lots in the RU-1 district may be reduced to 4,500 square feet; in the other four districts ZLL lots may be reduced to 4,000 square feet. Maximum lot coverage has been increased to 50 percent for ZLL development, in comparison to a maximum of 35 percent for conventional development in the RU-1 district. In addition to allowing one side wall to abut a side lot line, the ordinance allows a front yard setback of as little as five feet. There is no minimum rear setback.

The new ordinance includes provisions that help ensure privacy, access to the rear of the lots, maintenance of side yards, and maximum outdoor space. To gain privacy, walls abutting side lot lines cannot have any openings. For maintenance and access, a perpetual four-foot easement must be provided on the lot adjacent to the ZLL property line.

To make the best use of limited outdoor space, the ordinance requires that 15 percent of the wall area of each unit must open onto a patio. For each lot two offstreet parking spaces are required and at least three trees must be provided. The ordinance requires a site plan review and a public hearing for ZLL developments.

Builder response

Response to the new ordinance from the development community has been exceptional. In the year since passage of the Dade County ordinance in February 1981, 35 applications for five-to-10-acre developments had been filed. Nineteen of those applications have been approved, although permits have been issued for only about 100 units.

Since the first of the year, ZLL applications have slowed. But according to Walter Geiger, chief of the development division of the county planning department, the slowdown is due to the overall slump in the housing industry, not to any ZLL shortcomings. Truly Burton of the Builders Association of South Florida says builders like both the flexibility the new ordinance provides, and the possibility of cost savings, which she puts at $7,000 to $15,000 for each ZLL house.

What such figures mean to the buyer depends on how much of the savings developers are able or willing to pass on. Most of the ZLL developments approved to date in Dade County are for houses in the $100,000 range. Some observers say that price is low for Dade's competitive housing market and would be even higher if interest rates came down. Nevertheless, at least one moderately priced ZLL development has been approved. It offers nearly 200 houses at an average price of $65,000, a real bargain for the South Florida housing market.

Local homeowners have been less enthusiastic. Many of the new developments are being proposed for parcels adjacent to existing single-family-detached housing, and opposition has come from residents of the surrounding neighborhoods. One Miami attorney and homeowner, who is leading a fight against a ZLL development, was quoted in the *Miami Herald* as calling ZLL housing a cancer that will destroy single-family neighborhoods.

What this irate citizen and others fear most is that ZLL housing will lower the value of their houses. Their fear is probably unfounded, since most of the ZLL houses proposed will sell for higher prices than the existing housing in the area. J.J. Della Porta, a Miami zoning consultant who helped design Dade's first small-lot, zero lot line development, examined sales and tax records of the standard single-family houses surrounding the first ZLL development and found no reduction in their value as a result of their ZLL neighbors.

Another complaint is that the houses are too close together and look too much like rowhouses. Yet Della Porta points out that zero lot line houses don't have to look like rowhouses. "Once they become more common," he was quoted as saying, "we will find developers studying the better ones and learning from them."

In the meantime, county planners have developed additional design guidelines for ZLL development. One important new requirement is that lots on the periphery of any ZLL development must have a 50-foot minimum frontage, thus creating a buffer between new ZLL development and existing housing. Another requirement is that, in RU-1 districts, all ZLL houses must have a minimum frontage of 45 feet.

Other design guidelines developed to supplement those contained in the original ZLL ordinance recommend that the size of ZLL developments be limited to 10 acres and that new ZLL sites should not be approved if they are contiguous to other ZLL sites. The guidelines set maximum density at 5.6 units to an acre. They also recommend that zero lot line housing be considered as a transitional use between higher density uses (townhouses, for instance) and conventional, single-family-detached housing.

The future looks good for zero lot line housing in Dade County, especially if local officials continue to refine the ZLL ordinance. Acceptance in many other parts of the country has been slow. Lately, though, with the examples of Dade County; Nashville; Jackson, Mississippi; Norman, Oklahoma; and Beaumont, Texas, ZLL is getting more widespread attention. To realize its full potential for reducing housing costs, however, local officials will have to enact carefully drafted ordinances and make developers aware of the new standards.

Welford Sanders is an associate research director of APA.

Carving Up the American Dream

Patrick H. Hare
(July 1981)

Suppose a planner had a magic method of developing invisible rental units in single-family neighborhoods. Suppose the planner knew that a public proposal to permit development of the units would probably be opposed by neighboring homeowners. Suppose the planner also knew that if nothing were said, the units would be developed anyway—in violation of the town's zoning and building ordinances.

Roughly speaking, this is the only course of action open to a planner who feels there are benefits to "single-family conversions"—subdividing large, single-family houses to create small "accessory apartments," or "mother-in-law apartments." There is a catch, however. If nothing is done, illegal apartments may spread until they become so common they have to be made legal. But, if planners propose legalization, they may trigger strict enforcement, which could delay or even stop development of the units.

It's clear, though, that interest is growing. Led by the articles of Andree Brooks in the *New York Times*, newspapers in Long Island, Connecticut, and New Jersey have begun to follow the spread of accessory apartments. Phyllis Santry of the Tri-State Regional Planning Commission in New York City surveyed the communities her commission serves and estimated that over 70 percent of them have noted the existence of legal or illegal conversions. Many communities estimate that 10 to 20 percent of their single-family housing stock contains conversions.

George Sternlieb of Rutgers University says that accessory apartments are the wave of the future. In newspaper interviews, he has talked about turning "onesies into twosies." "Whoever invented the split-level ranch must have been clairvoyant," he says. "It converts overnight."

In today's housing market, single-family conversions offer practical advantages to both owners and tenants. The owner trades unused space and a small investment for rental income. The tenant gets an apartment in a single-family neighborhood at below-market rent, because the apartment can be created at lower cost than a new unit. According to Frank Thompson, the building inspector of Babylon, Long Island, which has about 4,000 conversions, the cost of conversion varies from $1,000 to add a kitchen to the lower level of a ranch house to over $30,000 to add a double dormer and make other modifications to a Cape Cod.

Obviously, the less expensive a house is to convert, the more likely it is to be converted. Plainfield, New Jersey, which has a model program designed to help older homeowners convert, estimates the costs at about $10,000 per unit. The monthly income from the rental units varies widely but can easily be two or three times the monthly cost of the additional investment, even if that investment reflects today's interest rates.

In addition, older homeowners can bargain with tenants about reductions in rent in return for such services as helping with home maintenance and occasional transportation. Tenants may be able to provide these services fairly easily, and both landlords and tenants benefit. Finally, tenants add security just by being there. They alleviate two common fears of older homeowners: the fear of break-ins and the fear of being alone in an emergency.

There goes the neighborhood

However, according to Santry's survey, many homeowners view single-family conversions as the beginning of a movement to change the single-family character of the neighborhood. Some express fear that speculators will buy up houses for conversion to rental duplexes. They worry about absentee landlords, increased traffic, and code violations.

How does the planner deal with such a politically controversial housing trend? Proposals to legalize single-family conversions have met with strong resistance. On Long Island, for example, where it's generally accepted that illegal conversions are widespread, only one town, Babylon, has taken steps to legalize them. Town planner Richard Spirio has an inch-high stack of news clippings devoted to the public outcry over Babylon's ordinance. Mel Barr, the town planner of Westport, Connecticut, is caught between 4,650 accessory apartments that zoning officials can't shut down without controversial evictions and the opposition of homeowners who fight any proposal to legalize the illegal apartments.

Ironically, it appears to be in almost everybody's interest to "keep them on the QT," according to Santry. For homeowners who have installed illegal apartments, making them legal means higher assessments and the risk of being caught if rental income is not reported on tax returns. Even neighbors concerned about deterioration of their area have a stake in keeping quiet about the apartments, because the fact that they are illegal makes landlords take special care to keep their tenants in line.

A few years ago, Hartford's West End Civic Association considered trying to legalize the apartments in its large single-family houses and then decided against it. Members reasoned that, if the apartments were illegal, an anonymous call to the building department could shut down an undesirable landlord. A proposal to make them legal in an adjoining West Hartford neighborhood was roundly defeated.

There are ways to deal with many of the objections to conversions. One is to permit conversions only by owner-occupants, who presumably will not want to see the neighborhood they live in deteriorate. This provision also keeps speculators from entering the single-family market and creating investment properties. Another approach is to pass regulations that minimize such exterior changes as additional front doors that could change the visual character of the neighborhood. A third approach is to grant permits on a case-by-case basis so each conversion can be checked out.

Yet another means of dealing with opposition is to point to a nearby town where accessory apartments are already legal. Babylon surrounds the incorporated village of Lindenhurst, where accessory apartments have been legal for years; and Babylon could easily use the stability of Lindenhurst's housing stock as an example. Even so, there was still substantial opposition in Babylon, as noted earlier.

Some towns make the occupants' age a criterion for granting conversions. Westport permits conversions if either the owner or renter is 62 or over. Another common approach is to permit apartments only for relatives of homeowners; these apartments often are referred to as in-law apartments.

Policing problems

The problem with these two approaches is enforcement. What happens when the relatives move out? What happens when the old people die? What happens when the property is sold? The extra units tend to be rented to someone who is neither elderly nor related.

In other words, legalizing apartments for specific groups tends to seed a crop of illegal apartments available for use by anyone. Fairfax County, Virginia, has responded to this threat by making homeowners who install apartments for relatives sign an agreement making them liable to pay a $1,000-a-day fine for every day the apartment is used by someone other than relatives.

Short of such a regulation, there isn't much that can be done to stop a legal apartment from becoming illegal. The homeowner has very little to lose by trying to rent an apartment that is already installed. Assuming the neighbors don't complain, the building inspector's only recourse is what one planner calls a "search and destroy mission." The resulting evictions are less than ideal from everyone's point of view. Also, as a study by the Metropolitan Area Planning Council in Boston points out, provisions restricting use to relatives or older people may inhibit homeowners from creating apartments. They fear that their investment will become worthless if their relative no longer lives in the apartment.

Nonetheless, regulations that subtly sow the seed of conversions may be the planner's only politically feasible choice. When zoning to legalize accessory apartments was proposed to a midwestern planning director, his reaction was, "It's happening anyway, so let's just let it happen." Letting it happen, either by nonenforcement of existing regulations or partial legalization, may build a constituency for eventual legalization, if only to permit inspection and correction of code violations.

It also may build in a problem that has to be solved later. Now that conversions are legal in Babylon, the town is considering offering low-interest loans to owners who are willing to legalize their two-family arrangements; the loans would help pay for the upgrading now required before a two-family permit can be issued.

One of the carrots often held out to taxpayers is the tax revenue that accessory apartments would provide. But this benefit may be illusory. In Babylon, the average assessment increase has been only $115, and a report on mother-in-law apartments by the Portland, Oregon, Growth Management Task Force suggests that new revenue would, at best, be offset by administrative and enforcement costs.

Clearly, advocates of legalization can't promise too much. Large tax increases will substantially reduce the incentive to create accessory apartments or even to bring existing illegal apartments under the auspices of the law.

Closely related to the question of assessments is the possibility that families in accessory apartments will add to the school population, thus leading to an increase in property taxes to meet school costs. Barbara Dietz, a real estate agent and active member of the North End Civic Association of Floral Park, Long Island, estimates there are about 500 accessory apartments in her town, 60 of them with children. She feels that it is particularly unjust that owners of houses occupied by school-age children don't pay increased assessments for their illegal apartments.

On the other hand, the lack of children might make some older suburbs feel a sense of loss of community. These towns might bend over backwards to be lenient toward families with children.

How big?

Children also raise the question of the size of accessory apartments—an area in which regulations vary greatly. Boston's Metropolitan Area Planning Council surveyed 23 communities with accessory apartments. It found that only 10 towns regulated apartment size and five specified a maximum, usually 600 square feet.

This inconsistency persists in ordinances in other regions. It reflects local residents' competing concerns about the quality of the apartments to be created as opposed to the desire to maintain the single-family character of the neighborhood. The Weston ordinance avoids the issue by using subjective language. It permits one accessory apartment in a "single family owner occupied dwelling. . . . provided it is . . . clearly a subordinate part thereof."

However logical it may seem to some, to others planning for the creation of accessory apartments seems to be planning for the subdivision of the American dream. This may be the real cause of the controversy surrounding the legalization of accessory apartments, not practical matters like apartment size.

Such feelings may also explain the lack of enthusiasm in towns where accessory apartments have been made legal. Two months after Portland, Oregon, began its Add-a-Rental program, no applications to create legal accessory apartments had been received. When Lincoln, Massachusetts, legalized accessory apartments several years ago, it included a provision in its zoning bylaws restricting the apartments to a maximum of 10 percent of the houses in the town. This restriction was removed in 1978 because nowhere near that number of apartments was created.

And in Babylon, which legalized accessory apartments in February 1980, almost every one of the 900 applications received within the first 10 months were to legalize existing apartments. "Only five or six applications for new apartments have come in since the program started," says Ed Thompson of Babylon's building division.

It's clear that simply legalizing accessory apartments will not necessarily result in the creation of large numbers of them. On the other hand, prohibiting them may not do much to keep them from spreading. Apparently, they involve a planning issue on which the curtain is only beginning to rise.

Partrick Hare is a planning consultant in Washington, D.C.

A Room of One's Own
William Fulton
(September 1985)

Andy Raubeson got into the single-room-occupancy (SRO) housing business almost literally through the side door.

A burly man with a salt-and-pepper beard—he looks more than a little like a retired seaman—Raubeson thought he was setting out to handle social problems when he was appointed director of the nonprofit Burnside Consortium in Portland, Oregon, back in 1979. Social services for the city's poverty-stricken Skid Row had been identified as a priority in Portland's downtown plan, and Burnside had been organized by civic leaders to coordinate and deliver them.

Almost as soon as he arrived on the job, however, Raubeson saw that the real problem on Skid Row was housing. At best, the old residential hotels in the neighborhood were in pitiable condition, with alcoholics, drug addicts, and the mentally ill living in squalor. At worst, they had been abandoned by their owners, torched by evicted residents, and subsequently claimed by transient squatters. "It just seemed so obvious to me that we had to champion the housing stock," he says.

So Burnside took a lease on a hotel that another nonprofit had walked away from. Starting with no experience, Raubeson and his colleagues at Burnside quickly learned the basic facts of SRO management. (Lesson number one was a first-hand experience: They slept in the hotel to protect it from arson.) Soon, Burnside leased a second hotel, then a third, and eventually started trying to figure out how to buy them.

Although downtown housing for all income groups was also a priority under the general plan, help was not easy to come by. Because each room usually lacks its own bathroom and kitchen facilities, SROs traditionally have been defined as "substandard"—and therefore ineligible for federal subsidies—by the U.S. Department of Housing and Urban Development. "There was an inventory of old, run-down residential hotels, and there were thousands of single individuals in need of assistance to afford decent housing," recalls Sam Galbreath, director of housing at the Portland Development Commission, the city's redevelopment agency. "But they didn't qualify for help under available HUD rules."

Civic leaders in Portland began to rally around the cause of SRO housing, including U.S. Rep. Les AuCoin (D-Ore.), who in 1980 persuaded Congress to amend the Housing Act of 1936 to make SROs eligible for federal housing assistance under certain conditions. After requiring the city to make a finding that SROs were needed because other housing wasn't available for poverty-stricken individuals, HUD then gave the Portland Development Commission a Section 8 demonstration grant to help purchase and renovate SROs.

The renovations proved to be remarkably cost-effective. With loans from the demonstration grant, the city was able to rehabilitate 247 SRO units downtown for less than $2 million—an average of $7,500 per unit, or a mere fraction of the cost of providing units under traditional Section 8 pro-

grams. Ensuing federal subsidies are about a third of what they have been in other Section 8 projects in Portland, according to Galbreath.

Since then, the Portland Development Commission has renovated 500 additional SRO units, with funding from such diverse sources as the federal Department of Energy, the Federal Emergency Management Administration, and the National Trust for Historic Preservation. Andy Raubeson, who now heads up the SRO Housing Corporation in Los Angeles, has become known as one of the nation's experts on SRO hotels. And, as the problem of homeless people gets more and more attention, cities around the country are rediscovering and renovating their residential hotels.

Growing interest

With each tenant limited to a small room, SRO hotels constitute housing in its most basic form. And, under the right purchase-and-renovation program, SRO hotel rooms may rent for $200 a month or less, with little or no monthly subsidy—a key point in an era of scarce federal housing subsidies.

Only a few years ago, interest in residential hotels was limited to a few large, expensive cities, notably New York and San Francisco. But now, interest is growing so rapidly that when Raubeson organized a conference on the topic in Los Angeles last spring, 103 people attended from all over the country—including representatives from states, cities, neighborhood groups, and nonprofit organizations interested in rehabbing and owning SROs.

Seattle, for example, has helped to rehab more than 1,000 units, and the city is now using such methods as development fees and development rights transfers to help salvage, renovate, and operate SROs in downtown areas. In Los Angeles, Raubeson's SRO Housing Corporation was created by the city's mammoth Community Redevelopment Agency, which is required by state law to use 20 percent of its "tax increment" profits for affordable housing. The agency has staked Raubeson's small operation to $10 million, and he expects to purchase and renovate more than 700 SRO units in the city's Skid Row section in the first two years of operation.

And, as the homeless issue has received more publicity, even HUD has shown more interest in SROs. Secretary Samuel Pierce, Jr., recently announced that the department would be willing to waive restrictions on the use of Section 8 rental certificates by individuals (as opposed to families)—an action that undoubtedly will bring more Section 8 tenants into SROs. (A waiver would allow twice the allocation of rental certificates to individuals, from 15 to 30 percent.) . . .

The fate of SRO hotels first became an issue in the 1970s, when their disappearance in San Francisco and New York began to displace thousands of people, particularly the elderly. In New York, the Mayor's Office of SRO Housing was established in 1973 to do social service work with SRO tenants, and the nation's strongest SRO tenant protection laws soon followed. But demolitions and conversion continued on a massive scale. According to the National Trust, the number of lower priced hotel rooms in New York dropped from more than 50,000 to less than 20,000 between 1975 and 1981, as the hotels were demolished for more profitable commercial or residential use.

New York's city council approved an 18-month moratorium earlier this summer to ban the conversion, alteration, or demolition of most SRO buildings. And, according to Judith Spektor, director of the Mayor's Office of SRO Housing, a number of funding programs are in place to assist SROs. City officials have estimated that 13 percent of New York's homeless formerly lived in SROs, so SROs will get some of the city's new $25 million capital fund to house the homeless. The SRO Loan Program, which makes federal block grant money available to hotel owners at one percent interest, already has led to restoration of 800 units, with 500 more in the pipeline. The city itself owns many SRO hotels through tax foreclosure and so far has rehabilitated 379 of these units. The capital fund for the homeless will encourage more nonprofit groups to get involved in SRO ownership and management. Furthermore, a controversial tax abatement program that led to the loss of many SRO hotels has been changed to permit abatements only for the restoration of SROs, not for their demolition or conversion.

In San Francisco, SRO hotels historically have made up more than 12 percent of the city's housing stock—for decades they served sailors on shore leave—and eventually became the primary source of low-income housing for the elderly. But in the 1970s, these hotels began disappearing: The Yerba Buena redevelopment project alone eliminated more than 4,000 SRO rooms, and the city's booming tourist trade caused hotel owners to convert thousands more to expensive rooms for tourists, particularly in the Tenderloin and Chinatown areas.

A moratorium on SRO hotel conversions was passed at the urging of neighborhood leaders in 1980. As in New York, a whole slew of funding measures has been used to assist nonprofit and private owners, including a fee imposed on builders of high-rise hotels in the Tenderloin as part of an urban development action grant (UDAG) deal. And the National Trust's Inner City Ventures program has assisted several SROs in Chinatown.

San Francisco has benefited as well from the state of California's decision to earmark $4.7 million for SRO assistance, to be distributed among eight projects, located mostly in the Bay Area. The financing can get quite complicated. The Arlington Hotel in San Francisco's Tenderloin, for example, is being purchased jointly by the St. Vincent de Paul Society and developer Robert Lurie, who also owns the San Francisco Giants baseball team. The financing includes $900,000 from Lurie (in exchange for permission to do other development work in the city), a large loan from the sellers, a $1 million loan from the state, operating subsidies from the city's Department of Public Health, $850,000 from a consortium of savings and loans put together to finance affordable housing, and about $500,000 from the city's affordable housing fund.

A question of management

As with any low-income housing project, however, the mere infusion of money does not guarantee success. Many hotels are located in crime-ridden neighborhoods, and their tenants are often in need of welfare, alcoholism recovery programs, and other social services. Thus, say SRO experts, management is the real key to making SROs work.

"You have to work to stabilize the tenants as well as house them," says Andy Raubeson. "Management has to be an advocate for the tenant if he is, say, going to get cut off of SSI [supplemental security income]." Raubeson says this can even mean making appointments for tenants at a social service agency and making sure the tenant goes: "You have to remember we are working with a fragile and vulnerable tenant load."

Raubeson says the single most important element in good management is a resident manager, paid by the owner, who must live through the ups and downs of the hotel's existence just as the tenants do. Other SRO experts agree that managing SROs is not like managing any other type of housing.

In San Francisco, for example, the North of Market Planning Coalition—a neighborhood group that played a big role in getting the UDAG subsidies for four SRO hotels—has consistently criticized management of those hotels by Goldrich and Kest, one of the largest builders of subsidized housing in California. Brad Paul, North of Market's executive director, says the Goldrich and Kest managers didn't understand the importance of having a desk clerk on duty 24 hours a day because the Tenderloin can be dangerous—or even the significance of attractive lobby furniture, an important feature to elderly tenants. Although the four hotels are being subsidized by the profits from a high-rise Ramada Inn nearby, they are reportedly losing money, and the city and banks have discussed restructuring their loans.

Because of this need for sensitive management, local governments and neighborhood groups are turning, increasingly, to ownership by nonprofit groups. Private owners, and particularly absentee owners, often fail to maintain their buildings well—sometimes even after receiving low-interest governmental loans for rehabilitation. Raubeson said the CRA in Los Angeles lent money to three private owners before establishing the nonprofit SRO Housing Corporation. It is now calling in all three loans.

San Francisco's Tenderloin area has probably been the leader in nonprofit ownership. The first nonprofit owner in the area was Reality House West, which purchased the Cadillac Hotel in 1977. According to Brad Paul, who lived at the Cadillac for three years, approximately 15 percent of the Tenderloin's 15,000 housing units—6,000 of which are SRO units—are already in nonprofit hands.

But some SRO experts see problems with nonprofit owners as well. Russ Schmunk, who works on SRO housing at the California Department of Housing and Community Development, suggests that, while nonprofits are often enthusiastic when they are first formed, they sometimes become so bureaucratized in succeeding years that they are insensitive to SRO needs. "The zealots tend to be replaced by people who are more cautious," he says. And Portland's Galbreath cautions against investing too much faith in nonprofits unless they are "hard-nosed and business-based."

Nevertheless, Schmunk and other SRO experts believe nonprofits are often better SRO managers than private owners, who, in Schmunk's words, "tend to cheat a lot." Of the eight SRO grants Schmunk's department is making now, seven involve nonprofits or governmental agencies.

And, as funds for SROs become more precious, nonprofits are likely to get the nod over private owners. In Portland, only six of the 14 SRO hotels are owned and operated by private individuals or groups. Says Sam Galbreath, "In a time of limited resources, the most efficient permanent solution is ownership by nonprofits."

Like others involved with low-income housing, SRO advocates don't argue that they can solve the entire problem themselves. In New York's rabid real estate market, says Judith Spektor, "we can't compete with the development bucks, no matter how much one-percent loan money we have." And Brad Paul in San Francisco believes that, as land prices elsewhere in the city rise, Yuppie tenants will eventually begin to push the elderly out of SROs in the Tenderloin.

Nevertheless, SROs seem to provide some inexpensive low-income housing for groups of people in some cities. In a report to the National Trust, Brad Paul wrote that SROs may prove to be the "appropriate technology solution" for affordable housing in the 1980s. As he put it, the SRO movement is proving that, in a time when money for big low-income housing programs just isn't available, "less space is still less space—but it can be pleasant, affordable, and enriching."

William Fulton is a contributing editor of Planning.

Sheltering the Homeless

Jim Schwab
(December 1986)

Times are changing for the homeless. No longer dismissed as drunks or derelicts, "street people" are getting new attention—fitting on the eve of 1987, proclaimed by the United Nations as the International Year of Shelter for the Homeless. Nationally, there are charges that federal economic and social policies have created the homeless phenomenon—an issue that last surfaced during the depression.

Local response has varied from the election of a mayor in Tucson, Arizona, on a platform of "running the bums the hell out of town" to initiatives in major cities aimed at preserving an adequate supply of low-income housing.

If homelessness is narrowly defined as lacking a roof over one's head, the numbers of homeless in the U.S. are quite low. Even the most classic street people often find temporary shelter at night. But most experts find this definition too narrow because emergency shelters are nobody's idea of "home." The definition also sidesteps the real question: the causes of homelessness.

Charles Hoch, assistant professor in the School of Urban Planning and Policy at the University of Illinois in Chicago, says that the total absence of shelter is merely the extreme end of "a continuum of uncertainty." Along the same continuum—though not as desperate—are people living in single-room-occupancy hotels, and those who double up with relatives or cannot find suitable housing when the supply of low-cost apartments diminishes due to abandonment or redevelopment.

What emerges from this approach is not a single number of homeless but several levels of jeopardy. Still, the debate over numbers is intense. The largest figure—over two million—was a thinly documented 1980 estimate by the Community for Creative Non-Violence, in Washington, D.C. At the other end of the scale, the U.S. Department of Housing and Urban Development estimated that there were 250,000 to 350,000 homeless in the U.S. in 1984.

The HUD report drew fire in congressional hearings. Richard P. Appelbaum, sociologist at the University of California at Santa Barbara, noted that it ignored homeless populations in smaller cities like Santa Monica. Chester Hartman, a fellow of the Institute for Policy Studies, in Washington, D.C., criticized the report as merely "aggregating lots of guesswork" rather than being a rigorously designed survey.

Earlier this year, the University of Chicago's National Opinion Research Center, in collaboration with the Social and Demographic Research Institute of the University of Massachusetts, undertook such a survey, with funding by the Robert Wood Johnson Foundation. Teams of researchers were deployed to count and interview the homeless both on Chicago streets and in shelters between midnight and 6 a.m. Despite earlier estimates of 15,000 to 25,000 Chicago homeless, NORC found a nightly average of only 2,000 to 2,300, many with serious physical and mental health problems.

Once again, critics objected. Hoch, who serves as a pro bono consultant to the Chicago Coalition for the Homeless, charged that the study's sampling methods (based on police estimates) were faulty, that some of the survey questions were naive, and that its definition of homelessness suggested a serious conceptual bias. . . .

Ensuring an adequate supply of low-income housing is one planning response to the potential displacement of the working poor, the low-income elderly, and others unable to complete for shelter in an inflated market. With the decline of federal housing subsidies, some cities have taken new interest in single-room-occupancy hotels as a viable source of low-cost housing.

In Cincinnati, for example, the city council last year made preservation of 1,300 low-income housing units, mostly SRO hotels, a priority in its downtown plan. Under pressure from the local Legal Aid Society, which pointed to a 79 percent drop in SRO units between 1970 and 1980, the city planning department worked with the University of Cincinnati's planning school to develop a strategy for saving the SRO hotels.

In May 1985, the plan was amended to include a commitment to replace some lost SROs with low-rent units, using a $250,000 community development block grant. Senior planner Charlotte Birdsall says the city is now considering the acquisition of a YMCA building that, ironically, had once been home to many elderly people, displaced because the Y wanted a more affluent clientele. Most of the building is now empty, except for a health club on the main floor. The new facility would provide 99 SRO rooms and 113 efficiency apartments. The council also amended its antidisplacement law to make residents displaced by development anywhere in the central business district eligible for relocation benefits.

Minneapolis and St. Paul have joined with Hennepin and Ramsey counties to provide their own low-cost downtown housing through the vehicle of the Minneapolis/St. Paul Family Housing Fund, a nonprofit corporation funded by the McKnight Foundation, that has created some 5,000 low-income housing units. A year ago, the foundation provided some $2.7 million for Phase I of the "More Than Shelter" program; total Phase II outlays, including public funds, are expected to reach $8.5 million by May 1988. The family housing fund is now developing 76 units in St. Paul's Hamline Hotel as part of the program. The goal, says president Tom Fulton, is to provide an additional 50 new SRO units in Minneapolis, to rehab 100 existing SRO units in each city, and to provide 90 units of transitional housing and 500 "board-and-lodging beds." The people served, notes Fulton, are those who, in the past, have fallen through the cracks due to their social or emotional problems.

In addition, in St. Paul, the historic American Beauty Macaroni Company building in Lowertown has been converted into a 56-unit SRO facility. The developer contributed nearly 40 percent of the cost of the $2 million project, while local foundations, the project architect, and the city supplied the rest.

Denver has also seen a downtown development boom but, unlike Cincinnati, it has also seen the bust. The boom, says Mitzi C. Barker, former executive director of the Denver Emergency Housing Coalition, attracted unemployed people seeking work in Colorado's oil industry. Barker, who recently moved to Anchorage, notes that the oil jobs actually were in western Colorado, not Denver, and that most of the migrants lacked the skills necessary for such employment. But, once in Denver, they often lacked the resources to move on. Meanwhile, redevelopment removed much of the low-cost housing.

In 1978, the Denver Department of Social Services, various churches, and traditional nonprofit service providers formed the housing coalition and offered to provide emergency housing, using $50,000 in city funds to enable member agencies to rent 10 vacant units belonging to the Denver Housing Authority. The coalition staff became property managers while also providing referral services for its clients. Its housing stock eventually increased to its present 32 units.

The use of public housing units, rather than traditional shelters, stems from the coalition's mission to serve families with children, says Barker.

Changes in the city's real estate market have opened up new opportunities for the coalition. Several property owners who were saddled with empty apartments allowed the coalition to occupy their buildings for a dollar a year. In return for insurance and security, the coalition gained a supply of short-term units that could be used for transitional housing. Barker says the city funded the project for two years, after which the local United Way provided a grant. The coalition also had a contract with the city social services department.

The coalition bought its first property this fall. A combination of city and private money subsidized the purchase of a $450,000 21-unit building at below-market interest. The Park Ogden building will provide low-income rental housing until the coalition needs it for transitional or emergency housing. If that happens, the coalition will assist tenants in relocating, acting executive director Les Jones says.

Cutting the red tape

In the popular view—if not in actual fact—New York City has the nation's biggest problem with homelessness. Everyone has read about welfare hotels where the poor suffer substandard conditions and the owners get bonuses for warehousing them.

Earlier this year, *New York* magazine reported that Leonard Stern, chairman of the Hartz Mountain pet food company and owner of *The Village Voice,* visited the hotels and shelters and labeled them "Auschwitz with plenty of food and changed linens and no work."

Stern was so upset that he provided $1 million in seed money for a new group, Homes for the Homeless, organized under the auspices of Manhattan's Episcopal Cathedral of St. John the Divine. Stern has already underwritten the purchase of two buildings by guaranteeing notes totaling $18 million. Homes for the Homeless executive director Sister Joan Kirby says the group is also committed to redistribution of New York's homeless, now primarily concentrated in midtown Manhattan near the Port Authority bus terminal. To that end, all of Stern's apartments are located in the outer boroughs. The group has already rehabbed the former Prospect Hospital, now the Prospect Interfaith Family Inn, which accommodates some 80 families in the Bronx, mostly women with children. Another facility in Queens, to be ready January 15, will have 260 units. Sister Kirby says the group is preparing to buy a third building elsewhere.

Sister Kirby says the city has smoothed the way for her group because it is desperate. Homes for the

Homeless is reimbursed by the state Department of Social Services for the services it provides. Although Sister Kirby credits the city with gaining approval of the shelters in the outlying boroughs, she criticizes some aspects of the city's performance, in particular its $2.10-per-person daily food allowance.

Homes for the Homeless will do far more than warehouse the poor. "We use job training and housing specialists to empower families to find permanent housing," says Sister Kirby, noting that the facilities will offer cottage industry experience and function as "client cooperatives." Residents even provide security, with some trained and employed as "peacekeepers." . . .

Homelessness is not just an urban problem, notes Paul Namkung, executive director of Rural Human Services in northern California's Del Norte County. His coastal outpost in Crescent City, 250 miles north of San Francisco, offers shelter and services both for local homeless people and for transients, many of whom are agricultural workers.

Namkung's nonprofit agency started modestly six and a half years ago. Namkung, a social worker, says he noticed that many needs went unmet as clients turned to specific agencies for particular kinds of assistance. In Del Norte County, heavily dependent on the lumber industry, unemployment often reaches 20 percent, and over one-third of its residents are below the poverty line.

At first, Namkung organized a volunteer hotline that offered counseling on a variety of social problems. When it became apparent that more was needed, Namkung left his mental health position to launch his own one-stop social service agency. He went to Sacramento, knocked on state agency doors, and returned with $1.8 million in grants for Rural Human Services' first year of operation. While providing social services, it also rents 16 rooms in a string of roadside motels for use as homeless shelters.

Namkung, who now has a staff of 18, supplemented by 40 to 60 volunteers, acknowledges that these units do not meet all the needs. Some homeless, mainly Vietnam veterans, camp out in the nearby Klamath National Forest. There is also community resistance to making the area too attractive for transients. For this reason, the county planning commission recently blocked a $900,000 state grant to convert a local church into an SRO.

But his program has drawn praise elsewhere.

Last year, the California chapter of the National Association of Social Workers named Namkung its outstanding social work administrator for the year. And the program continues to attract outside funds.

Nuts and bolts

Where exactly do planners fit into solutions to the problem of homelessness? A precise answer is difficult, but the fact that private agencies rely on city funds, services, and permits suggests that planners can facilitate the *process* of serving the homeless and preventing the problem. In Chicago, for example, the city council three years ago eased the way for shelters by making them special uses in certain zoning districts. APA's *Zoning News* editor Tom Smith notes that liberalized zoning in White Plains, New York, within the past year has allowed two new shelters to open, and another change in October permitted daytime "social service centers." But he also notes that community opposition has worked against many such proposals elsewhere. According to Alan Heskin, associate professor at the UCLA school of architecture and urban planning, planners can also play an important role by, in effect, making life easier for nonprofit service providers.

Along those lines, UCLA planning students last year won an AICP award for an action guide outlining physical planning issues, management needs, resources, and relevant legislation. The guide concludes with recommendations for a broad-based political movement to seek local housing reform, which Heskin says is necessary to offset a potent real estate lobby.

Jim Schwab is the assistant editor of Planning. *James Peters, formerly of the* Planning *staff, assisted with research for this article.*

Housing '87
Sandra Olivetti Martin
(January 1987)

It has come to this: More Americans need housing than there are houses.

Overall, 1986 was a good housing year, and it

followed on the heels of three other good years. Over 1.8 million new housing spaces were begun last year, according to the National Association of Home Builders. With lower mortgage rates, more houses went up.

Still, new starts did not keep up with need. And that means disappointment for American families, particularly low-income and minority families. It also means less revenue for those communities that depend on housing construction to supply jobs and on the property tax to build schools and roads. (The home builders association reports that the annual return on 100,000 homes is $1.5 billion in taxes and $3.25 billion in wages.)

Today's median-priced house costs above $86,000. Some, of course, cost less. In St. Louis's Central West End, on Mayor Vincent C. Schoemehl's block, one family has found a $70,000 bargain ripe for restoration. Their gain is the previous owner's loss. Newly divorced, she couldn't manage payments at 12 percent, let alone restoration, on one income.

Many houses cost far more than the median. In central New Jersey, for example, a median-priced house costs a whopping $140,000. To move in, a family would have to earn $50,000 a year. "That's discouraging news here, where the median family income is $40,000 a year," says state assemblyman David C. Schwartz. . . .

For the average American—whose real earnings are likely to have stayed flat since 1973—price is the central problem. Despite the increase in two-income families, an affordability gap of about $10,000 a year separates the average family, earning $28,000 a year, from the median-priced home. The gap becomes a chasm for the growing number of Americans who aren't average—single people, female heads of households, ethnic minorities, even young families.

Since the late 1970s, mortgage interest rates have created a big part of the gap. Although down from an all-time high of 16 percent in 1981–82 to some 10 percent today, they have been counterbalanced by other costs. Land and construction materials continue to rise. The demand for housing as investment and tax shelter has driven prices up. And property taxes have increased under pressure from states and local governments struggling to meet growing demands for service.

With costs so high, many would-be homeowners need a partner. Traditionally the federal government, but increasingly cities and states, add that leverage.

New Jersey, for example, is supporting lease-purchase partnerships to bring ownership within more of its citizens' reach. The state's Housing and Mortgage Finance Agency lends money both to developers of lease-purchase housing and to first-time buyers, and since 1984, 8,000 average Jerseyites have received assistance. Under their lease-purchase agreements, a portion of each month's rent for the first two years accumulates as down payment on a state HMFA mortgage.

Washington, D.C., whose housing is among the nation's most expensive, is one of many cities experimenting with partnerships to produce affordable housing. In November, 10 residents of the Wiley Court Project became owners of modern HUD-financed condominiums. The new owners pay a maximum of 30 percent of their monthly income in mortgage, taxes, and utilities for their units, priced from $60,000 to $72,000. "It's always been a fantasy of mine, but it never appeared possible to me, being a single parent and a poor parent," says one new owner, Evon Musgrove. . . .

Like their city cousins, many country dwellers need help in paying for housing. Kentucky is promoting rural homeownership by bankrolling community developers. Instead of federal money, the state relies on a new housing trust fund capitalized by revenues from tax-exempt bond sales. And in the nation's first statewide homesteading program, Virginia has used a $400,000 HUD grant to buy 26 vacant rural houses from the Federal Housing Authority's inventory of surplus properties. The properties, each needing up to $15,000 in repairs, are sold to low-income winners of a lottery drawing. . . .

New rules

With tax reform, renters may be less able and investors less willing to satisfy housing demand. Under the Tax Reform Act of 1986, the federal government has written new rules for the partnerships that previously accounted for much of rental housing. The new tax bill reduces the profitability of rental housing in three ways:

• Capital gains will no longer be taxed at a lower rate.

• Depreciation schedules for new residential property will be lengthened to 27.5 years from 19 years.

• Losses on rental real estate—formerly an attractive part of its tax advantage—can no longer balance gains in other income except for very small investors.

The effect, investment analysts say, will be higher rent. "As a result of incentives lost in the tax bill, we foresee tighter supply and higher rents until building apartments becomes economical again," says Jay Shackford of the National Association of Home Builders. "We project a 15 percent increase in rents over the next five years, above and beyond ordinary inflation."

In contrast, home ownership will remain a rather good deal under tax reform. Mortgage interest and property tax deductions on first and second homes remain untouched. For middle-income people, that makes ownership a major tax advantage—and the only one with any "economic oomph," experts say.

The fate of rental housing may also give home ownership a boost. "As scarcity forces rents up, renters may accelerate their buying plans," says Jay Shackford. More young families may choose to invest in a home sooner as rising rents compete with mortgage payments for a larger share of their income.

If so, they'll find money easy to borrow. Mortgage interest rates continue to fall from their 1981–82 high. Fixed rates could be as low as 9.5 percent by the middle of the year, and adjustable rates are expected to fall sooner, dropping to seven percent.

At the bottom end of the income scale, however, housing continues to disappear, despite occasional David-over-Goliath victories.

In Alexandria, Virginia, where pressure from land-poor Washington, D.C., puts a high price tag on property, a black middle-class community has won HUD's support in forcing the city to negotiate a discrimination complaint. Residents had charged that their neighborhood was under assault; demolished or renovated houses were not replaced, schools were closed, and a highway was planned to bisect the community.

More often Goliath wins. In Alexandria's largely Hispanic district of Arlandria, 1,500 low-income residents must find new homes because of a developer's plans to remodel the 416-unit Dominion Garden complex, raising rents for a two-bedroom apartment from an average of $460 to $650 a month. Affordable housing is as hard to find in the Washington, D.C., area as "platinum and gold,"

says Mitch Snyder of the Community for Creative Nonviolence, an advocate for the homeless.

The national stock of low-income housing has fallen by 10 million units in the last decade, according to estimates by the National Low Income Housing Coalition. As a result, the very poor pay up to three-fourths of their income in rent.

Further, federal assistance for housing has plummeted. "Today, housing seems to have fallen off the national agenda altogether," says David Maxwell, chairman of the board of the Federal National Mortgage Association (Fannie Mae).

After reaching a multibillion dollar peak in the late 1970s, federal housing aid has been cut by 70 percent—"more deeply than any other major federal activity," according to Allen Fishbein, director of the Neighborhood Revitalization Project of the Center for Community Change in Washington, D.C.

Until October, the tax law was a last haven of federal protection, although the system had its limitations. "The old tax law was terrific for builders but lousy for low-income people," says Barry Zigas of the National Low Income Housing Coalition. But even if the gravy went to the rich in tax write-offs and development subsidies, the poor at least got a bone. In 1984, for example, 50,000 units—about 1,000 per state—were added to the low-income stock, according to National Low Income Housing Coalition estimates. The group's 1980 study noted that over 21 percent of families whose income is less than half of their area's median live in subsidized housing.

The new law introduces a system of three tax credits for investors in low-income housing. Like the residential energy credit, each dollar of credit wipes out a dollar of owed taxes. The credits were hard won and will be granted sparingly. What's more, they promise only a three-year reprieve until they disappear on December 31, 1989.

The credits allow developers to subtract nine percent of the costs of building or rehabilitating low-income housing from their tax bill. The credit drops to four percent if other federal subsidies are used in construction or rehabilitation. The acquisition of existing low-income housing also earns four percent credit. This credit can be used for 10 years, but the project must continue in low-income use for 15 years.

The new system is full of such "buts." A project can still combine market-rate and low-income housing. But to earn credit, it must include more lower-income households than ever before. Roughly 20 percent of the units must be rented to families with an income of less than half the community's average. Higher poverty-level incomes are permitted, but they increase the project's percentage of low-income housing. For example, families with an income of 60 percent of the area average raise the low-income set-aside to 40 percent of the project.

Those "buts" give tax analysts pause. A major worry is whether there will be enough credits to go around. In order to balance what it "spends" and what it loses, the federal government has kept the figures low: $2.7 billion for the three years. Shares of that amount are to be allocated to the states on a per capita basis, with each citizen "earning" $1.25 in credit each year. Densely populated cities must get their share of the credit from their states.

The District of Columbia, which is on its own, shows how far the credit will go. Paradise Manor, a 672-unit project in need of renovation, would by itself use up $272,000—a third of the city's credit of $775,000, according to Marilyn Melkonian of Telesis, a small development group.

Other analysts worry that the credit will have few takers. For one thing, the allocation system means new bureaucracies in each of the states. That's a hurdle for developers and nonprofit organizations that are used to making their deals directly with communities. Political problems may crop up, too. Strategist Farley Peters of Washington's National Center for Policy Alternatives foresees squabbles in some states over which agency gets the credits, while other states will argue about who takes responsibility.

Some planners fear tax reform will dry up low-income housing as investors default and developers switch to high-rent uses. "Developers who built market-rate housing with low-income assistance will kiss the low-income tenants goodbye," predicts Barry Zigas of the National Low Income Housing Coalition. According to a June 1986 report by the General Accounting Office, much privately owned federally subsidized housing is nearing the end of its 20-year obligation to serve low-income renters. A million units—half the existing stock—may be lost by 1995. Without the old incentives, the units will lose their profitability, and massive displacement could result.

A last-minute amendment to the tax law pushed by Rep. Richard A. Gephardt (D-Mo.) may avert some of the expected defaults. Under the "transition rule" lobbied for by a coalition that included the American Planning Association, low-income investments made by August 16, 1986, will get eight more years of shelter. This rule, worth $500 million, is the biggest exception in the new tax code. "The exception was necessary to preserve existing housing and housing stock that is in the pipeline," Gephardt explained afterward. "With it, Congress showed its commitment to low-income housing. If that doesn't help enough, we'll go back and do more."

There is another roadblock in the way of low-income rental housing. The new tax code limits the states' powers to issue bonds. That means less money for city and state projects in 1987, when the bond cap (opposed by APA) will be $75 per capita, and still less in 1988, when the cap will be $50. As a result, low- and moderate-income rental housing must compete with all the other services citizens expect—roads, water and sewers, fire departments—as well as the convention centers and sports stadiums politicians crave.

"With states forced to cut the issuance of bonds by upwards of 80 percent in some instances, how will rental housing come out? Construction and rehabilitation would simply be far less attractive," Frank Shaforth, federal relations director for the National League of Cities, complained in *Nation's Cities Weekly.*

Not all are fearful, however. "Sure, the benefits here may not produce low-income housing, but that's no surprise; the old tax law didn't either," says Jack Kerry, a developer with Washington's Winn Company. "We're going to have to be creative to make it work."

Whatever their disagreements, interpreters of the tax code agree on one thing: It has made low-income housing a whole new ball game.

"In the past, tax-sheltered development was dominated by a few big corporate developers, whose investors had incomes above $250,000. They dealt in volume and predictability. Now the big guys have been chased off the playing field," says Sara Johnson of Telesis. Her firm is one of a new generation of small developers interested in combining social responsibility with profit.

Low-income housing advocates hope corporations and nonprofit organizations will pick up the slack. Low-income housing remains a potentially profitable investment for corporations, for they may continue to balance their "passive losses" against other gains. And nonprofits, with their social goals, are guaranteed 10 percent of every state's tax credit. Linking the will to the way will be the trick.

In general, all the indicators agree: The housing business is now state business. A new proposal before the U.S. Senate, the Evans-Durenberger bill (which APA is closely analyzing), would increase state and local responsibility for housing and community development and cut federal responsibility by $22 billion by 1994. The National Governors Association is urging states to accept the challenge of "full partner[ship] with the federal government and local governments in augmenting private-sector housing activities." The National Conference of State Legislatures is adding housing to its list of standing committees.

Post-federal age

Eastern states with an older housing stock—Massachusetts, New York, Connecticut—are the pioneers. Illinois with its new, 45-member Statewide Housing Action Coalition, is just moving into the field. Others are playing a full-court game—creating new models of state reliance for what may be housing's post-federal age.

Populous California is a model. It has long maintained the largest state-sponsored housing program in the nation and, since 1982, has had a comprehensive state housing program. The plan's linchpin: Local governments must plan housing for "all economic segments of the community."

To nudge plans into reality, the state provides dollar support. It helps lower rents through secondary financing and encourages self-help by funding nonprofit developers who organize building cooperatives. Funds come from tax-free mortgage revenue bonds, state grants and loans, and now the California Housing Trust Fund, set aside for low-income citizens.

Other parts of the plan are aimed at increasing the efficiency of scarce resources through high-density development and accessory apartments. "Despite the difficulty of keeping programs on track through changing political administrations, our program has made a difference. By making housing a unitary concern that local governments have had to address with the public and special interest groups, we've increased sensitivity as well as

our central ability to produce housing," says Christine Minnehan of the office of the California senate president pro tem.

A dozen states—and some innovative local governments—have housing trust funds on the books or under consideration. The *Wall Street Journal* estimates that $1.7 billion a year—enough to build 39,000 units or rehab 170,000—could be generated nationwide for trust funds from tenant security deposits, sales, and mortgage escrow interest alone. As state or local initiatives, the funds are independent of federal whim—an important status these days.

Trust fund capital comes from many sources: offshore oil production in California; interest on real estate escrow deposits in Maryland; real estate transfer taxes in Maine and Dade County, Florida; surplus cash from past bond issues in Kentucky. Some states, typically the smaller ones, use the funds to support housing purchases. Others subsidize low-income multifamily rental housing. Maine has used its housing fund to build four shelters for the homeless.

"Housing trust funds are a flexible model for creating permanent, annually renewable revenues for low-income housing construction, rehabilitation, and finance," says David Rosen, whose Oakland, California, firm promotes the trust fund idea.

Other promising innovations: In Kentucky, statewide nonprofit corporations provide technical assistance and development financing to community organizations all over the state. In Wisconsin, mutual housing associations and cooperatives are seeded with state matching grants. And a number of states—California, Colorado, Connecticut, Illinois, Indiana, New York, Massachusetts, South Carolina, and Utah among them—invest increasing amounts of their pension funds in banks that lower mortgage interest rates for first-time homebuyers.

Maryland mounted an ambitious housing program in 1986 despite federal cutbacks. The state's housing trust fund is expected to raise $1 million a year to support the Rental Housing Resource Corporation, a private nonprofit organization that develops and maintains low-income and special-need rental housing. The state also gives special attention to disabled citizens—the frail elderly, handicapped and developmentally disabled, abused children and spouses, and the homeless. Group homes and shelters are supported and housing subsidies provided for people who fall outside federal eligibility requirements. Additionally, home ownership gets a boost with a cooperative program under which local governments and nonprofits compete for a share of some $3 million in 7.75 percent mortgage money.

In New York, a state housing trust fund, which operates on a one-time grant of $25 million, has combined with other resources to provide $2.5 billion over five years, producing 50,000 housing units. Behind the construction are state-backed low-interest mortgages, variable-rate financing, interest-free construction loans, and—from the trust fund—infrastructure grants of $5,000 per unit. . . .

Grass roots

New ideas and designs abound in the private sector. Nonprofit corporations are putting money and thought into affordable housing. Developers are experimenting with mixes to meet special needs. And citizens are participating in housing decisions.

The Enterprise Social Investment Corporation of Columbia, Maryland, expects to be one of the first to try out the new tax credits, according to Helen Szablya. Founded by successful developer James Rouse, the corporation forms partnerships with nonprofit groups to develop housing for the poor.

The Enterprise Corporation currently has projects in 25 cities. For example, it helped a grass-roots group determine what steps were necessary to provide fit and livable housing for all the city's residents within a decade. On Enterprise's recommendations, Chattanooga Neighborhoods, Inc., has raised enough money for the first three years of the planned housing blitz. With 700 housing starts to its credit in 1986, Enterprise calculates that it can leverage every dollar it invests in a community with eight more dollars.

Housing partnerships also provide intangible benefits, as in downtown Seattle. Pricey new highrise offices, condos, and apartments have replaced much of the low-income housing and many of the people—population dropped from over 30,000 to about 12,000 between 1980 and 1983. But low- and middle-income tenants at Pike Place Market are holding tight to an island of affordability. The 87-unit Stewart House includes both rent-restricted units and market-rate single room occupancy units.

Seniors on fixed incomes, deinstitutionalized mental patients, and middle-income professionals are a self-governing community, says journalist Peggy Boyer, who last year paid $165 a month to the Pike Place Market Preservation and Development Authority for her single room (with bath down the hall).

Citizens are also pioneering tenant management in public housing. In 1976, HUD turned over the 18-acre, 25-year-old Comran Gardens near downtown St. Louis to the people who live there. Besides managing the 12-building project, a tenant board has hustled $42.5 million dollars for much-needed restoration.

"Connected as it is to development and the quality of life in communities, housing is a very important part of the planning process," says APA researcher Welford Sanders. "But planners probably have not been as effective in dealing with it as they could be. They may feel that once they have reviewed a new housing proposal for its consistency with their community's zoning ordinance, their responsibility has ended."

Yet for planners with social goals, housing remains a wide open field in which creative ideas abound. As the role of the federal government shrinks, states, local governments, citizens, and the "nonprofits"—foundations and special interest groups—take on even more responsibility.

But no matter how much states, local governments, nonprofits, and citizens can do—with planners' help—they cannot carry the whole weight of affordable, available housing for the nation. "We have to hope that what we're doing will eventually bubble up to the federal level, because that's the only source of resources big enough to deal with the critical state of housing," concludes Mary Nenno of the National Association of Housing and Redevelopment Officials. "At some point the federal government is going to have to come back in a bigger way."

Sandra Martin is a writer living in Dunkirk, Maryland.

Public Housing: A Status Report

(February 1985)

A CHEER FOR THE AGENCIES

Say the words "public housing" and even professional planners see images of Pruitt Igoe—the infamous St. Louis high-rise project that was demolished in the mid-1970s—and bureaucrats controlling empires of dilapidated residential real estate. Unfortunately, the popular image belies the creative activity that is going on in public housing programs around the country—programs that are correcting some of the problems that have traditionally plagued public housing developments.

One problem is the structure of public housing agencies. Although ostensibly independent public bodies, PHAs' institutional relationships with state and local governments, HUD, labor unions, and tenants' organizations preclude real autonomy. For instance, while PHAs can issue their own tax-exempt bonds, they are often hampered by local officials, fearful of an unsympathetic public response.

Further, PHAs' financing idiosyncracies, coupled with their rising expenses, have steadily increased their dependence on the federal government. Tenant participation in planning for modernization, required by HUD, creates another set of constraints. And in some PHAs, aggressive labor unions have taken advantage of bargaining opportunities, further reducing the agency's flexibility in the day-to-day management and maintenance of public housing developments.

Understanding such constraints helps us understand the environment in which PHAs must operate. Except perhaps for the homeless, public housing residents in large urban areas represent the population in greatest need of social support. And because of their social problems, public housing residents often make heavy demands on management. The public housing program is, after all, the only substantial aid program, other than direct welfare payments, that serves so poor a population. Most of the tenants are either elderly and living alone, or young mothers and their children. Their needs will not disappear.

Federal cutbacks in development, modernization, and operating subsidies and diminishing congressional support could easily demoralize public housing officials. Yet, despite these pressures, PHAs continue to search for new approaches. Here is a sampling from cities across the country.

Hartford, Connecticut. The city housing authority has employed an all-female construction crew to renovate 16 units in two of the buildings in its scattered-site program, which now includes 267 scattered-site units. Half of the construction workers are public housing residents; they are part of a program sponsored by foundations (Ford and Hartford Foundation for Public Giving); business (Hartford Insurance Group, Cigna Corporation, Connecticut Bank and Trust Company); labor (Greater Hartford Building and Construction Trades Council); and public agencies (Hartford's employment and training unit, Connecticut Commission on the Permanent Status of Women, Connecticut Department of Labor). The Hartford PHA is one of six participants in a national program called "Women's Ventures in Community Improvement."

New Haven, Connecticut. A technique more often applied to purely architectural problems, the charette, was used by the city's housing authority to garner support for the revitalization of a large, seriously deteriorated project called Elm Haven, which lies between the campus of Yale University and a subsidized high-tech industrial park near downtown. PHA director Linda Evans assembled a team of nine experts in December 1983 that included an architect, a site planner, a legal services attorney, a human services administrator, an educator, a development finance specialist, a housing planner, and a housing management expert. Its mission was to produce, in four days, a report outlining solutions to Elm Haven's persistent social, fiscal, design, and management problems.

Following up, the New Haven PHA garnered the necessary political support from local community leaders to form the Elm Haven Coalition, chaired by Mayor Biagio DiLieto. The coalition is now working on an action plan to present to HUD and other public and private funding sources. Its recommendations will include demolition of the project's six high rises; integration of the low-rise portion of the development with the surrounding street system; the use of scattered-site housing to replace the demolished units; reorganization of the

PHA's management and maintenance system; job training for tenants; and increased health, social service, and educational programs.

Springfield, Massachusetts. In 1980, the local housing authority received funding from the Massachusetts public housing program ("Chapter 705") to construct 22 units of scattered-site housing. It used the services of a local nonprofit organization, Springfield Inner City Rehab, Inc. (SICR), to plan the sites and buildings. SICR formed a Screening and Recommendation Committee that included neighborhood representatives and was successful in convincing state officials that kitchens should afford a view of play areas and that functional basement space was important.

Eleven duplex units were completed in 1982, and last year, the Springfield PHA received funding for 16 additional units.

Greensboro, North Carolina. This public housing authority, which adopted a scattered-site housing development policy in 1969, is known both for its excellent preventive maintenance program and for the design of its units. Each of the city's first three scattered-site developments has been planned to preserve the natural features of its hilly and wooded site and to harmonize with the surrounding neighborhood. Staggered rooflines, varied color schemes, and a variety of housing types eliminate the monotony that once characterized public housing. The three sites developed have 107, 39, and 11 units each. Four new approved sites are scheduled for 50 units each.

Pittsburgh. The public housing authority consciously fosters community spirit in neighborhoods where public housing developments are located. It works with tenant groups to promote food banks, job programs, and, in one case, a community learning center. The authority has built some 145 scattered-site units. The latest acquisition, a turnkey (developer-built) project called Renova/Sunnyside, includes 18 units tucked away on three different streets in the Hazelwood-Glenwood-Glen Hazel area of Pittsburgh.

San Diego. The San Diego Housing Commission is a partner in a creative joint venture with the California Housing Finance Authority and the Bank of America. In one development, the partners have leased land to a private developer for 55 years. Profits from the development are being used for a neighborhood park.

Cleveland. The Cuyahoga Metropolitan Housing Authority is planning to demolish 82 vacant public housing units and replace them with 25 new townhouses. Management and maintenance will be turned over to a community organization. Residents will also participate in construction—aided by funds from the federal Job Training Partnership Act.

Ruth Price
Price was formerly a housing development planner for the Housing Authority of the City of New Haven.

20 YEARS AFTER GAUTREAUX

Almost 20 years after a landmark suit was filed in Chicago in a 1966 case pitting a group of public housing residents against HUD and the Chicago Housing Authority, only 322 scattered-site units have been completed and occupied in the city. (The case is known as *Hills v. Gautreaux,* 425 U.S. 284 [1976].)

Yet housing agencies in 87 other cities have enthusiastically adopted the scattered-site approach to public housing.

The *Gautreaux* suit resulted in a 1969 federal court order, upheld by the Supreme Court in 1976, to end segregated public housing policies in Chicago; it was followed by orders in 1970, 1979, and 1982 that set specific goals for numbers of units—2,223 in all. The 1982 order specified that half of all new units were to be built or acquired in all-white areas while the rest could be located in "revitalizing" fringe areas.

Before *Gautreaux,* until 1975 in fact, all of Chicago's more than 30,000 public housing family units were located in all-black areas, and racial integration was a prime impetus for the local suit. But housing agencies in other cities had been moving toward scattered sites even before *Gautreaux,* according to a recent study for James Hogan, associate professor of political science at Seattle University in Washington, and Dorothy Lengyel, who oversaw the start-up of the Seattle Housing Authority's scattered-site program and is now a housing development specialist with the city's community development department.

Of the 333 metropolitan-area housing agencies in their survey, about a third had scattered-site programs. The typical program in their study consisted of 98 units on 15 sites and accounted for 9.5 percent of the authority's total number of subsidized housing units.

"The after-effects of the *Gautreaux* case gave the impression to other communities that the better part of wisdom would be to disperse housing opportunities for low-income people throughout the city," Hogan says.

One impetus was the 1968 Housing Act, which set a goal of deconcentration of public housing and changes in HUD allocations and regulations dealing with site decisions. HUD's experimental Area-wide Housing Opportunities Program (AHOP) further encouraged scattered-site programs, as did the increased availability of rehabilitation funds, which allowed public housing authorities to acquire and renovate single-family units outside of the central city core.

And, he adds, "by the late 1960s and early 1970s, the perception of planners, housing advocates, and housing specialists was that dense, concentrated public housing development projects were unsuccessful."

Whether to have scattered-site housing or not remains a local decision, under the terms of HUD's handbook. However, HUD has barred the construction of high-rise buildings for families since 1968 and, under the 1983 Housing Act, it now requires housing authorities to acquire existing housing unless they can prove that building new housing would be cheaper.

Last July, a suit similar to the *Gautreaux* suit, combined with the possible loss of $10 million in federal funds, forced Yonkers, New York, to select two sites for low-income housing in white neighborhoods.

The Hogan and Lengyel study gives a generally favorable picture of the scattered-site approach. Twenty-six percent of the officials surveyed reported that the overall public impression of scattered-site housing was very favorable, and 64 percent said it was favorable. Only eight percent said the public impression was unfavorable. Forty-six percent assessed their programs as very successful, and half said they were successful. Only three percent labeled them unsuccessful. Almost all said that future units would be scattered-site.

Community opposition was reported as the greatest problem by many of the agency directors. Lengyel herself notes that Seattle's scattered-site program encountered local opposition when it was initiated in 1978. The housing authority's response was to develop a formal citizen participation plan, which, Lengyel says, was effective in winning support. "We took our plans to each community group, and they worked with us through the design," she says. "We explained our budget constraints, although we did negotiate over density and siting. We didn't ask for variances or rezones. And we made a strong attempt to make sure our units looked like the rest of the community."

In all, some 240 sites (a total of 632 units) were located in 76 census tracts; thus community services were not overwhelmed, and tenants could easily integrate into the community, Lengyel says.

In Pittsburgh, one of several cities with scattered-site programs visited by Lengyel, and in Seattle, some maintenance chores have been assumed by residents, thus keeping a lid on costs, even though economies of scale have been eliminated. However, Seattle has still had to provide a satellite maintenance facility to serve its North End scattered units. And Tom Sheridan, director of HUD's Office of Public Housing, points out that higher administrative costs are typical of scattered-site developments.

The Chicago Housing Authority has had serious problems with both management and maintenance of its scattered-site units and has hired outside managers for half of them under a two-year experimental program, which Sheridan says HUD is following with interest. The experiment is also being monitored by Business and Professional People for the Public Interest (BPI), a group that has been associated with the *Gautreaux* case. Its director, Alexander Polikoff, filed the original suit while an American Civil Liberties Union attorney.

Polikoff still strongly supports the concept of scattered-site public housing, despite the Chicago Housing Authority's poor record. After building 11,200 high-rise units in the 1960s, it completed only 322 units during the past 15 years, with another 550 units under construction or rehabilitation or awaiting the start of rehabilitation.

"There had been incompetence within the CHA and no impetus from the mayor's office to get things done," Polikoff explains. "But now, after an awful lot of delay and misconduct, I think that for the first time the CHA has an administration in place that's capable of doing the job."

The bottom line for Polikoff is that scattered-site developments are far more suitable for low-income families than high rises. "You put 100 to 300 poverty-stricken families together in one building, as the critics of scattered-site argue, and to me, it's a prescription for disaster," he says.

Jerry DeMuth
DeMuth is an urban affairs writer in Chicago.

SCATTERED-SITE HOUSING
NO PANACEA

George Velez and his family live in a three-flat in the Humboldt Park neighborhood on Chicago's near west side. Velez, a truck driver, earns about $15,000 a year, and his wife brings in another $2,000 to $4,000. Until recently, when the Chicago Housing Authority bought their building as part of its scattered-site housing program, the Velezes had been paying George's brother-in-law $200 a month for the three-bedroom apartment they have occupied for five years. They love the neighborhood, which is largely Hispanic—their relatives all live nearby—and they are pleased with the local public school attended by their three children.

Today, the Velezes, who, because of their income level, are ineligible for the scattered-site program and face possible eviction. Their situation is one of the most egregious cases of a minority family being forced to move out of a unit acquired by the CHA to make way for another minority family, probably one with only a slightly lower income. There are many more such families. In fact, such displacement has been the rule rather than the exception in Chicago's scattered-site rehabilitation program.

In Chicago, unlike other cities, scattered-site housing has come to mean clusters of two to 12 units of either new or rehabilitated housing placed blocks, often miles, apart, and primarily designed to carry out the racial integration mandate of the *Gautreaux* decision and avoid the ills of huge institutional projects such as the Robert Taylor Homes. Since 1955, the *Gautreaux* lawyers charged in federal court, the CHA had refused to build in white, or even mixed, areas, but continued to build high-rise family projects in all-black areas—a practice that segregated the city as much or more than private housing policies had done earlier. Not only were low-income blacks excluded from white areas, but whites were effectively blocked from access to public housing. The *Gautreaux* plaintiffs charged the CHA with racial discrimination in its selection of sites and of tenants and in its management policies.

The federal district court decided in favor of the plaintiffs, but its "remedies" plus the inaction of the CHA, instead of providing additional low-rent housing for both blacks and whites, had the unintended effect of halting any further public housing for 15 years. By specifying that developments could have no more than 120 residents, the decision severely limited project size. And by allowing children only on the first three floors of a building, it effectively ruled out high rises for families.

The prime concern of the *Gautreaux* lawyers was to ensure racial integration. They were concerned only secondarily with the original objectives of the national housing acts—to clear slums, house low- and moderate-income families, revitalize the building industry, and aid in the rebuilding of city neighborhoods.

Generally, the target of the decision was the city of Chicago and the local public housing authority. However, during the past decade, HUD has adapted its general regulations to the restrictions of the *Gautreaux* decision, which has resulted in a national emphasis on scattered-site housing of the same Lilliputian variety. Even so, only some 10,000 to 13,000 units have been built nationwide, representing less than one percent of all public housing.

The dominant perception on the part of the CHA has come to be that scattered-site housing is not only one answer, but the *only* answer, to public housing needs. Yet a survey my colleagues and I conducted last year leads me to a different conclusion.

We studied 630 scattered units either built, acquired, or proposed by the CHA, and in them we found serious problems in siting, construction, and maintenance.

The neighborhoods chosen for the scattered sites in Chicago have been, by and large, areas where blacks and/or Hispanics already predominated or areas undergoing a population transition. Deteriorating buildings are the rule. One resident told us: "This neighborhood has changed so much that a few more changes can't make any difference." Another said, "I don't see the great need for CHA to bring in low-income black families, since they're already on the next block in conventional housing." CHA planners have made no serious attempts to coordinate with the city planning for these areas or to consider the potential for stimulating neighborhood revival. Instead, they simply scan current real estate listings and choose the better, if not the best, buildings in the selected neighborhoods. The dominating, if not the sole, idea seems to be to find sites that can be bought or built without neighborhood opposition.

One useful function of a housing authority, points out Paul Roldan, an executive of the Hispanic Housing Development Corporation, is to pick out deteriorated buildings in blocks with a good prognosis and help the areas along by renovation. In contrast, buildings bought for rehab by the CHA are often the neighborhood's best buildings—buildings that were doing just fine as private property and should have been left on the tax rolls.

A primary reason for *Gautreaux* was that public housing was mostly confined to the worst slums. In far too many cases, scattered sites have not changed this situation. Units are still likely to be built or bought in highly deteriorated areas like Chicago's Uptown, Englewood, or Woodlawn. In addition, the specific sites chosen are frequently uninspiring in exactly the same way public housing sites have always been uninspiring; they're next to a rail line, for instance, or in a heavily industrialized area, shoehorned between two deteriorated three-flats, or surrounded by vacant lots and boarded-up buildings. In a number of cases, buildings have been acquired and then left unfinished and unoccupied for two or more years.

Maintenance becomes much more difficult and more costly when relatively few units are dispersed in a vast area. Many of the tenants we surveyed in Chicago expressed dissatisfaction with the slowness of the CHA's response to maintenance requests. And considering the short time they have been in existence, the scattered-site units in Chicago are hardly in tip-top shape. Mailboxes are often in disrepair, vestibules and stairhalls are dirty, and landscaping is rudimentary at best. Often, maintenance standards dropped drastically when CHA took over an existing building. In the view of the professional management firms we talked to, scattered-sites are simply an inefficient method of operation. . . .

Even cities that are touted as scattered-site successes report problems. For example, Fred Lamont, executive director of the Seattle Housing Authority, which operates 600 scattered-site units, complains that the units are particularly expensive to construct and to maintain. He points out that maintenance men spend 40 percent of their time traveling from site to site.

"I really see little point to the whole scattered-site program for our city," he told me.

Alternatives

Where scattered-site housing has worked, it has been in larger agglomerations than the two to 12 units that resulted from the *Gautreaux* decision. According to public housing director John Tatum, Philadelphia has, for the most part, rejected the two-to-12-unit scattered-site concept in favor of 300-unit, racially integrated family developments in essentially white areas. Greensboro, North Carolina, which has an extensive scattered-site program, has also stuck to larger projects—in this case slightly under 50 units. Public housing director Elaine Ostrowsky says most of the projects are racially integrated and well accepted by the neighborhoods in which they have been placed—suggesting again that the *Gautreaux* principle is not only overly cautious, but also counterproductive.

New York City, long a leader in public housing, continues to scatter developments throughout the city. But "scattered-site," in New York's definition, means a minimum of 40 units, and most projects are much larger. One successful example is the Forest Hills Housing Cooperative, the 400-plus unit project built by the city housing authority after a bitter fight in which Mario Cuomo made an early mark as a mediator for then-mayor John Lindsay.

And in Chicago, in the 1950s, very successful 150- to 250-unit developments were built by the CHA as part of state and city public housing programs. Some of these projects won architectural awards, and they provided outstanding living for low-income citizens.

Also in Chicago—and all over the country—private developers have made good use of subsidies authorized by sections 223, 236, and 8 of the U.S. housing acts. In Chicago alone, private builders have provided some 33,000 low- and moderate-income units since 1968, most in 50- to 300-unit developments. Most are in satisfactory condition, and most are racially integrated. According to Elizabeth Warren of Loyola University, chronicler of Chicago's public housing, they have served about 20,000 black families, many more than were served as a result of the *Gautreaux* decision. The HUD-subsidized homeownership programs known as Section 235 and homesteading were equally successful—before much of their funding was withdrawn.

By substituting public ownership for private—when it buys existing housing—the scattered-site program dislocates the very people it is supposed to serve and costs taxpayers some half-million dollars in property taxes annually.

Thus, after 17 years of legal bickering, the widely hailed *Gautreaux* decision has produced few benefits and has in no way helped the neighborhoods in which the units have been placed.

J.S. Fuerst

Fuerst teaches social welfare policy in the Loyola University School of Social Work in Chicago. He is a former research director for the Chicago Housing Authority (1945–53).

Is Public Housing on Its Last Legs?

Stanley Ziemba
(September 1988)

Anyone who even occasionally reads a newspaper or listens to the news on radio or television is aware by now that much of this country's public housing system is in shambles. Conceived more than 50 years ago as a means of providing poor but upwardly mobile families with temporary, decent, low-rent living quarters, America's public housing projects, especially those in the largest cities, have evolved, instead, into a home for a permanent underclass of nearly four million people.

Public housing has burgeoned over the last five decades into some 1.3 million apartment units nationally, many of them contained in aging, poorly maintained, and densely populated developments. In too many cities, public housing has become the embodiment of virtually all the ills that plague urban America: broken families, poverty, unemployment, crime, racial and economic segregation, and deteriorating housing.

Chicago's public housing program, the nation's second largest, houses nearly 37,000 poor families, 70 percent of them headed by women. Ninety-five percent of the families are black and almost all subsist on some form of public welfare assistance or social security benefit.

Crime within Chicago's housing projects is significantly higher than in the surrounding city. Public housing residents make up about 4.5 percent of the city's population of three million. Yet 9.1 percent of all the homicides in the city, 8.3 percent of the rapes, and 8.6 percent of the aggravated assaults occur on Chicago Housing Authority property, according to a recent report by the Metropolitan Planning Council, a civic organization that conducts studies on urban issues.

Meanwhile, the deterioration of the authority's family housing stock—1,262 buildings, including 168 high rises—has reached epidemic proportions. Because of overcrowding, a lack of funds, and poor maintenance by the authority, several structures are virtually unlivable.

In fact, one-sixth of the housing authority's apartments—more than 6,000 units—are so deteriorated that they lie vacant despite a waiting list of 40,000 people in need of public housing units. "The problem is critical," says Vincent Lane, the CHA's executive director and board chairman since June. "It's like a cancer eating away."

CHA officials estimate that it would cost $1 billion to bring all of its residential buildings up to minimum standards. That's almost one-fifth of the funds that the federal government currently provides annually for repairs and operating subsidies to housing authorities nationwide.

To someone living in a small city or town where public housing is generally well run, or to someone familiar with the Chicago Housing Authority's long history of mismanagement—which nearly resulted in a federal takeover of the agency last year—the CHA's maintenance woes may seem atypical. However, the problem in some other large cities is even worse.

In Detroit and Providence, Rhode Island, it's estimated that roughly one-fourth of the public housing units are vacant. In Washington, D.C., some buildings have been completely abandoned or torn down because repairing them would be too expensive.

The U.S. Department of Housing and Urban Development estimates that about 70,000 public housing units currently are boarded up and that about 1,000 units are being demolished each year nationwide. And even in cities where the deterioration of the public housing stock has not yet become severe, housing administrators are concerned about their ability to maintain buildings in light of the lack of funds for repairs. The Council of Large Public Housing Authorities, a Boston-based organization representing some three dozen of the country's largest public housing agencies, estimates that $18 billion to $20 billion is needed to bring public housing nationwide up to snuff.

Can the system be saved?

Many public housing officials contend that the Reagan administration's budget cutters have already dealt the program, if not a mortal blow, at least a crippling punch. Over the last eight years, funding for day-to-day public housing operations, rehabilitation, and new construction has declined 80 percent to $7 billion in fiscal 1988 from $35 billion in 1980. It's obvious, says Robert McKay, executive director of the Council of Large Public Housing Authorities, that President Reagan's intent was to get rid of the program. The cuts, he said, "really put our backs up against the wall."

Federal housing officials, however, have repeatedly denied that the Reagan administration has attempted to get the federal government out of the business of housing the poor. The decision to reduce funding for public housing was justified in light of the program's poor track record prior to Reagan's presidency, they say. The alternative adopted by the administration turned out to be a housing voucher program, by which low-income families seek out an apartment in the private market and pay 30 percent of their annual income in rent.

Public housing advocates point out, however, that the voucher system, while perhaps a good idea on paper, in reality does little to meet the housing needs of very poor people, for whom conventional public housing was meant in the first place. What good is a voucher to a welfare mother with three or more children in a private rental market that, for the most part, refuses to rent apartments to large families, rich or poor, the housing advocates ask.

Despite the severe funding cutbacks and its myriad problems, most public housing administrators insist that the nation's public housing system remains salvageable. It must be saved, says McKay of the public housing council: "It's the only national housing program left that's available for the poor. To tear it all down and put some four million people out on the street would be unthinkable."

Moreover, it's estimated that the total value of the nation's existing public housing buildings is $75 billion to $85 billion. Demolishing them all is not likely to set well with the taxpaying public.

What should be demolished, almost everyone agrees, are the high-rise public housing projects. In Chicago, where almost half of the city's public housing units are contained in high-rise structures, a mayoral advisory council recently recommended the gradual demolition of most, if not all, of the city's high-rise public housing buildings.

In an unusually candid report, the advisory group of business leaders, civic officials, and private developers noted that "high-rise [public housing] buildings per se are not a problem. Rather, the problem is the intense concentration of large, poor, primarily single-parent families in buildings poorly designed to support their needs. This is further compounded by the concentration of such buildings in close proximity to each other while being racially and economically segregated and isolated from viable neighborhoods."

The advisory group concluded that it would cost the city's housing authority between $20 million and $48 million to replace about 800 high-rise units a year with new or rehabilitated low-rise public housing units, but argued that it would be cheaper than trying to rehabilitate many of the high rises. Part of the funds needed for replacement housing could be realized through the sale of CHA properties to private developers, the group added.

In Chicago, as in many cities, high-rise public housing complexes are located near or within neighborhoods undergoing revitalization. Consequently, private real estate developers undoubtedly would welcome the opportunity to bid on the land under several existing projects, if not on the buildings themselves.

Just recently, a highly successful, long-time Chicago developer publicly requested the CHA's permission to demolish six high-rise public housing buildings on Chicago's South Side lakefront to make way for a complex of economically mixed low-rise housing units. The project was put on hold in August, when the CHA announced plans to renovate two of the buildings, at a cost of $14 million.

"There is nothing sacrosanct about keeping high-rise buildings standing," the Chicago Urban League stated in a July report endorsing the idea of replacing CHA family high rises with low-rise units on scattered sites throughout the city. The notion of tearing down or selling off buildings "is not radical but virtually conservative," given decades of evidence that the buildings fail to provide a decent living environment, the league added.

However, it's unlikely that the sale of high-rise public housing projects in Chicago or elsewhere would generate sufficient funds to provide all the new public housing apartments that would have to be built to replace the high-rise units. Moreover, once new low-rise units were built, a continuous source of money would be needed to maintain them.

In addition, new sources of funding are needed now to upgrade existing low-rise projects, which make up the bulk of the nation's public housing stock, and which, unlike the high rises, are generally in good condition and harbor fewer social problems. Also, a source of revenue is needed to provide at least basic repairs for the high-rise complexes until they can be gradually replaced.

"What it all boils down to is that the federal government needs to set up a capital improvement fund for public housing, a set-aside of $1 billion to $1.5 billion annually for maintaining and eventually replacing the existing stock of public housing units," McKay says. His proposal is similar to the proposed National Housing Trust Fund for the repair and replacement of low-income housing that is currently being advocated by the U.S. Conference of Mayors.

The decision on any new funding vehicles, and on the future of the nation's public housing program in general, however, rests with the new administration and legislators that will be coming to Washington in January. Planners, local political decision makers, and public housing advocates have until then to impress on the current presidential contenders and congressional candidates the importance of maintaining and upgrading the nation's public housing program, not only for the sake of the poor who have no other housing alternatives, but also for the continued viability of our cities.

Stanley Ziemba is a reporter for the Chicago Tribune.

5

Special Places

"He is no true town planner . . . who sees only the similarity of cities." Cities in Evolution, *Patrick Geddes, 1915*
To be "special" implies that a place exhibits at least one unique characteristic or attribute—a geographic or topographical condition, for example, or an economic, political, or sociological circumstance. In a list of such places in American cities, few would fail to include New York's incredible site on Manhattan Island, bounded on the west by the sheer rock cliffs of the Hudson River Palisades, or San Francisco's incomparable site on the bay, or the immense geometry of L'Enfant's Washington, or the Paseo del Rio in San Antonio, or the fine-grained mixture of townhouses and squares in Savannah. Perhaps we might also add the devastation of the South Bronx.

Uniqueness probably exists far more in theory than in practice, however. In reviewing a number of 701 plans in the early 1960s, I was particularly impressed by the products of one well-known consultant. In the introductory material to each plan, he noted that every city was a "unique challenge, requiring a custom-designed response." Those same words appeared in every plan by the consultant; only the name of the city was changed (except in the plan for one Ohio city where the firm slipped, failing to remove the name of the last city for which it had worked).

The message in that is clear: Although we may be tempted from time to time to look for the unusual, most often we fall back on what we know, or suspect, worked elsewhere, thus contributing to the homogenization of America. But some special circumstances just can't be ignored. How, for instance, does a community ignore losing more than a quarter of its population and the abandonment of one-quarter of its housing stock as residents flee to the suburbs (as in Cleveland)?

Special in another way is Chicago, a city with particular meaning to American planners. Here, on

July 4, 1909, Daniel Burnham unveiled the nation's first metropolitan plan, the plan that gave the Chicago region its extensive park system, and wide roadways. But by the mid-1980s, Chicago's earlier leadership in planning was scarcely remembered, and the city seemed once again more than ready for, and in dire need of, reform. As neighborhood groups squared off against the downtown business interests, the climate for planning in America's "Second City" was being carefully monitored (see John McCarron's article) as a bell-weather for planning in older cities throughout the country.

Pittsburgh has been special to planners since the first decade of this century, when the Russell Sage Foundation selected it as the site for the first systematic statistical city survey. How well has "Steel City, U.S.A." weathered the demise of the American steel industry? Pittsburgh lost 30 percent of its population in three decades, and the last of its blast furnaces came down in 1983. Ruth Eckdish Knack describes what can happen when a city loses its reason for being.

Houston has always been somewhat special in American planning circles, if for no other reason than constant reference to it by antiplanning conservatives: "If Houston doesn't need planning and zoning, then neither do we!" Well, there are planners in Houston (as James Peters notes). But, lacking the zoning power, how well have they dealt with the city's problems during a period of economic slow-down? (One way, it turns out, is by imposing some 10,000 private deed restrictions enforced by more than 600 civic clubs.)

Austin, Texas, was the fastest growing major metropolitan area in the country in the early 1980s. To constrain skyrocketing growth, a long-term plan for land conservation was established for the land most hungrily eyed by developers. Proponents of managed growth nationwide carefully watched Austin's efforts. They also kept an eye on

San Diego, which set aside an area of over 20,000 acres for future urban growth, while concentrating on redevelopment of the city center. The question in both places: How well does managed growth co-exist with the forces that stimulate growth? (See the stories by Kaye Northcott and George Colburn.)

Seattle has always been special, with its magnificent site on Puget Sound and a reputation for both planning innovation and leadership. In October 1974, the city created an office of policy planning that was the envy of planners throughout the country. This office, which cut across all the departments of city government, had direct lines to political power through the office of the mayor. At last, in one city at least, the American planner would have political clout. But, as Jane Hadley reports, that direct line ran both ways, not only planners-to-political-power, but also political-power-to-planners. Did the political experiment in Seattle empower comprehensive planners, or did it make comprehensive planning an exercise in executive politics?

Politics is also the issue in Charles Whiting's article on the Twin Cities Metropolitan Council, generally acclaimed as the nation's most innovative and effective metropolitan regional organization. It, too, is special for planners.

Los Angeles is a special city in spite of itself. Lacking a recognizable city center and boasting a freeway system conducive to widespread urban sprawl, there is little that is public about the "City of the Angels." It has long had a reputation as heaven for real estate speculators and hell for public administrators. William Fulton tells how public-interest-focused planners operate in a society dominated by private interests, where political authority is fragmented in a multitude of neighborhoods and in the 80-odd cities within Los Angeles County.

Nearby Irvine presented a different sort of challenge, the opportunity to plan an urbanizing area that is three times as large as San Francisco. That challenge, described by Gladwin Hill, would appear to have been met with less than optimal fulfillment of its potential.

Until the early 1950s, Baltimore was considered special in a negative sense—as its Inner Harbor area was a hodgepodge of abandoned industries and warehouses. In the 1980s, Baltimore's Inner Harbor became a symbol of creative urban rebirth, lending vitality and beauty to the once-written-off-as-hopeless city center. As David Wallace notes, Baltimore was made a special place by diligent effort and by a creative imagination that enabled key players to see the city's potential beneath the grime.

History puts some cities on the list of special places. Kansas City is one such place, thanks to George Kessler's metro parks plan of 1893 and the contributions of J.C. Nichols at Country Club Plaza. Another is Cincinnati, the birthplace of modern comprehensive planning in the 1920s.

John Herbers's report on the New Jersey shore of the Hudson River raises other issues. Although a scant few hundred feet west of Manhattan Island, the old river towns were thought of, if at all, as a jumble of decaying freight terminals and rotting piers. But this problem area became an opportunist's paradise, and today high-rise offices and apartment towers rise out of the flotsam of the Hudson, making the river's western edge no longer a boundary but a centerpiece for the New York cosmopolitan center.

SMALL SCALE

Small communities sometimes become special by virtue of the relative scale of the challenges they face and by their creativity in the face of catastrophes that their limited municipal and human resources are asked to address. Babbitt, Minnesota, was built by the Reserve Mining Company in 1951. Thirty years later the firm closed, leaving the town with an 85 percent unemployment rate and loss of one-third of its population. Jim Schwab describes what happens under special conditions that one hopes never to have to confront, let alone plan for.

Yet another small community offers us a case study of populism in action. Santa Monica, California, described by Bill Fulton, installed a "progressive" city council in 1981. Planning was the centerpiece of this administration, which addressed itself to affordable housing, controlling the influx of large new office buildings, increased citizen participation, tenant ownership programs, and rent control. Santa Monica spearheaded a national movement to gain exactions from developers seeking the right to profit by land development.

Many foreign visitors comment on how similar American cities are. Is this the product of a homogeneous society, instant nationwide communications, and a materialistic culture, or of a lack of

Baltimore's massive waterfront urban renewal project, begun in the early 1960s, set the style for similar efforts in other cities. See ''An Insider's View of the Inner Harbor.'' Photo: Raquel Lavin.

In the mid-1980s, managed growth became a hot topic in the nation's eighth largest city. Voters decided the ''urban reserve'' in the northern part of the city should remain undeveloped until the 1990s. See ''San Diego: Beyond Spit and Polish.'' Photo: Robert Burroughs.

In the early 1980s, Santa Monica was awash in innovative ideas—most of them putting limits on property owners. The Paseo del Mar on Ocean Avenue (left) was negotiated down from a nine-story office building to a three-story complex of offices and shops. See "On the Beach With the Progressives." Photo: Victoria Torf Fulton.

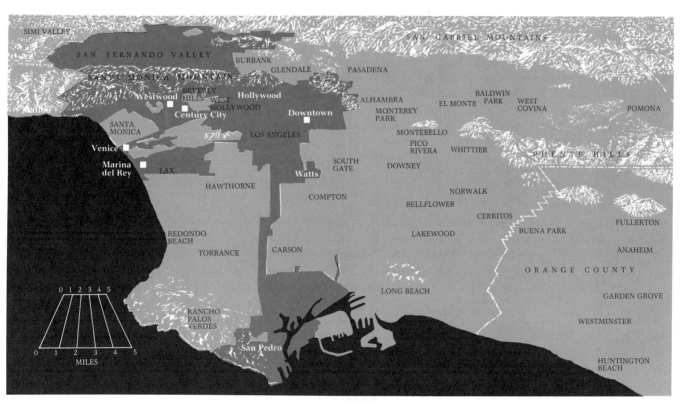

The Los Angeles metropolitan area, second largest in the nation after New York, is a pastiche of low-density communities connected by freeways. Simon Rodia's Watts Towers (right) are a symbol of the city's individuality. See "Los Angeles: Prime Time." Map: Dennis McClendon; photo: Los Angeles Department of City Planning.

Admired from afar, sometimes maligned at home, the nation's most innovative regional authority is at a crossroads. See ''Twin Cities Metro Council: Heading for a Fall?'' Map: Dennis McClendon.

Minnesota

ANOKA

WASHINGTON

HENNEPIN

RAMSEY

Lake Minnetonka

St. Louis Park

Minne-apolis

St. Paul

St. Croix River

CARVER

Minnesota River

Bloomington

Grey Cloud Island

Mississippi River

SCOTT

DAKOTA

Well known for its laissez faire approach to development, the nation's fourth largest city is beginning to rethink its methods. Above, a view of the city's downtown skyline from a near west side neighborhood. See ''Houston Gets Religion.'' Photo: James Peters.

San Antonio's Paseo del Rio presents many charming vistas. This masterpiece of design has inspired communities across the nation. See ''Sons of Riverwalk.'' Photo: The Waterfront Center.

A depressed farm economy and industrial decline have taken their toll in the Midwest, but a few places like Babbitt, Minnesota, have launched a comeback. See ''Small Towns, Big Dreams.'' Photo: *Babbitt Weekly News.*

Two Chicago legacies: 26 miles of public parkland along Lake Michigan—and machine politics. See ''Is Chicago Ready for Reform?''
Photo: Richard Sessions.

Before the Texas economy went bust in the late 1980s, high tech drew thousands to the state capital. See ''Austin: The Perils of Popularity.''
Photo: Dennis McClendon.

imagination that draws everything down to the lowest common denominator? We praise individualism, but fail to act as individuals. We deny the totalitarian imposition of limited choice, yet, in our freedom, we limit ourselves to narrow choices. We tout our freedoms to the world, yet choose not to act on them. Every place should be a "special place," optimizing its unique characteristics and potentials. We crave it on vacations elsewhere; we seek it in selecting colleges for our youth; we cross oceans to experience it in other countries. Yet we fail to recognize specialness and to preserve it when it is in our own backyard.

When all things are the same, there is no freedom of choice. A major role for planning must be to expand opportunities in a world where options are increasingly being closed. When diversity is threatened, it becomes society's job to restore it, to offer a wider array of choices, a greater variety of environments and life styles. In our rush to get individually wealthy, Americans get communally poorer each day. Is it so difficult to walk to a different drummer? To forsake the safe and sorry for the untested and the exciting? The death of civilizations lies not in the clash of barbarian hordes but in the numbness of the human spirit, in the grayness of human lives. In each of the selections that follow something special is recognized: a special opportunity, a special challenge, an out-of-the-ordinary condition or response. We are the richer for them.

Laurence C. Gerckens, AICP
Professor Emeritus, Ohio State University
President, On-Call Faculty Program

An Insider's Story of the Inner Harbor

David A. Wallace
(September 1979)

When Gerald Johnson said, "Baltimore might make it" in the *New Republic* in 1966, his emphasis was on *might*. To allow even that much was a major concession to optimism for Johnson and other native Baltimoreans, whose skeptical response to city plans has always been, "It won't happen in my lifetime." No more!

Today Baltimore clearly *has* made it, and the Inner Harbor is the centerpiece of the city's renaissance—a renaissance that fully meets historian Arnold Toynbee's theory of challenge and response, on which Gerald Johnson cautiously rested his supporting argument.

The success of city plans in general (and Baltimore's in particular) can be measured partly by comparing the outcome with how bad things were before. But the measurement is only partial, for in the long run plans must be judged by the quality of the new environment they create and by their impact on people. Who cares today about what a terrible place the Inner Harbor was a short 15 years ago? It was ringed with noisy traffic, the water was polluted and inaccessible, the decayed piers were used only for overspill parking from the CBD. The Inner Harbor in fact had been abandoned by port planners as being too small to have a major role in the region's maritime future, and it was surrounded by obsolete and deteriorated buildings.

All that was true in 1963, when a civic leader named Abel Wolman returned from Europe with glowing tales of Stockholm's harbor. Wolman advised Mayor Theodore R. McKeldin that, with Charles Center already a demonstrable success (the credit having gone to McKeldin's predecessor, Thomas D'Alessandro, Jr.), with the downtown emerging as a focus of investment interest, and with engineering for the perennially delayed Jones Falls Expressway supposedly well along, it was high time the mayor set in motion plans for the neglected harbor as the next step in downtown revitalization. At the urging of William Boucher III, executive director of the Greater Baltimore Committee (GBC), McKeldin reassembled D'Alessandro's winning Charles Center partnership with GBC to raise the funds. Wolman is reported to have suggested, "Get that young fellow who did Charles Center back down here from Philadelphia to do the Inner Harbor." Enter your humble servant and his design partner, Thomas A. Todd.

The Inner Harbor had had its share of plans but none had clicked. Arthur McVoy, head of D'Alessandro's planning department, had done a concept plan in 1956. A year later, Pietro Belluschi did a plan for GBC in an unsuccessful attempt to prevent D'Alessandro from putting the Civic Center in Druid Hill Park. Fortunately for both the park and the harbor, D'Alessandro ultimately agreed to have the Civic Center put next to Charles Center; however, while GBC was still enraged, Bill Boucher got the mayor to designate the entire MetroCenter a redevelopment area as a gesture of appeasement. The gesture cost the mayor nothing and was a lucky move because it obviated argument and extra steps when Charles Center, the Inner Harbor, and half a dozen other MetroCenter projects later surfaced as urban renewal plans.

The Charles Center urban renewal project had just been adopted in 1959 when Baltimore's benchmark CBD plan was published. The CBD plan wisely chose to mark the Inner Harbor as an area that needed further study, keeping the city's and investors' eyes focused on Charles Center. The temptation to follow McVoy's example with "wouldn't-it-be-nice-if" sketches for the harbor was hard to resist, but we knew the harbor's time was not yet ripe. In fact, it was not ripe for another four years.

Practical cats

At least three things made Tom Todd's 1964 Inner Harbor master plan different from earlier efforts: the fundamentally solid economics it was based on (skeptics' arguments to the contrary); the readiness of success-hungry city and federal programs to back a clear winner; and Todd's elegantly persuasive urban design and conceptual graphics.

The major design decisions made in 1964 have largely stood the test of time. They include the nature and location of the harbor's edge, Constellation Pier and the West Promenade as a pedestrian extension of Calvert Street; a major tower to anchor the harbor's northwest corner (which turned out to be the U.S. Fidelity and Guaranty Building); the World Trade Center, with its "prow" symbolically in the water; buildings on the piers (e.g., the aquarium) designed as "objects-in-space"; and the harbor's frame defined by the more or less continuous cornice lines of the surrounding facades. The McCormick spice factory on the west suggested the height limit—a principle that has sometimes been abandoned as market pressures have mounted. But by and large these principles of urban design were public policy and guided development throughout.

Adoption as policy was one thing, but implementation was another. Implementation depended, finally, on broad civic and business support and on

a lucky stroke of funding. Tom and I remember a key meeting of the client group at which James W. Rouse played the crucial role, as he had in the earlier Charles Center days. He admitted that he was skeptical about the numbers, but then he said, "Gentlemen, we must not fail to do this!" Heads nodded and belief in the plan spread like wildfire.

At that point, as luck would have it, the voters rejected a bond issue for construction funds for a new police administration building, and the money for site acquisition was available for diversion to the Inner Harbor. We shortly translated the central portion of Tom's master plan into an urban renewal plan for Project I, and the Inner Harbor was off and running. That happened in the summer of 1967.

Jim Rouse had good reason to be leery of our numbers. The front-end public investment of $29 million that would be needed to rebuild the harbor's edge, acquire property, and clear land was formidable. The size of the site that was assembled would have challenged the market absorption rate of much larger metropolitan areas. Nevertheless, Project I received a sizable federal grant, and a mixture of public and private development was well under way by 1971.

Project I dealt only with the one-block deep area along the harbor's edge, however. Money was tight, and HUD Secretary Robert C. Weaver had given priority for residential project grants to cities that would promise that at least 51 percent of the units would be for moderate- or low-income families.

In our 1964 Inner Harbor master plan, we had run out of short-range market potential long before we got to what is now Inner Harbor West (Project II). So we had just colored Inner Harbor West yellow for residential. Luckily, Edgar M. Ewing recognized that this situation and his relation to Weaver provided a rare opportunity for action.

Edgar who?

Edgar Ewing had worked for Baltimore's Department of Housing and Community Development, its predecessor BURHA, and BURHA's predecessor, the Redevelopment Authority, for many years. Most recently, he had been head of Baltimore's public housing program. A black civic leader and a friend of Weaver's, Ewing saw the chance to make Inner Harbor West a racially and economically integrated community. He felt that, if integration could be made successful anywhere, it could be done here because of the inherent attractiveness of the location. Also, since nobody lived in the Inner Harbor, the site did not start with the detriment of being somebody's turf. Inner Harbor West would be the capstone of Ewing's career.

The city and the Charles Center-Inner Harbor Management (CC-IH) (created first to carry out Charles Center, with responsibilities later expanded to include the Inner Harbor) somewhat reluctantly agreed to the preparation of an urban renewal plan, without any commitment to fund it. But they hadn't taken Edgar Ewing into account.

Ewing held a lot of chits at HUD. He had done many favors for Weaver and for Lawrence M. Cox, Weaver's assistant secretary, such as the thankless chairing of the Pruitt-Igoe [St. Louis] Housing Study Committee. With Weaver's blessing, Ewing showed our illustrated urban renewal plan to Cox, whose reaction was, "That's the best project Baltimore's got. Why doesn't the city submit it?"

Ewing explained that the housing and development commissioner at the time, Robert W. Embry, and the city had allocated all the available funds to other neighborhoods and had no intention of applying. Cox's response was to tell Ewing to keep the grant requirement below $19 million and submit the urban renewal plan two weeks before the end of the fiscal year; he'd get the money. Ewing did submit the plan, and he got the grant. Cox left HUD ten days later.

Embry and the city were fit to be tied, but what could they do? They had a project. Tragically, Edgar Ewing did not live to see the Garmatz Federal Building, the convention center, homestead housing, the Equitable Building, and Louis Sauer's Inner Harbor Village (now starting construction)—all in Ewing's project. It didn't turn out quite as Ewing had envisioned it, but it's not a bad memorial.

Edgar Ewing's opportunity, a lucky break for the Inner Harbor, made possible a much broader and more comprehensive development than otherwise could have occurred. The recently announced proposals for reuse of the Chesapeake & Ohio/Baltimore & Ohio railroad yards are testimonials to Ewing. But the harbor would not have had such impact had it not been for a series of fortuitous events related to transportation.

Try as we would, the 1964 planning effort could not shake the expressway engineers from their bulldog grip on the harbor. Public pressure in favor of the concept of housing on the piers forced the interchange out of the harbor itself, but it was not until five years had passed and $3 million had been spent that the Skidmore, Owings and Merrill design concept team was able to persuade everyone that the low-level Inner Harbor bridge would have to be 16 lanes wide and wouldn't work anyway. The bridge became patently impossible and fell of its own weight, so to speak.

With the expressway diverted by SOM to the south and no low-level bridge, the U.S.F. *Constellation* could be stationed in the harbor (and moved in and out for repairs), the playing fields in front of Federal Hill and the old houses in the homesteading area no longer would be part of a highway acquisition alignment, access to MetroCenter could be achieved via an expressway spur with a carefully designed touchdown at Pratt Street, and most of the truck traffic could bypass the harbor entirely. The Inner Harbor was freed at last.

The transportation planning included the Pratt Street Boulevard, another essential element of the 1964 master plan that Edgar Ewing's stroke of luck made possible. Originated by David W. Barton, City Planning Commission chairman at the time, the idea of the boulevard was often in jeopardy in the early days. The boulevard was intended as an integrating concept, to link the western part of the CBD to the harbor and to give definition to the CBD's southern boundary. Only a few blocks of it were located in the first project area. Without Project II to extend it, the boulevard would not have been long enough to be effective. This is a design idea that has finally proven tremendously effective. Thank you, Dave Barton!

Rouse, Boucher, Barton, and Ewing all had an important influence in the early planning; but, as the proverb says, success has a thousand fathers, and so does the Inner Harbor. My partner, Tom Todd, has been the guiding design force, both behind the overall urban design and at the intimate scale of *where* you walk, *what* you see, and *what* you walk and sit on: the promenade, Constellation Pier, the marinas, the bulkhead, and (now in process) the environment surrounding Harborplace. Decisions such as the marvelous simplicity of the stage that has been set for the harbor's activity, on down to the choice of brick as the rich, primary material, are evidence of careful and restrained design in the face of frequent pressure for overdesign. The seamen from the Tall Ships in the 1976 Bicentennial said Baltimore's was the best harbor of all.

But who could have predicted the aquarium (Embry's idea), or the proposed recycling of the old Gas and Electric Company's steam plant? And Rouse's Harborplace, although conceived by us as part of the 1967 urban renewal plan, in shifting north has achieved a closer relation to the CBD.

As we all know, carrying out ideas is as important as, if not more important than, the ideas themselves. The Inner Harbor has been fortunate to have the strong marketing and managerial hand of Martin L. Millspaugh and the production genius of Al Copp. They are the senior officers of CC-IH. And in Sandy Hillman the harbor has had a city-sponsored impresario of programs and events who has brought the harbor into every Baltimorean's life and every Baltimorean into the harbor.

But the city really should put up a statue to Edgar Ewing, and perhaps it will. I hope Gen. Sam Smith, the hero of the War of 1812 whose statue was removed from the harbor to Federal Hill in 1964, also will find his way back to the harbor.

Also on the list of those who deserve a statue is Mayor William Donald Schaefer. Every city should have such a mayor. The city is his family, and the Inner Harbor is his living room. With respect to the Inner Harbor, he showed a genius and a willingness to take political risks. Examples: his support of the unifying City Fair after the 1968 riots, of the construction of the clipper ship *Pride of Baltimore* in the teeth of a financial crisis, of the convention center and equity participation by the city in the new Hyatt convention hotel, and his engineering of the successful referendum for Harborplace. There is no question but the mayor is the principal reason for the Inner Harbor's success. His personal commitment has been crucial.

As interesting as all of the above may be to those who went through it in Baltimore, or to those who look for lessons to take home to other cities, the experience still does not explain fully the magic of the Inner Harbor today. What makes the place marvelously unique among cities is that it looks inward on itself, is intimate in scale, is enclosed, framed, and yet opens provocatively to the Outer Harbor and to the world. Lacking the skill to capture the soul of a city in words, I can only challenge each viewer to be aware that, in the Inner Harbor, Baltimore has rediscovered a crucial reason for its being and a way to enjoy it.

David A. Wallace, AICP, FAIA, Philadelphia is an archi-tect/planner/urban design partner in the Philadelphia firm of Wallace, Roberts and Todd, authors of the 1964 Inner Harbor master plan, the 1969 Project I urban renewal plan, the Inner Harbor West urban renewal plan, and the design of the harbor's public infrastructure.

Where Planning Counts
Ruth Eckdish Knack
(October 1980)

It's early morning on a market day, and Cincinnati's Findlay Market is a good place to be—to look, smell, touch, and find bargains on all sorts of fruits and vegetables, fresh meat, and spicy sausages. The frugal Cincinnatians who crowd the renovated, city-owned market, spilling over into the side streets of the Over-the-Rhine neighborhood, know a good buy when they see one.

Such frugality—a tradition here, especially among the descendants of the German immigrants who once crowded into Over-the-Rhine's red brick rowhouses—has helped Cincinnati make a graceful transition into the era of fiscal limits, according to a new Urban Institute report. The report lauds the city administration for having decided several years ago to emphasize upkeep rather than additions to its capital plant. "We do not build things we cannot maintain," the city's budget director said recently, explaining his opposition to a new riverfront park. So it's not surprising that the "coordinated city plan" now in the works is called a plan for the "mature city."

Frugality, prudence—the trusty old virtues just now being rediscovered by city watchers—may help Cincinnati accept such hard realities as population decline. The 1980 Census is expected to show fewer than 400,000 people, down by over 120,000 from 1960.

As in other northern cities, it's primarily the middle class that has left, abandoning inner city neighborhoods like Over-the-Rhine, a traditional port of entry, to the poor, the elderly, the black, and—in this case—the Appalachian, a reminder that this city is part of a geographical region with common characteristics and problems. Even though Cincinnati has a diversified employment base (from the family-owned Queen City Barrel

Company to Procter and Gamble, the city's largest employer), the diversity has not alleviated the problem of minority unemployment.

But Cincinnati has a lot going for it as it enters the eighties. Its neighborhoods never lost their identity, thanks to strong ethnic traditions and the blessings of topography. The city lies in the northern portion of a large, shallow bowl, split by the Ohio River. The first settlers lived in the area known as the basin, which was cut into the surrounding plateau by the actions of rivers and the glaciers, whose southbound movement ended here. The sides of the basin are defined sharply at first by steep hillsides, then more gradually as the slopes ease to the north. . . .

Edmund Bacon, the former director of the Philadelphia planning commission and a long-time Cincinnati observer, says the city was less brutal than many others in its approach to urban renewal. As a result, the downtown core has remained fairly intact and continues to attract businesses and shoppers. A number of significant landmarks also remain, including the Carew Tower-Netherland Hilton complex, which anticipated Rockefeller Center.

A second-level skywalk connects the downtown hotels, department stores, and some office buildings with the convention center and, at the river, hooks up with Riverfront Stadium and the coliseum (where 11 people died at a rock concert last year) and the curvy promenade called the Serpentine. All roads and skywalks lead to Fountain Square, which Bacon calls one of the most successful urban spaces in the United States.

The Urban Institute study cited above accurately observes that there is a relationship between Cincinnati's budgetary health and its government. Ever since 1926, when the Charter Committee threw out the remnants of Boss Cox's machine and instituted a city manager form of government, and despite a scandal or two since then, the city's political reputation has remained untarnished.

The current city manager, Sylvester Murray, says he accepted the job a year ago because "people here really do believe in good government." Murray, who came here from Ann Arbor, Michigan, is black—a fact worthy of note because he was hired by unanimous vote of a city council with only one black member (Mayor Kenneth Blackwell) out of nine.

Although Murray is outspoken, he steers clear of partisan politics. "I have communications open with *all* sides," he says. That position has helped him work out agreements that led to the passage this spring of two significant pieces of legislation: a historic preservation ordinance and an antidisplacement ordinance.

It's interesting, too, that, in a city where planners have reason to rest on their laurels, veteran planning director Herbert Stevens emphasizes change: "City planning changes as our economy and our society change, and planners must adjust."

Stevens himself did so. He came to Cincinnati in 1955, when parts of the 1948 master plan (a revision of the Bettman-Segoe plan of 1925) were being implemented. The plan reflected the needs and perceptions of the time, says Stevens, and the urban physical form it proposed was suitable for a "machine generation" brought up to dream of the "disposable city." Stevens stresses that "great things" were accomplished under that plan, which led to the redevelopment of the central riverfront and clearance of the slums of the West End.

But today, he says, "we see values in blighted areas that we didn't see then"; and instead of large redevelopment projects, his staff is working on smaller scale projects, particularly the community plans that he is credited with originating. Without Stevens, there would have been no community plans in Cincinnati, says neighborhood leader Patricia Crum. "Most bureaucrats realize instinctively that knowledge is power, but he wasn't afraid to give the neighborhoods the information they needed."

He's the journeyman of our profession, says a planner on his staff. "He's down to earth, and he doesn't shy away from the daily tasks that have to be done." Stevens says that he has lasted so long in one position because he has stayed backstage, remaining politically neutral. That stance fits in with his view of planners as initiators and coordinators, not implementors. "Somebody has to initiate proposals," he says, "and if planners didn't think they had to see their plans accepted the first time around, they wouldn't get so discouraged." In his view, the planning commission provides the political link between the planning staff and the voters, and implementing can be done by an operating agency.

The bag of tricks

At least in part because of Stevens, planners in Cincinnati have some good tools to work with: for example, the Planning and Management Support System (PAMSS), a computerized information service that catalogs data on every proposal and project city agencies are involved in. "We invented it," says Stevens proudly. There were some embryo efforts elsewhere, but they didn't encompass social planning, and Stevens wanted a true clearinghouse.

As innocuous as PAMSS seems, it met with opposition at first, especially from the city manager at the time, who saw himself rather than the planning department as the city's primary coordinator. But Stevens plunged ahead with an initial $50,000 in 701 funds, and now PAMSS is accepted by all but the most suspicious.

More controversial are the two zoning overlays created in the mid-seventies to protect special areas. Getting the city council to pass the Environmental Quality District zoning ordinance over the strong opposition of business and construction interests took four years and 15 drafts, says senior planner Sanford Youkilis. In an EQD—which could be a hillside, a neighborhood business district with an urban design plan, or any area where the city has made major improvements—all permit applications must include an environmental statement and be reviewed by a hearing examiner.

Lined up in support of the EQD zoning were environmental groups, the Women's City Club (which has sponsored several hillside forums), and—this was the key, Youkilis says—the neighborhoods. Since then, EQDs have been created for such areas as the steeply sloped East Price Hill, the College Hill business district, and Findlay Market, renovated by the city in 1972 at a cost of over $1 million.

Almost in tandem with the EQD, the city created an Interim Development Control overlay, a device that Sandy Youkilis says is unique to Cincinnati. The IDC is a way to protect an endangered area temporarily while the planners attempt to get EQD or historic district zoning. This summer, the city council upheld the planning commission's recommendation for IDC zoning for the Over-the-Rhine neighborhood, which was recently nominated to the National Register of Historic Places. The nomination aroused a storm of protest from those in and out of the neighborhood who fear . . . displacement of current residents. The IDC gives everyone a chance to consider the situation in some tranquility.

The planners' most important tool may not be an ordinance at all, however, but rather a process—the Herb Stevens process, some call it. That's the tradition of "working review committees," task forces made up of city council members, business representatives, and neighborhood leaders, which have been used for every planning project from the 1964 central business district plan on. The planning department provides a staff member to assist each task force. "Now every planner knows there must be citizen participation in planning," says Stevens. "We've been practicing it since the early sixties."

All this is not to say that the course of planning always runs smooth in the Queen City. For example, there were philosophical differences between the planning department and former city manager, William Donaldson, who left the city last year to become director of the Philadelphia Zoo. "The trouble with the planning department," he says, "is that it can't sell anyone on what it's doing. It was a great department 20 years ago. Now it's become irrelevant." To Donaldson, who is known for his candor, the basic problem is clear: The planning department doesn't work for the city manager and thus is not part of the general city government structure.

On another front, the relationship between the Department of City Planning and the Department of Development also has been marked by differences—characterized as much as anything by their contrasting styles of operation.

"Planning tends to be cautious, conservative," says University of Cincinnati planning professor Samuel Noe. "It has a longer range outlook. The people in Development are entrepreneurial types with a different temperament."

Development director Nell Surber admits that her department and Planning don't always see eye to eye about how the city should work and look. For example, she opposed the new historic preservation legislation, which was supported by Planning. "We don't need *more* regulations," she says. "The bottom line is that legislation to protect buildings doesn't get them renovated." Surber, who herself lives in a rehabbed Mt. Auburn townhouse, argues that she is not against anything but rather is *for* the "balanced city"—one that provides both housing and jobs.

Pointing out that her department would have been more aptly named Economic Development when it was reorganized in 1976, Surber speaks with assurance of the economic feasibility of continued office expansion downtown. A miniboom in the last few years has, in fact, seen four new buildings go up: Central Trust's 27-story building; Federated Department Stores' striking triangular tower; Cincinnati Bell's headquarters building; and Fountain Square South, an $80-million office-hotel-retail complex rising, over the protests of preservationists, on the site of the demolished Albee Theater. . . .

Camaraderie

Development and Planning are not always at odds, however. There's evidence of that in the effective industrial planning process, a cooperative effort by both. Thirteen industrial "clusters" have been formed by the industrial development division of the planning department with technical assistance from the development department; four more are in the planning stage. In Madisonville, for example, a neighborhood development corporation has been helped to obtain a $7.8 million UDAG to convert the site of some World War II barracks into facilities for U.S. Shoe and Coca-Cola, providing jobs for local residents.

A prime mover behind the industrial cluster activity is Ralph Grieme, Jr., a Covington developer who is a consultant to the development department and also president of the Ohio-Kentucky-Indiana council of governments. Grieme's focus in his industrial planning work is on retaining the small industries that the city is known for rather than attracting large new industries. The city simply doesn't have the vacant land needed for big plants, he points out.

In other respects, Grieme is an interesting study in contrasts. He expresses impatience with the planning commission's penchant for public hearings and with the city's new antidisplacement ordinance ("it usurps too many property rights from individuals"). But he is also a strong planning advocate who emphasizes the need for a regional plan because of the many separate jurisdictions in the OKI region. As OKI president, he wants the agency to be "less low profile" and to get more involved in energy planning, especially. "Planning *is* the success of Cincinnati," he says. "But *our* [the development department's] plans are being developed with implementation in mind."

Out in the neighborhoods

Six cable television companies have been competing furiously this year to win Cincinnati's lucrative cable franchise. One of the big issues in that competition is "public access," particularly for neighborhood groups. And those groups are well organized and vocal in this city.

No one is more vocal than Pat Crum, the energetic director of the community development corporation in Bond Hill on the northern edge of the city—a "bellwether neighborhood," she calls it, where every urban problem surfaces early on. The neighborhood was redlined in the late sixties when blacks started moving in. In a "greenlining" counter-offensive to attract new investment into the neighborhood, a development corporation was formed, the first of 25 in the city.

A current issue is neighborhood recognition, a subject that has received attention lately with the convening of the first charter review commission in seven years. While the Charter Committee tradition is one of at-large government, some black neighborhood leaders and others have expressed frustration with their inability to elect representatives directly.

But Crum, who chairs a Congress of Neighborhood Groups task force on neighborhood recognition, disagrees. She remains a strong supporter of the present system, although she doesn't rule out some type of formalization, and she does feel that decisions about street cleaning and similar matters should be made at the neighborhood level. She is one of those calling for the assignment of community support workers to every neighborhood in the city to replace or supplement the community assistance teams (CATS), which, as part of the Office of Community Administration, report directly to the city manager. Says Crum, "The responsibility for community planning should return to the planning department."

Impartial assessment

Cincinnati's adherence to tradition—its contentment with *not* always being first—means Oktoberfest and Music Hall. But it also means provincialism. Pat Crum says she's still considered a newcomer—after 20 years.

And it means conservative responses to social issues. This year the neighborhoods finally got together and got a small increase in the school levy passed, the first in 11 years. No Section 8 housing has been built yet in Cincinnati, although in June the city council adopted an advance site selection policy that allows the city to buy options on sites and gives the city manager, instead of the council, the authority to determine whether a proposal conforms to the city's housing policy. When it comes to planning, conservatism means no one-stop permitting and a long wait for an effective PUD ordinance (one is now being contested in the courts).

But that is quibbling. It doesn't take the luster off Cincinnati's good reputation. The results of good planning are everywhere. Edmund Bacon was a consultant to the city in the 1970s and visited this spring to work with planning students. So he's knowledgeable, yet, as an outsider, presumably impartial. And in his assessment, the city comes off rather well.

By refurbishing a beloved artifact, the Tyler-Davidson fountain, and giving it a fine, modern setting in a rebuilt Fountain Square, Bacon says, the city made a significant statement about the importance of urban life.

But he also warns that the outcome of many of the city's redevelopment projects "is still hanging in the balance." For example, the skywalks. "The effort was admirable, but their function hasn't yet been fully understood by the city. There is some question, for instance, whether they should be run down the alleys rather than through the buildings as in the much more successful effort in Minneapolis."

Moreover, Cincinnati has not yet realized the potential of new residential construction downtown. But its biggest failing, in Bacon's view, is in not understanding the value of infill development, which could be used to extend the character of such revitalizing areas as West Fourth Street.

Bacon realizes, though, that projects like the skywalks take a long time to mature. "There is still a chance for them to fulfill their full potential." Given the record of the city's "earnest citizens" and its "marvelous physical inheritance," he says, the prognosis is good.

Ruth Knack is the senior editor of Planning.

The Politics of Planning in Seattle

Jane Hadley
(February 1983)

Almost 10 years ago, Seattle embarked on an optimistic experiment in comprehensive planning that set it apart from most American cities. The experiment—the Office of Policy Planning (OPP)—is over, and today Seattle does its planning in much the same way that other large cities do: by finding immediate solutions to immediate problems. For political and economic reasons, though, planning in Seattle may be in better shape now than during the glory days of the mid-1970s.

The late 1960s and early 1970s saw a wave of closely connected developments in Seattle's politics and government. In April 1967, a group of young, forward-thinking citizens formed a group known as CHECC (for Choose an Effective City Council), whose immediate goal was to get two new city council candidates elected that November (which it did). Reflecting one of its key themes, the group issued a set of recommendations that called for centralizing planning in the city and passing city charter amendments that would increase the mayor's power to centralize departmental work.

CHECC and other good government groups such as the Municipal League and the League of Women Voters recognized that, for all the prosperity and relative homogeneity of its 500,000 residents, Seattle faced the same challenges as other central cities (namely, urban sprawl, housing abandonment, racial tension, and disinvestment). There was a growing consensus among these groups and others that the city government needed to be shaken out of its old-fashioned, business-as-usual method of operating.

Evolving directly out of this mood was a massive citizen participation effort known as the Seattle 2000 Commission, which over a six-month period in 1972 produced a 330-page book known as *Goals for Seattle for the Year 2000.* Hundreds of citizens participated in the numerous task forces, discussion groups, and meetings set up by the commission. The goals were adopted by the city council in 1973 and today still are included in environmental impact statements as legitimate, adopted public goals and policies against which proposals can be judged.

The central theme, stated repeatedly throughout the goals, is that of citizen participation: "A citizen participation process shall be a requirement in policy making . . . . The city should establish a citywide citizen participation system that allows the city and its citizens to interact on policy and program decisions."

Three other themes emerged as well:

• Comprehensive planning;

• Reorganization of city government to strengthen the accountability of departments to their directors and directors to the mayor and to enhance the mayor's executive powers and those of the city council as the city's policy-setting body;

• Neighborhood preservation, to be achieved by deferring to neighborhood groups and by limiting densities and encouraging mass transit.

Seattle 2000 explicitly called for the creation of an Office of Program Planning within the executive department of government that would have "responsibility for comprehensive planning and overall priority setting, coordinating the formulation of departmental action plans, and coordination with other government entities."

Although it was not always articulated in documents like *Seattle 2000,* a key factor in the push for a policy planning office was the increased infusion of federal dollars through such programs as Model Cities and revenue sharing. The mayor's office and several members of the city council, in arguing in 1972 for the creation of an Office of Executive Policy (a precursor of the Office of Policy Planning), said that such an agency was "a virtual mandate" from the federal government so that the city could handle federal grants.

The experiment

In mid-1974 Mayor Wes Uhlman proposed that an Office of Policy Planning (OPP) be created with a staff of 70. The city council established OPP in October 1974 with a staff of 38, about 35 of whom would come from other departments.

In announcing the head of the department, Uhlman noted that the new agency would have responsibilities far beyond the traditional land-use planning functions of city planning offices. "Planning is a lot more than drawing lines on a map and coloring them in," the mayor said. "It is much more than land use—it involves people problems and services." The purpose of OPP, he said, was to consolidate and coordinate planning activities taking place throughout the city departments.

City council member Michael Hildt, who as city council policy director in 1974 helped write the ordinance creating OPP, says today of the atmosphere then: "Planning was the key word. Anything could be solved if it was just planned." But Hildt identifies a second impetus for comprehensive planning besides *Seattle 2000.*

"Uhlman [after his election in 1969], was terribly frustrated by the Board of Public Works," Hildt recalls. The board, composed of the major department heads, made decisions on big public projects. The mayor, being outside that process, formed OPP in part to gain power over the board.

Uhlman's political motives regarding OPP were an issue from the very beginning. Even back in 1972 when Uhlman was arguing for creation of the Office of Executive Policy with a staff of five, several city council members said they were worried that the council's role could be slighted if policy authority were concentrated in the mayor's office.

This tension between mayor and council was to plague OPP throughout its rocky, four-year existence. During his battle to create the policy office, Uhlman had to compromise with the council on control: OPP was to be accountable to both the nine-member city council and the mayor. The mayor appointed the OPP director, subject to council confirmation, but the council held the purse strings and adopted a policy planning agenda or work program for OPP each year.

"It was not a workable compromise to have OPP reporting to both the mayor and the council, to have it reporting to 10 different politicians," says Barbara Dingfield, OPP director from March 1977 to mid-1978 and today a project manager for a major downtown developer.

Dingfield says that Uhlman used OPP to get control over programs just as he created the Office of Management and Budget to get budgetary control over city departments.

Hildt adds, "OPP never had any direction from the mayor that had anything to do with planning. OPP staff became project managers for the mayor. Some of them were answering phone calls and mail for him."

Another irritant in OPP's makeup: Its staff—predominantly young, bright, Ivy League-educated—had a reputation for arrogance with the council, the line departments, and ordinary citizens. As a result, the OPP staff was in constant tension with the staff and heads of the line departments.

As for what was actually produced by OPP staffers, the quality was mixed. Some projects were simple errand-running for Uhlman. Other work was almost comically abstract (such as a paper on citizen participation that drew on phenomenology and Hegelian theory to explain why participation was best accomplished by letting the mayor run things.)

Nevertheless, OPP had bright and ambitious people who often did good work. The office produced a solid report on the city's changing demographics. (It noted a dramatic increase in households occupied by young, single people and childless couples, an increase in the proportion of minorities in the population, and the loss of white families.) OPP recommended policies to respond to the change. The staff also produced a useful report on business migration from the city.

Hildt says certain OPP staffers were extremely helpful in working (to a certain extent, behind Uhlman's back) with a citizens advisory committee that was fighting City Light, the municipal electric utility, over whether the city should participate in the construction of two nuclear power plants, which were abandoned when the Washington Public Power Supply System ran out of money. The citizens committee recommended a strong 'no' and, fortunately for Seattle, the council went along with the citizens committee. OPP also began what appears to be a successful overhaul of the city's land-use plan and zoning code.

At its peak in 1978, OPP had 87 employees and a budget of $2.3 million. It was involved in utility planning, planning for law and justice, land-use planning, development of a capital improvement plan, block grant programs, transportation planning, economic development, intergovernmental relations, parks planning, and other areas. It was a powerful agency and, as current Mayor Charles Royer was to learn, a useful one. Royer had campaigned for the mayor's office in 1977 against OPP, charging that there were too many planners and that department heads, who had their feet on the ground, so to speak, should have more say in the development of policy.

But Hildt says, "Barbara Dingfield had Royer

eating out of her hand within a week or two after he took office." Dingfield adds, "We had an expertise there that he didn't have. We were small. We knew what the different departments were doing. We became an important resource for him."

In late 1978, a faction of the city council threatened to abolish OPP altogether. Furious lobbying by Royer managed to prevent its total elimination, but the council in a five-to-four vote did cut OPP's staff by a third.

In 1979 OPP became a slimmed down OPE, the "Office of Policy and Evaluation." The next year it lost more staff members, some of whom were transferred to city departments, some of whose positions were eliminated.

Finally, in 1981, the council struck the final blow and abolished the office altogether, transferring some of OPE's 40 employees to the Office of Management and Budget and about 12 to the mayor's office as the Land Use and Transportation Project.

The experiment in centralized planning was over.

Royer, whom the planners had won over so quickly and who fought vigorously to protect OPP and OPE from the council's budget ax, did not weep over the OPE/OPP corpse. Instead, a mere month after the council's budget action, Royer said, "I don't believe that I have diminished my ability to get things done. The underpinnings of that system were rotten before I got into office. It would have collapsed at one point or another."

Such a philosophical attitude is surprising, since the city's 1982 adopted budget shows that the number of positions in the executive department went from 320 in 1980 to 157 in 1981 to 138 in 1982 and that the budget slipped from $11.2 million in 1980 to $5.2 million in 1982. Why then is Royer smiling?

Two reasons, perhaps. First, many OPE/OPP staff members were transferred to line departments between 1979 and 1981, by which time Royer had firmly established his control over them. Virtually all of the department heads were appointees of Mayor Royer. A city charter revision in 1977 stripped the Board of Public Works of its charter authority, in essence subordinating the board to the city council and lessening its independence.

Second, cuts in staff and budgets were not restricted to the mayor's office; they were epidemic at the local government level. Like other cities, Seattle was hit by recession just when its federal funds started to dry up. The city's federal block grant allocation went from a high of over $17 million in 1980 to less than $14 million in 1982.

Others were not quite as serene as Royer about the loss of OPE/OPP. Council member Paul Kraabel put it this way during the 1978 budget wars over OPP, "You don't put planning into 16 different departments and expect coordinated results. You don't put the Army in charge of deciding whether you go to war."

How it works today

Although OPP or OPE are gone, there still are executive department planners reporting directly to Mayor Royer. John Howell runs a group of 15 planners within the Office of Management and Budget, an executive department office. And James Parsons is in charge of the 12 land-use planners in the Land Use and Transportation Project (LUTP).

Howell's group advises the mayor on how community block grant funds should be spent and has been involved recently in electricity and energy planning, a review of the city's housing policy, and planning for infrastructure repairs. "We consider Howell to be our utility infielder on policy," says Carol Lewis, an adviser to Royer on housing and land-use issues.

LUTP is finishing up the complete overhaul of Seattle's land-use policies and zoning code that has been going on for about four years.

There is no question that Mayor Royer has direct control over both these planning operations. Although Howell is in OMB and not in the mayor's office, Carol Lewis says that OMB is in effect "an extension of the mayor's office." . . .

The department that received the biggest increase in planners as OPE shrank was engineering. It has planners for solid waste, transportation, and some other long-range physical planning. City Light also has a sizeable forecasting and planning staff, and the city council staff increased in size as well.

Both the management team and the land-use cabinet are attempts by the Royer administration to compensate for the loss of OPP by "building a tighter system of accountability" says Lewis. "We use the departments but they are coordinated by the mayor's staff."

Another development that may have increased Royer's control over the line departments is a reorganization involving the Department of Commu-

nity Development (DCD) and what used to be called the Building Department and is now called the Department of Construction and Land Use (DCLU).

In the reshuffling that took place about two years ago, all of DCD's environmental analysts were transferred to DCLU. DCD's planning functions were either eliminated or subordinated to LUTP. Most neighborhood planners in DCD have been cut from the budget. There is no doubt that DCD was the loser and DCLU and LUTP the winners in this reorganization.

Today DCD performs two main functions: economic development (small business assistance and Urban Development Action Grants) and housing development (administering about $1.5 million for low-income housing development and producing various housing reports). The department has developed a distinct chamber of commerce flavor, to the distaste of some of its employees who remember its fighting days.

DCLU is clearly today's super department. It handles almost every aspect of development, from demolition licenses to zoning variances and from environmental analyses to use and building permits. Despite—perhaps because of—its power, the department has cloaked itself in procedures to suggest orderliness and neutrality. In fact, its director, William Justen, an engineer, has cultivated the persona of an administrative law judge—stressing procedures and denying the political side of his decisions.

Even so, neighborhood activists recently showed up at a little publicized city council hearing to excoriate Justen for acting like a king and being prodevelopment in his administration of the rules. These neighborhood activists say they now feel left out at city hall. Where are their beloved DCD neighborhood planners?

Asked earlier this year about the whereabouts of these neighborhood advocates, Justen responded that they were gone and good riddance to them. They had never performed a productive role, he said. They were guerrillas who stirred up anti-city hall sentiments.

Mayor in control

The upshot of the reorganization is that Royer's control over the bureaucracy has increased. No longer do city staff members forge their own political constituencies in the neighborhoods. A more consolidated and clear-cut division of duties makes it easier for Royer to identify and influence the progress of development projects. Further, Royer appears to be cultivating the public impression that he has little control over what Justen does.

This posture that the administration of land-use and development policies and rules is nonpolitical may be necessary to smooth over what appears to be a change in some of Royer's views since he first was elected in 1977. Royer campaigned as a champion of the neighborhoods against city hall and against the developers. His opponent, Paul Schell, now a major downtown developer, was seen by many neighborhood groups as being too sympathetic to developers, too cozy with the downtown establishment and the city hall bureaucracy. (Schell, a lawyer, was formerly head of DCD.)

To the extent that Royer has changed his views, it is useful for him to distance himself from the bureaucracy that implements the change. It must be said, however, that Royer took a strongly pro-neighborhood position three years ago on the land-use policies for the city's single-family residential areas (which cover an enormous proportion of the city's usable land area). Royer also has held firm recently in opposing legislation that would allow mother-in-law apartments in the single-family neighborhoods. Both of these issues loom large with the neighborhood councils.

But whether Royer has changed his views or not, development is a politically explosive issue in Seattle. Besides the neighborhood councils, activists include a group called Allied Arts, concerned mainly with urban design and architectural issues; the League of Women Voters; several groups representing the housing, displacement, and other social concerns of low- and moderate-income residents; and the Shorelines Coalition, which supports height limits and other strict controls on shoreline development. All of these groups have expressed the view that Justen does not regulate development as forcefully as he ought.

Much of the recent dissatisfaction with Justen has arisen since the new land-use and zoning codes for the city's residential areas went into effect. Disparities are showing up between the new code and development projects that got their permits under the old zoning. The neighborhoods are furious that DCLU has given these developments (some with three-year-old permits and blatantly out of scale with the new code) the green light.

The disparities have put the limelight on Justen's tendency to apply regulations timidly and perhaps to the benefit of developers. Shortly after the outpouring of neighborhood resentment about Justen's lack of even-handedness, his department reversed itself and revoked permits for several nonconforming projects that had not followed the rules.

In the future, DCLU is likely to be thrust even further into politics because it has taken on some sensitive planning tasks (revision of Seattle's shoreline master plan) that may not mix well with its essentially regulatory mission.

Despite the power of DCLU, it appears that Royer has a strong hold on the line departments. Carol Lewis, the mayor's adviser, says, "If we had the planning staff we had then [with OPP] and the management techniques we have now, we could really do it right." She adds that the best way to go in policy planning is to have a mix: some planning staff directly responsible to the mayor and some planners in the departments with coordination by the mayor's office.

Dingfield agrees for the most part. She says that if she were to start with a clean slate today, she probably would create an OPP as part of the executive department, but it would not be nearly as large. Instead, it would be a policy and issue management group of 10 to 15 people that would help focus the programs for the department, setting the agenda and then dealing with some of the policies that arise in the process of working on it. "But," she adds, "I would still give the departments the nitty-gritty stuff."

Jane Hadley regularly covers planning issues as a reporter for the Seattle Post-Intelligencer.

Twin Cities Metro Council: Heading for a Fall?

Charles C. Whiting
(March 1984)

The Twin Cities Metropolitan Council, widely admired—even envied—as the nation's most innovative and successful experiment in regional government, is in trouble. Seventeen years after its creation, the council is firmly enough established that its survival as an institution seems secure. But some of its best friends fear it may be losing effectiveness as an instrument for guiding regional growth and services in the seven-county Twin Cities area. Beset on one side by local governments jealous of their own authority, on the other by a governor and state legislature with little memory of why the council was created, and from within by a controversial chairman, whose actions and proposals have alarmed council friends and foes alike, the Metropolitan Council is at a crossroads.

Created by the Minnesota legislature in 1967, the council replaced a largely ineffective, council of governments-type body called the Metropolitan Planning Commission. The Metropolitan Council's basic charge is "to coordinate the planning and development of the seven-county Twin Cities area"—a function that has expanded over the years to include not just physical development and transportation issues but social programs as well. Thus, the council has been engaged in health planning, cable television coordination, A-95 review of federal grant applications, a planning and grant program for the elderly, an arts planning and grant program, and criminal justice planning.

But the council is not a level of general government. Its taxing power is set by the legislature and its responsibilities generally are limited to functions that cannot be performed by city and county governments. Actual regional services are provided by other metropolitan agencies—a transit commission, an airport commission, and a waste control commission—under the council's coordination.

Much of what happens to the council depends on what will happen after the Minnesota legislature convenes for its 1984 session in early March. To some extent, new legislative sessions always pose a threat. Hardly one has gone by since the council was authorized without some attempt being made to dismantle or undercut regional authority. Rarely, however, has that recurring urge to undo one of Minnesota's most notable governmental achievements been as serious as some think it is now. Former council chairman John Boland, once a legislator himself, predicts: "Metro Council stuff will be hot in the '84 session. A lot of people are saying we should just start over. What they're going to do is turn it into a council of governments."

Boland's certainty may be overstated. He is, after all, a member of a Citizens League committee that has been studying the Metropolitan Council with an eye toward proposing reforms in its duties and make-up. The Citizens League, a broadly based and respected research organization that was an early champion of metropolitan legislation, will fight hard to protect the council and is unlikely to be ignored on the issue. Ted Kolderie, a former director of the league and now a senior fellow at the University of Minnesota's Hubert H. Humphrey Institute of Public Affairs, also serves on the committee. He thinks the worst that will happen is that a bill to undercut the council will pass one legislative house, thereby causing enough alarm to prevent passage in the second house. . . .

Like Gov. Rudy Perpich and the present council chairman, Gerald Isaacs, Boland would prefer that council members be popularly elected. But that idea, which has been around as long as the council, has never been able to overcome legislative resistance, which seems stronger than ever this year.

The problem, as Boland and others see it, is that virtually no one is left in the legislature who remembers the 1967 debate about the form regional government should take or the then-compelling reasons why the council was insulated from local-government control.

Boland's Republican successor as council chairman, Charles Weaver, tried to do something about the problem in the summer of 1982. Weaver also once served in the legislature, where he was author of Minnesota's other nationally renowned metropolitan innovation, the tax base-sharing fiscal disparities law, explained below. Worried that retirements and 1982 election results might produce as much as a 50 percent turnover in legislative composition, Weaver organized a well-attended bipartisan seminar for metro-area candidates. Speakers included former legislative leaders from both political parties, who tried to explain—as one of them put it—"why those idiots passed those laws."

Why indeed? And how? Other places have attempted to enact metropolitan reform in one giant step—by what Robert Einsweiler, the former Metropolitan Council planning director, refers to as the "great happening" approach. The Minneapolis-St. Paul area moved in incremental steps.

With two major cities standing side by side, the Twin Cities metropolis had been forced to address some problems on a regional basis even before post-World War II suburban growth created a multiplicity of local governments. By the mid-1960s, Minneapolis and St. Paul jointly operated regional sewer and airport systems. Six counties surrounding the two cities had formed a metropolitan mosquito control district. And the Metropolitan Planning Commission, with seven-county representation, had begun drawing up a regionwide land-use and transportation plan in cooperation with 12 other city, county, and state agencies.

But what was in place in 1967 was not so much the skeleton of a regional system as a pile of disconnected bones, with some of the key parts missing or incomplete. The Metropolitan Planning Commission had regional planning responsibility but no authority to see that its plans were carried out. The sewer system operated by the Minneapolis-St. Paul sanitary district primarily served the central cities. Many suburbs, where septic tanks were creating groundwater pollution problems, started putting together their own independent sewer districts, one of which planned to dump its effluent into the Mississippi River near the Minneapolis water intake.

Meanwhile, interstate highways were opening up new areas to suburban sprawl. The privately owned bus company was cutting back on service, which was already largely confined to the central cities. The airports commission was beginning to think about building a huge new international airport 20 miles north of the Twin Cities. The number of municipalities in the seven-county area had grown to more than 100, all of them competing for a larger share of the tax base, some much more successfully than others.

One big family

But if there were regional problems, there also was a will to address them cooperatively. The existence of two central cities—which were themselves suburban in character—helped keep suburban distrust of "the big city" to a minimum. And, although the central cities were long-standing rivals, their business and civic leaders had recently learned how to work together to bring major league sports to Minnesota. The area was also the home of several major national corporations, which shared a tradition of civic involvement and tended to see the region as a single economic entity. And the area had a history of political moderation and responsible government, fostered and advised by such respected private organizations as the Citizens League. Finally, legislative leaders were growing weary of a multiplicity of divergent voices coming out of the metropolitan area—particularly on the sewer issue. . . .

The result, after a session-long debate, was a council that would take over the staff, property tax base, and planning functions of the existing Metropolitan Planning Commission. The council also was given new powers to suspend the long-range plans of sewer and other special districts if they conflicted with the comprehensive regional plan and to review and comment on municipal and township plans. A council member was to serve on each of the other regional commissions and on any new ones that might be created later.

Instead of representing local governments and special districts, as Metropolitan Planning Commission members had done, the council's 15 members (now 17) were to be appointed by the governor. Except for the chairman, who was to represent the area as a whole and serve at the governor's pleasure, each member would serve a four-year term and represent—on a one-person, one-vote basis—a district roughly coterminous with two state senatorial districts. The idea, said Professors Arthur Naftalin and John Brandl in a 1980 report prepared for the Humphrey Institute, was "to ensure that the council would not be the captive of local governments." (Naftalin is a former Minneapolis mayor and Brandl is a state representative; their report, *The Twin Cities Regional Strategy,* was published by the Metropolitan Council.) . . .

Two new operating agencies were formed at the start. One, the Metropolitan Transit Commission—also established by the 1967 legislature—soon purchased the struggling private bus company. And in 1969, relying heavily on council advice, the legislature resolved the troublesome sewer issue by creating what is now called the Metropolitan Waste Control Commission. The council was given power to appoint commission members and to prepare a regional sewer plan for the new commission to carry out. The transit commission was similarly directed in 1971 to carry out the transit elements of the council's transportation plan.

Tax-base sharing

The 1971 legislature also passed the fiscal disparities law, which the council's first chairman, former law professor James Hetland, has called "probably the best piece of legislation that has been adopted in any urban area of the United States." Although the law is not directly related to the Metropolitan Council, without it, according to Hetland, there would be "no way in which land-use controls or any sensible development controls could be imposed at the regional level."

That's because the law, by dividing the commercial-industrial tax base among the communities in the area, reduces their incentive to compete for such development. Designed mainly to close the gap in revenue-raising ability between "have" and "have-not" communities, tax-base sharing requires each municipality to put 40 percent of its commercial-industrial tax-base growth since 1971 (including new development and growth caused by inflation) into a metropolitan pool, which is then redistributed according to each community's population and overall tax base.

The fiscal disparities law was contested all the way to the U.S. Supreme Court. But it survived and, with $2.5 billion of commercial-industrial tax base now accumulated in the metropolitan pool, has reduced the per capita disparity between the area's richest and poorest communities from what would otherwise be a 13.3-to-1 ratio to just 4.3 to 1. But because the sharing is of the tax base, not the actual tax revenues, the law's financial impact is hard to measure in terms of improved services or reduced tax levies.

The Twin Cities regional strategy (Naftalin and Brandl's phrase) really began to take form in 1974, after the transit commission asked legislative approval of plans for a $1 billion rail rapid transit system that conflicted with a council proposal for a system relying on buses and small vehicles. To resolve the conflict—not only over the transit issue but over which agency had dominant planning authority—the legislature passed the Metropolitan Reorganization Act. The council gained power to name all members of the transit commission except the chairman and to approve transit and waste control development programs as well as the capital expenditures of the Metropolitan Airports Commission.

The reorganization act also gave the council new, far-reaching power to review the metropolitan significance of major public and private projects, which meant that it could block new housing developments, shopping centers, and other major development proposals that conflicted with its

regional plan. In addition, the act gave the council two new members, the right to act as a metropolitan housing authority, and the right to issue bonds for regional park acquisition and development.

The final step was the 1976 Metropolitan Land Planning Act, which required local governments to prepare comprehensive plans consistent with the council's metropolitan "systems plans" for sewers, parks, transit, and airports. Einsweiler, who is now on the Humphrey Institute faculty and recently conducted a study of the land planning act, says it's too soon to determine whether the law is achieving more rational development. But, he adds, as a "lever that forces local governments to plan," the law has given new status to planning and appears to be affecting local development decisions.

Minneapolis planning director Oliver Byrum helped put the law together as the council's director of comprehensive planning in the mid-1970s. From his dual perspective, he thinks the law is working, but not the way it was planned to work. "What the cities were required to submit should have dealt much more fundamentally with the items of regional importance that the council was interested in, not with details," Byrum says. "That would have produced better statements that would have fit together better."

Byrum says it is hard to point to any "tangible" effects the land planning act has had on development in Minneapolis or elsewhere. But he thinks the law was a factor in stopping plans for a major shopping center east of St. Paul, where expected residential development seemed unlikely to provide an adequate retail market. The law's main impact, he believes, has been to redirect investment away from the urban fringes toward the central cities—"and that's a benefit."

Over in St. Paul, city planning director Jim Bellus sees the requirements of the land planning act as "much more useful for suburban and rural areas than for a city like St. Paul where we had already done our planning and where the impact of metro systems such as sewers was fairly limited."

Bill Thibault, planner for St. Louis Park, a suburb on the west edge of Minneapolis, feels that the law is working "because the process provides for review and adjustment." For example, when provisions for light rail transit in the comprehensive plan St. Louis Park submitted for council approval in 1980 conflicted with the metropolitan transit policy that was then in effect, the council approved the plan anyway, apparently in anticipation of expected changes in the regional transit policy.

What, then, has the Twin Cities regional strategy accomplished? Naftalin and Brandl said in 1980 that the "gains are real and positive" but for a process as complex as metropolitan development "cannot be measured with any degree of precision." They questioned, for example, the council's claim that the Metropolitan Development Framework (the council's name for its regional plan) would save the region $2 billion in infrastructure costs over 20 years.

But they cited six directly attributable outcomes: (1) a mechanism for resolving complex regional problems; (2) coordination of basic metropolitan services; (3) development of a comprehensive regional plan; (4) the vetoing of such costly and unneeded capital undertakings as a heavy rail transit system and a new international airport; (5) the establishment of a regional focal point; and (6) a constantly expanding source of information about the region and its needs. Also, Ted Kolderie of the Humphrey Institute credits the council with doing exceptionally well in such "little-noticed second-level" areas as stormwater runoff, an areawide 911 emergency telephone system, and emergency medical service planning.

Ignoring history

All of this has led the Metropolitan Council's present chairman, Gerald Isaacs, to assert that the council's planning work and development controls are largely in place and that it is time to undertake new regional initiatives, especially in economic development. Isaacs, a Perpich appointee who took office in January 1983 and recently announced his resignation, effective on or before May 1, has a background in public and private development, including service as director of economic development for St. Paul and head of that city's port authority. One of his proposals is that the council act as a metropolitan port authority, issuing bonds for job-producing developments. (A search committee appointed to nominate a new council chairman to replace Isaacs was to report about March 1.)

Many, including local governments, the Citizens League, and area chambers of commerce, have argued that such a role for the council is unneeded and would conflict with its basic function, to control growth. Kolderie calls Isaacs's port authority

proposal "a profound effort to redirect the council—ignoring history, tradition, and the law—by trying to fit the thing to his personal interests."

Einsweiler agrees that Isaacs is going about it the wrong way. "Direct involvement in development is to growth control as spending is to investing," he says. Rather than money, Einsweiler would like to see the council provide what he believes local governments and developers really need: technical assistance, coordination, and help in reducing front-end risks on large-scale projects—"entrepreneurial coordination." But he sees virtue in the council emphasizing economic development—"It should have been done from the start." And he thinks the Isaacs proposal responds to "the regional agenda"—real needs as defined by the community, as opposed to what Einsweiler thinks has too often been a council tendency to define its work program in terms of its internal organization.

Take-over attempt

In response to continuing criticism, Isaacs deferred implementation of his economic development package. He also stopped pushing his other controversial proposal—to have an elected council take over the operating functions of the transit, airports, and waste control commissions. That idea drew a sharp letter of reprimand from Harry Sieben, Jr., and Roger Moe, respectively Minnesota's house speaker and senate majority leader, who told Isaacs that his job is to carry out the law as the legislature passed it, not to lobby for changes in the metropolitan structure. Others also have taken Isaacs to task on both the economic development and take-over issues, for seeking to involve the council in operating functions to the potential detriment of its basic planning and coordinating role.

Einsweiler agrees that "operations will always drive out planning." But he thinks Isaacs's take-over plan at least addresses a legitimate and long-standing problem of the council's relationship to other metropolitan agencies. "The talk," he says, "is about the council and other agencies, not about the sum of regional government and the pattern of shared relationships. The commissions operate as separate agencies while the council gets more and more remote from them. There is too much emphasis on who does what rather than on the process. It's not a collective metropolitan government; the units have retreated into little boxes.

"The real weakness," says Einsweiler, "is the

lack of understanding of the planning-operations relationship—who has the last word and where." To Einsweiler, the ideal relationship—in the case of transit, for example—would be for the Metropolitan Transit Commission and the Metropolitan Council to work out transit planning and policy together, with the council having the last word. Then both agencies would work out transit operations together, with the transit commission having the last word. . . .

Amid all of this turmoil, the council often seems distracted from its basic responsibilities. Minneapolis planning director Byrum, for example, criticizes it for inaction on the plans of Bloomington, a big suburb to the south, to redevelop the site of the area's vacated major league sports stadium (replaced by the Hubert H. Humphrey Metrodome in downtown Minneapolis). Byrum believes a new stadium would produce a third downtown that would undermine the vitality of the two existing downtowns. "The council hasn't understood the metropolitan issues involved," he says. "It has failed to look at the socioeconomic impacts or the long-range impacts on transportation. It's treating one of the largest development proposals in the area's history as a question of whether we do or don't need another freeway interchange."

Kolderie notes that both the council and the transit commission remained essentially on the sidelines as a legislative study commission pondered basic changes in the way transit service is organized and delivered—even though "that's the sort of thing the council itself was supposed to do." The legislative commission, says Kolderie, is doing an excellent job of addressing the need to find better ways of providing transit service in the suburbs. On the other hand, the council is "so screwed up with internal junk that it can't get at it. It dropped the ball completely and is now trying to catch up."

But the council is involved in another, more publicly visible transit issue. Having recently abandoned a long-standing policy that excluded fixed-guideway transit from consideration, it is now, at least officially, open to the idea of light rail transit. And it is pursuing a proposal, promoted by Isaacs, for private construction of a high-speed transit link between the Minneapolis and St. Paul downtowns. At the same time, however, the council is participating in a joint study of transit options—including light rail—along approximately the same corridor. This apparent conflict has led another participant in the options study to urge the council to drop the fast-link proposal, which he said would only waste time and distract attention from the study's more carefully thought-out approach.

The council is also involved in the selection of sites for the disposal of solid and sewage-sludge wastes. Having rejected some of the sites chosen by Hennepin County, the council is now conducting its own search for more acceptable locations. And it is reviewing proposed sites for a metropolitan-area horse racing track to be built under Minnesota's new parimutuel law.

The council also reviewed potential sites for the new Metrodome and actually issued the bonds for its construction—the first time it had exercised such authority. Otherwise, though, the 1977 state law authorizing a new sports stadium represented a significant step backward in legislative reliance on the council to resolve regional issues.

The choice of a site for the proposed new stadium was the subject of heated controversy, particularly between Minneapolis and Bloomington. To resolve it and to build and operate the facility, the legislature created the Metropolitan Sports Facilities Commission. But it did not put the commission directly under the council's umbrella. Sports commission members were appointed by the governor and were given the final say on what kind of stadium to build and where. Later legislation transferred the power to appoint commission members to the Minneapolis city council and narrowed the financing base from a seven-county liquor tax backing construction bonds to a Minneapolis-only tax.

Another example of legislative backsliding was the 1982 Surface Water Management Act, which required the metropolitan area's 44 secondary watershed districts to draw up plans for reducing surface-water runoff, a major source of pollution in the region's rivers and lakes. Although paralleling in many respects the 1976 land planning act, the surface water management act took away council review authority over watershed districts, which dated back to the 1967 law creating the council.

The question for the council, and for the Twin Cities metropolitan strategy in general, is whether the Minnesota legislature's stadium and watershed planning decisions were isolated incidents or the beginning of a trend away from coordinated solutions to regional problems. The 1984 legislative session may tell.

Charles C. Whiting, an editorial writer for the Minneapolis Star and Tribune, *was public information officer for the Metropolitan Planning Commission and the Metropolitan Council from 1962 to 1968.*

Is Chicago Ready for Reform?

John McCarron
(September 1984)

Chicago, long known as the "City That Works," is trying to shake a new reputation as the "City on Hold."

That's the status of several major urban redevelopment projects the city has undertaken. Almost everywhere one looks, from the big North Loop renewal area to the underused Navy Pier in Lake Michigan, city-sponsored redevelopment efforts are marking time, awaiting action, or "in committee." This semi-paralysis, a decade in the making, can hardly be blamed on Mayor Harold Washington, who is now in his second year as Chicago's first black mayor. The dilemma does present Washington with a serious challenge, however. For it is widely acknowledged that his administration must get the stalled projects moving—and soon—if he intends to win a second term against the still-powerful regular Democratic (don't call us a "machine") organization.

To that end, Washington has assembled a planning and development team unique in the city's modern history. The new people in charge of planning, housing, and economic development come from outside political circles, own impressive academic and civic credentials, and share a decidedly pro-neighborhood, rather than downtown, bent.

But while long resumes might carry weight in "planning" towns like Minneapolis or Portland, they are of dubious value in Chicago, the city that gave the word "clout" a new meaning. Planning here has traditionally been a weak sister of the political apparatus. Daniel Burnham's 1909 "Plan of Chicago" may have saved the city's lakefront from becoming a grimy industrial strip, but his successors have been meek fellows, summoned on occasion to bless deals cut in private between pols and developers. "Chicago ain't ready for reform," was

the way one ward-heeler put it, and he might have added "or for planning, either."

The godfather

All this was particularly true during the 21-year reign of the late Mayor Richard J. Daley. A consummate politician, Daley and his planning and public works czar, Lewis Hill, muscled through projects like O'Hare International Airport, McCormick Place (a huge lakefront exhibition center), the State Street Mall, a giant waterfront filtration plant, new transit lines, and fire and police stations.

Favored developers were given free rein, so long as they used politically influential law and consulting firms and, of course, hired union workers. Developer-politico Charles Swibel, former chairman of the Chicago Housing Authority (CHA), put deals together using union pension funds and government office tenants (as at Swibel's Marina City office-apartment tower) or by using his influence with Daley to help out-of-town developers swing urban renewal deals, as at the never-built Place du Sable housing complex on the Near West Side. The role of the city council, plan commission, and planning staff involved little more than watching for signals flashed by "Hizzoner," while the mayor built his political empire on concrete and the roar of jackhammers.

All this wheeling and dealing produced better and more lasting results than one might have expected. The city's downtown office construction boom, now 20 years old, roars on, defying experts' predictions of saturation. Big-league architects like Helmut Jahn are still recasting Chicago's impressive skyline, especially along hot spots like Wacker Drive and LaSalle Street. North of the Chicago River, an outright land rush has gripped Michigan Avenue, with skyscraper office-hotel-shopping malls sprouting on both sides of the street. (Interestingly, Charles Swibel was not such a permanent fixture after all. He was forced off the CHA board in 1982, during Mayor Byrne's reign, by HUD officials who were unhappy with conditions at the local agency.)

The near-absence of planning principles had its inevitable effects, to be sure. A stilted zoning code helped deaden large sections of the Loop with barren office plazas and useless sidewalk arcades provided by developers in return for extra stories. And no effort was made to preserve the airy, European charm of North Michigan Avenue once the high-rise builders moved in. Out in the neighborhoods, racial turnover and the attendant flight of people and jobs to suburbs went unchecked. During the 1970s, the city lost an average of 5,000 housing units a year to fire and abandonment.

Despite it all, the private-sector side of Chicago's downtown thrived during and after Daley's reign, especially when compared to downtowns in other Frost Belt cities. Projects involving city hall, however, haven't fared as well under Daley's successors: Michael Bilandic (1976–79), Jane Byrne (1979–83), and now, Harold Washington.

The current list of projects on hold is enough to make a Libertarian cackle. The six-block North Loop redevelopment area is fast becoming a planner's Vietnam. Ten years and $65 million worth of city planning and land acquisition have produced but one building, an elaborate parking structure. Repeated false starts (including a flirtation with the Hilton Hotels Corporation, which had proposed to build a $250 million hotel there) have hurt—not only because the decaying area lies smack between the Michigan Avenue and LaSalle Street booms, but because failure there calls into question whether Chicago has the wherewithal to execute a big public-private development a la Boston's Copley Place. . . .

Just why the private boom continued after Daley while public efforts stumbled is a question with several answers. Lacking sure-handed signals from the mayor's office, city planners recently have had to think and act on their own—an unaccustomed role. The city's potent business community has done little to fill the void. Kept outside the commander's tent by Daley, Chicago's corporate leaders are still groping for a meaningful role in civic affairs, with mixed results.

Business groups such as the nonprofit Central Area Committee, whose 1973 "Chicago 21" plan contained some solid ideas about improving downtown, recently updated their map with Nero-like proposals for decorative canals on the city's crumbling South Side and a new civic monument out in the lake. Corporate Chicago's ultimate pet project, though, is to stage a universal-class 1992 World's Fair on the downtown lakefront—a billion-dollar project considered frivolous by a growing number of neighborhood groups in the city's long-neglected interior.

Hatfields and McCoys

Under these circumstances, effective planning in Chicago would be tough even without the city council split, a royal political battle that pits 29 regular Democrats, led by Alderman Edward R. Vrdolyak, against 21 councilors loyal to the mayor. Blame here is a matter of opinion. Both sides have held the other's pet projects hostage at one time or another. Vrdolyak's forces, for instance, nixed a Washington proposal to have the Rouse Company redevelop Navy Pier, the city's cavernous, half-mile-long municipal dock, into a shopping and dining attraction. Most of the same aldermen endorsed the idea, in which the city was to put up $60 million of the $280 million project cost, when it was first proposed in 1980 by their ally, Mayor Byrne. Washington, in turn, has killed plans for a soccer field in Vrdolyak's ward and for a new branch library in the Daley clan's Bridgeport neighborhood.

Such is the battlefield confronting Mayor Washington's handpicked crew of planning professionals: planning commissioner Elizabeth L. Hollander, former head of the nonprofit Metropolitan Housing and Planning Council; economic development director Robert Mier, formerly an urban science professor at the University of Illinois at Chicago; and housing commissioner Brenda J. Gaines, formerly a special assistant with the U.S. Department of Housing and Urban Development.

Unquestionably, this trio is better versed in the theory of planning and urban development than any cabinet-level group within civic memory. The problem, of course, is that government Chicago-style bears little resemblance to the world of the weekend seminar, where city building is sometimes reduced to neat overhead projections of goals, objectives, and strategies.

A big question for Chicago, then, is: Can Washington's team make planning work? Or will they simply work on plans?

Here the posture of the city council is key, for the majority bloc can, if it chooses, make life all but impossible for the Washington team. Already it has demanded—though not yet won—council review of all city contracts in excess of $50,000, a potential bottleneck in that the city will parcel out $312 million for all of its contracts during this fiscal year. (Fiscal year 1984 began July 1.) Housing rehab loans exceeding $75,000 also must be run through the council. Gone, too, are rubber-stamp approvals, so typical of the council in the Daley era, of everything from bond issues to redevelopment agreements.

One could argue that city councils are supposed to review planning decisions, but one mayoral aide has a different reading of the council's motive: "There is a consistent interest in who gets the contracts and who gets the jobs."

"There's nothing wrong with council review if the time frame can be kept workable," says Hollander. "But we've got to be able to make decisions in a timely way. It's especially a problem working with the private sector, where time is money."

If the "council wars" can somehow be overcome, the mayor's development team may yet fully implement an ambitious set of programs announced last April on Washington's first anniversary in office. Called "Chicago Works Together," the plan includes 90 new and redesigned projects aimed at creating or saving 10,000 permanent jobs and 60,000 housing units. Common to many of the programs is a new emphasis on neighborhood needs and an effort to involve community organizations in renewal efforts by, for instance, providing them with planning grants.

This reach toward the neighborhoods could prove enormously popular in a city where the late Saul Alinsky's tradition of community activism still burns hot. Failure to do likewise was probably the political undoing of former Mayor Jane M. Byrne. She challenged the regular Democrats in 1979 on a pro-neighborhood platform, claiming an "evil cabal" of politicians and downtown interests was carving up the city for itself. Three months into her administration, all that changed. Byrne allied herself with the regulars and flipped to a pro-downtown strategy, explaining that the neighborhoods would benefit indirectly from growth of the Loop's financial and service districts.

Neighborhood leaders watched in anger as Byrne obtained UDAG money for downtown enterprises in questionable need, such as an addition to the Chicago Board of Trade. One year she diverted a third of the city's community development funds to pay overdue snow removal bills. A major planning function was yanked from the Chicago Rehab Network, an umbrella group for community-based rehabbers, and the work turned over to patronage workers in the city's housing department.

Against that recent history, anything the Washington team might do to empower neighborhoods (a Washington campaign pledge) will be hailed as a marked improvement. And it appears it intends to do quite a bit.

Under Brenda Gaines, the housing department is refocusing its effort toward rehabbing multiunit, walk-up apartment buildings—the city's biggest housing headache. Fortunately for the Washington administration, several of the city's major banks have recently kicked off multi-million-dollar rehab loan programs, and Gaines has moved quicky to dovetail those funds with her department's programs. Loan commitments have already been made on 1,600 housing units, she says, and community-based housing groups have been chosen to do much of the work.

"We try to leverage our money to the max," Gaines says. "The idea is to choose the deals that will do the most for low- and moderate-income families."

As for economic development, Mier is trying to breathe life into Chicago's moribund inner-city industrial parks and to link downtown developers with neighborhood projects. The idea, he explains, is to have developers of public-private projects downtown adopt a companion project out in the neighborhoods, lending their technical and financing enterprise.

Skeptics point out that Chicago's public-private projects aren't doing so well downtown and that another city requirement may turn developers off entirely. Mier counters that the Washington administration, by moving the entire development process into the open (on top of the table, as it were) will cut developers' costs by eliminating quid pro quos like campaign contributions. Requirements for "linked development," he argues, will be infinitely more palatable to developers than was the political arm-twisting of old.

Sorting things out

A common problem faced by Hollander, Gaines, and Mier is that the city's planning apparatus was drastically reshuffled under Byrne, with confusion over duties lingering still. The shakeup began in 1979, when Byrne created a department of neighborhoods, actually an elaborate citizens information service that the mayor's critics said functioned more as a propaganda mill. A year later the department of housing was formed by pulling the urban renewal section out of the department of planning.

And in 1982 the planning department was raided twice, first to create a new department of economic development and then to set up an over-arching office of city development under Ira J. Bach, a veteran Chicago planning executive.

The big loser, of course, was the planning department, which was also stripped of its role in transportation planning (to public works) and community development programming (to the mayor's office of budget and management). And, finally, another 51 people were let go early in Mayor Washington's term, when the planning department lost most of its federal community development funds. At last count, planning had 108 staffers, down from 600 in the Daley years.

To compensate for these losses, Hollander is concentrating on informational and process approaches rather than hands-on design work. She has kept the department's three-division organizational framework (development, zoning administration, and comprehensive and neighborhood planning) but added new functions and, in some cases, leadership to each.

To run her planning division, Hollander recruited David Mosena, former research director of the American Planning Association. He has set up two new subgroups: one to provide planning services to neighborhoods, another to get a handle on city-wide capital facilities planning. For the development division, Hollander hired Lucille R. Dobbins, a banker with strong accounting and financial credentials. As first deputy commissioner, Dobbins will have her hands full getting the North Loop and other big-ticket projects back on track.

And there have been other initiatives. The department's research unit recently turned out a Chicago Statistical Abstract superior to any previous compilation of federal census data. Hollander has also set up an urban design review unit to guide developers and their architects toward desirable public goals, such as including active retail uses rather than sterile plazas at sidewalk level. Other subdepartmental groups are working on changes to the city's labyrinthian building and zoning codes, planning for the 1992 World's Fair, and the first-ever set of procedural guidelines for the Chicago Plan Commission.

"We're doing more and more with less," Hollander recently said of her skeleton crew. "Every section has a management plan. There is motivation. . . . People are beginning to voice their opinions on things, something they were never encouraged to do before."

Whether these changes will have an effect out in the street—especially on those "on hold" projects—remains to be seen. Much depends, of course, on the political vagaries of "council wars."

"It's a period of adjustment," says Hollander, who insists Chicago may indeed finally be ready for reform, and maybe even a little planning.

John McCarron is an urban affairs writer with the Chicago Tribune.

Austin: The Perils of Popularity

Kaye Northcott
(November 1984)

Austin is Texas's most cerebral and least materialistic city. Where a Houstonian might ask, "If you're so smart, why aren't you rich?" an Austinite asks, "If you're so rich, why aren't you smart?" Virtually everyone who lives here, newcomer or old hand, loves the lakes, the spring-fed swimming pools, the cedar-scented hills, the live oaks, the pale violet sunsets, and the mellow ambiance that once earned Austin the nickname of the hippie Palm Springs.

The business community believes that Austin can protect its special qualities even while embracing the current boom, which last year made the three-county Austin area the fastest growing major metro area in the United States and which increased the metro-area population from 537,000 in 1981 to 671,000 today. The boom is sending land values and the once-low cost of living into the stratosphere. Many neighborhood leaders and environmentalists already see Austin as Paradise Lost. Although Austin is one of the few major cities in this free enterprise state that has seriously attempted to direct growth instead of simply allowing market forces to determine its destiny, the results have been mixed at best.

Austin politics are volatile; the balance of power tilts from neighborhood groups one year to developers the next. Growth pains and uncertainty about the future make city hall a revolving door type of place. In 1981, Dan Davidson, a planner by training and the strongest city manager in recent history, was eased out by a newly elected, neighborhood-dominated council. Many of the council believed Davidson was following his own pro-developer agenda rather than implementing the council's policies. Davidson's supporters countered that Austin wasn't acting as a council-manager form of government should, that the council members were acting like city managers. Given the choice of quitting or being fired, Davidson quit and went to work for the Nash/Phillips-Copus Company, Austin's largest homebuilder.

Where Davidson had been criticized for having too strong a hold over city departments, his successor, Nicholas Meiszer, was fired early this year for lack of initiative and failure to gain the respect of his staff. Meiszer's replacement was the deputy city manager, Jorge Carrasco, who so far has received good reviews.

In addition to Meiszer, Austin so far this year has lost an assistant city manager, human services director, director of water and wastewater, utilities director, parks and recreation director, vehicle and equipment director, finance director, city attorney, police chief, and a covey of planners. Some staffers resigned in Meiszer's wake. Others were fired for personal pecadillos or incompetence. Many found more lucrative employment with development companies. This administrative instability may simply reflect the anguish of a city seriously trying to deal with its future. But, nationally, Austin is developing a reputation for making mincemeat of its bureaucrats. When Davidson resigned three and a half years ago, there were 300 applications for his job; this time around, there were only 60 applications and those mainly from administrators in smaller cities.

Reconfiguration

Planning director Dick Lillie, who had been with the city for 19 years, left when Carrasco decided to divide the planning department into a 45-position Planning and Growth Management Department (for long-range planning) and a 125-position Office of Land Development Services (for zoning and permits). Lillie insisted that he had not resigned because of the reorganization but because "at the age of 53, I had reached that point in a career where you either stay until retirement or you go off and do something else." Shortly after his resignation, Lillie went to work for former Texas gov-

ernor and Nixon cabinet official John Connally and former lieutenant governor Ben Barnes, whose Austin-based partnership is building shopping centers, offices, and housing in various Texas cities.

Two new planners were brought in from Broward County, south Florida's sprawling boom county. James B. Duncan was hired to oversee land development services for Austin, a job similar to the one he held in Florida, where he is given credit for streamlining permit processing and computerizing the system, thereby reducing development application time from 90 to 30 days. Council members hope that Duncan can loosen the permit logjam in Austin's overworked and underorganized planning department.

Austin's new director of planning and growth management is Norman Standerfer, who was in charge of Broward County's long-range planning for the past four years. Standerfer and Duncan have been friends and colleagues since they attended the University of Oklahoma in the early 1960s. Together, they say, they hope to use their experience to help Austin avoid some of the mistakes made by Broward County. Standerfer told the *Austin American-Statesman,* "There's an opportunity to sit down with the population of Austin and say, 'Austin is about to explode. If growth is going to happen, just don't shut your eyes and let it happen. If there is no plan, you're going to end up like Broward County, and that's the pits.'"

In Austin, however, the new planning twosome will not have as many growth control tools at hand as it did in Florida, which authorizes local and regional development controls. Texas does not even give its counties ordinance-making authority. And Austin, for all its good intentions, has never enacted the controls necessary to force compliance with its master plan. In zoning cases, neighborhoods and developers battle to win over the city's planning commissioners, political appointees all. The city council has the final say on zoning, and each week it spends precious hours refereeing disputes.

Austin's master plan is based on goals enunciated in the Austin Tomorrow Goals Program, which retiring planning director Lillie counts as one of his major accomplishments. Between 1973 and 1975, the planning department brought 3,500 residents together to think about the future of Austin. (These planning sessions stimulated the growth of neighborhood groups, which today number close to 200.)

The plan adopted by the council in 1979 on the heels of the goals program was the city's first substantial revision of its 1961 master plan. It called for commercial and industrial projects to be located on a north-south axis defined by Interstate 35, which cuts through the center of the city. The hills, the lake shores, and the Edwards Aquifer recharge zone, all to the west, were flagged as the least desirable for growth because of the high cost of extending services and the danger of polluting the water supply and scarring the natural beauty of the hills.

Although the plan's intentions were good, neither it, nor the 1961 plan for that matter, has had much effect on the form of the city. Many would agree with the assessment of Robert Cullick, who reports on growth for the *American-Statesman,* and who says, "The Austin master plan has been effectively shelved." The western hills, for example, where intense growth was proscribed by the 1979 plan, are the latest target for heavy development.

As part of the Austin Tomorrow effort, an "Ongoing Committee" was appointed to "help guide city government in the direction of citizens' goals." But the plan has not been implemented through growth control or zoning ordinances. The nine-member planning commission recently sent the refined master plan to the city council for adoption, but attorney Jim Butler, a member of the commission, says, "I don't think the master plan is being looked at very seriously. I think our recommendations are fairly useless."

John P. Watson, a prominent developer, who, in a recent, much-publicized move, helped bring the Microelectronics & Computer Technology Corporation and the 3M Company to Austin, speaks for the business community when he says, "You can't absolutely draw a line in the dirt and say, no, this is nondevelopable." Indeed, 3M has announced it will build a research campus in the northwest hills near lakes Travis and Austin, the source of the city's water supply. The council seems to have given up on growth prohibitions, but it may choose to offer economic incentives—lower water connection fees, for example—to encourage north-south corridor growth.

Cataclysmic growth

For most of its recent history, Austin grew at a heady but potentially manageable three to 3.5 percent a year. Last year, its growth rate shot up to 9.6 percent, according to the Austin-based Population Research Service. At least a dozen new hotels are planned. Thousands of apartments are going up, as is a new generation of downtown office high-rises. Speculators are making quick millions by flipping both raw and developed land. Where traditional Austinites built modest houses that hugged the contours of the land or renovated old houses in the inner city, developers are now building pretentious $500,000, even million-dollar, speculative houses on the top of the western hills and over the Edwards Aquifer recharge zone. "No city can sustain this growth rate and not have problems," says council member Sally Shipman, a planner who also served on the APA board of directors.

Dowell Myers, who teaches community and regional planning at the University of Texas, recently issued a disturbing report on Austin. Myers noted that rapidly rising housing costs are putting a strain on all sectors of the community, that crime has doubled since 1970, and that the quality of the water supply has deteriorated significantly. He also observed that, while Austin has the lowest unemployment rate in Texas (3.6 percent in August), real income has risen far less for minorities than for the general population. In 1970, for instance, the per capita income for Austin blacks (12 percent of the population) was 52.3 percent of the average; for Hispanics (18 percent of the population), it was 59.3 percent. . . .

Schisms

Up until the mid-seventies, the Austin city council, which is elected at large, was populated by owners of small local businesses. They were not particularly interested in attracting new industry to the city or in opening up the governing process. Being the capital city and the premier campus of the University of Texas also has created problems. It's hard for a city to gain control of its own destiny when two of its major components remove land from the tax rolls and carry out independent building programs. Revenue from the university's two-billion-dollar endowment is used primarily for extravagant construction, which is not subject to city ordinances.

During the seventies, UT began increasing its enrollment (today the Austin campus has 47,500 students), but failed to build new dormitories. Thousands of politically active students were cast out into the community. In 1975, a coalition of students, white-collar liberals, and minorities gained control of the city council. City boards and commissions began reflecting the true diversity of the city and people began talking about growth control. Simultaneously, the Austin Tomorrow goals program was helping to nurture the fledgling neighborhood movement. By the time the activist students had graduated, the environmentalists and the neighborhood groups were ready to take their place as the standard bearers for growth control.

Since then, the city council majority has seesawed between the business establishment and the neighborhoods. The black and Hispanic council members sometimes vote with the chamber of commerce, sometimes with the neighborhoods. Even before the current growth crunch, it was hard to set long-term goals for the city because of the shifting consensus.

In 1981–82, the council tilted toward the neighborhoods. With two exceptions, city planner Sally Shipman and environmentally oriented Roger Duncan, the current council is more developer-oriented. (However, a quirk in Texas zoning law allows Shipman and Duncan to block some upzoning proposals: It takes a six-to-one majority to approve a zoning change when the owners of 20 percent of the property surrounding the site in question oppose the change.) Next year, it's possible that the neighborhoods will regain control of the council when districts are instituted as the result of a lawsuit filed by the NAACP. Only the mayor will be elected at large, and the council will be expanded from seven to nine members. . . .

Austin's early efforts in the direction of growth control fall into the category of benign neglect. In the 1970s, the city refused to annex new land and declined to provide the infrastructure needed for new suburbs. This strategy backfired when developers turned instead to a form of state-authorized special district known as a "municipal utility district" (MUD), which has the power to issue bonds and levy taxes to pay for services. (Under state law, if a city turns down a developer's request for services, the state water resources board can authorize a MUD—and usually does.) Twenty-three MUDs have been created so far within Austin's five-mile extraterritorial jurisdiction. (Texas gives cities subdivision approval, but not zoning, powers within their ETJs—the size of which vary by population.)

Although MUDs, by their nature, are outside direct city control, negotiations usually bring them into general compliance with city policy, and in many cases they agree to future annexation. Annexation gives Austin influence over a MUD, but it also means that the city eventually absorbs the MUD's debt for building in an area the city was reluctant to serve in the first place. . . .

This summer, Austin imposed limited-purpose annexation on 10,000 acres northwest of town. Limited-purpose annexation allows the city to implement zoning controls without providing city services and without levying taxes. The city has never used limited annexation on so large an area, and the legal staff anticipates a court challenge. Mark Rose, the council member who sponsored the annexation, wants the city to prepare a comprehensive land-use plan for the area, specifying densities and types of allowable uses. That's expected to provoke heated debate between environmentalists and builders. The former say density limitations are the way to prevent pollution of the lakes and the aquifer; the latter insist the filtration systems provide adequate protection.

Council member Sally Shipman expresses doubt that the city has the clout to protect the area. She says she fears that most of the land-use planning will be done by developers and rubber-stamped by the majority of the council.

Another sensitive question is how much of the infrastructure costs the developers will bear. Although Austin has adopted a capital recovery fee that requires builders to finance some of the cost of city services, growth is by no means paying for itself. City manager Carrasco is negotiating with Nash/Phillips-Copus and 3M on how much of the $15 million bill for laying sewer lines through the western hills the developers would pay.

Meanwhile, city taxes are increasing steadily. Between 1983 and 1984, the total appraised value of real estate in Austin increased by 52.8 percent. Almost 94 percent of the increase was due to revaluations, rather than growth. Last year, the average home was valued at $60,000; this year it will be valued at $92,000, increasing the homeowner's bill by $51. In addition, Austin will be imposing double-digit increases in utility bills. (The city owns its electric utility, and Austin residents bear the highest debt per capital in the state. But proponents of the recent bond package argued that the debt is not out of line when you understand that 68 percent of the debt is for the city-owned electric utility.)

Despite its staggering size, this September's bond package will not come near to providing the new infrastructure the city needs, including new sewage treatment plants, water lines, and roads and bridges, a new city hall, and a bigger airport. The Chamber of Commerce is also pushing for a new convention center.

The test of a city plan is whether it passes from the book to the earth. Many here believe that standard planning processes are simply too slow to cope with the traumatizing rate of development confronting Austin's neighborhoods and natural environment. Yet planner/council member Sally Shipman is optimistic. "The people who live here are here by choice," she says, "and they will demand the preservation of Austin's assets."

Kaye Northcott is a former editor of the Texas Observer.

On the Beach With the Progressives

William Fulton
(January 1985)

Last November, almost four years after its nationally publicized sweep to power, a coalition of rent control activists in Santa Monica, California, narrowly lost control of the seven-member city council because of a campaign technicality.

During those four years, the efforts of the group known as Santa Monicans for Renters' Rights (SMRR) had been hailed as the liberal answer to Reaganite populism by *Mother Jones* and the *Village Voice* and ridiculed as "suburban radicalism" by the *Wall Street Journal.* Local public officials had been subjected to death threats and described as socialists or worse ("The People's Republic of Santa Monica") by landlords and conservatives.

Yet, while Santa Monica's rhetoric and reputation may have been far to the left of most city gov-

ernments—the rent control people are closely allied to Tom Hayden and his Santa Monica-based Campaign for Economic Democracy—planning, not El Salvador or the nuclear freeze, was the centerpiece of their "progressive" administration.

"We're not going to be taking trips to Havana or renaming Main Street Ho Chi Minh Boulevard," quipped planning professor Derek Shearer, the rent control group's campaign manager, shortly after the 1981 election. And, indeed, although the goal of the new administration was a high-sounding commitment to "democratize" urban life for the city's residents, its agenda was hardly unusual for a Southern California beach town at a time when all the beach towns in the Los Angeles area were being inundated with expensive condominiums and high-rise office developments. They were concerned with maintaining affordable housing in a skyrocketing market, controlling the influx of large office buildings, and increasing citizen participation in the planning process.

What made Santa Monica unusual was the fact that the city's wide-open political atmosphere allowed the administration to go far beyond conventional methods in almost every area of planning—to become, in short, a test tube for such progressive planning ideas as developer exactions and tenant ownership. City officials didn't invent very many of the tools they used; rather, their creativity lay in borrowing ideas from all over the country. Where they ran into trouble was in trying to translate these ideas into practical planning tools—and in that, there are lessons for other cities, no matter what their politics.

How did they do? It's probably fair to say that they pulled planning practices in the city to the left and in the process moved toward the center themselves.

For one thing, they succeeded in halting high-rise development and even encouraged construction of some attractive low-rise, mixed-use projects. "We stopped the march to the sea," says Shearer, now chairman of the city planning commission and head of the urban affairs program at Occidental College in Los Angeles, referring to the line of high-rises heading down Wilshire Boulevard toward the ocean. "The bottom line is that Santa Monica will not become another Westwood or Century City. No way." (Westwood and Century City are Los Angeles neighborhoods not far from Santa Monica where 20-story office towers have prevailed in a previously low-rise environment.)

They also increased neighborhood participation and acted on the theory that developers owe a debt to the city in which they build. For three and a half years, while they prepared new development guidelines, the ruling group used open-ended zoning negotiations to extract promises from office and hotel developers to help solve the city's social ills—wresting such concessions as low-income housing, money for social services, hotel vouchers for battered women, and preferential hiring for minority residents.

In doing so, however, they stumbled over the problem of how best to involve neighborhood residents in the planning process. The project-by-project negotiations alienated developers and bankers, who considered the city's demands arbitrary, and also created a "generation gap" between the rent control group and the city's old-line planners, who in any other place would be regarded as liberal. Two SMRR appointees—city manager John Alschuler and Mark Tigan, director of the community and economic development department— emerged as the administration's top negotiators. At the same time, the influence of long-time planning director James W. Lunsford waned, and he took early retirement last year.

Commenting on what happened, Frank Hotchkiss, a former Santa Monica planning commissioner, said before last November's election: "The rule of law has been set aside and the rule of arbitrariness has been in effect since 1981. They [SMRR] retain that discretionary power at all costs—it's a real threat to the underlying system of government." Hotchkiss is director of planning for the Southern California Association of Governments.

Finally, SMRR made peace, of a sort, with the business community, which was actively involved in revising the city's overall land-use plan. And the ongoing war between landlords and tenants led to an innovative tenant ownership program. Gentrification continues to occur in Santa Monica, but the new program stands a good chance of protecting some relatively low-cost housing in an increasingly high-cost city.

In the end, SMRR lost power not because its members had not pleased the electorate, but because one of the incumbent council members failed to collect enough valid signatures to be placed on the ballot. The other three incumbents won reelection handily.

Jane and friends

In the 1960s, the completion of the Santa Monica Freeway brought the city, a middle-class suburban beach town, within easy driving distance of downtown Los Angeles and touched off a surge of apartment building. Now, though still mostly white and middle class, Santa Monica is much more crowded, with a population of 88,000 compressed into eight square miles; 80 percent of the city's residents are renters.

In the 1970s, Santa Monica was near the epicenter of the amazing Los Angeles real estate boom. Speculation in apartment buildings was brisk, the rush for condos hit the city in force, and old retail and manufacturing areas were being recycled as office developments. Moderate planners and politicans—including Frank Hotchkiss and Christine Reed, who became mayor a few weeks ago when SMRR lost power—had already begun to win some battles against the growth-oriented business establishment. In the mid-1970s, they downzoned the city and imposed height limits and later called on the city council to impose a moratorium on condo conversions.

But the population in Santa Monica was changing dramatically, thanks to the apartment construction. A city that had voted for Goldwater in 1964 was carried by McGovern eight years later. In 1973, Tom Hayden and Jane Fonda moved to Santa Monica, closely followed by Shearer and his wife, consumer activist Ruth Yannatta Goldway. Soon, an enclave of 1960s activists was redefining the city's political landscape.

When the real estate boom hit, the activists joined the burgeoning rent control movement. Under the umbrella name Santa Monicans for Renters' Rights, the activists, with the assistance of the city's many elderly renters, passed one of the toughest rent control laws in the country and elected three members to the city council, including Goldway. SMRR activists did not like even the moderate planners, believing them too strongly linked to the business community. As proof, they pointed to approval of such buildings as Lawrence Welk's 11-story project near the ocean, which they denounced as too tall.

"At first I was considered a thorough radical," says architect Herb Katz, who served on the planning commission at the time and won the decisive seat on the city council last November. Then, after SMRR emerged, "I went from the far left to the far right, and I didn't move."

In 1981, SMRR captured a ruling majority on the nonpartisan city council, and Goldway, who had earned a reputation as hard-nosed, was selected mayor by her colleagues.

The first action the new council took in 1981 was to place a six-month moratorium on all construction in the city, a move that outraged local builders. (Almost as controversial was the appointment of Shearer, the mayor's husband, to the planning commission; opponents called it nepotism, despite his undeniable qualifications.) Sixty-one projects were stopped by the moratorium, but soon builders began to come before the council to request exemptions.

The new council members had made production of affordable housing their top priority, particularly since the Reagan administration had begun to dismantle federal housing subsidies. They also knew that, because of Proposition 13, property taxes on new office buildings wouldn't do much to fill the city's coffers. And they had seen the environmentally oriented California Coastal Commission negotiate all sorts of concessions, including low-cost housing, from beachfront developers in exchange for the necessary building permits.

Thus Santa Monica began a three-year period during which it was almost impossible to build a big project without first negotiating with the city and offering considerable concessions. Out of this peculiar set of circumstances—one that gave the city enormous leverage over developers in a hot real estate market—emerged a series of innovative housing and planning programs that worked with varying degrees of success.

The city already had tight control over landlords because of the rent control law. Rent increases and other matters were determined by a powerful, independently elected rent control board, all of whose members had been elected on the SMRR slate and which was continually at odds with local landlords. Shortly after the election, SMRR turned its attention to revising the city's housing element, one of the nine general plan elements required by California law. With tension mounting in the city, the new council was eager to find ways to produce new housing units and allow tenants to buy their apartments from landlords, but they were opposed to the construction or conversion of condominiums because of the city's history of speculation.

The planning commission proposed such solutions as limited-equity cooperatives and ownership by nonprofit corporations. But the housing element got caught up in a bitter imbroglio over another housing production idea: allowing granny flats, or second units in existing, single-family houses. Homeowners, whose political power had been dissipated by the tenant movement, closed ranks to fend off what they saw as a tenant attempt to harm their neighborhoods. As a result of the homeowners' attack, the council was forced to eliminate the granny flat idea. Debate over many of the other innovative proposals the planning commission had introduced dragged on into late 1982.

Thereafter, SMRR's focus shifted from producing new affordable housing to simply trying to protect the low-cost housing that was already available. Two neighborhood groups banded together to create the Community Corporation of Santa Monica to buy and renovate run-down apartment houses.

Meanwhile, the pressure to allow some sort of condo conversion continued to build. In 1983, a group of homeowners and affluent tenants drew up a ballot proposition to allow condo conversion in certain circumstances and, hoping to appeal to tenants, included provisions that would allow renters to sell their right to purchase their units. Despite SMRR's vigorous opposition—and a visit by Ralph Nader on the coalition's behalf—the proposal was defeated only narrowly, and, in the same election, an extremely bitter one, Ruth Goldway lost her bid for reelection to the council. After the election, landlords continued their practice of choosing mostly young, single, and upscale tenants for rent-controlled apartments, and a landlord attorney began punching big holes in the rent control board's powers.

When the pressure for condo conversions did not abate, SMRR agreed for the first time to negotiate with landlords and affluent tenants on a tenant ownership proposal. The resulting plan, approved by voters last June, allows tenants to buy their apartments at below-market rates if most of the renters in a building express interest in doing so; protects renters who don't want to buy (senior citizens and handicapped people get lifetime leases at controlled rents); and places a six-percent tax on purchases to help poor people (or nonprofits like Community Corporation) buy apartments in the city. Though still untested, it has been hailed by all parties in the city as a way around the rent control stalemate.

Making deals

For three and a half years after SMRR came to power, the city council and top staff members negotiated design changes and exactions on almost all large projects on a case-by-case basis. Eventually the land-use element laid out new rules that incorporated many of the exactions used in the negotiated cases.

The biggest project halted by the moratorium was a $150 million hotel-office-retail complex designed to house the international headquarters of Welton Becket Associates, the largest architecture firm on the West Coast. Excavation for the buildings, on the site of a former garbage dump in an area of the city zoned for manufacturing, had already begun, although no building permit had been granted. Fearing they might lose a court case based on their vested rights, Becket officials proposed to negotiate a "development agreement" with the city to allow construction to continue.

Development agreements—in essence, zoning contracts between local governments and developers—were authorized by the California legislature in 1979 at the instigation of real estate interests, who were angry about antideveloper court decisions in vested rights cases. The agreements were designed to assure builders that, once started, their projects couldn't be stopped by a change in government. Even in Santa Monica, it was often the developer who proposed use of a development agreement. But the city used the process as a way of exacting concessions in exchange for the right to build.

After months of acrimonious negotiation, Becket got its building permit and also permission to exceed the height limit for the hotel portion of the development. In return, the firm agreed to pay for: 100 units of on-site low-income housing, a community room, an on-site day-care center, a three-acre park (the entire site is 15 acres), traffic management and energy conservation measures, job training and affirmative action programs, and an arts and social services fee equal to 1.5 percent of the cost of the project.

Development exactions are not unusual in Cali-

fornia (they are supposed to be "reasonably related" to the project at hand), but the nature of the Welton Becket deal was unprecedented. Subsequently, the city lifted the moratorium and adopted interim development guidelines that allowed builders to proceed as long as they paid the same kind of price. In the months that followed, the city negotiated two more development agreements and settled a lawsuit with a developer who agreed to similar conditions and also promised to give the city $275,000 to restore the famous Santa Monica carousel, featured in the movie *The Sting.*

There were some success stories. Goldway and developer Herb Kendall, for example, negotiated an attractive Mediterranean-style project just across from the Santa Monica Pier. Kendall had planned an eight- or nine-story office building, but Paseo del Mar was built as a two- and three-story complex of offices, shops, restaurants, and apartments for low- and moderate-income people. Both developer and mayor expressed pride in the project.

But not everyone was happy. The president of Welton Becket, while acknowledging that the development agreement process was his best alternative given the situation, told "60 Minutes" that the city had the power to engage in extortion. Lawrence Welk's attorney claimed that city officials were playing "Let's Make a Deal" ("You build some affordable housing, and we'll give you what's behind curtain three"). The moderate planners from the 1970s also complained that the negotiation process was destroying the integrity of the city's zoning. "If we hadn't had strict enforcement of zoning in the M–1 [manufacturing] zone, the Becket site wouldn't have been available," says James W. Lunsford, who stepped down last year after 13 years as Santa Monica's planning director and is now a consultant to local developers.

In June 1982, the council decided it couldn't rezone the city, as it had hoped, until it had revamped the land-use element of the general plan, a process that eventually took two and a half years. In the meantime, developers had to follow the stiff interim development guidelines or negotiate a development agreement with the city. Lunsford says it is these "social exactions" that separate the older generation of physical planners like himself from the younger group that was running the city by that time. "To me," he says, "if a 12-story building is wrong, it's wrong no matter who lives in it."

"They made these deals for what they thought society should be," says Herb Katz, another of the "old school" planners. "They were trying to dictate on a block-by-block basis what will happen."

But the new city government believed, as then-city manager John Alschuler put it at an APA workshop in 1983, that Santa Monica had to avoid the temptation to worship office construction and its $80-per-square-foot prices as a "false idol" because it destroys the diversity of the city's employment and population. "If you alter the employment base, you're trading off the rich heritage of that diversity for the sterility of most of western Los Angeles," he said.

In the face of a court challenge to the exactions, the city commissioned a study from Hamilton, Rabinowitz & Szanton, which concluded that exactions are legal because new office buildings create increased demand for housing and, because of Proposition 13, don't provide enough revenue to pay for the cost of the city services they demand. (Alschuler left the city manager post last September to open a New York office for the same consulting firm. His top aide, Mark Tigan, will leave Santa Monica next month to become director of the Community Development Trading Group in Newport, Rhode Island.)

Alschuler and Tigan said they disliked negotiating on a project-by-project basis because the deal making was exhausting and expensive. (In early 1984, the city adopted a minimum processing fee of $10,000 for development agreement applications, based on studies of how much staff time they had spent on them.) But they defended the idea as an interim measure until the land-use element provided clear rules.

Alschuler, who himself received a $14,000-a-year housing subsidy from the city in order to live in expensive Santa Monica, made another point as well at the 1983 workshop referred to above: "We don't have much choice without federal housing programs. We've gotten 250 new units of low- and moderate-income housing with no federal subsidy in the last year. I think that's a remarkable accomplishment for a city of 90,000 people."

Delicate balance

A basic tenet of SMRR's philosophy of democratizing urban life is the notion of bringing local residents into the planning process. Even before the 1981 election, the council, at the SMRR's insistence, had given large chunks of federal block grant money to neighborhood groups and encouraged them to speak out. And among SMRR's first reforms was the extension of planning commission notification to tenants as well as property owners.

"We balance off the interest groups," said Vivian Rothstein, who was hired by the SMRR-dominated council to serve as the city's liaison to neighborhood groups. "The more articulate they are, the better we can balance them off. We do whatever we can to make them more articulate."

Alschuler and Tigan, however, sometimes came into conflict with the aggressive neighborhood groups the city had so deliberately created. While recognizing that the city did not want high-rise development, they saw their roles as deal makers who could lure tax-rich development into Santa Monica to help support the many social services that SMRR wanted.

But in negotiating development agreements, the city staff felt it got little guidance from the council or from the interim development guidelines.

"There was a lack of general consensus about what the project objectives were," says Paul Silvern, who succeeded Lunsford as planning director. "We were negotiating in the dark." As a result, the staff often engaged in heavy private negotiations, and neighbors and even the planning commission felt dealt out. The question of who was to participate in the negotiations, and how, collapsed into confusion on more than one occasion.

In one instance, a proposed hotel expansion, the city staff negotiated a development agreement with many unusual exactions—room vouchers for use by social service agencies, provision of a shuttle tram to the beach, and a special bed tax to help the civic auditorium—only to have neighbors come along later and raise a completely different set of concerns about traffic and parking. It took six additional months of negotiation to mollify the neighbors.

The next time, apparently worried that the same thing might happen again, Tigan encouraged an office developer to consult the neighborhood group first. This group was more aggressive, however, and negotiated its own exactions, including a two-percent limited-equity partnership in the building. Though some described it as enlightened community partnership, the business community was enraged. Only the collapse of the project for other reasons saved the city from a rough battle with the neighborhood group over control of the exaction money.

The last straw seemed to come when Alschuler pushed hard to bring one of the largest Cadillac dealerships in the country—and its rich trove of sales tax money—across the line from Los Angeles. First, the city alienated neighboring homeowners by committing more than $300,000 a year of the tax money to housing programs while leaving them uncertain about new traffic lights and street signs. Then the planning commission objected to the deal because the building's five-story height was higher than the imminent land-use element was likely to allow. Finally, the city council overruled the planning commission and mollified the neighbors, but again the deal fell through for other reasons.

Ironically, a city administration committed to neighborhood participation never did find a satisfactory way to bring neighborhood groups into the negotiated development process.

Finally, last October, the city council approved a new land-use element that had been two and a half years in preparation. For the first time since the moratorium, Santa Monica has clear rules for development.

New office development is to be concentrated downtown. Hotels—considered good tax generators and employers of unskilled, low-income residents—are being encouraged near the ocean, much to the dismay of some of the old-line planners. The old manufacturing district is to be split in two, with the eastern half set aside for "garden offices" such as research and development parks and the western half designated as an "industrial conservation district" that bans most office uses but provides a bonus for factories that include artists' studios.

Office developers still must pay a housing and parks fee of $2.25 per square foot for the first 15,000 feet and $5 per square foot after that. But some of the socially oriented requirements of the interim development guidelines—day care centers, for example—have been dropped.

After the planning commission approved the land-use element, some business people, including property owners on Wilshire Boulevard—where projects were limited to three or four stories and floor-area ratio was held to between 2.0 and 2.5—complained that the restrictions were too severe. Alschuler negotiated a compromise, subsequently adopted by the city council, that raised allowable heights (four–six stories) and FARs (3.0–3.5) slightly.

Development agreements, the subject of so much controversy over the last years, are expected to be used only with projects expected to be built in phases or large, complex projects, such as the Rand Corporation property, a big and attractive piece of land near the beach (Rand's headquarters are in downtown Santa Monica). Some neighborhood leaders wish they had the leverage negotiation provided, but city officials are pleased. "Instead of negotiating 90 percent of the world, the city can now sit down and negotiate for 10 or 20 percent," says former city manager Alschuler.

Some city officials already feel burned by the outcome of the Welton Becket project. After building the office buildings, Becket claimed it could not get financing for the project's second phase, which included the hotel, the three-acre park, and many of the amenities the council had negotiated for. (The city applied for a UDAG to assist phase two but was turned down.)

As SMRR leaves power and the land-use element is translated into zoning regulations, the rent control activists feel they've achieved many of their objectives, the moderates promise no major changes in the way the city is run, and others are glad the city is entering a time that promises more stability and fewer headlines.

"We got the message across," says Derek Shearer.

"Many people want to put this behind them and move on to other things," adds planning director Paul Silvern, who was a neighborhood activist before joining the city. "But land-use issues will always be a focal point for debate in Santa Monica."

William Fulton is a contributing editor of Planning.

Houston Gets Religion

James Peters
(August 1985)

For two decades now, Houston has played the part of planning's whipping boy. Media observers periodically troop down to this Gulf Coast metropolis to file their dire reports about the nation's largest boomtown, the city without zoning.

"It's spreading like a spilled bucket of water." (French magazine writer)

"A cluttered dime store, a garage sale gone wrong, a leaking sewer pipe." (*Atlantic Monthly*)

"Unzoned, unfettered, and mostly unrepentant." (*Planning,* March 1982)

The criticism sharpened in the last two years as the city's most recent boom began slowing, a victim of the same forces that launched it in the early 1970s—shifting international oil prices. Thousands of newcomers began rehitching their U-Haul trailers to head back to the Rust Belt or to other Sun Belt states. Although the city's population (roughly three million) has continued to grow, albeit much less rapidly, its housing vacancy rate has soared to 18 percent, with enough vacant units (some 200,000) to meet market needs until 1988. And the glut of office space—at 25 percent, second only to Beirut—could last up to 12 years, according to one real estate research group. In fact, Houston has more unoccupied office space than either San Francisco or Denver has *total* office space.

Yet, in the years following what one developer calls "our drunken stupor of prosperity," Houston also has been quietly working on something else— something it historically hasn't done much of— public planning. And, although almost no one claims that Houston will ever adopt zoning, many of the city's recent planning efforts do seem similar to things other, more "progressive" cities are doing.

Its achievements include: a three-year-old development ordinance that sets standards for minimum building setbacks and maximum block lengths; strong ordinances for billboards and mobile homes; regulations establishing a minimum distance (1,000 feet) between sex-oriented businesses; one of the nation's first controls for helicopter pads; a dozen scenic districts and roadways; a new historic landmarks commission; and under consideration now, off-street parking requirements for commercial businesses in residential areas.

In addition, the city's planning department has been overhauled and strengthened under a new director. This reorganized Department of Planning and Development has been a lead agency in the passage of a five-year capital improvements program—the city's first; the establishment of several new economic development initiatives; and the ini-

tial steps in the formulation of a series of area comprehensive plans.

At the same time, Houston's already-aggressive private sector has begun to pay more attention to planning issues. All in all, says city council member Eleanor Tinsley, "We've come a long way from planning being a nasty word."

Most long-time observers say the time is ripe for a variety of reasons. First, severe problems of traffic congestion and overdevelopment that no longer can be ignored. Second, a city administration, headed by Mayor Kathryn Whitmire, that strongly supports the need for some degree of public planning. And, last, interestingly enough, the economic downturn itself. Says George Greanias, a city council member who has been a proponent of several of the recent planning initiatives: "The slowdown has reminded people that the city's future is not God-given. So there's more of a willingness to face up to difficult issues."

In fact, many developers view the slowdown— or, more accurately, "decline in the rate of growth"—as a blessing in disguise, a way to cull the good from the bad. . . .

New blood

An even more important reason for the new development attitude may be the local political situation. Traditionally, most Houstonians will tell you, the real estate industry called the shots when it came to local government. Until six years ago, all seven members of the city council were elected at large, which resulted, in the words of one local political observer, in a council often composed of "six old white men and a token minority." Needless to say, land-use and neighborhood issues were seldom high-priority agenda items.

A major change occurred in 1979, when a federal judge ordered district election of council members. Soon after, the council was expanded to 14 members, only five of whom were voted on at large. In 1981, the same year that former city controller Whitmire was first elected mayor, the council election brought in several people who had come up through neighborhood politics, including attorneys, such as Greanias, with strong land-use interests.

About the same time, Mayor Whitmire also began to change the composition of the city's planning commission, long a bastion of real estate and development interests. In her two two-year terms as mayor, Whitmire has replaced 11 of the 14 commissioners she inherited. The commission, now more representative of neighborhood interests, is headed by Burdette Keeland, a local architect who has taken a strong stand on development issues.

Soon, the council and commission began to tackle some of the city's long-ignored public issues. Most of those dealing with land use would never have been brought up for public hearing a few years before, notes *Houston Post* reporter Emily Grotta.

One of the first things approved—"and in some ways the roughest thing yet," recalls council member Eleanor Tinsley—was a citywide sign ordinance. Passed in 1980, it sets size and height standards and bans any new billboards, beginning next year.

Whitmire's presence has also been felt at the department level where at least 14 of the 22 department heads are her appointments. One of those selections is Efraim S. Garcia, head of the newly expanded department of planning and development.

Under Garcia's authority, the community development and economic development divisions have been moved from the mayor's office to the planning department. The move helped to increase the size of the planning department from 78 to 133.

By late this summer, Garcia says, most of the city's planning-related agencies should be under one roof. The department's development branch will handle project management of backlogged community development block grant cases, as well as all permits and plat review. "We've got the fastest plat processing in the country," brags Garcia, noting that all plats, by law, must be evaluated by the city within 10 days.

A second branch of the planning department, redevelopment, includes the divisions of community development, economic development, and neighborhood revitalization. The latter handles the city's estimated 10,000 private deed restrictions and helps train the "civic groups" that help enforce them.

Finally, the department's new long-range planning branch includes comprehensive planning and "Metrocom" (a citywide data base). By reducing the planning staff of the old community development office from 160 to 50, Garcia has been able to double the number of planners in other divisions, such as comprehensive planning.

The shift is part of an effort to reorganize the present unwieldy system for administering federal community development block grants—a task that Garcia views as one of his toughest. The city has 25 community development commissions, whose elected representatives make up a "citizens advisory group" responsible for divvying up the city's yearly CDBG allocation (last year $25 million). However, much of the funding has been spent for staff, and many approved projects have never been carried out, leading to an $85 million backlog at present, says Garcia. The new arrangement, he says, should allow planners to assist the citizens group in establishing priorities. "There no longer is the adversarial relationship that used to exist between planning and community development," he adds.

The planning department also is working in areas that generally have been foreign to Houston's public sector, including the five-year capital improvements program, industrial revenue bonds, a new industrial development corporation, and rehabilitation tax abatements for the city's three new historic districts.

First step

The biggest accomplishment thus far is the passage three years ago of the development ordinance. "It was the first instance of our saying to the world we are interested in planning," says Eleanor Tinsley, a city council member who spurred the regulations, along with former assistant planning director Kerry Gilbert.

Five years before, a similar proposal had been voted down, without even a public hearing, says Tinsley. This time, the development industry was again strongly opposed, but after nearly a year of negotiations, the city gained its approval.

A refrain heard throughout the negotiations was: "We don't want another Woodway Canyon," a reference to a strip of office buildings in the Galleria-Post Oak area that abuts directly on Woodway Avenue, a relatively narrow and crowded thoroughfare.

In response to such problems, the ordinance establishes a minimum setback, varying from 10 to 25 feet, for buildings outside the central business district. It also establishes a minimum road right-of-way and a maximum length for blocks, ranging from 1,400 to 1,800 feet. The reduced block length is intended to prevent the type of congestion that is occuring near such office-retail clusters as Galleria-Post Oak. Because of a lack of such controls in the past, 40 percent of the city's 207 arterial streets are shorter than two miles.

The new controls "are nothing more than what responsible developers have been doing all along," Garcia told the *Houston Post.* "They're a way to eliminate the undesirable by-products of growth."

Says planning consultant Vernon Henry, who has worked with developers in Houston for some 25 years, "We're getting just the gut necessities, not all the various bells and whistles of some ordinances."

And, finally, as if to confirm to outsiders that Houston is not totally abandoning its laissez-faire view toward land-use controls, council member Tinsley says of the new regulations: "We're not telling people what to put where, as zoning does. What we're doing is letting the free market go where it wants but helping to guide it."

On top of this, the city council has designated 12 areas as "scenic districts and roadways." This designation includes stricter sign controls than the citywide ordinance. The most recent of the bunch: Galleria-Post Oak, Greenway Plaza (an office-retail area near the Summit sports arena), and a strip along the new Hardy Toll Road, which will link downtown with the airport. . . .

In addition to zoning, there's one other planning technique Houston will probably never see, and that's a citywide comprehensive plan. "Our jurisdiction is just too big," says Garcia, noting that, with its extraterritorial jurisdiction (ETJ), the city covers more than 2,000 square miles—about the size of Delaware—and stretches about 70 miles from east to west. Texas state law permits cities of over 100,000 population to review all development proposals within their ETJ, which extends five miles from their city limits. No other entity can issue building permits in that area without the city's concurrence.

So, instead of a citywide comprehensive plan, Garcia is developing plans for specific areas of the city, starting first with the most distressed parts of the center city. (In Houston, curiously enough, the center city is often defined as anything inside Loop 610, the 44-mile-long highway that surrounds the city; see map.) The goal is to compile a "compendium of plans" or, as Garcia has said on occasion, partly in jest, "to sneak up on the city with a comprehensive plan."

But, as if to reinforce the traditional focus of power in Houston, many of the area plans will be prepared jointly with various private planning associations.

One long-standing misconception about Houston, many local planners say, is that no land-use planning has taken place. The reality is that it just hasn't been done by the public sector. Since the 1940s, many neighborhoods have controlled local land uses and, consequently, property values through the use of deed restrictions. Some 630 private "civic clubs"—not unlike zoning boards—administer these deed restrictions, with some assistance from the city.

The problem is that most deed restrictions expire after 25 years and must be extended if the neighborhoods are to remain protected. In older, changing neighborhoods, extension—or creation in the first place—is often difficult, if not impossible, since 70 percent of the property owners must approve the deeds. Not surprisingly, the most effective civic clubs are those in the wealthiest areas, since enforcement (read court) costs are steep.

Besides the neighborhood associations, Houston has another type of planning forum in some of its suburban "employment centers," the dozen or so satellite downtowns to the north, south, and west.

The most famous of the satellites is the Galleria-Post Oak area, which roughly surrounds the popular Galleria indoor shopping mall. Located about six miles west of the city's downtown, this cluster of high rises has more office space than all but 10 U.S. downtowns. Its new landmark structure, the 64-story Transco Tower, designed by Philip Johnson and John Burgee, is the tallest building outside a downtown in the country.

Similar centers include: the aforementioned Greenway Plaza, the Texas Medical Center near Rice University, the North Belt-Greenspoint area south of Intercontinental Airport, the Sharpstown Mall cluster southwest of the city, and—one of the fastest-growing concentrations—the West Houston Energy Corridor, which lies some 20 miles west of downtown.

Several of the areas have formed their own planning associations, and today there are at least nine. Most have their own planning staffs, drawn primarily from the city's planning department or one of the area's university research centers.

The creation of these private planning associations, and the work they do to help guide development, was a natural evolution for Houston, says

Jack Linville, a former research director for the American Institute of Planners, who, until a few years ago, headed one such group, the West Houston Association. "When things were booming in the 1970s, it didn't matter what you put up. Everyone was successful. The only controls here were whether you could get the financing.

"But the market today is more sophisticated, and the competition is a lot tougher. Consequently, this more mature market is paying more attention to circulation, flood control, and design issues."

One illustration of how private development has changed is apparent on newly developing stretches of Westheimer Boulevard, a major east-west thoroughfare. There, some 12 miles west of downtown, one sees the best and worst of the city's strip development. The more recent commercial projects boast landscaped parking lots, earth berms along the frontages, and small, discreet business signs. The older projects, often just next door, suggest a more familiar strip mix: numerous curb cuts, portable signs, and no landscaping.

Despite the growing sophistication of the city's planning efforts, however, most developers and planners see a continued role for the private planning associations. The West Houston Association, for instance, last year had half the budget of the city's planning department, says Garcia. He hopes to use the efforts of the private associations as adjuncts to the city's own efforts—particularly in preparing area comprehensive plans.

A backdoor to zoning?

No planner could ever get through a discussion of Houston without asking the big question: What about zoning?—will it ever be adopted? In fact, Garcia says that some city council members think the various planning resolutions he has been getting approved are little more than "a backdoor to zoning."

But Garcia insists that neither he nor the mayor has any intention of pushing for a zoning ordinance. "It's just not in the cards," he flatly states. Says Eleanor Tinsley, one of the more pro-planning council members, "I think we've gone too far and too long without it."

"Everyone attributes what's wrong in Houston to not having any zoning," says Garcia. "But zoning doesn't affect the number of roads, the traffic congestion, the flooding, or the sewage problems."

In fact, some local planners fear that zoning would simply encourage the sprawl.

Nonetheless, consultant Vernon Henry says he still wishes Houston residents had adopted zoning in 1962, the last time it came up for a vote. "Despite the problems we would have had with it," Henry says, "we could have prohibited some of the ills from the rapid development in the 1960s."

Garcia says his staff has looked closely at what has happened in the city's previous attempts to institute zoning. The first time was in 1927, when both a master plan and a zoning ordinance were proposed. Both were strongly opposed by developers and property owners. Another master plan and zoning ordinance were defeated in 1938, although, two years later, the city did adopt its first subdivision regulations. In 1948, zoning was brought before the voters in a citywide referendum, when it failed by a two-to-one margin. The 1962 vote was closer—53 to 47 percent.

Despite this legacy, many observers say that if zoning came up for a public vote tomorrow, it might pass. "But the council still wouldn't go for it," says council member Tinsley.

Instead, Garcia says his staff is looking at various types of performance-based controls, such as the system discussed in the APA Planners Press book by Lane Kendig, *Performance Zoning*. Many local planners feel some type of land-use control is essential to protect some of the city's older neighborhoods. Many of these areas have become attractive to young professionals, both because of their distinctive housing stock and because of their proximity to downtown. Yet, without some type of controls, investment is often a risky proposition.

Mayor Whitmire has bought a house in one such area, recently designated as one of the city's first historic districts.

A newly proposed ordinance would require off-street parking for commercial uses in residential areas. Such a law would be of particular value in the trendier mixed-use sections like the Montrose area. The city's new "sex-oriented business" ordinance also should help protect property values. It prohibits such businesses from locating in an area with 75 percent residential concentration.

But more serious problems also continue to plague Houston—notably, traffic and flooding.

A subtropical area at the same latitude as New Delhi and Cairo, Houston at times—every other year, in fact—gets as much as a foot of rain during a 24-hour period. Consequently, many of the city's streets actually are designed to channel off floodwaters. And every now and then some unlucky motorist who ventures into a deluged underpass drowns in his car.

With increased development, flooding has become an even more severe problem, compounded by the soil subsidence caused by pumping underground water. The ritzy Galleria is alleged to sink a couple of inches each year.

A related problem is sewage. Half of the city's sewage treatment plants are operating at capacity, a condition that has effectively halted construction for most of the last decade in several sections of the central city.

The sewer moratorium has given rise to an interesting black market in permits ("actually a gray or green market," one developer told the *New York Times,* "since it costs a lot of cash.") "Brokers" have been known to sell unused sewer permits—often for undeveloped sites such as parking lots or cemeteries—to prospective developers for as much as $5,000. "Every realtor in town has got a briefcase full of sewer letters," a developer told the *Times* reporter.

Until 1983, the city didn't charge a fee for the permits, though now it charges $1.61 per gallon. It also has established fees for developers to reserve capacity in new treatment plants, and that has helped speed construction. Two years ago, voters approved a series of bond packages totaling $560 million to be used for various capital facilities, including new and expanded treatment plants. As the plants have been finished, the moratorium has been lifted in several sections of the city. Garcia estimates that most work will be finished in the next three years.

Finally, earlier this year, the city council approved a new flood management policy that, in effect, requires most new developments to provide detention ponds.

Freeway city

The one thing most people think of when they think of Houston is traffic. In recent years, it has gotten heavier; the "peak period" zoomed from two hours in 1969 to seven-and-a-half hours in 1981. That's no worse than most large cities, but in Houston the freeways are the only way to get around and they have, in fact, become a prominent magnet for new land uses and congestion.

Loop 610, which originally was intended as a bypass, has essentially become the city's main street—a thoroughfare whose frontage roads are lined with commercial and retail uses. What Broadway is to New York and Main Street is to small towns everywhere, Loop 610 is to Houston. It's busy at all hours, and it is the city's truest public open space.

To alleviate the congestion, several new loop roads are under construction or on the drawing boards. Beltway 8, which will be one of the city's first toll roads when it's finished, will circle the city about six miles outside of Loop 610. Farther out, repairs are scheduled for F.M. (farm to market road) 1960, and beyond that—about 24 miles from downtown—plans are under way for something called the Grand Parkway.

The issue of mass transit is also making its way back into the news. Two years ago, Houston voters, by a wide margin, defeated a proposed $2.35 billion bond issue for a heavy rail starter line that even its supporters now admit was a bit ill conceived. A couple of months ago, after numerous public hearings and committee reports, the Metropolitan Transit Authority announced a revised proposal, which it hopes to put before the voters in a year or two.

The "Option C" scheme calls for a 23-mile light rail loop that would run west from downtown along Interstate 10 to Loop 610, south through the Post Oak area, and east again along U.S. 59 to downtown, with spurs to the Texas Medical Center and the University of Houston. It would be less expensive and would cover a greater area than the single corridor line proposed two years ago. The downtown portion would be a subway.

In addition, the proposal calls for busways to run along the medians of the freeways radiating out from Loop 610. Eventually, transit planners say, some of these routes could be converted into light rail extensions.

Meanwhile, MTA has been actively promoting its improved bus service, long a joke around Houston for its labyrinthine routes, inconsistent schedules, and poorly maintained equipment. But, under a new general manager, Allan Kiepper, formerly head of Atlanta's MARTA, MTA has upgraded its fleet and reworked most of its routes. It also has busways under construction or in operation along three major freeways and is running an assortment of slick advertisements ("Metro Works for You") on local radio and television. The ad campaign is crucial, most transit planners agree, if MTA is to gain public acceptance for its next rail transit proposal. (Bus ridership has increased over a third in the last two years, MTA says.)

This November, Mayor Whitmire comes up for reelection to her third term. Her major challenger, thus far, is former mayor Louie Welch (1964–74), who announced last May after much prodding from the city's still-active "Network" of business leaders and developers, which still holds regular breakfast meetings. Many Network members say the 38-year-old Whitmire has not been the strongly visible leader they feel is necessary to help diversify the city's economy.

The 66-year-old Welch, most recently president of the local chamber of commerce, held office during the early stages of the city's local boom period, but before the fallout from rapid growth hit the city.

The difference between Welch and Whitmire comes out in their attitude to such public amenities as parks. Welch once opined that Houston didn't need many public parks, "because Houstonians have big yards." Whitmire, meanwhile, has made parks a priority item, having announced plans earlier this year for a 10,000-acre park on the city's far west side.

What effect Welch's record as mayor will have on the election is unclear, particularly because many of the current residents didn't live in Houston when he was in office. Moreover, the most pressing issue of the election is not likely to be traffic, flooding, or sprawling development, but rather something else—gay rights. Welch has made an issue of Mayor Whitmire's support last year of two initiatives that would have prohibited discrimination against gays in city hiring practices. The initiatives were roundly defeated in a referendum last fall.

According to a recent newspaper report, Welch's campaign already has raised $1.5 million, Whitmire's less than half of that. And, despite what many City Hall observers say is a solid gain in budgeting and the like, Whitmire's support for public planning and smoother administrative practices may not matter to enough voters.

"Who, after all, can really see the difference made by the new sign controls, minimum setbacks, and the like—particularly when they've been in place for such a short time?" asks one local planning consultant. Still others assume that Welch's forces will try to pin the economic slowdown somehow on the Whitmire administration. Nevertheless, a recent newspaper poll showed Whitmire slightly ahead of Welch.

Many years ago, Houston publisher Oveta Culp Hobby remarked of the city: "I think I'll like it if they ever get it finished." Today, Houston still is not finished. But, as it makes its way from ill-defined adolescence to self-assured maturity, it must grapple with some long-ignored problems.

Exactly what form the city will finally take will either be an affirmation or indictment of its unique mix of public and private planning. In any case, as local writer Doug Milburn says, "We'll never be some urbanologist-architecture critic's private little vision of the Ideal City."

James Peters was formerly the associate editor of Planning.

Comeback City

Charlene Prost
(October 1985)

Just four years ago, St. Louis was being described as a city with so many problems that nothing short of a miracle could guarantee its survival into the twenty-first century.

The 1980 census figures had been released, and St. Louis—the nation's fourth largest city in the early 1900s, the city of beer, baseball, and the shimmering Gateway Arch—had just attained a new distinction. According to the census, the city's population had dropped 27 percent in the 1970s, from 622,000 to 453,000—down from a peak of about 880,000 in the early 1950s. It was the largest percentage decline of any major city in the United States. And, to the dismay of the local politicians, civic leaders, and many of the residents, the national press had a field day.

"Some parts of St. Louis now resemble a ghost town," proclaimed *Time* magazine in a May 4, 1981, story on the city's downward spiral. The city had lost not only people, *Time* reported, but roughly a fourth of its housing stock—mostly because of abandonment as people began moving out to the suburbs.

But St. Louis survived the journalistic hard knocks and gloomy predictions, just as many local people and the politicians said at the time that it would. And today, the old city founded on the banks of the Mississippi River in 1764 is once again emerging as a thriving metropolis.

The outward migration, while continuing, has been slowed considerably. And city officials, and many others too, are optimistic that it will soon level off.

No doubt the flight of whites and many businesses to the suburbs, together with the decreasing family size, accounted for much of the city's population loss over the years, just as it did in other large old cities. St. Louis County, which surrounds the city, has continued to grow, as have such outlying areas as St. Charles County and Chesterfield, on the fringe of St. Louis County. Many middle-class blacks also have moved from the city, mostly to northern and northwestern St. Louis County. Today, officials estimate the city's black population at roughly 46 percent.

Those who expect the outward-bound trend to be reversed believe that most city residents who wanted to "escape" to the suburbs probably are already there. In their view, the vigor of development under way in the downtown, the widespread housing rehabilitation in the neighborhoods, and the city's keen interest in keeping up the momentum will continue to bring residents back.

Despite the city's budget problems over the last several years, it has managed to spend roughly $10 million each year to assist housing developers who are filling in many of the desolate, empty lots where deteriorating buildings were cleared away as part of urban renewal back in the late 1950s and early 1960s.

Most of that money has come from the city's federal block grant allocation, which is distributed by its main planning body, the Community Development Agency. While the agency has been criticized in the past for not doing enough to plan for future development, it has excelled in creating innovative programs to channel federal money into the neighborhoods and in working with developers and neighborhood groups.

The agency also has been involved in a highly successful effort begun in 1981, under the current administration of young (39), second-term mayor Vincent C. Schoemehl, Jr., to try to obtain even more federal money for development. A main tar-

get is the Urban Development Action Grant program. Back in November 1980, the city was trailing behind its peers. It had received only four UDAGs, totaling $4.7 million, out of more than $1.7 billion that had been awarded to larger cities since the program began three years earlier. By July 1983, the city had received seven more grants, totaling more than $20 million. Today, the city receives as much if not more than other cities its size. It has gotten a total of 22 grants, amounting to roughly $65 million.

That's not to say that the picture is completely rosy. The city still has thousands of vacant lots and derelict buildings, particularly on the north side, where the black community has traditionally lived, in parts of the near south side, and in the west end. The city continues to battle residual fears, particularly on the part of suburbanites, that coming downtown means instant mugging, or worse. But that, too, is changing, as the revitalization continues and word of it spreads.

Good news

Last fall, Lomas & Nettleton, a national mortgage banking company, released a well-publicized report saying that, while in many cities the movement to revitalize inner-city neighborhoods has lost much of its vigor, in St. Louis rehab activity was alive, well, and growing.

"Developers here believe in quality work," says Leon Strauss, a local developer who has become a sort of guru for neighborhood rehab in St. Louis. "We don't just patch 'em up. We basically rebuild, from the inside out. People come here from out of town, and they are shocked at the quality they see."

The National Trust for Historic Preservation also considers St. Louis a leader in the use of investment tax credits for rehabilitating its older buildings. "St. Louis has more certified projects under the investment tax credits, and more dollars invested, than any other city in the country," says Tim Turner, director of the agency's Midwest regional office in Chicago.

Last year alone, according to figures compiled by the Landmarks Association of St. Louis, Inc., a nonprofit preservation group involved in much of the rehab activity, more than $51 million—most of it private—was spent to renovate properties individually listed on the National Register of Historic Places, with an additional $35 million being invested in the city's historic districts, in older, blue-collar, south side neighborhoods like Carondelet and Soulard, in more fashionable, yuppie-populated areas like the Central West End, and even in Murphy–Blair, a large, badly run-down area on the north side with just enough life left in its once-fine, old brick buildings to capture developers' interest.

Barbara Geisman, executive director of the city's community development agency, estimates that roughly seven percent, or nearly 12,000 of the 170,000 occupied housing units, have been replaced or substantially renovated over the last several years. "There probably are more than that," she notes. "It's just hard to keep tabs on all of them because of the large numbers of people, the urban pioneers, who are coming in and redoing houses on their own, without coming to us for financial help." At the same time, however, it's clear that more work is needed. The 1980 census showed that the city still has another 20,000 units that were either vacant or in such bad condition that they should not be occupied.

Developers, meanwhile, have been discovering the city's downtown with its ample supply of sturdy, old, commercial structures, particularly in the one-time garment district along Washington Avenue where the red brick loft buildings, with terra cotta and masonry decoration, are grossly underused and perfect for renovation.

Roughly $979.6 million in new construction and renovation projects were completed or started in the downtown in 1984, according to figures supplied by Downtown St. Louis, Inc., a private business group. An additional $247.4 million is going into projects being started this year, some by local firms, others by out-of-towners like the Metropolitan Life Insurance Company, which is putting up a speculative, $100 million office building. At 41 stories, it will be the city's tallest.

The Rouse Company's newest project—the $135 million transformation of Union Station, the city's grand old railroad terminal building and 11.5-acre train shed, into a festival marketplace with shops and restaurants and a 550-room Omni International Hotel—drew local and national applause when it opened a few weeks ago, although some skeptics still wonder whether the market is there to support it.

And in early August, the opening of the retail portion of the $177 million St. Louis Centre shop-

ping mall complex in the heart of downtown drew an enthusiastic response. Some 40,000 residents packed the streets to watch a ribbon-cutting production that featured thousands of pink, green, and white balloons and a giant, two-story-tall curtain that drifted upward, on cue, to unveil the big glass-covered main entrance. The new mall, which connects downtown's last two remaining department stores with a four-level galleria, is said to create the largest enclosed shopping center in any downtown in the country.

Finally, too, the decade-long controversy over whether to tear down a group of more than a dozen old office buildings to complete the 21-block Gateway Mall through the southern section of downtown has died down—although not to the pleasure of preservationists. The most important buildings in the stretch—one listed on the National Register of Historic Places and two others certified as eligible for listing—are down now. And the first new building planned there, an undistinguished 15-story office structure, is rising out of the ground.

The neighborhoods

Mayor Schoemehl pointed out to the crowd attending the St. Louis Centre opening that it was witnessing the culmination of a decade of planning by civic leaders, the business community, and two previous city administrations.

And in many respects, the mayor's observation applies also to rebuilding the city's neighborhoods. For while housing rehab activity in St. Louis got started a bit later than in some other cities and proceeded relatively slowly in the beginning, its roots go back to the late 1960s. . . .

Two of the often-pointed-to urban pioneering successes are Lafayette Square and, to a lesser extent, Soulard. Lafayette Square is just about the earliest of the areas discovered by the urban pioneers. Way back in the 1960s, they began noticing its long-neglected nineteenth-century townhouses, some pre–Civil War. Many of the houses surround and face Lafayette Park, established in the 1850s and to this day enclosed with its original, ornate cast-iron fence, which the city helped restore several years ago.

Soulard is about the same vintage but is more of a working class neighborhood that over the years has been home to waves of different ethnic groups—German, French, Lebanese, Polish, Czech, Croatian. They left behind their solidly constructed, deep-red brick houses and elaborate churches and community buildings.

In both areas, many buildings had been cut up into rooming houses. But they had survived well over the years, their handcarved woodwork and stained glass well-preserved under layers of paint and grime—just waiting to be uncovered by the young couples and single people, delighted at the thought of picking up a house for a bargain $20,000.

Other areas illustrate another phenomenon that is showing up more and more often in St. Louis. That is the joining together in a housing rehab project of a private developer and a neighborhood group. In the DeSales area on the south side, for example, a neighborhood group formed a community housing corporation, which has joined with a private firm, the Westminister Development Company, in a $3.3 million project to renovate housing in two adjacent areas, Tower Grove East and Fox Park, both rather severely deteriorated. The coventurers recently received a $720,000 low-interest loan from the city through the Urban Development Action Grant program to help finance the $3.3 million project.

Also on the near south side, in the LaSalle Park neighborhood, is the first large-scale project to take advantage of Missouri's generous, and sometimes controversial, tax abatement law, Chapter 353, which enables the city to give developers substantial tax breaks for a period of up to 25 years. Under the law, the city can freeze assessed valuation for 10 years. At that point, the property is reassessed, and the owner is taxed on half the valuation of the land and improvements for the next 15 years. Chapter 353 also permits the city to allow private developers to use its power of eminent domain within city-approved redevelopment areas. That tool allows developers to file condemnation suits in circuit court to force property owners to sell their property for what court-appointed commissioners decide is a fair market price.

LaSalle Park is significant for another reason as well. The private developer in the partnership was the Ralston Purina Company, a multimillion-dollar conglomerate whose main headquarters are in the LaSalle Park neighborhood.

Unlike many other firms that had left the city in the 1960s to get away from the urban problems, Ralston decided to stay. And later, several other large institutions followed Ralston's lead.

In 1971, Ralston officials and the city put together a plan to rejuvenate the entire 144-acre neighborhood around the Ralston complex. The original scheme, a classic urban renewal plan, called for demolishing many of the nineteenth-century structures that characterized the neighborhood. But before Ralston and the city had gotten around to doing that on a large scale, people like Carolyn Toft, now executive director of the nonprofit Landmarks Association of St. Louis, Inc., and John Roach, formerly director of the city's community development agency, now a vice-president for the Pantheon Corporation, managed to convince Ralston of the advantages of historic preservation. As a result, the original plan was changed, and many of the old buildings have been renovated, with some infill of apartment buildings, condominiums, and commercial buildings.

While not problem free—federal redevelopment money was so slow in coming that many long-time residents moved out—the LaSalle Park project was, in many respects, a model for other large-scale neighborhood projects that were to follow.

In 1975, the city approved a revitalization plan by the Washington University Medical Center and several neighborhood institutions for a 185-acre section west of the downtown. That same year, the late Alfonso J. Cervantes, a former mayor, announced an ambitious, 11-acre development project in the once-prosperous central west end, abutting the Washington University project area. While Cervantes's redevelopment corporation hasn't yet fulfilled all its promises for Maryland Plaza, it has managed to fill empty storefronts with new shops and restaurants, and the area has become trendy, particularly for young couples and singles. So trendy, in fact, that some of the residents in the surrounding neighborhood have complained about too much noise and activity coming from the bars and restaurants.

In the 1970s, developer Strauss won city approval for the redevelopment of 100 acres of probably the most deteriorated section of all, in the west end. And the Laclede's Landing Redevelopment Corporation was formed to redo some large, mostly vacant, nineteenth-century warehouses and commercial buildings on the waterfront, adjacent to downtown, as an office, entertainment, shopping, and residential complex.

Also in the 1970s, the St. Louis University Medical Center undertook a $73 million plan to revitalize a 274-acre area on the south side. Since 1978, the Midtown Medical Center Redevelopment Corporation, the vehicle established to carry out the effort, has rehabbed some 200 rental housing units, constructed a small number of new units, and rehabbed and sold some 40 single-family houses. In addition, the corporation has encouraged private developers working in the neighborhood to produce another 86 units of rental housing. Many of the units created have been set aside for low- and moderate-income tenants, says corporation director John Abramson.

The redevelopment corporation also operates a variety of social, self-help, and recreation programs for neighborhood residents. . . .

Besides tax abatement, the city has been involved in the neighborhood revitalization effort primarily through the Housing Implementation Program (HIP), which was devised in 1977 as a way of channeling federal block grant funds to make grants and low-interest loans to developers—including neighborhood groups and individuals—who wanted to build or renovate housing.

"At first," recalls community development director Barbara Geisman, who joined the agency about that time, "we had difficulty getting applications for the money. The development industry had not grown up yet. But by 1981, we were getting $12 million in applications for a program that had $6 million a year in funds."

At that point, she says, the agency decided to use the HIP program to create something new, a For Sale Incentives Program, through which some of the block grant money could be funneled to developers who would build or renovate for-sale housing units.

"Then several years ago, we added another new program, for the urban pioneers who wanted to buy a house, rehab it, and live in it. Every year, we fine-tune our programs to some degree, depending on what is happening in the market."

Geisman and Myles Pomeroy, head of strategic planning for the community development agency, recently put together a list of some of the housing redevelopment projects for which the agency's money has been used over the last several years. Some excerpts from selected years:

• In 1979, nearly $3.8 million in HIP money was spent to help develop (mostly through rehab) 656 housing units, with a total development cost of more than $23 million.

• In 1982, nearly $8.5 million in HIP money was spent on 745 units, with a total cost of nearly $40 million.

• In 1984, figures for the HIP program and housing units created with the help of the UDAG program were combined. During that year, more than $7 million in HIP money and another $5.7 million obtained through UDAG were used to produce 1,022 units of housing, with a total development cost of more than $62 million.

• Between 1982 and 1984, the agency's assistance to developers through the For-Sale Housing Implementation Program resulted in 368 additional units, with a total development cost of more than $22 million.

Also, says Geisman, the agency helped developers get funding through other federally sponsored programs, including the Section 312 program for development of multifamily housing and Section 202, which assists in the development of housing for the elderly and the handicapped. In addition, the agency makes low-interest loans to homeowners for emergency repairs or improvements to bring dwellings up to city code standards.

"I think city government here has a good relationship with the people who are doing redevelopment," says Geisman. "If a developer has problems, or if we are having problems here, we all sit down and figure out what to do to keep the ball rolling. That's important over the long haul.

"We also have a good corps of developers—a lot of local people who got into the business early and have grown up with it, including some who live in the neighborhoods where they are working. And there's still a lot of stuff out there for us to do."

Charlene Prost is a reporter for the St. Louis Post–Dispatch *who specializes in urban issues.*

San Diego: Beyond Spit and Polish

George A. Colburn
(November 1985)

In San Diego, everyone in a position of power must cope with the legacy of Pete Wilson, mayor for 11 years of this sun-drenched city on America's southwestern tip. The main element of that legacy is a political and governmental policy of "managed growth" that was supposed to settle for at least a generation the emotional matter of new construction in the city's undeveloped areas.

Thought by some to be a precise roadmap that would validate the city's long-time boast of being "America's Finest City," the growth policy was seen by others as merely a set of flexible guidelines that could be changed whenever local governing bodies recognize new realities.

The battle over these conflicting interpretations of managed growth will come to a head November 5 when the city electorate votes on an initiative proposition aimed at stopping encroachment by city council action into the northern part of the "urban reserve," 20,000 acres that were to remain undeveloped until 1995. [And, in a late-breaking development, the current mayor has been hanging on to his job by a thread.]

Another major aspect of Wilson's legacy was his vision of a revitalized downtown, including a new convention center on San Diego Bay. Wilson set events in motion that have pushed that vision close to reality, and today all elements of the city seem to be united on the desirability of dramatically changing the downtown landscape. In a frenzy of self-congratulation, these elements joined hands in August to open the Horton Plaza Shopping Center, a bold, $180 million, six-block development that the architect refers to as nothing less than an attempt "to reinvent the American city."

All around the shopping center, development abounds—new housing, a historic district, hotels, office buildings, and the like. Under the smooth and innovative leadership of Gerald M. Trimble, the Centre City Development Corporation (the city's redevelopment agency) has invested some $120 million in incentives to stimulate $3.5 billion worth of projects in its 300-acre domain over the past 10 years. Assessed valuation has grown from $92 million to $559 million, while the tax take has increased from $1 million to $6 million and is expected to rise another 30 to 40 percent by 1990.

Trimble, who says he thinks of himself as a developer rather than a bureaucrat, refers with pride to the business deals he has made for CCDC with developers who take advantage of city incentives. As part of the deal on Horton Plaza, for example—where the city invested some $40 million—the developer is giving the city 10 percent of the average rent for the 170 shops, 25 percent of parking revenue, and 10 percent of net cash flow on office space.

By 1988, the new convention center will be opened. Already dubbed by city boosters in national ads as "The Meeting Place of Your Dreams," the dramatic structure on the bay, by Canadian architect Arthur Erickson, will have more than 340,000 square feet of exhibit space and could draw up to 400,000 convention goers into the city annually—spending some $200 million and creating 4,500 new jobs. The new center will allow San Diego to compete with cities like San Francisco and Atlanta and to go after big events like the national political conventions—finally putting behind the memory of the loss of the 1972 Republican convention even though Richard Nixon considered it his "lucky city." Despite all that, though, city voters have made it clear on several occasions that they didn't want to pay for a convention center. Finally, the cash-rich San Diego Unified Port District came up with a plan to build the center and lease it to the city for $1 a year.

In fact, the entire city is booming, giving the impression to an outsider that San Diego will have to work hard to avoid being overwhelmed by the success of its own publicity campaign to the rest of America. With a population of almost 900,000 and annual growth of about 2.6 percent, it's already the nation's eighth largest city, second in California only to Los Angeles. Unemployment is a respectable 6.2 percent, while employment rose last year by 55,600 jobs—a hefty increase compared to national averages—and a figure of particular interest to the city's 150,000 Hispanics, most of whom live in the southern sections closest to the Mexican border. . . .

The politicians

But dealing with the forces that stimulate growth while keeping faith with the managed growth philosophy has not been easy since Republican Wilson got himself elected to the U.S. Senate in 1982. His successor, Roger Hedgecock, 39, a first-rate politician (also a Republican) and environmental activist, and a supporter of Wilson's policies, was thought by many the perfect man to handle the pressures and demands of the mayor's job in the 1980s.

But only a few months into his term, the new mayor was accused of taking $350,000 in illegal campaign assistance from a group of friends who were involved in an investment scam that rocked the city last year. Mastermind of the bogus operation that swindled some 1,000 San Diegans of $80 million over a six-year period was J. David Dominelli, already sentenced to 20 years in federal prison.

Although under indictment, the mayor won election to a full term over almost token opposition in 1984. Then, last February, his trial ended with a jury locked 11 to one for conviction on charges of conspiracy and perjury. The trial obviously weakened Hedgecock's standing with the voters and led, at least indirectly, to the November 5 ballot issue, which seriously divides city residents.

With almost daily publicity on the charges against him—and the Dominelli scandal fascinating the entire city—Hedgecock could not deliver the votes in the summer of 1984 to stop council approval of a scheme allowing 5,100 acres of the urban reserve to be opened for the construction of a graduate-level Christian university and a linked 750-acre industrial park. The council's five-to-four vote to approve the La Jolla Valley development in a remote northeastern section of the city also provided approval for a major residential development on the site—after 1995, the earliest date set for opening the reserve.

The council action—which in one stroke allowed development of one-sixth of the total urban reserve—dismayed many residents, including the environmental coalition that proved its clout in the Wilson era and during the Hedgecock campaigns.

As far as planning director Jack Van Cleave is concerned, the entire urban reserve should be left alone until at least 1995. Of the city's total 211,000 acres, almost 81,000 are considered "urbanized" for general plan purposes. Another 67,500 are planned for urbanization. The entire urban reserve currently consists of almost 31,000 unplanned acres plus another 32,000 acres controlled by the military.

Van Cleave, who has been director for the last six years (and with the department 38 years), says the staff recommended denial of the La Jolla Valley project "because the case boiled down to [the developers'] argument that there was a need for industrial land in the city. Our study indicated that such land was not needed." The proposed university, Van Cleave points out, may be considered by city agencies at any time in any area under a conditional use permit. Van Cleave also notes that the

ongoing controversy over La Jolla Valley puts a considerable strain on the already overtaxed resources of the $5 million planning department and its staff of 120, including 45 planners.

While Van Cleave's position puts him in league with environmental groups like the Sierra Club, which led the drive for an initiative, he is bothered by the fact that planning decisions for the urban reserve will be in the hands of the voters rather than the city council if voters approve Proposition A on November 5. The mayor, however, had no such qualms. A bad eight-to-one loser in the city council on the issue of approving more development in the already sprawling Mission Valley (which includes the recently enlarged San Diego Stadium, home of the football Chargers and baseball Padres), Hedgecock vehemently endorsed the proposition.

He expressed outrage, for example, at the fact that in the six years since the growth management plan was adopted, the council has changed more than a third of the northern urban reserve to the status of "planned urbanizing" area—thus allowing development to move forward in those areas.

Like Mayor Wilson before him, Hedgecock couched his position in economic terms so as not to unduly alarm Republican backers. He claimed, as Wilson did, that the city's budget could not handle the strain of providing services in outlying areas without damaging services in built-up areas. He and his citizen allies, who gathered more than 75,000 signatures in a few weeks to force the November 5 ballot issue (which would reverse the city council approval of La Jolla Valley), said there was plenty of room in the city's designated "urbanized" and "planned urbanizing" areas to accommodate steady growth over the next decade.

If voters didn't take a hand in the planning process, the mayor said, the council would continue its "slaughter of the urban reserve," making it likely that San Diego would become "just a slightly smaller version of Los Angeles." Indeed, that thought became the slogan of the proponents of the November 5 initiative vote: "No LA; Yes on A."

Then, on October 9, initiative backers almost lost their main supporter. The mayor's second trial ended in a conviction on 13 counts, several of them felonies. California law ordinarily would have forced him to resign his office. Soon after the conviction, however, allegations of jury tampering became public, and the mayor said he would stay in office until the issue was resolved.

Still, most political observers believe the initiative proposition will pass, despite a well-financed "education campaign" organized by building industry leaders. Before Hedgecock's conviction, a private poll showed Proposition A leading by three to one. With the most visible backer of the proposition now preoccupied with the effort to overturn his conviction and the "anti–A" forces readying a counterattack, the final vote could be close. No one expects the initiative to lose, however.

The development gang

Hedgecock had claimed openly that the campaign to defeat the initiative proposition was being financed "by the usual gang of developers who have so successfully controlled city council decisions" and don't want to lose that control to the voters.

A key player has been Louis Wolfsheimer, Pete Wilson's planning commission chairman and a leading architect of the growth management concept and plan. A lawyer for the church group seeking to build the university in La Jolla Valley and a member of the San Diego Unified Port District Commission (which is building the long-awaited convention center), Wolfsheimer believes that Wilson's concept of "in-filling" the city's developed areas "has worked too well." In his view, the intensity of development (fueled by city incentives) has led to a breakdown of public services in the older parts of the city. He also notes that land is so scarce in these older areas that many of the canyons that give San Diego a special topographical beauty are being destroyed by new construction.

Wolfsheimer argues that the mayor and his allies see the growth management plan as something "set in concrete." Yet, he says, when the plan was developed in the mid–1970s and finally incorporated into the general plan in 1979, it was intended to be flexible. "Now we are short of industrial land, and if we cannot accommodate those who want to build here, we will have missed the boat," and the tax base and jobs that could be provided by such industrial development will merely "leap-frog" to the unincorporated areas.

Wolfsheimer, who came to San Diego from Baltimore 22 years ago, says he perceives an "elitist mentality" among anti–La Jolla Valley forces that

work to keep out newcomers. "And some politicians pander to this attitude," he claims.

In the wheeling and dealing that led to council approval for La Jolla Valley after the planning staff and commission turned it down, Wolfsheimer and his client—Campus Crusade for Christ—agreed to postpone the residential element in the plan until 1995. Still, he thinks it makes no sense for the city to stop residential growth while housing is being built all around it in the unincorporated areas of San Diego County. "North County residents come into San Diego, where the jobs are, but the city gets no tax money from this growing commuter population, which clogs our main highways every day."

Allied with Wolfsheimer on the La Jolla Valley project is another city resident with clout, William Rick, chairman of the port commission and head of Rick Engineering, the company begun by his late father, longtime planning director for the city until the mid–1950s. Rick's firm directed a study for Campus Crusade that claimed there was a pressing need in the northern part of the city for industrial land such as that proposed by his clients. Rick contends that, had it not been for the distraction of the area's previous owners, the Teamsters Pension Fund, when the city revised the general plan in 1979, the La Jolla Valley would not have been part of the urban reserve at all.

Another advocate of La Jolla Valley is Mike Madigan, the senior vice-president of the Pardee Construction company, a division of Weyerhaeuser Real Estate and a major builder of residences in San Diego. Madigan, a former aide to Mayor Pete Wilson, helped cut the deals that led to Wilson's solution of the growth issue that divided the city in the 1970s. But today, he says, "growth is no longer the issue. The issue is *how* the city will grow." Madigan claims that the city's plans for its developed areas are no longer valid. "Unless you build on steep hills, in the canyons, and tear down a lot of older structures, the development potential in the urban areas is now severely limited," he says.

And, according to Madigan, the city has failed badly in the urban reserve because it has not figured out what to do with it—despite the passage of six years since growth management became official city policy. The general plan, he notes, is a compilation of 30 or so community plans that represent the thinking of small subareas, all with their own limited views of what the city should do.

Thus, it represents "macro-thinking" and is outdated. Instead of allowing itself to get in the position of reacting to someone else's plan for the La Jolla Valley, he adds, the city should be considering how the area fits into the broader picture. Madigan suggests that the general plan should be updated every five years if San Diego is to cope coherently with the reality of ongoing growth.

Downtown blooms

While the urban reserve issue threatens to tear the city apart, there appears to be total unity over the issue of downtown redevelopment. Twenty years after virtually killing off downtown retail through city approval of a major shopping and commercial center in Mission Valley a few miles to the north, the power structure now celebrates the rebirth of the city's core. The mastermind of the reorientation is Ernest Hahn, developer of the Horton Plaza shopping center, the heart of what prominent San Diegans want to believe will make San Diego into "a real city," not just a large place.

It's ironic that Hahn, a major developer of suburban shopping malls nationwide, should be the creator of downtown San Diego's renaissance. For his Fashion Valley Shopping Center in Mission Valley and his University Towne Center in the Golden Triangle contributed significantly to the after-five center city exodus. In the last 20 years, downtown after dark has been populated almost exclusively by military men seeking a good time and by an assorted variety of street people. All that makes these recent activities all the more remarkable.

Horton Plaza. Hahn's greatest achievement, many believe, is that he has brought four major department stores to a downtown that no longer had any. The complex, by Los Angeles architect Jon Jerde, whose firm coordinated design for the 1984 Los Angeles Olympic Games, will have 170 stores and restaurants, seven movie theaters, two legitimate theaters, and three specially commissioned pieces of outdoor art. It's all divided into Disneyland–like "neighborhoods" of tenants with similar interests, and so far people have been incredibly enthusiastic about it. Nevertheless, there's some uncertainty about how Horton Plaza will do, for downtown still carries a strongly negative image for many local people.

Horton Plaza is the fruit of 10 years of enormous effort by all sorts of groups and individuals that began when Wilson convinced the local power

structure to make downtown redevelopment a priority. Along the way, it had to overcome such obstacles as Proposition 13, which severely limited local government spending; a major recession; and skyrocketing bank interest rates. But Wilson's priority remained in place.

Housing. Downtown backers believe that the success of Horton Plaza and of other new projects hinges on the development of downtown housing. And housing has, in fact, become the focus of the Centre City Development Corporation.

CCDC residential projects already in place include a federally funded twin-tower low-income housing complex, a 27-story luxury residential tower (with penthouses selling for more than $1 million), and two low-rise projects with units selling in what Californians consider the "moderate range," i.e., from slightly under $100,000 to more than $200,000. Near Horton Plaza, construction is about to begin on a 180-unit, block-square, market-rate project by award-winning architect Rob Quigley. And on another full block, the $40 million City Plaza will provide three floors of condominium units, three floors of office space, and ground-level retail outlets.

Also about to break ground downtown is Market Street Square, almost 200 lower income and market-rate family rentals, subsidized with a $3.7 million federal grant.

Hotels. The opening in early 1988 of the convention center, while long anticipated, also has some people worried, both at the port district commission and at the Convention and Visitors Bureau, San Diego's highly successful sales machine. For one thing, design changes have added millions to the overall cost of the center and delayed its opening by several months.

Besides that, the luxurious Inter-Continental Hotel, which is on port district property near the convention center, has lost several hundred thousand dollars a month since its opening a year ago. If the developer doesn't find financing soon for a planned second tower, the port district will revoke his option for a third hotel in the vicinity, also on port district land. And if the two additional hotels are not ready for the opening, the center will be in serious trouble. For the port district is counting on the revenues from the anticipated 2,200 rooms to pay the bills for the center. . . .

A priority item in the CCDC agenda is to clean up two pockets of seedy businesses that are constant reminders of the old days. One such area is along Horton Plaza on Fourth Avenue. Another is lower Broadway leading to the Bay, between Horton Plaza and a large new Santa Fe Railroad redevelopment project—two blocks of bars, tattoo parlors, sex shops, and the like. The Santa Fe development, valued at $800 million over the next two decades, will include high-rise offices, retail outlets, a hotel, and an extension of San Diego's highly successful trolley line.

Finally, with the vitality of downtown seemingly assured by the end of the decade, design is becoming more of a local issue. There is nothing really outstanding about the new downtown skyscrapers (held to a 31-story maximum by the Federal Aviation Administration because of the close-in airport), but that could change in the next round of building, particularly since design is now the highest priority for the CCDC.

George A. Colburn is a free-lance writer and television producer based in New York City. He spent eight years of the Pete Wilson reign as a resident of San Diego.

Pittsburgh's Glitter and Gloom

Ruth Eckdish Knack
(December 1985)

There was plenty of scoffing last spring when Pittsburgh was named number one livable city in Rand McNally's *Places Rated* poll. But even hardened skeptics might be won over by David Lewis's lyrical descriptions. The Pittsburgh architect and urban designer, who came here from England 20 years ago, has written of "a city whose urban form is more clearly and richly articulate than any I have seen," whose "hilltop neighborhoods . . . are linear girdles of green," and where the sunset "transform[s] the rivers into paths of gold and sheath[s] the skyscrapers in silver."

But there's a downbeat note in the imagery. The shuttered upriver steel mills—the industrial heart of the Monongahela River Valley—"their slim black stacks serried silently against the sky"—look to Lewis like "World War I dreadnaughts wrecked in a sea of goldenrod," and the "neat frame houses" of the Mon Valley mill towns "harbor the hope-

lessness of steelworkers whose lives have been shattered by the closings." . . .

Certainly, these contrasts are not unique to Pittsburgh. But they are more vivid there than in most other places. In addition, local public and private groups have taken a particularly active role both in directing downtown development and in searching for solutions to the region's economic problems. All of this merits a closer look.

Downtown lovers in flatland cities think of places like San Francisco and Cincinnati—and Pittsburgh—as having all the luck because their topography keeps them relatively compact. And to geographers, the 57-square-mile Pittsburgh peninsula, squeezed into a triangle where the Monongahela and Allegheny rivers join to form the Ohio, is an authentic "central place."

Often noted is the fact that the city has the third largest concentration of *Fortune* 500 companies (16) in the U.S. Those firms and others occupy over 26 million square feet of downtown office space. And, according to a recent survey by the Urban Investment and Development Company, Pittsburgh is eleventh in office square footage built in the last 35 years, with six million square feet added since 1980. Not bad for the nation's thirty-third largest city (1984 pop. 402,583) and fifteenth largest metropolitan area (2,372,000). Moreover, Pittsburgh has kept its downtown retailing base, with the local department store chains reporting their highest volume of sales in their central locations.

To David Lewis, the glistening skyscrapers of downtown's "Golden Triangle" make Pittsburgh a "mini-Manhattan," though without Manhattan's overwhelming social problems. But a century ago, to Charles Dickens, it was "hell with the lid off."

What happened in the meantime was the city's famous post–World War II smoke control effort and, more recently and more sadly, a regional economic depression that has done in almost all the remaining steel mills. The air cleanup was the cornerstone of a major renewal effort—"Renaissance I"—engineered by the Allegheny Conference on Community Development, the nonprofit civic group that has played an enormous role in charting the course of Pittsburgh's development since its founding in 1943.

Those who have studied the conference often point out that the corporate chiefs who make up its board had—and have—the clout to get things done, and their commitment to the city's downtown is reflected in figures like the office space construction noted above. They started with the tip of the triangle, where the three rivers join and which, 40 years ago, was a ramshackle warehouse zone. The old buildings were cleared under urban renewal powers, to be replaced by the Gateway Center office-hotel complex, a state park at the "point," and, some blocks away, a park-topped garage modeled after San Francisco's Union Square. . . .

In 1977, city council president Richard Caliguiri, the city's former parks and recreation department head, captured the mayor's office with a promise of equal time to downtown and the neighborhoods. Under the rubric "Renaissance II," some dozen new office buildings have gone up or are under way, along with a recently completed light rail downtown subway (replacing the old trolley lines), a convention center, and a revamped concert hall.

By all rights, the central business district of an extremely depressed Rust Belt region shouldn't have glittering Gothic cathedrals (Philip Johnson's Pittsburgh Plate Glass complex—PPG Place), or, for that matter, an apparently increasing supply of yuppies. Clearly, part of the reason for Pittsburgh's success is the cooperative climate established by the Allegheny Conference. Its current director, only the third in the organization's history, is Robert Pease, a civil engineer by training, who was also the city's urban renewal director in the 1960s (the "halcyon days" of urban renewal, he calls them). Once again, says Pease, the conference "has reverted to what we do best—economic development"—including a number of projects related to downtown development.

What's the magic?

"Pittsburgh is perceived by developers as a place that's good to develop in," says Donald Elliott, a former New York City planning director and now a lawyer for a New York firm that specializes in land development projects. For one thing, says Elliott, local officials know when to stop making demands on developers. "They don't go back after an agreement is signed and say, 'Oh, by the way, we want a plaza here.' " In short, "the word is out; Pittsburgh is a place where you can make a project work," and that, he adds, is why "every developer in the country is willing to come in here."

Some of the credit for that popularity must go to the head of the Urban Redevelopment Authori-

ty, Paul Brophy, a veteran at 40 of one other city post (housing director) and one nonprofit one (director of ACTION-Housing, Inc.). Last December, Brophy was listed in the *"Esquire* Register," the magazine's round-up of "the best of the new generation."

In Brophy's view, Pittsburgh "works" because its tradition of public-private partnership is "very much intact," and—very important for him—"is becoming a neighborhood partnership, too," a point that is also stressed by Mayor Caliguiri. The backdrop for the partnership is a basic agreement that "development is good." What other stance is possible, Brophy asks, in a city that has lost a third of its population over the last 20 years and is "working like crazy" to make the transition from a manufacturing-based economy to one that is more diversified?

Brophy sees his job as "helping to develop a level of expertise in city government that puts us in a position to work creatively with the development and lending communities." That means recognizing a developer's constraints and "need for profit," but also knowing when to make demands on behalf of the public. And sometimes it means helping the developer revise a proposal to make it more "politically salable."

Noting that he comes from a "fairly straightforward" city planning background (with a master's from the University of Pennsylvania), Brophy puts himself into a "new generation of planners," people whose experience with the community development and urban development action grant programs taught them how to negotiate and "how to tell the difference between a grant and a soft loan"—and to whom "private is not a dirty word."

That's not to say that Pittsburgh is a laissez-faire town. In fact, while the URA has been pushing development forward, the city planning department has been reemphasizing its concern with urban design—a situation that Brophy says he approves of.

For several years, the planning department has been working on a series of zoning code revisions that substantially change the existing code, enacted in 1958. For example, a new residential provision allows townhouses in certain single-family neighborhoods, while still keeping out multifamily apartments. Other recently adopted provisions permit sidewalk cafes in commercial districts, regulate advertising signs, make group homes a special conditional use category, and create "specially planned districts" for areas that require special attention. The department is nationally known for its community planning division, which has taken an active role in housing rehabilitation and neighborhood commercial development.

But it's downtown where the changes are most clearly related to aesthetic concerns. Considered most important by city planning director Robert Lurcott is the change in calculating open space to fulfill the code's open space requirement. Developers must now supply 20 percent of usable open space in almost all the downtown, whereas before they could count surrounding streets and other peripheral space. A carefully worked out open space study, done by the planning department, was based on William H. Whyte's pioneering work on Manhattan's streets and plazas. The standards were refined further by New York-based urban designer Jonathan Barnett, who has been a consultant to the Pittsburgh planning department since 1978.

A further change is a complicated new method (a little like San Francisco's) of figuring allowable height—an attempt to keep tall buildings in the downtown core with a gradual slope down to the riverbanks. The first project to be affected by this provision is Allegheny International's new two-tower complex, which also gained considerable additional density by transferring development rights from an adjacent theater.

Such changes are made possible, Lurcott says, by a mayor "who conveys a positive attitude about getting things done and who is particularly sensitive to neighborhood needs, but who also says, 'Let's make sure we do it right.'" Lurcott recalls that several years ago, Mayor Caliguiri visited Detroit's fortress-like Renaissance Center and came back vowing, "not here." The result is an emphasis on maintaining a lively street life, particularly along such traditional shopping streets as Smithfield, where a retail mall is part of the big new Oxford Center development.

Above all, though, Lurcott believes the flexibility of its development plan review process—worked out with Barnett's help—is the key to Pittsburgh's considerable success in getting a good measure of amenity in new development. For example, planners were able to bend the rules to allow the glass-enclosed winter garden at PPG Place to count as open space. Lurcott, a native of Westchester County, New York, with architecture and planning degrees from Cornell, has been city planning director since 1977, when he replaced Robert Paternoster, now planning director of Long Beach, California.

A locally popular example of negotiation at work is the agreement worked out among the city, Allegheny County, and the Urban Redevelopment Authority regarding the Allegheny International project, which ventured into new development territory by crossing rather scuzzy Liberty Avenue. As part of the development rights transfer deal referred to above, the developers, Allegheny International and Chicago-based Urban Investment and Development, got a big density bonus, the right to demolish at least one historic building, and a $17 million UDAG.

The city got a rehabbed Stanley Theater, an old movie house that now becomes the Benedum Center for the Performing Arts, complementing Heinz Hall down the street, and the prospect of continued funding through a mechanism established with the help of the Allegheny Conference—the Pittsburgh Trust for Cultural Resources. The theater is viewed as the nucleus of a new performing arts complex with other spaces a possibility in the future, and the whole project is seen as the salvation of the down-at-the-heels Penn-Liberty district.

Symbols

For renowned urban geographer Brian Berry, who has been at Carnegie–Mellon University for five years, the downtown building boom is a symbol of a major transformation that has taken place in the Pittsburgh region. He points out that manufacturing, which used to provide half the area's jobs, now accounts for only 18 percent, less than the figure for the U.S. as a whole. Meanwhile, employment has continued to grow in the service sector. And a key component of that sector is the concentration of corporate headquarters in the downtown.

Other important components of the service economy are biomedical research and computer-oriented research and development. And in both, Berry says, Pittsburgh has an edge because of its strong university presence. "After all," he notes, "the base of this sort of transformation is ideas."

And just as the downtown skyscrapers symbolize the faith in corporate growth, other sites have come to stand for the local optimism—tinged with some anxiety—about the sort of transformation Berry describes. They represent what national columnist Neil Peirce has called America's "armpit opportunities."

The most striking is the site of the almost-abandoned Jones and Laughlin steel company, some 50 acres along the Monongahela River just a mile from the downtown and adjacent to the Penn–Lincoln Parkway. Some 5,000 jobs were lost in 1980 when J&L closed the rolling mills and blast furnaces where it had produced steel auto bumpers. The property then was bought by a Cleveland company and later sold to the city for some $4 million as a potential industrial park. The problem was—and still is—where to get the money for the necessary improvements.

A year ago, an Urban Land Institute advisory panel, sponsored by the URA, visited the J&L site and agreed with the local people that it was an ideal location for advanced technology firms. That idea got a big boost last summer when the U.S. Department of Defense announced the award of a $103 million, five-year contract to Carnegie–Mellon University to create a "software engineering institute." The institute will be built on the CMU campus, half a mile from the J&L site, and local officials are confident that it will make J&L a hot property. In the meantime, the URA is continuing to look for research firms and light industry, particularly in the fabricated metals field, since a fabricating firm still occupies a portion of the site and intends to stay. The planning department has put the property in a "specially planned district" zoning category, allowing considerable leeway in meeting traffic and design requirements.

"Obviously," said Paul Farmer, the city's deputy planning director in charge of comprehensive planning, at a national urban design conference held in Pittsburgh last year, "it would be best to redevelop industrial sites for industrial use. But if you can't, ..." Farmer was referring to Herr's Island, a 42-acre sliver of land in the Allegheny River just over two miles from the downtown and once the smelly location of the area's meat packing and processing plants. Since there seem to be no new heavy industry takers, the URA, which owns the land, is now marketing it as a site for offices ("advanced technology," of course), a marina, housing, and a conference center. Part of the redevelopment strategy in this case is to get the public to start thinking of the rivers as recreational and development resources—in the planning department's terms, "a high-value amenity."

Yet another riverfront site being heavily promoted by the city is 30 acres just west of the Three Rivers Stadium, where plans call for more high tech (a science and technology center) and an international trade mart, hotels, another marina, and maybe a festival marketplace—all connected to the downtown via people mover or aerial tramway. A couple of years ago, the city assumed development rights around the stadium from the Pittsburgh Pirates, and it has since become more and more enthusiastic about its potential. Recently, the state pledged $2 million for road improvements, which will provide access to the river. (A related development is the recent sale of the baseball team for $22 million by a consortium composed of the city, Allegheny County, and some 15 local businesses, with the city's share coming from the sale of stadium bonds. The Pirates management had threatened to sell the team to outside interests.)

Finally, the city's warehouse district, the long and narrow piece of underused railroad land at the edge of downtown and adjoining the new convention center, is also up for redevelopment. In this case, the city planners hope to bring people downtown to live—not an easy task in a neighborhood-oriented city. A start is being made at Daniel Burnham's magnificent Pennsylvania Station, whose office tower is being converted into rental apartments by a Philadelphia firm capitalizing on the federal preservation tax credits. The next target is a former Armstrong Cork factory building farther down on the strip, near the newly renovated wholesale produce market.

Clearly, the city has decided that high tech—robotics, biomedical research, and particularly computer software—is where its future lies, and its land-use plans are being developed with that aim in mind. City officials caution, however, against assuming that the recent projects represent a conscious effort to shift from one specialized economic base—steel—to another. "The city's strategy is a diversification strategy," says economic development planner Steven Branca, "and it's building on the very solid high tech infrastructure that's already here in the corporations and in the universities."

Meanwhile, a very successful local entrepreneur thinks it is overlooking another, less obvious opportunity, but one that could bring in just as many dollars as another software firm—which is likely to employ very few people anyway.

That opportunity is tourism, and the entrepreneur is Arthur Ziegler, Jr., the co-founder of the 20-year-old Pittsburgh History and Landmarks Foundation and the developer of the profitable Station Square project just over the Smithfield Bridge from the Golden Triangle. The new light rail system, which runs across the Monongahela River and then stops at Station Square en route to the southern suburbs, has increased business to the already-thriving, 41-acre development, which includes a fancy restaurant in the marvelously restored Pittsburgh and Lake Erie railroad terminal, two warehouses recycled into Ziegler's own version of a festival marketplace, and an architecturally mundane but successful hotel. A second hotel and new housing are in the works.

"Are we creating the kind of industry that will create jobs?" asks Ziegler, gesturing out the window at the downtown. "We can have glittering buildings across the way and talk all we want about reusing steel mill sites. But the fact is that we are very weak in creating new businesses." Ziegler is still burning from the rebuff city officials gave him when he first proposed to reuse the P&LE terminal. "We had an idea for an industry that would create jobs, at a time when people said no one could attract tourists to this town. Then we went out and created that industry, and it worked." And, in fact, Station Square, which is owned by the landmarks foundation and leased to concessionaires, is taking in upwards of $3 million a year.

Ziegler also warns of the city competing against itself, a danger if it carries out plans for festival marketplaces on the stadium site or in the Strip District. "I think we need a planning policy that treats the city as an economic organism that competes in the national market but not with itself," he says. "And we can only compete if we're unique,"—which, to Ziegler, means emphasizing the area's natural assets (the rivers) and the more romantic aspects of its industrial past. To some extent, he has done that at Station Square, where the last of the city's giant Bessemer converters occupies a star position, although inside the shopping mall, uniqueness is harder to pin down.

Upriver

After a morning's drive up the river through the boarded-up centers of the Mon Valley steel towns, it's hard for a visitor to settle down to talk of robotics and marinas. One wants to believe in the promise of the "information economy," but knowing that up to half the work force in Homestead—to cite just one example—is out of a job doesn't make it easy to do so.

Nor are there many believers among the members of the Tri-State Conference on Steel, the group that, along with the steelworkers union, is leading the drive to reopen the Dorothy Six blast furnace, a plant that employed up to 8,000 people at a time in the decade before it closed last year. U.S. Steel argues that the site is unprofitable. The workers reply that's because the company refuses to modernize. In the middle is the Allegheny County Community Development Department, which has brought in consultants to study the situation; so far it is stalemated.

The county is also a partner in the much-touted "Strategy 21" program, a $2 billion package of economic development projects for which some $425 million state funding is being sought and, in two cases, was recently received. The projects include the science and technology center and a 360-degree-screen Omnimax theater at the Three Rivers Stadium site ($2 million granted); the Herr's Island redevelopment; Strip District improvements ($1 million granted); the J&L site development; a variety of university-related advanced technology research projects, including some in metals research; highway and airport improvements; and a countywide "Metals Retention/Reuse Study" to look at ways in which government can help the faltering metals industry and, where it's too late for help, figure out how sites can most profitably be reused. Recently, Mayor Caliguiri proposed the creation of a regional "Mon-Ohio Reconstruction and Development Commission" to study just such issues. The rationale for the funding request is Pennsylvania's traditional, if unwritten, tit-for-tat legislative funding formula: If Philadelphia gets something big (a recent convention center), then Pittsburgh gets something big, too.

But for city planning director Robert Lurcott, the significance of the Strategy 21 document goes far beyond finances. "It's the first time," he notes, "that the city and the county have gotten together with the universities to work on a common agenda and common goals." And that, he adds, bodes well for the future.

Strategy 21 is also a document produced primarily by the public sector—the planning department put out the report itself—and, to some observers, that indicates the extent to which the public side has grown in aggressiveness over the past few years. Lurcott notes, though, that the document builds on an economic development strategy report published last year by the Allegheny Conference, which made many recommendations along the same lines, including suggestions for a seed capital fund and for a regional job retraining strategy.

The conference's recommendations are based on the work of nine task forces, which summed up their findings in a huge volume. But, while the background material is invaluable, the cautious nature of the recommendations was disappointing to some. Joseph Plummer, an editorial writer for the *Pittsburgh Post–Gazette* who has followed the conference for several years, suggests that the major corporations who supply it with brainpower may have lost some of their commitment—victims themselves of economic woes that have put them in a "contracting mode."

Shot-and-beer town

A favorite local sport since that Rand McNally livability rating has been trying to figure out just why Pittsburgh won. The coauthor of the ranking, David Savageau, has been quoted as saying that the reason was simply that Pittsburgh was "not awful" in any of the nine categories examined. Its highest score was in education where it came in seventh out of the 329 metro areas rated—not surprising considering the reputation of Carnegie–Mellon University and the University of Pittsburgh, the latter, incidentally, the area's largest employer. It also netted a seventh place in the arts category (thanks in large part to Andrew Carnegie, whose legacy includes *the* library and a huge museum and whose one-hundreth-fiftieth birthday is being celebrated this year). The numbers slip drastically in housing (186) and economics (185).

But Clark Thomas, a *Post–Gazette* columnist, suggested recently that Pittsburgh is "livable" not because it has museums and hospitals (it got a 14 in health care) but rather because it has an extremely stable population of "belongers." Thomas was reporting on a talk by a University of Florida researcher, Jack Detweiler, who said Pittsburgh's stay-at-homers—particularly the mill workers—account for half the population and give the city's neighborhoods their small-town characteristics—including a relatively low crime rate.

Will the city remain so livable if the people who gave it its character are forced to move to find work, Detweiler wondered. In short, will the wine cooler set be as loyal and as stable as the shot-and-beer crowd it's replacing? It's a good question to contemplate while riding the Monongahela Incline from the foot of Mount Washington (which was called Coal Hill in the days when German immigrants commuted by incline to their mill jobs). At the bottom is Station Square, whose many bars sell more wine than whiskey. Across the river is the Golden Triangle, symbolic center of the corporate city. And at the top is the old ethnic neighborhood that is gradually being discovered by an early wave of gentrifiers.

The city's future looks good, says Brian Berry—at least for those who can adjust to an "information economy." And for the romantics who mourn the passing of the open hearth furnaces (and the slag heaps and the soot), there's still a product. After all, says Berry, "computer software is as much a product as a lump of steel."

Ruth Knack is the senior editor of Planning.

Big But Not Bold: Irvine Today
Gladwin Hill
(February 1986)

It sounded so simple when the idea was broached 25 years ago. Here, 35 miles southeast of Los Angeles, was the country's biggest expanse of undeveloped single-ownership land in an urban setting: 144 square miles of variegated terrain, from oceanfront and farmland to mountain foothills. Six times as big as Manhattan Island, three times the size of San Francisco. Prepared, after more than a century of seclusion, to take the leap into development.

A planner's dream. Especially when the owners of the acreage known as the Irvine Ranch spurned the standard pattern of chopping up the land and selling it off piecemeal, electing instead to shape it, like a world-class diamond, according to a unified scheme.

The master plan for Irvine, the biggest private development on record, materialized rapidly. It looked in outline like something out of a storybook—an array of communities, spaced by parklands, greenbelts, and farmlands. Homes. Light industry. Business. Commercial and cultural centers. Even a university.

All that remained was to build it. The ceremonial first spadeful of earth was turned and Irvine was off to write new pages in the annals of urban planning.

This was the era of planning's great expectations. The federal government was about to launch its New Communities program. Of 16 such federally incubated "new towns" of the 1960s, only one—The Woodlands, near Houston—is now officially counted as a success. Irvine was a contemporary venture, but an entirely private one.

A quarter-century after its inception, the master plan proceeds. Like a motion picture "lap dissolve," in which one scene fades into quite a different one, the erstwhile Irvine Ranch, with its herds of cattle and miles of crops, is turning into a bustling mosaic of urbanization—too big to be encompassed visually in any way but from the air, too variegated and complex to be digested except in pieces.

The Irvine property, extending from the Pacific Ocean inland to the Santa Ana Mountains, fell naturally into three segments. The master plan's author, the late Los Angeles architect William Pereira, envisioned the seaward southern portion as the initial development area, the central agricultural segment as a greenbelt (at least temporarily), and the northern portion as something to be developed perhaps a generation hence. . . .

Some of the conceptual magic implicit in a 144-square-mile unified development has been vitiated by freeways. At the outset it was segmented by two, the San Diego and the Santa Ana, and now four more cross or abut the property. While these are mere threads in such an expanse, they have the psychologically if not aesthetically divisive effect of old-time railroad tracks. Nor is there much sense of unity in the vast reaches of open land dotted with occasional residential complexes and futuristic clusters of high rises.

The transformation from an old-West fiefdom has proved to be anything but simple. Almost from month to month, for more than 20 years, the evolution has been marked by corporate upheavals, zigs and zags in strategy and policy, zoning and taxation problems, community-relations crises, fluctuations in the real estate market, and some commercial and institutional disappointments.

Many details of these vicissitudes will never be known. Unlike most ventures of its size, the Irvine project, as a privately owned entity, has been shrouded in something of an informational Iron Curtain. The curtain has been parted only intermittently, to divulge facts the company chose to release or that have emerged in litigation and government records.

Regional newspaper coverage of Irvine has consisted principally of occasional announcements of plans for individual buildings, buried in the real estate sections. (Only a few years back, an inquiring reporter for the *New York Times* was rebuffed with the cryptic corporate statement that "our policy has become one of not having any coverage outside of California if we can help it.") Today a new brigade of executives is more communicative. But much basic corporate data remains, as an official put it, "proprietary."

Not to scale

Irvine's customary "not-to-scale" maps make the massive development look as cozy as your average subdivision. The realities are that the Irvine spread is roughly rectangular, 10 miles wide and extending inland nearly 25 miles, narrowing to a point as it approaches the Riverside Freeway. Small chunks of the property lie within the boundaries of a half-dozen adjacent municipalities. Over the years, odd bits of Irvine land have been legally annexed for one reason of convenience or another.

Three-quarters of the ranch is still largely undeveloped. Forty thousand of the original 92,000 acres are still in "agricultural" status, affording a tax break; 14,000 acres are actually in crops.

Development has been concentrated on the seaward portion of the property, south of the Santa Ana Freeway. The central city of Irvine now encompasses 42 square miles. The University of California's Irvine campus, initially an anchor feature of the master plan, occupies 1,000 acres donated by the Irvine Company and 500 more bought from it. There is a big Hilton hotel (owned by the Irvine Company) and a Four Seasons hotel near completion. In addition, several hotels on the coast and beside the freeways are planned.

Much of the developed area—some of it within Irvine city limits, some in unincorporated parts of the county—has been subdivided into 15 manicured communities with names like Wildwood and Windwood, generally of one to three square miles.

Concurrently, in other areas, there has been industrial and commercial development.

Early quasi-official projections estimated 300,000 people would be living and working in the Irvine development by 1980. Five years past that benchmark, the total population is 80,000, in 30,000 residential units. Overall employment in the development stands at about 115,000, according to the company. The early predictions for 1980 have been revised downward, and the achievement time moved up to "early in the twenty-first century."

What happened to the dream? To begin with, such projections are congenitally overoptimistic. In reality, there was no way to predict how long it would take such an extraordinary undertaking to mature.

The Irvine property constitutes one-sixth of Orange County, which has been one of the fastest-growing areas in the nation, doubling in population to two million people since the 1960s. Real estate developments have been myriad, and no one could tell whether newcomers would be attracted to Irvine or someplace else.

Orange County ordained in the 1970s that between 10 and 20 percent of new housing had to be affordable to people of moderate income, defined by a complicated formula. As interpreted by the Irvine Company, this meant domiciles in the $80,000–$150,000 bracket. Seventy-five percent of the firm's residential building planned for the next five years is in this category. (The median household income in Irvine is $45,000.)

Irvine started with an emphasis on upscale housing, mixed with moderate-priced houses. Before long, the company was so short of lower-bracket homes that it had to dispense them by lotteries. This was only the first of a number of shifts in basic strategy—some impelled by outside forces like the fluctuating regional real estate market, others occasioned by corporate perturbations.

Irvine attracted wide attention when, in 1974, it became an early target in the takeover craze, with the Mobil Corporation tossing out a then-spectacular $200 million bid.

Formed in the Civil War era by a syndicate headed by James Irvine, an Irish-born Forty-Niner, the ranch had remained in the hands of his descendants for a century. By 1960, protracted family feuding over management of the property culminated in a decision to develop it. Architect William

Pereira, designer of the Los Angeles International Airport and the Cape Canaveral rocket complex, was engaged to produce the plan.

Mobil entered the picture after a 1969 federal tax law forced the James Irvine Foundation to dispose of its controlling interest. Mobil's bid was tentatively accepted, then blocked by a suit by an heir, Joan Irvine Smith. She then joined forces with a syndicate of investors who bought the property in 1977 for $337 million.

The group included Alfred Taubman, a Detroit developer; Max Fisher, a Detroit industrialist; Henry Ford II; Milton Petrie, the merchandising magnate; Herbert Allen, Sr., Wall Street financier; and a dark horse, Donald Bren. Bren was a youthful California entrepreneur who had parlayed a small grubstake into a phenomenal series of home-development successes, including Mission Viejo near San Diego. Six years later, in 1983, after numerous management problems, Bren bought out the other participants for $518 million.

The Taubman syndicate's initial idea was to phase out the extensive in-house construction program under way and simply wholesale land to other developers, while adhering to the master plan. A year later, that policy was reversed, and the company started a new program of building luxury homes. But within two years it became apparent that the possibilities there were limited, and in another shift the company added "low-end" housing to its program. Three years later, in 1983, the decision was made to phase out luxury-home construction and put the emphasis on "affordable" homes for first-time buyers.

A recent Irvine advertisement reflected these shifts in strategy. It offered units in 21 different developments, at prices ranging from $90,000 to $300,000, with home sites in one elite area priced at $320,000. Eight of the 21 developments were Irvine company projects, four of them developments of a separate Bren company, and nine projects of other developers.

Architectural styles vary from Spanish-colonial and ranch to California modern and sleek ultramodern condos and apartments. Home design in each development is prescribed by the company, even to an owner's options in paint colors.

The largest of the 15 communities, scattered over a distance of 12 miles, is Woodbridge, a 1,700-acre tract. ("Over 30 beautiful parks . . . 2 lakes to choose from . . . trails for walking, jogging, and biking . . . Village center—50 shops and services . . .") Started in 1975, with a planned population of 25,000, a decade later it is still in development, with some 15,000 residents.

All the developments share the glossy, overly neat but inanimate look through which developers subliminally seek to conjure up images of idyllic, uncomplicated living—a counterpart to those decorator living room photographs that would be ruined by the presence of a rumpled magazine. There are no architectural innovations that would jar the bourgeois sense of security.

The company established three commercial/industrial enclaves, well separated from the residential areas. They share a goodly portion of the high-tech and electronics business that has given Orange County the sobriquet of "Silicon Valley South."

The biggest of these industrial areas covers some three square miles at the intersection of the San Diego and Santa Ana freeways, eight miles east of the Irvine municipal center. Originally it was divided into four segments, dedicated respectively to clean industry, technology, biosciences, and general business.

But this neat scheme produced problems. Prospective tenants preferred locations outside their categories; industrial applicants complained of segregated "third-class citizenship"; others objected to arbitrary exclusion of convenience enterprises, such as restaurants and stores. So in 1984 the company was impelled to "repackage" the 2,200-acre complex under the umbrella name of "Spectrum," opening up the tracts to mixed development.

The company's original idea was to sell industrial and commercial sites outright, and 80 percent of the development was on this basis. Donald Bren recently reversed this concept; now the policy is to keep land in company ownership and develop it in joint ventures with outsiders.

Hundreds of companies are represented in this area, and new buildings have been sprouting by the month. The biggest employer is the Fluor Corporation, an international engineering concern, with a payroll of 4,000.

Downscaling

From the beginning, implementation of the grand plan has been recurrently jarred by unexpecteds, inevitable in such a big undertaking. . . .

The late 1960s brought a stunning unexpected:

the dawning of the Environmental Revolution. While much of Irvine's planning had been environmentally idealistic, the ensuing avalanche of development strictures hit the company particularly hard in regard to its ocean frontage. It originally had ideas of implanting a population of 100,000 in the area of its "Irvine Coast" project, encompassing 10,000 acres between Corona del Mar and Laguna Beach. But static from 22 official agencies and environmental and civic groups over the years has decimated this scheme. To obtain needed development approvals, the company had put 4,000 acres into state and county parklands, and the population projection has been scaled down to 6,000. Current figures are hard to come by, but they obviously don't total more than a few thousand.

Civic pressures were intensified by the company's protracted battle with several thousand tenants in the Newport area. In the 1950s, before the master plan was mounted, the tenants had signed long-term leases at low rents for choice oceanfront sites. When these leases started expiring in the late 1970s, the tenants were confronted with rent increases, based on current market values, of as much as 3,000 percent, or purchase options on the same scale. A class-action suit, spearheaded by a tenants' "Committee of 4,000," forced the company, for the sake of community relations, to scale its demands way down.

One of the company's early major undertakings was a big shopping center in the Newport area dubbed Fashion Island. In its 17 years it has experienced stiff competition from the South Coast Plaza in nearby Costa Mesa, and the Irvine Company is now pumping $84 million into a major facelift aimed at more than doubling Fashion Island's menu of 72 shops.

No one is under the impression that the Irvine Company is feeling any financial pains. The last annual profit figure to be reported unofficially was $20 million in 1982. The price escalation since Mobil's $200 million bid in 1974—$337 million when the property turned over in 1977, some $500 million when Donald Bren got control in 1983—hardly suggests fiscal anemia.

Recently, the company put a valuation of $7 million on a six-acre parcel adjacent to the university—land worth only a few thousand dollars an acre 30 years ago. The site was the company's contribution to the $20 million research center given to the

National Academies of Sciences and Engineering by industrialist Arnold Beckman.

California's famous Proposition 13, passed in 1978, virtually freezes county tax valuations until a property changes hands. For 1983, the Irvine Company paid a $14 million tax, based on a valuation of $1.1 billion. But in 1984 the county, holding that Donald Bren's 1983 move from minority partnership to principal owner constituted a change in ownership, revalued the property at $3 billion and reckoned Irvine's new tax bill at $42 million. The company is appealing, contending that a change in corporate stockholding is not the same thing as transfer of title.

Not quite Valhalla

Crass figures aside, what about the quality of life at Irvine? No opinion polls have been publicized, but it seems reasonable to presume that most residents like their relatively sequestered environment, their lakes, golf courses, boat basins, riding and hiking trails, and other recreational opportunities, their serene vistas of ocean, mountains, and greenbelts.

But there also has been some disillusionment on the part of those who were bemused enough to expect a Valhalla.

The Irvine company at the outset abjured social dynamics. Early in the project's history, an official noted that its goal was "just to make the community a pleasant place to live, and not get involved in sociological planning as some other new planned communities have done."

What many settlers have discovered is that, apart from uncommon amenities, there is no psychic magic in living in an extraordinary enclave.

Harsh realities such as juvenile drug busts, school-tax squabbles, and an Irvine mayor shooting at his wife recurrently intrude. Ironically, for such a thoroughly planned settlement, Irvine's most pressing current problem is traffic. The Santa Ana and San Diego freeways are principal cross-country arteries. They have become so congested with through traffic at times that many motorists escape them by using parallel Irvine community streets. This traffic is threatening to interfere with some development plans. To remedy the situation, Orange County is planning to build three peripheral through-traffic arteries.

With all the residential elegance, one inhabitant summarized, "you still have the problems of earn-

ing a living, commuting, raising children, and paying taxes. A satisfying life still depends on a person's imaginative resources."

Some, amid the diffusion of communities, have voiced the familiar complaint that "there's no *there* there." The *Los Angeles Times* urban affairs critic, Sam Hall Kaplan, has remarked that Irvine is "a planned new city without one really major focus or activity center, but rather, a collection of satellite centers." And a sociologist at the university says, "It's like someone had a fantasy that the perfect city was just green lawns and big houses and safe stores to shop in. Well, they made it—and found that the dream actually was very boring."

But to such views the Irvine Company's current planning director, Roger Seitz, engaged after a prestigious career in Chicago, rejoins: "I'd heard that people thought Irvine was somewhat boring, too well planned. But now that I'm here I find that those who feel the city is boring are a small minority. The great majority like the tranquil atmosphere, and they want it to remain that way."

William Pereira, Irvine's designer, was contemptuous of conventional city planning, calling it "a two-dimensional thing that tends to freeze a problem as much as to solve it. The tax assessor has become a de facto city planner. Here we're trying to do something in 30 years that could take 300 by random growth."

Some time before his death last November, Pereira, whose role in Irvine activities had tapered off by the 1970s, took a ride through the development. He expressed gratification with the implementation of his master plan. Acknowledging that there had been inevitable amendments and problems, he commented: "We aren't gods. We could only try to predict trends and wants that would affect our future. We did a fair job, if I can say so."

Los Angeles: Prime Time

William Fulton
(February 1986)

Carey McWilliams, the late editor of the *Nation,* who probably understood Los Angeles better than anyone who has ever written about it, once called it "a very special city in spite of itself." And, in fact, Los Angeles has prospered by flouting traditional ideas of what a great city ought to be.

Cities are supposed to be dense; Los Angeles is geographically diffuse. Cities are supposed to have as their spine great mass transit systems; Los Angeles had one once and tossed it aside. Cities are supposed to have grand public spaces. Los Angeles has none, priding itself instead on its distinctly private way of life.

While many planners and sociologists find this attitude disturbing, the people of Los Angeles see nothing wrong with it. For one thing, most of them rarely think of themselves as residents of the city of Los Angeles. They speak of living in Hollywood or Sherman Oaks or Venice or one of the dozens of other relatively small, low-density communities that make up the metropolitan area. For another, even after you discount all the cliches about "autopia," Los Angeles can truly be described as one of the few large metropolises in the world where the automobile is thought of as a given. It is useful to remember, too, that this city of global importance is only 100 years removed from its origins as a dusty cowtown.

Not surprisingly given this environment, "planning" as most people understand it has been something of an afterthought. It is true that many of the tools of urban planning were put to impressive use in such megaprojects as the 230-mile Los Angeles Aqueduct, the freeway system, and, in the early part of this century, the interurban railway system. The Los Angeles area has also produced some of the most magnificent real estate developments in the country—from the high-rise Century City on a former movie lot near Beverly Hills to the recreation-oriented, county-owned Marina del Rey along the ocean to the 90,000-acre suburban city of Irvine in Orange County. But planning techniques have usually been used only to stimulate or respond to demand, not to shape a great city. "Urban planning" in its best sense—an overarching vision that can transform a mere collection of people and buildings into an inspiring metropolis—has only rarely played an important role in shaping Los Angeles.

Yet Los Angeles is changing—in fact, showing signs of approaching middle age. After struggling for years to gain recognition as a world-class metropolis, it has seen its international reputation improve greatly—with the aid of the 1984 Olympic Games. In terms of population, with just over three million residents, Los Angeles recently surpassed Chicago as America's "second city." Now it is engaged in a struggle of a different sort: coming to grips with the consequences of such success.

Los Angeles today is deluged by a remarkable influx of immigrants from Asia and Latin America, and an equally startling inflow of capital from around the world. This has given the city its now-famous racial diversity, but it has also turned L.A. into a kind of economic melting pot.

The greater metropolitan area has surpassed San Francisco as the financial capital of the West Coast and now challenges the Silicon Valley for leadership in the high-tech area. But it has suffered noticeably as a manufacturing center: Automobile production in Los Angeles, at one time second only to Detroit's, has virtually disappeared over the past 10 years, as have major concentrations of rubber, steel, and glass manufacturing. In short, Los Angeles has become both a Sun Belt city and a Rust Belt city.

It is also becoming more like other cities in terms of density. In the central parts of the metropolis, and some of the suburban centers too, the endless, low-rise plains are being replaced with concentrations of high-rise office buildings, apartments, and shopping centers. As a result, the city must put up with more of the everyday annoyances of urban living that local residents have always felt belonged in Chicago or New York or San Francisco but not in Los Angeles.

All this has raised questions about urban life that might seem commonplace elsewhere but, until recently, have seemed remote in Los Angeles: Are our commercial centers getting too crowded? Can we build an effective mass transit system? What will happen to our commuting patterns if the geographic distribution of jobs and housing gets too far out of balance? Should developers have to mitigate the environmental side effects of their projects?

Almost by coincidence, just as the city begins to grapple with those problems, two key urban planning posts are opening up at the same time. Last summer, city planning director Calvin Hamilton announced his retirement after several years of waning effectiveness. He will leave in June. Then, in December, the board of the powerful Community Redevelopment Agency surprised the entire city by forcing out longtime administrator Edward Helfeld. The vacancies give Los Angeles an opportunity to refocus its planning efforts in a new and perhaps more effective direction. . . .

Myths

Its sheer vastness has given rise to two myths about Los Angeles, neither of which has much truth. One is the idea that the famous "sprawl" is the result of one city—Los Angeles—moving relentlessly outward. In fact, Los Angeles as we know it today is a collection of dozens of small and medium-sized communities, most of which started life independently and then blended into what remains a multicentered region.

The other myth is that Los Angeles is a city designed with the automobile in mind. In fact, the multicentered region was spawned and strengthened by the Pacific Electric "Red Car" system, the nation's largest interurban rail system. The freeway system, which so often seems to define L.A. in the media, did not take hold until the 1960s, and even then it was laid out following the course set by the Red Car lines. It is true, however, that today the freeways provide a spine for a region that might otherwise have none.

While the Southern California megalopolis extends across several counties and includes more than 10 million people, the heart of what we think of as L.A. is really the Los Angeles basin—a valley-like area bounded by mountains on the north and east, and the ocean on the south and west. The basin contains most of the city of Los Angeles as well as a number of the suburban coastal communities.

It also contains L.A.'s "Manhattan": the Westside, a strip of land about 15 miles long (from downtown L.A. to the ocean) and about six miles wide (from the Hollywood Hills to the Santa Monica Freeway) that includes almost everything outsiders think of when they think of Los Angeles: the

downtown financial center, Dodger Stadium, Hollywood and many of its studios, the famous hillside houses, Beverly Hills and Bel Air, the Century City office complex, UCLA, fast-growing "Koreatown," and the smog-free Santa Monica beach. Here the tremendous "densification" of Los Angeles is most in evidence, and low-rise neighborhoods find themselves fighting daily battles with construction financed by the inflow of capital from around the world.

But the rest of the L.A. area is changing rapidly, too. The San Fernando Valley, once a quiet collection of suburbs, has seen so much construction (some of it high-rise) that its major freeway, the Ventura, is now the busiest in the country. Immediately to the east, the influx of Asians and Hispanics is dramatically changing the demographic makeup of the San Gabriel Valley; 50 miles beyond that, Riverside and San Bernardino are among the fastest growing areas in the country—and the last refuges of the inexpensive house in Southern California. To the south, Orange County, with more than two million people, has shed its redneck image and emerged as a virtual metropolis unto itself, driven largely by rapidly growing high-tech industries.

The political system, like the urban form, is a collection of many parts that don't always fit together. Thanks to a series of water-related annexations early in the century, the boundaries of the city of Los Angeles look like a bizarre 500-square-mile attempt at gerrymandering. Heavily populated areas a mile from downtown fall outside the city, while low-density suburban neighborhoods 40 miles away fall within its boundaries, and a thin strip of land straddles the Harbor Freeway for 20 miles to connect the city with its deep-water port in San Pedro.

Filling the political gaps are many of Los Angeles County's 83 other cities, including several outposts of forceful local government that engage in some innovative planning, making it all the harder for the city of Los Angeles to do a good job of planning on its own. Imagine the residents of Greenwich Village, the Upper West Side, and the Upper East Side in New York incorporating into independent cities and doing their planning separately, and you'll get an idea of what it's like for L.A.'s planners to deal with West Hollywood, Santa Monica, and Beverly Hills.

As if that weren't enough to make coordination

difficult, the system of local decision making is unusually fragmented too. As the *Los Angeles Times*'s chief local correspondent, Bill Boyarsky, wrote not long ago: "Separate government agencies going their own ways without communicating is an old story in Los Angeles, as old as traffic jams."

Transit, for example, is the responsibility of the Southern California Regional Transit District, which runs the regional bus system and is planning to build the Wilshire Boulevard subway—except that the purse strings to the county's $250 million-a-year transportation sales tax fund are held by the Los Angeles County Transportation Commission, which is planning a light rail system of its own.

The Los Angeles City Planning Department is particularly trapped by this fragmented system. The department is directly responsible for the land-use planning in the city, except close to the ocean (then the state Coastal Commission gets involved) or in a redevelopment area (in which case the planning department is likely to butt heads with the immensely powerful, largely autonomous Community Redevelopment Agency) or at a proposed transit stop (in which case the aggressive RTD often tries to step in). Of course, crucial areas of the community—and not just outlying areas—are planned for either by smaller cities or by the Los Angeles County Regional Planning Department, whose territory includes Malibu and Marina del Rey.

The most important piece of this puzzle, however, lies within city hall itself. By charter, Los Angeles has a "weak mayor–strong council" system, meaning that the 15 members of the city council have a lot more control over what the city does than Mayor Tom Bradley. Bradley, who has generally maintained a low-key profile on controversial issues, has rarely taken the lead on planning in the city.

The result is often described as a city with "15 little planning directors." Council members have great control over what goes on in their districts, and most are afraid to challenge a project in someone else's district for fear of reprisals. This means that even when council members are interested in doing good land-use planning, they usually can do so only on a spot basis within their own districts. This system—plus the traditional power of the real estate industry, dating back to the early boom days—has done much to render traditional planning efforts in Los Angeles irrelevant.

In 22 years as director of city planning, Calvin S. Hamilton has managed to forge a master plan that includes many inspired concepts, particularly the idea of clustering development to reinforce the city's multicentered nature. The land-use sections of the plan were put together as locally based community plans by thousands of homeowners and residents.

But implementing the plan would require a massive reduction in the city's zoning, which was established in the 1940s to accommodate a population of more than 10 million. Vast portions of the city are zoned for dense apartment or office development, but Hamilton has never had the political clout to persuade the city council to proceed with the downzoning, and until last year the planning commission has rarely reviewed individual projects to determine their effects. As a result, developers have routinely received permits for projects that far exceed the master plan's guidelines—projects that would almost certainly require an environmental impact statement and extensive public hearings in a city like San Francisco.

"This kind of government can be very destructive," says Dan Garcia, a downtown lawyer who has chaired the city planning commission for the past eight years. "Sometimes it makes you feel like you want to give up."

The flashpoint

In the last few years, such pressures as the Westside building boom have pushed this fragmented system of planning to the limit. At the urging of several members representing the Westside, the city council has imposed a series of restrictions. For example, a one-year ban on construction around Los Angeles International Airport led to a fee on new development for traffic improvements. A three-story height limit has been imposed on major boulevards in West Los Angeles, and a moratorium now covers commercial development in the crowded Westwood area around UCLA. And Michael Woo, a trained urban planner who was elected to the council from Hollywood, has begun pushing for control over the Community Redevelopment Agency's proposal for a redevelopment district there.

All these actions, however, amount to fighting fires. With the council reluctant to act on a city-wide rezoning, intense development still occurs without review or mitigation in many parts of the city, and tension among residents has continued to build. The whole issue finally reached a flashpoint a little over a year ago, when a coalition of homeowner groups from the Westside and the San Fernando Valley sued the city, demanding that it be rezoned to conform with the master plan drawn up by the planning department.

"Many of the homeowner groups were surprised and amazed and dismayed when they found out that all the work they had done on community plans made no difference whatever," says Carlyle Hall, an attorney with the Center for Law in the Public Interest who represented the homeowners.

Over the past year, that lawsuit has done what many years of persuasion by Calvin Hamilton had failed to do: It has pulled the Los Angeles City Council, kicking and screaming sometimes, into the age of real land-use planning.

The lawsuit hinged on a state law passed in 1978—at the urging of a state legislator who didn't like the president of the city council—requiring Los Angeles to change its zoning to conform with its master plan. The law gave L.A. until 1982 to comply, but the city proceeded slowly, completing only a fourth of the job by 1984. Hamilton asked the council for money to hire additional people for the task but didn't get any.

"Hamilton was trying," says Hall. "He did try to get the council to face up to the problem. But he was finding it extremely difficult to get the council to do anything."

Then, in September 1984, a state bill that would have given the city until 1987 to comply was vetoed by Gov. George Deukmejian, who probably will run for reelection in a rematch with Mayor Tom Bradley. When the city council moved slowly after the veto, homeowner groups filed the suit. In January 1985, Superior Court Judge John L. Cole gave the city 120 days to complete the rezoning.

Once the court order was issued, the council did move to deal with the rezoning. Although it stopped short of the citywide moratorium advocated by some council members, it established, for the first time, planning commission review power over projects that do not conform to community plans. When the homeowners subsequently returned to court, claiming the city was moving too slowly, Judge Cole fashioned an agreement allowing the city to keep the new ordinance in place until 1988 while it finished the rezoning. He also appointed prominent Los Angeles planning consultant Francine Rabinovitz to oversee the city's work on his behalf.

Last July the council allocated more than $5 million to do the job. A consultant has been working on a survey of parcels since last fall.

Whether or not the rezoning lawsuit eventually forces basic changes in Los Angeles's attitude toward planning, it has had several immediate effects.

For one thing, the suit has given the planning department greater clout in dealing with other agencies that work on land-use planning. One provision of the consent decree approved by Judge Cole gives the planning commission review power over big downtown projects—power that previously had rested exclusively with the Community Redevelopment Agency.

The CRA is generally given high marks for transforming downtown from a lackluster, low-rise office area into the center of the burgeoning Pacific Rim financial network. But as the downtown redevelopment area has grown, so has the amount of money CRA has received from tax increment financing mechanisms. (The state Community Redevelopment Law gives local agencies broad powers to condemn and to use tax increment financing in order to revitalize blighted areas.)

Although Edward Helfeld, who served as CRA administrator until December, says Hamilton and other city hall officials are part of the planning process, the fact is that with the tax increment money and the enthusiastic support of Gilbert Lindsay, the 85-year-old-black council member who represents downtown, the agency has had the power to plan for development downtown that the planning department lacks.

Over the past few years CRA had independently approved several downtown developments that exceeded the size allowed in the master plan (though not the zoning). This angered planning commission chairman Dan Garcia, who tried to work out a deal with CRA to bring the commission into the process. In particular, Garcia disliked CRA's approval of a transfer of development rights from the historic central library to a proposed 75-story building across the street.

But Garcia had no leverage until the zoning lawsuit was filed. Now, thanks to homeowners in outlying areas, the planning commission will review downtown projects that previously would have required only CRA approval.

Another important bit of fallout from the zoning lawsuit is the impending departure of Hamilton himself. Although the planning director says he was pleased that the homeowners filed the suit and forced the council to face rezoning, the incident seemed to point up his ineffectiveness, and after considerable discussion he decided to retire next June.

Hamilton was already under fire when the rezoning question arose. In 1984, Mayor Bradley suspended him without pay for six weeks after he was accused of using his position to promote a nonprofit tourism firm he helped organize. Although he was cleared of criminal charges by the state attorney general's office, the incident was still fresh in everyone's mind when the zoning lawsuit came along.

In the midst of the rezoning controversy, Hamilton lost support both of the homeowners, who blamed him for not implementing the master plan, and the developers, who began to fear that he would indeed implement it at last. Further, several prominent local politicians said that Hamilton, though highly regarded as a thinker, was rather out of date in an era when implementation was so important.

After members of the council began calling for his retirement in July, Hamilton conferred with Bradley, who, the planning director says, "sort of decided for me." But Hamilton decided to stay on until after the APA conference in April.

For his part, Hamilton believes he has not been ineffective. He says the master plan is the best in the country. "They blame me for not doing anything about implementing it, but that's not true," he adds. "It was the council's decision, and most of them didn't really want to do it."

Hamilton does concede this, however: "My early time was spent selling planning and visualizing what could and should be done. A lot of that has been done, and now it's a matter of putting together agencies and actors to implement plans."

Shortly after Hamilton decided to retire, another key player in Los Angeles's planning game departed more hastily. In December, CRA administrator Edward Helfeld left in what was billed as a contract dispute with his board of directors, which is appointed by the mayor and which includes influential downtown business and labor leaders. Helfeld, who had headed the powerful agency for almost a decade, was regarded with suspicion by some planners because he saw his job as "facilitating" development, particularly massive projects downtown, even at the cost of the city's master plan. Since his ouster, however, he has become a kind of martyr among local planners, who talk of his devotion to the Skid Row section of downtown.

The whole incident raised anew the question of who controls the city—particularly since Bradley, who will need contributions from businesses and developers in his coming run for governor, was out of town at the time and said nothing about the incident for weeks later.

The future

There is more, of course, to planning in Los Angeles than the problems of the city planning department and CRA. Smaller cities such as Santa Monica and Long Beach have undertaken innovative programs. And environmentalists and homeowners are fighting hard to drag the pro-development Los Angeles County Board of Supervisors into modern times. (So far they have fought mostly losing battles on coastal-area plans in Malibu and Marina del Rey.)

But the rezoning case symbolizes the larger challenges that the Los Angeles area is facing as it copes with the consequences of success and the onset of middle age.

Some local planners suggest that nontraditional solutions—such as more "telecommuting," for example—might be the answer to the region's traditional planning problems.

Yet even nontraditional solutions require a constituency for good planning—a constituency that Los Angeles has traditionally lacked. It seems likely that the upcoming search for a new city planning director and the selection of a new CRA administrator will rivet the attention of the public—or, at least, the politicians—on the challenge of building such a constituency. The events of the last few years seem to prove that support for more aggressive planning is growing in Los Angeles. But, in a city that has always prided itself on being different, it remains to be seen whether the planning constituency can grow big enough, and work effectively enough, to make a difference.

William Fulton is a contributing editor of Planning.

New Jersey Gets the Last Laugh

John Herbers
(March 1987)

On a clear day, from almost any Jersey City street leading to the Hudson River, the Manhattan skyline looms large and close. From that perspective, it seems like a grotesque attachment to northern New Jersey's urban complex, for decades considered a decaying backwater in the nation's largest metropolitan area.

From the twin towers of the World Trade Center in lower Manhattan, the view is, of course, quite different and more revealing. There, one looks across the wide mouth of the river at the long-familiar railroad yards, junkpiles, and dilapidated docks and warehouses. But there is also something new emerging—something that many New Yorkers find surprising. Gleaming high rises, manicured parks, and acres of cranes and other construction machinery are fast transforming a historic eyesore into what some planners expect to be one of the most exciting and expansive waterfront developments in the nation.

New Jersey Gov. Thomas H. Kean described the scope of it in his annual message to the state legislature earlier this year. From the George Washington Bridge to Bayonne—a distance of 16 miles and encompassing Hoboken, Weehawken, West New York, Fort Lee, and Edgewater, as well as Jersey City—22 waterfront projects are either under way or on the drawing board. "Taken together," said the governor, an active supporter of the development, "they involve more than $10 billion in investment. They could create 20 million square feet in office space, 36,000 residential units, and two million square feet of commercial development by the turn of the century. This will create 100,000 new jobs."

Some of the planners involved foresee an urban strip that will offer homes for rich and poor alike, a wide array of business and industry, one of the nation's most advanced public transit systems, and amenities ranging from bike and jogging trails to cultural centers.

All that is far from assured, however. In Man-hattan, the Regional Plan Association, the citizens group that monitors development throughout the metropolitan area, is keeping a skeptical eye on what is taking place across the river. Its fear is that the projects will take jobs from New York and do little to alleviate the region's middle-income housing shortage.

There are also environmental concerns, particularly about the future of the Palisades, those vertical columns of diabase rock that rise above the river plane along the northern part of the strip under development. And there is skepticism about the ability of the transportation plan to meet the needs of an area whose past decline was due in part to being squeezed between land and water.

It's the possibilities for success, though—possibilities that in many ways exceed those elsewhere in the metropolitan area—that excite both critics and promoters.

Surprise

What is happening on the waterfront today was on no drawing board a decade ago. New Jersey's suburban areas had long attracted commuters, but it wasn't until the late 1970s, when New York residential costs began to skyrocket, that real estate people discovered that, in return for lower living costs and spectacular views of the Manhattan skyline, people working in Manhattan would also be willing to commute to the New Jersey river towns.

Young couples began to buy and restore old rowhouses in decaying neighborhoods of Jersey City and West New York, and a few daring developers put up high rises on the cliffs of Fort Lee and Hoboken, offering quick travel to the city via the George Washington Bridge or the Port Authority Trans-Hudson (PATH) subway line. Settlement of the Penn Central Railroad bankruptcy case in the late 1970s put acres of waterfront property on the market for the first time.

A catalyst for commercial development was the rehab in 1982 of a huge, old Jersey City warehouse. In what was then considered a risky venture, two builders paid $25 million for the 2.5-million-square-foot property, which they began converting into the Harborside Financial Center. Last fall, they sold the project for $120 million. Now partially occupied and still undergoing renovation, the old building is only one of many riverfront construction sites.

Although the idea of affluent New Yorkers settling on the New Jersey waterfront seemed radical a decade ago, in retrospect, it seems clear that the unfolding development simply filled a vacuum caused by changing economic conditions and population patterns. In years past, the old waterfront cities comprised one of the nation's largest and most varied manufacturing centers. Thousands of factories made products ranging from boiler tanks to castor oil and shipped them by rail and water to consumers and corporations around the world.

In the 1970s, the whole region's manufacturing complex went into steep decline, accompanied by a parallel loss in population. Left behind on the waterfront were decaying old neighborhoods, idle office buildings, docks, and rail yards, and a disproportionate share of the poor, minorities, and the elderly.

The Jersey waterfront remained depressed long after New York's economy had begun its revival—a revival based not on manufacturing but on finance, communications, and other white-collar, service-sector endeavors. In Manhattan, the boom was so rapid that expansion room was needed. New Jersey in many ways offered better alternatives than New York City's outer boroughs, although they too have experienced some spillover development.

Samuel J. LeFrak has been one of New York City's most prolific developers, builder of Lefrak City in Queens, the largest privately financed housing project in the country. Now LeFrak is building a new community for 30,000 people in Jersey City, a project that so angered New York City officials that they tried to derail a $10 million Urban Development Action Grant earmarked for the development.

LeFrak's development, called Newport, offers a good example of the economic and procedural reasons for the massive shift of construction across the river to New Jersey. In New York, LeFrak says, there are so many political entanglements and requirements that it can take a quarter of a century to complete a large project. And in New Jersey, the labor and land costs are so much lower that an apartment built to rent for $1,250 a month in Manhattan can be built to rent for $900 in Jersey City.

Although New Jersey has its own political idiosyncrasies, developers say that compared to New York City, it has less militant labor unions, less regulation, and generally lower taxes, a combina-

tion that leads to faster construction and higher profits.

Yet the waterfront development is much more than a spillover from Manhattan. It is part of a remarkable wave of growth sweeping the rural areas of New Jersey and, to some extent, even the old industrial centers like Newark, long the ultimate example of the decaying central city.

The growth has three main centers: the highway corridors around Princeton and Trenton, the Meadowlands west of the Hudson, and the rural area along Interstate 78 in the vicinity of Morristown. Long derided as a confusing stretch of decaying old cities and sprawling suburbs between New York and Philadelphia, New Jersey is suddenly known as the place to be.

A key reason is that the state happens to lie in a high-growth corridor extending along the Eastern Seaboard from the Carolinas to New Hampshire. Moreover, it has an abundance of open land—most of it away from the old cities but close to interstate highways and airports—that is ideally suited for the high-technology enterprises, sprawling shopping centers, and scattered residential subdivisions that dominate the new development of the 1980s.

Much of this development is, of course, speculative, driven by tax advantages and the desire of foreigners to put their money in long-term investments in a politically and economically stable nation. The sprawling office parks out along the freeways are considered the wave of the future, almost certain to continue. What's interesting about the New Jersey waterfront development is that its density and style are so different from what is happening over most of the state and across the nation.

Major projects under way or scheduled for construction include:

• Newport (the name was recently changed from Newport City at the request of Jersey City, which didn't want it to be mistaken as a separate municipality). It will cost some $10 billion by completion in 1995. Built on 400 acres of former railroad land at the mouth of the Holland Tunnel, Newport will include several high-rise apartment buildings, three hotels, a convention center, a shopping mall, an 80-story office building that, with others, will provide 10 million square feet of space, and a 1,000-slip marina. The city-approved master plan is by RTKL Associates of Baltimore, with certain revisions under way by Stanton Eckstut.

• Port Liberte, a mixed-use development in Jersey City designed by French architect Francois Spoerry, will offer 1,700 housing units, one million square feet of office space, a shopping mall, hotel, marina, and restaurant set on more than two miles of canals within close view of the Statue of Liberty.

• Lincoln Harbor, a development by Hartz Mountain Industries (of pet supply fame), will offer 1.6 million square feet of office and retail space in Weehawken, adjacent to the Lincoln Tunnel. Paine Webber, the brokerage house, is moving part of its operation from Manhattan; it will employ 2,500 people in the complex by late next year. The master plan, by the architectural firm of Wallace Roberts & Todd, noted for its work on Baltimore's Inner Harbor, calls for townhouses, retail shops, and a variety of amenities.

• Port Imperial in Weehawken and West New York promises to be a "European-style" community of 30,000 with its own ferry to Manhattan. Arcorp Properties, headed by trucking company owner Arthur Imperatore, who said he had a "cosmic vision" of the project, is planning almost 10 million square feet of office and retail space, a hotel, and a marina on a 365-acre site, with elements borrowed from Venice, Copenhagen, and Paris. Last December, a ferry service linked Arcorp's property with West 38th Street and the Javits Convention Center in Manhattan.

Enough planning?

In all, there are more than 20 big projects under construction or approved for some stage of development. This, along with ambitious plans for rail-bus-boat transportation connections and a walkway the full length of the riverfront, has, of course, raised questions about adequate planning.

Most of the development is in Hudson County, which besides being a money-poor jurisdiction, has little authority to coordinate the development that is encouraged by the cities and towns that make up the waterfront. And the municipalities' plans and zoning sometimes conflict with the initiatives of the metropolitan-area agencies such as the Port Authority of New York and New Jersey.

For several years, the Regional Plan Association has been urging New Jersey to set up a riverfront commission with authority to act as overall planning agency and to make sure that plans of individual municipalities "add up to an accessible and attractive waterfront." In a December 1985 report,

the association said: "Here is an area which cries out for cooperative, comprehensive planning. The New Jersey riverfront is virtually an island, cut off by the Palisades to the west and the river to the east, with few connecting 'bridges' and without a continuous north-south roadway. If this area is not carefully planned, initial development will inhibit rather than stimulate additional projects because of the lack of amenities and excessive traffic."

But legislation for a riverfront commission has languished in the New Jersey legislature, and James Wunsch, associate director of the Regional Plan Association, noted in a recent interview that even as ground is broken for many of the planned waterfront projects, the need remains for a strong overall agency to guide the growth.

The closest New Jersey has come to such a commission is the public-private advisory committee appointed by Gov. Kean, who has also opened a waterfront development office in Jersey City. Herman Volk, the director of the governor's office and a planner by profession, says that the arrangement has worked out more smoothly than some had anticipated. "The local governments have really welcomed our help," he says. A staff member of the Regional Plan Association suggests that might be because there has been little state pressure to conform, not surprising in light of Gov. Kean's often-expressed belief in local self-government.

The governor's initiative, however, has resulted in some broad requirements intended to serve the overall guidelines agreed to by most of the public and private interests involved. For example, the state environmental protection department, which by law must approve each project, requires public access to the waterfront and assurance of adequate transportation. The requirements are part of the "linkage" program that the state and the local governments are imposing on developers as a means of obtaining a new transportation system and an unbroken public walkway along the river.

All has not been smooth sailing, however. There is ongoing controversy, for example, over Liberty State Park, a beautiful, 750-acre expanse of waterfront plazas, walkways, and picnic groves built on abandoned rail yards. Bordering on New York Harbor and less than half a mile from the Statue of Liberty and Ellis Island, the park is one of the region's most prized recreational areas.

The Kean administration wants to see more intense development there, including a walkway on the seawall, a new science and technology museum, and an aquarium. The governor proposes that all be built and operated by private developers, and to that end appointed a nonprofit development corporation, a sharp departure from the state's traditional practice of administering public parks through the Division of Parks and Forestry.

When the development corporation moved on a plan to build a 600-boat marina on 57 acres of the park, the Jersey City city council unanimously adopted a resolution calling the marina a "reckless giveaway of public parklands" and demanded public hearings on the proposal. Construction of the marina has been delayed and the matter placed under negotiation.

Such a controversy seems minor, however, when compared to the prospects of chaos in the overall transportation system, regarded by all concerned as the key to success or failure of the waterfront development. Currently, the Port Authority estimates that a quarter of a million commuters cross the river between 6 a.m. and 10 a.m. every weekday by way of tunnels and bridges. By 1990, the agency expects another 50,000.

Gov. Kean's plan to meet that demand is both costly—estimates run close to $1 billion—and complicated. The proposal calls for construction of new PATH lines on abandoned rail and trolley rights-of-way as well as on rails now used by Conrail for carrying freight; for extensive new highways and bus routes; and for huge new commuter parking lots near the tunnels and rail terminals. A key element is the proposed shift of Conrail lines a few miles to the west so as to permit more passenger service along the waterway.

At this writing, negotiations on the transfer had been bogged down for many months, but New Jersey planner Volk said the parties involved were "very close to reaching an agreement" under which the state would pay most of the relocation costs.

The Port Authority and the New Jersey Department of Transportation are cooperating with the governor's plan by enlarging the PATH stations, ordering new cars, and preparing for construction of new rail lines. Overall, the transportation costs are to be covered by the public bodies involved and by contributions exacted from the developers—part of the linkage agreement—with no new direct tax on residents.

At the same time, plans are being laid for ferry service that would, at best, supplement rail, bus, and automobile transit between New York and New Jersey. Early in this century, ferries were a major mode of commuter transportation in the New York region. But in 1967, the last trans-Hudson ferry ceased operation—until last December's resumption of service by Arcorp Properties.

As Sigurd Grava, professor of urban planning at Columbia University, pointed out in an article in the July 1986 edition of *Transportation Quarterly,* new technology in water transportation, which permits such innovations as a bus-carrying ferry, enhances the opportunities for moving large numbers of commuters by water. Experience with new ferries elsewhere, however, suggests to planners in the New York area that the possibilities of water vehicles are limited and that the demand for ground transportation will increase.

Environmental concerns are also many. The New Jersey Department of Environmental Protection is said to be diligent about such matters as requiring adequate sewage treatment plans as the construction proceeds and the population grows.

The Regional Plan Association remains concerned, however, about protection of the Palisades, which could be totally obscured from both sides of the river if high-rise construction continues unchecked. It is important, notes the RPA's Wunsch, that the contrast of the Manhattan skyline on one side and the natural splendor of the Palisades on the other be retained.

Jerseyite worries

Of even more concern to the Jerseyites is the possibility that they will be crowded out by the new development or left isolated in decaying neighborhoods. This concern was the chief reason that Jersey City elected a new mayor in 1985, Anthony Cucci, who charged the previous administration with promoting development at the cost of low-income residents.

One of the new mayor's first actions was to appoint Rick Cohen, a young urban planner with a history of developing low- and moderate-income housing, as director of the city's Department of Housing and Economic Development. Cohen has since obtained pledges from most of the big developers either to include affordable housing units in their projects or to donate to a housing trust fund. In Newport, 18 percent of the units now under construction are being reserved for lower income people, with rents substantially below the average.

Yet Regional Plan Association staff members say that while Jersey City is making progress on housing the needy, other jurisdictions are lagging in that regard.

Whatever the concerns, development of the New Jersey waterfront has created a rare sense of excitement. One reason is that it promises greater density than the thinned-out suburbs—or even the thinned-out cities. Moreover, it once again brings to the central cities residential construction affordable by the middle class.

Virtually every large American city has experienced some downtown revitalization as the new service economy takes hold and the manufacturing economy declines. But the middle class has not returned in numbers, even when there has been substantial gentrification. Baltimore's much-proclaimed Inner Harbor redevelopment, for example, has not stemmed the city's population losses. The trend almost everywhere is to deconcentration—fewer occupants per housing unit and fewer housing units per acre of land.

The Regional Plan Association said a decade ago that the New Jersey waterfront should go one of two ways. Either there should be extensive development, coupled with a vastly improved transportation system, or growth should be drastically limited. The association said it much preferred the high-density alternative both for the convenience of the residents and for the making of an attractive city.

The waterfront is now, in fact, moving in the direction of very high density. Roughly half a million people live there now, and entire new communities of many thousands soon will be imposed alongside the old neighborhoods. And the transportation system now in the making could well become a model for other urban areas.

The remaining question is whether the New Jersey waterfront will turn out to be a little Manhattan, with highly skilled, affluent people living and working near enclaves of the unemployed—a "dual city" as the U.S. Advisory Commission on Intergovernmental Relations, a nonpartisan government agency, has termed many of the nation's old industrial cities that have lost their blue-collar populations.

The new jobs opening on the waterfront are mostly like those that have fueled the recovery of Manhattan in recent years: jobs in banks, brokerage firms, communication companies, accounting firms, and so on that require skills that most of the chronically unemployed do not have.

Between the cliffs and the new development on the waterfront are the old neighborhoods, their blocks of rowhouses filled with poor blacks, Hispanics, and elderly whites—and an increasing number of yuppies from across the river.

Some authorities such as Rick Cohen, the Jersey City housing director, believe it is possible with the right kind of planning for the new development to accommodate all of these people and to build a new city on old industrial ruins that will not be divided between the rich and poor. That seems to be the largest challenge facing the New Jersey waterfront.

John Herbers was formerly the national correspondent for the New York Times, *based in Washington, D.C. He is the author of* The New Heartland: America's Flight Beyond the Suburbs and How It Is Changing Our Future, *published by Times Books.*

Small Towns, Big Dreams

Jim Schwab
(November 1986)

Babbitt's dream evaporated almost overnight five years ago. The Minnesota Iron Range community, 90 miles north of Duluth on a two-lane country road, began for just one reason: a low-grade iron ore called taconite. The Reserve Mining Company built the town in 1951 expressly for its workers, who earned good wages, financed their houses on easy terms through an employee credit union, and often had money to burn.

For years, Reserve's taconite mine, a joint venture of the Armco and Republic steel companies, was the most productive in the world. But decline in the U.S. steel industry and competition from other taconite sources finally closed the mine in 1981, decimating the town that at its peak was home to 3,700 people. Lacking proximity to anything but its iron mines, Babbitt had to scramble for economic survival. So did its residents, many of whom left as unemployment soared to 85 percent. The rapid exodus cut the population to today's 2,300, and the average housing price plummeted to under $10,000.

Babbitt should have become a ghost town. When the mine reopened in 1983, it recalled just 300 of its 1,500 former workers. What has kept the town alive—and optimistic—is the tenacity of its citizens and of the mayor they elected in 1982, Don Cole, 66, a retired mine foreman. Taking office at the peak of Babbitt's crisis, Cole also brought to his job a self-effacing humor that masked enough of the gloom at city hall to get things done. "I was crazy enough to be talked into running, and people were crazy enough to elect me," he tells visitors.

Babbitt's civic entrepreneurs

A smile and an easy laugh are part of the salesman's repertoire, and Cole is a salesman for Babbitt. His first priority was to train Babbitt to sell itself through Minnesota's Star Cities program. The state's Department of Energy and Economic Development launched Star Cities in 1981 to highlight and strengthen the state's most aggressive local development programs.

The certification requirements would daunt many small cities: forming a local development corporation; compiling labor statistics, a community profile, and a fact book; completing a five-year economic development plan, a five-year capital improvement plan, and a one-year work program; producing a video presentation for prospective businesses; developing a local business retention strategy; and handling a mock presentation for industrial site-seekers.

But the town had one key asset: a pool of unemployed volunteers who combined their talents to make Babbitt a Star City in a record four and a half months. Its 37 volunteers outpaced the paid staff of many larger communities, producing a quality slide show for only $87. In contrast, says Harry Rosefelt, the state's director of development resources, most of the 40 cities that have been certified took 12 to 18 months. The town's achievement won it visibility among state officials that paid handsome dividends later.

The city council also formed the Babbitt-Embarrass Area Development Association (BEADA), inviting joint efforts with a nearby township that shared Babbitt's school district. But Cole and the council never intended to settle for a passive role while a small appointed board assumed control of economic development efforts. The same civic enthusiasm that achieved a speedy Star Cities designation enlisted 435 individual and 29 business members to sustain BEADA's projects and committees.

Cole joined the search for funding sources to augment BEADA's membership dues and bond sales. He recalls a 1983 effort to solicit foundation officials who had not heard of Babbitt and had no idea where it was or why they should care. Cole says foundation grants ultimately added $55,000 to a revolving loan fund that targeted small business loans to local people who could not qualify for bank credit. Babbitt's skilled but largely unemployed work force would become its main source of entrepreneurial talent.

Because the city had relocated its offices to the Bryant Center, an office and retail complex in a converted school building, the old city hall became an ideal trial site for BEADA's efforts. A $134,000 community development block grant financed renovation of the building, while BEADA loans allowed a pool table manufacturer and a small novelty products firm to occupy it. BEADA has relied heavily on board members' personal knowledge of loan applicants and has taken risks. Yet, Cole says, BEADA's 19 loans have shown a perfect repayment rate thus far.

The city did less well, at first, in trying to attract new businesses from other areas. It struck out in its courtship of a Yugoslavian furniture manufacturing firm that exported most of its goods to the U.S. A junket in the governor's airplane to court a hazardous waste reprocessor led to a proposal that met considerable local protest.

On the bright side, Reserve Mining's steady disengagement from Babbitt offered new opportunities for the reuse of abandoned buildings. Learning of an inventor with a patented process for rubber tire recycling, Cole arranged to buy a 33,000-square-foot building formerly used by a pneumatic drill manufacturer and the five acres it sat on. Total price: $5,001. Two state agencies had poured over $1 million into the rubber company to encourage its development, but Minnesota Waste Management Board rules required that a county own the building the company would use.

Aware of this restriction, Cole arranged sale of the site to St. Louis County for $30,000. When the company's attorney found a last-minute legal obstacle to the city's proposals, the mayor lobbied for an enabling law that passed the Minnesota legislature in a head-spinning 10 days. Then, aware that the inventor was the key to the success of Rubber

Research Elastomerics, Cole insisted he buy a $500,000 life insurance policy with the city as beneficiary. The new plant is expected to eventually create 60 new jobs but two firms that will also locate in Babbitt to make use of the unique product may add twice that number. Babbitt's daring strategies finally seem to have paid off.

In its heyday, Babbitt billed itself as the "town at the end of the road." Its remote location posed problems for business recruitment, but, says *Babbitt Weekly News* publisher Audie Austreng, it also provides attractions for an American public turned on to outdoor sports.

Austreng heads BEADA's tourism committee, which won the Minnesota Office of Tourism's 1985 tourism marketing award. He and his volunteers have produced a slide show, "The Roaring Stony River," and sent local people to seven major sports shows in a bid to publicize Iron Range lakes, ski trails, and rivers.

Still, Austreng says that tourism is something that Babbitt cannot afford to promote without regional cooperation, which only recently has begun to emerge. Grants from the state Department of Iron Range Resources and Rehabilitation have spurred tourism. Austreng also brings up a touchy subject for many former mine workers: The new jobs in tourism will not support the standard of living that miners were used to.

A new crisis has added to the ranks of unemployed miners. A year ago, LTV Corporation bought Republic Steel's half of Reserve Mining Company. In August, LTV filed for reorganization in federal bankruptcy court, leaving Armco with complete financial responsibility for the mine. Layoffs of the remaining 300 workers resulted, and state negotiators began talks to find ways to reopen the mine. Once again, Babbitt seems "at the end of the road." But its leaders at least know what they can achieve with a committed citizenry.

Iowa's flower lady

Karen Merrick, the mayor of Guttenberg, Iowa, is immensely popular there precisely because of her personal determination to assure Guttenberg's future. In the late 1970s, while serving on a new economic development committee, she led other local women in planting flowers, shrubs, and trees along state Highway 52 on the western edge of the Mississippi River town. She believes that "to attract anyone here—be it tourists, industry, or good teachers—the community must be presentable."

Skeptics then called her the "flower lady." But Merrick, now 39, won her second race for mayor in 1981. She has won easily ever since, but says this is her last term. Her supporters expect her to seek higher office.

The foundation of her popularity is a high-energy style of leadership. Convinced that an attractive community, not tax favors, is the way to attract and retain business, she has Guttenberg's property tax bumping up against its state-imposed limits while providing a variety of amenities and infrastructure improvements. A populist who cochaired the "rural caucus" at the 1984 Democratic national convention, she stresses broad citizen participation.

Aware that a 150-year-old river town has the history and scenic qualities to attract tourist dollars, Merrick secured $10,000 for facade restoration from a state cultural grants program. The city earlier got all 62 buildings in a three-block business district listed on the National Register of Historic Places.

There is urgency to Merrick's task. Shortly after she took office, a local manufacturer of recreational vehicles closed due to a business slump, laying off 200 workers. In Dubuque, some 40 miles south, John Deere, the big farm implement manufacturer, was cutting its 6,000-person work force in half. The Dubuque Packing Company was laying off meat cutters. By early 1984, Guttenberg's unemployment rate had climbed to 21 percent as Merrick struggled to get her economic revival on track.

The city committed $120,000 from general obligation bonds and $53,000 from municipal electric system profits to purchase 10.6 acres on a bluff north of town and to grade the land for an industrial park. It gave this land to its development group, which sold it to two out-of-town firms: Illinois Tool Works, an auto parts manufacturer, and Products Unlimited, a maker of electronic relays and switches. Meanwhile, Ertl Toy Company took over the facility of a defunct Chevrolet dealership.

The three firms added 250 new jobs, a gain of some consequence in a town of 2,400 people. The two firms in the industrial park expect to add at least 100 new jobs by next fall.

Finding the firms was not pure luck. Terry Ackley, a former Guttenberg resident, was working at Products Unlimited in Sterling, Illinois, when the mayor called. Ackley put her in touch with the owner, and the development commission took over from there.

Tourism has also become a priority in Guttenberg as the city seeks to capitalize on its riverfront scenery and German heritage. New retail outlets are proliferating: Diamond Jo's Warehouse, in a nineteenth-century warehouse, opened a gift shop in 1978, added a restaurant three years ago, and last year opened a bar and lounge at river level. Charles Lawson, a former Peoria insurance company employee, restored a 63-year-old paddle-wheeler—the oldest on the Mississippi—to begin river cruises this summer at Lawson's Landing. He and his wife, Angie, are using the city's $10,000 restoration grant to reroof a former pearl button factory, which they expect to convert into a riverfront inn.

Evidence of a substantial payoff for these efforts came this spring, when the Iowa Development Commission sponsored a tourist ad in three out-of-state metropolitan Sunday newspapers. Of 57 Iowa cities featured in the ad, Guttenberg attracted inquiries on 32 percent of all the coupons the commission received, ranking fourth. Local development commission chair Mary Bess Goeppinger reports another sign of success: A "tagging" system she initiated among retailers indicates that 50 percent of all sales are to visitors.

Merrick estimates that with the recent industrial expansions, unemployment has fallen to 15 percent. And Goeppinger notes that city sewer improvements have allowed the development commission to attract a third company to the industrial park.

Most of these improvements will survive Merrick's administration, but the mayor is taking no chances. She notes the city is hiring a project planner to "put our plans on paper." She adds, "We know what we want: an urban renewal plan for industry and for downtown revitalization." The planner's job will be to answer the technical questions about how Guttenberg can best achieve its vision.

College town

Vernon Deines, who teaches community and regional planning at Kansas State University, suggests that college towns have an intangible bonus that can overshadow other criteria for small town economic survival: a highly educated faculty that can provide a core of community leadership and vi-

sion. And, he says, the college is a stable major industry.

Grinnell College, with some 1,200 students, provides a sizeable payroll in Grinnell, Iowa. Even more important, the student body creates jobs in local retailing. Nevertheless, "town-gown" antagonisms are common in rural areas, and Grinnell is no exception. The difference here is that community leaders are recognizing the college as a key part of their economic development plans—and as an amenity to build on.

That amenity and the stability it brings Grinnell are likely to be crucial in coming years in offsetting the lingering effect of the surrounding farm economy, which is drying up the town's major outside source of retail dollars. Hard-pressed farmers now have difficulty paying their feed, fertilizer, and equipment suppliers, and have cut back on much of their consumer spending.

Sharp Lannom, owner of Grinnell-based DeLong Sportswear, admits that the town has not always gone out of its way to make its downtown attractive to students whose campus is located just six blocks away. The students—few of whom come from the rural Midwest—tend to view Grinnell as alien territory. They come because of the school's reputation for academic excellence.

Lannom was the founder and is now the first president of a broad-based planning vehicle unique in the Grinnell area: the Grinnell 2000 Foundation. It began with a small organizing board two years ago, raised some funds within the business community, and hired Benjamin Webb, formerly with the Iowa Development Commission, as its executive director.

Webb promptly contracted for a planning study of Grinnell's future with the Naisbitt Group of Washington, D.C., and scheduled a town meeting in November 1985 to launch its membership drive and seek community input.

In the view of some Grinnell residents, however, the foundation got off to a rocky start by choosing an all-male board of directors. In response to criticism from the local League of Women Voters and other groups, the group later elected a 20-member board that, according to the bylaws, must include eight women, eight men, and four people from outside the city limits. But even with the handicap of some bad first impressions, including some created by hiring the firm of *Megatrends* author John Naisbitt, the foundation's membership got off to an impressive start. Of the 2,300 residents who attended the town meeting, 300 signed up. Webb says 129 nominated themselves for board service.

By Labor Day, the foundation had nearly 1,200 members in a city of 8,800 people. Foundation membership is not cheap—$52 per year, or $1 a week, guaranteed through a payroll deduction plan.

Two big tasks have been accomplished: Getting Grinnell named a Main Street community and establishing a low-interest revolving loan fund for commercial improvements in the downtown business district.

The National Trust for Historic Preservation launched the national Main Street program several years ago to promote small-town preservation. Governor Terry Branstad introduced the Iowa version of the program in January. The state development commission invited nearly 50 communities to apply for the inaugural class, and 18 did so. Grinnell was one of five accepted. Each town received a $15,000 grant plus consulting services paid for by the development commission.

According to development commission director John Schaffner, Iowa is one of only two states that provide chosen cities with a cash grant and paid services. Grinnell's part of the bargain is to pay for a Main Street manager for its program, which shares an office with the Chamber of Commerce.

But Grinnell and its new foundation did not stop there. Several local corporations have teamed up with Grinnell College to provide $250,000 for low-interest loans to support downtown improvements. That program, too, will be coordinated by newly hired Main Street manager Matthew Hussman, a Grinnell College graduate.

Main Street, the foundation, the Grinnell Chamber of Commerce, and the Greater Grinnell Development Commission, which owns land for future industrial use, are all private organizations. Where does the city fit it?

There is ample opportunity for duplication of efforts, says assistant city manager Gary Goddard, but it is the city's role to prevent it. To maintain close cooperation, the city provides the foundation free office space in its civic center. The city also provided $10,000 toward the Main Street budget and will increase its commitment as the state grants decline. Two council members sit on the Main Street board. And the Main Street grant application

to the state was a cooperative project between the city, the foundation, and the chamber.

Meanwhile, the Grinnell 2000 Foundation may adopt or modify many ideas from the Naisbitt Group report, whose suggestions include attracting catalog companies to capitalize on the city's access to Interstate 80, building an airport, marketing the city as a retirement center, encouraging local farmers to diversify crops, attracting a "first-rate" restaurant, and forming a student advisory board for retailers. Grinnell has won approval of federal funds for its airport and is beginning construction.

The foundation also knows how to start small in its improvements, not unlike Guttenberg's Karen Merrick. Just before Labor Day, its volunteers began to plant trees and shrubs at the I-80 interchange south of town. In four years, Webb says, they hope to have planted a continuous four-mile stretch into downtown Grinnell.

Kansas State's Vernon Deines says that about 10 percent of small towns have three advantages that allow them to stabilize their local economies in the face of industrial decline and a depressed farm economy. Those advantages are the quality of life, including the housing stock and access to cultural amenities; a skilled labor force, especially if there is a nearby training facility such as a community college; and most important, the infrastructure to serve the new industry.

What the leaders of Grinnell, Guttenberg, and Babbitt have shown is that none of those advantages merely happen: They are developed with imagination and careful planning—and no small amount of popular civic involvement. For towns that do not develop or acquire these advantages, Deines sees mostly "further decline." Such towns, he says, will not "dry up and blow away overnight," but they will fade away.

Jim Schwab is the assistant editor of Planning.

Sons of Riverwalk

Ann Breen and Dick Rigby
(March 1988)

By any criteria—use of the water, originality of design, quality of execution, contribution to the city's social and economic life, successful fit into context—the San Antonio Riverwalk is a classic. It is justly celebrated and often emulated. And, while it is impossible to copy exactly, the Riverwalk has many lessons to teach us, some obvious, others not.

In inspired American waterfront planning, the Riverwalk takes its place with Robert Moses' riverside promenades in New York, Burnham's Chicago lakefront, and Olmsted's "emerald necklace" of parks in Boston. In the 1960s, the Riverwalk achieved new popularity among San Antonians; it ranks with the transformation of the Ghirardelli chocolate factory overlooking San Francisco Bay as a milepost in the history of changing public attitudes toward waterfronts. San Antonio's Riverwalk was a "festival marketplace" before the phrase was invented.

A young local architect, Robert Hugman, spelled out his vision for the downtown riverfront in a 1929 speech to community leaders. Hugman spoke of shops, cafes, boats, housing, greenery, and lighting lining the banks of the San Antonio River, then little more than a drainage ditch. It would be an environment to delight residents and tourists alike, he said.

The process by which Hugman's vision was accomplished and the complex features that went into the original Riverwalk, as well as its unique configuration, make it a difficult installation to replicate. But the spirit of the enterprise is there to learn from, and that is what some of the more successful descendants of Riverwalk have done.

At the beginning

Often overlooked in discussions of Riverwalk is its context. The Paseo del Rio, the original, horseshoe-shaped section of the Riverwalk, is short (a mile and a half) and narrow, following a turn in the river as it winds through downtown. San Antonio developed around this horseshoe, known initially as the Big Bend. The river runs 16 to 18 feet below the streets and noise of the city, immediately establishing a separate environment, lush with vegetation, perfect for pedestrians, cooler by 10 degrees than the streets above.

While owing its commercial and popular success to initiatives of the 1960s, Riverwalk's remarkable design is a product of the 1930s. Robert Hugman's vision is credited with inspiring a general master plan for the Paseo del Rio, prepared under the auspices of the local chapter of the American Institute of Architects in 1938. Execution, overseen in large part by Hugman, came under the Works Progress Administration from 1939 to 1941.

Careful observation of the old Paseo del Rio section shows the artistry and craftsmanship involved. The WPA engaged the services of skilled local artisans to construct the paths, bridges, entry points, steps, arches, benches, and landscaping that today make the Riverwalk such an intriguing place. Despite all the intricacies of the different sections, the entire Paseo del Rio nonetheless fits together as a coherent whole.

The way all this came about is instructive. Individual artists and crafts people were set to work on separate sections of the walk, always working within Hugman's overall plan. No doubt, a spirit of competition affected the workers as well and contributed to the quality of the outcome. As noted by consultant Sherry Wagner, who with her husband was active in the Riverwalk rejuvenation in the 1960s, this approach directly contradicts today's conventional wisdom, which calls for detailed design guidelines and master plans for major urban projects.

The cultural fit of the Riverwalk, something every visitor senses, is one of the not-so-obvious factors contributing to its success. The lure of the Paseo del Rio, beyond its physical beauty, has much to do with the openness and warmth of San Antonio's large Mexican-American population, which is known for its hospitality. Thus, the city is a natural tourist and visitor center.

Another relatively unappreciated factor is the significance of the area's Spanish legal heritage. Intrinsic in Spanish law is the public's right to access to water, the "right of thirst." There was never any question in San Antonio of public accessibility along the riverfront, an emerging issue and point of controversy in many cities now seeking to redevelop their waterfronts.

Equally important and equally hidden to the casual visitor is the critical role played by citizens at important turning points in the river's history.

First was Emily Edwards. She argued forcefully to the city council against a 1920s flood protection plan that would have buried the San Antonio's Big Bend. The plan, although a logical approach to preventing major floods like the one that occurred in 1921, would have filled in the riverbed with concrete, turning it into a storm drainage area and parking lot. "Miss Emily" and three friends founded the San Antonio Conservation Society to oppose the channelization of the river. They didn't have the answer to the flood problems, they said, but they knew the engineers' approach was wrong.

Architect Hugman allied with the women and prepared his own visionary plan for what might be developed along the river. The stage was set for the Works Progress Administration to begin the transformation, which included a bypass canal, two dams, and a floodgate. The WPA improvements extended over 21 city blocks, with walkways covering 17,000 feet along both riverbanks and including 32 stairways and 21 bridges, built at a total cost of $430,000.

Over the next 15 years, the walk was sorely neglected. Isolated and lacking activity, it came to be considered so dangerous that in the 1950s the area was placed off limits to San Antonio's considerable military population.

In the early 1960s, citizen leadership came forward again. San Antonio architect Cyrus Wagner and local businessman David Straus had a strong vision of what the Riverwalk could be: a lively walkway, safe and inviting, with shops and restaurants and hotels. Through diligent salesmanship, meeting by meeting and slide show by slide show, they succeeded in promoting the concept.

A bond issue was passed in 1964 to provide improvements and encourage property owners adjacent to the river to orient the rear of their buildings toward the Riverwalk. When owners balked, Wagner and Straus sought out buyers who would cooperate. Today, key associations formed at that time—the Paseo del Rio Association, the Riverwalk Advisory Commission, and the River Corridor Committee—continue to pursue the preservation and development of the Riverwalk.

The advisory commission oversees developments along the Riverwalk, reviewing projects that will have visual as well as physical impact on the river. Its guidelines, spelled out in a 1977 manual, aim to preserve the Riverwalk's distinctive character by controlling such things as building awnings, street furniture, and noise. The Paseo del Rio Association is a business group, while the corridor committee is governmental.

Aggressive programming of events was critical to luring the public down to the river in the 1960s. Today there are festivals like the spring Fiesta week, which includes a barge parade, and month-long Christmas festivities. Linked now to the historic Alamo, the Riverwalk is also at the heart of the tourist trade. According to one estimate, tourism added $1 billion to the San Antonio economy in 1987.

On the downside, one now sees trash in the San Antonio River that would have been cleaned up in the past, and mud where the water was green. A lesson to be learned here is that a water resource must be continuously cared for.

The extensions to the Riverwalk also get mixed reviews. Praise is due for the skill with which those involved used a watercourse, winding through the lobby of a Hyatt hotel, to tie the Alamo historic site to the river. Significantly less successful is an extension to HemisFair Plaza. In contrast to the original Paseo del Rio, which is filled with vegetation and varied patterns and materials, much of the new walkway is sterile-looking and devoid of greenery, cafes, or other sources of liveliness.

The situation offers dramatic proof that a walkway along a water body does not by itself necessarily become an attraction. A barren downtown river walkway can be as deadly as any other place without social and commercial highlights. For people attract other people. Gathering places that combine natural resources with cafes, restaurants, galleries, hotels, theaters, and shops offer an unbeatable combination.

People from communities across the continent flock to San Antonio to study the Paseo del Rio. Among the many cities whose representatives have come to look are Dayton, Louisville, Minneapolis, Sacramento, Indianapolis, Phoenix, Reno, Santa Cruz, Houston, and Charlotte.

Some of these pilgrims have sought to duplicate what they saw; others have been more generally inspired. What many people seem to take away is a "can do" attitude. "If folks in San Antonio can clean up what was basically a polluted drainage ditch and create such an exciting hospitable riverwalk, we should be able to do something with ours" is a common reaction.

Denver is an example. In a book called *Returning the Platte to the People,* Joseph Shoemaker, chairman of Denver's Platte River Greenway Foundation and the Platte River Development Committee, tells how a 1974 visit to San Antonio inspired him. During the ensuing decade, Shoemaker and others oversaw the conversion of the much-abused South Platte River into a highly valued regional resource. Today, the Platte River Greenway boasts landscaped walks and bikeways, pocket parks, fishing areas, and boating facilities, and the system continues to be expanded.

A former project director for the greenway, planner Robert Searns, of the firm Urban Edges in Denver, showed slides of the Paseo del Rio to garner community support for the greenway in the early days. He finds the Riverwalk "prototypical," a "model in thinking."

More recently, Littleton, a town just south of Denver, has begun to implement a riverfront plan that is even more derivative of San Antonio's Riverwalk. The Arapahoe Greenway plan (which won an APA award in 1986) calls for mixed-use retail and office developments, housing, and recreational and cultural facilities abutting the river. Already in place is a 30-acre shopping mall, the Riverfront Festival Center. Its marketing director, Sally Rippey, says she arranged for a presentation on San Antonio to fire up Littleton residents about the kinds of improvements that are possible.

Although the Platte River Greenway is primarily a recreational trail for a sprawling, suburban area, in its transformation of a derelict and ignored resource it is akin to the San Antonio experience.

The Bronx

New York's Bronx River was also in a sorry state until a concerned local resident, Ruth Anderberg, helped by Anthony Bouza of the New York police department, mounted a highly successful all-volunteer river cleanup. A year later, in 1974, Anderberg founded Bronx River Restoration and became its first director. An earlier visit to the San Antonio Riverwalk expanded her vision of what could be done. The result was a 1980 master plan that called for no less than 37 different projects, including a 20-mile pathway, cafes, canoe rentals, fishmarkets, and cultural centers, all in one of the nation's most troubled urban areas.

Some progress has been made. A riverfront art center has been founded, a community garden established, part of an old riverside pathway unearthed, environmental education programs put in place, and detailed plans for a 20-mile hiking and bike trail drawn up. Nancy Wallace, the current director of Bronx River Restoration, recently announced the award of a $900,000 grant from the New York State environmental bond act to fund the first phase of the Bronx River Trailway. The funds will be matched by the city to acquire at least $1.8 million worth of additional parkland along the river.

The work to date has made at least a small dent in the beleaguered Bronx, while the ambitious plans now being implemented promise to contribute significantly to the turnaround of the area.

Florida versions

A plan for improvements along the New River in downtown Fort Lauderdale, Florida, has also been funded recently. The New River is already a popular haven for boats, and its banks are walkable in part. But the city wants to upgrade the area and provide strong linear connections between various activity centers. A riverwalk master plan was completed in 1985 by Sasaki Associates of Watertown, Massachusetts.

In 1986, a $7.5 million bond act was passed to bring about the changes, and last year, the National Endowment for the Arts awarded the city $40,000 to begin detailed design work by Edward Durell Stone, Jr. & Associates. Meanwhile, a delegation from Fort Lauderdale paid the requisite visit to San Antonio.

In north Florida, Jacksonville has its own variation on the riverwalk theme, although designer Carlos Cashio of Cashio, Cochran, Torre/Design Consortium, Ltd., in New Orleans, says the Southbank Riverwalk is in no way related to its namesake.

Nevertheless, Cashio's promenade along the St. John's River does what a good riverwalk should do: It provides access to the water, creates a major recreational facility, links existing and proposed neighboring uses, and generally celebrates the river as an urban resource. The contemporary design uses historic waterfront materials: wood and steel pipe.

Jacksonville's riverwalk is seen as a contributor to a hoped-for resurgence of the city's downtown, along with the recent opening, across the river, of Jacksonville Landing, a Rouse Company festival marketplace.

Smaller scale

On another scale and a different style altogether is the riverwalk in Naperville, Illinois, a Chicago suburb. This time the impetus was the town's sesquicentennial and a decision to tackle the long-neglected downtown portion of the DuPage River. Once again, the local architect in charge of the riverwalk design, Charles George, traveled to San Antonio for firsthand inspiration.

While not nearly as urban in feeling as San Antonio's, Naperville's Sesquicentennial Riverwalk is full of intricacies and carefully executed details, including observation pavilions, fishing platforms, wood footbridges, an amphitheater, and boating facilities. Once again, citizens played a key role in the riverfront development, and they continue to provide funds and donate labor for upkeep.

Citizen participation was also key to the success of Riverbank Park in downtown Flint, Michigan. Park designers used a community workshop process to come up with a scheme for 10 acres along the Flint River; the project now includes a manmade island, stalls for art fairs and bazaars, an amphitheater, and a series of pedestrian paths and bridges. Project architect Bill Hull of Amphion Environmental, Inc., in Oakland, California, says the raised bridge design was directly inspired by the arched bridges in San Antonio.

For Bill Barlow, from 1979 to 1986 chief architect for the National Park Service in Lowell, Massachusetts, the "high quality of execution" of the WPA portion of San Antonio's Riverwalk was a significant inspiration. Barlow cites the Paseo del Rio's integration of linear waterway, pedestrians, and boating as being particularly important to his thinking about the treatment of canals for Lowell's National Historic Park.

Three years ago, all 30 members of the city's historic preservation commission took a trip to San Antonio to see for themselves, and Barlow says that gave the park a real boost. Founded in 1979, the commission was to be phased out after 10 years; as a result of the San Antonio trip and the potential it showed for canal use, the commission's life was extended another seven years.

Like many others before them, those commissioners from Lowell benefited from an unlikely source of inspiration: a skimpy urban river that has become a mecca for vacationers and conventioneers. As the commissioners meandered along the Paseo del Rio, dined al fresco, and cruised along the river in one of the festive little boats, they absorbed ideas that are likely to affect their thinking in the years ahead.

We can only hope that such pilgrimages continue, that others travel to San Antonio and learn well the myriad lessons its exquisite Riverwalk has to teach us about citizen leadership, quality design and craftsmanship, compatibility of commercial and environmental values—and the importance of a little romance.

Ann Breen and Dick Rigby direct the Waterfront Center in Washington, D.C. Many of the insights in this article come from a presentation by Sherry Wagner at Urban Waterfronts '86, the center's annual conference in Washington, D.C.

6

Transportation

The actions of individuals and agencies that impact (and are affected by) transportation are very much like a complex balancing process. That is why, to understand transportation, one must work with this idea of equilibrium. We know, for instance, that water seeks its own level. Push it down, and it squirts up somewhere else. Try to scoop it up, and it runs through your fingers. Water can be lifted, but it requires a container. If the container leaks, the water tends to run back to where it was.

Conventional wisdom about transportation planning often ignores this idea of an equilibrium and follows what might be called an engineering approach: Fix it where it is broken. From this perspective, actions taken to make things better often seem to have unintended side effects—even perverse effects—and the interconnections are difficult to fathom. But if the connections were seen less as hard physical relationships and more as fluid or intangible forces, the consequences of various policy actions would be less difficult to comprehend and predict. Many of these real-life interrelationships occur through economic markets, such as travelers choosing when and how to travel and carriers choosing what type of service to offer. Other connections take place through political processes, such as choosing how much to subsidize transit or highways, and whether local airports can impose landing fees.

Because transportation is tied into almost everything else, it is often hard to know, when a transportation problem appears, whether the solution lies within the particular modal and geographic confines of the symptoms or somewhere else. Symptoms may be obvious ones, like congestion, or subtler ones, like run-down infrastructure. The source of the problem may be in another location, another transportation mode, or another sector (such as land use). This situation leads to a good deal of frustration because those who see the problem narrowly don't understand why the direct solution doesn't work.

Trying to build a waterproof barrier between, for example, subsidies to transit capital (to upgrade the quality of the vehicle fleet) and transit operating expenses (so the subsidy won't pump up labor costs) is almost impossible; the money inevitably leaks through. Subsidies to intercity passenger rail travel can reduce fares, but highways and airlines provide very attractive competition on both price and performance, so the impact of the rail subsidy is diluted. Preventing exurban sprawl is an uphill struggle because it is so easy to travel to (or develop) a nearby jurisdiction that has less stringent land-use controls. Travellers, private contractors, manufacturers, public agencies, and real estate developers are all seeking their own preferred solutions in this equilibrium. Each depends on the other, and no single party controls the outcome.

Unsettling as this may seem, the overall outcome can be designed and guided, so long as prejudices don't obstruct perception. The idea that building a bigger highway results in additional traffic was once so startling that it produced a new term: "induced" demand. This misnomer reveals a misunderstanding about the concept of demand, which says that if the price (in time and money) goes down, a larger quantity (volume of traffic) will be consumed. Economists refer to this phenomenon as "elasticity." There is a tendency to think demand is inelastic—that price has no effect on consumption—but inelastic demand is rare in the transportation sector; here, price always plays a part.

Failing to comprehend at least the outlines of the equilibrium can result in some odd proposals. For example, Bob Komives suggests in "Why Not Treat Transit Like a Utility?" that each new development be required to build its own transit system, complete with vehicles and an endowment for operating costs. The illusion here is that the developer would pay for this system and nothing else would be affected; in practice, the developer would either pass the costs on in the selling price of housing, or build somewhere that didn't require this extra cost. And in the end, the system would be unused because residents probably would prefer their cars.

A BALANCED PERSPECTIVE

Those who argue that transit is a money-loser undeserving of subsidy are partly right, as are those who claim that transit carries more people per "lane-mile" than autos. Those who object to the negative externalities of transportation (such as noise and pollution) are correct, as are those who observe that environmental concerns are not significant enough to warrant stopping the construction of needed facilities. Those who claim that land-use patterns are a source of suburban congestion are correct, as are those who assert that land-use controls will have little impact on solving them.

A truly comprehensive perspective is not easy to articulate. Traditionally, there have been two conflicting paradigms of how transportation systems should be managed. One suggests that everything should be centrally planned, with recognition of all the interdependencies and indirect effects. The other says that the system works best in an autonomous (market-like) fashion, and that decentralized planning is more effective. At the moment, transportation policy in the U.S. is an eclectic mixture of both paradigms and has little overall coherence. Roads are built both by local governments and developers, commuter bus services are often provided by independent private entrepreneurs, and the air traffic system is owned and operated by the Federal Aviation Administration.

The extremes of these two paradigms can be illustrated with two prevailing myths about autos and transit. The first is that transit creates external benefits, such as livable cities, that go beyond what the actual transit users derive. The second is that the market has chosen auto travel, so subsidies to transit are simply wasted effort.

Those who assert that a particular activity creates external benefits are in fact rejecting the market outcome and placing the burden of decision upon government. But the first clue that external benefit may be a slippery idea is its lack of guidance on what level of effort is enough. If transit creates external or community benefits, why don't

cars? Why not telephones, houses, power saws, and sliced bread? Why should anything have to make its way in the marketplace?

The confusion here is between indirect and external (nonmarket) benefits. Transportation always benefits the direct users: commuters, business travellers, vacationers, truckers, railroads, and other carriers. But it also benefits indirectly the shippers, retailers, grocery shoppers, and others that require transportation to accomplish some other activity. For indirect transportation users, the value of the good or service includes the transportation component and the cost of the transportation is included in the price. Therefore, one can see that transit may make cities more livable—but that such a result is indirect; it is a byproduct of user benefits, not of government subsidy. In other words, transit and attendant land-use patterns are not external benefits but are, rather, direct traveller benefits passed on to indirect consumers.

Now to examine the second myth: Drawing the conclusion that the market has chosen the private automobile as the best answer rests upon a demonstration that there is no bias in the process by which highways came to dominate transportation. But if consumers were to face the full costs—no more, no less—of their many alternatives, then the resulting equilibrium would provide the maximum benefits that can be obtained for the resources used up. If the resources are competed for fairly, in all markets, then the resources could not be put to better use in any other activity.

In reality, no market functions perfectly. Often as not, the distortions are produced by public policy as much as by private greed (sometimes for the same reason). Highway users do not cover the full costs of roads (less than one-third); they do not pay in relation to the costs they create (congestion, pavement damage); and they generate unpriced negative externalities (air and water pollution, noise, and danger to bicyclists and pedestrians). The bias in favor of autos is greatest in markets that are or could be contested by transit, notably urban commuting. The bias in favor of trucks for goods movement is similar ("Making Trucks Pay Their Way"), if perhaps less pronounced.

Because the private auto provides a service that will be preferred so long as it is cheap, low transit prices and greater convenience cannot make transit attractive. Only higher prices for highway use and parking ("No More Free Ride," and "What's New

Parking spaces are more expensive than ever—but so are cars. As a result, both are being built in smaller sizes. See ''What's New in Parking.'' Photo: Thomas Smith.

Some experts think the hottest real estate in America is within a half-mile of rapid transit and commuter rail stations. See ''Living the Good Life Near Transit Stations.'' Drawing: C. William Brubaker.

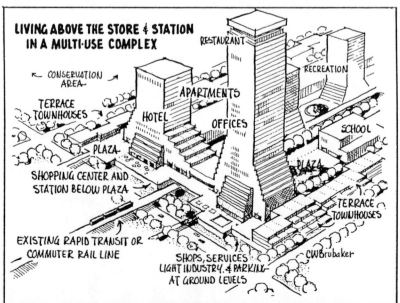

LIVING ABOVE THE STORE & STATION IN A MULTI-USE COMPLEX

RESTAURANT

← CONSERVATION AREA

RECREATION

TERRACE TOWNHOUSES

APARTMENTS

HOTEL

OFFICES

SCHOOL

PLAZA

PLAZA

SHOPPING CENTER AND STATION BELOW PLAZA

TERRACE TOWNHOUSES

EXISTING RAPID TRANSIT OR COMMUTER RAIL LINE

SHOPS, SERVICES LIGHT INDUSTRY, & PARKING AT GROUND LEVELS

CWBrubaker

The SkyTrain in Vancouver, British Columbia (far left), North America's first fully automated transit system, is integrated with the city's bus system and harbor ferry. SkyTrain passengers buy their tickets from automated vending machines (left). See ''Look Ma, No Hands.'' Photos: BC Transit.

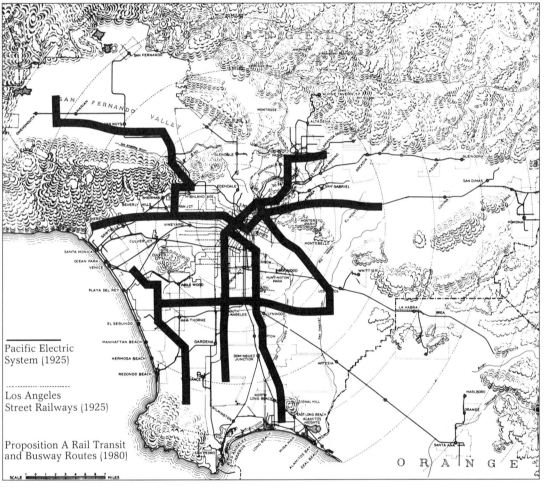

Pacific Electric
System (1925)

Los Angeles
Street Railways (1925)

Proposition A Rail Transit
and Busway Routes (1980)

Los Angeles wasn't always the car capital of the nation. In 1925, the Pacific Electric Railway and the L.A. street-car systems tied the region together. Voters approved a new regional rail and busway system in 1980. See ''To Live and Drive in L.A.'' Map: Dennis McClendon.

When the bus stops coming to small towns, local van service may be an option. In Coldwater, Michigan, Porter's Piston Pushers gets passengers to the nearest Greyhound depot, 35 miles away. See ''You Can't Get There From Here.'' Photo: Michael Morrissey.

in Parking") will stimulate transit use. Delay from congestion does have the effect of increasing the effective price to highway users, but it creates no incentive to increase vehicle occupancy. The car with four people suffers the same delay as the one with one person, so nothing is gained by carrying more people in the same vehicle (even though congestion would be eliminated if everyone did it). A money charge on the vehicle, in contrast, can be shared by putting more people inside it.

POLITICS VERSUS MARKETS

At the core of every transportation problem are two components: efficiency and equity. Efficiency is concerned with getting the most benefits from the resources consumed, while equity is concerned with who pays, who benefits, and whether some disadvantaged groups should be provided with increased mobility at someone else's expense.

Efficiency can be divided into two categories: utilization, which is getting the most out of the facilities we have, and investment, which is building new facilities when that is justified. Congestion, for example, is evidence of inefficient utilization because delay is incurred when it needn't be. Likewise, low usage levels are evidence of inefficient investment, meaning that the same resources might have produced more social benefits if deployed in some other form. Externalities imply that users are overconsuming transportation because they can export a share of their costs onto nonusers.

Components of the transportation system that are provided by the public sector are subject to a political review before they become reality. Efficiency does not guide the political environment, and equity often gets mangled along the way. Transit and rail passenger routes are laid out to serve the districts of political supporters, not just travel needs. Investments are chosen to balance porkbarrel formulas, not because the transportation benefits exceed the costs. Public managers must respond to political interests (unions, neighborhoods, developers) at least as much as those of users. So long as these activities are carried on in the public sector, a certain amount of waste is unavoidable. Whether transferring some of the activities to the private sector ("Leave the Driving to Us") will result in greater efficiency depends upon which activities are involved and how they are transferred.

DEREGULATION

Railroads, airlines, interstate trucking, and intercity bus service all used to be regulated with respect to both their routes and rate structures. Removal of that regulation—mostly between 1975 and 1985—led to major changes and much ferment. From being fixed and certain, the equilibrium became dynamic.

One issue frequently raised is service to smaller and more remote markets. As described in "You Can't Get There From Here," profitable air service from Dubuque to Chicago was abandoned by the carrier because the landing slots at congested O'Hare airport could be put to more lucrative use. This situation is blamed on deregulation, but the real cause of the problem is the monopoly of publicly created landing rights. If the carrier simply paid a landing fee, based on time of day, there would be no slot to monopolize. The carrier could run as much service as it wanted, scheduled during peak or off-peak hours, based on the willingness to pay of each of its market segments.

Likewise, deregulation of intercity bus service led to the bypassing of some small towns. While subsidized train service may not be the only cause behind the decline of bus service, the combination of rail, highway, and transit subsidies undoubtedly cut into the market. The inescapable conclusion, however, is that many services to small towns have been maintained in the past because of regulation (meaning that other taxpayers or ratepayers provided the subsidy), and the towns themselves are not economically viable. It may seem heartless to let them wither, but who should be taxed to support them?

TRANSIT AND LAND USE

In the early part of the 20th century, streetcar lines were a form of loss leader used by developers to open up tracts of suburban real estate. Some planners concluded from this bit of history that today's transportation investments can guide land-use development. In practice, the two are interdependent.

In "Build Here: Transit's Rallying Cry," Manuel Padron describes the real estate development taking place in the handful of North American cities that have built new heavy rail transit systems since 1950. His summary alludes to the two most basic issues regarding such systems. The first is the need to intensify land use around stations. Because new rail systems are placed in settings that already have a land-use and transportation equilibrium based on highway travel, the transit system must rearrange land-use patterns in order to be viable. Doing this requires increasing land-use density around stations, with major public sector effort in joint development and land-use regulation. To achieve efficiency, the two (transit investment and land-use intensification) must go together. In Los Angeles ("To Live and Drive in L.A."), where the existing land-use pattern is most strongly auto-oriented, attempting to insert a rail transit system creates strenuous conflicts.

The second issue is the mistaking of spatial redistribution of land use for net growth. When the existing spatial equilibrium is perturbed by a new transportation facility, some investment may be redirected to new locations. The net gain or loss, however, is much smaller than the amount shifted. If the facility is soundly designed and supported by land development efforts, then the net benefits of the investment will be positive. If the facility is poorly designed and implemented, some locations may gain but it will be at the greater expense of other locations.

DEMAND MANAGEMENT

Attempts to improve the use of existing facilities (as a complement to or substitute for new capacity) is called demand management ("Peak Performances") or TSM (for transportation system management). One of the objectives of such management is increased ridesharing, which can be marginally improved by providing free information about potential carpool participants through matching services. But the equilibrium level of ridesharing is determined by the options available to the traveller and their cost. When the price of fuel goes down, so does ridesharing. When the price of parking (money as well as time and walking) goes up, so does ridesharing. Anything that increases the cost to the vehicle in a way that allows that cost to shared among individuals will induce higher occupancy.

IMPACT FEES

One of the latest twists in road financing is the imposition of impact fees on new development. Traffic impact fees are sometimes imposed only if the expected number of trips will overload some link

in the system, and then the revenues must be spent to improve that link. This sounds reasonable. Consider, however, the following sequence. Developer A builds 2,000 dwelling units at a time and place where the trips will use up 100 percent (but no more) of the available road capacity; A thus pays no fee. Developer B adds 100 units, overloads the network, and is therefore liable for a large fee. Removing five percent of A's traffic would eliminate B's fee. Is this situation equitable?

To the lawyer, it matters a lot who got there first. To the economist, it doesn't; economists think the marginal cost is the responsibility of every consumer whose presence in the market gives rise to the cost. All vehicles in the congested traffic stream are equally the cause of the congestion, the economist says, and they should all face the same price. Only if they do will the road be wisely used and will society learn whether the road is worth expanding or not. If some get the use for free, their benefit is not revealed (and that benefit may be little or nothing).

Charging the developer for the peak traveller creates a rather tenuous link between the cause of the problem and the imposition of the charge. Ideally, the developer would levy a fee on each peak traveller, but this job should be done by the road authority, not the developer. If that happened, then carpooling, transit ridership, and off-peak travel would all increase. Without such actions by the developer, the impact fee is just a property tax in a slightly different form, and the uses of the revenues are irrelevant.

NOVEL TECHNOLOGY

Upbeat descriptions of the success or potential for new technologies are frequent, and have lots of appeal ("A Desire Named Streetcar"; "Look Ma, No Hands"; and "Speed Sells"). We like to believe that our problems will soon be solved by scientists, brilliant minds, and new hardware. In transportation, there has been much promise—automated vehicles that guide themselves, magnetically levitated trains, superconducting motors, air-cushioned vehicles, hydrofoils, vertical takeoff aircraft for intraurban travel, underground pneumatic tubes, telecommunications that do away with travel—but not much product.

Most of the novel technologies are feasible, but they seldom offer significantly higher performance and they usually require enormously higher costs.

In normal markets, technology is advanced and absorbed when it offers an advantage over what was previously in use. Because few transportation modes survive on their own merits in the marketplace, new technology must be forced. The result is that transportation technologies get pushed when they aren't advantageous and sometimes left on the shelf because there is no real market to express the need.

THE EFFICIENT CITY

Many of the results of transportation planning efforts are counterintuitive, because we use the wrong model to predict impacts. Once understood, the problems are not as insoluble as they may seem. Misunderstood, the problems are intractable.

A vision of the ideal city is described in "Living the Good Life Near Transit Stations," but there is no theory or evidence explaining why it is desirable, or even whether the parts are compatible. Perhaps we could all agree on this vision, or perhaps some people would want modifications, or prefer another outcome. Without a process for reconciling inevitably divergent preferences, however, any particular vision is simply an expression of the author's tastes. Even if we could all agree on a preferred result, it can't be achieved unless we understand the process for getting there. In fact, it might be better to seek agreement on the process rather than on the ultimate product.

Given the nature of the problems, is it possible to imagine what an efficient system of transportation and land use would look like? Here's one picture: There would be fewer roads, better transit, higher vehicle occupancies, higher prices to users for peak travel, and no congestion. Land uses would be more clustered into "nodes," and uses would be intermixed rather than segregated. There would be less parking, less sprawl, less pollution and noise, and fewer accidents. Hardware would not look all that different from today's, although more of it would be automated. Finally, there would be no subsidies to any form of transportation. All this, and mobility too.

Douglass B. Lee, AICP
Transportation Planner
U.S. Department of Transportation
Transportation Systems Center
Cambridge, Massachusetts

Why Not Treat Transit Like a Utility?

Bob Komives
(December 1979)

A city that is really serious about expanding its transit system would treat transit like sewers. The fact is that public policy makers show more respect for sewers and other utilities than they do for public transportation. Developers are required to provide utilities in new subdivisions, yet they are allowed to ignore transit.

It makes no sense to spend millions of local and federal dollars to provide or improve transit in existing urban areas while development on the fringes of urban areas still is being designed exclusively for automobiles. It would be easier to get new suburban residents into the habit of taking public transportation if the transit system were so convenient that it became one of the factors that attracted them to the area in the first place. If newcomers didn't think they would need two, three, or four cars to survive in the neighborhood, they would be more likely to use public transit from the beginning.

Installing transit in new developments would:
• increase the chances of transit investments being made in older sections of the city by improving the health of the entire system;
• reduce the automobile traffic generated by new developments;
• reduce air pollution and energy consumption in the region;
• improve mobility for carless young people, the elderly, and lower income residents in new developments;
• avoid the future costs and inefficiencies of trying to retrofit transit in neighborhoods that are poorly designed for it and whose residents already have acquired fleets of personal vehicles;
• provide people with a reasonable alternative to the private automobile for at least some of their travel.

Planners learned an important lesson from their experience with streets, sewers, electricity, and water: Don't saddle a community with the need to go back and install necessary utilities after a development is in place. When utilities are provided from the outset, the community saves money; less harm is done to the environment; and new residents have a more pleasant neighborhood. True, development costs go up, but at least all developers are operating under the same rules. Most important, the utilities usually work better, since they are carefully planned before housing construction gets under way.

For some reason, we don't treat transit the same way. Instead, each new fringe development degrades the existing transit system by restricting its usefulness to an ever-decreasing proportion of the metropolitan population.

Wouldn't it make sense to expand transit as we do other public utilities? Why not make it a part of the initial planning, financing, and marketing of new developments?

What kind of transit? Clearly, a streetcar or subway that ended at the property line of one development wouldn't be of much use. Besides, transit systems with fixed routes and schedules are too expensive and inefficient for all but very specialized high-density areas. So, when we consider installing transit in a new development, we should be thinking about road vehicles—buses, minibuses, and taxis. Of course, road vehicles can use the same roads as private autos; but, nevertheless, there are transit components to "install"—among them, design, financing, and administration.

Design

The design of modern subdivisions presents many problems for public transit. Low densities increase the distance between riders; cul-de-sacs discourage door-to-door service; the lack of sidewalks discourages riders from walking to bus stops; and there is usually no place to install shelters for riders.

A development planned with transit in mind will look different from one for which transit is not considered. Road area will be reduced; the vehicular circulation system will be simplified; cul-de-sacs will be connected by transit, pedestrian, and bicycle rights-of-way; special transit-loading stations will be built at central points of activity; pedestrian and bicycle circulation systems will converge on transit stops. In an industrial park or commercial complex, the parking and circulation system will be designed to give transit vehicles

convenient entry, loading, and exit opportunities and to reduce the amount of parking space.

Any sort of transit operation in a new development should pay for itself or at least require no greater subsidy than is provided for other parts of a community's public transit system. The developer would buy the vehicles or pay the local share if the system were eligible for federal subsidies. In addition, the developer would establish an initial operating fund. Long-term operating funds would be ensured by covenants established automatically with the sale of each lot or by taxing powers given to a special transit district. Fares could be charged for some or all of the services.

Administration

A transit system in a new development could become part of the communitywide public transit system, or it could serve only the residents of the new development.

A private transit system serving a specific development is simpler to operate. A representative body—perhaps part of the homeowners association—is established to set routes and schedules, arrange for maintenance, and decide on a fare structure. The advantage of such an arrangement is that the system can be tailored easily by the residents to their own needs.

But there are disadvantages as well. Economies of scale—in maintenance, personnel costs, or equipment purchase—are lost. There is bound to be duplication of service when adjoining neighborhoods send half-full buses to the same destinations. And private systems would not be eligible for federal assistance.

For some communities, it makes more sense to try to integrate the new transit service into the existing public system. Financing still could be guaranteed by the development, and a neighborhood group still could set routes and schedules, but other riders would be picked up en route. The income from the additional passengers would reduce the costs for residents. The public transit authority would maintain the vehicles and hire the drivers. The vehicles could either be owned by the development and rented by the transit authority for public service, or owned by the transit authority and chartered by the development for special service.

The local transit agency could develop a complete transit installation package for each new development. The package would include advice on planning the system, model covenants, suggestions for equipment, and sample administrative agreements between the development and the transit agency. . . .

A community that chooses to promote transit primarily for home-to-work trips may decide to lay most of the burden for installation upon new industrial rather than residential developments.

A key to the successful implementation of a transit installation program is to include transit installation in the approval requirements for any large-scale developments. A city might begin with a pilot project in one development. Then, if there is strong support, it should give serious consideration to applying the program to all new developments and allowing existing neighborhoods to take advantage of the improved transit system.

Bob Komives is a planning consultant in Fort Collins, Colorado.

Making Trucks Pay Their Way

David J. Forkenbrock
(July 1984)

Highway financing policy in the United States is undergoing gradual but significant changes. In general terms, these changes involve a shift in responsibility from the federal government to state and local governments and the establishment of user charges tied more closely than in the past to the size and type of vehicle.

The 1960s and 1970s witnessed an unprecedented expansion of the U.S. highway network, as federal funding was channeled into construction of the interstate system and other major highways. Limited consideration was given to preserving existing highways, and almost nothing was set aside for later rehabilitation. Today, more than half of the rural interstate mileage is in fair or poor condition; urban segments generally are in even worse repair, especially in the East.

Non-interstate highways, typically older and built to lower specifications, also are in bad shape. In Iowa, for example, the average pavement age of primary highways is 36 years—a figure fairly representative of most states. Forty percent of the nation's bridges are over 40 years old, and approximately 67,700 bridges on federal highways are considered deficient. According to the U.S. Department of Transportation, over 90 percent of the nation's primary rural highway mileage will need resurfacing within the decade—and the cost of rehabilitating the nation's highways and bridges will be $327 billion.

The level of federal funding for highway-related projects is growing, and an increasing portion of this funding is being applied to so-called 4R (resurfacing, restoration, rehabilitation, and reconstruction) projects. The fiscal year 1986 authorization for interstate and bridge rehabilitation projects constitutes 33.8 percent of the total authorization for highway programs, up from 27.9 percent in FY 1983. Annual federal authorizations for rehabilitation projects have risen by $1.65 billion between fiscal years 1983 and 1986, to a total of $5.1 billion—much of the increase due to the recent increase in the federal gas tax.

This figure still appears small, however, when compared to the magnitude of this country's highway rehabilitation needs. Moreover, as these needs mount, a large percentage of the associated costs will fall on state governments. States with deteriorated highway systems will experience new fiscal burdens that are as unfamiliar as they are unwelcome.

There is a lingering myth that highway financing has followed the guiding principle of "pay as you go." The fact is, most states have erred by holding their highway user taxes too low. If motor fuel tax rates had risen proportionally with highway construction and maintenance costs since 1970, the per gallon tax rate in most states would be 50 percent more than current levels. Consider Iowa, which has one of the highest motor fuel tax rates in the nation—13 cents per gallon for gasoline and 15.5 cents for diesel fuel. If those rates had been indexed in 1970 to keep pace with highway costs, today they would be 19.5 cents and 22 cents, respectively. Enough revenue would be available to fund a comprehensive rehabilitation program.

But most states have failed to raise fuel taxes significantly, and now a desperate need for revenue has precipitated a rush to increase those taxes. During the past three years, nearly half the states have raised their tax rates. Still, only eight states and the

District of Columbia have tied those rates to an appropriate index.

Motor fuel taxes and vehicle registration fees have been the principal mechanisms for financing highways at the state level. However, both methods have come under attack for being inequitable. Motor fuel taxes, it has been pointed out, do not adequately take into account differences in vehicle size and weight. Although a large truck-trailer pays about four times as much fuel tax per mile as an automobile, it causes far more than four times as much road wear.

Their critics note that registration fees are insensitive to usage rates. Two identical motor vehicles may pay the same registration fees, but one vehicle may travel 10 or 20 times as many miles as the other.

In an attempt to improve the equity of their highway financing methods, 11 states have adopted weight-distance taxes, and seven other states are considering them. Weight-distance taxes take into account a vehicle's registered (permitted) weight, as well as the distance the vehicle travels within a state. The taxes typically are applied to vehicles weighing over 26,000 pounds, and they replace traditional motor fuel taxes while lowering vehicle registration fees. Cost allocation studies, based on engineering data on the pavement damage caused by various axle loads and vehicle configurations, are used to determine the vehicle's relative cost responsibilities.

Determining the cost responsibilities makes it possible to assign an established budget figure to different types of vehicles, and to do so fairly. The budget level is dictated by how well preserved a highway system the state aspires to and how high a user tax schedule is considered acceptable to residents of the state.

Using Iowa as an example, suppose that annual user tax revenues are to be increased by a total of $100 million and that registration fees are to be reduced to a maximum of $100 annually. The resulting tax structure would range from just less than one cent per vehicle mile for autos and light trucks to almost 14 cents for large "combination" trucks weighing over 75,000 pounds. With a budget level of $100 million, the tax burden for vehicles under 26,000 pounds would not be increased; in some instances it actually would be reduced. However, an 80,000 pound combination truck operating 60,000 miles per year in the state would be required to pay

$8,487 in annual user taxes, up from Iowa's current $3,717.

At present, low user taxes amount to a subsidy to the trucking industry. Whether this subsidy should be continued is, of course, a policy issue. If society does, in fact, choose to subsidize motor carriers by underpricing their use of the highway system, other vehicles using the highway system will pay a higher rate or the costs will be shifted to future users, possibly in the form of higher vehicle operating costs.

My analysis shows that in Iowa the net economic impact of a weight-distance tax with rates set to generate $100 million in additional revenue annually would be relatively minor. If most of the cost burden were passed on to shippers, the effect would be approximately a half percent increase in shipping rates. This increase could slow economic growth slightly in the short run. In the long run, however, a well-preserved highway system is likely to lower shipping costs and thus bolster economic growth.

Weight-distance taxes are not new. Oregon has used this form of tax structure for over 30 years. But only now, with the serious fiscal squeeze of recent years, is this approach to highway user taxation receiving a broader level of attention. It is opposed by operators of long-haul trucks and supported by the American Association of State Highway and Transportation Officials.

The choices involved in charging higher user taxes and shifting more of the burden to heavy vehicles are important ones from a public policy standpoint. They are the sort of choices that decision makers at all levels of government will face more and more frequently as the nation's infrastructure crisis worsens.

David J. Forkenbrock, AICP, heads the Public Policy Center at the University of Iowa.

No More Free Ride

Donald C. Shoup and Don H. Pickrell
(April 1980)

Free parking is part of the American way of life. Three out of four cars driven to work are parked free in employer-provided spaces. When other free parking on the streets and in lots is added, 93 percent of all auto commuters park free at work, according to the most recent census data.

Free parking is not harmful in itself, but the increased driving it causes is. Because the cost of parking is highest in the densest areas, the offer of free parking, perversely, gives the greatest cost reduction to drivers headed to places where traffic congestion and air pollution are already worst and where public transit is best.

Our research turns up the surprising finding that, on average, free parking leads at least 25 percent more commuters to drive to work alone. This strong impact of free parking on the amount of driving is explained by the fact that parking subsidies are so big and go to so many people. Even an unthinkably high $1-a-gallon gas tax would raise the cost of driving to work for most commuters by less than free parking already decreases it. Since most workers travel 14 miles or less round trip to work (and in that distance a car that gets the national average of 14 miles per gallon would consume only one gallon of gas), a $1 tax would raise the cost of most auto commute trips by less than $1 a day, and free employee parking already lowers it by more than that for many, if not most, downtown workers.

With such generous subsidies given to so many employees, it is not surprising that 69 percent of all household heads in the United States (64 percent in central cities) drive alone to work. And while a tax to reduce driving would add to inflation, ending free parking would not. The cost of driving would be raised only for those who now park free, without in any way increasing the cost of living for anyone else.

The stimulus for employers to offer free parking to their employees is that its value is not taxed as income. Someone in the 40-percent tax bracket would need an increase in taxable salary of $1,000 a year to leave enough, after taxes, to pay $50 a month for parking. So offering employees free $50 parking spaces is equivalent to offering an annual $1,000 bonus to anyone who drives and nothing extra to anyone who doesn't. With a tax incentive like this, is it any wonder we "need" so much foreign oil?

Our proposal to undo the damage caused by income tax exemption of free parking benefits is to amend federal and state tax laws to permit employers to give tax-exempt travel allowances instead of free parking. Only employers who can certify to the IRS that they subsidize *no* employee parking would have the option of paying *all* employees a tax-free travel allowance. Non-driving employees of firms that offer free parking could then ask their employers: "How can you give free parking to drivers and nothing to me when you could give us all a tax-free allowance instead?"

If commuters were given money instead of free parking, many of them would soon decide to do what planners have long exhorted them to do—join carpools or ride the bus.

An important advantage of the travel allowance approach is that the government would not have to force employers to change their parking policies. Thus, there would be no interference with collective bargaining. The ones who would benefit from the tax change are those who do not now get a large parking subsidy, and this group consists disproportionately of low-paid, minority, and women workers.

The solution to the problem is simple: Pay people with money instead of parking spaces.

Copyright 1980 by Donald C. Shoup, AICP, professor of planning at the School of Architecture and Urban Planning at UCLA, and Don H. Pickrell, an economist with the U.S. Department of Transportation's Transportation Systems Center, Cambridge, Massachusetts.

What's New in Parking

Wilbur S. Smith
(June 1983)

Urban transportation has always had an important place in city planning, and parking is obviously an integral part of urban transportation. Thus, it seems a good idea to look at some of the changes that are likely to take place in the field as a result of new economic, environmental, and energy concerns.

First, let's consider some economic facts. The personal automobile (which, it should be noted, remains parked for 18 to 22 hours a day) continues to be the first choice for all trip purposes. At the same time, garage construction costs have increased dramatically, and operating and maintenance costs have generally doubled in the past 10 years. High interest rates have stymied many plans to build new parking.

A few land uses, surprisingly, need fewer parking spaces than they did 10 years ago. That's true of shopping centers and new, centrally located office buildings with access to public transit, for instance. Here, the changes are the result of higher parking fees, fuel price hikes, rising vehicle operating costs, and shifts in government policy. According to a recent study by the Urban Land Institute, shopping center developers are now willing to provide up to 18 percent fewer spaces in large regional centers than in years past. That means they will allow demand to exceed supply 19 hours a year (during the holiday rush), as opposed to the nine hours that once were considered a safe allowance.

More typical, however, is the increase in demand for parking space, seen particularly at community colleges, night schools, medical centers, and hospitals. In the case of hospitals, the reason for the increase is that the length of stay per patient is going down and more services are offered on an outpatient basis. Before 1965, two parking spaces per bed was a good rule of thumb for planning hospital parking. Now, a range of from 1.6 to 3.4 spaces is used.

Most airports are also experiencing significant changes in overall parking demand. Whereas the unit need is about the same as in years past (one space per 1,000 annual passengers), the total need is increasing—a result of the sharp rise in air passenger traffic.

Policies governing the supply and price of parking increasingly are undergoing revision in cities that are seeking to revitalize their economy and reshape development. Changes also are being made in response to federal clean air requirements. Many jurisdictions have amended their zoning regulations in response to changes in vehicle sizes and in unit parking demands (space requirements related to such variables as number of employees, amount of floor area, and number of patients). The changes affect both on- and off-street parking.

The most widely adopted new on-street parking policy is the residential parking permit program (RPPP). At least 10 U.S. cities currently use permits, which are intended to reduce long-term parking by commuters in residential areas. Before and after usage studies in Washington, D.C., and San Francisco have documented the success of the RPPP programs.

Portland, Oregon, and Seattle have gone further, giving preferential parking treatment to vehicles used in car- and vanpools. The response in each case has been favorable.

Some cities have placed a ceiling on parking supply in the central business district; others are specifying both minimum and maximum requirements aimed at balancing parking supply with street system capacity, controlling auto emissions, and increasing the use of public transit.

In a paper presented at a Transportation Research Board meeting in January 1982, Edward Barber and Raymond Ellis described some of the trends in central business district parking policies. They noted, for instance, that Portland, Oregon, San Francisco, and Seattle have restricted the construction of separate parking facilities and removed minimum parking requirements for new downtown development. Portland, along with Boston, also set a limit on total CBD parking supply. In Portland, the ceiling applied to all types of parking; while in Boston, it applied only to commercial spaces open to the public (but not to employee and customer parking). Toronto is another example of a city that controls the amount of new parking developed in order to encourage transit use.

Alternative help

Policies to reduce or control parking supply are most evident in cities where there are viable alternatives to automobile commuting. For instance, in Chicago, where transit use is relatively high, the zoning ordinance permits nonaccessory parking lots or garages downtown only as part of a planned development, which requires city council approval. The city allows 10 percent fewer spaces if parking is underground, if a building has a good transit connection, or if the development is located in the central business district.

Edmonton, Alberta, exemplifies the growing trend of linking transportation access to parking policies. In November 1981, Edmonton formally reduced its parking requirement for all downtown uses except residential to one space for every 2,152 square feet of gross floor area (about half of the old requirement). Developers who provide direct access to the city's light-rail transit can negotiate an even greater reduction.

A number of communities in the U.S.—following the lead of Canadian cities where the practice is more prevalent—have instituted or are considering policies that would permit a private developer to make "in lieu" cash payments to local governments instead of providing parking. The local government then uses the money to build new public parking facilities or to support existing facilities.

In sum, the tendency (especially in the larger cities) seems to be toward a more controlling position on off-street parking. It is interesting to observe that this movement toward restriction comes at a time when the incidence of joint public-private investment ventures is increasing, in some ways requiring public policy to become more flexible.

Pricing

Parking charges at many publicly owned facilities are substantially below true-market values and also substantially below what is needed to support the development of new facilities. In a competitive sense, these low rates often have a negative impact on the feasibility of providing needed new parking.

Much evidence suggests that parking price can affect both the use of spaces and the choice of travel mode. That means that pricing can be used to gain such objectives as a reduction of traffic congestion, greater transit use, ride-sharing, and compliance with clean air requirements. For these reasons, many cities, airports, and institutions have recently decided to increase parking fees significantly.

The Dallas-Fort Worth airport has increased daily parking fees in the terminal area by 40 percent. Meter rates in Portland have increased from 25 cents to 50 cents an hour. Last September Denver raised the meter rates of about a third of its CBD parking spaces from 20 cents to 50 cents a half-hour. Parking fees at municipal, off-street facilities in Wilmington, Delaware, increased 23 percent in 1981. New Haven, Connecticut, recently doubled CBD meter rates to 50 cents an hour.

The fall 1982 newsletter of the Institutional and Municipal Parking Congress (published in Fredericksburg, Virginia) also notes that at least four cities—Honolulu, St. Paul, San Francisco, and Portland, Oregon, have set parking rates in publicly owned facilities to discourage long-term parking. In Honolulu, doubling municipal parking rates meant that six percent more cars could be accommodated. The benefits were a doubling of available spaces during the lunch hour and a 36 percent increase in monthly parking revenues.

In some cases, rates have been lowered. Eugene, Oregon, and St. Paul, Minnesota, are among the cities that have instituted free downtown parking programs to attract shoppers and other nonwork travelers. Preferential parking rates for carpools and vanpools have been implemented in Montgomery County, Maryland, Portland, San Francisco, and Seattle.

Effective enforcement is the key to the success of most parking policies, particularly in the light of the kinds of policy changes I have been describing.

Washington, D.C., and New York City both have aggressive towing and "booting" programs—the latter a way of using a metal tire clamp ("the Denver boot") to prevent a parking violator from leaving a spot. Both also use computers to speed up the collection of parking fines from scofflaws, as do many other jurisdictions. Baltimore, Boston, Portland, Seattle, Washington, D.C., and Montgomery County, Maryland, have instituted a variety of enforcement programs for high-occupancy carpool vehicles, which get special parking privileges. Users are required to certify that they belong to carpools, and follow-up verification is required.

Garage design

Clear-span construction seems to prevail as the most used framing configuration for free-standing garages. Such construction allows quick changes in parking angles and stall widths to adapt to changing vehicle dimensions. Stall and aisle dimensions are being reduced in response both to rising costs and smaller, more maneuverable cars. Many new, efficiently designed, self-parking facilities (those with 40 percent small-car spaces) have a gross building area per parking space measure of 300 square feet per space or less, as compared to 350–400 square feet per space common only a few years ago.

Security concerns have dictated additional changes in garage design: greater use of closed circuit television, security fencing on ground levels, and greater use of open stairs and glass-walled elevators. We are seeing greater use of energy-conserving lighting systems and—a key development—more joint-use developments that include parking and other uses (office, hotel, retail, residential) within the same structure.

Some facilities are leaning toward more sophisticated ticketing and cashiering systems in which the cashier seldom, if ever, handles currency. Overall emphasis is being placed on reducing operating costs both through more efficient use of staff and through automation. In some places, it is now possible to pay for parking and transit at the same time. On the whole, parking system operations have been made responsive to state-of-the-art management and accounting techniques made possible by improved computer technology and applications.

Recent estimates indicate that the cost of providing a parking space in a well-designed surface lot ranges between $1,500 and $2,000. That puts the typical square-foot cost of a surface parking lot at $5.50 exclusive of land. This figure does not include the costs of gates, meters, cashiers, and other revenue collection expenses.

The costs of parking structures differ greatly according to site conditions, ratio of on-grade to elevated construction, and design efficiency. Last year, construction costs for parking structures ranged from $14 to $23 per square foot, with high-rise parking more likely to be at the top end of the scale. Operating expenses vary widely, from $160 per space to over $400, with labor expenses accounting for over half of the total.

High interest rates and limited investment funds have caused local governments to seek innovative methods of financing parking facilities. The recent emphasis has been on developing large, mixed-use projects in cooperation with the private sector. More traditional methods of funding public parking projects are also used. These include general obligation bonds, parking revenue bonds, lease rental revenue bonds, industrial revenue bonds, and special assessment district bonds.

In the private sector, the traditional, long-term, fixed-rate loan has nearly become extinct. The variety of alternatives includes variable, indexed, or renegotiable rate loans; shared appreciation mortgages; percent-of-cash-flow or presale agreements; and joint ventures. Some developers are using the condominium approach (selling individual spaces) to finance parking garages.

Public-private joint ventures are being used successfully in many areas. These ventures entail the use of tax-exempt bonds for long-term financing, with lease payments from the private sector used to pay debt service.

Clearly, the need for parking will continue to grow. But overall, parking needs are likely to fluctuate, depending on such variables as the extent to which transit systems are improved, the health of the central business districts, and the state of local economies. Different cities will continue to have very different needs. It is imperative that public officials recognize these differences, and that they base their programs on analyses of specific situations. Only that way will those businesses and activities dependent on automobile transportation not be penalized by a dearth of parking.

Wilbur S. Smith is the chairman of Wilbur Smith and Associates, a 30-year old, nationwide, transportation consulting firm with headquarters in Columbia, South Carolina.

Leave the Driving to Us

Robert Guskind
(July 1987)

As the architect of the Reagan administration's campaign to step up private involvement in mass transit, Urban Mass Transportation Administration chief Ralph Stanley made enemies. So it wasn't a surprise that a lot of people cheered when Stanley announced recently that, after nearly four years as UMTA administrator, he was stepping down to take a job with a New York development firm.

Stanley had outraged transit managers and labor leaders with directives that local transit agencies invite private operators to compete against them. And he had irritated politicians at the state and local level, and in Congress, with unrelenting attacks on public transit and Uncle Sam's part in bankrolling it.

"The federal government has spent $40 billion on transit since the 1960s and the program still doesn't work," Stanley said in an interview two weeks before he left his UMTA post at the end of May. "That's why I campaigned so hard to introduce some competition into the system."

Stanley got at least some of what he wanted. Transit agencies in Dallas, Houston, Los Angeles, and New Jersey, among others, are now contracting out large chunks of bus service. Elsewhere, cities are raising money for rail lines from developers and property owners. There is even discussion of privately built and operated rail lines and employee-owned transit systems.

Despite strong advocacy by the administration and some high-profile successes with contracting, however, privatization is still only a minor factor in the $14 billion a year transit industry, according to UMTA, accounting for about six per cent of public agency operating budgets last year. The practice remains concentrated in cities where private transit companies have always been strong players and many of the services public agencies are buying from private companies have traditionally been in private hands: vehicle maintenance, long-distance commuter hauls, small-town and suburban service, and such "demand-responsive services" as dial-a-ride and transportation for the handicapped.

"You can't say that there's been a lot of action or some ground swell of [support for] privatization," says Roger F. Teal, a transportation planner at the University of California at Irvine. "For many of the agencies, it's business as usual. Management accepts contracting at the margins, but they're trying to protect the core of their operations."

There are serious questions, as well, about whether privatization will survive the departure of its most ardent advocates in the federal transit bureaucracy.

Contracting out is only one facet of the administration's privatization policy, but it has sparked the most emotional debate of all. Unfortunately, the arguments on both sides are mostly anecdotal and are backed up by the most minimal systematic research.

Contracting's boosters showcase those arrangements that are actually cutting costs and, in some cases, attracting new riders. An often-cited example is Dallas Area Rapid Transit, which has been contracting for three years with a group of private companies for suburban express and local bus service. The arrangement has quadrupled ridership and saved the agency some $10 million a year. Under a $130 million contract, Trailways Commuter Services provides drivers, Ryder Truck Rental supplies some of the buses and maintains the vehicles, and ATE Management, a Ryder subsidiary, manages the system.

Another example is Westchester County, New York, which now contracts for its entire bus system. Liberty Lines Transit, the largest of the private contractors in the area, carries some 125,000 riders a day. One study comparing costs in Westchester to those of Long Island's Nassau County—whose system is publicly operated—found costs in Westchester of $3.18 per vehicle mile versus $4.09 a mile in Nassau. Those figures have been questioned, however, and observers note that the Westchester system includes many long express runs to Manhattan.

Westchester's subsidy to its system is $3.7 million a year, versus Nassau's $8 million, although the latter system carries fewer riders. One reason is fares: 90 cents for Nassau but up to $4 in Westchester. Nassau County officials also claim that local politics make it necessary to continue unprofitable routes. "They don't have the political hacks to take care of like we do," says one Nassau County transit official, referring to his Westchester counterparts.

Similarly, Phoenix claims it saves 62 percent on some of its contracted bus routes over comparable public operations. When it contracted with a taxi company to provide Sunday service on one route at a cost of $100,000, the city cut costs even further. Estimated tab for the old Sunday bus service: $900,000.

A recent UMTA study found contracting savings ranging from 18 percent for small agencies (under 25 vehicles) to 50 percent for large ones (over 300 vehicles). The study also concluded, however, that medium-sized agencies (100-300 vehicles) wouldn't save money by contracting and that savings are sometimes nil for agencies of any size.

Smokescreen?

Critics, mindful of the not-so-distant past when private transit firms folded by the dozen and precipitated public takeovers in the first place, argue that a handful of successful experiments and studies claiming savings is no reason for turning over transit services to private enterprise. Some, like Richard Bradley, executive director of the International Downtown Association and a former transportation official in Connecticut, suggest that "the industry saw privatization as a smokescreen for the elimination of public transit."

"In our judgment privatization is not a substitute for adequate funding for mass transit," says Jack R. Gilstrap, executive vice-president of the American Public Transit Association, a trade group representing transit agencies and some private operators. "Nor do I think there's much interest among private operators in taking over large hunks of transit service."

Unionists see attacks on their jobs and attempts to shift business to nonunionized firms. Privatization is "nothing but thinly veiled union busting," says an official of one of the nation's largest transit unions. . . .

Labor typically accounts for 80 percent of transit's operating costs. In Dallas, Trailways' nonunionized drivers have to work for three to four years before earning the starting salary of a regular city bus driver and nationally, one privatization expert estimates, private wages and benefits are a third to a half lower than public packages.

"The public sector doesn't have the same profit motive or responsiveness that says be cost-efficient," says M. Anthony Burns, president of Ryder System, Inc., which along with its subsidiaries, Ryder Truck Rental and ATE Management, is one of the nation's biggest private transit operators. "A private company can save them time, energy, and sometimes capital and provide a better quality system at a better price. Nobody's talking about taking over public transit; we're talking about the public and private sector working together."

Both management and labor question whether private providers would maintain less profitable services ("leaving us with the midnight bus to Watts," as one Los Angeles official puts it) and suggest business will cut corners in order to maximize profits.

Privatization proponents disagree. For example, Charles Lave, an economist at the University of California at Irvine, and editor of *Urban Transit: The Private Challenge to Public Transportation*, claims that by contracting for rush-hour service and suburban commuter runs, which use equipment and drivers that are idle the rest of the day, public agencies can eliminate operating deficits and serve more low-income riders.

Lave and others argue that charges of "cream-skimming" by private operators are misleading because public transit runs its biggest losses at rush hour, even though buses are often full. The Sacramento transit authority, for instance, estimates that peak riders are 250 percent more expensive to carry than off-peak riders. Opponents counter that, since accounting practices and cost estimates vary widely and public overhead costs—equipment, facilities, and supervisors—won't necessarily decrease, some agencies could end up losing relatively profitable routes to private operators.

Finally, admirers of privatization contend that the threat of competition, in and of itself, is a good thing. It's a strong incentive to public agencies to watch costs, they say, and a prod to labor to make concessions. Politicians, meanwhile, agree that competition may help keep costs down, although they also charge that the administration's privatization directive threatens local control over transit planning and operations. What will happen, they ask, if private providers decide that transit wasn't such a lucrative business venture after all. . . .

Politics

Any discussion of privatization eventually turns to Washington politics. On this front, even the Reagan administration's critics grudgingly admit that UMTA's policy of trying to cajole, and some would say threaten, public transit agencies into turning to the private sector have made their mark. The administration "got people to jump through hoops," says the Urban Institute's Ronald F. Kirby, who is generally supportive of privatization.

Stanley, who understood the power of UMTA's ability to make large discretionary grants, crafted a privatization strategy out of the "we'll try anything at least once" school of public management. In 1984, UMTA required public agencies seeking federal money to ask private firms to bid for contracts on new or reorganized bus service and periodically to review existing service to see if private operators would be cheaper. An Office of Private Sector Initiatives to spread the word about privatization soon followed. UMTA's 10 regional administrators were given two to three percent annual salary bonuses if they pushed privatization.

In 1985, UMTA announced that it would give "priority consideration" to those applicants for its $1.1 billion in capital grants "who demonstrated their commitment to competitive bidding and private-sector involvement," and that it would pay the full cost of plans for encouraging private involvement.

Critics charge that UMTA dragged its feet on grants where privatization plans didn't measure up. The agency "held up a lot of grants," says one transit union official. "And they did it because they were maniacs. Absolute, ideologically driven maniacs, who needed to make a point."

Others are more circumspect about the agency's approach. "UMTA provides us with a lot of funding," says Ronald L. Reisner, assistant executive director of New Jersey Transit. "When they speak we certainly listen very carefully. But we were favorably disposed in the first place. We didn't feel any strong-arming."

Perhaps because of, or perhaps despite, the new UMTA requirements, New Jersey Transit decided to contract out five percent of its bus service; it already pays $8 million a year in subsidies to private carriers. So far the agency has contracted out routes—to unionized private carriers—in two northern counties. One of the arrangements involves nine routes carrying 790,000 passengers annually in an affluent area; the other is for five routes with 1.6 million riders in poor, inner-city neighborhoods. The agency also leases some 700 buses to more than 130 private carriers at $1 a year.

"There were a lot of allegations that we were conditioning grants," Stanley says. "We were ceaseless promoters for privatization, but I never held up a grant."

Be that as it may, UMTA's actions provoked a congressional investigation and a firm congressional rebuke last fall. An unpublished investigative report by the House Appropriations Committee suggested the agency was attempting a "radical redirection" of federal policy that could be illegal and recommended that the privatization policy be suspended. The report also described as "questionable" several UMTA-funded studies showing cost savings from privatization.

The report was followed by the congressional equivalent of a cease-and-desist order, tied to last fall's transit appropriation. An UMTA proposal to require that 20 percent of federal money be set aside for contracting was turned down, along with a plan to weaken labor protection provisions that bar federal money from being used to eliminate union jobs. As a result, recent privatization guidelines are considerably softer in tone. The agency also appears to have shifted to carrots (voluntary demonstration projects and technical assistance) instead of sticks.

Down the line

There's a fair chance that contracting activity will abate now that Stanley and other advocates have left Washington and Congress has expressed its displeasure with the practice, but it's equally likely that private financing and planning—driven by more than politics—will thrive into the 1990s. Stanley puts it bluntly: "The federal money isn't going to increase. We're not going to build any more transit systems for developers. The bank's closed."

Los Angeles and San Francisco are probably typical of the money stream of the future. Los Angeles, which broke ground last year for the $1.25 billion, 4.4-mile first leg of a planned 20-mile subway system, will raise between 10 and 15 percent of the cost through assessment districts around its subway stations. The assessments were put on hold, however, until the line opens in 1992 because developers objected to paying before the system was running. San Francisco recently won a court fight (although an appeal is likely) to allow it to charge impact fees on new developments, with the proceeds going to the city's transit system. The money will help cover operating costs.

Maligned for its subway system, Miami helped finance its $148 million downtown people mover with a 50-block assessment district that will collect $20 million from an 18-cents-per-square-foot fee on office space in the district. Some observers say Miami's planning process for the people mover is a model for other cities. When the city realized it was short of government money, it negotiated a solution with the business community, which agreed to support the levies.

In other areas, business groups are assuming more responsibility for planning transit systems. Given the increased local cost of transit, says Gary L. Brosch, director of the Joint Center for Mobility Research at Rice University in Houston, a research organization funded in part by UMTA, "the business community has to be involved in finding the solution. If not, planners are going to face a rebellion."

Some developers have taken to volunteering transit facilities in the hope of winning approval for these projects. In Alexandria, Virginia, developers of a proposed 38-acre commercial center have offered to build a station on a nearby Washington Metro line. Local officials are now pressing additional demands that the developers widen an adjoining roadway and build a series of highway interchanges for the project.

There are also plans around the country for—mostly—privately financed, built, and operated rail lines. The most prominent is a plan in northern Virginia to build a $200 million, 16-mile, light rail line to connect the regional Metro system with Dulles International Airport. It would be financed through the sale of shares, developer fees, and the upfront investment by the company chosen to build and operate the system. The public contribution takes the form of industrial revenue bonds and other tax breaks (the system received a special exemption in last year's tax reform bill).

Such schemes are still highly experimental, however, and thus far have amounted to little more than interesting ideas. Developers have built or are building people movers for their own projects in Tampa, Florida, and suburban Dallas's Las Colinas

center. But in Orlando, a $361 million rail link between downtown and Disney World fell apart when Disney executives refused to provide a right-of-way on their property. Orange County had already approved $194 million in bond financing for the project, and a French transportation and aerospace firm that wanted to build and run the system was trying to raise $60 million in loans. . . .

Mass transit will never again be the business it was in the 1960s and 1970s. Even if some privatization experiments do not outlive the Reagan administration, the next president is likely to face calls from both liberals and conservatives for a radical overhaul of federal transit policy. There's also a chance that an administration that is perceived as less hostile to transit will have an easier time being heard in Congress.

A recent study by the Urban Institute for the National Council on Public Works Improvement, a congressionally sponsored organization, recommends a series of changes in transit policy—including the division of local transit authorities into policy/planning bodies and service providers who would compete on the open market, a shift to block grants, fewer federal guidelines, and local cost sharing of 75 to 80 percent. "The disappointing performance of mass transit in U.S. cities can be attributed primarily . . . to inappropriate governmental policies and programs," the study concludes. "It has failed to stimulate the widespread adoption of proven cost-effective strategies."

There is also discussion of such esoteric alternatives as employee ownership of public transit authorities, a route taken recently by a small operation in Lake Tahoe. Stanley thinks that giving public transit's employees a financial stake in their operation either through profit sharing or outright ownership is worth exploring. "There has to be a way to make labor's interest coincide with management," Stanley says. "All this bashing back and forth is striking out at the wrong enemy." . . .

Robert Guskind is a contributing editor of the National Journal *in Washington, D.C., and of* Planning.

You Can't Get There From Here

Jim Schwab
(July 1987)

Waterloo and Dubuque, Iowa, have a problem. Their airports, though not thriving, have remained viable since Congress deregulated the airline industry in 1978. Together, the two airports serve half a million people, enough to have lured Air Wisconsin to provide connector service to United Airlines at Chicago's O'Hare International Airport. That gave the cities good connections with virtually the entire country. Their problem is that they've put too many eggs in one basket.

O'Hare, the busiest airport in North America, is one of only four airports in the U.S. (the others are New York's Kennedy, Washington National, and Los Angeles) with a limit on landing slots. In April, Air Wisconsin announced that after July 7 it would discontinue service to Waterloo and Dubuque and use those valuable slots for other, presumably more profitable, markets. And other airlines can only start such service if they already have landing rights at O'Hare and are willing to take slots away from another community.

That competition for landing slots is symptomatic of the larger pattern in rural and small-city transportation. Regulation used to guarantee service of all kinds—rail, truck, bus, and air—to areas that often could not support such service economically. Federal subsidies supported air service to many small communities, while the Interstate Commerce Commission often refused permission for railroads, trucking firms, and bus companies to abandon unprofitable routes. The result of a decade of deregulation has been a shakeout in which some communities gain and others lose—and the results are not always predictable.

What's happening in Waterloo and Dubuque illustrates a peculiarity of the deregulation process, says John Coleman, director of the U.S. Department of Transportation's Office of Essential Air Service. The EAS office was created by the Airline Deregulation Act of 1978 to ensure air service to some 400 smaller communities. The law provided limited subsidies for 10 years to allow those communities to adjust to deregulation. Adequate service, according to the Civil Aeronautics Board, which was disbanded in 1985, consisted of 80 round-trip seats each weekday and weekend to a designated hub airport. It also required at least two daily trips, but limited subsidies to a maximum of 40 seats daily.

Dubuque and Waterloo, however, have not needed subsidies. Their markets were profitable—just not profitable enough for the highly competitive business at O'Hare. Dubuque, with a high percentage of O'Hare-bound passengers, took the lead in protesting the abandonment. In mid-May, local civic and business leaders took petitions bearing more than 35,000 signatures to Washington in an effort to convince the Iowa congressional delegation and the Transportation Department to allocate new landing slots at O'Hare. This time, though, they want the slots to belong not to an airline, but to the city. In response, Sen. Tom Harkin (D–Iowa) held a June 1 hearing in Cedar Falls.

That hearing also dealt with the fate of the Essential Air Service program itself, which expires next year unless Congress extends it. Without it, subsidies to the smallest airports will end—and so, too, may their service. It is a matter of concern to virtually all western senators, as well as many in the South and Midwest.

Overall, the federal subsidies have been modest—Coleman estimates about $30 million—in comparison to those in effect before deregulation, which were above $100 million by the late 1970s. The reduction came when small commuter airlines began serving markets from which major carriers had withdrawn, combining greater efficiency with more frequent service because the smaller planes fly fewer empty seats.

But not everyone is sympathetic to EAS or the special problems of airports whose major hub has a limit on landing slots. Francis Mulvay, an economist for the U.S. General Accounting Office, suggests that the alternatives are not always as bad as small city advocates claim. He notes that, while New Yorkers have better air access, it may well take a Bronx resident longer to travel to Kennedy International Airport than it would for Dubuquers to go to Cedar Rapids, Iowa, 70 miles away. Clinton, Iowa, which uses EAS subsidies to maintain service, is only a 30-minute drive from the Quad Cities airport in Moline, Illinois, which does not.

Critics of the EAS program argue that small airports have had 10 years to adjust to deregulation and that the only serious losers are likely to be residents of those communities so remote and so small that, without subsidies, they would be stranded.

A thesis completed this spring by University of Iowa graduate planning student Cathy Young supports that view. Young found that Cedar Rapids was monopolizing any regional gains in air traffic while other eastern Iowa airports were slowly losing market shares—a pattern experts have noted in other parts of the country. Passengers boarding at Waterloo fell from over 100,000 in 1978 to fewer than 80,000 last year. A depressed economy—Waterloo is heavily dependent on farm-related manufacturing—contributed to the decline. In thriving Cedar Rapids, during the same eight-year period, boardings rose nearly 50 percent to almost 400,000.

The cycle feeds on itself as busier airports get more competitive fares, notes Waterloo aviation director Bruce Carter, who monitors fares weekly to ensure that airlines keep Waterloo fares in line with those elsewhere in Iowa. Otherwise, the decline in local air traffic could become a collapse.

Ellen Lau, president of Travel Headquarters, a Dubuque travel agency, sells about 60 percent of her air tickets to leisure travelers and 40 percent to commercial travelers. Many of the former, she notes, "shop around" the region's airports for the best deals. Fares out of Cedar Rapids are often much lower than Dubuque's due to the heavy competition. Cedar Rapids, served by only two carriers until 1979, now boasts 12, including Continental, TWA, Northwest, and United.

What's left for Dubuque are the business customers, who are less willing to shop for fares because time spent traveling is money. And that is precisely why the anti-subsidy arguments are beside the point, says Arnie Honkamp, chairman of the Dubuque Airport Commission. The issue is not leisure travel, he says, but economic development.

Honkamp cites the example of CyCare, a Dubuque supplier of computer services for medical practice that relocated its sales office to Chicago and its headquarters to Phoenix. Honkamp argues that small city air service benefits metropolitan areas by mitigating the overdevelopment problems that plague some major airport corridors and by maintaining their access to smaller markets.

But few advocate repeal of deregulation because the new EAS program under deregulation has brought better service to most small airports. For those communities like Cedar Rapids that are big deregulation winners, the continuation of federal subsidies may be a minor issue. For the rest, including many in the rural West, their extension will be a crucial issue in 1988.

Bus stops

Unfortunately for the small towns of rural America, airline deregulation is only one factor in their increasing isolation. Deregulation, which in the 1970s spread from the rail industry to the airlines to the trucking industry, hit intercity buses in 1982.

Unlike air deregulation, bus deregulation had no interim subsidy program to ease the pain. The major bus companies, called Class I carriers by the Interstate Commerce Commission, were free to abandon routes and stops on two weeks' notice. Smaller carriers were completely free of any federal regulation.

Within three years, according to a 1986 ICC study, 15 percent of the communities previously served lost their bus service. Of these, more than 90 percent were towns of less than 10,000 population. Hardest hit was the Rocky Mountain region, where nearly 23 percent of the towns lost service.

Even before deregulation, American Bus Association figures show the Class I interstate carriers were losing passengers; between 1970 and 1985, the numbers were reduced by half to 89.8 million. As deregulated airline fares from major cities became more attractive in recent years, the bus industry grew increasingly receptive to its own deregulation.

In the wake of the 1982 deregulation, says GAO's Francis Mulvay, a former vice-president of the bus association, the completely unregulated Class II and III carriers, serving regional and local routes, have largely abandoned their fixed routes for the more lucrative charter services. But Mulvay also questions the adequacy of bus industry data, which he says is largely secondhand information from the ICC, an inadequate source now that only Class I carriers are required to report. As a result, he says, no one is absolutely sure what is happening to rural service, except that it is deteriorating.

Mary Kihl, associate dean of Iowa State University's College of Design, agrees. She questions whether many of the communities in the ICC survey had service even in 1982. Her survey, based on listings in *Russell's Guide,* the bus industry register of scheduled routes, suggests that many towns had been informally abandoned years before, without notice to the ICC. However, she also notes that much of the evidence was anecdotal, depending on whether a local source had "noticed" the bus coming through.

In such an environment, with no federal subsidies comparable to the airline program, replacement of abandoned bus service is often a matter of luck and timing. Until recently, new feeder lines attempting to start local service to connect with major routes have found little interest on the part of the big carriers—a distinct contrast to the attitude of the major airlines in dealing with commuter services.

Moreover, the new bus lines have often found it difficult to regain customers after a period of interrupted service, says Fred Fravel, senior associate at Ecosometrics, a Bethesda, Maryland, consulting firm specializing in transportation. A case in point is the experience of Jefferson Lines, an interstate carrier serving the Mississippi Valley, which tried a feeder line demonstration project in Iowa. Says Fravel: The vans failed to generate enough traffic "to make it worthwhile." He notes that Greyhound has also experienced difficulty in efforts to franchise local service. The parent Greyhound firm sold its bus lines to a new firm, called Greyhound Bus Lines, in Dallas, in mid-March. The new Greyhound has indicated it will soon pursue franchise efforts more aggressively. . . .

Many rural public transit services got started by offering service to a special clientele. Extremely rare just 20 years ago, such services are now common and have even formed their own advocacy association, the National Association for Transportation Alternatives, based in Washington, D.C. That location is no accident. From the beginning, most of the services have depended on federal money to operate, most of it from the Department of Health and Human Services. Federal interest in rural public transit needs began in the Johnson era in the Office of Economic Opportunity, says Jon Burkhardt, vice-president of Ecosometrics. There was a recognition, he notes, that lack of transportation reinforces the cycle of poverty.

A Federal Highway Administration demonstration project in the 1970s resulted in the creation of Section 18 funds administered by the Urban Mass Transportation Administration as part of the mass transit budget. A separate UMTA fund provides capital assistance to social service agencies for transit services to their clientele, while the HHS budget adds numerous special funds for operating aid for transit services to the elderly, handicapped, Medicaid patients, and other "transportation-disadvantaged" groups.

Section 18's three percent share of federal transit money for rural areas is producing about $60 million a year, though a special allocation raised last year's budget to $75 million. The National Association for Transportation Alternatives has persuaded Rep. Olympia Snowe of Maine to introduce a bill to raise that share to five percent. UMTA supports the increase. George Rucker, research director of Rural America, an advocacy group in Washington, D.C., notes that Health and Human Services funds, though not specifically differentiated along rural and urban lines, amount to over $1 billion—but in a multitude of smaller pots, all with their own regulations. That can be an accounting problem for small rural transit programs.

Many systems are quite small indeed. Marlene Gakle has been operating the Saline County Area Transit Services in Western, Nebraska, since 1972. With a population of under 10,000, the county, an hour southwest of Lincoln, uses just three vans and four staff people. Yet the funding sources for the $66,000 operating budget—and their guidelines—are no less complex than for larger systems. In southern Maine, the York County Community Action Corporation in Sanford serves some 140,000 people in an area of 1,000 square miles with 18 vehicles, funded by an amalgam of public and private sources. In fiscal 1987, the system took in $389,000 in public funds ($33,000 of that Section 18 money) and $67,000 from private sources, including the United Way and various sheltered workshops it serves.

David Raphael, executive director of Rural America, estimates that there are about 1,000 rural public transit systems nationwide, with another 4,000 services provided by human services agencies. Such numbers suggest a need for state-level coordination, says Patricia Weaver, director of the Transportation Center at the University of Kansas. Thirty-five states now provide funding and technical support for rural transit.

One state that wins high marks from rural transit experts is Iowa, which has been divided into 16 districts, each with its own coordinated rural transit services. Agencies that need special services for their clientele must cooperate within the districts to avoid duplication. Achieving that coordination was not easy, says J.P. Golinvaux, district representative for the Iowa Department of Transportation's Air and Transit Division, which established the system. "It took administrative courage" and "some head-knocking," says Golinvaux, to overcome turf rivalries among the various agencies involved.

In northeastern Minnesota, the state provides rural services through Arrowhead Transit Services in the town of Virginia, part of the Arrowhead Community Action Agency. The agency uses 50 vans and buses to serve a seven-county region of 21,000 square miles; a third of its $1.36 million budget comes from the state, with the rest from human services agencies and local government, which must contract with Arrowhead, according to agency transit director Judy Byman. . . .

More statewide efforts will be needed, says Iowa State's Kihl, if we are to ensure that people in rural areas can, in fact, get from here to there. And that means coordinating rural transit services with access to remaining intercity bus lines; perhaps combining freight and passenger van services; and even abandoning a few small airports in favor of better transportation to other, more economically viable, facilities.

The economic fate of the nation's rural areas and small towns will depend to a large extent on the quality of these efforts.

Jim Schwab is the assistant editor of Planning.

Build Here: Transit's Rallying Cry

Manuel Padron
(June 1984)

As federal funds for rail transit construction and operating subsidies become increasingly harder to get, cities are seeking creative ways to bring more capital into their transit systems. One method that has received a lot of attention is "joint development"—the shared use of a piece of property to the benefit of both a public transit agency and a private party.

Although it is being touted as a new concept, joint development, in fact, has a long history. In the mid- to late-1800s, private railroad companies received large grants of land from the federal government—substantially more land than was necessary to build their railroads. The sale of this excess land led to the development of cities and towns along the railroad lines and the creation of vast fortunes for the railroads. In this century, the federal interstate highway program has radically changed development patterns across the country, bringing profits to many a property owner.

Like the railroad barons and interstate highway planners, a transit agency often acquires more property than is necessary for building new rail lines and stations. Sometimes that is because extra land is needed as a staging area for construction; other times entire parcels are purchased in order to obtain a specific lot.

But, historically, government agencies, including transit authorities, have been inefficient in developing and managing these real estate holdings. Since public agencies are subject to political pressure and often ill equipped to negotiate real estate deals, it may be in an agency's best interest to enter into an agreement—a long-term lease for example—with a developer who is experienced in generating the most profit possible from a piece of property.

It should be noted that station-area development frequently is confused with the term joint development. Station-area planning and development may or may not occur on property owned by a transit agency and may or may not be coordinated with the agency.

A related point is that the term joint development often is used interchangeably with "value capture"—a concept that encompasses the various means by which a community shares in the economic benefits of publicly funded improvements. Yet joint development is just one of several value-capture mechanisms, albeit the most used, and successful, one to date. Other techniques include station cost sharing, connector fees, lease of advertising space and concession rights, and special transit tax districts. . . .

Toronto

Toronto offers the most extensive and best examples of joint development of transit facilities with private projects in all of North America. The pattern of cluster development along its rapid rail corridors—whose subways were largely built in the mid-1950s—is a classic of transit-related urban development.

Toronto Transit Commission (TTC) officials expect revenues from the leasing and sale of excess properties eventually to equal the cost of purchasing the system's rights-of-way—well over $100 million. Eight years ago, the leasing of property for joint use generated almost $825,000 annually. That trend continues today.

As an arm of Toronto Metro—the region's acclaimed metropolitan government—the TTC's land-development policies are designed to maximize development around most of the rail system's stations. The region's urban pattern attests to the effectiveness of this policy.

Although not all land-value benefits generated by the system are captured directly by the transit commission, they are in effect captured by the community at large through real estate taxes. And, indirectly, some of the land-development benefits also are plowed back into the TTC, since the local share of the system's expansion and some operating costs are supported by Metro through ad valorem taxes.

Directly, of course, the transit commission has benefited immeasurably from Metro's land-use policies because intensive use by Toronto's residents has ensured the success of the rail system.

All excess TTC properties are disposed of with the goal of promoting joint use. Since 1960, the commission has favored long-term leases over the sale or short-term rental of property. In disposing of excess property rights, the TTC must offer the rights first to the Metro government and then to the municipality in which the property is located. Only after local governments refuse the rights can the TTC offer them to private developers. Of the hundreds of short-term leases that have been granted, about half have gone to municipalities—for such things as parking and concession stands.

Washington, D.C.

The Washington Metropolitan Area Transit Authority (WMATA) now owns and controls rights-of-way for one of the nation's largest transportation projects—the 48-mile Metro rapid rail system that began operation in 1976. Several years ago, WMATA expanded its real estate program, originally limited to property acquisition, to include the increasingly important function of land management. The land-management activities are separate from land acquisition and relocation.

A report issued just three years after the first Metro segment opened estimated that even at that early stage Metro had generated over $970 million worth of private development. The report projected that an additional $5 billion in development would occur in the vicinity of Metro stations once the system was completed. It now appears that new local tax revenues from Metro-related development will total more than $50 million by next year.

. . .

Here are a few examples of Metro station-area developments:

• The Connecticut Connection is a $14 million, 200,000-square-foot, office-retail complex on a site originally purchased by WMATA for an entrance to the downtown Farragut North Metro station and for a construction staging area.

• The Rosslyn Metro Center is a 31,300-square-foot parcel purchased by WMATA to construct the mezzanine service area of the Rosslyn Metro station. It was joined with an adjacent, 37,000-square-foot, privately owned parcel in order to obtain higher density uses than permitted by existing zoning. This allowed the construction of a $22 million retail-office complex directly above and adjacent to the station.

• At the Van Ness station in northwest Washington, WMATA has selected the Prudential Insurance Company to develop a $28 million retail-office project on a 65,000-square-foot site. As part of its agreement with WMATA, the developer will provide a five-bay bus stop and a 25-car kiss-and-ride facility on the site. A similar agreement was worked out for the proposed Bethesda Metro Center complex, a $100 million office-hotel-retail center in Bethesda, Maryland.

• At the White Flint station near Rockville, Maryland, WMATA hopes to recover the acquisition cost of the 33-acre station site through the sale of 765 residential units being built as part of a $214 million mixed-use private development.

Atlanta

The Metropolitan Atlanta Rapid Transit Authority (MARTA) has emphasized the desirability of joint-use policies in planning and building the first phases of the city's three-year-old rapid transit system. For example, it encouraged the construction of the $100 million Southern Bell Building over the new North Avenue station, as well as two 20-story state office buildings over the Georgia Street station. Several other downtown MARTA stations also are tied into retail and office buildings; in fact, over 30 percent of downtown's private office space now is directly connected to the MARTA system.

From 1973—when property acquisition began—until recently, MARTA derived no direct financial benefit from the numerous instances of joint property use. However, there have been many indirect benefits from the downtown stations: higher potential ridership (i.e., the 5,000 Southern Bell employees atop the North Avenue station); a stronger local tax base, including revenue from a special one percent sales tax on transactions in the MARTA service area; and an improved station environment.

MARTA also owns a considerable amount of valuable excess property—both large and small parcels—in Atlanta. In August 1982, in response to interest by private developers, MARTA adopted a policy for disposing of excess property rights, patterned after Washington, D.C.'s policy. MARTA now favors long-term leases over outright sales and will use a competitive bid process for securing private developers.

Recently, MARTA leased the air rights over the Lenox station's south concourse (now under construction in north Atlanta) and a three-acre parcel south of the Arts Center station. The development of these two properties will bring MARTA its first revenues from long-term leases—starting at more than $300,000 a year from each of the properties.

Miami

Miami is actively pursuing joint development and has two major projects under way in connection with its new Metrorail rapid transit system, which is scheduled to begin operation this summer. Inter-

estingly, both projects involve land that otherwise would only be used for park-and-ride lots.

● At Miami's Dadeland South station, for example, the Green Development Company has leased five acres from the Metro-Dade County Transportation Administration to build three office towers with a total of 600,000 square feet of space, a 300-room hotel, and 50,000 square feet of retail space. The 99-year lease agreement calls for the developer to pay the transit authority four percent of the project's unadjusted gross revenue annually—an amount expected to equal $1 million by 1990. In addition, the developer will provide Metrorail, at no cost, with 1,000 of the 3,300 parking spaces in a new garage.

● Metro also has leased 494,000 square feet at its Dadeland North station site for a proposed 1.7-million-square-foot office-retail-residential-hotel private development. Also included is a parking structure for 4,880 cars, with 2,085 of those spaces reserved for Metrorail park-and-ride facilities, again at no cost to the county. The developer's lease payments will escalate to about $1 million a year by 1990.

Meanwhile, at the downtown Government Center station, a $138 million complex of city, county, state, and federal buildings is partly complete, including a new cultural arts center that opened earlier this year. The government center has helped spark a $2 billion construction boom in the area, city officials estimate. . . .

Baltimore

Maryland's Mass Transit Administration (MTA), which is responsible for Baltimore's new subway system, has worked with Baltimore city planners on an aggressive policy of station-area planning. The goal: to attract new industry, business, and housing to add jobs and broaden the city's tax base.

To encourage development around the stations, planners designated new urban renewal areas and modified existing urban renewal plans. In some cases, zoning was changed to promote certain types of construction, while discouraging unwanted uses, such as those depending on automobile access. The city also incorporated station-area road improvements into its capital improvements program. In exchange, MTA has given the city the first opportunity to buy land that is no longer needed for construction of the subway system.

Even before the first leg of the $797 million

Metro system opened last November, over $50 million worth of new office, residential, and commercial construction was under way within 2,000 feet of each of the nine stations on the eight-mile, northwest corridor route. (Another three stations are planned for the line's six-mile extension, which now is under construction.)

The city's planning department and MTA planners identified three of the nine station areas as specific sites to encourage development in, and the U.S. Urban Mass Transportation Administration granted $10 million for site planning and project assistance. The city also created a quasi-public agency, the Market Center Development Corporation, to oversee development within those station areas.

The highest level of activity is taking place around the Lexington Market station, where a $7 million addition to a 200-year-old market opened in 1982 and construction has begun on the first phase of an office-shop complex that will ring the market.

In addition, the city has budgeted $500,000 to construct an "urban farm village" near the station. The village will recreate an old-fashioned farmyard, with areas set aside for crafts and peddlers, a theater, and a gazebo for public events.

Among the projects proposed for other station areas in the city: a high-technology business park and $6.3 million district court complex near the Reistertown Plaza station and new housing near the Upton and Penn–North stations.

Los Angeles

The Southern California Rapid Transit District (SCRTD) is still in the preliminary design phase of its 18.6-mile, 18-station Metro Rail project. But, already, SCRTD has become a pioneer among U.S. transit agencies by officially establishing land-use and development policies at a very early project stage—even before property is acquired.

The environmental impact report prepared for the Metro Rail project estimated that SCRTD could realize $434.4 million (in 1982 dollars) from 65-year leases of air rights above the nine proposed stations offering the best development potential. SCRTD also was successful in getting state enabling legislation passed to establish special benefit assessment districts for areas near transit stations. Each district is subject to approval by at least 60 percent of the voters within the district. Assess-

ments can vary among districts; for instance, SCRTD can take into account such differences as benefits accrued to property owners, and the size and cost of station facilities in different areas.

The advantage of a special assessment district as a value-capture mechanism for financing the construction of a rapid transit system is that all or a major portion of the station construction costs can be recovered from property owners in the station area. The drawback is that taxes collected in the district can be used only to repay construction bonds and not to provide operating revenue. Also, the total value that can be captured from a special assessment district is limited to the amount of tax revenue required to repay the construction bonds, and that may be much less than the total benefit derived by property owners from the presence of the transit station.

Station-area master plans also have been prepared by the city's planning department for each of the three downtown stations. They define allowable development density and scale, land-use mix, and implementation mechanisms.

Manuel Padron, a transportation consultant based in Atlanta, is the former director of planning and marketing for the city's MARTA system. He has worked on joint development projects with transit agencies in Houston, Los Angeles, and several other cities.

To Live and Drive in L.A.

John Pastier
(February 1986)

It is almost axiomatic among planners that Los Angeles was the first great urban region to be shaped by the automobile. Yet in the early decades of the century, before the auto had made its staggering mark on the local landscape, greater Los Angeles had already been given the outlines of its far-flung form by a massive dose of the more traditionally urban technology of fixed rail transportation.

In its heyday during the 1920s, the Pacific Electric Railway system served 100 million passengers a year on 1,164 miles of track that stretched 87 miles from east to west and 58 miles from north to south, often in its own right-of-way. It was the busiest and most extensive interurban system in the country.

Concurrently, the trolleys of the Los Angeles Railways covered a 10- to 12-mile diameter in a far more closely woven web. They carried more than 255 million passengers in their peak year of 1924.

Both companies were controlled by traction magnate Henry Huntington, and both had real estate arms to sell town lots along their routes. Together, they formed the world's greatest electric railway empire, but the land sales were the more profitable aspect of the business.

What the automobile did, starting in the 1920s but working with fullest force after World War II, was to fill in the voids of the old rail-derived urban pattern, rather than substantially expanding its perimeter. Only in the last decade has rubber-tired transportation pushed the edge of development much past the ends of the early twentieth-century rail lines.

But for some inauspicious timing, Los Angeles might have been a more traditionally formed city. In 1906, a predecessor of the Pacific Electric announced a subway line to the west, but the Panic of 1907 killed that plan. At that point, the fledgling city of 200,000 could easily have restructured itself around such a fixed rail spine. An ambitious rapid transit plan was prepared in 1925, but it was shelved by civic leaders favoring the "decentralized" form Los Angeles was already developing. A 1939 proposal to leave transit rights-of-way in freeway medians was rejected in favor of freeway express buses, before Angelenos realized that freeways could suffer from congestion, too. A 1954 monorail plan and a 1960 proposal for "ultramodern," high-speed trains were also shelved. Bond issues for rail systems were defeated by voters in 1968, 1974, and 1976.

A short downtown subway, built in 1925 and since destroyed, and a short-lived experiment with median-strip transit in the Hollywood Freeway were among the PE's only steps toward true rapid transit. The system became less competitive with the auto: the ride to Long Beach stretched from 36 to 60 minutes as grade crossings multiplied. A syndicate of major bus, tire, and gasoline manufacturers bought up the interurban and streetcar systems and converted them to bus lines. With the market for its products thus expanded and a competing technology eliminated, the syndicate promptly lost interest in running the operation and sold it to local government, a tactic that was repeated throughout the country from 1932 to 1955. In 1949, a federal jury convicted General Motors of criminal conspiracy in this matter, but the court levied a token $5,000 fine and the syndicate's activities continued another six years.

Surprising density

Economics-centered planners, such as Melvin Webber at the University of California at Berkeley, argue that rubber-tired transport has prevailed because it is the form that makes most financial sense in our society. But cities are physical places as well as economic ones, and an automobile-based transportation system, even when augmented by buses, is not capable of comfortably supporting the residential and employment densities that occur in most major American urban centers.

In the process of becoming the nation's second most populous city, Los Angeles has evolved from a low-density to a high-to-medium-density settlement. The urbanized area has about 5,200 people per square mile—second only to New York—and its regional core averages 12,000 with a peak of 28,000 per square mile. While the latter two densities—those most relevant to rail rapid transit planning—do not reach the levels of older eastern and midwestern cities, they are still surprisingly high for an automobile-dependent Sun Belt city.

Consequently, Los Angeles has begun to feel the basic limitations of its rubber-tired circulation system. The problems are experienced most acutely on several freeways (and not only during rush hours), in the downtown core where gridlock sporadically occurs, and even in some outlying commercial and office centers such as Westwood, which boasts the nation's busiest street intersection in terms of daily vehicle count. The Southern California Rapid Transit District (RTD), one of several mass transit operators in the region, carries about 1.5 million bus passengers daily, making it the largest bus-only transport agency in the country.

The downtown business community is probably the strongest single-interest group in favor of rail rapid transit. Street and parking capacity is already strained in the city's financial district, but nonetheless, some 30 million square feet of office space are coming onto the market, under construction, or on the drawing boards. One project, the 73-story, 1,007-foot Library Tower, will be the tallest building west of Chicago.

All of this new office space is concentrated in a relatively small section in the western portion of downtown where the automobile has already exacted its due in land use and urban form. There have been major street widenings (and accompanying sidewalk narrowings) and the start of a one-way traffic network. One street in this financial district, Grand Avenue, is double-decked with its lower half serving underground parking and loading docks, while another, Fourth Street, is actually a short elevated freeway. Such concessions to the automobile have produced an inhumanly scaled environment resembling a movie set for a mechanistic science-fiction fantasy. The perception of large downtown employers seems to be that only high-capacity rail transport will be able to bring enough new workers into this congested district to match projected office space growth.

After turning down rail rapid transit bond issues three times, Los Angeles County voters approved a half-percent sales tax increase for public transportation in 1980. A legal challenge held up collections for two years, and the first three years' revenues were spent entirely on buses, but now about $100 million is available annually for rail transit. This includes two light rail projects of the Los Angeles County Transportation Commission (CTC), as well as the RTD's subway project, Metro Rail.

All of the CTC's funds are locally generated and controlled, but only 14 percent of present Metro Rail funding comes from the RTD itself. About 55 percent is federal money, and unfortunately for the RTD, its efforts to begin a subway system have coincided with a regime unsympathetic to rail transportation in general. For two years, the Reagan administration withheld $129 million of congressionally approved construction funds, claiming that it could not afford the project. As a result, the $3.3 billion, 18.8-mile "starter line," long intended as the first increment of an eventual 150-mile heavy and light rail system, has been cut back to an initial segment of a mere 4.4 miles. In December, President Reagan signed a bill authorizing $429 million for the project, but administration commitment to the project is still dubious.

This is just half of the "minimum operable system" originally defined by the RTD and would seem unlikely to serve any substantial trip demand unless it were extended. The RTD projects 55,000 boardings daily on this segment by the end of the century, an estimate that seems highly optimistic for a five-station fragment that runs from the not-very-busy Union Station, makes three stops downtown, and then terminates in the low-income, inner-city Westlake district. The route serves no white-collar residential areas. The latest construction estimate for this short segment, plus some support facilities scaled to serve the full 18.8-mile line, is $1.25 billion.

The trouble with rail

Optimistically assuming that the full starter line will be built with reasonable speed, there are still reasons to question Metro Rail's possible effectiveness in Los Angeles. For even when viewed from a pro-rail perspective, Metro Rail is a mixed bag. On one hand, it represents the best hope so far for rail transit in the nation's second-largest city, and even the unsympathetic Reagan administration has judged it to be the most cost-effective of the new systems. . . .

On the other hand, Metro Rail has some obvious flaws. The most conspicuous ones are related to its routing. Although popularly thought of as the "Wilshire Subway," the expression is largely a misnomer. The alignment begins logically enough by traversing downtown and heading westward under Wilshire Boulevard. But after less than 6.5 miles, it abruptly leaves the region's main street, making a right-angle turn and heading north. It misses such major Westside business centers as Beverly Hills, Century City, Westwood, Brentwood, and Santa Monica. As a starter line, it is not the best possible start, for its routing reflects political considerations taking precedent over urban transit needs.

When Tom Bradley successfully ran for mayor in 1973, his most memorable campaign promise was to begin construction of a subway line within 18 months of taking office. Under the best of circumstances he will be 11 years late, and even that sluggish timetable has required major political concessions.

The reason that the starter line swerves north is to reach North Hollywood in the innermost corner of the San Fernando Valley, a sprawling suburban district whose generally conservative residents make up more than a third of the city's population. Giving the Valley nominal subway service was meant to placate a large voting bloc that sees Metro Rail as primarily benefiting the central city.

As a further complication, the line does not go to North Hollywood with any directness, but rather meanders along an 18.8-mile path to cover the 11.5-mile straight-line distance between its termini, serving seven of the 15 Los Angeles city council districts in the process. At one point, the route actually doubles back on itself for two miles in order to serve the politically important Fairfax district. This detour may eventually be shortened, since a severe underground methane gas explosion in the neighborhood recently prompted a technical reexamination of that portion of the alignment.

One may argue that it makes sense for a starter line to serve politically symbolic areas rather than those with higher potential patronage, but if so, the routing ignores some important constituencies. The transit-dependent black community is served only marginally, as is the comparably dependent and even larger Latino population. One may therefore say that social needs have also been slighted.

When viewed from a perspective that is skeptical of rail transit, the objections multiply. Peter Gordon, a professor of planning and economics at the University of Southern California, and Donald Shoup, a professor of urban planning at the University of California, Los Angeles, argue that Metro Rail will cost too much and do too little to be worthwhile. They challenge the RTD's projections of 364,000 daily riders, pointing out that this figure represents "more passengers per mile of route than any other system in America, including New York's," and that it exceeds those of larger systems in denser cities such as Washington and San Francisco. . . .

These criticisms also apply to the CTC's light rail line from downtown Los Angeles to Long Beach. Ground was broken last fall for this $690 million, 22-mile link, which replaces a Pacific Electric line that was abandoned a generation ago. Ironically, 16 miles of its route will be on the old interurban right-of-way. Gordon calls the CTC's projection of 54,000 daily riders "an outrageous number. If they get a fifth of that," he says, "I'd be very surprised." He notes that only 1,600 Long Beach residents work in downtown Los Angeles and only 160 Angelenos work in downtown Long Beach. The CTC is also committed to building a purely suburban light rail line along the route of the future Century Freeway, but plans are too preliminary to analyze or even describe the project.

Gordon and Shoup argue that car and van pooling would do far more for traffic congestion than Metro Rail, at a fraction of the cost. Commuter vehicles in Los Angeles average 1.1 occupants, compared to 1.4 in Washington, and a national average of 1.25 in large cities. Just meeting the national average would remove 500,000 vehicles from the road, they say.

This critique of local transit proposals is convincing, for the plans seem to overstate their claims. But the planning professors' solutions of car pooling and bus subsidies, while more cost-effective and less grandiose, also seem to attack only part of the problem. Advocating more rubber-tired transportation on freeways and city streets can only be a short-term solution.

Road hogs

The region's freeway system, expensive and extensive as it is, is riddled with problems. The older, more central segments, such as the San Diego, Hollywood, Harbor, and Santa Ana freeways, are clogged well beyond normal rush hours. Newer outlying freeways fare better, but only because they are massive (as many as 10 lanes) and serve less intense needs. The logical spine of the system, the Beverly Hills Freeway running between and parallel to Wilshire and Sunset boulevards, was never built, and has been deleted from the state's highway plan as the result of massive political opposition. As a result, traffic in the regional core must either take a roundabout course on the freeways that were built or use very congested city streets for long distances.

This and increasing local traffic have created continuous pressure for street widening in the older, more urban parts of town. The result has been to narrow sidewalks and create major highways on what should have been civilized city streets. Los Angeles is planning to make more downtown streets one way, over the protests of merchants on Broadway, the region's most intense pedestrian and retailing street. Downtown's oversized blocks, about twice the size of other cities', will ensure that the detours caused by a one-way pattern will be longer than usual. . . .

But the worst aspect of a transportation system based on millions of individual vehicles is the chaos it creates. In a public transportation network, the operators are professionals focused on their work, and the vehicles are more or less systematically maintained. In a private system, the operators

394 The Best of Planning

are amateurs who are often inattentive or distracted on the road. Death and injury are the worst results of such a system; property damage, stress, lost time, and inconvenience are its more common and less drastic effects. . . .

All this suggests that Los Angeles has reached an awkward stage in its evolution. It is too big and dense to function well as an automobile city, but too auto-dependent and spread out to work well as a public transportation city. As its population grows, it intensifies at its core while spreading out at its edges, thus perpetuating its dilemma.

Perhaps someone will invent a vehicle as wondrous as the automobile was a century ago, one that will allow Los Angeles to continue to grow in its contradictory ways and yet find transportation and air-quality relief. Until that time, mobility will be the city's most pressing planning issue, and one that seems likely to elude solution through the mechanisms that operate today.

John Pastier is a Los Angeles-based critic of architecture and urban design. He is a contributing editor of Architecture *magazine.*

Peak Performances

William Fulton
(July 1987)

Once it was called "TSM"—transportation systems management—and it was mostly a means of squeezing a little extra capacity out of a highway system by using ramp meters, signal synchronization, and car-pool matching services.

Today, it's more often called "TDM"—transportation *demand* management. The effort is focused on lowering demand, and it concentrates mostly on ways of getting cars off the highway during rush hour, either by ride-sharing or flexible work hours. And, more and more, these techniques, which had some success when used on an uncoordinated basis, are becoming an integral part of overall land-use planning systems in jurisdictions around the country.

In Silver Spring, Maryland, for example, ride-sharing and transit subsidies are included in a central business district redevelopment plan; in Los Angeles, developers can reduce an expensive impact fee by using demand management to cut down on the number of trips.

And in Minnesota, where the state legislature limited the size of a new interstate link through the Twin Cities lanes, local officials have come up with a freeway design that requires a series of demand management methods to be taken.

By themselves, of course, none of these techniques is new. What's changing is the framework within which they are used. More and more, demand management techniques are being required as a condition of approval for a new development project, or worked into a land-use plan for an entire district. And the last few years have seen a rapid increase in the number of transportation management associations, or TMAs—groups of private-sector employers and developers that work together to reduce traffic demand.

The biggest reason for the new institutional arrangements is the rapid growth in suburban office centers, which have dramatically changed the commuting patterns of American metropolitan areas in the last five or so years.

"Demand management is much more feasible in self-contained suburban centers than in traditional downtowns," says transportation expert Kenneth Orski, president of the Washington-based Urban Mobility Corporation, consultant to many TMAs and local governments.

While the cities remain heavily dependent on mass transit, suburban demand management can make effective use of car pools and van pools, flexible work schedules, and other "soft" techniques. In addition, unlike urban areas, suburban business centers often have short peak commuting periods, so shifting traffic to off-peak periods is relatively easy to achieve. . . .

As one planner put it recently, "there's no incentive like a requirement." And Orski notes that the best way to ensure ongoing private-sector commitment is to impose demand management goals, as Pleasanton, California, has done as part of an overall growth strategy and as Los Angeles is about to do.

Experts in the field warn, though, that demand management can't work wonders. At best, it can hike the number of people not driving alone in suburban areas from around 15 percent (which seems to be the "natural" range) to about 25 percent. "We're really pressing our luck if we get more than one-quarter of all commuters," says Robert Cervero, who teaches transportation planning at the University of California, Berkeley and has been studying suburban commuting patterns.

Further, experts like Orski and Cervero say, ride-sharing—a key demand management technique—is extremely sensitive to factors beyond the control of local management efforts, notably the price of gas. As gas prices have dropped in the last few years, ride-sharing has also dropped.

There are various ways to measure the effectiveness of demand management, and cities have not settled on one as the most effective. The traditional method, of course, is to measure the number of employees who commute by alternative means. Some cities, however, are interested in raising the average number of riders per vehicle. This is the measure Los Angeles will use in its new ride-sharing program, which requires all large employers to participate.

Increasingly, cities are measuring demand management in terms of their own road capacity by using the so-called "level of service" ratings established by traffic engineers. These ratings classify roads and intersections from A (best) to F (worst) based on congestion. Intersection congestion, for example, is measured by average delay before proceeding. In some cities, if certain intersections deteriorate below a certain level of service—usually C or D—the situation can trigger demand management requirements or even building restrictions.

The most highly acclaimed demand management ordinance, that of Pleasanton, California, 30 miles east of San Francisco, uses both levels of service and employee commuting targets in an attempt to manage demand. The strategy has been successful so far, with about 35 percent of commuters either ride-sharing or traveling outside the peak hours.

Pleasanton is a small (30,000 or so) city that is experiencing enormous job growth, due mostly to Hacienda Business Park, which will eventually top out at 10 million square feet. Recognizing that their efforts alone could not solve the problem, Hacienda's developers at an early stage began lobbying the city for a demand management plan. The result is a plan, written in 1984, that has received wide attention throughout California.

The Pleasanton breakthrough is to make participation in demand management mandatory from the beginning. Major employers, developers, and landlords must design and implement individual TSM programs that, over a four-year period, will induce 45 percent of employees to use such alternative commuting methods as ride-sharing and driving outside the peak hours. The yearly targets for each new development start at 15 percent, rising 10 percent a year for the next four years.

At first, employers may choose their own methods for achieving the goals. But if the targets are not met, the city council can take over through a city TSM task force, made up of representatives of large developers and employers. The makeup of this task force was a compromise after the business community rebelled against the idea of a city-appointed "TSM czar," who could take control of individual employers' programs if necessary.

Pleasanton's problems are simplified by the fact that, because the area is strictly suburban office development, the peak hours are short. The TSM ordinance declares "peak hour" to be 7:30 to 8:30 in the morning and 4:30 to 5:30 in the evening, and most commuters who participate in the TSM program do so by driving during off-hours.

No miracle

Although widely talked about, the Pleasanton case is not a miracle. The national drop in ride-sharing was reflected in Pleasanton, when drive-alone commuters increased from 81 percent in 1985 to 84 percent in 1986. Pleasanton is so convenient to the homes of most commuters—47 percent live within 10 miles—that city transportation manager Gail Gilpin admits it is hard to lure many people out of their cars.

The program is now in its third year, meaning employers must reach the 35 percent level. Gilpin notes that only five of 40 employers failed to make the second-year goal of 25 percent. However, the city has not taken action against any of them. Gilpin is proud of the fact that 12 of the 40 exceeded 45 percent, and that the overall level was close to 35 percent—already beyond the "outer limit" that Cervero and Orski peg at around 25 percent. But the hard part is still ahead: Can Pleasanton reach—and hold onto—the ultimate 45 percent target?

In Southern California, Los Angeles, though typical of cities that impose "impact fees" to pay for new roads, now allows developers to use demand management to reduce the fees. At this point, the new arrangement applies only to the fast-growing coastal district around Los Angeles International Airport, where developers must pay $2,010 for every vehicle trip their project generates. They can save a substantial amount by reducing the number of trips generated.

The idea is becoming popular among developers. "If it saves them money and gives them good public relations, generally they'll do it," says L.A. city planner David Gay. . . .

Across the country, in Silver Spring, Maryland, the transportation problem was the same, but the demand solution proved to be somewhat different. Montgomery County officials wanted to redevelop the central business district in Silver Spring, but they also felt bound by their Adequate Public Facilities ordinance, which links new development to provision of infrastructure. They are currently in the process of setting up a Transportation Management District designed to bridge the gap between the traffic generated by the redevelopment effort and the traffic that existing roads and transit systems can bear. . . .

Downtown Silver Spring is the terminus for the Washington Metro's Red Line and for its feeder buses from that part of Montgomery County. Thus, the basis of the county's program is to subsidize transit fares. The county will sell a $12 monthly bus pass to employers for $10 and an $80 monthly rail pass for $60, hoping that employers will provide a further subsidy. (The program will cost the county $1.5 million a year, still far less than the cost of constructing new roads.)

Administration of the program, however, is not so different in Silver Spring than in Pleasanton. Each large employer must submit a demand management plan to the county, and each must participate in an annual survey designed to monitor progress.

In Minneapolis and St. Paul, demand management as an integrated part of a new highway was forced on the local government by the state legislature, responding to neighborhoods threatened by right-of-way acquisition. A state moratorium on interstate construction was lifted for Interstate 394, entering downtown Minneapolis from the west, but the new highway was limited to six lanes.

Steve Alderson, a transportation planner with the Twin Cities Metropolitan Council, says this limitation dictated demand management as a solution because successful use of I-394 "would be impossible without an increase in auto occupancy."

So demand management has been built into the interstate construction itself, with a combination of "hard" and "soft" techniques. During construction of the interstate, which won't be completed until 1992, a high-occupancy vehicle lane, associated with promotional ride-sharing programs, has been introduced along the route. Eventually, that HOV lane will lead directly to special downtown garages reserved for vans and car pools, which will be linked by skyways to nearby office buildings.

To succeed, the I-394 program must push what the experts believe is the upper boundary of demand management. In 1985, 20 percent of all rush-hour vehicles were car pools or buses; by 1993, that figure must rise to 29 percent. The increase in car pools and buses in proportion to traffic is much higher: Of the 1,200 additional vehicles that will be added to rush-hour traffic over the next six years, 75 percent must be car pools or buses to make the system work. . . .

Retrofits

While the public sector is working on demand management mandates, the private sector is busily setting up a network of independent organizations—known as transportation management associations, or TMAs—to work on demand and on other traffic problems. . . .

A granddaddy of the TMA business is Boston's 12-year-old Medical Area Service Corporation (MASCO), a coalition of medical institutions and colleges in Brookline's Longwood Medical Area. With five planners, 50 transportation employees, and a $14 million budget, MASCO serves as a mini-transit district. It owns 3,200 peripheral parking spaces, which it leases to its member institutions. It also runs shuttle buses to the parking lots, and to Harvard Square in Cambridge. Finally, it serves as a lobbying group, representing the institutions' interest in improving public transit in Boston.

Momentum has been a problem for a number of TMAs, but so far all the member institutions remain committed to MASCO, even though some are in competition with each other for health care services. Economies of scale outweigh competitive pressures, says Larry Christianson, vice-president for parking and transit services. . . .

Good sign

Perhaps the surest sign that TMAs and demand management are on the upswing, however, is the fact that the Silicon Valley in Northern California has finally latched on to the idea.

Recently, six of the cities along the congested Route 101 corridor, including San Jose, have been discussing possible solutions as part of the "Golden Triangle Task Force." Part of the reason is that the six cities are no longer competing with each other for industrial growth so much as they are competing with cities in Colorado, Oregon, and other areas seeking to become the next American high-tech capital.

The task force has proposed a four-part approach to regional growth problems, including creation of more housing, new means of raising capital funds, policies to manage and equalize job growth—and transportation demand management.

Those involved look longingly at nearby Pleasanton and its ability to force employers to deal with transportation demand from the beginning. The Silicon Valley, by contrast, is 85 percent built out.

"We don't have the leverage to get mitigation fees," says Edie Dorosin, executive vice-president of the Santa Clara Manufacturing Group, an industry organization that is coordinating the Golden Triangle effort. "Our focus is primarily existing employers."

Still, the group's approach is not likely to be much different from Pleasanton's: a mandatory reporting program for all large employers, then an evaluation after three years and—perhaps—a mandatory program after that if things don't improve.

. . .

Ultimately, the Golden Triangle group may come to grips with the larger land-use issues that are implied in the problems of transportation demand. Its members are currently talking about each city taking responsibility for providing a certain share of housing, while limiting the amount of industrial growth it will allow, in order to create more balance in commuting patterns. There's no guarantee that they'll reach an agreement, but so far they all seem to acknowledge that such land-use changes would constitute what might be called the ultimate transportation demand management measure.

William Fulton is a contributing editor of Planning.

A Desire Named Streetcar
F. K. Plous, Jr.
(June 1984)

Can streetcars save American cities? Can they revitalize decaying downtown commercial cores and nearby residential districts? Can they reduce auto congestion, air pollution, and the indiscriminate malling over of once diverse and interesting urban districts? And, even if they can't make a direct impact on the environment, can they at least make public transit more viable by attracting riders who insist on something faster and more comfortable than a bus?

Advocates of the latter-day successor to the electric trolley car, the Light Rail Vehicle (LRV), say they can. LRVs, they say, have the speed, comfort, and—let's face it—the plain old charm to attract large numbers of riders. And, they point out, LRVs can do the job at a fraction of the cost of heavy rail systems, which operate on expensive, grade-separated rights-of-way.

A cursory inspection suggests that some of these claims have merit. The cities that decided to keep their old streetcars or to introduce new ones report steadily increasing ridership and a significant positive impact on the area as a whole.

In San Diego, for example, ridership and revenue on the three-year-old, 16-mile Tijuana Trolley have exceeded all expectations. Planning for a second route is under way.

Calgary and Edmonton, two booming cities in Canada's growing West, have installed LRV lines; Edmonton, a 5.6-mile line in 1978 and Calgary, a 7.7-mile route in 1981. Right behind those pioneer LRV cities are 17 others in various stages of development—from just about to open (Portland, Oregon; Vancouver, British Columbia; and Buffalo) to under construction (San Jose and Sacramento, California) to serious studies (Dallas, Denver, Detroit, Long Beach, and Columbus, Ohio) to just looking thanks (Norfolk, Salt Lake City, and Milwaukee). There are short "tourist" lines in Seattle, Fort Worth, Detroit, Lowell, Massachusetts, and Birmingham, Alabama.

This boom in new LRV lines has been accompanied by the reconstruction and extension of most of the handful of streetcar lines that survived the post-World War II highway monopoly.

Toronto, which made a watershed decision in 1972 to preserve—and systematically expand—its streetcar system, now has the busiest fleet on the continent (92.2 million fares and 225 passenger miles). Its number of vehicles, 396, is second only to Philadelphia's 506.

Boston, Philadelphia, San Francisco, and Pittsburgh all have retained and modernized their streetcar systems during the last two generations, and now they are upgrading them again—this time to LRV status on substantial segments. Both Newark and Cleveland are upgrading their historic lines—Newark with a rebuilding of its entire 4.3 miles of track and several stations, and Cleveland with the purchase of 48 new Italian-built cars for its 13.2-mile system, much of it serving the prosperous suburb of Shaker Heights. Meanwhile, New Orleans hangs on to its popular 6.6-mile St. Charles streetcar line and its superbly maintained 60-year-old, heavyweight cars.

If light rail transit is enjoying some sort of renaissance in North America today, one good reason may simply be that it had nowhere else to go but up. Fifty years ago McGraw-Hill's annual Transit Directory reported that the North American streetrailway, or "traction," industry, had a total of 9,971 route miles operated by 51,920 powered vehicles. Last year, the New York–based consulting firm of Gibbs & Hill reported that the total light rail route mileage in North America was 297; 466 if all lines being planned or under construction were included. The total streetcar/LRV fleet, it said, numbered 1,586, with 449 units on order. . . .

Nothing of importance really happened in the streetcar industry until the mid-1970s, when a combination of municipal ownership of transit facilities, UMTA funding, and the 1973 and 1979 fuel crises forced a fundamental rethinking of the streetcar's potential for building—and rebuilding—cities.

Don't call it a streetcar

What emerged was something called the Light Rail Vehicle. Out the window went such turn-of-the-century nomenclature as streetcars, street railway, and traction company. The correct term for the whole operation now is Light Rail Transit (LRT).

The distinctions are not euphemistic. Streetcar and street railway are no longer appropriate terms,

since a major theme of new LRT technology is to get the car off the street and onto a private or semi-private right-of-way.

The car itself is the most noticeable improvement. Most of the LRVs now being supplied to North American cities are really two cars permanently joined—articulated, in rail parlance—over a common four-wheel truck at the center. The LRVs scheduled for delivery to San Jose in 1986, for example, will be 88 feet long and will carry 76 seated passengers and 91 standees. The last time streetcars operated in San Jose, in 1938, the standard car was 43 feet long and carried 36 seated passengers and perhaps 40 standees.

Additional operating economies are attained by combining LRVs into trains of one, two, or three such units, making it possible for one operator to carry nearly 1,000 passengers during peak travel times. Ten to 15 standard buses, each with its own driver, would be needed to carry the same load, a major reason why the LRV's higher initial cost is quickly compensated for by savings in labor costs.

Consequently, for little more than the price of a common streetcar line, medium-sized cities can attain a rush-hour, mass-transport capacity that approaches the volume of the much more expensive heavy rail transit lines. That means cities that have outgrown their bus systems can still make a quantum transit leap—if the right-of-way is available—without the expense of a new subway or expressway expansion.

Because the line between the "light" streetcar and the "heavy," grade-separated rapid transit train is beginning to blur, planners and transit boosters are learning to discard some of the conventional thinking about urban transit. Advantages once exclusive to heavy rail now, with a little ingenuity, can be made to work for light rail too.

Speed. Santa Clara County senior transportation engineer David Minister says that by keeping most of San Jose's new LRT system on a private or semi-private right-of-way, including a downtown transit mall (also a feature of Buffalo's new pseudo-light rail system), "overall speed will be about 23 miles an hour." South of downtown, Minister adds, four miles of grade separation will permit 50-mile-an-hour speeds. Those figures compare favorably with the performance of heavy rail systems. And, by running through a tunnel under the Golden Triangle, Pittsburgh's newly rehabilitated downtown streetcar line will avoid enough congestion so that a rush-hour crosstown trip will take only eight minutes instead of 45.

Capacity. Besides linking cars into trains, modern LRT managers are raising capacity in other ways. Pittsburgh's new LRVs, for instance, will have doors for high-level platform entry on one side and stairs for street-level use on the other. In the downtown tunnels, high-level station platforms permit rapid loading and unloading; in the less congested neighborhoods, the cars will continue to handle passengers at street corners. A similar system is already at work on San Francisco's Muni line.

Fare collection. Obviously, a single motorman can't collect fares from all the passengers in the multiunit train. So new systems like San Diego's use European-style honor-system ticketing and random inspections. Cheating has been minimal, and the losses more than made up by the operating economies. Additional economies come from automated ticketing at unmanned stations.

Rights-of-way

Whether to tunnel, create a mall, build a median strip, create a private LRT line, or share underused railroad right-of-way—and where to switch from one alignment to another—is usually dictated by local topography, land cost and availability, budget and local politics. Calgary and Edmonton both use surplus railroad right-of-way in outlying neighborhoods, but Calgary routed its LRVs through downtown on a 12-block transit mall while Edmonton built 1.5 miles of tunnel.

San Jose will use a transit mall downtown, a street running north of downtown, and an expressway median strip south of the city center. Buffalo, which had to scale back a planned heavy rail subway system, is getting a 1.2-mile downtown mall and—strangely enough—5.2 miles of streetcar subway in outlying neighborhoods. Boston, which understood as early as 1897 that Colonial–era streets are too narrow and crooked to accommodate streetcars, tunneled early and often. With 11.2 of its 32.6 miles of LRT lines underground, Boston leads the continent in buried light rail trackage.

But San Diego is probably the most ambitious advocate of the "get-the-streetcars-off-the-streets" philosophy. Only 1.6 miles of its 15.6-mile Tijuana Trolley line are on city streets. The remainder use the right-of-way of the abandoned San Diego, Arizona & Eastern Railroad.

Off-the-street definitely is the trend in LRT routing—and probably will remain so as long as fast, maneuverable private autos are permitted to overwhelm the larger, less maneuverable LRVs. . . .

The major difference between today's LRVs and the old street railways is that the new lines are being planned, sited, and financed with a precision the older installations never enjoyed.

One reason is government, which demands that all transit capital projects be justified economically if they are to receive federal assistance. With a single exception, the San Diego line, which waived UMTA participation because the distress sale of a prospective right-of-way offered substantial cost and time reductions, the U.S. Urban Mass Transportation Administration is deeply involved in the capital funding of all U.S. light rail projects. UMTA provides 50 percent of the capital for new systems and 80 percent for renovations or extensions of older ones—provided the project meets its criteria. With only about $0.5 billion in such funds available each year, U.S. cities compete vigorously for their piece of UMTA's capital grants, and any awards are preceded by several years of the intense, often agonizing "Alternative Analysis" required by UMTA.

Brian Cudahy, UMTA's Director of Capital and Formula Assistance, describes Alternative Analysis as a negotiated agreement that puts local planners and their consultants under pressure to keep their systems modest and their costs down.

The alternatives range from Transportation Systems Management (TSM), which might simply mean special bus lanes or encouragement of car pools, to new public works, such as a downtown bus terminal. A totally new heavy rail line like San Francisco's, Washington's, or Atlanta's represents the heaviest expenditure.

The critical consideration, says Cudahy, is the cost per passenger and, in particular, the added federal contribution per passenger. Anything a community can do to reduce that figure increases its chance of winning an UMTA grant. Buffalo, for example, scaled back its project to reduce costs, agreeing to reduce overall mileage and step down from heavy rail to light.

Building ridership

Pittsburgh's reconstruction and extension of its existing 25-mile trolley system is a good example. The $500 million project, which involves construction of 3.1 miles of downtown tunnel to replace surface lines, double track, and elimination of grade crossings on suburban routes, and the purchase of 55 new LRVs to supplement 45 older streetcars, began with discussions a dozen years ago. Formal planning started in 1977.

Once the decision for an improved LRT was made—after an earlier proposal for an overhead, rubber-tired people mover called "Skybus" was rejected—authorities from the Port Authority of Allegheny County began conducting informal community meetings. Among the developments announced at the meetings was the Port Authority's carefully calculated plan to build ridership inducements into the LRT system before the line was due to open.

First, residents were told that all-day parking rates at downtown, city-owned garages would be raised to discourage commuters from driving. At the same time, short-term rates were lowered to get suburban shoppers into the habit of going downtown. In 1981, a program was started to encourage commuters to park at Three Rivers Stadium just across the Allegheny River from downtown and to ride free Port Authority shuttle buses to work. Within a month, more than 2,000 auto commuters were using the shuttles, and despite a recent increase in the day-long parking rate, the popularity of the program continues. By the time the downtown streetcar subway opens this November, officials predict, the pro-transit psychology will have built a strong LRT constituency. . . .

Ironically, no development signals the success and acceptance of the LRT so much as the fact that it is being actively promoted in cities where it seems to be inappropriate. Orlando, a sprawling, Sun Belt city with no discernible corridors and a downtown with only five million square feet of commercial space is the scene of a sharpening battle between rival schools of thought.

On the one hand, Orange County commission chair Lou Treadway sees a light rail system as the answer to congestion, pollution, and what he feels is lagging growth. "I would hate to think that 25 years from now . . . people will be saying, 'Why didn't they plan for this?' " Yet [Boris] Pushkarev [author of the 1982 book, *Urban Rail in America*], who has examined the Orlando plan carefully, thinks the local promoters are fooling themselves. The patronage for an LRT is simply not there, he

says, and even when it arrives it will be relatively expensive to provide for.

If that's true, then Orlando and its sprawling, car-dependent analogues across the Sun Belt have a real dilemma: Many are just big enough to produce more auto traffic and pollution than the road system and the atmosphere can handle, but not big enough—and certainly not dense enough or linear enough—to justify building an LRT system. What that means is that the next phase of LRT growth may be in those industrially obsolete northern cities that are holding a valuable trump card in the fact that they sit on logistically rational maps. For the others, the Orlandos that aspire to a fleet of handsome LRVs but can't produce the riders, Pushkarev has this advice: "Reserve the right-of-way, introduce land-use controls that will cluster new development around it, but don't start building until a more reliable market develops."

F. K. Plous, Jr., is a Chicago writer who specializes in transportation, urban affairs, and real estate development.

Look Ma, No Hands
Dennis McClendon
(July 1987)

To the visitor watching an approaching SkyTrain in Vancouver, something looks vaguely wrong about the rapid transit cars moving overhead on an elevated guideway. There is no motorman's cab. In fact, there is no motorman.

Vancouver's 13.6-mile SkyTrain was North America's first fully automated transit system, carrying some 60,000 passengers a day. And it is making believers out of transportation planners who had dismissed automated guideway transit (AGT) as an impractical Buck Rogers fantasy. Besides Vancouver, automated systems are carrying passengers in Kobe, Japan; Lille, France; and Miami; and others will soon open in Detroit; London; and Berlin.

For planners, the positive implications of automation go far beyond specifying hardware. Freed from attendant labor costs, trains can run more frequently, and service need not be cut back at night and on weekends. The short headway (time between trains) is extremely important to the public's perception of convenience.

Moreover, frequent trains can be shorter and smaller. That lowers the cost of stations and guideways and cuts right-of-way costs. Frequent trains can also offer branch-line service, further increasing passenger convenience.

Despite these advantages, automation has been a long time in coming. The problems San Francisco's BART system encountered with unproven technology soured planners on high-tech transportation. San Diego, by contrast, enjoyed immediate success with its manned, no-frills light rail line. It was quickly emulated by Portland, Sacramento, and San Jose.

Automated systems built in the 1970s, at Morgantown, West Virginia, and the Dallas/Fort Worth airport were plagued by start-up problems. "It was a new technology and there were bugs in it," says Lawrence Fabian, publisher of *TransitPulse,* a Boston-based newsletter on people movers. "Morgantown was experimental, but it got a lot of publicity for its problems." The result, says Fabian, was a "feeling that we should get back to basics."

Morgantown's system, which links parts of the University of West Virginia campus with each other and the town, was dedicated in 1972 but not opened to passengers until 1975. Rebuilt and expanded in 1978, it now carries 22,000 passengers a day over a 3.3-mile route, at a per-passenger cost of about 80 cents. Reliability, as low as 47 percent before rebuilding, is now around 98 percent.

AGT development was also slowed by indecision in the Urban Mass Transportation Administration. UMTA spent a lot of money on AGT research in the 1970s, but Morgantown was the only system built. A downtown people mover program in the late 1970s attracted applications from 76 cities, but only Miami and Detroit ever reached the construction stage.

Meanwhile, almost unnoticed, small-scale people movers began to sprout in more localized settings such as airports, zoos, and mixed-use developments. Nearly 30 such systems are in service in the U.S. today. Most of them are simple horizontal elevator-type systems marketed by elevator vendors like Westinghouse or Otis.

However, AGT did begin to prove itself abroad. Kobe's system opened in 1981, although at first it carried crews. The most convincing example was Lille's 8.5-mile VAL system, whose first line

opened in 1983. The system carries nearly 100,000 riders per day, nearly 50 percent more than forecast. By 1986, the system was even turning a profit, with a 40 cent fare bringing in around 15 percent more than operating and maintenance expenses. A second line is now under construction, and a third is planned. Toulouse, Strasbourg, and Bordeaux have plans for similar systems.

Matra, the French company that developed VAL, is now trying to interest U.S. cities in automated transit. Last year, the company won a contract to build a line at Chicago's O'Hare International Airport, and Jacksonville, Florida, will soon begin construction of a VAL downtown people mover.

Vancouver's SkyTrain also has been an impressive success. The elevated guideways went up rapidly, with only minor disruptions of traffic. The system's small cars allow sharp curves, reducing the need for extensive property condemnation. In the downtown area, inbound and outbound tracks are stacked in a disused freight railroad tunnel. During Expo 86, the system carried more than 20 million passengers, reportedly with but a single hour of computer downtime. Part of the line hosted a special shuttle operation to a remote pavilion, with headways of less than 90 seconds.

Hawaii wants one, too

The success of the Vancouver and Lille systems has caught the eye of transit planners in Honolulu, where a traditional heavy rail system called HART was planned in 1979 but cancelled in 1981. That setback was "fortunate, in some ways," says University of Hawaii at Manoa professor Karl Kim, because in the meantime AGT technology has matured enough to merit serious consideration. Kim and Michael Schabas of the city-county transportation department recently prepared an "alternatives analysis update" that says AGT offers "dramatic improvements in service with substantial cost savings."

For example, instead of HART's 400-foot-long trains at four- to 20-minute intervals, an AGT system could carry the same number of riders in 160-foot trains at 90-second intervals. The smaller, lightweight trains mean smaller stations and guideways, says Kim, with far lower land acquisition costs than for a traditional system. The report estimates the cost of an AGT system at about $50 million per mile, compared to $100 million per mile for the HART proposal.

The report also notes that AGT's high frequency and cheaper stations make possible branch line service "to the doorstep" of major destinations, and separate stations in various downtown areas where HART could only afford one.

Hemmed in by mountains and sea, Honolulu is unusually well suited for rail transit. Moreover, roads are nearing capacity—with no room for expansion—and bus usage is high. A 1984 study by the Oahu Metropolitan Planning Organization confirmed that only grade-separated transit could have a measurable impact on traffic congestion.

Is it worth it?

But AGT might be less appropriate for other cities, says Boris Pushkarev, author of a 1982 book, *Urban Rail in America.* "AGT still requires very heavy capital investment because it has to be entirely grade-separated," he says. "Light rail, which can run in the street, requires maybe one-quarter or one-fifth the investment."

Pushkarev concedes that automation changes the cost-benefit calculations in two important ways: "It lowers the threshold at which transit becomes feasible, and it lowers the cost of increasing service frequency. Before, you had to assemble a trainload of people to justify the cost of one or two people to operate that train. But with automation, the marginal cost is zero, so you can increase service frequency and increase the attractiveness of transit. It makes rail more competitive with buses."

The Honolulu report found an average operating cost for what it calls "state of the art" rapid transit systems of eight cents per passenger mile, compared to 20 cents for older rail systems and 28 cents for bus systems. The biggest difference, of course, is labor costs. The Lille system, for example, has a staff of 160 for maintenance and other operating requirements; adding operators to the trains would require another 120 people. Some of those savings also result from barrier-free, self-service fare collection, well known in Europe but only beginning to be proven in North America.

Still, the Honolulu report says a new system "could well generate an operating surplus, possibly even paying a part of capital costs." Kim says the city is even considering "a franchise, as existed at the turn of the century" to build and operate the system, hoping in this way to avoid the cost overruns and delays that have plagued other rail transit projects.

Troubles galore

AGT has certainly not been immune from those. Detroit's downtown people mover has been a public relations debacle. Costs have soared from $137 million to more than $200 million, opening day has been pushed back from January 1986 to this August, and ridership projections have dropped from 70,000 to 20,000, with some UMTA pessimists saying 10,000 is more like it. However, Fabian and others are quick to point out that Detroit's problems are not related to the technology, which is the same as that used in Vancouver.

Miami's Metromover also has had cost overruns, and ridership has been lower than projections. That's mostly because the Metromover is the downtown distributor for Miami's heavy rail system, on which ridership has been far below expectations. But Metromover has had very few problems and little downtime in its first 16 months, according to Bob Good, program manager for Westinghouse, which built the system.

Westinghouse recently won a contract to build (and operate for five years) a similar system using smaller vehicles in the "urban center" of Las Colinas, a large suburban Dallas development. Guideways were constructed as office buildings were built, and the 1.25-mile first phase is to be in operation by October 1989.

The sweeping guideways in Las Colinas contrast sharply with the Spanish bell towers, one containing a station, through which they run. Miami's system is also accessible from some downtown buildings, but aesthetic reviews are mixed. Pushkarev characterizes the structure as "really not an aesthetic addition," and says his 1982 book's call for a lighter, less obtrusive guideway is still valid.

The other frequent objection to elevated structures is noise. That doesn't arise for rubber-tired systems such as Westinghouse's or VAL, which can also climb steeper grades, but switches and crossovers are more difficult to design. Vancouver thought steerable trucks and precision wheel grinding would make a steel-wheel system acceptable, but noise levels have been higher than expected, prompting citizen complaints.

Safety, which could be expected to be an issue, in fact, doesn't seem to be one. Westinghouse's Good says there has been "very little or no concern from the general public" in Miami. Acceptance of automation in France has been so good that existing transit systems such as Paris's are now retrofitting some operations for automated operation.

Before committing itself to automation, Vancouver's BC Transit studied 11 systems with computer-driven trains and found few problems. Uniformed attendants rove through the BC Transit trains to handle technical malfunctions, security, and fare enforcement. A similar policy will be followed on London's new Docklands Light Railway, which suffered embarrassment when a test train overshot the end of the track in March. No one was injured.

With so many systems carrying passengers, safety concerns recede every day. "Airport people don't even blink an eye," says Tom McKean, a transportation consultant in Annandale, Virginia. "They use automated transit just like an elevator. They don't even think twice about it." Fabian was amused to recently catch a colleague referring to "conventional people movers," until recently a contradiction in terms. As the technology proves its worth, he says, ideas such as personalized routing of vehicles and bypassing off-line stations—much touted by earlier AGT promoters—are again being discussed.

"Vancouver, Miami, and [Lille's] VAL have really convinced people that this is not a toy," says McKean. "It can really do a job."

Dennis McClendon is the managing editor of Planning.

Speed Sells

F. K. Plous, Jr.
(July 1987)

When Japan National Railways opened its 320-mile Shin Kan Sen (New Trunk Line) between Tokyo and Osaka in 1964, overseas observers quickly concluded that high-speed passenger trains were technologically feasible. Shin Kan Sen trains ran right—fast, frequently, reliably, and comfortably.

Moving at sustained—rather than mere top—speeds of 125 miles an hour on a totally grade-separated right-of-way barred to slower freight and commuter trains, Shin Kan Sen was an immediate hit with the traveling public. On opening day,

air traffic between Japan's capital and its second-largest city dropped 40 percent, a blessing in a tiny mountainous nation.

In the ensuing 23 years, Shin Kan Sen has proved that high-speed rail can be profitable, too. Despite heavy capital costs for its all new right-of-way ($640 million for the original 320 miles), Shin Kan Sen is the only component of the Japanese system to make money. In 1980, the total system—by then up to 640 miles—produced a net income of $1.3 billion.

A similar record has been established since 1984 when the French National Railways (SNCF) opened its own new line between Paris and Lyons, featuring electrified TGVs (*trains a grande vitesse*, or high-speed trains) cruising at 168 mph. Now being expanded to western France (TGV Atlantique) and into neighboring Belgium, the Netherlands, and Germany, TGV is France's acknowledged intercity people mover *par excellence.*

Like the Germans, now bringing their own high-speed Inter-City Express (ICE) trains on line, the French consider high-speed rail the only real transportation option for densely populated urban regions. They note that the fast trains bring quantum increases in passenger capacity while consuming relatively modest amounts of land, fuel, and labor. Two tracks occupying a strip about 50 feet wide can carry more passengers per hour than a six-lane expressway—and without the road's noise and air pollution.

Not surprisingly, high-speed rail has caught the attention of decision makers in the U.S. "More and more Americans have ridden fast trains in other countries," says Pennsylvania State Rep. Richard H. Geist (D-Altoona), "and they're saying, 'Why not here?'"

Geist is chairman of both the Pennsylvania High Speed Intercity Passenger Commission and the Washington-based High Speed Rail Association. HSRA, a North American alliance of vendors, planners, consultants, civil engineering firms, and real estate interests, promotes high-speed rail as the solution not only to logistical problems, but to allied questions of economic development, land use, and environmental quality as well.

Despite such enthusiasm, high-speed rail faces an uphill climb in North America. Funding is the most conspicuous problem. Although cheaper on a passenger-mile basis than interstate highways and airways, the infrastructure required for true high-speed rail service costs billions. It includes elevated or depressed rights-of-way, bridges, tunnels, stations, yards, sound-proofing structures, overhead electric structures, and computer-controlled signaling. Raising funds for such projects can be daunting in a nation that cannot yet distinguish high-tech railroading from the relic it replaces.

Faced with the frustrations inevitable in creating expensive new systems, some passenger rail advocates call for an incremental approach. Instead of a 21-jewel, high-tech railroad in some distant future, they argue, why not spend more modest amounts to upgrade existing rail lines for 90-, 100-, or 110-mile-an-hour service?

High-speed rail advocates reply that such thinking masks a failure to understand the preferences of today's spoiled travelers. To win the volume of passengers necessary for financial success, rail systems must beat the auto and jet airliner decisively, not just incrementally. Ridership studies show that a speed advantage of 10, 20, or 25 percent is not enough to lure the masses. Trains must move at least twice as fast as cars in order to convert substantial numbers of intercity motorists to train travel. The 125 mph top speed of the original Shin Kan Sen is now considered the bare minimum required for heavy passenger recruitment. The TGV's cruising speed of 168 mph is more like it.

Such speeds also make high-speed rail competitive with the airliner over distances of less than 400 miles. Chicago to Detroit (279 miles) is nominally a one-hour flight, but ground travel can easily eat up another hour at each end, with airport congestion adding still another. A high-speed rail trip of three hours (including stops) is truly a draw.

But to attract large numbers of passengers, trains need not only speed but frequency—at least 10 to 12 departures a day in most corridors. And at that density, fast passenger trains cannot safely mingle with the long, slow, heavy coal and grain trains now favored by U.S. railroads. Amtrak's second-busiest corridor, Los Angeles-San Diego, is considered to be at capacity with seven trains a day in each direction. California authorities would like more trains, but the single-track line's owner, Santa Fe Railway, says congestion already is interfering with the movement of freight.

At this time, a true, high-speed rail format (125 mph minimum) does not exist in the U.S. Trains exceed 90 mph only on approximately 16 miles of specially rebuilt track between Albany and Schenectady, and in the busy Northeast Corridor, rebuilt by Amtrak at a cost of $2.1 billion but able to handle trains at 125 mph only over designated stretches of straight track.

Moreover, part of the price Amtrak paid for its fancy railroad was an obligation to host slower freight trains between Washington and New York. Last January 4 at Chase, Maryland, 16 people were killed when an Amtrak Metroliner moving at 119 mph struck a Conrail freight locomotive that had violated a stop signal. The collision prompted renewed reminders that high-speed trains require dedicated (i.e., freight-free) rights-of-way for safe operation.

Who pays?

Complicating the questions of funding and format is a related political and logistical issue posed by no other form of transport: Because high-speed rail occupies a peculiar niche—distances of less than about 400 miles—it does not lend itself to the creation of a national system eligible for the same federal funding that builds highways and airports.

Instead, discrete interurban corridors—often in one state—are the rule. A "Texas Triangle" linking Dallas-Fort Worth, Houston, and Austin-San Antonio is one such scheme. So are Ohio's "Three-C Corridor" (Cleveland-Columbus-Cincinnati); Pennsylvania's projected Philadelphia-Pittsburgh route; and Florida's Miami-Tampa-Orlando system.

Even if planners succeed in linking their systems across state lines, as Ohio and Pennsylvania would like to do with a Cleveland-Youngstown-Pittsburgh segment, the scope of their efforts is at best regional. Nobody is counting on federal assistance, and after gaining eight years' experience at the state and regional level, high-speed rail planners are becoming convinced they can—and should—finance such systems closer to home, using private-sector money.

What's missing is the mechanism—and the answers to questions such as these:

• Who should own the right-of-way? State government (or a multistate authority where routes cross state lines)? A private corporation chartered by the state?

• Who should own and operate the trains? A state or multistate authority? A designated private-sector operator? Competing operators like the privately owned airlines that compete in government-owned airways?

- How should the service be priced? Can farebox revenue alone repay both capital costs and operating expenses and produce a profit? Or should the financing be designed to tap the larger revenue stream that flows from successful transportation projects—leasing or sale of air rights over tracks, participation in real estate developments around stations, fiber optic telecommunications lines buried in the right-of-way, concessions to purveyors of station services? . . .

Role models

Although 13 states have taken some sort of step toward the planning of a high-speed rail operation, only four projects—three intrastate and one bi-state—can be considered to have gone beyond the exploratory stage.

- Pennsylvania appears to have compiled the most rigorous and accurate ridership projections so far, a 75-page study by Gannett Fleming Transportation Engineers of Harrisburg, in collaboration with New York-based Parsons Brinckerhoff. The study, issued last July, embodies the criteria that emerged two months later in the High Speed Association guidelines. It says a high-speed route roughly paralleling the old Pennsylvania Railroad main line between Philadelphia and Pittsburgh should cut ground-travel time to three hours from the current seven. Intermediate points, such as Harrisburg, Altoona, and Johnstown, expensive to serve by trunk airline and tiresome to reach by auto, could be directly linked to the state's two largest cities, as could Pennsylvania State University at State College. Projected ridership by the year 2000: between 5.5 and 8.8 million.

- Ohio's original agency has been succeeded by the Ohio High Speed Rail Authority. It scaled back its route map to a 249-mile spine connecting Cleveland, Columbus, and Cincinnati and designed a novel funding plan signed by Gov. Richard Celeste last November. The authority can issue $2 billion in tax-exempt bonds, put the funds into escrow, and use the estimated $100 million in proceeds to finance market and engineering studies. The sponsor of the program, state senator Robert J. Boggs, has become chairman of the authority. Ohio says it will use either French TGV or German ICE technology, with cruising speeds of about 170 m.p.h.

- Florida wants to use fast trains to direct growth away from overpopulated coastal areas and into younger inland settlements. The state's chairman of the High Speed Rail Transportation Commission, David Blumberg, is a real estate developer, and the commission's financing strategy is an adaptation of methods used by nineteenth-century rail barons to open the West.

The state will acquire cheap land along the right-of-way and resell it to developers, who stand to benefit from the new rail service. Presumably, the state could even take an equity position in some of the projects expected to spring up around station sites. Last year, consultants Barton-Aschman Associates issued a report comparing three types of high-speed rail technologies. This March, the Florida Department of Transportation agreed to spend $250 million to $275 million to acquire its first stretch of right-of-way—a 76-mile portion of the CSX Transportation line from Homestead to West Palm Beach. The initial system, planned to open in 1995, would swing west from West Palm Beach to serve Orlando and Tampa-St. Petersburg.

- Los Angeles-Las Vegas promises the first project aimed almost exclusively at tourist travel. This 230-mile line is expected to cost between $2.2 billion and $2.5 billion, but a Phase II study headed by Barton-Aschman claimed it would earn a 20 percent return on investment, carrying 40 percent of all travelers between Southern California and Las Vegas and inducing about 28 percent in new travel. The median strip of Interstate 15 is envisioned as the basic right-of-way, with the western terminus at Ontario, 40 miles from downtown Los Angeles. Proposed financing methods include tax-free industrial revenue bonds and zero-coupon bonds.

The major obstacle now, the High Speed Rail Association report concludes, is "to find a private-sector franchisee who will have the financial capability to secure construction loans of approximately $3 billion over an eight-year time frame."

That's a big order. But Americans have spent big before when they wanted a better way to travel, and Pennsylvania representative Rick Geist thinks they're about ready to do it again. As he told a National Public Radio interviewer at the High Speed Rail Association's Fourth Annual Conference in Las Vegas in May: "Americans like speed, Americans like high technology, and Americans like comfort. High-speed rail has all three."

F. K. Plous, Jr., is a Chicago writer specializing in transportation, urban affairs, and real estate development.

Living the Good Life Near Transit Stations

C. William Brubaker
(April 1980)

Urban sprawl continued unabated through the decade of the 1970s despite recurring gasoline shortages that warned us to change our twentieth-century habits of low-density development; separation of homes from workplaces, shopping, and community facilities; and over-dependence on the automobile.

However, I believe we will change our habits. I believe that our older, more compact, and more accessible cities and towns will become more attractive places to live and work. They were the first places to be settled, and they are at the best locations. . . .

I believe we will take a fresh look at our older cities and towns and recognize some under-utilized resources. And I believe we will find that the good life doesn't depend on the consumption of vast quantities of oil. . . . Public transportation systems everywhere will be improved. People will demand it. As people change their life-styles and learn how to commute by train and bus, many will want to live within walking distance of rapid transit or commuter railroad stations. The logical response to this new need will be redevelopment of areas near existing stations.

Areas around rapid transit and commuter railroad stations are ripe for new development. Frequently, only low-density and obsolete buildings characterize station areas. I see a growing demand for townhouses and apartments, commercial and industrial buildings, and all kinds of community facilities near public transportation stations.

People who still depend on their automobiles to get to work, shopping, school, and recreation are going to be looking for alternative means of transportation. The alternatives will include walking and bicycling (still effective people movers), buses, and rail transit. As we have learned in recent decades, none of these alternatives works very well where density is low. However, they all work well in the older, more compact cities.

Soon, the hottest real estate in America will be within a half-mile of rapid transit and commuter rail stations. We can expect a revolution in real estate, planning, and architecture in response to this new awareness. We can expect revitalization of the blocks served by rapid transit.

I think that some of the redevelopment will be conventional, with vacant, long bypassed land and land cleared of obsolete buildings being used for townhouses, workplaces, commercial buildings, and community facilities. But immediately around stations, such zoned land use seems inappropriate. Instead, the mixed-use development concept offers maximum convenience and accessibility, creating a high-intensity node serving a broader, low-intensity area.

The mixed-use development either can bridge over or tunnel under the station and high-speed transit line, providing direct access from both directions. Apartment towers, hotels, and offices can rise above a multilevel base that integrates shops, restaurants, light industry, services, and community facilities along the main pedestrian ways. The new complex can include some existing structures, with a soft edge of townhouses that relate well to surrounding, lower density residential areas.

A good example of just such a mixed-use development is Sheppard Centre in suburban Toronto, which combines offices, apartments, townhouses, and stores near a transit station. Here, development occurred simultaneously with a new transit station, but this type of arrangement is also appropriate around existing stations.

Not everyone will want to live above a transit station. But some people will. With children in school, I wouldn't want to live there. But with the nest empty, I would happily sell the now-too-large house a half-mile away and move to the new center.

With stores an elevator ride away, with recreation only a bicycle ride away, and with the central business district only a fast train ride away, the good life will be possible without an automobile. Americans will discover that they are not quite as dependent on gasoline as they thought they were.

C. William Brubaker is president of the Chicago architecture firm, Perkins & Will.

7

Economic Development

Up through the early 1970s, the U.S. economy expanded at a quick pace, with real per capita personal disposable income rising from $2,700 in 1960 to $4,100 in 1973. While the tax-paying public in most parts of the country enjoyed a rising standard of living, there were relatively few complaints about taxes imposed to pay for federal programs to help the cities, aid the poor, and preserve the natural environment.

The national economy reversed course when the Vietnam War ended and the OPEC cartel was formed. Real income growth slowed, petroleum prices tripled, and, in the early 1980s, we entered the most serious recession since the Great Depression. The loss in income and jobs was particularly painful in those midwestern and northeastern industrialized states that had received a disproportionate share of defense expenditures and were already showing signs of losing investment to the South and West. These so-called Rust Belt states were further hurt by their concentration of employment in industries dependent on oil.

These changes in the national economy brought about dramatic changes in the political climate. Feeling the impact of a declining standard of living, taxpayers became sensitive to the share of federal, state, and local funds being spent on urban welfare and social programs. Urban renewal, Model Cities, and low-income housing programs came under attack, not completely unfairly, as ineffective and wasteful. Social programs and environmental regulations that had been acceptable when the public felt prosperous were viewed as luxuries when real income began to fall. In 1976, President Jimmy Carter made the first round of cuts in social programs. Further cuts, and the emasculation of environmental regulations, were carried out under President Ronald Reagan, and predictions are that austerity will continue under the Bush presidency.

Increasingly, responsibility for social programs was shifted to state and local governments, but such programs also lost support there, and for the same reasons. Studies of the tax limitation movement in the late 1970s indicated that residents wanted social programs cut at the local level as well as the federal level. Faced with a declining income, taxpayers were simply unwilling to allocate substantial tax dollars to help the poor.

Although the federal government adopted measures to help the national economy get moving again, local governments also took initiatives to stimulate job growth and enhance local tax revenues. Acceptance of this enhanced local government function came so quickly that it is easy to overlook the fact that 15 years ago, few planners thought of economic development as one of their major responsibilities.

Southern states had, in fact, used tax concessions, industrial revenue bonds, and advertising to attract industry since the 1930s, but at the local level, economic development had largely been the job of chambers of commerce. Further, until the mid-1970s, most economic development efforts had been limited to declining central cities and lagging rural communities. These early efforts had emphasized the provision of housing and jobs for the poor—although in many cases, the poor did not benefit as planned. The mid-1970s saw the expansion of local government economic development efforts to even the most prosperous states and communities.

The planning profession proved to be highly adaptable in shifting focus from more traditional fields of planning to economic development. Planners stepped into the newly created departments of economic development as directors, industrial recruiters, and researchers. (See "Setting Up Shop for Economic Development.") A 1984 survey of planners by the American Planning Association found that 13 percent considered economic devel-

Some waterfronts are going upscale, but in Portland, Maine, a recent zoning provision aims at protecting traditional maritime activities. See ''SOS for the Working Waterfront.'' Photo: The Waterfront Center.

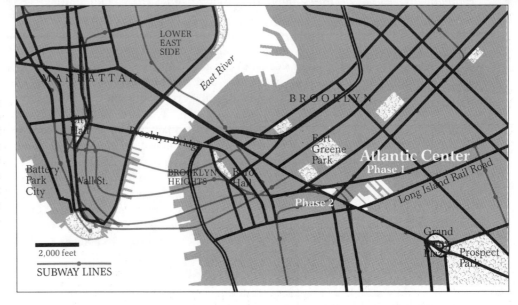

New York's development review process was meant to give citizens a voice in land use decisions. That's what happened to two mixed-use projects in downtown Brooklyn. See ''A Project Grows in Brooklyn.'' Map: Dennis McClendon.

Thirty years after its push to industrialize, Puerto Rico continues to battle high unemployment. Farming and manufacturing are staples, but so is the informal economy (left). See ''Beyond Operation Bootstrap.'' Photo: Philip Langdon; map: Dennis McClendon.

Lots of cities see a new ballpark as their ticket to world-class status, but the parks tend to overpower their neighborhoods. A Chicago architect's scheme (above) for fitting a new baseball park into a city site. See ''Stadiums: The Right Game Plan?'' Drawing: Philip Bess.

Los Colinas is one of a spate of ''new downtowns'' popping up across the country. See ''Office in the Dell.'' Photo: Dennis McClendon.

opment to be their major occupational responsibility. Only three other planning functions captured such large percentages: land use and regulation (30 percent); comprehensive planning (19 percent); and environmental planning (15 percent). More respondents were economic development planners than, for example, were transportation planners (12.5 percent). Planning schools also adapted by adding faculty and courses on regional and urban economic development.

CATCHING UP

The typical local economic development program includes a standard package of incentives, with periodic and often indiscriminate additions responding to the latest fad. Examples of the standard development tools are tax abatements, industrial revenue bonds, and industrial parks—and their use is reflected in the *Planning* articles included here. See, for example, "The Biggest Industrial Park of All," "Doing Deals," and "Beyond Operation Bootstrap."

Many traditional land-use planners and social planners who made the switch to economic development planning were faced with the need to acquire skills in both economics and finance. Planners had to learn, as indicated in articles like "How Planners Can Get Support from the Business Community," that companies were not going to invest or remain in distressed locations or hire disadvantaged workers unless government could make it worthwhile to do so. "Beware the Pitfalls of Fiscal Impact Analysis" offers another example of a basic economics lesson for development planners. This article lays out the use, advantages, and problems of the average and marginal cost methods of evaluating the expansion of public services. And Alan Rabinowitz, in "The Mysterious World of Finance," explains how private companies view long-term investments and describes the workings of the municipal bond market.

LOCAL STRATEGIES

One widely adopted local development strategy is the construction of stadiums and convention centers and the hosting of world's fairs. Often, the decisions are skewed because politics dominate the final decisions or because cost-benefit assessments fail to include community pride as a quantifiable benefit. Nevertheless, many medium-sized and small cities have embraced this approach to development even after economic analysis indicates there is insufficient demand to fill these facilities in all but the largest U.S. cities. "Convention Centers: Too Much of a Good Thing," "After the Fair," and "Stadiums: The Right Game Plan?" outline the few successes and many failures, in terms of short-term costs and benefits, of these ambitious economic development strategies.

In contrast, the public provision of industrial parks is a basic development strategy that has paid off in terms of job creation and increased tax revenues, if done in the correct context. But it was only after watching numerous expensive industrial parks sit idle that many development officials came to realize land and services are only two of the many factors that entice a business to an area; in the average manufacturer's location decision, these factors rank lower than wage rates, the quality of the labor supply, and the availability of raw materials. "The Biggest Industrial Park of All" outlines the planning of and expectations for an industrial park in New Orleans. And the widespread use of the media, particularly television and magazine advertising to lure tourists and business, is noted in "Bringing Madison Avenue to Main Street."

In all the competition, development agencies have come to realize that there are few large plant branches circling the U.S. looking for a place to land. Estimates are that only about eight large firms undertake open searches for new branch locations in a single year. Many development officials, therefore, have turned their attention toward retaining the jobs they already have and by encouraging home grown enterprises. The emphasis on encouraging local entrepreneurs gained credibility in the early 1980s, when widely touted research claimed that most new jobs in the U.S. economy are created by small businesses. The idea caught the imagination of development officials across the country despite the fact that later research found that small businesses (usually defined as those with less than 100 employees) account for only 36 percent of all jobs in the national economy and create roughly the same number of new jobs.

Strategies to encourage small businesses have been widely adopted. Business incubators, for example, provide low-cost overhead for fledging enterprises, and although they have not proved to be the panacea promised by early enthusiasts, in the correct location the incubators have helped small, locally owned firms get a foothold in the economy. And while small businesses have higher rates of failure, once established, they appear to provide a stable, long-term employment base. "Hatching Small Businesses" illustrates how incubator programs work in several communities.

The attraction and generation of high-technology firms has also generated enthusiasm among development officials and continues to shape both state and local economic development strategies in the 1980s. Communities everywhere came to believe that high-technology firms were the solution to local economic problems because these firms are supposedly "footloose," attract the most desirable workers, are environmentally clean, and provide good prospects for employment growth. Strategies for attracting these firms have been adopted indiscriminately, however, and the reality has not matched the promise.

It turns out that, far from being footloose, high-technology firms seek out locations where related businesses are situated, labor is highly skilled, public schools are good, and amenities abound. Communities are discovering that the footloose operations in the high-technology sector are the more routine assembly plants and that, like other low-skilled manufacturing plants, they offer low-wage assemblyline jobs with little opportunity for advancement. Moreover, high-tech firms are not necessarily environmentally clean. "Silicon Strips" reports that 20 percent of the hazardous waste produced in Massachusetts comes from high-tech firms; the article illustrates the environmental deterioration and traffic congestion that have accompanied the high-tech corridors in California's Silicon Valley, Route 128 outside of Boston, and numerous other areas, including Portland, Oregon; Austin, Texas; and suburban Washington, D.C.

RETHINKING STRATEGY

In the late 1970s and early 1980s, many communities, particularly those experiencing economic decline, overspent, missspent, and sacrificed environmental quality and social equity to attract new firms. The interjurisdictional competition for jobs was so intense that communities were afraid to ask much of industry for fear that industry would take its jobs and tax revenue elsewhere. Communities were willing to provide generous tax abatements, pay for infrastructure, float industrial revenue bonds, and reduce environmental and land-use regulations, even when there was little empirical evidence that these incentives influence locational decisions and when analysts determined that the community could not expect to recoup its investment for a very long time.

The situation is different today, as citizens have come to realize that economic growth is not without cost. "Office in the Dell" describes suburban citizens' anger over traffic congestion. And "SOS for the Working Waterfront" questions the displacement that occurs when small-scale marine activities are squeezed out of traditional dockyard areas in cities like Portland, Maine. More examples: Bellevue, Washington, which instituted strict design controls on new development, and Bethesda, Maryland, where local planners extracted a range of design and public amenities from private developers interested in building atop the new metro stop ("Bethesda Stages a Beauty Contest for Developers"). And in California, writes William Fulton in "Doing Deals," developer exactions include not only the provision of curbs, water and sewer lines, and street lighting, but child care, affordable housing, and job training.

This trend away from automatic giveaways requires a new set of skills. Economic development planners must learn how to drive a hard bargain with developers, which in turn requires an understanding of real estate finance and negotiation techniques.

One innovation that is blurring the line between the traditional planning role and economic development is the growth in public-private partnerships. Some local governments are becoming more active participants in the development process by tying zoning approvals to market assessments, by taking an equity share in development deals, by leasing government property to private interests, or by taking outright ownership. "The Profit Motive" offers innovative examples of city involvement in real estate deals in California, Virginia, and Illinois. The advantage of these partnerships is that government does not make investments until there is a proven developer for the site or market for the product. Industrial parks and urban renewal are two examples of development strategies that went astray because private firms did not invest even after government had spent large sums on the assumption that they would. One danger of public-private partnerships is the potential for conflict of interest. Where the city is part owner of the project, design and long-term comprehensive planning standards may be compromised to maximize profits.

These partnerships are not limited to government, however. "Off the Barricades Into the Boardroom" describes how community development corporations work with banks and developers to build low-income housing and revitalize distressed neighborhoods.

Planners are ending the decade of the 1980s as savvy players in the economic development field. Except in the most distressed communities, local governments are less willing to sacrifice environmental quality, social equity, and good planning for jobs and tax revenue. Communities increasingly are linking zoning and development permits to developer commitments for low- or moderately priced housing, construction jobs for local residents and minorities, improvements in project design, and other concessions. "A Project Grows in Brooklyn" describes the approval process in two mixed-use development projects. Both show how citizens and the local government have negotiated a range of concessions from developers to help low-income residents.

After more than a decade of incentives, state and local governments are realizing that economic development is a long-term venture. Educating politicians to consider the eventual consequences of development decisions is one of the most important roles planners can play. Investments in education, the natural environment, sound land use, and attractive urban design will yield higher payoffs in economic growth in the long run than will the automatic granting of tax abatements, low-interest loans, and concessions in environmental and planning regulations. In fact, communities that fail to tax their businesses and reinvest in worker skills may be abandoned for cheaper labor elsewhere ("Beyond Operation Bootstrap"). Areas that permit the deterioration of their physical infrastructure and natural and social environments may find that such strategies backfire as businesses and higher income residents relocate to cleaner, more attractive places.

Marie Howland
Associate Professor, Institute for Urban Studies
University of Maryland

Pamela Wev
Former Director of Economic Development
Loudoun County, Virginia

Setting Up Shop for Economic Development

Ruth Eckdish Knack
(October 1983)

Deciding what form an economic development organization should take—a hot issue right now—is a relatively new problem. Economic development used to be primarily the province of the local chamber of commerce, perhaps with some facts and figures supplied by a small economic development office within the municipal planning office. In the late 1950s, federally funded urban renewal offices took the lead in organizing development projects, which, throughout the next two decades, were almost exclusively real estate projects.

The connection between development and jobs strengthened some during the Model Cities era of the late 1960s, but the work of retaining and attracting the big industrial job producers was more often a state than a local responsibility. In the mid-1960s, the advent of the U.S. Economic Development Administration spurred the creation of economic development committees, and the Community Services Administration began to fund neighborhood development corporations. Other nonprofit corporations were formed to take advantage of Small Business Administration programs. Downtown business interests formed their own development corporations.

Philadelphia may have been the first city to establish a nonprofit corporation concerned with the economic development of the entire city, and a lot of places are looking to it as a model now. Today, some 50 citywide economic development corporations are listed in the directory published by the National Council on Urban Economic Development. Some of these groups evolved from Model Cities agencies. The Dayton City-Wide Development Corporation is an example. Others are creations of a local chamber of commerce or, like the Philadelphia Industrial Development Corporation, of the chamber and the city government. Some concentrate on financing and land development for industry, as PIDC did in the beginning. Later, it broadened its focus to include financial assistance for commercial enterprises—an emphasis of many of the newer corporations as well.

Some of the corporations have an extremely close relationship with the city government (the Baltimore Economic Development Commission, BEDCO, for one). Others are governed by boards completely composed of private sector representatives. A mixture may be more typical. For example, a new economic development commission in the small city of Aurora, Illinois, is sponsored equally by the city and the chamber of commerce. The salary of the single staff member is shared by both, with office space provided by the chamber. The nine-member board is appointed by the mayor, four from a list provided by the chamber of commerce, and five from a list drawn up by the city.

Although all the quasi-public corporations pride themselves on their no-strings approach to development, evidently this stance is not enough to allay private-sector frustration entirely. Recently, some 25 big corporations in Philadelphia each agreed to chip in $50,000 a year to support a new, completely private, economic development corporation, the Greater Philadelphia First Corporation. According to a planner in the Delaware Valley Regional Planning Commission, the new group grew out of the dissatisfaction of those who felt that economic development groups in the metropolitan area were working at cross purposes and that private contributions were not being invested according to a clearly defined strategic plan. The new corporation, which is directed by Ralph Widner, will fund specific projects in response to proposals by civic organizations and quasi-public agencies. Its board includes a representative of PIDC.

Staying put

At the opposite end of the spectrum from the private groups are those economic development departments that determine to remain an integral part of city government. The model in this case is Portland, Oregon, which in 1973 merged five bureaus and commissions into one umbrella agency, the Office of Planning and Development (which has since been disbanded). Other examples are St. Louis, which recently reorganized its planning department to include economic development, and Oakland, California, which in 1979, merged its

community development and employment and training offices into a super-agency—the Office of Economic Development and Employment.

In the view of Alan Gregerman, research director of the National Council for Urban Economic Development (CUED) in Washington, both options—the strengthened city department and the quasi-public corporation—have their own strengths and limitations. "The form that works best in a particular city," he suggests, "is a function of many factors, including community size, economic circumstances, local development objectives, and the level of commitment of the public and private sectors to economic improvement." In big cities," he adds, "it's reasonable to have a number of different economic development organizations—as long as they communicate and complement each other."

Gregerman believes the public approach works well in cities where the local government has given a high priority to economic development and the private sector is already actively involved—as it is in St. Paul. In contrast, he says, a quasi-public corporation may be more effective in communities where economic development is only one of many priorities competing for scarce public dollars, or where the private sector is uneasy about working directly with local government. (To put it more frankly, in a city where clout rules, a corporation, which can often bypass the city council, may get more done.)

Increasingly, Gregerman notes, communities are choosing the quasi-public route. He sees no reason to change, however, if an effective economic development department is already in place. In short, if it isn't broken, don't fix it.

The organizational issue came to a head this fall in Chicago, where a business-sector advisory group, Chicago United, pointing to Philadelphia as a model, was pushing for the creation of a strong, new quasi-public entity. However, Robert Mier, who was recently appointed economic development commissioner by new mayor Harold Washington, has expressed opposition to the idea of putting too much power in the hands of a private body. Mier, a planner, was the director of the Center for Urban Economic Development at the University of Illinois at Chicago. His confirmation by the city council, it should be noted, is by no means a sure thing in the city's politically turbulent atmosphere. Some business leaders have expressed fears that his interests are too slanted toward the neighborhoods, to the neglect of downtown.

"The major question," says Mier, "is the degree to which economic development gets privatized. The city must retain responsibility for policy making, and it must remain accountable for its use of public resources."

Mier does believe, however, that there is a place for an implementation organization "to take on things when the market fails." He has proposed, in fact, that the city create a new industrial development corporation—an idea that Mayor Washington made part of his platform. But Mier would make the new body responsible to the economic development commission rather than remaining independent, as Chicago United would prefer.

Rather than strengthening the private side, Mier wants to beef up the city's economic development planning—pulling development and employment training together in one agency along the lines of Oakland or San Antonio, both of which he often refers to as models. "In the past," he says, "economic development in American cities meant real estate development. I think we seduced ourselves into thinking that if we could solve the land problem, we could solve the economic development problem. What we ended up with is economic development in cities that were good at real estate development. What's needed now is to put jobs back at the center."

Ruth Knack is the senior editor of Planning.

How Planners Can Get Support from the Business Community

Kirk Hanson
(March 1977)

Many activists and urban planners exhibit a surprising ignorance of the reality of running a major corporation. In their attempts to persuade or embarrass business leaders into contributing more to the health of our cities, they often blunder badly.

For example, Episcopal Bishop Paul Moore of New York, in his 1976 Easter sermon, blamed the decline of New York on "immoral decisions on the part of political and economic leaders." And in a followup interview in *Planning,* he particularly criticized the many large corporations that in recent years have moved to Westchester County, New York, and to Greenwich and Stamford, Connecticut.

I have no quarrel with the notion that institutions as well as individuals have responsibilities to society, but I am most uncomfortable with blanket denunciations of corporations that either leave the city or fail to respond to a planner's or critic's notion of what business must do to help save the cities.

Unfamiliar with the pressures upon corporate executives, the process of corporate decision making, and often some aspects of basic economics, urban planners and activists sometimes conclude that such actions are necessarily insensitive and immoral. Unfortunately, this naivete often defeats the very purposes the critics espouse. The more unrealistic and uninformed the demands and criticisms against business, the easier it is for executives to ignore the charges.

I suppose some persons believe business somehow is less noble than other institutions, and so they neglect to develop an understanding of this dominant institution of American society. I would argue that such study is critical to success for anyone who would hope to influence corporate action. Planners must learn to speak the language of corporate executives and be able to spot critical considerations that can swing a corporate decision. And to be most effective, urban specialists also must know what they can reasonably expect and not expect from business organizations. . . .

For the past five years, I have consulted with several large urban-based corporations and for one year served on the staff of Chicago United, a coalition of 40 Chicago leaders, half of whom are chairmen or presidents of the city's largest corporations and the other half of whom are minority business and community leaders.

Working intimately with top corporate leaders, I came to a greater understanding of the corporate world view and of the institutional processes corporate leaders manage. I became increasingly frustrated with many urban officials and community leaders for their lack of understanding of these same phenomena.

Why don't business corporations contribute more to the city? The answer lies in the ideology and in the decision-making processes of business institutions. The way corporations make decisions differs little from that of most of our public bodies. All are complex, political, and sometimes irrational—and all are strongly influenced by the ideologies and the long-established routines ingrained in the culture of each organization. Consider these factors:

The business ideology. Business executives proclaim and appear to believe in a free enterprise system that no longer exists, if it ever did. While they operate in a mixed economy and would defend a number of incentives and regulatory arrangements with which they are most familiar, most executives nevertheless express an abstract belief in the complete separation of the functions of government and the private sector.

Corporate leaders contend that the sanctity of private property gives corporate managers the right to run their businesses without interference from urban officials, planners, or self-appointed activists. Confronting critics whose ideology often is as simplistic as it is hostile, executives take refuge in extreme free enterprise rhetoric.

There are, however, a few enlightened executives who realize that large business organizations are social as well as economic institutions. These individuals recognize that in a society as complex and interactive as ours, the functions of private and public sectors must overlap and complement one another. They also believe that only by the participation of business leaders and their institutions in the social and political life of the city can their viewpoints be appreciated and effective solutions to urban problems be found.

The corporate policy process. We all wonder at times at the apparent stupidity of American business. How could General Motors be so foolish as to have Ralph Nader shadowed by private investigators? How could Exxon have permitted a subsidiary manager to contribute millions illegally to Italian political parties? How could ITT have so blatantly offered $400,000 to the Republican party at the time it was lobbying the government concerning an antitrust suit?

The answer, most often, lies in the often irrational nature of the corporate policy process and not in a malevolent decision by an individual or a conspiratorial group. . . .

Too often, planners and activists think the corporation is a simple, hierarchical structure presided over by a president who can, by his order, mobilize all the resources of the firm to any end. In reality, corporate decision making is as slow and complex a process as public-sector decision making. The power wielded by top management in any organization with thousands of employees and many constituencies is greatly restricted. . . .

Performance measurement in the firm. Two characteristics of the modern corporate structure prevent a chief executive from ordering the immediate implementation of policies and programs. The typical large corporation produces many different types of products for different customers in different geographical locations. The top management cannot hope to have the expertise to direct and control such diverse businesses. Firms decentralize into product divisions run as semiautonomous "businesses" by executives who retain considerable freedom of action.

The second characteristic is the performance measurement system set up to evaluate and control these division executives. The standards set by top management in the parent company are predominantly and often exclusively quantitative, emphasizing the return on invested capital and the rate of sales growth. Such short-run, quantitative standards militate against the consideration of social and political concerns. Only at the top of the corporate structure can concerns other than numbers be freely integrated with economic considerations.

Most policies and programs, however, must be implemented in the divisions, where such flexibility does not exist. In deciding where to build a plant, for example, the division executive normally follows a standard procedure for assessing costs and quantitative outputs. This leaves little room for qualitative factors such as the impact on the community. Some firms now are experimenting with broader measures of performance, but these efforts are embryonic.

The overloaded executive agenda. Economic and social impacts, then, must be reconciled at the top corporate level. However, with the number of social and political concerns pressing upon business and demanding the attention of top management, the executive agenda has become badly overloaded. Most corporations are lagging badly in appointing sufficient staff to help top executives make these difficult decisions. Some management theorists are predicting that major corporations soon will have three senior executives where a single president performed well not so long ago.

The new executives will be a chairman solely to manage the affairs of the board of directors, a president to manage the operations of the corporate businesses, and a third executive of equal rank to handle all external relations and to translate sociopolitical concerns into effective corporate policy. Until this change occurs, there will be a critical shortage of executive time. Getting the attention of top management will be among the most difficult tasks facing urban officials.

Peer group orientation. Executives, like other individuals, are concerned about the norms of their peer group. When presented with an unusual decision, particularly regarding delicate social or policial issues, a major question will be, "What are other businesses and executives in the city doing?" This tendency is most institutionalized in corporate philanthropy. In most major cities, corporate contributions officials meet regularly to compare plans to support or decline various programs. In unfamiliar territory, executives tend to move as a group. . . .

What can be expected of business, then? The answers are specific to the individual firm. Its size, financial health, and other characteristics will determine to what degree it can incur the additional costs of locating or remaining in the city, participating in city-sponsored programs, and responding to other city needs. The largest companies have offices in several urban areas and must carefully divide their attention and resources. The smallest firms may not have the resources both to manage the business and participate in civic affairs.

There are several types of assistance urban officials and planners ought to expect from corporations. Among them are the following.

Partnership. Executives should be expected to work cooperatively and publicly with political and other urban leaders on major city problems, but the type of vehicle chosen for this partnership must be action oriented. Too many executives remember with horror and frustration the urban coalitions that disintegrated into debating societies.

Information. City officials badly need two kinds of information that business has access to. The first is data on economic and social conditions in the city. Banks and utilities can be most helpful in this regard. The second kind of information is prior notification to city officials of any corporate decision that will have substantial impact on the city.

Given sufficient notice of a firm's plans to leave the city, for example, it may be possible to work out an equitable package of incentives and assistance to enable the business to continue operations in the city. Other corporate plans may suggest city action to minimize social disruption or to capitalize on positive impacts. . . .

Public policy support. The future of the cities may depend most directly on success in gaining financial resources from state and federal governments and on efforts to expand local taxation and make politically difficult budget cuts. Business executives can be expected to aid appeals to Washington or the statehouse, as Detroit executives recently did, and to support unpopular but necessary budget measures.

Patterns of business life. The quality of working life within major corporations has a significant impact on the health of the city. Business patterns set the tone for many aspects of urban life. For example, businesses should end their support and patronage of discriminatory private clubs. That meetings of prominent officials discussing urban problems are held in restricted clubs is a particularly grotesque bit of humor.

Urban officials and activists must learn and speak the language of business. The business system can be made to work for the cities, not against them. We must understand how a proposal or issue affects a particular firm, how it would be implemented, and by whom. We must understand the power of peer group pressure and business's inordinate fear of adverse media attention. . . .

A dedicated urban official or activist can learn the unique attributes of each company's culture, gaining a tremendous advantage in persuading the firm to behave in ways most beneficial to the city. When it comes time for public criticism, the individual who understands the corporate policy process can most effectively phrase charges that pierce the corporate veil and make it more difficult for this and other firms to resist in the future.

Kirk Hanson, formerly a research associate at the Harvard Business School, served on the staff of Chicago United and was a consultant to several major corporations.

Beware the Pitfalls in Fiscal Impact Analysis

Richard B. Stern and Darwin G. Stuart
(April 1980)

More and more these days, local governments are confronted with development proposals that may require expansion of public services. At the same time, money for expansion is in short supply. The obvious solution is to determine the fiscal consequences of each development proposal. This is not to say that other criteria should be overlooked but that analysis of fiscal impact be a prerequisite for approval.

Planning agencies use fiscal impact analysis in four ways.

- As a growth management tool to evaluate areawide land-use alternatives. (Examples: Phoenix, San Diego, Tucson, San Antonio, and Minneapolis-St. Paul.)
- As an integral part of budget forecasting in central cities.
- As part of redevelopment programs in declining portions of central cities. (Here fiscal impact analysis is used to identify slack or under-utilized capacity and to streamline and improve established public services. It can also be used to find out the extent to which major projects will pay their own way through tax increment financing, value capture, and similar techniques.)
- As a way to evaluate the fiscal consequences of a specific development proposal. (In this case, the analysis is prepared either by a local government or a developer in response to local zoning, annexation, or subdivision requirements.)

Six fiscal impact analysis techniques—actually cost analysis techniques, since the method of evaluating revenues is the same in all cases—are defined by R. W. Burchell and David Listokin in *The Fiscal Impact Handbook.*

These techniques are:

- The per capita multiplier method, which applies only to residential development and considers average municipal costs per person and average school costs per pupil;
- The case study method, which projects future local costs associated with specific demands for services;
- The service standard method, which estimates manpower needs for specific services required by new development;
- The comparable city method, which estimates the impact of large-scale development by comparing the impacts of comparable developments on similar communities;
- The proportional valuation method, which assigns municipal costs to a proposed nonresidential development according to its proportion of total local property valuation;
- The employment anticipation method, which estimates costs associated with new employees generated by nonresidential development.

Three of these fiscal impact methods—case study, comparable city, and employment anticipation—use marginal costing; the others use average costing.

The pitfalls

Experience indicates that there are potential stumbling blocks in all six methods. In some cases, the danger lurks in the underlying assumptions; in others, it stems from a misunderstanding of method. Not all the pitfalls lie in wait for every fiscal impact analyst, but most analysts will encounter at least one; and each one could result in inaccurate or unintelligible results or severe misunderstandings when conclusions are conveyed to officials or the public.

Making inappropriate assumptions about the ratios of residential to nonresidential land uses. Homeowners in communities with lots of business and industry in general pay lower property taxes than homeowners in communities that are largely residential. In the first instance, nonresidential land uses produce tax revenue without making major demands on schools and other public services. Thus, the mix between residential and nonresidential land uses that is assumed as a context for analyzing any given development project is critical to the analysis of fiscal feasibility. The analyst needs accurate answers to these questions: What are the overall development trends within the community? Will the present ratios of residential to nonresidential land uses persist? Will pre-project and post-project land-use ratios be the same?

The intent here is not that every project produce a surplus of revenue but that land uses remain balanced. Nonresidential uses that have "carried" residential land uses in the past should continue to carry them in the future. In sum, the analyst needs an understanding of the entire range of projects taking place within the community so that the surpluses of some can offset the deficits of others. . . .

Perpetuating the mystique of computerized models. Too often, elected officials, planners, administrators, and citizen commissioners regard computer analyses as more precise and credible than analyses performed by hand. This assignment of magical powers is unfortunate, since all fiscal impact analyses require the same computations. Computers simply perform them faster.

Further, the use of computerized models tends to hide the high degree of uncertainty involved in all fiscal impact analysis. Fiscal impact methods are all ad hoc in nature, with very little in the way of statistical precision.

If the problems to be analyzed are massive and detailed, a computer can make sense. But for small-scale, relatively straightforward fiscal impact analyses—the great majority—such models tend to be cumbersome and inflexible. Data requirements tend to be too expensive, and the workings of the models are often difficult to understand.

Computer analysis does have a particular virtue, however. That is its potential for sensitivity analysis. Sensitivity analysis makes it possible to explore different land-use mixtures and to assess various revenue sources and the costs associated with different public service systems.

Neglecting to weigh fiscal impacts against other impacts. A common pitfall involves placing too much weight on fiscal factors and ignoring factors that are less easily quantified. Other kinds of impacts include those typically considered in environmental impact statements: environmental impacts on air, water, flora, and fauna; traffic impacts; social consequences for neighborhoods, housing markets, racial balance; economic impacts; land-use and transportation impacts.

One way to gain a better perspective on the relative importance of fiscal consequences is to relate all the impacts in a broader cost-effectiveness or cost-benefit framework. Monetary impacts—those involving public costs and revenues—then become only one of several important consequences that must be assessed, compared, and traded off.

Not knowing when to use average costing approaches. Average costing is by far the most com-

monly used approach in fiscal impact analysis. This approach assumes that the average costs of municipal services will remain stable in the future, with some adjustment for inflation. That assumption is fair in relatively slow-growing communities where the supply of public services matches demand and financing systems are stable. The most popular analysis method, the per capita multiplier technique, is based on this assumption.

However, in communities with population decline or rapid growth, a different situation pertains. Public service capacity is then likely to be either underutilized or deficient.

In these situations, marginal costing makes the most sense. Here, the costs associated with public services needed for new developments should reflect the amount of excess capacity available (in which case marginal costs will be relatively low) or the degree of overcrowding (in which case there will be higher marginal costs). Basic to the use of marginal costing is an understanding of the existing supply of and demand for local public services. Highly misleading results may emerge if the inappropriate fiscal impact technique is used. . . .

Risking the increasing skepticism of public officials by not using standardized methods. Many communities that have included requirements for fiscal impact analysis in their zoning codes or subdivision regulations have become disenchanted with the effectiveness of such requirements. The reason is that virtually every analysis has turned up a positive fiscal impact regardless of the type of development, density, or land-use mix. In other words, analysts have tinkered with the various techniques until they have found one that presents the development in a favorable fiscal light.

Public officials become skeptical when confronted with lack of standardization among the various fiscal impact methods. Depending on local growth and development conditions, as well as fiscal relationships and data, different methods can produce dramatically different cost-revenue ratios. It then appears that the methods have been manipulated to produce desired results. . . .

Neglecting to devote enough time to the presentation of conclusions. Most planners prefer the simplest methods of fiscal impact analysis. The per capita multiplier method, which is the easiest to understand and most logical, seems to be the most credible. But it is also the most simplistic, making many shaky assumptions about average costing, land-use mixes, and so on.

Because they are harder to understand, more sophisticated techniques require more effective communication of methods and results. It is particularly important to match the results of fiscal impact analysis with other pertinent impact analyses. Too often, local officials cannot determine how the results of fiscal impact analysis should be weighed.

Richard Stern, AICP, is a vice-president of the Balcor Corporation in Skokie, Illinois. Darwin Stuart is a consultant specializing in transportation.

The Mysterious World of Finance

Alan Rabinowitz
(July 1984)

Fifteen years ago, I wrote a book called *Municipal Bond Finance and Administration* (which the late Dennis O'Harrow, the sage of the American Society of Planning Officials at that time, recommended as bedtime reading for planners). Today, even though peace and human development are far more compelling concerns than bond issues, the subject of private and public money to implement community development is still important enough to keep planners awake. My objective in the first section below is to illustrate the differences between private and public views of long-term capital investment. The second section is an update on trends in the markets for public securities.

Two worlds

Planning has much to do with channeling money into socially desirable projects, so planners need to understand the ways of those who deal with money. As I write, it occurs to me that the worlds of finance and planning are physically and psychologically separate. The planner works in and on three-dimensional space and talks face to face with the multifaceted population such space contains.

In contrast, financial people look out at the world from their offices in central places and spend much of their time using telecommunications to deal with two-dimensional abstractions of interest rates, bidding syndicates, and bond ratings. The financier is primarily interested in discrete transactions in the here and now, the planner with a developing situation over a longish time.

Consider housing as a case that translates these different concepts of time into more concrete terms. The interest of the planner is in the creation of viable, interesting, amenity-packed neighborhoods, serving a balanced population and served by a range of public facilities. A planner sees the neighborhood as a home for generations of families, recognizing the dynamic potential of changes in land use and of in- and out-migration that might alter the flavor of the area. A planner must accept uncertainty.

The housing financier has a far different interest. His, or her, goal is to convert "housing" into a manageable investment that, at any point in time, can be bought and sold, slotted into investment portfolios, and given a market value. Thus the banker's interest is in (a) standardizing the housing unit through minimum-property and land-use-zoning requirements and (b) standardizing mortgages with respect to rates, maturities, collateral, and repayment schedules.

More and more, the banker's interest is a short-term one. Where formerly such mortgages remained the property of the originating bank until extinguished, changes in the structure of the banking industry now make it feasible for banking institutions to pass their mortgages off to the secondary market almost as soon as they are written.

Both planners and the financial community would like to see a steady flow of private and public money into community development, but they must work in different ways to ensure it. Financiers want to deal in short-term instruments—or at least with an uninterrupted flow of interest payments and profits. That means that developers must borrow on a short-term basis to produce long-term capital improvements.

These are some of the consequences of this emphasis on the short term:

- Those who hold land are forced to strive for quick speculative gains;
- There is continued agitation for a simple, quick permitting process;
- Developers yearn for government assistance to lower financial costs and risks; UDAG, below-

market-rate loans, and the old Title I urban redevelopment capital grants are examples;

• Developers put up strong resistance to any attempt to impose extra costs for environmental, housing, and other community needs.

The private side of urban development is slowly polarizing into two groups: (a) a small group of well-established venturers working in tandem with major financial institutions to create very large projects and (b) a significant number of investor/developers able to handle much smaller properties on an incremental basis as local opportunities arise. Equity capital remains a problem for both groups, and probably always will, but (as I observed in a book about such matters in the 1925–80 period, *The Real Estate Gamble*) the organized capital markets—"Wall Street"—have never been successful in providing long-term equity capital on a sustained basis for real estate and community development. . . .

The planner's world assumes that lots of money, private and public, will be available to make the "built environment" work well, but there may be a limit to how much public money taxpayers are willing to spend on it. It follows that the more is spent for "national defense," the less will be available for all our other needs, but, even if we take care of education, health, and social welfare, there remain the complex issues of how money should flow through the intergovernmental system and what role should be assigned to the central government in relation to the state and local governments.

Some automatic form of sharing of federal income-tax receipts with lower levels of government seems to be permanent, and there may be general agreement that the federal government should fund certain types of projects, mostly in transportation: interstate highways, airports, maybe railroads, and, traditionally, rivers and harbors. The question is often whether the taxpayers in Little Rock need to pay for local mass transit in Dubuque. The increasing concern over the degree of "national purpose" in such programs is best reflected in the studies by the U.S. Advisory Commission on Intergovernmental Relations, with which planners should be familiar.

Local financing

Over and above any federal assistance, local facilities are locally mandated and financed by a combination of current revenues and municipal bond

issues. . . . My own view is that the dominance of the property tax in local finance and the associated diversity of autonomous governments induces excessive competition among those government units and makes cooperation on such matters as land-use controls and provision of local services so tenuous an activity as to make each unit of government seek to maximize its property tax receipts and to minimize its responsibilities for lower-income citizens.

I also must note that the creation of privately owned "public" utilities, franchised by government to enjoy a local monopoly, was tantamount to giving away the best revenue-producing opportunities that local governments had. Imagine the planner's world if the public sector could set prices for essential utilities at a level that enabled them to finance all municipal services required without other taxes.

The inevitable result of these structural shifts was to make the property tax the primary source of revenue to pay for local public capital improvements, whether such expenditures were paid for by current revenues or by the proceeds of general obligation bonds. The extent of bond sales is limited by the severe restrictions largely imposed as a result of nineteenth-century peccadillos; these restrictions control use of the taxing power and the amount of debt that can be incurred. In any event, the capital markets are open at any time to an unregulated procession of local governments offering bonds for sale.

The investor-owned "public" utilities join the municipal corporations in the search for long-term financing. The private corporations offer corporate bonds, equipment-trust indentures, sale-leaseback agreements, and, when possible, the revenues to secure the special form of municipal obligation known as the industrial development bond. Increasingly, the theory as well as the practice of long-term finance in the public sector is taking on the characteristics of the public-serving corporations and partnerships of the private sector. . . .

The markets for public securities

The need for long-term financing for state and local capital projects will not disappear (and may even grow if we take seriously the call to rebuild our "infrastructure"). Public securities (otherwise known as state and municipal bonds) provide cash beyond the capacity of current revenue sources.

They also provide some degree of intergenerational equity, spreading the cost of the benefits over the lives of those both living and unborn who will enjoy them. If prospective users of the public facilities can be excluded from the benefits without too many socially repugnant consequences, bonds can be financed by user fees and excise taxes in addition to property taxes.

Since 1969, when I wrote my book, some things have changed in the field of public securities, but many of the concerns remain the same. States and their subordinate units of government still flock to the market on an unprogrammed basis. Holding municipal bonds is still attractive to some investors because the interest payments are generally free of federal taxes. While bonds represent only a portion of state and local capital outlays, they still claim an important share of the business of the organized capital markets.

According to the Federal Reserve, new private-market stocks and bonds issued in 1983 amounted to $98.5 billion. In that same year, the total amount of public securities issued, including both refunding and new capital issues, amounted to $84.8 billion, slightly more than half of the total being offered by special districts and authorities. Since 1976, more revenue-backed bonds than general obligation bonds have been offered in the market. A total of $70.8 billion in public securities for new capital projects were sold in 1983.

Four critical issues confronted the municipal-bond markets in 1969 and still do today: (1) bond ratings and their effect; (2) the drive by large commercial banks to regain the privilege of underwriting revenue bonds; (3) the use and abuse of industrial development bond issues; and (4) the future of the tax-exemption feature, to which we can add the general concern over the demand for such tax-exempt bonds. In the paragraphs below, I try to provide some sense of the current status of these concerns and some thoughts on other concerns that have emerged in the more recent past.

Originally ratings were bought and paid for by large investing institutions, but, in recent years, the cost of preparing the analysis that is the foundation for a rating has increasingly been placed somewhat incongruously on the credit-seeking government. In any case, the validity of a rating and its significance in establishing the relative value of a bond in comparison with all other bonds in the market continue as the subject of some controversy, al-

though computerized data bases and larger staffs have helped the rating agencies improve their products. I personally believe that much remains for the bond analyst to do (and a substantial portion of bond issues are still unrated). I am particularly interested in the present efforts of the rating agencies to measure "fiscal stress" in a given jurisdiction as a basis for issuing warnings, putting bonds on a danger list, and providing grist for the newspaper headlines.

The New Deal's Glass-Steagall Act prohibited commercial banks from further participation in the underwriting of all municipal bonds that were not general obligations backed by the "full faith and credit" of the issuing governments. All other tax-exempt bonds, collectively known as revenue bonds, were brought to market by a new class of securities dealers, the investment bankers. With the steady growth of non-general obligation issues in the postwar years, and now with the vast transformation of the financial industry, the pressure to repeal that portion of the Glass-Steagall Act and to permit banks to compete for the revenue bond business has reached a new level of intensity. Whether the change will be allowed and what its significance might be as the contending institutions merge into giant agglomerations of financial services are perhaps concerns more about concentration in the banking industry than about financial probity.

The nature of the debate about the role of bonds to finance facilities primarily owned by private corporations or for the benefit of private individuals has not really changed since public bond issues came under the scrutiny of the Treasury (and the Advisory Commission on Intergovernmental Relations) in the early 1960s. What has changed is both the volume of such issues and the extension of their use to provide pollution-control systems for industrial corporations, housing for middle-income families, tax increment financing of local improvements for developers, as well as facilities under the general rubric of economic and industrial development. In all such cases, revenue to service the bond issues comes from the firms and individuals benefited rather than from the general revenues of local governments and the states.

At issue is the concept of "public purpose" with respect to development and housing, and we can expect the debate to continue, especially when such bond issues seem to crowd out other forms of tax-exempt securities from a fairly narrow market in an economy that is said by some to be congenitally short of investable savings. At this writing, Congress may be in the process of reconsidering its prohibition on the use of bonds issued by state and local housing finance agencies for the construction of single-family houses.

The future of tax exemption

The Constitutional doctrine of "reciprocal immunity" constrains sovereign governments from taxing one another. Thus, states do not tax federal property and the federal government does not tax the states or their instrumentalities. Nevertheless, the Treasury has long considered such exemption a waste of potential revenue, agreeing with those who claim that greater savings could be arranged for state and local borrowings if the bonds were fully taxable and if direct federal subsidies were used to lower the effective cost of the borrowings. While that issue remains unresolved, attention has been focused on the Economic Recovery Tax Act of 1983, which appears to levy a tax on the tax-exempt interest received by Social Security pensioners.

Only a few years ago, the purchasers of state and local bonds were primarily casualty insurance companies and rather well-to-do individuals (and the trust companies that represented them). That's because the large pension funds were not subject to taxation, and many individuals found better shelter from taxation through investments in real estate, oil, and so forth. For about 15 years, however, strenuous efforts have been made to broaden the market for public securities in a number of different ways: increasing yields relative to corporate bonds; restricting alternative kinds of tax shelter; issuing bonds in smaller denominations; creating all sorts of "mutual funds" to enable small investors, even in relatively low tax brackets, to enter the market for tax exempts more easily; and creating various new forms of bonds (such as zero-coupon bonds). The market is still sensitive to the vagaries of demand, however, and fearful of incursions on its territory by competing government programs such as the "All Savers Certificates" of the early 1980s and the Individual Retirement Accounts (IRAs) of the moment.

Other happenings

Among the more newsworthy events of recent years are these:

• The commotion over the increased probabilities of default, beginning with the shock over the bankruptcy of the New York State Urban Development Corporation, the actual but undeclared bankruptcy of New York City itself, and the monstrous mismanagement of the Washington Public Power Supply System, not to mention a slew of threatened or voluntary municipal bankruptcies, all of which have made a characteristically nervous market even more suspicious;

• The requirement that all bonds issued after the start of 1984 be registered in the name of their owners, replacing the "bearer bond" system, which allowed anyone holding the coupon to receive the interest without having to be identified (the implication was that tax-exempt bonds could be useful in the so-called underground economy, far from the scrutiny of the Internal Revenue Service);

• The growth of insurance programs to guarantee payment of interest and principal on municipal bonds;

• The introduction of municipal bonds into the fast-developing options and futures markets.

Alan Rabinowitz, AICP, is the president of Territory Research, Inc., a Seattle consulting firm.

Convention Centers: Too Much of a Good Thing?

Dan McGuinness
(November 1982)

Since 1970, over 100 arenas, convention centers, or combinations of the two have been built in the United States. Once associated with major cities, visions of economic renewal combined with civic pride have brought convention facilities to smaller cities such as Dubuque, Iowa; Binghamton, New York; and Jamestown, North Dakota. While current high interest rates have dampened enthusiasm for major capital projects, the proliferation of arena-convention centers is likely to resume once interest rates come down.

Albany County, New York, is no exception. It already has one medium-sized convention center, "The Egg," on the Empire State Plaza in Albany and, surprisingly, an even larger arena-convention center in tiny Glens Falls (pop. 17,500). But periodically, public officials and private entrepreneurs in other cities and towns in the county trot out proposals for their own facilities. The lack of detailed information on the subject makes it difficult for county planners to evaluate these proposals. To fill the gap, the Albany County Planning Board has begun compiling its own information on capital costs, operating costs, facility size, and economic impacts.

Many of the figures that follow come from the industry profile survey conducted in 1978–79 by the International Association of Auditorium Managers in Chicago. Although somewhat dated now, the survey is the most comprehensive source of data available. The planning board's aim in collecting this information is to provide a framework for evaluating local proposals. We hope this summary also will be useful to planners elsewhere.

Costs

Even the most optimistic proponents of convention centers and arenas do not claim that the facilities will earn enough to cover the capital costs—which can be staggering. Construction costs of $2,000 per seat are common. At that rate, a 5,000-seat facility would cost $10 million. With 30-year bonds fetching 12 percent interest, the financing comes to $1,241,431 annually.

Occasionally, construction cost estimates have been way off. Louisiana voters, for example, approved a $30 million bond issue to finance the Louisiana Superdome. The final cost was $163 million.

Few facilities can meet operating expenses from revenues. According to the auditorium managers survey, of 156 facilities with arenas, only 69 had operating revenues greater than expenses. Of the 88 city-owned facilities, 58 operated at a loss.

In many cities, the losses are major. In 1978, for example, convention centers in Jamestown, North Dakota, lost $65,000; in Asheville, North Carolina, $238,000; and in El Paso, Texas, $480,000. While some cities have covered operating deficits with special hotel or entertainment taxes, others have had to meet the deficit from operating budgets, a procedure guaranteed to spark controversy.

Persistent operating deficits at the New Haven,

Connecticut, Veterans Memorial Coliseum recently led the city's mayor to call the facility a "white elephant." Utica, New York, where the arena has lost money every year since it opened in 1960, is attempting to sell its facility to Oneida County.

Too often, the size of a facility seems to be more a function of civic pride than of market area. For example, Hartford and New Haven, Connecticut, both built arena-convention center complexes in the 1970s. Although the population of the Hartford SMSA is 74 percent larger than New Haven's, the Hartford facility seats only nine percent more. Similarly, although the Huntsville, Alabama, SMSA has 37 percent more people than the Roanoke, Virginia, SMSA, Roanoke's civic center seats nearly 20 percent more than Huntsville's.

Impact

Increasing trade is often given as a major reason for constructing a convention center facility. Proponents speak glowingly of the millions of dollars that convention delegates will spend in the community and the multiplier effect of this spending on the local economy.

However, only big-city facilities are likely to draw major national conventions. Smaller places must rely on state and regional conventions. Also, according to a 1978–79 survey by the International Association of Convention and Visitors Bureaus in Champaign, Illinois, delegates to state and regional conventions spend 29 percent less, on the average, than delegates to national or international conventions.

Thus, smaller cities draw less lucrative conventions. And, since state associations stay in-state, smaller local facilities are left to compete against each other. So, unless the number of statewide conventions increases proportionately, each additional convention facility means less convention business for the others in the state.

Estimates of expenditures by convention delegates also must be kept in perspective. For example, the Richmond, Virginia, Convention and Visitors Bureau reports that, in 1980, the area hosted 278 conventions with a total of 261,229 delegates. The bureau estimates the total economic impact at $47 million—a substantial sum in absolute terms but still less than one percent of total personal income of the Richmond SMSA.

In contrast, the 1977 restaurant and bar receipts in the SMSA were $182,625,000—nearly four times the 1980 convention delegate expenditures. In short, the importance of the expenditures of convention delegates to the local economy is easily exaggerated.

Any type of convention facility represents a major investment for a community. Yet high capital and operating costs and uncertain revenues make it a risky proposition. Our tentative, preliminary estimates indicate, for example, that a new 5,500-seat arena in Albany County would cost upwards of $16 million. Depending on the assumptions made, the operation could result in an annual profit of $426,000 or an annual loss of $287,000.

Because of such inherent uncertainty, planners need to evaluate proposals carefully to determine whether a convention facility will make a direct, tangible contribution to the community coffers. Civic chauvinism should not overwhelm common sense.

Dan McGuinness is an associate planner with the Albany County, New York, Planning Board.

After the Fair: What Expos Have Done for Their Cities

James Peters
(July/August 1982)

Short of war, there's nothing that produces community effort more than a world's fair.—A Seattle fair planner, 1962. There was a time when the term "world class" wasn't bestowed on a city until after it had staged a world's fair. An international exhibition was considered the center of art and culture—a place for millions to "tour" the world, see the latest inventions and trade products, sample exciting amusements, and leave with a vision of the future.

Since the first international fair, London's Great Exhibition of the Works and Industry of All Nations in 1851 (the Crystal Palace), there have been 82 world's fairs, 17 of them major ones. In North America, the totals are 21 and six. Today's world's fairs still draw millions, but the reasons for holding one have changed considerably.

"A city has always received an enormous outburst of civic pride from a fair," notes John R. Mullin, a University of Massachusetts planning professor who has studied the legacy of world's fairs. "Banks loosen up. Private benefactors come forward, and there is a ready and willing electorate. In short, a fair has become a great tool for redevelopment."

In the past 20 years, Seattle has received a popular civic center from its Century 21 Expo. Spokane redeveloped an underused island as a riverfront park with Expo '74. And Knoxville is banking on a fair to clean up a downtown railroad yard. The jargon for these fair legacies is residuals.

Several foreign fairs—most notably the Paris exhibitions—have also left behind substantial site improvements, but this article will concentrate primarily on the physical legacy of North American fairs, as well as their influence on the planning profession.

The fairs of the late nineteenth century, urban designer Paul Spreiregen has written, "proclaimed a new hope and fresh image of our cities." None did more in that regard than Chicago's Columbian Exposition of 1893. The fair's "White City" inspired millions of Americans who saw or read about its gleaming white, neoclassical buildings and statuary, its broad boulevards, restful parks and lagoons, hidden utilities, and generous use of outdoor lighting. It provided a vision, the fair's master planner, Daniel H. Burnham, later wrote, "of the need for the unity of a general plan," rather than the piecemeal public works projects being undertaken by most of the country's formless, industrial cities.

This heightened interest in civic beauty and order, as most are aware, provided a new direction to American city planning, with a focus on building parks, civic centers, and boulevards. With the subsequent publicity given the McMillan Commission's Plan for Washington, D.C., and Buffalo's Pan-American Exposition, both in 1901, the City Beautiful movement in America was off and running.

Model city

The Louisiana Purchase Exposition in St. Louis in 1904 gave an additional boost to the formation of art clubs and civic improvement societies around the country. The Model City exhibit, one of the fair's most popular attractions along with such culinary inventions as the ice cream cone, hot dog, and iced tea, helped bring the City Beautiful movement to smaller cities.

The "ideal street" at the fair offered full-scale examples of town halls, libraries, hospitals, railroad stations, and schools, as well as street fixtures, public bathhouses, and park equipment—all designed in the over-wrought neoclassical style popularized by the Chicago world's fair. Hundreds of cities subsequently copied the models in their own public buildings and street designs. . . .

Ironically, one of the most obscure fairs, Seattle's 1909 Alaska–Yukon–Pacific Exposition, left one of the most interesting physical legacies—even though its 3.7 million attendance was a fraction of the Columbian Exposition's 27 million. The regents of the University of Washington offered their campus as the site of the fair, provided it would result in new buildings and improvements to the grounds of the new school. The campus core still bears traces of the exposition, including a campus drive, a boulevard vista of Mt. Rainier, one building, and several landscaping features.

Part of San Francisco's first world's fair in 1915 was built on landfill in the Marina section. After the fair, houses were built on much of the site, and the popular Palace of Fine Arts remained as a local landmark. The deteriorated stucco complex was recently reconstructed in concrete after a public fundraising drive. This fair is also viewed as a catalyst for the construction of a new civic center, and it helped renew interest in a master plan that Burnham had prepared shortly before the 1905 earthquake.

Gathering place

In terms of public use, perhaps the most substantial legacy can be found in San Diego's Balboa Park, the site of fairs in 1915 and 1933. "It's the most vivid residual," says Alfred Heller, editor of the quarterly journal, *World's Fair,* "simply because its result—a public gathering place—is so similar to the fairlike quality of the original exhibitions."

The 1,400-acre park had been set aside in 1868, but some 35 buildings, along with pools, formal gardens, and statuary, still survive from the two fairs, most notably the picturesque Spanish Colonial architecture of the Panama-California International Exposition in 1915.

Today, those buildings house museums, art galleries, concert areas, and public gardens. The world-famous San Diego Zoo was established in 1922 to exhibit animals that had been imported for the 1915 fair. Other exhibits formed the beginning

of the city's Fine Arts Society, the Museum of Man, and the Natural History Museum.

The 194-acre fairground itself was listed in the National Register of Historic Places in 1977. Ron Buckley, a planner who staffs the city's historic sites board, says rehabilitation of many of the fair structures, which in many cases are still built of the "temporary" redwood and stucco materials, is under way. The buildings have always been too popular and well-used to be torn down, he says.

As the planning profession took a more practical bent, with an emphasis on zoning and social issues, world's fairs began to look beyond the legacies of museums and parks. This was particularly true during the Depression, when three world's fairs were seen as economic recovery mechanisms.

Chicago's Century of Progress in 1933–34 celebrated the centennial of the city's incorporation, using a 427-acre site along Lake Michigan, south of downtown. The park's landfill construction and hundreds of temporary exhibit buildings employed thousands and created Northerly Island, since converted to an airport. Several major public improvements on the site, including an aquarium, planetarium, stadium, and natural history museum, were completed shortly before fair construction began.

In San Francisco, officials dove-tailed the need for a new airport and public works projects with a major celebration of the opening of the Golden Gate and Bay bridges. The result was the 1939 Golden Gate International Exhibition, set on the newly created, 400-acre Treasure Island, midway between San Francisco and Oakland. Several of the exhibition buildings were designed for conversion to airport hangars and an administration building following the fair, but the Navy took over the island for use as a base instead. The Navy still uses three fair structures.

Valley of ashes

An equally ambitious fair was held in New York City in 1939–40. Parks commissioner Robert Moses used the fair as an excuse to create a new city park, Flushing Meadow, out of what had been a refuse dump in Queens (described by F. Scott Fitzgerald in *The Great Gatsby* as a "valley of ashes . . . a grotesque garden"). The fair also enabled Moses to rush through the construction of billions of dollars worth of new highways and bridges throughout the New York metropolitan area.

Although the two-year fair piled up a large deficit, its exhibits influenced a generation of planners and architects. Its hit exhibit was General Motors' Futurama, which moved visitors around and over a Norman Bel Geddes-designed model of the "World of 1960." His plans for 100-mile-an-hour, limited-access highways captured the imagination of American transportation engineers.

The New York fair was the last one in the U.S. for nearly two decades, but as World War II ended, several cities saw a world's fair as a way of putting together quick redevelopment projects. That trend, inspired by a national fair in London in 1951 that redeveloped a decayed area across the Thames from Parliament, was finally realized in this country at the Century 21 Expo in Seattle in 1962.

Modest by world's fair standards—only 72 acres compared with St. Louis's 1,272 in 1904—Seattle's expo is still considered the most successful as a redevelopment tool. As one magazine of the day noted, "Under the surface glitter lies a unique and solid accomplishment in civic planning."

The glitter was indeed memorable. A monorail linking the site to downtown, a mile away, was billed as the mass transportation of the future. Although the idea didn't catch on as expected, except for similar systems in a few airports, amusement parks, and Japanese cities, the Seattle monorail is still running and still making a profit.

A 500-foot tower built for the fair instantly became a symbol of Seattle, just as the Eiffel Tower, built for a world's fair in 1889, became the symbol of Paris. For better or worse, Seattle's Space Needle also encouraged a generation of towers, all topped with restaurants, in other cities.

The fair's 12-block site was designed around an existing armory, high school stadium, and auditorium in a declining neighborhood north of downtown. A civic center had long been proposed in the city's master plan, and local leaders were quite upfront in stressing that the fair was primarily a tool for its development.

Fair planning was coordinated by local architect Paul Thiry, who worked with the city's planning department and an assortment of mostly local architects to reuse the existing buildings and add new pavilions. Throughout the fair, a civic center commission met regularly to discuss and plan for the site's future use.

Today, Seattle Center is a successful cultural and convention center for the city. The site was relandscaped in 1964 into an urban park almost too crowded, some would say, with ethnic food shops, arts and crafts shops, amusement rides, and museums. The U.S. Pavilion is now a science center, the Washington state pavilion is a sports arena and convention center, and the auditorium has become the city's opera house. Two bond issues have been approved since the fair for site maintenance, and another is scheduled later this year.

This same civic center formula was tried six years later at the San Antonio world's fair, with mixed results. HemisFair '68 was the keystone to a long-planned urban renewal project adjacent to the central business district—the first world's fair right downtown. And while it has left an assortment of permanent facilities—including a convention center–sports arena, the Institute of Texas Cultures, and a new federal courthouse—the site gives the impression today of an abandoned amusement park.

"As urban renewal it's been a bomb," says one local planner, who notes that the question of what to do with the site is a periodic item on the city council agenda. There has never been much development interest in the property, and the Tivoli-type amusement park never attracted the crowds it was supposed to. In fact, several smaller buildings, along with the skyride that loops the site, will be pulled down later this year.

Nevertheless, the fair did help revive a lethargic downtown. San Antonio's famed riverwalk was extended for the fair, several new hotels were constructed, and the city was able to clear a rundown residential area, while successfully relocating its tenants. In addition, as in Seattle, the fair left the city a symbol, the 622-foot Tower of the Americas.

Expensive failure

Two much larger fairs in the 1960s offer a split decision—one an expensive success, the other an expensive failure.

The New York World's Fair of 1964–65 lost millions of dollars, sullied the notion of world's fairs for many because of its rampant commercialism, and contributed to Robert Moses's fall from power.

Moses, the fair's master planner, saw it as another opportunity to develop Flushing Meadow Park, which had gone unimproved since its use for the 1939 fair. He and other fair leaders rejected the idea of using the site for a new town or university. Instead they opted for more park improvements, the new Shea Stadium, a $3 million marina, and $133 million worth of highway improvements. A visitor to the site today will see an eerie wasteland, with a few aging relics, including the Unisphere, the fair's symbol, scattered across hundreds of acres of largely unused parkland. "It's worse than the ash heap it was converted from," one critic said recently.

In contrast to this is Montreal's Expo '67, which set an attendance record for a six-month fair with 50.8 million. The city used the celebration as an excuse to pyramid dozens of public projects, including a new subway system (the Metro), highway expansion (finished 10 years ahead of schedule), and 745 acres of new parkland in the middle of the St. Lawrence River. (The fair's projected $50 million deficit eventually ballooned to $200 million. Unlike the largely private-financed U.S. fairs, however, all losses were covered by local, provincial, and federal agencies.)

Three-quarters of the fair site was built from scratch by adding on to an existing island in the river, extending a peninsula out from downtown, and creating a completely new island. The fair was based on a master plan that linked the four main fair sites with a network of monorails, express trains, and a subway line. The fairgrounds were organized according to theme, an idea borrowed from Disney, planners said.

The fair also introduced some avant-garde architectural designs, including Moshe Safdie's modular Habitat housing on the mainland and Buckminster Fuller's 20-story geodesic dome, the U.S. Pavilion.

Unfortunately, subsequent use of the fair site has not lived up to its grand expectations. Habitat, at $125,000 a unit in 1967 rates, proved too costly to be an acceptable prototype, and a recent fire seriously set back plans to rehabilitate the aviary in Fuller's dome.

Nor did flamboyant Montreal mayor Jean Drapeau's plans for a permanent fair on the site ever materialize; they were a victim, in part, of the city's serious fiscal problems. Many of the pavilions, which Drapeau lobbied to have donated to the city, rather than demolished, are in disrepair; several will be torn down later this year for a much-downscaled continuation of the "Man and his World" exhibition.

Hopes for a housing development on one of the islands have gone unrealized; instead an annual road race is held there. LaRonde amusement park,

however, which was built for the fair, has been a huge success and a historic city park still draws Montrealers from the nearby downtown, as it did before Expo.

Numerous plans for other fairs were never carried out. In the late 1960s, Victor Gruen proposed an international exhibition in suburban Maryland, outside Washington, D.C., whose site would be reused as a new town. Boston envisioned a Bicentennial fair in 1976 on its Harbor Islands; Philadelphia planners countered with a linear fair that would be located on air rights above railroad tracks. None of these fairs, including proposals for Detroit, Los Angeles, Miami, and St. Louis, ever gained the necessary support.

The most recent U.S. fair, Expo '74, in Spokane, Washington, was built for the purpose of turning the city's riverfront, mostly railroad yards and industrial buildings, into a city park. Most local officials will tell you that "it was the single most important event in the city's 100-year history."

In addition to Riverfront Park, which is located on two islands in the Spokane River, adjacent to downtown, the city gained a new convention center and opera house. The fair also provided the impetus to build a skywalk system downtown.

Several fair buildings remain on the island, including the U.S. Pavilion, whose large, tentlike structure once dominated the park. Its deteriorated canvas roof was removed several years ago, but the pavilion still houses an ice rink, theater, and science center. Dozens of other events, such as arts and crafts shows, a weekly farmers market, and free concert, are staged in the park.

Several million dollars were spent redeveloping the park after the fair in hopes that it would become self-supporting, but that hasn't happened. Park managers are now looking for a private operator who could develop other attractions, possibly a theme amusement park on 10 of the park's 50 acres. "Many people are disappointed that the park hasn't lived up to its potential," says one park official, "but overall we're probably still way ahead."

Some believe the whole notion of a world's fair is antiquated and question whether the massive expenditures for a fair should be made while there are more pressing urban needs. They point out that new housing, improved schools, and the maintenance of existing public services are far greater needs for today's aging cities than new parks and cultural institutions, which were the greatest needs of relatively young, turn-of-the-century U.S. cities. Still others complain that fairs are organized in a planning vacuum, that those who push for the fair often are not there to find a reuse for the site afterwards.

Despite these protests, fairs continue to be seen as a valuable planning mechanism and catalyst for public improvements. If future fairs are going to live up to their enormous redevelopment potential, however, they must be viewed as a means to an end, not a single-shot exercise in civic promotion. Most of the fairs described here have failed in that respect.

James Peters was formerly the associate editor of Planning.

Stadiums: The Right Game Plan?

Ruth Eckdish Knack
(September 1986)

The White Sox were doing so poorly in mid-August that many Chicago baseball fans were complaining that the question of a new playing field was more interesting than the action in Comiskey Park. A month earlier, the team owners had announced that they were pulling out of stadium negotiations with the city and were ready to talk seriously about a site in the suburbs or even elsewhere in the country. Will they move? Stay tuned.

Meanwhile, stadium connoisseurs are keeping an eye on the Miami area, where a new football stadium is nearing completion. It's the only one of a spate of recent stadium proposals that actually made it past the drawing board stage, and it offers hope for a new type of private financing.

Although it sometimes seems that there is no city in the country that is not talking about a stadium, about 20 have been identified as serious contenders by John E. Petersen of the Government Finance Officers Association, coauthor of a 1985 article on financing sports facilities. He notes that stadiums are seen as blue-chip civic investments that bring prestige along with revenue. "It's like having a first-class symphony, or a zoo, or any of the luxuries people expect from a big town," said a San An-

tonio stadium proponent quoted in a local newspaper.

Critics warn against viewing a stadium as an economic panacea, the most recent version of the pedestrian mall, convention center, festival marketplace, and revolving restaurant—all at one time touted as urban cure-alls. Noting that the interests of team owners, stadium developers, and the public do not necessarily coincide, others warn of the need for strict public scrutiny of stadium proposals.

But a city that's about to lose a team doesn't necessarily want to go slow. Not when franchises are footloose, as they have been increasingly since 1982, when the Oakland Raiders won their antitrust suit against the National Football League. The Raiders' departure for Los Angeles left Oakland with a $1.5 million annual debt service bill for its publicly financed stadium.

The older cities especially have learned to accept the reality that professional sports teams are business propositions for many owners. Not too many would echo the words of Detroit baseball owner John Fetzer, who in 1974 refused to desert Tiger Stadium for the new Pontiac Silverdome, saying, "This franchise belongs to the inner city of Detroit; I'm just the caretaker."

When desperation sets in, concessions by public stadium authorities become the rule. In Baltimore, for instance, where the loss of the Colts football team to Indianapolis in 1984 still rankles, the baseball Orioles now pay rent only if they have a profitable year. And the Oakland A's baseball team got an even better deal in a new lease that allows it to pull out without penalty in 1990 if it is losing a "life-threatening sum."

Philadelphia, trying to keep two teams happy in Veterans Stadium, has promised to build some 80 skyboxes for the football Eagles and "baseball-only" suites for the Phillies. The total package of freebies could cost the city up to $2.5 million a year.

Concessions can backfire, though. Anaheim lured the Los Angeles Rams with a promise that the team's owners could develop part of the parking lot adjacent to the stadium. The Los Angeles Angels baseball team sued, charging favoritism to the football team. The case is still in court.

If the old stadium won't do even with renovations, the city may promise a whole new field. San Francisco, after first insisting that no public money would be spent, now says it will commit itself to a $36 million "budget" stadium for the baseball Giants. But, in July, a consultant hired by the team said the downtown railyard site presented big problems and could double the stadium cost. Mayor Dianne Feinstein canceled a scheduled bond referendum and said she would study the alternatives, including a retractable dome for windswept Candlestick Park.

Such reluctance to commit public funds for stadium projects is not surprising, says the GFOA's Petersen, whose research (published in the June 1985 *Government Finance Review*) has convinced him of two things: That some form of public financing is involved in virtually every stadium project, even those billed as private, and that taxpayers are increasingly reluctant to ante up.

For instance, Cleveland voters turned down a stadium bond issue in a 1984 referendum. Yet the city continues to feel pressure from both its pro teams, the baseball Indians and the football Browns, to build a domed replacement for its lakefront municipal stadium. How to pay for it? One possibility: a share of a statewide "sin tax" on bar drinks and cigarettes, an approach that Petersen suggests may become more common.

In 1982, the Chicago city council approved a $5 million tax-exempt industrial revenue bond issue to pay for 27 "skyboxes" at Comiskey Park, the home of the White Sox baseball team. In return, the Sox owners reiterated the promise to stay put made when they bought the team the year before. Then, last year, citing the need for major repairs to their 76-year-old ballpark, the owners issued an ultimatum: Build us a new stadium or we split.

At the same time, the Tribune Company, owner of the Cubs, the city's National League baseball team, stepped up its call for a repeal of the legislative ban on night games at venerable Wrigley Field, the only major league park without lights. And the football Bears, in a good bargaining position after last year's Super Bowl win, renewed their complaints about the terms of their Soldier Field lease with the Chicago Park District.

The city responded by soliciting development proposals for a multipurpose domed stadium on 60 acres of vacant railroad land along the Chicago River, just south of the Loop. That plan fell through when none of the three teams would agree to share the facility. The developers came back with a scaled-down, open air, baseball-only stadium, adjoined by a smaller arena for basketball and hockey.

After months of negotiations, representatives of Chicago Mayor Harold Washington and Illinois Gov. James Thompson finally worked out a subsidy arrangement, only to see it fail because a draft bill didn't get to the state legislature until the final weekend of the session, when lawmakers were ready to go home. The Sox owners said at that point that they couldn't wait for the fall session and were giving up on the city. "We tried to keep the team in the city because we felt an obligation to Chicago," said co-owner Jerry Reinsdorf in announcing the decision. "We gave it our best shot."

But even before the city deal died, Reinsdorf and his partner had begun negotiating with suburban DuPage County officials about building a stadium on a 140-acre site recently bought by the team. Now they have given DuPage an end-of-the-year deadline for coming up with a financing plan. But this one, too, would probably have to go through the state legislature, which means another delay—and makes skeptics wonder whether the team was ever serious about staying in the city. Now Mayor Washington is trying to make sure that the pending federal tax reform law doesn't allow the suburbs to take advantage of a clause exempting Chicago and four other cities from a general ban on the use of tax-exempt industrial revenue bonds for stadium financing.

The Sox say a suburban stadium would be cheaper to build and easier to fill, since their marketing surveys show that half their fans live in the northwest suburbs. Both the Bears and Cubs also have or have had options on land in DuPage. Chicago urbanologist Pierre DeVise has suggested that all three teams might have a hidden agenda, a desire to escape the city's social and racial mix. "They're looking for a 'Smith' address—not a Grabowski one," said DeVise, paraphrasing a recent comment by Bears coach Mike Ditka about differences among football teams. If they move, they can't call themselves the Chicago White Sox (or, presumably Cubs or Bears), said Mayor Washington. Would that it were enough to keep them at home.

Siren cities

Or to keep them in the state for that matter, for the Sox, especially, have been eyed covetously by other cities, including Buffalo; Columbus, Ohio;

Denver; Indianapolis; Miami; New Orleans; St. Petersburg; Tampa; Washington, D.C. (which has an empty stadium); and Phoenix—the place every team threatens to move to when it doesn't get what it wants at home.

These are the cities that keep popping up on lists of siren cities waiting to lure a major league team. They're determined, too. St. Petersburg, for instance, is going ahead with its plans despite a strong statement by baseball commissioner Peter Ueberroth that the city "is not among the top candidates" for an expansion or relocation team.

In July, after a public hearing at which proponents turned out in force, the city council reaffirmed its support of a 43,000-seat domed baseball stadium that could also accommodate concerts and conventions. The 66-acre downtown site, part of a redevelopment area, has been cleared, state environmental approval is in hand, and an $85 million tax-exempt bond issue is in the works.

The bond issue was in doubt for a while because Pinellas County at one point reneged on its agreement to pledge tourist taxes to support the bonds. The city, which has pledged an excise tax, sued and won. "We're ready to go," says Robert Rowan, special projects director in the economic and community development department.

Meanwhile, across the bay in Tampa, another dome is on another architect's drawing board. "But ours is a diametrically different approach," says Ronald Short, director of the Tampa-Hillsborough County Planning Commission.

First, says Short, the promoters, the Tampa Bay Baseball Group, say they won't build until they have a team. Second, the plan calls for heavy private investment, so public risk is lessened. The site, adjacent to the Buccaneers football stadium, has been leased from the Tampa Sports Authority. Yes, says Short, the obvious proposal has been made: that the two cities get together and build one stadium for the region. Neither jumped at the chance.

One of the teams eyeing other cities is the St. Louis Cardinals football team. And concern about a possible loss last year prompted Missouri senators Thomas Eagleton and John Danforth to draft a bill that would give pro sports leagues a greater say in potential franchise shifts.

Specifically, the legislation, S.259, the Professional Sports Community Protection Act, would permit the leagues to promulgate rules regarding team relocation, with approval subject to a three-fourths vote of the franchise owners. The league's decision would have to be based on standards spelled out in the bill, including the extent to which the team had received public financial support.

In April, the bill was approved by the Senate Commerce, Science, and Transportation Committee, which is chaired by Danforth. The threat of a filibuster by Sen. Albert Gore, Jr., of Tennessee has kept it from the Senate floor so far. Gore contends that the measure would kill the chances of a football franchise for his state. He wants to include a requirement that the NFL add several new teams.

The legislation would apply only to the football, hockey, basketball, and soccer leagues—none of which now has clear legal authority to regulate franchise transfers. Baseball already has such authority, although, as the bill's proponents point out, expansion has not suffered. Ten major league clubs have been added since 1961.

In effect, S.259 would overturn the 1982 decision in the Oakland Raiders case. A federal court said then that a similar NFL rule requiring three-fourths of its members to approve a team move was an antitrust violation. This summer the NFL was again a defendant in an antitrust suit brought by the fledgling United States Football League. The USFL charged that the NFL impaired competition by monopolizing the television networks. But, while the court agreed with the monopoly charge, it rejected the network control charge.

Perhaps most hurt by the decision was New York City, eager for a new football team to replace the Giants and Jets, who now play at the New Jersey Meadowlands. "We were hoping for a settlement," says William Mattison, Jr., president of the Flushing Meadows Sportsplex Project, the state-sponsored authority that handled negotiations last year for the privately funded stadium proposed by developer Donald Trump, owner of the USFL New Jersey Generals and a plaintiff in the suit. Now, says Mattison, the best hope is to attract an existing franchise.

Privatization

Whoever plays in it, Mattison adds, any new stadium will have to be paid for privately. In fact, there's so much interest in alternative financing that it has led a 30-year-old entrepreneur named Mark Ganis to carve out a new area of business for himself: the privatization of sports facilities.

Working with an investment banking firm (Goldman Sachs), architects (HNTB), and marketing consultants, Ganis has helped package large private stadium deals for several cities. His year-old firm, Sportscorp, Ltd., is part of a development group that last month was chosen by Phoenix to build a downtown domed stadium for the football and baseball teams the city is counting on attracting.

"Privatization of stadiums is a new industry," says Ganis. "The public money just isn't there anymore. Yet a lot of cities are still in desperate need of new facilities.

"We recognized that this market was not being served, and we found a way to provide a stadium at little or no cost to the public. We look at stadiums very much like traditional real estate developments, which means that we try to maximize revenue and limit expenses. People don't realize how many revenue streams a stadium can generate. We have identified 14 different ones, and we use them to convince investors that a stadium is a good risk."

Apparently everything in a ballpark is a potential revenue source if it's marketed right. Ganis's design consultants create traffic flows that will take crowds past the maximum number of concessions and ensure "accidental" television exposure for the advertisers on ballpark signs and billboards—a popular ploy for cigarette ads, which are banned from TV.

In markets that are less attractive to investors, Ganis admits that some public subsidy may be necessary. In Phoenix, the subsidy will take the form of a land deal. In return for the developers' promise to build a 73,000-seat domed stadium at minimal public cost, the city will donate the stadium site and also acquire and clear the land around it, 66 acres in all. The developers have a seven-year option on the land, with plans to build some $153 million worth of office, retail, and residential space.

A new breed of private stadiums may change things, but right now it's hard to single out examples of financially successful stadiums. What one does find is stories of economic development successes generated by stadiums. Everyone's favorite example is the New Jersey Meadowlands sports complex. "There would have been development in the Meadowlands without the stadium, but we don't think it would have happened as quickly as

it has," said a spokesman for the Hacksensack Meadowlands Development Commission, the planning body for the region. The commission estimates that the sports complex has generated over $630 million in office, hotel, and residential development and 45,000 jobs since it opened in 1976.

But it's the racetrack, not the stadium, that's the real draw. The track produces six times the revenue of the stadium and arena combined, and it pays almost all of the $35 million debt service on the complex.

Busch Stadium and its two teams are considered such a boon to downtown St. Louis that local officials quake at the thought of losing them. The St. Louis County executive recently has been talking about building a surburban stadium for the football Cardinals. In response, a downtown business group commissioned a planning firm, Team Four, to consider what effects the team's loss might have on the downtown.

The figures were fairly predictable: a large loss of jobs (up to 3,250) and a decline in sales (up to $104.5 million a year). But the consultants also considered the effect on the city's poor, who couldn't get to jobs at the suburban site; the loss of patrons at new downtown attractions like St. Louis Centre; and the cost of duplicating infrastructure that already exists in the city. In all three areas, it concluded, the negative impact would be substantial.

Even worse: the potential psychological impact. "The prospect of losing such major crowd-gathering events as professional football and hockey . . . calls into question the image of the city that has evolved over the past 15 years."

Indianapolis planner Stuart Reller is talking about something similar when he recalls how local business people promoted the Hoosierdome as a way to shake the city's "Naptown" image." And it worked. It's given people confidence in the city and encouraged them to think that downtown is an OK place to be."

The Louisiana Superdome is often held up as an example of what not to do in financing a dome; its cost overruns are legendary. But a team of University of New Orleans professors found recently that the dome has had a healthy effect on nearby downtown development. "It's the most successful urban renewal project in the city," says finance professor Wayne Ragas, one of the authors of the report, a 10-year assessment commissioned by the state.

The researchers found a substantial impact—$17 million—on adjacent land. Surprisingly, they concluded that much of that effect was the result of the dome's parking garages. According to Ragas, the data suggest that office developers deliberately chose sites adjacent to the dome so they could take advantage of the low-cost parking. "No one ever realized that the stadium would be a catalyst for office construction," says Ragas. His final word is that building the stadium was a good decision, "but not necessarily for the original motives."

The skeptic

"Civic ego plays a tremendous role in all of this," says economist Robert Baade of Lake Forest College in Illinois, who has been studying the economic impacts of professional sports for several years. "Moon Landrieu, mayor of New Orleans when the Superdome was built, called it an 'exercise of optimism.' But is that enough of an argument for extensive public financial involvement? I'm not sure. Too often, a city starts with the idea that a stadium is a good thing and then tries to justify it."

In particular, Baade questions economic rationales that are based on the multiplier effect—spinoff spending on food, lodging, entertainment, local transportation, and so on. The multiplier, he notes, doesn't take account of what people are *not* spending money on when they're spending on sports. "The public sector may be helping to develop a particular segment of the economy at the expense of another." This fall, Baade will look at the "consumption function" in eight cities with stadiums to see whether total spending did, in fact, increase.

But what if the stadium is built without public funds? Does Baade still have reservations? "Privatization does seem to be the wave of the future," he answers. But to say that the public sector will be completely divorced from the project is overly optimistic. Who will provide the infrastructure, for instance?

Finally, Baade asks, "What does a private stadium in the suburbs mean for the people who can't afford skyboxes? To some extent, we're pushing the public out of spectator sports. Does the public sector want to be a party to this?"

There are other issues, too, besides the economic ones. For stadiums rank right up there with prisons and nuclear waste dumps as LULUs (locally unwanted land uses).

"There hasn't been a sports stadium built since the Roman Coliseum when the neighbors haven't objected to it," said Miami Dolphins owner Joe Robbie. Robbie was defending himself from the attacks of residents of two adjacent subdivisions, who have sued to ensure that all zoning regulations are adhered to. In Chicago, many residents of the emerging South Loop neighborhood, proposed site of the now-defunct stadium, say they're glad to see it go. And a siting controversy in Sacramento turned into a political brouhaha when stadium proponents pressured city officials to approve development in an area once earmarked for agriculture. The prize: One pro team, the basketball Kings, and the promise of a baseball team—someday.

If Chicago architect Philip Bess had his way, such controversies would never occur. Bess is a die-hard fan of the old city ballparks, and his first choice would be to keep teams where they are, especially when they play in an urban beauty like Comiskey Park, the oldest ballpark in the U.S. But if a new stadium were absolutely necessary, it would be a "textural" one that fit into its surroundings.

Bess has come up with a prototype for an urban ballpark that would, in his words, be "good for baseball and good for cities." Like the older parks, it would conform to the shape of the city blocks around it and thus might have an eccentric shape—in contrast to the standard donuts and ellipsoids of the recent parks. His stadium would not be a free-standing object. It would be part of a neighborhood, but a benevolent part, easily accessible by public transit, with parking handled in an aesthetically pleasing way.

Most important, in Bess's view, ballplayers would never again have to feel the way former Pittsburgh Pirates player Richie Hebner did when he said, "I stand at the plate in Philadelphia, and I don't honestly know whether I'm in Pittsburgh, Cincinnati, St. Louis, or Philly. They all look alike."

Ruth Knack is the senior editor of Planning.

The Biggest Industrial Park of All

Robert J. Marak
(May 1982)

New Orleans is putting a lot of faith in the development of the Almonaster–Michoud Industrial Corridor. Because it's the only large piece of relatively undeveloped land left within the city limits, it might represent the city's last chance to strengthen its manufacturing base. It's also the largest development of its kind in the U.S., a 12,000-acre industrial park within five miles of downtown.

A milestone in the four years of planning for this industrial park took place this spring, when the master plan for the area was adopted by the city council. The unusual site conditions made planning particularly difficult and necessitated an unusual degree of cooperation among planners, engineers, and environmentalists. Now the city is ready to prepare the site for that California high-tech firm and the others that are expected to follow.

In a 1975 essay called "Pro Bono Publico," University of New Orleans economics professor James R. Bobo attacked local politicians, public institutions, and the media for denying the truth about New Orleans's economy. Bobo cited the figures showing a loss of manufacturing jobs and challenged the city's leaders to take action.

The figures are hard to deny. In 1979, tourism accounted for 27.3 percent of the city's jobs, the port 11 percent, and manufacturing 7.7 percent. While the first two sectors are undeniably important (the port is number one in the U.S. in terms of tonnage), the jobs they create are often low-paying and dead-ended.

For a while in the 1960s, there was hope for diversification. That was when the Michoud Assembly Facility, part of NASA's Saturn program, employed over 11,400 people. But when the Saturn program ended, that number dropped to 1,622. Only recently, with the advent of the Space Shuttle program, has the facility's job roster begun to climb. It employs 3,700 today.

All that's left

In 1978, Ernest N. Morial, who that year became the city's first black mayor, centered his campaign around the issues of economic development and job creation. When he took office, Morial established an office of economic development, whose charge was to devise a development strategy. The result: the identification of some 12,000 acres in east New Orleans as appropriate for industry and office use.

The Almonaster Corridor was an obvious choice. New Orleans is surrounded by water, with Lake Pontchartrain to the north, the Mississippi River to the south, and wetlands to the east and west. The land is at or below sea level; an intricate system of levees, canals, and pumping stations keeps the city afloat. East New Orleans is one of the few areas left in the four-parish metropolitan area where land is available and suitable for development.

More than half of the Almonaster Corridor is vacant; the zoning ranges from heavy industry to commercial. It is in the adjacent areas, where land is zoned residential, that 40 percent of the metropolitan growth is expected to occur in the next three years.

Besides its availability, the corridor has several locational advantages that make it an ideal industrial park site. It is only five minutes by truck via Interstate 10 from downtown New Orleans. The tracks of the Family Lines Rail System form the northern boundary, connecting at Mobile, Alabama, with lines serving the entire Northeast.

The corridor also is served by the New Orleans Public Belt Railroad, whose primary function is to haul Port of New Orleans cargo; it originates and receives cars from the eight national railroads serving New Orleans.

On the south, the corridor is bounded by the Gulf Intracoastal Waterway and the Mississippi River Gulf Outlet. The former is part of a barge traffic network extending from Brownsville, Texas, to St. Marks, Florida. The latter provides deep water access to the Gulf of Mexico, offering a speedy alternative to the Mississippi River.

Why so few takers?

With all these advantages, why isn't the corridor fully developed?

The answer is relatively simple. First, the corridor lacks proper drainage and sanitary sewer systems and an adequate road network. Second, a large portion of the potential industrial market has already been won by outlying parishes in the metropolitan area.

To some extent, the corridor has been developing on its own, particularly in those areas where the roadways and drainage are most favorable. The Michoud Assembly Facility mentioned above covers some 825 acres, and firms like Folger Coffee, Georgia Pacific, TANO Corporation, Siemens-Allis Electronics, and Litton Industries occupy relatively large sites. With its adoption of Mayor Morial's economic development program, however, the city assumed the responsibility of providing infrastructure improvements and committed itself to developing the corridor as a planned industrial park.

As a first step toward fulfilling that commitment, the Morial administration successfully lobbied in 1979 for a state law establishing a 7,000-acre Almonaster-Michoud Industrial District and creating a board of commissioners. The legislation paved the way for a permanent funding source for the district by providing for an ad valorem real property tax of 20 mills. The tax was approved by voters in a citywide referendum last May.

There is a catch. Proceeds from the tax will amount to only about $165,000 a year initially. That's because of the low assessment values in the New Orleans area, an abundance of tax-exempt land in the district, and—most of all—Louisiana's 10-year industrial exemption program. Tax revenues are not expected to cover significant capital improvements, but rather will be used to staff the industrial district board and provide marketing services, increased sanitation, and security services. As the district develops industrially, land values will increase and the tax will become more important in providing improvements.

Most of the public improvements scheduled by the city and the district board will take place within the 7,000-acre district. The remaining acreage in the corridor will be improved by private developers or reserved for future use. Within the past four years, the district has received about $2 million from HUD, EDA, and the Port of New Orleans for planning, engineering, and environmental studies.

With the engineering studies nearing completion and the environmental impact statement in its final approval stage, construction of drainage improvements is scheduled to begin later this year. These first improvements will be funded mostly by the state and HUD's community development block grant program.

Potential

The city commissioned the Philadelphia firm of Wallace, Roberts and Todd to prepare a master plan for the Almonaster Corridor, including an assessment of capital improvement needs and recommendations for management and marketing.

The transportation element presented a particular challenge to the master planners. The economic practicality of retaining an open drainage canal network meant that the truck and rail transport system had to mesh with the drainage network while keeping a maximum amount of land available for industry. The master plan also played a key role in defining the organizational structure of the district's board of commissioners.

Projections by the planning firm indicate that an additional 4,250 acres of the Almonaster Corridor will be developed by 2000. The 26 industrial classifications viewed by the planners as most suitable for the corridor fall into five general categories: metal fabrication, electronics, chemicals and drugs, ship and boat building, and stone products.

According to the plan, development of the additional land in the corridor should create some 27,375 jobs by the year 2000. It would take a public investment of $103 million but would stimulate some $1.29 billion in private investment.

Planned or under way in the corridor are: a $200 million container facility for the Port of New Orleans; a 90-acre foreign trade zone; an asphalt and concrete facility; a budding electronics industry complex, with three firms already in place; and a state-organized regional food distribution center for southern Louisiana farmers. The center is expected to give a boost to the wholesale food industry in Orleans Parish.

The city has taken an active role in marketing the corridor. It also sponsors a program to aid prospective firms with permitting and financing; it has used industrial development bonds to finance the TANO Corporation expansion and has a UDAG for SFE Technologies. It is also hoping that the corridor might be eligible for designation as a federal enterprise zone.

The Almonaster Corridor won't be fully developed until well into the twenty-first century. The area is too big and its site too difficult for overnight action. From a planner's point of view, this situation might be construed as a natural form of land banking. The land will be there when it is needed. No matter what the schedule, however, development is likely to be carefully planned and programmed.

In 1982, Robert Marak was an industrial development coordinator in the Mayor's Office of Economic Development in New Orleans.

Bringing Madison Avenue to Main Street

Robert Guskind
(February 1987)

Sometime this spring, if all goes according to plan, residents of Los Angeles will be bombarded by $1 million worth of ads inviting them to spend a few days eating, drinking, and reveling in New Orleans. They'll also be hit with millions of dollars of sales pitches on behalf of gambling in Nevada and an equally well-financed campaign urging them to spend their vacation dollars at home. On the opposite coast, Gov. Thomas Kean, standing before a backdrop of mountains, lakes, and beaches, will smile into a camera and remind people that "New Jersey and you" are "perfect together."

These state and local promoters won't be the only ones hitting the airwaves, newspapers, and magazines. Borrowing a page from the Madison Avenue image makers, states and cities around the nation are leaping headfirst into the high-stakes, big-budget game of self-promotion, selling themselves the same way car dealers hawk used cars and fast food chains extol the virtues of their hamburgers.

Whether image making is as important as many local officials and their consultants contend, or is simply a passing, if costly, fad is almost a moot point. Rare is the state or major city that hasn't brought in an advertising agency or public relations firm to dream up a jingle or create a magazine and to secure an edge in the race for business and tourist dollars.

In an era of tightfisted government spending, marketing states and cities has become big business—a huge, politically popular growth area in budgets and a boon to the consultants hired to devise the sales pitch. Nationwide, somewhere between $3 billion and $6 billion was spent in 1986 to sell states and cities. The communities have two purposes in mind: increasing tourism and attracting new business.

Some of the more lavish efforts have all the trappings of major consumer media campaigns. Consulting firms are brought in to run opinion polls measuring public perceptions, and market research surveys identify potential customers and the appeals likely to sway them. Commercial advertising agencies are hired to write catchy slogans and upbeat jingles. Celebrities and alluring models are enlisted to deliver the pitch.

The tourist appeals range from glamorous to ambiguous. Miami uses a blonde dressed in a lavish evening gown, reclining before the city skyline, to invite would-be tourists to "see Miami the way we see Miami." The Four Tops urge people to take them up on their suggestion to "do it in Detroit" (whatever "it" may be). The business pitches tend to be more practical. Oklahoma offers itself as "the profitable place to be," while Tennessee promises "yesterday's values and tomorrow's jobs."

Other locales add well-oiled public relations operations to the ads, hoping to achieve what the consultants politely call "cosmetic surgery." In these efforts, millions are spent massaging the press and business leaders to win favorable publicity, preferably in the national media.

'Perception is reality'

"With the changing economy, people can live and work wherever they choose," says Cleveland Mayor George Voinovich. "A city's image is extremely important to its competitiveness."

Voinovich should know. He came into office in 1979 on the heels of one of the most protracted public nightmares of recent times—a period beginning with both the Cuyahogan River and a former mayor's hair going up in flames and ending with the first municipal default since the Depression. But Cleveland's public standing has rebounded in recent years, thanks largely to a healthier economy and renewed credit rating—and a $6.5 million business-sponsored public relations campaign to tell national newspapers and the television networks about the changes.

"Many of the actions that affect our economic progress are based on perceptions," says George Miller, executive director of the New Cleveland Campaign, which has run the public relations drive. "Perception is reality."

To sway those perceptions, New Cleveland, in addition to its national advertising, has commissioned polling firms to gauge the extent to which the attitude of business and the media toward the city has shifted. It hired one of the largest public relations firms in the country to run the News Bureau Cleveland, which circulates stories about the city to a "blue ribbon" direct-mail list of some 15,000 national and regional "opinion leaders."

In the South, states trying to lure high-technology and service businesses have gone to great lengths to shake their lingering rural image by publicizing education reform and the cosmopolitanism of their cities. Recent North Carolina ads assured readers—over a photo of a scene from the 1960s-vintage "Andy Griffith Show"—that the state has changed greatly since the show's heyday 25 years ago.

Many of the well-funded advertising efforts of the 1980s are aimed at potential tourists. Yet, as recently as a decade ago, most public officials took a dim view of promotion campaigns. And the state and local ads that were produced were crude in comparison to commercial product advertising.

Then came "I Love New York." In 1977, New York became the first state to undertake a full-fledged image-building promotion campaign, turning its modest $200,000 advertising effort into a $5.4 million extravaganza. In an early television ad, a cheerful fisherman, vacationing along the Hudson River, beamingly announced to millions of viewers that "I'm from Cape Cod but I love New York." Within the year, vacationers started rolling in, pouring billions of dollars in new travel spending into the state's economy. Officials credited the campaign with helping New York City recover from its near-bankruptcy.

Nearly a decade later, the tourist promotion binge by the states costs $216 million a year, compared to $98.1 million in 1979, according to the U.S. Travel Data Center in Washington. Many states have doubled or quadrupled their promotion budgets: New Jersey spent $1.7 million in 1982 and $6.4 million in 1986. California, where Gov. George Deukmejian has earned a reputation as a fiscal conservative, increased its promotion budget from $470,000 to $5.1 million in one year. Illinois, which spent $50,000 on tourist promotion in the late 1960s, led the field with a budget of $19.2 million last year, followed by Michigan ($11.8 million), Tennessee ($10.7 million), New York ($10.6 million), and Florida ($9.5 million).

Local governments have jumped into the tourist arena as well, spending hundreds of billions of dollars on new convention facilities, festival marketplaces, gleaming downtown projects, sports stadiums, and other attractions designed to lure both visitors and convention goers. To keep their facilities full and the dollars flowing, convention and visitors bureaus have increased their marketing outlays from $22 million in 1973 to $250 million today.

The bulk of the money is spent on television advertising, which typically eats up 60 percent or more of promotion budgets. Convention marketers, meanwhile, concentrate on reaching association executives and other meeting planners in trade publications. Gimmicks abound, too: Many states and cities offer reporters and other "opinion leaders" lavish, all-expense-paid, "get acquainted tours." Connecticut went so far as to offer travel writers hot air balloon tours of the state.

The painful, and long-lasting, economic shake-outs of the Reagan era have contributed to this governmental love affair with tourism. "In the last decade, political leaders and other decision makers finally began to recognize that there was some economic significance to the tourism industry," says John Hunt, head of the travel and tourism program at Washington's George Washington University.

Tourism has, in fact, become a major factor in the U.S. economy, employing nearly 15 million Americans last year. State and local leaders have come to view it as a clean, relatively recession-resistant industry that requires little in the way of infrastructure and that can help offset the leakage of manufacturing jobs.

"When you're pushed to the bottom, you have no choice but to get out there and sell yourself," says Ron Forman, chairman of the Greater New Orleans Marketing Committee, the group that commissioned the Los Angeles advertising campaign. Forman estimates that the $1 million the marketing committee plans to spend in California will generate some $30 million in new business for New Orleans's severely sagging economy.

But if the search for tourists seems aggressive,

it's mild compared to the intensity states and cities bring to luring new businesses. In this area, the leaders are the Sun Belt states, which in the 1970s began to peddle their tax breaks, "good business climate," and high quality of life in northern newspapers, magazines, and television stations.

Today, state governments spend over $100 million a year on economic development advertising. Michigan is the biggest spender, with a $3.3 million outlay last year. It's followed by New Jersey ($2.9 million), New York ($2 million), Arkansas ($1.7 million), and Maryland ($1.6 million). These figures generally don't count the cost of trade missions, hiring public relations agencies, and publicizing state programs in other bureaucracies.

The budgets of many of the 10,000 economic development groups operating in cities and counties dwarf the money spent at the state level. Spartanburg, South Carolina, has spent $2.5 million over four years to market itself to business. Mobile, Alabama, is in the process of spending $4 million. When cash flowed more freely in the city, Houston spent $2 million a year on economic development promotion.

"Million dollar programs are becoming more and more common" even in relatively small communities, says Ted Levine, president of Development Counsellors International, Ltd., an economic development consulting firm based in New York. The average local marketing program spends about $1 per capita annually, he estimates, with some spending as much as $5 per capita.

That's not to say that economic development promotion efforts must be big-budget extravaganzas. Anne Arundel County, Maryland, has run a national advertising campaign for $34,000 a year by contracting with a local community college for market research and using the results to target business executives likely to be attracted by the county's 400 miles of Chesapeake Bay shoreline. Half-page ads showing a businessman working at his computer aboard a sailboat have been run in *Sail* and *Yachting* magazines at a cost of under $3,000 each, as opposed to the more than $60,000 it costs to buy a quarter-page in the *Wall Street Journal* and other national publications.

Tactics

Such "lifestyle" approaches are particularly in vogue in economic development pitches. "Quality of life is the buzzword of the decade," says Lissa Brown, Anne Arundel County's director of marketing. San Antonio offers "the good life for business" in an ad picturing its downtown Riverwalk, and Loudoun County, Virginia, where a suburban real estate boom has already created alarming traffic congestion, still promises business "an idyllic lifestyle, with lush countryside, peaceful villages, and a community spirit."

The latest fad is the promotion of local school systems. Los Angeles County hired the polling firm used by Mayor Tom Bradley and San Francisco Mayor Dianne Feinstein to measure public opinion (negative) about its schools and then launched an image-building campaign. In Prince Georges County, Maryland, a business group shelled out $250,000 to saturate Baltimore and Washington television with commercials promoting the county's school system.

The school ads are directed as much to local people as to outsiders, and as such they suggest another significant trend—toward internal marketing for the purpose of generating public support among residents. "Institutional marketing can get people to see a vision and a future for the community," says Richard Fleming, former executive director of the nonprofit Denver Partnership, who recently became the head of the Denver Chamber of Commerce.

The state of Michigan, for example, spends 65 percent of its economic development advertising budget within its own borders. Polls show that residents consider the state to have an "unresponsive government and a lousy business climate," says Louis J. Glazer, deputy director of the Michigan Department of Commerce. "Until you get over that hurdle, anything else you do doesn't matter."

Most economic development ads, however, still aim at bagging plants and offices from beyond. Their pitches rely heavily on two time-tested industrial recruiting staples: tax breaks and lack of labor unions. Nevada promotes its "favorable corporate tax structure" and "strong work ethic labor force." Kentucky's mailing to interested businesses includes a four-page memo outlining favorable provisions in the state tax code and noting that businesses can recoup $10,000 from the state if they're unsuccessfully sued by the government. Georgia promises wage rates "among the nation's lowest."

In contrast to the relatively genteel tourist competition, the economic development footrace turns ugly from time to time. Illinois last year launched a $345,000 television, radio, and print campaign lampooning business owners who moved their operations to Texas only to have them fail. The ads featured a sheepish-looking businessman wearing a 10-gallon hat and standing next to a Cadillac sporting a steer horn hood ornament and "Hook-Em" license plates. Several Texas cities fired back with their own ads, including Fort Worth, which has a $350,000 sales campaign under way.

Those who find such spectacles, and their cost, unsettling question the propriety of spending public money on promotional ventures. More and more, however, tourism promotion programs are being paid for by hotel room occupancy or other dedicated taxes, which even in smaller cities raise millions of dollars a year. Some 80 percent of convention bureau budgets nationwide are supplied by hotel taxes, according to the International Association of Convention and Visitors Bureaus.

The private sector pays more directly as well. Businesses are donating half of the $1 million New Orleans will spend on its tourist ads, and a volunteer group of advertising executives spent nine months coming up with a new "get to know us" slogan, song, and commercials for Philadelphia. Local broadcasters donated $2.5 million worth of air time to run the commercials (in the hope, perhaps, of making people forget an earlier slogan: "Philadelphia is not as bad as Philadelphians say it is").

In other cities, business groups are running big-budget economic development marketing campaigns on their own. The Denver Chamber of Commerce is kicking off a four-year, $5 million marketing campaign that was organized after market research found fewer than one in five companies even willing to consider a move to the city. The campaign, heavily angled towards advertising and public relations, follows a two-year-old effort to tone down Denver's image as an Alpine ski resort and play up its role as a regional business center. Already gone is the city's old "mile high" slogan.

In Denver and elsewhere around the country, private involvement in marketing has led to some unusual alliances between natural enemies, including government agencies used to competing for money and authority. "People recognize that the transformation of the city's image accrues to everyone's benefit," says David Gillece, deputy director of the privately funded Greater Baltimore Committee, which does advertising and public relations for the region.

"Businessmen have a self-interest in promotion," says Ken Poole of the National Council for Urban Economic Development in Washington, D.C., "and they understand it better than public officials." A new image can take up to a decade to take root, and business groups are more likely to stick with a strategy than politicians operating from election to election, says Hans Wanflu, president and general manager of the Royal Sonesta Hotel in New Orleans and a prime mover in the city's new marketing campaign.

Does it pay off?

The big question is whether it's worth hiring jingle writers and spin doctors (Washington jargon for those who try to put the best "spin" on a situation) to sell states and cities with an enthusiasm usually reserved for selling laundry detergent. Backers of the practice have assembled a raft of strong arguments and data to show how well-planned marketing strategies can pay off.

Dozens of states, for example, have documented how tourist spending and tax revenue increase with their marketing budgets. Back when Pennsylvania was spending $60,000 a year on tourist promotion, vacationers spent $4.9 billion. In 1985, when the promotion budget hit $6 million, tourists spent $8.8 billion and generated $300 million in tax revenue.

The case for economic development marketing is less clear-cut. Says Cecele Frankel, a vice-president of DCI in New York, "You can't say you're going to land 6,000 jobs every so many months if you spend a given amount of money. But there's a definite correlation between areas that do a good job of marketing themselves and growth." And a post-image campaign follow-up poll in Cleveland in 1981 found that 48 percent of business executives surveyed believed the city had improved as a place to work and live versus only 15 percent in 1978.

The most telling evidence may come from New Jersey, which has been on a promotional roll for several years. Only 62 percent of residents surveyed in 1979 rated their state a "good" or "excellent" place to live. But when pollsters asked the same question in 1985, they found a dramatic improvement: 80 percent rated their home state good or excellent.

Looking at such results, many officials are convinced the millions they've spent in the 1980s will have a long-term payoff. "Image advertising is exactly the right place to be," says Michigan's Glazer. "We're absolutely convinced that if the nation views Michigan as the center of the Rust Belt, rather than the next high-tech frontier, it's going to make an enormous difference in the economic future of the state." Michigan did benchmark polling in 1984 when its $10 million "Yes! Michigan" campaign was getting under way and may do some comparative polling in the future to gauge the results.

Even when the idea of promotional marketing is viewed favorably, however, there is often considerable dissension over the methods used.

High-cost television and national ads generate the greatest controversy. "I'm suspicious of general advertising," says Dan Whitehurst, the former mayor of Fresno, California, and now executive director of the Fresno County Economic Development Corporation. "All you have to do is look and see how many thousands of people are doing the same thing." Far better, in his view, are ads placed in narrowly circulated trade publications, which "give you access to the decision-making loop."

In stressing advertising, states and cities are entering the realm of "psychoeconomics," says Robert Friedman, president of the Washington-based Corporation for Enterprise Development, which promotes public investment in internal job creation programs. "It's not as though they're squandering huge amounts of money on the prospecting they do, but at a time when government budgets are so tight, you have to wonder if those dollars might be better spent elsewhere."

Others wonder if the rush to promote is another manifestation of the herd mentality that seems to overtake economic developers from time to time. Marketing has become "a damned-if-you-do and damned-if-you-don't proposition," says George Washington's Hunt. "These people are caught in a situation where everybody's doing it anyway so they think they've got to do it, too."

Because many governors and mayors are featured prominently in ads, aggressive marketing also raises ethical concerns about the manipulation of marketing budgets for self-promotion. "Economic development marketing can get to be very

partisan and very dicey," notes Michigan's Glazer. New Jersey Gov. Tom Kean's frequent appearances in the state's television commercials actually prompted a court suit by Democrats during his 1985 reelection campaign. They charged that the promotional spots violated the state's campaign spending limits. The courts agreed and barred the ads from the air for a time.

State and local salesmanship raises concerns that go to the heart of public-policy decisions in the budget-conscious 1980s. Critics charge that more and more spending and planning decisions are being made on the basis of promotional value rather than on real economic and community needs. When states and cities are taken in by their own public relations, says California marketing expert Jivian Tabibian, "the attributes that are the most promotable become those that get the highest priority."

The tourist-promotion binge in particular is "a rat race," says Edward C. Neeble, a professor at the University of New Orleans, that has led many locales to sink millions of dollars into projects that may not be needed or adequately planned. "Most cities are caught in a vicious circle at this point," he says. "First they develop things and promote them to fill hotel rooms. If they're successful, developers build more rooms and the city has to do more promotion, build more facilities, and plan more events."

The most successful tourist promotions are sometimes the least expected. For example, Fort Mill, South Carolina, has benefited from television evangelist Jim Bakker's 2,500-acre religious fantasy land, complete with a $1 billion "Christian amusement park" that includes a trip to heaven and a ride through hell. The theme park drew some 4.9 million visitors last year.

But less successful examples abound. One Indiana town spent $700,000 of local and federal money to build replicas of the Egyptian Pyramids, the Great Wall of China, and a Mayan Temple—none of them ever completed. Johnstown, Pennsylvania, has invited tourists to see "a town hit by 22 floods." Kansas advertises the Barbed Wire Museum in La Crosse.

"This interest in smoke-and-mirrors tricks is tragic," says Cleveland State University professor Norman Krumholz, president of the American Planning Association and former planning director for Cleveland. "It's like a Third World country receiving American aid and spending it all on a big sports stadium instead of taking an intelligent look at its economy.

"There is a certain place for trying to change the pictures in people's minds about a place and the spiritual uplifting that goes along with that," he continues. "But we tend to overdose on that, just as we believe too thoroughly in the trickle-down effect. We have to look more closely at the reality of the notion."

There's little doubt that promotion can be effective. "Everything we can do to put our best foot forward means that we're better off as a city," says Cleveland's mayor Voinovich.

Nevertheless, there are fears that some states and cities may be frittering away money trying to shape images that only time will change. Media scholars use the term "channel noise" to describe the near-impossibility of cutting through deeply held public perceptions, whether or not they're rooted in reality. It has taken Chicago almost two decades, for instance, to live down the reputation it gained in 1968, when violent clashes between demonstrators and police horrified a national television audience. Dallas is still associated with the Kennedy assassination. Cleveland's hair-on-fire mayor may no longer be the source of amusement he once was, but he hasn't been forgotten, either.

The ability to temper a public relations disaster "depends on how significant and how emotionally charged an event is," says Hunt. "Natural catastrophes seem to wear off pretty quickly, but there are situations where dumping $2 million into a public relations campaign is like throwing money down a rathole."

Philadelphia may have taken that advice to heart in time to save some money and spare itself additional national embarrassment in the wake of the 1985 MOVE debacle. The city was planning to put the MOVE incident in an upbeat light by publicizing the rebuilding of the neighborhood the MOVE bombing destroyed, when the ads were vetoed at the last minute. "MOVE was bad news," says Bruce Shaeffer of the Philadelphia public relations agency of Shaeffer & Associates. "If you do bad things, you get bad press and there isn't a damned thing that all the king's horses and all the king's men can do to put it back together again."

Guskind is a contributing editor of the National Journal *in Washington, D.C., and of* Planning.

Hatching Small Businesses

Candace Campbell
(May 1984)

Small, homegrown businesses are becoming the focus of local economic development efforts. Whether the nurturing party is a city agency, a chamber of commerce, a private corporation, or a community group, the recipient is often an indigenous, fledging business rather than an established business recruited from elsewhere.

What a start-up business often receives is space in a "business incubator," a building that offers low rent, centralized services, flexible leases, and management advice—thereby acting as a hatchery for new businesses and new jobs.

In the past year we have studied several dozen of these business incubators around the country. Most of them are publicly owned or operated, and half of the total have been in operation less than a year. Most incubators arose from a collaboration between local government, universities, and private corporations.

Almost all of the incubators began in existing, often vacant, buildings—including office buildings, warehouses, schools, post offices, shopping centers, and storefronts. The Akron, Ohio, office of economic development found its incubator building, an old warehouse, after surveying 26 vacant and underused buildings. In several other cities, abandoned factories have been donated as incubator sites.

The purchase and rehabilitation of these structures have been funded by a variety of government loans and grants, including such sources as: the federal Economic Development Administration, the Appalachian Regional Commission, Urban Development Action Grants, and Community Development Block Grants. Some have been paid for by state or locally issued industrial revenue bonds. A few resulted from the donation or bargain sale of buildings and property by private corporations.

In several of the incubator projects we surveyed, Emergency Jobs Bill and Job Training Partnership Act funds were used to provide labor to rehabilitate the buildings. In other cities, low-interest renovation loans are available to tenants.

We have found that business incubators are like mother hens. They want their chicks to hatch, grow, and leave the nest. After a few years, successful new businesses are asked to pay market-rate rent or to leave the incubator building to make room for others. These incubators are set up so that it is easier to leave the nest than enter it. Business plans are screened, and potential tenants often must be interviewed by seasoned business people before being accepted.

The industrial incubator developed by the city of Akron, Summit County, and the University of Akron works this way. Akron's economic development office manages the facility but prospective tenants' applications are reviewed by a board with representatives from the city, the county, and the Private Industry Council's job training program. Applicants also are interviewed by representatives of the Small Business Institute of the university's business school, the Service Corps of Retired Executives, and the Regional Development Board.

"Each company is evaluated based on its business plan, financing, and job potential," explains Greg Balbierz, the project manager. "The aspiring new businesses are then given a punch list of things to do before admittance." Balbierz views the business plan as the start-up firm's "sweat equity—the blueprint, backbone, and foundation of the business."

Flexibility in the leasing and management of space is typical of most incubator buildings. At the Bennington County Industrial Corporation's incubator in North Bennington, Vermont, bigger operations are offered longer leases while smaller ones are often rented on a month-to-month basis. This arrangement allows the smaller firms to be relocated within the incubator as larger firms expand. "The larger the number of jobs at stake, the longer the lease," says BCIC's former executive director John Williamson (now head of the Springfield, Massachusetts, Economic Development Corporation).

Flexibility also means that when a business falls on hard times but the future looks promising, leases are renegotiated downward and the rent is spread out over time or deferred until cash flow picks up again. June Lavelle, director of Chicago's Fulton-Carroll Center for Industry, says, "We're out to encourage people to go into business without slaughtering them; therefore, we are very flexible."

But Lavelle and other managers of business incubators also speak of running the incubator itself in a businesslike fashion. Jerry Mahone, director of the Rensselaer Polytechnic Institute's incubator program in Troy, New York, says of the fledging entrepreneurs, "You must be able to hold their hands when needed and give them a push when they need pushing." Balancing flexibility and skill in business management appears crucial to the success of an incubator.

Centralized services

The centralized services available in the incubators help to reduce the overhead costs of the new businesses located there. These services may include telephone answering, typing, copying, data processing, bookkeeping, and legal assistance. Some incubators provide computers and software specially designed for small businesses, bulk mailing equipment, WATS lines, TELEX, satellite communications, laboratories, classrooms, furniture, office equipment, libraries, conference rooms, and lunchrooms.

Some of these services and facilities are included in the rent while others are offered for a fee. For example, tenants in the Control Data Corporation's Business and Technology Centers may use the centers' conference rooms without charge eight hours a month. Most of the other services available in Control Data's centers are offered at market rate.

There is some disagreement among incubator managers on the need for centralized services. June Lavelle says the Fulton-Carroll Center in Chicago developed centralized services only after tenants expressed a strong demand for them. "Only the basic type of service is important," she adds, noting particularly phone answering and limited secretarial assistance.

Overall, the most common comment from those involved in business incubation is that "the people are more important than the building." Thus a close rapport between the building's managers and its tenants is vital.

The incubator's unique social atmosphere encourages trading relationships. In Buffalo's industrial incubator, one firm makes parts for another's assembly operation. Similarly, Chicago's Fulton-Carroll Center has five or six tenants that buy and sell from each other.

Resident managers or management teams help with business plans, product development, marketing, personnel, and the technical aspects of the incubator's businesses. Many incubators strive to maintain a mix of new and established businesses, since the best source of advice for new businesses often is other established firms. Another advantage is purely financial; the higher rents from established businesses help subsidize the start-ups.

As with a mother hen, an incubator's organizers must have the ability to meet the diverse needs of its fledgings. Says John Toon of Georgia Tech's incubator: "It takes more than a building with low rents. It takes business development people, it takes financing people, and it takes a close relationship with the companies."

With the exception of those that have established venture capital funds, most business incubators act as brokers between new businesses and investors. Sometimes this means simply providing introductions to lenders and venture capitalists; other times it means developing proposals and packaging loans to suit particular needs. The Georgia Tech center sponsors an annual two-day venture capital conference at which incubator tenants and others can meet Georgia investors.

In most locations, small businesses can take advantage of the Small Business Administration's low-interest loans through a business development center. The SBA-backed Small Business Investment Corporations (SBICs) and Minority Enterprise Small Business Investment Corporations (MESBICs) also provide equity capital in some areas. In addition, several states and local governments have developed small business revolving loan funds for new businesses. These local sources of financial assistance, if not offered directly by the organization that manages the incubator, are often located within the incubator building itself.

In Chester, Pennsylvania, the city's development office can provide incubator tenants and other small businesses with up to $15,000 in low-interest loans from a revolving loan fund. The development office controls disbursement of the loan by endorsing the checks to the business owner and each of its suppliers during the life of the loan. John Fitzgerald, the director of the development office, explains, "You have to baby-sit them. These entrepreneurs have no concept of accounting. If they are in the red for nine months and you find out on the tenth, it's too late. To help new businesses you *have* to intrude into their business for the first few months."

This intrusion sometimes takes the form of periodic reviews, which are required in the lease agreements. During these reviews, the progress of each firm is weighed against its business plan and job targets. If a firm fails to meet the targets, its lease can be terminated for cause.

The Innovation Center at Ohio University in Athens negotiates an equity position in each firm along with the tenancy agreement. The center can maintain its part-ownership forever but offers the right of first refusal to the business should the center want to sell its shares.

Public efforts

Creating jobs by creating employers is the main objective of publicly sponsored business incubators. Their organization and management are centered in city economic development departments, urban renewal authorities, and regional planning and development commissions. With some exceptions, public incubators tend to shy away from high-technology tenants and toward light assembly, manufacturing, and sometimes retail and service businesses.

One of the oldest publicly sponsored incubators is Buffalo's Incubator Industries Building, which was constructed by the city's urban renewal agency in 1978 with the aid of a $2.3 million Economic Development Administration grant. It offers no centralized services, but the tenants do have access to city loans and assistance programs.

More common than new construction is the conversion of existing vacant buildings. The East End Manufacturing Center in Chester, Pennsylvania, for example, is in an old knitting yarn factory, converted with the aid of $1.3 million in EDA and Community Development Block Grant funds.

St. Paul, home of two Control Data business and technology centers, has just opened its first public incubator as part of its "Homegrown Economy Project." The idea is to diversify the local economy by encouraging the growth of light industry, thus reducing the amount of goods and services imported from outside the city. This public incubator is unusual, by the way, because the city does not own the building. Instead, it has worked out a deal with the owner-developer of a recently renovated, 60,000-square-foot building in the Midway industrial area. In return for a city-financed low-interest mortgage, the developer has agreed to provide incubator space and also to use his profit to renovate other property in the same area. "From the city's perspective, it's a good deal," says Richard Mahony, who directs the Homegrown Economy Project. "We get a building rent-free, although not cost-free, and we get our money back in 10 years."

Many of the nonprofit incubators target development to a particular industrial area or neighborhood. The organizers are industrial development associations, chambers of commerce, and community organizations with broad local support and a good real estate development track record.

The Bennington County (Vermont) Industrial Corporation, for example, has been developing real estate since 1957. In 1978, the group bought an old mill complex, renovated it in two years at a cost of $1.2 million (paid for by an EDA grant and state loans), and offered space to small businesses. The building presently houses 22 firms, ranging from a company that refashions laboratory beakers into gourmet cookware to a firm that manufactures Teflon-coated fabric (some of which was used to cover the Humphrey Metrodome in Minneapolis). Another tenant is a sheltered workshop for the mentally retarded, which provides lunch service for the building's tenants. The industrial corporation's former director, John Williamson, estimates that 250 jobs have been created at the center since 1978.

Another example, also mentioned above, is the Fulton-Carroll Center for Industry, which was started by the Industrial Council of Northwest Chicago in late 1980. Presently leasing its 340,000 square feet to 25 businesses, the center has created a net increase of 249 jobs and graduated seven firms in three years. Its director, June Lavelle, estimates that 50 percent of the jobs created are low-skilled and the rest semi-skilled. . . .

The corporations

Private corporations establish business incubators for two reasons: the chance to make a profit and the chance to contribute to the community. For example, Control Data, which has developed its business and technology centers in some 20 cities, both in the U.S. and abroad, sells computer, library, and secretarial services. "Control Data has made the development of new businesses part of its product line," says company representative Sharon O'Flannigan.

Another private-sector developer of incubators is Loren Schultz, president of Technology Centers

International, Inc., who has five "technology enterprise centers" in operation and six in the development stage. Like other incubators described in this article, TCI offers below-market rents, centralized services, and equipment rental in its incubator buildings. An unusual feature is TCI's "champion"—a subcontractor with extensive business experience who helps incubator firms with business planning and financing. Initial consultation is free, but follow-up assistance is on a retainer or fee basis. Each of Schultz's centers has a locally developed venture capital fund of $3 to $5 million and the possibility of financing through TCI's larger master venture fund.

One of Schultz's newest centers is in a former high school in Minneapolis two blocks from the University of Minnesota campus. This incubator is unusual in that the building will be operated as a cooperative and the mix of enterprises will include two dance companies, a sculpture school, and 30 to 40 high-tech firms.

In Rockford, Illinois, where unemployment has hovered around 20 percent the last two years, the Barber-Coleman Corporation started the Business Center for New Technology in 1982 in an idle textile machinery plant. The company does not offer any financial assistance itself, but it has donated space in the incubator to the local business development agency.

Barber-Coleman's approach may signal a trend if other corporations pick up on the idea and offer surplus manufacturing space for use as business incubators. John Dixon, the incubator coordinator, already has met with corporate representatives from two other states considering similar centers.

While it's clear that most incubators are still in the fledging stages, their early experiences offer some suggestions to potential developers:

● Evaluate the potential entrepreneurs. Is there a market for their ideas and products?

● Compare the cost of renovating an old structure with the price of building new.

● Enlist qualified people with business experience to manage the incubator.

● Select a mix of new and established businesses.

● Don't waste money on unnecessary services.

● Avoid conflicts by developing explicit lease agreements, but be flexible.

Candace Campbell is a former planner for the Neighborhood

Development and Conservation Center in Oklahoma City.
She surveyed business incubators for a research study at the
University of Minnesota's Humphrey Institute of Public
Affairs and is now a partner in a St. Paul consulting firm,
Pryde Roberts Development Services.

Silicon Strips

William Fulton
(May 1986)

In central New Jersey they call it the "zip strip"—
the band of land alongside Route 1 that qualifies
for a prestigious Princeton zip code. In the last couple of years, this area has given new meaning to
the term "high-tech corridor."

In California's Silicon Valley and along Route
128 near Boston, the term describes highway strips
that have evolved from breeding grounds for fledgling high-technology research businesses—usually
spawned by major universities—into a profusion
of industrial and office development that no planning effort can keep up with. But along the zip
strip, the corridor and its problems seem to have
arrived *before* the high-tech businesses.

Princeton University's Forrestal Center is just
beginning to spin off research firms, but large corporations and speculative office buildings are
flocking to the area, creating traffic congestion and
driving up the cost of housing. Route 1 suggests
that even the likelihood of a future Silicon Valley
near a major university is enough to generate more
development than planners can keep up with.

The first high-tech corridors were isolated phenomena: Route 128 in the East—which began
sprouting entrepreneurs from MIT in the late
1940s, and Silicon Valley on the West Coast, with
few in between.

Now, however, the Route 1 story is being repeated all over the country—in areas as diverse as
Route 202 near Philadelphia (less than 50 miles
from Princeton); the "Sunset Corridor" outside of
Portland, Oregon; Austin, Texas; and the suburban
counties around Washington, D.C. Almost every
large metropolitan area, it seems, has a "Silicon
Forest," a "Silicon Desert," or a "Silicon Mountain." Some are popping up more or less by accident, while many others are being created

deliberately by state and local governments.
Sprawling along a major highway, the typical corridor often passes through a half-dozen or more
suburban jurisdictions, leading Frank Popper of
Rutgers University to dub it a "one-road Los Angeles."

The high-tech corridors may not represent a
large part of the national real estate market, but experts at the Urban Land Institute and other research organizations agree that they are among the
fastest-growing segments of the market. As a result, they are stirring up familiar questions about
the impact of economic growth on the quality of
life and the issue of control over development.

"These things are being looked at exactly like big
power plants were in the 1970s, or hazardous waste
in the early 1980s," Popper says.

But the analogy isn't quite right. Unlike traditional industries or nuclear power plants, high-tech
businesses are footloose, able to locate just about
anywhere. This means that high-tech firms place
a premium on the very quality of life that the corridors are destroying.

Footloose

The footloose nature of high-tech firms also has
led to intense competition among cities eager to attract them. This competition makes the current situation far different from the 1970s, when growth
control was also an issue in many places. Local
planners today are concerned more with economic
development and less with land-use regulation,
and they are expected not just to plan but to produce results. Most of the research and writing on
the high-tech industry deals with how to attract it,
not how to plan for it.

"High tech is harder to deal with [than growth
control in the 1970s] because everybody wants it
so much," says Florida growth control expert John
DeGrove. "If you have a chance to get it, you'll
take it and hope to hell you'll figure out the infrastructure problems later."

But around the country, both in mature high-
tech corridors and emerging areas, local planners
are beginning to face up to the problems. In Silicon
Valley and along Route 128, communities that
rarely cooperated in the past are getting together
to discuss common problems. In emerging areas,
some planners are looking ahead to identify potential problem areas. And everywhere, state and local
governments are becoming aware that high-tech

industry might not be the clean solution to economic development it has been touted as. For too long, says Michael Greenberg, a toxics expert who teaches at Rutgers, planners have regarded high-tech industry as a no-lose proposition.

In fact, the production processes of the electronics industry involve a number of toxic materials. A recent study by a Tufts University professor revealed that about 20 percent of the hazardous waste in Massachusetts was produced by high-technology firms. Groundwater contamination from leaky underground hazardous waste storage sites in Silicon Valley also is a major concern. When the Environmental Protection Agency recently added 20 Silicon Valley sites to its Superfund cleanup list, 18 were sites used by high-tech firms.

Greenberg and other experts in the field agree that local planners are just beginning to talk to developers about their role in preventing and solving the problem of high-tech toxics. More typical till now has been the response of the Silicon Valley area, which has relied on a governmental solution, lobbying the state legislature—unsuccessfully, so far—for regional groundwater protection.

Apart from the toxics question, most of the planning problems associated with high-tech corridors arise from an underlying land-use imbalance. In particular, poor distribution of employment centers and affordable housing has led to severe traffic congestion.

High-tech research and development concentrations are typically housed in small (20,000–50,000 square feet) buildings spread out into a number of different suburban jurisdictions. Each of the suburbs typically protects its own interests first, zoning the land along the corridor for industry to the exclusion of housing, or vice versa.

In the 1970s, several states appropriated some of the land-use authority traditionally held by local governments in order to preserve special areas that were growing rapidly. California created the Coastal Commission, New York the Adirondack Park Agency, and New Jersey the Meadowlands and Pinelands commissions. Other fast-growing states, such as Vermont, Oregon, and Florida, adopted more general land-use laws designed to protect the environment.

In this decade, local governments have begun to rebel against state land-use efforts. Thus, in high-tech corridors, it has been difficult to gather a con-

sensus on issues other than building new highways. There are signs of change, though.

Route 128

Nowhere in the country are local governments more fiercely independent than in New England. But on the periphery of the Route 128 high-tech corridor outside Boston, some communities are getting together for the first time to try to deal with land-use questions, particularly those involving traffic congestion.

Part of the reason is that new roads are no longer an easily available option. "Almost every road-building program will result in significant opposition," notes Rosamond DeLori, chair of the Lincoln Planning Board.

In three areas near Route 128, three groups of towns have set up joint voluntary review committees to examine development proposals and make recommendations to the locality involved. The cooperative groups have no legal authority now, but if the review process—which local officials compare to Florida's Development of Regional Impact system—succeeds, the local governments may ask the state legislature to give them statutory power.

The towns are not on Route 128 proper, but along radial corridors spreading to the east and north, where development is just beginning to hit in a big way. Traditionally, says DeLori, "the towns haven't even talked to each other." In fact, with the onset of high-tech development, they began suing each other over projects.

The miniregional effort began when the women selectmen from Burlington, Bedford, Lincoln, and Lexington began to meet informally. "So there was a nucleus of people who trusted each other," says DeLori. The other two subregional groups were created with assistance from the chambers of commerce.

Silicon Valley

The same thing is happening, to a certain extent, in Silicon Valley, where the maldistribution of industrial and residential land is the major issue. Historically, Silicon Valley cities have competed for high-tech development by zoning large amounts of land for industrial use—at the expense of land for housing.

Most of the employment centers are strung along the south rim of San Francisco Bay from San Jose to Palo Alto, about 15 miles to the northwest. Far from being the hub of the metropolitan area, San Jose—the fifteenth largest city in the country—serves as a bedroom community for such high-tech suburbs as Sunnyvale, Santa Clara, and Mountain View. Although it has a little over half of Santa Clara County's population, San Jose contains only 31 percent of the county's jobs.

Silicon Valley is a good illustration of the way high-tech corridors try to deal with their problems. The area has been more than willing to provide transportation improvements and to push the state for groundwater protection. Santa Clara County currently has two half-cent sales taxes, one to build a light rail transit system and another for freeway construction. But the cities traditionally have been unwilling to do anything about the jobs/housing imbalance.

"If it's a choice between more housing density and importing workers, they'll import the workers," Santa Clara County Supervisor Susanne Wilson says of Silicon Valley residents. "They'll take the crowded freeways."

But this year, for the first time ever, at the urging of San Jose Mayor Tom McEnery, five of the major industrial cities in the valley, including San Jose, have gotten together to talk about the possibility of converting some prized vacant land from industrial to residential use. Gary Schoennauer, planning director for San Jose, says that, because of the extent of Silicon Valley's traffic problems, cities are getting more "nerve."

"I didn't think we'd ever get to this point—five cities meeting in the same room," he says. Though not even Schoennauer is willing to predict that the cooperative effort will yield any results, he says the fact that they are meeting at all "tells me that there is a political constituency out there."

Of course, not everyone is convinced that this kind of bottom-up planning can work. "We're not counting on bottom-up in Florida," says John De-Grove, who oversaw the state's land-use program as director of Florida's Department of Community Affairs. (DeGrove is now director of the Joint Center for Environmental and Urban Problems in Boca Raton, which deals mostly with growth management issues.) He adds: "By the time things get bad enough that local governments are willing to get together, they're pretty damn bad."

DeGrove may be right. The cooperative approach seems to hold the most hope for the mature areas such as Silicon Valley and Route 128, where land-use and traffic problems have become monstrous. In the emerging areas, state or regional land-use controls may be the only way to go.

Perhaps the nation's leading state-control success story is the "Sunset Corridor" outside Portland, Oregon. In the 1970s, Oregon passed state laws directing all local governments to draw up urban growth boundaries—lines that would represent the outer limit for urban development for a 20-year period. The law did a great deal to help the state manage growth and maintain the quality of its environment.

But when Oregon's leading industry, the timber business, was hit particularly hard by the recession in the early 1980s, the land-use law was called antibusiness, and in 1982, it barely survived a repeal effort.

But after that, Oregon was able to use the law to its advantage in actually encouraging high-tech businesses along the Sunset Corridor. The urban growth boundaries don't just require cities to determine where growth *won't* grow. They also demand that they determine and plan for where growth will go.

"Companies building new plants mainly want to know what the rules are," Henry Richmond of 1,000 Friends of Oregon, a citizens' watchdog group, was quoted as saying last year. "They find that our land-use programs, tough on saving the countryside, are pro-housing and pro-industry. We've found ways to aid industry by identifying and making accessible more industrial sites within the urban growth areas." Included within the growth boundaries are 60,000 acres zoned for industry.

The result: In 1983 and 1984, the electronics industry's two boom years after the recession, the number of electronics manufacturing firms in Oregon grew by 80 percent—the highest figure in the nation.

Recently, however, some Portland-area developers have sought a loosening of the boundaries. According to Jill Hinckley, land-use coordinator for the Portland-area Metropolitan Services District, several industrial developers have asked for amendments so they can construct more high-tech buildings in the Sunset Corridor. Even if local officials oppose the changes in industrial land, Hinckley adds, they may push for boundary changes to provide land for housing. . . .

William Fulton is a contributing editor of Planning.

SOS For the Working Waterfront

Ann Breen and Dick Rigby
(June 1985)

While it is difficult to generalize where literally hundreds of communities are involved—at different stages of development, in all sections of the country, and on bodies of water ranging from giant lakes to small streams—we think it's safe to predict that there will be many a fight over waterfront use in the coming years.

An examination of four communities thought to be in the forefront on the issue suggests an increasing concern about the potential disappearance of traditional, often small-scale, marine businesses—commercial fishing and related wholesale and retail operations, boat building and repair, ship chandlers, tugboat bases, marinas, sail makers, tour operations, boat rentals.

The issue is whether these enterprises will be forced by market pressures to vacate areas that are increasingly being eyed by commercial interests. For them, and often for the city's economic development establishment, the working waterfronts occupy land that is ready for redevelopment with such "higher" economic uses as offices, housing, festival marketplaces, and stadiums.

Meanwhile, the business owners themselves are starting to organize to resist displacement. And they're gaining allies in city government and elsewhere. The examples that follow tell more.

The point at which the Miami River meets Biscayne Bay is where the city began—at a trading post where settlers swapped goods with the Indians who traveled by canoe from Lake Okeechobee. The narrow river (only 90 feet wide in some spots) is five and a half miles long from the bay to the point inland where it is blocked by a dam. Thus, in the shadows of downtown skyscrapers, one is treated to a most unusual urban scene: ocean-going freighters parked in rows alongside commercial fishing boats, tugs, yacht storage and repair yards—all strung out along the river in varying stages of upkeep.

The clash of competing interests is clearly visible along the river. It is dramatized by the juxtaposition of the gleaming, $90-million Knight conference center and, just opposite, Tommy's Boatyard, which has been at this site since 1930. Operator Tommy Curry is worried that his lease won't be renewed when it runs out soon and notes that downtown development has pushed his taxes up to $30,000 a year. At last report, Tommy's was hanging on, barely, having been granted some tax relief by the city.

In 1978, the city's planning and community development departments commissioned a riverfront study from Wallace McHarg Roberts & Todd and Economics Research Associates. The consultants recommended three parcels along the east end of the river, close to downtown, as sites for housing. The sites adjoin Miami Shipyards, a large and successful repair business, and thus the question was raised as to whether heavy marine industry can coexist with townhouses.

More recently, the marine businesses themselves have begun to speak up, spurred by rising concern about abandoned boats, crime, dredging, and commercial pressures. Last year, the Miami River Revival Committee and the Marine Council, which represents the boating community and related marine industry, persuaded Florida governor Bob Graham to appoint a task force to study conditions along the river. That group, headed by Miami lawyer Robert Parks, reported to the governor last December with a variety of recommendations. Among them: tax relief for river-related businesses, including fishing fleets, boat repair yards, and freighter loading operations.

The committee also proposed the establishment of a "blue belt," or marine zone, a district similar to an agricultural green belt, where a ceiling would be put on marine business property taxes. Statewide, the idea is strongly supported by boating interests, including marina operators, who say they are being squeezed out by waterfront condominiums.

Working Marin

On the West Coast, in Marin County, California, there is similar competition for control of a working waterfront in Sausalito's Marinship area. Marinship is the name of a 200-acre portion of the waterfront that was used for World War II Liberty Ship construction. Today, it's a hodgepodge of boatyards, houseboats, shacks, and salvage yards. It's adjacent to Sausalito's popular downtown tourist district.

Instead of a governor's task force, as in Miami, the key actors in Sausalito are members of a grassroots organization known as "Art Zone." The group includes artists and writers, as well as those working in marine-related businesses. Organized in 1980 by Stewart Brand, publisher of *The Whole Earth Catalog* and adviser to former California governor Jerry Brown, the group was a response to the dawn bulldozing of Bob's Boatyard, a beloved, though bedraggled, local institution.

Art Zone's mission is to educate the community about the working waterfront and develop support for local maritime arts and crafts. Its name is meant to contrast with the idea of a "war zone," which is what Art Zone's members fear the waterfront is becoming. The group has sponsored a Maritime Day, published a newsletter and a column in a local paper, and monitored the town government—thus becoming a factor in local politics.

A recent focus of conflict is the Marina Plaza development, a two-building office complex that happens to be right next door to Gate 3, a particularly rundown section of Marinship, an area, in fact, that looks like a 1960s commune. The Marina Plaza developers sought city condemnation of Gate 3 on the grounds that it "endangered the health and safety of the general public."

The developers also charged the city with neglecting to enforce its own ordinances. And, in fact, city zoning prohibits residential uses along most of the waterfront. That zoning was passed in the late 1960s to prevent condominium development along the shoreline, but it had the effect of making most of the current waterfront residences illegal. Until the Marina Plaza challenge, the city had done little to enforce the law.

In an attempt to balance the conflicting values represented by Gate 3 and Marina Plaza, the city, last year, hired local architect Walter Stewart to prepare a master plan for the entire Marinship area. Stewart, whose task has been summed up as trying to legislate funk, is trying to balance the community's extremes. He anticipates including a new mixed-use zone that would allow some limited office development along the waterfront, while at the same time preserving the marginal marine businesses and making some provision for existing residences.

In Seattle, as in Sausalito, a high-minded shoreline policy had an unfortunate side effect, at least in the eyes of those interested in retaining a working fishing fleet on Lake Union, a mile north of downtown.

The policy in question, the Seattle Shoreline Master Program, adopted in accord with Washington State's 1971 Shoreline Management Act, placed the highest value on public access to the waterfront, preserving views, and maintaining open water—not on commercial ventures.

In accord with this policy, the city, in 1982, approved three restaurant proposals for Lake Union. One of the restaurants, with an adjacent marina and retail space, was to be built on Henry Pier on the south end of Lake Union. The pier looked unkempt and disorderly, but its five marine businesses employed 84 people in 1981 and did about $4.3 million worth of business. Waterfront observers pointed out that the Henry Pier was unique in its ability to handle certain kinds of heavy repairs. The zoning dispute took over two years to resolve.

Despite the restaurant approval, Lake Union's working waterfront may have won out in the long run, for the fishing industry has coalesced for the first time on land-use issues. In 1982, the Seattle Marine Business Coalition, a group of some 120 firms, was organized, and it commissioned a study to document the value of marine businesses on Lake Union and the adjoining ship canal in the Ballard area. The study's report, prepared by Natural Resource Consultants of Seattle, placed the overall value of the 1,400-vessel, ocean-going fleet based in the city at about $1 billion. The 1979–80 catch was worth $307 million.

And finally, in 1983, the city council voted to make restaurants conditional waterfront uses, noting that they "shall not usurp land needed for and better suited to water-dependent and water-related industrial and commercial use."

"We have lost the southern end of Lake Union," said attorney Thomas Malone, who heads the marine business coalition, "but we have won the war to save the lake. We have succeeded in altering the political consciousness of the city."

Currently, the city is debating its entire shoreline policy. The staff of the land-use division has been heading in the direction of recommending an "urban maritime zone" where priority would be given to maritime businesses. It's not yet known if the city council will approve such a zone for the south end of Lake Union, where offices and marinas now compete with industrial and marine businesses.

Down east

While Seattle is in the throes of working out a new regulatory approach to the preservation of marine businesses, Portland, Maine, has already acted. Its city council voted, in April 1983, to permit mixed, commercial use of a portion of the central waterfront along Casco Bay—but to preserve the territory on either side for industrial waterfront uses.

Portland has a rich maritime history, blessed as it is with a natural deepwater harbor. The city is small, with a population of only 61,500, and the central waterfront is immediately adjacent to the downtown core. The fact that the downtown is extremely compact means that what happens on one block has an immediate impact elsewhere. In the last decade, numerous structures have been restored in the area called the Old Port Exchange. Boutiques, chic restaurants, and offices have moved into the several-square-block area.

Meanwhile, the central waterfront, a mile and a half along Commercial Street, continues to function as a working waterfront. The fishing fleet numbers about 200 boats. The atmosphere along the 15 wharves—most privately owned—is informal and rents are low. Commercial Street is busy with trucking, warehouses, and related businesses.

The city and state governments have made major investments at both ends of the central waterfront. At the east end, they invested heavily in the $50 million Bath Iron Works dry dock, one of the largest such installations on the East Coast. The dry dock could employ up to 1,000, depending on the vagaries of Navy contracts and the ship repair business in general. At the other end of the waterfront is a new, municipal fish pier, built with $15 million in public funds.

It is the part of the central waterfront between the Bath works and the fish pier that is the major focus of controversy in Portland. In 1981, the city hired the American City Corporation, the consulting arm of the Rouse Company, to prepare recommendations for this area. Its market analysis indicated that the waterfront could support housing, offices, and a hotel, requiring some $11 million in public investments. Several wharves were slated for removal.

American City has said repeatedly that the uses it proposed were compatible with a working waterfront. It pointed to the examples of Boston, Baltimore, and Oakland, California, where, it said, higher income uses coexist with industrial waterfront uses. Others, it should be noted, have cited those examples as proving the opposite.

The recommendations aroused the ire of owners of the waterfront businesses. They charged that American City had not talked to them, although, for its part, the firm says it talked to more people in Portland than it usually does in making an analysis of an area's potential.

"We were pretty vocal in attacking the plan," says Robert Snyder, Jr., of Blake Supply Company, president of the Waterfront Preservation Association, a group of about 45 firms organized in opposition to the American City plan. The group has since virtually disbanded, in part because of certain actions taken by the city and in part because some waterfront business owners have come to see the suggestions of the American City report as either sound or inevitable.

What the city did was to create two new zoning districts along the waterfront. At both ends, covering 11 of the 15 wharves, it created a restructured waterfront zone (W–2) where permitted uses are marine (16 specific activities,), commercial (including restaurants and marine retail), and, public. Everything else—boutiques, hotels, condominiums—is barred.

The second, much smaller, new zone is mixed use (W–1). It allows a range of 14 commercial activities—including offices, hotels, boutiques, and residential on the upper floors along the north (city) side of Commercial Street. Other housing is possible as a conditional activity so long as it doesn't displace fishing berths. All marine uses are also allowed.

Ironically, some of the property owners in the more restricted zone who were most vociferous in urging protection of the working waterfront are now contemplating selling their property to commercial developers. The new uses would, however, require zoning exceptions.

Others are adamant about staying. "I don't talk to real estate people," John MacGowan, manager of Custom House Wharf in the center of the mixed-use zone, told the Portland *Evening Express.* "I don't like this stuff where you drive out a lot of people who can't afford these improvements." MacGowan is planning to build a new $100,000 packing plant for R&S Seafood Company, a major tenant on his wharf.

Despite such activity—including a $1 million investment in a boatyard in the restrictive zone—it's not certain that Portland's waterfront can withstand the commercial pressure described in the American City report.

Summing up

These four cities, of course, are only a small sample of what's happening to working waterfronts across the country. But certain conclusions that can be drawn from them may help in understanding the situation elsewhere.

Character. We note, first, that marine businesses may make a major contribution to a city's character. The question is whether a city values that character. If it does, it must deal with the fact that many of the waterfront businesses, customarily low-margin operations, may need financial subsidies.

The question of character came into play in Seattle, where many questioned whether the city would indeed be better off if the Lake Union shoreline lost its houseboats and marine businesses. It also was an issue in Portland, where the city government has, for the moment, made a conscious decision to encourage the lobster and fishing fleets to stay downtown.

Perception. A related factor is that marine businesses may look unkempt and disorderly—even when they are successful. Thus, for example, Plato Cox's Auto-Marine Engineers yard in Miami is frequently dubbed a junkyard when, in fact, it is a busy and profitable repair facility known worldwide. Similarly, the local fishing industry was, to some extent, dependent on the repair operations of the Henry Pier on Seattle's Lake Union; others dismiss these and similar marine businesses as marginal.

Blue-collar question. Any study of working waterfronts must also deal with the issue of blue-collar employment. Do blue-collar jobs deserve protection in an age of high tech? Are restaurant jobs equivalent to ship repair jobs? Some communities are answering no; they are placing a high value on employment diversity. The trick now is to translate that value into job protection.

We often refer to a "fishing industry." But a closer look shows that most marine businesses are small and their operators are fiercely independent—even idiosyncratic. They cannot always be counted on to unite politically to protect themselves, although, in the cases presented here, there are signs of an awakening.

Regulation. All four cases reflect the difficulty of enacting appropriate regulations to protect marine businesses. In Portland, the situation is particularly ironic in that the owners of leading waterfront businesses are having second thoughts about the restrictive nature of the new marine protection zone that they helped to enact.

In Seattle, we see the difficulty of defining "water-dependent" uses, protected under the city's shoreline policy. Is it appropriate to describe a seafood restaurant as a water-dependent use simply because it offers public access to the waterfront?

Ultimately, shoreline communities must decide whether to view their waterfront as simply a commodity or as a community resource. If it's viewed as a commodity like any other piece of real estate, there is little justification for a city to intervene in the workings of the marketplace, any more than government steps in to save small drugstores or corner groceries.

The other, more complicated view is that a waterfront is a community resource and that it differs from other potential development sites by virtue of its proximity to what is inherently public, the adjacent body of water. This view holds that what happens to the waterfront should not be left only to private developers, and that other values besides strictly economic ones should be considered. Such values might include protection of blue-collar jobs, retention of marine enterprises as tourist attractions, and preservation of the community's individuality.

This broader view of the waterfront provides a rational basis for intervention, beyond standard zoning and police controls, to curb the excesses of development. But exactly what this intervention should be is not easy to decide. Miami's "blue-belt" notion of taxing on the basis of present marine use, not development potential, is one avenue. Another is the suggestion, also aired in Miami, that development rights be assigned to waterfront tracts; those rights could then be sold and applied elsewhere, with the sales benefiting existing waterfront businesses.

Ann Breen and Dick Rigby head the Waterfront Center in Washington, D.C.

Office in the Dell

William Fulton
(July 1986)

Thirty miles northeast of midtown Manhattan, Stamford, Connecticut (pop. 102,000), has become one of the leading corporate headquarters cities in the world. In Houston, the Galleria-Post Oak area would be the ninth-largest downtown in America—if it were a downtown, instead of a quasi suburb 10 miles away. In California, the Orange County city of Costa Mesa, 35 miles from Los Angeles City Hall, is building a $65 million performing arts center to complement a forest of office buildings and one of the largest shopping malls in the country. And outside Dallas, a former ranch called Las Colinas, strategically located close to the Dallas-Fort Worth Airport, is rapidly becoming the most prestigious corporate address in the region.

All across the country, a new kind of "downtown" is emerging. Like the traditional urban downtown, it is a center for employment, commerce, and culture. But it's usually located far from the center of the old city, in an area that until recently was thought of as a bucolic suburb. Some of these centers are emerging almost overnight in older, traditionally low-rise suburban shopping areas. Others are being planned from scratch on raw land, much as the new towns of the 1960s were. And planners and researchers are puzzled about what they represent and how to deal with them.

In fact, experts in the field haven't even been able to agree on what to call them. Terms like "suburban activity centers," "urban villages," "outer cities," and "megacenters" have been kicked around, but nothing has caught on.

Where the jobs are

Whatever they should be called, suburban downtowns are everywhere, from New Jersey and Michigan to Texas and California. "The suburban downtown phenomenon is very widespread," says Peter Muller, a University of Miami geographer, who has been researching them. "And it's not restricted to the Sun Belt."

In simplest terms, suburban downtowns are employment centers, representing a shift of jobs away from central cities. Office employers—the lifeblood of the postwar downtown—have been heading for the suburbs in increasing numbers. As one builder in Las Colinas was quoted as saying, "Corporations are attracted to the same amenities as residential buyers"—fresh air, grass, and proximity to a growing percentage of the labor force.

In fact, the unprecedented pace of office construction in the last five years has dramatically altered the shape of suburban America. While the suburban population is growing slowly, employment is mushrooming. According to The Office Network of Houston, which tracks construction and leasing of office space nationally, 57 percent of all U.S. office space was located in traditional downtown areas in 1981, while 43 percent was elsewhere. In the last five years, so much construction has gone on in the suburbs that the figures have flipped—57 percent is now located outside of urban downtowns and only 43 percent is in the old central business districts.

The nature of suburban employment also is changing rapidly. When the rush to the suburbs began just a few years ago, it was made up mostly of "back office" workers like clerical employees in banks' credit card operations. But real estate location experts say that middle management is heading for the suburbs now, too. For example, Merrill Lynch's large new operation in Princeton, New Jersey, includes 50 money-market managers. Only a few years ago, such a move from Wall Street would have been unthinkable. Following the middle managers to the suburbs are large accounting and law firms and other service-oriented businesses traditionally found only in big-city downtowns.

"All the stuff that doesn't *have* to be downtown is moving to the suburbs," says David Dowall, professor of urban and regional planning at the University of California, Berkeley.

Because of this massive employment shift, a whole new kind of city is being created in the suburbs. But as real estate consultant Christopher Leinberger, managing partner of California-based Roberts Charles Lesser, Inc., puts it: "Nobody has an image of what that city should be." Developers want to build at urban densities. Planners demand suburban-style height and parking requirements. And residents often rebel at the resulting traffic congestion.

The result, says Leinberger, is something that is "neither fish nor fowl." The new downtowns aren't really suburban. They employ up to 100,000 people, often in tall office buildings. And even when they're located close to commuter rail stations, they're frequently characterized by massive traffic jams.

But new downtowns aren't really urban, either. Most are designed for the automobile, with little concern for pedestrians or transit riders and with few of the urban characteristics that can make a downtown job enjoyable. And some of the businesses are reporting difficulty finding employees for lower paying jobs. Having moved to the suburbs partly to draw upon the attractive suburban work force, they're inaccessible to the urban working class—a group that, ironically, could become more important as the number of suburban women looking to reenter the work force dwindles. "It's increasingly difficult to find housewives in the suburbs sitting at home not working," says Dowall.

In short, as Houston developer Giorgio Borlenghi put it at a conference on the subject not long ago: "Satellite areas perform a city's urban functions, but they don't become downtowns."

Why not? Why have whole new cities sprung up in front of us over the last 10 years without much attention from planners or designers? They've been ignored partly out of snobbishness—as if the suburbs weren't worthy of serious attention, even while they were capturing two-thirds of all office construction, as they have been doing over the past few years.

"We've been ignoring a major part of our urban landscape," says J. Thomas Black, staff vice-president of the Urban Land Institute, which is just beginning to research the subject. "There is a tremendous bias among urban designers, who don't like to admit that the suburban centers exist. There's a real shortage of concepts as to what the alternatives are."

"Suburban planners are used to dealing with smaller scale development problems, what to do with a commercial strip, for instance," notes APA deputy director Frank So, who helped organize the "Suburbs Becoming Cities" workshop being presented this month in Philadelphia. "I don't know how many of those planners realize that they are on a new plateau, where they're going to be faced with 20-to-30-story office buildings."

Many researchers and consultants who have been looking at the suburbs agree that suburban planners—used to dealing with subdivision regulations and shopping malls—may not be up to the office invasion.

Talking about the mishmash of development around Princeton, Ingrid Reed, the university administrator who chairs the Mercer County Planning Board in New Jersey, complains: "I have not seen any planners who can tell me how to do it better."

One of the reasons few suburban downtowns have done better is that, as suburban buildings have gotten bigger, the underlying assumptions about suburban development—auto orientation, campus settings, low scale—haven't changed.

"When you take certain things for granted, such as the use of the automobile, that implies a certain pattern," says ULI's Black. "You get a driveway and a parking lot and a building, and they don't relate to each other in some sensible way." Moreover, say some experts, suburban areas are willing to accept greater density—temporarily ignoring side effects like traffic jams—but they often won't accept taller buildings.

"A building is just like a balloon," says John Kriken, a partner with the architecture firm of Skidmore, Owings & Merrill in San Francisco. "It blows up to fill out the envelope allowed by law." In many suburban communities, Kriken adds, allowable floor area ratio is high—four, five, even eight to one—but height is limited to between three and six stories. That means buildings will be low and bulky, leaving designers little room to create "people spaces."

In Leinberger's view, the low-rise approach is not in the suburbs' best interest. Campus settings, he says, are no more useful than surface parking lots in creating a downtown atmosphere. "Even with a lot of grass, it's the same basic thing—there's no way you can actually walk from building to building." And in Westport, Connecticut, once the archetypal affluent suburb, local residents are, in fact, not worried about "Manhattanization" so much as encroaching "Stamfordization"—the onslaught of large, corporate-type office campuses.

Worries

Among suburban dwellers, there is fear that the suburban downtown is bringing the city and its problems—particularly traffic congestion—to the tranquil areas they moved to in order to escape the city in the first place. And so they are organizing themselves to resist the commercial growth of the suburbs.

"This is the hottest political issue in the country," says Leinberger. "The suburbs are trying to hang on to the image of what they were 20 or 30 years ago."

"I think we're revving up for the next growth control era," adds David Dowall. "Only this time they'll be commercial and industrial growth controls."

In Northern California, where the residential growth control movement reached its zenith in the late 1970s, there is now a renewed effort to restrict commercial growth through ballot initiatives. Even in North Carolina, traditionally a state with few restraints on economic growth, growth-control advocates have been elected to local office in several cities in the fast-growing Research Triangle area.

Interestingly, the commercial development that many suburbanites believe will choke them has been partly self-induced. In the 1970s, commercial growth often was favored over residential growth by communities eager to boost sales tax revenues, reported Cynthia Kroll, a regional economist with the Center for Real Estate and Urban Economics at the University of California, Berkeley, in a recent study on the issue. Since 1980, however, commercial development growth management measures have surged.

A good example is Walnut Creek, an affluent suburban community in Contra Costa County, 20 miles east of San Francisco. Office space in Walnut Creek grew from 400,000 square feet in 1970 to 2.3 million in 1980. In 1975, the city's downtown plan set a height limit of 10 stories near the BART transit station and six stories elsewhere in the downtown. But it proposed living with the current street system, while clustering commercial growth around the BART station, near a charming old part of the downtown.

Since 1980, however, office space in Walnut Creek has doubled to five million square feet, and six to eight mid-rise office buildings have grown up around the BART station. However, BART has not picked up many of the new commuters, and significant development has occurred outside the downtown. The number of workers driving into Walnut Creek from nearby communities has doubled. At the same time, the neighboring city of Concord has been encouraging the construction of large commercial developments, such as Bank of America's four-building, million-square-foot complex, a redevelopment project that opened this spring, and that has created more through traffic in Walnut Creek. As the in-commuting increased, traffic at major intersections in Walnut Creek deteriorated to what traffic engineers call the "E" level of service—just short of gridlock. The response from the residents was to look aggressively for ways to slow or freeze development.

"This used to be a community that had a sense of place," says Cynthia Kroll. "Now all of a sudden it's urban, and it never expected that to happen."

In response, city residents last year passed two growth control initiatives reminiscent of the Bay Area's residential growth-control measures of the 1970s. One initiative, passed in March 1985, froze height limits on all parcels of land within the city and reduced the overall height limit to six stories. In November, voters approved a second measure banning all commercial construction until traffic flow at major intersections improved to the "D" level of service. At the same time, two growth control advocates were elected to the city council.

For the moment, commercial construction is stopped, but in the long run it is unclear whether the measure will lead to less construction or more highways. "We'll never be able to achieve these service levels," says Gary Binger, Walnut Creek's director of community development. "It's forcing us into the mode of building more highways."

Going with the flow

Not every suburb is fighting commercial development. Some older, close-in suburbs have accepted the fact that they will inevitably become more urban and have planned accordingly. Thanks largely to the Washington, D.C., Metro rail system, Bethesda, Maryland, has been transformed from a quiet suburb to a booming "outer city" with 10-story hotels and 20-story office buildings—but is using strict design and development controls in hopes of creating a lively, urban atmosphere.

Bellevue, Washington, outside Seattle, has taken a similar approach. Faced with a large amount of suburban-type commercial development scattered all over the city, Bellevue decided to concentrate construction in its central area, converting it into a true "urban downtown." Strict design controls require pedestrian orientation for all buildings, and parking requirements have been reduced to urban levels (2.5 to three spaces per 1,000 square feet). The downtown is being tied by pedestrian walkways to a transit (bus) hub, and independent parking garages and lots are prohibited in the downtown.

"We've decided we are going to be an urban place, at least downtown," says Mark Hinshaw, Bellevue's staff urban designer.

Other new suburban centers, such as Las Colinas, have taken advantage of the vast land ownership and high ambitions of private developers to create an idyllic environment that seeks to be both urban and suburban.

Geographer Peter Muller calls Las Colinas, a 12,000-acre former ranch just five miles from the Dallas-Fort Worth airport, "the first city of the twenty-first century." It is the brainchild of Dallas developer Ben Carpenter, whose family assembled the ranch and has lived there for decades. Las Colinas is a new town in conception, with residential, cultural, and employment areas all contained within the development. But it has been constructed with attention to amenities; every time Carpenter found a drainage problem, for example, he solved it by creating a small lake or creek, rather than building a concrete culvert. And the core of its commercial area—called the urban center— could become a prototype for suburban downtowns.

The urban center focuses on a lake, created at a cost of $1 million. A huge parking garage is hidden from a pedestrian "canal walk" by a row of old world fake fronts and is topped by a two-acre landscaped plaza. Water taxis carry passengers from place to place within the urban center. Carpenter has built a ramp to accommodate a future people-mover and has joined a group of developers offering a right-of-way for Dallas's future light rail system. Blessed with the 1980s version of a "great location" (proximity to a nationally significant airport), Carpenter is clearly selling a suburban downtown by giving it a sense of place.

But most of the new suburban downtowns are neither Bethesda nor Las Colinas. Most are stuck somewhere in between, usually in a traffic jam— the case of Tyson's Corner, Virginia, or the corporate campuses of Westchester and Connecticut. Traffic is perhaps the most visible side effect of intense suburban development—and, suburban

planners say, traffic is what riles up suburban residents more than anything else.

"The thing that drives all the negatives—it's all transportation," says Binger, who notes that most of the Walnut Creek disputes have been prompted by traffic concerns.

In some suburbs, important strides have been made through transportation systems management (TSM) techniques. In Pleasanton, California, 20 miles south of Walnut Creek, the massive Hacienda Business Park (which will contain more than 10 million square feet of space when completed) has reduced commuting trips by more than 40 percent in a single year through TSM measures such as free shuttle buses to the nearest BART station. And at Warner Center in Los Angeles's San Fernando Valley, about 20 percent of employees either take the bus or carpool—an amazing statistic, considering that the center is 25 miles from downtown Los Angeles and surrounded by low-density residential neighborhoods.

New roads?

Increasingly, construction of new highways is being considered as a serious option, despite the cost. Local developers are being asked to pick up more of the cost in roads, and local governments are putting up more money as well. Santa Clara County, California, home of Silicon Valley and San Jose, recently passed a half-cent sales tax—in effect for 10 years only—to construct new highways.

"The only answer is new expressways," says Peter Muller, reflecting on his visits to a dozen or more suburban downtowns. "That's anathema to everything in planning, I know. But, with the suburban majority in the House of Representatives, I can see it as a big issue in the 1990s."

Narrowly focused transportation measures may keep traffic barely under control around the suburban downtowns. But in the long run, they are not likely to succeed in improving the environment of suburban downtowns. Without broader measures to improve function and design, suburban centers might find themselves in the same kind of vicious traffic circle that characterized cities in the 1950s and 1960s.

Many of the planners researching and working in the suburbs today agree that the potential for lively and interesting suburban downtowns exists, if only the suburbs had the cohesiveness and political will to be creative.

The answer might be deceptively simple if the underlying assumptions of suburban development are challenged. "Bring the buildings closer together," says Hinshaw, the urban designer from Bellevue. "Unless you have a concentration of some level of intensity, you're not going to have anything going."

In fact, many of the suburban downtowns, such as Houston's Galleria-Post Oak area, are so densely built up that the critical mass for better planning and design already exists. "In Post Oak, you actually feel as though you could walk and not be ridiculed," says Dowall.

The trick in design terms is to accommodate cars, transit riders, and pedestrians all in the same space. And an increasing number of planners and designers are talking about turning parking, that old nemesis of good urban design, into a positive aspect. Parking garages, they say, can help to create good urban spaces. "It's crazy from an economic point of view to build a parking garage unless the land values are high," says Dowall, "but it may be very important for urban design."

The question remains, however, whether the political will exists in the suburbs to take such bold steps. One planner, when told of innovative design efforts in a project in Washington's northern Virginia suburbs, responded by saying: "The concepts that bind Fairfax County together are the roadway networks. I wonder if the people spaces will work."

And Ingrid Reed, the planning commissioner from Princeton, admits that while aesthetic disasters in the suburbs bother her, they probably don't bother many of her constituents. "It's the traffic issue that bugs people. I'm not sure that there is any consensus on making suburbs better."

William Fulton is a contributing editor of Planning.

Bethesda Stages a Beauty Contest for Developers

William Fulton
(January 1985)

In recent years, downtown Bethesda, Maryland, just north of Washington, D.C., has taken on the look of a typically lackluster, older suburban center. Rows of nondescript strip commercial buildings crowd the streets and too many cars chase too few parking spaces. A unique "beauty contest" for developers, sponsored by the Maryland-National Capital Park and Planning Commission (Montgomery County's planning staff), is expected to change all that, converting the downtown into an area with a strong sense of place, filled with plazas, walkways, courtyards, and, according to one consultant, the biggest array of public art outside of New York's Rockefeller Center. If all goes as planned, the process will stand as a monument to the ability of public planners to negotiate tough deals with private developers.

The beauty contest—a public competition that rewarded well-designed projects with extra square footage—was devised by the planning commission when it realized the potential for explosive office growth around a new downtown Metro subway stop. "We saw it [the explosive growth] coming," says John Westbrook, a former architect with the Rouse Company and now chief of urban design for the county planning commission. "And, in order not to be in a first-come, first-served situation—where time and not quality decided who got to build—we had to set up a procedure to deal with it."

To be sure, the planning staff was dealing from a position of strength in Bethesda. A radical downzoning during the 1970s, which later was upheld by the courts, left allowable floor-area ratios in the county's four central business districts so low (3.0 or less) that it was hardly worth the effort of developers to build there. In order to give the cities some leverage, the county planning staff devised an "optional method of development" based on density bonuses. Under this system, the county would allow much higher FARs (up to 8.0) in exchange for certain concessions from developers that would help carry out the goals of the four CBD sector plans.

Still, a problem arose in Bethesda. While development was being carefully phased within the central business district, construction just outside the CBD roared on. The result, Westbrook says, was a donut, and the challenge was to how to fill it. "What we wanted was a jelly-filled donut, with something sweet in the middle," he says.

The sweet treat Westbrook envisioned was what he calls "animation," a lively atmosphere reminiscent of Rouse's festival marketplaces in such places as Baltimore and Boston, but transferred to a growing suburban community. In Westbrook's view, it is the sense of place that counts. "The buildings should be secondary," he says.

The solution came in two stages. First, in 1980, the county placed what amounted to a moratorium on building in the CBD outside the immediate area of the Metro stop. Meanwhile, proposals were sought for development on the Metro-owned land above the station. The result was the three-building Metro Center complex, some 17 stories high with well over one million square feet of office, hotel, and retail space, and a public plaza surrounding the subway entrance. Plans were approved by the county in October 1983, with construction expected to be complete later this year.

Then the moratorium was lifted. But the county made the decision, based on traffic studies, to limit future CBD development to about three million square feet of space, an amount produced by about 2,100 vehicle trips during the peak afternoon rush hour. The projects would be equally divided between office and residential use. The bulk of the 2,100 trips—1,675—were set aside for office/retail construction that employed the optional method of development. Residential builders were allotted 225 trips, while office builders who declined to use the optional method were given 200 trips.

Ranking

Unfortunately, the number of projects seeking approval under the optional method would have produced more than the allowed number of trips. So the "beauty contest" was launched for a three-block area around the Metro stop. This is how it worked. Projects tentatively approved on an individual basis were ranked according to four criteria: residential use, enhancement of the pedestrian environment, functional use and visual compatibility, and management organization. Projects were then to be approved in order of their ranking until the number of trips produced totaled 1,675. Lower ranked projects simply wouldn't make the cut. With these incentives, developers began scrambling to find ways to get high marks.

"In the past we had to beat them over the head to get amenities," says Westbrook. "Now they were coming to us and saying, 'What does it take to win?'"

Amenities alone were not enough, however. Westbrook's urban design staff juggled various de-

velopment proposals against one another in an effort to come up with a varied downtown environment, rather than just a bunch of tall buildings with plazas.

Some developers offered to build (and maintain) theaters, art galleries, and parks. And, in one case, the planning staff persuaded two developers with plans to build across the street from one another to alter their projects so as to create a set of complementary "gateways" to the CBD.

In another case, Westbrook and his staff persuaded the developer of a building across from the Metro station to forego the standard plaza and retain the existing street-level edge instead. All projects, in accordance with the downtown's streetscape plan, will provide new paving, lighting, and landscaping. The planning staff also brought in Ronald Lee Fleming of the Townscape Institute in Cambridge, Massachusetts, to work with developers to make sure that their new public art and plazas don't go unused—an "animation strategy" it is called. The result is an ambitious program of public art that's integrated into the streetscape.

For example, one building offers a sculpted glass drinking fountain and also three glass-and-copper columns that serve as the northern CBD gateway. Other proposed art includes murals, ceramic insets, and stained glass. The planning staff gave higher rankings to Rouse-like management schemes that emphasized programs for keeping the plazas filled with people.

Few losers

As it turned out, there weren't many losers in the beauty contest. The only proposal that needed to drop out was the bottom-ranked project, a 400,000 square-foot office building that was much bigger than the other proposals. All of the eight other proposals, plus one that had been approved before the competition, apparently are going ahead.

Not that the downtown Bethesda plan is entirely without potential problems. Fleming fears that some of the developers will change their public art plans, perhaps for the worse. And Westbrook acknowledges that some of the developers' "urban housekeeping" concessions—such as private security and promises to book festival events—have caused concern among the police and the chamber of commerce, the traditional providers of such services.

Developer Robert Eisenger of Bethesda, whose

three proposals were ranked at the bottom of the list by the planning staff, says other developers may have promised too much in order to win approval. He predicts they will return to renegotiate. Two of Eisenger's projects were approved, while the third was the only one that didn't make the cut.

In addition, Eisenger, who says he spent $250,000 preparing for the competition, complains that the planning staff's requirements were too detailed, considering that approval was not certain.

Attorney Michael Glosserman of JBG Associates in Washington, D.C., whose two projects finished third and fifth, fears that the county's tight schedules might kill some projects. All projects must start construction within 18 months of the competition.

"The planning process is going to dictate what market forces would ordinarily dictate," Glosserman says. "We would not start either of our projects unless market conditions were right," he adds, even if that meant his firm's "trips" would be doled out to someone else.

Nonetheless, most observers praise the competition. "If everything develops the way it is on paper, it'll be a terrific space," says Glosserman. Fleming, who has worked with dozens of other downtown projects, calls the Bethesda effort "an act of will on the part of a talented and aggressive planning staff."

And John Westbrook says the experience in downtown Bethesda proves that public planners can play a major role in shaping large-scale development. "The private sector could never do it," he says. "Only the public sector can say, 'We have the big picture,' and stay in and negotiate it."

William Fulton is a contributing editor of Planning.

Doing Deals

Ana Arana
(February 1986)

In 1978, California's cities and counties suffered a severe financial blow when voters approved Proposition 13, the antitax measure that limited property tax increases. Almost overnight, localities were forced to reevaluate their spending practices and cut costs. When subsequent federal cutbacks further undermined their financial situation, California localities knew they had to find other ways of financing new development.

The upshot was that the cities and counties concluded that they would raise additional revenue by becoming more effective managers of their public assets. First, they made growth pay for itself, by exacting certain concessions from developers in exchange for building permits. Second, they entered the development business, by becoming partners in commercial and industrial real estate projects and getting a percentage of the profits.

Tax increment financing

TIF is one of the most common and most recent such methods. Forty percent of all TIF districts in the state were established after 1973, although the mechanism was made legal by the Federal Housing Act of 1949. TIF is politically popular because it revitalizes urban areas without raising taxes. But its biggest attraction in California is that it allows the generation of revenue bonds and circumvents Proposition 13's restrictions on general obligation bonds.

A locality sets up a TIF district by declaring an area blighted and zoning it for redevelopment. The locality unilaterally freezes the amount of taxes the area pays into the general fund, and the redevelopment agency receives all future tax increments. The redevelopment agency then floats bonds against the increases in tax revenue expected in future years.

Los Angeles has made effective use of TIF, particularly downtown. And in recent years, the city's Community Redevelopment Agency has expanded its use into 14 other areas. It's now involved in 16 projects and operates with an annual budget of $150 million.

In fiscal year 1984–85, the agency expects $55 million in revenue, over 80 percent of it from two high-density commercial sites in the downtown area, Bunker Hill and the Central Business District Redevelopment Project.

"What we've learned in our 30-odd-year history is that only high-density projects bring in high profits," says Ed Helfeld, who was the CRA administrator until his forced resignation in December. Thus, the agency has used the revenues earned downtown to strengthen the 14 other TIF sites, which bring in only modest increments because they are in depressed residential areas.

Since California law requires 20 percent of all TIF revenue to be used to build or refurbish affordable housing, Los Angeles has invested some of its TIF money in housing programs for the homeless people who frequent downtown's Skid Row.

But while Los Angeles has had success with TIF, Helfeld warns other localities to be sure of the economic situation before declaring an area blighted. "In the early days, there was the assumption that all we had to do was empty out the land and then private enterprise would come in. But sometimes the market was not there," says Helfeld. He notes that Los Angeles's first TIF site became successful only when the city began to emerge as a regional financial center.

A report by the California Debt Advisory Commission also cautions that TIF districts can depress the local tax base. About 3.5 percent of the property value in California is now channeled into TIF districts, souring relations between TIF and other taxing entities such as the state government, county governments, and school districts.

Los Angeles County sues every locality that sets up or expands a TIF district. And California school districts have become the fiercest opponents of TIF districts. Their opposition stems from the fact the schools ordinarily would get part of the tax increments the TIF district keeps.

At this point, at least 30 California school districts have fought successfully for a share of the TIF revenue. The Southern California city of Thousand Oaks had to promise its local school district $31 million in redevelopment aid over 60 years to clear the way for a TIF project.

Says Peter Detwiler, a consultant to the state senate committee on local government, "Localities like to think the state has nothing to do with TIF districts, but in essence, the state ends up giving the schools the funds that a TIF district takes for redevelopment. And the state's general fund gets shortchanged."

Exactions and fees

After the passage of Proposition 13, exactions became much more common. Short of public funds to pay for the impacts of growth, localities first required developers to pay for curbs, street lighting, and other physical needs. These days, however, the list of exactions has been expanded to include such services as child care, affordable housing, and job training programs.

Defending such social service exactions, local government officials argue that the benefits and burdens of development should be shared by the community and the developer. "Santa Monica looks at exactions from an environmental point of view. Our long-range objective is finding what the community really needs and evaluating whether development puts a burden on or delivers services," says Paul Silvern, the former planning director for the city of Santa Monica.

Development agreements

Development agreements came into being because developers wanted a law to protect their interests when negotiating over exactions with a locality. The agreements are authorized by a 1979 California state law. The agreements permit localities to negotiate each development project from scratch. In return for agreeing to certain exactions, the developer gets a written guarantee that his project will be built as agreed, no matter what change of heart the community may have.

Some analysts think development agreements destroy local governments' police power and decision-making ability. In fact, many cities have derived benefits from them—although localities with the most aggressive and knowledgeable staffs win the most favorable and profitable agreements.

Affluent Irvine, for example, recently entered into a development agreement with the Irvine Company, the real estate concern that built the city in the 1960s. City officials were concerned that a retail and office complex planned by the company was not developing its retail uses as rapidly as expected, thus costing the city sales tax revenue.

After two years of negotiation, the Irvine Company agreed to guarantee the city up to $1 million a year in tax revenue for 25 years, whether the commercial part of the complex was developed or not. In return, the city promised not to rezone the property and not to restrict nearby residential development.

Equity participation

Equity participation may be the most profitable revenue-raising method being used by Southern California localities today. It allows public entities to earn inflation-free revenue while giving them a measure of control over what is built on their land.

The method involves two types of agreements: participatory leases, which allow local governments and redevelopment agencies to lease public lands, and equity participation agreements, which allow them to invest redevelopment money or federal grants in real estate projects. In both cases, the locality gets a percentage of the profits.

Participatory leases have been a common practice in the private sector for years; in the public sector, port authorities have used them to avoid surrendering control over profitable beach property.

Redevelopment agencies have also used participatory leases in TIF districts. The Los Angeles Community Redevelopment Agency, for example, worked such a deal on the California Plaza project on Bunker Hill a few years ago and is now getting 15 percent of all net profits. That project has been so successful that agency officials say they will be doing more of these leases in the future.

In recent years, more and more Southern California localities have used participatory leases independent of redevelopment—in effect, playing a role that's much closer to that of a private developer.

Los Angeles County has set up an entire agency, the Community Development Commission, to explore the market for participatory leases. For starters, the agency is examining and cataloging all underutilized or vacant county property and has begun work on one participatory lease project. By next year, it expects to have six or seven projects under way.

The current project is a $50 million mixed-use development on the former site of the Long Beach General Hospital—a 24-acre property. In payment, the county is getting $1 million a year in rent on a 66-year lease, a percentage of the project's gross revenue, and a percentage of the profits in case of resale or refinancing. At the end of the lease period, the county expects to earn up to $1.3 billion from this project.

Besides providing extra revenue, participatory leases are more flexible. "You know that at the end of a certain period, the land can be turned around and put out for another use, if need be," says Allan Kotin, a principal with Kotin, Regan & Mouchly Inc., a real estate market analysis firm that advises local governments on participatory leases.

The best example of an equity participation agreement is the one the city of Lawndale carried out in 1983. A working class suburb surrounded by upper-middle-class beach towns, Lawndale struck a deal with a developer who was building a shopping center in the adjacent city of Redondo Beach. The city received an Urban Development Action Grant and lent the developer $8 million at six percent interest, while Redondo Beach set up a TIF district in the area where the shopping center was going to be built.

Lawndale won a job participation agreement from the deal—50 percent of the jobs were guaranteed for its residents—plus 25 percent of the shopping center's net profits, and 25 percent in case of resale or refinancing. Redondo Beach, meanwhile, revitalized a rundown area and kept the traditional revenue provided by a TIF district.

"Other cities could carry out this type of deal. Whether they use UDAG money or redevelopment money, they can always cut 'everyone wins' deals," says Mark Winogrond, the former director of community development in Lawndale, who now works for the newly incorporated city of West Hollywood.

Sales tax participation

A danger of sales tax participation is that local governments could give preference to development that brings in a lot of sales taxes to the detriment of residential development. But, if used properly, this method could bring in a steady stream of revenue.

Of all the types of commercial development available, auto dealerships provide the highest profits. And in Southern California the most successful auto mall is one run by the city of Cerritos, a former dairy valley that incorporated in 1956.

"We were lucky to have lots of vacant land adjacent to a main freeway and across the way from a commercial center," says Dennis T. Davis, director of environmental affairs. The city used redevelopment money to acquire the land, which it then sold to the dealers at a much lower price. Twelve dealerships share space in the 87-acre auto mall.

Although the city receives only the traditional one percent sales tax, the profits are monumental. "One percent of the price of one car is considerable," says Davis.

Although local governments are enjoying success with many of these new revenue-raising methods, government officials agree that the risks are high. "The worst is to get overly excited and work on your dreams rather than on market analysis," says Winogrond.

Others note that local governments must understand where they lack expertise. "The success of a project depends on the type of people who negotiate it. Redevelopment people can't be planners, and planners can't be financial advisers," says Keith Breskin of Katz, Hollis, Coren & Associates, a firm that advises California localities on redevelopment matters.

Other observers pose even more difficult questions. "We don't know where this whole new way of operating a government is taking us," says Peter Detwiler. "As public officials and planners, we need to ask ourselves some questions. Are we putting too much emphasis on short range goals, in exchange for more revenue? And are we contracting away the public interest in the process?"

Ana Arana is a Los Angeles-based writer.

The Profit Motive

William Fulton
(October 1987)

In early August, the board of supervisors in Fairfax County, Virginia, just outside Washington, cut a deal that it hopes will save its constituents some money. Instead of floating some $80 million in bonds to pay for a new county government center, the supervisors decided to have private real estate developers build it for them.

In return, the county agreed to give the Charles E. Smith Companies and the Artery Organization $24 million in cash, $16 million in other considerations—and 116 acres of land, which would be zoned for commercial and residential development. On that land, the development partners expect to build $400 million in private projects, including 1.2 million square feet of office space, a 250-room hotel, and 600 residential units. The county will get back title to just over half the land in 75 years.

Top county officials, who trumpet the deal as a prime example of public entrepreneurship, say they are simply cashing in on the increased value

of the property, which cost the county only $4 million eight years ago but is now worth 10 times that amount. As board chairman John F. Herrity told the *Washington Post:* "The basic question is: Does it make sense to take a $4.1 million investment and turn it into an $83 million government center?"

Meanwhile, citizen groups and others charge that this is a giveaway. They say the county could realize a far greater profit by hanging onto the land, which will certainly appreciate in value after the government center is built. "To give it away at this point makes no sense," says Maya Hubert, an aide to Audrey Moore, the only supervisor who dissented.

That's not all. In the negotiations with the developer, the winning entry in the county's design competition for the new government center was scrapped. And rival local developers say the county has given this project preferential treatment, allowing higher density and ignoring potential traffic problems.

For better or worse, Fairfax County has joined the growing number of communities around the country that have become active players in the world of real estate development. Strapped by financial problems, determined to gain more control over their community's future—and their treasuries—these local jurisdictions aggressively and unabashedly use every ounce of power at their disposal.

Some, like Fairfax County, seek to cash in on their real estate assets, just as private corporations do. Many become equity partners in real estate ventures—or, by issuing infrastructure bonds, become "silent" partners. And just as many transform the zoning process into a battle over market analyses and financial feasibility studies, determined to make sure their town doesn't get stuck with an unsalable turkey.

They do it to save money, generate profits, protect their own interests, and gain a larger role in shaping the local economy. "Almost every city in the country is going to come to understand how important real estate development is to the city's economic health," says Rick Pederson, research director for the Frederick Roth Company in Denver, which has helped many cities to learn about the real estate market. "They can't afford not to understand."

In taking this tack, however, cities often risk controversy, litigation—and the integrity of the planning process. Many of the brightest young planners in the nation have jumped on the real estate bandwagon, believing that cities and counties have to look out for number one. But to many older planners, the trend toward active involvement in the real estate market is a scary one. They say it deemphasizes comprehensive planning in favor of deal making and compromises the city's role as an impartial arbiter of land-use decisions.

Turning a profit

By its very nature, planning affects real estate development patterns. And it's not exactly news that cities sometimes zone property or favor particular developers because of a desire to revitalize an area, to gain revenue, or, in some cases, to exclude certain uses.

But in the last few years, the planning process and the real estate market have become more intertwined than ever. It's a long way from *Euclid v. Ambler Realty Co.,* the 1926 U.S. Supreme Court ruling upholding zoning, to the growing practice of demanding market studies as part of a project's review.

It's also a long trip from the land write-downs and tax abatements of the 1960s and 1970s to the current attitude in Los Angeles, where the county government (after getting state laws changed to define turning a profit as a "public purpose") aggressively develops its vast surplus land holdings purely to raise revenue.

All this has come about for several reasons—but undeniably the most important is the fact that cities are far more "on their own" than they have been in decades. Unable to count on substantial federal or state support, reined in by taxing limitations, local governments recognize they are responsible for creating jobs, tax revenue, and other elements of their future prosperity.

"We can't even think of what's happening in the public sector any more as public administration," says John Kirlin, a professor at the University of Southern California's Public Affairs Center in Sacramento. "The issues of service delivery that once dominated local government—those are still issues. But there's been a shift in the thinking of local governments. Now they're concerned with job creation, economic growth, quality of life—things very tied in to the development process."

For planners, this means more power, more prestige, more attention, and—in many instances—more trouble. As the resident experts on land, planners are the ones city managers and elected officials turn to when dealing with the issues Kirlin talks about. Increasingly, planners are becoming deal makers, focusing more on short-term real estate development and less on long-term comprehensive planning.

And, as their attention focuses more narrowly on real estate development, planners are confronting two new issues. The first is the relationship between planning decisions and the real estate market. It is a hard-learned lesson of the recent office glut that developers don't always know the market best.

"The traditional concept was that the private sector was responsible for establishing the need for that use," says Dean Macris, planning director in San Francisco, which takes the market into account in assessing proposals for office buildings. "Today that no longer holds. Cities are far more sensitive toward understanding that an excessive amount of anything can pull down the whole economy."

The second issue planners are dealing with is the strategic importance of the real estate owned by their own city or county.

"There's no such thing as surplus land anymore," Peter Detwiler, principal consultant to the California senate's local government committee, declared to a group of local planners and developers at UCLA not long ago. And, indeed, local governments from New York to California are becoming equity partners in private real estate development—sometimes to create jobs, sometimes to balance the local economy, and sometimes solely for profit.

The public entrepreneur

When James Hankla came to the Los Angeles County bureaucracy five years ago, he brought with him an idea called "asset management." Thanks to his experience as the hustling director of redevelopment in Long Beach (where he is now city manager), Hankla quickly realized that the financially strapped county had hundreds—maybe thousands—of acres of surplus real estate that could be developed, not just sold, to assist in the county's long-term fiscal planning.

In three years as head of the L.A. County Community Development Commission and two as the county's chief administrative officer, Hankla made real estate development a top priority for the county government. During his tenure, the county worked out several deals involving leasing land to private developers in exchange for a long-term share of the profits. The site of a former county hospital in the Long Beach area will become a business park. A small park downtown, across the street from city hall, will become a 20-story office building in which the county, the city, and the state will share the profits. Now the county is working on commercial developments for three parking lots strategically situated between the L.A. Music Center and Bunker Hill.

Each one of these real estate deals will probably net the county no more than $1 million to $3 million a year—a drop in the bucket in its multibillion-dollar budget. But top county executives say such money, coming with no strings attached, can be of tremendous strategic importance in the county's budget making.

Though L.A. County's purely financial motives are still a little unusual, its general approach isn't. Local governments, in many cases led by their planning or community development directors, are recognizing that they can achieve strategic objectives by understanding the true value of their surplus real estate, particularly if it is located in prime areas like downtowns or waterfronts.

"Cities traditionally have had a 'use' view of real estate, rather than a 'market' view," says Merrilee Utter, a former banker who now serves as Denver's director of asset management. "If they need a fire station, they build a fire station without thinking about the market. They need to know there's a market they can interact with."

Aggressive smaller cities are already doing this. An example is Fairfield, California, which is reaping profits (and sales tax revenue) from a regional shopping mall it helped bring into town. In a way, it's a sophisticated version of urban renewal: Instead of subsidizing developers to persuade them to build, as they did in the 1960s and 1970s, cities are demanding a piece of the action for their entrepreneurial efforts.

The danger is that overall planning objectives may be lost in the process. For example, New York under Mayor Edward Koch has aggressively pursued a policy of selling off such "surplus" real estate as the Coliseum site at Columbus Circle. The $455 million sale has raised tremendous objections from local citizen groups, which fear the ensuing office tower will cast long shadows over Central Park.

Market zoning

Like a lot of formerly sleepy suburban towns, the village of Deerfield, Illinois (pop. 17,000), just north of Chicago, has undergone a dramatic metamorphosis in recent years. First it was pounded with office development and then, in the last two years, with business-oriented hotels hoping to seize on the opportunities those offices presented.

At first Deerfield went along with the hotel projects. But after four hotels had received approvals, the village stopped short of giving a fifth one the go-ahead. The reason had nothing to do with sound land-use planning, or whether a hotel should someday be built on the land. The reason was that Deerfield didn't believe the market was there to support another hotel.

"You'd like to say these guys are professional," says Barbara Houpt, Deerfield's planning director. "But you get a market study. The thing is two years old, when we had no hotels. It doesn't reflect construction of two large all-suite hotels. We've got to say to them, 'You've lost your credibility.'"

"We have an investment in our community," Houpt adds. "It does us no good to have these things fail."

"Market zoning" is not in the traditional repertoire of even the most sophisticated city planner. But the Deerfield experience is being repeated all over the country. Increasingly, city administrations expect planners to use permit approvals with discretion—turning down projects when they're likely to stand empty, letting them through easily during a slump.

"With the approval process, the public sector can control the amount and location of space out there," says Bill Whitney, acting assistant director for development and urban design at the Boston Redevelopment Authority. "We don't want to allow too much space on the market at one time, so that we don't have a bunch of 600-foot-tall office buildings standing vacant."

In adopting a more skeptical attitude toward the market savvy of real estate developers, planners are, to a large extent, simply reacting to the office glut of the early 1980s, which left many cities in the lurch. They have learned, as real estate economist Anthony Downs once put it, that "if lenders will give the money, someone will build" no matter what the market conditions are. So in many cities, the planners themselves have learned more about the market.

Predictably, much of this market-driven planning occurs in Boston and San Francisco, which probably regulate and negotiate with developers more aggressively than any other cities in the county. In Boston, says Whitney, the BRA has used its understanding of real estate markets—and tenant needs—to identify opportunities private developers might overlook.

"By understanding the nature of the users, we are able to identify sites and areas where height might be required, where different floor plans might be required, where back-office uses might be appropriate." In particular, he adds, the BRA has been successful in getting developers to build smaller buildings geared to smaller financial and professional service firms.

In San Francisco, market zoning arrived with the adoption in 1985 of a new downtown plan that limited office growth to 950,000 square feet per year. (That number was subsequently cut in half by Proposition M, a citizen initiative.) Although the competition that downtown developers must go through is often described as a "beauty contest," market factors are, in fact, just as important as aesthetic ones.

"The criteria force us to look at the need for space," says Amit Ghosh, the city's director of comprehensive planning. "There is no way to avoid it."

Last year, the planning commission rejected all proposed office buildings, partly because of the high vacancy rate. This year, three projects were approved—but evidence of preleasing and marketability played an important role in their selection.

As the Deerfield story shows, market zoning is not limited to cities like San Francisco and Boston. Planned unit development ordinances often require market studies as part of the application. And a recent experience in Folsom, California (pop. 18,000), shows that even small cities are willing to challenge a developer's marketing assumptions.

In this case, a local developer was seeking a zone change (and comprehensive plan amendment) to allow a shopping center and a senior housing project. The developer insisted that more retail, and particularly a new supermarket, could be supported; local merchants disagreed. The city hired Angus McDonald & Associates, a financial analysis firm from Berkeley, to do a retail market study.

McDonald concluded that Folsom could support many new retail outlets, though not necessarily another supermarket. The city planning commission turned the project down. Political pressure played a role, but so did the market analysis.

In ignoring market forces up to now, McDonald says, "from a planning standpoint we [planners] have been doing our jobs wrong."

A good mix

In some cases, market awareness has clearly led to better planning, and to a more stable local economy. Local officials in places like Denver and Oklahoma City regularly salivate at the highly regulated—and prosperous—office markets in San Francisco and Boston. They recognize that no local action could possibly have kept the bottom from falling out of their local economies. But they also believe that if they had been more sensitive to market pressures, they could have shaved the peaks and filled the valleys to a certain extent.

Further, Bill Whitney of the BRA—which is sometimes criticized for encouraging enormous downtown developments—also believes that identifying the market for smaller office users has aided the urban environment in Boston. Whitney says the needs of smaller users have helped shape "smaller, more characteristically Boston buildings," which lease well, in the areas just outside downtown.

In many other instances, market-oriented planning may lead to trouble if it is not accompanied by sensible comprehensive planning. For instance, there is the possibility that a city or county will become so deeply involved as a player in the local real estate market that it will lose its ability to fulfill its role as referee.

Whether cities can get caught in an antitrust-related legal bind is open to question. Three years ago, Congress exempted local government from liability for damages under antitrust laws. But local governments still could be enjoined legally from engaging in anticompetitive practices. According to Christopher Duerksen, a lawyer with the Enterprise Foundation who tracks zoning and planning cases closely, few lawsuits are likely to be filed—they're too expensive and cities can easily reject projects on other grounds—but a developer with a grudge and a lot to lose could win an injunction.

The pall of anticompetitive practices looms over "market zoning." In particular, say some observers, the increasing trend toward issuing bonds to pay for infrastructure for new projects could lead cities to protect certain developers as a means of protecting their own bond rating.

In California, development finance expert Dean Misczynski, who wrote *Windfalls for Wipeouts* with the late Donald Hagman, fears the worst. The use of infrastructure bonds to support new development has grown from $20 million a decade ago to about $1.5 billion today. Most are used to handle roads, sewers, and schools in new residential subdivisions.

Misczynski points out that when a city floats an infrastructure bond to support a private development, it becomes a silent partner in that development—and may not look favorably on other development proposals, fearing that they might harm the marketability of the subdivision it's supporting and thus cause the bonds to default.

"At some point, if you start protecting Project A because the bonds have your name on them, you're probably going to run into an antitrust problem," says Misczynski, principal consultant for the California senate's Office of Research. Even if antitrust damages aren't available, with a huge subdivision at stake—California subdivisions can have several thousand houses—a developer still might be willing to put up a court fight. . . .

In times like these—when the availability of capital drives construction as much as market demand, when cities must look out for themselves, when sleepy suburbs stand in the so-called "growth path"—there's no question that an understanding of the real estate market is essential to good planning. But it's also clear that planners can't afford to narrow their work so much that they become nothing more than real estate deal makers. In the long run, a healthy local real estate market and good long-term planning may not be incompatible. It remains to be seen how well planners can learn to accommodate the one without losing sight of the other.

William Fulton is a contributing editor of Planning.

Off the Barricades Into the Boardrooms

William Fulton
(August 1987)

Nine years ago, when he first started fighting redlining on Cleveland's east side, Patrick Kenney didn't expect to wind up in a partnership with the city's biggest banks. But today, the one-time VISTA volunteer runs the Buckeye Evaluation and Training Institute, a nonprofit group, and serves on the board of the affiliated, for-profit Buckeye Woodland Community Development Corporation in the neighborhood where he once worked as an organizer. The corporation is capitalized and partly owned by four local banks.

In a way, this turn of events makes Kenney sad. Sometimes he feels coopted, he says. "When you have your banks walk in and be partners, it's a little more difficult to say to them, 'Stop redlining,'" he says. Moreover, the organization Kenney came from, the Buckeye-Woodland Community Congress, is basically out of business today.

At the same time, the efforts of the Buckeye-Woodland CDC have paid off in a satisfying way. In an old Hungarian neighborhood devastated by racial blockbusting, Kenney and his coworkers have essentially created a housing market where one did not exist 10 years ago. They have forged a stable community where residents who want to add on to their houses can obtain bank loans to do so, where real estate appraisers looking for "comparables" can find a neighboring house that actually has market value, and where some private buyers pay more for rundown buildings than Kenney himself would.

Further, the group has done it not as an arm of the government, but as a private, for-profit development company. The "comparables" exist because the Buckeye corporation put them there by buying the houses, renovating them, and selling them—sometimes at a loss simply in order to establish a market for their future efforts.

And when Kenney somewhat wistfully ponders a renaissance of community organizing in the Buckeye-Woodland area, he thinks about it in terms of the development corporation's interest. Better city services to the neighborhood are just as important now as they were 10 years ago—but today, if you see Kenney out in the streets protesting, it would be because his development corporation needed those services to make its renovated houses marketable.

In other words, though he hasn't lost the idealism that brought him to the neighborhood in the first place, Pat Kenney is not a neighborhood organizer any more. He's a developer.

And he's not alone. The trend toward nongovernmental community development corporations, which began in the 1960s, has now come to full maturity. Despite the paucity of federal dollars—or maybe because of it—this mostly nonprofit activity (the for-profit Buckeye is an exception) is flourishing as never before. With entrepreneurial zeal, these groups are building and renovating housing, refurbishing commercial strips, and setting up jobs programs.

Growing numbers

Neighborhood groups are at the core of the community development corporation movement, but throughout the 1980s an increasingly varied set of other organizations have become involved in development: social service groups, settlement houses, ethnically oriented organizations, even a few outfits that started out as civil rights groups. That may explain why so many different names are used: local development corporations, neighborhood development organizations, and—most often—community development corporations, or CDCs.

For financial support, CDCs are turning to new sources. In New York State, for example, upwards of 180 community-based development groups are funded by an ambitious state program. In Chicago and elsewhere, including Pat Kenney's Buckeye neighborhood in Cleveland, neighborhood groups have used the threat of blocking bank mergers and expansion under the federal Community Reinvestment Act to force antiredlining agreements. Though the financial results of these agreements are sometimes small (the banks' stake in Buckeye so far is only $150,000), in Chicago three agreements have led to a $170 million commitment to community development.

Perhaps most important is the part philanthropic, part investment-oriented approach of the Local Initiatives Support Corporation. LISC, which was organized in 1980 as part of a national Ford Foundation community development effort, has raised over $100 million from more than 400 foundations and corporations. The money has been used for both grants and investments. Right now LISC is putting together a $30 million real estate syndicate, with corporations nationwide taking advantage of a low-income housing tax credit—one of the few tax shelters left after passage of the federal tax reform act last year.

Nobody knows for sure just how big this local development sector is, but the best estimates suggest that between 2,000 and 5,000 groups are in operation nationally, doing as much as $1 billion in business per year. Many are designed to bring low-cost housing and economic revitalization to the nation's poorest neighborhoods. But CDCs have also become common in lower middle-class neighborhoods, where they are sometimes used in hopes of averting real disaster. LISC's success, in particular, suggests that they must doing something right.

"There's a hell of a lot of initiative that's locally based that's beginning to show results," says Michael Swiridoff, formerly with LISC and now head of an 18-month study at the New School for Social Research in New York to determine just how big and influential the local development sector is. If LISC has raised $100 million, he adds, "there must be a product out there that catches the eye."

The continued survival and growth of CDCs in a period of public-sector cutbacks confirms one of the basic lessons of the 1980s in community development: If you want something done, learn how to do it yourself.

Even though they're not getting much backing from the U.S. Department of Housing and Urban Development, the CDCs do get help from a number of institutions that have sprung up in recent years. They include the National Training and Information Center in Chicago, the Development Training Institute in Baltimore, and Pratt Institute's Center for Community and Economic Development in Brooklyn. These groups provide information, training, and technical assistance to local development corporations; like the corporations, they are funded by a crazy-quilt combination of government funds, foundation grants, and fees for services rendered.

Groups like these have also kept the local development corporations stocked with a well-trained and aggressive cadre of leaders who keep in touch with each other and see themselves as hard-nosed deal makers. And, although their relations with local government are sometimes as acrimonious as those of any other developer, local political leaders increasingly see them as efficient organizations that can get things done.

"It's not just a matter of your heart being in the right place," says Ronald Shiffman, executive director of the Pratt Center, which has assisted innumerable community development corporations, large and small, in the Northeast. "You have to know how to crunch the numbers and make the deals."

Fighting city hall

Paul Brophy, the highly regarded former director of Pittsburgh's Urban Development Authority, who saw a thriving local development sector spring up there, identifies three stages in the evolution of neighborhood groups into community development corporations. First comes the negatively oriented group, born in crisis. Its agenda, and its talent, lies in stopping something.

In the second stage, the group has advanced to a positive agenda, which it lobbies city hall to fulfill. Often, though, the groups feel that "there's a limit to pushing city hall toward doing things," says Neil Mayer, economic development director in Berkeley, California, who studied 100 local development groups nationwide as a researcher with the Urban Institute.

That's when the group enters the third stage of evolution and becomes a development corporation. And, say several leaders in the field, the dissatisfaction with city hall often found in stage-two groups usually carries over to stage three.

The conflict between city hall and the neighborhoods was evident even in the earliest days of CDCs, which first emerged from the Kennedy-Johnson administration's antipoverty efforts. In the late 1960s, that conflict was manifested in debates over whether the Model Cities program ought to be based in the neighborhoods or controlled by city governments. Today, essentially the same debate continues.

According to Joseph B. McNeely, director of the Development Training Institute and formerly head of the HUD Office of Neighborhood Self-Help, the conflict between city hall and neighborhood-based development groups doesn't begin at the top or the bottom of the government bureaucracy, but in the middle.

"Good politicians learn to adapt to whoever has staying power," he says. "And people at the real low levels of the bureaucracy may be the instigators of these groups by leaking them information." But the middle-level bureaucrats—including planners—see neighborhood development groups as competition, McNeeley says. "The local director of community revitalization would rather have his own person out on the commercial strips."

Dan Cohen, who served as executive director of Los Angeles's Route 2 Housing Corporation for four years, recalls that he had a love-hate relationship with the city's community development department, which provided the organization's operating budget. "They loved us because we produced; on the other hand, we were taking funds away from them," says Cohen, whose corporation built almost 300 units of housing in four years.

In fact, he recalls, "they hated us so much that even after we gave them all those units they put us on six-month contracts. We didn't get paid for four months at a time." Inability to draw a regular paycheck was part of the reason Cohen left Route 2 and joined the city of West Hollywood, where he has helped establish a city-sponsored CDC.

Likewise, Floyd Lapp, executive director of the Kingsbridge-Riverdale-Van Cortlandt Development Corporation in the Bronx, says he and his counterparts have had an uneasy relationship with the state and federal bureaucrats who dole out the funds. "It's a real uptown-downtown split," he says.

Still, Lapp says, he must play the game. "After all, city hall has the money, so you have to be nice."

This rivalry exists even though, very often, the professionals on both sides—the city bureaucrats and the community development staff people—are professional planners. Lapp, for example, is active in the New York Metro APA Chapter, while Cohen received a master's degree in planning from the University of California, Los Angeles. Anita Landecker, LISC's California director, studied planning at Harvard.

Geography can play an important role in a CDC's success. In Cleveland, Pittsburgh, or Baltimore, development groups are almost always organized around established neighborhoods defined by geography, simply because the social structure is so firmly rooted. In California, it's a different story.

According to Landecker, local development corporations in the state are much less likely to follow geography, being arranged instead along ethnic lines or other common interests. Particularly in Los Angeles, inner-city neighbors are in such a state of flux that roots are rarely put down. Typical of successful CDCs in Los Angeles is El Pueblo Community Development Corporation, which works on low-income housing for Hispanics in various parts of the city.

Their kind of town

Probably no city in the country has a stronger network of community development corporations than Chicago. The reasons seem to lie not only in the city's strong ethnic neighborhoods, but its history as the center of confrontational community organizing pioneered by the late activist, Saul Alinsky.

On the commercial revitalization side alone, some 75 groups belong to CAN-DO (Chicago Association of Neighborhood Development Corporations), which provides a remarkable range of services. Among them is an annual "retail fair," partly underwritten by real estate agents, which promotes the attributes of various neighborhoods for businesses considering relocation or expansion.

CAN-DO's member groups often serve as local chambers of commerce and, with the umbrella organization's help, they've had success in recruiting retail businesses for their commercial strips. Some, like the effective Lawrence Avenue Development Corporation, even tax their own member property owners to raise funds. One affiliated CAN-DO organization, the City-Wide Development Corporation, has packaged some $15 million in business loans over the last three years.

The Chicago network is particularly adept at finding money for housing. The highest-profile effort to bring money into neighborhood housing in Chicago—and probably the entire country—was that of the Chicago Reinvestment Alliance, which used federal banking laws to break redlining and bring private mortgage money into depressed areas.

The Chicago Reinvestment Alliance was put together in 1983 by the Woodstock Institute and the National Training and Information Center, whose director, Gail Cincotta, is a near-legendary figure in neighborhood development circles. The alliance quickly saw that the surge in bank expansions and mergers under federal deregulation could be used as a lever to get more bank money into the neighborhoods.

The law that gave the alliance this leverage was the Community Reinvestment Act of 1977, which made public the lending records of major banks and allowed community groups to challenge mergers and expansions based on proof of redlining. The breakthrough case was that against the First Chicago Corporation, which in 1983 sought approval to acquire the American National Bank. Using CRA, the alliance showed that, in 1982, two-thirds of First Chicago's mortgage loans had gone to just three affluent lakefront neighborhoods in Chicago.

These embarrassing statistics forced First Chicago to negotiate with the alliance in an attempt to stave off opposition to the merger. The result was remarkable: an agreement to make $120 million in loans in Chicago neighborhoods over the next five years, about two-thirds for housing and about one-third for commercial development. The alliance has since forged similar agreements for $35 million with Harris Bank and $18 million with Northern Trust.

Cincotta says some $60 million of the money has made it to "the street" so far, with almost half earmarked for multifamily housing, about 12 percent for single-family housing, and the rest going to assist small business expansions.

The alliance's success under CRA has not been replicated elsewhere. Part of the reason is Chicago's long history as a national center for neighborhood organizing, which makes it easier to put deals together there. Neighborhood efforts always have high visibility, and, even before the CRA negotiations, the banks paid attention.

LISC's Chicago office is the largest in the country, doing as much as a third of the organization's business nationwide. The Chicago Equity Fund, involving LISC and other organizations, raised $11.5 million the first year from Fortune 500 corporations in Chicago alone; that money leveraged $45 million in loans to build 950 low-income housing units, all sponsored by CDCs. As Andy Ditton, a LISC vice-president who until recently ran the Chicago office, puts it, the Chicago environment "creates an atmosphere in which organizations and relationships thrive."

Not everyone agrees, however, that the LISC approach of focusing on the most down-and-out neighborhoods such as New York's South Bronx is the best idea. Floyd Lapp notes that his development corporation was created to bolster a fading commercial strip in a middle-income part of the Bronx. In his view, the foundations would do better to work on saving marginal neighborhoods than to pour all their money into really desperate situations.

Because they are grass-roots organizations, it is hard to quantify the impact that community development corporations have had on urban neighborhoods nationwide. Money from LISC or CRA agreements is almost always used as leverage to acquire much larger amounts of private funds. What's indisputable is that some of the most successful groups—at least in the post-Carter era—are the small ones. Pratt's Ronald Shiffman says large CDCs with big overhead, such as Brooklyn's Bedford-Stuyvesant Restoration Corporation, were wracked by budget cuts, but smaller ones managed to cope.

"They grow from the bottom up rather than the top down," Shiffman says. "They're more rooted, more able to deal with cutbacks, and have a bigger constituency." This is good news for the grass roots, although it may hamper the efforts of city-sponsored CDCs, which are becoming increasingly popular but sometimes do not have a broad constituency.

Leaders in the neighborhood development field believe that CDCs have reached a new level of maturity in the '80s. But they also believe only so much progress can be made without the federal government's involvement.

Andy Ditton predicts that LISC's $30 million syndication "will be the major resource available this year. But saying $30 million is the largest thing happening nationally is kind of sad."

Adds Joseph McNeely, "We're talking about successes, but on the margin." Even with all this activity going on, he says, "we're losing more [low-income housing] units than we're gaining, net. There has to be a federal response."

On the positive side, Ditton says, lack of federal money makes the groups more efficient—able to do more with less. "You can afford to be lazy and inefficient when you have a lot of money thrown at you," he says. "Being forced to earn revenue forces a certain business discipline.

"If more federal money becomes available," he adds, "and it is put on the street in a different way than before, a lot more could be done. People have developed skills they didn't have before."

William Fulton is a contributing editor of Planning.

A Project Grows in Brooklyn
Jennifer Stern
(March 1987)

An odd-looking acronym spelled ULURP (pronounced YOU-lurp) may not mean much to the rest of the country, but to some New Yorkers at least, it's almost a household word. It stands for the Uniform Land Use Review Procedure, which was established in the 1975 revision of the city charter to streamline land-use decision making.

Each year, some 1,200 applications for zoning changes, capital projects site selection, urban renewal projects, and a variety of special permits make their way through the several ULURP steps, finally winding up at the Board of Estimate. The city's final arbiter of zoning and planning decisions, the board is made up of the mayor, the borough presidents, and other top officials.

On the whole, the process has been judged a success despite some grumbling from developers about project delays and from the city's 59 community boards about their limited, advisory role in the process.

In fact, most ULURP applications pass through the charter-mandated steps—from the city planning commission to the appropriate community board, back to the planning commission, and through the Board of Estimate—with hardly a hitch. Where ULURP comes to citywide attention is in the review of the biggest projects—those that will have a major impact on the life of the city.

Two examples are adjacent mixed-use projects (both with the same developer) on 27 acres in downtown Brooklyn: Atlantic Center and Brooklyn Center. Although they completed their almost-two-year trip through ULURP in October, both continue to be controversial, provoking challenges to the city agencies and the community board that approved them.

It has been almost 20 years since 104 acres of downtown Brooklyn were first set aside for urban renewal. The site was designated the Atlantic Terminal Urban Renewal Area (ATURA) after the now shabby railroad terminal that still stands there. In the late 1960s, some 20 acres were cleared and 2,500 mainly black and Hispanic residents forced to leave. Although 2,400 affordable units were originally planned as replacement housing, only 800 units were built—all in high-rise buildings completed in the late 1970s.

Plans came and went for the rest of the site. One called for a new campus for Baruch College, part of the City University of New York, another for a new major league baseball stadium. Atlantic Center represents the eighth amended urban renewal plan for the site. The adjacent Brooklyn Center Urban Renewal Area (BCURA), smaller and historically more commercial, has had a less turbulent history.

In 1984, New York City's Public Development Corporation (PDC), the city's quasi-public real estate development agency, turned its attention to the ATURA site. The PDC has statutory power to find developers for city property, and one of its goals is to stem the flow of back-office functions out of the city by encouraging commercial development in the outer boroughs. According to senior planner Hardy Adasko, the PDC considered the Atlantic Terminal area a prime site because of its unparalleled access to public transit.

The site includes the corner of Flatbush and Atlantic avenues, two of the borough's busiest streets. Atlantic Terminal, still used by the Long Island Rail Road, is also one of the city's largest subway stations, where 10 lines intersect. Next to the renewal area is the landmark Williamsburgh Savings Bank, the tallest building in Brooklyn. Nearby are the gentrifying neighborhoods of Boerum Hill, Fort Greene, Clinton Hill, and Prospect Heights.

The PDC used its powers to bypass the usual request-for-proposals process in picking its developer, Rose Associates, a Manhattan firm that has built mixed-use projects in Washington, D.C., and Boston. PDC officials insist that limiting its negotiations to one potential developer was necessary for such a complex project, but critics have questioned the procedure, citing the Rose family's substantial 1985 campaign contributions to New York Mayor Edward Koch, to Brooklyn borough president

Howard Golden, and to then deputy mayor Kenneth Lipper.

In any case, Rose Associates and the PDC submitted the ULURP applications in August 1985. There were 13 separate applications, covering the various aspects of the project subject to review under the ULURP provisions of the city charter: the acquisition and disposition of city-owned property, amendments to the urban renewal plan, changes in the city map, changes in the zoning map and text, and special permits for modifying setback and violating sky exposure plane regulations.

Nuts and bolts

The development package put together by Rose and the PDC called for three million square feet of office space, more than half in two Skidmore, Owings and Merrill-designed 25-story towers; some 400,000 square feet of retail space, including a large supermarket; two parking garages; a 10-screen movie theater; a health club; and 643 townhouse condominiums, priced for families with an annual income between $25,000 and $48,000.

The project's $530 million price tag includes a wide range of subsidies, among them a $10.7 million federal urban development action grant, a $2.5 million grant from New York State's Affordable Housing Fund, almost $5 million in surplus Municipal Assistance Corporation funds, a 22-year city property tax abatement, and a reduction in the city occupancy tax.

The UDAG award also raised a few eyebrows. Because the U.S. Department of Housing and Urban Development first rejected the UDAG application for lack of a major tenant, the PDC, which also has an equity interest in the projects (25 percent of the profits above the base return), helped arrange for the city's Health and Hospitals Corporation to move to Atlantic Center when it's completed sometime after 1989. The move will mean a tenfold rent increase—to $8 million a year—for the financially beleaguered health corporation.

ULURP was meant to speed up the review process. To do that, it sets a six-month deadline for land-use decisions. However, the 180-day clock doesn't start running until an application is certified as complete by the city planning commission. At that point, it is passed on to the community board, which has 60 days to hold a public hearing and then to approve or disapprove.

Then it goes back to the planning commission, which must hold a public hearing and vote on the application within 60 days. The final step is the Board of Estimate, which casts the only binding vote. The community board only advises and, although the planning commission can effectively stop a project, an applicant may appeal a negative vote to the mayor and the Board of Estimate.

It's the precertification phase that raises the ire of developers. They complain that the requirements for certification of applications are too vague (the city planning department may request "any additional information necessary") and that the process is extended still further by the City Environmental Quality Review, which requires environmental impact statements for many projects submitting ULURP applications.

"For the small builder, there's almost no way to get decisions made," says Steven Spinola, president of the Real Estate Board of New York and a former president of the PDC. "Clearly there should be a time limit set on precertification."

Frustration

Rose Associates partner Jonathan Rose calls the process "extremely frustrating." He's particularly angry about the many times the city's department of environmental protection asked for revisions in the environmental impact statement. For example, he says, after the traffic study was completed, the department brought up the idea of cold starts—that auto pollution produced in the first hour or so that a car is running is different from that produced later.

"We had to go back and survey drivers as to how long their cars had been running when we had already surveyed them on where they were coming from and where they were going. This happened with every aspect of the EIS," says Rose. "It's a waste of time and money."

Like all community board members, the 50 members of Community Board 2 are volunteers, appointed by the borough president on the recommendation of the area's city council representatives. Each board has an annual budget of $121,000 to operate a central office. In addition to their land-use review responsibilities, the community boards also make recommendations for the city budget and municipal services and serve as local clearing houses for the concerns of district residents.

Jerry Renzini, a five-year board veteran just elected to his fourth term as chair, says Community Board 2 has been overwhelmed recently with ULURP applications for large-scale developments in downtown Brooklyn. Atlantic Center and Brooklyn Center were among the most time-consuming. As soon as the projects came to the board's attention, Renzini says, its planning and district development committee set up a subcommittee to review them. By the time they were certified, the subcommittee had met 15 times and the board had also held several public information meetings on the projects.

The seeds of the still-active controversy over the projects were planted during the subcommittee meetings. At its final session on May 28, the members recommended approval by the full board if the developer agreed to several conditions:

● To build rental and condominium units affordable to low- to middle-income families.

● To develop affirmative action programs for construction contractors, for businesses in the completed projects, and for other jobs created by the projects.

● To scale down the retail portion of the project, move the supermarket, and reduce by half the size of the movie complex.

● To use the sales tax escrow account (made up of developers' payments in lieu of sales taxes on construction materials) for the housing and affirmative action programs.

"It's impossible to predict when a project will be certified," concurs Adasko of the PDC. "Most projects submit what they think is a complete application, only to find that more information is required. I'm not saying it's all the fault of the review agencies," Adasko adds. "Until [they have] something in hand, it's hard to judge what is complete."

According to Robert Alpern, chair of the Civic Charter Review Coalition, the drafters of the city charter did not foresee that precertification would be such a long process. He and others say its length stems in part from the city's attempt "to solve problems internally before they go to the community." Both developers and communities resent this approach: developers because it extends the precertification process, communities because it presents them with projects whose plans seem set in stone.

Start the clock

Altogether, says Rose, it took 16 months from the time the projects were first announced to certification. Adasko notes that the city sought and got many changes in the projects during that time. The buildings were set back to permit street widening. One parking lot was redesigned. A detailed open space plan was produced, and the developer was required to demonstrate in the environmental impact statement the impact of the building heights and how much off-street parking would be required by the residents.

When the department of city planning was satisfied with the applications, the planning commission voted last April to certify the package—finally starting the ULURP clock.

At that point, the applications went to Brooklyn's Community Board 2, which represents some 90,000 residents in the northwest section of the borough. The neighborhoods included in its district range from historic Brooklyn Heights, with its expensive brownstones, to the borough's ailing downtown. In 1980, according to U.S. Census figures, almost half of the district's residents were black and almost a fifth Hispanic. Over 25 percent of the population was below the poverty level. Some 85 percent of the housing units were rentals.

These demands resulted from concerns that the upscale projects would not benefit community residents and merchants; that the planned condominium units would be affordable to only 13 percent of the local residents; that the stores in Atlantic Center would take business away from reviving local shopping strips; and that all the jobs generated by the projects would go to people outside the community.

Neither the planning and district development committee nor the full board agreed with the subcommittee's demands. On June 18, the full board, after several public hearings, passed the 13 ULURP applications by a wide margin. It did, however, ask the planning commission to recommend that the developer pursue affirmative action, spend the sales tax escrow account exclusively within the district, and agree to convert the 10-screen movie theater to office space if it proved not to be economically viable.

The board also told the commission that it was concerned about a lack of parking for residents and that it wanted the city to develop some of the abandoned housing it owns in the district for low- and moderate-income residents so as to preserve the community's economic mix.

Opponents of the projects contend the board's vote is proof that the board does not represent the community. Ted Glick, a subcommittee member but not a board member, notes that few of the board members have low incomes and few are tenants, and that most of the planning and district development committee members are white. Board chair Renzini counters that the board's make-up is representative of all the neighborhoods in the community district.

Final steps

The package of applications moved next to the city planning commission. Although community board votes on ULURP applications are not binding, board chair Renzini feels the city planning commission and the Board of Estimate take his group's recommendations very seriously. He estimates that city planning commission and Board of Estimate votes have concurred with those of Community Board 2 at least 95 percent of the time.

At the planning commission's public hearing on July 9, eight speakers testified for the Atlantic Center proposal and four against certain aspects of it, including the potential traffic congestion and the lack of parking for the residential complex. According to Ted Glick, who also heads the ATURA Coalition, a group of 51 local organizations, politicians, and community leaders still fighting for changes in the projects, only a handful of opponents showed up at the hearing because his group did not learn of it in time. Instead, they submitted written comments on the projects' lack of affordable housing and their threat to local commercial strips.

In mid-August, the planning commission approved the applications and filed its lengthy report on the applications with the Board of Estimate. The report echoed the community board's recommendations on affirmative action. It also recommended that the sales tax escrow funds be used to create more low-income housing in the surrounding neighborhoods.

The opponents came out in force for the final step in the ULURP process, the Board of Estimate hearings and vote. Four state assemblymen and a state senator spoke against the projects, along with dozens of renters. Speakers for the projects included the local city council representative, the chair of the Regional Plan Association, and the president of the PDC. The final hearing, on October 9, went on late into the night before the 13 applications were finally approved, along with a resolution that the sales tax escrow account be dedicated to affirmative action and job training programs.

The fight over the Atlantic Center and Brooklyn Center projects is still not over. At the Board of Estimate hearing, a staff attorney for the South Brooklyn Legal Services Corporation announced that his group was filing suit in federal court on behalf of local low-income residents against HUD, city officials, and Rose Associates. The suit seeks to require HUD to withdraw approval of the $10.7 million UDAG on the ground that it had not adequately considered "secondary displacement," the substantial rise in rents—and evictions—likely for residents of the 25 percent of local housing units that are not rent-regulated.

Three additional lawsuits may be filed against the projects, according to Glick: a second South Brooklyn Legal Services suit charging that the EIS did not adequately address secondary displacement, an ATURA Coalition suit on the increase in air pollution that would result from the development, and a local block association suit concerning increased traffic and air pollution.

Over the past several years, civic leaders have unsuccessfully proposed a variety of changes in the way ULURP works. The suggestions include adjusting the length of time for community review according to the complexity of the application and requiring developers to pay a fee that would enable community boards to hire consultants to evaluate projects. But in the case of the Atlantic Center and Brooklyn Center projects, the complaints did not concern ULURP's structure so much as the way it is implemented, particularly the drawn-out precertification process and the make-up of the community board; changes in these areas are not likely to come soon.

Moreover, despite the complaints, many of those involved feel this ULURP episode was quite successful. "It was not rushed, and the public comments were all put back into the EIS and the planning commission's report," says Victor L'Eplattenier, senior planner for the Brooklyn office of the Department of City Planning. He calls it "a display of the procedure at its best."

On its tenth anniversary, ULURP still rates high as a viable method for giving citizens a voice in land-use decisions.

Jennifer Stern is a free-lance writer in New York City.

Beyond Operation Bootstrap
Philip Langdon
(June 1987)

In the 1950s and 1960s, every government economic planner in the U.S. had heard of Puerto Rico's "Operation Bootstrap," the celebrated program to transform a poverty-stricken Caribbean island into a manufacturing center. The development program initiated by Gov. Luis Munoz-Marin in 1947 ranks as one of the most extensive economic planning efforts ever carried out under the U.S. flag. With the encouragement of the mainland government and the guiding hand of planning expert Rexford Tugwell, among others, the Munoz-Marin administration built an array of industries that attracted millions in private investment from U.S. companies.

As a result of this early experiment in centralized industrial planning, Puerto Rico quickly advanced from one of Latin America's poorest regions to one of its highest in per capita income—from $296 in 1950 to $4,301 in 1985.

But in the last 15 years, the island has suffered setbacks, and today it offers a less promising vantage point for considering the success of a national industrial policy. Compared with state governments in the continental U.S., Puerto Rico's government (the former unincorporated territory became a commonwealth in 1952) continues to exercise an extraordinary degree of influence over economic affairs. Yet there's growing recognition that despite good intentions and sizable financial resources, the government has often acted inefficiently and, partly as a result, has had trouble overcoming the obstacles that face a partly modernized economy.

In response, the island's planners are now adding new strategies to the ones that once lured American apparel, textile, pharmaceutical, and electronics companies to a sunny land where the wages were low and the laborers abundant. Increasingly, the commonwealth is fostering locally owned businesses, encouraging service industries, and forging ties outside the U.S. While carrying out these initiatives, planners—nearly all of them working at the commonwealth level—must also oversee major improvements in infrastructure, especially waste disposal and highways.

Contrasts

How effective all these efforts will be is an open question, for Puerto Rico is a complex and contradictory place—a land of Fortune 500 subsidiaries with well-trained local personnel but also of tens of thousands of people who lack the skills to find work to keep themselves above poverty level. It is the home of both a style-conscious, Master-Charging consumer society and of crime so rampant that even residents of suburbs feel compelled to cage their windows, doors, porches, and carports with heavy metal grills.

Puerto Rico was visited by Columbus in 1493 and settled in the 1500s under the leadership of Spain's Juan Ponce de Leon. By the time the 3,435-square-mile island (about two-thirds the size of Connecticut) was seized by the U.S. during the Spanish-American War, it had developed a plantation economy based on sugarcane, coffee, and tobacco. A limited quantity of coffee is still harvested in the beautiful mountains that form the island's dramatic east-west spine, and the foothills and coastal plains grow sugarcane, pineapples, bananas, and plantains.

Today, though, Puerto Rico is a predominantly urban, industrial society. Some 423,000 of its 3.4 million people live in the city of San Juan on the island's northeastern coast. Another 167,000 live in Ponce on the relatively dry southern coast. Much of the rest of the population inhabits smaller cities and suburbs close to San Juan or spread along the northern coast.

Travel Puerto Rico's 8,000-mile network of well-paved roads today, and you'll find enclosed shopping malls as glossy as those in mainland America's most affluent suburbs—along with a profusion of Burger King and McDonald's outlets (where "drive-thru" comes out "auto expreso"). Yet at intersections near San Juan's Luis Munoz-Marin Airport—which is becoming a major Caribbean transportation hub—motorists stopping for traffic lights are approached by grown men who go from car to car selling Chiclets.

At the edge of San Juan's huge, campuslike Medical Center, which offers some of the best health care in the region, old junked trucks, painted fluorescent blue and yellow, squat permanently along an entrance drive, serving as makeshift refreshment stands. Jarring juxtapositions of sophistication and backwardness crop up frequently.

Some of those Chiclets peddlers are members of Puerto Rico's huge underground economy which, according to many economists, employs roughly a third of the commonwealth's workers. Business publications like the *Wall Street Journal* report that it's common for people who collect welfare or food stamp benefits—well over half the population receives some form of assistance—to earn income that's never reported.

In Puerto Rico, almost everything is built of concrete—from the now-empty 22-story DuPont Plaza Hotel, which looks remarkably intact and reclaimable despite the black stains from the New Year's Eve fire that took 96 lives—to the one-story houses in the San Juan suburb of Levittown, where Levitt Homes has adapted its tract home-building formula to the scarcity of wood. So dominant is concrete that the health of the construction industry is measured in bags of cement sold.

Among the most spectacular of the island's concrete buildings is an angular, four-story structure on busy Franklin D. Roosevelt Avenue near San Juan's high-rise banking district. This is the two-year-old headquarters of the commonwealth's Economic Development Administration, better known by its Spanish name, "Fomento," the agency that began Operation Bootstrap and continues to administer the economic programs set in motion during the Munoz-Marin era. The Fomento Building, like a knock'em-dead John Portman hotel, is arranged around a skylit atrium, with glass-lined elevators offering views of hanging vines, terraces with palm trees, and a ground-floor fountain.

The lavishness of the building symbolizes the importance the government attaches to economic development. "Creation of jobs is the number one priority of the administration," says Amadeo I.D. Francis, special adviser for economic affairs to Gov. Rafael Hernandez-Cohen.

In contrast, the Puerto Rico Planning Board, which oversees physical planning, occupies spartan offices in a government tower whose elevator lobby is laced with cobwebs.

Lately, some of the economic trends have been

encouraging. Though 17 percent of the island's labor force is officially listed as unemployed (a big jump from the 10 percent jobless rate that massive emigration and vigorous industrial growth had produced by the end of the 1960s), the 17 percent figure represents a substantial improvement over recession conditions four years ago, when the unemployment rate hit 25 percent.

Antonio J. Colorado, Fomento's forceful, pin-striped administrator, reels off statistical evidence of Puerto Rico's progress: "The average wage has gone from $2.86 an hour in 1976 to $5.27 in 1986. In chemicals and pharmaceuticals, it's gone from $3.90 in 1976 to $7.44 in 1986." But Colorado admits that this improvement has also created difficulties. "Some jobs cannot be done here anymore," he says. The islanders can no longer compete with unskilled laborers in the Far East or Haiti who are paid less in a day than a Puerto Rican expects to earn in an hour.

Work sharing

Fomento is responding to the wage-competitiveness problem by focusing on the type of manufacturing that combines relatively unskilled work in neighboring, low-wage Caribbean countries with higher skilled, better paid work in Puerto Rico. Westinghouse Electric, for instance, had intended to stop making a particular circuit breaker at a mainland U.S. plant because it couldn't compete with imports from the Far East. Fomento arranged for a Westinghouse supplier in Indiana to manufacture the circuit breaker in the Caribbean through the "twin plant" system, as it is called—using more than 300 workers to do the lowest paid routine work at a plant in the Dominican Republic and a smaller number to perform the skilled operations at a factory in Puerto Rico.

Another company, this one a shoemaker based on the mainland, saw the twin-plant program as an economical way to shift some of its manufacturing from the Far East to the Dominican Republic and Puerto Rico. "Companies that are fearful about possible trade restrictions are coming back [to Puerto Rico]," Colorado says. "We can manufacture at lower cost than anywhere else within the U.S."

The twin plant program is a keystone of the Reagan administration's Caribbean Basin Initiative, which allows products from Caribbean and Central American nations to enter the U.S. duty-free, just as products from Puerto Rico have done for decades. In 1986, the twin plant program generated more than 1,100 jobs in Puerto Rico.

Some of those jobs expanded the local labor force, but some represent mainly a holding action—a way of retaining some of the production that would otherwise desert Puerto Rico for nations where labor is cheaper. Despite a recent upturn in apparel manufacturing and a burst of activity in electronics, most economists do not expect manufacturing employment—currently 150,000—to grow substantially in the near future.

The commonwealth is continuing the Operation Bootstrap policy of enticing U.S.-based corporations with guaranties of exemption from federal income taxes (under section 936 of the Internal Revenue Code) and with substantial abatements on Puerto Rican taxes. Electronics, chemicals, and pharmaceuticals are among the industries that have established operations in Puerto Rico over the years, at least partly because of tax breaks.

Westinghouse alone operates 24 plants on the island, and some three dozen drug manufacturers, including Squibb, Pfizer, and Johnson & Johnson, turn out seven percent of the world's supply of pharmaceuticals in 84 Puerto Rican plants. "There's probably more pharmaceutical manufacturing per square mile than in any country in the world," Colorado boasts.

Unfortunately, just as in the continental U.S., advanced industry does not necessarily mean high employment. The electrical and electronics segment of the economy offers about 23,000 jobs, and pharmaceuticals employ slightly under 15,000—not huge numbers on an island where the government reports that the total labor force, including the unemployed, has just passed the one million mark.

"We were not that enchanted with the idea of giving away taxes to get mainland corporations," observes James Tobin, a Yale University economics professor who, in the mid-1970s, led a government-backed study of Puerto Rico's finances. "They weren't getting that many jobs out of it even then."

In effect, Puerto Rico uses federal tax breaks to offset some of the disadvantages of being located 1,000 miles from the U.S. market, of being heavily dependent on imported materials, and of having to meet costly federal requirements, such as the use of U.S. ships. Because companies with "936" operations can avoid commonwealth taxes on profits that stay on the island, several billion dollars have been deposited in Puerto Rican banks; these funds are being used for low-cost loans to spur further economic growth.

In January, the commonwealth enacted an industrial incentives act that exempts new business facilities from 90 percent of their Puerto Rican corporate taxes for periods ranging from 10 years in the San Juan area to 20 to 25 years in remote areas where unemployment is highest. Two offshore islands, Vieques and Culebra, and a large area of Puerto Rico's central highlands, are targeted for the greatest tax relief. Francis, in his high-ceilinged office in the governor's mansion, says, "We expect that the new act will be a major boon to continuing to attract investment from abroad."

In the past, "abroad" would almost certainly have meant the U.S. But no more. Says Colorado: "We have had to open our horizons not only to the U.S. but to Europe and the Far East." More than a year ago, as part of a Fomento trade mission to Japan, Gov. Hernandez-Colon announced that the commonwealth would float a $100 million bond issue in Japan, using the proceeds to help Japanese businesses start operations in Puerto Rico.

"One of the positive things Operation Bootstrap brought to Puerto Rico was the production of a large group of managers with a lot of experience," Colorado observes. Native Puerto Ricans, educated in the extensive university system, now administer more than 90 percent of the manufacturing plants owned by outside corporations.

The island's economic strategy now hinges partly on encouraging these administrators—and other ambitious local people—to start their own companies. In 1986, for the first time in Fomento's history, more than half the companies helped by the agency were owned by Puerto Ricans rather than outsiders.

Fomento's real estate arm, the Puerto Rican Industrial Development Company (PRIDCO), helps both locally owned and outside companies to start manufacturing operations. PRIDCO has built and leased manufacturing plants containing more than 18 million square feet of space.

In a corollary effort, the government is also attempting to reverse the island's decline in agriculture—the leading employer as recently as 1960, when it provided 23 percent of the island's jobs. The big push toward industrialization led farming

jobs to plummet to five percent of total employment at the beginning of the 1980s.

"Agriculture could emerge as an important sector in Puerto Rico again," says Hector Lopez-Pumarejo, president of Corplan, the largest independent corporate management consulting firm in Puerto Rico. The government has tried such innovations as using Israeli drip-irrigation techniques to grow melons and vegetables along the arid south coast.

Reforms

Historically, the same commonwealth that has offered a battery of economic assistance ranging from loans to tax abatements has also demanded money back through high personal income tax rates—up to 83 percent in 1978. The rate is lower now, but as of this writing remains a hefty 50 percent, applied to taxable income above $38,000. Taxes are one reason why some of Puerto Rico's most valuable professional workers depart for the mainland.

Lopez-Pumarejo's firm is involved in a government-supported tax reform study that is expected to result later this year in further reductions. "The tax package," he says, "will be geared to stimulate investment and saving, and to encourage high-income professionals to stay in Puerto Rico." An equally important goal is to reduce the rampant tax cheating.

A more equitable and effective tax system would provide a stronger foundation for the government's far-flung and, in some cases, expensive economic initiatives. The commonwealth invested huge sums to build an oil refining and petrochemical industry, most of which was put out of business by OPEC's price hikes in the 1970s. In attempting to stimulate economic development, the commonwealth over the years has also acquired a shipping line, a telephone company, and an electrical utility in addition to providing health, education, and other services.

"It's a government involved in many things, and not terribly efficiently," says Fuat M. Andic, a San Juan economist who directs management consulting services in the Caribbean and Central America for the accounting firm Arthur Young International. "The bus company has been losing millions. The education level is poor. Health is a monstrous setup."

When growth in the private sector lagged, the government loaded its own payrolls. As a result, public administration is now the largest single job category in Puerto Rico, accounting for nearly a quarter of the island's employment. Unlimited numbers of workers seem to be available to pick up the litter continually tossed onto highways and into parks and to direct traffic at government facilities.

Andic notes that many agencies have begun productivity analyses. "Employees will be used better," he says, "and there will be rational purchasing." But it's fair to wonder how much optimism is warranted. A dozen years ago, Professor Tobin's bluntly worded report emphasized that the government would have to exert strong discipline over its own appetite, over the wage rates that were making Puerto Rico uncompetitive, and ultimately over the Puerto Rican tendency to spend rather than save. Much of the payroll loading took place after that report was issued, and wages climbed so dramatically that some manufacturers departed for cheaper nations.

Infrastructure needs

Another challenge now facing the island is the need to improve its infrastructure. "Puerto Rico has the big advantage of having an industrial infrastructure—an adequate electrical generating system, a good communications network, a good air freight system, a labor force well acquainted with technical skills," says Francis. This puts it in stark contrast to some poorer Caribbean countries, where workers are less educated and electrical power is often interrupted.

But because some public projects have lagged, the government must now target some $1 billion a year for infrastructure improvements. Moreover, industrialization has brought environmental problems. "The federal clean water act has finally caught up with Puerto Rico," notes Lina M. Dueno, vice-president of the Puerto Rico Planning Board. For years, the government procrastinated—building large sewage treatment plants, for instance, but neglecting to install trunk lines, with the result that plants sit unused and rusting. Now, under court order, it must quickly remedy the situation, which has interfered with some industrial development projects.

The infrastructure crisis next in line is highways. The roads are generally smooth—better, in fact, than many in potholed parts of the mainland—but there aren't nearly enough of them to accommo-

date the rapid spread of the suburbs and the huge volume of (mostly Japanese) cars. Traffic jams are horrendous—not helped any by the Puerto Rican penchant for lunging into intersections and relying on horn honking and short blasts of auto burglar alarms to make headway.

In Arecibo, a city of 61,000 on the northern coast west of San Juan, Gov. Hernandez-Colon says the inadequacy of the highways has "strangled" economic development by discouraging industries from moving in. Lina Dueno points out that highway construction has long been limited by the fact that on a small island, acquisition of rights of way is expensive, accounting for up to four-fifths of the cost of every highway.

One bright spot for Puerto Rico is tourism, which has been on the upswing for the past three years and which seems to have been undeterred by the DuPont Plaza fire. From 1985 to 1986, the number of visitors rose 12 percent, to 1.7 million, and this year's figures point toward a further increase. A commission appointed by the governor has been studying what safety improvements are needed to prevent any more disasters like the DuPont fire.

Meanwhile, the government-owned Caribe Hilton is voluntarily installing sprinkler systems, which had not been required in Puerto Rican hotels.

The government continues to build new hotels, with plans to sell them to private investors once they're complete. Some 3,000 hotel rooms in both publicly and privately built hotels will be added in the next three years, according to Carlos A. Diago, deputy director of the Tourism Company, a government agency that commands a budget of about $18 million.

The Tourism Company has increased the number of cruise ships visiting Puerto Rico, strengthened its promotions to U.S. travel agents, fostered the development of small country inns, and granted economic incentives to hotels that comply with high maintenance and service standards. Tourism generates six percent of the gross national product, a figure that Diago hopes will rise to 10 percent within the next three years.

At the same time, PRIDCO is also considering selling several of the hotels it owns, and perhaps disposing of its convention center in the Condado, the beachfront tourist area near historic Old San Juan. Rafael L. Ignacio, president of the agency, explains that the hotels require an annual investment of some $20 million. "With that money," he says, "we could build 40 to 50 industrial buildings throughout the island, with an average of about 100 employees per building."

Using words familiar to observers of mainland economic development, Puerto Rican officials put their faith in the service industries. "We should be a Caribbean service industry center," says Andic in his thirteenth-floor office in the Scotiabank tower, located in the Hato Rey banking district where corporate modern buildings house Chase Manhattan, Citibank, Banco Popular, and other financial institutions from Puerto Rico, the mainland, Spain, and other parts of the world. "The increase in banks in the last 10 years has been tremendous," says Lopez-Pumarejo, who notes that "almost all the Wall Street brokerage houses have offices in Puerto Rico. The service industries can create a lot of high-income employment." . . .

There is seemingly a government program for everything in Puerto Rico, but the main thrust is toward mastering the most modern kinds of economic activities—the ones that require a literate, trained labor force. This means—though planners usually prefer not to be so blunt about it—that the uneducated will continue to have dismal prospects, while those who can profit from the emphasis on knowledge will ride the wave of the future.

At one point, Operation Bootstrap, abetted by huge emigration to the mainland, reduced the unemployment rate to what would now be considered a "mere" 10 percent. But that event is unlikely to happen again. Francis says the government finds it challenging simply to prevent the jobless rate from climbing back up above 17 percent.

In his book, *The Next Left: The History of a Future,* Michael Harrington writes, "The fact is, *the nature of economic growth has changed.* Investment can now create more national product but not more jobs, or at least not more jobs of the kind essential to upward mobility for the great mass of the people." We should be leery of judging the massive and ultimately disappointing Puerto Rican venture in centralized economic planning too harshly. East of Japan, solutions seem hard to come by.

Philip Langdon is the author of Orange Roofs, Golden Arches: The Architecture of American Chain Restaurants, *published by Knopf, and of* American Houses, *published by Stewart, Tabori & Chang.*

8

Urban Design

Urban design is an increasingly important issue in many American cities, as the articles in this chapter demonstrate. Citizens, elected officials, and business people are again seriously interested in the appearance and the physical quality of their cities and suburbs. Once more one can ask, without apology, "Why not a beautiful city?" "Why not a memorable and attractive skyline?" "Why not the harmonious integration of new buildings with old?" "Why not adjacent new buildings designed to be visually compatible with each other?" "Why not a careful relationship of public and private activities and spaces?" "Why not safety, amenity, and a sense of place for pedestrians?" "Why not a physical expression of civic pride?" The articles that follow show that we can have all of these qualities in our cities, if we want them—and if we are willing to work consciously and diligently to achieve them. That is what urban design is all about.

The term "urban design" first came into general use among architects and planners in the mid-1960s. But the basic ideas of urban design were consciously employed in American cities from the earliest days of settlement, as John Reps of Cornell University has shown us. True, in the 19th century, the inexorable grid was stamped like a branding iron across the urbanizing landscape. But for all its faults, the grid at least provided a coherent public framework and infrastructure on which to build.

Early in our own century, the virtues of what was called civic or group design were promoted by Werner Hegemann and Elbert Peets in their monumental pictorial concordance, aptly titled *The American Vitruvius*. The picturesque physical possibilities of town and suburban development were equally well demonstrated in numerous projects across the country by such planners as Charles Mulford Robinson, John Nolen, and Earle Draper.

Alas, these traditions were forgotten in the trau-

mas of the Great Depression and World War II. As a response to long pent-up demand, the building boom that occurred after the war was pragmatic, speculative, and generally undistinguished design. Moreover, it was made possible by and was oriented to the scale of the automobile. It was exactly what most Americans wanted. Urban or civic design was something you left behind in the cities and could return to anytime you wanted, if you needed that sort of thing. Of course, some people—mostly poor minorities—never did make it out of the cities. They could have civic experiences all the time, if they wanted them.

What happened, as any planner could have predicted (and some did), was that jobs and other urban activities followed the suburban residents out into the countryside. But since the only locations provided for such activities were, by default, along the highways, there they settled in endless strips. "A new form of city," the Pollyanna planners announced; "God's own junkyard," the Jeremiahs called it. Meanwhile, central cities were being denuded of vital activities while being made easy for the automobile—at the expense of the pedestrian. It didn't have to happen that way, said visionaries like Lewis Mumford, Charles Blessing, and Edmund Bacon, who pointed to other, far superior models. (See "Five Experts Describe Their Concept of the Ideal City.") Chaos or control were the choices we faced, wrote Christopher Tunnard and Boris Pushkarev in 1963.

Actually, the chaos was a result of a highly institutionalized land development process guided by and benefiting a close fraternity of speculators, politicians, and state highway departments eager to give us what we (and especially they) wanted. There really was control there. Perhaps that is why J.B. Jackson was later able to find an indigenous American order in all that chaos and why Robert

478

Venturi and Denise Scott Brown could tell us we could learn from the strip in Las Vegas.

In retrospect, it all seems inevitable. But so does our eventual disenchantment with it. Much of the American manmade landscape now manifests a de-civilizing sameness, the physical expression of our one-way, media-based culture. The Urban Land Institute tells us that suburban commercial centers like Tyson's Corners and Bailey's Crossroads are the new downtowns of America—lacking, the developers finally admit, only a public dimension and pedestrian connections—and these, they hope, can be sneaked in as an afterthought. Only they can't. They would have to have been planned in the first place as integrated, functioning elements. The thousands of shopping centers that dot the American landscape may be commercial successes but they are for the most part urban failures and we know it. Urban design is a response to these failures.

The term itself emerged as an identifiable concept in the United States only in the mid-1960s. The landmark event was probably the publication of Paul Spreiregen's 1965 book, *Urban Design: The Architecture of Towns and Cities,* one of the earliest and most influential pronunciamentos of the new doctrine. Other important works soon followed, including Design of Cities, by Philadelphia's city planning director, Edmund Bacon. These authors called for a return to three-dimensional design and denounced the prevailing two-dimensional approach to land-use planning that they said was neglecting the real spatial world in which we live. Compounding the problem, in the view of the urban designers, was the excessive inclination of planners and planning educators to rely on the abstract world of social science. Design, after all, could never be science; it is art. (The later contributions of anthropologists and environmental behaviorists would show that social science could indeed make a real contribution to design, but this appreciation would come only much later, after a decade of research.)

A vigorous debate ensued between the urban designers, who usually were trained as both architects and planners, and the growing numbers of planners who came out of nondesign backgrounds. (See "Staking a Claim on Urban Design.") A parallel debate, less intense but no less real, evolved between the proponents of urban design and conventional architects, who tended to be narrowly trained to create ego-gratifying masterpieces, often conceived as sculpture free-floating in space. Urban designers sought to occupy the middle ground increasingly being vacated by both planners and architects. Only the landscape architects held fast to their traditional claim to civic and park design, fields related though not quite equivalent to urban design.

Despite the vigor of the debate, discussion of urban design in the 1960s was largely confined to planning and design circles. But in the process of creating a self-conscious discipline, urban designers became increasingly aware that the clients for their skills would also have to be educated or even generated. As Jonathan Barnett later recalled, an urban designer was defined in those days as someone who knew the answers to a lot of questions that no one was asking. This was soon to change, however, as the urban design efforts initiated by Edward Logue and David Crane in Boston, David Wallace in Baltimore, and Edmund Bacon in Philadelphia began to bear fruit. In 1967 Jonathan Barnett, Jaqueline Robertson, Alexander Cooper, Richard Weinstein, and others persuaded the Lindsay administration in New York City that urban design could be good public policy. The Urban Design Group they created within the New York City Planning Commission, though relatively short-lived, awakened New York to new design possibilities. That approach was soon emulated in a number of other cities.

Back to the future

By the late 1970s high interest rates and growing energy costs slowed new construction and, with it, opportunities to practice urban design. But the historic preservation movement, developing momentum at this time, helped to foster urban design values. Thanks to relatively high costs for new construction, the less expensive and well-built older areas of cities offered attractive real estate investment opportunities. Historic preservation soon became a fashionable, and often profitable, form of nostalgia. No need to reproduce a Victorian main street a la Disney World. Some of it was still out there. And it was relatively cheap, or would be cheap until the supply of restorable buildings got used up or the area became gentrified. The historic preservation movement benefited urban design awareness by resensitizing us to the delights of the eye: detail, pattern, harmony, craftsmanship, and natural materials. Historic districts sensitized us to

Seven experts tackle the problems of the suburban commercial strip in a *Planning* roundtable. See "Zipping Up the Strip." Photo: Dennis McClendon.

Drawings help define the problem in a design charette. This is a huge mine in Butte, Montana. See "Visiting Firemen." Drawing: Butte R/UDAT.

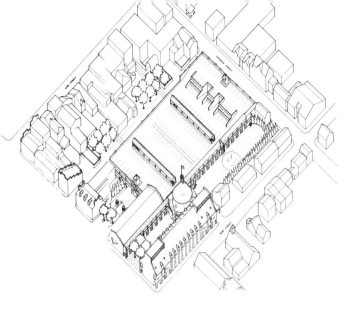

In 1987, the National Endowment for the Arts sponsored a design competition for a new town hall and parking structure for historic Leesburg, Virginia. See ''Stacking the Decks for Better Design.''

Downtown Kalamazoo in the 1950s (left) and today (below)—the after shot showing the nation's first permanent pedestrian mall. See ''Pedestrian Malls: Twenty Years Later.'' Photos: city of Kalamazoo (top) and Steve Deisler.

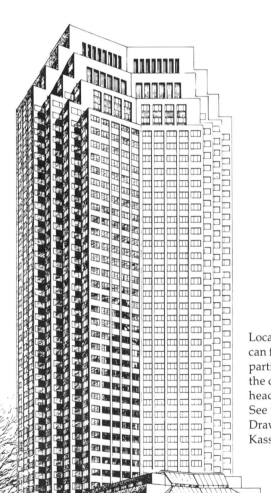

Local design review boards can force a change in particular proposals—as with the design for the Sohio headquarters in Cleveland. See ''Design by Committee.'' Drawing: Hellmuth, Obata & Kassabaum.

Buildings can be designed to fit into their context and to lend some interest to the surrounding skyline. What's needed is some variation in shape (below), but not too much (above). See "A Skyline Paved With Good Intentions." Drawings: Richard Hedman.

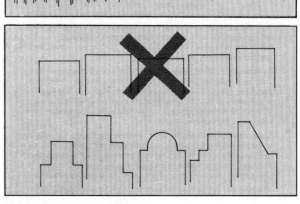

House of jazz musician Al Hirt in the French Quarter of New Orleans. Hirt removed the original stoop, prompting a city request for its restoration. See "Design by Committee." Photo: Matthew F. Kuluz, Jr.

No longer built only in winter cities, second-level walkways are found all over the nation. This one is built above an alley in Des Moines. See ''The Ins and Outs of Skyways.'' Photo: Des Moines Planning and Zoning Department.

Montreal's underground passageways provide a tie between downtown buildings and the transit system. See ''Critiquing the Underground City.'' Photo: Quebec Tourism.

the delights of walking in pleasant urban surroundings.

The message was clear: Since somebody had once designed and built all this, similar environments could be designed from scratch. Townhouses came back into vogue. Georgetown imitations were built in the Washington suburbs, pale reflections of the original but perhaps an improvement over the monotonous rows of detached housing previously in fashion. But though it stimulated an interest in urban design, the new suburban design left a feeling that something was missing: an authenticity, a grittiness, a cityness.

Postmodern architects understood the inherent problem of inauthenticity, but their answer was to turn imitation into a joke: Greek columns here, medallions there, fountains and statues galore. It is all great fun. But it is not urbanism. In fact, the postmodern conclusion is that there can be no real urbanism any more, only large buildings that can, at best, pretend to be fragments of urbanism. For postmodern designers, the struggle to relate new to old is often only a matter of superficial contextualism. For urban designers, in contrast, adroitly managing the relation of new and old is the essence of city building. Postmodernism is not itself urban design and, as a movement that delights in the arbitrary, may well be antithetical to urban design.

Despite the uneasy relationship with postmodernism, urban design in the late 1980s is alive and well. Robert McNulty's influential group, Partners for Livable Places, can now point to cities all over the country that have consciously used urban design techniques to improve their appearance, quality of life, and economic vitality. Indianapolis has learned from Boston, Chattanooga has learned from Indianapolis, and so on. The spread of awareness is uneven, of course, and there are many cities where proposals for better urban design still bring blank stares.

But many more cities have recognized that the urban design process can remedy a variety of problems. It can help to create lively public places ("Painting the Town Red"). It can bring dead streets back to life ("Why Don't We Do It in the Road?"). And urban design can help overcome the "spacification" of the city, as the geographer Edward Relph has called the spread of low-density, space-wasting, automobile-oriented development through city and suburb alike. This has been accomplished using new pedestrian facilities to connect urban activities, as has been done in Minneapolis/St. Paul with skyways ("The Ins and Outs of Skyways") and in Montreal with underground walkways ("Critiquing the Underground City"). The careful integration of parking facilities with existing urban fabric is another way to achieve better pedestrian movement and visual harmony ("Stacking the Decks for Better Design"). The urban design process has even been addressed to the visual and functional problems of an existing highway commercial strip ("Zipping Up the Strip"). It remains to be seen, however, how much remediation urban design can bring to a form that is so much a creation of automobile movement and scale.

How does the urban design process work? Under what conditions does it succeed? And what tools work best? Several of the articles in this section provide useful answers to these questions. One technique described is that of the charette where "visiting firemen," experts who come in to a city on a short-term basis, develop solutions to local problems through a short-term, intensive marathon. Another article describes the design review committees that are also widely used now to ensure better design outcomes. We are told that, for effective design review, we need guidelines in the form of an urban design plan, areas that are carefully chosen, early involvement in design decisions, and an effective review board embracing a mix of skills and outlooks. Also essential is the back-up of an adequate professional staff team, with planning, design, legal, and financial skills well-represented ("Design by Committee"). But as Hamid Shirvani has suggested, you can't simply legislate good urban design. You also need enlightened and informed public opinion. Like generals and war, city building is too important to be left to the architects, planners, and real estate developers, or even to urban design staffs. Urban design works best when vigorous, informed public debate occurs because the real options are fairly and openly presented. Just as good clients are required for good buildings, an informed public is required for good city-building. Fortunately, there is evidence that the public interest in urban design is growing.

The future of urban design looks promising. But to continue to evolve and gain further acceptance, urban design theory and practice must address three important issues:

• Can urban design processes be made relevant to the specific needs of low-income people in cities?

• Does the urban design process have any role to play in the restoration of deteriorating civility and civic order in American cities?

• Finally, how do we best relate the urban design process to the general planning process? Planners recognize that urban design cannot be undertaken in isolation from general comprehensive planning strategies. But we need to learn much more about how to make urban design an integral part of urban planning, and vice versa. The articles that follow, helpful as they are, only begin to suggest answers to these three difficult and critical questions.

David A. Johnson, AICP
Professor of Planning
University of Tennessee, Knoxville

Five Experts Describe Their Concept of the Ideal City

(December 1978)

As every planner knows, urban planning is an art occupied with details: zoning districts, transportation lines, population densities. Lest the forest get lost in the trees, *Planning* magazine asked five experts to consider a question concerning the city as a whole. What would the ideal city look like, we wondered?

Those who answered our question are Charles Blessing, professor of architecture at the University of Detroit and director of city planning in Detroit from 1953 to 1977; Edmund N. Bacon, former executive director of the Philadelphia City Planning Commission; Oscar Newman, architect and city planner and author of *Defensible Space* (1972) and *Community of Interest* (1979); Ian McHarg, chairman of the Department of Landscape Architecture and Regional Planning at the University of Pennsylvania and author of *Design with Nature* (1971); and George Ramsey, director of the graduate passive design laboratories at the College of Architecture, Georgia Institute of Technology.

Charles Blessing. The ideal city of the ancient Greeks—Plato and Aristotle—and of the Renaissance 2,000 years later, was a static, final design, rigidly laid out, rigidly bounded, hardly a dynamic blueprint for a vital, human environment. This is probably the reason why these theoretical exercises in geometry had so little impact on the urban forms actually created. The "ideal" designs left little room for the irregularities of natural settings or the free exercise of the imagination. What theoretical city pattern (such as the nine-sided Palma Nuova) could vie with the medieval Italian towns of Siena, Assisi, or Orvieto? Which rigid, idealized city could equal the diversity or beauty of Salzburg or Edinburgh?

As it turned out, the ancient Greeks built an actual city that far excelled even the most dramatic concepts of the "ideal" city. In terms of human scale, natural beauty, and design, Periclean Athens is the very opposite of the rigid concepts of the Greek philosophers or the Renaissance architects.

Ancient Athens, while approaching Plato's ideal city, with an acropolis in the center and a wall around the periphery, was vital. Its builders responded to the terrain and to the communal needs of the Greek people. For worshipers, they sculpted a flat platform on the hilltop of the Acropolis adequate to support the great size of the Parthenon. For the great orators such as Pericles, and for the citizens who assembled to hear them, the builders constructed the fan-shaped Pnyx, which offered dramatic views of the entire Acropolis.

Because of its mild climate, Athens was a city dominated by its public life. Outdoor areas such as the agora, the theaters, the stadium, and the Pnyx became outdoor living rooms. Linking these areas were processional routes or streets that offered constantly changing views of the Acropolis.

When one considers the possibility of creating an ideal city today, one must be more modest, for our vast metropolitan regions house millions of people. Even so, partial solutions show promise.

Our modern cities also can be redesigned to accommodate pedestrians and take advantage of the terrain, as was done in ancient Athens. It would be possible along the riverfront in Detroit, for example. With a sustained effort to build a pedestrian walk along the riverfront, people eventually could enjoy a walk of a mile or more without interference from vehicles. And the newly completed 100-acre civic and convention center is much larger than the agora of Athens.

A greater challenge for Detroit is building an extensive system of linked pedestrian greenways running perpendicular to the proposed linear parks along the riverfront. Eventually, these greenways could connect virtually the entire central city, an area of nearly 20 square miles. Four greenway links in the system already have been built—those of Lafayette Park, Elmwood Park, the Detroit Medical Center, and Wayne State University.

A more ideal city environment could emerge in this country within this century. At least we could be closer to it than at any time in our 200-year history. For this to happen, though, citizens must participate in developing the goals for an ideal environment; politicians must endorse these goals; and planners and urban designers must create the concepts to fulfill these goals.

Edmund N. Bacon. First, the downtown must be a vital place; it must serve as the focal point of the entire city and the region. It must be a place that everybody in the city identifies with and finds meaningful.

The whole experience of arriving in the center city must be rewarding, not deadening. Riding the subways must be dignified—an inspiring and pleasant experience. To accomplish that, we've introduced light and air into the subways, and we've built gardens into the subways. I think the world's first subway garden is in Philadelphia.

It is crucial, too, that the energy of the center city flow outward in all directions—into the residential areas—and that the center city not allow itself to be surrounded by a moat or wall that separates it from residential areas. This means no blight and no expressways around the center city.

As for the future of the city: The time has come when we must face the growing scarcity of fossil fuels and the resulting change in movement and transportation. Since we will have to move from a petroleum-based mode of transportation to an electrically based one, we will have to recluster cities on converging electrically driven transportation lines.

This fact will mean expensive changes in the form of the city. It will mean, among other things, that the suburban areas will deteriorate and die and that suburban centers will fade away. And it will mean that points of convergence of transportation lines, such as the centers of metropolitan areas, will have a tremendous resurgence and revitalization.

Oscar Newman. Architects and city planners no

longer can allow themselves the luxury of projecting social and physical utopias from the tops of their heads—dream worlds and great pieces of sculpture such as Minoru Yamasaki's Pruitt-Igoe in St. Louis and Ralph Rapson's Cedar-Riverside in Minneapolis. These are doomed to failure because they do not take into account how people live or answer residents' aspirations about the symbolic significance of their home environments.

The frequency and scale of past mistakes now make it mandatory for us to ask people about the nature of their visions. It is also necessary for us to study how people live and use their sociophysical environments. The forms and images we arrive at this way are likely to be different from those we were educated to espouse as architects and planners.

In the past, we too frequently have fast-talked community groups, housing agencies, developers, the federal government, and cities into building low-, moderate-, and middle-income housing projects that met only our criteria. They proved unusable because we had a vision of how people should live that was unrelated to their own needs and fantasies.

The project we designed for Newark, New Jersey, is a combination of high-rises for the elderly and walk-ups and row houses for families with children. The entire project can, however, still be built at a density similar to what was achieved by the high-rise Pruitt-Igoe development in St. Louis—which was torn down. In our scheme, the elderly and families with children are kept separated from each other in different buildings and groupings. Each grouping is designed to allow residents to provide for their own security. Each age group is provided communal space, both in and between buildings, that is directed toward the group's specific needs. With the dissolution of the extended family in today's society, we must find new means of bringing people together.

Another problem we face in our cities is the consequence of concentrations of low-income families in housing developments and particular neighborhoods. Such concentrations, coupled with abundant, federally assisted suburban housing, have served to send the middle class into the suburbs.

Now our central cities are dying hulks. We have polarized the poor in the urban core and the wealthy in the suburbs. It is clear that we no longer can afford to build housing that concentrates the poor. Rather, the poor should be housed in middle-income housing developments where no more than 20 to 30 per cent of all the units are assigned to low-income families. The low-income families should receive rent subsidies and be indistinguishable from their neighbors. The buildings should not be designed to stand out as publicly assisted developments; rather, they should blend in inconspicuously with the surrounding middle-income communities.

Ian McHarg. Environments are variable, so there is not going to be any universal solution. There are going to be particular solutions. We define all the environments in the world by the plants and animals that occupy them. Human adaptation should be as specific and variable, too. It should be possible to distinguish a city in a desert from a city in a tundra from a city in a tropical rain forest. By and large, modern architecture has never distinguished between environments. There's the same stupid inappropriateness of Lisbon, Glasgow, and San Francisco.

The differences among cities are so enormous that the word city has almost no utility. To use one solution in every environment by definition would be wrong. Because environments are variable, the idea that Phoenix is the same as Philadelphia, which is the same as Anchorage, which is the same as New Orleans, is madness.

The only place in the U.S. where you would know where you were, infallibly, without reference to any plants or animals, would be in the land of the pueblos. If you dropped from a helicopter and you couldn't see plants or animals but only buildings, and you saw these pueblos, you'd know absolutely that you had to be in a hot, arid climate; and the chances would be very, very good that you would be in either Arizona or New Mexico, not anywhere else. That should apply everywhere. There should be an appropriateness of the human adaptation to the place.

George Ramsey. What America needs is full recognition of its wasteful, inefficient urban systems and its resulting life styles—in other words, its very low quality of life. Basically, we have only two types of physical development: suburban sprawl and vertical, high-rise sprawl. Both systems are inefficient energy consumers. Both systems involve high dependency upon precious fossil fuels, are highly polluting, and fail in any type of evalua-

tion that measures crime, education, food production, water and air quality, or taxation.

Perhaps the worst aspect of sprawl is its linkage systems—the nightmare of highways, gaudy miles of commercial strip development, and concomitant taxes, plus the government agencies and environmental destruction involved in supporting and regulating such systems. American agribusiness uses 13 calories of petroleum for every calorie of food produced, and the low nutrient content of what we eat speaks ill of the whole setup. We face so many crises that they cannot be listed. What to do?

What we need is an exodus from our large cities. Twenty percent of the population of our large cities should move to small towns and rural areas. We must do this because it is very dangerous to have three percent of the population supplying all the food for the other 97 per cent. This exodus also would stop the ridiculous expansion of our large urban areas.

Further, the exodus should be assisted by the federal government. It should create the opportunity to build new, self-reliant villages in which all waste and water are recycled locally and where fresh food is grown in greenhouses and with hydroponics. What would evolve are new food systems, housing located near work, and pedestrian communities where typical transit is the bicycle. There life would be healthy, taxes low, and energy used efficiently.

Meanwhile, back in the cities, federal tax incentives should be used to urge people to move closer to work. City bicycle paths are urgently needed to provide a safe, inexpensive means of transportation. Automobiles should have 40 horsepower engines that obtain 100 miles per gallon. Urban food-growing systems should be employed where possible. Solar and other alternative natural energy systems—though not nuclear fuel—should be used throughout the nation. Finally, nearly all our giant parking lots should be converted to housing, gardens, or parks, thus permitting all of us to live near our work in a safe and more durable environment.

A Skyline Paved With Good Intentions

Richard Hedman
(August 1981)

There was a time when cities didn't need specialists in urban design. Architects handled it themselves and did a rather good job of it. The pinnacles of Lower Manhattan, the great escarpment of Michigan Avenue in Chicago, and the flowing form of San Francisco took shape in the first part of this century as if ordained by nature.

Then, during the 1960s and the 1970s, it all changed. The urban world was turned upside down by the unique convergence of four powerful forces: rapid population growth, an expanding economy, cheap energy, and a new, untested architectural vision.

In one generation San Francisco's graceful skyline was lost forever, a victim, you might say, of rationalized vandalism. The first interloper was the Hartford Insurance building on California Street. Then came the new Bank of America building, which began to take shape in 1967. At first, the growing skeleton did not appear threatening. Some who had seen the model thought that perhaps it might be too dark, but they were assured by the designers that the color had been carefully considered.

Architecturally, the Bank of America is a fine building. But in terms of how it affects the cityscape, it was and remains an urban disaster; too large, too dark, and—given those attributes—in the wrong place. The same building located at the center of the financial district would eventually have been integrated into the cityscape. Other large buildings would have clustered about it, minimizing the scale of its dark facades and providing a transition to the finely scaled hills of the city. Where it stands, however, it doesn't work.

The urban design plan coasted into official being on the wave of public concern provoked by the Bank of America building together with two enormous projects proposed for the waterfront. The plan was adopted by the city planning commission in 1971 and the height and bulk controls put into effect the following year. Assured by the planners that the controls would do the job, the commissioners felt confident they were providing the city with the protection it needed.

It wasn't enough.

The height and bulk controls did keep a Chicago-type monster building, a Sears Tower for example, from dominating the skyline and did prevent a blight of view-blocking slabs. But, even without that, a delicate skyline was fated to be coarsened and brutalized. True, relative to most American cities there is much beauty left. But now the scenes we call San Francisco must be carefully cropped with an editorial eye.

Form follows fashion

To discover why architects have done what they have done to San Francisco in spite of the urban design plan, and to many other cities without an urban design plan, it is necessary to understand the nature of their design bias and the design revolution that led them to the aesthetic approach known as the International Style. It was unique in that it claimed to be not just another style, but, more emphatically, the bedrock of architectural truth—an architectural religion, with architects cast in the role of high priests. The glad tidings brought to the sinful followed these lines:

• Where decoration was once a virtue, it is now an evil.

• Pure simplicity shall depose corrupt opulence, and ancient symbols shall be replaced by logic.

• That which most completely contrasts with the awful past is best.

Under an architectural philosophy that claims the new to be pure and the old to be degenerate, the old becomes something to be despised rather than sensitively related to. With contrast and newness the objectives, buildings could work only against each other, never with each other. Unlike the architecture taught by the Ecole des Beaux-Arts, where the subtle interaction of buildings in creating and defining space was an integral part of design, the new architecture had no urban design content beyond contrast. Not the kind of everyday contrast that exists between Mission and Colonial Revival or between Georgian and Art Nouveau—but a radically new kind of contrast that differed in every aspect. For ease let us call it High Contrast, although the most accurate name would be Revolutionary Contrast.

High Contrast can be an extremely effective device. Many superb examples exist throughout the world. The polished, machine-perfect pavilion set in a lush meadow is an archetypal example and a surefire award winner. The steel and glass prism surrounded by elaborately ornamented terra cotta confections produces an equally successful urban example.

An architecture born of the desire to contrast suffers mightily when the source of contrast is removed. Mies's and Johnson's Seagram building in New York City, once a stunning apparition in an old-fashioned and rather grungy setting, has in a few brief years been reduced to just another highrise set in just another plaza.

Contrast is not a balanced affair. It requires a minimum ratio of background to object so that the background presents a cohesive setting showcasing the sole exception. Pursued wantonly, contrast has a facile ability to destroy itself, translating into chaos, more irritating than interesting. Clearly, if contrast is the object, then the character and permanence of the setting must be an integral part of the design concept.

While our most acclaimed architects move from razzle to dazzle, lesser lights are designing the vast bulk of new construction in America without any clear objective to guide them, moving from one design fad to the next. Badly needed is an accepted body of architectural language that works well in both the city and suburbia and that can be mastered by minor talents on small budgets. The existence of such a unifying factor would not stifle creativeness any more than masonry construction limited good design in preceding eras.

There is one way in which modern high-rises do work in concert and that can be seen in the cumulative impact of the box-shaped tower. When the Chase Manhattan Bank first thrust its box-top form into New York's skyline, one architectural critic applauded its forthright honesty in dispensing with the foolish pinnacles, pyramids, and pediments that graced the tops of surrounding towers, for saying bravely and forthrightly, "This is what office floors look like." That humble beginning gave us today's Lower Manhattan, boxed in with architectural honesty. During the same span of years, San Francisco also gave up a poetic-but-corrupt skyline in exchange for an assortment of large, honest, functional boxes arranged with all the grace of a refrigerator showroom. From most directions, all traces of the pre-1960s skyline are obliterated. Building economics, not the height limits, have given us rows of buildings of similar height, producing an ugly, boring skyline.

Streetscape

San Francisco's old downtown possessed a tightly knit streetscape. Belt courses at the third or fourth floor lines were carefully referenced to one another. Subtle design games of reversed emphasis and substitution were played out, adding visual variety to the common thread tying the many parts into a coherent whole. The street space between the block fronts was positive in nature, not an empty void, filled with an almost palpable space.

The emerging streetscape is of quite different order. The new buildings ignore the belt courses of their older neighbors. The building skin, instead of giving a sense of weight and mass similar to masonry construction, expresses the new technology, rising sleek, smooth, and weightless. The space defined by such buildings tends to be indefinite in nature, and the new purity is underscored by ground floors for the most part devoid of shops, restaurants, signs, and other distracting features.

Small plazas and sidewalk arcades, rather than increasing interest and amenity, as was expected by the planners in 1967 when downtown San Francisco was rezoned, produced just that much more blank space to walk by and through. As more and more buildings were replaced, there was less and less contrast for the new buildings to feed upon. The result is a growing "no-man's-land": new, tidy, crisp, and boring.

Observation of pedestrian movements indicates that many people go out of their way to avoid using the new arcades. The fact that they have a remarkable sameness that borders upon the institutional charm of a hospital corridor must be a good part of the problem. The visual conflict between facades with all vertical patterns and all horizontal patterns, rather than inducing drama and interest, simply becomes just one more factor adding to a disjointed imagery.

The thin, lightweight-appearing facades coupled with too many bare plazas produce a street that gives little sense of three-dimensional space.

Clearly something basic is missing from modern rationalist architecture. Today's buildings simply do not aggregate well. The whole too often is less than the sum of the parts. The origin of the omission becomes obvious the moment you examine the rationalist architectural philosophy in a broader context: There is no urban design component. It isn't there for the simple reason that it would have required some recognition of the very architecture that yesterday's revolutionaries were so completely opposed to. Thus, we have an architecture satisfactory for suburban shopping malls and industrial parks but not for rebuilding the urban core. There is growing evidence that in a city good urban design is more important than what is currently considered good architecture.

How did it happen? Why didn't the much-vaunted urban design plan protect the city? What were the urban design professionals doing?

Certainly the urban design plan was comprehensive enough in its injunctions. But the very effort to cover all the bases in an even-handed way ironically may be responsible for some of the plan's weakness. The objectives and policies are so generally stated that it is difficult to make the intent stick when it comes to a specific design issue. When push comes to shove, a collection of bland good intentions is not enough. Like the Bible, there are always passages that can be quoted in a way to support the developer's proposal.

Lately, some local planners have been saying that the city needs a detailed design plan indicating precisely what should go where. But it is not the tactical position of the urban design plan that is at fault. The problem is not what was done but rather how it was done. The underlying assumption of the plan—that our ability to predict the future is quite limited—has in no way been disproved. The record of city planning over the past 30 years should be ample evidence. It continues to make sense to emphasize how things should be done. What was and is lacking is a clear statement of design objectives that positively link architecture to urban design. Any approach that avoids dealing with architecture will probably fail.

Architecture's victory

When the city planners were determining the scope of recommendations to be included in the urban design plan, they decided to stay within what they saw as the accepted bounds of urban design and to avoid prescribing specific architectural requirements. The local American Institute of Architects chapter made clear its opposition to anything faintly resembling design review, and the last thing needed at the public hearing was a clutch of angry architects launching a verbal barrage. Hindsight has revealed the lack of specifics to be no small omission.

Continuing to operate under the 1968 downtown zoning ordinance with its bonuses for plazas, arcades, side setbacks, multiple entrances (bonuses for just about everything a smart developer would want to do anyway) has not helped either. When the urban design plan was being prepared, it seemed unpolitic to undo what so recently had been adopted. Only now is the department of city planning finally beginning to redirect downtown zoning toward urban design objectives.

During the high-rise boom that accompanied adoption of the urban design plan, the urban design staff was dominated by the functionalist ideals of the International Style. The staff would consistently shy away from any urban design requirements that called for features that might be labeled decorative.

All, including the author, were weaned on the Truths of Modern Architecture, which made it difficult for the staff to oppose the urban design flaws inherent in the architecture itself. Time and time again, architecture triumphed over the objectives and policies of the urban design plan. Yes, there were battles and struggles, some well publicized, others hidden backstage, but it was amazing how quickly the staff would cave in when the great totem of architectural integrity was raised in sacred intonations.

Fortunately, all is not lost. There is room to correct many past mistakes, or at least to hide them. Downtown San Francisco is still rich in fine old buildings that can be integrated into the future. Proposed new urban design objectives, policies, and principles will sharpen design review and the environmental evaluation process of downtown buildings. If adopted, a new bonus system will require amenities that support, not undermine, the intent of the urban design plan. And a substantial revision of the bulk controls will assure that subsequent development will be in scale with the cityscape.

Further, there are many signals coming from the architectural world to the effect that designers are beginning to question the restrictions imposed by the International Style. A richer architectural vocabulary is beginning to emerge that appears capable of accommodating the concerns of urban design. Most important, the city now has a planning commission willing to say no to bad urban design, and in several recent instances the commission has been more aggressive than the staff in pursuing the objectives of the urban design plan.

In the past, great streets came into being because architects respected previous epochs and sensitively related their buildings to each other. Over time, they reinforced the positive features that evolved. While styles changed, there were sufficient common denominators to produce an ensemble effect. Today, a city is lucky if the architect considers the building next door, much less the block. When a good street does emerge, it is more likely to be the result of simple good luck than of sensitive design. That is why cities need urban design: to provide the coherence that used to come from tradition.

The role of urban design is to protect streets with positive characteristics and ensure that new development enhances each street's special qualities. Where a clear design direction is lacking, the urban designer must direct new development toward a coherent image for the street. Selecting an image for a street or block is a little like mixing paint. If too many colors are mixed, the result tends toward a muddy grey; one such mixture cannot be readily distinguished from another. Great streets are memorable because they have a specific color or flavor, and it is the clustering of great streets that makes a great city.

Unlike a flatland city where the viewer must remove himself to a distant highpoint to view the city, San Francisco is constantly on view within itself. In fact, views are San Francisco's most cherished open space. To a significant degree they offset the pressure and claustrophobia of living in a densely built city.

Change afoot

Here are a few basic urban design policies, proposed as part of a comprehensive revision of San Francisco's controls for downtown. They are not magical and will not effect an overnight cure, but in combination with planned revisions of the bulk controls they will help stem the erosion of the city's special qualities. Their effectiveness will be directly in proportion to the city's determination to enforce them.

1. Ban the box-top high-rise and approve only buildings thoughtfully shaped in relationship to their position in the skyline.

2. Require the first 40 to 65 feet of facade to be built to the street property line along the entire frontage in order to retain the traditional street pattern.

3. Demand that the lower portions of buildings that form the pedestrian environment—the first 40 to 65 feet—be visually interesting.

4. Make each new building work with its neighbors in defining street space.

5. Retain older buildings, or the significant portions of them, with architectural and urban design merit.

6. Insist that new buildings relate harmoniously to nearby buildings of architectural merit.

7. Where the existing character and quality merit changing, direct the design of buildings toward a specific design objective.

These policies are already being aggressively implemented under the city planning commission's unusual discretionary review power. They are part of the interim controls in effect while the total package of proposed changes undergoes environmental review.

During the preparation of San Francisco's urban design plan, one of my colleagues said to me, "The problem with architects is that they don't have any taste." At first I was offended—after all, I had a degree in architecture—but, as time passed, I had to admit he was right.

But since then, I have concluded that the problem is not so much an absence of taste as a distortion of values emanating from the prevalent architectural vision. As long as this vision leads architects to make rude public gestures, urban designers will be needed to set forth urban design rules for good public deportment. Such rules are at best a stop gap measure; their chief merit is that they make architects *consider* urban design. The ultimate solution is a new architecture that builds in urban design instead of tacking it on.

Richard Hedman, now retired, was the principal planner for urban design for the San Francisco Department of City Planning. As a cartoonist, he's known for And on the Eighth Day *and* Stop Me Before I Plan Again! *(both published by APA).*

Pedestrian Malls: Twenty Years Later

Ruth Eckdish Knack
(December 1982)

Some 150 pedestrian malls—including transit malls—have been built in the United States in the last two decades. Most haven't failed outright, but few have lived up to their billing as the salvation of downtown retailing. Just about as many department stores and first-run movie theaters have closed in towns with malls as without, and just as many wig stores, fast-food places, and video-game arcades have opened up.

What's different about the malls is the trees and grass and children's playgrounds—and the ubiquitous Muzak. Now some analysts are questioning whether the parklike atmosphere is conducive to retailing, and some places are going to the other extreme and ripping up their malls. Most, though, are sticking with the mall, while searching for ways to bring it up to date.

The late Victor Gruen, credited both with designing the first big suburban shopping center and with popularizing the downtown mall idea in the United States, said all along that it was no panacea. ("A mall is too small to be all.") In most places, however, the mall was exactly the part of the downtown program that was singled out for implementation.

Kalamazoo, Michigan, the first U.S. city to build a permanent pedestrian mall, is a case in point. The central business district of this small city in southwestern Michigan (85,000 in 1960; 79,000 today) was in relatively good shape when a civic group hired Gruen to prepare a downtown plan in 1956, but there was a threat of competition down the line from the outlying shopping centers that were beginning to crop up.

Gruen's master plan, which did not include a specific design for a mall, called for the creation of an entire pedestrian precinct—a series of covered walks, plazas, and landscaped malls ringed by a low-speed perimeter road feeding several giant parking lots at the edge of the core. In later phases, the pedestrian core was to be expanded by moving the perimeter road outward.

"We must think in terms of comprehensive long-range planning for Kalamazoo rather than in terms of temporary stopgap measures," Gruen wrote.

Mall City

Despite the warning, Kalamazoo decided to start at once with a three-block mall along Burdick Street, which opened in 1959. The city was so proud of itself that it took a new official nickname, "Mall City" (replacing "Debt-Free City," "Paper City," and "Celery City"). The only gesture toward the perimeter road was to make Kalamazoo and Michigan avenues a one-way pair.

Gruen complained that Kalamazoo "put the frosting on the cake before it built the cake," recalls architect Beda Zwicker, a Gruen associate since 1953. (He had higher hopes, Zwicker reports, for Fresno, California, which adopted more of a mall-centered Gruen plan a few years later.)

For a while, Kalamazoo's three-block mall was enough to keep a basically healthy business district going. "It really electrified downtown," says James Visser, now director of the newly created Downtown Development Authority (DDA) and former head of the planning department's economic development division. Carrying out the entire Gruen plan would have meant tearing down half the downtown for parking, Visser says, "and that would have been an unmitigated disaster."

(At this point, more by default than official policy, DDA is doing much of the planning for the central business district, including the mall. As the result of a recent agency reorganization, the planning department was reduced to a small section of the community development division of the office of public services. Both the original mall and later revisions were designed primarily by the parks and recreation department.)

In 1972, the mall was extended a block north and redone, this time from storefront to storefront (the first go-round was from curb to curb). Then in 1975, the Kalamazoo Center, a hotel, office, retail, and convention facility, was built near the north end.

Both the original mall, which cost about $100,000, and the 1972 expansion were paid for by local merchants, who formed an assessment district, and the city. Kalamazoo Center was a joint venture by the city and a private developer. More recently, the city used an urban development action grant to spur development of a high-rise apartment building now under construction. It's phase one of a hoped-for mixed-use complex a block past the mall's southern terminus.

Clearly, today, the mall is holding its own. It has a built-in lunchtime clientele from the nearby Upjohn research facilities, Bronson Hospital, and city offices. But the mall hasn't attracted large numbers of students from the city's four colleges, and it hasn't really been competitive with the area's five suburban shopping malls—particularly the large new one in Portage to the south—and there are vacant stores. The bleakest stretch is the north end, closest to the low-rent section of town and the "Multimodal Center"—a historic railroad station remodeled for use by Amtrak, Greyhound, and local taxis.

A year ago, four out-of-town architects were invited to town to lead a student charette aimed at coming up with new ideas for revamping the area around the mall's north end. This fall, the four came back to present their ideas to a local forum. The schemes were farout: a hotel topped with a dirigible by Chicagoan Stanley Tigerman; a two-block-long glass "Winter Garden" by New Yorker Robert Stern; a fish-shaped apartment building by Greg Walsh of Los Angeles (standing in for Frank Gehry); and a lake in the shape of the Great Lakes by Merrill Elam of Atlanta. The point, each architect stressed, was to give Kalamazoo some oomph.

"The mall is antiquated in terms of the expectations of people today," said Stern. "You need something decisive, bold, big in scale, to draw people back."

"It's too wide," added Tigerman, "and too boring." Why not, he suggested at one point, put back the cars?

"You must create a sense of place, something to make downtown different from the suburbs," said Greg Walsh, who, as a young architect, worked in Gruen's office when the Kalamazoo plan was being prepared. The feeling then, said Walsh, was that the mall idea was at the forefront of planning theory. "But now things have changed. The mall isn't enough."

Local planners seem to have taken the proposals with more than a grain of salt. (Dirigible City? "No way," said one.) There is interest, however, in unchanneling the now-hidden Arcadia Creek, as proposed by all four architects, and using it to create a new focal point for the downtown.

The Downtown Development Authority also is exploring the possibility of using tax increment financing to stimulate housing development near the mall. A recent analysis by Economic Research Associates indicated that there was, in fact, a market for downtown housing. Another idea being toyed with is a skywalk system connecting the second stories (mostly empty now) of mall buildings.

Is transit better?

Mall fashions have changed over the years. Although full pedestrian malls continue to be built, the more recent trend seems to be toward some sort of limited transitway. Minneapolis's Nicollet Mall was the first in 1964, with other well-known transit malls in Philadelphia; Portland, Oregon; and Chicago; and a new one just opened in Denver—a total of about 35 to date.

Part of the reason for the trend is money. Since the Urban Mass Transportation Administration was created in 1964, 80 percent federal funding has been available for malls that fulfill transit purposes. At the same time, competition has increased for the community development block grant funds used for some of the more recent pedestrian malls. That has forced communities still interested in a full mall to look to such other sources as tax increment financing, local bond issues, and, of course, the assessment districts that were a funding mainstay of the earliest malls, along with urban renewal funds.

Glen Weisbrod, a planner who has studied transit malls for Cambridge Systematics, a Massachusetts consulting firm, says they can be a good compromise design for merchants who fear the effects of cutting off Main Street traffic. He also notes that transit is a way of bringing a sense of activity to a too-wide mall, and he predicts that we will begin to see more "semi-malls" (street widenings of one sort or another), which will be open to general traffic as well as buses.

Another obvious trend is toward the enclosed downtown shopping center. A recent example is the Rouse Company's Grand Avenue complex in Milwaukee, a combination of old and new buildings, connected by an arcaded mall, and from all accounts doing well. Muskegon, Michigan, has roofed over four downtown blocks, with a Sears store at one end and a 1930s bank at the other.

Other examples are numerous: the Uncle Sam Atrium in Troy, New York, and Midtown Plaza in Rochester (an early one); the Gallery in Philadelphia; Santa Monica Place; Chicago's Water Tower Place; and, of course, the Kalamazoo Center.

Bruce Heckman, a consultant with Robert Teska Associates in Evanston, Illinois, predicts that the advent of the inflatable, fiberglass roof, like that used on domed stadiums, will produce even more enclosed centers. He warns, though, that roofing over can take away from the architectural flavor of the old downtowns.

Enclosed centers also may siphon activity from other parts of the downtown, notes Fred Kent, director of the Project for Public Spaces in New York, the group founded by William Whyte to study the ways in which people use cities. One the other hand, observes Kent, enclosed shopping centers may simply be a way of reinventing the department store—"and that was a good idea."

What the mall watchers say

It's hard to tell from the literature exactly why pedestrian malls haven't been more successful. Books and articles on the earlier, full malls tend to be mere compendiums of mall projects, often based on information supplied by downtown associations rather than objective analyses. Several of the more recent transit malls have been studied in some depth, however. And there is no shortage of mall watchers with strong opinions about the reasons for success or failure. Here are some of their conclusions:

Don't do too little, too late. Trying to get retailers back after they've left the downtown is an uphill struggle, says consultant Robert Miller of the Real Estate Research Corporation in Chicago. Kalamazoo is relatively successful, in his view, precisely because it built its mall before suburban retailing got a strong foothold and then continually added more ingredients to the downtown mix.

Too little can mean too short a mall (as Gruen said of Kalamazoo), or it can mean going ahead with cosmetic improvements without considering the whole range of downtown needs. "Think of the mall last," says Bruce Heckman, "after you've thought about how you're going to draw people to the area—and how you're going to move them around once they get there."

Don't copy. There's no recipe for downtown success, writes Basil Rotoff in *International Experiences in Creating Livable Cities* (Norman Pressman, ed.; 1981; University of Waterloo, Ontario). Rotoff, who teaches planning at the University of Manitoba, makes the point that European cities, often the model for North American planners, have far different social and cultural traditions. Assuming that North Americans will use the mall for an evening stroll in the European style is a big mistake, he suggests.

That's true within the U.S., too. What works in Kalamazoo may not work elsewhere, particularly in smaller places. Thus, Tom Moriarity does not recommend malls for the towns he advises for the Main Street Project of the National Trust for Historic Preservation. And, it turns out, none of the 48 towns now involved in the program had built malls. "In a little town, it's simply not worth the expense," says Moriarity. "It doesn't address the real problem of why people are not coming downtown."

The best bets. Malls have the best chance of success in towns with large numbers of workers downtown and in university towns—places with built-in pedestrian volume. Thus, the malls rated highest by those we talked to are in Boston, Madison, Boulder, Santa Cruz, Ithaca, Eugene, and Burlington, Vermont. One observer notes that residents of university towns are often philosophically inclined to support public places.

Modify when needed. Kalamazoo, we've noted, revamped its mall twice. But it didn't do enough, says Fred Kent of the Project for Public Spaces. He believes that most malls need drastic changes, including adding traffic if they are over 40 feet wide. The better malls, in his view, are those, like Boston's Downtown Crossing, that concentrate pedestrians in a relatively narrow space.

Design counts. Harvey Rubenstein, a Pennsylvania landscape architect and author of *Central City Malls* (John Wiley & Sons, New York; 1978), says good malls use good materials: brick or granite paving, for instance, instead of concrete. He notes that new—and very expensive—techniques have been developed to ensure longer life for mall trees and shrubs.

Is the cost worth it? Main Street adviser Tom Moriarity believes "it's contradictory to the nature of a retail street to try to turn it into a park."

A new mall planned for downtown St. Paul (described in the October 15, 1982, *Downtown Idea Exchange,* a good source of mall news) may well avoid such design pitfalls. Each of its five blocks will be different, with a mixture of open, partly covered, and enclosed spaces. At midpoint is the existing Town Square shopping center.

Branch out. More important than what a mall looks like is what goes in it. Every mall needs a major anchor, says Bruce Heckman; but instead of the traditional, big department store, it may be a group of speciality stores, restaurants, or even a performing arts center. "In small towns, trying to keep Sears downtown may no longer be a valid goal," says Tom Moriarity. "In fact, looking at downtown as a retailing center alone is myopic. We want to keep everything there: stores, city government, entertainment, and housing."

Office use is beginning to rival retailing on Winston-Salem's recently demalled Trade Street, but in other cities, including Kalamazoo, strengthening downtown shopping remains an important goal. Encouraging downtown housing is seen as a way of expanding the retail clientele.

Take a lesson from the shopping center. Hire a promotion manager, says Tom Moriarity. And don't forget maintenance. "A well-designed mall that's falling apart won't be worth much," adds Bruce Heckman. It may be necessary to form a special taxing district or amend an existing one to come up with additional funds.

Ruth Knack is the senior editor of Plannng.

The Ins and Outs of Skyways

Carol Morphew
(March 1984)

Skyways, skywalks, and pedways are different names for elevated, enclosed walkways connecting buildings in the city core. Crossing above congested streets, skyways offer pedestrians a safe, weather-protected alternative to city sidewalks. The earliest systems were developed in the 1960s in the northern states and Canada.

But skyways are no longer simply makeshift solutions to winter city miseries. They have given an economic boost to both cold- and warm-weather communities—and some in between. Louisville, Charlotte, Cincinnati, and Des Moines are devel-

oping major systems. And skyways are in place as far north as Edmonton, Alberta, as far east as Rochester, New York, and as far south as Dallas, Texas. Seattle and Fargo are far along in the planning stages.

Skyways now link new downtown hotel, apartment, and condominium complexes to the rest of the city core. They connect many retail businesses, thereby attracting shoppers back downtown. And they are even reaching to the outskirts of the downtown to bring motorists in from outlying parking ramps.

The physical form of the skyway bridge also has evolved over the years. The older, simple, glass-enclosed footbridges have given way to climate-controlled, expensively detailed runways, sometimes stacked two stories high. Early skywalks seemed to leap across the street from one building to another. More contemporary skywalks often give the impression of being a building within buildings, a growing organism that winds through existing downtown structures. A major concern is whether the skyways' design will enhance or detract from the architectural integrity of the buildings they connect.

Planning problems have also evolved. Minimum building standards must be observed to ensure safe interbuilding passage as well as adequate vehicular clearance. Security becomes an issue when retail shops front on the skyways or when foot traffic is light.

Our study of the largest privately built skyway system in the country (in Minneapolis) and our proximity to other Upper Midwest systems (in St. Paul, the nation's largest public system, and Duluth, an excellent small city system) have led us to formulate a generic planning framework for skyway development. Our framework presupposes that most future skyways will be incorporated into existing city patterns of buildings, streets, and open spaces. It is intended to achieve the following goals:

● To build and maintain a pedestrian network that provides a safe and efficient means of foot travel throughout the downtown core;

● To coordinate a system of bridges and interior pathways that grows in an orderly manner, linking the most heavily traveled areas of the downtown first and not leapfrogging to the edges of downtown in order to spur speculative development;

● To encourage a well-designed system that complements existing buildings, open spaces, and streets.

Economic issues

Like many other cities, Minneapolis and St. Paul have lost many downtown shoppers to suburban malls. But the cities' skyway systems are playing a significant role in bringing shoppers back downtown. In both cities, skyways now connect all major department stores and hundreds of smaller shops and retail services. Minneapolis city planners estimate that two to three million square feet of downtown retail space is now accessible via the city's 21 existing skywalks.

But while skyways have boosted retail sales on the stores' second and third levels, they also have created a wasteland for street-level shops. In St. Paul—where there are 27 skywalks—a full 90 percent of the city's downtown retail business is now located on the second level; street-level shops are a rarity. Only in Minneapolis have street-level shops thrived, and that is because of Nicollett Mall. (Third-level skyways, a reality in Calgary, Alberta, and now being discussed in Minneapolis, remove shoppers even further from the street.)

The result of an extensive and unchecked skyway system can be a downtown comprised exclusively of large department stores and major corporate businesses that can afford the high rents that the skyway system has inadvertently created. One solution is for the community to restrict skyway expansion with the aim of safeguarding traditional commercial areas and street-level shopping patterns.

New skyway bridges cost between $2,000 and $3,000 per linear foot. The total cost of recent bridge additions in Minneapolis was $500,000. Information on the costs involved in inserting an interior pathway through an existing building is harder to come by, mostly because this type of installation is often undertaken as part of a larger remodeling, making segregation of skyway costs difficult. Estimates published in the mid-1970s ranged from $150,000 to $200,000 per corridor.

Architectural issues

The major architectural problem facing city planners today is how to insert a skyway bridge between preexisting structures of different architectural styles. In St. Paul and Duluth, where the skyway systems were developed by public agencies, a single prototype design has evolved. It is made of glass and steel and is lighted and heated by an internal system that is independent of the attached buildings. In Duluth, all skywalk floors are paved with quarry tile.

A major refinement in recent years involves the slope differential between buildings. In hilly St. Paul and Duluth, the newer bridges remain parallel to the streets below, and the interior path is inclined to guide pedestrians from one building to the next. Instead of turning corners or angling across streets, bridges take the shortest route from building to building.

In Minneapolis, where skyway bridge design for the most part is the responsibility of the individual developer or renovator, the bridges come in all shapes and sizes. The most recent bridges slope across the streets, falling and rising to meet existing floor levels. One newly built bridge turns a corner as it crosses over a public street to connect a new office tower with the county government center. Minneapolis's newer bridges are often twice as wide as the bridges of the 1960s; bridges now vary from nine to 29 feet in width. The extra girth relieves morning and midday congestion, but it also increases the dark space underneath at street level. Some bridges in Minneapolis are transparent, some are covered with reflective glass, and one includes a wall embedded with neon artwork.

Where the bridge enters a building is also an important design issue. Downtown Des Moines is crisscrossed with alleys, and the city's 1980 skyway planning report recommended that the skyway bridges enter the buildings over the alleys. That means the least developed side of the building is pierced by the skyway, leaving the more monumental and ornate facades untouched. Unfortunately, most downtown alley systems are no longer extensive enough to coordinate with skyway placement.

Another question is the effect the skyway system will have on the architectural character of downtown. Historic buildings can rarely accept a skyway link without aesthetic damage. The alternative may be an underground passage or no link at all. Further, an elaborate skyway system may create an overwhelming new megastructure. The skyway bridges can become too dominant, forcing the character of individual structures to recede and creating the illusion of one endless mass instead of separate, distinct shapes. Ideally, skyway bridges should be simple links to more complex structures.

Some local planners argue that the Minneapolis skyways are too disparate and the St. Paul skyways too regimented and architecturally confining. A proposed alternative is to develop bridge designs particularly suited to specific locations. Thus, a bridge connecting two historic structures would take on a different character from a bridge connecting two glass office towers or a bridge connecting a restaurant to an Art Deco theater. Design guidelines, properly formulated and applied, can encourage consistency without stifling creativity.

Operational issues

Signage. An important and often neglected aspect of skyway systems is appropriate signage. While many skyways have some sort of interior signage, often there is no family of signs to guide the downtown traveler through the entire system. As an example, the Minneapolis system (which began in 1962) has only recently been retrofitted with a complete skyway map system, but there is no skyway system reference map anywhere in the huge IDS Center, a network hub where four major links converge. In contrast, the St. Paul and Duluth systems have carefully designed illuminated signs, appropriately placed at points where pathways enter buildings and cross.

Pedestrians also need signs directing them to public services such as telephones, restrooms, emergency exits, and security offices. For vision-impaired pedestrians, audio directions may be useful.

Security. Interior passages that allow open shops bordering the walkway are an easy mark for shoplifters. Design solutions are needed to allow merchandise to be displayed to skyway travelers but secured from theft.

Incidents of personal assault have been reported in skyway systems, especially in segments that are poorly lit or unused for long periods. With more cities planning outlying parking lots that are linked to the city center by long skyways, the dangers will increase and additional security measures will be needed.

Skyway paths should be designed to minimize blind corners and dark alcoves. Longspan bridges ideally should be designed with large transparent areas to allow observation from the street level.

Running lights and corner mirrors also add to personal safety.

Operating hours. In Minneapolis, where skyways are privately owned and operated, their hours vary. The result is confusion about the availability of the whole network. Department store bridges are open only during store hours (mid-morning to mid-evening), which effectively shuts off major segments of the system to downtown office workers coming to work early in the morning. Office building skyways are closed evenings, preventing shoppers from reaching all stores. And downtown residents of high-rise apartments cannot use the skyways to reach stores, theaters, and restaurants on Sundays and holidays.

In St. Paul, the skyway system is publicly operated. All skyways are open from early morning to late evening. Operating on this schedule has meant more expensive security, however, as police patrols have been stepped up to prevent loitering and assaults.

Whether privately or publicly built, skyway networks are *public* transportation systems. A planning process is needed to help guide development for the benefit of downtown shoppers, employees, and the general public.

Carol Morphew is coauthor of Skyway Typology: A Study of the Minneapolis Skyways, *which is available from the AIA Press.*

Staking a Claim on Urban Design

Ruth Eckdish Knack
(October 1984)

Trying to define urban design is like playing a frustrating version of the old parlor game, Twenty Questions, in which the answer to every question (Is it animal? vegetable? mineral?) is no. Most people find it easier to say what urban design is not (architecture, engineering, landscape architecture, city planning) than what it is. The term "is still as much a presumption as it is a description," wrote New Yorker Jonathan Barnett in a 1982 article.

In the absence of a solid definition, the way has been left open for almost anyone who chooses to order a letterhead stamped "urban designer." The ambiguity has also led to flare-ups of long-standing rivalries among planners, architects, and landscape architects over who should take the lead in the emerging field.

A major difficulty in getting a handle on urban design is that it encompasses such a range of work, from the multibuilding-complex plans prepared by giant architecture firms like Skidmore, Owings and Merrill to the "streetscape guidelines" compiled by the lone urban designer on the staff of the Little Rock, Arkansas, planning agency. Michael Pittas, the former director of the National Endowment for the Arts' Design Arts Program, aptly calls urban design the "grey area" between architecture and planning; that is to say, the area of common concern. But he, like many others, notes that, as planning moves farther from the physical and architecture becomes more formalistic, the gap between the two widens and the grey area runs the danger of disappearing.

Several years ago, the late Kevin Lynch, noting that the term "urban design" had been "captured" by large-scale project design, came up with a new label, "city design"—a name he said he chose in desperation since it implied incorrectly that the city is the only focus of attention. (At about the same time, APA substituted "community design" for urban design in its policy statement.) Lynch's term doesn't seem to have stuck, but his definition is as good as any in distinguishing urban design from planning: "I think of what I call city design as skill in creating proposals for the form and management of the extended spatial and temporal environment. . . . In a sense, this is a return to that old-fashioned field of physical (or land-use) planning, but it is simultaneously more focused and yet also more amply connected to other concerns, and given a sharper sense of humanistic purpose."

Add to that this list of the ways in which urban design differs from architecture, suggested by Michael Pittas, and the picture begins to get less hazy:
- Urban design has a more public focus.
- Its time frame for action tends to be longer than an architect's (and shorter than a planner's).
- It values process as much as product.
- It is more interested in enabling change than in authorizing it.
- Its practitioners generally remain anonymous (no architect of record).
- It recognizes a pluralistic client.

Questions of turf are even more important than definitions. Does urban design fit into a university planning department, for instance, or into an architecture department? And where do public practitioners belong? Planning? Public Works? Stuart Pertz, head of APA's urban design and historic preservation division, has proposed that the field be elevated to the status of a profession and that some sort of licensing or credentialing procedure be established. If that were to happen, who would administer the fledging programs?

Grady Clay contends that it's landscape architects who are the true inheritors of the urban design mantle, for they alone never abandoned the field. Historically, says Clay, the recently retired editor of *Landscape Architecture* magazine, landscape architects have always been involved with the public interest, using public spaces to shape the city. "In the 1960s and 1970s, when planners were spinning themselves off into 'process' and architects were spinning themselves off into an egotistical preoccupation with 'my building,' landscape architects were there to fill the physical planning gap, often intervening in the development process on behalf of nature."

The architects' view

"The most serious urban design is done by architects," said Alexander Cooper in a recent lecture, although some of what Cooper does is far removed from the architect's traditional province. His firm, Cooper Eckstut of New York City, has produced "master plans" for big project areas like New York's Times Square and a huge tract in downtown Chicago known as the Chicago Dock and Canal property. "What we do as urban designers," he says, "is to fix the public spaces and then come up with guidelines for the buildings." Cooper, in short, practices what has come to be called "contextual architecture"—an activity that has more than a little resemblance to the physical planning of old.

Similarly, David Lewis, head of a Pittsburgh firm called Urban Design Associates, advises budding urban designers to become architects. Lewis was one of the founders in 1979 of the Institute for Urban Design, the nonprofit group that publishes *Urban Design International* magazine and sponsors periodic conferences on the topic; he is also a former chair of the American Institute of Architects' urban design and planning committee.

Lewis sees architecture as a generalist profession whose mainsprings are a city's economics and inherited infrastructure. His firm has built a reputation for developing a community participation process, using techniques developed by Kevin Lynch and Donald Appleyard, two acknowledged mentors. Lewis's staff of 20 are all architects, although he and several others are also members of AICP, "which gives us enough expertise," he says, "to be able to dovetail with public planners."

Planning's shift

"As far as I'm concerned," says Allan Jacobs, former head of San Francisco's planning department and now a professor at the University of California, Berkeley, "almost all of city planning was what we now call urban design. When city planning became 'urban planning' and later just plain 'planning,' the part of it that was concerned with the physical environment became one part of a bigger general profession."

In a 1980 "urban design manifesto," Jacobs and Donald Appleyard chastised both architecture and planning—the former for having become a "narcissistic pursuit" and the latter for being too immersed in program administration "to have a clear sense of direction with regard to city form." Jacobs's strong words stem from his frustration at the marked shift in the planning field over the last 30 years, a shift that Rutgers planning professor Donald Krueckeberg describes as a "land rush away from design." There are signs that a growing number of planners are, in fact, sympathetic to Jacobs's implied wish for a rebalancing of the field.

"The planning profession needs urban design greatly; it shouldn't be left to outsiders," says Jonathan Barnett, an urban design consultant and teacher in New York and one of the founders of the landmark urban design group established in the city's planning department in 1967. Barnett says that, because planning agencies often need assistance in handling site selection, design review, and other urban design-related activities, he has been able to carve out a niche for himself as a consultant. In recent years he has worked for such cities as Pittsburgh; Kansas City; Charleston, South Carolina; Bridgeport, Connecticut; and Louisville on a variety of downtown and neighborhood projects.

Another urban design claimant is the historic preservation movement, which in the view of James Marston Fitch, who founded Columbia University's historic preservation program 20 years ago, "has completely transformed the field of urban planning"—a field that Fitch believes had fallen into disrepute. Pressure to save landmark buildings and districts "has compelled planners to regard cities as organisms rather than as things that have to be bulldozed and rebuilt," says Fitch, "and it has compelled designers to come up with more interesting solutions to urban planning problems."
. . .

As a public planner, it's not surprising that Richard Hedman thinks that public agencies should have in-house urban designers rather than relying solely on consultants. "Otherwise," he says, "you get a little bit of urban design here and a little bit there, with no consistent viewpoint represented." He makes the point . . . that good urban design does not require every planner to be a designer. What it does require, he says, is "that people involved in important design decisions know what to look for and the questions to ask." And for those directly involved in design, he adds, an architecture background is important.

Hedman himself was trained as an architect at the University of Florida and then became one of the first students, in the late 1950s, in the University of Pennsylvania's Civic Design Program (which gave him a combined master's in architecture and city planning). After several years of varied practice (consulting, downtown planning in Miami, design work for two world's fairs, a preservation project for Sacramento, the Market Street design project in San Francisco), he was hired, in 1968, by then-planning director Allan Jacobs to do an urban design plan for San Francisco. His title was principal planner for urban design, a first-time use for the city. The urban design section, which he heads, now has two other urban designers besides Hedman.

For about eight years, HUD official Andrew Euston had been proselytizing to get people to accept the idea of a new profession—urban environmental design administration (translated from HUD-speak, someone who administers the design of cities and towns). Urban environmental design is an activity that is eligible for community development block grant funding, but, according to Euston, it has not gotten the attention it deserves.

Under the UED category, HUD has helped fund such things as a planning charette in New Haven and conferences on regional resource themes by

University of Wisconsin landscape architecture professor Phil Lewis.

Although similar to planning in its emphasis on process, Euston says there are major differences. For one thing, an urban environmental design administrator is not tied to a particular public agency, and he or she could come out of any number of backgrounds. The point is that he is able to implement urban decisions. To help clarify, Euston offers an example of "a paragon of an urban environmental design administrator—the Zen Master of the field": Weiming Lu of St. Paul.

In fact, as director of the Lowertown Redevelopment Corporation, Weiming Lu does show how a planner can take a lead role in urban design administration. Operating with a tiny staff out of an office in a renovated warehouse, Lu searches out developers, helps them finance their projects, and exercises an informal sort of design control. The nonprofit Lowertown corporation was created by the city of St. Paul in 1978, backed by a $10 million grant from the McKnight Foundation. The result today is some $200 million in investment, with 25 projects completed or under way.

Lu's forte is gentle persuasion. "You don't have to dictate a design," he observes. "But you can give advice without acting in the architect's role. You can say things about the rhythm of the design, for instance." For some Lowertown projects, design guidelines have been written into loan agreements.

Lu, the son of an architect and trained as a civil engineer in China and as a planner at the University of North Carolina, credits his work as a planner for the city of Minneapolis in the 1960s with teaching him how to work with different kinds of people and how to "marshall his forces" to get measures approved. Later, as urban design director for Dallas, he was effective in getting a controversial sign control law—part of a more comprehensive urban design program—passed by using the same combination of technical skill and political astuteness. In a speech to the American Institute of Architects last year, Lu said, "The public sector has the leverage to ask developers to pay more attention to urban design."

The schools

Donald Krueckeberg says he finds it telling that several members of the Rutgers planning faculty have degrees in architecture yet express no interest in teaching design-related courses. "They don't find their architecture training applicable to the problems they are interested in solving," he says.

Recently, however, Krueckeberg has observed some change. Some of the "nondesign planners," he notes, are once again talking about design. "Even some of the Marxists, those most involved with theory, are beginning to look at the practical problems of design." Certainly, Krueckeberg adds, the architects are not solving them, and that leaves things open for a fresh approach.

In the meantime, here is a brief survey of several academic programs that suggest the range of urban design offerings currently in place.

• Harvard's 25-year-old design program is often described as a "big architecture" program, partly because of the reputation established under Moshe Safdie, who was director from 1978 to 1982. However, current acting director Richard Krauss stresses that there is a strong effort to broaden the designers' education by offering courses in planning, law, and economics. Krauss himself has an interest in social policy (he has an undergraduate degree in anthropology from Harvard and a graduate degree in architecture from MIT).

The core of the Harvard program is five design studios, one of which, for the past three years, has taken a group of students to Jerusalem to work on a design problem in the Old City. In recent years, about half of the 22 students in each incoming class of the two-year program have been from foreign countries. Part of the reason is that Harvard requires an architecture or landscape architecture degree for admittance, and it's harder, apparently to attract recent U.S. grads.

The news from Harvard is that it is organizing a new, more planning-oriented urban design program, headed for the interim by Jose A. Gomez-Ibanez, a professor of city and regional planning in Harvard's Kennedy School of Government. According to Krauss, the new program will, to some extent, fill the gap left by the shift of city and regional planning from the School of Design to the Kennedy School in 1980. Although details are still up in the air—for instance, no one knows yet whether the new program will offer a first or second professional degree—Krauss believes "it will look a lot like what physical planning used to look like."

• At the University of California, Berkeley, says Allan Jacobs, urban design, to some extent, has become the province of the landscape architecture department, which moved in to fill the void in environmental planning and large-scale project planning created by the decision of the Department of City and Regional Planning to shift its emphasis to policy and quantification.

Berkeley's informal urban design program is largely based, Jacobs says, on advice given by Kevin Lynch. It consists of four courses, offered by both planning and landscape architecture, and taken, as Jacobs puts it, by "a floating crap game of students." The courses cover the theory of urban form, environmental planning, and the legal and administrative techniques needed to implement urban design. One studio is required. Students can elect an urban design concentration in either of two joint master's degree programs: architecture and planning or landscape architecture and planning.

Largely as a result of the activities of the late Donald Appleyard and carried on by Peter Bosselmann, Berkeley is strong in environmental simulation. "It's a highly quantitative approach to the physical environment," says Jacobs, "and an immensely important part of urban design." Such work, he adds, contributed to San Francisco's yes vote last June in a referendum to limit height in parts of the downtown.

• At Kansas State University in Manhattan, Ray Weisenburger, the first president of APA's combined urban design and historic preservation division, heads the program of graduate studies in community urban design in the College of Architecture and Design. Some 10 students get graduate degrees in planning, landscape architecture, or architecture with an emphasis on urban design—a typical arrangement for many schools.

What is less typical about the Kansas State program is that many of the student projects have a small-town focus. Some are undertaken jointly with students in the planning department's historic preservation concentration.

• At the University of Illinois at Urbana, there are no urban design requirements in the Department of Urban and Regional Planning. The one course offered started out as a service course in urban design implementation for architecture students. It is taught by Lachlan Blair, who, surprisingly, says that he would not recommend that urban design studies be made a requirement for planning students. "Planners need to get design appreciation," he says, "but not not necessarily hands-on design." Nor does Blair put much stock

in urban design programs that are offshoots of those architecture schools that don't offer much planning. "They stumble because they don't teach students how to get things done—which is the province of planning."

In general, Blair, who has some 40 years of experience in architecture, planning, and urban design, "finds suspect" people readily identified as urban designers. "The best urban design is an anonymous product," he says.

• Pratt Institute in New York offers a rare evening urban design program, headed by Stuart Pertz. Although the program is housed in the architecture school, Pertz stresses that he wants to show "that you don't have to be an architect to be an urban designer," and his program does, in fact, admit non-architects. Pertz is a partner in a large New York architecture, engineering, and planning firm.

• Since 1970, the Massachusetts Institute of Technology has had an environmental design program within the Urban Studies and Planning Department (part of the architecture school). Its head, Gary Hack, says the program's concerns cover both the design of places and the design of organizations that are capable of managing those places (a philosophy similar to HUD's urban environmental design administration). Like Illinois's Lock Blair, Hack says he is not sure that urban design should be a separate program (MIT students get joint degrees in architecture and planning). But he does believe that public planners should have a basic understanding of design so that they can deal with outside architects. Hack, who has master's degrees in architecture and in planning and a Ph.D. in urban studies, is in practice with the planning consulting firm of Carr, Lynch.

• Hamid Shirvani, who directs the urban design program in the landscape architecture school at the State University of New York-Syracuse, says, "We didn't want to have a separate program because we didn't want to spend all our time debating what it was." About a dozen graduates a year think of urban design as their special area of expertise, Shirvani says.

Syracuse is developing a new program to educate developers, and Shirvani says the curriculum will include material on both site planning and urban design. Shirvani's special interest is research; he is editor of *UD Review,* published by the APA urban design and historic preservation division. "We shouldn't blame practicing planners for bad urban design," he says. "We should blame the academics for not doing enough research and writing in this area."

• At the University of California, Los Angeles, says Dolores Hayden, "we are particularly interested in the social issues connected with urban design." Hayden is coordinator of the Built Environment Program in the Graduate School of Architecture and Urban Planning at UCLA (which also has another advanced program in urban design).

Hayden has founded a nonprofit group called the Power of Place, whose goal is to "redefine preservation" by investigating the history of the various ethnic and minority groups that have settled in Los Angeles. The organization will search out sites that are significant to these groups, prepare a "social agenda" for each, and try to come up with ways that "designers and artists can use the locations (many now parking lots) to suggest an alternative vision of the city." The organization's headquarters will be in a historic firehouse leased from the city.

In her practice, Hayden, an architect, is working on new housing that incorporates a day-care center—an interest carried over from her recent book, *Redesigning the American Dream*. It is in housing, she points out, that women may have made their strongest contribution to urban design, although, of course, women like Raquel Ramati, Denise Scott Brown, and the late Jacqueline Tyrwitt have been involved in other aspects as well.

• Urban design's only work-study program is housed in the School of Architecture and Environmental Studies of City College, City University of New York. The 14-year-old program, organized by Jonathan Barnett, leads to the degree of Master of Urban Planning (Urban Design). Its focus is on urban design as a separate discipline, not simply an offshoot of planning and architecture. Instead of studio courses, students work part-time in local firms and agencies. Barnett stresses legal and real estate issues—"the media," he notes, "through which urban design occurs." One of the original ideas behind the program was to provide staff for the New York City urban design group (Barnett was one of the founders), but the urban design group has since been dissolved and the program has broadened its focus.

After years as a practitioner, Barnett has some very definite ideas of what an urban design educa-

tion should be like. "Urban design students today need a practical education," he says, "in which they're presented with real situations rather than hypothetical studio problems. And above all, they need to know how to make design proposals so that there is a reasonable chance that they will be carried out.

"We began with a bias in favor of teaching people what urban designers need to know to work effectively in a planning agency. That included an understanding of how cities work and some familiarity with real estate law. We devised the case study method to show how urban design problems could be solved.

"Over time, we have modified the original curriculum, doubling the number of credit hours of real estate and experimenting with a more extensive law course as well. The case-study course has evolved from an emphasis on how others have solved problems into a process where students are given the data describing a real situation and asked to draw up a proposal. Then the professionals who dealt with the real life situation come to class to show what they did and comment on the students' work. Our internship has changed from placing most students in public agencies to putting almost all of them in private offices."

Graduates of the program go into government agencies, architecture offices, consulting firms and—more and more frequently—into real estate, a phenomenon that, Barnett hopes, will have a salutary effect on the quality of the environment in the future.

Ruth Knack is the senior editor of Planning.

Critiquing the Underground City

David Brown and Pieter Sijpkes
(March 1985)

Surprisingly, considering the attention focused in recent years on Montreal's "underground city," the city never had a shopping arcade of the sort that was common in Europe at the turn of the century. Certainly, though, the conditions were right for such an enclosure: A compact CBD, temperatures ranging from 90 degrees Fahrenheit in summer to 30 below in winter, and an average annual snowfall of almost seven feet.

It was the 1960 opening of Place Ville Marie, Canada's first large mixed-use complex, that pointed the way to Montreal's current multilevel city. The project was constructed over a wide trench left over from the building of a Canadian National Railway tunnel in the 1920s to provide suburban commuter service to Central Station, just south of Place Ville Marie.

The developer of the project, which includes a grade-level shopping center and several floors of parking below, saw the potential of an underground link to supply his shopping mall with customers from the massive flow of commuters. That first underground link has served as a prototype for the entire system, which now includes nearly nine miles of pedestrian walkways, linking two railway stations, seven hotels, three department stores, 1,015 shops, 128 restaurants, 25 bank branches, 26 cinemas and theaters, 1,400 apartments, and 10,000 indoor parking spaces.

But, while the underground system has drawn praise from numerous visiting planners and architects, it is not without its critics. What many of those critics have noted is the lack of any formal development plan or guidelines for the system. Initiated by developers, rather than the city administration, the underground city remains a loosely strung together federation of private fiefdoms, each with its own rules. The municipality's role in extending the system has been limited to reviewing development proposals. It offers no clear incentives or disincentives for extension. Developers are responsible for construction, maintenance, and security. And, generally, the hours of operation are the same as those of the Metro, the city's subway system, 5:30 a.m. to 1 a.m.

As a result of this haphazard arrangement, certain key linkages—between the McGill Metro station and the recently opened Banque Nationale de Paris building, for instance—have never been completed. Moreover, developers who do provide links often attempt to funnel pedestrians past as many stores as possible, thereby lengthening travel time and adding to an already confusing pattern of retail corridors. The problem shows up clearly in the link between the Place Bonaventure Metro station and the south side of Central Station, where pedestrians are unnecessarily diverted into the Place Bonaventure shopping mall.

Anti-street?

A frequent criticism that may *not* be entirely true is that, by siphoning people from the street, indoor pedestrian systems lead to a decline in street activity and, thus, safety. A 1980 study by a McGill University planning student confirmed that shops moved inside when the opportunity presented itself; enclosed shops represented 36.1 percent of the total number of downtown stores in 1980 as opposed to 2.7 percent in 1961. But the student, Ian Cross, also noted that the indoor environment boosts the central area's overall retail viability. Assured of convenient, protected shopping opportunities, a larger segment of the population regularly shops downtown.

To us, the debate between indoor and street shopping seems to be mostly an ideological one. The effect of underground links need not be deleterious if indoor and outdoor systems are designed to be complementary and easy transitions are provided—and if street frontage is not given over to service entrances, as has occurred on President Kennedy Avenue in Montreal.

Nor do we share the fear of second-level pedestrian systems voiced by the more dogmatic adherents of the underground system. While the below-grade option maintains clear street views and provides an easy link with the Metro, it also makes it difficult to provide indoor parking space. . . .

A major disadvantage of the underground system is the lack of natural lighting, a problem solved to some extent by the atriums included in recent additions to the system, such as Complexe Desjardins and Place Guy Favreau. Uneven architectural design makes some of the long corridors, like the one between Place Bonaventure and the Metro, confining and frightening.

Signage is also an issue. While storefronts and circulation areas are clearly marked inside, the lack of consistent exterior signage makes it hard for a visitor to get around. Public orientation maps, which do not include an overall view of the system, are not much help.

Also, accessibility is hampered both by temperamental escalators and a lack of elevators to the underground passageways.

Who Rules?

The underground city consists of several domains under different jurisdictions. The Metro System, a public domain, is patrolled by a special section of the Montreal police force, while the parts under the jurisdiction of private developers are responsible for their own security.

However, the boundaries between these domains are not always clear to the public. The confusion that can result was shown clearly in a 1983 court case in which street musicians won the right to be allowed to play in parts—but not all—of the indoor environment. (They are allowed in the tunnels leading to and from the subway but not beyond the turnstiles of the Metro or on private property.)

The case brought into focus a key issue concerning the underground network. Is it a true (public) part of the city? Or is it a glorified network of private shopping centers? Our own systematic, "post-occupancy evaluation" of the underground city has shown that many people—and particularly, the elderly, the poor, and the unemployed—use the system for recreation. Yet the operators of the "private" parts of the system sometimes take measures to prevent such use—removing seating, limiting access to toilets, intimidation by guards, and so on.

Now that we've outlined some of the problems, what do we suggest as solutions?

• Use the Metro police to patrol the whole indoor environment, applying a uniform set of rules.

• Adopt a standard system of signs that would show visitors where they are in relation to the streets, the subway, and other landmarks.

• Construct public indoor parks linked to the Metro and the existing underground system.

• Provide movable seating to create an atmosphere of friendliness and informality rather than hostility.

Only when the indoor passageways function as a true urban system, with consistent hours, arrangements, and orientation, will the indoor environment deserve the title "indoor city."

David Brown teaches urban planning and Pieter Sijpkes teaches architecture at McGill University in Montreal.

Zipping Up the Strip
Ruth Eckdish Knack and
Dennis McClendon
(July 1986)

Early on a Sunday morning, Firestone Boulevard in the Los Angeles suburb of Downey is deserted. But it isn't hard to imagine what this strip of six-lane highway is like during a weekday rush hour. That's what Planning asked a group of planners to do last April during the national APA conference.

The six out-of-towners were taken on an early morning tour by Downey community development director James Cutts and his assistants, Ronald Yoshiki and Gregory Shaffer. Then the group assembled in a city hall conference room to talk about what they had seen.

THE PARTICIPANTS
(Titles correct as of 1986)

James Cutts. Downey community development director.

Ena Dubnoff. Los Angeles architect and faculty member, University of Southern California.

Calvin Hamilton. Former Los Angeles planning director.

Bruce Heckman. Executive vice-president of Teska Associates, a planning consulting firm in suburban Evanston, Illinois.

James D. Meehan. Developer with CM Properties in Santa Ana, California.

Dennis Ryan. Chair of urban design and planning program, University of Washington, Seattle.

Richard Tustian. Montgomery County, Maryland, planning director (suburban Washington, D.C.).

In the post-World War II suburban boom, Downey prospered as a primarily residential, blue-collar suburb some 20 miles southeast of downtown Los Angeles. Its major east-west artery, Firestone Boulevard, attracted auto dealers, small industrial shops, and an assortment of retail establishments, some clustered in an open-air shopping center called Stonewood.

But in the late 1960s, Downey began to feel threatened on the residential front by the plethora of new developments in Orange, Riverside, and Ventura counties and by commercial competition from adjacent communities. Commerce, to the north, is known for having no property tax, and Cerritos, to the south, has lured auto dealers to its 35-acre "auto mall." Downey's population also began slipping, from 88,000 in 1970 to 82,000 a decade later.

Meanwhile Downey, whose motto is, after all, "Future Unlimited," began looking for ways to upgrade its image and deal with such problems as a growing number of elderly residents. Part of the 3.2-mile Firestone Boulevard corridor was declared a redevelopment area in the late 1970s, and two years ago, the city commissioned a revitalization plan from two Los Angeles consulting firms, Archiplan and Economics Research Associates. They recommended such streetscape improvements as a blocklong sidewalk canopy.

Cutts noted that the consultants described Firestone Boulevard as a "museum of fifties architecture," and such streamlined structures as Simpson Buick impressed our panel as well. Just off Firestone, on Lakewood Boulevard, is one of the original McDonald's drive-in restaurants. The city is now assembling land for two "auto centers," one of which will include Simpson. It is also attempting to attract retailers to several small shopping centers, or "promotional centers." In an effort to intensify the strip's commercial nature, Downey planners are looking for ways to relocate the few remaining residences scattered along it and to rationalize the zoning, further separating commercial and industrial uses.

The civic center area, which includes what's left of Downey's original downtown, was described as a special concern of local planners. A new Embassy Suites hotel has added some vitality, and now, said Cutts, the city is aiming for a parking garage, movie theaters, and new restaurants. Cutts noted that, while Downey has a design review procedure, it is only now developing a list of set standards.

Recognizing that the problems of Firestone Boulevard are replicated in thousands of suburban areas throughout the country, we asked our panel first to comment on this particular strip's strengths and weaknesses and then to suggest directions for the future.

Planning. We began with the premise that Firestone Boulevard is a problem area. Could we be wrong? After all, this is a classic bit of strip. Perhaps we should just leave it alone—learn from Las Vegas, in effect.

Heckman. That might be a viable alternative—although not necessarily one I approve of—if, in fact, Downey were more like Las Vegas. But it's not. Firestone would have to be a lot more intense, a lot more glitzy, and a lot more economically healthy even to come close. I suppose you could identify a portion of the strip as a place where anything goes, where there's no sign control, for instance.

Tustian. A lot of people who live here probably like Firestone just the way it is. I think it's important to look at the strip from a macroscale perspective and ask who except the architects and planners really wants things to change. But you've also pointed out that residents are beginning to perceive that their main street, their front parlor so to speak, is getting shabby. Before you decide what to do about that, however, you need to know more about what's happening. You need an economic analysis of this retailing climate and a good picture of the demography and travel patterns. You need to understand the behavioral forces that condition the way people use this area. To change the form, you have to understand the functional elements.

Heckman. If this strip has a problem, it's the old one: There's no there there. It's hard to see a pattern as you drive up and down the corridor. It's like what the political scientist Norton Long called a series of inconsequential decisions that have built to a massive calamity. A whole series of things have happened through the years, and the result is a lack of coherence.

I see that you're beginning to get a vertical core in the older downtown area, with the Bank of America building, the hotel, and the new office buildings that are going up. But I'm very concerned about how the new buildings are going to link together. Without a good plan, you get a lot of ad hockery. For example, you're adding more parking, but I'm not sure that that won't be counterproductive to the interlinking of some of those buildings.

Hamilton. What I see here is a place that has no real center. Right now, you seem to be about 95-percent auto-oriented. It seems to me you've got to decide if you want a pedestrian environment or not, and if you do, you have to take some actions to promote it. A filling station on one corner of your commercial core and the high school parking lot on another is not going to do it. You've got to analyze the pattern of existing land uses and of parking. And you've got to consider whether Firestone could, in fact, become a pedestrian shopping street. Maybe not, since it is a major highway. If you decide it can be, you need to make clear, through good urban design, which portions are pedestrian and which are not. Then you can set appropriate requirements for use, height, parking, and so on.

To get that kind of analysis, it seems to me, you need to do something like what we did in Los Angeles in connection with our centers plan. We identified the specific functions within each of 52 centers, and now we're thinking about what incentives and disincentives we can provide to get more of the functions we want.

Dubnoff. If you're going to serve the local community, including the people who don't drive, there's going to have to be some kind of concentration of community activities. The big problem now is that there's no easy way to cross the strip.

Heckman. I see some real strengths here in your plans for the civic center area and in the idea of developing automobile centers close to the freeway. But I'm concerned about what happens in between. How are you going to deal with the rest?

Tustian. Yes, you have to ask how well the strip functions as a strip. How well can you get around on it by car? And how does it look to the person in the car?

Ryan. I'd like to extend the discussion of land planning into the area of design. I was struck this morning by the fact that you don't use the local Southern California landscaping possibilities in a dramatic way. You have a great opportunity to use those big palm trees in a powerful design way. I saw some huge ones, but there aren't enough yet to define places or mark boundaries. It's great that Firestone has distinguishable entries at both ends. But they should be more identifiable.

Cutts. We're working on that. We have plans to delineate the entrances to the city with palm trees and new signs.

Heckman. But don't stop with the entry signs. Carry the same theme through to the public parking lots and the signage around the civic center. If you're going to start hammering on people about improving their signs, set a good example yourself.
. . .
Meehan. The problem is who's going to do all this. What you have here are major landowners who are reluctant to spend dollars on their property. They need a push from the city, which has to

provide the entrepreneurship that's been missing so far. And that means the city has to support its staff so that it can create a climate for development. Now some of that has already happened, and we're beginning to see a perceived quality increase in Downey. People from outside who are looking for a place to invest are beginning to consider Downey. In fact, our firm, which has built office buildings and shopping centers in Texas, Nevada, and California, is now looking at a site here. One thing a lot of people are considering now is what are called "promotional centers," small shopping centers with a supermarket and a soft goods store like a Loehmann's. Developers are beginning to realize that places like Downey are underserved by soft goods outlets.

The new hotel will help attract new businesses. Now you need some more restaurants around it. Then you'd have a hook. But you've also got to stimulate the businesses that are here already. For example, I think Stonewood is out of date. I'd gut it, cover it, and bring in all new tenants. But the present owners aren't going to do that. To really get things moving would require creating a massive special assessment district, and politically that would be tough.

Tustian. As a way of mobilizing support, it might be a good idea to present people with a scenario of what the strip would be like if the government took no action.

Heckman. Instead of an assessment district, you might be able to do it with a joint-venture development corporation, which would make the property owners partners with a developer. There are a lot of creative tools that you might be able to use. But before you worry about a tool, you need some public consensus.

We know that redevelopment used to be a dirty word in Downey. But now that attitude is beginning to change. So maybe you can get some public discussion of these issues. And maybe it would be a good idea, as somebody already suggested, to work on one segment of the corridor at a time. Pick out the part that's the highest priority for you and try to get a consensus on it.

Hamilton. That might work for the auto row. You don't need redevelopment there at all. Instead of buying the properties, the city could set up a joint development corporation and then work with developers to move ahead.

Heckman. And if you can pyramid on the auto

dealers' cooperation with tax increment financing, you can create a thing that will nurture itself. It's easy for the public to see that the dealerships are a strong economic force in the community and that you really have to do something to keep them. So assembling the land for the auto centers shouldn't be all that controversial.

One of your fundamental tenets ought to be to try to keep what's good here. And part of that is the auto dealerships. You want to be sure they don't steal away in the dead of night and wind up in a neighboring community.

Tustian. I'd like to ask Jay Meehan why the private market doesn't seek to use the excess zoning capacity that's here already. Why does the city have to be the engine of change?

Meehan. The reason is that, while there is a lot of desire for investment, it's also true that investors are looking for the least risky opportunities. Downey is still perceived as a marginal location, and that's because it has had such helter-skelter development in the past. In some areas, it reminds me of Houston, because of the lack of clearly set out development standards.

What this town really needs is more political support of the planning staff. The tools are here, the balls and bats are on the field. Now we've got to get some guys in city hall who will say, "Play ball."

I agree that Downey is a good place for offices. The trouble always comes back to image. Downey isn't perceived as a document-intensive city, like Los Angeles, for instance, a place where documents have to be hand delivered for recording or to bring to a judge. But it's not a people-intensive city either because there aren't a lot of places for people to meet. It needs some more offices to provide people to eat at those restaurants you want to put in.

You've got an opportunity to provide a lot of the services that other places around here don't provide. Why not think of yourself as the provider of services for the surrounding communities? You could fill up an office building with lawyers and accountants and travel services and so on. But to attract an office building, you have to help out with some sort of subsidy, or agree to lease some of the space for five years or so to remove some of the speculation.

Dubnoff. I'm concerned that we seem to be talking primarily about serving the region. Wouldn't it be of value to find out what the people who live here might need in the central area? There should be a connection between the business opportunities and the housing provided. Is the housing too expensive for those who work here? Can they get child care? It seems to me you should be looking at these things together.

Ryan. It's a planning truism that good plans come from good processes, and that's what we're hearing now. But to have good processes you've got to feed in good information. You can't just get people together for coffee and talk about what you need. What you have to do is bring in people like Jay, who understand the economics of doing business in a place like this.

And then, it seems to me, you should look at the strip as a microcosm of the whole city. There are special places on it and there are also ordinary places. In a sense, the ordinary places are support areas, background areas, and as such they're very much needed. But not every place should be a special place. Maybe what happens in the in-between places on the strip should simply be allowed to happen as long as there's some sort of general framework for considering circulation and linkages.

Ruth Knack is the senior editor and Dennis McClendon the managing editor of Planning.

Design by Committee
Ed Zotti
(May 1987)

In New Orleans, they told noted jazzman Al Hirt to put back the stoop on the house in the French Quarter that he had removed during a remodeling. In Los Angeles, they convinced a developer who wanted to build a subdivision along scenic Mulholland Drive to reduce the density, drop plans for a ridgetop restaurant, and donate part of another ridge to the city for use as an archaeological park. In Cleveland, they held up approval of the new Sohio headquarters and forced a variety of design modifications at a time when the city's downtown was starved for new construction.

"They" in each case is a local design review board. Nobody knows exactly how many boards there are, partly because they take so many different forms in different cities. But most observers believe their numbers are on the increase.

The term *design review* is of relatively recent vintage, and much of the current interest in it is the result of popular disenchantment with modern architecture. But the concept has been around a long time.

One of the first boards was New Orleans's Vieux Carre Commission, established in 1936 to protect the special qualities of the French Quarter. Cleveland set up its Fine Arts Advisory Committee in 1959 to review projects planned for the mall, the focal point of downtown. San Antonio created the River Walk Advisory Commission in 1962.

Review boards are created for all sorts of different reasons. Some are concerned with historic preservation, while others focus on the natural environment. Some are intended to implement an urban plan, while others simply wish to foster "good design."

Board members may be design professionals, ordinary citizens, or a combination of the two. Their jurisdiction may cover an entire city or be limited to a district or to certain types of projects. The opinions they hand down may be mandatory or advisory.

But whatever their makeup and whatever they're called, design review boards have a common mission: to evaluate development proposals on aesthetic and/or urbanistic grounds. Only secondarily are they concerned with issues like density, use, and safety, which traditionally have been the province of zoning and building departments.

Not all design review boards work equally well. The fact that they focus on such slippery qualities as "human scale" and "respect for the urban context" sometimes makes them controversial. Developers and public officials often regard them as a nuisance, and some architects and planners think they stifle creativity.

"Design review eliminates the most egregious bad buildings, but it also eliminates the exceptional building that departs from the norm. It guarantees a pleasant environment, but not necessarily a distinguished one," says Jonathan Barnett, the New York-based planning consultant, author, and teacher.

"What can happen is that architects trim their designs to what they think are the prejudices of the review board," says Robert Campbell, architecture critic for the *Boston Globe* and a practicing architect who recently served on a review panel in San Francisco. "Another problem is that the review board can be a group of tin-pot dictators.

"But that's not a sufficient reason to abandon the concept. The idea that constraints stifle creativity is nonsense. Constraints stimulate creativity. It's like a sonnet or a fugue—the rules give you a net and a court to play on. It's only since World War II that we've had this architectural free-fire zone where anything goes. Most great cities of the past had regulations, not just written plans but tradition and limits on skills and resources."

Horror stories

Opponents of design review tend to cite the same stories to illustrate how boards can get out of hand. One prominent example is the controversy over the design for the headquarters of the American Institute of Architects in Washington, D.C., in the late 1960s.

The city's presidentially appointed Commission of Fine Arts felt architect Romaldo Giurgola's design would overwhelm the historic Octagon House, which was next to the site. During the long review process, Giurgola made a number of modifications in an effort to satisfy commission members. But Gordon Bunshaft, the head of the New York office of Skidmore, Owings & Merrill, remained a holdout. He announced that as long as there was a notch at the point where the building's two wings met, he would never approve it.

With that Giurgola walked out in a huff. Another firm, the Boston-based Architects Collaborative, was brought in—and produced essentially the same design, minus the offending notch. The commission approved the plans and the building was built. The practical result? In some eyes, a three-year delay, a duplication of architectural fees, and little else.

But most observers agree such episodes are the exception. "It's rare for a fine arts commission to veto a project," Barnett says. "Usually a compromise is worked out." A more common problem is that arts commissions don't have enough staff to be able to do a thorough job.

Recently, the city most often cited as an example of design review run amok is San Francisco. Because the city now has a downtown development cap of only 475,000 square feet annually, developers must compete fiercely to win approval of their projects by the city's planning commission. To help the commission decide which projects are most worthy, the city decided to appoint a three-member panel of architectural experts to review proposals.

The process had its maiden run last year. Three developers made elaborate presentations; all three were rejected. The developers howled; the local chapter of the American Institute of Architects complained. *San Francisco Chronicle* architecture critic Allan Temko calls the effort "a fiasco," noting that the developers spent huge amounts on their presentations.

"Design review came at the end of a very long and expensive process," Temko says. "The planners really put the developers through the hoops."

To reduce the burden on developers and make the procedure more "constructive," as one city staffer puts it, this year's review is a two-step process. Seven developers have made presentations and heard oral comments from the panel. They are then to resubmit their drawings, presumably having made some effort to meet the panelists' objections. Finally the panel is to make written comments to the planning department.

And then there's Boston. For a brief period it appeared that a design review board would help dispel the city's reputation as the "toughest city in America to build a high rise in," as the *Wall Street Journal* put it. But so far that hasn't happened.

Boston has a history of ensnarling projects in controversy. The Boston Redevelopment Authority, which must approve most downtown projects, typically responds to opposition by appointing ad hoc investigating committees. The result is often an interminable review process.

For a long time, the city had no design guidelines, and now has them only in sketchy draft form. Developers complain that they have no idea what sorts of design issues they'll be expected to address. There were high hopes when the city created the Boston Civic Design Commission, a panel of architects and lay people headed by John deMonchaux, dean of the school of architecture and planning at the Massachusetts Institute of Technology. But no other members have been appointed yet because of a dispute between deMonchaux and the mayor's office regarding the commission's makeup.

"Ten days ago, the city was about to announce the composition of the commission without having come to a final resolution with me," deMonchaux said in mid-March. "When I heard about it, I said they'd better leave my name off the list. I'm especially concerned about the qualifications of the design professionals. It's not that the people chosen by the mayor aren't capable; it's just that some of them may not have experience with the issues that are going to be critical."

Although deMonchaux declined to speculate, many believe the real issue behind the delay is control over the development process. "Mayors tend not to like [boards and] guidelines because they reduce their power," Campbell says. "In San Francisco, you have a unique situation where the citizen rebellion reached such heights that the mayor was delighted to be able to cop out and toss the decision to the planning board. You don't have that situation in Boston."

Waffling

Politics sandbagged design review altogether in Minneapolis, which on two occasions has considered establishing a review board, only to reject the idea both times. In the early 1970s, the city got state legislation passed that enabled it to create design review boards for specific districts. The immediate motive was to establish a district for the Whittier neighborhood, an area of large Victorian-era houses that were gradually being replaced by nondescript apartment buildings.

But design review proponents were unable to persuade the public. "A lot of it was what I call the 'you-mean-I-can't-paint-my-house-purple?' syndrome," deputy planning director Richard Heath says. "People were afraid a design review board would infringe on their right to do what they wanted with their property." The ordinance was dropped.

The issue arose again in 1983 following the construction of a large and intrusive downtown skyscraper complex. A city council task force spent a year studying whether a review board would be an appropriate way to prevent such development in the future. This time, says Heath, "there was furious opposition from those who felt that review would place a heavy hand on developers and stall efforts to redevelop downtown." Although the review board had its advocates as well, in the end the matter was tabled once again.

Discouraging though such news can be, there are also many signs that design review boards can work well. By common consent, one of the best is

Portland, Oregon's design commission. The commission is one element in a review process that has won praise for several reasons: It is relatively fast, there are well-defined development guidelines, and it has a tradition of reasoned debate. Virtually every downtown project in Portland is subject to design review.

"From a developer's point of view, it's good to have a process where you get to a yes-or-no vote within a reasonable time," says commission member Harriet Sherburne. "That's better than if you have some amorphous process with people bickering and getting themselves quoted in the press."

Sherburne, who is also vice-president of the Seattle-based Cornerstone Columbia Development Company, has had a chance to view things from both sides. Before joining the commission she was project manager for RiverPlace, a Cornerstone mixed-use project in Portland. A large project by Portland standards, RiverPlace occupies an urban renewal site on the Williamette River. It includes a marina, restaurants, riverfront shops, and condominium apartments. (A planned 13-story tower was cancelled.)

The review process from initial submission to final approval took six weeks. Only some covered boat moorings were disallowed. "Part of the reason it went so smoothly was that the city had very explicit standards, and we designed very closely to those standards," Sherburne says.

"There were still some questions and catty remarks. Some people wondered whether wood frame construction was appropriate for an urban site. A few thought the project was too Disneylandy, too cute. One of the things inherent in a review process is that it lets people state their tastes. But when we got down to it, they said it's not necessarily what I would have done but it does meet the standards, so it's approved."

However, the consensus that makes Portland's process work doesn't necessarily prevail in other Pacific Northwest cities. Seattle, for instance, also has a design commission. But it doesn't have the broad powers that Portland's does (its jurisdiction is limited to public projects), partly, one gathers, because nobody can agree on what course development should take.

"In Seattle, obstreperous behavior is well entrenched," Sherburne says. "You have people with the attitude that I'm going to lie down in front of the bulldozers and you'll never get your permits."

David Hewitt, an architect and former chairman of the Seattle Design Commission, notes the commission has had its successes, but he admits that its voice is often lost amid the shouting. "It's such an open process, everything is public reviewed to death. Everybody gets their three minutes before the city council. I guess that's good, but the people from the community are often very self-serving."

Adds Hewitt: "You have public officials taking on serious design issues without professional advice, which opens the door to a lot of pitfalls." He points to a recently enacted land-use plan, which architects have protested as being unnecessarily prescriptive regarding design.

"If we had a more candid dialogue with the mayor and the city council we could be more effective," Hewitt says.

Hanging tough

But even under adverse political circumstances, some boards have managed to make a difference through a combination of diplomacy and stubbornness.

Cleveland is a case in point. Although not usually thought of as being in the forefront of urban design, it was one of the earliest cities to empower public officials to pass on aesthetic questions. A 1942 city charter amendment gave limited design review authority to the city plan commission.

In 1959, the city created a Fine Arts Advisory Committee made up of architects, artists, and the like to review development within the "public land protective district," which centers around the downtown mall designed by Daniel Burnham. Later, the committee's purview was extended to include urban renewal areas elsewhere in the city. Its role is limited, however. Often it gets involved at a late stage of the design process (although this is changing), and its opinions are merely advisory to the plan commission. Until recently, the committee had no formal design guidelines to fall back on and had to rely on the memory of its long-term members to provide continuity of decision making. Its most notable achievement has been ensuring a modicum of good taste in downtown signage.

But in the early 1980s, the committee had a moment of glory during the brouhaha over the new headquarters for Sohio, Cleveland's largest company. The building was to be the state's largest office building and the city's largest single project since the 1920s.

"It was fated to be controversial from the beginning," says city planning director Hunter Morrison. "There were an awful lot of aspirations riding on it. Coming as it did right after the disastrous era of Dennis Kucinich, it was a sign that a major corporation had faith in the city. For the new administration [of Mayor George Voinovich], it was a statement to the business community that we can in fact do business with you.

"The design community was also extraordinarily interested," Morrison notes. "The building was planned for the most sensitive site in the entire city, at the terminus of the mall, facing on Public Square. Many hoped that after the long firestorm of mismanagement and incompetence, this would put Cleveland on the map."

The initial design by the St. Louis firm, Hellmuth, Obata & Kassabaum, which called for a very long, thin building, was a disappointment. "It looked like a Chinese wall that rose out of the ground 600 feet to a flat top," Morrison says. "The main impression was that this obelisk out of '2001' had been plopped on Public Square."

Other complaints were that the five-story glass entrance atrium on Public Square was out of place among its stolid masonry neighbors and that the ground-floor shops turned their backs to the street.

The Fine Arts Committee objected strongly to the proposal. There followed what Morrison tactfully describes as "an honest exchange of views," tempered by the city's fears that Sohio, which was in the process of being sold to British Petroleum, might kill the project altogether.

"The mayor's position was get the best deal you can, but get the project," Morrison says. "He was not willing to let this thing die for lack of consensus."

To hasten things along, the city brought in Jonathan Barnett as a consultant. He suggested a series of design modifications that satisfied the most serious objections. The top of the building was sculpted to reduce its bulk, more masonry was added to the atrium, and the building's "footprint" was squared off.

The building that resulted "turned out pretty well," in Morrison's view. Most important, he notes, is the fact that the arts committee stood its ground, as it did a year or so later in a controversy involving a state rehabilitation center. "We showed that we wanted good design and that we would stick to our guns to get it."

Most likely to succeed

What makes the difference between an effective design review board and one that just goes through the motions? In discussion with officials and observers around the country, some common elements emerge:

Political support. Ideally the review process should have both official and grass-roots support, but experience suggests that if you've got the latter, the former will follow.

In Los Angeles, for instance, after a long battle with city and state officials, citizen activists were able to convince the city to create the Mulholland Scenic Parkway Citizens Advisory Committee in the early 1970s. The activists first got involved in the late 1960s when they feared the state would take over Mulholland Drive, which runs along the crest of the Santa Monica Mountains, and rebuild it to freeway standards.

That idea having been laid to rest, the advisory committee helped formulate development guidelines for a mile-wide corridor along the drive. The guidelines were adopted by the Los Angeles city council, which later gave the committee design review power. The committee's opinions are advisory to the city's director of planning.

Hearings are expected to begin soon on a detailed "specific plan" to guide future development along the Mulholland corridor. The Los Angeles city charter provides for the creation of such plans for designated districts within the city, each overseen by a review board, usually appointed by local city council members.

The Mulholland plan would regulate everything from streetlights to drain pipe color ("All . . . shall be painted an earth tone brown"). No buildings would be permitted to penetrate the Mulholland "viewshed," meaning they must be invisible to people driving along the parkway.

"It's a battle to keep ahead of developers," says Patricia Rosenfeld, a longtime member of the advisory committee. "In the beginning we lost more than we won, but we've finally turned the climate around. The idea of a design review board has now been generally accepted."

A shared goal. No design review board can succeed without a rough consensus on what the city is to look like when it is "done." In the absence of a clearly articulated architectural vision—and there have been few since the demise of the City Beautiful master plans popular in the early part of the century—many design review efforts have focused on preservation, usually of historic areas or the natural environment.

If the value of what is being preserved is widely appreciated, it is possible to generate public support for very restrictive controls. Such is the case in Santa Barbara, California, which has a wealth of Spanish colonial architecture in a beautiful natural setting. The city's Architectural Board of Review evaluates all major developments with respect to such things as color, landscaping, and even stucco texture (it should have a "smooth, lightly troweled finish"). Board approval is required before a building permit is issued. A separate landmarks committee reviews projects within the historic El Pueblo Viejo district.

Guidelines. Producing clear, detailed, comprehensive design guidelines takes time and talent and can be politically difficult. But without them a review board is simply expressing off-the-cuff opinions about the projects that come before it.

"In many cities, design review is just part of the permitting process," says Hamid Shirvani, dean of the school of architecture and planning at the University of Colorado at Denver. "They don't establish any parameters beforehand.

"For a design review board to be effective, you first have to identify what kind of city you want and what goals you want to achieve. Then you come up with policies and guidelines to implement those goals."

Without guidelines the review process can be abused by people who simply wish to halt development or who are pursuing some other agenda of their own. The lack of guidelines also means that achieving long-term physical planning goals, e.g., a continuous riverfront walkway, depends entirely on veteran review board members who remember to bring up the issue as projects come along over the years.

Finally, guidelines make life easier for developers, who can get an idea what the city is looking for before they spend a lot of money on architects' fees.

Board makeup. Shirvani recommends that boards include a mix of design professionals, concerned citizens, and a couple of planning department staffers.

"A design review board with only lay members isn't worth a damn," he says. "Ordinary citizens

don't know design and don't know how to translate their ideas into specific recommendations. An all-designer board doesn't work either because the designers end up talking to each other."

Districts. Except in very small jurisdictions, the powers of most review boards are best limited to clearly defined districts. This serves the dual purpose of keeping the board's workload to a manageable level and making it easier for developers and permit clerks to determine which projects require review. It also makes design review more politically palatable by eliminating potential sources of opposition. Developers who would object to a blanket review of downtown, for instance, might have fewer problems with a smaller district covering a corridor or waterfront.

The question of workload is especially important in jurisdictions that contemplate a very broad review process. Bellevue, Washington, opted for staff review rather than a board because it subjects 50 to 60 projects a year to a full-scale review that can take from six weeks to a year. Other cities permit staff review for small projects while sending larger ones to a board.

Limited scope. Aesthetic review in parts of town without well-established historic character or natural features worth preserving may be particularly controversial. Some jurisdictions have found it useful to limit review to such urban design considerations as street-level facades, orientation of retail space, and the like. Seattle, for instance, is considering empowering its design commission to review amenities provided by developers in return for zoning bonuses.

Los Angeles's "specific plans"—16 have been adopted so far, with many more pending—often take on aesthetic issues, but their ambitions are usually modest. The purpose of the Park Mile plan, for example, is to "protect the low-density, single-family residential nature" of a stretch of Wilshire Boulevard where deed restrictions on commercial development have expired. According to local observers, that goal has largely been achieved. New commercial construction consists of offices rather than traffic-generating retail projects, and the corridor's park-like quality has been maintained to some extent.

Early involvement. "Many fine arts commissions only get one shot at reviewing a project, and it often comes too late to do much good," Barnett says. "Ideally there should be both a preliminary and a final review."

In Portland, developers must attend a preapplication conference with staff from various city departments to outline their plans and get an idea of what the review process involves. Then they submit a formal application, complete with detailed drawings. The staff prepares a written report and, if the project is large enough, schedules a public hearing and notifies neighboring property owners and other interested parties.

The staff report is made available to the public 10 days before the hearing. The design commission hears testimony and votes on the project immediately afterward. The decision may be appealed to the city council. The whole process, from preapplication conference to public hearing, usually takes just 90 days.

Not every review board can be expected to work as well as Portland's. But many think the concept is still worth fighting for.

"I believe in planning," Campbell says. "I believe that the public has the right to determine what the city is going to look like, and that the city has the right to enforce that determination."

Barnett agrees. "Developers often don't pay much attention to off-site considerations. Review boards can make them adhere to some minimal standards of urban design. Sometimes the board may be the only spokesman for urban design that the community has."

Ed Zotti is a Chicago writer specializing in planning and design.

Visiting Firemen

Ruth Eckdish Knack
(May 1987)

In pop psych terms, it's called "bonding as a group." It's what happens to sequestered jurors, kids at summer camp, soldiers in battle—and, in this case, 11 men and a woman huddled around a drawing-filled table in a Fort Myers, Florida, motel suite. Although most of them met for the first time just days before, they're trading banter like old friends.

It's after midnight on the final day, last January, of a five-day blitz by an Urban Land Institute advisory panel, and the group is working against the clock—*en charette*—to finish its recommendations for redeveloping Page Field, the area's outmoded airport. The week was crowded with interviews, receptions, and tours, including a helicopter survey of Lee County and, for some, a ride in the Learjet owned by panel chair Peter Bedford, a California developer.

Another panel member, planner Jeffrey Wingfield, Jr., had flown into Page Field from Atlanta in his own Cessna two-seater, and two other panelists also were pilots—a plus for understanding the problem they were faced with: how to reconcile the demands of general aviation and development on a 638-acre site four miles from downtown Fort Myers. A detailed history of Page Field, which lost its commercial flights when a new regional airport opened in 1983, was included in the fat briefing book prepared by the panel's sponsors, the Lee County Board of Commissioners and the Business Development Corporation of Southwest Florida.

In the morning, the "experts" will make their formal presentation to the area's business and political leaders. They've already rehearsed. Now they've got to fill in the blanks, anticipate questions, and churn out an array of land-use maps—a job that falls to the landscape architect in the group, Miles Lindberg of Minneapolis. For him and a few of the others, it will be an all-nighter.

Parlez-vous charette?

At 40 this year, ULI's Panel Advisory Service is the granddaddy of the programs that organize "advisory panels" or—in what has become increasingly common parlance—"charettes." The term comes from the Ecole des Beaux Arts in Paris, where art and architecture students used small handcarts (charettes) to rush their work to their assigned critics. Often, the students would be drawing away while the carts were moving, giving the word the meaning of a last-minute burst of activity to meet a deadline—a usage common in architects' offices. In turn, the architects on panels like ULI's found it a convenient term to describe what they were doing: going to a place to look at a specific problem and offer a solution in a very short period of time.

Of course, that definition covers a lot of ground, and a lot of variations among the groups that sponsor charettes. They include:

American Institute of Architects. AIA's Regional/Urban Design Assistance Team program also celebrates an anniversary this year—its twentieth. The first R/UDAT was in Rapid City, South Dakota, in 1967; the most recent in Naples, Florida, last month. Named for two AIA committees, Regional Planning, and Urban Planning and Design, R/UDATs are more design-oriented than some of the other panels described here, although the teams always include other disciplines as well. In July, the program will receive the Sir Patrick Abercrombie Prize for Town Planning at the conference of the International Union of Architects in Brighton, England.

American Society of Landscape Architects. Two years ago, ASLA inaugurated a Community Assistance Team program to do once-a-year charettes in conjunction with the annual ASLA conference. The first effort was a plan for a series of stepped-down parking structures to create "hills" along Eggleston Avenue at the west edge of downtown Cincinnati. Last year's CAT offered a "cooperative decision-making framework" for San Francisco's Presidio, an army base that lies entirely within the Golden Gate National Recreation Area. . . .

Institute for Urban Design. The institute also has started holding charettes in connection with an annual conference. In 1985, the subjects were the Chicago River and a near south side Chicago neighborhood called "the Gap." Last year, in Dallas, visitors joined local people in evaluating Dallas's pedestrian circulation system. The institute is in Purchase, New York.

International Downtown Association. Focusing on downtown management programs, the nonprofit IDA in Washington, D.C., offers a series of visits through its Panel Advisory Service. Clients can sign up for any part: an overview with two or three speakers, a retreat, or an intensive on-site visit with three or four outside experts. "It's a flexible and customized approach," says president Richard Bradley.

National Main Street Center. The center sends Resource Teams to towns affiliated with the National Main Street Program, part of the National Trust for Historic Preservation. Program associate Kennedy Smith stresses that the team is part of a larger framework of services.

Partners for Livable Places. The Washington-based Partners offers "brain-storming sessions" as part of its for-fee consulting services, which cost between $15,000 and $30,000. "We thought we could design something less capital-intensive, more emotional-intensive than ULI or AIA," says president Robert McNulty. Examples: a session on the uses of public art in Glendale, California (sponsored by a local savings and loan); a one-day "mental groundbreaking" requested by New Jersey developer Arthur Imperatore; and a "cultural planning charette" in downtown Hartford.

Project for Public Spaces. PPS, in New York, conducts two- and three-day on-site workshops on management problems. "We describe them as intensive direction-finding," says vice-president Stephen Davies. The team is usually composed of staff members.

Waterfront Center. The Washington-based group brings in speakers for a one-day Ideas Forum ($3,000 plus expenses) and two-day Design Workshops, full-fledged charettes with five outside experts, including center codirectors Ann Breen and Dick Rigby ($6,000 plus expenses). Past charettes the center is proud of include a 1985 design workshop in St. Paul that helped raise $500,000 for a riverfront plan and one in Rock Island, Illinois, that produced plans for a Mississippi River walkway.

Other charettes are organized by universities, community design centers, consultants, business groups, and ad hoc coalitions like the one (including the Maryland APA chapter) that recently sponsored an urban design charette in Baltimore.

Pittsburgh architect David Lewis, a veteran R/UDAT panel member and coauthor of the 1986 book on the program called *Urban Design in Action,* . . . ties the interest in charettes to the citizen participation movement of the 1960s—a movement that's far from dead, judging from the response to the "design-in" sponsored by the Community Design Center in Knoxville to help generate alternatives to a controversial highway proposal. In Orlando recently, a charette was used to involve inner-city neighborhood residents in a streetscape project. And in Chicago, the park district and the local AIA chapter had a turnout of over 100 at a "park charette" to make big plans for three classic city parks. A $5 registration fee bought drawing paper and a box lunch. The drawings that resulted were displayed at the Museum of Science and Industry.

At the other end of the scale—but useful because it shows the range of the term—is the charette used by consultants to get a project off the ground. A planning team created by Sasaki Associates and Barton-Aschman went into a "charette mode" for three weeks while it worked on urban design guidelines and a master plan for Parkway Center, a huge area in far north Dallas. According to Sasaki landscape architect Rick Leisner, the intensive session was unusual for a publicly sponsored project. "It meant," he says, "that we could work through the process in a short time."

At its best a charette can galvanize an audience into action. For example, in Jacksonville, Florida, last January, Philadelphia planner Edmund Bacon was part of a team invited to help prepare a downtown plan. With a few strokes of a pen, he showed how two downtown "nodes"—Jacksonville Landing, a soon-to-be-opened riverfront marketplace, and Hemming Plaza, the city's historic town square a few blocks to the north, could be connected with a second-level walkway. It took an outsider to do that, Bacon believes. "It gave a different perspective," he says, "a clear vision of how these projects could be connected. Many people didn't see that before."

A charette's virtue, says urban observer William H. Whyte, is that it offers a "full inventory of ideas—outrageous and otherwise." The downside is suggested by Louisville critic Grady Clay: "It sometimes invites posturing, when participants are asked to make believe they have the power to make decisions."

"People think fastest when they work fast," adds Whyte, pointing to the feature that above all sets charettes apart. They're for people who work well under a deadline. "I like that about them," says Whyte, "although it does tend to reward a certain amount of glibness."

An AIA publication describes a 24-hour nonstop work session, starting at dawn on the third day when most of the work on the final report takes place. Similarly, the ULI panelists in Fort Myers began each day with a 7:30 breakfast meeting and continued long past midnight. Built into both the R/UDAT and ULI schedules is a frantic last-minute rush to prepare the final presentations. "They're all weary, and they have deadlines, and I think that is not conducive to the production of ideas," said former Denver planning director Alan Canter, commenting on a R/UDAT in his city several years ago.

On the other hand, every procrastinator knows

that deadline pressure has its advantages. Sometimes it's the only thing that makes a researcher stop collecting and start writing. Weiming Lu of St. Paul agrees that charettes can be a stimulus. "Sometimes the compacted time and the need to produce a visible result can be quite useful," he notes. Yet Lu cautions that "charettes can never replace a more thoughtful kind of community-based and long-range kind of planning. A lot of issues can't be aired so quickly. And implementing some of these things requires a great deal of effort. It can't be done overnight."

Besides procrastinators, charettes are also good places for dreamers. Lu notes, correctly, that few planners ever get a chance to plan a city. Charettes are a way to get their feet wet. "The danger," he says, "is that a lot of people go in with a lot of ego. They have the illusion that they can go into a town and solve problems that have been building up for years." . . .

New blood

Recently, ULI has begun broadening its panels by adding more people from other fields outside of real estate development. There were three planners in Fort Myers, for example: Jeff Wingfield of Hammer, Siler, George in Atlanta; William Lacy, the planning director of the Jefferson County planning office in Birmingham, Alabama; and Emil Malizia, a planning professor at the University of North Carolina in Chapel Hill, one of the first academics to serve on a ULI panel. The cross-fertilization may have produced some results. During the rehearsal for the final presentation in the Fort Myers motel, Wingfield said *sotto voce* to Malizia, "The developers are starting to sound more like planners, and the planners are starting to sound more like developers."

Looking back later, Wingfield said his first experience on a ULI panel was a good one. "It was a terribly stimulating experience, meeting a bunch of fellows in different disciplines than my own. I felt comfortable with them because a lot of the work I do is with developers. At the same time, I found myself looking out for the public interest more often than they did." His one reservation? "That you won't get the depth of analysis out of the panel that you need to sustain the effort. In this case, the clients were sophisticated, but some place else, they might assume that one week is a substitute for the eight or nine months of hard work that a consultant puts in."

An AIA mainstay is Boston architect Charles Redmon. He took part in his first R/UDAT in 1975 in Long Branch, New Jersey, and soon after became active in the urban planning and design committee, which oversees the program. A few years ago, Redmon had a chance to contrast the ULI and AIA approaches to charettes when he took part in a joint venture in Tucson.

The city, he explains, had asked for both a R/UDAT and a ULI study in an effort to find a way to smooth city-county relations. Recalls Redmon: "They thought the R/UDAT could do the visualizing, and ULI could tell how to implement the ideas. We also discovered that there were two factions: the developers, who felt they could talk only to ULI, and the architects, who said they could talk only to AIA. We pointed out that the recommendations could differ. Then the city would be left with the problem of unraveling them."

Opposed to the idea of two charettes for one problem, Redmon proposed a pathbreaking joint study to ULI advisory service director Jerry Church. Church agreed, and the resulting "hybrid" became the first united effort of its kind. It was cochaired by Redmon and Robert Nahas, a developer from Castro County, California.

It was also "fancier," in the view of R/UDAT staff director Bruce Kriviskey, than the AIA people were used to. The ULI panels travel first class, for instance, and stay in better hotels. "I felt isolated from the community," Kriviskey says. The AIA ground rules, which require participants to agree not to take commissions from the charette, applied in this case.

R/UDAT teams are put together by the R/UDAT Task Group of AIA's Urban Design and Planning Committee. First the task group selects a project manager. Then the task group and the manager pick a team chair, and finally the team. Team leaders tend to be architects, in part for obvious reasons, and in part because architects traditionally manage interdisciplinary teams for specific projects. Minneapolis architect Ben Cunningham noted several years ago, discussing the Kansas City "Northland" R/UDAT, which he chaired, that "architects can also offer real world, physical solutions." But he added that his colleagues are also often shortsighted, tending to focus on near-term solutions. "That's why," he added, "you have to

have a team". (And why, he might have added, planners should be on it.)

Generally, the ULI panels, with eight to 12 members, are larger than the other groups'. R/UDATs, for instance, usually have five members. According to Sumner Myers, the former director of technology and transportation for the Institute of Public Administration in New York, that's closer to the mark. Seven is the ideal number, says Myers, basing his opinion on his experience in setting up "product planning groups" for the Department of Energy in the late 1970s.

"When panels are large, there's a tendency for everything to sink to the lowest common denominator," he says.

One reason for keeping size down is cost. ULI's set fee is $75,000 to $80,000, depending on exact size of the panel. About 60 percent of that amount covers expenses, says senior associate James Van Zee. The rest goes to ULI. Private companies pay more than public agencies. The private developers can also request closed-door presentations if they prefer.

New at ULI is the "public service panel" that was inaugurated last fall at the annual conference and will be repeated in July in Los Angeles. The Chicago panel went to North Lawndale, perhaps the city's most depressed neighborhood, and made recommendations for developing two sites. Van Zee says expenses were paid out of conference membership fees.

Van Zee notes that ULI does not do "heavy marketing" of its panel advisory services because it doesn't want to compete directly with consultants. "Actually," he says, "we think the panels open up opportunities by pointing out things that need to be followed up on. When a consultant complains, we invite him to join a panel."

R/UDATs cost less, in part because they are generally a more grass-roots operation. Whereas ULI staff does much of the preparatory work for a panel visit, AIA's Kriviskey describes himself as a "wholesaler," who makes the contacts for the charette and then turns it over to a committee member. Typical R/UDAT expenses run from $20,000 to $25,000, a figure that includes the obligatory helicopter or light plane flyover. Since the late seventies, it also includes a setaside for follow-up meetings. The AIA urges potential R/UDAT hosts to seek contributions from a wide range of sponsors, the best way, the R/UDAT handbook notes, of ensuring broad community support.

"I think charettes work only when the problem that's being addressed is at a point where the people involved either have to or really want to make it work," says University of Washington urban design professor Dennis Ryan, a veteran of several R/UDATs.

The trick, adds Ryan, is preparation—on both sides—a point raised by practically everyone I talked to. "The better prepared the community was for the charette, and the more information they could provide to the team, the better the process itself is." Ryan recalls fondly the Chamber of Commerce representative who was "a real ball of fire" and whose working committee put together all the information the team needed.

Sometimes it's good to hear from the other side, the one who's being called on to put together all that material for the visitors. Chicago city planner Patricia Gallagher filled that role for the Institute for Urban Design Chicago River charette in October 1985. "It was a lot of work," she says: "Getting the people together, preparing the background reports, focusing the activities. I think it's an extremely useful planning tool—but it took an enormous amount of time."

The outsider issue

A major question in evaluating charettes is whether an outside opinion is the best opinion. "Outside" doesn't necessarily mean "out of town," but it does describe someone who doesn't have to deal with the problem tomorrow morning—who can go home and forget about it—leaving the implementation and the headaches to those who can't.

To avoid the problem, the American Society of Landscape Architects says it uses local people at its annual conference charettes. Kennedy Smith of the National Main Street Center says having an on-site project bridges the gap between the outsiders and the community. But Smith also notes the "strange dynamic" that occurs when someone comes from outside. "People tend to listen."

Similarly, Canadian architect Brian Eldred, cochair of last year's Winter Cities R/UDAT, praises the "fresh eyes approach" as offering a new perspective on old problems. The Winter Cities panel was AIA's second "generic R/UDAT," a program aimed at dealing with broader problems, in this case, "How to make a city center in a winter

region more livable." The charette took place during the first Canadian Winter Cities Forum, itself a prelude to the big Winter Cities '88 meeting February 14 to 19, 1988, in Edmonton.

Nor was there much doubt about the effectiveness of an outsider in Jacksonville, where Edmund Bacon dramatically showed local officials and business people how development could be rerouted to create a north-south connector through the downtown, away from the St. Johns River. "Hiring people like Bacon, [retailing expert] Jack Gould, and [transportation planner] Fred Gorove to come in gave people faith in the downtown project," says Stephen Kelly, vice-president of SPG, the consulting firm that is directing the downtown plan together with a local architecture firm, KBJ, under the sponsorship of the Downtown Development Authority.

But we're not just bringing in outsiders, Kelly says. "We got all the movers and shakers—the developers, landowners, city staff—together in one room. And we're building consensus. There's a lot of support for the plan we're proposing."

Bacon himself acknowledges that consultants sometimes "ride roughshod" over the feelings of local people. "But this is different. This time, we really are working with the mayor and local administrative agencies. Most important, the consultants and the architects will be there to carry the ideas forward."

One more charette is scheduled for Jacksonville, in mid-July after the election, which will give the city a new mayor and city council. In the meantime, the planners and architects are working on their promised implementation plan, including a five-year downtown marketing program.

In contrast, a resident of the Chicago neighborhood that was the site of one of the Institute for Urban Design charettes two years ago still has bad memories. "I thought there was a certain insensitivity in the whole process," she says. "I tried to put it in perspective, but I was upset when they said, 'We'll just pick up that statue and move it over here.' They didn't pay any attention to what the people who live here would think about that." Another observer suggests that charettes—generally development-oriented—are inappropriate in very poor areas where development is not likely to take place—an observation that might apply to the ULI panel's shopping center proposal for North Lawndale.

But even that exercise—which seemed well meaning but not particularly astute to some onlookers—gains support from Chicago planning commissioner Elizabeth Hollander, who is a fan of charettes. "It sent a national signal to ULI that I thought was very important," Hollander says, adding that she regularly uses the charette process to stimulate thinking in her department.

Richard Bradley, president of the International Downtown Association, acknowledges that charettes like ULI's and AIA's can serve a purpose. "I bought them when I was back in Hartford [as head of the downtown council]. They bring stature and credibility.

"But much of the time," he adds, "nothing happens. There's no obligation on the part of local parties to go ahead." That's why, Bradley suggests, many communities are turning away from the charette approach. "The instinct is right—get a group of bright people in and articulate a vision. But I find people don't listen."

Bradley likes to quote a friend, a systems analyst, who says, "The solution is always within the system. One or two speakers can probably do the same catalyzing as a full charette. You're better off getting four or five of you in a plane and visiting another town than calling in a group of outsiders and taking them up to see your town from the air.

"Yes, the charette process does release energy. But I think you have to unlock the energy within the community, within the system. You have to involve the stakeholders in the community."

Bradley's words are backed up by Hal Mason, community development director of Shelby, North Carolina, one of the towns in the original Main Street program. Charettes work best, says Mason, when the problem to be dealt with is very immediate—downtown revitalization—and when the community is interested. "If the local people haven't been brought into the process," he warns, "they listen and then they ignore."

James Duncan, the development director of Austin, Texas, and new president of APA, does believe in bringing in outside consultants, particularly in a group—charette-style. And he believes in it so strongly that he did it himself when the timing proved wrong for a ULI panel. "In early January," he recalls, "the city manager said we needed an objective appraisal of our development procedures. That's become a political issue here.

"We had to move fast. The manager wanted to put a package together by March. ULI said it would take three months. So we went out and put together our own team."

The five-member team was headed by California management consultant Paul Zucker and included Michael Shibley, of the National Association of Home Builders, and Richard Counts, former Phoenix planning director. They spent three days in Austin and later issued a 30-page report.

"It was the best $13,000 we ever spent," says Duncan. The amount covered team expenses for the three-day visit. "The outside consultants reinforced a lot of the things we were doing. The gist of their recommendations was that we should build trust in our system and rely more on our staff."

After his experience, Duncan is sold on the idea of APA doing something similar for its members. He suggests that APA could serve as the "middle man" for communities that want to put together their own teams.

Taking stock

According to a recent survey by a planning graduate student at Memphis State University, towns that have hosted R/UDATs are generally pleased with the results. Kelly Shannahan conducted phone interviews with officials in 32 towns, almost all of which had charettes between 1975 and 1980. Forty-four percent of his sample reported some success, and 78 percent said the charette had beneficial spinoffs—e.g., "it focused attention on problems." Shannahan found that the most important ingredient of success was approval by city staff, elected officials, and citizens groups.

Shannahan also did case studies of several towns, including one, Bellaire, Texas, that had scored a miserable one (out of 10) in an evaluation survey published by the AIA in 1980. Surprisingly, Shannahan found that most of the Bellaire recommendations have now been implemented. "Apparently, they just took a little time to cook," he says. In Stockton, California, he found a distinct lack of success in sprucing up a transient-filled downtown. "The R/UDAT isn't very helpful with social problems," he concludes; "yet the physical recommendations made in Stockton can't be implemented until the social problems are addressed."

In one case, New Orleans, critics say the R/UDAT was a waste of time because it didn't produce a design for a park adjacent to city hall. Shannahan suggests the local people probably needed a design competition instead of a charette.

The 1980 evaluation led to some changes in the R/UDAT program. Communities were advised to seek funding from several sources, not just city hall; to involve various local actors in the charette process; and to make a commitment to implementation. "There was a naivete in the late 1960s and 1970s about instant gratification," says Charles Redmon. "In the early 1980s, things began to change."

A major innovation in 1980 was the follow-up program, which calls for a team "debriefing" four to six weeks after the R/UDAT and a "revisit" six months to a year later. The chair and several key members are involved in both visits. 1980 was also the year in which the number of R/UDATs peaked at 10, suggesting both the popularity of charettes and the availability of federal funds to help pay for them.

Last month, San Diego hosted the 94th R/UDAT, and staff director Bruce Kriviskey suggests that it's a good time to take stock. "We've grown tremendously from the old days when it was just an informal discussion with local folks. Now we seem to be at a threshold. We may have gone as far as we can go with the kind of nationally organized R/UDATs we have been doing. We want to encourage local AIA chapters and universities to put together their own teams. On the national level, we'll focus on generic, transferrable R/UDATs like the Winter Cities one in Edmonton," says Kriviskey.

"R/UDAT was born in the crucible of the civil rights movement," says David Lewis. "The times changed, and so did the needs of the towns that asked for the charettes. We're going to smaller and smaller places, for instance.

"But even with the changes, I think R/UDAT is the single most compelling professional instrument that has occurred in the last three or four decades. It's had a deep impact on my practice. For the future, the next major thrust must be one that affects policy, and the way to do that is to make R/UDATs deal with the intellectual and political themes."

Now back to Fort Myers to see that charette in action. The panel members are lined up on the stage of the Edison Community College auditorium, ready to spell out their recommendation for the piece of land that they've come to know intimately over the past week—to the exclusion, it seems to some of them—of everything else in their lives.

"This site offers a unique opportunity," says Peter Bedford. "It shouldn't be developed piecemeal." The others flesh out the plan: Separate the field into three planning areas. Use part of the site to improve road connections. Develop the northwest corner into a high-quality commercial park within five years. Set aside 411 acres as a "great asset"—to be developed into something all county residents can enjoy. Start looking for an alternative general aviation site, and create an airport authority.

The flack begins to fly when pilots in the audience object strongly to any future abandonment of the airport. A local businessman says he's unhappy that the plan isn't more specific. A county commissioner questions the proposal's economic feasibility.

But the panel holds its own, responding cogently and often humorously. A woman in the audience moves for the creation of an airport authority. Later, the local newspaper publishes the results of its survey, asking, "What do you think should be done with Page Field?" 185 wanted to leave it as it is, while 36 said to do what the experts say. The response suggests that the battle for the hearts and minds of Fort Myers's residents is still not won. But clearly they've been put on the right track.

Ruth Knack is the senior editor of Planning.

Why Don't We Do It in the Road?
Grady Clay
(May 1987)

In the beginning was the path, and lo it became the road. And in the fullness of time, it became a wide place in the road.

When, in the course of human events, people discovered the horse and invented the saddle and the stirrup, they took all space to be their domain. And so it came to pass that the earth and all its lands were transformed.

And, in the passage of time, someone invented the railroad and said, "It is good." And with it, perfected the art of waging war at great distances, the commanding of colonies far away, and the satisfying of wants and desires by canvassing the whole earth for treasure.

In due course, the automobile found its way into the family pocketbook, attached itself to the male ego, and covered the countryside with things called suburbs, drive-ins, and mortgages.

Meanwhile, the United States began to evolve a new life form, "the Insulated Society." In the nineteenth century, early sanitation laws and social reforms had swept off the streets and into institutions millions of beggars, peddlers, kids, and tramps. Prostitution and other forms of sidewalk salesmanship were licensed or forced off the sidewalk. By the early twentieth century, the department store and elevators had further conspired to pull adults off sidewalks and into tall buildings.

Air conditioning moved two generations of families indoors, especially in the Sun Belt. Local bond issues made possible the indoorsing of sports arenas, superdomes, and local versions of Madison Square Garden—"garden," they still call those things!—all across the land.

Today, funerals have moved into funeral parlors; "graveside" has become a room in a temporary prefab. Grief—an ancient form of disturbing the peace—is discouraged in public. Drinking has been perfected as an indoor art form, and sidewalk cafes are permitted only after strenuous local politicking. State and county fairs, those last remnants of the carnival spirit and practices of the Middle Ages, are now structured and warehoused and franchised from one city to the next. To parade or to pilgrimage—get a permit.

Each new age of confinement takes its toll: Traditional architects and their buildings are so inward-directed, their designers so motivated to produce single, isolated, photogenic, tight-security structures, that street life around buildings becomes a second-class activity. Louis Kahn immortalized buildings by declaring grandly that "a street wants to become a building"—an architect's self-serving declaration if I ever heard one. Only the radical fringes of architecture students, mostly in Europe, are left to carry on that crusade for street-life revival fought so bravely but briefly in the U.S. during the sixties.

The multiuse complex is born, proliferates, and sets up its own private street system. Watching this privatizing, we take note of "down time"—

stretches of the urbanized environment where learning is at a minimum, where street frontage gives over to parking lots and garages with impenetrable street frontages, to buildings that turn blank walls to the street (that form of design called "Riot Renaissance") with no shops, few doorways, no access, no learning.

Here we observe the rise of the new citadels, those multipurpose megastructures containing convention halls, hotels, indoor race tracks, sports arenas, and parking ramps, self-consciously designed to capture customers and keep them spinning around, spending time and money indoors, off the street. These are our new zones of confinement.

Skyways get added, with closing hours, television surveillance, and private police, a separate, quasi-public circulation system, subject to more-or-less private regulation.

The indoorsing of America flourishes as well in the suburbs. Millions of families have been subsidized into buying freestanding houses, as far back from the street as possible, as far from the old city as feasible. Modern merchandisers assure us that for every car, a carport; for every party, a party room; for every garden, a garden room. By now, two generations have been induced to move into the "rumpus room," the "family room," the "great hall," or what in England is called "the snug," so that the secondhand image industry by way of television can take over six hours of family time per day.

Looking inward

In all this, the public deserts the sidewalk, retreats from the real world of the out-of-doors. Instead of stepping out, we snuggle down. In the process, we depopulate the street, isolate ourselves from foreign experience, from accidents and incidents, surprises and comeuppance, strangers and oddities, cut-and-thrust—the school-and-testing-ground of the street.

And so, with fewer eyes available to penetrate street life, Jane Jacobs's prediction in 1963 in *The Death and Life of Great American Cities* comes to be: Streets are reopened to hustler, lawbreaker, pimp and prostitute, drug dealer, and hot merchandiser. And the residents? They take off if they can. Nobody's left to run about and scream and shout, to call police, or even to break up a brawl—in short, to represent middle-class values.

All this adds up to a drastic shriveling of what

poets and historians like to call "the American experience." In nineteenth-century novels and plays, the street epitomized democracy-in-action. It stood for an open society, with freedom of access at its very core and foundation. How could it be so quickly transformed?

For one thing, we were mesmerized by a century of cheap energy, as though God Himself had signaled us out to be the repository of His beneficence. We were brainwashed by a half-century of self-serving "research" designed to prove that getting from here to there quickly by personal automobile was the fundamental human activity of the twentieth century.

In the process of setting up our insulated society, we have put down the street as an educational device. The street speaks a universal language. Its signals are part of everyday learning; its rules for movement are among the most widely understood of all public codes of conduct; and even its most bizarre variations offer, upon close examination, familiar goings-on in the School of the Street.

The street as teacher

To matriculate in this school, one must start with the sidewalk of one's own street. Jane Jacobs showed masterfully what a large curriculum is offered by any complex street system—and how much is to be learned in front of one's own house. Her pre-Toronto location, Hudson Street in New York's Manhattan, has gone down in urban history as one of the great learning streets. . . .

Marshall McLuhan tried to write off the street in his 1964 book, *Understanding Media.* He lumped the road together with the printed word as "our older media." But today, 23 years later, television has not, as McLuhan predicted, replaced the street. The television screen's truncation of places-in-the-round to places-on-a-flat-surface leaves out feeling, smell, movement, experiment—all the elements of "being there" that are the essence of there-ness. But it is clearly not enough to condemn secondhandedness. We have to be able to defend the value of the street as an ever-present educational device.

And so it falls to us to approach the street-as-school in a structured way; to organize it as a replicable experience; and to record it in ways useful beyond the classroom—first, as a mode of communication in which the language we use is an essential part; second, by suggesting special methods of

examination; and finally, by speculating upon the street, the road, and the highway as laboratories for universities.

Lamentably, our language is still imprecise and deficient in dealing with the street. For present purposes, I define it this way: "a generally leveled, linear, artificially lighted, and paved surface, extended across territory in a continuous and often straight direction, bounded on either side by curbings or other tangible limits, and offering to adjoining properties unlimited or partial access to and from its surface."

But what about all those unpaved, rocky, potholed lanes and alleys that admit to no such rigidities—dusty in summer, muddy in winter, impassable after rains, of random width and direction? And what about all those variations and subspecies? What of those things called Main Street, Main Drag, Shopping Strip, Back Alley (Laneway in Toronto), Front Street, Back Street, Side Street, Dock Street, Structural Street (a nice example from Allan Jacob's book, *Looking at Cities)?* All this nomenclature suggests that the School of the Street properly begins with the language of the street.

Looking at the street as an educational enterprise means considering it as part institution and part open to the most outrageous assumptions and interventions. It is the great common carrier of information in a democratic society, exuding volumes of lessons, examples, warnings, and admonitions.

Its rules of movement are among the most widely understood of all codes of public conduct. Within this broad context, one should view the trip and the walk—together with our language for them—as mechanisms to help us learn to cope with experience and to generalize from it.

Linneaus, the great Swedish botanist, spoke of "the sovereign order of nature," which he organized with his naming system for vegetable and animal life. If the study of urban objects and processes is to advance beyond its present contentiousness, then we too will need all the discrimination of nomenclature that we can muster.

One of the more intriguing aspects of studying streets is that their evolutionary order is far more apparent than was the evolution of plants and animals. One day's commute from suburb to downtown, one eye-filling trip to the airport, one strongly held gaze at a roadside uncovers more historical evidence of evolution than the mind can digest. However, the evidence is scattered among many disciplines. Street researchers come in all creeds and colors, including traffic management and historic preservation. Environmental psychologists, planners, and architects hustle their own deals, using their special lingo.

What we need is a multidisciplinary university course in visible evidence and the same intensity of scholarly gaze that is regularly fastened upon single buildings of renown. We need a fully documented and logical order, a Linnean-type guide to thinking about streets.

Such a guide might suggest that we think of the street as the link between today's multiuse complexes and the ancient pathways—Indian paths through North America, for example—that persist within the structure of most cities. In the evolution of those paths—once sufficiently recorded—there lies a new form of evolutionary theory waiting to be discovered. When such a theory finally develops, I suspect it will revolve around a single vital criterion: access and accessibility, from which all other attributes flow.

There is hope in the new wave of road historians who began publishing observations on road, highway, motel, and tourist facilities in the 1970s, encouraged by the essays of J.B. Jackson in *Landscape* magazine: Henry Manny III, columnist in *Road & Track* magazine, and more recently, William H. Whyte's marvelous movies of people on the street.

The cross-section

Beyond learning the language of the street, I suggest that a cross-section trip through a metropolitan area is as revealing to the modern observer as the first cross-section of human tissue was to the anatomist Vesalius, or as the valley section was to the great Scottish botanist-ecologist-planner Patrick Geddes. Future theorists of street meanings can find no better mentor than Geddes and no better model than his cross-section of a typical eighteenth-century valley—brought up to date in metropolitan context.

But the Geddes diagram can tell only part of the story of the modern city and its street system. Geddes's town was an old-fashioned processor of raw materials. Today's American city has become a processor of power and information, and to understand that power firsthand, one must traverse the whole city, the whole metropolitan area, as a continuous experience from outer trail to path to road

to street, into the very city center, and out the other side. Such an experience forces the student-learner to confront the "city" as a complex educational enterprise, with various forms of learning available at each stage.

This kind of cross-section trip forces lessons on us. In a single hour's journey across a city, we pass 10 generations of cars, 100 generations of advertising fashions, and 1,000 variations in roadside building styles. The evidence is so thick it emerges into a razzle-dazzle of street-road-highway. But behind the blue, an order exists, waiting to be found, through time-lapse photography, historical studies, and maps.

To make the most of a cross-section analysis as a learning device, one must plot out a route that follows one general direction, not doubling back upon itself, and that spans the full range of the "commutershed." The route must deal with the center, whether the historic city center, the civic center, or the geographic center where all the roads once came together. It must cope with the zone or neighborhood from which come major sources of exportable goods and services. It must explore a dying area—slums beyond recall, an abandoned warehouse district, a mill district undermined by foreign competition.

My ideal cross-section would encounter at least one growth area where roadside billboards announce new construction and zoning changes to come. It would include "best" addresses, where the Volvo and Mercedes agencies cluster. And it would bring us into at least visual contact with the area's major geographic features. It would include at least one Main Drag, preferably that special variation I call Alpha Street—the one that starts down by the original town landing, meanders through the dying mill district, then through the city center, office district, and courthouse square, proceeds uphill along the decaying Mansion Row. . . .

We need to view the street from the reformist tradition. It is not just the inevitable byproduct of our latest mode of transport, but a vital part of the learning and testing system for the larger society.

One thing we should avoid is more outpouring of public funds into repetitive traffic/transport/movement studies—an expensive exercise in single-purpose thought. I have just given away a huge personal library of such documentations and shudder at the way they flog dead horses from one intersection to the next.

Instead, I suggest that we—as a society—do these things:

● Find, save, and improve those outdoor places that invite the public, that offer outdoor experiences the public is ready to enjoy and build upon.

● Resist the widespread efforts to privatize public streets, to take over parts of the public street for private buildings, private events, parties, anniversaries—to deny the public's access to its own properties.

● Write the walk, the saunter, the parade, the promenade, the pilgrimage, or the cross-section into agendas for local events.

Examples abound. Baltimore uses the public spaces of the Inner Harbor for parades, competitions, marathons—all under the direction of an events coordinator in the mayor's office. Boston's well-mapped Patriot's Walk is often a part of convention tours. River Walks have spread from much-imitated San Antonio, to Minneapolis, Jacksonville, Norfolk, New Orleans, Miami.

We need to find other ways to drag into the out-of-doors—kicking and screaming if necessary—those human activities too long subsidized and sequestered inside, so they become accessible to all.

We must do what we can to break out of the cocoon of insulation, the cotton batting of second-hand experience, the narcotic effect of warmed-over images. And we must do it by steadying our own gaze, venturing our own original and perhaps revolutionary theses, perfecting our own filters, drawing our own conclusions. Who knows, there may be a new Linnaeus among us, drawing on evidence that right now, is right before our very eyes.

Grady Clay is the former editor of Landscape Architecture *magazine. He is the author of* Close-Up: How to Read the American City *(University of Chicago Press, 1980);* Alleys: A Hidden Resource *(Grady Clay & Co., Louisville, 1978); and* Right Before Your Eyes *(APA's Planners Press, 1987).*

Stacking the Decks for Better Design

Ed Zotti
(October 1987)

Planners who fret about the impact of traffic and parking on American cities had better brace themselves. According to a recent industry survey, the U.S. is in the middle of a boom in parking garage construction. Nearly 1,200 garages containing more than 1.1 million spaces will be built by 1990, says the Parking Market Research Company of Alexandria, Virginia. Total cost: $8.5 billion.

Much of the construction is concentrated in California, specifically Los Angeles. But nearly every city of any size is getting its share, with mid-sized cities like Indianapolis, Orlando, and Raleigh included in the top 10.

The special problems that parking structures present have long been recognized. In addition to sometimes snarling traffic, they're often considered a blight on the landscape. In downtown areas, they can create dead spots on pedestrian streets. Most cities have done little to combat these failings in the past. Now an increasing number of jurisdictions are taking a firm hand in regulating parking garage design. They're requiring or at least encouraging ground floor retail in garages on key thoroughfares. According to Tom Smith, APA's associate director of research, they're also asking for more landscaping, more attractive facade treatments, even rooftop planting so the sight of a garage won't offend nearby high-rise occupants. . . .

Judging from projects around the country, such efforts are starting to have an impact. In Kansas City, a garage was recently constructed behind the facade of two older buildings. In California, parking decks in the Old Pasadena historic district are faced with stucco to harmonize with their surroundings. In Chicago, which is becoming to parking structures what Rome is to churches, there are musical garages, theatrical garages, and one garage that looks like a classic automobile.

Here's a look at how several cities around the country are coping with the latest wave of parking construction.

Orlando

Described as "a sleepy little southern town" until the advent of Disney World, Orlando has seen considerable high-rise construction since the late 1970s. After a few unhappy experiences in which shops were replaced by blank-walled garages, the city completely revamped its land development code in 1985, adding stringent regulations governing garages. An important goal was "an active, pedestrian-oriented downtown," says senior planner Bruce Hossfield, who wrote much of the code.

On primary streets downtown, at least half of a garage's street frontage must be given over to retail, and the facade must achieve "architectural unity" with the structure the garage is intended to serve. The code requires perimeter landscaping and flower boxes or hanging planters on the lower stories. Adjacent sidewalks must be rebuilt according to a prescribed streetscape plan.

Only a handful of structures have been built under the new requirements, Hossfield reports, but indications so far are encouraging, even though developers and architects aren't always enthusiastic at first. On one project, a new parking deck for the First Union Bank, "I had to field several calls from the architect in Tampa wondering why we were requiring all this," he says. But in the end all the requirements were met—everything from flower boxes to ground floor shops and compatible architectural treatment.

"Admittedly, Orlando is in a situation where we can demand more," Hossfield says. "We have a growing downtown, and we're not begging for people to come in. If we were, perhaps we'd make fewer demands. But I would still say downtown is well served by this type of regulation."

The fact that the code was written in cooperation with Orlando's downtown development board, which represents local business interests, has helped win public acceptance. "The things we're asking for make the area more attractive to the building tenants and their employees, thereby increasing the value of the building," Hossfield says.

Irvine

Not every city is out to preserve its downtown pedestrian environment, as Orlando is. Irvine, California, for one, doesn't really have much of a downtown pedestrian environment; for that matter, it doesn't have much of a downtown. Instead, it's got something called the Irvine Business Complex, a 2,500-acre mixed-use center whose zoning was changed a few years ago to permit high-rise office construction.

But Irvine's zoning code also includes stringent provisions forbidding blank walls and requiring streetscaping around all parking structures. The idea is to create an attractive street scene, but the beneficiaries won't be pedestrians so much as passing motorists. One recently proposed parking structure at a key intersection is designed to look like a smaller version of the office tower it's intended to serve.

Irvine does hope to create an attractive pedestrian environment eventually, not so much because it has ambitions of becoming another Paris but because every office worker who stays on the premises at noon instead of driving somewhere for lunch is one less motorist adding to congestion on the area's overburdened streets. As part of a strategy that includes bonus points for on-site restaurants, the local code requires that no more than 65 percent of any site be covered by garage and office building combined. Fifteen percent of the remainder must be plazas, and "amenity credits" are offered for parks and the like. The hope is that attractive grounds will encourage workers to brown-bag it outdoors.

Irvine would also like developers to incorporate some greenery into the parking decks but hasn't hit on a totally practical way for them to do it. Planners have tried to convince developers to plant vines on horizontal trellises on garage roofs, both to reduce heat gain and to make the structure more attractive from above, but the results so far haven't been very satisfactory. The code requires a tree in a 15-gallon planter every 30 feet around the perimeter of each structure and encourages the use of the taller varieties of trees so that the building eventually will be partially hidden by greenery.

Kansas City

When developer Paul Copaken was planning the AT&T Town Pavilion, a 1.2-million-square-foot office and retail complex in downtown Kansas City, he decided to build a 2,200-space parking garage next door. But clearing the entire block would have meant destroying two turn-of-the-century buildings with handsome terra cotta trim. After negotiating with city officials and preservationists,

Copaken agreed to preserve the facades of the buildings and construct the garage behind them.

After the front of the eight-story Jenkins building was reinforced with steel, the back portion was demolished, leaving a slice about 30 feet deep. Around the corner, the two-story Bonfeils building was cut back to 60 feet in depth. Though such "facadism" might offend purists, Copaken says the only alternative was destroying the buildings altogether. The Bonfeils building is currently occupied by offices and shops, and the lower floors of the Jenkins building could be in the future.

From the standpoint of leasing space in the adjoining office tower, preserving the buildings has proved beneficial, Copaken says. "Looking into a parking structure is not always the most beautiful view in a downtown environment. On the other hand, it was extremely expensive to do." Costs on the Jenkins building alone were over $1 million.

Chicago

Chicago has few formal rules for parking garage design, but a determined effort by public officials working with several enlightened developers has resulted in an unusual, even whimsical collection of structures that mesh well with the urban fabric. Two of the more notable garages were built in a downtown urban renewal district after lengthy consultation with the city's planning staff.

The first, originally called the Transportation Center and now known by its address, 203 North LaSalle, was envisioned as a garage atop a collection of transportation-related shops (rental car agencies, airline ticket offices) adjacent to a newly extended rapid transit line to O'Hare airport. But developer Richard Stein went the city one better by adding a 15-story office building on top of the garage. The wisdom of the concept was briefly called into question when prospective tenants expressed concern that they were being asked to lease space in a glorified parking deck, but adroit marketing seems to have minimized that problem.

The parking portion of the structure, which features glass-enclosed elevators, cannot be readily distinguished from the office part, at least from a distance. A handsomely finished, two-story retail arcade occupies the ground floor. Eventually the building will have direct connections to the subway, the Loop elevated train, and the city's downtown pedestrian tunnel system.

The feature of the garage that has attracted the most notice, however, is a musical floor-reminder system dreamed up by Myron Warshauer, president of Standard Parking Corporation, the garage's operator and codeveloper. Each floor is identified with the name of a city associated with some catchy song—for example, Frank Sinatra singing "New York, New York"—a great help for patrons trying to remember what floor they parked on. The patented system has since been incorporated into several other parking decks in Chicago and on the West Coast.

Planners, along with many of Standard Parking's competitors, have tended to dismiss the tunes as a gimmick. But Warshauer contends that the music helps to make his garages "people-friendly."

Stein and Warshauer have collaborated on another Chicago garage now nearing completion, the 12-story, 950-space Theatre District Self-Park. The facility is meant to serve the downtown "theater row" that the city has been trying to get rolling for several years. Accordingly, the musical reminders are famous show tunes, and the entrances are highlighted with marquees. Several thousand square feet along a narrow street now used as an alley have been reserved for what planners envision as an intimate, shop-lined lane connecting theaters on State and Dearborn streets.

Such architectural niceties add considerably to the cost of a parking structure. Warshauer estimates that the fancy facade on the Theatre District Self-Park accounted for $1.5 million of the project's $24 million total cost. The developers have agreed to contribute an additional $350,000 toward the eventual redevelopment of the alley.

Because of competition from nearby garages, the extra costs can't be reflected in higher parking rates, Warshauer notes, but he hopes to gain by attracting additional parkers drawn by the pleasant ambiance. He and Stein are now working on another structure near the Art Institute that will feature a $1 million limestone facade. The floor reminders? Famous paintings coupled with appropriate music, such as Toulouse-Lautrec's "Jane Avril" and the cancan. Elsewhere in the Loop, architect Stanley Tigerman, noted for his tongue-in-cheek approach, has designed a parking garage intended to recall the grille of a vintage car, complete with headlights and fenders.

What else is new

Some cities aren't content merely to regulate parking construction; they want to build the facilities themselves, a policy that can sometimes lead to trouble. For instance, Calgary, Alberta, limits the number of parking spaces that downtown developers can build on site and requires them to contribute to a "cash-in-lieu" fund that's later used to build public garages.

Unfortunately, during the boom years of the late 1970s, parking construction tended to lag behind office construction, upsetting developers and their lenders, who feared the lack of parking would threaten the viability of their projects. The recession of the early 1980s rendered the question temporarily moot, and officials say parking construction has now caught up with demand.

Pasadena hit on a slightly different way to pay some of the costs of the two municipal parking structures it's building in its Old Pasadena historic district. After an attempt to impose a parking assessment on local property owners met with strong resistance, the city came up with a concept known as "zoning credits."

The scheme allows the developers of nearby retail and office structures to satisfy their off-street parking requirement by "claiming" spaces in the municipal garages, paying the city an annual fee per space. The program, which was inaugurated just a few months ago, is voluntary; developers who would rather satisfy their parking requirement some other way are free to do so.

Pasadena is also concerned lest garages detract from the district's historic character. The two new decks, approved following an extensive review process, will be finished in stucco with rooftop trellises and trees and shrubs at the base. One garage even features a mission-style tower. To reduce the profile, two levels in both structures are below grade. A total of 14,000 square feet of retail space is provided, and planners say they've already had inquiries about leasing space.

Pleasant though the amenities are, it's not certain how much longer they're going to remain affordable. According to the Parking Market Research study, garage construction costs are escalating rapidly, with a 50 percent increase projected from 1986 to 1990.

What's more, changes in the federal tax laws are making garages tougher to finance. Public-private joint ventures are particularly threatened, since the new laws sharply limit the use of tax-exempt financing to pay for private ventures. That means a municipality can no longer sell industrial revenue bonds on behalf of a developer who wants to build a parking deck to serve a new office tower—even if part of the facility is open to the public.

"No more than 10 percent of the spaces can be on long-term lease to a private party," says E. Carlton Heeseler, senior vice-president for Shearson Lehman Brothers. "Nor can a private entity assume more than 10 percent of the garage's annual debt service." To finance such projects, local governments instead are turning to commercial paper pools offering low-interest taxable financing.

Still, with 25 million more cars expected to be on the road by the year 2000, more parking decks will have to get built somehow, and they might as well get done right. "I think ingenuity rather than big bucks is the answer," says Myron Warshauer. "Imagination can go a long way."

Ed Zotti is a Chicago writer who covers planning and architecture issues.

Painting the Town Red
Ruth Eckdish Knack
(May 1988)

In the 1960s, Mel Brooks narrated a short and very funny film called "The Critic" in which abstract paintings flashed on the screen as Brooks kept asking, *This is art?* What, one wonders, would our confused critic make out of the "artwork lake" Helen and Newton Harrison have created for a Pasadena floodplain; or the fanciful sculptural benches being readied for downtown Minneapolis sidewalks; or *Steam Shuffle*—bursts of steam activated by passersby and accompanied by snippets of poetry—on display last fall in Philadelphia during the first national conference on American public art.

All of the above, and far more curious examples as well, are encompassed in the current broad and forgiving definition of art in public places. Not only is public art no longer necessarily commemorative; now the artwork is as likely to be a landscape or a building top as a piece of sculpture.

Recently, too, artists have begun collaborating with architects, landscape architects, and occasionally planners—with predictable conflicts at times. And the amount of money involved continues to grow as "percent-for-art" programs expand to cover private development and local governments explore the potential of art-zoning tradeoffs.

In the works are changes in selection procedures and policies for maintenance and removal, some stemming from the continuing flap over Richard Serra's *Tilted Arc* in New York, which has prompted much soul searching from the top levels of the General Services Administration on down. One result is a growing recognition of the value of integrating public art with development plans, and of planners as fitting coordinators for such projects.

Togetherness

As the program for last fall's national public art conference made clear, the image of the lonely artist slaving away in a garret rarely applies today. "Public art has come of age," said Penny Balkin Bach, executive director of Philadelphia's Fairmount Park Art Association, which sponsored the meeting. And coming of age in this case means a new definition of art that is likely to require collaboration among a broad range of professions.

Examples abound. In Philadelphia, sculptor Jody Pinto worked with an architectural engineer to create *Finger Span*, a steel pedestrian bridge in Fairmount Park. In New York, teams of artists, architects, and landscape architects are collaborating on projects for Battery Park City, encouraged by the area's redevelopment authority. "I didn't want to see one more piece of public sculpture in New York City, even if I designed it," says sculptor Jennifer Bartlett, who is working with a landscape architect and an urban designer to produce a series of theme gardens.

Collaborative works range in scale, too. Environmental sculptors like Michael Heizer and Robert Morris work on "earthworks," huge land reclamation schemes that require the involvement of engineers, geologists, and other technical experts. In Houston, though, five artists designing a small park in an historic area near downtown pride themselves on the "human scale" of their project. "We thought about the park as a piece of art rather than a place for art," said photographer Paul Hester at the Philadelphia conference.

Seattle is often cited as a model of cooperative

arts activity. In 1979, three artists helped design the city-owned Viewlands/Hoffman electrical substation to fit in with its residential neighborhood. More recently, five artists worked with the National Oceanic and Atmospheric Administration on a shoreline walk that required much interaction with city departments.

Local artist Buster Simpson is gaining a national reputation for his offbeat functional art, including a composting toilet for the homeless and a self-watering drainpipe planter "to make the alleys green," projects that often depend on city agencies for approvals. All of this activity is guided by a city arts plan, the result of a 1984 study called "Artwork/Network," which includes criteria for analyzing potential public art sites.

Nationally, cooperation is much in evidence in the growing number of transit art programs. For example, Arts on the Line, a program of the Massachusetts Bay Transit Authority and the Cambridge Arts Council, has involved artists in the design of new stations on the Red Line Extension. The East-West Gateway Coordinating Council has sponsored a similar program in St. Louis; its competition announcement specifically states that "artists to be considered should be open to collaboration with other artists, engineers, and architects."

Recent trends in funding for public art suggest that we're moving full circle from private funding to public and back again. In the old days, of course, artists were paid by their patrons. The federal Works Progress Administration took over in the 1930s, leaving a rich legacy of murals, sculpture, and decorative public works. The next big federal funding push came in 1963 with the General Services Administration's Art in Architecture program, which provided one-half of one percent of construction funds for art. In 1967, the National Endowment for the Arts made its first local matching grant: $45,000 to the city of Grand Rapids for an Alexander Calder stabile.

Meanwhile, cities and states, through "percent-for-art" ordinances, began to require public agencies to use one or two percent of their construction budget for art. A recent study for the NEA counts 99 percent-for-art programs nationwide. About three-fourths of those are city programs, with more and more counties joining in.

The news is that percent programs are being extended to cover private development as well as public. San Francisco has already changed its guidelines to require private developers in the area covered by the downtown plan to spend one percent on project art; the guidelines also note that art will be a factor in evaluating projects competing for approval under the city's annual growth cap. The catch, says city planner Eva Liebermann, is that no buildings have been built since the plan passed, which of course means no new art.

Now Los Angeles is considering its own version of private tithing. City council member Joel Wachs has introduced legislation that would require all development to include a percent contribution for art. "Art is good for the city," said Wachs at the Philadelphia conference. "It's time that municipal governments begin to recognize what assets their cultural resources are."

Wachs is proposing that the city's current one-percent art requirement for public construction be extended to all buildings except single-family houses. At least 40 percent of the total would be deposited in a trust fund, which could be used to finance performing arts or temporary installations as well as permanent artworks—a significant departure from most percent-for-art programs and a feature that is opposed by some visual artists, the primary beneficiaries of such programs in the past.

The trust fund, recommended by a blue-ribbon task force, would be similar to a fund created in 1985 by the city's Community Redevelopment Agency, which used percent-for-art funds to help finance a new contemporary art museum. CRA allows developers to make an eight percent trust fund donation and eliminate on-site artwork altogether or to do both.

Wachs estimates that the funding changes would net Los Angeles an additional $25 million a year for the arts. Part of that sum would come from a new eight percent hotel tax. His bill is now being reviewed by his own recreation and cultural affairs committee. Wachs aide Lee Ramer says hopes are high that the legislation will pass the council this summer, "even though it includes an arts fee, and nobody likes an arts fee."

Instead of a fee, the percent requirement, a few places are holding out the lure of density bonuses or even project approval in return for public art. A notable example is Bethesda, Maryland, where the Maryland-National Capital Park and Planning Commission weighs public art among other criteria in doling out building permits. Several years ago, Bethesda held a one-time "beauty contest" to

choose projects for its burgeoning downtown. The competition resulted in a wide array of public art, including a trellis and gazebo by sculptor Martin Puryear and a garden cafe by Howard Ben Tre and Jim Sanborn. The art agreements with the developers were negotiated by the planning commission's urban design staff, headed at the time by John L. Westbrook II.

In 1986, Westbrook assessed the Bethesda experience in an article in *Place*. "No one knew in advance if the risks of singling out public art as being of major importance would pay off," he wrote. Clearly, he noted, it did, fulfilling his intention "to bring a little delight into the public realm."

Love and hate

That delight is not universal, however, as the horror stories recited by artists and arts administrators at the Philadelphia public art conference make clear. Artist Andrew Leicester of Golden Valley, Minnesota, described the continuing controversy over his modern "gargoyles" at a Colorado prison. State legislators, he suggested, used the issue to push for an end to the state percent-for-art program.

Sandra Percival, Art in Public Places program manager for the state of Washington, told of two sets of murals commissioned for the house and senate chambers of the state capitol in Olympia. The paintings so offended legislators that they ordered them removed—in the case of the senate paintings by Michael Spafford, simply covered. Both Spafford and the house muralist, Alden Mason, are University of Washington professors who were chosen in a competition organized by the state arts commission.

In fact, only two of the four Spafford panels, depicting the "Twelve Labors of Hercules," were installed. The legislators contended that some of the scenes were pornographic, and a decorator hired to redo the chambers said the paintings would clash with the new color scheme. Not surprisingly, Spafford sued, charging breach of contract; since the work was created specifically for the site, he contended, removal would be tantamount to destruction. Seattle arts groups organized a mural defense fund, and their members sported buttons with the slogan "Art Outlives Politics." But in October 1987, as the public art conclave was taking place in Philadelphia, a King County superior court judge ruled that the artist's contract did not ensure permanent display and thus there was no breach of contract. The work remains covered.

Other places, other stories: Artist Billie Lawless said the abstract neon figures he did for a piece in Buffalo, New York, represented life. Critics said they looked more like male genitals. The mayor agreed and ordered *Green Lightning* dismantled. It's now part of an ad hoc sculpture park in downtown Chicago.

In Cleveland, Standard Oil canceled plans to install a giant rubber stamp by Claes Oldenburg on the plaza of its downtown building while the piece was being fabricated. "I don't think the symbolism is appropriate," said the company chairman. In St. Louis, last November, the head of the city's parks department ordered removal of a sculpture by Alan Sonfist, which she called a "public eyesore." The $100,000 piece had been dedicated just a year earlier.

In Chicago, it was a roomful of murals on the theme of Virgil's *Aeneid* in a new public library branch that brought out the protesters. The murals remain, but the city has revised its selection policy to allow more public input.

But no case has been publicized more than that of *Tilted Arc* by minimalist sculptor Richard Serra. Installed in a plaza in front of New York's federal building in 1981 at a cost of $175,000, the 12-foot-high, 120-foot-long curved sheet of Cor-Ten steel was reviled by workers in nearby buildings, who charged that it prevented use of one of Lower Manhattan's few open spaces. A *New York Times* critic called it "an awkward, bullying piece that may conceivably be the ugliest outdoor work of art in the city." Others defended Serra's vision.

Although originally commissioned by the federal General Services Administration, *Tilted Arc* drew the particular enmity of the regional GSA administrator, William J. Diamond, who said the selection was "a typical case of an elite choice without public input." Diamond and the acting GSA administrator in Washington insisted on removal even after artists and art scholars showed up en masse at a public hearing to defend the work. "The like-it-or-lump-it theory of public art is dead," Diamond gloated.

It turned out not to be so simple. Last December, a review panel organized by the National Endowment for the Arts at GSA's request agreed with Serra's argument that the work was "site-specific" and recommended that it stay. However, a federal judge turned down Serra's claim that his First Amendment right of free speech was violated. Serra warned that the GSA decision would have a chilling effect on public art. And he might be right. When the controversy was at its height, a St. Louis alderman introduced a bill to allow a referendum on removal of a Serra piece on the downtown Gateway Mall. The piece is still there, but the threat remains.

"I don't think it is the function of art to be pleasing," Serra has said, raising the hackles of those who think *Tilted Arc* ruins Foley Square. But even without the emotion, the question remains, "Whose public space is it anyway?"

Richard Sennett, a professor of urban sociology at New York University, testified in the Serra case "on behalf of the space." At the public art conference, Sennett talked about the conflict between modern art and the classical idea of a public place. For the Greeks, he noted, "togetherness" was the most important social value. In contrast, the modernist movement in art most values autonomy and speaks of the artist's "right" to a space.

Given this conflict, is it possible to get a great modern public place? People like Los Angeles councilman Joel Wachs say that the public art can be the needed catalyst. But urban designer Jacquelin Robertson, dean of the University of Virginia architecture school, disagrees. Robertson, like Wachs, was a member of the NEA panel that reviewed the Serra case.

"To have a great public space, you need a willing public," he told the Philadelphia conference. "We don't have that. We have developed a voyeur culture that no longer requires public gathering places." And all the public art in the world won't create a public realm for a public that isn't interested, he added.

"I'm not sure it's even a good idea to use art for such purposes," said Richard Kahan, now a New York developer but formerly chairman of the Battery Park City Authority. "Mixing art and economics simply results in bland art." (And in fad art, others might add. It's apparent to anyone doing research on public art that the same names pop up over and over again, and even the same types of art. "Gateways" are big now, and so are benches. But woe to the traditional sculptor who works in a representational style—unless he's someone like super-realist Seward Johnson, a perennial favorite.)

Help is on the way

For all its acrimony, the Serra controversy had one positive result: the publication this spring by the National Endowment for the Arts of a new handbook for artists and arts agencies. Pam Korza, a staffer with the arts extension service of the University of Massachusetts continuing education division, coordinated the Public Art Policy Project.

Asked originally to help GSA develop new administrative procedures, NEA's Visual Arts Division soon decided to broaden its study, Korza says. The division organized several task forces to review existing procedures and recommend changes. The result is a 304-page book called *Going Public: A Field Guide to Developments in Art in Public Places,* written by Korza and Jeffrey L. Cruikshank. . . .

The book's key recommendation is to allow a 10-year grace period before removing any controversial work. The suggestion is part of a suggested "public artwork review process" included in the publication. The authors warn, however, that "there is a danger in the codification of public art processes." Thus, the book is billed not as a guidebook but as a source book of case studies and observations. A lengthy appendix includes documents from programs viewed as models—the Washington State, Seattle, and King County arts commissions; Fairmount Park Art Association; Arts on the Line in Cambridge; and the Art in Public Places program of Metro Dade County, Florida.

The section on the administration of public art programs analyzes percent-for-art programs and discusses procedures for commissioning a work. A model contract developed by the New York City Bar Association is included. Noting that responsibility for existing public art is an area that needs attention, the book devotes a section to preservation and maintenance. Here the model is King County's conservation policy, which covers such topics as what to do with site-specific works when the community around them changes.

One section of *Going Public* presents case studies of places that have integrated public art programming with community planning, a trend that the authors view as promising. What's not always clear, however, is who will do the planning.

The turf questions involved were made explicit in a November 1986 article in *Landscape Architecture* by a San Francisco landscape architect named Mary Margaret Jones. Jones was part of a committee es-

tablished to set public art guidelines for San Francisco's new downtown plan. "If Richard Fleischner, Michael Heizer, Isamu Noguchi, and Scott Burton indicate a movement in public art—the art is the plaza, garden, or landscape—the landscape architects may find themselves in the wings," she wrote.

While the overlap is not as great for planners, they are also likely to experience conflict as artists and arts administrators become more involved in community planning. "Cultural planning," for example, seems to be a growth area today (although the seed was planted years ago by the late Harvey Perloff). Yet Chicago's recent cultural plan wasn't prepared by a planner; nor is a new one being done for Lowell, Massachusetts. . . .

It's clear from recent grant lists that the NEA has fallen hard for "planning." Projects range from a plan for a "unifying art element" along a Baltimore street by sculptor Martin Puryear to a streetscape plan for Cleveland's warehouse district by Seattle artist Buster Simpson. In St. Paul, the NEA has helped fund a program that grants year-long fellowships to artists to work with planners, architects, and engineers under the aegis of the city's Department of Planning and Economic Development.

Yet to be seen is whether the artist-planners can translate their often idiosyncratic style into a field that requires a high degree of cooperation—and whether they can deal with the inevitable bureaucracy. Rather than encouraging artists to do planning, some suggest, we should be encouraging planners to become more knowledgeable about art in public spaces and about the needs of artists.

Rob Wilkinson of Seattle, who himself bridges the gap between planner and art consultant, suggests that planners have a real advantage in their skill at dealing with the complexities of permitting. "Artists are becoming more and more dependent on people who can help them over these hurdles," he says.

Wilkinson developed an interest in public art as a community planner for the University of Washington; many of the small towns he worked with saw public art as a way to improve their downtowns, he says. About four years ago, Wilkinson and a partner started Art on File, a mail-order slide library specializing in architecture, urban design, and public art. He also consults with communities that are setting up percent-for-art programs.

Planners are in a unique position to put some

balance back into public art, says Ronald Fleming, a consultant in Cambridge, Massachusetts, and a frequent critic of NEA's Art in Public Places Program, which he feels often ignores the views of the public. Fleming has devised an environmental profiling technique for communities to use in evaluating a public space, and he suggests that planners are the ideal leaders of such a process, starting with an "awareness walk" to get an idea of the texture of the place.

To bring them up to speed on public art, Fleming proposes local and national charettes, organized, he suggests, by APA. "Planners are constructive, pragmatic types," he says, "and they're more likely than arts administrators to recognize that the public has certain rights in public art." In short, says Fleming, planners understand context, and that makes them the best advocates for public space.

Ruth Knack is the senior editor of Planning.

Planning Issues: Parcels and Panoramas

One of the earliest discoveries of the practicing planner is the intimate connection between the large and the small. Controversies involving the rezoning of a parcel or two of land often turn out to be inescapably related to broader issues of race and class, suburbanization and density, amenities, and national and regional real estate trends. And the process works equally smoothly in reverse. National transportation, environmental, and housing policies have direct impacts on dozens of local land uses. For this reason, the reader will find a loose unity in the following chapter, which combines a detailed examination of a decade of land-use litigation with a parallel exploration of demographic trends, offers a brief excursion into a massive regional dilemma, and attempts to assess planning past and future.

If there is one truism in planning, it is that the dust never settles. New programs, funding and staff changes, and political turnover all assure a degree of turbulence in most planning jurisdictions. One of the exceptions to this rule used to be local land-use planning. Zoning and rezoning, subdivision control, and appeals for variances and special exceptions seemed to be relative constants in an unsettled universe. While the waters were roiled by fair-share housing litigation in the 1970s and 80s, the impact was limited to a handful of states where activist courts intervened in land-use arrangements that had the effect of excluding poor and minorities from suburbs.

That's no longer true. Now, all across the nation, local land-use issues involve just as much turmoil as other aspects of planning—as the article on the U.S. Supreme Court's 1987 landmark planning decisions makes clear.

PROPERTY RIGHTS AND EQUITY

Over the years, *Planning* magazine has published landmark articles on the controversies relating to alleged inequities in land-use planning. Prominent examples include the contributions by Donald Hagman and John Costonis. Real estate activity has historically been the source of more American millionaires than any other sector of the economy. Hence Hagman's discussion of windfalls and wipeouts is not only timely but is also timeless. What is increasingly clear is that in an age of exponential litigation, apparent governmental discrimination on behalf of one landowner or group of landowners to the detriment of others presents us with operational problems as well as profound legal questions concerning the nature of fairness. Hagman offers legally defensible solutions to these dilemmas, ranging from transfer of development rights to transfer taxes and compensable regulation.

In "A New Approach to the Taking Issue," John Costonis offers schematic proof of the spectacular financial benefits that could accrue from government constraints on land-use intensity. Approval of a zoning change that would allow a site to be used for a hotel was worth $4 million to the lucky landowner, while relegation to wetlands conservancy resulted in a loss of $75,000. Costonis stresses the need to offer modest remedies in order to provide "fair compensation" to afflicted landowners, and he recommends that existing tools of governance be expanded accordingly.

As it happened, these two articles, written in the 1970s, foreshadowed a storm that broke in the late 1980s. In 1987, the U.S. Supreme Court took on two cases involving California court decisions concerning the taking of private property without just compensation to the owners. In one California case, concerning a church-owned campground that was devastated by fire and flood, the Court overturned a county government ruling that held that the site should remain an undeveloped floodplain. In the second case, the Court struck down a California Coastal Commission ruling pertaining to public access to the shoreline across private property.

In "Takings Stir Up a Storm," Robert Guskind predicts that the two decisions will lead to more careful drafting of land-use regulations, to a corollary need for more and better lawyers—and serious legal challenges to increasingly popular linkage programs. The latter are likely to undergo closer scrutiny to prove a direct connection between the proposed development and requirements for day care centers, low-income housing, or other public purposes that the linkage programs are set up to foster. Indeed, the entire area of development exactions, one of the hottest planning fields of the 1980s, may be open to legal challenge.

GROWING DEMOGRAPHIC CHALLENGE

Planners are familiar with the cow-in-the-python population model used to explain the baby-boom generation born between 1946 and 1962. The baby boomers started by overcrowding the hospitals and nurseries and proceeded to impose enormous demands on schools and colleges and thence—decade by decade—to exert pressures on the job and housing markets. The next act in the drama will be a boom in retirement homes and geriatric care and finally, presumably, increasing demand for well-located grave sites in conveniently located cemeteries.

Within this vast tidal sweep of population change are a number of sectoral changes of considerable import to planners. Sylvia Lewis summarizes key trends in "Changing Times." In addition to substantial growth in the numbers and proportion of the elderly, there are significant gains in the immigrant population, largely of Oriental and Hispanic extraction, and a decline in family size linked to divorce and rising female employment. Also linked to this situation is a growing, and thus far mainly unsatisfied, demand for acceptable and affordable day care, and for heightened attention to children's well-being, including environments that increase the chances for better health and improved learning.

Lewis reminds us that these are not women's issues but rather challenges that have a major impact on the functioning of communities and the economy. She also suggests that problems are not geographically movable; they cannot easily be transferred someplace else no matter how much a community may yearn for its poor, high-service-level populations to go away. The reasons are clear enough: Most elderly people age in place, and most broken families lack the incomes to move to the suburbs. Foreign immigrant populations may be a partial exception, although there is little consolation for troubled cities in the fact that upwardly mobile Asians do not linger in the slums because they quickly earn enough to move to the suburban communities that offer safer environments and better schools for their children.

Other facets of suburbanization are considered by Ruth Eckdish Knack, whose "Once and Future Suburb" points to a startling diversity in the communities that fall under the general rubric of suburbs. While many older suburbs face the kind of poverty, slum, and tax base problems that confront central cities, newer communities are developing into employment and commercial centers surrounded by varying combinations of low-to-high density residential development. The less fortunate towns can be seriously afflicted: Just over a fourth of U.S. poverty families live in suburbs, including a sprinkling tucked away in the more affluent communities.

Knack includes a discussion of the communities beyond the traditional suburbs—in the catchall territory generally termed exurbia. With the massive suburban growth of employment, those in search of low-cost housing have moved out to "suburbs of suburbs." In planning terms, infill has again been displaced by leapfrogging.

In "Take Me Home, Country Roads," John Herbers offers convincing evidence that the "new heartland" or "countrified cities" outside metropolitan areas account for a sizable proportion of urban development, especially in the nation's fastest growing counties. Densities are extremely low, and the new, high-income population is expensive to service. The good news is that most of the development is taking place on marginal rather than prime farmland. The bad news is that serious planning is poor or virtualy nonexistent because the growth sprawls across numerous jurisdictions, many of them ill-equipped to deal with the new

Two signs of change in the the suburbs: racial mix (top) and an abandoned shopping center. See ''The Once and Future Suburb.'' Photos: Brent Jones.

Yesterday's immigrants, like these Hungarians arriving at Ellis Island around 1910, were likely to be European; today an increasing proportion comes from other continents. See ''Changing Times.'' Photo: National Park Service.

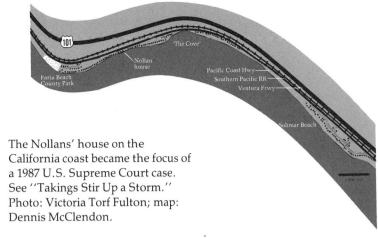

The Nollans' house on the
California coast became the focus of
a 1987 U.S. Supreme Court case.
See ''Takings Stir Up a Storm.''
Photo: Victoria Torf Fulton; map:
Dennis McClendon.

Rural and semi-rural
areas like Idaho's
northern panhandle
(left) and Boyne City,
Michigan (above), have
become magnets for
city people seeking
land and privacy. See
''Take Me Home,
Country Roads.''
Photos: David Frazier
(left) and R. Randolph
Frykberg.

challenges. One limited response has been the creation of special districts to provide needed services. In some regions, the states have entered the picture, but overall, Herbers suggests, the prospect seems to be for more of the same formless communities, temporarily (and only barely) slowed by various kinds of development moratoriums or growth management initiatives.

In an earlier article, "The Future of Nonmetropolitan America," Niles Hansen underscored the trend toward the expansion of "urban fields," zones that he defined as lying about a two-hour drive from a large central city. He also reminded us (as Herbers does, 14 years later) that poor people often get the worst of it when more affluent migrants take over. There is, in fact, an inescapable parallel between the impact on the poor of gentrification in cities and in the gentry invading semirural slums and near-slum areas.

Hansen took up a topic that rarely receives attention in a profession oriented toward cities and suburbs, the plight of the rural poor. Some economic improvement is taking place in a few rural counties thanks to "industrial filtering"—plants moving to outlying areas—and, implicitly, through outmigration of the poor coupled with inmigration of the prosperous. But in a prescient passage, Hansen raised the possibility of industrial filtering "spreading to foreign countries rather than major lagging regions of the United States," leaving the U.S. as a service and professional center with much of its low-end manufacturing relocated abroad.

THE POPPERS' PROPOSAL

Most Americans (planners included) have grown up with a romantic image of intrepid pioneers in covered wagons turning vast areas of the virtually uninhabited Great Plains into productive farms. With the help of substantial federal crop subsidies, costly demand irrigation projects, and outright welfare, a small population in this huge region has hung on through recurring droughts, killer blizzards, locusts, dust storms, and overgrazing. In the face of a generally disastrous public and private policy, Deborah Epstein Popper and Frank Popper in "The Great Plains: From Dust to Dust" point to a modest success: In the 1930s, 7.3 million acres of largely abandoned farms were purchased for "national grasslands." Rising commodity prices and a shortlived energy boom resulted in a brief period of buoyancy, only to be followed in the 1980s with

"a deep depression" in the region's farm, ranch, and mineral economies. The aquifers have been depleted, soil erosion is spreading, and the nation is in no mood for big new irrigation projects. Further, the rise in temperatures caused by the greenhouse effect points to worse disasters ahead. Since depopulation is already well under way, the Poppers offer a simple solution: Deprivatize much or most of the region and turn it back into grassland, a huge "national commons" for wild life, hunting, and other recreation. The Poppers have a name for it: Buffalo Commons.

They also point to the likelihood of resistance to the proposal from private landowners and other vested interests. They were right: After the magazine article appeared in 1987, a Billings, Montana, newspaper responded to the proposal with amused outrage, calling for the Poppers' home state of New Jersey to be converted into a paved parking lot and for Frank Popper to be stuffed, mounted, and presented to the Smithsonian Institution as an artifact.

It is conceivable that the recommendation would have met with less resistance had Popper done what he proposed a decade earlier in "We've Got to Dig Deeper into Who Owns Our Land." In that article, Popper examined a number of ownership surveys and discovered a surprising amount of concentration in large holdings, especially in rural areas. If such is the case in the Great Plains, then buying out a relative handful of landowners to create the Buffalo Commons might not be such a pipedream after all.

REAGAN AND BEYOND

In "Living with Hard Realities," an aptly named article on economic policy, Richard Nathan points out that our current era of government retrenchment in domestic affairs predates President Reagan. The sea change in U.S. politics occurred with Reagan's huge budget deficits, which forced liberals to expend their energies on forestalling further cuts rather than on advancing new initiatives. Nathan faults Reagan government policy (which he traces back to the Carter administration) for neglecting the immobile poor in distressed areas (particularly in older cities), on the false supposition that they can pick up and move and for concluding that place-oriented programs like the Economic Development Administration are ineffective. Nathan's remedy? A variety of federal initiatives focused on human resources, including schools, health, and job training. The need is especially urgent, he says, because states and cities have not managed, and cannot manage, to fill the chasm created by severe federal cutbacks. Perhaps it is no accident that elements of enhanced federal human resource programs emerged in both parties during the 1988 presidential election.

One of the hallmarks of President Johnson's Great Society was the creation of the U.S. Department of Housing and Urban Development. Symbolically, it was a major achievement: Not only did HUD represent a broad national commitment to confronting urban problems, but Robert Weaver, its director, was the first black to be appointed to a cabinet position. Subsequently HUD, like other Johnson initiatives, ran into stormy weather.

William Fulton took stock in 1985, two decades after HUD's creation. As noted in "HUD at 20 Faces a Midlife Crisis," he found a profoundly troubled agency, low on the federal totem pole, with genuine agency achievements in housing and renewal obscured by an unending barrage of criticism. Further, the deep Reagan cuts in HUD's budget seemed to indicate that the agency lacks effective constituencies to defend its interests. Fulton sees the 1968 Housing Act, with its establishment of the Section 235 and 236 subsidy programs, as the agency's high point, but the escalation of the Vietnam War quickly moved domestic reform programs to the back burner. President Nixon surprised many of his liberal detractors by supporting the urban programs he had inherited and even launching a new initiative, the ill-fated "Operation Breakthrough," which focused on manufactured housing and market aggregation as the surest road to cutting the cost of shelter.

The turning point in federal policy came in 1973, with the Nixon impoundment of domestic funds and the appointment of an enthusiastic budget cutter as HUD administrator. But the cut did not mean that there was no progress in the Nixon years. While the wobbly Model Cities and New Communities programs and Operation Breakthrough were terminated, the Community Development Block Grant program was initiated, and the Section 8 program produced a substantial amount of new housing. Similarly, the Carter administration's record was mixed (but mostly negative): Urban Development Action Grants (UDAG) came in, but the heralded major initiative, a national urban policy, proved farcical. Overall, (as a preview of things to come in the 1990s), Fulton reminds us that the Carter administration was so fearful of budget deficits that it resisted any new initiatives that seemed to require significant expenditure.

Reagan's policy toward HUD, Fulton says, is "to ignore it," except as a handy source of budget cuts. The few new ideas proposed by the Heritage Foundation and other conservative think tanks proved abortive. HUD staff has shrunk; funding is down by 70 percent in the Reagan years, and block grants have diminished. Overall, the Reagan record is one of abdication, but Fulton underscores the fact that many of the cities and states have managed to fill part of the gap with their own resources of money and skills. And the recent rescue of UDAG from the Reagan budget cutters suggests that the constituency for HUD efforts has not entirely disappeared.

The last article in the chapter is my own vision of things to come, "A Nod to the Nineties." Not surprisingly, I foresee more of the same ahead: tight budgets and a need for local and state resourcefulness (including relatively small amounts of funds) to fill the gap left by a diminished federal presence. One aspect of this effort would be to package effective planning as a fundamental element in responding to current imperatives. In the 1990s, effective planning is likely to take the form of economic development, although other targets of opportunity may appear if we have spectacular collapses of bridges or other newsworthy crises.

While planners are no longer in peril as an endangered species threatened by budget extinction, they still have to be exceedingly careful about activities that seem to threaten established social values. (Such confrontations may well include efforts to extend fair share housing.) The article also underscores a conclusion I have stressed elsewhere, the recognition that most planning is performed on a small, incremental scale, with rare opportunities to engage in large programs with soaring objectives. Moreover, to achieve substantial progress, planners are likely to need a crash course in business techniques, including the mysteries of spread sheets and business plans.

The article also touches briefly on another legacy of the pre-Reagan and Reagan years, the sorry consequences of two decades of denigrating federal bureaucrats. To planners, this means that an activist administration will have to replace lost talent at HUD and other relevant agencies or devise bypass mechanisms such as task forces or new agencies.

Finally, as we look forward to the new decade, we take comfort in one basic change in the political landscape, the maturation of the nation. By this I do not refer to the aging of the baby boomers. I suggest that we—planners, politicians, media, and business—have progressed toward a state of adulthood in which self-delusion gives way to confrontation with reality. As professed problem solvers, planners in past years often faced attacks from interests that believe, sincerely or otherwise, that the problems we identify are exaggerated and that our proposed solutions are absurd or dangerous. In an era when business journals and planning journals use the same sober language, we can discuss and even argue substance without rancor, at least much of the time. In such an era—the New Realism, I call it—planners have a special responsibility to ensure that the needs of the poor and other urgent priorities will not be forgotten.

Melvin R. Levin, AICP
Professor of Urban Studies and Planning
University of Maryland, College Park

A New Deal: Trading Windfalls for Wipeouts

Donald G. Hagman
(September 1974)

Suppose we want to make a tradeoff in real estate ventures. We want to use windfall profits to offset the losses of those who get wiped out by government or community action related to land deals. We already have asked ourselves two questions: Should real estate owners be allowed to keep increases in land values they have not earned themselves? Likewise, should society be able to impose losses on real estate owners without paying damages? To both questions we have answered, No.

Consider Jones, who is none too bright. Exercising no particular investment savvy, he buys a parcel of land in 1965 for $5,000. It is zoned for single-family use. Today he sells it for $500,000 because a transit station for a new subway line has been opened on adjacent property or the property has been zoned for 100-story skyscrapers. Without lifting a finger, Jones has a $495,000 windfall.

In this case, government caused the windfall by building the transit station or by rezoning. But if the transit system has been built previously, Jones may have had the same windfall. And the rezoning, while necessary to Jones's windfall, was not sufficient. Property can be rezoned for more intensive use and not enjoy any windfall unless there is market demand for that use.

Thus, while one can conceptually separate windfalls caused by government from those caused by the community, they are very hard to disentangle and measure. Nevertheless, since Jones's windfall was not caused by Jones, it may not be unfair to make him share it. Windfall, then, is a real increase in the value of real estate, except that primarily caused by the owner.

Jones could have been less fortunate. His $5,000 parcel might now be worth $5 because the city acquired adjacent land for a garbage dump, or because adjacent property was zoned for 100-story high-rise buildings, or because Jones's property was downzoned into a conservation or historic area. The market value of Jones's property, located between a garbage dump and a highrise, is $5.

This time Jones suffered a wipeout. Wipeouts are the opposite of windfalls. Should government or the community be able to wipe out Jones without paying any compensation? In fairness, perhaps he should be paid.

Why the sudden interest?

I note a quickening of interest these days in the ageless windfalls and wipeouts problem. It is not because governmental development is suddenly creating windfalls and wipeouts, since government development activity has slowed down from its pace of the 1950s and 1960s. Also, fewer wipeouts result lately from the externalities of governmental development because what does occur is being done more sensitively as a result of the National Environmental Policy Act of 1969 (NEPA) and similar laws.

Some increased interest stems from changes in attitude. Society now feels somewhat more strongly that windfall profits from speculation in land is wrong and that something should be done about it. Still, wipeouts of unprecedented magnitude and frequency result from governmental regulation that is being upheld by the courts. If this were 1964, there would be no NEPA—that workhorse for delay and obfuscation—nor any state environmental policy acts. We would not have celebrated NEPA's first birthday with the Clean Air Amendments of 1970, which permits the air pollution fraternity to control land use with implementation plans for transportation and indirect sources. Under the Clean Air Act, development can hardly occur where air is bad. But then it can hardly occur where air is good, either, due to the nondegradation rule. The water pollution types, too, muscled in on land-use control under the Water Pollution Control Act Amendments of 1972. That act has powerful effects on location and hence on land use by prohibiting point source discharge any worse than the best attainable, by moratoria on sewer connections where governmental sewage disposal plants are not providing secondary treatment, and by reliance on land-use plans and controls to eliminate the nonpoint sources of pollution. Meanwhile, HUD slipped through the Flood Disaster Protection Act of 1973, as close to federal zoning of flood plains as one could come. Indeed, it's high time that HUD, always a source of succor for traditional land-use planners and controllers, got a piece of the environmental action.

I call all these acts the quiet federalization of land-use controls, a process far more revolutionary than the resumption of control powers by state and regional bodies. This is not to say state and regional bodies have been quiescent. Tough state and regional controls have been enacted, many now financially assisted by another important federal statute, the Coastal Zone Management Act of 1972. These acts apply from sea to polluted sea.

The various states also have enabled or required localities to get tougher. Since the beginning of the 1970s, for example, California has required every city and county to have a general plan that must have several provisions, including one on open space. These plans must be complete by a statutorily set date, and there must be zoning and open space zoning and subdivision control. The controls, as well as the construction of capital improvements, must be consistent with the plans.

Localities, too, have been using traditional controls in a tough new way. St. Petersburg, Florida, has attempted to outdo Boca Raton's "cap" by fixing a population limit less than the number of people already in the city. In Petaluma, California,

with a building permit quota system, tough new regulations are ubiquitous. Mention Ramapo, Fairfax County, and dozens of other local governments across the nation and planners smile while developers frown.

Obsequious to environmentalism, and made bold by public policy arguments for limiting growth, the courts generally have upheld tough new regulations that emanate from all levels and subdepartments of government. This spring, the U.S. Supreme Court upheld the right of a municipality to limit the number of unrelated persons living in each household in a single-family zone.

The effect of all these tough regulations is a paralyzing mishmash. Windfalls and wipeouts abound, but the market is so confused with the numerous signals that it doesn't know how to react.

Recapturing windfalls and mitigating wipeouts

So who cares that windfalls and wipeouts abound? I care, because I believe that the public considers a planning system that ignores the windfall and wipeout problem to be inequitable, and no planning system so perceived can survive. Second, this is bad planning.

Consider the experiences of Australia, England, and New Zealand.

Australia's Commission of Inquiry into Land Tenures, headed by jurist R. Else-Mitchell, in its first report in November 1973, noted that witnesses identified the "lottery" aspect of planning as one of its major defects. Australians apparently conclude that the public, not private individuals, should benefit from increases in value from rezoning or other development permissions. They also conclude the public should bear the costs of reductions in value resulting from planning decisions.

Second, the Australians say, whenever there is a prospect of private profit or loss from planning decisions, planning tends to be done in secret—and that can lead to corruption of the sort common in this country. Third, since permissions to develop are scarce, when a landowner obtains one he is in a quasi-monopoly position and can be expected to seek monopoly profits, thus increasing land costs.

Fourth, the Australians ask, as Henry George did in this country: Why should the community put in facilities that increase land values at its own expense and let landowners in the area capture the increased value? Surely the Australian observations are valid issues here, too.

Winston Churchill had similar ideas more than 50 years ago. A landlord, he said, can do nothing and still watch his land increase in value. Roads are built, services improved, water piped in, and the land value improves. The greater the population in the surrounding area, the higher the profit. In fact, the more the city does to improve houses and streets, the more it must pay to buy the land of the landlord who has done nothing.

In New Zealand, J. Pope wrote in 1970 that the New Zealand Town and Country Planning Act 1943, S. 44, requires compensation for downzoning. He then asked a good question: Why not charge for rezoning for more intensive uses? Pope said such a charge would prevent speculators from sitting on their planning permissions, would provide funds to replace reserve fund contributions such as dedications and exactions on development permissions, and might provide general funds. He also observed that industrial users could be exempt from charges for betterment recapture. No doubt this suggestion stems from a keen desire to industrialize New Zealand, but such a tax expenditure subsidy could be used for other purposes—for example, to lower land costs for low-income housing.

To these observations about windfalls and wipeouts, I add my own:

• The environmental movement will soon be dead. Environmentalists cannot expect a long-term, healthy movement unless they address the wipeout problem. Increasingly, developers are fighting bankruptcy.

• Members of the real estate industry are unduly interested in public service. The real estate industry should be represented on planning bodies. Society needs their expertise. But too many are there with private interests in public clothing.

• There is no planning. Exhausted by resolving neighborhood squabbles over windfalls and wipeouts, planning bodies have no time to deal with the larger public interest—theoretically the duty our public planning bodies are paid to do.

• Plan-making invites its own destruction. A city plans and zones some areas for intensive development, others for less intensive use. It places infrastructure accordingly. As a result, land prices are lower in the area scheduled for less intensive use. Meanwhile, the multiple family developer reaps his windfall after obtaining a rezoning.

• Sprawl abounds. There is never enough money to acquire property for open space use. It

is usually impossible, either politically or constitutionally, to regulate it so severely that no use is permitted. The compromise is regulation for unintensive use, a euphemism for sprawl.

• Horsetrading is the order of the day, especially in windfall recapture devices in cottage industries. They might be called exactions on development permission and are subject to considerable haggling between developers and planning bodies that confer development permissions. Often the amount of the exaction depends on what the traffic will bear, whether the developer is a resident or an outsider, the relative state of the local government fisc this month, and the growth or nongrowth proclivities of the body currently in power.

Methods for recapturing windfalls have been used in the U.S. to recoup public capital costs associated with private development. If public infrastructure is financed entirely by the community at large, the property receiving the benefit of that infrastructure reaps a windfall. By imposing the cost on the development, the windfall is reduced. Five windfall recapture techniques of this sort have evolved in this century.

Until the Depression, the special assessment was the most heavily used windfall recapture device. In 1913, Los Angeles, Kansas City, Portland, and Oakland derived over 20 percent of their revenues from special assessments. Nationwide, cities derived about seven percent of their revenues from special assessments in 1930. In 1971, they produced $598 million in revenue for state and local governments.

There is nothing inherent in the special assessment that limits it to its usual role of recapturing costs of local improvements. Nothing precludes its use for recapturing benefits conferred by general improvements. Special assessments could be used to finance fixed-rail mass transit, or freeways, or oversized sewers.

During the development splurge following World War II, the special assessment was still under a shroud of disfavor, and local government increasingly insisted on the dedication and improvement of public facilities as a condition for final acceptance of subdivisions. Such exactions are windfall recapture devices. No aspect of subdivision law is as heavily litigated, with developers resisting strenuously as communities continually shrink the subsidy to private development. In 1949, the landmark case of *Ayres v. City of Los Angeles* established that developers could even be required to dedicate and improve lands where a considerable portion of the benefit accrued to the general public.

The next method for imposing costs on new development came when communities realized that in some cases fees in lieu of dedication and improvement would be appropriate. In a sense, this was more like a special assessment, but paid in advance.

By the mid-1960s, municipalities had discovered that the exactions that worked so well on subdivision permissions also could be used with variances, conditional use permits, rezonings, even building permits. Dedication, improvement, and fees in lieu of them were imposed as conditions on other types of permissions. Needless to say, dedication and improvement exactions on subdivision approval is still novel in some parts of the country. On the other hand, the increasing use of these devices is hardly novel in Western countries.

The most recent step in the evolution that began with special assessments is less well known than the earlier steps. In the mid-1960s, cities and developers of subdivisions in California bargained to reach an agreement on the relative shares of the infrastructure to be provided by subdividers and the community. The agreement, changing almost yearly, took the form of a statute that the lobbyists for the two groups had been able to exact from the legislature. Similar statutes existed in almost every state, though cities generally evaded them. The statutes told the cities what they could ask for in exactions for approving subdivisions, but the laws did not say that subdivisions had to be approved. Often a developer either did what the city said or took his subdivision elsewhere. Some cities, however, sought to opt out of the pesky agreement set up by the statute by inventing what I call development taxes.

In one of the most obscure yet significant land-use cases of the 1970s, the Associated Home Builders of Greater East Bay took on the city of Newark, California, on its development tax and lost. California Government Code §37101 permitted cities to license businesses, and the Newark ordinance put a tax on the business of constructing housing units based on the number of bedrooms in each unit. The tax had to be paid before the building permit was issued, and the fees received were to go into a capital outlay fund. The city had argued that residents require greater fire and police protec-

tion and street use than commercial and industrial buildings do.

The decision might well represent the proposition that revenues from the license tax are general revenues and could be used for any purpose. If the business of constructing dwellings can be licensed, so can the business of subdividing, the tax being measured by the number of lots, for example. The case might stand for the proposition that all public costs associated with the new development can be loaded on the development itself. Perhaps it even means that, if the property with a development permission is worth more than it was without the development permission, the tax can reach the amount of the increase. In effect, the license tax could constitute a buy-in fee to existing community infrastructure. The Newark scheme has swept California. And as California goes in city planning control, so goes the nation.

But not yet. Arizona cities got wind of the California practice. Tempe collected $400,000 before the Arizona Supreme Court held the tax was invalid. Nevada cities and developers entered into one of those statutory agreements over the use of the new device. Having won in the trial courts in Florida, developers there are now girding for legal battles over the technique in the appellate courts.

The Australians knew about the English act. In 1970 the state of New South Wales adopted an unearned increment tax in designated areas that were declared capable of development. Enacted to provide funds to pay for infrastructure built by the community, and to hold down land prices, the act became unpopular even with the Liberals, the more conservative party, which had secured its adoption, and it was repealed late in 1973.

One would be hard put to classify a transfer tax, a sales tax on land transactions, as a windfall recapture device. Traditionally, the tax is imposed whether or not the property sold has increased in value since its acquisition. Nevertheless, transfer taxes are a potential source of revenue, used in all Western countries. In Florida, a 0.3 per cent tax resulted in revenues of $88.5 million in 1972. While that amount included transfer taxes on other property as well, it does not appear to have included Florida's typical $.55/$500 of consideration tax the federal government used to impose. Now abandoned, it has been picked up by states and localities. A New York State tax at that rate produced $6.8 million in 1972.

If enforced, the transfer tax can be made difficult to evade by preventing transfer of title until the tax is paid. And if the tax is limited to increases in value, the result might be a hybrid law such as the unearned land value transfer tax law proposed this year in a California bill.

Whoever is interested in windfall recapture must at some point acknowledge a debt to Henry George. His ideas about the right of the community to increased land value have made the land value taxation movement potent for reform. Yet while many accept the concept of the community's right to at least some part of the increment, land value taxation wins few converts.

Windfalls, however, have generated less interest lately than wipeouts. There are only a few ways of avoiding wipeouts in this country, partly because courts have traditionally invalidated land use regulations that excessively depress land values. Invalidation of governmental action is less important for avoiding wipeouts than other, positive, methods.

Compensable regulations are one way to avoid wipeouts. Land-use regulations in the U.S. are either held valid or invalid. There may be a need for a middle course under which severe regulations can be upheld if some compensation is paid. Other Western countries are more generous than are governments in the United States in compensating for wipeouts from regulation. In England, for example, if a planning permission is revoked or modified before building operations are complete, the developer can claim damages for construction expenses and for loss or damage attributable to the change.

Unlike special assessments, capital gains taxes are not usually considered windfall recapture devices. Capital gains are taxed because they are income. But a capital gains tax, when it is heavier on real estate than on other capital assets, also can be a windfall recapture device. The English Conservative party said in 1967 that a special capital gains tax on land is the best way of recapturing betterment. But it dallied when it came to power and failed to enact such a tax before it lost in this spring's elections.

Vermont's Land Gains Tax, effective May 1, 1973, became the first capital gains tax on land to be adopted in a Western country. Motivated primarily by the desire to discourage speculation and development by out-of-state residents, the tax also was touted as a windfall recapture device that would raise funds to permit lower taxation on open space lands, though as enacted the gains tax instead funds homeowner property tax relief.

A similar tax, the New Zealand Property Speculation Tax Act of 1973, was aimed at curbing land speculation. And as of April 9, 1974, a lien was put on all property sold in the Province of Ontario, Canada, pending passage of a 50 percent land speculation tax. The legislation is motivated by rising land costs partly resulting from land speculation.

It appears that the ideas for these four capital gains taxes on land were not exported from one jurisdiction to another. They arose spontaneously. That they did suggests the tax idea is well worth watching as a windfall recapture device.

Betterment levies or unearned increment taxes differ from capital gains taxes in one major respect: the tax is imposed not because the gain is income but because the increment is unearned. It belongs to the community because the community created the increment. Further, the grant of development permission or the start of development, as well as a sale or transfer, may be a taxable event. These betterment recapture devices date back to the 1909 Housing Act, regarded as the first English planning law. The concept was exported to other Western countries, save the United States. But the other countries did not have early capital gains taxes, and some still do not. The capital gains tax in this country thus might be a surrogate for betterment recapture.

Returning to power in 1964, England's Labor government implemented a new experiment for recapturing betterment, the 1947 experiment in nationalization of development rights having been ended by the Conservative government. The Land Commission Act of 1967 created a 40 percent betterment levy. But the commission created by the act was empowered to acquire land by compulsory purchase, and that feature of the act was its undoing, for the conservatives repealed it almost immediately upon resuming power in 1971.

The U.S. law is clear

In the United States, the law is black or white. Either the developer has or has not a vested right. If vested, the development can be completed. If the right has not vested, the developer's losses are not covered by government. Compensation is also payable in England if planning permission is refused or made conditional for development within the concept of existing use. A landowner has no right to maintain an existing use in the United States. An existing use can be made nonconforming and can eventually be terminated without compensation.

The American Law Institute's Model Land Development Code, finally nearing completion, has provisions for compensable regulation. A California bill introduced in April provides for payment for losses in property values due to a rollback in zoning. Compensation is limited to the amount of the previous year's property taxes.

Nuisance law is another vehicle for encouraging neighborliness. Landowners can be forced to mitigate wipeouts through damage payments. However, nuisance law has not evolved much since society gave public land-use controls monopoly over externalities.

Even the king has been found to do wrong. Particularly in airport cases, governmental activity has been ruled a nuisance because of noise. The English, though, have taken the most outstanding step toward encouraging neighborliness by governmental land users and developers. Under the Land Compensation Act 1973, the governmental builder of public works is made liable for effects such as noise, vibration, smell, fumes, smoke, and artificial lighting. The landowner can recover for damages to property merely located near the public improvement.

To use windfalls for eliminating wipeouts, one or more of the windfall recapture methods could be coupled with one or more of the wipeout mitigation methods. Both methods could be used simultaneously.

The transfer development rights (TDR) concept is new and indigenously American . . . The basic idea is that a landowner whose development right on land is restricted can nevertheless be permitted to use that development right on other land that can be developed beyond what ordinarily would be permitted. Alternatively, the landowner may be permitted to sell the development right to someone else who can then develop other land to an intensity beyond what is ordinarily permitted. The landowner's wipeout is mitigated either by permitting him a windfall on other land or by permitting him to sell the development rights that have been taken. At first glance it seems the scheme will not work unless the demand for land is greater than the supply. Therefore, supply will likely have to be constrained by public land-use controls.

TDRs have been authorized and used in New York City, but a trial court decision on their use was not favorable. They also have been authorized for use in Los Angeles. The number of areas considering TDR use are now legion.

Zoning by eminent domain is also a windfall-wipeout device as American as TDR. It is almost 60 years old and may be ready for a comeback. Minnesota has had a statute that permits zoning by eminent domain since 1915. The concept might be more fully called Zoning by Special Assessment Funded Eminent Domain, ZSAFED, a more descriptive acronym than TDR.

ZSAFED is based on the assumption that, when some land is restricted and suffers a wipeout, other land somewhere enjoys an offsetting windfall. This happens because demand for land utilization is not affected by a change in the location of usable land. Demand merely seeks a supply elsewhere. Assume A and B each own half of an unzoned island. It is decided to zone A's land for agriculture and B's land for urban development. That decision represents the use of a zoning concept, but not zoning itself, as police power, since the right to develop A's land for anything but agricultural uses is taken by eminent domain. As a result of the taking, A's land is damaged. But since B's land is benefited by the taking because the demand for urban development has now been shunted there, B is specially assessed up to the amount of benefits received. The resulting funds are used to pay off A's damages. Windfalls for wipeouts.

In conclusion, I offer a revised version of a story told by Robert Merriam, chairman of the Advisory Commission on Intergovernmental Relations.

A small bird was walking along a road across the cold steppes of Russia. Along came a horse and dropped a huge pile all over the bird. You might think it was a wipeout, but the bird was warmed and also had the windfall of a long-term food supply. The bird began chirping happily. A cat heard the chirping, peeled off the windfall, and wiped out the bird.

There are three morals to this story: First, he who externalizes on you is not necessarily doing you a disfavor. Second, he who removes the externality is not necessarily doing you a favor. Third, if you're full of externalities, don't chirp about it.

The late Donald G. Hagman was professor of law at the University of California at Los Angeles.

A New Approach to the Taking Issue

John J. Costonis
(January 1976)

Although it is hardly the subject of television talk shows, the taking issue has enjoyed a sudden popularity that land-use professionals no doubt find flattering. But the popularity of the issue also exposes the fraternity to the charge of harboring what Alfred North Whitehead called "inert ideas . . ., ideas that are merely received into the mind without being utilized or tested or thrown into fresh combinations." Learned discussion of the taking issue abounds with precious distinctions that, because they retain little or no cutting edge, can only puzzle the public.

Consider the premise that the only tools for dealing with the taking issue are the police and eminent domain powers. Most professionals assume that land-use measures must fall under one or the other rubric. Valid police power measures, they say, advance the public health, safety, and general welfare—and too bad for the landlords. But tradition and the courts have convinced the fraternity that measures that go too far in restricting private land use are acceptable only under the eminent domain power. Regrettably, certain features of eminent domain put it beyond reach as a feasible land-use tool in all but rare instances. For example, compensation must be keyed to the restricted land's highest and best use (fair market value), which leads to extravagant awards. Compensation must be paid in dollars, of which there are relatively few in public fiscs these days. Further, in most states awards may be determined only by a condemnation jury working under limits adopted in earlier Populist times to curb abusive use of eminent domain by railroads and other powerful groups.

Contenders in the debate about the taking issue pursue it to one of two predetermined outcomes. Those committed to more vigorous public governance strain to enlarge the police power at the expense of eminent domain. Some even say that, whatever its private economic consequences, emi-

nent domain should no longer function as a constraint on other wise commendable public regulation. Opponents of this argument make similarly broad claims for private landowners, urging that government should pay for the right to regulate (that is, to use eminent domain) whenever it encroaches on their supposed rights.

So pursued, the debate is unprincipled, coming down to little more than you pays (or don't pay) your penny and you takes your pick. As in all such arguments, the proposed solutions are stilted. Police power advocates, for example, give short shrift to compelling legal, equity, and political considerations. Despite deft legal arguments for extending police power, confiscation remains a stumbling block to ambitious public governance. Witness the spate of recent decisions in New York, Virginia, and California invalidating landmark, environmental, and open space preservation measures based on the police power. As Donald Hagman has noted, the ethics of wiping out a few private landowners to benefit the many are troublesome at best. Besides, it is politically naive to push for an indiscriminate police power approach. Even assuming—which I do not—that this approach is legal and ethical, it does not face up to the political realities surrounding land use. Whether we speak of landmark attrition in Chicago, the Vermont legislature's refusal to approve a state land-use plan, or congressional neglect in failing to pass a national land-use bill, the result is the same. Systems that ignore possible financial costs to politically powerful groups will have little chance of practical success.

Fans of eminent domain also have problems. Their real purpose is to bump government as the dominant force in land-use regulation and to substitute the private market. Updating Adam Smith, William Blackstone, and John Locke, they advance a bloated view of private property rights and indict public governance as being bungling and antisocial. With private choice their king, they are mute before Ada Louise Huxtable's charge that "if there were no other way than to let sound business practice take its course, there would be little hope for the urban environment." But this fey conception of private rights bluntly ignores the fact that the dollar value of private land often derives from public regulation, public capital improvements, and general community growth. That value does not result from man's having seized property from the state of nature and invested it with the fruits of his own labor.

In short, it is futile to try to resolve the taking issue by relying exclusively on police power and eminent domain. The real estate community pronounces eminent domain as the sole antidote to stern public governance. This course is impractical and inappropriate, since it virtually guarantees that judges and legislatures instead will opt for the police power, even when its use is blatantly unfair. Environmentalists and advocates of strong central planning, on the other hand, mistakenly applaud sweeping expansion of the police power. Dramatic victories in the courts or legislatures are all very well; but, to have any decent chance of success, programs must respond to the legitimate concerns of all interested groups, particularly those with the political clout of the real estate community.

Administrators, courts, and legislatures, too, are in a bind. Officials on the firing line, be their mission protection of landmarks, coastal areas, or open space, do battle with failing weapons. Not surprisingly, they seldom prevail against competing market or political pressures. Similarly, courts are struck with an inferior choice. Either they must sustain land-use restrictions and ignore their potential or actual unfairness, or they must invalidate the restrictions altogether, forcing government to use the eminent domain extreme. While the courts are leaning toward accepting police power restrictions, it is less because of a new mood in land use than because of choosing the lesser of two evils. Hence the inelegance, if not downright confusion, of judical efforts to fix the point at which the two powers diverge. Meanwhile the legislatures sit on their duffs, doing little to relieve the agony of courts and administrators by prescribing useful criteria for fixing that point or devising creative measures and modes by which fair compensation might be afforded. . . .

The two horns

In law as in life it sometimes helps to step back from a dilemma to ask whether it has been created artificially by its premises. In examining the taking dilemma, one can see that the premises underpinning the current debate inevitably torpedo a fair, practical solution. One premise holds that government can use only the police power or eminent domain in adopting specific land-use measures. The other premise holds that compensation must be made in dollars and measured by the highest and best use of the land.

The source of the taking dilemma, in short, is that the type of regulation now causing all the fuss cannot be handled adequately under the two existing powers. Common sense suggests, however, that the framework for public governance be enlarged to include a third power and that a different kind of compensation be devised to be used with it. Hence my proposal for the "accommodation power" and its sidekick, "fair compensation."

The accommodation power would join with, but not displace, the police power and the power of eminent domain. Accommodation would be unnecessary when government's pursuit of health, safety, and general welfare does not impinge unfairly on private property owners. Nor would it come into play when government acquires private land outright for public works. But accommodation would be required in borderline cases—where stringent regulation is needed to protect community values but would be likely to be neither fair nor effective if imposed without some compensation.

How might legislatures define borderline cases, and how might courts identify them? The scope of the accommodation power might be illustrated by a model showing the varying levels of development potential in a private parcel. Consider a parcel subject to wetlands protective zoning.

SPECTRUM OF LAND-USE INTENSITY

Intensity	Use	Value
Highest and best use unrestricted by public regulation	Hotel	$4,000,000
Allowable use	Single-family housing, 10 dwelling units per acre	1,000,000
Reasonable beneficial use	Single-family housing, 2 dwelling units per acre	200,000
Resource protection use	Wetlands conservancy (aquacultural uses only)	−75,000
Zero-intensity use		−50,000

Increasing Development Potential →

The first and last categories, highest and best use unrestricted by public regulation and zero-intensity use, need little explanation. The first is simply the use promising the greatest dollar return from an unregulated parcel. Zero-intensity use allows no use at all. It would represent a negative return, because the owner must pay real estate taxes and the other carrying costs of land ownership. Few commentators seriously urge that landowners are entitled legally to the first category. And only the most rabid police power enthusiasts would insist that, absent some severe threat to community welfare, government can deprive a property owner of the entire development potential of his land without compensation.

An example of the resource protection use category is the wetlands conservancy: tight land-use controls, typically adopted to protect environmental amenities. But two qualifications are needed. First, this category is plotted below the reasonable beneficial use category on the table only for illustration. In some cases, resource protection could permit a greater economic return than that possible under reasonable beneficial use. A negative value is assigned to resource protection use on the table to reflect both the private land's carrying costs and possible costs from adapting the land for the uses permitted under the conservancy designation. Second, this category may apply to measures serving such ends as growth management, nonconforming-use amortization, or airport zoning, which are environmental only in the broadest sense.

The allowable use category denotes a level of development potential that is substantially more liberal than necessary to prevail against a court challenge charging unfair confiscation. In fact, the vast majority of private land is zoned this way in the United States today. Accordingly, it usually corresponds to what, in eminent domain terminology, is the standard of "highest and best use under existing land-use controls." (Eminent domain doctrine further provides that, if the condemnee can show that more favorable zoning of his land is "reasonably probable," he must be compensated for this additional increment of development potential. Thus his award would fall somewhere between the allowable use and the highest and best use unrestricted by public regulation.)

The reasonable beneficial use category is most important here because it defines the border line between measures that are sustainable under the police power and those that must rely on the accommodation power. This category implies suffi-

cient economic return on private land to escape invalidation on confiscation grounds. Behind the category lies the premise that land-use controls can bar a parcel's most profitable use without being confiscatory if the controls allow the landowner a reasonable economic return.

Land-use controls may be enacted under the police power if they permit an intensity of use that equals or is greater than that prescribed by reasonable beneficial use. If the permitted intensity is less, government must use the accommodation power. Accordingly, as the table indicates, accommodation, not police power, would be the proper tool, because the economic return possible under resource protection falls below that plotted for the parcel's reasonable beneficial use. When such discrepancies occur, government would have two options. If it lacks the wherewithal for fair compensation, it must liberalize the challenged restriction. But, in doing so, it need allocate only enough additional density to satisfy the reasonable beneficial use standard. If it has the resources and wants to save the measure, it must provide fair compensation.

Money not needed

What, then, is "fair compensation"? Basically, it is a device that splits the difference between the absence of compensation under the police power and eminent domain's "just compensation." Based on reasonable beneficial use, compensation should fall substantially below the highest and best use while also honoring the property owner's legitimate claim to fair treatment. Second, compensation need not be made only in dollars. It may take the form of any marketworthy alternative whose dollar value can be determined reasonably through accepted appraisal methods.

The first of these differences, which is quite straightforward, is the subject of Section 5–303(5) of the American Law Institute's Model Land Development Code. This provides for the valuation of condemned property, not at its highest and best use, but at the level of "minimum development necessary to eliminate the unconstitutional taking." But the code fails to explain how to defend legally a valuation measure that is at odds with the constitutionally compelled standard of highest and best use. The fair compensation and accommodation power concepts advanced here afford a legal rationale for this deviation.

The idea that compensation need not be made in dollars, however, may raise some eyebrows. Underlying this concept is a premise ignored by both sides in the taking debate. As allocator and frequent creator of lucrative private development opportunities, government has various non-dollar but marketworthy alternatives that it can and should use to compensate those who would otherwise be wiped out by strict regulations. The premise is two-edged. It rejects the argument that the lack of public dollars justifies private wipeouts. If government can prevent wipeouts, it should do so. The premise also rejects the contention that only the landowner has an economic stake in his land.

To the extent that these expectancies are publicly authored, they should not be immune to some degree of recoupment if recoupment provides government with the resources to deal fairly with true wipeout situations.

Given the idea that compensation need not be made in dollars, is it likely to be accepted? At first, no. The real estate community undoubtedly will applaud compensation but vilify recoupment. The reverse is true for the environmentalists. Nonetheless, I am confident that the premise will eventually catch on, if it hasn't already. The ironies of the nation's land-use quandary ought to prove to both sides that they cannot have it all one way. The question they should ponder is whether their interests are better served by their polarized positions or by an approach such as the one offered here that splits the difference between the extremes favored by each.

How might the proposal offered here work in practice? It is working already through devices such as zoning bonuses and nonconforming-use amortizations that lighten the burden of stringent public measures by offering the landowner economic tradeoffs. The developer who provides a plaza or galleria with his building receives in return additional density in the form of a zoning bonus. The landowner required to remove his billboard need do so only after he has recouped his investment, a period moreover during which he enjoys a governmentally created monopoly.

A more elaborate example of the use of the accommodation power and the fair compensation concept is contained in the Puerto Rican Plan, a proposal which Robert DeVoy and I prepared in 1974 on behalf of the Conservation Trust of Puerto Rico and which is now under consideration by the Puerto Rico Planning Board. In the plan, the transferable development rights (TDR) technique is used to protect Puerto Rico's environmentally sensitive areas. The plan is a three-step undertaking that involves (1) designation and regulation of these areas, referred to as protected environmental zones (PEZs); (2) designation of transfer districts in which development rights originating in the PEZs may be sold to create an environmental trust fund; and (3) compensation from the fund for meritorious claimants in the PEZs.

The accommodation power comes into play in the plan's requirement that the commonwealth compensate PEZ landowners who demonstrate their inability to enjoy a reasonable beneficial use return under the PEZ (resource protection use in the table). The fair compensation concept is reflected on two levels. First, compensation payable under the plan is keyed to the difference, if any, between the reasonable beneficial use and PEZ returns. It is not tied to highest and best use. Second, although meritorious PEZ claims are paid in dollars, these dollars in turn derive from the sale in a transfer district of their equivalent in development rights. That government can properly compensate in marketworthy development opportunities, as well as in dollars, is therefore acknowledged indirectly. The plan contrasts in this respect with other TDR schemes, such as the New York City and the proposed Chicago landmark preservation programs, which authorize compensation in the form of development rights alone.

Enlarging the framework of public governance by adding the accommodation power to existing tools raises a bevy of questions of its own. When does regulation bar a reasonable beneficial use return in specific cases? What are the appropriate roles of legislatures, courts, and administrative bodies in using accommodation power? Will planning—heretofore focused on controlling physical development—be distorted if it is used deliberately to address fiscal questions as well? Do planners have the knowledge and public officials the integrity and perseverance to manage such governance? Difficult questions all, and disagreements on their proper resolution are inevitable. Less subject to doubt is the need to break free of the altogether too narrow police power/eminent domain merry-go-round. This is an imperative first step in strengthening public governance in the United States.

John J. Costonis is dean of the law school at Vanderbilt University. This essay is derived from a lengthier article, " 'Fair' Compensation and the Accommodation Power: Antidotes for the Taking Impasse in Land-Use Controversies," which appeared in the Columbia Law Review, *October 1975.*

Takings Stir Up a Storm

Robert Guskind
(September 1987)

When the U.S. Supreme Court decides to take on a land-use case—a rather rare event—the planning community definitely takes note. So it was no surprise that the High Court's two June rulings in California land-use cases have both public-sector planners and developers buzzing.

At first glance, the long-awaited decisions appeared to confirm the worst fears of planners and local officials, who saw them as severely hampering a range of practices from growth moratoriums to historic preservation efforts to development linkages that raise money for roads, low-income housing, day care, and dozens of other programs. Meanwhile, developers, property owners, and builders were reported to be "dancing in the streets" because they saw new openings for lawsuits challenging state and local regulations.

But now that both the initial fears and the euphoria are fading, it's clear that there is less to the rulings than first thought. Neither ruling is a sweeping legal judgment on the planning tools used nationwide to control development.

Key in both cases was the constitutional question of how far government regulation of property can go before running afoul of the Fifth Amendment to the Constitution, which prohibits the "taking" of private property without "just compensation" to its owners. While the high court defined several important nuances, it neither altered governmental authority to regulate land use nor eased the difficult test of proving that a regulation has actually gone "too far" and "taken" property.

In *First English Evangelical Lutheran Church of Glendale v. County of Los Angeles* (107 S.Ct. 2378), the Supreme Court ruled June 9, by a vote of six to three, that if a zoning ordinance prevents "all use" of property, the government must compensate the owners

for the loss—contrary to the California practice of limiting the remedy to an order overturning the offending regulation. Significantly, Justice William Rehnquist, who wrote the majority opinion, noted that damages apply to temporary prohibitions on use.

Two weeks later, in a decision that received minimal public attention because it was announced the same day as the retirement of Associate Justice Lewis F. Powell, the high court struck down a California requirement that property owners allow public access along beaches in return for building permits. Such permit conditions, the Court ruled in a five-to-four-vote in *Nollan v. California Coastal Commission* (107 S.Ct. 3141), must be directly related to the burden created by the development in question. California's regulations did not meet that standard, they found.

Much ado about nothing?

According to Brian Blaesser, a land-use attorney with Siemon, Larson, Mattlin & Purdy in Chicago, the "heightened reaction" to the two cases has not been merited. "These decisions don't end the ability of local government to devise and implement sophisticated regulations," says Blaesser. "It remains within their grasp to fashion responses to the opinions without having to go backwards in time to an earlier era of less sophisticated regulations."

Gus Bauman, litigation counsel for the National Association of Home Builders, takes a similarly low-key view. "Some people seem to believe that public treasuries are about to be raided" by property owners who will now automatically win damage suits against state and local governments. "That's simply not going to happen," says Bauman, who has been active on behalf of property owners in many of the land-use cases that have reached the federal judiciary.

That's not to say that the Supreme Court decisions won't exact a toll on land-use regulations. At a minimum, most legal and planning experts agree that until further litigation clarifies the issues the *First English* and *Nollan* rulings raised but did not fully answer, their psychological impact is bound to inhibit state and local governments. "The power relationships between the community and the developers are more equalized than they were before," says Donald Connors, an attorney with Choate, Hall & Stewart in Boston, who represents both local governments and developers. "And that will have profound implications for land use."

The issues raised in both decisions have already been introduced into pending lawsuits in at least two states, California and New York. There are likely to be other results, too. Many experts are predicting that local governments will rely more heavily on the advice of planners and consultants to ensure that their regulations stay within the bounds of both court decisions. Linkages and exactions will be more closely scrutinized to make sure they are clearly related to a project's impact. And the decisions may encourage greater use of such techniques as transfer of development rights and cluster development that allow some use of property.

The fallout will not be felt equally around the nation, though, since many state courts already adhere to the principles the high court set out in the two decisions. California, where both cases originated, will be hardest hit because it has not only some of the nation's most stringent land-use requirements but also a body of state law that favors local governments on takings issues. Metropolitan areas experiencing rapid growth will have to make the most changes because burgeoning areas tend to apply building moratoriums and to impose exactions on developers.

There are also glimmerings in both cases of a gradual shift in philosophy on the Court. Some observers think the justices will view land-use regulation more skeptically when they hear new cases—as these decisions all but guarantee they will. The Court "is turning more towards property rights," says Robert Best, a lawyer with the Sacramento-based Pacific Legal Foundation, which has assisted lawsuits brought by developers and owners. Recent rulings indicate the Court "is concerned that governmental entities have been overstepping constitutional bounds in regulating property rights," Best adds. If the Court takes on a more conservative tenor with the confirmation of U.S. Court of Appeals Judge Robert Bork as its new associate justice, that balance could shift decisively.

To planners in Los Angeles County, the issue that ultimately sparked the *First English* litigation was simple: Since 1957, the church had owned a 21-acre campground for handicapped children in an area of the Angeles National Forest that was prone to floods. In 1977 a forest fire destroyed some 3,860 acres of vegetation upstream, and early

the next year a rainstorm caused severe flooding, destroying the campground's buildings and killing 10 people in the area.

In response, citing the "public health and safety," the county moved to restrict development with a temporary ordinance declaring the area a floodplain and banning new construction or reconstruction of buildings. Later, when the measure was adopted permanently, the county qualified its restriction, saying some structures could be rebuilt in the flood protection area if they met a strict building code. While the new regulations meant the church could build—within limits—on the campground site, it did not do so.

Instead, the church continued its suit, claiming that the temporary ordinance denied it all use of its property and that it was entitled to compensation from the county for its loss. The California courts ruled against the church, citing a 1979 California Supreme Court decision in *Agins v. Tiburon* (upheld in 1980 by the U.S. Supreme Court on procedural grounds). The *Agins* decision limited the remedies available to property owners to a court order overturning unconstitutional land-use regulations.

Ultimately, the U.S. Supreme Court rejected the California court's reasoning that "the need for preserving a degree of freedom in the land-use planning function" mitigated against money damages. Chief Justice Rehnquist wrote that the Court was "not unmindful of these considerations," but that they did not relieve government of the burden of compensating owners who lose "all use" of their property.

The Court assumed that the church's allegation that it had lost all use of its property was true and noted that the holding in this case did not pertain to "the quite different questions that would arise in the case of normal delays in obtaining building permits, changes in zoning ordinances, variances, and the like." The case was sent back to California for an eventual state court ruling on whether the floodplain ordinance is an unconstitutional taking.

The ruling also embraced the 1981 dissent of Justice William Brennan in *San Diego Gas & Electric Co. v. City of San Diego,* another case in which the majority refused to rule on the substantive issues involved. Brennan, in a dissent that was used by many lower courts as a guidepost to what the high court's position would be when it finally reached a decision in a land-use case, had argued forcefully for the "temporary taking" concept and for damage awards. His opinion posed a now well-known question: "After all, if a policeman must know the Constitution, why not a planner?"

Placing bets

Does the *First English* ruling mean a new wave of lawsuits and court findings that land-use regulations are "takings" of property? Probably not, say most legal experts. "As long as the threshold for finding a taking remains as high as it has been," says attorney Jerold S. Kayden, a lecturer in real estate at the Harvard University Graduate School of Design, the issue of compensation will arise in "relatively few cases."

While legal precedents vary, state courts—which handle the vast majority of land-use cases—generally require an owner to show a complete deprivation of the use of property before finding a taking. In fact, the decision might lead to even fewer damage awards, writes William Fulton in the July issue of *California Planning & Development Report.* "With financial compensation at stake," says Fulton, "judges will be very reluctant to find that a taking has occurred as the result of a zoning ordinance."

"If the Court had come to a new definition and found that removing 50 percent or 60 percent of the value of property was a taking there might have been some problems," says Terrence E. Moore, executive director of the New Jersey Pinelands Commission, a state agency that oversees strict land-use controls on more than a million acres of environmentally sensitive land. Relying on New Jersey case law, the commission allows transfer of development rights, sale of property to a state land bank, and other mechanisms that have generally allowed it to steer clear of the takings controversy. "Agencies that have total restrictions on use were probably susceptible to this kind of decision anyway," Moore believes. "It's quite clear you can't come in and say that you can't do anything at all on that 1,000 acres you own."

While such obstacles will limit *First English's* impact on the vast majority of down-zonings and historic preservation efforts, growth control measures such as building moratoriums or annual building limits could come under attack if courts apply the new "temporary takings" rule in those cases. "The most extreme forms of growth management are at risk," says Douglas R. Porter, director of development policy research at the Urban Land Institute in Washington. "But even moratoriums will still be possible because generally they are declarations of emergency for a short period of time."

Measures designed to halt growth while infrastructure planning studies are under way or to allow time for added sewage capacity—all related to public health and safety—are probably least vulnerable. "If it's a one-year moratorium to do a certain kind of planning, it's probably not a problem and it might hold up for an even longer period," says Porter. He cautions, however, that communities that keep development bans in place "year after year after year" will face "more risk every year the restriction is in place."

Wetlands and environmental protection measures will also be prone to litigation. In New York's six-million-acre Adirondack Park, property owners subject to regulations enacted in 1973 are planning new damage suits over density limits in some areas that limit construction to one building per 47 acres. While the litigation isn't welcome, officials are relatively confident their regulations will pass constitutional muster. "Public perception is a factor, but as a strictly legal matter these cases are not a big deal," says Adirondack Park Authority counsel Robert Glennon. "An owner still has to prove the only possible use for his land is more buildings. How the hell is anybody going to prove that?"

On the beach

If the *First English* decision is the equivalent of a blunt instrument whose uses are somewhat unclear, the *Nollan* ruling is likely to have immediate and well-defined effects.

The case grew out of a large-scale planning effort, endorsed by California voters when they passed the Coastal Act in 1972. The ballot measure produced a coastal plan, detailed land-use regulations, permit conditions—and the California Coastal Commission, which regulates development along the 1,000-mile-long coastline. Since then, the commission's efforts to increase public access to the coast and restrict commercial and residential development have led to frequent political clashes and much litigation.

It is against this background that Patrick and Marilyn Nollan applied for a permit to tear down a beachfront bungalow in an unincorporated part of Ventura County and replace it with a two-story house. Before granting the building permit, the coastal commission required the owners to file a deed allowing the public to cross their beach (generally, shorelines are publicly owned up to the high tide line, while the beach beyond is privately owned). The Nollans took the commission to court, contending the state wanted to take part of their property without compensation.

In court, the coastal commission argued that the permit condition eased access between public parks and beaches north and south of the Nollan home and that such conditions were necessary because coastal development was creating "a wall separating the people of California from the state's tidelands." In fact, thousands of other coastal property owners had agreed to similar conditions. When the California courts upheld the requirement as being "reasonably related" to state planning objectives, the Nollans appealed to the Supreme Court.

The high court rejected the coastal commission's reasoning that allowing public passage across the Nollans' beach would help break down the "psychological barrier" caused by coastal development that blocks views of the shore. The beach access requirement, wrote Justice Antonin Scalia, did not directly address the problem of construction obscuring the shoreline.

"The building restriction is not a valid regulation of land use but an out-and-out plan of extortion," Scalia wrote. "The commission may well be right that [public access] is a good idea" and "is free to advance its 'comprehensive program,' if it wishes, by using its power of eminent domain." But, "if it wants an easement across the Nollans' property," he wrote, "it must pay for it."

Justice William Brennan dissented, arguing that the majority was insisting on "a precise accounting system" that is "insensitive to the fact that increasing intensity of development in many areas calls for farsighted comprehensive planning."

In broad legal terms, the *Nollan* decision works "a radical change" in the way courts will view development conditions in the future, says Boston attorney Donald Connors. And it could become a major problem for officials around the nation.

"*Nollan* says that the courts should use a higher level of scrutiny than that which land-use lawyers have assumed for the last 50 years should be employed," says Jerold Kayden. The Court said regulations "must 'substantially advance' the legitimate state interest. Everyone had thought that it was

sufficient for the regulations to be 'conceivably related' or to 'reasonably advance' that interest."

"Linkages used to be limited only by the imagination of government officials," says the home builders' attorney, Gus Bauman. "Now there's an outer limit."

Will some of the more creative linkage programs hold up in court? What about San Francisco's requirement of day care facilities in new office buildings or developer contributions of $1 per square foot to a child care fund? Or Boston's low-income housing linkages?

Such arrangements may very will prevail, but the *Nollan* decision also means more cities will be conducting detailed studies such as the one San Francisco did to prove the "nexus" (close tie) between its $5-per-square-foot transit impact fee on new developments and the additional demands those buildings make on the city transit system. The arrangement was recently deemed legal by California's courts.

"Linkage programs are at the outer extreme of the exaction process in terms of what is demanded and how directly connected it is to the development," says ULI's Douglas Porter. "Developers will continue to negotiate deals based on business judgment, but there will be more questions about unrelated conditions." Particularly vulnerable, many believe, are requirements of contributions to off-site projects or to special funds that collect money from hundreds of developers.

The reliance on impact studies, says Bill Fulton, will result in "green eyeshade planning" practiced by "a new cadre of planners-slash-accountants conducting statistical studies to find these direct links."

It's no accident that so many crucial land-use cases have percolated up to the federal judiciary from California. Since the 1970s, California voters and officials have enacted progressively stricter land-use regulations, growth controls, and development conditions. More than 100 California towns have passed measures to restrict growth; even Los Angeles, which may have invented the concept of urban sprawl, last year limited construction in residential neighborhoods.

Pushed by Proposition 13, which requires a public vote to lift a cap on property tax increases, California also has led the nation in imposing wide-ranging linkage fees and exactions that shift more of the cost of funding government services and programs to developers.

"Politically, development has been the safest target," says the Pacific Legal Foundation's Robert Best, but that may change. The Supreme Court decisions "have unsettled a lot of California land-use law," he adds. "We are facing an era where the courts will be reconsidering previously settled cases."

There are many unknowns. Chief among them is California's Supreme Court, which took on a decidedly more conservative tone after voters deposed Chief Justice Rose Bird, an avowed liberal, last November. The new Chief Justice, Malcolm Lucas, appointed by Republican Gov. George Deukmejian, will have a major role in shaping the future of California land-use law.

Already, the California Coastal Commission is reassessing its permit requirements, although it has not yet decided how it will respond to *Nollan.* San Francisco Mayor Dianne Feinstein cited the *First English* decision in rejecting a five-block construction moratorium passed by the Board of Supervisors. For its part, the Pacific Legal Foundation is now scouring the state for a growth moratorium, or perhaps an annual building cap, that it can challenge under the *First English* "temporary takings" doctrine.

These California issues highlight the dilemma governments around the country will continue to grapple with. "Local governments must accommodate growth while at the same time preserving their community's character and must do it all without much federal revenue," says Chicago attorney Brian Blaesser. "So they're looking to those perceived to have deeper pockets. It's difficult to fashion mechanisms that don't raise the question of whose ox is being gored."

The greatest irony of all for the California conservatives who have supported this generation of property rights litigation may be the political and fiscal pressures the *Nollan* ruling will set in motion. Even without the new impediments to linkage and development fee programs, support has been building to scrap Proposition 13.

If those pressures intensify now that alternative development arrangements are open to new attack, the conservatives' most treasured achievement—which spawned the nationwide tax revolt of the late 1970s and early 1980s—could be the first victim. And just as the spirit of Proposition 13 spread

across the nation, tax limitations coast-to-coast could begin to unravel in the years to come.

Robert Guskind is a contributing editor of Planning.

Changing Times
Sylvia Lewis
(September 1985)

Let me introduce you to my neighborhood—census tract 2413 in the city of Chicago. While older and poorer than most of the U.S., this neighborhood shows, in miniature, where the country is and where it may be heading. On my block alone, we have an immigrant Vietnamese family, couples with new babies, single parents, a three-generation family presided over by a widowed grandmother, and several households consisting of adults who are more than friends but less than spouses. Down the street sit 41 units of newly built Section 8 family housing, and around the corner in both directions are a nursing home and a high rise for the elderly.

Investors looking at this area see a gentrifying inner-city neighborhood filled with old mansions and brick bungalows, while demographers and planners might note the high proportion of elderly residents, the immigrants, and the working women and single-parent families. These three groups seem to be growing in number and importance nationwide, as well as in my neighborhood.

The elderly

To put the elderly in perspective, consider that the membership of the American Association of Retired Persons is 15 million—700 times larger than the membership of the American Planning Association. Further, the number of individuals 65 and over is growing—from seven percent of the population in 1940 to 12 percent in 1984—and, if recent trends continue, reaching 17 percent by the year 2020.

Still, the key for planners is not the sheer volume of those over 65 but the fact that elderly people are part of the community and likely to remain so. Only five percent live in nursing homes, while another five percent a year move to a new community. Most of the rest stay put in the towns and cities (even the very houses) they occupied in middle age.

Retirement communities, subsidized housing for the elderly, and "life-care" communities house relatively few of our elderly citizens. Even Sun City, Arizona, the largest of the retirement communities, and one that is fully developed, has a population of less than 50,000. Federally assisted housing shelters only eight percent of all elderly households—a total of 1.5 million people. And life-care communities (where large initial fees are paid to guarantee long-term health care) house 150,000 individuals.

Further, all three options are likely to remain limited. Experts on the topic say Sun City may be the last giant of its kind. Most life-care facilities are so expensive that only a quarter of the 28 million elderly could afford them. And, according to Aaron Rose, national director of retirement centers for the accounting firm of Laventhol and Horwath, of these seven million, only 10 percent would be likely to choose this type of housing even if enough were available. At the moment, Rose says, there are 600 to 700 of the communities, with the largest concentration around Philadelphia, where 27 facilities offer 6,600 housing units at entrance fees ranging from $15,000 to $160,000.

Finally, subsidized housing for the elderly has been taking some knocks, despite its popularity in local communities. HUD last February proposed a two-year moratorium on funds for Section 202—the only federal housing program exclusively for the elderly and handicapped. The agency suggested to Congress that money already in the pipeline from previous years be spent on Section 202 units and that no new funds be appropriated for fiscal years 1986 and 1987.

Congress balked. At the end of July, when budget issues were still being debated, congressional committees agreed that Section 202 should be funded at approximately the FY 1985 level of $600 million. HUD estimates that 14,000 units will be built under the program in FY 1985, which ends September 30.

Meanwhile, it should be noted that Section 202 is a small potato compared to other assisted housing programs. It has built 100,000 units for the elderly (all sponsored by nonprofit organizations), whereas Section 8 has created 800,000 elderly units and public housing funds, 650,000.

Among the elderly, homeownership is by far the most common living arrangement: 75 percent own their own homes. Phyllis Myers, a senior associate at the Conservation Foundation, calls this tendency of the elderly to stay put "aging in place"—which is also the name of a 1982 report she wrote that looks at ways to help keep the elderly in their familiar neighborhoods. . . .

"Even in the best of times, before we cut back on assisted housing, advocacy groups took the position that there was a vast unmet need for assisted housing for the elderly," Myers says. "But we shouldn't jump to the conclusion that the elderly want to live that way."

In a survey done for the report, Myers and her colleagues found that 80 percent of the older people interviewed had been in the same residence for 18 years and overwhelmingly indicated that they wanted to stay. "They were attached to their neighborhood, though they wanted it to improve," she says.

Leo Baldwin, coordinator of special projects for the American Association of Retired Persons, agrees. "We're seeing projections that 90 percent of the elderly population won't get into specialized housing," he says. "They'll continue to live in the community, just as when they were younger." What the elderly want, he says, is independence, security, and permanence. "At 70, you're not looking to move again at 75."

Many of the innovative programs planners have been discussing for the last few years are, in fact, aimed at allowing the elderly to age in place. That is true of accessory apartments, granny flats, shared housing, and home equity conversion, to name some techniques that have gained currency. . . .

Meanwhile, interesting programs are cropping up to help the elderly in other ways. All of the profits from the Pennsylvania state lottery are earmarked for programs that benefit people over 65 and with less than $15,000 family income. Among those benefits: partial funding of nursing home care; free rides on public transit; discounts on prescription drugs; property tax and rent rebates. The tax and rent rebates are also available to younger widowed and disabled people who meet age and income guidelines.

Between 1972, when lottery sales began, and mid-1985, the Pennsylvania state lottery made over $6 billion in sales and spent over $2 billion on programs for the elderly. The tax and rent rebate programs alone cost over $1 billion.

In New Jersey, with an elderly population of 922,000 (about 12 percent of the total), a condominium conversion law allows elderly and disabled renters to remain in place. The state has also experimented with home repair and weatherization programs, a granny flat demonstration, and reverse annuity mortgages, which allow the elderly to borrow against the equity in their houses.

Barbara Parkoff, a specialist on living environments for the New Jersey Division on Aging, has been involved in many of these projects and now is helping to set up the New Jersey Shared Housing Association, which she says may be the first incorporated association of its sort in the U.S. Programs that match up unrelated adults who want to share housing now exist in 11 of the state's 21 counties.

Still, a lot remains to be done to accommodate the elderly. Here are some of the issues, as outlined by the U.S. Senate Special Committee on Aging:

• Older women are more numerous and more likely to be living alone than older men. Seven out of every 10 women over 75 are widowed but only three out of 10 men are. Nearly half of the women live alone, while only one in five of the men do so.

• The elderly are concentrated geographically. At the time of the 1980 census, nearly half the elderly in the U.S. lived in just eight states. Florida had the highest percentage (17 percent) and Alaska the lowest (three percent).

• Almost two-thirds of the elderly lived in metropolitan areas in 1980, but for the first time, more than half of them lived in suburbs instead of central cities.

• Overall, the elderly are not as poor as they were in 1960, but poverty is unevenly distributed among them. In 1982, about eight percent of elderly white men lived in poverty, defined as $4,775 or less for an individual living alone. The rate was twice as high for white women, four times as high for black men, and five times as high for black women.

• Younger people have misconceptions about the elderly. According to a survey conducted by the National Council on the Aging in 1981, younger people perceive the problems of the elderly to be more severe than the elderly themselves do. For example, nearly half of the younger people thought that the elderly have serious problems with poor

housing, whereas only five percent of the elderly felt that way.

• On the other hand, the elderly do, in fact, have problems. One in six said they did not have enough money to live on, and one in seven said they could not find transportation to stores and basic services.

This last point is the flip side of helping the elderly to age in place. As Leo Baldwin of AARP notes, "What we're seeing is a need not only for diverse housing, but for diverse services that people can reach easily." Among the needs he cites: neighborhood activity centers, perhaps including health monitoring services. He suggests that surplus schools would be perfect in this role.

As they become more numerous, the elderly are exerting more political muscle, with unusual results in some places. Everyone expects special retirement communities to have age restrictions, but now at least one non-retirement community has established a special zoning district that favors the elderly. Mesa, Arizona, this year passed a provision allowing an "age overlay zone," and surrounding Maricopa County has allowed such zones since 1979. If all the owners in such a district agree, they can prohibit children under 18 and require that each household contain at least one adult aged 50 or over. Dwelling units that don't meet the requirements are considered to be nonconforming occupancies.

To date, the city has received six applications for overlay zones and approved two, both in mobile home subdivisions—one with about 100 units, the other 1,200. Mesa's planning director, Wayne Balmer, is sure that more applications are on the way because many of the city's 25,000 elderly (11 percent of the total population) are concentrated in areas with deed restrictions that are the same as the city's requirements for overlay zones. The city is also trying to annex two retirement areas that were granted overlay zones by the county.

Balmer notes that such discriminatory zoning may be difficult to enforce if the city has to determine the age of individual homeowners and if city officials don't make it clear up front that they intend to follow their ordinance to the letter.

"At this point," says Balmer, "we're suggesting that people put age restrictions in their deeds. That makes them responsible for enforcement and gives them parallel protection if the ordinance is overturned."

Families

One day, it's possible that historians looking back at the twentieth century will take note of all our medical and social advances and conclude that the change in the lives of women was the single most important change of all. Not only are women marrying later and having fewer children than their mothers and grandmothers, but they also are working outside the home in much greater numbers than their predecessors did. In 1940, one in four women over the age of 16 (and one in six married women) were in the labor force. By 1984, a majority of women were working.

In 1960, only one in five mothers of children under six years worked; by 1984, a majority did so. Further, the U.S. Bureau of the Census predicts that 60 percent of women will be in the labor force by 1995.

Increasingly, women are shifting for themselves—or for themselves and their children. Divorce rates rose from 47 to 114 per 1,000 married individuals between 1970 and 1982, and the growth of single-parent families has been remarkable. According to the Census Bureau, the vast majority (88 percent) of single-parent families with children under 18 are headed by women. Women headed one in five families with children in 1970; within 12 years, the proportion had nearly doubled. In black families with children, nearly one of every two is maintained by the mother alone. Arthur Norton, a Census Bureau demographer, was quoted in *American Demographics* magazine to the effect that three of every five children born in 1983 will live with only one parent at least part of their lives before reaching the age of 18.

"Clearly these changes in the composition of the labor force pose a challenge to many basic planning assumptions," says Eugenie Birch, associate professor in the urban affairs department of Hunter College in New York City. At the APA conference in Montreal last spring, she outlined some of the questions planners are now asking:

- What problems have land-use patterns and transportation systems created for American workers?
- How can neighborhoods and communities be organized to relieve these problems?
- Should Euclidean zoning (separating residential, commercial, and industrial uses) be broken down?

- Can investments be redirected toward neighborhoods so that more jobs are available there?
- Should neighborhoods have a range of housing types of varying cost? . . .

Experts say that high-quality child care is the working mother's single most important need, though they also point out that the demand for affordable child care still far outpaces the supply. As one measure of need, the Census Bureau notes that 36 percent of mothers of young children who are not working and have an income of less than $15,000 would look for work if child care were affordable.

In a recent report on women's employment needs, the League of Women Voters fixes the blame for lack of affordable child care on the federal government, noting that recent budget cuts have squeezed 150,000 children out of subsidized child-care programs. "In 1983, more than 23 million children in the U.S. required day- or after-school care," says the League. "Federal support in meeting this demand has been grossly inadequate and continues to decline. . . . The federal government seems sadly out of step with radically changing needs."

The Child Welfare League (a national children's advocacy group) takes a less strident tone in condemning federal cutbacks, noting that "the diminishing supply of adequate day care is a major problem," but the group also estimates that by 1990, the number of preschool children with working mothers will reach 10 million (up from 7.5 million in 1980).

Meanwhile, private, for-profit child-care services are prospering. There are, for example, 900 Kinder-Care Learning Centers in the U.S. and Canada, serving 95,000 children. Officials of the 16-year-old company have been quoted as saying that their industry has just scratched the surface because for-profit child-care providers serve less than one-fifth of all children under the age of five.

Employers also offer child-care services, either on site or by giving cash payments or vouchers to employees. According to a report published this summer by the Conference Board (a business research association in New York), more than 1,800 companies nationwide offer their employees some help with child care. Still, the report says that for working families, child care is the fourth largest budget item, after food, housing, and taxes. At a cost of $3,000 per year per child, child-care expenses typically eat up 10 percent of a family's budget.

What can cities do to make sure that affordable child care is available? For one thing, they can make child care a zoning consideration. Several speakers at last spring's APA conference pointed out that many zoning ordinances fail to distinguish between small and large child-care facilities, requiring special permits even for small, home-based centers serving fewer than seven children.

Edith Netter, assistant director of the Boston Redevelopment Authority, suggested that such small centers be permitted as of right. "People can look at zoning as an obstacle," she said. "We've got to consider it as a means to achieve our policies." Netter also pointed out that some communities have successfully encouraged child-care facilities by giving floor-area bonuses to developers who provide on-site child care or by allowing child care in industrial space.

Tradeoffs are possible, too. San Francisco's new downtown plan, which was adopted in July, requires downtown developers to donate a square foot of day-care space for each 100 feet of office space in new or rehabbed buildings of over 50,000 square feet. Alternatively, they may make a cash contribution of one dollar per square foot of office space, to be used anywhere in the city. If downtown gains one million square feet of office space annually—the limit allowed under the new plan—the city could gain as much as 10,000 square feet of space for day care. Developers are under no obligation to run day-care centers, however; that function is being left to employers leasing space in the office buildings or to private day-care operators.

Beyond child care is a whole range of needs arising from changes in family patterns. For one thing, children have become a factor in planning. . . .

"Transitional housing" is a development worth noting. The term refers to multifamily dwellings that include shared spaces, usually for women and children who are in some sort of crisis situation and need more than temporary shelter. The usual stay is between six and 24 months. Joan Sprague, executive director of the Women's Institute for Housing and Economic Development in Boston, calls transitional housing a "bridge between emergency and permanent housing." It's appropriate, she says, for unwed pregnant teenagers and some of the elderly, handicapped, and drug-dependent.

Sprague's organization has helped set up transi-

tional housing in Massachusetts and elsewhere. And in a manual to be published this winter by the institute (179 South St., Boston, MA 02111), she cites over a dozen examples, ranging in size from a six-family residence to Warren Village near downtown Denver, which has room for 202 families. Two points of interest: transitional housing is more than a new-fangled boarding house, since the residents may share a variety of common spaces as well as life experiences. Further, the limited data on transitional housing suggest that it does help residents stand on their own feet.

A study of Warren Village conducted in 1981 showed that, while fewer than half the residents were employed when they first entered, 94 percent of those who had left were still working after two years. In addition, the number on public assistance dropped by 90 percent.

The two Warren Village complexes differ from some other examples of transitional housing in that they have no shared residential spaces. In addition, although the buildings are open only to single-parent families, parents of both sexes are welcome. Of interest to planners is the fact that Warren Village II is a planned unit development with commercial space (currently vacant) on the first floor. Child care and job training are provided on the site.

One caveat from Joan Sprague: Because neighborhood groups may object to transitional housing, it may be most feasible in marginal neighborhoods that are being redeveloped and "have a vision of a better future rather than vested interests."

Immigrants

Less numerous than either the elderly or working women, immigrants living in the U.S. may be the greatest "X factor" in America's demographic picture. First, no one knows exactly how many immigrants live here and how many more may arrive in the future. The Census Bureau estimates the current number at 14.1 million, but that figure does not account for all the illegal aliens—estimates of their number vary from three to 12 million. Second, the immigrants' presence here is partly determined by federal policy, making birth and death rates inaccurate predictors. Third, the ethnic mix of recent immigrants is changing. Since 1960, an increasing proportion comes from Asia and South America and a smaller proportion from Europe.

As noted in a 1982 Rand Corporation report, if the U.S. economy remains relatively strong and the population stable in number and advancing in age, there is every reason to expect that the U.S. will continue to act as a magnet for people living in countries where the opposite conditions apply.

In a telling statistic, the report noted that the average Mexican earns only one-seventh of what the average American earns. At the same time, the Mexican fertility rate is much higher than ours. So the U.S. can expect continued immigration from the south. According to the Census Bureau, more than a third of the 3.3 million immigrants who came here between 1975 and 1980 came from Latin America—more than half of those (726,000) from Mexico.

In other words, the U.S. population cannot be viewed in isolation. The Vietnam War, for example, sent over 200,000 Vietnamese to the U.S. Nine of every 10 Vietnamese immigrants living here in 1980 had arrived since 1975, as had 97 percent of all Laotian immigrants and three of every four Iranians.

Since 1921, when it first imposed immigration quotas, the U.S. government has always controlled the immigration picture. But besides the 600,000 or so admitted legally each year, some experts add in another 500,000 *illegal* immigrants annually. Congress has been struggling with the illegal alien problem for several years. Bills that would grant legal status to those who arrived before 1980 have failed twice. But another such bill was introduced in the Senate this spring by Alan K. Simpson (R-Wyo.), a perennial sponsor. A new twist in this latest bill would delay amnesty until the federal government set up programs to control both the ingress and hiring of illegal aliens. A comparable bill has not yet been introduced in the House.

Local drama

Meanwhile, the drama behind the numbers is being played out on the domestic scene. "Single Mothers Are Targets in Marriage Fraud" was the title of a recent *New York Times* article about American women who make marriages of convenience with foreigners seeking permanent status and are then left high and dry when their new husbands fail to deliver the promised dowries.

Movies, too, reflect the times. "Alamo Bay," released this year, tells the story of Vietnamese fishermen battling for survival in Texas. And "El Norte," the saga of a brother and sister from Guatamala who sacrifice everything they have to

enter the U.S. illegally, gives a vivid picture of what it takes to make it in the promised land. On her death bed, the young woman sees a vision of her dead mother, who says, in effect, that the trip to Los Angeles may not have been worth the price.

The lesson is the same in all three cases: Individuals, not governments, make the biggest difference. For the clash of cultures may be too great and community resources too limited to make assimilation a smooth process. . . . The situation may be exaggerated by the fact that foreigners are more "exotic" than they used to be. Before 1960, three of every five immigrants to the U.S. were European; by 1980, Europeans accounted for less than one in eight. Conversely, between 1975 and 1980, three-quarters of the immigrants were from Asia and Latin America.

In a few places, though, the local community goes all out to welcome newcomers. For example, Monterey Park, California, a city of 59,000 seven miles from downtown Los Angeles, was chosen an All America city this year partly because of the services it offers to newcomers—most of them Chinese immigrants. Its programs include English-language lessons conducted by volunteers; translators working with the police department; job training; and referral and counseling services.

According to an article in the *Los Angeles Times*, Monterey Park is called "Little Taipai" in the Orient because it has become a destination for so many Chinese. In fact, the city changed from 85 percent Caucasian in the 1960s to 75 percent Asian and Hispanic now, and Bob Dawson, a planner with the city's community development department, says immigrant Chinese investors are responsible for most of the city's new development. To accommodate the newcomers, city hall prints its quarterly magazine, *Monterey Park Living*, in both English and Chinese. The community development department's handouts on sign regulations and development procedures are also bilingual.

While these trends aren't universal, communities can't afford to ignore them because what happens nationally often appears in a miniature version at their own front door. The elderly may be concentrated in eight states right now and the immigrants visible mostly in metropolitan areas, but the numbers and the people they represent are constantly shifting.

Monterey Park is instructive because immigrants completely changed its ethnic composition in 20 years. On a wider scale, the 1980 census showed that, for the first time, more elderly people were living in suburbs than in central cities. And working women and single parents are, of course, everywhere.

As for the neighbors in Chicago's census tract 2413, we've had a most interesting turn of events. The local elementary school, closed three years ago, became the scene of a pitched battle between developers who wanted to convert it to condos and neighboring residents, who saw it as a neighborhood center. The school board vacillated between selling and retaining the property. Finally, after much ado, the school reopened last fall—as a school. Could this, too, be the wave of the future?

Sylvia Lewis is the editor and associate publisher of Planning.

The Once and Future Suburb

Ruth Eckdish Knack
(July 1986)

The unhappy protagonist of "The Man Who Loved Levittown," the title story of a recent prize-winning fiction collection, became so unhinged by the changes in the community he had moved into as a young World War II veteran that he finally set his house on fire. And the Levittown he remembered is what many of us still have in mind when we conjure up the image of a suburb. Tract house with lawn and/or crabgrass, 2.5 children, and a daddy who catches the 7:55 for his job in the city. In fact, though, as countless newspaper series and a recent *Newsweek* cover story have made clear, suburbia has become a place that's increasingly hard to categorize—and to plan for.

"Suburbia is a squishy term," says Census Bureau geographer Richard Forstall, explaining that the bureau talks about metropolitan statistical areas and urban areas, but not suburbs per se. Some "central cities," he notes, include many areas that look like suburbs, and some areas that are considered suburban look suspiciously urban. For example, Los Angeles's San Fernando Valley, which gave us the quintessentially suburban valley girl,

is part of the city, while industrial areas to the south are not.

Nor can suburbs be pigeonholed by function as bedroom communities, for today they're as likely to be office centers and even cultural and recreational centers. Exurban Lake County, Illinois, for example, has just attracted a major new Chicago-area racetrack, a replacement for a closer-in suburban track that burned last year. And a suburban area north of Miami is the site of the new Dolphins stadium. "The suburbs are usually defined as being in the shadow of the city," says longtime Westchester County, New York, planning consultant George Raymond. "But all the new development has created real suburban centers—and a more complete way of life."

Demographic stereotypes won't do, either. Because of the vagaries of terminology, the Census Bureau's Forstall can't tell us exactly how many people live in the "suburbs." But he can say that 105 million people live outside the central city boundaries, as opposed to 74 million inside. And those people are more and more likely to be poor, elderly, and members of minority groups. They're also likely to work in the suburbs, as almost 60 percent of the residents of the high-growth northwest Chicago suburbs do.

What all this adds up to is a citylike entity but without the traditional core. Freed from dependence on rail lines that limited the location of the earliest suburbs, the new ones are spreading into the countryside. "Ring cities," Rutgers University's George Sternlieb aptly calls them. The newest developments attract the jobs, while the older suburbs are left with such city-type problems as homelessness, substandard housing, and decaying commercial strips.

Meanwhile, planners play catch-up in understaffed municipal agencies and in county offices, which are assuming greater planning responsibilities. (Case in point: Gwinnett County, Georgia, which just issued an impressive new master plan.) We thought it was a good time to look at some of the problems these planners are facing and some of the ways that they're dealing with them.

In *Pride of Place,* his recent book and television series, architect Robert Stern waxes lyrical about the early planned suburbs like Olmsted's Roland Park outside Baltimore. And, as well-to-do enclaves, many of these communities are thriving. But other older, inner-ring suburbs, not so well-favored to begin with, are showing signs of residential and commercial decay.

Quoted recently in an article about the old blue-collar suburbs, University of Miami geographer Peter Muller noted that they face stiff competition from the new downtowns—"the outer city," in his phrase. "Entire communities are considered used up," he said, "and they're being discarded like so many beer cans." He could have been talking about Highland Park, Michigan, which nearly went bankrupt in 1983, or Harvey, an almost all-black community south of Chicago, whose long-abandoned shopping mall made the news when a group of investors proposed to convert it into, of all things, "the world's largest mausoleum."

More conventional solutions have been offered for the shopping center woes of such places as Park Forest, Illinois, the postwar new town made famous by William H. Whyte's *Organization Man.* In the Washington, D.C., area, the Montgomery County, Maryland, Planning Board is looking at older suburbs' retail centers as part of a master plan for the Kensington-Wheaton area. In fact, county planner Patrick Hare was hired by the agency two years ago specifically because of his interest in older suburbs.

"I look for ways of marketing what we have here," he says, "because we're competing with the newer areas to the north. The Sunday papers have big ads for the new subdivisions, and an area like this one tends to get overlooked—despite the fact that we have a good, solid housing stock and fine parks." Hare proposes that the county acquire additional land to create "billboard parks," which would be visible from the road.

But his primary interest is in the problems of the county's growing elderly population. In 20 years, he points out, the number of residents over 75 is expected to more than double to 7.5 percent of the population, and many of them will continue to live alone in single-family homes. A study just starting will consider various siting strategies for elderly housing units and will also look at ways of adapting single-family houses for the disabled elderly.

An irony, Hare notes, is that the "young elderly"—those under 75—are often opposed to land-use changes that would benefit the "frail elderly." Thus, the first group, which doesn't like to think of itself as "old," may oppose added bus service, new sidewalks, and even code changes to allow accessory apartments and senior citizen centers.

Nevertheless, provisions must be made. "These are Peter Pan suburbs," says Hare. "No one ever thought people would grow old here." But clearly they have, and provisions must be made, as they must at the other end of the age spectrum for children who need day care. Says Hare: "The image of the mother staying home taking care of her kids was so strong we didn't provide for day care space. A land-use planner from the moon would assume that day care *should* be in a basement."

Diversity

The first Levittown was all white. Developer William Levitt was quoted by Herbert Gans in his classic study, *The Levittowners,* as fearing the project wouldn't sell if it were opened to blacks. Today, the Levittowns are integrated—a symbol perhaps of the growing ethnic diversity that's apparent in suburbs all over the country. Indian children are no longer an oddity in the Montgomery County, Maryland, schools, and a DuPage County, Illinois, commercial strip caters to recent arrivals from Hong Kong.

Progress toward racial integration has been slow, however. Richard Forstall of the Census Bureau notes that 47 percent of all whites live in the suburbs but only 22 percent of all blacks. In the inner-ring suburbs where blacks are likeliest to move, resistance often stems from a fear of "resegregation," a complete white-to-black turnover.

To counter this fear, the Chicago suburb of Oak Park has taken a number of steps that have gained it national publicity in the past few years. First, to make monitoring possible, Oak Park required apartment owners and managers to report their buildings' racial mix. It also instituted a rigorous code enforcement program and a tenant referral service, operated through a nonprofit housing service. About six years ago, Oak Park added an "equity assurance program," which guarantees homeowners against a decline in property values because of integration. "It's a security blanket," says village community relations director Sherlynn Reed, who notes that the program has never been used. Finally, just last year, the village inaugurated its "diversity assurance program," intended to maintain integration in apartment buildings, which constitute half of Oak Park's housing stock.

Under the new program, owners who allow the housing center to show apartments on a nondiscriminatory basis are eligible for rehab grants and low-interest loans. An earlier proposal to give cash incentives to tenants who integrate buildings was dropped. Reed says the programs have worked "because we're up front about what we're trying to do. We want to maintain diversity all over the community." After climbing from zero to 11 percent in the 1970s, Oak Park's black population has remained stable for several years.

Although tagged "too integrationist" by some and "segregationist" by others, Oak Park's programs have generally been viewed as successful. More important, they've been upheld in court. Meanwhile, though, much of the rest of the Chicago suburban area remains virtually closed to blacks, which means, of course, that many of the suburban jobs are also inaccessible.

That's why so much attention was paid to the news that the suburb of Cicero had signed a U.S. Justice Department consent decree eliminating the village's residency requirement. The rule on Cicero's books was that only residents could be hired for municipal jobs, yet the community was known as a bastion of segregation. A Catch-22 situation.

"With the impetus of this settlement, there should be no exclusively white community any place in our metropolitan area," said a jubilant Kale Williams. Williams heads the Leadership Council for Metropolitan Open Communities, a group formed 20 years ago when Martin Luther King, Jr., came to Chicago to lead a civil rights march. Since then it has opened several fair housing centers, gained a reputation as an effective lobbying group, and had considerable success with a program that has placed some 3,000 public housing families in suburban housing. But that program depends on federal subsidies, and with the loss of Section 8 new construction funds, it must be scaled back. . . .

An alternative, and apparently effective approach, is the one taken by Washington, D.C., which has organized van pools to transport city residents to suburban jobs. The city has formed the Washington Area Jobs Council to recruit and refer workers, and provide job training and day care. Originally involving only Fairfax County, the program has since expanded to other jurisdictions. . . .

Housing in exurbia

Exurbia, for the Census Bureau's Richard Forstall, is another "squishy term." Once the refuge of the horsey set, semirural areas some 50 miles from the central city are now the locale of choice for the mixed-use megacenters as well as for those seeking relatively affordable housing. But, while some local people welcome the chance to make a real estate killing, others resent being squeezed out of scarce housing.

That's the situation in upstate Orange County, New York, where—as planning consultant Robert Ponte puts it—"suburbs of suburbs"—are springing up as housing and commercial development push ever farther from New York City. Commuters have indicated their willingness to travel up to two hours from their jobs in the city or close to it in order to live in the mid-Hudson region. The area is most familiar to generations of vacationers, who passed through it on their way to Catskill Mountain resorts, but it's also known for its manufacturing centers like Newburgh.

Recent *New York Times* articles have noted that commuters make up over 90 percent of the buyers in many developments along Route 17, the area's major artery. The average home price rose 22 percent between 1984 and 1985; this year it is expected to be over $90,000. Few rental apartments are being built, and those that are go for up to $700 a month, out of reach for many noncommuters. In addition, population projections suggest that the elderly and other needy groups are growing rapidly. . . .

To guarantee a supply of moderately priced units, the consultants suggest that the county give density bonuses—more units per acre if they sell or rent below a certain price. Tied to this recommendation is the idea of a housing trust fund, which would allow builders to make in-lieu payments instead of providing low-income housing. The consultants' report suggests that the county set up a nonprofit corporation to administer such a trust fund. However, Ponte notes that the trust fund idea is controversial and may not survive.

Another suggestion is to establish a "floating" planned unit development zone, which would allow a developer to dedicate only part of a site to moderate-income housing. The report also suggests that the county consider a new planned unit development category—for manufactured housing.

The common assumption of those making the two-hour commute to Orange County is that the suburbs closer to the city are all filled up, that there simply is no room for more building. Yet, according to George Raymond, whose consulting firm, RPPW, Inc., has been a Westchester County fixture for many years, that's a misconception. In his view, the inner suburbs still have a lot of vacant and buildable land. What they're lacking is an effective housing policy. "Had such a policy been in place when the jobs first began spreading into the suburbs, the pressure might have been less." Eight years ago, Raymond notes, Westchester did adopt a policy encouraging the production of 50,000 housing units. "On paper it sounds good. In fact, though, the county has no power to enforce the policy and only about a third of the goal has been reached."

Nevertheless, the land is there, a surprising amount of it, Raymond says, and "if the outer suburbs continue to resist residential development and if the courts don't upset their zoning policies, then I see an intensification in the inner ring. To be sure, some people will object to the additional housing, but they're the ones who would have liked the suburbs to remain the way they were 30 years ago."

Raymond is not, he stresses, advocating a reduction in the amount of open space that Westchester developments are known for. He was an early proponent of the notion of clustering housing units to provide common open space and to preserve environmentally sensitive areas. But he's disturbed by the current trend of municipalities to eliminate all land considered environmentally sensitive from the gross area of the site when establishing the number of units that will be allowed.

That, says Raymond, is a perversion of the cluster concept. "If the municipality wants 20 percent of the site in open space, it should say so. But it should allow the developer to decide where to build."

Design issues

In other contexts, too, standards have become a major suburban issue. And the big news here is the renewed interest in design.

The early garden suburbs were, of course, known for their graceful architecture and pleasant site plans, and those qualities were emulated by such prewar new town experiments as the federal Greenbelt towns and, to a lesser extent, by the more recent new towns like The Woodlands, Texas.

More often, though, the postwar suburbs just grew, with stock housing plans—and street plans—the rule. And faced with what they perceived as

hopeless tackiness, architects, and planners too, tended to throw up their hands and give up. (Or to go off in another direction entirely as Paolo Soleri did. It has been 15 years now since he started building Arcosanti, his megastructure alternative to suburban sprawl, in the desert outside Phoenix.) "The planning community has been slow to appreciate the suburban traditions and to provide good models," says Robert Stern—admittedly not an impartial observer.

But Stern sees hope in greater consciousness of quality on the part of both planners and the public and in such developments as Seaside, a much-praised, pedestrian-oriented resort—a suburb of sorts—in the Florida Panhandle. Similarly, urban designer Jonathan Barnett writes in his new book, *The Elusive City,* of the "revival of interest by real-estate developers in creating suburban development comparable in architectural interest and landscape quality to older garden suburbs."

Design sophistication has come to suburban downtowns, too. We note that a Los Angeles suburb, Glendale, won a 1985 *Progressive Architecture* urban design and planning citation for its downtown urban design study. And on a larger scale, Bellevue, Washington, has attracted national attention for its effort to focus development in the downtown core and to ensure pedestrian amenities.

Five years ago, Bellevue made a policy decision to concentrate development in the downtown. It followed up by lowering permissible floor area ratios outside the downtown, cutting downtown parking requirements in half, and eliminating the setback requirement for downtown buildings. Those efforts have received national publicity—including an article by nationally syndicated columnist Neal Peirce, lauding Bellevue for making itself over into a "Class A municipality."

Bellevue's newest wrinkle is a "CBD perimeter design district ordinance," designed to control development on the edge of the downtown. The spur, says Mark Hinshaw, the city's urban designer, was a proposal for a 22-story mixed-use project adjacent to a neighborhood of three- and four-story apartments. "Neighborhood transition" became an issue in the 1984 city council election. In response, the council enacted a development moratorium and gave the planning commission a year to come up with a new policy.

During that time, downtown property owners

argued that reducing building size on the perimeter would hurt economic growth. Their claims were countered by an environmental impact statement that showed not only that the downtown would remain strong but that a new ordinance was needed to protect adjacent neighborhoods.

The ordinance passed last fall sets a series of height limits in a stairstep, or wedding-cake, configuration, with the tallest buildings in the core. It also offers developers a height bonus and a higher floor area ratios if they provide downtown housing. The FAR limit is further relaxed for builders who provide neighborhood-type retail in the perimeter areas.

Design is being used in a different way in Opa-Locka, Florida. The Miami suburb, now mostly black and with 13 percent unemployment, was developed in the 1920s by the aviation pioneer Glenn Curtiss, who adopted an Arabian Nights theme. Several of the public buildings and a number of the private houses are decked out in minerets and towers, and the streets have such exotic names as Aladdin and Ali Baba.

Opa-Locka's idea is to redevelop itself as a tourist attraction, using its unusual architecture as a draw and creating a festival bazaar to lure spin-off trade from the new football stadium under construction two miles north.

Gridlock

But design, as important as it is to many of us, is not the issue that raises the blood pressure of suburbanites. Traffic is. Kenneth Orski, a former federal transportation official and now head of a Washington, D.C. consulting firm, notes that in several recent surveys suburban residents put traffic at the top of their list of concerns, before crime, housing, and pollution, which headed the list in the 1960s. (Meanwhile, another recent survey, by the National Association of Home Builders, indicates that 70.9 percent of prospective homebuyers want to live in a suburban setting—17 minutes from work.)

Traffic congestion has also become a ballot box issue. In Fairfax County, Virginia, for instance, it is expected to be the primary issue in this November's council election. The war cry: "We don't want another Tyson's Corner in our backyard." Tyson's Corner is the area's booming megacenter—a crossroads with gas station in the 1960s, now a minicity with about 12 million square feet of office space

and 25,000 cars a day. Says Orski: "I really believe traffic congestion will drive politics in the suburbs for years to come."

The culprit is, of course, the suburban office boom. The traffic it generates is being superimposed on an essentially static road network, with little prospect of expansion. Orski points out that total highway mileage in the U.S. increased by just over one percent between 1978 and 1984, while average traffic volume on the urban interstates grew by nine percent. Moreover, the new traffic "has lost its directional lines," so that inbound and outbound congestion are the same. "The days of the leisurely reverse commute are ending," says Orski.

The fact that huge numbers of people are affected may, in fact, be good news, in Orski's view. "Traffic congestion used to be a concern only to those who commuted downtown. Now people who never go downtown get stuck in hour-long traffic jams." So a much broader cross section is exposed to the problem, and their frustration has led to a growing acceptance of the principle of cost sharing—impact fees for roads, for instance.

It has also given new importance to the concept of Transportation Systems Management—an idea that Orski promoted at the Urban Mass Transportation Administration in the 1970s. TSM is a flexible approach to providing transportation that can include organized van pooling, stricter parking regulations, and a variety of other measures.

TSM, says Orski, was conceived of as "basically a public-sector responsibility." It became increasingly clear to him, however, that many of the suggested activities were not in the purview of government agencies. "Public agencies can exhort, but it's the private sector that influences behavior—by charging for parking for instance." So Orski came up with the idea of a "transportation management association" to facilitate areawide private-sector activities. The first TMA was launched in 1977 in Tyson's Corner. Now there are about 20 scattered throughout the country.

The TMAs' basic function is to coordinate—setting up ride-sharing arrangements and staggered work hour programs, for instance. They also lobby county and state governments for road and transit improvements. And some TMAs actually provide transportation. In Princeton, New Jersey, for example, a TMA runs a shuttle between several office parks, the downtown, and the Amtrak station. Some provide bicycles for lunchtime use by employees. Others have talked about providing a short-term car rental service for people who don't drive to work.

"The beauty of a TMA," says Orski, "is that it can tailor a transportation program to the needs of a specific group." And that, for him, is what makes the private-sector approach more practical than a public transportation system. Even the new rail systems, he notes, have had the paradoxical result of contributing to congestion by stimulating development around transit stations rather than relieving it. He cites recent surveys showing that fewer than four percent of the commuters in the Washington, D.C., and San Francisco metropolitan areas—locations of new subway systems—travel to work by rail.

Public transportation was efficient as long as people lived in the suburbs and worked downtown, he concludes. "The dispersed travel patterns we see today make it virtually irrelevant."

Politics

As suburban planning grows in complexity, political pressures increase as well. Montgomery County, Maryland, is a case in point. In a continuing controversy, the elected county executive, Charles Gilchrist, has accused the county's planning agencies of being ineffective and insufficiently attuned to long-range issues. Gilchrist contended that the county executive was excluded from planning decisions, and he was backed up by a blue-ribbon committee—which he appointed.

The state legislature agreed and gave Gilchrist—who is retiring this year—part of what he wanted. The county executive may now appoint two members of the planning board, although the county council still appoints the chair. Even more important, the county executive now has the power to veto master plans, zoning text amendments, and subdivision regulations.

According to one local observer, the debate has had the healthy effect of forcing the county executive and the county planners to work together more. And that's worth noting in a suburban context where counties are assuming ever greater responsibilities. So even in a state like New Jersey, where municipal powers are the rule, we find an example of a county gearing up to take on a new planning role. Two years ago, a surprising combination—the county chamber of commerce and the Regional Plan Association—worked together with

a consultant, Lawrence O. Houstoun, Jr., to produce a countywide plan for Morris County, New Jersey, a semirural area in the northern part of the state, which is expected to draw 150,000 new jobs in the next 15 years. The result, published last fall, was "Morris 2000," which calls for the county government to "take the lead in creating an effective growth management system."

In particular, the report recommends that the county planning board be given the power to approve site plans on projects large enough to have a regional impact. Legislation proposing just such power has been introduced in the state legislature by Assemblyman Barry McEnroe.

And that seems to us a sign that interjurisdictional cooperation is not as hopeless as it once seemed, and that indeed there may be a constituency for long-range planning in the suburbs.

Ruth Knack is the senior editor of Planning.

Take Me Home, Country Roads
John Herbers
(November 1987)

San Luis Obispo County on the California coast halfway between Los Angeles and San Francisco is a beautiful land of majestic mountains, beaches, sunbathed valleys and vineyards, and attractive small towns. Over the past two decades, the county has grown twice as fast as the state itself; since 1970, the number of residents has doubled to about 200,000. During that time, the county's economy—thanks to natural attractions, freeways that permit long-distance commuting, and the presence of California Polytechnic State University—has more than kept pace with the population growth.

Now it must cope with the consequences of growth: whole towns without water and sewer services, traffic jams on what used to be lonely country roads, and a huge unmet demand for public services. In response, beleaguered county officials talk about the need for growth-management policies, but such policies are so controversial that they would seem to have little chance of success.

Growth problems, of course, are nothing new on the American development scene. What is new is the kind of growth that is taking place in hundreds of areas like San Luis Obispo—a scattered growth that is occurring outside established towns and cities, and that is, in fact, a mixture of urban, suburban, and rural. It is posing special problems for planners, policy makers, and local governments because most of it is happening in a complicated web of political jurisdictions that seem ill-equipped to guide or control the new development.

The new-growth areas are different from any kind of settlements we have known in the past. Although they contain suburban and exurban elements—subdivisions, shopping centers, and highway sprawl—they are much more likely to preserve the small towns, landmarks, and features of the natural environment. Unlike most suburbs, the new communities usually have an economic base of their own. They are far less dominated by the cities, even though they frequently lie within officially classified metropolitan areas. For many of their residents, they offer an alternative to the crime and congestion of cities and the sterility of the suburbs.

For want of a better term, I call these new communities "the new heartland." Joseph Doherty, a former federal official who has tracked the phenomenon all over the country, coined the label "countrified cities" to describe it, and Jack Lessenger, writing recently in *American Demographics,* uses "penturbia." All these terms describe communities of such low density that they make the old "suburban sprawl" seem dense. Subdivisions, single-family housing on five-to-10-acre lots, shopping centers, retail strips, schools, and churches, all separated by farms, forests, or other open spaces, are characteristic.

Those who live in the new heartland are predominantly young adults, many with children, who moved there either because they were seeking a more relaxed life style than they know in the cities and suburbs or because they could find affordable housing or employment nowhere else. But many of the new communities also contain large numbers of elderly people—retirees attracted by the open spaces, low-cost housing, and outdoor recreation. Overall, the population is generally white, with higher than average income and educational achievements.

The young adults I interviewed in these places over a period of eight years almost invariably said they liked living there because the new communities reminded them of small towns of the past and because they could enjoy a higher standard of living at lower cost than in the cities or suburbs.

"Centerless, soulless"

The new, scattered development is not occurring without criticism. For example, Barbara Boggs Sigmund, the mayor of Princeton, New Jersey, noting the commercial and residential growth taking place for many miles across the New Jersey countryside and putting a traffic burden on her small university town of 12,000, calls the new, low-density communities "centerless, soulless, and anticity." Virtually all of them are indeed without any all-purpose center and sprawl unplanned over many square miles of land.

New heartland communities are found in every region, on the outer fringes of metropolitan areas; around small towns far removed from the large cities; along rivers, coastlines, and reservoirs; near retirement and recreation areas; on marginal farmland; around state capitals and college communities; along interstate highways; and in many mountain valleys. They are seldom found on flat, rich farmland, which continues to lose population in all regions. Nor are they part of the back-to-the-land movement of the 1970s that drew those disenchanted with American civilization to rural communes. Rather, the new communities are made up of a prosperous, adventurous middle class superimposed over small towns and countryside in a way the suburbs never were.

While the new, dispersed communities resemble exurban places of the past in many respects, they are fundamentally different in that they have their own economy and are less likely to be filled in with development. In the late 1960s and 1970s migration, most of the new communities were found in nonmetropolitan areas removed from large urban centers. In the 1980s, the migration is largely to exurban areas that lie within metropolitan areas, which cover some one-fifth of the land area in the United States, land that includes vast rural tracts. Some observers have mistakenly concluded that this spurt of growth in metropolitan areas signals a return to the cities. And it's true that many of the old industrial cities have indeed undergone a revival, mostly in their downtowns.

But that is not where the greatest growth is occurring. Both Census Bureau and private estimates (from Dun and Bradstreet, for example) for the first half of this decade show the greatest growth to be in the farther reaches of the exurban areas— 60 to 70 miles in all directions from New York, two and three counties removed from such cities as Atlanta, Philadelphia, San Francisco, and Chicago— and in small metropolitan areas that are in themselves low-density, anticity developments that few Americans ever heard of: places such as Ocala, Florida, Edinburg-McAllen, Texas, and Chico, California.

The five fastest-growing counties of 100,000 or more in Florida—Marion, Seminole, Lee, Brevard, and Palm Beach—together gained 380,000 people between 1980 and 1986 for a total of 1.7 million. Yet within those five counties, only West Palm Beach, with a population of 68,000, could be considered a sizeable city.

Perhaps the best example is North Carolina. Although it has a strong industrial base, most of its six million people live in outlying areas between the small cities that dot the state from the tobacco-growing lowlands in the east to the Appalachian Mountains in the west, a pattern of development encouraged by both political and business leaders in hopes that the state will never entirely lose its rural image.

There is much evidence to suggest that the new kind of low-density growth will continue into the next century. It is a product of what some authorities call a post-industrial society. With the decline of heavy industry and the rise of a service economy, neither factories nor office buildings need to be clustered near sources of raw materials and water or rail transportation. For the first time in American history, both businesses and workers can settle pretty much where they please. And where they please is not the large city. Americans have never become urbanized in the way Europeans are. In fact, the big industrial cities are a relatively new phenomenon in the U.S., with many of them going into decline only a generation or so after they matured. A Gallup poll taken in 1986 showed that fully half of American adults would like to move to towns of under 10,000, a finding consistent with other public opinion surveys taken over the last half century. In one sense, the new communities are a new version of the small town, even though they are spread over many square miles.

Problems ahead

Now, however, there is growing concern about the ability of our existing government structures and policies to deal with the new growth in a way that will prevent the new communities from repeating the mistakes of our old cities and suburbs.

In many ways, widely scattered growth poses more problems for planners and government officials than more traditional growth within a municipality or confined suburbs. For one thing, the scattered growth usually occurs over a complex of overlapping and conflicting jurisdictions—one or more counties, an array of small municipalities, and scores of special taxing districts. San Luis Obispo County, for example, is suffering from what local officials call "patchwork growth," caused by the inability of the county government and a dozen or more small municipalities to coordinate their planning efforts.

In keeping with the trend nationally for such places, about 65 percent of new housing construction has been outside the municipalities. People prefer to settle in the country, not in town. Those outlying settlements have not built the infrastructure—water, sewer, and other facilities—required in the incorporated places. As a result, says councilman Robert Griffith of the small city of San Luis Obispo (pop. 36,000), there is a "brown, ugly ring around each municipality, kind of like a bathtub ring. We need a real collaboration in land-use policy between what the city says ought to go on outside its city limits and what the county is allowing meanwhile." Griffith was referring to the lack of cooperation among jurisdictions, a common failing in the new dispersed communities.

In some other areas, however, it is the municipalities that are frustrating county planning. In the northern part of Montgomery County, Maryland (near the District of Columbia), the overall county plan bans certain types of development felt to be harmful to citizens—heavy commercial development next to residential neighborhoods, for instance. But this has not stopped some developers from getting what they want by whipsawing the municipalities—that is, inviting them to compete against one another in lowering requirements, a practice that is not uncommon among places hungry for economic development.

In the Puget Sound area of Washington, where there is an abundance of new low-density growth, planners say they are hampered by, among many other things, 72 separate taxing districts in one county alone, Pierce, where Mount Rainier with its scenic attractions seems to be pulling to it people and jobs. Somehow, officials there say, all these districts have to be drawn into a master plan, a feat that so far they have not been able to accomplish.

The problem of multiple jurisdictions can be seen even more clearly in central Texas. A few miles north of the Lyndon B. Johnson ranch near Austin is an area of dry scrubland that is selling for as much as 100 times the price it would bring for cattle grazing. The largest towns, scattered over hundreds of square miles, have names like Marble Falls and Llano.

There is not much there to set off a land rush except artificial lakes, state parks—and the fact that the area happens to be on the edge of the corridor of economic development that stretches from Dallas to San Antonio. People from cities and suburbs along Interstate 35 rush in on weekends and at vacation time for recreation. Others are buying arid land to turn into "ranchettes" and big estates, and housing complexes are going up for retirees.

Special districts

Because both housing and commercial establishments are scattered, the area of development laps over political jurisdictions established when the population was a few thousand ranch hands and townfolks. Neither the towns nor the counties have the capacity to provide the services that are in demand. As a result, special districts or authorities with taxing power have been set up over wide areas—each to provide a particular service. One problem in Texas as in many other states is that the counties do not have the authority to enforce their plans over the multiple jurisdictions authorized by the state constitutions.

Similar practices have become common in many other areas of the United States. Between 1962 and 1982, the number of special districts, not including those for schools, increased from 18,323 to 28,733, a rise of 57 percent, according to the Census Bureau. Most of the new districts, formed to provide such services as water, sewage disposal, libraries, fire protection, and flood control, are in newly developing areas and are independent of the general service governments that spawned them. They are in effect shadow governments run by officials, who may be appointed or elected. Once established

to provide a single service, they usually operate outside the public spotlight that is focused in most communities on elected general governments.

Because the county or municipal governments, set up in a simple era when towns were towns and country was country, were not equipped to deal with the new spread development, the special districts are usually viewed as a necessary invention. Yet in the opinion of J.C. Doherty, they have preempted such a range of services that they have weakened the authority of general governments to deal effectively with growth and to govern in the comprehensive way that they should.

Long-range planning is particularly difficult for new heartland communities. In Palm Beach County, Florida, with over 37 municipalities and 20 special service districts, officials and planners a few years ago thought that planned unit developments offered a solution to patchwork growth. Wellington, for example, is a private project of spacious homes, clubs, and other facilities with its own schools and services that seemed when it was started to put no burden on the governments in the area. But the population of Wellington is now approaching 20,000 and it, along with other such projects, is contributing to massive traffic jams over the county. "No one at the time they were approved thought they would ever cause any problem," says Jan Winters, the county administrator.

Under Florida's 1985 growth management act, such new projects are to be required to pay impact fees to help finance whatever facilities will be needed to serve project residents outside their boundaries. But the law is untested and even if it proves effective for new projects, those approved before its enactment are exempt. The population of exempt projects in Palm Beach County alone could reach 60,000 and continues to grow, according to local officials.

A further problem for planners is that in most of the newly developing areas there is a sharp and frequently bitter division among residents, with some wanting to stop the growth and keep the landscape in a pristine state while others encourage growth, largely for economic reasons. In San Luis Obispo County, for example, some residents and public officials are preparing a ballot initiative that, if approved by voters, would substantially slow or stop the growth.

The history of such initiatives in California, however, is that they seldom prevail, and the prospect is for continued growth and heightened tensions exacerbated by demands of new residents for the same services they enjoyed in the cities and suburbs. "The first thing newcomers to these areas do is join environmental groups to preserve the countryside and the next thing they do is join an anti-tax group, all the while putting demands on the local governments for more services," says one Florida planner.

Nevertheless, some progress is being made toward controlling and guiding the new growth, even in the absence of any coherent policy from the federal government. States such as Florida and Massachusetts are moving to use their powers to achieve a more rational approach to growth, and in counties ranging from Pierce in Washington, to Palm Beach in Florida, officials of the local governments involved are coming together—"out of desperation," some of them say—to adopt countywide plans for all to follow.

The department of city and regional planning of California Polytechnic State University recently sponsored a conference on the aesthetics of the new growth, appropriately held in a hotel-shopping complex adjacent to a large spinach field and attended by planners and others from across the nation and Canada. There was agreement that much new research is needed if planners are to deal intelligently with the new growth. Edward J. Ward, chairman of the conference and a professor of planning at the university, noted that "fundamental change in how we use and view rural and small town lands and resources" is needed.

"To what extent is it possible to integrate the ideals of city, small town, and rural models of the good life?" Ward asked. "We are going to have to discover what constitutes an acceptable planned and designed countryside." Then to achieve the goals intended, he added, may even require "a reinventing of local government. . . . Local governments, especially counties, are going to have to become much more involved actors in the land development process." One urgent requirement, he said, is that the new communities make way for a larger diversity of income classes than is now being achieved in many areas, a chance for low, middle, and high-income groups to enjoy an environment that includes access to both the natural environment and the amenities of urban development.

Achieving such a diversity may be the silver lining in what otherwise seems a most difficult period ahead. For what the new areas all have is space. Space provides a buffer between groups that clash when forced to live in close proximity, as now seen most dramatically in large cities like New York. We may yet see a recreation of the small town environment that so many Americans seem to be yearning for, where rich and poor mingle in the marketplace but go home to their own houses in the country.

John Herbers, formerly national correspondent for the New York Times, *is the author of* The New Heartland *(Random House, 1986).*

The Future of Nonmetropolitan America

Niles M. Hansen
(August 1973)

During the past several decades the entire population increase of the nation has been absorbed by urban areas. By 1970 nearly three-quarters of the total population was living in cities of 2,500 or more. All but one of the 50 largest standard metropolitan statistical areas (SMSAs) showed substantial growth during the 1960s. Meanwhile, over one-third of the counties in the United States, mostly rural, lost inhabitants. Nonmetropolitan America exists within the context of an essentially urban—and urbanizing—society.

Economic activities are attracted to cities because of the economies of agglomeration and concentration. People are drawn to cities because cities offer improved incomes and a diversity of career and life-style options. Nevertheless, the forces at work in the urbanization process are tending to be offset—at least in part—by the widespread feeling that the quality of life in big cities is deteriorating. The city is associated with increasing congestion, slums, violence, welfare costs, and suburban sprawl.

On the more positive side are two countervailing forces favoring nonmetropolitan areas. One is the extension of "urban fields"—interdependent rural-urban living spaces extending up to 100 miles or more from metropolitan cores. The other is the decentralization of manufacturing from metropolitan to nonmetropolitan areas.

In the past Americans gave little thought to the distribution of the nation's population and economic activity. Whatever the validity of the traditional faith in the market system, the trend of public sentiment is toward the development of small towns and cities as an alternative to metropolitan growth. This has been borne out by public opinion polls and by recent congressional and executive actions. . . .

Perceptions

Although economists have formulated abstract models—usually based on unrealistic assumptions—of optimal ways to allocate resources spatially, there seem to be few places where the people believe themselves to be living under these conditions. City dwellers have their urban crises, and country folk find no end of information on how disadvantaged they are relative to their more affluent cousins. Today, the legislative pendulum appears to be swinging in favor of "doing something" for rural areas.

The case for development policies for rural or nonmetropolitan areas is based on two related phenomena. First, nonmetropolitan counties consistently have had lower per capita personal incomes. In 1968, the value was $2,614 for all nonmetropolitan counties; for metropolitan counties, it was $3,811. Nonmetropolitan areas also experience a disproportionate number of persons living in poverty. For all races, 17.1 percent of the nonmetropolitan population was in poverty status in 1969, compared to 9.5 percent in SMSAs and 13.4 per cent in central cities. However, while about a third of all blacks were below the poverty level, over half the blacks living in nonmetropolitan areas were poor.

Another rationale for rural development policies concerns population loss. In the past 50 years the urban population has increased from 54 million to 149 million. The rural population has remained steady, at around 54 million. However, the farm sector of rural population has declined from 32 million in 1920 (or three-fifths of the rural total) to fewer than 10 million today (less than one-fifth of the rural total). Continuing outmigration of the farm population remains high, a result of declines in agricultural employment, especially where nonfarm jobs have not taken up the slack. In some areas the outmigration of young adults has produced something rare in American history, a natural decrease in population. In 1950 only two counties experienced natural population decrease; in 1960 there were only 38. In 1970, however, over 500 counties fell into this category. In particular, there have been fewer births than deaths in large groups of contiguous counties in Missouri, Kansas, Nebraska, Illinois, and Texas.

While some counties have been unable to hold people and others have continued previous growth patterns, quite a few nonmetropolitan counties have demonstrated remarkably improved population retention. The nature of this growth and its significance for policies that might be applied to other areas are noteworthy. It is not assumed here that population growth is necessarily desirable or that population decline is necessarily bad. Nevertheless, an examination of the factors behind the reversal of stagnation or decline has obvious relevance to the formulation of national manpower and growth policies encompassing all kinds of urban and rural places. Indeed, this reversal can only be understood in the context of a national system of forces involving both metropolitan and nonmetropolitan areas.

The counties studied were chosen on the basis of a classification system of population retention made available by Calvin Beale of the Economic Research Service, U.S. Department of Agriculture. In this system, there are three groups of counties: counties of inadequate and declining population retention ability; counties with improved retention ability; and counties with population growth and net immigration in both the past two decades. The two kinds of counties that are the focus of this article are subgroups of Beale's second group. The first, called *turnaround-reversal* counties here, consists of counties that gained population in the 1960s after losing in the 1950s. The second, *turnaround-acceleration* counties, consists of counties that gained population in both decades, but grew rapidly in the 1960s after relative stagnation and net outmigration in the 1950s. The regions studied were Northern Vermont and New Hampshire, the Tennessee Valley, the Ozarks, Central Wisconsin and Minnesota, the Colorado and New Mexico Rockies, and Central Texas.

As I have implied above, the population of the United States is becoming increasingly concentrated not only in metropolitan areas, but also in relatively few metropolitan regions, of which the northeastern megalopolis is the most familiar.

While some view this phenomenon with alarm, others find it to be consistent with the objective of increased opportunities for most of the nation's population: William Alonso points out, for example (and this is only a kernel of his complex idea), that per capital income in the United States rises sharply with urban size.

Nevertheless, federal policies with respect to the development of a national growth policy continue to emphasize small towns and rural areas. These include extension and expansion of the activities of the Economic Development Administration and the Appalachian Regional Commission, executive espousal of special revenue sharing for rural development, liberalization of farm credit and development of new public and private rural community development sources, financing of new rural telephone systems, and incentives to get professional health manpower to locate in rural areas. . . .

The metropolitanization of the American population may be perfectly consistent with population growth in previously stagnant or declining non-metropolitan counties. The fundamental reason is that for many people a metropolitan life means more than merely living and working in an SMSA. Just as the compact nineteenth-century city gave way to the metropolitan area, so today the SMSA is giving way to urban fields which may include whole regions within a two-hour driving radius of the central cities. Increased incomes, leisure, and accessibility have permitted a growing number of persons to avail themselves of opportunities and amenities throughout their respective urban fields. Thus, many persons who work in SMSAs may reside in nonmetropolitan areas where residential amenities are more agreeable, and many persons who live and work in SMSAs regularly go to non-metropolitan areas for tourism, recreation, second homes, and retirement. Indeed, this broader spatial framework has made it ever more difficult to distinguish "rural" from "urban."

Moreover, urban fields need not be limited to areas contiguous to SMSAs. Areas with attractive recreation-tourism-retirement-second home features may expand because of demand generated by metropolitan residents who live well beyond commuting range.

The phenomena described here are clearly seen in all the regions studied. Turnaround-acceleration counties in particular cluster around major SMSAs and many smaller ones. Moreover, while employ-ment expansion in these counties includes a considerable amount of manufacturing activity, it also includes a relatively large number of workers in non-goods-producing sectors usually associated with metropolitan areas. The interstate highway system has helped to expand urban fields, but its primary role has been to squeeze recreation opportunities that they once took for granted, as more and more territory falls into the "off limits" domain of the more affluent. There is also widespread concern over damage to the environment caused by increased population. One hope is that this concern for the environment will be translated into effective controls for preserving scarce resources. In any event, it is apparent that although the omnivorous appetite of metropolitan residents for non-metropolitan amenities may cheer local chambers of commerce, the blessings are at best mixed.

Role of industry

In addition to the expansion of urban fields, the principal cause of reversal of nonmetropolitan decline or stagnation is the decentralization of manufacturing. Wilbur Thompson's hypothesis of industrial filtering in the national system of cities maintains that invention, or at least innovation, takes place more than proportionally in the larger metropolitan areas of industrially mature regions. However, as industries age and their technology matures, skill requirements fall and competition forces the industries to relocate to lower wage areas. The lower an urban area in the skill and wage hierarchy, the older the industry it tends to attract. Its national growth rate also slows. Intermediate level places tend to develop growth rates somewhat above the national average by getting increasing shares of slow-growing industries; but in smaller places, the positive change in shares weakens and may even erode to zero, leading to slower than average growth and net outmigration—even to absolute employment and population decline in the smallest places. . . .

Although industrial growth in rural hinterlands is by no means a universal phenomenon, its occurrence in some regions has given rural development advocates some cause for rejoicing. But what appears to be "success" must be qualified. First, it could be argued that many of the turnaround-reversal counties are at best only nominally successful by any standard. A net loss of fifteen people in one decade and a net gain of a dozen in the next is scarcely an impressive performance.

This last point would be telling with respect to one or a few counties, but loses credibility when urged against whole regions, such as the Tennessee Valley, the Ozarks, and northern Wisconsin and Minnesota, where large blocks of counties have experienced significant reversal of often severe population decline. Growth, even small growth, must be acknowledged as significant when it occurs over such large areas. Nevertheless, it remains true that these regions do not have the relative security that characterizes metropolitan areas with more diversified economic activities. Agricultural employment still is considerably above the national average in these regions, and the few manufacturing sectors are frequently in the low-wage, slow-growth (and often heavily subsidized) class.

Moreover, rural workers have been among the most neglected in terms of manpower and other domestic policies. Rural manpower programs remain hampered by a scarcity of manpower experts, low population densities, limited training facilities, and an urban bias in manpower legislation and programs. It is estimated that in 1971 rural areas accounted for 31 per cent of the national population and an even larger proportion of all poor persons, yet they received only 23 per cent of manpower outlays. In addition, the rural employment service staff amounted to only 16 per cent of the total. However, some efforts are being made to obtain a greater share of manpower funds for rural areas from the Department of Labor.

Yet regional development must begin somewhere. And there are indications that, despite deficiencies in public policies and programs, the process of industrial filtering eventually leads to the upgrading of both manpower qualifications, types of industry, and incomes. These phenomena are clearly in evidence in the South. The industrialization of the South was initiated in large measure by the movement of textile mills from New England and other northern areas into the Piedmont region of the central Carolinas. The textile mills in turn generated other activities, such as chemical plants and dye suppliers.

The growth of manufacturing in the Carolinas, and especially North Carolina, was followed by similar expansion into Georgia. Decentralization spread next to the Tennessee Valley, which has managed to achieve a higher degree of industrial diversification than either the Carolinas or Georgia. More recently, Mississippi and Arkansas have entered the lower rungs of the filtering process.

Although Georgia is actively recruiting northern industrial firms, it is not attempting to sell the state on the basis of a cheap labor force; that era has passed. Tennessee officials are proud that they no longer need to tempt firms with the kinds of subsidies available in Arkansas and Mississippi. Arkansas and Mississippi are gratified with industrial growth based on low-wage, slow-growth industries, though they are itching for something better.

The southern turnaround counties that have been the primary beneficiaries of industrial decentralization are overwhelmingly white in racial composition. The largest block of turnaround-reversal counties in the nation is in the Ozarks. The remarkable industrial growth taking place in Mississippi is concentrated in a few counties in the northeastern part of the state. Similar expansion is occurring in northern Alabama. Some of the most impressive manufacturing growth in the nation is in Tennessee (apart from some southwestern counties), northern Georgia, and the Piedmont. Yet a fact even more striking than their industrial expansion is that these southern counties have proportionally fewer blacks than the nation as a whole.

This lack of extension of employment opportunities to areas with a high proportion of blacks has been rationalized on a number of grounds. Many employers believe that blacks are less productive and more prone toward organization by unions. A prominent local official in northeastern Mississippi, commenting on the failure of the industrial growth characteristic of his area to spread to the Black Belt, stated that firms seeking a large pool of relatively cheap labor may need to go as far south as northeastern Mississippi, but no farther. Whatever superficial merit these arguments may have, it cannot be denied that racial discrimination plays a part in the failure of firms to locate in black areas.

However, overt racism by potential employers is not the only cause. Past and present discrimination against blacks in the provision of manpower services and health, education, and other human resource investments has created a labor force that may really be relatively less productive. Marginal firms in particular cannot afford experiments based on social concern. In view of the continuing migration of large numbers of blacks from the rural

South, it clearly would be in the national interest to upgrade substantially the development of the region's black human resources.

This is not to suggest that manpower and related programs would be a panacea for the problems of rural blacks or other groups concentrated in economically lagging regions, and especially not for those who choose to remain in these regions. There is a tendency for better educated and better trained workers to leave poor rural areas for more attractive opportunities elsewhere. Even in the case of the turnaround counties, outmigrants improved their economic status in relation to nonmigrants. Turnaround counties also tend to provide relatively little economic advantage to immigrants, though there are regional differences in this regard.

In the Minnesota-Wisconsin and Vermont-New Hampshire regions, the nonmetropolitan labor forces have clearly benefited from a relatively long process of mutual upgrading of education and manpower training on the one hand, and industrial composition on the other. The South, though it is rapidly rejoining the rest of the nation economically, retains its uniqueness. Nevertheless, capital deepening and higher wages have accompanied the simultaneous industrial filtering and labor-force upgrading process that has moved through the Piedmont, northern Georgia, Tennessee, and the white counties of Arkansas and northern Mississippi and Alabama. . . .

Without subsidies on a scale not likely to be politically feasible, lagging rural areas with large concentrations of minority groups will remain poor. Yet the people of these areas can be given the option of employment in viable urban growth centers, preferably not too big or too distant from the regions where the relocatees feel they have their roots. If a federal subsidy can accelerate growth in a center that is already growing, and if this subsidy is made conditional on providing opportunities for residents of lagging areas, then it would be more efficient to try to tie into the growing area than to attempt to create growth in stagnant areas that are basically unattractive economically. Assisted labor mobility also would have an important role in such a strategy. The lack of a permanent program of comprehensive worker relocation assistance is one of the greatest deficiencies in public policies directly affecting spatial resource allocation.

A related manpower issue is whether rural workers should receive training in their home areas or in urban places. No simple answer can be given because of the wide variety of possible circumstances. Nevertheless, the case for coordinating training in rural areas with local economic development activities is strong where such areas are benefiting from manufacturing decentralization. A study of relocation projects in Michigan and Wisconsin, for example, indicated that while migrants apparently received little benefit from training, workers who remained at home were helped considerably by training. South Carolina's efforts to integrate a manpower inventory system and worker training program with industrial expansion has succeeded. When a firm demonstrates an interest in a given locale, the recruitment, selection, classification, and training of the local labor force are carried out to meet the specific requirements of the firm. On the other hand, training in urban areas would be more feasible when rural areas lack the facilities and employment opportunities.

Whatever the merits of these approaches, they would affect a relatively small proportion of the nation's total population. The turnaround regions that are now growing spontaneously as a result of the extension of urban fields and manufacturing decentralization also involve only a fraction of the total population. Thus, even if the nation's largest cities are too big in some meaningful if not yet quantifiable sense, it seems clear that solutions to problems of the spatial distribution of population and economic activity will have to be explicitly urban—broadly defined to include urban fields. This is not to say that the people living in hinterlands of urban fields and in-between areas must either construct high-rise buildings and international airports or else move to metropolitan areas. But they should learn to cooperate in at least simulating some of the advantages that firms find in metropolitan areas.

It is significant that the turnaround regions lie wholly or mostly within the areas covered by the regional commissions created in 1965 by the Public Works and Economic Development Act and the Appalachian Regional Development Act. In addition, the turnaround regions have profited in varying degree from the activities of the Economic Development Administration and from planning efforts carried out within the context of state-designated multi-county planning units. Few would claim that these federal and state initiatives have been responsible for the growth of the relevant regions. The agencies involved have had too little money, too little time, and no coherent and systematic strategies for development. In many cases they also have neglected the human resource and manpower development needs of the poor.

Nevertheless, their presence has undoubtedly been a positive factor in inducing and orchestrating the growth that has taken place. In the future it may be hoped that they will concentrate their efforts not only on *regional* development, but also on the plight of those disadvantaged persons whose economic status remains deplorably low, even by the most modest standards of equity.

Niles Hansen is Leroy G. Denman, Jr., Regents Professor in Economics at the University of Texas at Austin. This article is excerpted from his book by the same title (now out of print).

The Great Plains: From Dust to Dust

Deborah Epstein Popper and Frank J. Popper
(December 1987)

At the center of the United States, between the Rockies and the tallgrass prairies of the Midwest and South, lies the shortgrass expanse of the Great Plains. The region extends over large parts of 10 states and produces cattle, corn, wheat, sheep, cotton, coal, oil, natural gas, and metals. The Plains are endlessly windswept and nearly treeless; the climate is semiarid, with typically less than 20 inches of rain a year.

The country is rolling in parts in the north, dead flat in the south. It is lightly populated. A dusty town with a single gas station, store, and house is sometimes 50 unpaved miles from its nearest neighbor, another three-building settlement amid the sagebrush. As we define the region, its eastern border is the 98th meridian. San Antonio and Denver are on the Plains' east and west edges, respectively, but the largest city actually located in the Plains is Lubbock, Texas, population 179,000. Although the Plains occupy one-fifth of the nation's land area, the region's overall population, approximately 5.5 million, is less than that of Georgia or Indiana.

The Great Plains are America's steppes. They have the nation's hottest summers and coldest winters, greatest temperature swings, worst hail and locusts and range fires, fiercest droughts and blizzards, and therefore its shortest growing season. The Plains are the land of the Big Sky and the Dust Bowl, one-room schoolhouses and settler homesteads, straight-line interstates and custom combines, prairie dogs and antelope and buffalo. The oceans-of-grass vistas of the Plains offer enormous horizons, billowy clouds, and somber-serene beauty.

During America's pioneer days and then again during the Great Depression, the Plains were a prominent national concern. But by 1952, in his book *The Great Frontier*, the Plains' finest historian, the late Walter Prescott Webb of the University of Texas, could accurately describe them as the least-known, most fateful part of the United States. We believe that over the next generation the Plains will, as a result of the largest, longest-running agricultural and environmental miscalculation in American history, become almost totally depopulated. At that point, a new use for the region will emerge, one that is in fact so old that it predates the American presence. We are suggesting that the region be returned to its original pre-white state, that it be, in effect, deprivatized.

Last settled

As the U.S. spread into Indian territory in the late nineteenth century, the Plains became the last part of the nation to be settled by whites. The 1862 Homestead Act marked the beginning of sharp cycles of growth and decline, boom and bust. Federally subsidized settlement and cultivation repeatedly led to overgrazing and overplowing (sodbusting, in Plains terms). When nature and the economy turned hostile again, many of the farmers and ranchers were driven out—and the cycle began anew. Most of the post-Civil War homesteaders succumbed to the blizzards of the 1880s and the drought and financial panic of the 1890s. Homesteading flourished again in the early 1900s, crested during World War I as European agricultural productivity fell, and once more slumped in the early 1920s when drought and locusts hit.

For much of the Plains, the Great Depression began before it struck Wall Street. By 1925, Montana had suffered 214 bank failures, and the average value of all its farm and ranch land had dropped by half. As the depression intensified, the Plains were perhaps the most afflicted part of the country. In 1935, the five states with the largest percentage of farm families on relief were New Mexico, South Dakota, North Dakota, Oklahoma, and Colorado, and conditions were far worse in the Plains portions of each of those states.

Thus the Plains had undergone a dozen years of depression before the onset of the Dust Bowl in 1934, which in turn was the ecological consequence of earlier decades of too-assertive agriculture. The shortgrass Plains soil in places was destroyed by an excess of cattle and sheep grazing and of cultivation of corn, wheat, and cotton. When drought hit with its merciless cyclicality, the land had no defenses. By the late 1930s, the Dust Bowl covered nearly a third of the Plains. It kicked up dirt clouds five miles high and tore the paint off houses and cars. It sent the Okies west to California, inspiring both John Steinbeck's famous novel, *The Grapes of Wrath,* and Dorothea Lange's stark photographs.

The federal government responded by abolishing homesteading in 1934. The next year it established the Agriculture Department's Soil Conservation Service, which built windbreaks and shelter belts. Beginning in 1937, the federal government bought up 7.3 million acres of largely abandoned farm holdings of the Plains (an area bigger than Maryland), replanted them, and designated them "national grasslands." Today the national grasslands, which are administered by the Agriculture Department's Forest Service, are used primarily for low-intensity grazing and recreation. Often thick with shortgrass, they rank among the most successful types of federal landholdings.

After the trauma of the Dust Bowl, much of the recent history of the Plains seems anticlimactic. A measure of agricultural prosperity returned during World War II and after, although the Plains remained a poor region, falling further behind most of the rest of the country economically and continuing to suffer depopulation. To some extent, the picture looked rosier. New technologies came in— custom combines, ever-larger irrigation pumps, center-pivot irrigation sprayers—and the average size of farms and ranches grew steeply. Droughts persisted; after one in the 1970s, the National Oceanic and Atmospheric Administration estimated that, had it continued another month, the Dust Bowl might have returned.

The federal government found new ways to in-

tervene. The crop subsidy programs introduced experimentally in the thirties were greatly expanded in the forties and fifties. The dam and irrigation projects begun in 1902, primarily in the intermountain West, accelerated in 1944 with the adoption of the $6 billion, 100-dam, Pick-Sloan plan for the Missouri River, an effort aimed primarily at the Plains portion of the watershed. It meant that Plains farmers and ranchers could, like their competitors farther west, get federal water at below-market prices.

With the creation in 1934 of the Interior Department's Grazing Service and its evolution after the war into the Bureau of Land Management, the federal government established public land grazing districts that rented grazing rights to ranchers at below-market rates. More recently, the Plains benefited from the energy boom of the middle and late 1970s, which quintupled prices for oil and natural gas. Some 200 energy boomtowns suddenly sprouted in the Dakotas, Montana, Wyoming, and Colorado. The lessons of the 1930s were forgotten as agricultural commodity prices rose rapidly. Plains farmers and ranchers once again chopped down their windbreaks, planted from fencepost to fencepost, and sodbusted in the classic 1880s-1910s manner. This time, though, the scale was much larger, often tens of thousands of acres at a time.

The 1980s punctured the illusion of prosperity. Today the pressures on the Plains and their people are as ominous as at any time in American history. The region's farm, ranch, energy, and mineral economies are in deep depression. Many small towns are emptying and aging at an all-time high rate, and some are dying. The 1986 outmigration from West and Panhandle Texas, for instance, helped make the state a net exporter of population for the first time ever.

Soil erosion is approaching Dust Bowl rates. Water shortages loom, especially atop the Ogallala Aquifer, a giant but essentially nonrenewable source of groundwater that nourishes more than 11 million acres of agriculture in Plains Colorado, Kansas, Nebraska, New Mexico, Oklahoma, and Texas. Important long-term climatic and technological trends do not look favorable. Government seems unable to react constructively to these trends, much less to anticipate them.

In fact, the agricultural crisis is more serious on the Plains than in its more publicized neighbor region to the east, the Midwest's Corn Belt. Plains farmers and ranchers have always operated under conditions that their counterparts elsewhere would have found intolerable, and now they are worse. Farm bankruptcy and foreclosure rates are higher in the Plains than in other rural areas, as are many of the indices of resulting psychological stress: family violence, suicide, mental illness. In 1986, there were 138 bank collapses in the U.S., the largest number since the Depression. Texas had the most, 26, followed by Oklahoma with 16 and Kansas with 14. In contrast, the two Midwestern states in the most agricultural difficulty, Iowa and Missouri, had 10 and nine, respectively.

A series of mid-1980s federal agricultural initiatives—new subsidies, such as the Payment in Kind (PIK) program; additional tax breaks; a national conservation reserve where farmers and ranchers are paid not to cultivate erodible soil (that is, not to sodbust)—seem to have little impact in the Plains. The national conservation reserve, for instance, can at most cover a quarter of any one county. The only federal measure that appears effective is a 1985 law that makes it easier for farmers and ranchers to declare bankruptcy.

The situation is comparable in the energy sector. Oil prices have fallen drastically since 1983. Many large Plains oil and natural gas companies have laid off most of their employees. The energy boomtowns have long gone bust. Between 1985 and 1986, the number of active oil rigs in West Texas's Permian Basin dropped from 298 to 173, reducing local income by an estimated $50 million.

Ripple effect

The local collapses reverberate. When local banks fail or are endangered, the remaining ones lend more conservatively and charge higher interest. When a heavily agricultural county's farmers and ranchers cannot make a living, neither can its car dealers, druggists, restaurants, and clothing stores. Local public services, which have never been exactly generous in the Plains, fall off. Items like schools, roads, law enforcement, and welfare are always relatively expensive to provide and administer in large, lightly populated areas; they are especially expensive because of the traditional Plains pattern of many comparatively small local governments, which cannot take advantage of economies of scale.

Faced with a choice between higher local taxes

and fewer services, most Plains localities chose the latter. In the late 1970s, for example, Oklahoma towns rode the oil boom to become early leaders in school reform; now a tenth of the state's teachers have lost their jobs, many others have had their salaries frozen, classroom size has grown, buses are not repaired, and textbooks go unreplaced.

The quality of life also declines. The service cutbacks fall hardest on the poor: Montana farm laborers, South Dakota Indians, Mexican-Americans along the Rio Grande, clients of social work and public health agencies across the Plains. Agricultural market towns get smaller, older, and poorer. Already modest downtowns become gap-toothed streets of increasingly marginal businesses. Entire counties lack a single doctor or a bank, and many more are about to lose them.

The long-term outlook is frightening. Climatologists note that, over the last 50 years, rainfall in the Plains has actually been comparatively stable. Future droughts are inevitable, and they're likely to hit harder and more often. The greenhouse effect—the buildup in the atmosphere of carbon dioxide from fossil-fuel combustion—is expected to warm the Plains by an average of at least two to three degrees, making the region even more vulnerable to drought. The longstanding attempts to seed clouds or otherwise artificially induce rain continue to be unavailing.

Water supplies are diminishing throughout the Plains, primarily because of agricultural overuse. Farmland has already been abandoned for lack of water in the Pecos River Valley of New Mexico and between Amarillo and Lubbock in Texas. In 1950, the Kansas portion of the Ogallala Aquifer was 58 feet deep; today in many places it may be less than six feet. As parts of the aquifer approach exhaustion within a decade or so, Plains water prices are sure to rise steeply. Moreover, our huge national and regional agricultural surpluses argue against further irrigation initiatives to stimulate yet more agriculture.

Some farmers and ranchers and some localities are undertaking serious water- and soil-conservation measures, but it may already be too late to halt the erosion. Such counties as Gaines in Texas and Crowley and Kiowa in Colorado appear to be nearing Dust Bowl conditions. The federal Council on Environmental Quality has classified the desertification of West Texas and eastern New

Mexico and parts of Colorado, Kansas, and Oklahoma as "severe."

Already today, when Plains farmers and ranchers, small or large, give up land, the big agribusiness corporations are usually unwilling to buy it, even at a bargain price. Because the big companies are not interested—in clear contrast to their behavior elsewhere in the country—the price of Plains land drops lower still. The brute fact is that most Plains land is simply not competitive with land elsewhere. The only people who want it are already on it, and most of them are increasingly unable to make a living from it.

The tragedy of the commons

"Grass no good upside down," said a Pawnee chief in northeast Colorado as he watched the late-nineteenth-century homesteaders rip through the shortgrass with their steel plows. He mourned a stretch of land where the Indians had hunted buffalo for millennia. It grew crops for a few years, then went into the Dust Bowl; farmers abandoned it. Today, it is federal land, part of the system of national grasslands. Like most of the Plains, it is an austere monument to American self-delusion. Three separate waves of farmers and ranchers, with increasingly heavy federal support, tried to make settlement stick on the Plains. The 1890s and 1930s generations were largely uprooted, as the 1980s one soon will be.

Our national experience in the Plains represents a spectacular variant on the tragedy of the commons, Garrett Hardin's famous ecological fable of how individual short-term economic rationality can lead to collective long-term environmental disaster. To the Indians and the early cattlemen, all of the Plains was a commons. The Homestead Act and the succeeding federal land subsidies for settlers amounted to attempts to privatize the Plains, to take them out of the federal domain and put them permanently in individual or corporate hands. Today's subsidies for crops, water, and grazing land amount to attempts to buttress the privatization.

But private interests have proved unable to last for long on the Plains. Responding to nationally based market imperatives, they have overgrazed and overplowed the land and overdrawn the water. Responding to the usually increasing federal subsidies, they have overused the natural resources the subsidies provided. They never created a truly stable agriculture or found reliable conservation devices. In some places, private owners supplemented agriculture with inherently unstable energy and mineral development.

Now that both the market imperatives and federal subsidies seem inadequate to keep the private interests on the Plains, these interests are, as Hardin would have predicted, rapidly degrading the land and leaving it, in many places perhaps forever. As a nation, we have never understood that the federally subsidized privatization that worked so well to settle most of the land west of the Appalachians is ineffective on the Plains. It leads to overproduction that then cannot be sustained under the Plains' difficult economic and climatic conditions.

It is hard to predict the future course of the Plains ordeal. The most likely possibility is a continuation of the gradual impoverishment and depopulation that in many places go back to the 1920s. A few of the more urban areas may pull out of their decline, especially if an energy boom returns. And a few cities—Lubbock and Cheyenne, for example—may hold steady as self-contained service providers. But the small towns in the surrounding countryside will empty, wither, and die. The rural Plains will be virtually deserted. A vast, beautiful, characteristically American place will go the way of the buffalo that once roamed it in herds of millions.

Little stands in the way of this outcome. New mineral or energy sources might be discovered on the Plains. New crops might be developed, such as the cereal triticale (a high-protein cross between wheat and rye) or a Plains equivalent of the Southwest's jojoba bush, whose oil is now finding applications ranging from facial creams to industrial lubrication. Several groups in Kansas are exploring uses for oils from amaranth and rapeseed plants. Other Plains states are trying to create a llama or donkey industry that will meet the demand for horse substitutes, unconventional pets, or exotic wool. But most conceivable replacement crops for the Plains do not yet exist or are more economically and abundantly produced elsewhere, usually in the Midwest.

For some parts of the Plains, tourism and recreation might be plausible options. Growing numbers of ranchers offer their land for hunting, wildlife photography, backpacking trips, and wilderness expeditions in addition to the usual dude-

and-tenderfoot packages. In places within three or four hours' drive of big cities—most noticeably in West Texas—ranches are being carved into ranchettes for weekend cowboys. But tourism cannot offer much to the Plains as a whole. Farmers typically cannot tap the recreation market, and many ranchers feel that tourism demeans them, compromises their independence.

Bring back the commons

The most intriguing alternative would be to restore large parts of the Plains to their pre-white condition, to make them again the commons the settlers found in the nineteenth century. This approach, which would for the first time in U.S. history treat the Plains as a distinct region and recognize its unsuitability for agriculture, is being proposed with increasing frequency. Bret Wallach, a University of Oklahoma geographer and MacArthur fellow, has suggested that the Forest Service enter into voluntary contracts with Plains farmers and ranchers, paying them the full value of what they would cultivate during each of the next 15 years but requiring them not to cultivate it. During this time, they would instead follow a Forest Service-approved program of planting to reestablish the native shortgrasses. Afterwards, the service would, as part of the original contract, buy out their holdings except for a 40-acre homestead.

Similarly, Charles Little, former editor of *American Land Forum,* suggests that by expanding the national grasslands, the grazing districts operated by the Bureau of Land Management, and the anti-sodbusting national conservation reserve, we could retire enough agricultural land to slow the depletion of the Ogallala Aquifer. Robert Scott of the Institute of the Rockies in Missoula, Montana, urges that 15,000 square miles of eastern Montana, about a tenth of the state, be transformed into an East African-style game preserve called the Big Open. With state and federal help, fences would come down, domestic animals would be removed, and game animals stocked. According to Scott, the land could support 75,000 bison, 150,000 deer, 40,000 elk, 40,000 antelope. A ranch of 10,000 acres (nearly 16 square miles), by now a normal size for the area, would net at least $48,000 a year from the sale of hunting licenses alone. Some 1,000 new jobs—for outfitters, taxidermists, workers in gas stations, restaurants, motels—would develop in this sparsely settled area.

Scott's approach, unlike Wallach's and Little's, lets ranchers and farmers keep all their land by treating it as free range. Yet all three proposals would be costly and provoke great resistance from the landowners because they would constrain their property rights.

We believe that despite history's warnings and environmentalists' proposals, much of the Plains will inexorably suffer near-total desertion over the next generation. It will come slowly to most places, quickly to some; parts of Montana, New Mexico, South Dakota, and Texas, especially those away from the interstates, strike us as likely candidates for rapid depopulation. The overall desertion will largely run its course. At that point, the only way to keep the Plains from turning into an utter wasteland, an American Empty Quarter, will be for the federal government to step in and buy the land—in short, to deprivatize it.

If the federal government intervenes late rather than early—after the desertion instead of before it—the buy-back task will, ironically, be easier. The farmers and ranchers will already have abandoned large chunks of land, making it simpler for the government to reassemble the commons (and to persuade the holdouts to sell). Those parts of the Plains where agriculture, energy development, mining, or tourism remains workable will have become clear, and here government would make no deprivatization attempts. We suspect, however, that there won't be many such places.

In practical terms, a federal deprivatization program would have two thrusts, one for Plains people, the other for Plains land. On the people side, government would negotiate buy-backs from landowners—often under distress-sale circumstances. Some of the landowners will be in a position to insist on phased sales or easements that allow them to hold on to their land somewhat longer.

It will be up to the federal government to ease the social transition of the economic refugees who are being forced off the land. For they will feel aggrieved and impoverished, penalized for staying too long in a place they loved and pursuing occupations the nation supposedly respected but evidently did not. The government will have to invent a 1990s version of the 1930s Resettlement Administration, a social work-finance-technical assistance agency that will find ways and places for the former Plains residents to get back on their feet.

On the land side, the government will take the newly emptied Plains and tear down the fences, replant the shortgrass, and restock the animals, including the buffalo. It will take a long time. Even if large pieces of the commons can be assembled quickly, it will be at least 20 to 30 years before the vegetation and wildlife reassert themselves in the semiarid Plains settings, where the land changes so slowly that wagon-trail ruts more than a century old are still visible. There may also be competing uses for the land. In South Dakota, several Sioux tribes are now bringing suit for 11,000 square miles, including much of the Black Hills. The federal government might settle these and other long-standing Plains Indian land claims by giving or selling the tribes chunks of the new commons.

The federal government's commanding task on the Plains for the next century will be to recreate the nineteenth century, to reestablish what we would call the Buffalo Commons. More and more previously private land will be acquired to form the commons. In many areas, the distinctions between the present national parks, grasslands, grazing lands, wildlife refuges, forests, Indian lands, and their state counterparts will largely dissolve. The small cities of the Plains will amount to urban islands in a shortgrass sea. The Buffalo Commons will become the world's largest historic preservation project, the ultimate national park. Most of the Great Plains will become what all of the United States once was—a vast land mass, largely empty and unexploited.

Creating the Buffalo Commons represents a substantial administrative undertaking. It will require competent land-use planning to identify acquisition areas, devise fair buyout contracts, and determine permitted uses. It will demand compassionate treatment for the Plains' refugees and considerable coordination between huge distant, frequently obtuse federal agencies, smaller state agencies whose attention often goes primarily to the non-Plains parts of their states, and desperate local governments. To accomplish these tasks, the federal government will, for the first time, have to create an agency with a Plains-specific mandate—a regional agency like the Tennessee Valley Authority or a public-land agency like the Bureau of Land Management, but with much more sweeping powers.

By creating the Buffalo Commons, the federal government will, however belatedly, turn the social costs of space—the curse of the shortgrass im-mensity—to more social benefit than the unsuccessfully privatized Plains have ever offered.

Deborah Epstein Popper is a graduate student in geography at Rutgers University in New Brunswick, New Jersey, and Frank J. Popper chairs the university's urban studies department.

We've Got to Dig Deeper Into Who Owns Our Land

Frank J. Popper
(October 1976)

Although planners deal with how the country's land is used, zoned, and subdivided, they also should be concerned with the basic question of who owns the land in the United States. The long-range consequences of land ownership are staggering, not only from a political viewpoint but from the standpoint of how land is controlled for ulterior motives, by whom, and how it might—or might not—be developed.

It's not that information on land ownership doesn't exist. It does, and it's on file in every assessor's and recorder's office in every city and county courthouse in America. But few individuals have bothered to collect and analyze it. The few researchers of this information are mainly a handful of Naderish citizen-advocates, government agencies, and investigative reporters willing to do the tedious work of sifting through dusty local records and then chasing after reluctant, often dummy, corporations and suspicious public agencies for confirmation.

Since the results of such studies rarely are pulled together in one place, and since planners seem largely unaware of them, it is well worthwhile to examine some sample findings. These results are presented with the caveat that landowners—whether individuals, corporations, or government agencies—all too often underreport or conceal the extent of their holdings.

From the report of the Nader study group on California land use, *Politics of Land* (Grossman, 1973): California's top 10 private landowners controlled 11 percent of the state's total private acreage. If separate government agencies were counted as separate owners, 250 owners held about two-thirds of the state's total land area. About 43 per cent of the state's private timberland was controlled by 20 firms, and 29 firms held about 21 per cent of its private cropland. In 1920 the average size of a California farm was 250 acres; in 1969, with fewer farmers, it was 627 acres. In some rural counties, the top 20 private landowners held as much as half the private land. . . .

From the report of New York State's temporary study commission on the future of the Adirondacks (1970): In Adirondack Park, which is roughly the size of Vermont and comprises a fifth of New York State, one percent of the landowners held more than half the private land. Three timber companies owned more than 125,000 acres apiece. About three-fifths of the private land was held by nonresident individuals and corporations.

From the *Report to the People* of the Hawaii State Land-Use Commission (1975): In 1968, 39 persons and corporations owned about 44 percent of Hawaii's total land area. Eighty-seven per cent of all private lands were held by interests that controlled 1,000 acres or more. Eleven trusts held 17 per cent of all private lands. Major private owners, along with state and local governments, held 85 per cent of the state's total area. The private owners held nearly all the land that could be developed.

From the Kansas Farm Project's paper, "Concentrated Land Tenure in Kansas in the 1960s" (Center for Rural Studies in San Francisco, undated): Twenty-eight corporations and 164 individuals each owned at least 5,000 acres of Kansas agricultural land. Their holdings totaled about 2.1 million acres. . . .

Other studies of the concentration of land ownership have been conducted on DuPont corporate and family holdings in Delaware; steel, coal, and railroad company ownership in West Virginia; agribusiness holdings in Nebraska; and coastal ownership in Hawaii and South Florida.

What the studies show

Beneath the statistics of all these studies, the main patterns of ownership are fairly clear. American land ownership is highly concentrated, especially in rural areas.

- Large timber-and-paper, oil, coal, agribusiness, and utility companies own much of the country's private land and undoubtedly much of the best, most productive portions of it.

- Financial institutions, development companies, manufacturing concerns, and railroads are surprisingly underrepresented, although they still own a great deal of valuable property.
- Nonlocal, absentee ownership is widespread. It may well be that most of the private land in America is absentee-owned.

These findings show—or rather confirm—that the Jeffersonian vision of a nation composed largely of small land-owning farmers and rural artisans of relatively equal wealth has long since dissipated. The findings are important because they suggest that a disconcertingly large number of land-use planners are working in areas with a high concentration of land ownership and are largely unaware of the possible effects.

This lack of knowledge can make planners less able to deal with many issues they must face. A city, county, or region whose land ownership is highly concentrated or becoming so is likely to be one where planning and environmental laws are subverted by political influence, where assessments unfairly favor large landowners, and where unresponsive absentee ownership often can thwart the government and the people of the community. If the large ownership happens to be locally based, it may attempt to manipulate planners.

An area with highly concentrated ownership is vulnerable to extremely rapid changes in land use that can bring painful consequences to community residents. A comparatively small number of transactions, made by large outside interests dealing among themselves, can overwhelm local planners and quickly change the community for the worse. Only a few owners need sell out or convert the uses of their land to transform a settled rural community into one suffering from all the ills of excessively fast urban growth.

Today, the best examples of this local vulnerability come from energy development in the West. In 1970, for instance, the land around the town of Rock Springs in rural Sweetwater County, southwest Wyoming, was mainly owned by a subsidiary of the Union Pacific Railroad (headquarters in Omaha, 700 miles away) and the federal government. The town's population was 12,000, and it was a pleasant place. But when two utilities— Pacific Power and Light and Idaho Power—bought or leased most of this land to build the $400 million Jim Bridger Power Plant, the big out-of-state coal and oil companies moved in.

The town was never the same again. By 1974, writes Joan Nice in *High Country News,* the town's population had swelled to 26,000. It had an overloaded sewage system, high prices, large school and hospital bonded indebtedness, traffic congestion, a high crime rate, and nasty drug and prostitution problems. There was no housing available, and highly paid construction workers were sleeping in tents, campers, and trailers. Mental health caseloads had multiplied by 10. Small farmers and ranchers were being squeezed out of business.

Similarly, a good deal of the voracious growth of Sun Belt cities as well as suburbs in the Northeast since 1945 has been made possible by the fact that large landowners on the urbanizing fringes of these areas have been able to sell off their holdings in huge chunks. For example, the explosive urbanization of what may be the fastest-growing area of Florida, the coast of Pasco County north of Tampa, came about largely as a consequence of the sale of a single ranch.

In many cases new private industry and public projects have strengthened local economies. But too often unchecked development has resulted in thousands of miles of sprawl, immense strains on local governments and public services, irretrievable desecrations of beautiful land, and permanent loss of some of our best farmland. We haven't seen the end of this growth yet.

Before the recent recession, second-home and residential developers were buying up tracts in units of tens of thousands of entirely rural acres, again overwhelming local planning and governmental capabilities and irreparably damaging communities. The most spectacular example was probably the Palm Coast development near St. Augustine, Florida, where the development subsidiary of International Telephone and Telegraph Corporation was planning to build a new community of three-quarters of a million people in Flagler County, population 4,500. Palm Coast's hundred thousand acres accounts for a third of the county's land. Although the Palm Coast project is now in abeyance, these sorts of huge developments may materialize again if the economy continues to recover. And more local residents will suffer the social consequences of rapid conversion of highly concentrated landholdings. . . .

Much to learn

But for all the importance of land ownership concentration, there are vast areas about which we know virtually nothing. Is concentration increasing over time? It seems likely, but direct, hard evidence is meager. The Nader studies of Maine and California suggest that timber and agricultural holdings have become more concentrated, but most of the studies cited so far have very little to say about changes in concentration over the years. There is no concrete proof that overall concentration of land ownership across the country is increasing.

Then there is the intriguing matter of the identity of the large landowners. We know that certain kinds of corporations own a great deal of valuable land. Large timber, energy, agribusiness, and development companies—along with well-known and anonymous wealthy individuals—may not be white knights, but most of them are respectable. What about the ones that aren't? Shady union pension funds and organized crime fronts are visible in many Appalachian coal fields and in Florida, California, and Arizona land development projects. And what about those faceless trusts legalistically based in Liechtenstein, the Cayman Islands, or other clumps in the fathomless ooze of international dirty money? We are almost totally ignorant about the American landholdings of domestic and foreign predators.

There's an even bigger gap in our knowledge. The existing studies of land ownership concentration focus nearly exclusively on rural areas. We know very few details about most ownership in urban and urbanizing areas. This neglect is unfortunate because more people are directly affected by concentration patterns in these areas, and land values are higher. Thus the political stakes in concentrated ownership are higher as well.

There is some information on urban areas. The Nader study of California land use, the touchstone of American concentration studies, is the best investigation I know of urban landholdings. Its data on acreage and assessments in San Francisco, Sacramento, San Mateo, and Ventura counties suggest that urban ownership is usually somewhat less concentrated than rural ownership. And manufacturing concerns, development companies, and financial institutions own substantially higher percentages of land in California urban areas than they do in rural ones.

However, we need much more research on urban land concentrations. Nobody knows how much of the Detroit area is owned by the auto companies or how much of Houston is owned by oil interests. Underassessment of large holdings, which the Nader groups found in California, is a common problem in cities and suburbs, yet we know very little about it. Nor do we know much about the extent of the tax-exempt holdings of educational, religious, charitable, and other nonprofit organizations.

If we had more good studies of urban land concentration, I suspect the results could be disconcerting. The tax-exempt organizations could emerge as major depressants of many city treasuries. The educational, religious, and charitable institutions, as well as other corporate and individual specialists in human redemption, might turn out to own embarrassing amounts of slum property. The holdings of organized crime might be revealed. The real estate activities of public works and urban renewal agencies could come to light. So could the dealings between such agencies and the friends of politicians.

Perhaps the task of uncovering land ownership is best left to independent study groups which can operate despite the wrath of political interests and land-baron manipulation. However, the task is so immense that no planner—whether citizen-advocate, academic, elected official, or public agency employee—should be unaware of the ramifications of the concentration of land ownership. Planners of all kinds should pay more attention to who owns the land.

Frank Popper chairs the urban studies department at Rutgers University.

Living With Hard Realities

Richard P. Nathan
(October 1983)

A common refrain in current discussions of U.S. domestic policy is that government programs don't work and that we should rely on the private sector to solve public problems. This notion often gets translated into vague political statements about the need for an "industrial policy," or if it is more specific, into discussions of new economic development programs such as urban enterprise zones. At the root of such carryings on is the belief that government programs can harness private energies to stimulate the economy, create jobs, aid distressed areas and industries, enhance the tax base—in short, do everything but part the Red Sea. The purpose of this essay is to bring this discussion down to particulars. This is not an easy task. One of the dangers for policy analysts of being relevant—that is, working on current issues—is getting too close to events as they are unfolding and failing to understand long-range trends and more basic issues.

Economists often discuss four major types of economic development policies: sectoral, regional, rural, and inner-city. The problem is that the objectives of these four types of policies often conflict, and, for that reason, programs tend to be confused and unsatisfying.

Sectoral policy refers to aid for firms in new and growth industries. Presumably, these firms should be located in the places where they are most likely to take root and prosper, i.e., economically strong and growing areas. In contrast, the aim of regional policy is to encourage industries—both new and old—to start up or remain in places where they otherwise would not be located. Rural development and inner-city policies are more site-specific, though not necessarily compatible, variants of regional policy.

Note that the four types of economic development policies listed here do not include "industrial policy," now in high fashion as a cure-all for the nation's economic and social ills. Industrial policy is similar to sectoral policy but not identical. As described by one of its foremost proponents, Robert B. Reich of the Kennedy School of Government at Harvard, industrial policy is designed to deal with one essential problem. "We are losing the competitive struggle because we cannot work together," Reich says in his book, *The Next American Frontier.* It is obvious that, in a mature industrial democracy, institutions must adapt to external conditions and technological developments. Nevertheless, Reich's evangelical approach—and that of other aficionados of industrial policy—does not tell us how we should change our political and economic institutions to achieve greater flexibility and cooperation. This oversight must be frustrating to practitioners in the economic development field who are engaged in the day-to-day work of industrial and land-use planning at the regional, state, and local levels.

Ten years ago, David Kennedy, a state senator from Minnesota, cut through all of these niceties in setting forth "the law of appropriateness." Although directed to American federalism as a whole, Kennedy's law brings this discussion of economic development policies into the right focus. Kennedy's law of appropriateness is: "The level of government most appropriate to deal with a given problem is that level by which one is employed." A derivative of Kennedy's law for the economic development field is: "Any government official's definition of economic development policy depends on the type of jurisdiction for which he works."

This situation—a cacophony of voices—is unlikely to change, grounded as it is in the pluralistic and decentralized character of our governmental system.

Still, for the purposes of this article, I would like to restrict the term "economic development," as it applies to the policies and programs of the U.S. government, to rural and inner-city policy and discuss the way in which (and the degree to which) we should target economic development subsidies to different types of distressed areas. The dominant trend in the federal government's economic development policies and programs over the past 10 years has been to spread subsidies more widely—rather than to target them to the most needy places. Readers of this magazine do not need proof that tax incentives for job creation, grants and loans from the Economic Development Administration (EDA), and block grant funds are being ever more widely dispersed. I don't like this situation; I think it is inefficient. But one man's notions of distributive justice and efficiency are but a stone thrown into the sea of domestic policy making. What, in short, do current governmental and economic trends indicate for the planners and managers of these kinds of programs?

The Reagan cuts

The United States is in a period of retrenchment in domestic affairs that predates Ronald Reagan. It is a natural reaction to the substantial growth of domestic social spending over the long period from the New Deal until the adoption in 1978 of California's Proposition 13. This current mood is likely to persist for a long time. We have to get used to the new politics of limits in domestic affairs.

Taking advantage of the momentum of the 1980 presidential election, Ronald Reagan in his first year in office used the congressional budget process in a skillful and dramatic way to obtain substantial cuts in domestic programs in fiscal year 1982, which began October 1, 1981. Soon thereafter, a reduction in federal income taxes, coupled with increases in defense spending, had the effect of creating huge federal deficits. Although the administration was not successful in obtaining further cuts in domestic spending for fiscal years 1983 and 1984, the mood in Washington has been fundamentally changed. Those who favor domestic programs are on the defensive. Instead of advancing initiatives, they are busy forestalling cuts.

On the whole, federal programs to stimulate local economic development have not been as hard hit as social programs for the poor. However, the success of the changes wrought by the administration in the welfare system has important implications for economic development. The heaviest burden of federal welfare cuts falls on precisely those highly distressed communities that, in my opinion, should be the target of the federal government's rural and inner-city development policies.

The Reagan philosophy for economic development is similar to that of the Commission for a National Agenda for the Eighties, appointed by President Jimmy Carter at the end of his presidency. David Stockman, the federal budget director, and the commission—headed by William J. McGill—argued that the federal government should aid needy people (presumably on a uniform basis) and that the free market should be relied on to determine where new jobs are created. According to this nice, neat theory, people then can move to the places where the jobs are, with the certainty that they will be protected in the event of adversity by a "safety net" with the same sized holes everywhere. Although the Reagan administration is cutting aid programs aimed at *both* people and places, the debate continues to be waged in terms of a false dichotomy that tries to distinguish between them.

My own view is that we have no choice but to use both kinds of programs to aid distressed areas. As a practical matter, the combination of cash and in-kind welfare benefits to needy people has reached levels in many industrial states that the public regards as "adequate" or "near-adequate."

(Reagan's policies do not cut benefits for people on welfare who do not work.)

Under these conditions, if we want to do more to help those places in which poor people are concentrated—and as a practical matter, poor people's mobility options often are limited—then we have no choice but to use programs that aid communities in providing services and facilities to rehabilitate disadvantaged people. The answer will be to improve our schools and to have employment and public works programs—as well as economic development—in these troubled communities. This practical point is often overlooked in simplistic pronouncements about social policy.

Early in Reagan's first year in office, David Stockman chose the urban development action grants, along with the loans and grants of the Economic Development Administration, to make the point that place-oriented programs are an inefficient way to stimulate local economic development. Both programs were "zeroed out" in the proposals the Reagan administration sent to the Congress to amend the fiscal year 1982 federal budget.

The outcome was a near-win on EDA and a setback on the Urban Development Action Grant program. UDAG ended up with a 35 percent cut in budget authority in 1982, while EDA was cut by 68 percent. For UDAG, the lobbying efforts of business people and local officials (both liberal and conservative), and the quiet, persistent efforts of HUD Secretary Samuel Pierce, saved most of the program. But, to reiterate my point about proponents of domestic policy having been forced into this defensive stance, victory consisted not in getting more, but in keeping what there was—or at least most of what there was in UDAG.

Two other types of federal aid programs are important for practitioners in the economic development field—programs that support state and local planning agencies and those that provide aid for public infrastructure. For federal grants that support planning, the main story line is one of decline and lost interest. Reagan's revisions of the fiscal year 1982 federal budget targeted a wide array of planning grants as programs to be eliminated.

The other type of federal aid program important to local economic development efforts is capital grants. Here, the picture is brighter. Federal cuts in this area were not deep and in a number of cases have been restored by later federal legislation. The Surface Transportation Act signed by President Reagan in January 1983 raised the gasoline tax by five cents a gallon to provide funds for highways and mass transit. A similar job-creation bill, the Emergency Jobs Act passed in March 1983, provided $4.6 billion for a wide range of programs—including $1 billion for community development block grants.

A major question of our recent research at Princeton is the extent to which cuts in social and other domestic spending programs have been replaced by state and local funds. The main finding to date is that replacement has been minimal. Hit by the recession and tax and spending limits, states and localities on the whole have ratified the Reagan cuts, i.e., passed them along to the recipients of the federally aided services and activities.

What will be the result? By doing less to help impoverished people, governments at all levels are guaranteeing that distressed communities slide further into decline.

All things considered, though, there is reason to be bullish about the U.S. economy and labor market as a whole and particularly about the prospects of the West as a region and for smaller cities and nonmetropolitan places in general. Data from the 1980 census show that smaller cities and towns (under 50,000 population) grew much faster in the seventies than larger urban places did. But the older and most troubled cities face grim prospects.

This category includes big cities like Detroit, St. Louis, Newark, and Buffalo; smaller cities like Camden, New Jersey; Gary, Indiana; and Chester, Pennsylvania and older suburbs like Robbins, Illinois. I believe—but it is hard to prove—that the growing problem of an isolated and alienated American underclass is becoming increasingly concentrated in these older, distressed cities.

This is also increasingly true of cities in the South (like Birmingham, Miami, and Atlanta), according to new research we are doing. Southern cities did very well in the sixties and early seventies, but economic data from the Census Bureau show that they fell off in a consistent and decided way in the middle and late seventies. Paradoxically, the political case for targeting federal aid for economic development that I made earlier is strengthened by the fact that urban distress is not limited to the East and Midwest.

Another reason for targeting federal aid is that economic research indicates that tax incentives to attract industries to needy areas are much more efficient if provided by higher levels of government—the federal government and the states—than if provided by local communities, the latter being, unfortunately, the predominant practice in the United States. This, in my view, is the reason why Reagan's urban enterprise zone approach is an attractive one.

A brighter note

Finally, the overall jobs situation is brighter as far as efforts to reduce unemployment are concerned. In the next decade, the average annual growth rate of the labor force is likely to be half (maybe less than half) of what it was in the past decade. Although many jobs are changing, Marc Bendick, Jr., of the Urban Institute concludes (and his analysis is convincing) that "there is no reason to believe that technological change—or any other form of structural economic change—threatens the American labor force with cataclysmic readjustment problems over the next decade." Bendick's analysis suggests that there are no secret formulas for identifying industrial winners and losers. Sound analysis and flexibility on the part of local officials are the keys to successful economic development planning. High tech and robotics are not always going to be the right approach to local job creation.

The special social and economic problems of the United States are increasingly focused in older places, both rural and urban, and especially those with concentrations of racial and ethnic minorities—people who for practical reasons are not mobile. These problems are getting more serious at precisely the time that the federal government is doing less about them. Will Rogers once said, "Things will get better despite our efforts to improve them." For domestic policy in the United States in the current period, I'm not so sure. In short, the situation is grim.

For economic development programs, the lessons are multiple. We cannot think narrowly about economic development policies and programs for the most distressed places. We must consider both their industrial and human resources. We need to be concerned about schools, health, job training—as well as subsidies that can be used to attract and hold industry.

Practitioners in the economic development field are aware of many of these hard realities. They preach the gospel, but the congregation is losing

faith. Maybe Will Rogers was right. Maybe we can look forward to a renewed period of concern and commitment to community social and economic needs, but history seems to teach otherwise—namely, that mood shifts of the depth and scope of the one we are now experiencing tend to be long lasting.

Richard Nathan is professor of public and international affairs at Princeton University.

HUD at 20 Faces a Midlife Crisis

William Fulton
(November 1985)

Twenty years ago this month, on November 10, 1965, federal workers undertook the first construction project arising from the creation on that day of a new, cabinet-level department dealing with urban affairs. Typically, something went wrong. The department's first official act was to remove the Housing and Home Finance Agency's metal plaque from the front of the Lafayette Building on Vermont Avenue in Washington and replace it with a sign designating the new headquarters of the Department of Housing and Urban Development. But the sign's specifications turned out to be wrong, and it was removed almost immediately. The new department, which still lacked a secretary, now appeared to lack a name as well.

Two months later, though, President Lyndon Johnson called a surprise press conference at the White House—his first in several months—to announce that Robert C. Weaver, the administrator of the HHFA, would become the first HUD secretary. It was truly a historic moment. Never before had the federal government made a broad national commitment to urban problems, and never before had a black been appointed to a cabinet position. And through two decades, five presidents, and seven secretaries, HUD has faced the remarkably difficult task of carrying out its charge of assuring "sound development of the Nation's communities and metropolitan areas in which the vast majority of its people live and work."

To the disappointment of its creators, however,

the existence of a cabinet seat did not succeed in keeping housing and urban matters high on the national agenda. Even under Johnson, with the memory of violent riots in U.S. cities still fresh, the department had difficulty competing with the Vietnam war for the president's attention and energy. And it wasn't long before the national economy and federal deficit became far more important issues to every presidential administration, Republican and Democratic, than the nation's urban ills.

"There has never been a secretary anybody paid any attention to," says Robert Embry, who worked for two of them as an assistant secretary in the Carter administration. "HUD was low on the totem pole."

To be sure, HUD's 20-year history includes many significant achievements. Its housing assistance programs have provided decent housing for millions of Americans, though sometimes at great cost. A series of grant programs laid the foundation for reviving many now-vibrant urban centers. And the department has helped train a cadre of urban professionals, many of whom continue to do good work on the state and local levels.

But the national commitment to urban problems has disappeared—so much so that the Reagan administration has greatly reduced the department's staff, budget, and influence without so much as a peep from the American people. The conventional wisdom in Washington is that HUD simply doesn't have a constituency any more. Ironically, there seems to be a tremendous constituency for these same issues on the local level, where innovative leaders—mayors and top staff people—are trying to link economic development and solutions to social problems. Many urban experts, noting that the era of big-budget federal departments is clearly past, believe that this downshifting of power to localities has created a whole new range of opportunities for HUD in monitoring, coordinating, and encouraging the local innovations.

But HUD under Reagan has shown absolutely no interest in seizing the day. Secretary Samuel R. Pierce, Jr., who has become the longest-serving HUD chief, is also the most passive. Around Washington he is known as "Silent Sam," and the rest of his department is hardly more vocal than he is. To critics like Anthony Downs, a senior fellow at the Brookings Institution, it is not the HUD staff and budget cuts that are disturbing—those were inevitable—but the sheer invisibility of the

department. "HUD is an impressive demonstration that stealth bomber technology works on federal bureaucracies," says Downs, one of the nation's most respected urban analysts.

Strong start

Such disappointments were certainly not foreseen when a HUD-type agency was first talked about in the early 1960s. President John F. Kennedy gave the idea its first public airing in his State of the Union address in 1961 when he called for the creation of such a department. Though it was almost five years before HUD was born, the consensus at the time was that something like it was long overdue. For more than 40 years, after all, census figures had shown that the U.S. was a mostly urban nation.

In setting up HUD, Weaver and his aides had, at least at first, a strong commitment from the Johnson White House, which wanted HUD to succeed as part of the "Great Society." Jay Janis, who served as Weaver's executive assistant and later as undersecretary in the Carter administration, recalls that at least once a week Weaver would get a call from the White House—sometimes from Johnson himself—demanding "a big housing bill." The result was the Housing Act of 1968, which established the Section 235 and Section 236 subsidy programs, both run by the Federal Housing Administration, and which authorized the FHA to use its programs in older, declining areas, adding a social aspect to that agency's work for the first time.

The 1968 housing act represented the high point of national commitment to urban affairs. Builders, civil rights groups, mortgage bankers, church and social reform groups all lobbied for its passage. Weaver describes the bill as one of his greatest achievements, and Janis recalls that Johnson wanted it as his "last great coonskin." The Johnson/Weaver years were also a time of federal initiative in special, innovative programs, including Model Cities, which targeted federal aid to distressed urban areas, and the New Communities program, which was meant to encourage orderly suburban development.

From the beginning, however, the federal effort was undermined by the fact that many important urban programs remained outside HUD and were not coordinated with each other. The department absorbed all of HHFA's units, including the FHA, the Public Housing Administration, the Urban Renewal Administration, the Federal National Mortgage Association, and the Community Facilities Administration. (The amalgamation of federal programs known as HHFA was so unwieldy that even its director, Weaver, called it an "administrative monstrosity." It was described in *Federal Government and Urban Programs,* a 1978 book by former HUD official N. Carter McFarland.)

But other programs, just as important, were not included, largely for political reasons. Johnson refused to transfer the Community Action Program out of the Office of Economic Opportunity, believing it would be more independent there. Urban mass transit programs were left out because Johnson had plans to create a federal Department of Transportation. VA housing programs stayed in the Veterans Administration, and the Federal Home Loan Bank also remained independent.

One of the new programs that did seek to coordinate all federal urban activities, Model Cities, failed because the White House would not take a strong role in knocking cabinet-level heads together and—a problem that would come up again and again—because Congress increased the number of "targeted" areas to include more of its members' districts. "At the time, we did as much as could be done," recalls Weaver. "Where we missed was in getting a greater amount of coordination from the White House."

Given the Johnson administration's commitment to urban affairs, why was this coordination lacking? "I'll give you the answer in one word," says Janis. "Vietnam. Because of the escalation of the Vietnam war, Johnson did not want to take on the task. But it would have been his next priority."

But the Great Society's moment soon passed. And during Richard Nixon's first term, federal spending and the national economy overrode urban problems as the country's leading domestic issue—a state of affairs that continues to this day.

The Nixon years

Though he was elected by a largely suburban constituency, Nixon did maintain a vigorous department during his first administration by appointing a strong secretary, his former political rival, George Romney. Romney, who had been governor of Michigan during the riots in Detroit a few years earlier, was by all accounts clearly committed to HUD's programs. He gave high priority to the ill-fated "Operation Breakthrough," a program de-

signed to nurture ideas that could increase the volume of housing production and decrease its cost. "Breakthrough" emphasized greater use of manufactured housing, leading Weaver to characterize Romney, the former president of American Motors, as "well intentioned, although he wanted to produce housing like automobiles."

Late in 1972, however, Romney became so frustrated by Nixon's indifference to housing issues and by the condescension shown him by White House aides that he decided to resign at the end of Nixon's first term. Shortly before Romney left at the beginning of 1973, Nixon impounded domestic funds and suspended HUD's subsidized housing programs. He then appointed James Lynn, who had been general counsel and undersecretary at the Commerce Department. Lynn concentrated on reducing HUD's expenditures, even though the department had never accounted for more than two percent of the federal budget. Under Lynn, the HUD budget stopped growing for the first time in 1973, holding steady at $3.6 billion.

Lynn's appointment marked the end of the agency as a forceful presence in the White House; no secretary since has been as visible as Weaver and Romney were. According to some HUD staffers, the Lynn years also marked the end of HUD as an exciting young agency at which to work. By the time Lynn departed in 1974, many of the best and brightest staffers had either retired or left.

The shift in federal priorities during the Nixon administration was reflected in the fate of the New Communities program. Inspired by attempts to construct private "new towns" in the 1960s, the program was meant to encourage innovative suburban development, mostly through federal loan guarantees but also through meaningful urban growth policies. The Nixon administration never took the program seriously, however, and did not produce the growth policies that were required by the new towns legislation. Moreover, at a time when finance was becoming extremely important in federal circles, a consultants' analysis found that the New Communities staff "was thin or altogether lacking in large-scale real estate business experience, including management, finance, construction, and marketing." Eventually HUD was stuck with over $300 million in defaulted loans—effectively killing the new towns program and chances for similar programs in the future.

Block grants

Despite the financial problems, the Nixon and Gerald Ford years did bring a new, more streamlined approach to housing and community development that has proved effective over the years. The Community Development Block Grant program, approved by Congress in 1974, folded seven HUD grant programs to local governments into more general "block grants." The idea was part of Nixon's "New Federalism" proposal to return greater control to state and local government, and it quickly became the department's largest community development program—rising from $38 million in 1975 to $2 billion in 1977 and almost $4 billion by 1980.

Some critics contended that block grants subtly redistributed a greater share of federal urban aid to the suburbs at the expense of distressed inner cities. But Floyd Hyde, an assistant HUD secretary during the Nixon administration, says the intention was not to abdicate federal responsibility for urban problems. "The idea was that the federal government should set some broad standards for communities and provide broad resources," says Hyde.

The other streamlined policy that came out of the Nixon years was the Section 8 housing program, which was also established by the 1974 act. Section 8 was meant to correct the weaknesses the Nixon administration had found in other housing assistance programs by providing subsidies directly to apartment owners on behalf of low-income tenants.

Although Lynn had shepherded the block grant and Section 8 proposals through Congress, it was up to his successor, attorney Carla Hills—appointed by Gerald Ford in 1975—to implement them. "When I arrived, I found the regulations [for Section 8] were not drafted," she recalls. "I had to testify at a budget hearing 11 days after arriving." She says that, although Lynn had promised Congress that HUD would produce 200,000 housing units during the first year of Section 8, "it was my happy chore to go up and testify that we would get only 20,000."

However, Hills, who also had little experience in urban affairs, worked hard to learn the subject and raise morale, and she says HUD was able to produce 500,000 units the following year, despite the constraints imposed by a president who freely used the budgetary veto.

The Carter administration might have represented a return to a Democratic presidency, but it did not mark the return of a White House commitment to urban affairs. Carter did appoint a strong-minded secretary, the late Patricia Roberts Harris, and HUD did embark on a few innovative programs, such as the Urban Development Action Grants and a national urban policy designed to make sure that all federal actions reinforced the strength of cities. But Janis, who was undersecretary at the time, recalls that Carter was so beleaguered by the budget deficit that he "was scared to death that we'd send over a proposal that would cost money"—a clear contrast to the Johnson years.

Under Reagan

By the time Ronald Reagan took office in 1981, it was obvious that the political forces that had created HUD and given it importance in the late 1960s and early 1970s had been dramatically weakened.

The most important change, of course, was financial. The federal government no longer had the dollars to spend on domestic programs that it had in HUD's early days. Moreover, there was no longer the unified constituency of interest groups that Johnson and Weaver had built. "The civil rights groups have found a different agenda," Janis says. "The builders have no interest in assisted housing any more. The cities believe HUD can no longer deliver. And the administration has adopted the decentralization strategy. Most people see HUD as a lost cause."

It's true that some groups that were part of the original coalition—such as the National Association of Housing and Redevelopment Officials, the National Low-Income Housing Coalition, the National League of Cities, and the American Planning Association—still see themselves as HUD's constituency. They still lobby Congress about HUD's budget and programs, and often they are able to restore funds that the administration has proposed cutting.

But, Americans as a whole no longer seem so interested in urban problems—at least in part because fewer of them are affected by them. By 1980, almost half of all Americans lived in suburbs, and only a third lived in the central cities. In Anthony Downs's words, "Reagan's constituency is mostly suburban and rural, so why bother?"

Under Reagan, the national "urban policy" required under the Housing and Community Development legislation has had three priorities: national economic recovery; a transfer of responsibilities to state and local governments; and public-private partnerships. Translated into political reality, this has meant that Reagan has dealt with HUD mostly by ignoring it.

His HUD secretary, Samuel Pierce, is a wealthy New York lawyer with little experience in urban matters, although he was one of the original members of the Battery Park City Authority. Pierce has probably been the most low-profile HUD secretary yet appointed—so much so that, at a White House reception for urban leaders in 1981, Reagan did not recognize him, addressing him instead as "Mr. Mayor."

Pierce notes that HUD is now in a position of trying to do more with less. "A lot of people, like [Robert] Weaver, were in government when government was spending a heck of a lot of money. We are at a point now where we have to be very parsimonious. Our number-one problem is the deficit. We have to use our heads and work out ways of getting the most we possibly can for what we spend."

Pierce's credibility at HUD was undermined during Reagan's first term by a slew of embarrassing mini-scandals involving his political appointees. Several top administrators, including first undersecretary Donald Hovde, resigned over questionable travel expenses. Hovde agreed to repay $2,800 for illegally commuting in government-owned chauffeured cars. Assistant secretary Emanuel Savas resigned after it was revealed that HUD employees had typed and proofread a manuscript of his book, which was titled *Privatizing the Public Sector*. And Baker A. Smith, the department's director of labor relations, left amid allegations that he had dismissed employees because of their union background. Pierce himself, who is black, was accused of racial discrimination by four high-ranking black officials, who claimed they had been transferred to positions of less responsibility.

On the occasions when Pierce has taken the initiative, he has not always been effective. For example, he defended the UDAG budget, which the Office of Management and Budget wanted to eliminate. But its preservation (at a reduced level of funding) may have been attributable more to the lobbying of hotel interests than the secretary's elo-

quence. And even though Pierce is also a big supporter of enterprise zones, arguing that they would contribute to the federal treasury in the long run, no enterprise bill has passed Congress. The federal income tax break the zones would include could kill the idea, at least as long as Congress is interested in tax reform.

Earlier this year, Pierce did show initiative by coming out in favor of unprecedented federal funding for fair-housing "testers"—people who pose as prospective renters or home buyers in order to determine whether racial discrimination is occurring.

But the efforts of the Reagan administration to reduce HUD's role have taken their toll. The staff has been significantly cut back, from a high of 15,600 full-time employees in 1980 to only 12,437 in 1984—and morale is said to be low. "The programs just went to hell and the department is in chaos for the most part," suggests former secretary Weaver.

Not everyone is critical of Pierce. Carla Hills says, "Sam Pierce has done some good things," pointing to his emphasis on rent subsidies over new construction in low-income housing programs.

When Pierce first took office, one of his biggest concerns was the increasing HUD debt (almost $250 billion) created by federal low-income housing construction programs—primarily because of the Section 8 new construction program, which most housing experts agree has not been cost-effective.

"I knocked that out because I figured that program was excessively expensive and we didn't get out of it what we should," Pierce says. "And so we push more on Section 8 existing housing and, of course, we started the voucher program."

Pierce is a longtime advocate of housing vouchers, although at this point the program is still in the early stages. Through expanded use of the Section 8 existing program, the number of assisted units has increased from 3.2 million at the beginning of the Reagan administration to 3.9 million in 1985. But the number of new units has been dropping every year—from 550,000 units in 1976 to 225,000 in 1981 to a little over 100,000 this year.

Seeking another way to fund new construction of subsidized rental housing, the Reagan administration created the Housing Development Action Grant (HoDAG) program, which sought to encourage private investment in rental housing. But it was so ineffective that, after a $315 million commitment in 1985, it was killed in the 1986 budget.

And on the community development side, administration budget proposals have repeatedly sought to terminate, suspend, or cut programs local governments regard as important. Block grants, the biggest community development program, continue to survive at a slightly reduced level. From a high of around $4 billion in 1981, they were cut last year to about $3.8 billion. Reagan proposed slightly less, $3.5 billion, for 1986.

Similarly, UDAG has been proposed for termination by the administration, but has been rescued by Congress more than once. Other areas have suffered, too. The HUD research budget has been cut from more than $60 million to less than $20 million. The Section 701 program, which gave local governments grants for comprehensive planning, had a $52 million budget in 1980 but has been terminated since; many local community development directors say they cannot afford to do long-term planning anymore as a result. The Solar Energy and Conservation Bank, established in 1980 with the expectation of a $3 billion federal commitment, was zeroed out in the 1986 budget after expending only $150 million from 1982 to 1984.

Given the federal budget deficit, many of these reductions were inevitable—and, indeed, some of them started during the Carter administration. But the bottom line is that the Reagan years have not seen a blossoming of the "new federalism" at HUD but, rather, what Floyd Hyde, who set up the block grant program under Nixon, calls an "abdication" of federal responsibility in urban affairs. And despite the administration's rhetoric about giving powers to lower levels of government, HUD has succeeded in transferring only one small program—small cities block grants—to the states.

"Instead of being a partner with local governments in seeking solutions," says one senior HUD official who dates back to the Weaver days, "we're really attempting to disconnect ourselves and say, 'You folks can solve your own problems.' "

Growing up

To a certain extent, in the view of many urban experts, this is the right thing to do. They note that the Reagan budget cuts have forced many cities to, in a sense, grow up. "As difficult as the Reagan years have been, there have been benefits," says

Hyde, now a Washington lobbyist for several cities. "The cutbacks in federal aid have forced local governments really to assess what they ought to be doing. Cities have become better performers."

And there is considerable evidence that HUD's efforts over the years have helped foster the skills cities need to survive on their own. The UDAG program turned many community development directors into tough negotiators able to cut deals with private developers, which will allow their cities to recoup some federal losses. And HUD veterans such as David Michel, now community development director in Syracuse, New York, believe that cities that once had to be prodded on such matters as affirmative action and citizen participation are now more likely to take the initiative on their own.

"If there is less of a need for HUD today," says former New Orleans mayor Moon Landrieu, who served as Carter's HUD secretary from 1979 to 1981, "it is only because the federal government and HUD developed the standards and applied them in the first place."

And there is just as much evidence that these local successes still depend to a great extent on the continued leadership and support of the federal government. "One of the real ironies of this administration," says the senior HUD official, "is that it points to the success 'on their own' of cities like Baltimore—when, in fact, there is $35 million in federal aid in that success."

Almost no one outside of HUD is willing to suggest that all state and local governments have the money and the sophistication to deal with urban problems on their own. John Tuite, who was HUD area manager in Los Angeles from 1980 to 1983, estimates that only about 40 percent of the nation's large cities—and fewer small ones—have learned the sophisticated negotiating skills they need to survive without HUD.

At a conference on rental housing in Los Angeles a few weeks ago, Henry Felder, HUD's deputy assistant secretary for policy development and research, asserted that state funds are often available to fill the breach for local communities when federal funds are not forthcoming. On the same panel was California housing director Susan DeSantis, who was appointed, incidentally, by budget-conscious Republican governor George Deukmejian. Asked whether the state of California could fill the gap, DeSantis looked at Felder and said, "It's not likely."

On its twentieth anniversary, after all the different presidents, all the different secretaries, and all the ups and downs, it's clear that HUD still has a role to play, although it may not be the active, money-driven role that Lyndon Johnson and Robert Weaver envisioned. Moon Landrieu sees HUD as a sort of "senior partner" in cities' efforts to rejuvenate themselves. That role means some selective financial pump-priming—but, at a time of local initiative and creativity, it also means the important job of coordinating, researching, and evaluating what's happening on the local level. In this view, HUD could do a good job even without massive funding.

Right now, HUD is not doing much coordinating or monitoring, and a number of urban observers believe that this means cities will not be able to benefit from each other's experience as much as they should: "You've got this innovative, creative activity going on locally," says Janis, "but where is the 'technology transfer'?"

Moreover, not everyone agrees that the federal government can be an important actor in housing and community development if it isn't ready to put cash on the line. George Sternlieb of Rutgers responded to the "senior partner" idea with characteristic bluntness: "No tickee, no washee." And even Janis is not sure that HUD can be effective without a big budget, if only because Americans associate money with power.

It's clear, though, that the opportunities are there—at least on the local level, where mayors from Boston's Flynn to San Francisco's Feinstein are running on planning and development platforms. The big question now is whether HUD has the political will to play any significant role at all.

William Fulton is a contributing editor of Planning. *Researcher Steven Webber assisted in gathering data for this article.*

A Nod to the Nineties

Melvin R. Levin
(June 1988)

Almost 10 years ago, *Planning* published "Bumpy Roads Ahead" (July 1979), my attempt to gauge the future of the profession in the new decade. Looking back, it seems that my track record as a seer was not too bad. A year before Ronald Reagan's election as President, I wrote that, not only were no large new planning programs in the offing, but existing programs would be cut back—as indeed they were. I was also on target in predicting the waning influence of both the new left and the new right, noting that self-righteous fringe elements make a lot of noise but that real power remains close to the mainstream.

Where I erred was in predicting that other professions, most notably lawyers, would make inroads on planning. It has not happened. We have not only solidified our hold on traditional planning work but have made minor incursions into new fields such as corporate planning and appraising. Buoyed by that two-out-of-three batting average for the 1980s, I am ready to hazard another round of predictions—this time for the post-Reagan nineties.

Don't count chickens. First, it seems clear that, regardless of how compassionate the next presidential administration is, no new large-scale federal initiatives can be expected. Indeed, we will do well to retain most of what's left after the cuts of the last eight years. The budget deficit, trade imbalance, shaky foreign debtors, and other fiscal worries virtually guarantee another dozen years of belt tightening.

Rather than urban paymaster and pacesetter, its role between 1935 and 1970, the federal government will continue to function primarily as a not wholly reliable source of supplementary funds and occasional inspiration. (By this time, we should be used to federal drift and cutbacks, which began 15 years ago with the impoundments of the Nixon administration.)

Some may argue that funds can be freed up by shifting funds from military to civilian programs.

But those of us old enough to remember the "peace dividend" after the Vietnam War know that the iron law of military expenditure will come into play: Any savings from a reduction in one set of weapons will immediately be absorbed by expenditures for others. Money saved on missiles is likely simply to be allocated to conventional weaponry, higher military salaries, and base revampings—the latter a popular political item. In no case will the money be available for the urban slums.

Local initiatives. One byproduct of the fading away of the feds has been the resurgence of states and localities. The days of haunting federal bureaucracies for funding, of hiring Washington consultants as grantsmen and rainmakers, are over. We no longer listen to HUD officials pontificating to planning audiences on the art and science of qualifying for federal allocations—and we're not likely to do so in the nineties, either.

The engine. Cities have long focused their attention on jobs and taxes, the two pillars of economic development—and even more so as fiscal pressures increase. The same pressures affect the states and the federal government. The upshot is that 1960s-style social activism based on a combination of equity, noblesse oblige, and huge federal resources has been replaced by an investment ethic: Save, invest, generate new wealth. Redistribution is out (as was made clear in the 1986 federal tax reform); competitiveness is in.

The implications for urban policy are clear. Requests for program expenditures must be marketed politically as components of economic growth, not as charitable endeavors. Planners can convincingly argue, for example, that enriched day care, by laying the groundwork for a lifetime of schooling, will improve the quality of the labor force, thereby increasing income and production. . . .

A realistic analysis of planning programs offers ample grounds for packaging most of them as crucial elements of a successful economic development effort. And even the most backward areas, those whose policies seem indissolubly linked to their long-term poverty, may be open to forceful arguments that innovative planning can prevent economic obsolescence—particularly if the neanderthals are regularly outperformed by domestic and foreign competitors.

There's life yet. Fears in the early 1980s that planning agencies would disappear have been pleasantly confounded by reality. After the federal tap was half turned off, the cities and towns made three vital discoveries. First, the problems remained, even if less federal money was available to address them. Then, despite much initial anguish, the states and localities found that they had the money to do much of what needed to be done.

Last, local governments learned that in many respects life was easier with a greatly diminished federal presence; programs moved faster, were more flexible, and often had greater assurance of multi-year funding. Time and money were saved by not having to deal with lumbering federal agencies.

In sum, planning has finally been accepted as a permanent feature of the political and budgetary landscape, rarely any longer today described as a "wasteful frill" or a dangerous tool of meddling socialism. The question is no longer survival but content and direction.

Social engineering. The decisive turn taken by planning in the 1960s was reflected in a variety of new programs such as Model Cities and the War on Poverty and in a new awareness of the social implications of what planners do to land uses. Clearly, there is no going back to the days of innocence and insensitivity. But it is also true that the broadening of planning concerns has not been a trouble-free experience.

Two decades after the Johnson-era Great Society programs, conservatives argue that intervention proved ineffective; that social problems are best solved by a combination of economic growth and adaptation of the poor to mainstream standards; that anti-poverty programs simply wall off the poor and enrich the "povertycrats" rather than those they are intended to serve. In general, they say, the programs cost too much and deliver too little.

Meanwhile, the remaining social planning activists maintain that the gloomy statistics are exaggerated and misleading and that the faulty programs have either been discarded or improved. They also note that in the context of total government and private-sector budgets, social-sector spending is miniscule, and that this funding disproportion is part of the reason some results are negative. Like it or not, they add, social problems won't go away; many of the poor cannot compete in the mainstream and their problems constitute a serious drag on economic progress. In short, there is no alternative to government intervention.

Insofar as one can predict the public mood over the next dozen years, it seems likely that both sides will get support. Most people agree that something needs to be done—but not if it requires a substantial public outlay. The skepticism is deep and pervasive; the blind faith of the mid-1960s is long gone. As a result, we must be able to show that social programs are accountable, can be monitored for substantive progress, and are clearly linked to economic growth.

Guerrilla war. By temperament, Americans are impatient, attracted to the big push, the all-out offensive, followed by a victory parade. Vietnam-style conflicts are anathema, the invasion of Grenada the ideal: 7,000 troops, 8,000 medals, and victory in less than a week.

In this context, the Great Society programs and the War on Poverty offered the civilian equivalent of a Marine Corps invasion: a ringing declaration of intent and a frenzy of activity followed by apparent success. The civilian model was Roosevelt's 100 days, the early months in office when a new, activist administration, after putting down token resistance by panicked conservatives, devised a glamorous rescue operation for a stricken nation.

From the planner's standpoint, there is an illusory quality about promises to achieve a lot quickly. Most real reform is, after all, incremental. The wave of New Deal legislation was followed by successive wavelets of reform bills in the late 1940s and through the 1950s and 1960s, with a final flurry in the 1970s.

Even in this decade, the receding of federal initiatives has not changed the basic outlines of the planner's job. It was and is a mosaic of the prosaic: zoning referrals, land-use studies, and transportation impact analyses—with an overlay of modest-to-significant program initiatives. Between 1989 and 2000, incrementalism—overlaid with flashes of inspiration and transitory opportunities for innovation—will be the name of the game.

The business connection. An interesting byproduct of this era of struggling and coping is the new relationship between the local public sector and the developer. To a significant degree, the planner has become a kind of entrepreneur as government jurisdictions seek to expand their tax base and create jobs by direct intervention into the private sector. The new arrangements go far beyond the customary tax concessions into partnerships, leasing arrangements, and risk capital.

One of the happier, unintended consequences of the Reagan years and the business-government partnership has, in fact, been the demystification of real estate finance. Planners have discovered that business skills are necessary, interesting, and not particularly difficult to master. As a result, we'll be seeing more planners move into private-market jobs. They'll be following the precedent of architects like John Portman as well as all the MBAs, public administrators, and economists who learned the ropes as government employees and then moved on to the other, more lucrative side of the table. It is no accident that many real estate courses have been added to planning curriculums in the last five years.

Permanent problems. Faddishness is as much a danger in planning as it is in other fields. In the 1990s, the plight of the homeless, the decrease in affordable housing, the drug problem, the AIDS epidemic, and the portents of economic recession will be high on the concern agenda.

They replace such earlier worries as high crime rates, deteriorating public schools, environmental pollution, the collapse of the central cities, the decaying public infrastructure, and the travails of the underclass. In general, urban problems have lost their priority crisis status as the public learns to tolerate and adapt to conditions that seemed in earlier, freer spending years to require urgent remedy.

A change in focus does not, of course, mean that the older problems have been solved or even substantially alleviated. It is simply another sign of the public's tendency to focus briefly on the latest foreground drama that clamors for attention.

It's not hard to predict the attention-getting crises of the next decade: at least one major business recession, several spectacular collapses of rusted infrastructure, a few scandals involving badly housed and mistreated elderly, horror stories about the consequences of laissez-faire day-care. If we do our thinking now, we can be prepared to convert disasters into progress. But it will take a combination of common sense, business sense, and conscience.

New blood. In 1976, the incoming Carter administration was greeted by still-hopeful survivors at HUD and other agencies who had kept the faith during the lean Nixon-Ford years. Those hardy souls are long gone. Between 1980 and 1987, the HUD budget took a 70 percent hit, the largest decrease of any cabinet agency. Year by year, a combination of Reagan cutbacks and generous federal retirement benefits has left its mark. Many disenchanted employees have taken their pensions and gone, leaving behind all too many time-servers.

A new, activist administration will require restaffing. Also needed will be new agencies that do not depend on huge infusions of funds and that can bridge the gap between the old administration and the new.

Planners have done it all before. The New Deal in its early phases was faced with the challenge of converting small federal agencies into administrative structures capable of coping with a national emergency. And in the 1960s, the redevelopment authorities and poverty agencies were created to fill a vacuum until moribund planning agencies could be resuscitated. It can happen again.

Facing reality. The lopsided results of the 1984 presidential election sent a clear message to political candidates: Avoid such grim realities as trade deficits, fiscal equity, the need for tax increases, and stick to the feel-good issues. Bearers of bad news—and planners are often in their number—are as unwelcome as long-faced divorce lawyers at a wedding reception. Incumbent mayors hate to be reminded of their unfinished business: slums, homelessness, tax favoritism, traffic congestion, a shortage of affordable housing.

It is no accident that planners spend more time on problems than on celebrations, on putting out fires in the neighborhoods and dealing with disgruntled developers, merchants, and homeowners. Planners and planning agencies face a daily agenda of multiple choices, complexities, and variables. They recognize that compromise is inevitable, that victories are starting points for coping with new problems. They understand what it means to face reality.

The next decade will call for much imaginative effort to compensate for chronic shortages of funds. Creativity and political savvy can take us a long way. But first we need more A students to feed into the profession. As I have indicated on occasion, we have more than our share of Bs. It doesn't help our cause when professors in planning schools encourage promising applicants to look elsewhere, to law or other disciplines. . . .

We have two planners in the U.S. House of Representatives and others serving in state legislatures and city and county councils. We can use more. If we are to move into an age of increasingly generic, converging specializations, there is no reason why planning and planners should not have substantial representation among elected officials.

Most important, we must avoid the pitfalls underscored by David Halberstam in *The Best and the Brightest;* he described arrogant technical experts with no political experience making policy with much brilliance and very little wisdom. We must round out our A grades with maturity and humility—while also being cautious of following the lead of those academic theorists who fashion high-minded programs that combine stirring rhetoric with built-in failure. Model Cities (which owed much to this intellectual mutation) should not be our model; urban development action grants, the Head Start program, and clean water legislation should.

Luckily, the working planner (as distinct from many academics) practices in a political arena where the arts of coalition-building, pragmatism, and budget constraints are learned by doing.

Finally, we need vision. We need to cull the best examples of planning, here and abroad—the Best of Breed—clone them, modify them, and build them into the political landscape. But first we have to be sure that we have filled in the two missing pieces: a grasp of the whole and a care for the poor. We must ensure that economic realism does not put planning in a reactive posture—geographically and functionally fragmented and linked to the economy and not much else. In the title of his final chapter in *American City Planning,* Mel Scott aptly termed our quest "The Search for a New Comprehensiveness." We didn't find it in the 1960s or 1970s. We have another chance in the 1990s.

Melvin Levin, AICP, is professor of urban studies and planning at the University of Maryland.

Index